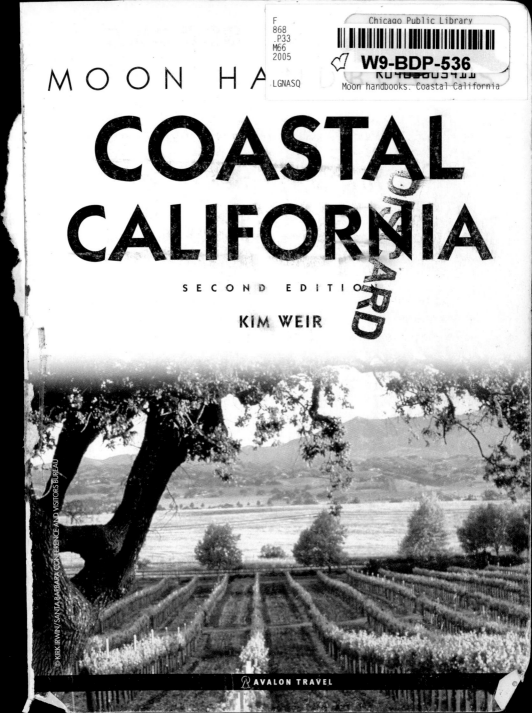

MOON HA

COASTAL
CALIFORNIA

SECOND EDITION

KIM WEIR

AVALON TRAVEL

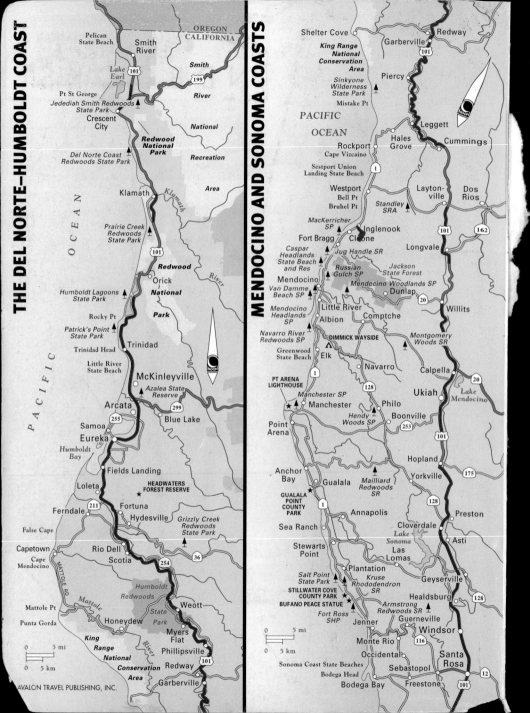

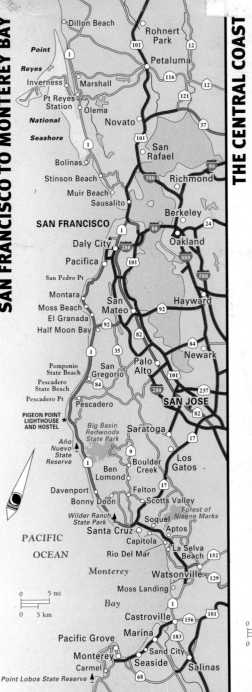

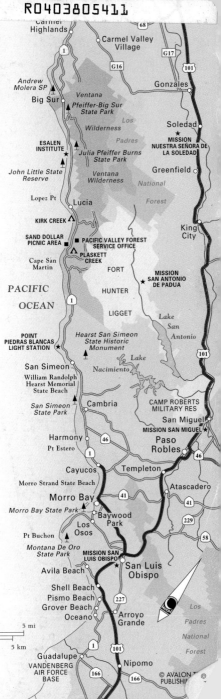

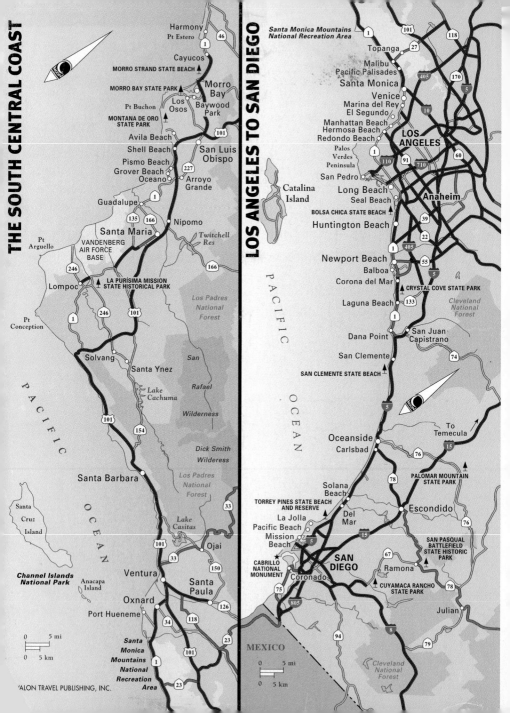

CONTENTS

Discover Coastal California

Explore Coastal California

Know Coastal California

MAPS

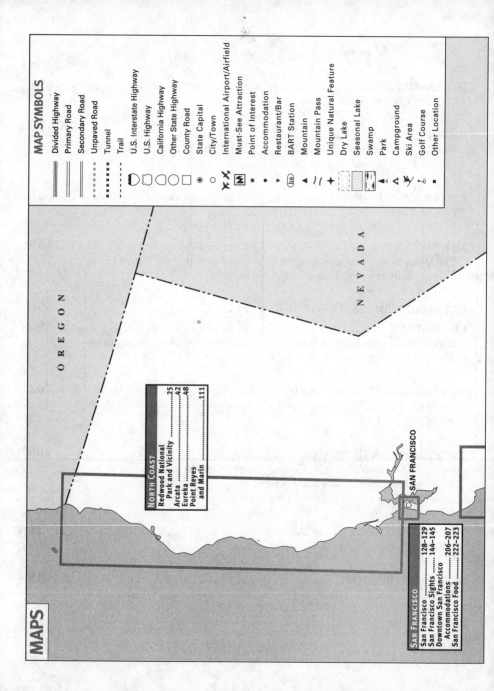

MAP SYMBOLS

Divided Highway
Primary Road
Secondary Road
Unpaved Road
Tunnel
Trail
U.S. Interstate Highway
U.S. Highway
California Highway
Other State Highway
County Road
State Capital
City/Town
International Airport/Airfield
Must-See Attraction
Point of Interest
Accommodation
Restaurant/Bar
BART Station
Mountain
Mountain Pass
Unique Natural Feature
Dry Lake
Seasonal Lake
Swamp
Park
Campground
Ski Area
Golf Course
Other Location

OREGON

NEVADA

SAN FRANCISCO

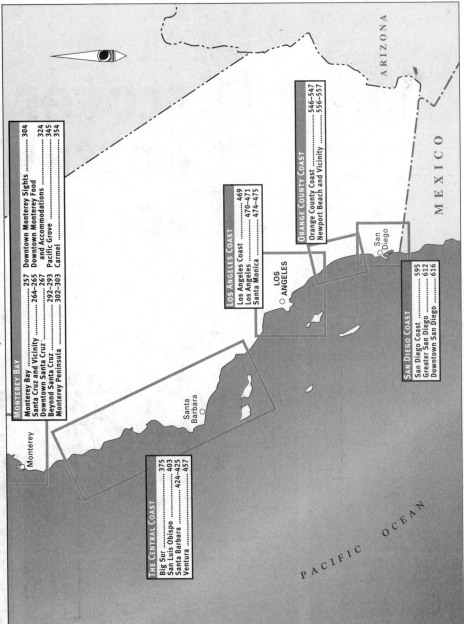

ARIZONA

MEXICO

San Diego

LOS ANGELES

Santa Barbara

Monterey

PACIFIC OCEAN

Discover Coastal California

California is a myth—a myth in the sense of a traditional tale told to impart truth and wisdom, and in the fanciful sense of some extravagant storybook fiction. Californians happen to like the quirky character of the state they're in. Whether or not they realize it, California as myth is exactly why they're here—because in California, even contradictions mean nothing. In California, almost everything is true and untrue at the same time. In California, people can pick and choose from among the choices offered—as if in a supermarket—or create their own truth. Attracted to this endless sense of creative possibilities— California's most universal creed, the source of the ingenuity and inventiveness the state is so famous for—people here are only too happy to shed the yoke of tradition, and traditional expectations, that kept them in harness elsewhere.

Californians tend to think life itself is a California invention, but "lifestyle" definitely is: people come to California to have one. Coming to California, novelist Stanley Elkin observes, "is a choice one makes, a blow one strikes for hope. No one ever wakes up one day and says, 'I must move to Missouri.' No one chooses to find happiness in Oklahoma or Connecticut." And according to historian Kevin Starr, "California isn't a place—it's a need." Once arrived in California, according to the myth, the only reason to carry around the baggage of one's previous life is because one chooses to.

But it would be naive to assume that this natural expansiveness, this permission to be here now, is somehow new in California. It may be literally as old as the hills. Native peoples, the first and original laid-back Californians, understood this. Busy with the day-to-day necessities of survival, they nonetheless held the place in awe and managed to honor the untouchable earth spirits responsible for creation. The last remembered line of an ancient Ohlone dancing song—"dancing on the brink of the world"— somehow says it all about California.

As a place, California is still a metaphor, for Shakespeare's "thick-coming fancies" as well as for those awesome mysteries that can't be taken in by the five senses. People come here to sort it all out, to somehow grasp it, to transform themselves and the facts of their lives—by joining in the dance.

California is crowded—both with people trying to live the dream on a permanent basis and with those who come to visit, to re-create themselves on the standard two-week vacation plan. Summer, when school's out, is generally when the Golden State is most crowded, though this pattern is changing rapidly now that year-round schools and off-season travel are becoming common. Another trend: "mini-vacations," with workaholic Californians and other Westerners opting for one- to several-day respites spread throughout the year rather than traditional once-a-year holidays. It was once a truism that great bargains, in accommodations and transport particularly, were widely available during California's nonsummer travel season. Given changing travel patterns, this is no longer entirely true. Early spring and autumn are among the best times to tour the Northern California coastline, for example.

Official holidays, especially during the warm-weather travel season and the Thanksgiving-Christmas–New Year holiday season, are often the most congested and popular (read: more expensive) times to travel or stay in California. Yet this is not always true; great holiday-season bargains in accommodations are sometimes available at swank hotels that primarily cater to businesspeople. Though most tourist destinations are usually jumping, banks and many businesses close on the following major holidays: New Year's Day (January 1); Martin Luther King Jr. Day (the third Monday in January); Presidents' Day (the third Monday in February); Memorial Day (the last Monday in May); Independence Day (July 4); Labor Day (the first Monday in September); Veterans Day (November 11); Thanksgiving (the fourth Thursday in November); and Christmas (December 25). California's newest state holiday is César E. Chávez Day, in honor of the late leader of the United Farm Workers (UFW), signed into law in August 2000 and celebrated each year on the Friday or Monday closest to March 31, Chávez's birthday. In honor of the nation's most famous Latino civil rights leader, all state offices close but banks and other businesses may not.

Spontaneous travel, or following one's whims wherever they may lead, was once feasible in California. Unfortunately, given the immense popularity of particular destinations, those days are long gone. Particularly for those traveling on the cheap and for travelers with special needs or specific desires, some of the surprises encountered during impulsive adventuring may be unpleasant. If the availability of specific types of lodgings (including campgrounds) or eateries, or if transport details, prices, hours, and other factors are important for a pleasant trip, the best bet is calling ahead to check details and/or to make reservations. (Everything changes rapidly in California.) For a good overview of what to see and do in advance of a planned trip, including practical suggestions beyond those in this guide, also contact the chambers of commerce and/or visitor centers listed. Other good sources for local and regional information are bookstores, libraries, sporting goods and outdoor supply stores, and local, state, and federal government offices.

California's missions are the beleaguered icons of the earliest days of settlement history. After decades of neglect, state and federal leaders are just now beginning to take action to preserve them from the ongoing ravages of time (and earthquakes). This being the case, it's almost miraculous that it's still possible to visit all 21 of the original missions—or, in some cases, reasonable facsimiles—and trace the 18th-century "royal road" (El Camino Real) of Spanish explorers, soldiers, and missionaries. The missions mentioned below are found along or near the coast.

Mission San Diego, California's first mission, founded in 1769, gave rise to California's first city. The modern Mission San Diego owes much of its present appearance to the reconstruction work of 1813.

Moving north is Mission San Luis Rey de Francia near Oceanside, the "King of the Missions," founded in 1798 but not completed until 1815. In 1893 the mission became a Franciscan seminary.

Its crumbling church walls steadied by scaffolding and surrounded by very contemporary California, Mission San Juan Capistrano, is impressive nonetheless. The mission's original Serra Chapel is the only one remaining in California in which Father Serra said mass.

Mission San Buenaventura, the ninth mission established in California, was the last founded by Father Junípero Serra, in 1782. Now a shining star in Ventura's charming downtown, the mission was destroyed by the earthquake in 1812, rebuilt in 1816.

Mission Santa Barbara, founded in 1786, was originally a collection of simple adobes. Despite centuries of earthquakes and floods, Santa Barbara's "Queen of the Missions," California's 10th mission, still stands.

Mission Santa Inés just east of Solvang off Hwy. 246, was

Mission Dolores

SUSAN SNYDER

established in 1804, the 19th of the state's 21 missions and the last in the region.

La Purísima Mission State Historic Park was the 11th in California's chain of coastal missions, originally built in 1787 in what is now downtown Lompoc. Now it's California's only complete mission complex.

Mission San Luis Obispo de Tolosa, founded by Father Junípero Serra, is still an active parish church. This, the fifth in the mission chain, was originally built of tules and logs, then of five-foot-thick adobe, crowned with tiled roofs to prevent native peoples from torching the place.

Mission San Miguel, 16th in the chain, was founded in 1797 by Father Fermin Lasuen. Located about nine miles north of Paso Robles, the mission suffered severe damage in the December 2003 earthquake that rocked the area, and is currently closed to the public.

Farther north near the Fort Hunter-Liggett military reservation, is the 1771 Mission San Antonio de Padua, not the biggest nor most ravishingly restored mission, certainly not the most popular, but somehow the most evocative of Spanish California—definitely worth the lengthy detour from Hwy. 101.

The 1771 Carmel Mission is California's second, and onetime headquarters and favorite foreign home of Father Junípero Serra, who is buried here. Most of the buildings are reconstructions. The mission gardens are evocative and inviting, featuring some rare and old-fashioned plants.

Over the hill from Monterey and beyond Salinas is Misión Nuestra Señora de la Soledad, founded in 1791. This, the 13th mission, was quite prosperous until 1825, but then crumbled into ruin. The chapel was reconstructed and rededicated, and another wing has since been restored.

Santa Cruz Mission was destroyed long ago—there is a replica and a state historic park in the vicinity now—but there is another, very evocative mission town nearby. Mission San Juan Bautista and adjacent San Juan Bautista State Historic Park, just north of Salinas via Hwy. 101, evoke the spirit of Spanish California. The mission scenes from Alfred Hitchcock's *Vertigo* were filmed here.

Mission Dolores is San Francisco's oldest structure, completed in 1791. This is the sixth mission established in California by the Franciscan fathers. The sturdy mission chapel—the small humble structure, not the soaring basilica adjacent—survived the 1906 earthquake due largely to its four-foot-thick adobe walls. In 2004, an entire wall of original Native American art, hidden from view since 1796, was discovered.

The most northerly and last of California's missions, founded in 1823, is Mission San Francisco Solano de Sonoma. The mission itself is included as part of appealing Sonoma State Historic Park.

It's easy to tour nature—more accurately, to participate vicariously in nature's grand, ongoing tours of Coastal California. Biologically speaking, the vast Monterey Bay National Marine Sanctuary is very "productive." Due to the bay's deep submarine canyon and the upwelling of nutrient-rich waters, life here is abundant. In fact, Monterey Bay serves either as migration corridor or permanent home for 26 species of marine mammals, 94 seabird species, 345 specific types of fish, plus sea turtles, invertebrates, and marine algae.

GRAY WHALES

Most famous of the year's whale migrations is the annual sojourn of the gray whale. Early in October the fat and sassy gray whales—with an extra 6–12 inches of blubber on board, following months of dining in rich arctic seas—start south, a 6,000-mile journey to winter in the warmer waters of Baja in Mexico. Pregnant females leave first, traveling alone or in small groups. Larger groups make up the rear guard, with the older males and nonpregnant females engaging in highly competitive courtship and mating rituals along the way—quite a show for human voyeurs. On the way home the rear guard becomes the frontline: males, newly pregnant females, and young gray whales head north from February to June, followed by cows and calves between March and July.

To watch migrating whales from land, there are prime "whale vistas" all along the Santa Cruz, Monterey, and Big Sur coastlines, starting near **Añ Nuevo** and continuing south to **Point Lobos** and **Big Sur**. Ocean-going commercial whale-watching tours are also offered in various locales.

As a historical reminder of just how and why whales became endangered, see the old two-story adobe **Whaling Station** near the Custom House in Monterey. Note—and walk softly upon—the sidewalk in front of the house, which is made of whalebone. Once a common sight in the country, whalebone sidewalks are now quite rare.

NORTHERN ELEPHANT SEALS

Like the gray whale, northern elephant seals were hunted to the edge of extinction for their oil-rich blubber, and numbered only 20 to 100 at the turn of the 20th century. All these survivors lived in Mexican waters, on Isla de Guadalupe off the west coast of Baja California. Their descendants eventually began migrating north to California in winter, and now show up in vast numbers every year along the San Mateo coast.

Male northern elephant seals start arriving at the **Año Nuevo State Reserve** in December, followed in January by the females, ready to bear offspring conceived the previous year. The males battle over status, the successful alpha bulls fighting to protect harems of 50 or so females from marauders. (Because these are wild, aggressive animals, keeping a 20-foot minimum distance between you and the seals is important.) During mating season, public access to the reserve is allowed only on guided tours. Yet the first males begin to arrive in November, before the official docent-led tours begin, so it is possible to tour the area unsupervised. Visit the dunes without a tour guide in spring and summer also, when many elephant seals return here to molt.

Though Año Nuevo was the first northern elephant seal rookery established on the California mainland, northern elephant seals are now establishing colonies elsewhere up and down the state's coastline. A significant colony of "e-seals" can be observed just south of **Piedra Blancas**, about 4.5 miles north of Hearst Castle. Docent-guided tours are available there, too.

MONARCH BUTTERFLIES

Pacific Grove is the best known of the 20 or so places where monarch butterflies winter—so no wonder the town is nicknamed Butterfly City U.S.A. Here, there's a big fine—and/or a sentence of six months in jail—for "molesting" monarch butterflies. Stop by the **Pacific Grove Museum of Natural History** to see the facsimile butterfly tree. Come in October for Pacific Grove's delightful, absolutely noncommercial **Butterfly Parade**, in October, part of **Welcome Back Monarch Day**, a community bash complete with carnival and bazaar to herald the return of the migrating monarchs, all to benefit the PTA. Not coincidentally, from October to February the most popular destination in town is the **Monarch Grove Sanctuary** on Ridge Road (just off Lighthouse), where docent-led tours are offered.

Here and elsewhere up and down the coast, adult monarch butterflies arrive in late October and early November. They first alight on low shrubs, then meet at certain local "butterfly trees" to socialize, sun themselves, and mate. In one of the more complicated of known migrant reproductive cycles, their offspring—actually, their offspring's grandchildren—make their way back to the California coast, without ever having been here.

MONTEREY BAY BIRDS

Winter is prime time to appreciate the grand brown pelican, for example, a fish-eating species known for its spectacular, 60-foot dives into coastal waters. Once endangered by DDT, the brown pelican has made a dramatic comeback in recent decades. More than 90 species of seabirds have been observed here. Best places for bird-watching include **Elkhorn Slough,** a protected federal and state estuarine sanctuary, where you can also observe the California clapper rail and the California least tern; and **Carmel River State Beach,** a bird sanctuary for hawks, kingfishers, cormorants, herons, pelicans, sandpipers, snowy egrets, and sometimes migrating ducks and geese.

The Monterey Bay area is productive for literature, too. Moments standing on the shores of Monterey Bay, or a first glance off the edge of the world from Hwy. 1 in Big Sur—that's all it takes to understand why writers would be drawn to this area.

ROBERT LOUIS STEVENSON

Stevenson was among the first to discover Monterey. Stevenson was in town a very short time, waiting for his love Fanny Osbourne to disentangle herself from an unhappy marriage so they could marry and return to Scotland, where the writer would pen the works that later brought him fame. The writer lived for several months in 1879 at the French Hotel adobe boardinghouse on Houston Street, now included in Monterey State Historic Park. Stevenson did some writing in Monterey, but most significantly he collected material—including grand landscapes, real and imagined, which would later appear in *Treasure Island*. Point Lobos inspired *Treasure Island*'s Spyglass Hill, for example, according to local lore.

Robert Louis Stevenson

COURTESY HAWAII STATE ARCHIVES

JOHN STEINBECK

More famous is Pulitzer and Nobel Prize–winning John Steinbeck, author of *The Grapes of Wrath* and *Of Mice and Men*. He was born and raised in nearby Salinas, though his depictions of Cannery Row and adjacent Pacific Grove resonate powerfully. Steinbeck was reviled in his hometown during his lifetime, though today two must-see destinations—the National Steinbeck Center and the Steinbeck Home—pay suitable homage. Also in Salinas is the one-room 1897 Old Lagunita School House featured in the John Steinbeck story "The Red Pony."

The Steinbeck family also had a summer cottage in Pacific Grove, where he started his life as a writer. A number of area sights are associated with Steinbeck, including El Carmelo Cemetery, Point Pinos Lighthouse, and Holman's

Department Store on Lighthouse Avenue, where the writer bought supplies. Then there's Cannery Row. In Steinbeck's day, Cannery Row was home to Monterey's sardine industry. In his novel by the same name, Steinbeck described the Row as "a poem, a stink, a grating noise, a quality of light, a tune, a habit, a nostalgia, a dream," though most would have recognized it as a corrugated collection of sardine canneries, honky-tonks, whorehouses, and waterfront laboratories. The then–American Can Company produced cans for local packing houses, and is now home to the American Tin Cannery Factory Outlets. The former Hovden Food Products/Portola Packing Co. is now the famed Monterey Bay Aquarium.

CARMEL BOHEMIANS

Carmel, too boasts a dazzling literary past, especially given the "Carmel bohemians" who once called this community home — Mary Austin, Sinclair Lewis, and Upton Sinclair among them. The poet Robinson Jeffers was also a bohemian, though from the start he stood apart, making his home outside the city limits. Jeffers and his wife Una built their grand medieval-looking, granite home, Tor House (open on weekends for tours), to overlook the ocean, with Jeffers assisting the stonemasons and horse teams in dragging the boulders up from the ocean. Working singlehandedly for four years, Jeffers later completed adjacent Hawk Tower, a retreat for his wife and sons.

BIG SUR BEATS

Much later Big Sur attracted its own bohemians — the Beat variety. Lawrence Ferlinghetti, who published Allen Ginsberg's poetic anthem *Howl* and later founded San Francisco's City Lights Books, owned a cabin beneath the Bixby Bridge — the focus of the 1962 novel *Big Sur* by Jack Kerouac. Ferlinghetti had encouraged Kerouac to retreat to the cabin, to regroup.

More famous as a Big Sur literary icon was Henry Miller, author of *Tropic of Cancer* and *Tropic of Capricorn,* who made his home there from 1944 to 1963. Today visitors can stop by the Henry Miller Memorial Library, a friendly array of Miller memorabilia and writings collected by his good friend Emil White, now also a community cultural arts center operated by the Big Sur Land Trust.

Big Sur's Nepenthe restaurant pays at least indirect homage to another great American writer — and actor and director and producer — Orson Welles, of *Citizen Kane* fame. Welles bought a cabin for actress Rita Hayworth that stood on almost the exact spot now occupied by Nepenthe.

The phrase "Ag's My Bag" is more common farther down the coast near San Luis Obispo, where you'll see it, in the form of bumper stickers pasted on pickups. Yet the agricultural heritage of the Monterey Bay and Santa Barbara areas is equally rich.

MONTEREY BAY

To taste agriculture in Santa Cruz, plan your trip around local certified farmers' markets, and pick up a copy of the *County Crossroads* farm trails and wineries map. Outstanding in the Field is a program of events in which local organic farmers and noted winemakers pair up with visiting chefs to offer organic farm tours and unique regional multicourse meals—these well-laden tables, yes, are out standing in the farmer's field. Ag Venture Tours specializes in winery tours and vineyard picnics in the Santa Cruz Mountains, Salinas Valley, Monterey, and Carmel Valley.

You can also tour on your own. Castroville, the "Artichoke Center of the World," grows 75 percent of California's chokes. Come for the annual Artichoke Festival and parade every May. Watsonville is the mushroom capital of the United States, though berries are a better reason to stop. An almost mandatory stop is Gizdich Ranch, famous for berries and apples. Another you-pick best bet for berries is Emile Agaccio Farms. Come to Watsonville in early August for the annual Monterey Bay Strawberry Festival. Or party hearty in Gilroy, home of the world famous Gilroy Garlic Festival, held on the last full weekend in July. Garlic ice cream, anyone?

Big in Salinas since 1911 is the four-day California Rodeo, held on the third weekend in July—one of the world's largest. Some of the local homage to the West is quite artisticsome of it associated with The Farm, on Hwy. 68 just west of town. In September comes Taste of the Valley, a food and wine festival serving as centerpiece for the annual local Salute to Agriculture.

In Carmel Valley is an outpost of organic produce—Earthbound Farm—whose 60-acre showcase farm here includes just-picked local produce as well as veggies, fruits, herbs, and flowers from other locales.

Get your deep-fried artichokes in Watsonville.

MELISSA SHEROWSKI

CENTRAL COAST

In San Luis Obispo is California State Polytechnic University (Cal Poly), a jewel in the community's crown, though the college is still snidely referred to as "Cow Poly" or "Cow Tech" in some circles. The biggest and best of area farmers' markets is the San Luis Obispo Higuera Street Certified Farmers' Market, held downtown every Thursday evening, weather permitting. Particularly worth it, too, from late summer into early November, is the 13-mile apple tour of the half-dozen or so 1900s-vintage orchards in the narrow canyon southwest of town.

Southern San Luis Obispo County wineries shine in both the Edna Valley and Arroyo Grande appellations just inland from the California coast. Another of California's newer small winery regions is the Paso Robles appellation, in the general vicinity of Paso Robles, Templeton, and Atascadero.

Come to Santa Maria in April for the annual Santa Maria Valley Strawberry Festival. The Elks Rodeo and Parade is the big event in late May or early June. Otherwise, people come here to track down world-famous Santa Maria–style barbecue.

In Lompoc, La Purísima Mission State Historic Park offers some perspective on the hard agricultural work that created mission wealth—from the olive press and grain mill to the bakery, the soap and tallow factory, and weaving rooms.

In the Santa Ynez Valley near Solvang, horse ranches are big business. Monty Roberts of *The Man Who Listens to Horses* fame, is headquartered in the valley at 110-acre Flag Is Up Farms, a thoroughbred racing and training ranch and event center.

Santa Barbara County wineries are becoming big business, and a major regional attraction. Among impressive local wineries—those working to preserve, not bulldoze, native oak trees—is Gainey Vineyard in Santa Ynez, noted for its sauvignon blanc, chardonnay, riesling, and merlot. Also notably conscientious—early on—with its oak trees is Firestone Vineyard in Los Olivos, the first in the country to produce estate-grown wines.

LOS ANGELES COAST

Agriculture thins to a wisp, the closer you get to L.A., but avocados are big around Carpinteria, lemons near Santa Paula. Two-lane Hwy. 126 between Hwy. 101 and I-5 is one of the few remaining "citrus scapes" in all of Southern California—groves of Valencia and navel oranges and lemons.

Particularly good for a start to a kid-oriented trip is San Francisco's grand Exploratorium, inside the Palace of Fine Arts, declared by the *Scientific American* to be the "best science museum in the world." Truth is, adults also adore the Exploratorium, a wonderfully intelligent playground built around the mysterious natural laws of the universe. The original interactive science museum, exhibits delve into 13 broad subject areas: animal behavior, language, vision, sound and hearing, touch, heat and temperature, electricity, light, color, motion, patterns, waves and resonance, and weather. Everything here is experiential, but in the Tactile Dome, your sense of touch gets a particular workout.

Then head for Monterey. As far as best places to both amaze and amuse kids, the Monterey Bay Aquarium is a winner. And grownups love it here, too. The aquarium's philosophy, "endorsing human interaction" with the natural world, means visitors get a fish-eye view of kelp forests, octopus gardens, drifting sea nettles, galloping seahorses, anchovies going off to "school," and sharks. Kids can "pet" velvety bat rays and starfish, watch sea otters feed and frolic, and begin to understand the powerful kinship they share with all life on earth. In summer, the aquarium offers two-hour guided Fishing for History Walking Tours are offered in conjunction with the Maritime Museum of Monterey.

Discover other kid's stuff along Monterey's Cannery Row, where the Monterey Bay Aquarium is anchored. The Monterey County Youth Museum on Wave Street offers hands-on adventure—interactive exhibits on science, art, and more—of greatest appeal to younger youngsters. These days older kids will be drawn like so many techno zombies to the Edgewater Packing Company Family Fun Center nearby, packed to the gills with classic and high-tech amusements—from the NASCAR simulator and the virtual-reality batting cage to the Dance Dance Revolution Extreme video game.

Special-effects amazements come and go, but it's still true that if the kids need to let off some steam, nothing beats fresh air and exercise. Try a long walk or bike ride on the Monterey Bay Recreation Trail. Or hit the playground. Locally loved but lesser known among visitors is the colorful Dennis the Menace Playground at El Estero, designed by cartoonist Hank Ketcham and first opened to the public in 1955. Recently renovated, the park is a wonder—from the hedge maze and new giant roller slide to the unique climbing wall.

Looking for an attraction with still more giddyup? Hightail it to Molera Horseback Tours at Andrew Molera State Park in Big Sur, where you can sign on for one- to three-hour naturalist-guided rides along the beach and through the redwoods.

Also fun for family play is Gilroy's fantastic, $100 million Bonfante Gardens theme park. The 40 rides and other diversions here are great, from the cool antique car ride and 1927 carousel to the roller coaster, yet what's truly impres-

Monterey Bay Aquarium

sive is the way all attractions here are artfully woven into the landscape—a relaxed atmosphere, and an inspired horticultural feat.

The three-ring circus of California theme parks presides over Santa Cruz at the Santa Cruz Beach Boardwalk, the West Coast's answer to Atlantic City. Open daily in summer and on weekends the rest of the year, the Boardwalk is an authentic amusement park—with dozens of great carnival rides, good-time arcades and other cheap thrills, and quirky shops and eateries. If your kids' primary relation to reality is virtual: One of the best roller coasters in the nation is the historic 1924 Giant Dipper, a gleaming white wooden rocker 'n' roller—truly impressive when lit up at night. Also impressive, also a national historic landmark, is the 1911 Charles Looff carousel, one of a handful of Looff creations still operating in the United States. This one has 70 handcrafted horses, two chariots, and a circa-1894 Ruth Band pipe organ—all lovingly restored to their original glory. Tell the kids not to worry. There are plenty of virtual thrills at the Boardwalk. For more actual reality—before it all disappears—take the kids bowling at the Boardwalk Bowl bowling alley across the street.

Before or after the Boardwalk, head for the Roaring Camp and Big Trees Railroad. Visit Roaring Camp and ride the rails on one of two different trips. Hop aboard a 100-year-old steam engine and make an hour-and-fifteen-minute loop around a virgin redwood forest, or take a 1940s-vintage passenger train from Felton down to Santa Cruz. There's a year-round calendar of special events, too, including October's Harvest Faire and the Halloween Ghost Train, and December's Holiday Lights Train. The railroad offers daily runs (usually just one train a day on nonsummer weekdays) from spring through November and operates only on weekends and major holidays in winter.

Despite generally high prices, everyone can afford to travel in California—even the fairly marginal, including self-supporting college students and the burgeoning ranks of the nickle-and-dimed. Along California's sublime coastline, exceptional hostels make truly low-budget travel possible.

Not just "youth hostels" anymore, hostels welcome travelers of all ages, certainly anyone willing to throw a sleeping bag down on a bunkbed. Many of California's hostels offer private rooms to couples and families, too. Hostels feature some sort of shared living space, often with TV, VCR, and/or computers to retrieve and send email. Most also include laundry and full kitchen facilities, so travelers can prepare their own meals—another huge travel savings. Not only are hostels practical, they're perfectly located—in some of the most beautiful areas along the California coastline, and in the heart of big cities. In addition, more than any other travel option, hostels offer the opportunity to meet a wide range of travelers, of all ages and backgrounds, from all around the world.

How can you beat all that for about $20 a night?

For obvious reasons, advance reservations are strongly suggested.

NORTH COAST

Starting in the north, right on the coast but also in the heart of Redwood National Park, is the fabulous, wheelchair-accessible Hostelling International USA (HI-USA) **Redwood National Park Hostel,** known locally as the De-Martin House.

Best bet for noncamping budget travelers in Point Reyes is the HI-USA **Point Reyes Hostel.** Considerably closer to urban Marin County but also an excellent choice is the HI-USA **Marin Headlands Hostel** within the Golden Gate National Recreation Area, just minutes from the Golden Gate Bridge.

SAN FRANCISCO

San Francisco is full of shoestring-priced hostels renting dorm-style bunks. The HI-USA **San Francisco City Center Hostel** is centrally located just a stroll away from the new Asian Art Museum and Civic Center. Near all the downtown and theater district hubbub is the HI-USA **San Francisco Downtown Hostel.** The HI-USA **San Francisco Fisherman's Wharf Hostel** is just west of the wharf at Fort Mason. Other popular hostels include the **Green Tortoise Guest House** and the recently remodeled **Pacific Tradewinds Guest House** near the Transamerica Pyramid.

Just south of San Francisco are two spectacular lighthouse hostels, both affiliated with HI-USA. Farthest north and closest to San Francisco, between

Not just a light house, Pigeon Point Lighthouse is also a hostel.

Montara and Moss Beach, is picturesque **Point Montara Lighthouse Hostel**. Closest to Santa Cruz is the **Pigeon Point Lighthouse Hostel** near the Año Nuevo State Reserve in Pescadero.

MONTEREY BAY

In Santa Cruz proper, the wheelchair-accessible HI-USA **Santa Cruz Hostel** occupies the historic 1870s Carmelita Cottages downtown. Monterey's onetime Carpenter's Union Hall turned hostel—**Carpenter's Hall Hostel**—is just four blocks from Cannery Row.

CENTRAL COAST

San Luis Obispo also has a great HI-USA hostel—**Hostel Obispo,** close to downtown and Amtrak, and less than an hour away from Hearst Castle. Santa Barbara offers the **Santa Barbara Tourist Hostel,** just two blocks from the beach and a block from State Street.

LOS ANGELES AND ORANGE COUNTY COAST

One of the best bargains in Los Angeles is the HI-USA **Los Angeles/Santa Monica Hostel** in downtown Santa Monica—a budget traveler's bonanza, just blocks from the beach, pier, and Third Street Promenade.

In San Pedro's Angels Gate enclave is the quiet HI-USA Los Angeles/South Bay Hostel. A best bet for budget travelers—especially surfers—in Huntington Beach is the Colonial Inn Youth Hostel, just blocks from the beach, housed in a circa-1903 three-story colonial. Another option, though not on the coast, is the excellent summers-only HI-USA Fullerton Hostel.

SAN DIEGO COAST

Affiliated with HI-USA, the San Diego Downtown Hostel is in the heart of the Gaslamp Quarter—and all those restaurants and clubs—on the corner of Fifth Avenue and Market. Just a stroll to the ballpark, too.

San Diego boasts three hostels at, or very near, the beach. Thoroughly renovated and affiliated with the American Association of International Hostels, bustling Banana Bungalow San Diego is right on the beach—and right in the middle of the way-cool, way-young Pacific Beach scene.

San Diego's newest place is also classic—the Ocean Beach International Hostel, at home in the historic Hotel Newport. The quieter HI-USA San Diego Point Loma Hostel is in a pleasant residential neighborhood—close to the ocean but not particularly close to San Diego's other attractions.

Explore
Coastal
California

North Coast

*Note: Please see color maps
at the front of this book*

Fog created California's north coast, and still defines it. Fog is everywhere, endless, eternal, *there*. Even on blazing, almost blinding days of sunshine when the veil lifts, the fog is still present somehow, because life here has been made by it. Stands of sky-scraping coast redwoods need fog to live. So do many other native north coast plants, uniquely adapted to uniformly damp conditions. The visual obscurity characteristic of the coast also benefits animals, providing a consistent, year-round supply of drinking water and, for creatures vulnerable to predators, additional protective cover.

Fog even seems to have political consequences. As elsewhere in the northstate, the secessionist spirit is alive and well on the north coast, but the fog makes it seem fuzzy, and the urge is taken less seriously here than it is elsewhere. When, in the mid-1970s, for example, some Mendocino County citizens banded together to form their own state (they called it Northern California), the response from Sacramento was off-the-cuff and casual: "The county's departure, if it ever goes, would scarcely be noticed, at least not until the fog lifted."

People often find fog disquieting, depressing. Some almost fear it. If only momentarily, in fog we become spatially and spiritually bewildered. Our vision seems vague; we hear things. We fall prey to illusions; we hallucinate: trees walk, rocks smile, birds talk, rivers laugh, the ocean sings, someone unseen brushes our cheek.

Must-Sees

M Redwood National Park: The most spectacular reserve on earth for the rare coast redwood offers a 30-mile coastal hike, tidepools, fern canyons, and perfect summer swimming holes and herds of Roosevelt elk (page 28).

M Arcata Bay and Marsh: This wonderful wildlife preserve is home to more than 200 bird species, river otters, muskrats, and pond-raised trout and salmon (page 44).

M Old Town Eureka: Eureka's onetime skid row is all spiffed up these days, home to the **Carson Mansion,** folk-art **Romano Gabriel Wooden Sculpture Garden, Clarke Memorial Museum.** Eureka's amazing **Blue Ox Mill Works** is the only mill of its kind remaining in the country (page 49).

M Ferndale: is a perfect rendition of a Victorian village. Especially fun here is the **Kinetic Sculpture Museum,** which displays noble survivors of the famed annual kinetic sculpture race that starts in Arcata and ends here (page 57).

M Humboldt Redwoods State Park: This is home to more than 40 percent of the world's remaining redwoods—a delightful place to wander, along trails and old logging roads alike (page 62).

M King Range National Conservation Area: What was once lost has now been found, at least by intrepid hikers (page 68).

M Mendocino Headlands State Park: The key advantage of Mendocino Headlands is that it also introduces the picturesque town of Mendocino, and the trail to Big River (page 76).

M Fort Ross State Historic Park: This is the place called home by Russian-American Fur Company trappers for 40 years (page 102).

M Point Reyes National Seashore: The sublime Sonoma Coast State Beaches and charming Bodega

Bay segues into the wide-open vistas of Point Reyes, famous for its **whale-watching** (page 113).

M Golden Gate National Recreation Area: This vast sweep of national parklands begins immediately adjacent to Point Reyes near Olema then wraps around various parks—Tomales Bay, Samuel P. Taylor, and Mount Tamalpais State Parks; Muir Woods National Monument; the Point Bonita Lighthouse—and extends across the bay to San Francisco's Presidio (page 114).

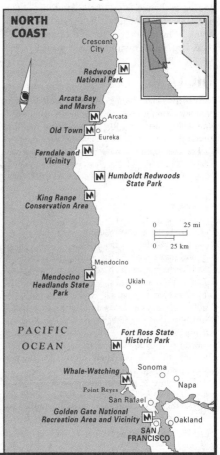

All of a sudden, we don't know where we are and haven't the foggiest notion where we're going. Life as we know it has changed. We have changed.

Dense coastal fog occurs along this cool-weather coast, according to meteorologists, as a result of shoreward breezes carrying warm, moist oceanic air over colder offshore waters. The air's moisture condenses into fog, which rolls in over the coastal mountains in cloudlike waves. As the marine air moves inland and is warmed by the sun, it reabsorbs its own moisture and the fog dissipates.

But science doesn't really explain fog at all—not fog as change, as creator, as fashioner of fantastic forms, as shape-shifting summoner of strange sounds, or protector of the primeval purpose. Fog, in the mythic sense, is magic.

THE LAND

California's northern coastline has few sandy beaches, even fewer natural harbors. Land's end is rugged and inhospitable, with surging surf and treacherous undertows. Because of this—and because of zero-visibility coastal fog—shipwrecks are part of the region's lore. Bits and pieces of hundreds of ships have washed up on these unsympathetic shores.

Offshore west of Eureka, some 4,000 feet below the surface, is a formation known as the Mendocino Ridge. In 1994, researchers from Oregon State University discovered 100 miles of extensive beach deposits near the now-sunken ridge, which itself is a feature of the Mendocino Fault Zone. (The meeting here of the Pacific and Gorda tectonic plates with the North American continent creates the Mendocino Triple Junction—one of the most active earthquake zones in the world.) These scientists now speculate that when the ridge was young, some three to five million years ago, it had risen as a 200-mile-long east-west "fold" of islands offshore from what is now San Francisco. These islands profoundly changed the regions' climate—deflecting the cool California Current to the west, and allowing warm, subtropical waters from Mexico to surge north along the coast—before receding. This,

STANDING ON SHAKY GROUND

Because of the gale-force winds driving storms against the western edge of California for half the year, most north coast settlements are in more protected inland valleys. But some of these areas, including those near the Eel, Garcia, and Mad Rivers, parallel major northwesterly earthquake fault zones. As it turns out, even the redwoods, those gentle giants of the north coast, stand on shaky ground. The seismically active San Andreas Fault (responsible for San Francisco's devastating earthquake and fire in 1906 and again in 1989) runs north from the Bay Area on the seaward side of the mountains before veering back out to sea at Point Arena. Other faults related to the 1992 Eureka-area quake cluster farther north.

According to recent geologic speculations, a massive earthquake is likely somewhere along the Pacific Northwest's offshore Cascadia subduction zone within the next 50–150 years. Such a quake, expected to register as high as 9.5 on the "energy magnitude" scale (considered more accurate than the Richter scale for major quakes), could occur anywhere from Vancouver Island in British Columbia to Mendocino in California. Such an event would be more powerful than any earthquake the San Andreas Fault could generate, much more powerful than any quake ever measured in the mainland U.S., and roughly equal in destructive force to Chile's 1960 earthquake (so far, the century's most devastating).

Before arriving at this ominous conclusion, Humboldt State University geologists studied the Little Salmon Fault near Eureka. Their preliminary findings, announced in 1987 at the annual meeting of the Geological Society of America, suggest that the fault slipped 30–33 feet in separate earthquakes occurring roughly every 500 years during the past half-million years—suggesting quakes of "awesome, incomprehensible" power.

researchers say, would explain evidence that California's coastal climate was once quite warm—a trend that ended rather abruptly about three million years ago.

The region's major features on land are the Coast Ranges, consecutive ridges angling north to Eureka, where they meet up with the westward edge of the Klamath Mountains. Geologically, the Coast Ranges (with few peaks higher than 8,000 feet) are composed of once-oceanic, uplifted, and relatively "soft" Franciscan Complex sedimentary rock. The deep soils covering the bedrock were produced over eons by humidity (gentle but constant enough to crumble rock) and, augmented by forest humus, are generally protected from erosion by the ancient forests themselves. The thick coastal soil gives these mountains their gently rounded shape. When saturated with water, and especially when atop typically weathered bedrock, coastal hillsides have a tendency to slide. Landslides are even more common in areas where extensive logging or other removal of natural vegetation occurs, since intact native plant communities make good use of soil moisture.

Federal Wild and Scenic River status has finally been extended to the north coast's Eel, Klamath, Smith, and Trinity Rivers, protecting them from dam projects, other water-diversion schemes, and logging within their immediate watersheds. The Smith is now protected as a national recreation area. Other major north coast rivers include the Garcia, Mad, Navarro, Noyo, and Russian.

Climate

The north coast has a Mediterranean climate cooled in summer by the arctic California Current. Heavy rainfall, 80–160 inches per year, and winter's endless overcast days compete with thick fog the rest of the year for the annual let's-make-a-gray-day award. The sun is most likely to make its chilly appearance during early spring, but September usually brings balmy weather. Often at the end of February, "false spring" comes and stays for a week or more. North coastal temperatures are moderate year-round, but can *feel* cold anytime, due to bone-chilling fog and moist air whisked ashore by steady ocean breezes.

A rarity along the southern Sonoma County coast but nonetheless widely observed is an offshore floating mirage resembling Oz's Emerald City, with towers, minarets, the whole show. This strange-but-true phenomenon is vaguely attributed to "climatic conditions." Also rare is the earthquake-related weather phenomenon of tsunamis, or giant coast-crushing waves. Radiocarbon dating of Native American cultural remains (which happen to coincide with dates of major Cascadia earthquakes) suggest that ancient tsunamis were so powerful they tossed canoes into the tops of trees. The most recent tsunami came in 1964, when a 13-foot wave generated by an 8.5-magnitude earthquake in Alaska smashed ashore in Crescent City on the Northern California coast, killing 11 people and destroying much of the town.

FLORA AND FAUNA
Trees to Trillium

In one of his more famous gaffes as governor of California, Ronald Reagan reportedly once cut redwood trees with the old saw, "If you've seen one, you've seen 'em all." (Reagan was misquoted, actually. What he said was, "A tree is a tree—how many more do you need to look at?") Despite Reagan's opinion on the subject, the north coast is noted for its deep, dark, and devastatingly beautiful forests of tall coastal redwoods, or *Sequoia sempervirens*—sadly, a tree most often appreciated as construction timber for suburban sun decks. Another regional tree with commercial value is the Douglas fir, *Pseudotsuga menziesii,* faster growing than redwood so often replanted by foresters on clearcut lands. Still another is the yew, whose bark contains components that have been used to treat breast cancer.

Yews, Sitka spruces, cedars, and lowland firs reach to the coast. Maples, sycamores, and alders add contrast and color in mixed streamside forests. Foothill woodlands—scattered oaks and conifers in a sea of grasses and spring wildflowers—are common north of San Francisco. Introduced groves of Australian eucalyptus trees—planted now primarily as windbreaks, though at one time intended as timber trees—are common along the Sonoma County coast, inland, and up into Mendocino County.

Coastal shrublands have no true chaparral but share some of the same species: fragrant California laurel (bay) trees, scrub oak, dogwood, ceanothus, and purple sage. The least favorite shrub here, as elsewhere in California, is poison oak, usually found in shaded areas. Among the most beautiful coastal "shrubs"—sometimes growing to tree size—are the native rhododendron species, both the western azalea and the California rose bay.

Red elderberries, blackberries, salmonberries, raspberries, huckleberries, and gooseberries all grow wild along the north coast. Wildflowers are abundant, primarily in spring. Unusual are the creeping beach primroses, beach peas, and sea rockets on beaches and sandy dunes. Beneath redwoods grow delicate fairy lanterns, oxalis, and trillium.

Oceangoing Animals

California gray whales are a stunning presence, offshore, during their annual migrations. Among other ocean animals, sea otters or "sea beavers" fun to watch. The large (1,200-2,000 pounds) northern sea lion can be spotted along rugged far northern shores, but more common is the barking California sea lion. Coastal tidepools harbor clams, crabs, mussels, starfish, sand dollars, jellyfish, sponges, squids, sea anemones, and small octopi. (Look but don't touch: eager collectors and the just plain curious have almost wiped out tidepool communities.)

For those who enjoy eating mussels—steamed in butter, herbs, white wine, or even fried—find them on rocky sea coasts. People pry them off underwater rocks with tire irons, pickaxes, even screwdrivers. Keep these bivalves alive in buckets of cool, fresh seawater until you're ready to eat 'em. But *no* mussel collecting is allowed during the annual "red tide" (roughly May–Oct., but variable from year to year), when tiny red plankton proliferate. These plankton are fine food for mussels and other bivalves but are toxic to humans. (The red tide is less of a problem for clams, but to be on the safe side, just eat the white meat during the annual mussel quarantine.)

North coast salmon, steelhead, and American shad are all anadromous, living in the sea but returning to freshwater streams to reproduce.

Landlubbing Animals

On land, deer are common mammals, found everywhere along the coast and inland. Protected colonies of Roosevelt elk can be seen far to the north in Redwood National Park. Smaller mammals include dusky-footed woodrats and nocturnal "pack rats," which nest in trees and rarely travel more than 50 feet in any direction. More common are gregarious California gray squirrels, black-tailed jack rabbits, raccoons, and skunks. Aquatic land mammals include muskrats or "marsh rabbits" and the vegetarian beaver.

Here, as elsewhere in California, gray foxes are common; characteristically clever red foxes are less so. From more remote areas, particularly at dusk or dawn, comes the lonely howl of coyotes. Bobcats (truly "wildcats" when cornered) are fairly abundant but rarely seen, though mating squalls can be heard in midwinter. Very rare are mountain lions, which usually discover people before anyone discovers them. Black bears, found even at sea level though they range up into higher elevations, usually won't attack humans unless frightened or protecting their cubs.

A common nonnative Californian along the coast is the nocturnal opossum, the only native U.S. marsupial. Also nonnative, and preferring the cover of night for their ferocious forays through the world, are wild pigs—an aggressive cross between domesticated and imported wild European hogs.

A surprising variety of birds can be spotted along the shore: gulls, terns, cormorants, egrets, godwits, and the endangered brown pelican. Mallards, pintails, widgeons, shovelers, and coots are common waterfowl, though Canada geese, snow geese, sandhill cranes, and other species fly by during fall and winter migrations. Great blue herons are nearly as common along inland rivers as they are near the sea. If unseen, mourning doves can still be heard (a soft cooing), usually near water or in farm country. Families of California quail scurry across paths and quiet roadways, sadly oblivious to the dangers of traffic.

Great horned owls, keen-eyed nocturnal hunters with characteristic tufted "ears," usually live in wooded, hilly, or mountainous countryside. Their evening cries are eerie. The magnificent ravens, which seem to dominate the terrain as well as the native mythology of the Pacific Northwest, are quite territorial, preferring to live inland at higher foothill and mountain elevations. The American kestrel or sparrow hawk can often be spotted in open woodlands and meadows or near grazing lands. More common is the red-tailed hawk, usually seen perched on telephone poles, power lines, or fences along the road—getting a good view of the countryside before snaring rabbits, ground squirrels, or field mice (though they're not above picking up an occasional roadkill). Speaking of roadkill: Least appreciated among the birds of prey are the common redheaded turkey vultures.

In rugged coastal canyons are some (but not many) golden eagles, a threatened species wrongly accused by ranchers and tale-spinners of attacking deer and livestock. Even rarer are endangered bald eagles, usually found near water—remote lakes, marshes, large rivers—primarily in inaccessible river canyons.

HISTORY

A Portuguese sailor first sighted Cape Mendocino in 1543, but explorers avoided setting foot on the foreboding, darkly forested coastline due to the lack of natural harbors. According to some historians, Sir Francis Drake dropped anchor at Point Reyes in 1579, that landing most likely pivotal in convincing the Spanish to extend their mission chain from Mexico up the California coast to Sonoma.

But after Drake's "discovery" of the north coast, it took nearly three centuries for substantial settlement to occur. Misery was the common experience of early explorers. The intrepid Jedediah Smith nearly starved while trailblazing through the redwoods, called "a miserable forest prison" by other unlucky adventurers. The Russians arrived on California's north coast in the early 1800s to slaughter sea otters for fashionable fur coats and hats. Their Fort Ross complex

on the coast north of the Russian River (now a fine state historic park) was built entirely of redwood. After the otters were all but obliterated, the Russians departed. So desperate for building materials and furniture was Sacramento's founder John Sutter that he traveled all the way up the coast to Fort Ross, purchasing (and dismantling) entire buildings for the lumber and carting off rooms full of Fort Ross furnishings and tools.

With the California gold rush of 1849 and the sudden onslaught of prospectors throughout the territory came new exploratory determination. The first settlements in California's far north, including the coastal towns of Eureka and Trinidad, started out as mining pack stations for inland gold mines. Then came redwood logging, a particularly hazardous undertaking in the early days, from felling to loading finished lumber onto schooners anchored off the rocky shoreline. (Most of the original logging towns and lumber "ports" have long since vanished.) Tourism had a respectable early start, too, particularly with the

YUROK TIME

I like time before Darwin
and von Humboldt. I like Yurok
time, for example, when Umai
(a lonely girl) could sing herself
across the ocean into the world-
beyond-the-world

to visit the sunset and find
Laksis (Shining One), her nightly friend.
I like names without Latin:
seagull rather than *Larinae*,
stories without explanations,
a song for no reason,

a journey through the horizon
to unknowns without fear or shadow.
I like the sun going down
just now, a moment of gold
spraying out, a stunned instant when words go
back before books.

—*Gary Thompson*

advent of drive-thru redwood trees and take-home knickknacks.

Now that the "harvesting" of the region's vast virgin redwood forests is all but complete, tourism will increasingly become a mainstay. Redwoods in isolated protected groves, a few redwood state parks, and Redwood National Park, not to mention the spectacular coastline, offer ample opportunity for increased tourism.

THE ECONOMY

Depending upon the year, who's running for office, and whom you talk to, illicit marijuana growing pumps somewhere between $110 and $600 million into the north coast's economy each year. According to NORML, the National Organization for the Reform of Marijuana Laws, California leads the nation in pot production

with an annual crop estimated at $2.55 billion. Traditionally, though, the lumber business has been the reigning industry, booming and busting along with construction and the dollar. Fluctuations in demand mean frequent unemployment and localized economic depressions.

Agriculture—sheep and cattle ranching, dairy farming, and commercial fishing—is less important overall, but dominant in certain areas. Recreation and tourism, especially "green" tourism, along with related small businesses and service industries, are growing in importance. Locals tend to view these inevitable incursions of "outsiders" as both a blessing and curse. There's begrudging gratitude for the money visitors spend yet at times also thinly disguised disgust for the urban manners and mores, not to mention increasing development and higher prices, that come with it.

Redwood National Park and Vicinity

Pointing north to Oregon like a broken finger is Redwood National Park, California's finest temple to tree hugging. Although well-traveled Hwy. 101 passes through the park, away from the highway much of the park is remote and often empty of worshippers. Those visitors just passing through to the Trees of Mystery are likely unaware that they're witnessing a miracle—forests being raised (albeit slowly) from the dead. Redwood National Park is complete, yet unfinished. Standing in the shadow and sunlight of an old-growth redwood grove is like stepping up to an altar mindful only of the fullness of life. But elsewhere in the park—out back toward the alley, looking like remnants of some satanic rite—are shameful scars of sticks and scabbed-over earth, the result of opportunistic clearcutting during the political wrangling that accompanied the park's formation. Today, these areas are still in the early stages of healing. Yet Redwood National Park features some magnificent groves of virgin old-growth redwood. Three of the world's 10 tallest trees grow here—one of the reasons for UNESCO's

1982 declaration of the area as a World Heritage Site, the first on the Pacific coast. Redwood National Park is also an international Man in the Biosphere Reserve.

But other people call it other things. When the sawdust finally settled after the struggle to establish this national park—the costliest of them all, with a total nonadministrative price tag of $1.4 billion—no one was happy. Despite the park's acquisitions to date, purists protest that not enough additional acres of old-growth redwoods have been preserved. Philistines are dismayed that there is so little commercial development here, so few gift shops and souvenir stands. And some locals are still unhappy that prime timber stands are now out of the loggers' reach, and that the prosperity promised somewhere just down the skid roads of Redwood National Park never arrived—or, more accurately, never matched expectations.

Though federal and state lands within the boundaries of Redwood National Park are technically under separate jurisdictions, as a practical matter the national and its three associated state

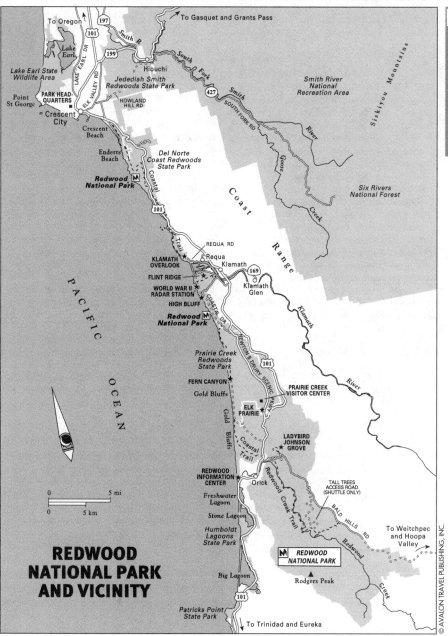

North Coast

REDWOOD
NATIONAL PARK
AND VICINITY

© AVALON TRAVEL PUBLISHING, INC.

COASTAL REDWOODS

Though they once numbered an estimated two million, the native population of coastal redwood trees has been reduced through logging and agriculture to isolated groves of virgin trees. The tallest trees in the state but only the fourth oldest, *Sequoia sempervirens* are nonetheless ancient. Well established here when dinosaurs roamed the earth, redwood predecessors flourished throughout the Northern Hemisphere 60 million years ago. Isolated from the rest of their kind by thick ice sheets a million years ago, the redwoods made their last stand in California.

The elders among today's surviving coastal redwoods are at least 2,200 years old. These trees thrive in low, foggy areas protected from fierce offshore winds. Vulnerable to both wind and soil erosion, shallow-rooted redwoods tend to topple over during severe storms. Redwoods have no need for deep taproots since fog collects on their needlelike leaves, then drips down the trunk or directly onto the ground, where the equivalent of up to 50 inches of rainfall annually is absorbed by hundreds of square feet of surface roots.

Unlike the stately, individualistic Sierra big trees or *Sequoiadendron giganteum,* the comparatively scrawny coastal redwoods reach up to the sky in dense, dark-green clusters—creating living, breathing cathedrals lit by filtered flames of sun or shrouded in foggy silence. The north coast's native peoples religiously avoided inner forest areas, the abode of spirits (some ancestral). But in the modern world, the sacred has become profane. A single coast redwood provides enough lumber for hundreds of hot tubs, patio decks, and wine vats, or a couple of dozen family cabins, or a hefty school complex. Aside from its attractive reddish color, pungent fragrance, and water- and fire-resistance, redwood is also decay-, insect-, and fungus-resistant—and all the more attractive for construction.

Despite the fact that downed trees are being floated overseas to Japan and Korea for processing as fast as the ships can load up, coast redwoods never really die. Left to their own devices, redwoods are capable of regenerating themselves without seeds. New young trees shoot up from stumps or from roots around the base of the old tree, forming gigantic woodland fairy rings in second- or third-growth forests. And each of these trees, when mature, can generate its own genetically identical offspring. Sometimes a large, straight limb from a fallen tree will sprout, sending up a straight line of trees. In heavily logged or otherwise traumatized forest areas, tiny winged redwood seeds find room to take root, sprout, and eventually flourish, blending into a forest with stump-regenerated trees.

parks—the Prairie Creek Redwoods, Del Norte Coast Redwoods, and Jedediah Smith Redwoods State Parks—are cooperatively managed. In general, the visiting weather is best in late spring and early autumn. August and September are the busiest times here (the salmon fishing rush), but September after Labor Day offers fewer crowds and usually less fog.

Some of the lush terrain included within the borders of Redwood National Park is so strange that filmmaker George Lucas managed to convince much of the world it was extraterrestrial in his *Return of the Jedi.* The park's dominant redwood forests host more than 1,000 species of plants and animals. Sitka spruce, firs, and pines grow on the coast. Leather-leaved salal bushes, salmonberries, and huckleberries con-

trol the forest's understory. Rhododendrons and azaleas bloom in May and June, followed by flowering carpets of oxalis or redwood sorrel, whose tiny leaves fold up like umbrellas when sunlight filters down to the forest floor. Mushrooms, various ferns, lacy bleeding hearts, and other delicate wildflowers also flourish here. In the meadows and along coastal prairies are alders, bigleaf maples, hazels, and blackberries.

Roosevelt elk, or wapiti, survive only here and in Washington's Olympic National Park, though they once roamed from the San Joaquin Valley north to Mt. Shasta. Black bears, mountain lions, bobcats, deer, beavers, raccoons, and porcupines are fairly common. Offshore are gray whales, seals, sea lions, porpoises, and sea otters, and you'll find creatures large and small in the tidepools. Trout and salmon are abundant in all three of the park's rivers.

The park is also home to 300 species of birds, including Pacific Flyway migrants, gulls, cormorants, rare brown pelicans, raptors, and songbirds. Redwood-loving birders listen for the mysterious marbled murrelet, a rare black-and-white seabird often seen but seldom heard and believed to nest in the treetops. If it can be established unequivocally that murrelets nest in old-growth forests (like the now-famous spotted owl), then their habitat will have to be protected from logging.

THE POLITICS OF PARK PRESERVATION

Before settlement, the land here was home to the Yurok, Tolowa, and Chilula peoples. These native residents thrived on an acorn-based diet supplemented by abundant deer, salmon, shellfish, berries, seaweed, and the occasional beached whale. The settlers who later arrived appreciated the landscape not as an intricate web of life, but as a resource ripe for harvest.

Logging in areas now included within Redwood National Park began in the 1850s but peaked after World War II, when annual harvests of more than one million board feet were the rule. By the early 1960s, the redwoods' days were clearly numbered. Lumber mills were closing and only 300,000 of the state's original two million acres of pristine coast redwood forest remained. Just one-sixth of that total was protected, thanks to persistent urging and financial contributions from the Save-the-Redwoods League, the Sierra Club, and other environmental organizations. As demands for redwood lumber increased, it was also increasingly clear that the time to save the remaining old-growth redwoods and their watersheds was now—or never.

One Park, Two Compromises

The establishment of Redwood National Park by Congress in 1968 consolidated various federal, state, and private holdings along the coastline from Crescent City south to the Redwood Creek watershed near Trinidad. The park totalled only 58,000 acres, half of which was already protected within the Prairie Creek, Del Norte, and Jedediah Smith Redwoods State Parks. Included were only a small portion of the Mill Creek (Del Norte Redwoods) area and less than half of the important Redwood Creek watershed (including the Tall Trees Grove). This unsatisfactory settlement cost almost $200 million, more than the U.S. government had ever spent on land acquisition in one place.

In August 1969, President Richard Nixon, former president Lyndon B. Johnson and his wife, Lady Bird, California governor Ronald Reagan, and other bigwigs bunched together for dignified dedication ceremonies in the Lady Bird Johnson Grove. But even then, the shortsightedness of the compromise was all too obvious; bulldozers and logging trucks were making clearcut hay on the ridgetops and unprotected watersheds beyond. Despite adequate bureaucratic procedures, the Reagan administration didn't believe in regulating the timber companies.

With devastation of even the protected groves imminent due to the law of gravity—the onrushing impact of rain-driven erosion from clearcut sites on areas downhill and downstream—environmentalists initiated another long round of legal-and-otherwise challenges. "Think big" U.S. Congressmember Phil Burton of San Francisco proposed an additional acquisition of 74,000 acres, countered by the National Park Service's think-small suggestion of just 21,500 acres. A final compromise, this one engineered by the Carter administration in 1978, added a total of 48,000 acres of new parklands (much of it already clearcut and in desperate need of rehabilitation) at a cost of $300 million more, not to mention $33 million for resurrecting the destroyed slopes of Redwood Creek or the millions set aside to compensate out-of-work lumber-industry workers. In addition, the compromise included a political coup of sorts, giving the National Park Service regulatory authority in a 30,000-acre Park Protection Zone upstream from Redwood National Park proper.

The Park Today

Redwood National Park's regional influence, if not the park itself, continues to grow. Save-the-

Redwoods League and other groups consistently seek to arrange or encourage the purchase of essential new redwood parklands. Witness the establishment of the Smith River National Recreation Area in 1990, for example, a preserve for more than 300,000 acres of Six Rivers National Forest. And in 2002, more than 25,000 acres of the Mill Creek watershed were purchased by the State of California in conjunction with Save-the-Redwoods League for $60 million, providing permanent protection for some of the state's healthiest watersheds. The Mill Creek property, the size of San Francisco, links Jedediah Smith and Del Norte Coast Redwood state parks and also connects coastal and inland forests.

The rehabilitation of clearcut lands remains a top park priority—more important than recreational development. Because of the immensity of the task and the slow healing process, Redwood National Park will probably not be "finished" for decades. Nonetheless, the park attracts some 400,000 visitors per year, and park facilities and private-sector developments related to park use (accommodations, restaurants, and recreation-related companies) are slowly growing.

M REDWOOD NATIONAL PARK

The main thing to do in Redwood National Park is simply *be* here. Sadly, "being here" to many area visitors means little more than pulling into the parking lot near the 49-foot-tall Paul Bunyan and Babe the Blue Ox at Klamath's Trees of Mystery, buying big-trees trinkets, or stopping for a slab or two at roadside redwood burl stands in Orick.

Though fishing, kayaking, surfing, and rafting are increasingly popular, nature study and hiking are the park's main recreational offerings. For those seeking views with the least amount of effort, take a drive along Howland Hill Rd. (one-lane dirt road) through some of the finest trees in Jedediah Smith Redwoods State Park. (Howland Hill Rd. transects the park and can be reached via South Fork Rd. off Hwy. 199 just east of the park or via Elk Valley Rd. south of Crescent City.) Or try a sunny picnic on the upland prairie

overlooking the redwoods and ocean, reached via one-lane Bald Hills Rd., eight miles or more inland from Hwy. 101.

Hiking

The together-but-separate nature of the park's interwoven state and federal jurisdictions makes everything confusing, including figuring out the park's trail system. Pick up a copy of the joint *Trails* brochure published by the Redwood Natural History Association available at any of the state or national park information centers and offices in the area. *Trails* divides the collective system north and south, provides corresponding regional trail maps, describes the general sights along each trail, and classifies each by length and degree of difficulty. Fifty cents well spent.

Among the must-do walks is the easy and short self-guided nature trail on the old logging road to **Lady Bird Johnson Grove.** Near the grove at the overlook is an educational logging rehabilitation display comprised of acres of visual aids—devastated redwood land clearcut in 1965 and 1970 next to a forest selectively logged at the end of World War II. At the parking lot two miles up steep Bald Hills Rd. (watch for logging trucks) you'll find a picnic area and restrooms.

The traditional route for true tree huggers, though, is the long (but also easy) 11.5-mile roundtrip hike (at least five hours one-way, overnight camping possible with permit) along **Redwood Creek Trail** to the famous **Tall Trees Grove.** The grove's **Howard Libby Redwood** was once 368 feet tall and claimed the title of the world's tallest tree. But in 1999, a storm blew off the top 10 feet, and the tree lost its tallest-tree crown, as it were, to another redwood (unmarked, for its own protection) in Montgomery Woods State Reserve in Mendocino County. The easy way to reach the grove involves taking a shuttle from the information center near Orick; buses leave four times a day in summer, otherwise thrice-daily (small fee). For those shuttled in, the guided tour includes a ranger-led discussion of logging damage and reforestation techniques.

Another possibility is coming in via the shuttle, then walking back out on the longer trail.

The longest and most memorable trek in Redwood National Park is the 30-mile-long **Coastal Trail,** which runs almost the park's entire length (hikable in sections) from near Endert's Beach south of Crescent City through Del Norte Redwoods State Park (and past the HI-USA hostel there), inland around the mouth of the Klamath River, then south along Flint Ridge, Gold Bluffs Beach, and Fern Canyon in Prairie Creek Redwoods State Park. A summers-only spur continues south along the beach to the information center.

If the entire coast route is too much, the **Flint Ridge Trail** section from the east end of Alder Camp Rd. to the ocean (primitive camping) is wild and wonderful, passing beavers and beaver dams at Marshall Pond. Easy and exquisite is the short **Fern Canyon Trail,** just off the Coastal Trail in Prairie Creek Redwoods State Park; it's less than a mile roundtrip through a 60-foot-high "canyon" of ferns laced up the sides of Home Creek's narrow ravine. To get there by car, take Davison Rd. from near Rolf's west over the one-lane bridge—watch for cattle being herded home—for six miles to the Gold Bluffs Beach Campground, then continue 1.5 miles to the parking lot. Even better is the four-mile hike west on the **James Irvine Trail** from the visitor center (or via the **Miners Ridge Trail,** which connects to Irvine by means of the **Clintonia Trail**). However you get there, the trip is worth it for the jeweled greenery—sword, deer, five-fingered, chain, bracken, lady, and licorice ferns—clinging to the canyon's ribs along the chuckling stream.

The **Revelation Trail,** just south of the visitor center in Prairie Creek Redwoods State Park, is a short self-guided nature trail for blind and sighted people, with rope and wood handrails the entire length and "touchable" sights. Trailside features are described on signs, in brochures also printed in Braille, and on cassette tapes available at the visitor center. Also special, rarely visited, and especially rich in rhododendrons is the short **Brown Creek Trail,** east of Hwy. 101 and north of the Prairie Creek visitor center.

JEDEDIAH SMITH REDWOODS STATE PARK

Though the competition is certainly stiff even close by, this is one of the most beautiful places on earth—and almost unvisited. Few people come inland even a few miles from Hwy. 101 near Crescent City.

Once Tolowa tribal territory, the Smith River, which flows through the park, was crossed by mountain man Jedediah Smith on June 20, 1828, after his grueling cross-country effort to reach the Pacific. The subsequent arrival of trappers, miners, loggers, fishermen, and farmers led to changes in the landscape and the rapid destruction of native populations. Yet this 10,000-acre stand of old-growth redwoods, Douglas fir, pines, maples, and meadows seems almost unscathed.

Historic **Howland Hill Road,** once a redwood-paved thoroughfare, is now graveled and meanders like a summer river through the quiet groves. The **National Tribute Grove,** a 5,000-acre memorial to veterans of World Wars I and II, is the park's largest. Tiny **Stout Grove** includes the area's largest measured redwoods. For an easy two-mile loop, walk both the **Simpson** and **Peterson Trails** through primeval redwoods and ferns. Even shorter is the combined walk along the **Leiffer** and **Ellsworth Trails,** something of a Jedediah Smith sampler. The 30-minute **Stout Grove Trail** offers trees and access to some of the Smith River's excellent summer swimming holes (complete with sandy beaches). Take the **Hiouchi Trail** for rhododendrons and huckleberries. More ambitious are hikes along both forks of the **Boy Scout Tree** and **Little Bald Hills Trails.** Also among the Smith River redwoods are excellent developed campsites.

Day use is $5. For more park information, contact the **Jedediah Smith Visitor Center** on Hwy. 101 in Hiouchi, 707/464-6101 ext. 5113, open from late May through September, 9 A.M.–5 P.M., or the **Hiouchi Information Center** on Hwy. 199 in Hiouchi, 707/464-6101 ext. 5067, which offers area natural history exhibits.

STORY WITHOUT END: THE POLITICS OF HARVESTING REDWOODS

Along the north coast, the politics of logging are as universally explosive as the issue of off-shore drilling. The battle to preserve redwoods, especially the remaining first-growth stands, has been going on for decades. So strong are the economic forces in support of logging and related industry that without the untiring efforts of the private Save-the-Redwoods League, Sierra Club, and other environmental organizations, most of the coast redwood groves now protected from commercial "harvesting" would be long gone. The fact that Redwood National Park north of Eureka was established at all, even if late, is something of a miracle. And the recent battle over the old-growth Headwaters Forest echoes all the wars that came before.

Environmentalists adamantly oppose the accelerating practice of clearcutting, the wholesale denuding of hillsides and entire watersheds in the name of efficiency and quick profits. "Tree huggers" have argued for years that anything other than sustained yield timber harvesting—cutting no more timber than is grown each year—not only destroys the environment by eliminating forests, wildlife habitat, and fisheries but ultimately destroys the industry itself. Someday, they've been saying for several decades, the forests will be gone and so will logging and lumber mill jobs. "Someday" has arrived. The timber business has harvested its own industry into oblivion.

The failure of both the 1990 "Green" and Forests Forever initiatives, statewide ballot propositions in favor of forest protection, has only served to increase local furor. Earth First! and other activist groups subsequently took on Pacific Lumber Company and other timber firms—taking the battle into the forests and surrounding communities, as in 1990's "Redwood Summer." Timbermen and truckers also took to the streets defending their traditional livelihoods with community parades and other events accented by yellow solidarity ribbons. The fight became so intense, philosophically, that the Laytonville school board was publicly pressured to ban *The Lorax* by Dr. Seuss because of the book's anti-clearcutting sentiments. (The book banning failed, ultimately.)

A further blow to business as usual came with a 1990s admission by the California Board of Forestry that the state has allowed timber companies to cut down so many mature trees—old growth and otherwise—that there now looms a serious "timber gap," a substantial reduction in future forest harvests. The "statewide emergency" is due to "past failure" to regulate industrial timberlands and "has resulted in long-term overharvesting, drastically reducing both the productive capability of the land and maintenance of adequate wildlife

DEL NORTE COAST REDWOODS STATE PARK

Del Norte is a dense and foggy coastal rainforest comprised of 6,400 acres of redwoods, meadows, beaches, and tidepools. It's so wet here in winter that the developed campgrounds close. The **Damnation Creek Trail,** crossing Hwy. 1 en route, leads through magnificent old-growth *Sequoias,* spruce, Oregon grape, and seasonal wildflowers to a tiny beach with offshore sea stacks and tidepools. Or, take the **Coastal Trail** from Wilson Creek to the bluffs. Easier is the short walk to the north coast's finest tidepools (and the Nickel Creek Primitive

Camp) at the end of **Enderts Beach Trail,** accessible from Enderts Beach Rd. south of Crescent City. To see the park's second-growth redwoods, and for exceptional bird-watching, take the almost four-mile **Hobbs Wall Trail.** Beyond Del Norte Coast Redwoods as the highway descends to Crescent City is the **Rellim Demonstration Forest,** which offers a well-maintained self-guided nature trail and a comfortable lodge for fireplace-warming after your hike. Day use is $5. For more information about Del Norte Redwoods State Park, contact the **Redwood National and State Parks Information Center,** 1111 Second St. in Crescent City, 707/464-6101.

habitat." This new crisis has further shocked the California timber industry, long accustomed to the board's regulatory sympathies.

The most recent chapter in the redwood wars began when the north coast's Pacific Lumber Company (PALCO) was acquired in a junk bond-financed deal by Maxxam Corporation. The original PALCO was well regarded by environmentalists as a responsible, sustained-yield logger, but with Maxxam CEO Charles Hurwitz at the helm, PALCO began clearcutting on its 202,000 acres in Humboldt County, for the first time in its history—to pay the price of Hurwitz's purchase. Among PALCO's holdings: the 60,000-acre Headwaters Forest, the largest remaining stand of privately owned old-growth redwoods in the world.

When the PALCO chain saws threatened to fell the roadless 3,000-acre Headwaters Grove at the heart of the vast old-growth redwood forest, environmentalist activists went to war with Hurwitz. For more than 10 years, Earth First! and other environmental groups stopped at nothing—public protests, guerrilla theater, tree-sitting, lawsuits—to prevent the harvesting of the Headwaters Forest. After years of forest warfare and hot tempers in nearby north coast communities, a deal brokered in 1998 by U.S. Senator Dianne Feinstein seemed destined to provide the political solution. Feinstein's compromise allowed the federal and state governments to purchase the core Headwaters acreage and a surrounding watershed buffer—a total of 7,500 acres—and required a "habitat conservation plan" for the remaining PALCO acreage, in an attempt to balance logging and wildlife protection.

But Hurwitz balked. The federal funding authorization was set to expire, negotiations were stalled, and the Headwaters' future looked grim. Yet on March 1, 1999—with just *seven minutes* left on the funding clock—the deal was struck and signed, and the Headwaters Forest became public property—for a hefty price tag of $480 million.

After the dramatic conclusion to the Headwaters conflict, most area residents were relieved. At least some of the Headwaters Forest is now preserved, the state and federal governments will regulate logging and wildlife habitat protection on the remaining acreage, and PALCO loggers can return to work.

Some environmentalists, though, say it was a bad deal—not going far enough to protect the Headwaters ecosystem as a viable whole. They are particularly concerned about the probable loss of several pristine old-growth groves, and the threat to the Coho salmon run due to damage to the Elk River watershed.

The saga continues.

KLAMATH AND VICINITY

This area was once the traditional fishing and hunting territory of the Yurok people. But when settlers arrived, the Yuroks were doomed; the native people were hunted by miners for sport, their villages burned, their fisheries ruined.

In 1964, when 40 inches of rain fell within 24 hours in the Eel and Klamath River basins, the entire town of Klamath was washed away—and not as easily replaced as the gilt grizzlies on the remnants of the Douglas Memorial Bridge outside town. The grizzlies' gold cement den mates, frequently defaced by graffiti artists, decorate the new Klamath River Bridge.

The 263-mile-long Klamath River—California's second-largest—drains 8,000 square miles and is fed by more than 300 tributaries, including the Salmon, Scott, and Trinity Rivers. Despite the shocking die-off of 33,000 salmon along the river's lower reaches in 2002, the Klamath is still one of the world's finest fishing streams. Anglers line the Klamath and the lagoon from late fall through winter for the salmon run, though fishing for cutthroat trout downstream from town is good year-round.

Among sights along the primarily unpaved **Coastal Drive,** which starts on the south side of the Klamath River—great views on a sunny day—is a World War II-vintage early-warning radar station cleverly disguised as a farmhouse (with false windows and dormers) and barn.

In late June, Klamath's **Salmon Festival** attracts mostly locals for an unforgettable salmon barbecue, traditional Yurok dances, singing, basketry displays (not for sale), stick games, and logging skills contests. For more information about the area, contact the **Klamath Chamber of Commerce,** 800/200-2335, www.klamathcc.org.

Trees of Mystery

The site of old Klamath is now overgrown with blackberries. New Klamath is dominated by the Trees of Mystery, 5500 Hwy. 101, 707/482-2251 or 800/638-3389, www.treesofmystery.net, made famous by Robert Ripley's *Believe It or Not!* Chainsawed redwood characters are the featured attraction along Mystery's Trail of Tall Tales. The free End of the Trail Indian Museum is worth some time, though, with its end-of-the-line artifacts from everywhere in the U.S. and Canada. New and definitely different—a

Klamath, Trees of Mystery, Paul Bunyan

new way to explore a forest—is the **Sky Trail** aerial gondola. The gondola ride begins halfway along the walking trail and glides through the forest for 8 to 10 minutes, climbing to an elevation of almost 750 feet and allowing visitors to get the "big picture" of oceans, mountains, and forest. Some transfer assistance may be required for visitors in wheelchairs; a motorized cart is available for transport to the gondola loading site; call for details. Trees of Mystery admission is $17 adult, $10 kids age 4–10 (under 3 free), Sky Trail included.

Just south of Klamath is the **Tour-Thru-Tree,** 430 Hwy. 169, 707/482-5971, this one some 700 years old and chainsawed in 1976. To tour thru, take the Terwer Valley exit off Hwy. 101 and go east a quarter mile on Hwy. 169. The tree is open year-round. Admission is $2 per car, 50 cents for walk-ins and bike-ins.

PRAIRIE CREEK REDWOODS STATE PARK

An almost dangerous feature at Prairie Creek is the permanent and photogenic herd of Roosevelt elk usually grazing in the meadow area right along Hwy. 101. Whether or not a loaded logging truck is tailgating, drivers tend to screech to a halt at the mere sight of these magnificent creatures—which, despite their technically wild status and correspondingly unpredictable behavior, have that bemused and bored look of animals all too familiar with humankind. A separate herd of elk grazes in the coastal meadows along 11-mile **Gold Bluffs Beach,** also noted for its excellent whale-watching, sand dunes carpeted in wild strawberries, and a primitive campground with solar showers.

Elsewhere in 14,000-acre Prairie Creek Redwoods State Park, heavy winter rainfall and thick summer fog produce rainforest lushness. Redwoods rub elbows with 200-foot-tall Sitka spruce, Douglas fir, and Western hemlock above an amazing array of shrubs, ferns, and groundcover, not to mention 800 varieties of flowers and 500 different kinds of mushrooms. **Fern Canyon** is unforgettable. Also particularly worthwhile at Prairie Creek: beachcombing, surf fishing, nature walks and photography, picnicking, and camping. Prairie Creek's **Revelation Trail** loop, which includes a rope guide for the blind, has been proposed as the national standard for trail accessibility.

Near the visitor center/museum are some fine family campsites with flush toilets and hot showers. The more primitive beach campsites are first-come, first-camped, as are the adjacent hike-and-bike sites. Walk-in campsites are available at **Butler Creek Primitive Camp**. Register first with the office at Prairie Creek.

The park day-use fee is $5. For more park information, contact the **Prairie Creek Visitor Center** here, 707/464-6101 ext. 5300, open 9 A.M.–5 P.M. March through October 31, until 4 P.M. otherwise.

Orick and Vicinity

The privately owned wide-spot-in-the-road of Orick, mostly a strip of souvenir stands and supply stops (including a good little grocery), is the first outpost of civilization north of the park's excellent **Thomas H. Kuchel Visitor Center** at the mouth of Redwood Creek, 707/464-6101 ext. 5265. The center features a massive relief map of the park, wildlife and cultural displays, an excellent bookstore, plenty of videos, and complete information about the national park and the three state parks. It's wheelchair accessible and open daily 9 A.M.–5 P.M., closed Thanksgiving, Christmas, and New Year's Day. "Patio talks" and coast walks are offered in summer.

For more information on Orick, contact the **Orick Chamber of Commerce**, 707/488-2602, www.orick.net.

ACCOMMODATIONS

Camping

Each of the three state parks in the area offers developed family-type camping, with hot showers and other very basic comforts ($14–19). Disposal stations for RVs are available but hookups are not. These campgrounds are popular in summer, so advance reservations are advised; contact ReserveAmerica, 800/444-7275, www.reserve america.com. Though the Del Norte Camp-

ground is closed off-season due to very wet conditions (sometimes washouts), winter drop-in camping at the other campgrounds is usually no problem.

Primitive sites are also available at **Nickel Creek**, Endert's Beach; **Flint Ridge**, west of Klamath; **DeMartin**, between Damnation and Wilson Creeks along the Coastal Trail; and along the **Redwood Creek Trail**. Obtain the required permits at information centers or at park headquarters in Crescent City. Primitive camping at the national park sites is free, though there is a small fee for environmental campsites within the state parks.

Mystic Forest RV Park, about five miles nouth of Klamath at 15875 Hwy. 101, 707/482-4901, offers both grassy and wooded sites for RVs and tenters, $14–20. Abundant amenities, from hot showers and laundry to grocery and gift shop. At the north end of the Klamath River Bridge is the **Camper Corral**, 707/482-5741, offering 100 pull-through sites, most with full hookups and about half with cable TV (RV and tent sites, $14–23). Other amenities include heated swimming pool, hot showers, a Laundromat, rec hall, shuffleboard courts, and other recreation facilities. The **Chinook RV Resort**, 17465 Hwy. 101, 707/482-3511, $18 per night, is another angler's favorite.

Hostels and Motels

Accommodation prices in and around Orick are reasonable, partly because Redwood National Park is too far north for most visitors to California, but also because it's foggy here during peak tourist season. Most people follow the sun. Within national park boundaries but right on the coast—about 12 miles south of Crescent City at the Hwy. 101 junction with Wilson Creek Rd.—is the fabulous HI **Redwood National Park Hostel**, 14480 Hwy. 101 N. (at Wilson Creek Rd.), 707/482-8265 or 800/909-4776 #74 for reservations, www.norcalhostels.org, known locally as the DeMartin House. This is the grandly restored onetime home (circa 1908) of one of Del Norte County's pioneer families. The 30-bed hostel is perfect even for small group retreats, with a dining room, small dorm rooms, a common room cozied up with a woodstove, outdoor redwood decks with fine views, and good kitchen facilities. The hostel is wheelchair accessible. Couple and family rooms are available with adequate advance notice. The rate is $16 per night adults, $8 children.

Choice in area accommodations may seem meager, but the price is definitely right. Expect tariffs in the $50–100 range. One possibility is **Prairie Creek Motel,** next to Rolf's Park Café in Orick, Hwy. 101 at Davidson Rd., 707/488-3841. The **Motel Trees,** 15495 S Hwy. 101 (across from Trees of Mystery) in Klamath, 707/482-3152 or 800/848-2982, offers amenities including a tennis court, in-room color TV with movies, and an adjacent restaurant. Or try the comfortable **Ravenwood Motel** in Klamath at 151 Klamath Blvd., 707/482-5911 or 866/520-9875. The **Historic Requa Inn,** 451 Requa Rd., 707/482-1425 or 866/800-8777, www.requainn .com, is nothing fancy on the outside but quite appealing—an English country-style inn first opened in 1885. Some rooms have great views. The inn's **dining room** is open to guests for breakfast and dinner, to nonguests for dinner only (by reservation). **Rhodes End Bed & Breakfast,** 115 Trobitz Rd. in Klamath Glen, 707/482-1654, www.rhodes-end.com, offers three romantic rooms, great food, and an outdoor hot tub. Massage available, too.

FOOD

Most people camp, and bring their own provisions—the Eureka-Arcata area being the last best supply stop before heading north. Supplies are also available in Crescent City, just north of the park.

Best bet for a fascinating meal in Orick, not to mention friendly people, is **Rolf's Park Café,** 123664 Hwy. 101, 707/488-3841, on the highway north of Orick proper (take the Fern Canyon exit), open only in spring and summer. Tables are set in the solarium and (weather permitting) outside on the deck. Rolf Rheinschmidt is known for his exotic dinner specialties, like wild turkey, elk and buffalo steaks, wild boar and bear roasts, even antelope sausage, plus chicken and pasta dishes, vegetarian dishes, and forest fare like fiddlehead ferns and wild mushrooms. Rolf also cooks up some great breakfasts, including the house specialty German Farmers Omelette—a creation of eggs with ham, bacon, sausages, cheese, mushrooms, potatoes, and pasta topped with salsa and sour cream—as well as fine and filling pancakes. Lunch features Rolf's special clam chowder, grilled German sausage sandwiches, smoked salmon and sweet onions on rye, hot chicken and mushrooms, burgers, and salads. Wash it down with beer or wine, and have some linzertorte for dessert. Great place.

Other possibilities include the basic diner fare, giant cinnamon rolls, and good cream pies at the **Palm Cafe** in Orick, 121130 Hwy. 101, 707/488-3381, or a quick grocery stop at the **Orick Market,** 121175 Hwy. 101, 707/488-3501. Or try the **Historic Requa Inn,** 451 Requa Rd. in Klamath, 707/482-1425 (reservations advised). Ask locally for other possibilities.

INFORMATION AND SERVICES

In addition to the national park proper, three state parks—Prairie Creek, Del Norte, and Jedediah Smith, all covered above—are included within the larger park boundaries, protecting more redwoods (160,000 acres total for the four parks) and offering additional recreation and camping possibilities. Distinct though they are, the state and national parks are managed cooperatively. The centralized information source for all the parks is the **Redwood National and State Parks Information Center,** 1111 Second St. (at K St.) in Crescent City, 707/464-6101, www.nps.gov/redw. The center's telephone number includes recorded information on each of the individual parks in the system, and you can also reach a human during office hours; to contact each state park directly, dial the given extensions listed below. There is no fee for admission to Redwood National Park, but the day-use fee for the state parks is $5. Park headquarters and other visitor centers are closed on Thanksgiving, Christmas, and New Year's Day.

The **Thomas H. Kuchel Visitor Center,** near Orick at the old lumber mill site at the mouth of Redwood Creek (north of Freshwater Lagoon and west of the highway), 707/464-6101 ext. 5265, is an imposing, excellent interpretive museum. The enthusiastic staff is very helpful. Open daily 9 A.M.–5 P.M. Pick up a map for the park's trail system. Members of the Yurok tribe occasionally demonstrate the traditional brush dance; call for current information.

Other centers include the **Hiouchi Information Center,** on Hwy. 199 west of Hiouchi, 707/464-6101 ext. 5067, open 9 A.M.–5 P.M. mid-June to mid-September, where members of the Tolowa tribe sometimes offer a renewal dance demonstration, and the **Jedediah Smith Visitor Center** on Hwy. 101 in Hiouchi, 707/464-6101 ext. 5113, with history and natural history exhibits as well as campfire programs, junior ranger activities, and ranger-guided walks, open 9 A.M.–5 P.M. mid-May–Sept. The **Prairie Creek Visitor Center,** 127011 Newton B. Drury Scenic Parkway in Prairie Creek State Park, 707/464-6101, ext. 5300, open 9 A.M.–5 P.M. (4 P.M. in winter), features a natural history museum as well as a nature store.

Park Field Seminars

Redwood National Park Field Seminars, sponsored by the College of the Redwoods Del Norte campus, 883 W. Washington Blvd. in Crescent City, 707/464-9150, include kayak instruction for both the Smith and Klamath Rivers and workshop topics such as local Native American culture, birdlife, freshwater stream ecology, astronomy, and basic outdoor photography. Most field seminars are offered in summer.

Getting Here

Most people drive—and the immense size of the park makes a personal vehicle quite handy. **Greyhound,** 1603 Fourth St. in Eureka, 707/442-0370, or 500 E. Harding in Crescent City, 707/464-2807, stops on its way between those two cities at the Shoreline Deli just south of Orick, at Paul's Cannery in Klamath, and at the Redwood National Park Hostel north of Klamath. To fly into the area, nearest is the Arcata-Eureka Airport in McKinleyville, 3561 Boeing Ave., 707/839-1906. Rental cars are available there.

CRESCENT CITY AND VICINITY

Most of the world's Easter lilies, that ultimate modern-day symbol of resurrection, are grown north of Crescent City, the only incorporated city in Del Norte County. A proud if historically downtrodden town laid out in 1853 along the crescent moon harbor, Crescent City is a grim weatherbeaten gray, pounded so long by storms it has become one with the fog. Grim, too, is life for prisoners locked up just outside town at **Pelican Bay State Prison,** the state's largest maximum-security prison. The prison primes the community's economic pump with some $40 million per year and was the focus of California senator Barry Keene's Name That Prison contest. Among the unselected but otherwise superior suggestions from clever north coast minds: The Big Trees Big House, Camp Runamok, Dungeness Dungeon, Saint Dismos State (a reference to the patron saint of prisoners), and Slammer-by-the-Sea.

Crescent City still suffers from the 1964 tsunami that tore the town off its moorings after the big Alaska earthquake, as well as a freak typhoon with 80-mile-an-hour winds that hit in 1972. Life goes on, however; the once devastated and denuded waterfront is now an attractive local park and convention center. Crabbing from the public **Citizens' Wharf,** built at Crescent Harbor with entirely local resources and volunteer labor when government rebuilding assistance fell through, is especially good. The French-designed harbor breakwater is unique, a system of interlocking, 25-ton concrete "tetrapods."

Come in February for Crescent City's **World-Championship Crab Races,** an event that includes a world-class crab feed, Dungeness crab races, children's games, and an art fair. March brings the annual **Aleutian Goose Festival,** with more than 80 events, workshops, and guided wilderness excursions celebrating area nature reserves, birding, and cultural heritage. Crescent City's **July 4th** festivities include everything from

© ROBERT HOLMES/CALTOUR

Crescent City Harbor

cribbage and kite flying to sandcastle sculpting. At Smith River just north, the local **Easter in July Lily Festival** celebrates the lily bloom, the festivities including sunrise church services, a lily float contest, and food and crafts booths decked out with you-know-what. Also fun the last weekend in July is the two-mile **Gasquet Raft Race** on the Smith River, with contestants limited to rafts and other crafts paddled only by hand. The local pronunciation is "GAS-key," by the way, in the same vein as "Del-NORT" County.

Sights

See the **Battery Point Lighthouse** near town, originally known as the Crescent City Lighthouse and first lit in December of 1856. Weather and tides permitting walk out to it on a path more than 100 years old and visit the island museum, 707/464-3089, open Wed.–Sun. 10 A.M.–4 P.M. (small donation); call for the Apr.–Sept. tour schedule. Decommissioned in 1953, though it was 12 more years before they turned the light out, the Battery Point Lighthouse was restored in 1981 by Craig Miller, with local donations of materials. The Del Norte His-

torical Society has operated the light as a private navigational aid since 1982. Spend some time in the **Del Norte County Historical Society Museum,** 577 H St., 707/464-3922, to appreciate its collection of Native American artifacts, quilts and kitchenware, and logging and mining paraphernalia—and to get the local lighthouse story. Open Mon.–Sat. 10 A.M.–4 P.M. (admission by donation). Notable at the museum is the first-order lens—over 18 feet tall—taken from the **St. George's Reef Lighthouse,** the town's second and known as the nation's most expensive, built after the tragic loss of the sidewheeler SS *Brother Jonathan* at North Seal Rock in 1865. Restoration of the now-retired St. George's, one of the most dangerously situated lighthouses anywhere, is now beginning; helicopter tours will one day be offered. Stop by the historic **McNulty House** nearby, 710 H St., 707/464-5186, to take in exhibits of antiques, old clocks, and works of area artists.

Another place to find just the right memento is the gift shop at the **Northcoast Marine Mammal Center** in Beachfront Park, 424 Howe Dr., 707/465-6265, www.northcoastmarinemammal.org, a nonprofit rescue and rehabilitation center (donations always appreciated).

Smith River

North of Crescent City, just shy of the Oregon border, is the town of Smith River, where the river flows to the sea. If you wind up here at the end of the day, check out the **Ship Ashore Resort**, 12370 Hwy. 101 N, 707/487-3141 or 800/487-3141, www.ship-ashore.com, with motel rooms $50–100, or its popular steak and seafood restaurant, the **Captain's Galley**. The bizarre Ship Ashore Museum and Gift Shop by the highway—a 160-foot-long ship beached in the parking lot—clues diners in to the turnoff. Campers can stay at the Ship Ashore's RV park.

Camping

Nothing in Crescent City beats camping at Jedediah Smith Redwoods State Park, though four national park or national forest campgrounds lie northeast of town near Gasquet, others are to the southeast via Southfork Rd., and still more are scattered through the Smith River/Six Rivers region.

Expect rates of $15–30 at private RV campgrounds. Options in town include the **Harbor RV Anchorage**, 159 Starfish Way, 707/464-1724, paved parking right on the beach at the north end of town; the **Bayside RV Park** near the boat harbor, 750 Hwy. 101 N., 707/464-9482; and the **Crescent City Redwoods KOA**, 4241 Hwy. 101 N., 707/464-5744 or 800/562-5754, www.koa.com, with both tent and RV sites as well as cabins. Another attractive possibility, a 20-acre wooded site, is the **Village Camper Inn RV Park,** 1543 Parkway Dr., 707/464-3544. You can also park the Winnie at the **Del Norte County Fairgrounds**, 421 Hwy. 101 N., 707/464-9556, where facilities include showers and a covered driving range ($8–10 per night).

Accommodations

Motel rates in Crescent City drop markedly in winter. Otherwise decent rooms can be found for $50–100. The only motel on the beach is the aptly named **Crescent Beach Motel**, next to the Beachcomber restaurant at 1455 Hwy. 101 N, 707/464-5436, www.crescentbeach motel.com, with appealing refurbished rooms—almost all of them opening out onto the beach. Appealing in a more introverted way is the **Curly Redwood Lodge**, 701 Hwy. 101 S (a half mile south of town on the highway, near the marina), 707/464-2137, www.curlyredwoodlodge.com, a definite blast from the past—1957, to be exact. That was the year the motel first opened, built from the wood of one massive "curly" redwood; the spectacular wood grain is still proudly exhibited throughout. The motel also features large rooms, color TV with cable, and coffee available in the lobby.

The **Crescent City Travelodge,** 353 L St., 707/464-6124 or 800/578-7878, www.travelodge .com, offers 27 rooms, TV (with HBO, ESPN, and CNN), a sauna, and complimentary continental breakfast. The **Super 8,** 685 Hwy. 101 S., 707/464-4111 or 800/800-8000, offers in-room coffeemakers, cable TV with HBO, a coin-op laundry, and fax service (incoming faxes free). The **Best Value Inn,** north of town at 440 Hwy. 101 N, 707/464-4141, features both a sauna and indoor hot tub. **Econo Lodge,** 725 Hwy. 101 N., 707/464-6106, also offers a sauna and hot tub, as well as complimentary breakfast.

Just south of town and also across from the marina is the **Best Western Northwoods Inn,** 655 Hwy. 101 S., 707/464-9771 or 800/557-3396. Amenities here include in-room hair dryers, irons, and coffeemakers, along with high-speed Internet service, a guest laundry, and spa. Good onsite restaurant, free breakfast. Nearby is the fairly new **Anchor Beach Inn,** 880 Hwy. 101 S. at Anchor Way, 707/464-2600 or 800/837-4116, with microwaves and refrigerators, coffeemakers, hair dryers, free continental breakfast.

The historic 18-room **Patrick Creek Lodge** 13950 Hwy. 199 east of Gasquet, 707/457-3323, www.patrickcreeklodge.com, offers fabulous Smith River trout fishing in summer, salmon and steelhead fishing from fall through spring, and rooms with antiques year-round.

The Victorian **White Rose Mansion Inn** in Smith River near the Oregon border, 149 S. Fred

North Coast

Haight Dr., 707/487-9260, www.whiterose mansion.com, offers something for bed-and-breakfast fans—specifically, seven nicely decorated guest rooms, including a cottage suitable for families with children. Most are $100–150. Two rooms with two-person whirlpool tub are $150–250. There's also a three-bedroom beach house, $150–250.

Food

Standard grocery chains, like Safeway, exist in Crescent City. Better for replenishing the picnic basket, though, is a stop (and plant tour) at the north coast's noted **Rumiano Cheese Company,** 511 Ninth St. (at E St.), 707/465-1535 or 866/328-2433.

Some restaurants here don't take credit cards, so bring cash. A basic for breakfast is **Glen's Bakery & Restaurant,** 722 Third St., 707/464-2914, where you can get a sticky bun for breakfast and a mean bowl of clam chowder or fresh fish dishes for lunch. **Thai House,** 105 N St., 707/464-2427, is the place for noodle dishes and spicy seafood. The **China Hut Restaurant,** 928 Ninth St., 707/464-4921, serves Cantonese, Mandarin, and Szechuan. **Da Lucianna Ristorante,** 575 Hwy. 101 S., 707/465-6566, is elegant for Italian.

For seafood, head for the **Beachcomber Restaurant,** 1400 Hwy. 101 S. (at South Beach), 707/464-2205, right on the beach. **Harbor View Grotto,** 150 Starfish Way, 707/464-3815, offers no-frills "view dining" along with fresh seafood and steaks.

For hearty prime rib, seafood, and fabulous Sunday brunch served up with a scenic drive, head for the **Patrick Creek Lodge** on Hwy. 199 east of Gasquet, 707/457-3323. North along the coast in Gold Beach, Oregon, and offering the most sophisticated dining for miles around is **Chives,** 29212 Hwy. 101, 541/247-4121.

Information and Services

The **Crescent City-Del Norte County Chamber of Commerce Visitor Center** is at 1001 Front St., 707/464-3174 or 800/343-8300, www.northerncalifornia.net. **Greyhound,** 500 E. Harding St., 707/464-2807, has two buses heading north and two heading south daily. The **post office** is at 751 Second St. (at H St.), 707/464-2151. The **public library** is at 190 Price Mall, 707/464-9793. For medical care and emergencies, contact **Sutter Coast Hospital,** 800 E. Washington Blvd., 707/464-8511 (information) or 707/464-8888 (emergency room).

South from Redwood National Park

HUMBOLDT LAGOONS STATE PARK

The community of **Big Lagoon** just off the highway north of Patrick's Point is also the site of Big Lagoon County Park with its dirty sand beaches and camping. Humboldt Lagoons State Park includes Big Lagoon itself and the miles-long barrier beach separating it from the sea, along with three other lagoons, a total of 1,500 beachfront acres best for beachcombing, boating, fishing, surfing, and windsurfing (swimming only for the hardy or foolhardy).

Next north is freshwater **Dry Lagoon**, five miles of sandy beach and heavy surf particularly popular with agate fanciers and black jade hunters. Camp beside this marshy lagoon at one of six environmental campsites: outhouse, no water, no dogs. Ocean fishing is possible in winter only, but there's no fishing at Dry Lagoon, which lives up to its name most of the year. **Stone Lagoon** two miles north is prettier but smaller, with boat-in primitive campsites. A half mile farther north is part-private, part-public **Freshwater Lagoon,** planted with trout for seasonal fishing (no official camping here, though RVs are a permanent fixture along the highway). The **Harry A. Merlo State Recreation Area,** 800-plus acres named for a noted Louisiana-Pacific executive, entwines throughout the lagoon area.

Boat-in campsites are $12, Dry hike-in sites $12. There is no day-use fee. The small **Humboldt Lagoons Visitors Center** is at Stone Lagoon, open summers only. For more information and to reserve campsites, contact **Humboldt Lagoons State Park,** 15336 Hwy. 101, 707/488-2041.

PATRICK'S POINT STATE PARK

The Yuroks who for centuries seasonally inhabited this area believed that the spirit of the porpoises came to live at modern-day Patrick's Point State Park just before people populated the world—and that the seven offshore sea stacks that stretch north to south like a spine were the last earthly abode of the immortals. Most impressive of these rugged monuments is **Ceremonial Rock,** nicknamed "stairway to the stars" by fond rock climbers.

Old trails once walked by native peoples lead to and beyond rocky **Patrick's Point,** one of the finest whale-watching sites along the coast. "Patrick" was Patrick Beegan, the area's first white settler and a warrior after Indian scalps. Stroll the two-mile **Rim Trail** for the views, but stay back from the hazardous cliff edge. Sea lions are common on the park's southern offshore rocks near **Palmer's Point.** The short trail scrambling north from near the campground (steep going) leads to long, sandy, and aptly named **Agate Beach,** noted for its many-colored, glasslike stones.

For all its natural wonders, Patrick's Point is also fine for people (good picnicking). Except for mushroomers and whale-watchers, best visiting weather is late spring, early summer, and fall. **Whale-watching** from Ceremonial Rock or Patrick's Point (weekend ranger programs offered in January and February) is best from November to January but also good on the whales' return trip, February to May. Dress warmly and bring binoculars. Call the park for current whale-watching information. The **museum** here features natural history and native cultural exhibits. The park's day-use fee is $6. The park's **Sumêg Village** is a reconstructed traditional Yurok village, with native plant garden adjacent.

Patrick's Point has three developed campgrounds: **Agate Beach, Abalone,** and **Penn Creek** (west of the meadows), with 124 naturally sheltered tent or trailer sites and hot showers ($15–20 per night). ReserveAmerica reservations, 800/444-7275, www.reserveamerica.com, are mandatory during the summer. In addition, there are two group camps (complete with covered picnic areas and propane barbecues) also reservable for day use and 20 hike-and-bike campsites ($10–12). For more information, call the park at 707/677-3570.

TRINIDAD AND VICINITY

A booming supply town of 3,000 in the early 1850s and later a whaling port, Trinidad is now a charming coastal village recognized as the oldest incorporated town on California's north coast. Impressive **Trinidad Head** looms over the small bay, with a white granite cross at the summit replacing the first monument placed there by Bodega y Cuadra for Spain's Charles III.

The **Trinidad Memorial Lighthouse** on Main St. was the village's original light tower and was relocated to town as a fishermen's memorial. It features a giant two-ton fog bell. The **Trinidad Museum,** 529-B Trinity St., 707/677-3883, offers displays about the region's natural and cultural history. It's open in summer, Fri.–Sun. 1–4 P.M. Humboldt State University's **Fred Telonicher Marine Laboratory,** 570 Ewing St., 707/826-3671, has an aquarium open to the public, as well as a touch tank for getting intimate with intertidal invertebrates. It's open year-round, weekdays 9 A.M.–5 P.M., and also weekends 10 A.M.–5 P.M. when school is in session.

Besides solitary beachcombing on **Trinidad State Beach,** 707/677-3570 (good for moonstones and driftwood, day-use only, no day-use fee); surfing at rugged **Luffenholtz Beach** two miles south of town; and breathtaking scenery, the area's claim to fame is salmon fishing. Commercial and sport-fishing boats, skiffs, and tackle shops line Trinidad Bay.

For more information on the area, contact the **Trinidad Chamber of Commerce,** Main St. and Patrick's Point Dr., 707/677-1610.

Accommodations

For the most reasonable accommodations, head north on Patrick's Point Dr. to the state park and its excellent camping (see below). A lovely alternative is **Azalea Glen RV Park & Campground,** 3883 Patricks Point Dr., 707/677-3068, http://azaleaglen.com, a serene, lush garden-like setting complete with lily ponds, azaleas, and ducks. RV and tent sites are $24–30 in summer. No generators. Quite nice for cabins (most have kitchens) is the recently refurbished **Bishop Pine Lodge,** 1481 Patrick's

© ROBERT HOLMES/CALTOUR

Memorial Lighthouse, Trinidad

Point Dr., 707/677-3314, www.bishop-pinelodge.com, also featuring two-bedroom units and cottages with hot tubs. Most are $50–100. Playground area, well-equipped exercise room. Pet friendly, too. The new **View Crest Lodge,** 3415 Patrick's Point Point Dr., 707/677-3393, www.viewcrestlodge.com, also offers comfortable cabins with all the modern comforts; some have whirlpool tubs; most are $100–150. RV and tent camping are available, $16–20.

In town, across from the lighthouse, the **Trinidad Bay Bed and Breakfast,** 560 Edwards St., 707/677-0840, www.trinidadbaybnb.com, is a Cape Cod–style home circa 1950. It offers two standard rooms and two suites, all with king or queen beds and private baths (one suite with fireplace). Closed Dec.–Jan. Most rates are $150–250. About five miles north of Trinidad proper and adjacent to the state park is the **Lost Whale Bed and Breakfast Inn,** 3452 Patrick's Point Dr., 707/677-9105 or 800/677-7859, www.lostwhaleinn.com, a contemporary Cape Cod with eight guest rooms (all with private baths, most with great ocean views), full breakfast, hot tub, and afternoon refreshments. Rates are $150–250. Ask about the Farmhouse, a two-bedroom house on five acres, also available for rent. Nearby is the, very nice **Turtle Rocks Inn B&B,** 3392 Patrick's Point Dr., 707/677-3707, www.turtlerocksinn.com, which offers six guest rooms on three oceanfront acres. Each room has a private bath, private deck, and modern amenities. Rates, $150–250 (lower rates in the off-season), include a gourmet hot breakfast.

Food

In April or May each year, the town hosts a massive **crab feed** at Town Hall. Otherwise, *the* place to eat in Trinidad is the very relaxed and rustic **Seascape Restaurant** (once the Dock Cafe) at the harbor, 707/677-3762, which serves hearty breakfasts, excellent omelettes, and seafood specialties (good early-bird specials). Open 7 A.M.–9 P.M. daily. Reservations are a good idea at dinner. Other dining choices include the **Trinidad Bay Eatery & Gallery,** at Trinity and Parker, 707/677-3777, open Wed.–Sun. for breakfast and lunch. But best of all, just north of town, is the excellent **Larrupin Cafe,** 1658 Patrick's Point Dr., 707/677-0230, a friendly and fine place noted for things like barbecued cracked crab, barbecued oysters, steamed mussels, and chicken breast wrapped up with artichokes and cream cheese in phyllo dough. Or try the mesquite-grilled portobello mushroom on slices of Spanish cheeses and potato bread. Excellent desserts, too. No credit cards. Open Thurs.–Tues. nights.

South from Trinidad

Off Hwy. 101 via Clam Beach Drive is **Clam Beach County Park,** a good place for collecting agates and moonstones; camping is available for $8 a night. Adjacent is **Little River State Beach,** where Josiah Gregg and company arrived from Weaverville in December 1849, exhausted and near starvation. Little River has broad sandy beaches backed by dunes, and offers clamming in season and good surf fishing. For more information, call 707/488-2041.

Heading south is **McKinleyville,** something of an Arcata suburb "where horses still have the right of way." Stop in for pub grub and a frothy pint of Black Bear Stout at **Six Rivers Brewing Co.,** 1300 Central Ave., 707/839-7580. The town is adjacent to the Azalea State Reserve and offers good whale-watching from **McKinleyville Vista Point.** For more information on the area, contact: **McKinleyville Chamber of Commerce,** 2196 Central Ave. 707/839-2449.

EXCURSION INLAND: WILLOW CREEK

In the Mad River Valley just northeast of Arcata on Hwy. 299 is **Blue Lake,** a tiny town in farm, dairy, and timber country. One thing *not* in Blue Lake is a lake, due to the Mad River changing its course some time ago—the original lake is now a marsh. Among things that are here: the **Blue Lake Museum,** 330 Railroad Ave. (in the old Arcata and Mad River Railroad Depot), 707/668-4188, which is stuffed with historic memorabilia (open limited hours). The old railroad itself—known locally as the Annie and Mary Railroad, after two company bookkeepers—was originally called the Union Wharf and Plank Walk Company and boasted 7.5 total miles of track. Plank Walk employees proudly declared: "We're not as long as other lines, but we're just as wide." Come in July or August (call the chamber for exact date) for **Annie & Mary Day,** with a parade, barbecue, music, and theater. Summer also brings the fabulous **Dell'Arte Mad River Festival,** performances of physical theater, music, comedy, storytelling, clowning, puppetry, and more, hosted from mid-June through July by Blue Lake's famed **Dell'Arte International School of Physical Theatre,** 707/668-5663, www.dellarte.com. For more information on the area, contact the **Blue Lake Chamber of Commerce,** 431 First St. in Blue Lake, 707/668-5345.

Willow Creek, east from Blue Lake on Hwy. 299, serves as Northern California's Bigfoot headquarters. The legendary man-ape is everywhere, including the **Big Foot Golf and Country Club,** 530/629-2977. Stop in at the **Willow Creek-China Flat Museum,** on Hwy. 299 at Hwy. 96, 530/629-2653, to see historical exhibits and a Bigfoot Center, with casts of Bigfoot footprints, literature about the mythic creature, and other Bigfoot memorabilia. Open Fri.–Sun. 10 A.M.–4 P.M. Continue east on Hwy. 299 to follow the Trinity River back to its source near Weaverville and the Trinity Alps. If the turbulent Trinity looks too inviting to pass up, arrange to raft it with **Bigfoot Rafting Company,** Hwy 299 (at Willow Way), 530/629-2263 or 800/722-2223, www.bigfootrafting.com. For more information on the area, contact the **Willow Creek Chamber of Commerce,** Hwy. 299 and Hwy. 96, 530/629-2693, www.willow creekchamber.com.

Arcata and Vicinity

Arcata is Eureka's alter-ego, no more resigned to the status quo than the sky here is blue. In 1996, Arcata made national news when a majority of Green Party candidates was elected to the city council. Environmental activism is an everyday concern here, and far-from-the-mainstream publications are available even at the visitor center. In addition to Arcata's world-famous **Cross-Country Kinetic Sculpture Race** on Memorial Day weekend, popular annual events include April's **Godwit Days Spring Migration Bird Festival;** the **April Fools Income Tax Annual Auction,** a benefit for the North Coast Environmental Center; and the September **North Country Fair,** one of the West Coast's premier craft fairs. A relaxed and liberal town, Arcata is determined to make a difference.

It would be easy to assume that the genesis of this backwoods grass-roots activism is the presence of academia, namely Humboldt State University, the only university on the north coast. But the beginnings of the Arcata *attitude* go back much further. When Arcata was still a frontier

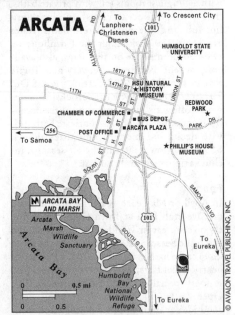

© AVALON TRAVEL PUBLISHING, INC.

trading post known as Union Town, 24-year-old writer Bret Harte set the tone. An unknown underling on Arcata's *The Northern Californian* newspaper between 1858 and 1860, an outraged Harte—temporarily in charge while his editor was out of town—wrote a scathing editorial about the notorious Indian Island massacre of Wiyot villagers by settlers and was summarily run out of town, shoved along on his way to fame and fortune. Besides activism, general community creativity, and education, farming and fishing are growing concerns. Appropriately enough, the popular semipro baseball team, a proud part of the community since 1944, is called the Humboldt Crabs.

SIGHTS

The presence of **Humboldt State University** keeps things in Arcata lively. Humboldt State, east of town on Fickle Hill near 14th St. and Grant Ave., 707/826-3011, www.humboldt.edu, emphasizes the study of forestry practices, fisheries and wildlife management, and oceanography. On campus, worthwhile sights include the arboretum, fish hatchery, and art gallery. Off campus, the **HSU Natural History Museum,** 1315 G St., 707/826-4479, features local natural history displays, an impressive fossil collection, and lots of hands-on exploration. Open Tues.–Sat. 10 A.M.–5 P.M. Admission is free (donations appreciated).

Phillip's House Museum, Seventh and Union Sts., is one of Arcata's oldest buildings, offering great views of Humboldt Bay and, inside, a peek into 19th- and early 20th-century life. The local Historical Sites Society, 707/822-4722, www.arcatahistory.org, offers tours every Sunday 2–4 P.M. and by appointment.

Arcata's downtown **Arcata Plaza,** with its memorial statue of President McKinley and out-of-place palm trees, is custom-made for watching people come and go from surrounding cafés and shops, or for resting up after a tour of local Victorian homes—if you don't mind hangin' out with the hang-out crowd. Several of the historic buildings framing the plaza are worth a look, including the **Jacoby Storehouse** on the south

side at 791 Eighth St., 707/822-2434, a stone-and-brick beauty with iron shutters that now houses a railroad museum, restaurants, shops, and bank. Also admire the striking **Hotel Arcata** on Ninth and the restored 1914 **Minor Theatre** at 10th and H Streets, 707/822-3456 and 707/822-5177, www.minortheaters.com, the nation's oldest operating movie theater built specifically for feature films—and still *the* place to catch art-house, classic, and current films.

Many local businesses exemplify Arcata's fairly elevated and imaginative environmentalism, such as **Fire & Light,** 45 Ericson Ct., 707/825-7500 or 800/844-2223, www.fireandlight.com, which produces hand-poured, hand-pressed recycled glass—dinnerware, glassware, dipping dishes, footed candlestands, and more—in a translucent rainbow of "green" colors, from aqua and cobalt to celery, citrus, and copper. The amount of recycled clear glass in each piece varies by color but averages 85 percent. Tours by appointment.

To get away from the crowds, visit Arcata's parks. Arcata's pretty 20-acre **Redwood Park** is off Park (head east on 11th St.). Just beyond is the town's beloved 600-acre **Arcata Community Forest,** with its second-growth redwoods, educational **Historic Logging Trail,** hiking and mountain-biking trails, and picnicking. For more information and maps, contact or stop by the city Environmental Services Department, in City Hall at 736 F St., 707/822-8184. To get to **Mad River Beach County Park** in the Arcata Bottoms, with its beach, miles of dunes at the mouth of the Mad River, and good ocean fishing, take Alliance Rd. from K St. to Spear Ave., turn left onto Upper Bay Rd., then left again.

Azalea State Reserve

This 30-acre preserve just north of Arcata on North Bank Rd. (Hwy. 200) is famous for its cascading, fragrant pinkish-white western azalea blooms (good in April and May, usually best around Memorial Day) and other wildflowers, all in the company of competing rhododendrons. Good steelhead fishing can be found in the area along North Bank Rd. near Hwy. 299's Mad River bridge. Open daily for day use only, sunrise to sunset. For more information, call 707/488-2041.

SCULPTURE RACE: A MOVING TRIBUTE TO "FORM OVER SUBSTANCE"

If you're in the area for Memorial Day weekend, don't miss the exuberant 38-mile, three-day transbay **World Championship Great Arcata to Ferndale Cross-Country Kinetic Sculpture Race.** Founded in 1969 by Ferndale artists Hobart Brown and Jack Mays, the race is a moving display of "form over substance." It's an almost-anything-goes tribute to unbridled imagination, but it does have a few rules. The mobile "sculptures" must be people-powered (though it is legal to get an assist from water, wind, or gravity); amphibious; and inspired by the event's high moral and ethical standards—such as "cheating is a privilege, not a right." (Kinetic cops patrol the course and interpret the rules.) Otherwise, anything goes—and rolls, floats, and flounders, through sand, saltwater, and swamp slime—in this ultimate endurance contest, also known at the Triathlon of the Art World.

Coming in first, even dragging in last, is not the point of this race. The contest's most coveted award is the Aurea Mediocritas, for the entry finishing closest to dead center—because, as the founders explain, winning and losing are both extremes, therefore "perfection lies somewhere in the middle." However, losing has its virtues, too, so the much-coveted Loser Award has been reinstated. Even spectators are part of the competition, thanks to the Most Worthy Fanatical Spectator Award.

Favorite recent entries have included the the Worry Wart, Grape Balls of Fire, Prince of Tides, Megasoreass, and Duane Flatmo's six-person Tide Fools. Some race survivors are on display at the sculpture museum in Ferndale. Prerace festivities include the **Kinetic Kickoff Party** and the **Rutabaga Queen Pageant** at Eureka's Ritz Club. For information about the race, now managed by the **Humboldt Kinetic Association,** call 707/845-1717 or see www.kineticsculpicturerace.org. Honorable former sculptures are exhibited at the **Kinetic Sculpture Museum,** 580 Main St. in Ferndale, open daily.

M Arcata Bay and Marsh

Walk along Arcata Bay to appreciate the impromptu scrap wood sculptures sometimes in bloom. The most fascinating bayside sights, though, are at the Arcata Marsh and Wildlife Preserve at the foot of I Street. This was one of the first wildlife preserves in the U.S. to be created from an old landfill dump and "enhanced" by treated sewage water. The aesthetic settling ponds offer excellent bird-watching. In fact, more than 200 bird species, river otters, muskrats, and pond-raised trout and salmon can all be viewed here. Facilities are well-designed for nature voyeurs, featuring trails, benches, interpretive displays, and bird blinds. Central to the reclaimed marsh's success is the Arcata Wastewater Aquaculture Project, which hatches and raises steelhead trout, coastal cutthroat trout, chinook salmon, and sturgeon. The project's T-shirt logo, Flush with Pride, depicts a fish jumping out of a toilet. For more information—and to get your T-shirts—stop by or call the **Arcata Marsh Interpretive**

Center, 600 S. G St., 707/826-2359, open daily 1–5 P.M. The Redwood Region Audubon Society, 707/826-7031, offers guided walks of the preserve at 8:30 A.M. every Saturday morning, rain or shine, leaving from the end of I St.; Friends of the Arcata Marsh offers guided walks every Saturday at 2 P.M., leaving from the interpretive center. Birders can call the Birdbox hotline, 707/822-5666, for information on recent sightings.

Lanphere-Christensen Dunes Preserve

Just east of Arcata, on the Samoa Peninsula near the Mad River Slough, is the 300-acre Lanphere-Christensen Dunes Preserve, managed by the U.S. Fish and Wildlife Service. It's open to the public by permit, obtained from the office at 6800 Lanphere Rd., 707/822-6378. No camping is permitted.

The Wiyot people once camped in summer on the pristine dunes and beach here, gathering berries in the coastal pine and spruce forest, and clamming, fishing, and hunting. Settlers later grazed cattle in this fragile ecosystem, which today is noted for its many well-preserved plant communities, from vernal pools and salt marsh to forest.

First purchased and protected in the 1940s by the Lanpheres, biologists at the university, the area is unique for another reason. At this latitude, the northern and southern dune floras overlap, meaning rare and typical plantlife from both are present as well as more than 200 species of birds and other animals. The best dune wildflowers come in June, but every season holds its attractions. From April to September, bring mosquito repellent. Rain gear is wise during the rest of the year, and always wear soft-soled shoes.

Friends of the Dunes leads nature tours at the dunes and sponsors environmental projects there. Tours begin at the Pacific Union School parking lot, 3001 Janes Road. For more information and to receive the organization's quarterly *Dunesberry* newsletter, call 707/444-1397.

ACCOMMODATIONS

Camp at Patrick's Point if at all possible. If not, the **Mad River Rapids RV Park,** 3501 Janes Rd. (north of town at the Giuntoli Ln./Janes Rd. exit), 707/822-7275 or 800/822-7776, www.madriverrv.com, is thoroughly civilized full-service facility offering paved sites with full hookups and cable TV, heated pool and spa, restrooms, showers, a laundry, minimart, video arcade, fitness room, tennis and basketball courts, playground, and fish-cleaning station. Each site has a patio, picnic table, and lawn. Rates are $29 and up.

Very nice—and right on the plaza, close to everything—is the refurbished and welcoming 1915 **Hotel Arcata,** 708 Ninth St., 707/826-0217 or 800/344-1221, www.hotelarcata.com, with most rooms $50–100, two-bedroom suites $100–150. If you'd prefer a B&B, equally affordable just a few blocks' stroll from Arcata Plaza is the **Lady Anne,** 902 14th St., 707/822-2797, an 1888 Queen Anne Victorian which features five guest rooms and the Writers Retreat suite, some with fireplaces, all with abundant antiques and plush guest robes. Full breakfast,

bikes to borrow, too. The modest **Fairwinds Motel,** 1674 G St., 707/822-0568, $50–100, also offers easy access to campus.

Most local motels are fairly inconveniently located along Valley West Blvd., off Hwy. 101 north of town; take the Giuntoli Ln./Janes Rd. exit and turn right. All offer rooms in the $50–100 range, though some also have higher-priced options. Reliable choices include **Arcata Super 8,** 4887 Valley West, 707/822-8888 or 800/800-8000, and good ol' **Motel 6,** 4755 Valley West, 707/822-7061 or 800/466-8356, www.motel6.com. There are solid, somewhat pricier options, all featuring a heated indoor pool and whirlpool spa, including the pet-friendly **Best Western Arcata Inn,** 4827 Valley West, 707/826-0313 or 800/528-1234.

FOOD

First stop for those just passing through should be **Arcata Co-op,** Eighth and I Streets, 707/822-5947, a natural-foods store, bakery, and deli with an abundance of organic everything, open 9 A.M.–9 P.M. (until 8 P.M. on Sunday). Healthy groceries, vitamins, and health-care products, as well as a juice bar, deli/café, and a Ramone's Bakery outpost, are all available at **Wildberries Marketplace,** 747 13th St. (at the top of G), 707/822-0095, open daily 7 A.M.–11 P.M. Wildberries is also the site of the **Arcata Certified Farmers Market,** held June–Oct. on Tuesday, 3–6 P.M. The **Arcata Plaza Certified Farmers Market** is held May through November at the Arcata Plaza (Eighth and G Sts.) on Saturday, 9 A.M.–1 P.M., For details on both, call 707/441-9999.

Basics

Los Bagels, 1061 I St., 707/822-3150, is largely a student hangout but every bit as popular as the Eureka shop, serving mostly coffee, bagels, and bread items with south-of-the-border flair. The **Wildflower Cafe and Bakery,** 1604 G St., 707/822-0360, has fresh bakery items, veggie food, homemade soups and salads, and "macrobiotic night" every Wednesday. **Café Mokka,** 495 J St. (at Fifth), 707/822-2228, serves decadent, incredibly good pastries, good coffee, excellent espresso, and—this is different—Finnish Country Sauna and Tubs out back, private outdoor hot tubs and sauna cabins for rent. Another great java joint, serving a variety of "organic varietals" and special blends, is **Muddy Waters Coffee Co.** at 1603 G Street, 707/826-2233, www.ilovemud .com, also an immensely popular local jazz, blues, and bluegrass venue. But don't miss **Sacred Grounds Organic Coffee Roasters,** 686 F St., 707/822-0690, www.sacredgroundscoffee.com.

Immensely popular for breakfast and lunch and everyone's favorite for brunch is **Crosswinds,** 860 10th St., 707/826-2133. If you're in the mood for coffee and some spectacular dessert, head for **Ramone's Bakery & Café,** 600 F St., 707 826-9000.

Frequent winner of local Best Burrito awards is **Rico's Tacos,** 686 F St., 707/826-2572, a best bet for inexpensive lunch. An all-around Mexican favorite is **Luzmila's,** 1288 G St., 707/822-5200. Immensely popular near the Minor Theatre is the **Arcata Pizza & Deli,** 1057 H St., 707/822-4650, which features a good variety of vegetarian choices among its pizza, sandwich, soup, and salad selections. Other lunch hotspots include the **Hole in the Wall** sandwich shop, Sixth and G Sts., 707/822-7407, open daily 10 A.M.–6 P.M., and **Japhy's Soup and Noodles,** 1563 G St., 707/826-2594.

Best burger bet is **Stars Hamburgers,** 1535 G St., 707/826-1379. For homegrown brew and good basic pub fare (a bit heavy on the grease) along with pool tables and Oakland Raiders football memorabilia, try the **Humboldt Brewing Co.,** 856 10th St., 707/826-1734, www.humbrew .com, owned and operated by Super Bowl champ Mario Celotto and his brother, Vince.

Higher End

Abruzzi in Jacoby's Storehouse, facing the plaza at 791 Eighth St., 707/826-2345, is a long-running slice of real Italiana here in the foggy north. Fresh daily are the baguettes, breadsticks, and tomato-onion-and-fennel-seed bread, along with Humboldt-grown veggies and seafood specialties. Good calzones, wonderful pastas. And do try the 14-layer torte. Now, however, Arcata also boasts a stylish branch of beloved **Mazzotti's** on the plaza

at 733 Eighth St., 707/822-1900, featuring everything from Sicilian pizzas to pasta primavera with bay shrimp and scallops. For friendly, family-style Italian and fabulous fresh pastas, those in the know head for **La Trattoria,** 30 Sunny Brae Centre, 707/822-6101. How will you ever choose?

Another relative newcomer is super-sophisticated **Jambalaya** American bistro, 915 H St., 707/822-4766, www.thejambalaya.com, an open-kitchen setup serving up fresh seafood and regionally raised meats, fresh vegetables, and organic local produce in dishes such as portobella Napoleon and fresh Humboldt Bay oysters with smoky chipotle aioli. Open weekdays only for lunch, Mon.–Sat. for dinner (extended hours in summer). Kids menu too. Dinner-only **Folie Douce,** 1551 G St., between 15th and 16th, 707/822-1042, www.holyfolie.com, is regionally famous for its exotic and stylish wood fire-baked pizzas—everything from Thai chicken to green coconut curried prawns with fresh mango, jalapeño, and cilantro. Reservations wise.

INFORMATION AND SERVICES

The helpful **Arcata Chamber of Commerce** is in the new California Welcome Center at 1635 Heindon Rd. (near the Hwy. 101./Hwy. 299 junction), 707/822-3619, www.arcatachamber .com, open weekdays 10 A.M.–5 P.M. in tourist season, shorter hours in winter (call for current schedule). Stop to find out about special events, such as the **Bebop & Brew** jazz and microbrew festival and the **Arcata Bay Oyster Festival,** both held in June. Among the free publications available here are the ***Tour Arcata's Architectural Past*** brochure, ***Arcata Outdoors,*** and the free ***Welcome to Arcata*** map, in addition to a tidal wave of free local newsletters and newspapers. The very good annual ***Humboldt Visitor*** and the monthly ***North Coast View*** are particularly worthwhile for travelers. The Bureau of Land Management's **Arcata Field Office** is nearby at 1695 Heindon Rd., 707/825-2300, www.ca.blm.gov/arcata, a worthwhile stop for information on exploring Samoa Dunes, camping in the King Range, or hiking the Headwaters. Local semipro ball games are held at the **Arcata**

Ballpark, Ninth and F Sts., in June and July. For details and tickets, contact **Humboldt Crabs Baseball,** 707/839-1379, www.crabsbaseball.org.

Like most college towns, Arcata has a decent supply of bookstores. A good place to start exploring them is **Northtown Books,** 957 H St., 707/822-2834, www.northtownbooks.com. In addition to various local publications, keep an eye out for copies of the **Arcata Eye,** headquartered in Jacoby's Storehouse, www.arcataeye.com, "America's most popular obscure small-town newspaper," which often boasts headlines such as "Some Moron Burned Down the Porta-Potty at the Marsh." Pretty darned profound.

Arcata & Mad River Transit System, 707/822-3775, bases its buses at the Transit Center, 925 E St. (between Ninth and 10th). Fare is $1, certain discounts available. The Transit Center is also the local stop for **Greyhound,** 707/825-8934 or 800/231-2222, which offers service to and from Eureka as well as points north and south.

Eureka

When James T. Ryan slogged ashore here from his whaling ship in May of 1850, shouting (so the story goes) *Eureka!* ("I have found it!"), what he found was California's largest natural bay north of San Francisco. Russian-American Fur Company hunters actually entered Humboldt Bay earlier, in 1806, but the area's official discovery came in 1849 when a party led by Josiah Gregg came overland that winter seeking the mouth of the Trinity River (once thought to empty into the ocean). Gregg died in the unfriendly forests on the return trip to San Francisco, but the reports of his half-starved companions led to Eureka's establishment on "Trinity Bay" as a trading post and port serving the far northern inland gold camps.

While better than other north coast harbors, Humboldt Bay was still less than ideal. The approach across the sand bar was treacherous, and dozens of ships foundered in heavy storms or fog—a trend that continued well into the 20th century. In 1917, the cruiser USS *Milwaukee,* flagship of the Pacific fleet, arrived to rescue a grounded submarine and ended up winching itself onto the beach, where it sat until World War II (when it was scrapped and recycled). But ever-imaginative Eureka has managed to turn even abandoned boats into a community resource. Before the Humboldt Bay Nuclear Power Plant was built here in 1963, the city got most of its energy from the generators of the salvaged Russian tanker *Donbass III,* towed into the bay and beached in 1946.

Oddly expansive and naked today, huge Humboldt Bay was once a piddling puddle at the edge of the endless redwood forest. Early loggers stripped the land closest to town first, but the bare Eureka hills were soon dotted with reincarnated redwoods—buildings of pioneer industry, stately Victorians that still reflect the community's cultural roots.

No matter how vibrant the colors of the old homes here, at times it seems nothing can dispel the fog in these parts. When the fog does finally lift, in wet years the rains come, washing away hillsides and closing roads, trapping the locals behind what they refer to affectionately as the Redwood Curtain. That sense of being isolated from the rest of the human world—something harried visitors from more urban locales long for—and the need to transform life into something other than *gray* may explain why there are more artists and performers per capita in Humboldt County than anywhere else in the state. Sunshine is where one finds it, after all.

SIGHTS
Humboldt Bay
Eureka's 10-mile-long Humboldt Bay was named for the German naturalist Baron Alexander von Humboldt. So it's fitting that the extensive, if almost unknown, **Humboldt Bay National Wildlife Refuge** was established on the edge of the bay's South Jetty to protect the black brant, a small migratory goose, and more than 200

other bird species. (Some 36,000 black brants showed up in 1951; some 10,000 come now, up from a recent low of 1,000, and their numbers are still increasing.) Other harbor life includes sea lions, harbor seals, porpoises, and gray whales, seen offshore here in winter and early spring. Humboldt Bay's **Egret Rookery** and other refuge features are best observed from the water. The Humboldt refuge administers the offshore **Castle Rock NWR,** a 14-acre island which serves as rookery for the largest breeding population of common murres in California and offers a migratory roost for Aleutian Canada geese, and also includes the **Lanphere Dunes** near Arcata.

The new refuge headquarters and visitor center, 1020 Ranch Rd. (off Hookton Road) in Loleta, 707/733-5406, pacific.fws.gov/humboldtbay, was named in memory of Richard J. Guadagno,

former refuge manager, who was aboard United Airlines Flight 93 on September 11, 2001. Interpretive trails include the three-mile (round-trip) **Hookton Slough Trail,** and the seasonal 1.75-mile **Shorebird Loop Trail.**

To get a look at the refuge from the bay, take the **Humboldt Bay Harbor Cruise** or sign on for a kayak tour with **Hum-Boats.** Human wildlife includes fishing crews, sailors, and the Humboldt State University crew teams out rowing at dusk (the best bird's-eye view is from the Cafe Marina on Woodley Island).

Fields Landing, where the last Northern California whaling station operated until 1951, is the bay's deep-water port, the place to watch large fishing boats unload their daily catch; the rest of the fleet docks at the end of Commercial St. in downtown Eureka. Fields Landing is also the place to pick up fresh Dungeness crab, usually

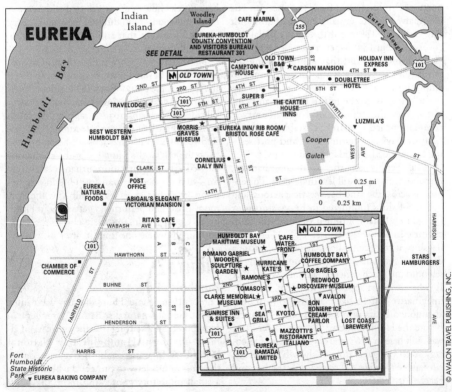

available from Christmas to February or March. Stop when the flag's flying at **Botchie's Crab Stand,** 6670 Fields Landing Dr. just off Hwy. 101, 707/442-4134.

The **Samoa Bridge** connects the city of Eureka with the narrow peninsula extending south from Arcata (almost across Humboldt Bay) and the onetime Simpson Lumber Company town of **Samoa,** the name inspired by the bay's resemblance to the harbor at Pago Pago. The entire town was bought in 2000 by locals who plan to spruce things up, and perhaps convert the old manager's mansion into a bed-and-breakfast. (Stay tuned.) Almost the same as always, though, is the **Samoa Cookhouse,** noted rustic restaurant and the last logging camp cookhouse in the West, also a fascinating museum. The **Eureka Municipal Airport** and **U.S. Coast Guard** facilities occupy the fingertip of Samoa Peninsula, near county-owned fishing access (very basic camping, restrooms, boat ramps).

Carson Mansion, Eureka

© ROBERT HOLMES/CALTOUR

Old Town

Part of Eureka's onetime skid row—the term itself of north coast origin, referring to the shantytowns and shacks lining the loggers' "skid roads" near ports—has been shoved aside to make room for Old Town. Most of the fleabag flophouses, sleazy sailors' bars, and pool halls along First, Second, and Third between C and G Streets were razed and others renovated to create this bayside concentration of new cafés, art galleries, and trendy shops. A new phase of waterfront redevelopment was unveiled in early 2002: the $7.9 million, 1,300-foot boardwalk between C and G Streets. A roster of events, from the annual spring **Taste of Main Street** and **Redwood Coast Dixieland Jazz Festival** to the **Old Town Fourth of July Celebration,** also define Old Town.

Most people stop first for a look at the gaudy, geegawed Gothic **Carson Mansion,** 143 M St., at the foot of Second St. (locals say "Two Street"), once the home of lumber baron William Carson. Those in the know say this is the state's—perhaps the nation's—finest surviving example of Victoriana. Now home to the exclusive all-male (how Victorian) Ingomar Club, even unescorted men are not welcome inside or in the club's palatial gardens. So be happy with a look at the ornate turrets and trim of this three-story money-green mansion built of redwood. Inside are superb stained-glass works, handworked interiors of hardwoods imported from around the world, and fireplaces crafted from Mexican onyx.

Better, though, and much more accessible despite the protective plate glass, is the fabulous folk art at the **Romano Gabriel Wooden Sculpture Garden** just down the street at 315 Second St., a blooming, blazing, full-color world of delightful plants, people, and social commentary, crafted from packing crates with the help of a handsaw. This is "primitive art" (snobs say "poor taste") on a massive scale, one of two pieces of California folk art recognized internationally (the other is Watts Towers in Los Angeles). Gabriel, a gardener who died in 1977, said of his work: "Eureka is bad place for flowers—the salty air and no sun. So I just make this garden." He worked on this garden, which includes likenesses of Mussolini, the Pope, nosy neighbors,

MORRIS GRAVES MUSEUM OF ART

Dazzling new star in Humboldt County's fine arts galaxy is the Morris Graves Museum of Art, at home in the historic, newly restored Carnegie Library. The completely accessible museum, also headquarters for the county arts council, features fine arts galleries, courtyard sculpture garden, a performance rotunda, and a young artists' academy. **Saturday Nights at the Morris Graves,** a performance series offered from September through May, offers everything from jazz, folk, gospel, and accordion concerts to poetry, dance, and theater. The Graves Museum is open to the public Wed.–Sun., noon–5 P.M., and during special Saturday night events.

The Humboldt Arts Council office is inside the museum, located in Eureka at 636 F St., 707/442-0278, www.humboldtarts.org. Pick up the arts council's annual magazine **The Palette** (free) wherever you find it around town, or at www.thepalette.com. To learn more about Morris Graves, the artist who endowed the museum, visit www.morrisgraves.com.

and tourists amid the fantastic flowers and trees, for 30 years. After Gabriel's death, it was restored, then transplanted downtown from his front yard.

Well worth it, too, is a stop at the fine and friendly **Clarke Memorial Museum,** 240 E St. (at Third), 707/443-1947, where you'll feel as though you're stepping into a 19th-century parlor. The museum was founded in 1960 by Cecile Clarke (a history teacher at Eureka High 1914–50), who personally gathered most of the collection. This is the place for a look at various Victoriana, including toys and dolls; glassware and jewelry; pioneer relics, including antique guns and other frontier weaponry, even a signed first edition of *The Personal Memoirs of General Grant;* and the incredible, nationally noted Nealis Hall collection of Native American artifacts, basketry, and ceremonial dance regalia. The museum building, the Italian Renaissance onetime **Bank of Eureka,** is itself a collector's item with its stained-glass skylight and glazed terra-cotta exterior. The building is listed on the National Register of Historic Places. Open Tues.–Sat., noon–4 P.M. Admission is free.

Eureka's family-friendly **Discovery Museum,** Third and F Sts., 707/443-9694, explores science, art, culture, and technology, with interactive exhibits and displays appealing to children of all ages. A recent big exhibit was the Whole Tooth. Open Tues.–Sat. 10.am.–4 P.M., Sunday noon–4 P.M. Admission $4.

The **Humboldt Bay Maritime Museum,** 423 First St., 707/444-9440, chronicles the area's contributions to Pacific seafaring heritage with original photographs, ship models, maritime artifacts and library, even an old Fresnel lens from the Table Bluff lighthouse and a refurbished Coast Guard lifeboat. Open daily 11 A.M.–4 P.M. Admission is free (donations welcomed).

The museum also owns and runs the **MV Madaket,** a former Humboldt Bay passenger ferry now providing sightseeing tours of the bay, daily May–Oct. Built in 1910, the *Madaket* is the oldest passenger vessel in continuous use in the United States, with the smallest bar. The harbor cruises depart from 122 I St. in Old Town. For more information, call **Humboldt Bay Harbor Cruise** at 707/445-1910.

Fort Humboldt and Sequoia Park

Reconstruction continues at Eureka's **Fort Humboldt State Historic Park,** 3431 Fort Ave., 707/445-6567. This outpost of the U.S. military's 1850s Indian Wars was onetime stomping grounds of the young Ulysses S. Grant. As depressed in Eureka as he was elsewhere in California, Grant spent six months here then resigned his commission to go home and farm in Missouri. The fort museum tells the story. Also here: an excellent (and wheelchair-accessible) indoor/outdoor museum display of early logging technology, along with picnic tables (good view of Humboldt Bay) and restrooms. Guided tours available on request. Park admission is free. From May through September, "Steam Ups" of historic steam-powered logging equipment are held on the third Saturday of the month. Come in April for the Dolbeer Donkey Days. Get here via Highland Ave. off Broadway. (Call for actual directions—it's tricky to find.)

There's something a little sad about Sequoia Park, the last significant vestige of the virgin redwood forest that once fringed Humboldt Bay, though the summr flowers here can be spectacular. The park is situated southeast of downtown at Glatt and W Streets, 707/443-7331, and is open Tues.–Sun. 10 A.M.–8 P.M. May–Oct., until 5 P.M. the rest of the year. Enjoy the peaceful melancholy of these dark woods laced with walking paths, a rhododendron dell, and duck pond. The five-acre **Sequoia Park Zoo,** 3414 W St., 707/441-4263, is home to animals from six continents, though the native river otters are best. The zoo is open Tues.–Sun. 10 A.M.–5 P.M. (until 7 P.M. in summer). Admission is free. In summer there's also an immensely popular seasonal petting zoo, open 11:30 A.M.–3:30 P.M.

ENTERTAINMENT AND EVENTS

Come in January for the unique **Almost-Annual Humboldt Pun-Off,** a delightful display of tasteless humor, benefit for Easter Seals (immensely popular, so get your tickets early). March brings **A Taste of Main Street** and the **Redwood Coast Dixieland Jazz Festival.** Fog or no fog, almost everybody crawls out in April for the annual **Rhododendron Festival.** In May, over Memorial Day weekend, comes the famous **Kinetic Sculpture Race,** starting in nearby Arcata. From June to August, count on **Summer Concerts in the Park,** at Clarke Plaza in Old Town. Come in June for the **Old Town Cattle Drive** At the top of the lengthy regional calendar of July 4 events is the annual **Humboldt Bay Festival.** Also in July: **Blues by the Bay.** Later in July, rodeo fans can head north to the annual **Orick Rodeo** or east to the **Fortuna Rodeo.**

In July and August, the **Humboldt Arts Festival** keeps the area jumping with concerts, plays, exhibits, even special museum displays. August is hot for history, what with **Fort Humboldt Days** living history and **Steam-Up** (the monthly cranking up of ancient logging locomotives) at Fort

Humboldt State Park and the **Civil War Days** reenactments in Fortuna. The annual **Humboldt County Fair** also comes in August, held in Ferndale. But there's also **Blues by the Bay.** In September, come for the **Festival on the Bay** and **Sights, Sounds & Tastes of Humboldt.** In December, the **Trucker's Christmas Convoy** parade is quite the shindig. For a detailed events calendar, contact local visitor bureaus.

Popular arts events include the monthly **First Saturday Night Arts Alive!** in the galleries and shops of Old Town and Downtown, the **Eureka Summer Concert Series** in Clarke Plaza at Third and E Sts., and the annual October **Maskibition** international competition of handmade art and performance masks. For information about what's happening arts-wise, stop by the new **Morris Graves Museum of Art,** also performance arts and gallery venue as well as headquarters for the Humboldt Arts Council at 636 F St., or try 707/442-0278, www.humboldtarts.org. **The Ink People Center for the Arts,** 411 12th St., 707/442-8413, www.inkpeople.org, is another

ALL WORK AND NO PLAYS?

The **Redwood Curtain,** a program of the Ink People Center for the Arts, promotes itself with this simple justification: Because Life Shouldn't Be All Work and No Plays. Indeed it shouldn't, especially when those plays are so good. Past Redwood Curtain plays include *Scotland Road* by Jeffrey Hatcher, *The Cripple of Inishmaan* by Martin McDonagh, *Crumbs from the Table of Joy* by Lynn Nottage, and *Two Rooms* by Lee Blessing.

Redwood Curtain's curtain goes up at the Eureka Mall, 800 W. Harris St., behind Staples and next to Six Rivers Bank, on the mall's Henderson St. side. Performances are usually scheduled Thurs.–Sun.; evening performances begin promptly at 8 P.M., Sunday matinees promptly at 2 P.M. Order advance tickets online at www.redwoodcurtain.com, or call the theater at 707/443-7688 for day-of-performance tickets.

BLUE OX MILLWORKS

Endlessly compelling, Eureka's time-honored Blue Ox Millworks complex is located at the foot of X St., 707/444-3457 or 800/248-4259 (for tour reservations), www.blueoxmill.com. The antithesis of all things high-tech, the Blue Ox pays hands-on homage to the beauty of craftsmanship, and particularly the craft of old-fashioned woodworking. In this going concern—a de facto living history environment, the only mill of its kind remaining in the U.S.—the machines date from 1850 to the 1940s. (Blue Ox recently acquired the late-19th-century Barnes Equipment Company Human-Powered Tool Collection, which includes the only complete and original mortising machine in existence.) There's an aromatic whirl of sawing, chipping, turning, grinding, and sanding as custom orders are filled.

Customers include the National Park Service—which once ordered 400 custom planters for the White House—and endless couples in the midst of Victorian restorations. Victorian replication is the specialty here, though the Blue Ox can duplicate or restore just about anything. The stunning Eureka Trolley built for Old Town merchants is a Blue Ox creation.

Self-guided tours of the mill—visiting the main shop, sawmill, moulding plant, blacksmith shop, "logging skid camp," and more—and the adjacent Blue Ox Craftsman's Village are offered Mon.–Sat. 9 A.M.–4 P.M. Weekday tours are usually more action-packed, if you want to see the craftsmen at work, and Saturday tours more personally guided. Admission is $7.50 adults, $6.50 seniors, children 6–12 $3.50, under 5 free.

arts locus. The Eureka chamber of commerce offers an extensive list of local galleries.

The most comprehensive source of information on the local music scene is **HumboldtMusic.com**, www.humboldtmusic.com. Among good bets for live music are local coffeehouses, the art-deco **Ritz Club,** 240 F St. in Old Town, 707/445-8577; **Club West,** 535 Fifth St. (at G St.), 707/444-2582. The **Eureka Symphony Orchestra,** 1437 Russ St., 707/444-2889, presents several concerts each year; call for schedule and ticket information.

For something more theatrical, try **Redwood Curtain,** 800 W. Harris St., 707/441-6965, www.redwoodcurtain.com, or the **North Coast Repertory Theatre,** 300 Fifth St., 707/442-6278. Also look for performances of the renowned **Dell' Arte Players,** 707/668-5663, www.dellarte.com.

INFORMATION AND SERVICES

Find out what's going on from the **Northcoast Journal Weekly,** www.northcoastjournal.com, which includes a good calendar. The **HumGuide,** www.humguide.com, is a great online general information source for Humboldt County. The **Greater Eureka Chamber of Commerce,** 2112

Broadway, 707/442-3738 or 800/356-6381, www.eurekachamber.com, is the best stop for visitor information. Pick up Old Town information (including a listing of local antique shops) and the free Victorian walking tour guide. (*Really* taking the Victorian tour, though, means getting some exercise, since Eureka boasts well over 100 well-preserved Victorian buildings and homes, and more than 1,000 "architecturally significant" structures.) Or stop by the **Eureka Main Street Information Bureau,** 123 F St. #6, 707/442-9054, www.eurekamainstreet.com. The **Eureka-Humboldt County Convention and Visitors Bureau,** 1034 Second St., 707/443-5097 or 800/346-3482, www.redwoodvisitor.org, is the central source for countywide visitor information. Nature appreciation resources, for example, include the free *Humboldt Bay Beaches and Dunes Map and Guide* and, for an introduction to the plants and animals of the local dune ecosystem, the laminated pocket *Beach and Dune Field Guide* ($6).

For books, head to the **Booklegger** in Old Town, 402 Second St., 707/445-1344. Eureka's main **post office** is at 337 W. Clark St., 707/442-1768, though a convenient downtown branch is located at the corner of Fifth and H Streets, 707/442-1828. **Eureka General Hospital,** 2200

Harrison Ave., 707/445-5111, offers 24-hour emergency medical care (707/441-4409). The local **California Dept. of Fish and Game** office is at 619 Second St., 707/445-6493, and provides regulations and licenses. Headquarters for **Six Rivers National Forest** is at 1330 Bayshore Way, 707/442-1721, www.r5.fs.fed.us/sixrivers, a good place to stop for camping information and forest maps. The regional **California Dept. of Parks and Recreation** office is at Fort Humboldt, 3431 Fort Ave., 707/445-6547.

ACCOMMODATIONS

Camping

Camping throughout Humboldt County is best in the wilds, but in a pinch, campers can head to **Redwood Acres Fairgrounds,** 3750 Harris St. (south off Myrtle), 707/445-3037, www.redwoodacres.com, full hookups and showers $15; the **Eureka KOA,** 4050 N. Hwy. 101 (a few miles north of town), 707/822-4243 or 800/562-3136, with facilities including "kamping kabins" ($40–50), tent and trailer spaces ($20–30), laundry room, rec room, showers, heated pool, and playground; or the **E-Z RV Park & Marina,** 1875 Buhne Dr. (south of town on Humboldt Bay) at King Salmon Resort, 707/442-1118, $19 with all hookups (RVs only).

Motels

Broadway is "motel row," and you'll also find reasonable motels on Fourth Street. Most Eureka motels offer substantially cheaper rates Oct.–Apr., and even the cheapest places usually have color TV and cable and/or free HBO.

There are decent motels for $50–100, including (at the low end of that range) the ubiquitous **Motel 6,** 1934 Broadway, 707/445-9631 or 800/466-8356, www.motel6.com; Eureka's **Travelodge,** 4 Fourth St. (at B St.), 707/443-6345 or 800/578-7878, with a pool and cable TV with HBO; and **Sunrise Inn & Suites,** 129 Fourth St., 707/443-9751. Options at the high end of the $50–100 range include **Days Inn,** 4260 Broadway, 707/444-2019 or 800/329-7466, which has an indoor pool and whirlpool tub. Some rooms have kitchenettes;

all have cable TV with HBO. Among others are the **Eureka Ramada Limited,** 270 Fifth St., 707/443-2206 or 800/233-3782, with sauna and indoor whirlpool tub; the **Holiday Inn Express,** 2223 Fourth St., 707/442-3261, with indoor pool, exercise room, and continental breakfast buffet; and the **Eureka Super 8,** 1304 Fourth St., 707/443-3193 or 800/235-3232, with indoor pool, sauna, whirlpool tub, and cable TV with HBO.

Motels in the $100–150 range include the **Best Western Humboldt Bay,** 232 W. Fifth St. (at Broadway), 707/443-2234 or 800/521-6996, with spacious rooms, large outdoor pool, whirlpool, and rec room. The large and attractive **Red Lion Inn,** 1929 Fourth St. (between T and V Sts.), 707/445-0844 or 800/733-5466, features amenities such as a swimming pool and spa, laundry and valet service, business center, and good onsite restaurant. The **Best Western Bayshore Inn,** 3500 Broadway (Hwy. 101), 707/268-8005 or 888/268-8005, offers an indoor/outdoor pool and spa, whirlpool tub suites, and a Marie Callender's restaurant. **Quality Inn Eureka,** 1209 Fourth St. (between M and N Streets), 707/443-1601 or 800/772-1622, features an outdoor heated pool and an indoor sauna and whirlpool tub.

Carter House Inns

Definitely "new Eureka" but full of Victorian charms are the Carter House Inns, 301 L St., 707/444-8062 or 707/445-1390, or 800/404-1390, www.carterhouse.com. What has become known at The Carter House is actually a complex of four properties—The Hotel Carter, The Carter House Inn, The Carter Cottage, and Bell Cottage—under unified management. The hotel and inn are vintage-1980s facsimiles, while the later cottages are renovations of the original 19th-century structures.

It all began with the 1981 construction of three-story **The Carter House,** built of fine rustic redwood following the very authentic (and very exacting) original design specifications of Carson Mansion architects Samuel and Joseph Newsom. Structurally, The Carter House is a stately re-creation of an 1884 "stick" Victorian home built in San Francisco and lost in the 1906 earthquake and fire. But otherwise it's quite modern, with very un-Victorian sunny rooms and suites (one with fireplace and whirlpool) and an uncluttered, almost contemporary air. That Carter House synthesis of "contemporary good taste with the elegance of a bygone era" extends also to still more luxurious **The Carter Hotel** across the street, and to the two inviting cottages. Homey **Bell Cottage** features three rooms and shared common areas, perfect for a small group traveling together. Romantic and sunny, **The Carter Cottage** is also known as "the love shack." Most high-season rates at the Carter House Inns are $150–250, though there are a handful of pricier suites. The Carter Cottage is about $500. In any accommodation, expect luxurious amenities, a breathtaking full breakfast, evening wine and hors d'oeuvres, and beforebed cookies and tea.

The outstanding restaurant at the Carter House Inns, **M Restaurant 301,** is a 1998 recipient of the coveted *Wine Spectator* magazine Grand Award. Restaurant 301 is supported by the extensive, organic **301 Gardens**—guests can help harvest vegetables, fruits, and herbs before dinner—and the **301 Wineshop.** Quite special, too, are the **Winemakers Dinners at Restaurant 301.** To get you there in style, at last report Mark Carter's 1958 Bentley was still available for limo service to and from the airport.

Bed-and-Breakfasts

Eureka's showplace inn, a destination in its own right for connoisseurs of high-Victorian style, is the award-winning **Abigail's Elegant Victorian Mansion,** 1406 C St., 707/444-3144, www.eureka-california.com. This elegant Victorian mansion offers more than four comfortable rooms, two with private baths (the other two share three baths and a Finnish sauna), fabulous breakfasts, and vintage auto tours. Guided by the inn's irrepressible innkeepers, Doug ("Jeeves") and Lily Vieyra, visitors could easily spend an entire day just touring *this* eclectic place, which is a spectacular de facto museum of authentic Victorian substance and style. Old movies and music add yet another delightful dimension to a stay

here. Don't miss the Victorian gardens and croquet field. Rates are $150–250.

The 1905 **Daly Inn,** 1125 H St., 707/445-3638 or 800/321-9656, www.dalyinn.com, offers three inviting antique-rich rooms (two share a bath) and two suites in a 1905 colonial revival. Guests enjoy a spectacular full breakfast, afternoon tea, phones, TV, a library, and gardens with a fish pond. Be sure to peek into the third-floor Christmas Ballroom. Rates are $100–150, though Miss Martha's room, with two antique twin beds, is $80.

The **Old Town Bed and Breakfast Inn,** 1521 Third St., 707/443-5235 or 888/508-5235, was the original redwood home of William Carson (of Carson Mansion fame), built in 1871. The hot tub came later. Rates for most rooms are $100–150. The **Campton House,** 305 M St. in Old Town, 707/443-1601 or 800/772-1622, is managed by the Quality Inn Eureka. The 1911 Arts & Crafts-style house features redwood interiors and abundant antiques. One room has a private bath, others share (two rooms are typically rented as a suite). Guests can use the pool, sauna, and whirlpool tub at the Quality Inn. Rates include continental breakfast and afternoon tea. Rooms are $50–100; the whole house can be rented for $250–400.

Quite special at the waterfront is **Upstairs at the Waterfront,** 102 F St., 707/444-1301 or 888/817-5840, www.upstairsatthewaterfront.com. Listed on the National Register of Historic Places and a recipient of the 1994 Governor's Award for Excellence in Design, "Upstairs" was once a brothel. These days it's a more sedate Victorian, offering two elegant, period styled bed-and-breakfast suites (yet with all the modern comforts) above the popular Café Waterfront (full breakfast included in a stay). Rachel's Room is $125, Sophie's Suite $175; combine the two for a great getaway apartment.

FOOD

Markets

Eureka hosts two certified farmers' markets, both held June–Oct. Fresh veggies, fruit, and other local products abound at the **Eureka Old Town**

Certified Farmers Market, Second and F Sts., held on Tuesday 10 A.M.–1 P.M. The **Eureka Certified Farmers Market** at the Henderson Center on Henderson St. (at F), is held Thursday 10 A.M.–1 P.M. For details on both, call 707/441-9999. **Eureka Natural Foods,** 1626 Broadway, 707/422-6325, is a year-round supply, veggie, fruit, and sandwich stop.

Old Town

Everyone will tell you that **Stars,** 2009 Harrison Ave., 707/445-2061, is the best bet for burgers. **Luzmila's** at 946 West Ave., 707/444-2508, serves great Mexican, from chiles rellenos to papas con chorizo. Or try immensely popular **Rita's Café & Taqueria,** 107 Wabash Ave., 707/268-0700.

Otherwise, Old Town offers just about everything. For the best bagels anywhere—infused, here, with Mexican flavors and traditions—try **Los Bagels,** 403 Second St. (at E), 707/442-8525, open daily for breakfast and lunch. (The original Los Bagels is in Arcata.) The **Eureka Baking Company,** 108 F St. and also 3562 Broadway (Hwy. 101), 707/445-8997, is wonderful for croissants, muffins, sourdough baguettes, and other fresh-baked fare. **Ramone's Bakery & Cafe,** 747 13th St., 707/826-1088, is excellent for pastries and fresh breads, light lunch, handmade truffles, and exquisite desserts, not to mention espresso and other good coffees. Ramone's has another location in Eureka, at 2225 Harrison, and outlets also in McKinleyville and Arcata. A great choice, too, for fresh-ground coffees (by the pound or by the cup) is **Humboldt Bay Coffee Company,** 211 F St., 707/444-3969, which offers live music on Friday and Saturday nights and outdoor seating in good weather. Another good stop for soup and sandwiches—and quite possibly the best ice cream anywhere on the north coast—is **Bon Boniere Ice Cream Parlor,** 215 F St. in Old Town, 707/268-0122.

Artsy, minimalist **Hurricane Kate's,** 511 Second St., 707/444-1405, serves up some great wood-fired pizzas, "world fusion," and meat-and-potatoes specialties, most everything served tapas style. Full bar. Open Tues.–Sat. for lunch

and dinner. **Avalon,** Third and G Sts., 707/445-0500, offers "Old World Food" with quite contemporary style, from the grilled rib-eye steak and local lamb chops to the cedar-planked salmon. Jazz on Saturday nights. Open for dinner only, Tues.–Sun. nights. Hugely popular **Lost Coast Brewery,** in the historic Knights of Pythias Hall at 617 Fourth St., 707/445-4480, is the place to go for eccentric decor and original art by Duane Flatmo, locally handcrafted ales like Alley Cat Amber and 8-Ball Stout, and good pub fare, served until midnight. Specialties include Lost Coast Vegetarian Chili, Stout Beef Stew, and Chicken Lips (really).

Justifiably famous (especially among lovers of the stinking rose) for its tomato and spinach pies, calzones, and other straightforward selections—one slice of the Sicilian pizza makes a meal—**Tomaso's,** 216 E St. (between Second and Third), 707/445-0100, is open for lunch and dinner weekdays and Saturday. Expect a wait—and however long that is, it'll be worth it. For something a bit dressier, the best Italian for miles around is served at **Mazzotti's Ristorante Italiano,** 301 F St., 707/445-1912, where specialties include linguini and white clam sauce, pasta Florentine, and Al Capone Calzone. Kid's menu, too. **Café Waterfront,** 102 F St., 707/443-9190, everybody's favorite for Sunday brunch, also features a small bed-and-breakfast upstairs—the aptly named Upstairs at the Waterfront, 707/444-1301. Other Old Town hot spots include **Kyoto** Japanese restaurant, 320 F St., 707/443-7777, and **Roy's Club Italian Seafood Restaurant,** 218 D St., 707/445-2511.

Seafood

The hands-down favorite for dress-up seafood is the Victorian **Sea Grill** in Old Town, 316 E St., 707/443-7187, where you'll find sophisticated selections like salmon with garlic wine butter sauce as well as hearty clam chowder. Many other local restaurants—above and below—also offer seafood specialties. Now that the beloved Old Eureka standard, the Eureka Seafood Grotto has closed for good, you have to actively seek real-deal seafood stupor. The **Cafe Marina** on Woodley Island, 707/443-2233, is a popular local fish house, open daily for breakfast, lunch, and dinner. The only place to buy fresh crab is **Botchie's Crab Stand,** 6670 Fields Landing Dr. just off Hwy. 101, 707/442-4134, open for business when the white flag (with orange crab) is flying. Crab season usually runs Dec.–Mar., weather permitting.

Samoa Cookhouse

Everyone should eat at the Samoa Cookhouse on the Samoa Peninsula, 707/442-1659, at least once. The Samoa is a bona fide loggers' cookhouse oozing redwood-rugged ambience. The phrase "all you can eat" takes on new meaning here: portions are gargantuan. No cuisine here, just good ol' American food—platters of thickly sliced ham, beef, turkey, and spare ribs (choices change daily), plus potatoes, vegetables, fresh-baked bread—all passed around among the checkered oilcloth–covered tables. Soup and salad are included in the fixed-price dinner ($12.95 when last we checked), not to mention homemade apple pie for dessert. Come early on weekends, particularly in summer, and be prepared to wait an hour or so. Equally hearty are breakfasts and lunch; a leisurely breakfast here is the best. No reservations are taken but all major credit cards are accepted—and there's a gift shop. To get to the cookhouse, head west from Eureka over the Samoa Bridge, turn left, then left again at the town of Samoa (follow the signs).

Restaurant 301

The Hotel Carter's elegant and small Restaurant 301, 301 L St., 707/444-8062, is open nightly for candlelight, classical music, and quality dining. In fact, Restaurant 301 has become something of an international dining destination since it won *Wine Spectator* magazine's coveted Grand Award in 1998. Fewer than 100 restaurants in the world have been so honored. According to *Wine Spectator,* Restaurant 301 is a "wine-and-food oasis. . . where a superb wine list is complemented by the culinary talent of Chef Rodger Babel." Menus here are created from fresh, local ingredients, from Humboldt Bay seafood to the fresh vegetables, fruits, and herbs harvested daily from the restaurant's own extensive organic gardens.

Entrées might include marinated and grilled quail breast medallions with fresh corn waffles, pecan-crusted Pacific salmon, or fennel-roasted sturgeon. The exceptional wine list features "unusually fine and reasonably priced wines," including treasured California wines and rare French wines. The cellar here boasts more than 23,000 bottles. Reservations are a must. The Hotel Carter also offers a famous four-course breakfast. To take the experience home with you, pick up a copy of the *Carter House Cookbook,* available for sale at the hotel.

GETTING AROUND

Get around town on the Humboldt Transit Authority's **Eureka Transit Service,** 133 V St. (catch most buses at Fifth and D Sts.), 707/443-0826, which runs Mon.–Sat.; regular fare is $1. The V St. station is also headquarters for **Humboldt Transit Authority,** same phone, www.hta.org, which serves the area from Scotia north to Trinidad Mon.–Sat. (including bicycle transport—call for details) with **Redwood Transit Service** buses. **Greyhound,** 1603 Fourth St. (at P St.), 707/442-0370, runs north to Crescent City and beyond, also south on Hwy. 101 to San Francisco. To fly into the area, the **Arcata-Eureka Airport** actually lies north of Arcata, in McKinleyville, at 3561 Boeing Ave., 707/839-1906. Rental cars are available there.

Tour the bay on the **Humboldt Bay Harbor Cruise MV** *Madaket* (once the Eureka-Samoa ferry); call 707/445-1910 for information. Rent a sailboat or kayak from **Hum-Boats,** 707/444-3048, www.humboats.com, or join a guided tour with Jay Dottle ("Captain Jay"). Local historian Ray Hillman, 800/400-1849, offers various **guided history tours.** The walking tour explores the waterfront historic district ($18 for two); the three-hour driving/walking tour ranges from an island in Humboldt Bay and Victorian wonders around Eureka to the antique logging equipment at Fort Humboldt; and the redwood park day trips (heading erther north or south) include a picnic lunch created from all-local products. Per-person rates are $9–60.

Eel River Country

Just south of Eureka is the Victorian village of Ferndale, well worth an excursion. From the Ferndale-Fortuna area, the aptly named Eel River accompanies Hwy. 101 south through Humboldt Redwoods State Park. Hwy. 101 continues south into California wine country, but at Leggett Hwy. 1 reclaims its independent identity, jogs seaward, then slips through Westport and Rockport on the way south to Fort Bragg and Mendocino. Not reachable by state highway is the rugged, almost inaccessible King Range.

⋈ FERNDALE AND VICINITY

Ferndale (pop. 1,400) is a perfect rendition of a Victorian village, the kind of place Disneyland architects would create if they needed a new movie set. Ferndale, however, is the real thing, a thriving small town where people take turns shuttling the kids to Future Farmers of America and 4-H meetings, argue about education at PTA meetings or ice-cream socials, and gossip on street corners.

The town was first settled in 1864 by Danish immigrants; at that time, the delta plain was heavily forested. The Danes were followed by Portuguese and Italians. Today, quaint and quiet Ferndale values its streets of colorfully restored Victorians.

For more information, contact the **Ferndale Chamber of Commerce** 707/786-4477, www .victorianferndale.org/chamber.

Sights

Lovers of Victoriana, take the walking tour; for a free guide to historic buildings (almost everything here qualifies), pick up the souvenir edition of the *Ferndale Enterprise* at the Kinetic Sculpture Museum or elsewhere on Main Street. Or take a Victorian-paced carriage ride. The horses and carriages of the **Ferndale Carriage Co.,** 707/786-9675, pick up guests at Main and Washington daily in summer, weekends only otherwise. To fully appreciate the town's history, visit the small **Ferndale Museum,** 515 Shaw Ave. (just off Main at the corner of Third),

707/786-4466, which also includes an Oral History Library, written histories, and old *Ferndale Enterprise* newspaper archives on microfilm. The museum is closed the entire month of January but otherwise open Wed.–Sat. (also Tuesday in summer) 11 A.M.–4 P.M. and Sunday 1–4 P.M. Small admission.

Most of Ferndale's historic commercial buildings are concentrated on three-block-long Main St., including the Roman-Renaissance **Six Rivers National Bank** building at 394 Main, originally the Ferndale Bank. The **Kinetic Sculpture Museum,** in the Ferndale Art & Cultural Center at 580 Main St. (no phone) displays a decidedly eclectic collection of survivors of the annual kinetic sculpture race, as well as works in progress. The Kinetic Sculpture Museum is usually open weekdays 10 A.M.–5 P.M., shorter hours on weekends. In the same building, along with various other galleries, is the **Ferndale Arts Cooperative Gallery,** 707/786-9634, with its impressive array of watercolors, wood work, pottery, sculpture, paper art, and jewelry. Open daily. Worth a stop, too, is the 1892-vintage **Golden Gait Mercantile,** 421 Main St., 707/786-4891, a squeaky-floored emporium of oddities and useful daily items, from sassafras tea and traditional patent medicines to butter churns, bushel (and peck) baskets, and treadle sewing machines. There's a museum on the second floor.

While touring the town—probably the best-preserved Victorian village in the state—travelers will be relieved to find that Ferndale has public restrooms (next to the post office on Main). Once off Main, most people head first to the famous **Gingerbread Mansion,** a Victorian built in a combination of Queen Anne, Eastlake, and stick styles. Tucked into its formal English gardens at 400 Berding and virtually dripping with its own frosting, the Gingerbread is one of the most photographed and painted buildings in Northern California.

Take the scenic drive to small **Centerville County Park & Beach** at the end of Ocean, which provides access to the 10 miles of beaches

© ROBERT HOLMES/CALTOUR

Gingerbread Mansion Inn

between False Cape and the Eel River lagoon: good beachcombing, driftwood picking, and smelt fishing in summer. On the way you'll pass **Portuguese Hall,** a popular event venue, and also the historic 1865 Victorian **Fern Cottage,** family farmhouse of state Senator Joseph Russ, open for tours by appointment only, 707/786-4735 or 707/786-4835. On the short drive along Ocean in the opposite direction from Main, on the way to 110-acre **Russ Park** (trails, forest, bird-watching), you'll pass **Danish Hall** (built in the late 1800s, still used for community events); Ferndale's striking **pioneer cemetery;** and the former **Old Methodist Church,** built in 1871, at the corner of Berding.

Arts and Events

The **Ferndale Repertory Theatre,** 447 Main St., 707/786-5483, offers weekend performances by both its adult and youth troupes most of the year—everything from *Blithe Spirit* and *Our Town* to *One Flew Over the Cuckoo's Nest.* In March, come for the big **Foggy Bottoms Milk**

Run, when whole families and serious runners alike participate in a footrace around the farm and back to Main Street. The Portuguese **Holy Ghost Festival** is in May, with a parade, dancing, feasts. Also in May is the annual **Tour of the Unknown Coast Bicycle Ride,** which starts at the county fairgrounds and can be ridden in 10- to 100-mile increments. On Memorial Day, the **Kinetic Sculpture Race** from Arcata ends on Main St., the surviving sculptures proudly paraded through town. Some also take up residence at the Kinetic Sculpture Museum here (for more information about the race, see Arcata and Vicinity). Come in June for the children's **Pet Parade,** in July for Ferndale's all-American **July 4th Parade and Picnic.** In August, the **Humboldt County Fair** and horse races come to the fairgrounds.

In September, **Tastes of Ferndale & Friends** bring a food and music sampler to Main Street. The annual **Victorian Village Oktoberfest & Harvest Day** is the main event in October. In December, come for the town's month-long **Victorian Christmas** celebrations, which include lighting up the world's tallest living Christmas tree (the 165-foot Sitka spruce on Main), a lighted-tractor parade, and the arrival of Santa Claus by horse and carriage. For more events information, contact the chamber office.

Practicalities

Camp at the handsome **Humboldt County Fairgrounds,** 1250 Fifth St. (off Van Ness), 707/786-9511, www.humboldtcountyfair.org, available for both tent camping and RVs, $15. Water and electricity hookups are available, along with access to restrooms and hot showers.

In the B&B department, the local star is the unabashedly luxurious 1899 **Gingerbread Mansion Inn,** 400 Berding St., 707/786-4000 or 800/952-4136, www.gingerbread-mansion.com, which offers 11 truly unique, antique-rich rooms in a refurbished 1899 Victorian mansion. Amenities include generous full breakfast and afternoon tea. Most rooms and suites are $150–250, four are $250 and up. Also quite fabulous is the **Victorian Inn,** 400 Ocean Ave. (at Main), 707/786-4949 or 888/589-1808, www.a-victorian-inn.com, 12 B&B rooms in a gorgeous downtown 1890 Victorian. All rooms feature private baths and extra amenities, from cable TV and CD players to in-room phones. Full breakfast Most rooms are in the very reasonable $100–150 range, several are $175. Curley's Grill and Silva's Fine Jewelry are other Victorian Inn jewels.

Ferndale offers other Victorian B&Bs, including the romantic **Shaw House Inn,** 703 Main, 707/786-9958 or 800/557-7429, www.shawhouse.com, an 1854 Carpenter Gothic Victorian with three parlors and eight guest rooms, all with private baths. Fabulous full breakfast included. Room rates are $100–150, suites $155 and $185. There are also some very small motels, including the **Francis Creek Inn** on Shaw Ave., 707/786-9611, the **Fern Motel** on Ocean, 707/786-5000, and **Ferndale Motel & Laundromat** on Main, 707/786-9471.

Picnickers can stop in at the **Ferndale Meat Company,** 376 Main, 707/786-4501, to pick up sandwiches, handmade smoked sausages (and other meats from the two-story stone smokehouse), and fine cheeses. For a sit-down meal, try immensely popular, family-friendly ◪ **Curley's Grill** downstairs in the Victorian Inn, 400 Main St., 707/786-9696, a California-style tavern open daily for lunch and dinner and also breakfast on weekends. Menu ranges from grilled portobella mushrooms or jumbo prawns to pasta primavera and grilled rib-eye steak, and the daily pasta and seafood specials are always worth a look. Stop by **Sweetness & Light,** 554 Main next to the post office, 707/786-4403, for truffles and other traditional chocolates.

Fernbridge

Between Eureka and Ferndale is Fernbridge, the name for both a community and a stately seven-arch Romanesque bridge called "the queen of bridges" up here in the north. Caltrans once nearly started a local armed rebellion when it announced plans to tear the bridge down. Fernbridge is home to the **Humboldt Creamery** dairy co-op, 572 Fernbridge Dr., 707/725-6182, as well as **Angelina Inn,** 281 Fernbridge Dr., 707/725-3153, locally loved for its Italian dinners and prime rib, steaks, and seafood. Open daily for dinner, full bar, live music on weekends.

Loleta

Dairies account for nearly half of Humboldt County's agricultural income. Since the pasturelands near Loleta are among the richest in the world, it's only natural that the region's first creamery was established here in 1888. Because of difficult shipping logistics, much of the milk produced here is processed into butter, cheese, and dried-milk products. Big doin's here is the **Loleta Antique Show** in October, not to mention **Swauger Station Days** in July. For more information about these and other events, call the **Loleta Chamber of Commerce,** 707/733-5666.

Loleta today is still a bucolic village of wood-frames and old brick buildings. For genuine hamburger and other quality meats, head for the **Loleta Meat Market** at 350 Main, 707/733-5319. Most of the action in town is at the award-winning **Loleta Cheese Factory,** 252 Loleta Dr., 707/733-5470 or 800/995-0453, famed for its natural Jersey milk cheeses, tasting room, and retail sales of cheese and wine. Step inside to sample and buy cheese right out of the display case. The company's famous creamy jack cheese comes in garlic, green chili, caraway, jalapeño, and smoked salmon variations. The cheddars also tease the palate—try the salami or smoked salmon versions. Watch the cheesemaking, too. The Loleta Cheese Factory is open Mon.–Fri. 9 A.M.–5 P.M., Sat. 9 A.M.–4 P.M., Sunday noon–4 P.M. Call to request a mail-order catalog.

If you decide to spend the night, try the four-room **Southport Landing Bed and Breakfast,** 444 Phelan Rd., 707/733-5915. This 1890s colonial revival mansion overlooks the Humboldt Bay National Wildlife Refuge. Guests have use of kayaks, bicycles, pool table, and a nature library. Rates, $50–100 and $100–150, include full breakfast and evening beverages/hors d'oeuvres.

FORTUNA AND HWY. 36

The largest city in southern Humboldt County, Fortuna was originally called Springville and established in 1875. Logging is officially the major industry in these parts, but tourism is catching up fast. Come in late March for the **Spring Daffodil Show,** one of the state's three major daffodil

HEADING FOR HEADWATERS

So intense was public interest in visiting the 7,500-acre Headwaters Grove after its 1999 purchase by California and the U.S. that state officials decided to limit initial access. Only those willing to hike a rugged 10 miles got an early look. Botanists feared—and still fear—that tourism will threaten the fragile old-growth redwood ecosystem.

No trail leads into the reserve's 3,000-acre core, but visitors can drive to the north edge of the forest, just south of Eureka, via Elk River Rd., then hike in some five miles along an abandoned logging road to reach an overlook into the unperturbed heart of the Headlands. Plan to be hiking all day. Limited visitor access is also available from south-east of Fortuna; guided half-day, four-mile roundtrip hikes are offered from mid-May to mid-November.

For current information on Headwaters access and to make reservations for guided hikes, contact the U.S. Bureau of Land Management's **Arcata Field Office,** 1695 Heindon Rd., 707/825-2300, www.ca.blm.gov/arcata. The website includes basic maps of the area. For background information on the battle to protect the Headwaters Grove, updates on current skirmishes, and details on other regional environmental activism, contact: **Environmental Protection Information Center (EPIC)** in Garberville, 707/923-2931, www.wildcalifornia.org.

shows, and in early April for the **Paddle to the Headwaters** Eel River canoe, kayak, and outrigger marathon and race, 877/837-0902, www.paddletotheheadwaters.com, fun for fiends and casual paddlers alike. Try July for the long-running **Redwood Fortuna Rodeo,** the oldest rodeo in the West; October for the **Apple Harvest Festival;** and December for the **Christmas Music Festival.**

The **Fortuna Depot Museum,** in Rohner Park at 4 Park St., 707/725-7645, occupies the old 1893 rail depot and exhibits the history of the Eel River Valley—everything from logging memorabilia and barbed wire to high school yearbooks and fishing lures. It's open in summer, daily 10 A.M.–4:30 P.M.; the rest of the year, Wed.–Sun. noon–4:30 P.M. Admission is free (donations appreciated).

Area motels have rooms $50–100, some higher. The **Best Western Country Inn,** close to the snazzy River Lodge conference center at 2025 Riverwalk Dr., 707/725-6822 or 800/679-7511, www.bwcountryinnfortuna.com, offers an indoor heated pool and whirlpool tub. For fresh regional produce, show up for the **Fortuna Certified Farmers Market,** 707/768-3342, held May–Oct. at 10th and L Streets, on Tuesday, 3:30–6 P.M. Otherwise, **Clendenen's Cider Works,** 96 12th St. (next to the freeway), 707/725-2123, open daily Aug.–Feb., is *the* place for half-gallons of homemade apple cider and fresh local produce. The **Eel River Brewing Company,** 1777 Alamar Way, 707/725-2739, offers around half a dozen homemade beers, including Ravensbrau Porter and Climax Amber. Order from a fine menu of steaks (organic Black Angus beef) and seafoods, pastas, and burgers. For the best biscuits and gravy around, head for **Hansen's Coffee Shop** and truck stop, south of Fortuna proper at 2404 Sandy Prairie Rd. (west of Hwy. 101, north of the Hwy. 36 turnoff), 707/725-2206. Some days the biscuits are gone by 9 A.M., so get there early.

For more information about Fortuna and vicinity, contact the **Fortuna Chamber of Commerce,** 735 14th St., 707/725-3959, www.sunnyfortuna.com.

Van Duzen County Park

Humboldt's largest county park, Van Duzen harbors four groves of nearly undisturbed redwoods along the Van Duzen River east from Hwy. 101 via Hwy. 36. Georgia-Pacific donated these groves, as well as Cheatham Grove farther west, to the Nature Conservancy in 1969, a very large corporate conservation gift. The land was subsequently deeded to the county and the Save-the-Redwoods League. You can hike, swim, fish, picnic, and camp ($12) at both **Pamplin** and **Swimmer's Delight** groves. **Humboldt Grove** is pristine old-growth forest open only for hiking. **Redwood Grove** was severely damaged by windstorms in 1978, but hikers can still walk the old roads. Day-use fee $3. For more information, contact Humboldt County's Parks and Recreation Division in Eureka, 707/445-7651.

Grizzly Creek Redwoods State Park

Gone but not forgotten is the now-extinct California grizzly bear, exterminated here by the late 1860s. The smallest of all the redwood parks, Grizzly Creek Redwoods State Park, 35 miles southeast of Eureka, was once a stagecoach stop. It's surrounded by mostly undeveloped forests along the Van Duzen River (visited now by an occasional black bear), among which are a few redwood groves. The main things to do: hike the short trails, swim, and fish for salmon, steelhead, and trout in winter when the river's raging. "Grizz Creek" (as the locals say) also has a natural history museum inside the restored stage stop.

The campground here (30 campsites, 30 picnic sites) is open year-round. Developed campsites are $20. ReserveAmerica reservations, 800/444-7275, www.reserveamerica.com, are a good idea in summer. Bring quarters for the hot showers. Grizzly Creek also features environmental campsites ($12) and hike-in/bike-in sites ($3). The park day-use fee is $6 per car. For more information, contact: Grizzly Creek Redwoods State Park, 16939 Hwy. 36 in Carlotta, 707/777-3683. A few miles beyond the park is the tiny town of **Bridgeville,** sold on EBay at the end of 2002 for $1.77 million then—when that deal fell through—sold again in 2004 for $700,000.

SCOTIA AND VICINITY

Scotia is a neat-as-a-pin town perfumed by the scents of apple pie, family barbecues, and redwood sawdust. A company town built (to last) from redwood and founded on the solid economic ground of sustained-yield logging, picture-perfect Scotia is one of California's last wholly owned company towns. Generations of children of Pacific Lumber Company (PALCO) loggers happily grew up in Scotia, then went to work in the mills—or went away to college on

PALCO-paid scholarships before returning to work as middle managers in the mill offices.

Scotia's serenity has been obliterated, to a large degree, by major economic and political events. One round of trouble started in 1985, when PALCO was taken over in a Michael Milken–related stock raid by the Maxxam Group. Environmentalists loudly mourned the passing of the old PALCO—friend of the Save-the-Redwoods League and sympathetic to conservationist thought, opposed to clearcutting as a forestry practice. Maxxam's Charles Hurwitz began his tenure at PALCO by clearcutting old-growth redwoods on the company's land. When Hurwitz directed his chainsaws toward the Headwaters Grove—in the midst of PALCO's 60,000-acre Headwaters Forest, one of the last privately held stands of virgin redwoods left in the country—it sparked an environmental and political battle that has taken a decade to resolve, to less than unanimous satisfaction. The agreement, among PALCO and the federal and state governments, saved the core groves of redwoods—for which PALCO received a hefty sum from the taxpayers—but left PALCO free to harvest the rest of its holdings, under what environmentalists contend are token environmental restrictions.

As if such stresses weren't enough, the town's business district was lost in April 1992, when fires started by a massive north coast earthquake destroyed the entire business district and damaged many area homes. (The mill was saved.) The quake's total regional price tag: somewhere in the neighborhood of $61 million. In this millennium, two sawmills tooled for now-rare old-growth logs stand idle, and local layoffs have begun.

Still, the big event in Scotia is taking a tour of the **Pacific Lumber Company redwood sawmill** and manufacturing facility, 125 Main St., 707/764-2222, www.palco.com, the largest in the world. The company's self-guided tour (free) is offered weekdays 8 A.M.–2 P.M., year-round except the weeks of July 4th and Christmas. Also stop by the **Scotia Museum** and visitor center on Main, a storehouse of local logging history housed in a stylized Greek temple built of redwood, with logs taking the place of fluted columns. (Formerly a bank, the building's sprouting redwood burl once had to be pruned regularly.) Open summer and early fall only, weekdays 8 A.M.–4:30 P.M.

About five miles south of town is the company's **demonstration forest,** open daily in summer (also free), and a picnic area with restrooms. **Rio Dell** across the Eel River is a residential community, its main claim to fame being good fossil hunting on the shale-and-sandstone Scotia Bluffs along the banks of the Eel.

The town holds a **Wildwood Days** festival in August. The **Rio Dell/Scotia Chamber of Commerce** is at 715 Wildwood Ave. in Rio Dell, 707/764-3436.

Practicalities

While in Scotia, consider a meal or a stay at the spruced-up **Scotia Inn,** directly across from the mill at 100 Main St. (at Mill), 707/764-5683, www.scotiainn.com, a classic 1923 redwood hotel now served up bed-and-breakfast style. The hotel includes a good restaurant—the **Redwood Room,** serving very American and more worldly fare—plus a separate café and several bars, one known as the **Steak and Potato Pub.** With its second story remodeled and reopened, the Scotia Inn now features18 rooms rich with antiques and four suites, all with private baths and classic claw-footed bathtubs. Continental breakfast included. Rates for most rooms are $100–150; for some rooms and suites, $150–250. **Cinnamon Jack's Bakery,** 341 Wildwood in Rio Del, 707/764-5858, is a coffee stop locally famous for its cinnamon rolls and muffins. Rio Dell's relaxed **Al's Diner,** 337 Second Ave., 707/764-3445, serves fabulous fresh fish, chops, steaks, and other wood-fired specialties.

ⓜ HUMBOLDT REDWOODS STATE PARK

This is the redwood heart of Humboldt County, where more than 40 percent of the world's redwoods remain. The Save-the-Redwoods League and the state have added to the park's holdings grove by grove. Most of these "dedicated groves," named in honor of those who gave to save the trees, and many of the park's developed campgrounds are along the state-park section of the Avenue of the Giants parkway.

Humboldt Redwoods State Park is one of the largest state parks in Northern California and the state's largest redwood park, with more than 51,000 acres of almost unfrequented redwood groves, mixed conifers, and oaks. The park offers 35 miles of hiking and backpacking trails, plus 30 miles of old logging roads—and surprising solitude so close to a freeway. Down on the flats are the deepest and darkest stands of virgin redwoods, including Rockefeller Forest, the world's largest stand of stately survivors. The rolling uplands include grass-brushed hills with mixed forest. Calypso orchids and lilies are plentiful in spring, and wild blackberries and huckleberries ripen July–September.

As is typical of the north coast, heavy rainfall and sometimes dangerously high river conditions are predictable Nov.–Apr. But the rampaging Eel River shrinks to garter snake size by May or June, its emerald water fringed by white sand beaches good for swimming, tubing, fishing, and for watching the annual lamprey migration. The wild and scenic stretches of the Eel are also known for early-in-the-year white-water rafting and kayaking. The **Avenue of the Giants Marathon** run through the redwoods happens in early May.

Humboldt Big Trees

At almost 13,000 acres, **Rockefeller Forest** is the main grove here and among the most valuable virgin stands of redwood remaining on the north coast (yes, donated by the John D. Rockefeller family). In **Founder's Grove,** the Founder's Tree was once erroneously known as the World's Tallest Tree; the park's Dyerville Giant is—or was—actually the park's tallest at 362 feet, when last measured in 1972 (the Giant toppled over in a 1991 storm and now lies on the forest floor), and even taller trees reach skyward in Redwood National Park north of Orick. But the Founder's Tree and Dyerville Giant are two mindful monuments to the grandeur of the natural world. After exploring Founder's Grove, consider the nearby **Immortal Tree,** which has withstood almost every imaginable onslaught from both nature and humanity—a testament to this tree's tenacity, and perhaps the forest's.

Not the largest tree or most martyred but a notable one nevertheless is the *Metasequoia,* which you can see near Weott (and south down the highway at Richardson Grove State Park). It's a dawn redwood native to China, kissing cousin of both species of California redwoods.

Camping

Camping is easy at Humboldt Redwoods, which offers hundreds of campsites and four picnic areas. **Burlington Campground** near Weott is fully developed (hot showers, restrooms, tables—the works for outdoor living), $20. Ditto for the **Albee Creek Campground** not far to the south, and **Hidden Springs Campground** near Miranda. All three of these campgrounds are popular, so make advance reservations in summer through ReserveAmerica, 800/444-7275, www .reserveamerica.com.

Unusual at Humboldt Redwoods State Park are five backcountry backpackers' camps, reserv-

able in advance (first-come) at park headquarters. These camps each have piped spring water (but no fires are allowed, so bring a campstove). Only one of the five—**Bull Creek Trail Camp**—is easily reached by nonhikers. Closest to the road but an uphill climb are **Johnson Trail Camp,** a collection of four backwoods cabins used from the 1920s to 1950s by "tie hacks" (railroad tie makers), and the **Whiskey Flat Trail Camp,** a tent camp named for the Prohibition moonshine still once tucked among these massive old-growth redwoods. **Grasshopper Trail Camp** is among the grasshoppers and deer on the meadow's edge below Grasshopper Peak (great view from the fire lookout at the top), and **Hanson Ridge Trail Camp** is tucked among firs and ferns.

In addition to the outback pleasures of these backcountry camps, the park features two walk-in environmental campgrounds: **Baxter** and **Hamilton Barn** (pick apples in the old orchard), both with convenient yet secluded campsites ($12); sign up at park headquarters, where you can get the particulars). Group camps and horse

AVENUE OF THE GIANTS

This scenic 33-mile drive on the old highway, a narrow asphalt ribbon braiding together the eastern edge of Humboldt Redwoods, the Eel River, and Hwy. 101, weaves past and through some of the largest groves of the largest remaining redwoods in Humboldt and Del Norte Counties. Get off the bike (the avenue's very nice for cycling, but wear bright clothing) or out of the car and picnic, take a short walk, and just *appreciate* these grand old giants.

The part-private, part-public Avenue is dotted with commercial attractions—tourist traps offering redwood knickknacks and trinkets manufactured overseas and trees transformed into walk-in or drive-through freaks of nature. But the curio shops and commercial trappings barely distract from the fragrant grandeur of the dim, dignified forest itself, sunlit in faint slivers and carpeted with oxalis and ferns.

Among the tiny towns dwarfed still more by the giants along the Avenue are **Phillipsville,**

Meyers Flat, and **Redcrest.** Phillipsville is home to the **Chimney Tree,** 707/923-2265, open 8 A.M.–8 P.M. from May to mid-October, and the Tolkienesque **Hobbitown U.S.A.** Meyers Flat boasts one of the state's oldest tourist attractions, the **Shrine Drive-Thru-Tree & Gift Shop,** 707/943-3154. Wagon-train travelers heading up and down the Pacific coast once pulled *their* vehicles through it. The tree stands 275 feet tall, measures 21 feet in diameter, and people can see the sky if standing inside the eight-foot-wide tree tunnel. These days, though, everyone worries every time a storm blows in, because most of the Shrine tree is dead and the behemoth is seriously listing. Visitors can also sample the **Step-Thru Stump** and (the SUVers favorite) **Drive-On Tree.** Food is available at the **Drive-Thru-Tree Cafe,** 707/943-1665. In Redcrest you'll find the **Eternal Tree House,** a 20-foot room inside a living tree, 707/722-4262 (gift shop) or 707/722-4247 (café).

camps are also available. Should all the state facilities be full, the area also includes a number of private campgrounds and RV parks.

Accommodations

The **Miranda Gardens Resort,** 6766 Ave. of the Giants, 707/943-3011, www.miranda gardens.com, is tops in the condo/cabin department, offering comfortable single or duplex cabins—some with two bedrooms, some with kitchens (all cookware and essentials supplied), several with fireplaces, two with whirlpool tubs. Heated pool, continental breakfast, onsite grocery. Most rates are $100–150, but some units are as low as $65 (one double bed), some as high as $175 and $225.

The **Myers Country Inn,** 12913 Ave. of the Giants in Myers Flat, 707/943-3259 or 800/500-6464, www.myersinn.com, is an 1860-vintage two-story hotel now functioning as a country-style 10-room bed-and-breakfast. Amenities include private baths, separate entrances, a fireplace in the lobby, and complimentary continental breakfast. Rates are $100–150.

Another best bet for cabins, on the north side of Humboldt Redwoods, is pet-friendly **Redcrest Resort** in Redcrest at 26459 Ave. of the Giants, 707/722-4208. Most cabins are $50–100; RV sites are also available.

Food

Great for a quick all-American meal, from biscuits and gravy to homemade pies, the place is the **Eternal Treehouse Café,** 26510 Avenue of the Giants in Redcrest, 707/722-4247, open daily for breakfast, lunch, and dinner. For American and international cuisine and fine wines, head toward Myers Flat and **Knight's Restaurant,** 12866 Ave. of the Giants, 707/943-3411. Worthwhile within driving distance are the restaurants in Garberville-Redway and at the Benbow Inn and the Scotia Inn in Scotia.

Information and Services

The day-use fee at Humboldt Redwoods is $6 per car. For maps and more information about the park, stop by or contact: Humboldt Redwoods State Park headquarters (at the Burlington Camp-

ground), also the district office, at 707/946-2409. Alternatively, call 707/946-1807 or 707/946-1814. The **Humboldt Redwoods Interpretive Association Visitor Center,** between headquarters and Burlington Campground, 707/946-2263, www.humboldtredwoods.org, is open daily 9 A.M.–5 P.M. in summer, Thurs.–Sun. 10 A.M.–4 P.M. in winter, and offers excellent natural history exhibits. In summer park rangers offer guided nature walks, campfire programs, and Junior Ranger activities for kids.

GARBERVILLE AND VICINITY

A former sheep ranching town, Garberville is *not* an outlaw enclave paved in $100 bills by pot-growing Mercedes Benz owners, as media mythology would have it. The town was once considered the sinsemilla cultivation capital of the world, an honor most locals are fed up with. The general belief today is that the big-time Rambo-style growers have gone elsewhere. But don't expect people here to share their knowledge *or* opinions on the subject, pro or con. With annual CAMP (Campaign Against Marijuana Production) invasions throughout the surrounding countryside, discretion is the rule of tongue when outsiders show up.

Not far north of Garberville is **M. Lockwood Memorial Park,** a popular rafting departure point also offering good fishing. Two small southerly outposts of Humboldt Redwood State Park are just north of Redway; **Whittemore Grove** and **Holbrook Grove** are both dark, cool glens perfect for picnicking and short hikes. Another area attraction is the famous **One Log House,** associated with Bear Meadow Espresso, 705 Hwy. 101, 707/247-3717, the hollowed-out "house" relocated here from Phillipsville and remodeled.

In June, the annual **Rodeo in the Redwoods and Bull-O-Rama** is the big to-do in these parts, followed in July or early August by the West Coast's largest and usually most impressive reggae festival—the **Reggae on the River** concert—which attracts top talent from Jamaica and America. For concert and other events information, contact the **Mateel Community Center** in Redway, 707/923-3368, www.mateel.org.

For more area information, contact the **Garberville-Redway Chamber of Commerce,** 773 Redwood Dr. in Garberville, 707/923-2613 or 800/923-2613, www.garberville.org, open daily 9 A.M.–5 P.M. in summer, and weekdays 9 A.M.–5 P.M. in winter.

Practicalities

Just about everything in Garberville is on Business 101, called Redwood Drive. The 76-room **Best Western Humboldt House Inn,** 701 Redwood Dr., 707/923-2771, has rooms with air-conditioning, color TV, movies, and phones. Some rooms have kitchens. Other extras here include a coin-op laundry, heated pool, whirlpool, and complimentary continental breakfast. Rates are $100–150. The smaller **Sherwood Forest Motel,** 814 Redwood Dr., 707/923-2721, www.sherwoodforestmotel.com, is quite a find, with abundant amenities. Rates are $50–100.

For farm-fresh fruit, veggies, flowers, and herbs, show up at the **Southern Humboldt Farmers Market,** 707/923-9209, held June–Oct. in Garberville at Locust and Church on Fridays, 11 A.M.–3 P.M., and in "uptown Redway," Tuesday 3–6 P.M. The laid-back **Woodrose Café,** 911 Redwood, 707/923-3191, is beloved for its fine omelettes, tofu specials, good vegetarian sandwiches, and like fare, everything locally and/or organically grown. Open daily for breakfast, for lunch only on weekdays. A good choice for wheat-bread-and-sprouts-style Sunday champagne brunch. For straight-ahead Italian food and pizza, not to mention impressive quantities of Mexican and American fare, try **Sicilito's,** 445 Conger St. (behind the Humboldt House Inn), 707/923-2814, open Fri.–Tues. for lunch and dinner, and Wed.–Thurs. for dinner only. For fresh fish in season and good family-style Italian and American fare, the place is the **Waterwheel Restaurant,** 924 Redwood Dr., 707/923-2031, open daily for breakfast, lunch, and dinner.

Just northwest of Garberville, across the highway in Redway, is the **Mateel Cafe,** 3342-3344 Redwood Dr., 707/923-2030, a fine-food mecca serving everything from Thai tofu to seafood linguine and stone-baked pizza. Vegans, carnivores, low-protein or high-protein dieters—there's something for everyone on the eclectic menu. And check out that Jazzbo Room. Open Mon.–Sat. for lunch and dinner.

BENBOW TO LEGGETT

Benbow Lake State Recreation Area

This state recreation area in the midst of open woodlands two miles south of Garberville is aptly named only in the summer, when a temporary dam goes up on the Eel River's south fork to create Benbow Lake. The lake itself is great for swimming, sailing, canoeing, and windsurfing, with pleasant picnicking and hiking in the hills nearby. (No fishing, no motorized boats.) Day use is $6. The lake area is also center stage for several summertime events, including the annual **Jazz on the Lake** festival, **Shakespeare at Benbow Lake,** and the **Summer Arts Fair.** For more lake information, call 707/923-3238 in summer, 707/247-3318 in winter, or call Humboldt Redwoods State Park, 707/946-2409.

The lake may disappear at summer's end, but the campground remains open all year. It's popular in summer, so reserve campsites ($20, or $23–30 with hookups) through ReserveAmerica, 800/444-7275, www.reserveamerica.com. The private **Benbow Valley RV Resort & Golf Course,** 7000 Benbow Dr., 707/923-2777 or 866/236-2697, www.benbowrv.com, which offers 112 sites with full hookups, $25–40 (discounts available), as well as a golf course.

Benbow Inn

Also open year-round is the elegant four-story Tudor-style Benbow Inn, 445 Lake Benbow Dr., 707/923-2124 or 800/355-3301, www.benbowinn.com. Designed by architect Albert Farr, the Benbow Inn first opened its doors in 1926 and over the years has welcomed travelers including Herbert Hoover, Charles Laughton, and Eleanor Roosevelt. A National Historic Landmark, the inn has been restored to a very English attitude. Complimentary scones and tea are served in the lobby every afternoon at 3 P.M., mulled wine at 4 P.M. when the weather is cold, and hors d'oeuvres in the common rooms between 5 and 7 P.M. The inn's dining room serves a good breakfast, lunch during the summer only, and staples like steak-and-kidney pie for dinner. Full bar. The inn is closed from early January until late March.

In addition to the summer activities staged at the lake, the Benbow Inn hosts a Teddy Bear Tea and Luncheon in May, special Thanksgiving festivities, a theme Christmas party, and a New Year's Eve Champagne Dinner Dance to the big-band tunes of Tommy Dorsey and Glenn Miller. Most rooms are $150–250 but some are $100–150; garden cottages are over $250 (starting at $325). Ask about off-season specials, which include three-nights-for-two and $99 main building room rates.

Richardson Grove State Park

Richardson Grove south of Benbow Lake, with more than 800 acres of fine redwoods, was named for 1920s California governor Friend W. Richardson, noted conservationist. Richardson Grove is popular and crowded in summer, though few people hike the backcountry trails. The Richardson Grove Nature Trail is fully accessible. Picnic near the river or camp at any of three developed campgrounds (Huckleberry/ Madrone is open all year). Developed campsites are $20, and the park's day-use fee is $6. Hike-and-bike campsites are also available ($3), and environmental camps ($12). The **Seven Parks Natural History Association,** in the visitor center at Richardson Grove Lodge, 1600 Hwy. 101, 707/247-3318 (if no answer, call 707/946-2311), offers a variety of redwood-country publications (open summers only). For more information, contact Humboldt Redwoods State Park, 707/946-2409. For camping reservations, contact ReserveAmerica, 800/444-7275, www.reserve america.com. Reservable in summer only.

Piercy to Leggett

At last report the historic lodge at the former Hartsook Country Inn in Piercy, 900 Hwy. 101—part of 33 acres purchased by the Save-the-Redwoods League to prevent logging—was serving as a summers-only visitor center. Piercy's **World Famous Tree House,** 707/925-6406, is a living redwood with a rotted-out hollow that's

home to the "the world's tallest single room." Just south of Piercy along the Eel River is the state's 400-acre **Reynolds Wayside Camp,** offering picnicking and 50 unimproved campsites. For details, call Humboldt Redwoods State Park, 707/946-2409.

Four miles north of Leggett on Hwy. 101, the lovely Frank and Bess Smithe Grove of redwoods at **Smithe Redwoods State Reserve** can be reached only from the west side of the highway, though most of the 665-acre park's protected trees are to the east. A quarter-mile hike here, once a private resort with cabins and restaurant, will take you to a 60-foot waterfall. For more information, call the park at 707/247-3318.

Nearby is **Confusion Hill,** 707/925-6456, one of those places where gravity is defied and water runs uphill, etc. Open year-round. You can also take the kids on a train ride through the redwoods (summers only) and view the world's largest redwood chainsaw sculpture. A logging museum, petting zoo, gift shop, and snack bar round out the facilities.

The **Standish-Hickey State Recreation Area** is 1.5 miles north of Leggett, this 1,000-acre forest supports second-growth coast redwoods, firs, bigleaf maples, oaks, and alders. It's also thick with ferns and, in spring, water-loving wildflowers. Camp at any of the three developed campgrounds here ($20, reservations necessary in summer) or at one of the hike-and-bike campsites, then go fishing, swimming, or on a hike to the 225-foot-tall **Miles Standish Tree,** a massive mature redwood that somehow escaped the loggers. The trail to the tree continues on to a waterfall. The **Mill Creek** trail is a steeper, rugged five-mile loop. Park day use is $6. For more information, contact the park at 69350 Hwy. 101 in Leggett, 707/925-6482. For campground reservations, necessary in summer, contact ReserveAmerica, 800/444-7275, www.reserveamerica.com.

Leggett's big attraction, the **Drive-Thru-Tree Park,** is as schlocky as it sounds, but for some reason humans just love driving through trees. They carved this car-sized hole in the Chandelier Tree in the 1930s, and for a small fee people can "drive thru" it (RVs won't make it). For more information, call 707/925-6363 or 707/925-6446.

The Lost (and Found) Coast

Dust off the backpack, get new laces for those hiking boots. This is the place. California's isolated "Lost Coast," virtually uninhabited and more remote than any other stretch of coastline in the Lower 48, has been found. Here steep mountains soar like bald eagles—their domes tufted with chaparral, a few redwoods tucked behind the ears—and sink their grassy, rock-knuckled talons into the surf raging on black-sand beaches. Local people, of course, snort over the very idea that this splendid stretch of unfriendly coast was ever lost in the first place, even if area highways were intentionally routed away from it. *They* knew it was here. And others have known, too, for at least 3,000 years.

Finding a Lost Culture

Much of the Lost Coast is included in two major public preserves: the **King Range National Conservation Area** in Humboldt County, and the **Sinkyone Wilderness State Park** in Mendocino County. Central to the decade-long battle over expanding the Sinkyone Wilderness, which since 1987 has doubled to include 17 more miles of Mendocino coast, was the fate of 75-acre Sally Bell Grove along Little Jackass Creek. The prolonged political skirmish between former property owner Georgia-Pacific (which planned to clearcut the area) and various private and public agencies focused first on the value of these thousand-year-old trees to posterity. But the war was also over preserving reminders of a lost culture.

Archaeologists believe that a site in the middle of Sally Bell was occupied by proto-Yukian people 3,000 to 8,000 years ago. Chipped-stone tools, stonecutting implements, milling tools, the remains of two houses, and charcoal from long-ago campfires have been discovered at the site. Since those ancient days, for at least 2,500 years up until a century ago, the Sinkyone and Mattole peoples lived permanently along this vast seaside stretch, though other groups came here seasonally when the valleys inland roasted in 100-degree heat. The living was easy, with abundant seafood a dietary staple.

The beaches fringing the King Range were sacred to the Mattole. Descendants talk about the legendary wreck of a Spanish ship along the coast from which the Mattole retrieved triangular gold coins for their children to play with. The coins were lost, however, when their caves along the coast collapsed after the 1906 earthquake. Ancient shell mounds or middens (protected by the Archaeological Resources Protection Act) still dot the seashore. Archaeologists with the U.S. Bureau of Land Management are active throughout the area each summer, and volunteers can occasionally join in on digs. More intriguing, though, is work now underway to establish the nation's first Native American-owned wilderness park, on uplands adjacent to Sinkyone, as a retreat for reestablishing traditional culture.

Getting Here (and Not Getting Lost)

Visiting the Lost Coast requires first getting there, something of a challenge. Roads here are not for the faint of heart nor for those with unreliable vehicles. Unpaved roads are rough and rugged even under the best weather conditions; some wags refer to driving the area as "car hiking." Though Lost Coast road signs usually disappear as fast as they go up (the locals' way of sending a message), existing signs that state Steep Grade—Narrow Road: Campers and Trailers Not Advised roughly translate to "Prepare to drive off the end of the earth, then dive blindly into a fogbank."

From Humboldt Redwoods State Park, take Bull Creek Rd. west through the park and over the rugged mountains down to Honeydew. There turn north on Mattole Rd. and continue north to Petrolia, near the north end of the King Range National Conservation Area. Lost Coast hikers "going the distance" south along the King Range beaches to Shelter Cove often start outside Petrolia, near the squat old lighthouse (reached via Lighthouse Road). Arrange a shuttle system, with pickup at Shelter Cove, to keep it a one-way trip (paid shuttle services are available).

The easiest path to the sea is steep, narrow, and serpentine Shelter Cove Rd., which ends up at the hamlet of Shelter Cove, roughly midway down the Lost Coast; from Garberville, take Frontage Rd. one mile to Redway, and go west 26 miles on Briceland/Shelter Cove Road. Off of this road, you can turn north on wild Wilder Ridge Rd., which connects with Mattole Rd. near Honeydew, or turn south on either Briceland Rd. or Chemise Mountain Rd. to reach Sinkyone Wilderness (the last nine miles are unpaved, 4WD-only in winter and never suitable for RVs or trailers). At Four Corners junction, you can take Bear Harbor Rd. down to the ocean at Needle Rock and Bear Harbor, or head south on Usal Rd., which eventually joins Hwy. 1.

From the south, reach Sinkyone Wilderness via Usal Rd., which turns north off Hwy. 1 a few miles north of Rockport (watch carefully—it's easy to miss, especially heading north).

Practicalities

The Lost Coast isn't nearly as "lost" as it once was. Expect company along the coast and on the trails, especially during the peak summer and fall seasons. September and October, when the weather is typically mild and fog-free, are often ideal. It's rainy and very wet here from late October to April; the area receives 100 to 200 inches of rain annually. The land itself is unstable, with landslides common during the rainy season. Fog is common much of the rest of the year. So in any season, come prepared to get wet. But dress in layers, since in mid-summer it can also get quite warm—in the 80s to 90s—and windy as well.

Mountain bikers will be in heaven here, provided they have strong legs, since "what goes down, must come up." To hike or backpack the Lost Coast, bring proper shoes. For coastwalking (often through sand but also over rocks), lightweight but sturdy shoes with good ankle support and nonslip tread are best. For hiking the inland backcountry—more grassland than forest due to the thin mountain soil, but also supporting chaparral, mixed stands of conifers and oaks, and omnipresent poison oak—heavy-duty hiking boots are wise. Also bring current maps of the area since hikers here are on their own, sometimes (though not always) trekking for days without meeting another human soul. You may meet

up with bears, however, which is why **bear canisters** (hard-sided, bear-proof storage containers) are required for backcountry camping; canisters are available for rent at local BLM offices and elsewhere (see King Range listing, below). Ticks and rattlesnakes can also be problematic here, and if you're planning to hike the beach, bring a tide table (some sections are impassable at high tides). Given the area's remoteness and rugged road conditions, come with a full tank of gas and bring adequate emergency supplies, food, and drinking water.

Other useful items include the Wilderness Press *Trails of the Lost Coast* map, featuring the roads and trails of both the King Range and Sinkyone Wilderness; the BLM map of the area, *King Range National Conservation Area Recreation Guide* (available at BLM offices); and the very enjoyable *An Everyday History of Somewhere* by Ray Raphael (Real Books), available from local bookstores.

To make your hike or backpack a one-way adventure, **King Range Outfitters,** 707/786-9637, will pack your gear in on mules—and will also accompany and accommodate equestrians (bring your own horse or mule). Or sign on with a shuttle service such as **Lost Coast Trail Transport Service** in Whitethorn, 707/986-9909, or the **Shelter Cove RV Campground, Market, and Deli** in Shelter Cove, 707/986-7474. If you'd rather sightsee from sea, whale-watching charters along the Lost Coast can be arranged through **King Salmon Charters** in Eureka, 707/441-1075.

KING RANGE NATIONAL CONSERVATION AREA

The northern reaches of the Lost Coast stretch 35 miles from south of the Mattole River to Whale Gulch. Much of the BLM's King Range National Conservation Area, a total of about 60,000 acres of rugged coastal mountains jutting up at 45-degree angles from rocky headlands, is being considered for federal wilderness protection. Despite the fact that most beaches are already closed to motorized vehicles, rebel offroaders are becoming a problem.

Most people come here to "beach backpack," hiking north to south in deference to prevailing winds. The trailhead begins near the mouth of the Mattole River. Get there from Mattole Rd. near Petrolia via Lighthouse Rd., then head south on foot. After about three miles, you'll come to the red-nippled relic of the Punta Gorda light station; the rocks nearby harbor a seabird colony and a rookery for Steller's sea lions. It's possible to continue hiking all the way south to Shelter Cove, a two- or three-day trip one-way (five days roundtrip), but a longer trek for those heading on to Sinkyone.

The trail saunters along miles of sandy beaches, around some tremendous tidepools, and up onto headlands to bypass craggy coves where streams flow to the sea. In wintry weather, this makes for quite the wild walk (check conditions before setting out); in any season, watch for rattlesnakes on rocks or draped over driftwood. Between self-protective downward glances, look around to appreciate some of the impressive shipwrecks scattered along the way. Also just offshore (in proper season) are gray whales, killer whales, porpoises, and harbor seals. Inland, forming an almost animate wall of resistance, are the mountains, their severity thinly disguised by redwoods and Douglas fir, forest meadows, chaparral scrub, and spring wildflowers. Make camp on high ground well back from the restless ocean, and always adhere to the backpacker's credo: if you pack it in, pack it out.

The 16-mile **King's Crest Trail** starts near Horse Mountain Camp and offers spectacular ocean views on rare sunny days, as does the **Chemise Mountain Trail.** Another fine inland hike is the **Buck Creek Trail** from Saddle Mountain, a challenging near-vertical descent through the fog to the beach. (Before taking the challenge, consider the comments scratched by survivors into the government's signs: "It's a real mother both ways" and "This hill will kill you.") Four primitive BLM campgrounds dot the King Range along both main access roads. It's five miles from Four Corners via Chemise Mountain Rd. to **Wailaki Camp,** picnic tables and 16 campsites on Bear Creek's south fork. (From Wailaki Camp, it's a steep 3.5-mile scramble

down to the wooden bench below, another half-mile to the mouth of Chemise Creek and the beach.) A bit farther is **Nadelos Camp,** with 14 sites. The smaller **Tolkan** and the very pretty, very private **Horse Mountain Camp** are on King Ranch Road.

The camping fee for the various campgrounds is $5–8 per night, and the day-use fee is $1 per day. Permits are required for building fires and using campstoves in the backcountry. All organized groups also need BLM permits. For more information, contact: **King Range Project Office** in Whitethorn, located .25 miles west of the Whitethorn Post Office on Shelter Cove Rd., 707/986-5400; the U.S. Bureau of Land Management's **Arcata Field Office,** 1695 Heindon Rd.707/825-2300, www.ca.blm.gov/arcata; and the **BLM Ukiah Field Office,** 2550 N. State St., 707/468-4000.

Rent bear canisters (required) locally for $5 each at the above offices, and also at the Shelter Cove RV Campground, Market, and Deli and the Petrolia Store. Canisters have a 600 cubic inch capacity and can hold no more than three days' worth of food, trash, and toiletries (soap, toothpaste, sunscreen) for one person. A $75 credit card deposit is also required for each canister.

SINKYONE WILDERNESS STATE PARK

Sinking into Sinkyone is like blinking away all known life in order to finally *see.* Named for the Sinkyone people, who refused to abandon their traditional culture and hire on elsewhere as day laborers, this place somehow still honors that indomitable spirit.

More rugged than even the King Range, at Sinkyone Wilderness State Park jagged peaks plunge into untouched tidepools where sea lions and seals play. Unafraid here, wildlife sputters, flutters, or leaps forth at every opportunity. The land seems lusher, greener, with dark virgin forests of redwoods and mixed conifers, rich grassland meadows, waterfalls, fern grottos. The one thing trekkers won't find (yet) among these 7,367 wild acres is a vast trail system. Many miles of the coast are accessible to hikers, and much of the rest of the 40-mile main trail system includes a north/south trail and some logging roads. The trail system connects with trails in the King Range National Conservation Area around the Wailaki area, but you can't reach Sinkyone from Shelter Cove by hiking south along the coast.

Sinkyone Wilderness State Park is always open for day use. The park also offers limited camping at more than 22 scattered and primitive environmental campsites, rarely full. To get oriented, stop by the park's **visitor center** at **Needle Rock Ranch House,** named for an impressive sea stack offshore just beyond the black-sand beach. (Take shelter in the cottage in bad weather—rooms here are now available for rent—otherwise camp under alders and firs nearby.) **Jones Beach** features a secluded cove and an acre of eucalyptus trees at an abandoned homestead (steep trail). Easier to get to is **Stream Side Camp,** two campsites in a wooded creekside glen, with a third perched atop a nearby knoll (with great ocean views, fog permitting). Farther inland is **Low Bridge Camp,** by a stream 1.5 miles from the visitor center.

Beautifully rugged **Bear Harbor** in the Orchard Creek meadow was once a lumber port serving northern Mendocino and southern Humboldt counties. All that's left of the nine-mile-long railroad spur that served the area from the mid-1880s until 1906 is a short rusted section of narrow-gauge track. Fuchsias cascade over the small stone dam. In late summer, harvest a few apples from the homestead's abandoned orchard before the deer do.

Energized after the beach trails with no place else to go, hike unpaved Usal Rd., which runs north to south and passes through Bear Harbor. Most cars can't make it past the gully in the road just over a mile south of Bear Harbor, but it's an easy walk from there to Bear Harbor campsites (excellent beach also). Other camp possibilities include a secluded seaside campground at Usal Creek, and two backpackers' camps at Jackass and Little Jackass Creeks.

Campsites are first-come, first-camped ($10 May–Sept., $7 Oct.–Apr.), and the day-use fee is $2 per car. Solitude seekers, please note that Sinkyone is particularly crowded on summer

holiday weekends. For more information, contact **Sinkyone Wilderness State Park** in Whitethorn, 707/986-7711 (recorded). You can also pick up a park map at the **Humboldt Redwoods State Park Visitor Center** on the Avenue of the Giants in Weott, north of Garberville.

LOST (AND FOUND) TOWNS

People in **Briceland** once made a living as bark peelers. There was a plant here built for the purpose of extracting tannic acid from the bark of the tan oak. The spot called **Whitethorn** near the headwaters of the Mattole River was once a busy stage station, then a loud lumber camp with five working sawmills. East of Honeydew is old **Ettersburg,** now posted as **Divorce Flat** and first homesteaded in 1894 by apple grower Alfter Etter.

Honeydew was named for the sweet-tasting aphid dew beneath cottonwoods down by the river. There's a gas station/general store/post office in Honeydew, usually but not necessarily open during the day. Head-turning from here, though, are the roadside views of King Peak and its rugged range. Perfect for picnicking is the **A.W. Way County Park** in the Mattole River Valley, loveliest in spring when the wild irises bloom. Day use is $2, campsites $12. For a roof over your head, **Mattole River Organic Farms' Country Cabins,** three miles outside Honeydew at 42354 Mattole Rd., 707/629-3445 or 800/845-4607, iansigman@hotmail.com, offers housekeeping cottages on a bluff overlooking the river. Rates are $50–100, depending on sleeping arrangements and options. All have kitchens with gas stoves, apartment refrigerators, pots, pans, and all the basics. By the way, all equipment on the farm operates on politically correct fuel—biodiesel.

Fishing is good on the Mattole River between Honeydew and eucalyptus-sheltered **Petrolia,** named for California's first commercial oil well, drilled three miles east of here in the 1860s. Just south of downtown Petrolia is a great place to eat—the **Hideaway** bar and grill, 451 Conklin Creek Rd. (at the Mattole River bridge), 707/629-3533. It doesn't look like much from the outside, but inside the locals gather for convivial conversation over glasses of Sierra Nevada Pale Ale on tap. The food is good, too. Petrolia also has a well-stocked general store, a gas station, and the deluxe, country-style **Lost Inn** in "downtown" Petrolia, 707/629-3394, actually a huge two-room suite in the front section of the family home (private entrance through a trellised opening and a private yard and garden). Inside you'll find a queen bed and a futon sleeper couch, a kitchenette, and a large glassed-in front porch perfect for capturing winter sun. An adjoining bedroom can also be rented—a perfect set-up for two couples traveling together. Guests enjoy fresh fruit and vegetables in season. Well-behaved pets are okay on the porch. Rates, including full breakfast, are $50–100. For a cabin stay, the place is **Windchime Cabins** (previously Ziganti's), 707/629-3582, with one studio cabin for $75 (two nights $125, three nights $175) and a two-bedroom cabin that sleeps four for $95 (two nights $135, three nights $195). Veggie garden onsite as well as equine overnight facilities (pipe fencing), $20 per horse per night with advance reservations.

Farther north, past the Mattole River lagoon and the road leading to the abandoned Punta Gorda Lighthouse, past the automated light tower atop Cape Ridge (built to replace the 16-sided pyramid tower built there in 1868), and past Cape Mendocino and Scottish-looking farm country lies the very Victorian town of Ferndale, just south of Eureka. As you come down to town, you'll get a great aerial view of the Eel River delta.

The big city on this lost side of the world, though, is **Shelter Cove**, a privately owned enclave within the King Range National Conservation Area once home to the Sinkyone and a major collecting point for the Pomos' clamshell money. Today, this is the place for soaking up some wilderness within range of humanity, for whale-watching, beachcombing, skin diving, and sport fishing. Stop by the **Shelter Cove RV Campground, Market, and Deli,** 492 Machi Rd., 707/986-7474, for current local information. Shuttle service to the Mattole Beach trailhead ($125) is also available. **Mario's,** at the marina, 707/986-1199, is open nightly for dinner and Fri.–Sun. for lunch. Declared one of the nation's premier fly-in dining destinations by *Private Pilot* magazine, the remote **Cove Restaurant** at 10 Seal Crt., 707/986-1197—is open Thurs.–Sun. for lunch and dinner. From well-prepared steaks and burgers to fresh fish and shellfish, just about everything's great. Luxury rooms and suites at the **Oceanfront Inn and Lighthouse,** 26 Seal Crt., 707/986-7002, are $100–150 and higher. The expanded coveside **Shelter Cove Motor Inn,** 205 Wave Dr., 707/986-7521 or 888/570-9676, offers rooms with abundant amenities (microwaves, refrigerators, coffeemakers, hairdryers); some have whirlpool tubs, fireplaces, and Internet access. Rates $50–150. The **Shelter Cove Beachcomber Inn,** close to the store and overlooking the campground at 412 Machi Rd., 707/986-7551 or 800/718-4789 (reservations only), offers six rooms and suites in three separate, fairly secluded buildings—various configurations with brass beds, private baths, kitchens or mini-kitchens, woodstoves, barbecues, and picnic tables. Rates are $50–100 for two, $10 each extra person. Call between 9 A.M. and 7 P.M. only. For more information on Shelter Cove, try the **Shelter Cove Business Directory,** www.sojourner2000.com.

To Mendocino

To reach Fort Bragg and Mendocino along an equally stunning stretch of coastline, head southwest on scenic Hwy. 1. This route hugs the coast past the small coastal towns of Rockport and Westport. Blink-and-you-miss-it Westport anchors itself around a couple of 90-degree bends in the highway, along a lonely and pristine stretch of coast near Westport–Union Landing State Beach. You have to slow down for the turns anyway, so pull over and explore. You may decide to stay awhile.

The **DeHaven Valley Farm,** 39247 N. Hwy. 1, Westport, 707/961-1660 or 877/334-2836, www.dehaven-valley-farm.com, is a large 1885-vintage Victorian farmhouse with a total of eight "view" rooms and cottages (two share a bath, five have fireplaces), serving full breakfast (dinner available in their restaurant). Most rooms are $50–100 (one is $119), and the four studio/cottage units are $100–150. Urbane accommodations are available at the cozy **Howard Creek**

Ranch bed-and-breakfast, 40501 N. Hwy. 1 (near the south end of Usal Rd., north of Westport), 707/964-6725, www.howardcreek ranch.com, a New England–style farmhouse and outlying cabins on 40 acres. Most of the 14 rooms, suites, and cabins (including one built around a boat) have private baths. Amenities include gorgeous gardens, a pool, sauna, and wood-heated hot tub. Full, hearty breakfast. Rates range $75–160.

Mendocino and the Coast

People just love Mendocino. They love it for a variety of reasons. Some are smitten by the town's Cape Cod architecture, admittedly a bit odd on the California side of the continent. The seaside saltbox look of the 19th-century wood-frame homes here, explained by the fact that the original settlers were predominantly lumbermen from Maine, is one of the reasons the entire town is included on the National Register of Historic Places. Others love Mendocino for its openly artistic attitude. Of course, almost everyone loves the town's spectacular setting at the mouth of Big River—and at the edge of one of the most sublime coastlines in California.

Everybody loves Mendocino—and as a result, people tend to love Mendocino to death, at least in summer. Not even 1,000 people live here, yet the community is usually clogged with people, pets, and parked cars. Mendocino-area rental homes are inhabited in summer and at other "peak" times, but in the dead of winter, locals can barely find a neighbor to talk to. Besides, almost no one who actually *lives* here (or lived here) can afford to now. Exactly when it was that things started to change for the worse—well, that depends on whom you talk to.

The Arts and "Culture Vultures"

In the 1950s, when nearby forests had been logged over and the lumbermill was gone, and the once bad and bawdy doghole port of Mendocino City was fading fast, the artists arrived. Living out the idea of making this coastal backwater home were prominent San Francisco painters like Dorr Bothwell, Emmy Lou Packard, and Bill Zacha, who in 1959 founded the still-strong Mendocino Art Center. Soon all the arts were in full bloom on these blustery bluffs, and the town had come alive. But even back then, as *Johnny Belinda* film crews rolled through Mendocino streets and James Dean showed up for the filming of *East of Eden,* old-timers and retirees could see what was coming. The town's possibilities could very well destroy it.

In the decades since, the costs of living and doing business in Mendocino have gotten so high that most of Mendocino's artists have long since crawled out of town with their creative tails between their legs—pushed out, locals say, by the more affluent "culture vultures" who consume other people's creativity. Though many fine artists, craftspeople, performers, and writers work throughout Mendocino County, most art, crafts, and consumables sold in Mendocino shops are imported from elsewhere. Even finding a local place to park is nearly impossible in Mendocino, a town too beautiful for its own good.

Mendocino at Its Best

Thankfully, in postage-stamp-size Mendocino, cars are an unnecessary headache. You can stroll from one end of town to the other and back again—twice—without breaking a sweat. So leave your car parked at the village lodging of choice. If you're staying elsewhere, take the bus. Or hike here, or ride a bike. Mendocino is at its best when seen on foot or from the seat of a bike. Note, however, that street addresses in Mendocino can be either three digits or five digits, all in the same block. Fortunately, the town is small and beautiful. So just find the street you need by name and wander along it until you find what you're looking for.

To stroll the streets of Mendocino or explore the headlands at the moodiest, most renewing time, come when most people don't—in November or January. This is the season when Mendocino is still itself, and seems to slip back to a

workers, an active fishing fleet, and many of Mendocino's working artists and much of their work. This friendly town offers an array of relatively urban services and amenities not found in smaller Mendocino. Just north of Fort Bragg is tiny **Cleone,** and at the south end of Fort Bragg is **Noyo Harbor,** with its bustling fishing fleet. Approximately halfway between Mendocino and Fort Bragg lies the little hamlet of **Caspar,** which makes Mendocino look like the big city.

Just a few miles south of Mendocino, near Van Damme State Park, is **Little River,** a burg boasting its own post office but most famous for the long-running Little River Inn that stands tall by the highway. A bit farther south is **Albion,** a miniscule coastal hamlet straddling the mouth of the Albion River—a natural harbor supporting a small fishing fleet. From just south of Albion and inland via Hwy. 128 is the attractive Anderson Valley and Boonville.

Mendocino Village

© ROBERT HOLMES/CALTOUR

time before this New Englandesque village was even an idea. A sense of that self blasts in from the bleak headlands, come winter, blowing rural reality back into town. In winter you can meet the community—the fishermen, fourth-generation loggers, first-generation marijuana farmers, apple and sheep ranchers, artists and craftspeople, even city-fleeing innkeepers and shopkeepers as they, too, come out of hiding.

The Mendocino Coast: Greater Mendocino

Given Mendocino's proximity to, and dependence on, a number of nearby coastal communities, any visit to Mendocino also includes the coastline for about 10 miles in either direction. The Mendocino Coast business, arts, and entertainment communities are so intertwined that they share a single visitors bureau.

Not counting Garberville, **Fort Bragg** north of Mendocino is the last community of any size before Eureka. Mendocino's working-class sister city to the north was named after a fort built there in 1855 for protection against hostile natives. Fort Bragg is now unpretentious home to working (and unemployed) loggers and mill-

MENDOCINO SIGHTS

Ford House, Kelley House, and the Joss House

Start your Mendocino explorations at the state park's **Ford House interpretive center,** near the public restrooms on the seaward side of Main, 707/937-5397. The center features a model of Mendocino as it looked in 1890, historical photos, exhibits on lumbering and the Pomo Indians, wildflower displays, local art, lots of brochures, free apple cider, and a store selling books and postcards. It's open year-round, daily 11 A.M.–4 P.M. (longer hours if volunteers are available).

Across the street, sedately settled into its old-fashioned gardens, is the 1861 **Kelley House** (entrance around the front at 45007 Albion), 707/937-5791, now housing the Mendocino region's historical society museum, library, and bookstore. In addition to taking in the exhibits of pioneer artifacts and historical photos, sign up for a guided walking tour of Mendocino (nominal fee) with **Mendocino Historical Research, Inc.,** mendocinohistory.org, which maintains and operates Kelley House as a historical research facility. The museum is open daily 1–4 P.M. June–Sept. (small admission), otherwise Fri.–Mon. only.

Also of historical interest, one of Mendocino's earliest buildings (1852), is the **Temple of Kwan Tai** joss house, a half block west of Kasten on Albion (between Kasten and Woodward), 707/937-5123, open to the public by appointment only. While you're out and about, also drop by **Crown Hall,** 45285 Ukiah St. (toward the west end), to see what's going on. The intimate theater hosts everything from local comedy troupes and community plays to big-name touring bands.

Mendocino Art Center

When you're ready to head off around town, a good first destination is the nonprofit Mendocino Art Center, 45200 Little Lake Rd. (between Williams and Kasten), 707/937-5818 www .mendocinoartcenter.com, open daily 10 A.M.– 5 P.M. This place is a wonder—a genuine *center* for countywide arts awareness and artistic expression. The organization sponsors apprenticeships in ceramics, textiles, and weaving, as well as fine arts programs; maintains an art library and a satellite center in Fort Bragg; and sponsors countless events. Whatever artistic endeavor is happening in Mendocino County, someone at the center knows about it.

Check out **The Main Gallery** and both the **Abramson** and **Nichols Gallery** here for exhibits of member artists plus special fine arts and crafts shows, and the gift shop. The center also houses three large studios, with the emphasis on textiles and fiber arts, ceramics, and fine arts, respectively. With extra time, sample the **Zacha Commemorative Sculpture Garden.** Since the belief here is that art should be accessible to everyone, the art center sponsors weekend art classes Sept.–June, and in summer offers three-week workshops. The center's **Schoeni Theatre** is home for the Mendocino Theatre Company. Very reasonable (shared) accommodations with kitchenettes are available in center-sponsored apartments; if that's not feasible, the art center staff will help with other arrangements.

Art Galleries

The number of art galleries in and around Mendocino is staggering. Some seem strictly oriented to the tourist trade while others are more sophisticated.

If you like the idea of supporting local artists, a good place to start is the **Artists' Co-op of Mendocino,** upstairs in the Sussex Building, 45270 Main St., 707/937-2217, showcasing the work of its owner-artists. A veritable fine furniture and woodworking emporium in town is the three-story **Highlight Gallery,** 45052 Main, 707/937-3132, which also displays handwoven textiles. The famed **William Zimmer Gallery,** Ukiah and Kasten, 707/937-5121, offers a large, eclectic collection of highly imaginative, contemporary fine arts and crafts, aesthetic homage to Mendocino Art Center founder Bill Zimmer. **Panache Gallery,** 10400 Kasten, 707/937-1234, has that, of course, but specializes in fine art, art glass, bronze, and wood, include works from Mendocino Coast Furnituremakers Association members (there's a second store location on Main, 707/937-0947). The intriguing **Partner's Gallery at Glendeven,** on the grounds of Glendeven Inn just south of the town, 8205 N. Hwy. 1, 707/937-3525, features changing exhibits by "partners" as well as guest artists.

Shopping and Entertainment

Despite its small size, Mendocino is stuffed with shops and stores, enough to keep shopping addicts happy for an entire weekend. **Alphonso's Mercantile,** 520 Main St. (between Kasten and Osborne), is a classical music store and smokeshop (even though Alphonso doesn't smoke anymore) with a million-dollar view of the coast. If you forgot to pack some summer reading, plan to spend some quality time at the **Gallery Bookshop & Bookwinkle's Children's Books** at Main and Kasten Streets, 707/937-2215, www.gallerybooks.com, a truly impressive independent bookstore. Just plain fun: **Out of This World** at 45100 Main, 707/937-3335, a megacollection of telescopes, microscopes, and binoculars.

Also fascinating and very Mendocino is **Mendosa's Merchandise and Market,** 10501 Lansing (at Little Lake), 707/937-0563 and 707/937-5879, one of those rare *real* hardware stores long gone from most California communities, accompanied by a decent local grocery. Quite the contrast but equally wonderful (with its "food for people, not for profit" slogan) is the collectively run **Corners of the Mouth** natural food store, 45015 Ukiah (between Ford and Lansing), 707/937-5345.

Venerable **Dick's Place,** 45080 Main St., 707/937-5643, with few concessions to the changing times, is still Mendocino's real bar. Inside, the locals drink beer, plug the jukebox (lots of good Patsy Cline), and play darts. Outside, the bar's sign, a 1950s-style martini glass grandfathered in despite local anti-neon ordinances, is visible from miles away through the regularly dense coastal fog. Next door, definitely a sign of changing times, is the **Fetzer Wine Tasting Room,** 45070 Main St., 707/937-6190, open daily 10 A.M.–6 P.M.

FORT BRAGG SIGHTS
Mendocino Coast Botanical Gardens
The nonprofit 47-acre Mendocino Coast Botanical Gardens, 18220 N. Hwy. 1 (two miles south of downtown), 707/964-4352, www.gardenbythesea.org, features native plant communities as well as formal plantings of rhododendrons, azaleas, fuchsias, and other regional favorites. Also here—in addition to some smashing views of the crashing coast—are a native plant nursery, picnic tables, the fine **Gardens Grill** restaurant, and summertime music concerts. A year-round calendar of special events and workshops are offered, too, from bird-watching tours to organic gardening classes. Wheelchair accessible. The gardens are open daily 9 A.M.–5 P.M. Mar.–Oct., and 9 A.M.–4 P.M. the rest of the year (closed Thanksgiving, Christmas, and the second Saturday in September). Admission is $6 general, $5 seniors (60 and up), $3 youths ages 13–17), and $1 children ages 6–12.

Guest House Museum
For the local version of redwood logging history, as told through photos, artifacts, and tree-mining memorabilia, stop by the Guest House Museum, 343 N. Main St., 707/964-4251, in an attractive 1892 redwood mansion that was once used as a guest house for friends and customers of local Union Pacific Lumber execs. Open Wed.–Sun. 11 A.M.–3 P.M., small admission. The only remaining **fort building** from the original Fort Bragg stands a block east of the Guest House on Franklin Street.

THE SKUNK RIDES AGAIN

In early 2003, the future of Fort Bragg's famed Skunk Train was in doubt, but after a brief hiatus a new owner climbed aboard. At last report, the Skunk was back on track, with Fort Bragg again the western terminus of everyone's favorite sightseeing railroad.

Though the Skunk may return to its longer Fort Bragg–Willits run, at last report the route ended at Northspur, the halfway point, where a little tourist village offers food booths, souvenir stands, and restrooms.

In summer 2004, the 3.5-hour Fort Bragg–Northspur trip was offered twice daily, at 9:30 A.M. and 2 P.M., with "Old No. 45" steam engine—a 1924 2-8-2 Baldwin Mikado—riding the rails on Tuesday, Wednesday, Thursday, and Saturday, the railroad's Super Skunk diesel locomotives or Skunk Motorcars (resembling city-style trolley cars) on other days. In fall and spring, one daily trip was offered, at 10 A.M. There's also a weekend-only schedule, with the steam locomotive scheduled on Saturday. Call or see the website for current schedule details. Also inquire about shorter Wolf Tree Turn outings. No trains run on Thanksgiving Day, Christmas Day, and New Year's Day.

Rates for 2004 Skunk Train excursions were $45 adult and $20 children ages 3–11 (toddlers free) for the steam train, $35 adult and $20 children for diesel or motorcar trains.

The Skunk strikes out from the station at Laurel Street. For current information and advance reservations, contact Skunk Train headquarters in Fort Bragg, 707/964-6371 or 800/866-1690, www.skunktrain.com.

Noyo Harbor

Fort Bragg's tiny fishing port lies at the south end of town, at the mouth of the Noyo River. It's a safe harbor for fisherfolk during stormy seas and shelters several fish restaurants popular with tourists, but fairly ho-hum in terms of cuisine and ambience. Don't miss Noyo's **Salmon Barbecue** festivities every July. It's a must-attend event for delicious fresh salmon and an intimate encounter with the local populace. Good folks, good food, big tradition.

Other Attractions

People think first of Mendocino when they think of art galleries, but Fort Bragg has at least as many—and more of the "working artist" variety. Not to be missed is the nonprofit **Northcoast Artists Collaborative Gallery,** 362 N. Main St., 707/964-8266, with everything from wearable art (weavings and handpainted silk scarves) and handcrafted jewelry to original art, prints, pottery, photographs, and greeting cards made by member artists. A very impressive enterprise. Fort Bragg's **Gallery District**—between Main and Franklin, and Redwood and Fir—so while you're in the area, see what else looks interesting. North Franklin St. between Laurel and Redwood boasts a number of **antique shops.**

Unique in Fort Bragg is **Adirondack Design,** 350 Cypress St., 707/964-4940 or 888/643-3003 (orders only), www.adirondackdesign.com. Founded by a group known as Parents and Friends, Inc., Adirondack Design provides jobs and services for the area's developmentally disabled adults. And what a job this crew does—crafting a high-quality line of redwood garden furniture and accessories, everything from Adirondack chairs, loveseats, rockers, and swings to garden benches and planters, cold frames, and a charming "bird chalet." Adirondack even produces a small footbridge.

STATE PARKS

Mendocino Headlands State Park

Start exploring the area's spectacular state parks in Mendocino proper. About the only reason there aren't shopping malls or condos and resort hotels between the town of Mendocino and its sea-stacked sandstone coast was the political creativity of William Penn Mott, the state's former director of Parks and Recreation. Mott quietly acquired the land for what is now Mendocino Headlands State Park by trading Boise Cascade some equally valuable timberlands in nearby Jackson State Forest.

The headlands and beach are subtle, more a monument to sand sculpture than an all-out ode to hard rock. The impressive stacks here and elsewhere are all that remain of sandstone headlands after eons of ocean erosion. Curving seaward around the town from Big River to the northern end of Heeser Dr., the park includes a three-mile hiking trail, a small beach along the mouth of Big River (trailheads and parking on Hwy. 1, just north of the bridge), sandstone bluffs, the area's notorious wave tunnels, offshore islands and narrows, and good tidepools. *The* peak experience from the headlands is whale-watching. (Whether watching the waves or whales, stand back from the bluff's edge. Sandstone is notoriously unstable, and the ragged rocks and wicked waves below are at best indifferent to human welfare.) For a map and more information, get oriented at Ford House, 707/937-5397, or call the state parks' Mendocino District Headquarters, 707/937-5804. You can easily walk here from town—it's just an invigorating and spectacular stroll away. Pick up the path at the west end of Main Street.

Van Damme State Park

This small state park just south of Mendocino is not famous but, despite the considerable competition, is one of the finer things about this stretch of the coast. The excellent and convenient camping here midway between Mendocino and Albion is secondary. Van Damme State Park is an 1,831-acre, five-mile-long preserve around Little River's watershed, pointing out to sea. Squeezed into a lush ravine of second-growth mixed redwood forest, Van Damme's pride is its **Fern Canyon Trail,** a 2.5-mile hiking and bicycling trail weaving across Little River through red alders, redwoods, ferns—western sword ferns, deer ferns, bird's foot ferns, and five-finger ferns, among others—and past mossy rocks, pools, and streamside herds of horsetails. A 1.5-mile trail offers a self-guided tour of the coho salmon's life cycle.

Though the Fern Canyon Trail is easy, the going gets tougher at the east end as the path climbs the canyon and connects with the loop trail to Van Damme's **Pygmy Forest,** a gnarly thicket bonsaied by nature. What makes the pygmy forest pygmy? Beneath the thin layer of darker topsoil underfoot is *podzol* (Russian for "colored soil")—albino-gray soil as acidic as vinegar. Iron and other elements leached from the podzol collect below in a reddish hardpan layer impossible for tree roots (even moisture, for that matter) to penetrate. Similar fairy forests are common throughout coastal shelf plant communities between Salt Point State Park and Fort Bragg, an area sometimes referred to as the Mendocino White Plains. It is possible to drive most of the way to this green grove of miniatures via Airport Rd. just south of the park, and the forest is wheelchair accessible. A short self-guided discovery trail here loops through dwarfed Bolander pine (a coastal relative of the Sierra Nevada's looming lodgepole), Bishop pine, Mendocino pygmy cypress (found only between Anchor Bay and Fort Bragg), and dwarf manzanita. Also noteworthy are the spring-blooming rhododendrons, which love acidic soils and here dwarf the trees.

Van Damme's tiny beach is a popular launch point for scuba divers and is usually safe for swimming, though no lifeguards are on duty. (The 1996 addition of Spring Ranch added more beach, and some spectacular tidepools.) The redwood-sheltered campground area is protected from winds but not its own popularity. Plan on making reservations for stays April 1–mid-October. A small group camp is also available.

After breakfast, stop by the visitor center and **museum** in the impressive Depression-era Civilian Conservation Corps rec hall built from hand-split timbers. Inside you'll find an overview of the area's cultural, economic, and natural history. Or take the short **Bog Trail** loop from the visitor center to see (and smell) the skunk cabbage and other marsh-loving life. For more information, including details on kayaking tours, call the state

ROLL IT ON, BIG RIVER

Eight miles of Mendocino's Big River estuary, 50 miles of the river and its tributaries, 1,500 acres of coastal wetlands, and nearly 6,000 acres of surrounding watershed are now protected as **Big River State Park,** thanks to the relentless fundraising of the Mendocino Land Trust and additional funds from state and federal agencies. California's longest remaining undeveloped estuary, the new Big River park is bounded on the north by Jackson State Forest and Mendocino Woodlands State Park; its southern boundary is near Comptche-Ukiah Rd., connecting in places with Van Damme State Park and other nature reserves.

Named not for its own size but the trees that shade it, Big River is a prime salmon spawning estuary and essential wildlife habitat. It provides the last piece of a 74,000-acre public-lands jigsaw, an effective wildlife corridor extending inland as well as along the coast. Big River alone provides protected habitat for 27 endangered, threatened, or "special concern" species, including the northern spotted owl, California brown pelican, and bald eagle. The river is a natural nursery for threatened anadromous fish species, including Coho salmon, steelhead, and Pacific lamprey.

Big River visitor facilities are scarce; no camping is allowed, and the only restrooms are located at Big River's beach area. Hikers (dogs on leash only), equestrians, canoers, and kayakers will still find the essentials here: land, water, and that big coastal sky.

The Big River Trail (Big River Haul Road) begins on the river's north side and meanders alongside its course, into Mendocino Woodlands State Park; more than 100 miles of public trails link the park to adjacent areas. Exploring by kayak or canoe is immensely popular. If you're not packing your own, call **Catch-a-Canoe & Bicycles Too** at the Stanford Inn, 707/937-0273.

For more information, call Mendocino State Parks, 707/937-5804, or stop by the Ford House visitor center in Mendocino, open year-round 11 A.M.–4 P.M. daily, 9 A.M.–5 P.M. in summer. For details on the Big River story, see the land trust's website, www.mendocinolandtrust.org.

North Coast

parks' Mendocino District Headquarters, 707/937-5804. Reserve campsites ($20) in advance through ReserveAmerica, 800/444-7275, www.reserveamerica.com. The park's day-use fee is $6.

Russian Gulch State Park

Just north of Mendocino on the site of another days-past doghole port, Russian Gulch State Park is 1,200 acres of diverse redwood forests in a canyon thick with rhododendrons, azaleas, berry bushes, and ferns; coastal headlands painted in spring with wildflowers; and a broad bay with tidepools and sandy beach, perfect for scuba diving. Especially fabulous during a strong spring storm is the flower-lined cauldron of **Devil's Punch Bowl** in the middle of a meadow on the northern headlands. A portion of this 200-foot wave tunnel collapsed, forming an inland blowhole, but the devil's brew won't blast through unless the sea bubbles and boils.

Russian Gulch is a peaceable kingdom, though, perfect for bird-watching (osprey, redtailed hawks, ravens, seabirds, shorebirds, and songbirds), whale-watching, even watching steelhead in their spawning waters. Rock fishing is popular around the bay, as is ocean salmon fishing and angling for rainbows in the creek (no fishing for spawning steelhead in fall or winter).

After a picnic on the headlands, take a half-day hike upcanyon. Make it a nine-mile loop by combining the southern trails to reach 36-foot **Russian Gulch Falls** (best in spring), then loop back to camp on the North Trail. (One of these trail links, the five-mile **Canyon Trail,** is also designated as a biking trail.) The far northern **Boundary Trail** is for hikers and horsebackers, running from the horse camp on the eastern edge of the park to the campground.

Camping at Russian Gulch is itself an attraction, with 30 family campsites ($20) tucked into the forested canyon; amenities include barbecue grills, picnic tables, food lockers, hot showers, and restrooms with laundry tubs. The separate group camp accommodates about 40 people. This close to the coast, campers often sleep under a blanket of fog, so come prepared for wet conditions. Reserve campsites in advance through

ReserveAmerica, 800/444-7275, www.reserve america.com. For more information, contact the Mendocino District Headquarters (located here, open Mon.–Fri. 8 A.M.–4:30 P.M.), 707/937-5804. The day-use fee is $6.

Caspar Headlands and Point Cabrillo Light Station

About two miles north of Russian Gulch, reached via Pt. Cabrillo Dr., are the spectacular Caspar Headlands, hemmed in by housing. Miles of state beaches are open to the public, though, from sunrise to sunset—perfect for whale-watching. The headlands are accessible only by permit (free, available at Russian Gulch). A particular point of interest is the historic 300-acre **Point Cabrillo Light Station and Preserve,** the preserve open daily to pedestrians (no dogs) 9 A.M.–sunset, the light station and gift shop open weekends 11 A.M.–4 P.M. Thanks to the restoration efforts of dedicated volunteers, in 1999 the light station's 20th-century technology was replaced by that of the 19th century—and the original third-order Fresnel lens once again casts its light seaward. It's about a half-mile walk to the lighthouse along the access road, from the entrance gate; paved parking is available off Pt. Cabrillo Dr., 9 A.M.–6 P.M. Guided 1.5-mile walks are offered every Sunday at 11 A.M., starting at the parking lot. Come in March for the **Whale Festival at Point Cabrillo Light Station.** Handicapped access parking is available at the lighthouse, in front of area residences.

For details about headlands access, call 707/937-5804. For information on guided walks, whale-watching weekends, and special events, call 707/937-0816 or see www.pointcabrillo.org.

Jug Handle State Reserve

For serious naturalists, the "ecological staircase" hike at this reserve just north of Caspar is well worth a few hours of wandering. The staircase itself is a series of uplifted marine terraces, each 100 feet higher than the last, crafted by nature. The fascination here is the *change* associated with each step up the earth ladder, expressed by distinctive plants that also slowly change the environment.

© KIM WEIR

tree at Jug Handle State Reserve

Jackson State Forest

Bordering Jug Handle Reserve on the east is this 46,000-acre demonstration forest named after Jacob Green Jackson, founder of the Caspar Lumber Company. Extending east along the South Fork of the Noyo River and Hwy. 20, the Jackson Forest (logged since the 1850s) has picnic and camping areas, and almost unlimited trails for biking, hiking, and horseback riding. The forest is accessible at various points east off Hwy. 1 and along Hwy. 20; a forest map is necessary to get around. **Forests Forever** and other citizens groups are now actively challenging logging here, promoting restoration plans. For more forest information (and a map), contact the **California Department of Forestry** office in Forth Bragg, 802 N. Main St., 707/964-5674.

Mendocino Woodlands State Park and Outdoor Center

Entwined with Jackson State Forest about nine miles east of Mendocino is this woodsy 1930s camp facility—actually three separate facilities and some 200 separate buildings constructed of wood and stone by federal Works Progress Administration and Civilian Conservation Corps workers. Available for group retreats, each of the three rustic camps includes a well-equipped kitchen, a dining hall complete with stone fireplace, cabins, and spacious bathroom and shower facilities with both hot and cold running water. For more information about this National Historic Landmark, contact the nonprofit **Mendocino Woodlands Camp Association,** 707/937-5755, www.mendocinowoodlands.org.

Directly south of Jackson State Forest and Mendocino Woodlands is the region's newest reserve, **Big River State Park.**

MacKerricher State Park

This gorgeous stretch of ocean and forested coastal prairie starts three miles north of Fort Bragg and continues northward for seven miles. Down on the beach, you can stroll for hours past white-sand beaches, black-sand beaches, remote dunes, sheer cliffs and headlands, offshore islands, pounding surf, rocky outcroppings, and abundant tidepools. Or you can stay up atop the low bluff

The first terrace was a sand and gravel beach in its infancy, some 100,000 years ago, and is now home to salt-tolerant and wind-resistant wildflowers. (Underwater just offshore is an embryonic new terrace in the very slow process of being born from the sea.) A conifer forest of Sitka spruce, Bishop pine, fir, and hemlock dominates the second terrace, redwoods and Douglas fir the third. Jug Handle is an example of Mendocino's amazing ecological place in the scheme of things, since the area is essentially a biological borderline for many tree species. Metaphorically speaking, Alaska meets Mexico when Sitka spruce and Bishop pine grow side by side. The phenomenon of the hardpan-hampered Mendocino pygmy forest starts on the third step, transitioning back into old-dune pine forests, then more pygmy forest on the fourth step. At the top of the stairs on the final half-million-year-old step, are more pygmy trees, these giving ground to redwoods.

The only way to get to the staircase trail is by heading west from the parking lot to Jug Handle Bay, then east again on the trails as marked, hiking under the highway. (Call for trail conditions before setting out.) The day-use fee is $6. For more information about Jug Handle, contact the Mendocino District Headquarters at Russian Gulch State Park, 707/937-5804.

paralleling the shore, where you'll revel in great ocean views and, in spring, an abundance of delicate, butterfly-speckled wildflowers—baby blue eyes, sea pinks, buttercups, and wild iris.

The park's usage is de facto separated into two areas: the tourist area (crowded) and the locals' areas (desolate). Tourist usage centers around the park's little **Lake Cleone,** a fishable freshwater lagoon near the campground and picnic area with a wheelchair-accessible boardwalk; waterfowl from Mono Lake often winter at the lake. Nearby are a picturesque crescent beach pounded by a thundering shore break, and the **Laguna Point** day-use area (wheelchair accessible), a popular place for watching whales offshore and harbor seals onshore. (Another good local spot for whale-watching is **Todd's Point,** south of the Noyo Bridge, then west on Ocean View). That's the tourist's MacKerricher. Not bad. And most visitors to the park don't venture far from it.

Which leaves the locals and savvy passersby to enjoy in blissful, meditative solitude the extensive areas to the south and north, which are connected to the lake/campground area by the eight-mile-long **Old Haul Road.** Once used by logging trucks, the now-abandoned haul road parallels the shore from **Pudding Creek Beach** in the south to **Ten Mile River** in the north. Only a short stretch of the road is open to vehicles, so it's a great path for bicyclists and joggers. North of the campground area, the asphalt road gradually deteriorates until it gets buried completely by the deserted and exquisitely lovely Ten Mile Dunes; if you venture up the coast this far, you'll likely have it all to yourself. South of the campground, the road passes a few vacation homes and a gravel plant before ending up just past a parking lot and a phalanx of beachfront tourist motels. (If you wander far enough south, you'll end up at Fort Bragg's **Glass Beach** just north of town, where if you're lucky you might find a Japanese fishing float or an occasional something from a shipwreck.) Either way, you'll get magnificent ocean views and plenty of solitude.

The fine campgrounds at MacKerricher are woven into open woods of beach, Monterey, and Bishop pines. Campsites are abundant ($20, no hookups), with the usual amenities. It's a popular place, so reservations are wise; call Reserve-America, 800/444-7275, www.reserveamericausa.com. The day-use fee is $6. For more information, call MacKerricher directly at 707/964-9112 or Mendocino District Headquarters, 707/937-5804.

RECREATION
Water Sports

For sightseeing afloat practically in Mendocino, catch a canoe (or kayak) from among the **Catch-a-Canoe & Bicycles Too!** fleet, at the Stanford Inn by the Sea (on the south bank of Big River), 44850 Comptche-Ukiah Rd., www.stanfordinn.com, 707/937-0273 or 800/331-8884. Birders especially will enjoy the serene estuarine tour of Big River. Catch a Canoe also rents bicycles and can offer tips on the best area rides. **Noyo-Pacific Outfitters** in Fort Bragg, 32400 N. Harbor Dr., 707/961-0559, www.noyopacific.com, offers guided kayaking trips, guided abalone diving, and kayak and dive rentals. **Lost Coast Adventures,** 707/937-2434, offers Sea-Cave Tours at Van Damme State Park in sit-on-top ocean kayaks. At last report **free, ranger-guided canoe trips** (for age 6 and older) were still offered in summer at **Navarro River Redwoods State Park** south of Mendocino. For details, call 707/937-5804.

Other Recreation

Ricochet Ridge Ranch, 24201 N. Hwy. 1, located north of Fort Bragg in Cleone, across the highway from the entrance to MacKerricher State Park, 707/964-7669 or 888/873-5777, www.horse-vacation.com, offers horseback rides along the beach at MacKerricher, as well as other rides (English/Western) by advance arrangement. **Back Kountry Trailrides,** about 14 miles east of Fort Bragg, 707/964-2700, www.bktrailrides.com, offers guided rides along redwood trails. Contact **Mendocino Village Carriage** on Little Lake Rd. in Mendocino, 707/937-4753 or 800/399-1454, for a tamer horsey experience—a carriage ride through town. For a guided llama trip, contact **Lodging and Llamas,** 18301 Old Coast Hwy., 707/964-7191, www.lodgingandllamas.com.

MOVIE-MAD MENDOCINO

Mendocino and the Mendocino Headlands have hosted countless movie crews, including the 1943 swashbuckling romance *Frenchman's Creek*—based on a Daphne du Maurier novel and starring Joan Fontaine, Arturo de Cordova, and Basil Rathbone—which took that year's Academy Award for Best Art Direction. In 1948 *Johnny Belinda* rolled into town. Jane Wyman, who played the tragic part of a deaf girl living on the Nova Scotia coast, left Mendocino to pick up an Oscar, later in the year, for Best Actress. But by the time film production ended, Jane Wyman and then-husband Ronald Reagan were in divorce court. "I think I'll name Johnny Belinda co-respondent," Reagan said.

In 1955 Mendocino's movie was Elia Kazan's version of *East of Eden*, the very-California John Steinbeck telling of the Cain and Abel story, starring James Dean as Caleb "Cal" Trask (Cain), the tragic loner, and Rochard Davolos as their father's favored son, Aron. Scenes from *Rebel Without a Cause* were also shot here. In 1966 the Cold War comedy *The Russians Are Coming! The Russians Are Coming!* rowed ashore, starring Alan Arkin in his first major role. In the 1970s came *The Summer of '42*, Herman Raucher's coming-of-age tale. The annual trysting place for Alan Alda and Ellen Burstyn in 1978's *Same Time, Next Year* was just south along the coast at Heritage House in Little River.

The popular 1980s TV series *Murder She Wrote* was also filmed largely in and around Mendocino; the house at 45110 Little Lake Street, now a bed-and-breakfast, was Jessica Fletcher's home in Cabot Cove, and Fort Bragg's Noyo Harbor starred as Cabot Cove's fishing harbor. Other movies made along the Mendocino Coast include *Overboard, Cujo, Forever Young, The Majestic, The Fog, Racing with the Moon, Slither, Island of the Blue Dolphins,* and *Humanoids from the Deep.*

Near Fort Bragg, MacKerricher's Haul Rd. is a cycle path par excellence. Rent mountain bikes, 10-speeds, and two-seaters at **Fort Bragg Cyclery,** 579 S. Franklin St., 707/964-3509.

Just south of Mendocino is the historic **Little River Inn,** 7751 N. Hwy. 1, 707/937-5667, www.littleriverinn.com, with a regulation nine-hole golf course and lighted tennis courts.

EXCURSION INLAND: ANDERSON VALLEY

South of Little River and Albion., Hwy. 128 snakes southwest through the Anderson Valley, a route that leads ultimately to Cloverdale and the northern fringe of the Sonoma County wine country. In addition to several appealing parks, the Anderson Valley boasts some excellent wineries—**Greenwood Ridge** (home to the annual California Wine Tasting Championships), **Navarro, Husch,** and **Handley Cellars** among them, outposts of the new north coast economy. The valley also boasts seasonal roadside produce stands and the intriguing small town of **Boonville,** home to the exceptional **Boonville**

Hotel, 707/895-2210, www.boonvillehotel.com; and the refreshingly noncommercial **Mendocino County Fair and Apple Show,** held in mid-September.

For more information on the Anderson Valley area, contact the **Anderson Valley Chamber of Commerce,** 707/895-2379, email: cofc@pacific.net, www.andersonvalleychamber.com, or the **Greater Ukiah Chamber of Commerce,** 200 S. School St. in Ukiah, 707/462-4705, www.ukiahchamber.com.

MENDOCINO ACCOMMODATIONS

The battle of the bed-and-breakfasts in and around Mendocino is just one aspect of the continuing local war over commercial and residential development. The conversion of homes to bed-and-breakfast establishments means fewer housing options for people who live here, but a moratorium on B&Bs may mean higher prices for visitor accommodations; the new Brewery Gulch Inn received the last "Mendocino village" bed-and-breakfast expansion permit allowed under the California Environmental Quality Act (CEQA). Most people here agree on one thing: only developers want to see large-scale housing or recreation developments in the area.

Avoid contributing to the problem altogether by camping. There are almost endless choices among the state parks nearby, and some very enjoyable, very reasonable alternatives inland along Hwy. 128 toward Ukiah. And that's not counting private campgrounds. More than 2,000 commercial guest rooms are available in and around Mendocino, but that doesn't mean there's room at the inn (or motel) for spontaneous travelers. Usually people can find last-minute lodgings of some sort in Fort Bragg, though the general rule here is plan ahead or risk sleeping in your car or nestled up against your bicycle in the cold fog.

To stay in style in Mendocino, there are some great places to choose from; the region is renowned for its bed-and-breakfast inns. Advance reservations are absolutely necessary at most places on most weekends and during summer, preferably at least one month in advance (longer for greater choice). Most bed-and-breakfasts require a two-night minimum stay on weekends (three-night for holiday weekends) and an advance deposit. In the off season (winter and early spring) and at other low-demand times, many inns offer three-nights-for-the-price-of-two and other attractive specials, particularly midweek.

A number of the inns listed below, in both the Mendocino and Fort Bragg areas, are members of the **Mendocino Coast Innkeepers Association,** 707/964-6725, and if one inn is full, it's possible that another can be accommodating. (Request a current brochure for full information.) **Mendocino Coast Reservations,** in Mendocino at 1000 Main St., 707/937-5033 or 800/262-7801, www.mendocinovacations.com, offers 60 or so fully furnished rentals by the weekend, week, or month, from cottages and cabins to homes and family reunion–sized retreats—"Fido-friendly" and "child-friendly" listings included. Mendocino Coast's "vacation stretch" policy gives you a third night free.

Mendocino Hotel

The grand 1878 **Mendocino Hotel & Garden Suites,** 45080 Main St., 707/937-0511 or 800/548-0513, www.mendocinohotel.com, started out as the town's Temperance House, a

Mendocino

sober oasis in a wilderness of saloons and pool halls. Later, Mendocino's grand dame slid from grace and did time as a bordello. These days the Mendocino Hotel has settled back into her Victorian graces. All 51 meticulous rooms and suites—24 Victorian rooms and two suites in the historic building, and 25 one- and two-story garden rooms and suites—are furnished in American and European antiques; many have fireplaces or wood-burning stoves and views of Mendocino Bay or the one-acre gardens, plus such not-like-home little luxuries as heated towel racks, fresh flowers from someone else's garden, and chocolate truffles on the pillow at bedtime. The hotel's parlor (note the 18th-century sculpted steel fireplace) is infused with informal Victorian coziness, more casual than the crystal-studded dining room. "European-style" Victorian rooms have in-room washbasins and shared baths (across the hall; bathrobes provided), $50–100; Victorian rooms with private bath are $100–150. Garden rooms are $150–250, suites $250 and up. Inquire about off-season specials, which can be quite attractive.

Bed-and-Breakfasts

Selecting "the best" bed-and-breakfasts in an area like Mendocino is like asking parents which of their children they love best. A new star in town, and amazingly elegant even for Mendocino, is **The Whitegate Inn,** 499 Howard St., 707/937-4892 or 800/531-7282, www.whitegateinn.com. This classic Victorian itself served as a star vehicle—in the classic *The Russians Are Coming* as well as Julia Roberts's *Dying Young* and Bette Davis's *Strangers*. But visitors don't stay strangers for long, once they step past that white gate and succumb to the Whitegate's charms—particularly if exquisite style and gourmet breakfasts served on bone china add up to the perfect escape. The entire inn, including the seven guest rooms, is impeccably decorated in French, Italian, and Victorian antiques. Amenities include fireplaces, European featherbeds and toiletries, down comforters, TVs, and clock radios—not to mention fresh-baked cookies and bedtime chocolates. Breakfast is also a sumptuous experience, with specialties such as pecan-and-date pancakes,

eggs Florentine, and—everyone's favorite—caramel apple French toast. But don't forget to smell the roses, and all the other flowers in the spectacular cottage garden. Rates are $150–250 and $250 and up. Ask about midwinter specials.

The charming **M MacCallum House,** 45020 Albion St., 707/937-0289 or 800/609-0492, www.maccallumhouse.com, is the town's most venerable bed-and-breakfast. This 1882 Victorian and its barn rooms and garden cottages, lovingly restored, still have a friendly quilts-and-steamer-trunk feel—like a fantasy weekend visit to Grandma's farm, if Grandma had some sense of style. MacCallum House features a total of 19 rooms—those recently remodeled feature sauna, hot tub, or jetted spa tub—and all have private baths. Six rooms are in the main house, some of these named after members of the MacCallum family; the master bedroom features a fabulous mahogany sleigh bed. Another six are in the barn, including the very special Upper Barn Loft. Of the seven cottages, the Gazebo Playhouse is most affordable, and the updated Greenhouse Cottage is wheelchair accessible. The spectacularly re-done three-story Water Tower features a glass floor, to view the original hand-dug well (still producing water). A king and a queen bed plus pullout sofa, two-person whirlpool tub, sauna, fireplace, ocean view—you name it, it's here. MacCallum rates, including full gourmet breakfast, are $100–300 (Gazebo Playhouse, $120; Upper Barn Loft, $265; Water Tower, $295), but ask about specials. Children and pets (in some rooms) are welcome. Also on the premises are the excellent **MacCallum House Restaurant** and the **Grey Whale Bar & Café,** 707/937-5763, owned and overseen by Chef Alan Kantor, a graduate of the Culinary Institute of America. Both serve regional cuisine (seasonally changing menu), including fresh seafood and shellfish, meats and poultry, organic produce, and north coast wines, and both are open from 5:30 P.M. nightly. And don't miss the house-made ice creams. Reservations highly recommended.

The fine **Joshua Grindle Inn,** Mendocino's first bed-and-breakfast, 44800 Little Lake Rd., 707/937-4143 or 800/474-6353, www .joshgrin.com, is a New England country-style inn with 10 exquisite rooms furnished with Early Americana. The historic main building, surrounded with stunning cypress, was built in 1879 by local banker Joshua Grindle. All have private bathrooms; most feature wood-burning fireplaces or woodstoves; and some have deep soak tubs or other special features. Particularly inviting, for a little extra privacy, are the two large rooms in the converted water tower out back (there's also a small room, $130) and the two "saltbox cottage" rooms. Rates include a delicious full breakfast. Rates are $150–250, but ask about the inn's various specials, including Bed, Breakfast & Beaujolais; A Rub and a Tub; Mendocino Golf Special; and festival-related Winemaker's Dinner Packages. Joshua Grindle also offers an ocean-view guesthouse, located near the Point Cabrillo Light Station, north of Russian Gulch.

The 1878 **c.o. Packard House,** a striking carpenter's gothic Victorian on Mendocino's "executive row," across from the Mendocino Art Center at 45170 Little Lake Rd., 707/937-2677 or 888/453-2677, www.packardhouse.com, was once home to the town's chemist. The chemistry these days is notably stylish. All four rooms and the Maxwell Jarvis Suite boast sumptuous bed linens, jet-massage spa tubs (some with separate showers), TV/VCR, CD players, phones, and appealing French furniture. The suite features a living room, kitchenette, fold-away twin bed, and bedroom with an antique painted French bed. Rates for all are $150–250.

The **Blue Heron Inn,** 10390 Kasten St., 707/937-4323, www.theblueheron.com, is a small charmer, a New England–style home just a half-block from the ocean. Two of the inn's stylish yet simple, cozy upstairs rooms share a bath, $95 and $105; the other has a private bath, $115. Great ocean views from the deck. Downstairs is the popular **Moosse Café,** open for lunch (brunch on Sunday) and dinner daily.

The John Dougherty House Bed & Breakfast, 571 Ukiah St., 707/937-5266 or 800/486-2104, www.jdhouse.com, is a Mendocino classic. This 1867 Saltbox, surrounded by cottage gardens and filled with Early American antiques, is included on the town's historic house tour. Its two light, airy suites and several other rooms

offer fabulous views. All six rooms (plus suites) have private baths, and some feature spa tubs and woodstoves. Two charming cabins are available. Bountiful hot breakfast. Rates are $150–250, with one room $135, another $145.

For something both contemporary and "country," try the blue-and-white **Agate Cove Inn,** just north of downtown at 11201 N. Lansing St., 707/937-0551 or 800/527-3111, www.agate cove.com. Agate Cove offers two rooms in an 1860s farmhouse (built by Mathias Brinzing, founder of Mendocino's first brewery) and a cluster of eight cottages, all on an acre and a half of beautifully landscaped grounds. Most rooms feature fireplaces, ocean views, and featherbeds; and; all have private baths, country decor, Scandia down comforters, hair dryers, TV/VCR, CD players, and irons with ironing boards. Enjoy a fabulous full country breakfast (cooked on an antique woodstove) of omelettes or other entrées with country sausage or ham, homebaked breads, jams and jellies, and coffee or tea. Rates are $150–250, with one room $119, two $269. The **Sea Rock Bed and Breakfast Inn,** 11101 Lansing St., 707/937-0926 or 800/906-0926, www.searock.com, is also a collection of country cottages and guest rooms, most of these with Franklin fireplaces; a few have kitchens, and all have private bath, queen bed, cable TV, and VCR. Breakfast buffet served in the lobby. Rooms are $150–250, suites $250 and up.

The **Headlands Inn,** at the corner of Albion and Howard Streets, 707/937-4431, www.head landsinn.com, is a fully restored 1868 Victorian saltbox with seven rooms, each with antiques, private bath, and fireplace. In-room extras include fresh flowers, fruit, and a city newspaper. Two parlors, an English-style garden, and complimentary full breakfast, afternoon tea, and refreshments round out the amenities. Most rooms are $150–250, some lower.

The **Mendocino Village Inn Bed and Breakfast,** 44860 Main, 707/937-0246 or 800/882-7029, www.mendocinoinn.com, is a New England–style Victorian circa 1882, with 10 guest rooms (two attic rooms share a bath), many with fireplaces or woodstoves. Full breakfast. Rates are $100–150 and $150–250. Guests also have full spa privileges at the affiliated and adjacent **Sweetwater Spa & Inn,** 44840 Main St., 707/937-4076 or 800/300-4140, www.sweetwaterspa.com, which offers water tower rooms and cottages, rooms in an 1870 Victorian elsewhere in the village, and accommodations south of Mendocino in Little River. All accommodations except one have private baths; most have woodstoves or fireplaces, many are pet-friendly. Some have hot tubs. Most rates are $150–250 (one room $295); most Little River rooms are $50–100 (one room $130).

Stanford Inn by the Sea

How organic can you get? To find out, head for the comfortably luxurious yet outdoorsy Stanford Inn by the Sea (known in a previous incarnation as the Big River Lodge), 44850 Comptche-Ukiah Rd. (at Hwy. 1, on the south bank of Big River), 707/937-5615 or 800/331-8884, www.stanfordinn.com. This is an elegant, friendly lodge with vast gardens. But here, the working certified organic garden and farm—Big River Nurseries—dominate the setting. The swimming pool, sauna, and spa are enclosed in one of the farm's greenhouses. The on-site **Ravens** restaurant is strictly (and deliciously) vegetarian and/or vegan, even serving organic wines. The inn may be organic, but it's not overly fussy—pets are welcome (and also pampered), for a fee, and "guest-friendly" dogs, cats, llamas, and swans are available for those who arrive petless. The Stanford Inn also provides exercise facilities and complimentary mountain bikes; canoe and kayak rentals are available.

The 33 guest rooms and suites are inviting and outdoorsy, paneled in pine and redwood, and decked out with big four-poster or sleigh beds and decent reading lights. Each features a wood-burning fireplace or Irish Waterford stove, as well as houseplants and original local art. Amenities include in-room coffeemakers and refrigerators, TV with cable and Cinemax, and stereos with CD players (on-site CD library, or bring your own). Rates are $250 and up, complimentary gourmet breakfast included; one-bedroom suites start at $320, two-bedroom suites, $630. But ask about the Stanford Inn's

Health Kick and other special packages. **Catch a Canoe & Bicycles Too,** 707/937-0273, is also based here, for kayak, canoe, and outrigger rentals (and sales), lessons, and guided trips. Mountain bikes, too.

Little River and Albion B&Bs

Heading north, the **Brewery Gulch Inn,** 9350 N. Hwy. 1, 707/937-4752 or 800/578-4454, www.brewerygulchinn.com, is a Mendocino phenom these days. The original pre-Victorian farmhouse has been supplanted by a dazzling new inn showcasing old-growth redwood felled in the mid-1800s but only recently fished up from the bottom of Big River as sodden, mineralized "eco-salvage" or "guiltless redwood." The new, redwood shake-sided Brewery Gulch Inn is elegant in its simplicity and craftsmanship. From the spectacular Great Room, with its soaring ceilings and skylights, immense glass-and-steel fireplace, and dramatic views of Smugglers's Cove to exquisite Arts and Crafts period–inspired furnishings and quietly luxurious guest rooms—every painstaking detail attests to the Brewery Gulch Inn's emphasis on quality. Rooms feature striking hardwood furniture, leather chairs fronting gas fireplaces, luxury linens, down comforters, TVs with DVDs, CD players, and dataports. Most have private decks, all have ocean views. Private bathrooms, with granite vanities and redwood cabinetry, come with terry bathrobes, hair dryers, quality toiletries, and tub-shower combinations; some have whirlpool tub or large soaking tubs. One room has been designed for disabled access. Most rates are $150–250, ranging as high as $295 (lower off-season rates Nov.–Mar.). And here, the idea of fashioning something new from the old applies to the land itself, since this is the site of Mendocino's first real farm and a perfect microclimate for vegetables, fruit trees, and roses. A veritable farm once again, thanks to proprietor Dr. Arky Ciancutti and his green thumb, both inn and 10-acre homestead have met standards of the California Organic Foods Act of 1990.

Or head south. **Auburge Mendocino and Seaside Village Cottages,** formerly known as

Rachel's Inn, 8200 N. Hwy. 1, 707/937-0088 or 800/347-9252, www.aubergemendocino.com, offers five rooms in the farmhouse, four suites in the adjacent barn—now the Vintner's Cottage—and several other options. Just north of Van Damme State Park, the inn abuts an undeveloped strip of the park just two miles south of Mendocino. Each room or cottage has its own bathroom, a big bed, fresh flowers and personal amenities, plus individual charm: a view of the ocean or gardens, a balcony, or a fireplace. Breakfasts and other meals are grand, and an Atkins Diet Retreat program has been added. Public areas of the inn function as a revolving local art gallery. Most rates are $150–250. Charming Chez Cremant Cottage on the inn grounds is $289; the Little River Cottage near the inn, $325–400; the luxurious Admiral's Retreat vacation estate varies in price, depending on how much space is occupied.

Across the highway is **Glendeven,** 8221 N. Hwy. 1, 707/937-0083 or 800/822-4536, www.glendeven.com, part inn, part art gallery, the latter featuring quilted paper and other textile works, abstract art, and handcrafted furniture. It has been declared one of the 10 best inns in the U.S. by *Country Inns* magazine. Glendeven's charms start with the New England Federalist farmhouse, continue into the secluded and luxurious Carriage House, and also the Stevenscroft annex. Many rooms and suites feature fireplaces and ocean views—not to mention exquisite antiques and linens, every imaginable amenity, and sumptuous breakfast. Most rooms are $150–250 (above $200), one is $185. La Bella Vista, a two-bedroom rental house, is available for $275–380 per night.

South of Mendocino are several other options. Notable among them is **Cypress Cove** on Chapman Point, 45200 Chapman Dr., 707/937-1456 or 800/942-6300, www.cypresscove.com—quite the place to get away from it all. The property's two luxury suites look out on Mendocino and the bay. Amenities include queen beds, fireplaces, and two-person whirlpool tubs. Among the plush extras: in-room coffee, tea, brandy, chocolate, fresh flowers, and bathrobes. One suite has a full kitchen, the other a kitchenette. High-season

rates (May–Oct.) are $250 and up, lower in the off-season.

In Little River, pet-friendly **The Inn at Schoolhouse Creek,** 7051 N. Hwy. 1, 707/937-5525 or 800/731-5525, www.schoolhousecreek.com, features a variety of restored 1930s country-style garden cottages looking downslope to the ocean. All have fireplaces, private baths, and TVs and VCRs; some have kitchens. Rates for cottages and suites are $150–250, including full breakfast, access to the welcoming lodge (books, games, and breakfast), and a chance to jump into that hot tub. The inn also offers attractive, motel-like rooms for $130; one has two queen beds. Be sure to ask about winter specials.

Farther south on the highway is the beautiful **Albion River Inn,** 3790 N. Hwy. 1 in Albion, 707/937-1919 or 800/479-7944, www.albionriverinn.com, offering 22 rooms in New England–style blufftop cottages, each one unique. Fireplaces, decks, and ocean views are par for the course here, and the inn's elegant gourmet restaurant draws visitors north from San Francisco, locals south from Mendocino and Fort Bragg—and raves from the likes of *Bon Appetit* and *Wine Spectator.* Rates include full breakfast, wine, coffee and tea, and morning newspaper. Standard rooms are $150–250, and "tub for two" and spa tub rooms are $250 and up.

The unusually charismatic **Fensalden Inn,** seven miles south of Mendocino and then inland, at 33810 Navarro Ridge Rd. in Albion, 707/937-4042 or 800/959-3850, www.fensalden.com, is a restored two-story stage station circa 1880, still straddling the ridgetop among open fields and forests. The eight charming rooms feature exquisite antiques; all have fireplaces. For the more rustically inclined, there's the weather-beaten, fully modern Bungalow beyond the inn, in a meadow. Hors d'oeuvres, wine, and full breakfast are complimentary. All rooms are under $200; one is $125, another $135 (lower in winter). The Bungalow is $225.

Mendocino Little River Inn

In "downtown" Little River, the classic stay is the family-owned Little River Inn, just south of Van Damme State Park at 7751 N. Hwy. 1, 707/937-

5942 or 888/466-5683, www.littleriverinn.com, originally just one rambling Victorian mansion built by lumberman Silas Coombs in the area's characteristic Maine style. (To get the whole story, buy a copy of *The Finn, the Twin, and the Inn: A History of the Little River Inn and Its Families*.) The Little River Inn has grown over the years. In addition to its classic fireplace cottages and updated lodging annex, it also includes fairly new romantic luxury suites just up the hill—complete with gigantic whirlpool tubs, wood-burning fireplaces, view decks and patios, and every imaginable amenity. The old inn itself is still a slice of Victorian gingerbread. Upstairs are several small and affordable rooms—and really the best, in terms of period charm: quilt-padded attic accommodations illuminated by tiny seaward-spying dome windows. The Little River Inn is a wonderful place, all the way around.

Tucked in behind appealing, locally loved **Ole's Whale Watch Bar**—from which, according to local lore, actor James Dean was once tossed for putting his feet up on a table—is the Little River Inn's **Garden Dining Room**. The restaurant serves great food, including simple and excellent white-tablecloth breakfasts with Ole's famous Swedish hotcakes, absolutely perfect eggs, and fresh-squeezed orange or grapefruit juice. The inn's restaurant is just about the only room in sight without an ocean view, but it does feature many windows—these opening out into lush and inviting gardens. If you arrive when the restaurant's closed, Ole's has a good bar menu. And great ocean views.

The inn also offers an **18-hole golf course**— the only one on the Mendocino Coast—and **lighted tennis courts**. For tee times, call 707/937-5667. In addition to full meeting and small-conference facilities, a recent arrival is **The Third Court Day Spa,** with a full menu of men's and women's body and facial massages, skin treatments, and hair and nail care. For spa reservations, call 707/937-3099.

Antique rooms upstairs in the main lodge are $110. Most rooms and suites are in the $150–250 range, including the older, motel-style units, both with and without wood-burning fireplaces or woodstoves, and most of the spacious

suites up the hill that feature wood-burning fireplaces and two-person whirlpool tubs (more in the high season). They all offer fabulous ocean views. Rooms in the inn's new, nautically-themed Mallory House, a restored 1890s farmhouse overlooking Buckhorn Cove just down the road, are named after three schooners built during Little River's Shipbuilding heyday—the **Electra,** the upstairs luxury suite; the ocean-view *Hannah Madison* downstairs; and the cove-view, handicapped-accessible *Johanna M. Brock*. Mallory House rates start at $250 in the high season. Additional luxury suites, with outdoor decks and hot tubs plus indoor whirlpool tubs and other luxuries, are available offsite, $250 and up, along with two cottages. White Cottage features dramatic views, and Llama Cottage offers gardens, forest—and llamas. All accommodations are lower in the off season. Inquire about specials and packages. Two-night minimum stay on weekends, three-night on holiday weekends.

Heritage House

South of Little River proper, the Heritage House, 5200 N. Hwy. 1, 707/937-5885 or 800/235-5885, was once a safe harbor for notorious gangster Baby Face Nelson, though things are quite civilized and serene these days. Heritage House itself is an old Maine-style farmhouse (now the inn's dining room, kitchen, and office) and the center of a large complex of antique-rich luxury cottages and suites—the best ones looking out to sea. Rates $150–250. Another major attraction is the exceptional yet reasonably relaxed **Heritage House Restaurant,** with its stunning domed dining room, open nightly for dinner—except when the entire establishment is shut down in winter, usually from Thanksgiving through Christmas and again January 2 to President's Day in February. The gardens (and garden shop) at Heritage House are also quite impressive.

FORT BRAGG ACCOMMODATIONS
Motels and Lodges
Mendocino has most of the bed-and-breakfasts, but Fort Bragg has the motels—in general the

BEELINE FOR SHORELINE

Looking for a fun, friendly, inexpensive stay on the Mendocino Coast? Fort Bragg's bright yellow **Shoreline Cottages & Motel** might be just the place. Welcoming cabins and motel rooms at this refurbished 1920s-vintage motorcourt, freshly painted inside and out, feature all kinds of homey touches—from stocked kitchens or kitchenettes (all have microwaves and microwave popcorn) to picnic tables and state-of-the-art propane barbecues.

Each of the seven two-person cottages has a theme, from birdhouses or seashells to dogs, and features a fully supplied kitchen (down to the wine glasses) with full-sized refrigerator, a table with two chairs, cable TV with VCR, and bath amenities. You'll sleep well, too, with a little assist from the quality pillow-top queen beds, each with a lovely quilt, and wooden window blinds. Year-round rates are $50–100. At last report cottages were

$75–85 per night in the summer high season ($55–65 at other times), and if you stayed for three nights the third was free. The four motel rooms are the same such-a-deal price, and feature two queen beds, mini-kitchen (small refrigerator, bar sink, microwave, and coffeemaker), and a dining table with four chairs.

Shoreline welcomes families and pets, and is just a stroll from a stretch of dog-friendly beach. Little extras include "borrowables," from beach chairs, toys, and kites to fully appointed picnic baskets. The snazzy propane barbecues in the central garden/picnic area are also a big hit with guests.

For more information and reservations, contact manager Suzanne Gibbs at the Shoreline Cottages & Motel, north of the botanical gardens and south of the Hwy. 20 turnoff at 18725 N. Hwy. 1 in Fort Bragg, 707/964-2977 or 800/930-2977, www.shoreline-cottage.com.

most reasonable accommodations option around besides camping. Most places have cheaper off-season rates, from November through March or April. Pick up a current listing of area motels at the chamber office.

Fisherfolk, you can stay in and near Noyo Harbor. **Harbor Lite Lodge,** 120 N. Harbor Dr., 707/964-0221 or 800/643-2700, www.harborlitelodge.com, overlooks Noyo Harbor from just off the highway. Most rooms (including view rooms) are $50–100, fireplaces extra. The **Anchor Lodge** in Noyo (office in The Wharf Restaurant), 780 N. Harbor Dr., 707/964-4283, www.wharf-restaurant.com, has 19 rooms, some right on the river, some with kitchens. Standard rooms are $50–100, apartment units $100–150. Pleasant **Surf Motel** is at 1220 S. Main St. (at Ocean View Dr., south of the Noyo River Bridge), 707/964-5361 or 800/339-5361, www.surfmotelfortbragg.com, with rooms $50–100. Across the way (on the ocean side) and open since 2001 is the 43-room **Emerald Dolphin Inn,** 1211 S. Main St., 707/964-6699 or 866/964-6699, www.emeralddolphin.com. Most rooms and suites are $50–100 or $100–150, though ask about specials and

discounts. Pets welcome in certain rooms ($10 extra).

You'll find a cluster of places on the beach side of the highway, just north of town past the Pudding Creek trestle. These places provide easy access to the Haul Road and beach, and all offer rooms in the $50–100 and $100–150 range. The very friendly **Beachcomber Motel,** 1111 N. Main St., 707/964-2402 or 800/400-7873, www.thebeachcombermotel.com ($50–100 and $100–150), sometimes welcomes pets. Shockingly urban, in such a remote setting, are the condo-like **Surf 'n Sand Lodge,** 1131 N. Main (Hwy. 1), 707/964-9383 or 800/964-0184, www.surfsandlodge.com, and across the highway, the **Beach House Inn,** 100 Pudding Creek Rd., 707/961-1700 or 888/559-9992, www.beachinn.com. Rates rangs $50–150.

Bed-and-Breakfasts

The boxy, weathered, clear-heart redwood **Grey Whale Inn,** 615 Main St., 707/964-0640 or 800/382-7244, www.greywhaleinn.com, was once the community hospital. If you're one of those people who don't think they like bed-and-breakfasts—under any circumstances—this place could be the cure for what ails you. The two-story whale of an inn offers peace and privacy, very wide hallways, 14 individually decorated rooms and suites (some quite large) with myriad amenities, a basement pool table and rec room, fireplace, and an award-winning breakfast buffet of hot dish, cereals, coffeecakes, fresh fruits and juices, yogurt or cheese, and good coffee. (And if you don't feel too sociable in the morning, load up a tray in the breakfast room and take breakfast back to bed with you.) A truly exceptional stay—and some of the rooms are quite affordable. All rooms are under $200. Four are under $125, including Fern Creek, a two-room suite with a queen bed, a twin, and a mini-kitchen. Another plus: from here it's an easy walk to downtown shops and galleries, Glass Beach, and area restaurants.

For fans of Victoriana, a particularly inviting local bed-and-breakfast is the 1886 **Weller House Inn,** 524 Stewart St., 707/964-4415 or 877/893-5537, www.wellerhouse.com—the only Mendocino Coast inn listed on the National Register of Historic Places. The seven Victorian guest rooms all have private baths; some have fireplaces or woodstoves, whirlpool tubs, or clawfoot bathtubs. "Very full" breakfast is served in the 900-square-foot ballroom, completely paneled in exquisite old redwood. All rooms are $100–150, several slightly higher on weekends.

The newly restored 1892 **Old Coast Hotel,** 101 N. Franklin St., 707/961-4488 or 888/468-3550, www.oldcoasthotel.com, is another great choice, a painstakingly restored Victorian hotel with decorative tin ceilings, polished oak floors, and granite fireplaces—a historic restoration recognized in 1997 with the mayor's award. The hotel's 16 rooms are "European style," but with private bathrooms, cozy quilts, and unique decor. Most rooms are $50–100, some slightly higher. And hey, sports fans: this may be the place for a getaway weekend. The handsome sports-themed bar and grill downstairs serves up regional microbrews and plenty of sports, from four TV sets. Restaurant fare is quite good, from award-winning clam chowder to peppercorn steak.

The two-story **Noyo River Lodge,** 500 Casa del Noyo Dr., 707/964-8045 or 800/628-1126, www.noyolodge.com, is a redwood Craftsman-style mansion (circa 1868) on a hill with harbor and ocean views, rooms and suites with private baths (some with fireplaces), a restaurant and lounge, big soaking tubs, skylights, and gardens. All rooms are under $200.

South of Fort Bragg and just north of Caspar, across from the state park, is **Annie's Jughandle Beach B&B,** 32980 Gibney Lane (at Hwy. 1), 707/964-1415 or 800/964-9957, www.jughandle.com, with five rooms featuring private baths and fireplaces, as well as a hot tub, ocean views, and excellent breakfasts. Rates range $100–250 (ocean-view rooms on the high end), including "Mendocino magic," Cajun-style gourmet breakfast.

MENDOCINO FOOD

For the **Mendocino Certified Farmers Market,** which runs May through Oct., show up on Friday, noon–2 P.M., at Howard and Main Streets. Otherwise stock up on natural foods, for here or to go, at **Corners of the Mouth,** 45015 Ukiah St., 707/937-5345, and get general groceries at **Mendosa's,** 10501 Lansing St., 707/937-5879. For gourmet goodies, bakery goods, and takeout, stop by **Tote Fete,** 10450 Lansing, 707/937-3383. Wander over to **Café Beaujolais** (see below) for fresh-baked bread.

For a hefty slice of pizza or quiche, a bowl of homemade soup, or just a good danish and a café latte, head for the **Mendocino Bakery,** 10483 Lansing, 707/937-0836. It's the locals' coffeehouse of choice and offers outdoor seating when the weather's nice. Open 7:30 A.M.–7 P.M. weekdays, 8:00 A.M.–7 P.M. weekends. The **Mendo Juice Joint,** on Ukiah a half block east of Lansing, 707/937-4033, specializes in fresh juices, smoothies, and healthy snacks.

Mendo Burgers, 10483 Lansing, 707/937-1111, is open 11 A.M.–7:30 P.M. and serves beef, turkey, fish, and veggie burgers, as well as ice cream. Also balm for that sweet tooth are the definitely decadent chocolates at **Mendocino Chocolate Company,** also at10483 Lansing, 707/937-1107. The **Mendocino Cookie Company,** at home in the old Union Lumber Company building, 301 N. Main, 707/964-0282, serves up more than a dozen delectable varieties, from peanut butter chocolate chip and white chocolate almond to Grandma Daisy's shortbread.

Herbivorous visitors will be right at home at **Lu's Kitchen,** 45013 Ukiah St., 707/937-4939, which serves "organic cross-cultural vegetarian cuisine" in a casual atmosphere. Garden seating and takeout, too. Look for salads, quesadillas, and burritos in the $4–7 range. Closed in January, part of Feb., and in heavy rain.

One of the best views in town is from the big deck at the **Mendocino Café,** 10451 Lansing St., 707/937-2422 or 707/937-6141, which has a great menu of Pacific Rim–inspired cuisine (try the Thai burrito) and a good beer selection. Another place for great views—but in a slightly more upscale atmosphere—is the **Bay View Cafe,** 45040 Main St. (upstairs), 707/937-4197, which serves south-of-the-border specialties and enjoys unobstructed views of the coast from its second-story bay windows.

Cafe Beaujolais

No one should come anywhere near Mendocino without planning to eat at least one meal at the noted Cafe Beaujolais, 961 Ukiah St., 707/937-5614, now under new ownership. The fresh-flower decor inside and on the deck of this old house is as refreshingly simple and fine as the food itself. Johnny Carson, Julia Child, Robert Redford, the food writer Elizabeth David, and food critics from the *New York Times* eat here when they're in town. But since Margaret Fox, once a baker in the back room of the Mendocino Hotel, first opened the café's doors more than a decade ago, it's been a people's place. Despite its fame, it still is—though some still haven't gotten over the fact that Cafe Beaujolais is no longer open for breakfast. (Beaujolais' famous blackberry jam, cashew granola, waffle mix, Panforte di Mendocino, and other take-home treats are available here and at various gift shops.)

Cafe Beaujolais begins with carefully selected ingredients—organic produce (visit the gardens here) as well as fresh local fish and seafood as well as chemical-free meat, poultry, and eggs from free-range, humanely raised animals. Dinner is a fixed-price French-and-California-cuisine affair featuring such things as local smoked salmon and roast duck with a purée of apples and turnips, still more decadent desserts, and an almost endless and excellent California wine list. Cafe Beaujolais is open for dinner nightly 5:45–9 P.M., though the restaurant is closed from late November through January. Reservations are necessary. Bring cash or personal checks; no credit cards accepted. The restaurant's bakery, called The Brickery, produces breads and pizzas from a wood-fired brick oven. Drop by for loves of country sourdough, Austrian sunflower bread, olive rosemary focaccia, and other signature breads daily, 11 A.M.–4 or 5 P.M.

Fine Dining

Neighbor to Cafe Beaujolais is **955 Ukiah St.,** 707/937-1955, difficult to find in the fog despite its numerically straightforward attitude. (The entrance is 100 feet off the street around a few corners.) The dining room is a former art studio. Dinners feature entrées including excellent fresh seafood—say, lightly smoked salmon, prawns, ling cod, and mahi mahi with tomatoes, roasted garlic, and basil, mixed with fettuccine—leg of lamb stew, peppercorn steak, unforgettable breadsticks, and Navarro and Husch wines from the Anderson Valley. For dessert, don't miss the bread pudding with huckleberry compote. No credit cards. Open Wed.–Sun. from 6 P.M. Also quite good in town is the **MacCallum House Restaurant,** 45020 Albion, 707/937-5763, open nightly for dinner (see bed-and-breakfast listing above for more information), and the **Moosse Café,** 390 Kasten St., 707/937-4323, featuring an eclectic menu of north coast fare—and sumptuous chocolate desserts. Open for lunch and dinner daily, and brunch on Sunday.

For prime rib, steaks, and seafood in a Victorian setting, consider the crystal-and-Oriental-carpet ambience of the **Mendocino Hotel,** 45080 Main St., 707/937-0511. At the hotel's more casual Garden Court restaurant and bar, the ceiling is almost one immense skylight—to keep the interior garden going. With that in mind, enjoy the salads and other greens with gusto. Open daily for breakfast, lunch, and dinner. For fine vegetarian meals, try **Ravens** restaurant at the **Stanford Inn,** Hwy. 1 and Comptche-Ukiah Rd., 707/937-5615.

Little River and Albion

You can always find a great meal at the grand white Victorian **Little River Inn,** looming up next to the highway south of Mendocino, 707/937-5942, which is famous for its Swedish hotcakes and other breakfasts and brunches but also offers fine American-classic dinners emphasizing steak and seafood. Another Little River classic, a tad fancier, is **M The Restaurant at Stevenswood** at Stevenswood Lodge, 8211 N. Hwy. 1, 707/937-2810, where dinner specialties range from herb-crusted lamb loin and prime dry-aged New York steak to pine nut–crusted salmon filet served with grilled parmesan polenta.

At the elegant **Ledford House,** 3000 N. Hwy. 1 (south of "downtown" Albion), 707/937-0282, even vegetarians can try the excellent soups because none are made with meat bases. Entrées include pasta picks like ravioli stuffed with ricotta cheese in sorrel cream sauce, and some definitely nonstandard seafood and meat specialties. The nearby **Albion River Inn,** 3790 N. Hwy. 1, 707/937-1919, serves up spectacular views, an outstanding wine list, and hearty California fusion, from grilled ginger-lime prawns to oven-roasted quail.

Another area dining destination is the **Heritage House Restaurant,** 5200 Hwy. 1 south of Little River, 707/937-5885, with a striking dining room, views, and an impressive seasonally changing menu.

FORT BRAGG FOOD

Finding a meal in Fort Bragg is usually a more relaxed task than in Mendocino, with less confusion from the madding crowds. Most restaurants are casual. For farm-fresh everything, show up for the **Fort Bragg Certified Farmers Market,** held May–Oct. on Wed. 3:30–6 P.M., at Laurel and Franklin. Call 707/964-6340 for details. The place for just-off-the-boat ingredients if you're cooking your own seafood is **Capt. Bobino's Mendocino**

Fresh Seafood in Noyo Harbor at 32440 N. Harbor Dr., 707/964-9297. For something different to take home as a memento, stop by Carol Hall's **Hot Pepper Jelly Company,** 330 N. Main, 707/961-1899 or 866/737-7379, www.hotpepperjelly.com, an inviting shop that sells intriguing jams and jellies, fruit syrups, mustards, herb vinegars, and unusual food-related gift items.

For a sweet treat, head for the **Mendocino Chocolate Company,** two blocks away at 542 N. Main, 707/964-8800 or 800/722-1107 (for orders), www.mendocino-chocolate.com, which serves up everything from edible seashells and Mendocino toffee to an amazing array of truffles and chews—including Fort Bragg 2x4s (peanut butter-flavored fudge "veneered" with dark chocolate) and Mr. Peanut Coastal Clusters. Though this is headquarters, there's another company outlet in Mendocino. Another possibility is **Cowlicks Ice Cream Café,** 250-B N. Main, 707/962-9271, or sample dessert at any number of wonderful local restaurants. **Headlands Coffee House,** 120 E. Laurel St., 707/964-1987, an artsy place famous for its "hot java and cool jazz," is not at all shabby for dessert either; sample the Cafe Beaujolais Amazon Chocolate Cake. Headlands serves espresso, coffee drinks galore, fountain items, and a selection of soups, salads, and hearty, inexpensive entrées along with an interesting crowd of locals. At breakfast, try the Belgian waffle with fruit and yogurt.

Breakfast and Lunch

In addition to local coffeehouses, a perennial favorite for breakfast is venerable **Egghead Omelettes of Oz,** 326 N. Main St., 707/964-5005, a cheerful diner with booths, the whole place decorated in a Wizard of Oz theme. (Follow the Yellow Brick Road through the kitchen to the restrooms out back.) Equally unforgettable, on the menu, are fried potatoes and omelettes with endless combinations for fillings, including avocado and crab. Good sandwiches at lunch. Open daily 7 A.M.–2 P.M. For organic everything—vegetarian fare in particular but also free-range chicken, seafood, and organic wines and beers—try **Cafe One,** 753 N. Main, 707/964-3309, open daily for breakfast and lunch, and (at last report) on Friday and Saturday in summer for dinner.

At lunch, locals line up for the Dagwood-style sandwiches at **David's Deli,** 450 S. Franklin St., 707/964-1946, but breakfast here is pretty special, too. For a unique atmosphere, head just south of town to the Mendocino Coast Botanical Gardens, where you can dine with garden views at the **Gardens Grill,** 18220 N. Hwy. 1, 707/964-7474. It's open for lunch Mon.–Sat., for dinner Thurs.–Sat., and for Sunday brunch.

Dinner

A Fort Bragg favorite is hip ℳ **Mendo Bistro,** 301 Main (at Redwood, upstairs in the Company Store), 707/964-4974, where the great food and reasonable prices share star billing. Here, you can pick a meat or seafood entrée and a style of preparation, then get it served just the way you like it for $8–15. Or choose from a half-dozen wonderful house-made pastas for $12, or entrées—such things as from free range–chicken pot pie to potato-crusted Alaskan halibut with roasted peppers, olives, and pesto—for $14–15. The monthly changing menu showcases the freshest possible ingredients. It really is affordable to eat here—so long as you don't carried away with the knock-out appetizers, including Mendo Bistro's award-winning crab cakes.

Otherwise, for a special dinner folks head to the **Rendezvous Inn & Restaurant,** just down the street from the Grey Whale Inn at 647 N. Main St., 707/964-8142 or 800/491-8142. This gorgeous homey bungalow with warm wood interiors serves marvelous crab cakes, jambalaya, vegetarian pasta and "beggar's purses," civet of venison, and other unusual entrées, starting from the freshest local ingredients. Open Wed.–Sun. for dinner. Upstairs are several guest rooms, each with private bath ($50–100, slightly higher in summer).

In a little less rarified atmosphere, good food is also available at ℳ **North Coast Brewing Co. Taproom and Restaurant,** 444 N. Main, 707/964-3400, a brewpub and grill pouring award-winning handmade ales to accompany pub grub (including Route 66 chili), pastas, steaks, seafood, and Cajun-inspired dishes. On a

sunny day, the outside beer garden—a genuine garden, quite appealing—can't be beat. Beer lovers take note: North Coast is among the finest of North American microbreweries, consistently producing brews that always satisfy and frequently astonish even the pickiest connoisseurs. All the offerings are outstanding, but don't miss the unique Belgian-style Pranqster or the positively evil Rasputin imperial stout. Open noon–11 P.M. daily except Monday. Across the street (at 455 N. Main) is the brewery itself, 707/964-2739, www.ncoast-brewing.com, offering free tours on weekdays, along with some memorable memorabilia and gift items.

A good choice for families is **The Restaurant,** 418 N. Main St., 707/964-9800, where the California-style fare might include delectable entrées such as poached halibut, calamari, scallops, shrimp, steak, and quail. Open for lunch and dinner (call for current schedule) and Sunday brunch. Children's menu. Reservations wise. The sports-themed restaurant at the restored **Old Coast Hotel,** 101 N. Franklin, 707/961-4488, is another possibility, with a steak and seafood menu. Open for lunch and dinner daily.

Seafood

Well-prepared seafood abounds at the area's finer restaurants, but Fort Bragg's favorite fancy seafood restaurant, open for dinner only, is **The Cliff House,** just south of the Harbor Bridge, 1011 S. Main St., 707/961-0255. Overlooking the jetty and the harbor, The Cliff House serves wonderful seafood, steak, and pastas—try the smoked salmon ravioli—along with specialties including chicken mushroom Dijon and pepper steak. On Friday and Saturday night, prime rib is also on the menu.

The place for seafood with a view in Noyo Harbor is tiny, unpretentious **Sharon's by the Sea** at 32096 N. Harbor Dr., 707/962-0680, open daily for fish tacos, fish and chips, and snapper piccata at lunch, and northern Italian dinner specialties such as cioppino, linguini alla vongole, shrimp scampi, and spinach torta. Angle for a seat out on the deck to take in the sunset.

Otherwise, the harbor is where the tourists go for fish. That said, **The Wharf,** 780 N. Harbor Dr., 707/964-4283, serves a creamy clam chowder and crispy-outside, tender-inside fried clams, and the prime rib sandwich is nothing to throw a crabpot at. Dinner specialties include seafood and steak. The specialty at the plastic-tableclothed **Cap'n Flint's,** 32250 N. Harbor, 707/964-9447, is shrimp won tons with cream cheese filling.

Ethnic

Yes, Fort Bragg has ethnic food, and most of it is pretty darned good. **Samraat,** 546 S. Main, 707/964-0386, specializes in the tastes of India. Humble as it may appear from the outside, it's worth seeking out.

Just north of town in Cleone, the legendary **Purple Rose,** 24300 N. Hwy. 1, 707/964-6507, prepares locally famous Mexican food in a bright, spacious, and casual atmosphere. The veggie burrito here is a work of culinary art. Open Wed.–Sun. for dinner. (Within walking distance from the campgrounds at MacKerricher State Park, the Purple Rose makes the perfect break from roasted weenies and marshmallows.) Mexican fare is also available in town at **El Sombrero,** 223 N. Franklin, 707/964-5780, and down in Noyo Harbor at **El Mexicano,** 701 N. Harbor Dr., 707/964-7164, which serves up authentic Mexican, down to the fresh-daily tortillas.

For Italian, everyone's favorite is **D'Aurelio's,** 438 S. Franklin St., 707/964-4227, which offers outstanding pizzas, calzones, and the like in a comfortable, casual atmosphere. Another possibility is **Bernillo's,** 220 E. Redwood Ave., 707/964-9314.

ENTERTAINMENT AND EVENTS

For most people, just being here along the Mendocino coast is entertainment enough. But if that's too quiet, consider the **Caspar Inn** between Mendocino and Fort Bragg, 707/964-5565, www.casparinn.com, "home of the blues in Caspar, California" and a venerable roadhouse—the last classic roadhouse in California. This boisterous tavern adheres to tradition, too, with packed houses dancing to big-name blues and touring bands. If the nightlife is the right life

for you, even on vacation, keep in mind that the Caspar Inn includes 10 rooms upstairs (shared baths down the hall), $60 including show admission, as well as **La Playa** Mexican restaurant.

Art

On the first Friday evening of the month, don't miss Fort Bragg's **First Friday,** when arts galleries and shops keep later hours, 5–8 P.M., during open receptions with wine and hors d'oeuvres. Festivities include coffeehouse concerts, street theater, and other surprises. Similar **Second Saturday** events are held 5–8 P.M. in Mendocino's galleries (you guessed it) on the second Saturday of every month, with more universal participation April through September. For the latest on this and other art events, stop by the Mendocino Art Center or contact the **Arts Council of Mendocino County,** 14125 Hwy. 128 in Boonville, 707/895-3680 or 888/278-3773 (hotline), www.artsmendocino.org, an umbrella for some 30 nonprofit arts groups that maintains a comprehensive calendar of events.

At home in Mendocino is the **Mendocino Theatre Company,** 45200 Little Lake Rd., 707/937-4477, which typically begins its performance season in the tiny Helen Schoeni Theatre every March. An eclectic mix of one-night or short-run acts—anything from local school plays to comedy troupes to touring world-beat bands—are presented at Mendocino's **Crown Hall,** 45285 Ukiah St. (down at the west end), a delightfully intimate venue with reasonably good acoustics as well. Mendocino's **Opera Fresca,** 707/937-3646 or 888/826-7372, www.opera fresca.com, has adopted Mendocino College's Center Theatre in Ukiah as its main stage, but is headquartered in Mendocino and does offer performances along the coast.

Fort Bragg is also quite theatrical. The **Gloriana Opera Company,** 721 N. Franklin St., 707/964-7469, www.gloriana.org, offers a six-week run in summer and special events throughout the year. The **Footlighters Little Theatre,** 248 E. Laurel St., 707/964-3806, performs Gay Nineties melodrama from Memorial Day through Labor Day. Fort Bragg is also home to the fine **Symphony of the Redwoods,** 707/964-0898. During its September to May season the orchestra plays three or four concert "sets," the first performance of each on Saturday night in Fort Bragg, the second on Sunday afternoon some 60 miles south along the coast at the Gualala Arts Center. The symphony also offers its **Opus Chamber Music Series** on Sunday afternoons in Mendocino's Preston Hall and performs at other events and venues, including the mid-July Mendocino Music Festival. The symphony and both area opera companies are working to renovate the 1914 redwood **Eagles Hall,** 210 N. Corry St. (at Alder), into a snazzy performance venue.

Events

Definitely hot in the chill of winter: **Mendocino Crab & Wine Days,** held from late January into February and featuring endless creativity in culinary and wine pairings. Down the coast, come February, is the annual **Gualala Chocolate Festival.**

Everyone celebrates the return of the California gray whale. The **Mendocino Whale Festival,** on the first weekend in March, celebrates the annual cetacean migration with wine and clam-chowder tastings, art exhibits, music and concerts, and other special events. The **Fort Bragg Whale Festival,** held the third weekend in March, happily coincides with the arrival of spring. Festivities include chowder tasting and beer tasting (the latter courtesy of Fort Bragg's own North Coast Brewing Company), a "whale run," doll show, car show, lighthouse tours, and more. On both weekends, **whale-watching tours** are offered from Noyo Harbor, and **whale-watch talks** are offered at area state parks. The **Whale Festival at Pt. Cabrillo Light Station,** held every weekend in March, also coincides with both festivals.

In April or May, come to Fort Bragg for the **John Drucker Memorial Rhododendron Show**—the granddaddy of all juried rhodie shows, with more thqn 700 entries. On the first weekend in May, Mendocino's **Annual Historic House & Building Tour** offers a self-guided tour of the town's historic treasures. In late May, Fort Bragg puts on its impressive annual **Memorial Day Quilt Show.** The annual **Mendocino Coast Garden Tour** in mid-June, sponsored by the Mendocino Art Center, includes some of the most spectacular gardens in and near Mendocino.

On or around July 4th, Fort Bragg hosts the **World's Largest Salmon Barbecue** down at Noyo Harbor. All proceeds support the Hollow Tree Creek Hatchery in Noyo Harbor. And Mendocino holds its old-fashioned **Fourth of July Celebration & Parade.** Starting in mid-July, Mendocino hosts the noted, two-week **Mendocino Music Festival,** 707/937-2044, www.mendocinomusic.com. At this gala event, held in a 600-seat tent set up next to the Ford House, the local Symphony of the Redwoods joins with talented players from Bay Area orchestras to perform classical works that might include symphonies, opera, and chamber music as well as the possibility of jazz, Big Band and show tunes, celtic harp, and other surprises. At Greenwood Ridge Vineyards in the Anderson Valley, come in late July for the annual **California Wine Tasting Championships.**

Usually held in July or August is the Mendocino Art Center's **Summer Arts & Crafts Fair.** In August is the Mendocino Coast Botanical Gardens' **Art in the Gardens** event and the Gualala **Art in the Redwoods Festival.** Fort Bragg's biggest party every year is **Paul Bunyan Days,** held over Labor Day weekend and offering a logging competition, parade, and crafts fair. The following September weekend, the **Winesong!** wine-tasting and auction takes place at the Mendocino Coast Botanical Gardens.

Come in November for the mushrooming **Mendocino Coast Mushroom Festival,** which started out as a simple display and lectures held at Mendocino's Ford House and now extends over two weeks. Regional restaurants and wineries celebrate Mendocino's edible fungi with "wild" meals and special mushroom walks. Come on Thanksgiving weekend for the **Thanksgiving Art Festival** at the Mendocino Art Center and, down the coast, the **Gualala Arts Studio Tour.**

December brings the Mendocino Coast's **Candlelight Inn Tours,** three consecutive nights when area inns dress up grandly for the holidays and host visitors for tours and refreshments; all proceeds support Big Brothers/Big Sisters of Mendocino County. In Fort Bragg, the yuletide spirit extends to special programs by the Symphony of the Redwoods, the Gloriana Theater Company, and the **Holiday Gift Show** at the restored Union Lumber Company Store, not to mention the **Hometown Christmas & Lighted Truck Parade** early in the month. This particular community party includes music, tree lighting, and truck lighting—a yuletide parade of logging trucks and big rigs all lit up for the holidays.

INFORMATION AND SERVICES

The **Fort Bragg–Mendocino Coast Chamber of Commerce,** 332 N. Main St. in Fort Bragg, 707/961-6300, www.mendocinocoast2.com, is a good resource. It's open Mon.–Fri. 9 A.M.–5 P.M., Sat. 9 A.M.–3 P.M. (closed Sun.). Among the free literature published by the chamber is the annually updated *Mendocino Coast* brochure and map, walking tours, and shopping guides. Also available here and elsewhere is the free annual *Mendocino Visitor* tabloid, the coast guide to state parks, the *Guide to the Recreational Trails of Mendocino County,* and local arts publications.

For books on the region—and just plain great books—plan to spend some quality time in **Gallery Bookshop & Bookwinkle's Children's Books** in Mendocino at Main and Kasten Sts., 707/937-2215, www.gallerybooks.com, a truly impressive independent bookstore.

The **Fort Bragg post office** is at 203 N. Franklin, 707/964-2302, open weekdays 8:30 A.M.–5 P.M. The **Mendocino post office** is at 10500 Ford St., 707/937-5282, open weekdays 8:30 A.M.–4:30 P.M. The **Mendocino Coast District Hospital,** 700 River Dr. in Fort Bragg, 707/961-1234, offers 24-hour emergency services.

GETTING AROUND

The **Mendocino Transit Authority** (MTA), based in Ukiah, 707/462-1422, www.mcn.org /a/mta, runs a daily north coast route (#60, The Coaster) between the Navarro River (Hwy. 1 and Hwy. 128 junction) and Fort Bragg on weekdays. Bus #65 (the "CC Rider") runs from Mendocino to Fort Bragg then on to Willits, Ukiah, and Santa Rosa. There's also a weekly route along the coast one bus each weekday between Ukiah and Gualala via the Navarro River bridge. At the bridge, you can transfer to or from the smaller vans of Fort Bragg's **Mendocino Stage,** 707/964-0167, www.mendostage.com, which run weekdays between Fort Bragg and Navarro, with stops in Mendocino and offers "custom" passenger service. The MTA also makes roundtrips between Point Arena and Santa Rosa. Connect with **Greyhound** in Ukiah.

Near Little River, a few miles inland from the coast, is the **Little River Airport,** 707/937-5129, the closest airfield to Mendocino. Private pilots flying into the airport can get a ride into Little River or Mendocino by calling Mendocino Stage.

Southern Mendocino Coast

The coast south from Mendocino is marvelously lonely in places, still a little greener (and wetter) than Sonoma County but with similar crescent coves and pocket beaches—one after the next, like a string of pearls. If the official distinction matters, the Gualala River forms the boundary between Sonoma and Mendocino Counties.

Beachcombers and hikers, a travel essential is Bob Lorentzen's *The Hiker's Hip Pocket Guide to the Mendocino Coast,* which keys off the white milepost markers along Hwy. 1 to the Gualala River. The book provides abundant information about undeveloped public lands along the southern Mendocino coast, such as the state's Schooner Gulch and Whiskey Shoals Beach. Also worthwhile to carry anywhere along the coast, though a bit unwieldy, is the *California Coastal Resource Guide* by the California Coastal Commission.

ELK

Aka Greenwood, the tiny town of Elk perches on the coastal bluffs well south of the turnoff to the Anderson Valley. Elk was once a lumber-loading port known as Greenwood, hence **Greenwood Creek Beach State Park** across from the store, with good picnicking among the bluff pines. The park is also a popular push-off point for sea kayakers. The **Elk Store,** 6101 Hwy. 1, 707/877-3411, whips up great deli sandwiches, and also carries gourmet cheeses and an impressive selection of wines and microbrews. In addition to the restaurants mentioned below, **Queenie's Roadhouse Café,** installed in a restored garage circa 1901, 6061 S. Hwy. 1, 707/877-3285, is open for breakfast and lunch; closed Tuesday.

Accommodations

The all-redwood Craftsman-style 1916 **Ⓝ Harbor House,** 5600 S. Hwy. 1, 707/877-3203 or 800/720-7474, www.theharborhouseinn.com, is a sophisticated bed-and-breakfast noted for its stylish, classic accommodations (six elegant rooms and four luxurious cabins, recently refurbished)

and fine dining (recipient of *Wine Spectator's* Award of Excellence). Rates, $250 and up, typically include full breakfast and fabulous four-course dinner plus private access to a strip of beach. Off-season rates for some rooms can dip as low as $95–125 (breakfast-only) and $145–175 (with dinner). Dinners emphasize Sonoma County seafood, meats, poultry, and produce, à la Tuscany or Provence. Open for dinner daily, at least most of the year. Beer and wine. No credit cards. Limited seating, advance reservations required—and be sure to request a window table.

Another area institution is the **Elk Cove Inn,** 6300 S. Hwy. 1, 707/877-3321 or 800/275-2967, www.elkcoveinn.com, where you get a spectacular view of the cove below from the inn's romantic gazebo. The Elk Cove Inn offers seven fine rooms in the main 1883 Victorian, plus four ocean-view cottages overlooking the cove. Fairly new at the Elk Cove Inn—and truly spectacular, just the thing for an extra-special weekend—are its four ocean-view luxury suites, housed in the new Craftsman-style annex. These sophisticated suites are certainly a fitting tribute to the era of craftsmanship, with a keen sense of style and every imaginable comfort, down to the fireplaces, whirlpool tubs, California king beds with both down and regular comforters, and mini-kitchens complete with microwave, small fridge, and coffee/cappucino maker. Floors in the bathroom feature heated floor tiles. Newer still are the day spa facilities. Inn rates include full breakfast, served in a delightful, cheerful, ocean-view breakfast room with intimate tables. Room are $150–250 (Swallow's Nest $130), and cottages and luxury suites are $250 and up (most $300–350). Inquire about off-season and midweek specials (particularly midweek stays in winter). The Elk Cove Inn also boasts a beer and wine bar—and a cocktail bar, including a menu of 23 different martinis. Dig those Z-shaped glasses.

More relaxed but equally charming are the seven cottages at **Griffin House at Greenwood Cove,** 5910 S. Hwy. 1, 707/877-3422, www.griffinn.com. The "house" is now **Bridget**

Dolan's Irish Pub & Dinner House, serving pub grub, soups and salads, Gaelic garlic bread, and hearty main dishes such as Irish stew, bangers and mash, and "very, very veg" specials. Out back are the flower gardens and cozy 1920s cottages; three feature sun decks and ocean views, and all have private baths (most with clawfoot tubs) and woodstoves. A hearty full breakfast is served in your room. Most cottages are $100–150, even in the high season—such a deal—and two are $150–250.

The **Greenwood Pier Inn,** 5928 S. Hwy. 1, 707/877-9997 or 707/877-3423, fax 707/877-3439, www.greenwoodpierinn.com, features eclectic cottages and cottage rooms perched at the edge of the cliffs above the sea, surrounded by cottage-gardenlike grounds. Most accommodations feature wood-burning fireplaces or woodstoves, and some also have in-room spa tubs; two rooms are pet-friendly. Continental breakfast is delivered to your room. (If you must have TV or a telephone, head for the main house.) Other amenities include the cliffside hot tub, in-room massage and facials (extra), and the on-site **Greenwood Pier Café,** noted for its house-baked breads and fresh garden veggies and herbs. Most rates are $150–250; one room is $130, two cottages are $250 and up.

POINT ARENA AND VICINITY

Point Arena was "discovered" by Capt. George Vancouver in 1792. Another good spot for whale-watching, Point Arena was the busiest port between San Francisco and Eureka in the 1870s. When the local pier was wiped out by rogue waves in 1983, the already depressed local fishing and logging economy took yet another dive. But today Point Arena has a new pier—folks can fish here without a license—and a new economic boon: the sea urchin harvest, to satisfy the Japanese taste for *uni*. In winter, come watch for whales. Or check out a movie at the art house **Arena Cinema,** 214 Main St., 707/882-3456.

Point Arena Lighthouse

A monument to the area's historically impressive ship graveyard, the Coast Guard's six-story, auto-

mated 380,000-candlepower lighthouse north of town is open to visitors (limited hours, small donation requested). Built in 1908, this lighthouse was the first in the U.S. constructed of steel-reinforced concrete; it replaced the original brick tower that had come tumbling down two years earlier. The adjacent **museum** tells tales of the hapless ships that floated their last here. Tours of the light tower and museum are offered daily, $4 adults, $1 children; call for current hours.

To help protect the lighthouse and preserve public access (no government support has been available), local volunteer lighthouse keepers maintain and rent out "vacation rental homes" (furnished three-bedroom, two-bathroom U.S. government-issue houses abandoned by the Coast Guard)—a good deal for families, with fully stocked kitchens, cozy wood-burning stoves, satellite TV, VCR, and stunning ocean views. Rates are $170–300.

For more information and reservations, contact **Point Arena Lighthouse Keepers, Inc.,** 45500 Lighthouse Rd., 707/882-2777 or 877/725-4448 (reservations only), www.pointarenalighthouse.com.

Manchester State Park

This 5,272-acre park north of Point Arena and the burg of Manchester is foggy in summer and cold in winter, but it presents dedicated beachcombers with a long stretch of sandy shore and dunes dotted with driftwood. Five miles of beaches stretch south to Pt. Arena. A lagoon offers good birding, and excellent salmon and steelhead fishing in both Brush and Alder Creeks. Also interesting here is the opportunity for some walk-in environmental camping, about a mile past the parking area. (Making an overnight even more thrilling is the knowledge that here at Manchester is where the San Andreas Fault plunges into the sea.) Once here, it's first-come, first-camped, with an opportunity to personally experience those predictable summer northeasterlies as they whistle through your tent. Group camp, too. For more information about Manchester and a camping map, contact the Mendocino state parks office, 707/937-5804, or call the park directly at 707/882-2463.

More private and protected is the **KOA** campground at 44300 Kinney Ln. (adjacent to the park office), 707/882-2375. Campsites start at $26; cabins and cottages also available.

Practicalities

If you don't stay at the lighthouse cottages mentioned above, consider the **Coast Guard House Historic Inn** at Arena Cove, 707/882-2442 or 800/524-9320, www.coastguardhouse.com, originally an outpost of the U.S. Life-Saving Service, precursor to the Coast Guard. This 1901 Cape Cod features six guest rooms (two share a bath), a cottage, and a boathouse. Queen or double beds, expanded continental breakfast. Most rooms are $100–150, cottages and other rooms $150–250.

For a superb five-course Italian meal and charming personal service, make reservations most Friday, Saturday, or Sunday nights at the already legendary **M Victorian Gardens,** an elegant farmhouse in nearby Manchester, 14409 S. Hwy. 1, 707/882-3606, one of the hottest dining destinations in Northern California. Stylish, very comfortable bed-and-breakfast rooms are available, too, $150–250.

GUALALA AND VICINITY

Though people in the area generally say whatever they please, Gualala is supposedly pronounced Wah-LA-la, the word itself Spanish for the Pomos' *wala'li* or "meeting place of the waters." Crossing the Gualala River means crossing into Sonoma County. On the way south to Sea Ranch from Gualala is **Del Mar Landing,** an ecological reserve of virgin coastline with rugged offshore rocks, tidepools, and harbor seals. Get there on the trail running south from Gualala Point Regional Park, a "gift" from Sea Ranch developers, or via Sea Ranch trails. The Gualala area is also known as the north coast's "banana belt," due to its relatively temperate, fog-free climate. At its heart is secluded Anchor Bay, just north of Gualala, enormously popular with rumrunners during Prohibition.

If you're not just blasting through town, stop off at the **Gualala Arts Center** galleries and stu-

dios, 46501 Hwy. 1, 707/884-1138, www .gualalaarts.org, to see what's up. Since 1961 Gualala Arts has served up a year-round menu of art, music, and theater. Come on Labor Day weekend (and the following weekend) for the annual **Studio Discovery Tour.** The center's **Dolphin Gallery** downtown is open daily 10 A.M.–4 P.M., and also serves as the **Gualala Visitors' Center.** For more area information, contact the **Redwood Coast Chamber of Commerce,** 707/884-1080 or 800/778-5252, www .redwoodcoastchamber.com.

Accommodations

Community life in this old lumber town always centered on the 1903 Gualala Hotel, where loggers and locals pounded a few after work, and where haute cuisine applied to spaghetti and steak and just about anything else served hot. Those days are gone, here and elsewhere, though it seems likely that the Gualala Hotel will remain a community draw. Along with new owners came serious efforts to rescue the hotel from dry rot and general decline—just in time for the hotel's centennial. Still a work in progress, the new, improved Gualala boasts new paint and new attitude, along with guest rooms gussied-up in old-fashioned style. Rates are quite reasonable; rooms with shared bathrooms are $50–100, with private baths $100–150. The dining room is pretty spiffy, too, whther you choose charbroiled burgers on foccaccia bread or pan-seared local salmon. Lunch is served Tues.–Fri., dinner Tues.–Sun., brunch on weekends. On Mondays, when the restaurant's closed, sample the saloon's café menu. For information or reservations, contact the **M Gualala Hotel,** 39301 S. Hwy. 1, 707/884-3441, www.thegualalahotel.com.

North of town is the **Old Milano Hotel,** 38300 S. Hwy. 1, 707/884-3256, www.oldmilano hotel.com, with five charming guest cottages and one genuine caboose. Cottages are each unique, rich with Victorian antiques, queen-size featherbeds, and stained glass; most offer an ocean view, whirlpool tub, or two-person shower. The caboose has a woodstove, terrace, and observation cupola. Rates are $150–250, including full breakfast and use of the ocean-view hot tub.

A stay at the ⋈ **Whale Watch Inn,** 35100 S. Hwy. 1, 707/884-3667 or 800/942/5342, www.whale-watch.com, is just this side of coastal condo heaven. Perched on the cliffs overlooking Anchor Bay (north of Gualala), the Whale Watch is the kind of place where decadence and decency both reign and Debussy pours out over the intercom. The 18 romantic, sometimes surprisingly formal retreats are collected in five separate buildings. Rooms and suites offer stunning views and amenities such as fireplaces, fresh flowers, decks, and whirlpool tubs; some have kitchens. Attendants bring breakfast to the door. Rates are $150–250 and $250 and up.

Just up the road is the **North Coast Country Inn,** 34591 S. Hwy. 1, 707/884-4537 or 800/959-4537, www.northcoastcountryinn.com, a onetime sheep ranch offering six hillside cottages rich in redwood, antiques, handmade quilts, wood-burning fireplaces, and other homey touches—not to mention the privacy and ocean views. All have private baths, some feature kitchens, whirlpool tubs, or private decks. The grounds include gazebo, deck, and a private hillside hot tub. Full breakfast. Rates are $150–250.

There are motels, too. Most rooms at the homey **Gualala Country Inn** on Center St. (at Hwy. 1) in Gualala, 707/884-4343 or 800/564-4466, www.gualala.com, are $100–150, a few slightly higher. You can even go international in Gualala, quite reasonably. The contemporary **Breakers Inn** on the bluffs, 39300 S. Hwy. 1, 707/884-3200 or 800/273-2537, www.breakers inn.com, features theme rooms with telling touches—the Denmark room has a steam bath—and abundant amenities, including large private decks overlooking the sea. Most rooms are $150–250, "garden view" rooms lower. Such a deal. Spa rooms are $250 and up. Check out mid-week and off-season specials.

Campers, head to **Gualala Point Regional Park** just south of town, 707/785-2377 or 707/527-2041, which offers coastal access and camping ($16 per night, no hookups). The park day-use fee is $3. Call 707/565-2267 for reservations. For more amenities, try privately operated **Gualala River Redwood Park,** 46001

Gualala Rd., 707/884-3533, www.gualalapark .com, in the redwoods on the north beach of the Gualala River, one mile east of town off Old Stage Road. The campground's 120 sites offer full hookups for $34–40 a night. Amenities include coin-op showers and restrooms. Abalone divers favor **Anchor Bay Campground,** down in a beachfront gulch just north of Anchor Bay village, 707/884-4222, www.abcamp.com. The small campground fills up often in spring and summer; reservations are accepted up to one year in advance. Rates start at $27 per night. Electrical hookups are extra; hot showers available. The campground also offers (for a small fee) access to Fish Rock Beach.

Food

If you're not eating at St. Orres (below), the fine-dining restaurant of choice in Gualala these days is the **Oceansong Pacific Grille,** next to the Breakers Inn at 39350 S. Hwy. 1, 707/884-1041, overlooking both beach and river. Since the kitchen has been under the direction of Swiss chef René Fueg, the restaurant has earned rave reviews from foodie magazines and locals alike. Seafood is one specialty, but you'll also find steaks, pastas, rack of lamb, and other entrées. For "downhome gourmet," try **The Food Company** just north of town at Robinsons Reef Rd., 707/884-1800, a combination café, deli, and bakery serving up fresh, wholesome fare. Sit outside on the sunporch or in the garden area, or pack your goodies to go. Open daily for breakfast, lunch, and dinner. To stock up on fresh local produce for the road, plan to arrive for the **Gualala Certified Farmers Market,** held May–Oct. on Sat., 3–5 P.M., at the Gualala Community Center, Hwy. 1 at Center Street. In Anchor Bay, services include a market and wine shop, as well as the **Fish Rock Cafe,** 707/884-1639, serving burgers, soups, salads, sandwiches (including veggie varieties), and Northern California microbrews. The café is open for lunch and dinner daily.

The ⋈ **Pangaea Café,** which first brought culinary note to Point Arena, is now at home in Gualala, 39165 S. Hwy. 1, 707/884-9669, arty and elegant and serving "eclectic" global, local, and organic cuisine. What that means varies from night to night, but might include temptations such as mahimahi with Lebanese couscous tabouleh, lentils, greens, and a cumin-scented lemon tahini sauce. Outrageous. Pangaea grows much of its own produce, bakes its own bread in a wood-fired oven, makes its sausage, and smokes its meats. The wine list highlights wines made from sustainably farmed grapes. Open for dinner only, Wed.–Sun. 5:30–9 P.M. Reservations recommended.

St. Orres

Continuing north from Gualala, you'll soon come upon a local landmark—the ornate onion-domed inn and restaurant of St. Orres, 36601 S. Hwy. 1, 707/884-3303 or 707/884-3335 (restaurant), www.saintorres.com. Some rock 'n' roll-literate wits refer to a sit-down dinner here as "sitting in the dacha of the bay." Dazzling in all its Russian-style redwood and stained-glass glory,

St. Orres is also a great place to stay. For peace, quiet, and total relaxation, nothing beats an overnight in one of the handcrafted redwood cabins (some rather rustic) scattered through the forest, or in one of the eight European-style hotel rooms (shared bathrooms). Hotel rooms are $50–100, cottages $100–150 and $150–250, full breakfast included.

Even if they don't stay here, people come from miles around to eat at St. Orres, known for its creative French-style fare. The fixed-price dinners ($40, not including appetizers or desserts) feature such things as a salad of greens and edible flowers from the garden, cold strawberry soup, puff pastry with goat cheese and prosciutto, venison with blackberries, wild boar, Sonoma County quail, salmon and very fresh seafood in season, eggplant terrine, and grilled vegetable tart. Wonderful desserts, and good wines (beer and wine only). No credit cards. Before dinner, sit outside and watch the sun set. Reservations are a must, a month or more in advance.

The Sonoma Coast

Northern California beaches are different from the gentler, kinder sandy beaches of the south-state. The coast here is wild. In stark contrast to the softly rounded hillsides landward, the Sonoma County coast presents a dramatically rugged face and an aggressive personality: undertows, swirling offshore eddies, riptides, and deadly "sleeper" or "rogue" waves. It pays to pay attention along the Sonoma coast. Since 1950, more than 70 people have been killed here by sleepers, waves that come out of nowhere to wallop the unaware, then drag them into the surf and out to sea.

October is generally the worst month of the year for dangerous surf, but it is also one of the best months to visit. In September and October the summertime shroud of fog usually lifts and the sea sparkles. Except on weekends, by autumn most Bay Area and tourist traffic has dried up like the area's seasonal streams, and it's possible to be alone with the wild things.

SEA RANCH TO TIMBER COVE

Sea Ranch

Almost since its inception, controversy has been the middle name of this 5,200-acre sheep ranch-cum-exclusive vacation home subdivision. No one could have imagined the ranch's significance in finally resolving long-fought battles over California coastal access and coastal protection. Sea Ranch hosted the first skirmishes in California's ongoing war over access to public beaches, battles that ended with the establishment of the California Coastal Commission.

From the start Sea Ranch architects got rave reviews for their simple, boxlike, high-priced condominiums and homes, which emulate weather-beaten local barns. The much-applauded cluster development design allowed "open space" for the aesthetic well-being of residents and passersby alike, but provided no way to get to the 10 miles of state-owned coastline without trespassing.

In 1972, Proposition 20 theoretically opened access, but the *reality* of beach access through Sea Ranch was achieved only in late 1985, when four of the six public trails across the property were ceremoniously, officially dedicated. Yet here, the public-access victory is only partial; Sea Ranch charges a day-use fee. So make it worth your while. From the access at Walk-On Beach, you can link up with the Bluff Top Trail that winds along the wild coastline to Gualala Point Regional Park some miles to the north.

There are other attractions. On the northern edge of the spread is the gnomish stone and stained-glass **Sea Ranch Chapel** designed by noted architect James Hubbell. Inside it's serene as a redwood forest. From the outside, the cedar-roofed chapel looks like an abstract artist's interpretation of a mushroom, perhaps a wave, maybe even a UFO from the Ice Age. What is it? Nice for meditation or prayer, if the door's unlocked.

Those who salivate over Sea Ranch and can afford the rates might consider an overnight stay (or maybe just a meal) at the 20-room **Sea Ranch Lodge,** 60 Seawalk Dr., 707/785-2371 or 800/732-7262, www.searanchlodge.com. Its pretty and plush accommodations look out over the Pacific, and some rooms have fireplaces and private hot tubs. Other amenities include pools, saunas, and an 18-hole links-style golf course (707/785-2468). Dine in the stylish Sea Ranch Lodge Restaurant or get simple breakfast or lunch at the Smokehouse Grill at the golf course. Rooms are $150–250 and $250 and up, though ask about specials. Vacation home rentals are also available.

Stewarts Point

Heading south toward Salt Point, stop at the weatherbeaten **Stewarts Point Store,** just to appreciate the 120-plus years of tradition the Richardson family has stuffed into every nook and cranny. You can buy almost anything, from canned goods and fresh vegetables to rubber boots and camp lanterns—and if they don't have it, they'll order it. Not for sale are items creating the store's ambience: the abalone shells and stuffed fish hanging from the ceiling, horse collars, oxen yoke, turn-of-the-century fish traps, and an 1888 Studebaker baby buggy.

Big news in Stewarts Point in 1996 was the completion of the 144-acre **Odiyan Buddhist Center,** the largest Tibetan Buddhist center in the Western hemisphere. Not a tourist attraction and largely hidden from view, the cultivated center of these 1,100 acres on Tin Barn Road includes six copper-domed major temples, a 113-foot gold stupa (a traditional monument to enlightenment), four libraries of sacred texts, 800 prayer flags, 1,242 prayer wheels, 200,000 clay offerings, 6,000 rose bushes, and 200,000 new trees. The center is the brainchild of exiled Tibetan lama Tarthang Tulku, founder of the Nyingma Institute in Berkeley and both Dharma Publishing and Dharma Press. The main building, the three-tiered Odiyan Temple, resembles a three-dimensional mandala—symbolizing balance and order. Tours are usually available, but you can visit online at www.odiyan.org.

Salt Point State Park

This 6,000-acre park is most often compared to Point Lobos on the Monterey Peninsula, thanks to its dramatic outcroppings, tidepools, and coves (this is one of the state's first official underwater preserves), wave-sculpted sandstone, lonely wind-whipped headlands, and highlands including a pygmy forest of stunted cypress, pines, and redwoods.

Though most people visit only the seaward side of the park—to dive or to examine the park's honeycombed *tafuni* rock (sculpted sandstone)—the best real hiking is across the road within the park's inland extension (pick up a map to the park when you enter).

Among Salt Point's other attractions are the dunes and several old Pomo village sites. In season, berrying, fishing, and mushrooming are favorite activities. Park rangers lead hikes and sponsor other occasional programs on weekends, and are also available to answer questions during the seasonal migration of the gray whales. The platform at Sentinal Rock is a great perch for whale-watching.

Among its other superlatives, Salt Point is also prime for camping—both tent and RV sites (no showers) are $20—especially the ocean-view campsites at Gerstle Cove, though Woodside Campground offers more shelter from offshore winds. Make reservations, at least for weekends during the summer high season, through ReserveAmerica, 800/444-7275, www.reserveamerica.com. Salt Point also has hike-in/bike-in and environmental campsites, as well as a group camp. Pleasant picnicking here, too. Day use is $6 per car. For more information, call Salt Point at 707/847-3221. For current dive conditions and information, call 707/847-3222.

Kruse Rhododendron Reserve

Adjoining Salt Point State Park, the seasonally astounding Kruse Rhododendron Reserve is an almost-natural wonder. Nowhere else on earth does *Rhododendron californicum* grow to such heights and in such profusion, in such perfect harmony—under a canopy of redwoods. Here at the 317-acre preserve, unplanted and uncultivated native rhododendrons up to 30 feet tall thrive in well-lit yet cool second-growth groves of coast redwood, Douglas fir, tan oak, and madrone. (Lumbermen downed the virgin forest, unintentionally benefitting the rhododendrons, which need cool, moist conditions but more sunshine than denser stands of redwoods offer.) The dominant shrub is the *Rhododendron macrophyllum*, or California rosebay, common throughout the Pacific Northwest. Also here is the *Rhododendron occidentale*, or western azalea, with its cream-colored flowers.

Most people say the best time to cruise into Kruse is in April or May, when the rhododendrons' spectacular pink bloom is at its finest. (Peak blooming time varies from year to year, so call ahead for current guestimates.) Another sublime time to come is a bit earlier in spring (between sweet-smelling rainstorms), when the rhododendron buds just start to show color and the tiny woods orchids, violets, and trilliums still bloom among the Irish-green ferns and mossy redwood stumps. But come anytime; the song of each season has its own magic note.

To get here from Hwy. 1, head east a short distance via Kruse Ranch Road. Coming in via the backwoods route from Cazadero is an adventure in itself, especially if the necessary signs have been taken down (again) by locals. To try it, better call ahead first for precise directions. Facilities at the preserve are appropriately minimal but include five miles of hiking trails, picnic tables, and outhouses. For bloom predictions, preserve conditions, and other information, call the reserve at 707/847-3222.

Timber Cove

Hard to miss even in the fog, the landmark eight-story **Benjamin Bufano** *Peace* **sculpture** looms over Timber Cove. Once a "doghole port" for lumber schooners, like most craggy north coast indentations, Timber Cove is now a haven for the reasonably affluent. But ordinary people can stop for a look at Bufano's last, unfinished work. From the hotel parking lot, walk seaward and look up into the the face of *Peace,* reigning over land and sea. The **Timber Cove Inn,** 21780 N. Hwy. 1, 707/847-3231 or 800/987-8319, www.timbercoveinn.com. offers fairly luxurious lodgings on a 26-acre point jutting out into the Pacific. Some rooms have private hot tubs, some have lofts, and most have fireplaces. Rates go as low as $78 and as high as $390, but most rooms are $100–150 and $150–250.

FORT ROSS STATE HISTORIC PARK

A large village of the Kashia Pomo people once stood here. After the Russian-American Fur Company (Czar Alexander I and President James Madison were both company officers) established its fur-trapping settlements at Bodega Bay, the firm turned its attention northward to what, in the spring of 1812, became **Fort Ross,** imperial Russia's farthest outpost. Here the Russians grew grains and vegetables to supply Alaskan colonists as well as Californios, manufactured a wide variety of products, and trapped sea otters to satisfy the voracious demand for fine furs. With pelts priced at $700 each, no trapping technique went untried. One of the most effective: grabbing a sea otter pup and using its distress calls to lure otherwise wary adults into range.

The Russians' success here and elsewhere in California led to the virtual extinction of the sea otter. Combined with devastating agricultural losses (due to greedy gophers), this brought serious economic problems to the region. Commercial shipbuilding was attempted but also failed. The Russians got out from under this morass only by leaving, after selling Fort Ross and all its contents to John Sutter. Sutter (who agreed to the $30,000 price but never made a payment) carried off most of the equipment, furnishings, tools, and whatever else he could use to improve his own fort. Sutter's empire building eventually required James Marshall to head up the American River to build a sawmill. Marshall's discovery of gold led to Sutter's instant ruin but also to the almost overnight Americanization of California.

The First Fort

The weathered redwood fortress perched on these lonely headlands, surrounded by gloomy cypress groves, was home to Russian traders and trappers for 40 years. The original 14-foot-high stockade featured corner lookouts and 40 cannons. Inside the compound were barracks, a jail, the commandant's house, warehouses, and workshops. At the fort and just outside its walls, the industrious Russians and their work crews produced household goods plus saddles, bridles, even 200-ton ships and prefabricated houses.

Perhaps due to the Russian Orthodox belief that only God is perfect, the fort was constructed with no right angles. Its Greek Orthodox chapel was the only building here destroyed by the 1906 San Francisco earthquake. It was rebuilt, then lost again to arson in 1970, though it's since been reconstructed from the original blueprints (fetched from Moscow). Outside the stockade was a bustling town of Aleut hunters' redwood huts, with a windmill and various outbuildings and shops. When the Russians at Fort Ross finally prepared to leave their failed American empire, the Pomo held a mourning ceremony to mark their departure—a testament to the visitors' amicable long-term relations with the native peoples.

Fort Ross State Historic Park, Sonoma County

© ROBERT HOLMES/CALTOUR

The Reconstructed Fort

A good place to start exploring Fort Ross is at its million-dollar **visitor center** and museum, which includes a good introductory slide program (shown throughout the day in the auditorium), as well as Pomo artifacts and basketry, other historic displays, period furnishings, and a gift shop. The free **audio tour** of the fort is itself entertaining (balalaika music, hymns, and Princess Helena Rotchev—namesake of Mt. St. Helena near Calistoga—playing Mozart on the piano).

The fort's only remaining original building (now restored) is the commandant's quarters. Other reconstructed buildings include the barracks—furnished as if Russians would sail up and bed down any minute—an artisans' center, and the armory.

The park's boundaries also encompass a beach, the ridgetop redwoods behind the fort, and other lands to the north and east. Thanks to the Coastwalk organization, hiking access (including a handicapped-accessible trail) has been added to the Black Ranch Park area south of the fort. Ask at the visitor center for current hiking information.

Practicalities

For more information, call Fort Ross at 707/847-3286 or 707/865-2391. Just 12 miles north of Jenner along Hwy. 1, the park is open 10 A.M.–4:30 P.M. daily (except major holidays). Day-use is $6 per car. Autophobes, get here via **Mendocino Transit** buses daily from the north, 707/462-1422.

On **Living History Day** in July or August, the colony here suddenly comes back to life circa 1836. History buffs can have fun questioning repertory company volunteers to see if they know their stuff.

For those who want to rough it, first-come, first-served primitive camping ($15) is possible at **Fort Ross Reef State Campground,** tucked into a ravine just south of the fort (20 campsites, no dogs); call for more information. Those who want to "smooth it" can instead try **Fort Ross Lodge,** 20705 Hwy. 1, 707/847-3333 or 800/968-4537, www.fortrosslodge.com, which offers all modern amenities and some great ocean views. Most rooms are $50–100 and $100–150, but those with private hot tub or whirlpool tub are $150–250.

Jenner

Perched like a sleepy sentinel on the steep, curvaceous hills overlooking the Pacific Ocean and the mouth of the Russian River, Jenner is primarily a pleasant collection of seaside shanties committed to watching the tourists roll by. If you, too, are just passing through, consider a meal stop at the locally popular **River's End,** 11051 Hwy. 1 in Jenner, 707/865-2484 or 707/869-3252. Also in Jenner is **Sizzling Tandoor,** 9960 Hwy. 1 (on the south side of the Russian River bridge at Willow Creek Rd.), 707/865-0625, serving mouthwatering East Indian fare.

South of Jenner and north of Goat Rock, at the mouth of the Russian River, a large population of harbor seals has established itself, attracting considerable human attention. Unlike sea lions, which amble along on flippers, harbor seals wriggle like inchworms until in the water, where their mobility instantly improves. On weekends, volunteer naturalists (members of Stewards of Slavianka) show up to answer questions, lend binoculars for a close-up look, and protect seals from unleashed dogs and too-curious tourists. Do keep your distance. When panicked, harbor seals will protect themselves by biting. Some carry diseases difficult to treat in humans—which is why sailors of old used to cut off a limb if it was seal-bitten.

"Pupping season" starts in March and continues into June. During these months, harbor seals and their young become vulnerable to more predators, since they give birth on land. Some worry that Jenner's large seal colony will attract other enthusiastic observers, like sharks and killer whales. Not known to attack humans (though no one will guarantee that), killer whales also consider harbor seals a delicacy. To avoid predators, harbor seals swim upriver as far as Monte Rio while fishing for their own prey: salmon and steelhead.

EXCURSION INLAND: RUSSIAN RIVER RESORT AREA

Most people think of the Russian River as the cluster of rustic redwood-cloistered resort villages stretching from Jenner-by-the-Sea east along Hwy. 116 to Guerneville, the region once a popular resort area for well-to-do San Franciscans. Today's colorful cultural mix, including loggers, gays, sheep ranchers, farmers, hippies, and retirees, is surprisingly simpatico despite occasional outbreaks of intolerance. After the devastating winter floods that regularly inundate the area, for example, locals accept the raging river's most recent rampage and set out, as a community, to make things right.

It's a mistake, though, to view the Russian River as strictly a Jenner-to-Guerneville phenomenon. The river's headwaters are far to the north, just southeast of Willits, though it's not much of a river until it reaches Cloverdale.

Roughly paralleling Hwy. 101 inland, this slow, sidewinding waterway—called Shabaikai or Misallaako ("Long Snake") by Native Americans, and Slavianka ("Charming One") by early Russian fur traders—uncoils slowly through Sonoma County's northern wine country, and multiple small wineries cluster like grapes. To find them—representing the Alexander Valley, Chalk Hill, Dry Creek Valley, Green Valley, and Russian River Valley appellations—pick up a free map and brochure at local chamber of commerce offices. Or contact **Russian River Wine Road,** 707/433-4374 or 800/723-6336, www.wineroad.com.

Contact the **Russian River Chamber of Commerce,** 707/869-9000, www.russianriver .com, for a current listing of resort-area lodgings, restaurants, and upcoming events. Stop off at **King's Sport & Tackle,** 16258 Main St. in downtown Guerneville, 707/869-2156, for current fishing information and supplies.

SONOMA COAST STATE BEACHES

Most of the spectacular 13 miles of coastline between Jenner and Bodega Bay is owned by the state. The collective Sonoma Coast State Beaches are composed of pointy-headed offshore rock formations or "sea stacks," natural arches, and a series of secluded beaches and small coves with terrific tidepools. Don't even think about swimming here, since the cold water, heavy surf, undertows, and sleeper waves all add up to danger. Never turn your back to the ocean. But for beachcombing, ocean fishing, a stroll, or a jog—well away from the water—these beaches are just about perfect. Rangers offer weekend whale-watching programs from mid-December through mid-April.

For a great hike, take the three-mile **Dr. David Joseph Trail,** starting at the Pomo Canyon Campground just off Willow Creek Road, south of the mouth of the Russian River. The route threads through the redwoods into the ferns, then on through the oak woodlands and grassland scrub down to the Pacific ocean at Shell Beach.

Four miles north of Jenner is the **Vista Trail,** which allows people in wheelchairs to come very close to the edge of a dramatic cliff for some fabulous views.

It's a spectacularly snaky road from Hwy. 1 down to dramatic Goat Rock, popular **Goat Rock Beach** just north, and the dunes just east. The craggy goat itself is an impressive promontory but illegal to climb around on: more than a dozen people have drowned in recent years, swept off the rocks by surging surf.

On Goat Rock Beach, near Jenner at the mouth of the Russian River, a large population of harbor seals has established itself, attracting considerable human attention. (No dogs are allowed on Goat Rock Beach, because of the seals and other wildlife, but Fido is permitted on Blind Beach south of Goat Rock.) Unlike sea lions, which amble along on flippers, harbor seals wriggle like inchworms until in the water, where their mobility instantly improves. On weekends, volunteer naturalists (members of Stewards of Slavianka) are here to answer questions, lend binoculars for a close-up look, and protect the seals from unleashed dogs and too-curious tourists. When panicked, harbor seals will protect themselves by biting. Some carry diseases difficult to treat in humans—which is why sailors of old used to cut off a limb if it was seal-bitten.

Harbor seal "pupping season" starts in March and continues into June. During these months, seals and their young become vulnerable to more predators, since they give birth on land. Some worry that Jenner's large seal colony will attract other enthusiastic observers, like sharks and killer whales. Not known to attack humans (though no one will guarantee that), killer whales also consider harbor seals a delicacy. To avoid predators, harbor seals swim upriver as far as Monte Rio while fishing for their own prey: salmon and steelhead.

Other Beach Areas

Sprinkled like garnish between the rocks and coastal bluffs from Jenner to Bodega Bay are a variety of public beaches, including Miwok, Coleman, Arched Rock, Carmet, and Marshall Gulch. **Shell Beach** is best for beachcombing and seaside strolls, with some tremendous tidepools and good fishing.

There's picnicking and camping at **Wright's Beach,** but also danger; **Duncans Landing,** just south, is most famous for **Death Rock;** a former offshore lumber-loading spot during the redwood harvesting heyday. Today it's one of the most dangerous spots along the Sonoma coast, due to "sleeper" waves that snatch people off the shore. The area is now fenced, and clearly marked as off limits. Believe it. Heads up anyway, though, since rogue waves have reached as far as the parking lot.

North of Bodega Bay is **Salmon Creek Beach,** part of which becomes a lagoon when sand shuts the creek's mouth. (If you must swim, try the lagoon here.) No dogs are allowed on Salmon Creek Beach, to protect nesting areas of the threatened snowy plover. **Schoolhouse** and **Portuguese Beaches,** best for rock fishing and surf fishing, are stunning sandy beaches surrounded by rocky headlands. Plan a picture-perfect picnic near **Rock Point** on the headland (tables available).

Practicalities

Along this stretch are plentiful pulloffs for parking cars, with access to beach trails and spectacular views. The day-use fee for the Sonoma Coast State Beaches is $6. Camp at **Wright's Beach,** with 27 developed campsites just back from the beach, $30; restrooms and some campsites are wheelchair accessible. Or try **Bodega Dunes,** a half mile south of Salmon Creek, with 98 developed sites secluded among the cypress-dotted dunes, hot showers, an RV sanitation station, and a campfire center, $20. (Wright's Beach campers may take hot showers at Bodega Dunes.) Developed Sonoma Coast campsites are reservable in advance through ReserveAmerica, 800/444-7275, www.reserveamerica.com. Primitive walk-in camping is available Apr.–Nov. at 11-site **Willow Creek Campground** along the banks of the Russian River (first-come, first-camped, $15); no dogs. Register at the trailhead, up Willow Creek Rd. (turn right at the Sizzling Tandoor restaurant). The walk-in **Pomo Canyon Campground** (also $15) is reached via the same route. About five minutes after turning off Hwy.

1, you'll reach the gravel parking lot marked Pomo Canyon Campground. From here, two trails run into the redwoods to the 20 walk-in sites, which feature a picnic table, fire grill, and leveled tent site.

The **Jenner Visitor Center,** 707/865-9433 or 707/869-9177, offering books, current information, and wraparound views from the deck, is staffed by volunteers and open spring through October. Or contact park headquarters at the **Salmon Creek Ranger Station,** 3095 Hwy. 1 (just north of Bodega Bay), 707/875-2603.

Bodega Head

Hulking Bodega Head to the north of town, protecting Bodega Bay from the heavy seas, is a visible chunk of the Pacific plate and the bulwark for the area's state beaches. Good whale-watching from here. Nearby is the University of California at Davis's **Bodega Marine Lab,** 2099 Westside Rd., 707/875-2211, www-bml.uc-davis.edu, a marine biology research center open to the public every Friday 2–4 P.M. for tours and at other times, in winter, for its special seminar series. Hike on and around the head on well-worn footpaths, or head out for an invigorating walk via hiking trails to **Bodega Dunes.** Five miles of hiking and horseback riding trails twist through the dunes themselves (access at the north end of the bay, via W. Bay Road). To get to Bodega Head, take Westside Rd. and follow the signs past **Westside Park.**

Doran County Park, on the south side of the bay, 707/875-3540, looks bleak, but its windswept beaches and dunes provide safe harbor for diverse wildlife and hardy plants. Due to the protected beaches, this is the only safe place to swim for many coastal miles. Good clamming, too. There's an excellent boardwalk, allowing people with physical disabilities to get close to the ocean. Day-use fee $3. Or visit the water-filled sump once destined for the nuclear age (called "hole in the head" and "the world's most expensive duckpond" by amused locals). With Hitchcock's nature-vengeance theme in mind, we can only shudder at what might have been if PG&E had built its proposed nuclear power plant here, just four miles from the San Andreas Fault.

EARLY BODEGA BAY

Though Cabrillo and his crew were probably the first Europeans to spot the area, the Spanish lieutenant Don Juan Francisco de la Bodega y Cuadra anchored the *Sonora* off Bodega Head in October 1775 and named it after himself—breaking with the more modest tradition of using saints' names corresponding to the day of discovery. Ivan Kuskov, an agent of the powerful Russian-American Fur Company, arrived in Bodega Bay from Sitka, Alaska, in 1809. He and his company grew wheat inland, hunted sea otters, then returned to Alaska with full cargo holds. Two years later, they built three settlements—Port Rumiantsov on the bay, and the towns of Bodega and Kuskov inland—before the construction of Fort Ross began farther north. American settlers first arrived in 1835, increasing after the Russians left in the 1840s. Bodega Harbor was a bustling seaport by the 1860s, though large oceangoing vessels haven't anchored here for more than a century.

BODEGA BAY AND VICINITY

Alfred Hitchcock considered this quaint coastal fishing village and the inland town of Bodega perfect for filming *The Birds,* with its rather ominous suggestion that one day nature will avenge itself. But people come to Bodega Bay and vicinity to avoid thinking about such things. They come to explore the headlands, to whalewatch, to kayak, to beachcomb and tidepool, to catch and eat seafood (including local Dungeness crab), to peek into the increasing numbers of galleries and gift shops, and to *relax.* Real life may intrude, even here. The **Children's Bell Tower** next to the Community Center, on the west side of Hwy. 1 about 1.5 miles north of the visitor center, honors seven-year-old Nicholas Green of Bodega Bay, shot and killed in 1994 while traveling with his family in Italy. His parents, Maggie and Reg Green, decided to donate Nicholas's organs to needy Italian recipients—a decision all but unheard of in Italy, and one that moved Italians and Americans alike.

Just wandering through town and along the harbor is fascinating. While keeping an eye on the sky for any sign of feathered terrorists, watch the chartered "party boats" and fishing fleet at the harbor; at six each evening, the daily catch arrives at the Tides Wharf. Bodega, just inland, is where visitors go to reimagine scenes from Hitchcock's movie, most particularly **St. Teresa of Avila Church** and **Potter Schoolhouse.**

Most people don't know, though, that Hitchcock's story was based on actual events of August 18, 1961, though they occurred in Capitola, Rio Del Mar, and other towns on Monterey Bay, farther south. That night, tens of thousands of crazed shearwaters slammed into doors, windows, and hapless people; the next morning these birds, both dead and dying, stank of anchovies. In 1995, researchers at the Institute of Marine Sciences at UC Santa Cruz suggested that a lethal "bloom" of a natural toxin produced by algae—domoic acid—present in Monterey Bay anchovies was probably responsible for the birds' bizarre behavior. Toxic amounts of domoic acid cause amnesia, brain damage, and dementia.

Inland are a variety of small spots-in-the-road, some little more than a restaurant or boarded-up gas station at a crossroads, all connected to Bodega Bay by scenic roller-coaster roads. Not far south of town in Marin County is **Dillon Beach,** known for its tidepools. Keep going south via Hwy. 1 to the sensational **Point Reyes National Seashore.**

Bodega Bay's **Fisherman's Festival and Blessing of the Fleet** in April attracts upward of 25,000 people for a Mardi Gras–style boat parade, kite-flying championships, bathtub and foot races, art shows, and a barbecue. Ochlophobes, steer clear. Or come in late August for the **Bodega Bay Seafood, Art & Wine Festival,** a benefit for the Chanslor Wetlands Wildlife Project (see www.sonomawetlands.org) showcasing seafood entrées, wine and microbrew tasting, entertainment, "recycled art," and children's crafts.

For more information on Bodega Bay and environs, stop by the **Bodega Bay Area Visitor Information Center,** 860 Hwy. 1 (next to Texaco), 707/875-3866, or see www.bodegabay .com. The visitor center is open Mon.–Thurs.

North Coast

10 A.M.–6 P.M., Fri. and Sat. until 8 P.M., and Sunday 11 A.M.–7.P.M., closed on major holidays.

Accommodations

Camp at Bodega Dunes just north of the harbor, at smaller Wrights Beach on the way to Jenner, or at primitive Willow Creek Campground near Goat Rock. (For more information on these state park campgrounds, see above). **Doran Beach County Park** to the south has first-come, first-camped primitive outdoor accommodations. Day-use fee is $3. Camping is $16 per night ($14 for county residents) for the first vehicle and $5 per additional vehicle, plus $1 per dog. No RV hookups. For information, call the park at. 707/875-3540, or call regional park headquarters at 707/527-2041. For reservations, call 707/565-2267. Another possibility is the private, full-service **Bodega Bay RV Park**, 2001 Hwy. 1, 707/875-3701 or 800/201-6864, www.bodegabayrvpark.com, $25–31.

In town, the hotspot is the fairly pricey **Bodega Bay Lodge & Spa**, 103 Hwy. 1 (off the highway at Doran Beach Rd.), 707/875-3525 or 800/368-2468, www.woodsidehotels.com, which offers full luxury amenities, including an ocean-view pool, spa, fitness center, and exceptional The Duck Club restaurant. Rooms and suites are $250 and up on weekends and holidays. It's also adjacent to the **Bodega Harbour Golf Links,** 21301 Heron Dr., 707/875-3538, an 18-hole Scottish links-style course designed by Robert Trent Jones Jr.

Another possibility is the **Inn at the Tides**, 800 Hwy. 1, 707/875-2751 or 800/541-7788, www.innatthetides.com, $150–250. Rates include full amenities (pool, sauna, whirlpool, TV and movies, and many rooms with fireplaces), great views, and continental breakfast. The Inn at the Tides also features a casual in-house restaurant and the very good Sonoma-style continental **Bay View** restaurant, and sponsors a **Dinner with the Winemaker** series of monthly dinners and wine-tastings. Also nice is the **Bodega Coast Inn,** 521 Hwy. 1, 707/875-2217 or 800/346-6999, www.bodegacoastinn.com, with rates $150–250. Much more affordable: old-fashioned, 14-room **Bodega Harbor Inn,** 1345 Bodega Ave., 707/875-3594, with rates $50–100. Cottages and houses are also available.

For spa services and pampering, head south six miles to plush **Sonoma Coast Villa,** 16702

SUSAN SNYDER

Bodega Harbor

Hwy. 1 (two miles north of Valley Ford), 707/876-9818 or 888/404-2255, www.scvilla .com. Indulgences include massage, a seaweed mud body mask, or an herbal body wrap. Enjoy a Mediterranean-inspired dinner, featuring fresh local produce (some right from the Villa's own organic garden) and the fine Sonoma County wines. Other amenities include a swimming pool and whirlpool tub, pool table, putting green, wood-burning fireplaces, beautiful Italian slate floors, stocked refrigerators (Sonoma county wines, soft drinks), organic in-room coffee, and unique furnishings throughout. Rooms and suites are $250 and up (some lower), including full country breakfast.

The inviting **Chanslor Guest Ranch,** 2660 Hwy. 1 (near Bodega Dunes, just north of Bodega Bay), 707/875-2721, www.chanslor ranch.com, is a working horse ranch that also boards people. Rooms feature quilts and homey comforts. Rates are $100–150 and include continental breakfast. Horseback riding is extra; for details, call 707/875-3333.

RUSSIAN BODEGA BAY

Though Cabrillo and his crew were probably the first Europeans to spot the area, the Spanish lieutenant Don Juan Francisco de la Bodega y Cuadra anchored the *Sonora* off Bodega Head in October 1775 and named it after himself—breaking with the more modest tradition of using saints' names corresponding to the day of discovery. Ivan Kuskov, an agent of the powerful Russian-American Fur Company, arrived in Bodega Bay from Sitka, Alaska, in 1809. He and his company grew wheat inland, hunted sea otters, then returned to Alaska with full cargo holds. Two years later, they built three settlements—Port Rumianstov on the bay, and the towns of Bodega and Kuskov inland—before the construction of Fort Ross began farther north. American settlers first arrived in 1835, increasing after the Russians left in the 1840s. Bodega Harbor was a bustling seaport by the 1860s, though large oceangoing vessels haven't anchored here for more than a century.

Farther north is the coastal town of Jenner, near the mouth of the Russian River. **Jenner Inn & Cottages,** 707/865-2377 or 800/732-2377, www.jennerinn.com, offers quite pleasing and private rooms and cottages—various buildings, all overlooking the ocean, the river, or both. In addition to unique features, many offer wood-burning fireplaces and/or whirlpool tubs. All have private sundecks. Find something for every price range, too, with rooms as low as $88 and cottages as high as $378 (the Osprey house), though most accommodations are $150–250 or $250 and up. Breakfast is served at the inn's **Mystic Isle Café,** also open to the public. Massage and yoga classes available. Ask about packages, some quite intriguing.

Food

Get fresh fish and chips, even hot seafood to go, at popular **Lucas Wharf Deli and Fish Market,** 595 Hwy. 1 (on the pier at the harbor), 707/875-3562. Or pick up a delicious seafood sandwich and microbrew, and take it out to one of the benches and tables overlooking a working dock. The adjacent sit-down **Lucas Wharf Restaurant and Bar,** 707/875-3522, is open for lunch and dinner daily and is known for its pastas and steaks as well as seafood. Great clam chowder, fisherman's stew, and sourdough bread. A bit more spiffy (and a *lot* more pricey) is the recently renovated **The Tides Wharf Restaurant,** 835 Hwy. 1 (just north of Lucas Wharf), 707/875-3652, which also overlooks the bay (and has its own dock and video arcade) and was featured as a backdrop in *The Birds.* The Tides is popular for breakfast, and you can count on fresh seafood at lunch and dinner. Open daily; there's a fresh fish market and bait shop here, too. For fine dining, head for **The Duck Club** at the Bodega Bay Lodge, 103 Hwy. 1, 707/875-3525, famous for its Sonoma County cuisine—everything from Petaluma duck with orange sauce and Hagemann Ranch filet mignon to grilled Pacific salmon with sweet mustard glaze. Open daily for breakfast and dinner (picnic lunch available).

The **Breakers Cafe,** 1400 Hwy. 1, 707/875-2513, is a good choice for breakfast (waffles, Benedicts, omelettes, breakfast burritos), lunch (good sandwiches like portobello mushroom or cold shrimp and crab), and dinner (pastas, soups, salads, steaks). The wholesome **Sandpiper Dockside Café & Restaurant,** 1410 Bay Flat Rd. (take Eastshore Dr. off Hwy. 1 and go straight at the stop sign), 707/875-2278, is a casual locals' place open daily for breakfast, lunch, and dinner.

To drive somewhere in order to totally enjoy sitting down again, head south on Hwy. 1 to Valley Ford, the town made famous by Christo's *Running Fence.* The frumpy white frame building is **Dinucci's,** 14485 Valley Ford Rd., 707/876-3260, a fantastically fun watering hole and dinner house. Study the massive rosewood bar inside, shipped around Cape Horn, while waiting for a table (folks are allowed to linger over meals). The walls in the bar are almost papered in decades-old political posters, old newspaper clippings, and an eclectic collection of lighthearted local memorabilia. The dim barroom lighting reflects off the hundreds of abalone shells decorating the ceiling. Dinucci's boisterous family-style dining room has close-together, sometimes shared (it's either that or keep waiting) checkerboard-clothed tables and a very friendly serving staff. Dinner starts with antipasto, a vat of very good homemade minestrone, fresh bread, and salad, followed by seafood or pasta entrées and desserts. For $15 or so, after eating here people can barely walk to their cars.

Point Reyes National Seashore

Some 65,000 acres of fog-shrouded lagoons, lowland marshes, sandy beaches, coastal dunes, and ridgetop forests, Point Reyes National Seashore also features windy headlands and steep, unstable, colorful cliffs, populations of tule elk and grazing cattle, and a wonderful lighthouse all too popular for winter whale-watching. A dramatically dislocated triangular wedge of land with its apex jutting out into the Pacific Ocean, Point Reyes is also land in motion: this is earthquake country. Separated from mainland Marin County by slit-like Tomales Bay, the Point Reyes Peninsula is also sliced off at about the same spot by the San Andreas Fault. When that fault shook loose in 1906—instantly thrusting the peninsula 16 feet farther north—the city of San Francisco came tumbling down.

Geologists were long baffled by the fact that the craggy granite outcroppings of Point Reyes were identical to rock formations in the Tehachapi Mountains some 310 miles south. But the theory of plate tectonics and continental drift provided the answer. The Point Reyes Peninsula rides high on the eastern edge of the Pacific Plate, which moves about three inches to the northwest each year, grinding against the slower-moving North American Plate. The two meet in the high-stress, many-faulted rift zone of the Olema Valley, an undefined line "visible" in landforms and weather patterns. In summer, for example, fog may chill the coastal headlands and beaches while the sun shines east of Inverness Ridge.

Seasonally, dogs are specifically restricted at Point Reyes—and people must also restrain themselves—because the northern elephant seals have returned to area beaches and established a breeding colony. To protect the elephant seals during the winter breeding and pupping season, some beaches are temporarily closed. Only leashed dogs are allowed on North Beach, Kehoe Beach, and the southern part of Limantour Beach. Contact the park office for current details.

To be fully informed about what's going on in and around Point Reyes while visiting, contact the park. A good free companion is the quarterly tabloid *Coastal Traveler,* published by the area's Pulitzer Prize-winning *Point Reyes Light* newspaper and available at area shops and businesses. For advance or additional information, contact the **West Marin Chamber of Commerce** in Point Reyes Station, 415/663-9232, www.pointreyes.org.

SIGHTS AND RECREATION

Get oriented at the park's barnlike **Bear Valley Visitor Center,** 415/464-5100, just off Bear

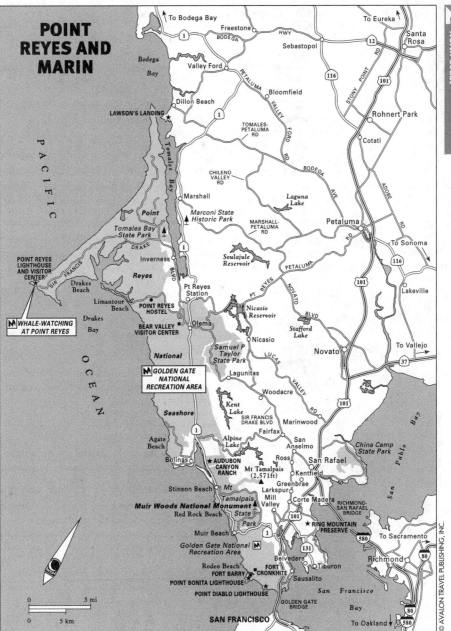

POINT REYES AND MARIN

To Bodega Bay

To Eureka

North Coast

Freestone
Santa
Rosa
BODEGA
HWY
Sebastopol
12

Bodega
Bay

Valley Ford
PETALUMA
116
101

Bloomfield
STONY POINT

Dillon Beach
Rohnert Park

LAWSON'S LANDING
TOMALES-
PETALUMA
RD
Cotati

To Tomales Bay
CHILENO
VALLEY
RD
BODEGA
AVE
ADOBE

Marshall
Laguna
Lake
Petaluma

Point
Marconi State
Historic Park
MARSHALL-
PETALUMA
RD
To Sonoma

Tomales Bay
State Park
DRAKE
Inverness
Soulajule
Reservoir
PETALUMA
116

POINT REYES
LIGHTHOUSE
AND VISITOR
CENTER
SIR FRANCIS
Reyes
Pt Reyes
Station
PT REYES
NOVATO
101
Lakeville

Drakes
Beach
BLVD
Limantour
Beach
POINT REYES
HOSTEL
Nicasio
Reservoir
BLVD

Drakes
Bay
BEAR VALLEY
VISITOR CENTER
Olema
Stafford
Lake
To Vallejo

WHALE-WATCHING
AT POINT REYES
Nicasio
Novato
37

National
Samuel P
Taylor
State Park
LUCAS

GOLDEN GATE
NATIONAL
RECREATION AREA
Lagunitas
VALLEY
101

Woodacre

Seashore
Kent
Lake
SIR FRANCIS
DRAKE BLVD
Marinwood
RD

Agate
Beach
Alpine
Lake
Fairfax
San
Anselmo
China Camp
State Park

Bolinas
AUDUBON
CANYON
RANCH
Ross
San Rafael
San Pablo Bay

Stinson Beach
Mt
Tamalpais
Kentfield
Greenbrae
Larkspur
RICHMOND-
SAN RAFAEL
BRIDGE

Muir Woods National Monument
Red Rock Beach
State
Park
Mill
Valley
Corte Madera

Muir Beach
RING MOUNTAIN
PRESERVE
580
To Sacramento

Golden Gate National
Recreation Area
Belvedere
131
Richmond
80

Rodeo Beach
FORT BARRY
FORT
CRONKHITE
Tiburon
POINT BONITA LIGHTHOUSE
Sausalito

POINT DIABLO LIGHTHOUSE
San Francisco
GOLDEN GATE
BRIDGE

SAN FRANCISCO
Bay
To Oakland
80
580

0   5 mi
0   5 km

© AVALON TRAVEL PUBLISHING, INC.

Valley Rd. (off Hwy. 1 near Olema), which, in addition to natural history and fine arts exhibits, includes a seismograph for monitoring the earth's movements. Near the picnic tables at the visitor center is the short **Earthquake Trail** loop (wheelchair accessible), which demonstrates the San Andreas seismic drama, from sag ponds and shifts in natural boundary lines to the old Shafter Ranch barn, a corner of which slid off its foundations during the 1906 San Francisco earthquake. Also near the Bear Valley Visitor Center are the short, self-guided **Woodpecker Nature Trail;** the **Morgan Horse Ranch,** where the Park Service breeds and trains its mounts; and **Kule Loklo,** an architectural re-creation of a Coast Miwok community. (When Sir Francis Drake purportedly arrived at Point Reyes in the late 1500s, he found more than 100 such villages on the peninsula.) The best time to see Kule Loklo is during July's Annual Native American Celebration, when this outdoor exhibit, complete with sweathouse, thatched and redwood bark dwellings, and dancing lodge, comes to life with Miwok basketmakers, wood- and stonecarvers, and native singing and dancing.

Limantour Estero near Drakes Estero and Drakes Beach is great for bird-watching; **McClures Beach** is best for tidepooling; and both **North Beach** and **South Beach** north of Point Reyes proper offer good beachcombing but treacherous swimming. Protected **Drakes Beach** and **Limantour Beach** along the crescent of Drakes Bay are safe for swimming.

For astounding views when the fog lifts above the ship graveyard offshore, head out to Point Reyes proper and the **Point Reyes Lighthouse and Visitor Center,** 415/669-1534 (open daily 9 A.M.–4:30 P.M. during whale-watching season, more limited hours at other times). The Chimney Rock Trail is wonderful for spring and summer wildflowers and, if you head west, is also a roundabout way to reach the lighthouse. On all Point Reyes hikes, carry water, wear proper walking shoes, and dress for sudden, unpredictable weather changes.

To experience the sound and fury of Coast Creek hurling itself into the Pacific via the "sea tunnel" at the **Arch Rock Overlook,** dress warmly, wear raingear and slip-proof shoes, and come (via the popular Bear Valley Trail) during a storm. For safety's sake, stay well back from the spectacle, and don't attempt to walk through the tunnel under any circumstances—though people often do in calm weather.

To make the most of a full moon at Point Reyes, head to the **Wildcat Beach Overlook** via the Bear Valley Trail from the visitor center, then south via the Coast Trail to the area overlooking the beach, **Alamere Falls** (most spectacular after heavy rains), and the southern stretch of Drakes Bay. An alternate route to Alamere Falls, about one mile south of Wildcat Camp, is via the Palomarin Trail from Bolinas or the Five Brooks Trail. For the best panoramic vista of Drakes Bay, take the Bear Valley, Sky, then Woodward Valley Trails to the bay (alternatively, take the Coast Trail from Coast Camp to the Woodward Valley Trail), then climb up the small hill overlooking the bay, just northwest of the trail.

COURTESY OF THE NATIONAL PARK SERVICE

Every view of Point Reyes National Seashore is breathtaking.

The **Randall Spur Trail,** created by the Civilian Conservation Corps, connects the Bolinas Ridge Trail with the various Inverness Ridge and Olema Valley trails—making Point Reyes's southern stretches more accessible for day hikers. Worth a stop on the way to the Palomarin trailhead in south Point Reyes is the **Point Reyes Bird Observatory,** 415/868-1221, www.prbo .org, established in 1965 as the first bird observatory in the country. Though it's a full-fledged research facility, the Palomarin observatory is open to the public, with bird walks, educational classes (call ahead for information), interpretive exhibits, and a nature trail. Field biology internships are also available. To get here by car, take the unmarked turnoff to Bolinas (near highway marker 17.00 at the north end of Bolinas Lagoon), continue two miles or so to Mesa Rd., then turn right and continue four miles to the observatory's bird-banding station.

These days, visitors can also horse around in Point Reyes, thanks to guided tours offered by **Five Brooks Ranch,** 415/663-1570, www.five brooks.com. The two-hour Fir Top Trail Ride is $50 per person, though one-hour and six-hours ride, overnight pack trips, and brief pony rides for the kids are also available.

Whale-Watching

Whale-watching, particularly fine from the lighthouse, is immensely popular at Point Reyes and best from about Christmas through January, when whales pass from one to five miles offshore. (Come on a weekday to avoid the crowds.) A hundred or more whale sightings per day is fairly typical here, though a 307-step descent to the lighthouse must be negotiated first. (Remember, what goes down must come back up.) You'll also get good views from the platform at the top of the stairs. The parking lot at the Point Reyes Lighthouse is fairly small, so in peak season—late December through April—whale-watchers park at Drakes Beach near the park entrance and take a shuttle bus to the lighthouse and Chimney Rock; the fee is $4 general, kids 12 and under free. National Park Service naturalists provide whale facts and whale-watching tips in January 10 A.M.–4 P.M. daily, both at the light-

house and the small information center near the viewing platform. For more information about Point Reyes whale-watching, including the complete shuttle schedule and special naturalist programs, call the Bear Valley Visitor Center at 415/464-5100 or see the park's website. The lighthouse is open to the public for self-guided and ranger-led tours Thurs.–Mon. 10 A.M.– 4:30 P.M. (closed in the event of high winds), as is the visitor center.

Not far from the lighthouse is the **Point Reyes Historic Lifeboat Station,** established in 1889 with a "surfcar" (like a tiny submarine) pulled through the surf on a cable, hand-pulled surfboats, and a Lyle gun and breeches buoy. The facility is open infrequently and is available for educational programs on marine biology and maritime history. For more information, call 415/464-5100.

INFORMATION AND SERVICES

For information about Point Reyes, including current trail maps, and to obtain permits for camping and backpacking, stop by any of the park's three visitor centers: the main **Bear Valley Visitor Center** at the park's Bear Valley entrance, 415/464-5100, open year-round Mon.–Fri. 9 A.M.–5 P.M., weekends 8 A.M.–5 P.M.; **Kenneth C. Patrick Visitor Center** at Drakes Beach, 415/669-1250, open weekends and holidays all year, 10 A.M.–5 P.M., and Fri.–Tues. 10 A.M.– 5 P.M. in summer; and **Point Reyes Lighthouse Visitor Center** at the end of Sir Francis Drake Blvd., 415/669-1534, open year-round Thurs.–Mon., 10 A.M.–4:30 P.M. Or contact Point Reyes National Seashore, 415/464-5100, www.nps.gov/pore.

There isn't any car camping at Point Reyes, but hike-in and ride-in (bicyclists and equestrians) family campgrounds are available; camping on the west side of Tomales Bay is boat-in only. Family campsites are $12 per night, group camps $25–35; for more details see the park's website. Call 415/663-8054 on weekdays for advance reservations and permit information.

For information about the year-round schedule of excellent classes and field seminars held at Point

Reyes (most offered for credit through Dominican College, some offered cooperatively through the Elderhostel program), contact **Point Reyes Field Seminars,** 415/663-1200, www.ptreyes.org, and ask for the current seminar catalog.

A very good guidebook to the area is *Point Reyes—Secret Places & Magic Moments* by Phil Arnot. Also by Arnot (and Elvira Monroe): *Exploring Point Reyes: A Guide to Point Reyes National Seashore.*

FARALLON ISLANDS

Visible from Point Reyes on a clear day are the Farallon Islands to the southwest. Protected as the Farallon National Wildlife Refuge, the largest seabird rookery south of Alaska, these islands are one of the five most ecologically productive marine environments on earth and now part of an international UNESCO Biosphere Reserve. Some 948 square nautical miles of ocean from Bodega Head to Rocky Point are included in the Gulf of the Farallones National Marine Sanctuary. These rugged granite islands 27 miles west of San Francisco are actually the above-sea-level presence of the Farallones Escarpment, which parallels the coast from the tip of Point Reyes to south of the Golden Gate. The natural but rare phenomenon of upwelling around the islands, with warm offshore winds drawing cold, nutrient-rich ocean water to the surface in spring, creates the phenomenal algae and plankton populations that support the feeding frenzies and breeding successes of animals farther up the food chain.

But during recent centuries, life has been almost undone at the Farallones. In the 1800s, "eggers" exploited the rookeries here to provide miners and San Franciscans with fresh eggs at breakfast. The islands have also survived assaults from sealers, whalers, gill netters, bombers, ocean oil slicks, and radioactive waste dumping.

In the summer, more than 250,000 breeding birds—from tufted puffins and petrels to auklets and murres—consider the Farallones home. Seals (including the once-almost-extinct northern elephant seal) and sea lions also breed here, and gray and humpback whales as well as northern fur seals are often spotted in the area. The nonprofit,

member-supported **Point Reyes Bird Observatory,** 4990 Shoreline Hwy. (Hwy. 1) in Stinson Beach, 415/868-1221, staffs a scientific study center at the Farallones (in addition to its center at Point Reyes), but otherwise people are not allowed on the islands—though the **Oceanic Society,** 415/474-3385, www.oceanic-society.org, sponsors one-day educational expeditions around the Farallon Islands June–Nov. and during the winter whale-watching season. (Bring binoculars.) The public is welcome, however, at the **Point Reyes Bird Observatory's Palomarin Field Station,** 415/868-0655, at the end of Mesa Rd. near Bolinas, to observe bird banding. The station is open daily May–Nov. and on Wed., Sat., and Sun. the rest of the year; call for hours and to make reservations for groups of five or more people.

For more information about the Farallon Islands and the surrounding marine sanctuary, contact the **Farallones Marine Sanctuary Association** headquartered at the Presidio in San Francisco, 415/561-6622, www.farallones.org.

GOLDEN GATE NATIONAL RECREATION AREA AND VICINITY

Beginning immediately adjacent to Point Reyes near Olema is the Golden Gate National Recreation Area (GGNRA), which wraps itself around various state and local parks inland, then extends southeast across the Marin Headlands and the Golden Gate Bridge to include the Presidio and a thin coastal strip running south to Fort Funston. The GGNRA also includes two notable tourist attractions in San Francisco Bay: Angel Island and Alcatraz. Most notable is the dramatic natural beauty of the Marin Headlands—sea-chiseled chilly cliffs, protected valleys, and grassy wind-combed hills rich with wildlife and wildflowers, all opening out to the bay and the Pacific Ocean. Protected at first by the Nature Conservancy until coming under national management in 1972, the vast Marin Headlands feature trails for days of good hiking and backpacking (stop by headquarters for a current trail map). Backcountry and group camps are scattered across the area.

COURTESY OF THE NATIONAL PARK SERVICE

View of San Francisco from Golden Gate National Recreation Area

Aside from the GGNRA's natural beauty, here also is historic scenery, from the 1877 Point Bonita Lighthouse to four military installations—Forts Barry, Cronkhite, Baker, and Funston—that protected the Bay Area beginning in the 1870s and continuing through World War II. The last U.S. Army post in the Bay Area was closed in late 2002 when Fort Baker was transferred by the military to the National Park Service.

For more information about the GGNRA, including trail maps, events calendars, and backcountry camping details, stop at the **Marin Headlands Visitor Center** at Fort Barry, in the historic Fort Barry Chapel at Field and Bunker Rds., 415/331-1540, open daily 9:30 A.M.–4:30 P.M., or the **Muir Woods Visitor Center** at Muir Woods, 415/388-7368, open daily 8 A.M.–sunset. The Golden Gate National Recreation Area offers two hike-in and two walk-in campgrounds in the Marin Headlands; inquire here for details and to make reservations (required). If you're still in San Francisco, get GGNRA information at: **Pacific West Information Center,** Bldg. 201 at Fort Mason,

415/561-4700, open Mon.–Fri. 8:30 A.M.–4:30 P.M.; the **Cliff House Visitor Center,** 415/556-8642, open daily 10 A.M.–5 P.M.; the **Fort Point Bookstore,** 415/556-1693, open only Fri.–Sun. 10 A.M.–5 P.M.; and the **William Penn Mott Jr. Visitor Center** at the Presidio, 415/561-4323, open daily 9 A.M.–5 P.M. Or see the park website: www.nps.gov/goga.

Several guidebooks published by the nonprofit Golden Gate National Parks Conservancy, 415/561-3000 or 415/657-2757, www.parks conservancy.org, are well worth buying—including the 96-page *Guide to the Golden Gate National Parks,* which covers every feature of the recreation area.

Tomales Bay State Park

Among the half-moon beaches and secret coves along the steep cliffs and shores of Tomales Bay are those protected within fragments of Tomales Bay State Park. One section is just north of Inverness, via Pierce Point Rd. off Sir Francis Drake Blvd., and others are scattered along Hwy. 1 north of Point Reyes Station on the east side of the bay. One of the prime picnic spots at Tomales Bay is

Heart's Desire Beach, popular for family picnicking and swimming, and usually empty on weekdays (parking $6 per vehicle). The warm, usually sunny, and surf-free inland beaches here are the main attraction, but hiking the forested eastern slope of Inverness Ridge is also worth it—especially in early spring, when trees, young ferns, and wildflowers burst forth from their winter dormancy. Unique is the park's fine virgin forest of Bishop pines. Walk-in campsites are available. For views and a great hiking trail, get directions to Inverness Ridge from Tomales Bay State Park personnel. The southern grasslands section of Tomales Bay, now included in the GGNRA after the federal purchase of the 250-acre Martinelli Ranch, is prime turf for hiking (best in March for wildflowers) and bird-watching. The trailhead and parking area is just off Hwy. 1, about 1.5 miles north of Point Reyes Station. For more information about the park, contact Tomales Bay State Park in Inverness, 415/669-1140.

Along the eastern edge of Tomales Bay, the **Marconi Conference Center,** 18500 Hwy. 1 in Marshall, 415/663-9020, www.marconi conference.org, occupies the 1914 Marconi Hotel once owned by Guglielmo Marconi, inventor of the wireless. This onetime communications center facility—taken over by the U.S. Navy during World War I, later operated by RCA, and more recently home to the much-praised then pilloried Synanon alcohol and drug abuse program—is now a state-owned conference center operated on the model of Asilomar on the Monterey Peninsula.

Samuel P. Taylor State Park

East of Point Reyes National Seashore and hemmed in by the Golden Gate National Recreation Area is Samuel P. Taylor State Park, 2,600 acres of redwoods, mixed forests, and upcountry chaparral reached via Sir Francis Drake Boulevard. The park offers an extensive hiking and horseback trail system, a paved bicycle path running east-west, family campsites, group camps, no-frills camping (including hiker/biker camps), picnicking, and swimming. Day use is $6. To reserve family campsites ($20), contact ReserveAmerica, 800/444-7275, www.reserve

america.com. For more information, contact Samuel P. Taylor State Park in Lagunitas, 415/488-9897.

East of Samuel Taylor near Nicasio is the vast Skywalker Ranch owned by Lucasfilms and George Lucas, film- and mythmaker in the tradition of mythologist Joseph Campbell and his *Hero With a Thousand Faces.* The public is not welcome. (And for the record, Lucas Valley Road, connecting Nicasio and Marinwood, was named long before Lucas bought property here.) Lucasfilms is now in the process of moving to new headquarters at San Francisco's Presidio.

Bolinas Lagoon and Audubon Canyon Ranch

Well worth a visit is the Bolinas Lagoon, as serene as a Japanese nature print, especially in spring, when only the breeze or an occasional waterfowl fracas ruffles the glassy blue smoothness of this long mirror of water surrounded by a crescent-moon sandspit. Reflected above is wooded Bolinas Ridge, the northwestern extension of Mount Tamalpais. In autumn, the lagoon is much busier, temporary home to thousands of waterfowl migrating south along the Pacific Flyway as well as the salmon offshore waiting for a ferocious winter storm to break open a pathway through the sandbars blocking their migratory path. At minus tide any time of year, the surf side of the sandspit offers good beachcombing.

Facing out into the Bolinas Lagoon several miles north of Stinson Beach is the Audubon Canyon Ranch, a protected canyon offering a safe haven and rookery for great blue herons and common egrets in particular, though more than 50 other species of water birds arrive here each year. By quietly climbing up the canyon slopes during the Mar.–July nesting season, visitors can look down into egret and heron nests high atop the redwoods in Schwartz Grove and observe the day-to-day life of parent birds and their young. Eight miles of self-guided hiking trails lead to other discoveries; picnic facilities also available.

The old dairy barn here serves as ranch headquarters and bookstore/visitor center. The ranch is wheelchair accessible and generally open to the public mid-March through mid-July only on weekends and holidays, 10 A.M.–4 P.M. Admission is free, though donations are greatly appreciated. Large groups can make tour arrangements for weekdays, though the ranch is always closed Mondays. For more information, contact: Audubon Canyon Ranch, 4900 Shoreline Hwy. (Hwy. 1) in Stinson Beach, 415/868-9244, www.egret.org.

Mount Tamalpais State Park

Though the park also stretches downslope to the sea, take in the views of Marin County, San Francisco Bay, and the Pacific Ocean from the highest points of Mount Tamalpais. This long-loved mountain isn't particularly tall (elevation 2,600 feet), but even when foggy mists swirl everywhere below, the sun usually shines atop Mount Tam. And the state park here has it all: redwoods and ferns, hillsides thick with wildflowers, 200 miles of hiking trails with spectacular views (plus access to Muir Woods), beaches and headlands, also camping and picnicking. The best way to get here is via Hwy. 1, then via the Panoramic Hwy., winding up past Pan Toll Ranger Station and park headquarters (stop for information and a map) to near the summit. From the parking lot, it's a quarter-mile hike up a steep dirt road to the fire lookout on top of Mount Tam.

The best way to explore Mount Tamalpais is on foot. Take the loop trail around the top. For the more ambitious, head downslope to the sea and the busy public beaches at Stinson Beach, still noted for its annual **Dipsea Race** held in June, a tradition since 1904. Rugged cross-country runners cross the still more rugged terrain from Mill Valley to the sea at Stinson Beach; the last stretch down the footpath is known as the Dipsea Trail. Or hike into the park from Marin Municipal Water District lands on the east (for information, call the Sky Oaks Ranger Station in Fairfax, 415/945-1181) and head upslope, via the Cataract Trail from just off Bolinas Rd. outside of Fairfax and past Alpine Lake—something of a steep climb but worth it for the waterfalls, most dramatic in winter and early spring but sublime for pool-sitting in summer.

Via the Matt Davis Trail, or the Bootjack Camp or Pan Toll Ranger Station routes, hike to the charming old (1904) **West Point Inn,** 1000 Panoramic Hwy., 415/388-9955, for a glass of lemonade and a rest in the porch shade. (Accommodations available; see below.) Four miles away is the **Tourist Club,** 30 Ridge Ave., 415/388-9987, a 1912 chalet where overnight stays are available only to members and their families, but hikers arriving via the Sun, Redwood, or Panoramic Trails can get snacks, cold imported beer, sodas, and juices. Open daily, great views of Muir Woods from the deck. More accessible for a picnic or snack stop (bring your own) is Mount Tam's Greek-style **Mountain Theater,** also known as the Cushing Memorial Theater, a 3,750-seat outdoor amphitheater on Ridgecrest Blvd. built from natural stone by the Civilian Conservation Corps. Rousing performances of the *Mountain Play* have been produced here each spring since 1913.

Mount Tamalpais State Park is open daily from 7 A.M.–sunset. Day use (parking) is $6. Limited primitive camping ($12–20) and rustic cabins ($60) are available. Make reservations for cabins through ReserveAmerica, 800/444-7275, www.reserveamerica.com. Campgrounds are first-come, first-camped; call the park for details. For more information, contact park headquarters at 801 Panoramic Hwy. in Mill Valley, 415/388-2070. For current information on Mount Tam's Mountain Theater productions, contact the **Mountain Play Association,** 177 E. Blithedale in Mill Valley, 415/383-1100, www.mountainplay.org.

Muir Woods National Monument

Muir Woods is peaceful and serene but quite a popular place—not necessarily the best destination for getting away from them all. Lush redwood canyon country surrounds Redwood Creek within the boundaries of Mount Tamalpais State Park, with a short trail system meandering alongside the stream, up to the ridgetops, and into the monument's main Cathedral and Bohemian redwood groves. For an easy, introductory stroll, the Muir Woods Nature Trail wanders through the flatlands, identifying the characteristic trees and shrubs. Fascinating at Muir Woods, the first national monument in the U.S., are the dawn redwood from China and the park's albino red-wood, the shoots from this freak of nature completely chlorophyll-free. But to avoid the crowds imported in all those tour buses clogging the parking lot, get away from the visitor center and the trails near the parking lot. Muir Woods is open daily 8 A.M.–sunset, $3 day-use fee, no picnicking or camping. No dogs. For more information, contact the Muir Woods Visitor Center in Mill Valley, 415/388-7368, www.nps.gov /muwo, or call 415/388-2595 (recorded information) or 415/388-2596.

Fort Barry

Just north of Point Bonita, Fort Barry includes an intact 1950s missile launch site and underground bunkers not usually open to the public; one of the bunkers is still home to a Nike Hercules missile.

The **Nike Missile Site** is open for self-guided tours Wed.–Fri. 12:30–3:30 P.M., and you can come out for a free guided tour of all areas of the site the first Sunday of the month 12:30–3:30 P.M. For information, call 415/331-1453.

Also at Fort Barry: Hostelling International's marvelous **Marin Headlands Hostel,** Bldg. 941, 415/331-2777, www.norcalhostels.org; the **Headlands Center for the Arts,** Bldg. 144, 415/331-2787, www.headlands.org, which explores the relationship of art and the environment (studio space for artists is provided, and public programs include lectures, installations, exhibits, and performances); and the **Marin Headlands Visitor Center,** 415/331-1540, open to the public 9:30 A.M.–4:30 P.M. daily and offering hands-on natural science exhibits, and educational and historical displays.

HYSTERICAL HISTORICAL HOAX: SIR FRANCIS DRAKE MYSTERY

The mystery behind one of the West's best historical hoaxes has finally been revealed. As it turns out, all along the joke was on a famed UC Berkeley professor—thanks to those merrily besotted pranksters of E Clampus Vitus, who in the 1930s cleverly faked "proof" that British privateer Sir Francis Drake came ashore north of San Francisco.

Historians agree that Drake explored coastal California. Tired of pursuing Spanish ships around the world, he beached the *Pelican* (later known as the *Golden Hinde*) and came ashore at "a fit and convenient harbour" somewhere in California in June 1579. Naming the land Nova Albion, here he made repairs, rested his tired crew, and claimed the area for Queen Elizabeth I with "a plate of brasse, fast nailed to a great and firme post." This much most historians agree on. The rest of the story has always been contentious, at best. Indeed, the desire to discover the truth about Drake's California adventure certainly created the context for a grand hoax.

Where exactly did Drake land? Since the main estuary at Point Reyes is named after Drake, as is the bay, the simple answer is that he came ashore here,

some 20 nautical miles north of San Francisco. But some contend that Drake actually landed at Bolinas Lagoon or explored San Francisco Bay and landed near Point San Quentin or Novato, near an old Olompali village site where a 1567 English silver six-pence was discovered in 1974. A more recent quest for remnants of Drake's visitation centers on Bodega Bay. Others say he stumbled ashore on Goleta Beach near Santa Barbara, where five cast-iron British cannons similar to those missing from the *Golden Hinde* were unearthed in the 1980s. But 70 pieces of antique Ming porcelain found near Point Reyes is proof enough, say true believers of the Point Reyes theory, since four chests of Chinese porcelain, which Drake stole from the Spanish, never arrived in England. Unbelievers counter that the porcelain washed ashore instead from the wreckage of the *San Agustin* off Drakes Bay.

In the midst of decades of speculation remained the mystery of a brass plate found on a beach near Point San Quentin in 1936. Was it genuine, or a clever forgery? Eminent UC Berkeley historian Herbert Bolton, who died in 1953, declared it to be authentic "beyond all reasonable doubt" and considered it "one of the world's long-lost treasures."

Point Bonita Lighthouse

The Point Bonita Lighthouse (call 415/331-1540 for hours and tour information) was one of the first lighthouses ever built on the West Coast and is still operating. Technically, though, this isn't really a lighthouse—there's no house, just the French-import 1855 Fresnel lens and protective glass, walls, and roof, with gargoyle-like American eagles guarding the light. Getting here is as thrilling as being here—meandering along the half-mile footpath to the rocky point through hand-dug tunnels and across the swaying footbridge, in the middle of nowhere yet in full view of San Francisco. Especially enjoyable are the sunset and full-moon tours conducted by GGNRA rangers. At last report the lighthousehouse was open to tours (free) Sat.–Mon. 12:30–3:30 P.M.

To get to the lighthouse, follow the signs to Fort Baker/Fort Cronkhite/Fort Barry from Alexander Ave. just off the north end of the Golden Gate Bridge, then turn left at Field Rd. and continue, following the signs. (For seaside barbecues, head to the picnic area at Battery Wallace near Point Bonita.) For more information about American lighthouses, contact the **U.S. Lighthouse Society,** 244 Kearny in San Francisco, 415/362-7255 or website: www.uslhs.org.

Fort Cronkhite

Just north of the Visitor Center is Fort Cronkhite, home of the **California Marine Mammal Center,** 1065 Fort Cronkhite (just above Cronkhite Beach), Sausalito, 415/289-7325, www.marine mammalcenter.org. Established in 1975, this hospital for wild animals returns its "patients,"

After years of controversy, in 1977 the British Museum declared the corroded placard an "undoubted fake" despite the Olde English ring of its language, and metallurgists said the plate was no more than 100 years old. But who would undertake such an elaborate hoax, and why? For years, no one knew.

In February 2003, four historians revealed the truth—or, as much of the truth as will likely ever emerge—in a heavily footnoted article in the California Historical Society's *California History* magazine. The "plate of brasse" discovered at San Quentin was just a practical joke played on Bolton by several of his colleagues, who (like Bolton) were members of the Ancient and Honorable Order of E Clampus Vitus, an organization that variously describes itself as a historical drinking society or a drinking historical society and is still known for its prankster tendencies. Bolton had long searched for Drake's plaque, proof that the explorer had come ashore at Point Reyes, so his friends decided to find it for him. They purchased a brass plate in an Alameda ship chandlery and carefully covered it with Elizabethan writing. Before they dumped it off at Point Reyes in the early 1930s, they also marked the back of the plate with transparent fluorescent

paint—spelling out the letters "ECV," for E Clampus Vitus.

Yet when the plate was discovered, to Bolton's delight, the "ECV" lettering escaped his attention, and everyone else's. The "inside joke" went public, in a big way—even a second fake brass plate, with an announcement by a Miwok "Great Hi-oh" failed to shake Bolton's certainty—so the friendly conspirators ultimately decided to keep their silence.

Mystery lingers, though. What became of Drake's journal, which supposedly documented his California sojourn as well as his discovery of the Northwest Passage? What happened to the gold, gems, and silver Drake stole from the Spanish ship *Cacafuego* and others, estimated in today's currency values as worth $50 million? Some say no treasure was buried along the California coast, that Drake would have jettisoned cannons, china, and other goods instead to lighten his ship's load. Drake, they say, took all his loot back to England, where he and his crew became millionaires, and the queen retired some of the national debt and started the East India Company. Others, however, are still looking.

once fit, to their native marine environments. The center, with more than 400 active volunteers and popular hands-on environmental education programs for children, is open to the public daily 10 A.M.–4 P.M. Wheelchair accessible. New members and financial contributions always welcome.

Hawk Hill

For views of the Golden Gate Bridge, San Francisco Bay, and the San Francisco skyline—not to mention exceptional birding opportunities—head to Hawk Hill (abandoned Battery 129, reached via Conzelman Rd.) on the north side of the Golden Gate above the bridge. Come in the fall (with binoculars and fog-worthy clothing) to appreciate the incredible numbers of birds of prey congregating here—100 or more each day representing 20-plus species. In spring, bring your kite—or keep watching. With any luck at all, Hawk Hill's Moby Vulture will still be flying. Any time of year, this is a great vantage point for watching huge cargo ships and other vessels make their way through the Golden Gate. For more information about the fall hawk migration, contact the **Golden Gate Raptor Observatory,** 415/331-0730, www.ggro.org.

Other Marin GGNRA Sights

The hands-on **Bay Area Discovery Museum** at East Fort Baker, 415/487-4398, www.badm.org, is designed for children ages 2–12 and their families. It offers a great variety of special programs year-round—"In the Dream Time" children's art workshops, for example. Open Tues.–Fri. 9 A.M.–4 P.M., Sat.–Sun. 10 A.M.–5 P.M., $7 admission for adults and children, 1 and under free. Two miles north of Muir Beach is the **Slide Ranch** demonstration farm and family-oriented environmental education center, 2025 Hwy. 1, 415/381-6155, www.slideranch.org, which offers special events (such as "Family Farm Day") year-round. Reservations are required for all events.

Also part of the GGNRA is infamous Alcatraz, offshore, onetime military outpost then island prison and federal hellhole—"The Rock"—for hard-core criminals. Alcatraz Island and its prison facilities are now open for tours. For current information, contact the Alcatraz Visitor Center, 415/705-1042, or see www.nps.gov/alcatraz.

Bolinas

Bolinas is noted for the locals' Bolinas Border Patrol, an unofficial group dedicated to keeping outsiders out by taking down road signs. Once *in* Bolinas, however long that may take you, the gravel beach here is clean and usually uncrowded. The colorfully painted **Bolinas People's Store,** 14 Wharf Rd., 415/868-1433, is a good stop for snacks and picnic fixings. **The Coast Cafe,** 46 Wharf Rd., 415/868-9984, is comfortable and cozy on a foggy or rainy day. (At lunch, try the fish and chips, made with fresh local halibut or salmon.) When you're ready for a casual pint of Anchor Steam, belly up to the bar at **Smiley's Schooner Saloon,** 41 Wharf Rd., 415/868-1311, a classic dive bar that's as local as it gets. Mind your manners and have some fun.

ACCOMMODATIONS

Camping

So popular that each has a four-day limit, the four primitive walk-in campgrounds at Point Reyes National Seashore are perfect for backpackers, since each is within an easy day's hike of the main trailhead and each other. Call 415/663-8054 for information and telephone reservations weekdays 9 A.M.–2 P.M.; permits required. Reservations can also be made in-person at Bear Valley Visitor's Center (on Bear Valley Rd. just west of Olema), 415/464-5100. Stop, too, for maps and wilderness permits.

Popular Coast Camp is most easily accessible from the parking lot at the end of Limantour Rd. and makes a good base for exploring the Limantour Estero and Sculptured Beach. Wildcat Camp is a group camp popular with Boy Scouts and others in Point Reyes's lake district (best swimming in Bass and Crystal Lakes). Glen Camp is tucked into the hills between Wildcat Camp and Bear Valley, and Sky Camp, perched on the western slopes of Mount Wittenberg, looks down over Drakes Bay and Point Reyes.

Other area camping options include the backpack and group camps of GGNRA, 415/331-

1540; the state campground at Samuel P. Taylor State Park, 415/488-9897; and the 18 primitive campsites plus backpack camps and group camp at Mount Tamalpais State Park, 415/388-2070.

Hostel

Best bet for noncamping budget travelers is **HI Point Reyes Hostel** on Limantour Rd. in Point Reyes Station, 415/663-8811 or 800/909-4776 #61, www.norcalhostels.org. Pluses here include the well-equipped kitchen (get food on the way) and all that beach. Advance reservations advisable. To get here: from Point Reyes Station, take Seashore west from Hwy. 1, then follow Bear Valley Rd. to Limantour Rd. and continue on Limantour for six miles. Dorm rooms under $16 per person. For information on getting to Point Reyes on public transit, call the hostel or Golden Gate Transit, 415/923-2000. The hostel's office hours are 7:30–10 A.M. and 4:30–9:30 P.M. daily; no check-in after 9:30 P.M. Considerably closer to urban Marin but also an excellent choice is the Marin Headlands hostel within the Golden Gate National Recreation Area.

Cabins and Retreats

The state's quite reasonable **Steep Ravine Environmental Cabins** on Rocky Point in Mount Tamalpais State Park, looking out to sea from near Stinson Beach, are small redwood-rustic homes-away-from-home with just the basics: platform beds (bring your own sleeping bag and pad), woodstoves, separate restrooms with pit toilets. Even with recent rate increases these cabins are still a deal: $60 per cabin per night (each sleeps five), a stay which includes an almost-private beach below in a spectacularly romantic setting. Before the state wrested custody of these marvelous cabins from the powerful Bay Area politicians and other clout-encumbered citizens who held long-term leases, photographer Dorothea Lange wrote about staying here in *To a Cabin,* co-authored by Margaretta K. Mitchell. Even the walk down to the bottom of Steep Ravine Canyon is inspiring, Lange noted, with "room for only those in need of sea and sky and infinity." One cabin (there are only 10) is wheelchair accessible; none have electricity, but they do have outside running water. Bring your own provisions. To reserve, contact ReserveAmerica, 800/444-7275, or make reservations online at www.reserveamerica.com.

Also notable and inexpensive in the area is the historic, rustic **West Point Inn,** built in 1904 as a traveler's stop for the Mill Valley/Mt. Tamalpais Railway. One of the five rustic cabins is wheelchair accessible, and there is a single-use restroom in the main lodge featuring a roll-in shower. Lodge rooms are coziest in winter months. Travelers with disabilities can drive in on an access road, but otherwise this is strictly a hike-in experience. (Bring your own food. Lodge cooking facilities available.) Rates are $30 per person. For more information and reservations, contact: West Point Inn, 1000 Panoramic Highway in Mill Valley, 415/388-9955.

Zen but not quite inexpensive is the San Francisco Zen Center's **Green Gulch Farm** or Green Dragon Temple near Muir Beach, where guests stay in the octagonal Lindisfarne Guest House. Rates are $75–105 per person or $125–155 for two, vegetarian meals included. Private Hope Cottage is available for private retreats, $200. For more information, call 415/383-3134 or see the website: www.sfzc.com/ggfindex.htm.

Inns

Even those without wheels can explore the seaward coast of Marin County in comfort and fine style—by hiking or walking the whole way from the Golden Gate Bridge with little more than a day pack and staying along the bay at a combination of hostels, campgrounds, hotels and motels, and the area's very nice bed-and-breakfast inns. (How far to go each day and where to stay depends upon time and money available.) For area lodging referrals and information, contact **Point Reyes Lodging,** 415/663-1872 or 800/539-1872, www.ptreyes.com; or **Inns of Marin,** 415/663-2000 or www.innsofmarin.com.

Especially for fans of the grand ol' days of the Arts and Crafts movement and invigorating wilderness lodges and, the most romantic place around is **M Manka's Inverness Lodge** on Argyle St. up on the hill in Inverness, 415/669-1034, www.mankas.com, famous for its "honest beds" and fabulous food. The lodge's four upstairs and four annex rooms—not to mention both the amazing Fishing Cabin and Manka's Cabin—serve up luxurious rustic charms. Room rates are $150–250 and $250 and up, higher on weekends (wonderful breakfasts included) and $100 more during certain holiday periods, due to exceptionally popular Thanksgiving–Christmas food fests. (Don't miss the restaurant here.) Cabins are $395 and up. Except for midwinter weekdays, make reservations *way* in advance.

The classic Craftsman **Ten Inverness Way,** 10 Inverness Way (on the town's block-long main street), 415/669-1648, www.teninvernessway.com, is comfortable and cozy. Rooms feature excellent beds, handmade quilts, and private baths; there's a stone fireplace in the living room, wonderful full breakfast, private hot tub. Standard rooms $100–150, deluxe rooms slightly higher.

In a woodsy canyon just outside town, welcoming **Blackthorne Inn,** 266 Vallejo Ave. in Inverness Park, 415/663-8621, www.black thorneinn.com, offers appealing furnishings in four-level "treehouse" accommodations with decks. Good buffet breakfast, great stone fireplace in the living room, fabulous setting. Hot tub available. The peak experience here is a stay in the Eagle's Nest, the aptly named octagonal, glass-walled room at the top of the stairs. Rates start at $225; most are $250 and up.

Also in Inverness Park is **Holly Tree Inn & Cottages,** 3 Silverhills Rd., 415/663-1554, www.hollytreeinn.com, which offers four charming rooms in the inn, plus a cottage on the premises (all $150–250), as well as the off-site **Sea Star Cottage** and **Vision Cottage** (both $250 and up).

Up on Inverness Ridge is **The Ark,** 415/663-9338 or 800/808-9338, www.rosemarybb.com, a very appealing cabin built from mostly recycled materials featuring bedroom, sleeping loft, woodstove, and fully equipped kitchen. Rates $150–250. Other cottages (all are "green") include the woodsy, two-room **Rosemary Cottage,** which has a cathedral ceiling, great light and windows, antiques, oriental rugs, well-equipped kitchen, woodstove, and garden hot

tub ($150–250); and **Fir Tree Cottage,** a spacious two-bedroom house perfect for families or two couples ($250 and up). Near Tomales Bay, **Marsh Cottage,** "a bed with a view" at 12642 Sir Francis Drake Blvd., 415/669-7168, www.marshcottage.com, features a fireplace and yes, a view, plus kitchen with make-your-own-breakfast supplies. Rates $150–250 per night, weekly rates available.

Olema offers a number of good choices. These include the **Olema Inn,** 10000 Sir Francis Drake Blvd. (at Hwy. 1), 415/663-9559, a onetime stage stop and World War II–era barracks now decked out in classic American furnishings (wonderful restaurant downstairs), and **An English Oak** on Bear Valley Rd. at Hwy. 1, 415/663-1777, www.anenglishoak.com, a bed-and-breakfast with with three cheery rooms and spacious separate cottage. Rates at both are $100–150.

For nostalgia with all the modern amenities (try to get a room away from the highway), the 1988 **Point Reyes Seashore Lodge,** 10021 Hwy. 1 (in Olema), 415/663-9000, www.pointreyes seashore.com, is an elegant re-creation of a turn-of-the-20th-century country lodge, a three-story weather-beaten cedar building with three two-story suites,18 rooms, and two private cabins, all with down comforters, telephones, and private baths, many with whirlpool tubs and fireplaces, most with a private deck or patio. Continental breakfast. Most rooms $150–250 (some are $135), suites $250 and up.

The restored 1885 **Olema Druids Hall** 9870 Hwy. 1, 415/663-8727 or toll free 866/554-4255, www.olemadruids.com, was originally built as a meeting hall for the Ancient Order of Druids (AAOD), a fraternal organization established in England in the late 1700s and in New York in 1830. The hall features expansive rooms and unique architectural details, three large guest rooms plus a master suite in the main house, and a separate cottage on the grounds. Rooms feature radiant-heated hardwood floors, down comforters, cable TV and VCRs; rates include complimentary continental breakfast. Rooms are $150–250, cottage $250 and up. Downstairs

San Francisco

"When I was a child growing up in Salinas we called San Francisco 'The City,'" California native John Steinbeck once observed. "Of course it was the only city we knew but I still think of it as The City as does everyone else who has ever associated with it."

San Francisco is The City, a distinction it wears with detached certitude. San Francisco has been The City since the days of the gold rush, when the world rushed in through the Golden Gate in a frenzied pursuit of both actual and alchemical riches. It remained The City forever after: when San Francisco started, however reluctantly, to conceive of itself as a civilized place; when

San Francisco fell down and incinerated itself in the great earthquake of 1906; when San Francisco flew up from its ashes, fully fledged, after reinventing itself; and when San Francisco set about reinventing almost everything else with its rolling social revolutions. Among those the world noticed this century, the Beatniks or "Beats" of the 1940s and '50s publicly shook the suburbs of American complacency, the 1960s and San Francisco's Summer of Love caused a social quake part of the chaos of new consciousness that quickly changed the shape of everything, and the 1990s dot-com revolution transformed the way the entire world works.

is the "store," Vita Collage, a commercial amalgamation of old and new.

The place to stay in Bolinas is **White House Inn,** 118 Kale Rd., 415/868-0279, www.thomas whitehouseinn.com, a New England–style inn with two guest rooms sharing two bathrooms in the hall; continental breakfast. Rates $100–150.

The original 1912 **Mountain Home Inn** restaurant, 810 Panoramic Hwy. (on Mount Tamalpais) in Mill Valley, 415/381-9000, www.mtnhomeinn.com, has been transformed into an elegant and striking three-story hotel with upstairs restaurant and bar. Fabulous views. Some of the rooms have fireplaces or whirlpool tubs. Rates include breakfast. Standard rooms $150–250, deluxe rooms $250 and up.

When Sir Francis Drake steered the *Pelican* to shore near here in 1579, he claimed everything in sight on behalf of Elizabeth I, Queen of England. For a taste of more modern true Brit on your way down from Mount Tam, stop at the  **Pelican Inn,** 10 Pacific Way (Hwy. 1 at Muir Beach Rd.) in Muir Beach, 415/383-6000, www.pelicaninn.com. This is a very British Tudor-style country inn, a replica of a 16th-century farmhouse, where guests sit out on the lawn with pint of bitter in hand on sunny days or, when the fog rolls in, warm up around the bar's fireplace with some afternoon tea or mulled cider or wine. Hearty pub fare includes meat pies, stews, burgers, homemade breads, various dinner entrées. Restaurant and pub open 11 A.M.–11 P.M. daily. Not authentically old (built in 1979), the Pelican is still authentic: the leaded-glass windows and brass trinkets, even the oak bar and refectory tables come from England. There's usually a months-long waiting list for the seven rooms here, which offer very appealing period charm (no phones or TVs). Rates are $150–250 and $250 and up.

FOOD

Inverness and Vicinity

After a relaxed afternoon spent reading in **Jack Mason Museum and Inverness Public Library** on Park Ave. (open limited hours, 415/669-1288

or 415/669-1099), head out Sir Francis Drake Blvd. from Inverness to **Johnson's Oyster Company,** 415/669-1149, for a tour and some farm-fresh oysters. Open Tues.–Sun. 8 A.M.–4:30 P.M.; free admission. **Barnaby's by the Bay,** 12938 Sir Francis Drake (at the Golden Hinde Inn just north of Inverness), 415/669-1114, open for lunch and dinner (closed Tuesday and Wednesday), has daily pasta and fresh fish specials, barbecued oysters, clam chowder, and crab cioppino.

Back in Inverness, **Gray Whale Pub & Pizzeria,** 12781 Sir Francis Drake, 415/669-1244, is the place for pizza, also salads, good desserts, and espresso in a pub atmosphere. Open 9 A.M.–9 P.M. daily. Or, try one of the town's two popular restaurants. At **Vladimir's Czechoslovak Restaurant & Bar,** 12785 Sir Francis Drake, 415/669-1021, expect good Eastern European food in an authentically boisterous atmosphere. (Yell across the room if you want dessert; that's what everyone else does.) The exceptional **Manka's** at Manka's Inverness Lodge on Argyle St., 415/669-1034, is a destination in its own right. Manka's serves sophisticated American-style dinners Thurs.–Sun. nights, carefully prepared from neighborhood produce, seafood, fish, fowl, livestock, and game.

Marshall, Point Reyes Station, and Olema

Popular in Marshall, along the east side of Tomales Bay north of Point Reyes Station via Hwy. 1, is **Tony's Seafood,** 18863 Hwy. 1, 415/663-1107. The food's quite fresh: they clean the crabs and oysters right out front.

Famous for its Pulitzer Prize–winning newspaper, the not-yet-too-yuppie cow town of Point Reyes Station is also noted for the mooing clock atop the sheriff's substation at Fourth and C. The bovine bellow, a technical creation of Lucasfilm staff, actually emanates—like clockwork, at noon and 6 P.M.—from loudspeakers atop the Old Western Saloon at Second and Main Sts. For "udderly divine" bakery items, from French pastries, bran muffins, and scones to cookies, stop by **Bovine Bakery,** 11315 Hwy. 1 (Main St.), 415/663-9420. The **Station House Cafe,**

North Coast

ANGEL ISLAND: THE WEST'S ELLIS ISLAND

Still sometimes called the "Ellis Island of the West," at the turn of the century what is now Angel Island State Park was the door through which Asian immigrants passed on their way to America. Japanese and other "enemy aliens" were imprisoned here during World War II, when the island's facilities served as a detention center. Explore the West Garrison Civil War barracks and buildings at the 1863 site of Camp Reynolds—built and occupied by Union troops determined to foil the Confederacy's plans to invade the bay and then the gold country. Among the buildings, the largest surviving collection of Civil War structures in the nation, note the cannons still aimed to sea (but never used in the war because Confederate troops never showed up). On weekends, volunteers in the park's living history program—with the help of apparently willing visitors—fire off the cannons, just in case the South rises again.

Though most visitors never get past the sun and sand at Ayala Cove (where spring through fall the Cove Cafe offers lunch, coffee, and beer), also worth a stop are the 1899 Chinese Immigration Center, quarantine central for new Asian arrivals, and World War II–era Fort McDowell on the island's east side near the Civil War battlements. Often sunny in summer when the rest of the Bay Area is shivering in the fog, Angel Island is particularly attractive to outdoorsy types for its hiking trails. (The eucalyptus trees being felled on Angel Island are nonnatives first planted in the 1860s and now being removed so natural vegetation can be reintroduced.) On a clear day, the view from the top of Angel Island's Mount Livermore is spectacular—with three bridges and almost the entire Bay Area seemingly within reach.

Park day use for most people is included in the ferry fee; otherwise (for private boaters) it's $10 for day-use, $20 for an overnight mooring. Contact the park for current ferry and private boating information. Maps are available in peak season, $1. Hiking and biking are popular; bring your own bike and helmet or, at least in peak season, rent them at Ayala Cove. Motorized island tram tours are offered daily April through October, on weekends only in March and November; call for details. Tours of Angel Island's historic sites are offered on weekends in peak season, and can be arranged for other times. For unbeatable scenery (and sometimes brisk winds), try a simple p nic atop Mount Livermore. Picnic sites are sca tered elsewhere, and group sites (fee) are als available. There's even a reservable baseball dia mond, at Fort McDowell. The intrepid can camp on Angel Island, which features nine hike-in environmental campsites, $10–13. For reservations contact ReserveAmerica, 800/444-7275, www.reserveamerica.com. (Campstove or charcoal cooking only—no fires.) If you're coming, pack light, since you'll have to manage the load on the ferry and pack it all into camp, up to a two-mike hike. For more park information, contact the **Angel Island Association,** 415/435-3522, www.angelisland.org, **Angel Island State Park headquarters** in Tiburon, 415/435-1915; and the **park ranger station,** 415/435-5390.

11180 Main (at Third St.), 415/663-1515, is the local hot spot, a cheerful country café serving breakfast, lunch, and dinner daily but particularly wonderful for breakfast, especially on foggy or rainy days.

Both a good restaurant and lodging stop, the **Olema Inn,** at Hwy. 1 and Sir Francis Drake Blvd. in Olema, 415/663-9559, is a grandmotherly kind of place serving basic good food and soups as well as California-style cuisine. Open for dinner Fri.–Sat. at 6 P.M. and for lunch and dinner during the summer. For plain ol' American food, head for **Olema Farmhouse,** 10005 Hwy. 1 in Olema, 415/663-1264: good burgers and hefty sandwiches, daily fresh fish specials.

SAUSALITO

Sausalito is a community by land and by sea, a hillside hamlet far surpassed in eccentricity by the highly creative hodgepodge of houseboaters also anchored here. Though, for a time, mysterious midnight throbbings from the deep kept Sausalito's houseboat community awake night after summer night—with some locals even speculating that these nocturnal noises came from a top-secret CIA weapon being tested underwater in Richardson Bay—it eventually turned out that the racket was simply due to romance. Singing toadfish have become to Sausalito what swallows are to Capistrano, migrating into Richardson Bay from the shallows each summer for their annual mating song—comparable, collectively, to the sound of a squadron of low-flying B-17 bombers. People here have adapted to this almost indescribable language of love, and now welcome these bulging-eyed, bubble-lipped lovers back to the bay every year with their **Humming Toadfish Festival,** a celebration conducted by kazoo-playing residents dressed up as sea monsters and clowns. Come over Labor Day weekend for the famed **Sausalito Art Festival,** www.sausalitoartfestival.org.

Aside from the pleasures of just being here—and exploring the nearby **Golden Gate National Recreation Area** (see above)—stop in Sausalito at the U.S. Army Corps of Engineers' **San Francisco Bay Model,** 2100 Bridgeway, 415/332-3870 (recording) or 415/332-3871 (office), a working 1.5-acre facsimile of the Bay and Delta built by the Corps to study currents, tides, salinity, and other natural features. We should all be grateful that the ever-industrious Corps realized it couldn't build a better bay even with access to all the bulldozers, landfill, and riprap in the world and settled, instead, for just making a toy version. Interpretive audio tours are available in English, Russian, German, Japanese, French, and Spanish. Guided group tours (10 or more people) can be arranged by calling 415/332-3871 at least four weeks in advance. Open in summer Tues.–Fri. 9 A.M.–4 P.M., weekends and holidays 10 A.M.–5 P.M.; the rest of the year, Tues.–Sat. 9 A.M.–4 P.M. Free. Get out and sample the bay on various boats and charters, particularly intriguing among them the 18th century–style *Hawaiian Chieftan,* 415/331-3214, www.hawaiian chieftan.com, with lunch sails offered from late April through December, $70 adults, $35 children. Sailing in the same fleet is the brigantine *Irving Johnson.* Saturday "adventure," Sunday brunch, and sunset sails are also offered.

Also in town, among Sausalito's armada of houseboat residents and bayside shops, is **Heath Ceramics Outlet,** 400 Gate 5 Rd., 415/332-3732, open Mon.–Sat. 10 A.M.–5 P.M. and Sun. noon–5 P.M., a wonderful array of seconds and overstocks for fine dishware fans.

For more information about Sausalito attractions and practicalities, contact: **Sausalito Chamber of Commerce,** 10 Liberty Ship Way, Bay 2, Ste. 250 in Sausalito, 415/331-7262 or 415/332-0505 (visitor information), www.sausalito.org, open weekdays 9 A.M.–5 P.M.

Must-Sees

Look for M to find the sights and activities you can't miss and N for the best dining and lodging.

M City Guides Walking Tour: Despite all the ups and downs, San Francisco is a superb city for walking. Among the best ways to orient yourself is by the free City Guides walking tours offered by the Friends of the San Francisco Public Library (page 136).

M Ferry Building: Walk along the Embarcadero connecting the San Francisco Maritime National Historical Park and museum, and stop by the Ferry Building, a foodie paradise (page 148).

M Asian Art Museum: Th new star of San Francisco's impressive Civic Center district is the venerable Asian Art Museum (page 150).

M Cable Car Barn: The free Cable Car Barn atop Nob Hill—peek into the grand hotels here—tells the story of Andrew Hallidie's great kinetic-energy invention (page 153).

M Telegraph Hill and Coit Tower: Crowning Telegraph Hill is Lillie Hitchcock Coit's monument to San Francisco firefighters (page 159).

M California Palace of the Legion of Honor: Art lovers most appreciate this 1920 French neoclassic palace, built in honor of American soldiers killed in France during World War I (page 168).

M San Francisco Museum of Modern Art: Blockbuster exhibits are always happening at SFMOMA, which began the transformation of the gritty South of Market into a hip neighborhood (page 178).

M Alcatraz: Walk The Rock, and tour the prison cells of American crime mythology (page 183).

M Presidio and Fort Point: Celebrate the San Francisco–side pleasures of the Golden Gate National Recreation Area (page 188).

M Golden Gate Park: Find refuge in Golden Gate Park, designed by Frederick Law Olmsted, and home to fine museums (page 190).

M Golden Gate Bridge: Stroll across the 1937 Golden Gate Bridge, the world's longest and tallest suspension structure at the time it was built (page 192).

M Año Nuevo State Reserve: This reserve along the coast just south of San Francisco is breeding ground and rookery for the enormous and unusual northern elephant seal. Guided winter tours require advance reservations (page 252).

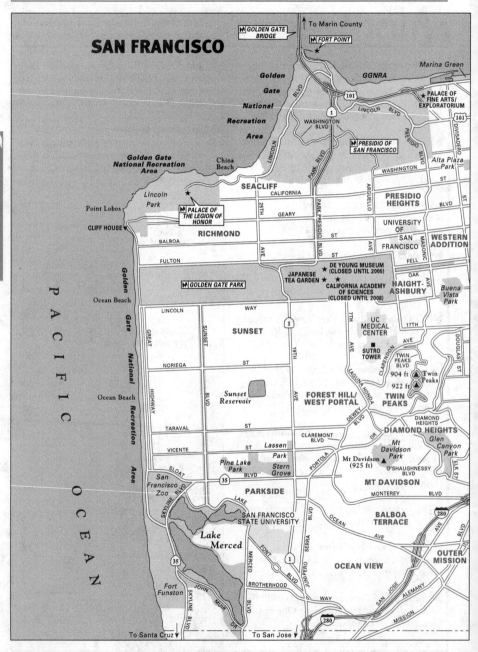

SAN FRANCISCO

To Marin County

GOLDEN GATE BRIDGE
FORT POINT

Golden
Gate
National
Recreation
Area

GGNRA

Marina Green

PALACE OF
FINE ARTS/
EXPLORATORIUM

WASHINGTON
BLVD

LINCOLN BLVD

Golden Gate
National Recreation
Area

China
Beach

PRESIDIO OF
SAN FRANCISCO

Alta Plaza
Park

Lincoln
Park

SEACLIFF

WASHINGTON
ST

Point Lobos

PALACE OF
THE LEGION OF
HONOR

CALIFORNIA

PRESIDIO
HEIGHTS

BLVD

CLIFF HOUSE

GEARY

UNIVERSITY
OF
SAN
FRANCISCO

WESTERN
ADDITION

RICHMOND

BALBOA

FULTON

FELL

DE YOUNG MUSEUM
(CLOSED UNTIL 2005)

OAK

JAPANESE
TEA GARDEN

HAIGHT-
ASHBURY

Buena
Vista
Park

Golden

Ocean Beach

GOLDEN GATE PARK

CALIFORNIA ACADEMY
OF SCIENCES
(CLOSED UNTIL 2008)

P A C I F I C

LINCOLN

WAY

UC
MEDICAL
CENTER

17TH

SUNSET

SUTRO
TOWER

TWIN
PEAKS
BLVD

904 ft   Twin
922 ft   Peaks

NORIEGA

ST

Ocean Beach

Gate

Sunset
Reservoir

FOREST HILL/
WEST PORTAL

TWIN
PEAKS

National

DIAMOND
HEIGHTS

TARAVAL

ST

CLAREMONT
BLVD

DIAMOND HEIGHTS

Mt
Davidson
Park

Glen
Canyon
Park

VICENTE

ST

Lassen
Park

Recreation

Pine Lake
Park

Stern
Grove

Mt Davidson
(925 ft)

O'SHAUGHNESSY
BLVD

San
Francisco
Zoo

PARKSIDE

MT DAVIDSON

MONTEREY

BLVD

SAN FRANCISCO
STATE UNIVERSITY

BALBOA
TERRACE

Area

Lake
Merced

AVE

OUTER
MISSION

Fort
Funston

O C E A N

OCEAN VIEW

BROTHERHOOD

WAY

To Santa Cruz

To San Jose

San Francisco

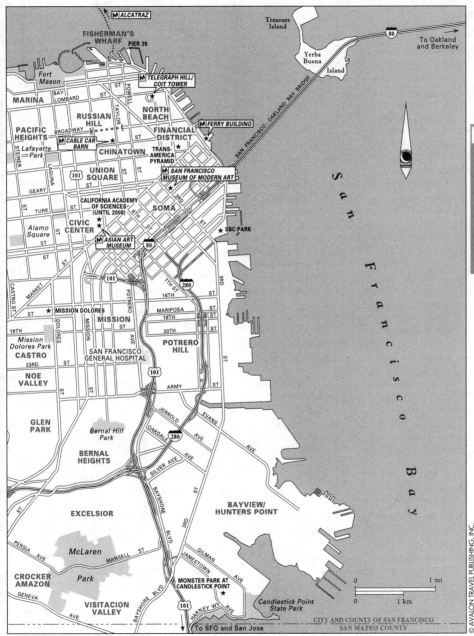

Of its many attributes, perhaps most striking is The City's ability, still, to be all things to all people—and to simultaneously contradict itself and its own truths. San Francisco is a point of beginning. Depending upon where one starts, it is also the ultimate place to arrive. San Francisco is a comedy. And San Francisco is tragedy.

As writer Richard Rodriguez observes: "San Francisco has taken some heightened pleasure from the circus of final things. . . . San Francisco can support both comic and tragic conclusions because the city is geographically *in extremis,* a metaphor for the farthest flung possibility, a metaphor for the end of the line." But even that depends upon point of view. As Rodriguez also points out, "To speak of San Francisco as land's end is to read the map from one direction only—as Europeans would read or as the East Coast has always read it." To the people living on these hills before California's colonialization, before the gold rush, even before there was a San Francisco, the land they lived on represented the center, surrounded on three sides by water. To Mexicans extending their territorial reach, it was north. To Russian fur hunters escaping the frigid shores of Alaska, it was south. And to its many generations of Asian immigrants, surely San Francisco represented the Far East.

The precise place The City occupies in the world's imagination is irrelevant to compass points. If San Francisco is anywhere specific, it is certainly at the edge: the cutting edge of cultural combinations, the gilt edge of international commerce, the razor's edge of raw reality. And life on the edge is rarely boring.

THE LAND

Imagine San Francisco before its bridges were built: a captive city, stranded on an unstable, stubbed toe of a peninsula, one by turns twitching under the storm-driven assault of wind and water, then chilled by bone-cold fog.

The city and county of San Francisco—the two are one, duality in unity—sit on their own appendage of California earth, a political conglomeration totaling 46.4 square miles. Creating San Francisco's western edge is the Pacific Ocean, its waters cooled by strong Alaskan currents, its rough offshore rocks offering treachery to unwary sea travelers. On its eastern edge is San Francisco Bay, one of the world's most impressive natural harbors, with deep protected waters and 496 square miles of surface area. (As vast as it is, these days the bay is only 75 percent of its pre–gold rush size, since its shoreline has been filled in and extended to create more land.) Connecting the two sides, and creating San Francisco's rough-and-tumble northern edge, is the three-mile-long strait known as the Golden Gate. Straddled by the world-renowned Golden Gate Bridge, this mile-wide river of sea water cuts the widest gap in the rounded Coast Ranges for a thousand miles, yet is so small that its landforms almost hide the bay that balloons inland.

Spaniards named what is now considered San Francisco Las Lomitas, or "little hills," for the landscape's most notable feature. Perhaps to create a romantic comparison with Rome, popular local mythology holds that The City was built on seven hills—Lone Mountain, Mt. Davidson, Nob Hill, Russian Hill, Telegraph Hill, and the two Twin Peaks, none higher than 1,000 feet in elevation. There are actually more than 40 hills in San Francisco, all part and parcel of California's Coast Ranges, which run north and south along the state's coastline, sheltering inland valleys from the fog and winds that regularly visit San Francisco.

City on a Fault Line

The City has been shaped as much by natural forces as by historical happenstance. Its most spectacular event involved both. More than any other occurence, San Francisco's 1906 earthquake—estimated now to have registered 8.25 on the Richter scale—woke up residents, and the world, to the fact that The City was built on very shaky ground. California's famous, 650-mile-long San Andreas Fault, as it is now known, slips just seaward of San Francisco. In the jargon of tectonic plate theory, The City sits on the North American Plate, a huge slab of earth floating on the planet's molten core, along the San Andreas earthquake fault line. Just west is the Pacific Plate. When earth-shaking pressure builds, sooner or later something has to give. In San Francisco, as elsewhere in California, a rumble and a roar and split-second motion announces an earthquake—and the fact that an interlocking section of the earth's crust has separated, a movement that may or may not be visible on the earth's surface. San Francisco's most recent major quake, on October 17, 1989, reminded us that The City's earthquake history is far from a finished chapter.

City in a Fog

San Francisco's second most famous physical feature is its weather—mild and Mediterranean but with quite perverse fog patterns, especially surprising to first-time summer visitors. When people expect sunny skies and warm temperatures, San Francisco offers instead gray and white mists, moist clouds seemingly filled with knife-sharp points of ice when driven by the wind.

Poets traditionally call forth all nine muses to honor the mysteries of fog. Scientists are much more succinct. Summer heat in California's central valley regions creates a low-pressure weather system, while cooler ocean temperatures create

higher atmospheric pressure. Moving toward equilibrium, the cool and moist coastal air is drawn inland through the "mouth" of the Golden Gate and over adjacent hills, like a behemoth's belly breath. Then, as the land cools, the mists evaporate. So even during the peak fog months of July and August, wool-coat weather dissipates by midafternoon—only to roll back in shortly after sundown. Due to microclimates created by hills, certain San Francisco neighborhoods—like the Mission District, Noe Valley, and Potrero Hill—may be quite sunny and warm when the rest of the city still shivers in the fog.

Weather

The coast's strong high-pressure system tends to moderate San Francisco weather year-round: expect average daytime temperatures of 54–65° F in summer, 48–59° F in winter. (Usually reliable is the adage that for every 10 miles you travel inland from the city, temperatures will increase by 10 degrees.) September and October are the warmest months, with balmy days near 70 degrees. The local weather pattern also prevents major rainstorms from May through October.

SUSAN SNYDER

the infamous San Francisco fog

Despite the water-rich imagery associated with the San Francisco Bay Area, the region is actually semiarid, with annual (nondrought) rainfall averaging 19–20 inches. Snow is a very rare phenomenon in the region.

HISTORY AND CULTURE

At its most basic, the recorded history of San Francisco is a story of conquest and curiosity. The region's original inhabitants, however, were generally content with the abundant riches the land provided quite naturally. Descendants of mysterious nomads who first crossed the Bering Strait from Asia to the North American continent some 20,000 or more years ago, California's native peoples were culturally distinct. The language groups—"tribes" doesn't serve to describe California Indians—living north of the Golden Gate were classified by anthropologists as the Coast Wiwok people. Though the barren and desolate site of San Francisco attracted few residents, the dominant native population throughout the greater Bay Area was called Costanoan ("coast people") or Ohlone by the Spanish, though the people called themselves Ramaytush.

In precolonial days, the region was the most densely populated on the continent north of Mexico, with a population of 10,000 people living in 30 or more permanent villages. Though each village considered itself unique, separated from others by customs and local dialect, the Ohlone intermarried and traded with other tribes and shared many cultural characteristics. Though dependent on shellfish as a dietary staple, the Ohlone also migrated inland in summer and fall to hunt game, fish, and collect acorns, which were valued throughout California for making bread and mush. Thousands of years of undisturbed cultural success created a gentle, gracious, unwarlike society—a culture that quickly passed away with the arrival of California's explorers and colonizers.

Early Explorations

Discoveries of dusty manuscripts, ancient stone anchors, and old coins now suggest that Chinese ships were the first foreign vessels to explore California's coastline, arriving centuries before Columbus bumbled into the new world. The Portuguese explorer Juan Cabrillo (João Cabrilho) was the coast's first official surveyor, though on his 1542 voyage he failed to discover the Golden Gate and the spectacular bay behind it. In 1579 the English pirate Sir Francis Drake took the first foreign step onto California soil, quite possibly near San Francisco, and claimed the land for Queen Elizabeth I. (Where exactly Drake landed is a subject of ongoing controversy and confusion. For a further discussion, see Point Reyes National Seashore.) And even Drake failed to see the Golden Gate and its precious natural harbor, perhaps due to the subtle subterfuge of landforms and fog.

The Arrival of Outsiders

In 1769, some 200 years after Drake, a Spanish scouting party led by Gaspar de Portolá discovered San Francisco Bay by accident while searching for Monterey Bay farther south. After Monterey was secured, Capt. Juan Bautista de Anza was assigned the task of colonizing this new territorial prize. With 35 families plus a lieutenant and a Franciscan priest, de Anza set out on a grueling trip from Sonora, Mexico, arriving on the peninsula's tip on June 27, 1776, just one week before the American Revolution. The first order of business was establishing a military fortress, the Presidio, at the present site of Fort Mason. And the second was establishing a church and mission outpost, about one mile south, on the shores of a small lake or lagoon named in honor of Nuestra Señora de los Dolores (Our Lady of Sorrows). Though the mission church was dedicated to Saint Francis of Assisi, it became known as Mission Dolores—and the name "San Francisco" was instead attached to the spectacular bay and the eventual city that grew up on its shores.

Though Spain, then Mexico, officially secured the California territory, underscoring ownership by means of vast government land grants to retired military and civilian families, the colonial claim was somewhat tenuous. By the 1830s, Americans were already the predominant residents of the settlement at Yerba Buena Cove (at the foot of what is now Telegraph Hill), the earliest version of San Francisco. Yerba Buena was first a trading post established by William Anthony Richardson, an Englishman who married the Presidio commandant's daughter. In the early 1800s, Russian fur hunters established themselves just north along the coast, at the settlement of Fort Ross. They sailed south to trade. English, French, and American trading ships were also regular visitors. By the 1840s, Yankees were arriving by both land and sea in ever greater numbers, spurred on by the nation's expansionist mood and the political dogma of "Manifest Destiny!" The official annexation of the California territory to the United States, when it came in mid-1846, was almost anticlimactic. After the 13-man force at the Presidio surrendered peacefully to the Americans, the citizens quickly changed the name of Yerba Buena to that of the bay, San Francisco—a shrewd business move, intended to attract still more trade.

The Gold Rush

Events of early 1848 made the name change all but irrelevant. San Francisco could hardly help attracting more business, and more businesses of every stripe, once word arrived that gold had been discovered on the American River in the foothills east of Sacramento. Before the gold rush, San Francisco was a sleepy port town with a population of 800, but within months it swelled to a city of nearly 25,000, as gold seekers arrived by the shipload from all over the globe. Those who arrived early and lit out for the goldfields in 1848 had the best opportunity to harvest California gold. Most of the fortune hunters, however, arrived in '49, thus the term "forty-niners" to describe this phenomenal human migration.

As cosmopolitan as the overnight city of San Francisco was, with its surprisingly well-educated, liberal, and (not so surprisingly) young population, it was hardly civilized. By 1849 the ratio of men to women was about 10 to one, and saloons, gambling halls, and the notorious red-light district—known as the Barbary Coast—were the social mainstays of this rootless, risk-taking population. Though early San Francisco was primarily a tent city, fire was a constant scourge. The city started to build itself then burned to the ground six times by 1852, when San Francisco was recognized as the fourth largest port of entry in the United States. And though eccentricty and bad behavior were widely tolerated, unrestrained gang crime and murder became so commonplace that businessmen formed Committees of Vigilance to create some semblance of social order—by taking the law into their own hands and jailing, hanging, and running undesirables out of town.

More Barbarians and Big Spenders

By the late 1850s, the sources for most of California's surface gold had been picked clean. Ongoing harvesting of the state's most precious metal had become a corporate affair, an economic change made possible by the development of new technologies. The days of individualistic gold fever had subsided, and fortune hunters who remained in California turned their efforts to more long-lasting development of wealth, often in agriculture and business.

The city, though temporarily slowed by the economic depression that arrived with the end of the gold rush, was the most businesslike of them all. A recognizable city and a major financial center, no sooner had San Francisco calmed down and turned its attentions to nurturing civic pride than another boom arrived—this time silver, discovered in the Nevada territory's Comstock Lode. Silver mining required capital, heavy equipment, and organized mining technology; this was a strictly corporate raid on the earth's riches, with San Francisco and its bankers, businesses, and citizenry the main beneficiaries. Led by the silver rush "Bonanza Kings," the city's nouveau riche built themselves a residential empire atop Nob Hill and set about creating more cultured institutions.

Confident California, led by San Francisco, believed the future held nothing but greater growth, greater wealth. That was certainly the case for the "Big Four," Sacramento businessmen who financed Theodore Judah's dream of a transcontinental railroad, a development almost everyone believed would lead to an extended boom in the state's economy. Soon at home atop

Nob Hill with the city's other nabobs, Charles Crocker, Mark Hopkins, Collis Huntington, and Leland Stanford also set out to establish some political machinery—the Southern Pacific Railway—to generate power and influence to match their wealth.

Bad Times and Bigotry

But the transcontinental railroad did little to help California, or San Francisco, at least initially. As naysayers had predicted, the ease of shipping goods by rail all but destroyed California's neophyte industrial base, since the state was soon glutted with lower-cost manufactured goods from the East Coast. A drought in 1869—a major setback for agricultural production—and an 1871 stock market crash made matters that much worse.

Legions of the unemployed, which included terminated railroad workers all over the West, rose up in rage throughout the 1870s and 1880s. They attacked not those who had enriched themselves at the expense of the general populace but "outsiders," specifically the Chinese who had labored long and hard at many a thankless task since the days of the gold rush. Mob violence and the torching of businesses and entire Chinese communities, in San Francisco and elsewhere, wasn't enough to satisfy such open racist hatred. Politicians too bowed to anti-Chinese sentiment, passing a series of discriminatory laws that forbade the Chinese from owning land, voting, and testifying in court, and levying a special tax against Chinese shrimp fishermen.

A near-final bigoted blow was the federal government's 1882 Oriental Exclusion Act, which essentially ended legal Asian immigration until it was repealed during World War II. San Francisco's Chinese community, for the most part working men denied the opportunity to reunite with their families, was further damaged by the Geary Act of 1892, which declared that all Chinese had to carry proper identification or face deportation. The failure of American society to support traditional Chinese culture led to rampant crime, gambling, and prostitution—acceptable diversions of the day for bachelors—and a lawless reign of terror by competing tongs who fought to control the profits. Only the gradual Americanization of the Chinese, which minimized tong influence, and the disastrous events during the spring of 1906 could change the reality of Chinatown. But the year 1906 changed everything in San Francisco.

Earthquake and Fire

By the early 1900s, San Francisco had entered its "gilded age," a complacent period when the city was busy enjoying its new cosmopolitan status. San Francisco had become the largest and finest city west of Chicago. The rich happily compounded their wealth in downtown highrises and at home on Nob Hill and in other resplendent neighborhoods. The expanding middle class built rows of new Victorian homes, "painted ladies" that writer Tom Wolfe would later call "those endless staggers of bay windows," on hills far removed from the low life of the Barbary Coast, Chinatown, and the newest red-light district, The Tenderloin. But the working classes still smoldered in squalid tenements south of Market Street. Corruption ruled, politically, during the heyday of the "paint eaters"—politicians so greedy they'd even eat the paint off buildings. The cynical reporter and writer Ambrose Bierce, sniffing at the status quo, called San Francisco the "moral penal colony of the world." But the city's famous graft trials, a public political circus that resulted in 3,000 indictments but shockingly little jail time, came later.

Whatever was going on in the city, legal and otherwise, came to an abrupt halt on the morning of April 18, 1906, when a massive earthquake hit. Now estimated to have registered 8.25 on the Richter scale, the quake created huge fissures in the ground, broke water and gas mains all over the city, and caused chimneys and other unstable construction to come tumbling down. The better neighborhoods, including the city's Victorian row houses, suffered little damage. Downtown, however, was devastated. City Hall, a shoddy construction job allowed by scamming politicians and their contractor cohorts, crumbled into nothing. Though a central hospital also fell, burying doctors, nurses, and patients alike, the overall death toll from the earthquake itself was fairly small. Sadly for San Francisco, one of the fatalities was the city fire chief, whose foresight might have prevented the conflagration soon to follow.

More than 50 fires started that morning alone, racing through the low-rent neighborhoods south of Market, then into downtown, raging out of control. The flames were unchecked for four days, burning through downtown, parts of the Mission District, and also demolishing Chinatown, North Beach, Nob Hill, Telegraph Hill, and Russian Hill. The mansions along the eastern edge of Van Ness were dynamited to create an impromptu firebreak, finally stopping the firestorm.

When it was all over, the official tally of dead or missing stood at 674, though more recent research suggests the death toll was more than 3,000, since the Chinese weren't counted. The entire city center was destroyed, along with three-fourths of the city's businesses and residences. With half of its 450,000 population now homeless, San Francisco was a tent city once again. But it was an optimistic tent city, bolstered by relief and rebuilding funds sent from around the world. As reconstruction began, San Francisco also set out to clean house politically.

Modern Times

By 1912, with San Francisco more or less back on its feet, Mayor James "Sunny Jim" Rolph, who always sported a fresh flower in his lapel, seemed to symbolize the city's new era. Rolph presided over the construction of some of San Francisco's finest public statements about itself. These included the new city hall and Civic Center, as well as the 1915 world's fair and the Panama-Pacific International Exposition, a spectacular 600-acre temporary city designed by Bernard Maybeck to reflect the "mortality of grandeur and the vanity of human wishes." Though the exposition was intended to celebrate the opening of the Panama Canal, it was San Francisco's grand announcement to the world that it had not only survived but thrived in the aftermath of its earlier earthquake and fire.

During the Great Depression, San Francisco continued to defy the commonplace, dancing at the edge of unreal expectations. Two seemingly impossible spans, the Golden Gate Bridge and

the Bay Bridge, were built in the 1930s. San Francisco also built the world's largest man-made island, Treasure Island, which hosted the Golden Gate International Exposition and "Magic City" in 1939 before becoming a U.S. Navy facility. (The Navy abandoned ship in the late 1990s and ceded the island to the city of San Francisco; the city will redevelop the island, after first completing earthquake stabilization. Meanwhile renovated buildings provide private housing as well as homeless assistance. The island is also a venue for occasional concerts and a regular flea market.)

No matter how spectacular its statements to the world, San Francisco had trouble at home. The 1929 stock market crash and the onset of the Depression reignited long-simmering labor strife, especially in the city's port. Four longshoremen competed for every available job along the waterfront, and members of the company-controlled Longshoremen's Association demanded kickbacks for jobs that were offered. Harry Bridges reorganized the International Longshoremen's Association, and backed by the Teamsters Union, his pro-union strike successfully closed down the waterfront. On "Bloody Thursday," July 5, 1934, 800 strikers battled with National Guard troops called in to quell a riot started by union busters. Two men were shot and killed by police, another 100 were injured, and the subsequent all-city strike—the largest general strike in U.S. history—ultimately involved most city businesses as well as the waterfront unions. More so than elsewhere on the West Coast, labor unions are still strong in San Francisco.

Other social and philosophical revolutions, for iconoclasts and oddballs alike, either got their start in San Francisco or received abundant support once arrived here. First came the 1950s-era Beatniks or "Beats"—poets, freethinkers, and jazz aficionados rebelling against the suburbanization of the American mind. The Beats were followed in short order by the 1960s, the Summer of Love, psychedelics, and rock groups like the legendary Grateful Dead. More substantial, in the '60s, the Free Speech Movement heated up across the bay in Berkeley, not to mention anti-Vietnam War protests and the rise of the Black Panther Party. Since then, San Francisco has managed to make its

San Francisco

place at, or near, the forefront of almost every change in social awareness, from women's rights to gay pride. And in the 1980s and '90s, San Franciscans went all out for unabashed consumerism. The dot-com boom met up with baby-boomer enthusiasms in the city's South of Market area, creating a new wave of high-tech style. But there are other styles, other trends. You name it, San Francisco probably has it.

Tourism

Tourism is the city's top industry these days, though even the tourist trade has been more difficult since September 11, 2001. It's not difficult to understand San Francisco's appeal. The city offers almost everything, from striking scenery and sophisticated shopping to fine hotels and restaurants. Even budget travelers can arrive, and stay, with exceptional ease, at least compared to elsewhere in California. And the city's multiethnic cultural, artistic, and entertainment attractions are among its most undervalued treasures.

Downtown San Francisco, which serves as the city's corporate and financial headquarters as well as tourist central, is a world of skyscraping office towers and imposed isolation. Surely it's no accident that the city's homeless live here. But the most authentic spirits of San Francisco live elsewhere, out in the neighborhoods. So do get out—out past the panhandlers and the polished glass buildings, past the pretty shops and the prettier shoppers—to see San Francisco.

Even out in the neighborhoods, though, San Franciscans have started to suspect that things aren't quite as wonderful as they once were. Their beloved city suffers from the same problems as other major cities, from staggering demands on urban services to worsening traffic problems and astronomical housing costs.

But at last report—and despite some notable historical lapses—the city's deepest traditions, liberalism and tolerance, are still going strong. And freedom is still the city's unofficial rallying cry.

Orientation and Tours

San Francisco is a walking city par excellence. With enough time and inclination, exploring the hills, stairways, and odd little neighborhood nooks and crannies is the most rewarding way to get to know one's way around. Helpful for getting started are the free neighborhood walking-tour pamphlets (Pacific Heights, Union Square, Chinatown, Fisherman's Wharf, the Barbary Coast Trail, and more) available at the Convention & Visitors Bureau Information Center downstairs at Hallidie Plaza (Powell and Market Streets), 415/391-2000. Also helpful: books such as Adah Bakalinsky's *Stairway Walks in San Francisco,* Rand Richards's *Historic Walks in San Francisco,* and Gail Todd's *Lunchtime Walks in San Francisco.*

Even with substantially less time, there are excellent options. A variety of local nonprofit organizations offer free or low-cost walking tours. Commercial tours—many unusual—are also

available, most ranging in price from $20 to $50 per person, more for all-day tours.

TOURS
City Guides Walking Tour

City Guides walking tours offered by Friends of the San Francisco Public Library, headquartered at the main San Francisco Public Library (Larkin and Grove), include many worthwhile neighborhood prowls. Call 415/557-4266 for a recorded schedule of upcoming walks (what, where, and when) or try www.sfcityguides.com. Most walks include local architecture, culture, and history, though the emphasis—Art Deco Marina, Pacific Heights Mansions, Cityscapes and Roof Mansions, the Gold Rush City, Landmark Victorians of Alamo Square, Haight-Ashbury, Mission Murals, Japantown—can be surprising. City

Guides tours are free, but donations are definitely appreciated.

Other Free and Low-Cost Walking Tours

Gold rush–era San Francisco is the theme behind the city's **Barbary Coast Trail,** www.barbarycoast-trail.com, a four-mile self-guided walking tour from Mission St. to Aquatic Park, marked by 150 bronze plaques embedded in the sidewalk along the way. Among the 20 historic sites en route are the oldest Asian temple in North America, the western terminus of the Pony Express, and the Hyde Street historic ships. Two different guides to the trail are sold at the Hallidie Plaza visitor information center (Powell and Market).

Pacific Heights Walks are sponsored by the **Foundation for San Francisco's Architectural Heritage,** headquartered in the historic Haas-Lilienthal House at 2007 Franklin St. (between Washington and Jackson), 415/441-3000 (office) or 415/441-3004 (recorded information), and offer a look at the exteriors of splendid pre-World War I mansions in eastern Pacific Heights. The **San Francisco Museum & Historical Society,** 415/775-1111, www.sfhistory.org, offers free historical tours and architectural walks conducted by Charles A. Fracchia, and includes details on these and other local heritage tours on its website.

Friends of Recreation and Parks, headquartered at McLaren Lodge in Golden Gate Park, Stanyan and Fell Streets, 415/263-0991 (for upcoming hike schedule), offers guided flora, fauna, and history walks through the park May–Oct., Sat. and Sun. at 11 A.M. and 2 P.M. Group tours are also available.

Precita Eyes Mural Arts Center, at 2981 24th St. (at Harrison), 415/285-2287, www.precitaeyes.org, offers fascinating two-hour mural walks through the Mission District on Saturday and Sunday starting at 11 A.M. and 1:30 P.M. Admission is $12 adults, $8 seniors/students, $2 youths 18 and under. Call for information on the center's many other tours. In addition to its self-guided Mission murals tour, the **Mexican Museum,** 415/202-9700, sponsors docent-led tours of San Francisco's Diego Rivera murals. The **Chinese Culture Center,** inside the Holiday Inn at 750 Kearny (between Clay and Washington), 415/986-1822, offers both a culinary and a cultural heritage walking tour of Chinatown.

The San Francisco Symphony Volunteer Council, San Francisco Opera Guild, and San Francisco Ballet Auxiliary combine their services to offer a walking tour of the three **San Francisco Performing Arts Center** facilities: Davies Symphony Hall, the War Memorial Opera House, and Herbst Theatre. The tour takes about an hour and 15 minutes; costs $5 adults, $3 seniors/students; and is offered every Monday, hourly from 10 A.M.–2 P.M. Purchase your ticket at the Davies Symphony Hall box office (main foyer) 10 minutes before tour time. For more information, call 415/552-8338.

Commercial Walking Tours

Helen's Walk Tours, 510/524-4544 or 888/808-6505, offers entertaining walking tours, with a personal touch provided by personable Helen Rendon, tour guide and part-time actress. Tour groups usually meet "under the clock" at the St. Francis Hotel (Helen's the one with the wonderfully dramatic hat) before setting off on an entertaining two-hour tour of Victorian Mansions, North Beach (want to know where Marilyn Monroe married Joe DiMaggio?), or Chinatown. Other options: combine parts of two tours into a half-day Grand Tour, or, if enough time and interested people are available, request other neighborhood tours. Make reservations for any tour at least one day in advance.

Dashiell Hammett Literary Tours, 510/287-9540, www.donherron.com, are led by Don Herron, author of *The Literary World of San Francisco and its Environs.* The half-day tours prowl downtown streets and alleys, on the trail of both the writer and his detective story hero, Sam Spade. They're usually offered Sundays in May and October, and other literary themes can be arranged. You can't make reservations; just show up or call to schedule a tour.

The personable Jay Gifford leads a **Victorian Home Walk Tour** (including a scenic bus trolley

San Francisco

ride) through Cow Hollow and Pacific Heights, exploring distinctive Queen Anne, Edwardian, and Italianate architecture in the neighborhoods. You'll see the interior of a Queen Anne and the locations used for *Mrs. Doubtfire* and *Party of Five*. While also enjoying spectacular views of the city, bay, and gardens, you'll learn to differentiate architectural styles. Tours meet at 11 A.M. daily in the lobby of the St. Francis Hotel on Union Square and last about two and a half hours. For reservations and information, call 415/252-9485 or visit www.victorianwalk.com.

Hob Nob Tours, 650/851-1123, www .hobnobtours.com, offers an absolutely scandalous historical walking tour of Nob Hill—one that lets guests in on lurid tales of high-society assignations and assassinations as well as the complex histories of the silver kings, the "Big Four" railroad barons, and opulent mansions, hotels, and other buildings and sights. The tour is $30 per person and includes a cable car ride up Nob Hill, appreciation of Huntington Park, and a tour of California's first cathedral. Optional (and extra): a full buffet breakfast at the Ritz Carleton ($25), a two-course luncheon at the Huntington Hotel's Big Four restaurant ($20), or high tea at the Renaissance Stanford Court Hotel ($20). Reservations are required. Tours start at the Fairmont Hotel lobby (Mason and California) at 9:30 A.M. and 1:30 P.M., respectively.

Cruisin' the Castro, historical tours of San Francisco's gay mecca, 415/550-8110, www .webcastro.com/castrotour, are led by local historian Trevor Hailey and offer unique insight into how San Francisco's gay community has shaped the city's political, social, and cultural development. Everyone is welcome; reservations are required. Tours are offered Tues.–Sat., starting at 10 A.M. at Harvey Milk Plaza, continuing through the community's galleries, shops, and cultural sights, then ending at the Names Project (original home of the AIDS Memorial Quilt) around 2 P.M. Brunch included.

San Francisco's coffeehouse culture is the focus of popular **Javawalk,** 415/673-9255, www .javawalk.com, a two-hour stroll through North Beach haunts on Saturdays at 10 A.M., $20 per person (kids half price). Group rates available.

Tours begin near the Chinatown arch in front of The Sak, 334 Grant Avenue. "Javagirl" Elaine Sosa also offers a **North Beach Beat** tour that concludes with three-course lunch, $35.

Culinary Walking Tours

No matter where else you walk off to, don't overlook San Francisco's fabulous food tours—most of which focus on Chinatown. **Wok Wiz Chinatown Walking Tours,** 654 Commercial St. (between Montgomery and Kearny), 415/981-8989, www.wokwiz.com, are a local institution. Reservations required. The small-group Wok Wiz culinary and historical adventures are led by founder Shirley Fong-Torres, her husband Bernie Carver, and other tour leaders, starting at 10 A.M. at the Wok Wiz Tours and Cooking Center and ending at 1:15 P.M. after a marvelous dim sum lunch (optional). Stops along the way include: Portsmouth Square; a Chinese temple; herb, pastry, and tea shops (where the traditional tea ceremony is shared); a Chinese open-air market; and a brush-paint artist's studio. Along with taking in the sights along Chinatown's main streets and back alleys, visitors receive a fairly comprehensive history lesson about the Chinese in California, and particularly in San Francisco. Wok Wiz also offers an "I Can't Believe I Ate My Way Through Chinatown!" tour, with an exclusive emphasis on Chinese foods and food preparation, and a shorter "Walk and Wok" shopping tour and hands-on cooking class. (Special group tours can also be arranged.) Serious food aficionados will probably recognize Fong-Torres, well known for her articles, books, and Chinese cooking television appearances. She is also the author of several books, including *San Francisco Chinatown: A Walking Tour, In the Chinese Kitchen,* and the *Wok Wiz Cookbook.*

Combining two cross-cultural tidbits of folk wisdom—"You never age at the dinner table" (Italian) and "To eat is greater than heaven" (Chinese)—**Ruby Tom's Glorious Food Culinary Walk Tours,** 415/441-5637, stroll through both North Beach and Chinatown, separately or on the same tour. Special walking tours include North Beach Bakeries (an early morning slice of life), North Beach Nightbeat (complete with cabaret, theater, or jazz entertainment), and Lanterns of Chinatown (a stroll under the night-lit red lanterns followed by a hosted banquet). A graduate of the California Culinary Academy, Ruby Tom is an award-winning chef herself. She conducted and organized the first professional chefs exchange between the People's Republic of China and the city of San Francisco. **All About Chinatown Tours,** 100 Waverly Place, 415/982-8839, www.allaboutchinatown.com, conducted by San Francisco native Linda Lee, also walk visitors through Chinatown's past and present; tours include a traditional Chinese lunch or dinner. Call for reservations and current schedule.

Over on the spaghetti-eating side of Columbus, *Chronicle* food writer GraceAnn Walden leads the **Mangia North Beach!** tour through the neighborhood's best trattorias, delis, and bakeries. Along the way, you'll pick up cooking tips, sample Italian cheeses, and learn some local history. The four-hour tour concludes with a multicourse lunch. Tours begin Sat. at 10 A.M.; for reservations, call 415/927-3933 or check www.sfnorthbeach.com/gawtour.

Driving Tours
A Day in Nature, 1490 Sacramento St. (between Hyde and Leavenworth), 415/673-0548, www.adayinnature.com, offers personalized half-day or full-day naturalist-guided tours (groups of just one to four people) of North Bay destinations like the Marin Headlands, Muir Woods, and the Napa Valley wine country, complete with gourmet picnic.

Gray Line, 415/558-9400 or 800/826-0202, www.grayline.com, is the city's largest tour operator, commandeering an impressive fleet of standard-brand buses and red, London-style double-deckers. The company offers a variety of narrated tours touching on the basics, in San Francisco proper and beyond. Unlike most other companies, Gray Line offers its city tour in multiple languages: Japanese, Korean, German, French, Italian, and Spanish. Much more personal is the **Great Pacific Tour Company,** 518 Octavia St. (at Hayes), 415/626-4499, www.greatpacifictour.com, which runs 13-passenger minivans on four different tours: half-day

city or Marin County trips plus full-day Monterey Peninsula and Napa/Sonoma wine country tours (foreign-language tours available). **Tower Tours,** 77 Jefferson (at Pier 43), 415/434-8687, is affiliated with Blue & Gold Fleet and offers tours of the city, Marin, Alcatraz, the wine country, Monterey Peninsula, and Yosemite; all tours leave from their office at Fisherman's Wharf. **Quality Tours,** 5003 Palmetto Ave., Pacifica, 650/994-5054, www.qualitytours.com, does a San Francisco architecture tour and a "whole enchilada" tour in a luxury seven-passenger Chevy suburban. **Three Babes and a Bus Nightclub Tours,** 415/552-CLUB or 800/414-0158, www.threebabes.com, caters to visiting night owls, who hop the bus and party at the city's hottest nightspots with the charming hostesses.

Many firms create personalized, special-interest tours with reasonable advance notice; contact the Convention & Visitors Bureau for a complete listing.

Though both are better known for their ferry tours, both the Blue & Gold Fleet and the Red & White Fleet (see below) also offer land tours to various Northern California attractions.

Water Tours
The **Blue & Gold Fleet** is based at Piers 39 and 41, 415/705-8200 (business office), 415/773-1188 (recorded schedule), or 415/705-5555 (information and advance ticket purchase), www.blueandgoldfleet.com. Blue & Gold offers a narrated year-round (weather permitting) **Golden Gate Bay Cruise** that leaves from Pier 39, passes under the Golden Gate Bridge, cruises by Sausalito and Angel Island, and loops back around Alcatraz. The trip takes about an hour. Fare: $19 adults, $15 seniors over 62 and youths 12–18, $9 children 5–11. The justifiably popular **Alcatraz Tour** takes you out to the infamous former prison. Fare is $16 adults with a self-guided audio tour, or $11.50 adults without the audio. Day-use fee on the rock is $1. (Also available is an evening "Alcatraz After Hours" tour, $23.50 adults, which includes a narrated guided tour.) Blue & Gold ferries also can take you to **Sausalito, Tiburon, Oakland, Alameda, Vallejo,** and **Angel Island.**

SUSAN SNYDER

Ferries offer a wonderful introduction to the City by the Bay

The **Red & White Fleet,** at Pier 43, 415/447-0597 or 800/229-2784 (in California), www.redandwhite.com, offers one-hour, multilingual Bay Cruise tours that loop out under the Golden Gate and return past Sausalito, Angel Island, and Alcatraz ($19 adults, $15 seniors/youths, $11 kids 5–11, not including the $1 day-use fee). Other offerings include weekend Blues Cruises in summer and a variety of land tours in Northern California.

Hornblower Cruises and Events, 415/788-8866, www.hornblower.com, docks at Pier 33 and elsewhere around the bay. The company offers big-boat on-the-bay dining adventures, from extravagant nightly dinner dances and weekday lunches to Saturday and Sunday champagne brunch. Occasional special events, from whodunit murder mystery dinners to jazz cocktail cruises, can be especially fun. And Hornblower's Monte Carlo Cruises feature casual Las Vegas-style casino gaming tables (proceeds go to charity) on dinner cruises aboard the M/V *Monte Carlo.*

Oceanic Society Expeditions, based at Fort Mason, 415/474-3385, www.oceanic-society.org, offers a variety of seagoing natural history trips,

including winter whale-watching excursions, usually late Dec.–May (about $50 per person), and Farallon Islands nature trips, June–Nov. (about $70 per person). Reservations are required. Oceanic Society trips are multifaceted. For example, only scientific researchers and trusted volunteers are allowed on the cold granite Farallon Islands, but the Society's excursion to the islands takes you as close as most people ever get. The Farallons, 27 miles from the Golden Gate, are a national wildlife refuge within the Gulf of the Farallones National Marine Sanctuary, which itself is part of UNESCO's Central California Coast Biosphere Reserve. The nutrient-rich coastal waters around the islands are vital to the world's fisheries, to the health of sea mammal populations, and to the success of the breeding seabird colonies here. Some quarter million birds breed here, among them tufted puffins and rhinoceros auklets (bring a hat). The Oceanic Society trip to the islands takes about six and a half hours, shoving off at 9:30 A.M. (Sat., Sun., and select Fri.) from the San Francisco Yacht Harbor on Marina Green. The 63-foot Oceanic Society boat carries 46 passengers and a naturalist. Contact the nonprofit Oceanic Society for other excursion options.

Self-Guided Tours

If you have a car, taking the city's **49 Mile Scenic Drive** is a good way to personally experience the entirety of San Francisco. The route is a bit tricky to follow, though, so be sure to follow the map and directions provided by the Convention & Visitors Bureau—and never try this particular exploration during rush hours or peak weekend commute times.

With enough time, design your own tour or tours, starting with the neighborhood and district information included in this chapter. Or, using a variety of special-interest books and other resources, design a tour based on a particular theme—such as "literary haunts," "bars throughout history" (best as a walking tour), "stairway tours," "musical high notes," "theatrical highlights," or even "steepest streets."

The **Steepest Streets Tour** is a particular thrill for courageous drivers and/or suicidal cyclists. (However you do this one, take it slow and easy.) As far as vertical grade is concerned, those all-time tourist favorites—Mason St. down Nob Hill, and Hyde St. to Aquatic Park—don't even register in San Francisco's top 10. According to the city's Bureau of Engineering, **Filbert Street** between Leavenworth and Hyde, and **22nd**

Street between Church and Vicksburg are the city's most hair-raising roadways, sharing a 31.5 percent grade. Coming in a close second: **Jones** between Union and Filbert (29 percent, plus a 26 percent thrill between Green and Union). So a good way to start this side trip is by shooting down Filbert (a one-way, with the 1100 block a special thrill), then straight up intersecting Jones. It's a scream. For more cheap thrills, try: **Duboce** between Buena Vista and Alpine (a 27.9 percent grade), and between Divisadero and Alpine, then Castro and Divisadero (each 25 percent); **Webster** between Vallejo and Broadway (26 percent); **Jones** between Pine and California (24.8 percent); and **Fillmore** between Vallejo and Broadway (24 percent). Whether or not you travel all these streets, you'll soon understand why hard-driving local cabbies burn out—their brakes, that is—every 2,000 miles or so.

A worthy variation is the **Most Twisted Streets Tour,** starting with one-way **Lombard Street** between Hyde and Leavenworth, a route touted as "The World's Crookedest Street," with eight turns within a distance of 412 feet. But San Francisco's truly most twisted is **Vermont Street** between 20th and 22nd Streets, which has six fender-grinding turns within a distance of 270 feet. Better for panoramic views in all directions is **Twin Peaks Boulevard,** with 11 curves and six about-face turns in its one-mile descent.

Sights Downtown

In other times, San Francisco neighborhoods and districts had such distinct ethnic and cultural or functional identities that they served as separate cities within a city. It wasn't uncommon for people to be born and grow up, to work, to raise families, and to die in their own insular neighborhoods, absolutely unfamiliar with the rest of San Francisco.

For the most part, those days are long past. Since its inception, the city has transformed itself, beginning as a sleepy mission town, then a lawless gold-rush capital that gradually gained respectability and recognition as the West Coast's most sophisticated cultural and trade center. The process continues. The city's neighborhoods continue to reinvent themselves, and California's accelerated economic and social mobility also erase old boundaries. Just where one part of town ends and another begins is a favorite San Francisco topic of disagreement.

Orientation

In San Francisco, "downtown" is a general reference to the city's hustle-bustle heart. Knowing just where it starts and ends is largely irrelevant, so long as you understand that it includes Union Square, much of Market St., and the Civic Center government and arts buildings. The Financial District and the Waterfront are also included. Six or seven blocks directly west of the Civic Center is the Alamo Square Historic District, one among other enclaves of gentrified Victorian neighborhoods in the otherwise down-and-out Western Addition, which also includes Japantown. Though purists will no doubt quibble, for reasons of proximity these are included with downtown. And while more "uptown" parts of the South of Market Area (SoMa) are essentially downtown too, as are Nob Hill and Chinatown, those areas are covered in more depth elsewhere below.

AROUND UNION SQUARE

Named after Civil War–era rallies held here in support of Union forces (California eventually spurned the Confederacy), San Francisco's Union Square is the oasis at the center of the city's premier shopping district and also parking central for downtown shoppers, since the square also serves as the roof of the multilevel parking garage directly below—the world's first underground parking garage, in fact. (Other garages within walking distance include the Sutter-Stockton Garage to the north, the Ellis-O'Farrell Garage two blocks south, and, across Market, the huge and inexpensive Fifth & Mission Garage.) Reopened to the public in late 2002 following a $25 million makeover, new, improved Union Square is paved in green and tan granite and includes Canary Island palm trees, pavilions, arbors, light sculptures, an orchestra-sized amphitheater, a café and espresso stop, and a discount theater ticket outlet. Large granite pedestals are custom-made for street performers. Be there and be square.

The landmark **Westin St. Francis Hotel** flanks Union Square on the west, near major stores like **Saks Fifth Avenue, Tiffany, Burberry, Macy's,** and **Neiman-Marcus** (which offers its popular **Rotunda** restaurant for après-shop dropping; open for lunch and afternoon tea).

Immediately east of Union Square along Post, Maiden Ln., and Geary, you'll find an unabashed selection of expensive and fashionable stores, including **Cartier, Dunhill,** and Euro-hip **Wilkes Bashford,** to more mainstream options such as **NikeTown USA** and **Eddie Bauer.** (Down in the basement at Wilkes Bashford is his new **Wilkes Home** store. Across Sutter is wobderful **Scheuer Linens.**) Or dress yourself up at **Ralph Lauren, Versace, Chanel, Escada, Gucci,** and several other designer emporiums. **Gumps** at 135 Post is the elegant specialist in one-of-a-kind and rare wares, where even the furniture is art. Don't miss a stroll down traffic-free, two-block **Maiden Lane,** a onetime red-light district stretching between Stockton and Kearny, chock-full of sidewalk cafés and shops. Here stands the spectacular brick V.C. Morris Building, now home to **Folk Art International Gallery.** Designed in 1949 by Frank Lloyd Wright, with its spiral interior this building is an obvious prototype for his more famous Guggenheim Museum in New York. Upscale houseware shops—**Sur La Table, Pierre Deux,** and **Christofle**—share the neighborood. **Crocker Galleria,** at Post and Montgomery, offers still more shopping.

Heading south from Union Square on Stockton, between O'Farrell and Market, you'll pass the **Virgin Megastore,** where music lovers can find just about anything to add to their CD collection. At Market St. is bargain-priced **Old Navy,** as well as a cheap thrill for shoppers—the eight-story circular escalator ride up to **Nordstrom** and other stores at **San Francisco Centre,** Fifth and Market, which was built in the late 1980s with the hope of attracting suburbanites and squeezing out the homeless.

Just down a ways from the theater district and skirting The Tenderloin at 561 Geary (between Taylor and Jones) is the odd **Blue Lamp** bar—note the blue lamp, a classic of neo-neon art. Once just a hard-drinkers' dive, now the Blue Lamp is a campy, hipsters', hard-drinkers' dive, most interesting late at night when the neighborhood gets a bit scary. But the real reason to come here is live music, just-starting band badness. A few blocks farther downtown, near Union Square at 333 Geary (between Powell and Mason), is another world entirely—**Lefty O'Doul's,** a hofbrau-style deli and old-time bar stuffed to the ceiling with baseball memorabilia. Lefty was a local hero, a big leaguer who came back to manage the minor-league San Francisco Seals before the Giants came to town.

THE TENDERLOIN

Stretching between Union Square and the Civic Center is The Tenderloin, definitely a poor choice for a casual stroll by tourists and other innocents. A down-and-out pocket of poverty pocked these days by the city signposts of human misery—drug dealing, prostitution, pornography, and violent crime—the densely populated Tenderloin earned its name around the turn of the century, when police assigned to patrol its mean streets received additional hazard pay—and, some say, substantial protection money and kickbacks. (The

extra cash allowed them to dine on the choicest cuts of meat.) The Tenderloin's historic boundaries are Post, Market, Van Ness, and Powell. In reality, however, the city's designated theater district (with accompanying cafés and nightspots), many newly gentrified hotels, even the St. Francis Hotel and most Civic Center attractions fall within this no-man's land, which is especially a no-woman's land. More realistic, better-safe-than-sorry boundaries are Larkin, Mason, O'Farrell, and Market, with an extra caution also for some streets south of Market (especially Sixth) as far as Howard. As a general rule, perimeters are safer than core areas, but since this is San Francisco's highest crime area, with rape, mugging, and other assaults at an all-time high, for tenderfeet no part of The Tenderloin is considered safe—even during daylight hours. Ask local shopkeepers and restaurant or hotel personnel about the safety of specific destinations, if in doubt, and travel in groups when you do venture any distance into The Tenderloin.

But the area has its beauty, too, often most apparent through the celebrations and ministries of the Reverend Cecil Williams and congregation at the renowned **Glide Memorial United Methodist Church,** which rises up at 330 Ellis (at Taylor), 415/674-6000, www.glide.org. Glide sponsors children's assistance and other community programs, from basic survival and AIDS care to the Computers and You program, which helps the economically disadvantaged learn computer skills. The Glide Ensemble choir sings an uplifting mix of gospel, freedom songs, and rock at its celebrations, held each Sunday at 9 and 11 A.M. Lines begin forming at the Taylor Street entrance 40 minutes before each celebration, plan on arriving early to get a seat. And feel free to contribute generously, and often. Surging hunger and homelessness in the new millennium make it hard for even Glide to keep up with community needs.

Yet some neighborhoods are cleaning up considerably, the indirect influence of commercial redevelopment and the influx of large numbers of Asian immigrants, many from Cambodia, Laos, and Vietnam. The annual **Tet Festival** celebrates the Vietnamese New Year. The Tenderloin also supports a small but growing arts community, as

San Francisco

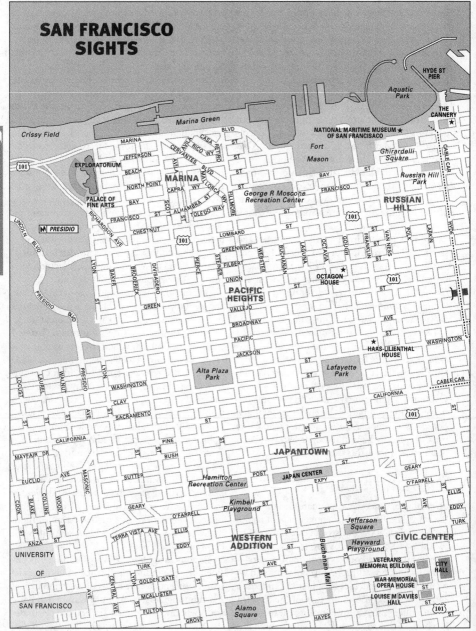

SAN FRANCISCO SIGHTS

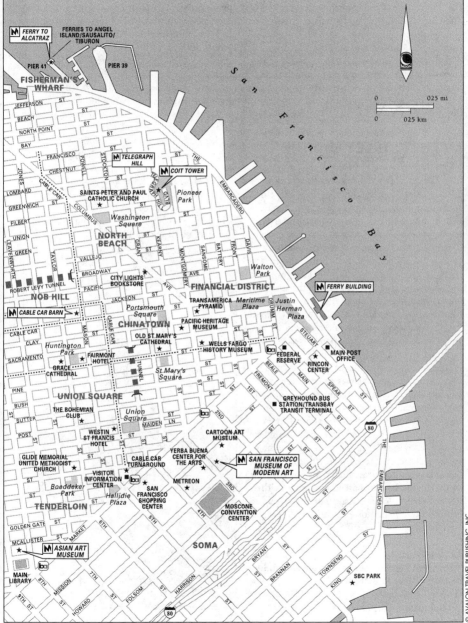

San Francisco

the 'Loin is one of the few remaining pockets of affordable housing in San Francisco. Among the neighborhood's many bars, the **Edinburgh Castle** at 950 Geary (between Polk and Larkin), 415/885-4074, stands out, drawing an interesting crowd of Scottish expatriates and young urbanites. The pub specializes in single malt Scotch, lager, fish 'n' chips, and literary events, including several signings by Irvine Welsh, author of *Trainspotting*.

MARKET STREET AND THE FINANCIAL DISTRICT

The Financial District features San Francisco's tallest, most phallic buildings, perhaps suggesting something profound about the global capitalist thrust. When rolling into town on the river of traffic, via the Golden Gate Bridge or, especially, Oakland's Bay Bridge, this compact concentration of law offices, insurance buildings, investment companies, banks, brokerages, and high-brow businesses rises up from the sparkling waters like some fantastic illusion, the greenback-packed Emerald City of the West Coast. Even if wandering on foot and temporarily lost, to get back downtown one merely looks up and heads off toward the big buildings.

The actual boundaries of the Financial District, built upon what was once water (Yerba Buena Cove), are rather vague, dependent upon both personal opinion and that constant urban flux of form and function. In general, the district includes the entire area from the north side of Market St. to the Montgomery St. corridor, north to the Jackson Square Historic District. Market Street is anchored near the bay by the concrete square of **Justin Herman Plaza** and its either-loved-or-hated **Vaillancourt Fountain,** said to be a parody of the now-demolished freeway it once faced.

Embarcadero Center

Above and behind the plaza is the astounding and Orwellian Embarcadero Center complex, the high-class heart of the Golden Gateway redevelopment project. Here is the somewhat surreal **Hyatt Regency Hotel,** noted for its 17-story indoor atrium and bizarre keyboard-like exte-

rior, as well as the **Park Hyatt Hotel.** But the main focus is the center's four-part shopping complex, **Embarcadero One** through **Embarcadero Four,** stretching along four city blocks between Clay and Sacramento. Inside, maps and information kiosks can help the disoriented. For a hands-on lesson in the **World of Economics,** including the chance to pretend you're president of the U.S. or head of the Fed, stop by the lobby of the **Federal Reserve Bank,** 101 Market (at Spear), 415/974-2000, open weekdays 9 A.M.–4:30 P.M., to play with the computer games and displays.

Robert Frost Plaza, at the intersection of Market and California, is a reminder that New England's poet was a San Francisco homeboy.

Heading up California St., stop at the **Bank of California** building at 400 California (between

the Transamerica building, once outrageous, now a landmark

Sansome and Battery), 415/445-0200, for a tour through its basement **Museum of the Money of the American West,** everything from gold nuggets and U.S. Mint mementos to dueling pistols. The **Wells Fargo History Museum,** inside Wells Fargo Bank at 420 Montgomery (near California), 415/396-2619, features an old Concord Stagecoach; a re-created early Wells Fargo office; samples of gold, gold scales, and gold-mining tools; and a hands-on telegraph exhibit, complete with telegraph key and Morse code books. It's open Mon.–Fri. 9 A.M.–5 P.M.; admission free. **Bank of America** at California and Kearny also has historical exhibits. In the 1905 **Merchants Exchange** building at California and Montgomery, the bygone boat-business days are remembered with ship models, now located on the third and eighth floors, and William Coulter marine murals along the bank's back wall. Mercantile action has entered a new era at the **Pacific Stock Exchange,** the former "temple of capitalism" at Pine and Sansome since 1930, which closed its doors in 2002 and transferred equity trading activities to its fully electronic Archipelago Exchange (ArcaEx).

People were outraged over the architecture of the **Transamerica Pyramid** at Montgomery and Washington, the city's tallest building, when it was completed in 1972. But now everyone has adjusted to its strange winged-spire architecture. Until recently it was possible to ride up to the 27th floor, to the "viewing area," for breathtaking sunny-day views of Coit Tower, the Golden Gate Bridge, and Alcatraz. These days, you'll get only as far as the lobby and the popular **Virtual Observation Deck,** with its four monitors connected to cameras mounted at the very tip of the Pyramid's spire. What's fun here is the chance to zoom, tilt, and pan the cameras for some fairly unusual views. The Transamerica lobby is open weekdays from 9 A.M.–6 P.M. Back down on the ground, head for Transamerica Center's **Redwood Park** on Friday lunch hours in summer for "Music in the Park" concerts.

Designated these days as the **Jackson Square Historical District,** the section of town stretching into North Beach across Washington St. was once called the Barbary Coast, famous since the gold rush as the world's most depraved human hellhole. Pacific St. was the main thoroughfare, a stretch of bad-boy bawdy houses, saloons, dance halls, and worse—like the "cowyards," where hundreds of prostitutes performed onstage with animals or in narrow cribs stacked as high as four stories. Words like "Mickey Finn," "Shanghaied," and "hoodlum" were coined here. Local moral wrath couldn't stop the barbarity of the Barbary Coast—and even the earthquake of 1906 spared the area, much to everyone's astonishment. Somewhat settled down by the Roaring '20s, when it was known as the International Settlement, the Barbary Coast didn't shed its barbarians entirely until the 1950s. Today it's quite tame, an oddly gentrified collection of quaint brick buildings.

ON THE WATERFRONT

San Francisco's waterfront stretches some six miles along the wide, seawall-straddling **Embarcadero,** which runs from Fisherman's Wharf in the north to China Basin south of the Bay Bridge. Remnants of bygone booming port days, the docks and wharfs here are today devoted as much to tourism as to maritime commerce. The area is much improved, aesthetically, now that the elevated, view-blocking Embarcadero Freeway is gone (it was razed after being damaged in the 1989 earthquake). Today the Embarcadero is lined with nonnative Canary Island palm trees—a landscaping strategy that initially irked some botanical purists who dismissed the trees as being "too L.A."

Just south of Broadway is the city's only new pier since the 1930s; 845-foot-long **Pier 7** is an elegant public-access promenade for dawdlers and fisherfolk, complete with iron-and-wood benches, iron railings, and flanking colonnades of lampposts, the better for taking in the nighttime skyline. At the foot of Market St. is the **Ferry Building,** completed in 1898. Formerly the city's transportation center, the Ferry Building today is largely office space. But the building still features its 661-foot arcaded facade, triumphal entrance arch, and temple-style clock-tower echoing the Giralda tower of Spain's Seville

San Francisco

cathedral. During commute hours, the area bustles with suits disembarking ferries from Marin. Hop one of the high-speed boats to Sausalito for lunch and you'll get there in about half an hour. Boats leave frequently daily, with extended hours in summer.

Across from the updated 1889 Audiffred Building at 1 Mission is city-within-the-city **Rincon Center,** incorporating the former Rincon Annex Post Office, which was saved for its classic New Deal mural art. Note, too, the **36,075-pound brass propeller** from a World War II tanker at 100 Spear St., introducing the waterfront exhibits inside.

The **Waterfront Promenade** stretches from the San Francisco Maritime National Historic Park at the foot of Hyde St. all the way along the bay to the new Giants ballpark. The promenade, built in stages over the last few years, replaces the waterfront's old piers 14 through 22. Named **Herb Caen Way** (complete with the dot-dot-dot) in 1996, for the late *San Francisco Chronicle* columnist, the seawall walkway features grand views of the bay. It's a favorite spot for midday runners and office brownbaggers; literary types enjoy the brass poem plaques embedded in the sidewalk.

A very long block south of Rincon Center is **Hills Plaza,** a fairly new commercial-and-apartment development with a garden plaza, incorporating the shell of the old Hills Brothers Coffee building. Farther south along the Embarcadero are more new developments also housing restaurants, including **Bayside Village** and the world-renowned drug rehabilitation program **Delancey Street.** Beyond, in China Basin, is **South Beach Marina Pier,** a public fishing pier with a good skyline view of the South Beach Marina.

Rising up at the foot of Second St. is the hugely popular **SBC Park** (formerly Pacific Bell Park), www.sfgiants.com, which replaced Monster Park (better known by its original name—Candlestick Park) as the home of the San Francisco Giants in 2000. SBC Park sits right on the waterfront, seats 42,000 fans, and offers sweeping views of the bay and the city skyline. Designed by Hellmuth, Obata & Kassabaum

architect Joe Spear, the fellow responsible for Coors Field in Denver and Camden Yards in Baltimore, the park combines the feel of an old-time ballpark with modern amenities. If you go, keep in mind that the popular games have 40,000 fans trying to drive and find parking downtown, and leaving the city by car takes two to three hours in traffic. Smart fans may find public transportation a better option, and in any case the ballpark is a fairly short walk from downtown.

Another corporate namesake is near SBC Park at the new Mission Bay campus of the **University of California, San Francisco.** Campus centerpiece is five-story, 435,000-square-foot **Genentech Hall,** one of 20 buildings planned here to lure biotech and drug companies. The campus will also include housing for students and staff, a campus community center, and parking.

Ferry Building

The 1903 beaux-arts Ferry Building designed by A. Page Brown, with its sky-scraping clocktower, is still a standout along the Embarcadero—and one of the city's most significant historic buildings. (The late *San Francisco Chronicle* columnist Herb Caen once observed that without the Ferry Building Tower, San Francisco would be like a birthday cake without a candle.) An enduring symbol of the days when ferries were almost the only way to get to San Francisco, the building survived the 1906 earthquake with nary a tremble, and still stood tall following the construction of both the Golden Gate and Bay Bridges. The Ferry Building is certain to survive gentrification, too: Fresh from a painstaking renovation, this grand bayside building of brick arches and steel trusses debuted in 2003 as the city's foremost food palace.

That's right. Just like the rest of San Francisco, at the new, improved Ferry Building it's all about hale, hearty, and happenin' food.

The building's vast interior, naturally lit by a skylight that extends the length of two football fields, is now home to a bumper crop of sophisticated food-related shops, restaurants, and related enterprises. In addition to specialty produce, meat, seafood, and sweets shops, the Ferry Building boasts the only other Bay Area outlet of Berkeley's famed **Acme Bread,** a **Cowgirl Creamery Artisan Cheese Shop,** and the **Miette** patisserie.

Stop into **Book Passage** for an impressive selection of books (about food and other topics) then settle into **Peet's Coffee & Tea** or **Imperial Tea Court** to dip into them. For something more substantial, try St. Helena–based **Taylors Refresher** for a grain-fed beef burger or fish taco; 25-seat **Hog Island Oyster Company** oyster bar; **Marketbar** Mediterranean bistro; and **Lulu Petite** and very North Beach **Mastrelli's Delis.** Flagship of San Francisco's very chic Vietnamese **M Slanted Door** restaurant family is here, too, in a spectacular setting overlooking San Francisco Bay.

Still, the Ferry Building's dominant food-related presence is the **Ferry Plaza Farmers Market,** sponsored by the nonprofit Center for Urban Education about Sustainable Agriculture (CUESA) and fast becoming the Embarcadero's (if not the city's) most enjoyable street scene.

One day soon the herb, produce, and flower vendors in the open-air arcades in front, facing the Embarcadero, will be open for business every day. At last report, though, farmers markets were scheduled Tues. 10 A.M.–2 P.M., Thurs. 3–7 P.M., and Sat. 8 A.M.–2 P.M., year-round. (On Saturday, the largest market, the rear plaza, is used as well.) Also offered is a special Garden Market, Sunday 8 A.M.–2 P.M., selling everything from vegetable starts to houseplants. With a permanent facility, CUESA also hosts conferences, classes, workshops, and exhibits about sustainable agriculture and other food and agriculture issues.

For more farmers market information, contact Ferry Plaza Farmers Market, 415/353-5650, www.ferryplazafarmersmarket.com. For more information about the Ferry Building and its businesses, contact **Ferry Building Marketplace,** One Ferry Bldg., 415/693-0996, www.ferry buildingmarketplace.com. The Ferry Building looms large along the Embarcadero at the foot of Market Street. It is accessible by ferry, MUNI, and BART; the historic trolley cars (Line F Market) stop right out front.

CIVIC CENTER AND VICINITY

Smack dab in the center of the sleaze zone is San Francisco's major hub of government, the Civic Center, built on the onetime site of the Yerba Buena Cemetery. (See cautions mentioned under The Tenderloin above, which also apply to almost any section of downtown Market St. after dark.) A sublime example of America's beaux arts architecture, the 1915 **San Francisco City Hall,** 401 Van Ness (at Polk), 415/554-4904, www.ci.sf.ca.us/cityhall, was inspired by a Parisian church, complete with dome and majestic staircase. Renaissance-style sculptures state the city's dreams—the not necessarily incongruous collection of Wisdom, the Arts, Learning, Truth, Industry, and Labor over the Van Ness Ave. entrance, and Commerce, Navigation, California Wealth, and San Francisco above the doors on Polk Street. After sustaining severe damage in the 1989 earthquake, the building was repaired and meticulously refurbished, and its interior stylishly redone, on the watch of equally stylish former Mayor Willie Brown, a project with a price tag of several hundred million dollars. Former state senator Quentin Kopp, never a Brown fan, has called this the "Taj Mahal" of public works projects. Decide for yourself whether that's true; free 45-minute tours are available daily.

The **War Memorial Opera House,** 301 Van Ness (at Grove), 415/861-4008, www.sfopera .com, is the classical venue for the San Francisco Ballet Company as well as the San Francisco Opera, the place for society folk to see and be seen during the September to December opera season. Twin to the opera house, connected by extravagant iron gates, is the **Veterans Building/Herbst Theatre,** home to the **San Francisco Arts Commission Gallery,** 415/554-6080, as well as **San Francisco Performing Arts Library & Museum,** 415/255-4800. The theatre hosts the noted **City Arts & Lectures** series, 415/392-4400, www.cityarts.net. The modern **Louise M. Davies Symphony Hall** at Van Ness and Grove, which features North America's largest concert hall organ, is the permanent venue for the **San**

Francisco Symphony, www.sfsymphony.org, 415/864-6000.

San Francisco's **New Main Library,** 100 Larkin (at Grove), 415/557-4400, is worth a browse, especially for the free Internet access offered at computer stations throughout the library. Free volunteer-led City Guides tours are headquartered here, 415/557-4266, schedules available at www.cityguides.org, and some depart from here. **Civic Center Plaza,** across Polk from the library, is home to many of the area's homeless, and also forms the garden roof for the underground **Brooks Hall** exhibit center and parking garage. **United Nations Plaza** stretches between Market St. and the Federal Building at McAllister (between Seventh and Eighth), commemorating the U.N.'s charter meeting in 1945 at the War Memorial Opera House. On Wednesday and Sunday the plaza reflects the multi-cultural face of San Francisco, bustling with buyers and sellers of fish, Asian greens, unusual fruits, mushrooms, and vegetables at the **Heart of the City Farmer's Market.**

Across Market St., technically in SoMa but allied in spirit with the Civic Center, is the stunningly refurbished former San Francisco Post Office and **U.S. Courthouse,** at Seventh and Mission. This gorgeous 1905 granite masterpiece, full of marble and mosaic floors and ceilings, was damaged in the 1989 earthquake but it's now back and better than ever after a $91-million earthquake retrofit and rehabilitation. The post office is gone, replaced by an atrium, but the courts are back in session here. The third-floor courtroom is particularly impressive.

On Sunday mornings, the solemn sound of jazz emanates from **St. John's African Orthodox Church,** which lost its lease on a storefront in the Western addition and currently operates as a guest of St. Paulus Lutheran Church at 930 Gough Street(at Turk), 415/673-3572. The tiny ministry devoted to celebrating the life of St. **John Coltrane,** and services are part celebration and part jam session. Lack of funds has delayed plans to renovate a space in the traditionally African-American Hunter's point area, so until then check for updates at www.saintjohn coltrane.org In addition to the area's many cafés,

restaurants, and nightspots, the **California Culinary Academy,** 625 Polk St. (at Turk), 415/771-3500 or 800/229-2433, is noted for its 16-month chef's training course in Italian, French, and nouvelle cuisine. For the curious, the academy is also an exceptionally good place to eat wonderful food at reasonable prices. The academy operates a bakery and café, the basement **Tavern on the Tenderloin** buffet, 415/771-3536, and the somewhat more formal **Careme Room,** 415/771-3535, a glass-walled dining hall where you can watch what goes on in the kitchen. Call for hours and reservation policies, which vary.

Ⓜ Asian Art Museum

San Francisco's venerable Asian Art Museum is now at home in one of its equally venerable buildings—both newly polished cultural stars in the city's revitalized Civic Center. A main attraction at the Civic Center since its early 2003 opening, the "new Asian"—officially known, now, as the **Asian Art Museum—Chong-Moon Lee Center for Asian Art and Culture**—has successfully relocated from the M. H de Young Museum in Golden Gate Park to the city's restyled 1917 beaux arts Main Library.

The old library's $160.5 million renovation—brainchild of renowned Italian architect Gae Aulenti, particularly adept in "adaptive reuse" techniques—left the dignified exterior intact yet radically transformed the once somber interiors into well-lighted, spacious galleries. And there's so much more space, about 75 percent more than the museum enjoyed in its wing at the de Young: some 29,000 square feet for the permanent collection, another 8,500 square feet for changing exhibits, enhanced at every turn with state-of-the-art interpretive exhibits and displays.

At the heart of the new Asian is an indoor sky-lit court that incorporates the library's prominent entrance and grand staircase, a dramatic focus for the museum's enlightened central space. The museum's overall "flow" encourages visitors to circulate through, above, and around the central court; a glass-enclosed escalator leads to upper floors, including a new second floor. Reworked interior walls allow art lovers to peer into galleries from a multitude of perspectives. Still, significant architectural history remains from architect George Kelham's original library design, including the interior's painted ceilings, skylights, great hall, stone floors, molded plasters, light fixtures, and inscriptions.

For all its new wonders, the true heart of the Asian Art Museum—the first museum in the U.S. dedicated solely to Asian art—is its permanent collection, an exquisite introduction to all major Asian cultures. Built from the renowned art collection of onetime Olympic athlete and Chicago millionaire Avery Brundage and his wife, Elizabeth, the museum now includes more than 13,000 art works representing 40 nations and 6,000 years of history. From the bronze *Seated-Buddha,* dated A.D. 338, the oldest known Chinese image of Buddha in existence, to the gilt bronze *White Tara* from Nepal, from illuminated Iranian manuscripts to exquisite Thai gilded-lacquer panels and Japanese bamboo baskets—this is the West's most spectacular Asian art collection.

The new Asian also features a café, store, and expanded educational facilities, which includes three classrooms and a ground-floor resource center allowing visitors to watch videos and listen to recordings.

Completion of the new Asian represents the final phase of San Francisco's 10-year renovation of its French neoclassical Civic Center complex, one of the nation's outstanding examples of the "City Beautiful" movement inspired by the Chicago World's Fair of 1893.

The Asian Art Museum is open Tues.–Sun. 10 A.M.–5 P.M., with extended evening hours every Thursday until 9 P.M. Museum admission, which includes a complimentary audio tour of the museum's galleries, is $10 adults, $7 seniors, $6 youths ages 12–17, free for children under 12. For more information, contact the Asian Art Museum at 200 Larkin St., 415/581-3500, www.asianart.org.

WESTERN ADDITION

These central city blocks west of Van Ness Ave. and south of Pacific Heights are certainly diverse. Settled in turn by Jewish, Japanese, and African Americans, the neighborhood's historical associations are with the Fillmore's jazz and blues bars, which hosted greats like John Coltrane and Billie Holiday in the 1950s and '60s.

The area is remarkable architecturally because so many of its 19th-century Victorians survived the 1906 earthquake, though some subsequently declined into subdivided apartments or were knocked down by the wrecking ball of redevelopment. The Western Addition's remaining Victorian enclaves are rapidly becoming gentrified. The most notable—and most photographed— example is Steiner St. facing **Alamo Square** (other pretty "painted ladies" with facelifts stretch for several blocks in all directions), though countrylike **Cottage Row** just east of Fillmore St. between Sutter and Bush is equally enchanting.

Today most of the Western Addition is home to working-class families, though the area south of Geary, considered "The Fillmore," was long composed almost exclusively of heavy-crime, low-income housing projects. Many of those boxy projects have been demolished, and redevelopment here is generally improving the aesthetics of the neighborhood.

The Western Addition's intriguing shops, restaurants, and cultural attractions reflect the neighborhood's roots. For an exceptional selection of African-American literature, Malcolm X marks the spot at **Marcus Books,** 1712 Fillmore (at Post), 415/346-4222, which also hosts occasional readings. Fancy dressing like a member of Run DMC? You'll find the country's biggest selections of Adidas clothing as well as vintage and retro wear at **Harput's,** 1527 Fillmore (between Ellis and Geary), 415/923-9300. **Jack's Record Cellar,** 254 Scott St. (at Page), 415/431-3047, is the perfect place to browse through obscure jazz and blues records.

Fillmore Street also creates the western border of **Japantown,** or Nihonmachi, an area encompassing the neighborhoods north of Geary, south of Pine, and stretching east to Octavia. This very American variation on Japanese community includes the old-style, open-air **Buchanan Mall** between Post and Sutter, and the more modern and ambitious **Japan Center,** a three-block-long concrete mall on Geary between Fillmore and Laguna. It's inaccessibly ugly from the outside, in the American tradition, but offers intriguing attractions inside, like karaoke bars and the **Kabuki Hot Springs,** 415/922-6000, a communal bathhouse on the ground floor.

Lined with boutiques selling clothing from independent labels, sidewalk restaurants, bookstores, and one-of-a-kind furniture stores, **Hayes Street** between Gough and Webster is an oasis of funky charm. Stroll the 300 and 400 blocks of Hayes for ornate and imported items. Browse **Worldware,** 336 Hayes Street, 415/487-9030,

for home decor; **Richard Hilkert, Bookseller,** 333 Hayes, 415/863-3339, for an independent selection of books; and **Zeitgeist** at 437 Hayes St. (between Gough and Octavia), 415/864-0185, for vintage timepieces from top manufacturers like Longines and Rolex. Farther up the street you'll find high fashion for feet at **Gimme Shoes,** 416 Hayes (at Gough), 415/864-0691, and **Bulo Women,** at 418 Hayes Street, 415/255-4939, with the matching **Bulo Men** at 437-A Hayes Street, 415/864-3244.

Sights Elsewhere

NOB HILL

Snide San Franciscans say "Snob Hill" when referring to cable car-crisscrossed Nob Hill. The official neighborhood name is purported to be short for "Nabob Hill," a reference to this high-rent district's nouveau riche roots. Robert Louis Stevenson called it the "hill of palaces," referring to the grand late-1800s mansions of San Francisco's economic elite, California's railroad barons most prominent among them. Known colloquially as the "Big Four," Charles Crocker, Mark Hopkins, Collis Huntington, and Leland Stanford were accompanied by two of the "Irish Big Four" or "Bonanza Kings" (James Fair and James Flood, Nevada silver lords) as they made their acquisitive economic and cultural march into San Francisco and across the rest of California.

Of the original homes of these magnates, only one stands today—James Flood's bearish, square Connecticut brownstone, now the exclusive **Pacific-Union Club** (the "P-U," in local vernacular) at 1000 California Street. The rest of the collection was demolished by the great earthquake and fire of 1906. But some of the city's finest hotels, not to mention an exquisite Protestant place of worship, have taken their place around rather formal **Huntington Park.** Huntington's central memorial status atop Nob Hill is appropriate enough, since skinflint Collis P. Huntington was the brains of the Big Four gang and his comparatively simple home once stood here.

Facing the square from the corner of California and Taylor is the charming, surprisingly unique red-brick **Huntington Hotel** and its exceptional **Big Four** bar and restaurant. The **Mark Hopkins Hotel** ("the Mark," as it's known around town) was built on the spot of Hopkins' original ornate Victorian, at 1 Nob Hill (corner of California and Mason). Take the elevator up to the **Top of the Mark,** the bar with a view that inspired the city's song, "I Left My Heart in San Francisco," and perhaps its singer, Tony Bennett, as well. Straight across the street, facing Mason between California and Sacramento, is the famed **Fairmont Hotel,** an architectural extravaganza built "atop Nob Hill" by James Fair's daughter Tessie (the lobby recognizable to American TV addicts as the one in the short-lived series *Hotel*). Inside, the Tiki-inspired **Tonga Room** is straight out of *Hawaii Five-O.* Kick back, enjoy a frozen cocktail, and soak in the strange ambience. Simulated rainstorms interrupt the tropical calm every half hour.

The **Stanford Court Hotel** at California and Powell, one of the world's finest, occupies the land where Leland Stanford's mansion once stood. For an artistic rendering of local nabobery, stop for a peek at the Stanford's lobby murals.

The **Bohemian Club** on the corner of Taylor and Post is a social club started by some of California's true bohemians, from Jack London, Joaquin Miller, and John Muir to Ambrose Bierce, Ina Coolbrith, and George Sterling. Though for old-time's sake some artists are invited to join, these days this very exclusive all-male club has a rank and file composed primarily of businessmen, financiers, and politicians. In July each year, these modern American bohemians retreat to the Russian River and their equally private Bohemian Grove all-male enclave for a week of fun and frolic.

Grace Cathedral

At the former site of Charles Crocker's mansion is Grace Cathedral, facing Huntington Park from Taylor St., an explosion of medieval Gothic enthusiasm inspired by the Notre Dame in Paris. Since the lot *was* cleared for construction by a very California earthquake, Grace Cathedral is built not of carefully crafted stone but steel-reinforced concrete.

Most famous here, architecturally, are the cathedral doors, cast from Lorenzo Ghiberti's Gates of Paradise from the Cathedral Baptistry in Florence, Italy. The glowing rose window is circa 1970 and comes from Chartres. Also from Chartres: Grace Cathedral's spiritual **Labyrinth,** a roll-up replica of an archetypal meditative journey in the Christian tradition. Since Grace is a "house of prayer for all people," anyone can walk the Labyrinth's three-fold path, just part of the cathedral's multifaceted **Veriditas** program. The indoor Labyrinth is open to the public during church hours, 8 A.M.–5 P.M. every day. The outdoor Labyrinth, outlined in stone, is an ancient Hopi/Cretan/Celtic design open 24 hours. Music is another major attraction at Grace Cathedral, from the choral evensongs to pipe organ, carillon, and chamber music concerts. Mother church for California's Episcopal Diocese, Grace Cathedral hosts endless unusual events, including St. Francis Day on October 6, which honors St. Francis of Assisi—the city's patron saint—and the interconnectedness of all creation. At this celebration all God's creatures, large and small—from elephants and police horses to dressed-up housepets, not to mention the women walking on stilts—show up to be blessed. For more information about Grace Cathedral's current calendar of odd and exhilarating events, call 415/749-6300 or see www.gracecathedral.org. And while you're in the neighborhood, take a peek into the modern **California Masonic Memorial Temple** at 1111 California, with its tiny scale model of King Solomon's Temple and colorful mosaic monument to Freemasonry.

▶ Cable Car Barn

Not just material wealth and spiritual high spirits are flaunted atop Nob Hill. Technical innovation is, too, and quite rightly, since this is where Andrew Hallidie launched the inaugural run of his famous cable cars, straight down Clay Street. A free stop at the **Cable Car Barn,** 1201 Mason (at Washington), 415/474-1887, open daily 10 A.M.–5 P.M. (until 6 P.M. during the summer), tells the story. No temple to tourist somnambulism, this is powerhouse central for the entire cable car system, energized solely by the kinetic energy of the cables. Electric motors turn the giant sheaves (pulleys) to whip the (underground) looped steel cables around town and power the cars. The idea is at once complex and simple. Feeding cable around corners is a bit tricky; to see how it works, hike down to a basement window and observe. But the "drive" mechanism is straightforward. Each cable car has two operators, someone working the grip, the other the brake. To "power up," heading uphill, the car's "grip" slides through the slot in the street to grab onto the cable, and the cable does the rest. Heading downhill, resisting gravity, the brake gets quite a workout. Also here: a display of historic cable cars and a gift shop.

CHINATOWN

The best time to explore Chinatown is at the crack of dawn, when crowded neighborhoods and narrow alleys explode into hustle and bustle, and when the scents, sounds, and sometimes surreal colors compete with the energy of sunrise. Due to the realities of gold rush-era life and, later, the Chinese Exclusion Act of 1882, this very American variation on a Cantonese market town was for too long an isolated, almost all-male frontier enclave with the predictable vices—a trend reversed only in the 1960s, when more relaxed immigration laws allowed the possibility of families and children. The ambitious and

JUSTIN MARLER

The Chinatown Gate was a gift from the Republic of China.

the educated have already moved on to the suburbs, so Chinatown today—outside of Harlem in New York, the country's most densely populated neighborhood—is home to the elderly poor and immigrants who can't speak English. It's still the largest community of Chinese anywhere outside China. And it's still a cultural and spiritual home for expanding Chinese communities in the Bay Area and beyond. Even those who have left come back, if only for a great meal and a Chinese-language movie.

To get oriented, keep in mind that Stockton St. is the main thoroughfare. Grant Ave., however, is where most tourists start, perhaps enticed away from Grant's endless upscale shops and galleries by the somewhat garish green-tiled Chinatown Gate at Bush, a 1969 gift from the Republic of China. As you wander north, notice the street-sign calligraphy, the red-painted, dragon-wrapped lampposts, and the increasingly unusual roofscapes. Grant goes the distance between Market St. and modern-day Pier 39. This happens to be San Francisco's oldest street and was little more

than a rutted path in 1834, when it was dubbed Calle de la Fundación (Foundation St. or "street of the founding") by the ragtag residents of the Yerba Buena pueblo. By the mid-19th century the street's name had been changed to Dupont, in honor of an American admiral—a change that also recognized the abrupt changing of California's political guard. But by the end of the 1800s "Du Pon Gai" had become so synonymous with unsavory activities that downtown merchants decided on another name change, this time borrowing a bit of prestige from Ulysses S. Grant, the nation's 18th president and the Civil War's conquering general. Despite the color on Grant, the in-between streets (Sacramento, Clay, Washington, Jackson, and Pacific) and the fascinating interconnecting alleys between them represent the heart of Chinatown.

Since traffic is horrendous, parking all but impossible, and many streets almost too narrow to navigate even sans vehicle, walking is the best way to see the sights. If you haven't time to wander aimlessly, taking a guided tour is the best way to get to know the neighborhood.

History and Museums

At the corner of Grant and California is **Old Saint Mary's Cathedral,** the city's Catholic cathedral from the early 1850s to 1891, still standing even after a gutting by fire in 1906. On Saint Mary's clock tower is sound maternal advice for any age: "Son, observe the time and fly from evil." (Saint Mary has a square, too, a restful stop just east and south of California St., where there's a Bufano sculpture of Dr. Sun Yat-sen, the Republic of China's founder.) Also at the Grant/California intersection is the **Ma-Tsu Temple of the United States of America,** with shrines to Buddha and other popular deities.

Packed with restaurants and tourist shops, Grant Ave. between California and Broadway is always bustling. Of particular interest is the unusual and aptly named **Li Po Bar** at 916 Grant, a former opium den and watering hole honoring the memory of China's notoriously romantic poet, a wine-loving warrior who drowned while embracing the moon—a moon mirage, as it turned out, reflected up from a river.

The **Chinese Historical Society of America,** 965 Clay (between Stockton and Powell), 415/391-1188, www.chsa.org, is the nation's only museum specifically dedicated to preserving Chinese-American history. Chinese contributions to California culture are particularly emphasized. Some unusual artifacts in the museum's huge collection: gold-rush paraphernalia, including a "tiger fork" from Weaverville's tong war, and an old handwritten copy of Chinatown's phone book. Open Tues.–Fri. 11 A.M.– 4 P.M., Sat. and Sun. 12–4 P.M., closed Mondays and major holidays. Admission is $3 adults, $2 students and senior citizens, $1 for children 6–17, and free for children under 5.

The **Pacific Heritage Museum,** 608 Commercial (between Montgomery and Kearny, Sacramento and Clay), 415/399-1124, is housed in the city's renovated brick 1875 U.S. Mint building. The museum features free rotating exhibits of Asian art and other treasures; open Tues.–Sat. 10 A.M.–4 P.M. To place it all in the larger context of California's Wild West history, head around the corner to the **Wells Fargo History Museum,** 420 Montgomery, 415/396-2619, open weekdays 9 A.M.–5 P.M.

Portsmouth Square—people still say "square," though technically it's been a plaza since the 1920s—on Kearny between Clay and Washington is Chinatown's backyard. Here you'll get an astounding look at everyday local life, from the city's omnipresent panhandlers to early-morning tai chi to all-male afternoons of checkers, *go,* and gossip—life's lasting entertainments for Chinatown's aging bachelors. Across Kearny on the third floor of the Financial District Holiday Inn is the **Chinese Culture Center,** 750 Kearny (between Clay and Washington), 415/986-1822, which has a small gallery and gift shop but otherwise caters mostly to meeting the needs of the local community.

The further actions and attractions of Chinatown's heart are increasingly subtle, from the Washington St. herb and herbalist shops to Ross Alley's garment factories and its fortune cookie company, where you can buy some instant fortune, fresh off the press—keeping in mind, of course, that fortune cookies are an all-American invention. Intriguing, at 743 Washington, is the oldest Asian-style building in the neighborhood, the three-tiered 1909 "temple" once home to the Chinatown Telephone Exchange, now the **Bank of Canton.** But even **Bank of America,** at 701 Grant, is dressed in keeping with its cultural surroundings, with benevolent gold dragons on its columns and doors, and some 60 dragons on its facade. Also putting on the dog is **Citibank** at 845 Grant, guarded by grimacing temple dogs.

Both Jackson and Washington Streets are best bets for finding small and authentic neighborhood restaurants. **Stockton Street,** especially between Broadway and Sacramento and especially on a Saturday afternoon, is where Chinatown shops. Between Sacramento and Washington, **Waverly Place** is referred to as the "street of painted balconies," for fairly obvious reasons. There are three temples here, open to respectful visitors (donations appreciated, picture-taking usually not). **Norras Temple** at 109 Waverly (at Clay) is affiliated with the Buddhist Association of America, lion dancing and all, while the fourth-floor **Tien Hau Temple** at 123 Waverly

San Francisco

primarily honors the Queen of Heaven, she who protects sojourners and seafarers as well as writers, actors, and prostitutes. The **Jeng Sen Buddhism and Taoism Association,** 146 Waverly, perhaps offers the best general introduction to Chinese religious tolerance, with a brief printed explanation (in English) of both belief systems.

For a delightfully detailed and intimate self-guided tour through the neighborhood, bring along a copy of Shirley Fong-Torres's *San Francisco Chinatown: A Walking Tour,* which includes some rarely recognized sights, such as the **Cameron House,** 920 Sacramento (between Powell and Stockton), a youth center named in honor of Donaldina Cameron (1869-1968), who helped young Chinese slave girls escape poverty and prostitution. Fong-Torres's marvelous and readable guide to San Francisco's Chinese community also covers history, cultural beliefs, festivals, religion and philosophy, herbal medicine (doctors and pharmacists are now licensed for these traditional practices by the state of California), and Chinese tea. It includes a very good introduction to Chinese food—from ingredients, cookware, and techniques to menus and restaurant recommendations.

Shops

To a greater extent than, say, Oakland's Chinatown, most shops here are aware of—and cater to—the tourist trade. But once you have some idea what you're looking for, bargains are available. Along Grant Ave., a definite must for gourmet cooks and other kitchen habitués is the **Wok Shop,** 718 Grant (between Sacramento and Clay), 415/989-3797, the specialized one-stop shopping trip for anything essential to Chinese cooking (and other types of cooking as well). The **Ten Ren Tea Company,** 949 Grant (at Jackson), 415/362-0656 or 800/543-2885, features more than 50 varieties of teas, the prices dependent on quality and (for blends) content. There's a private area in back where you can arrange for instruction in the fine art of a proper tea ceremony. (Notice, on the wall, a photo of former president George Bush, who didn't quite get it right when he tried it.) For unusual gifts, silk shirts, high-quality linens and such, **Far East Fashions,** 953 Grant (between Washington and Jackson), 415/362-0986 or 415/362-8171, is a good choice.

Finally, musicians and nonmusicians alike shouldn't miss Clara Hsu's **Clarion Music Center,** 816 Sacramento St. (at Waverly Place), 415/391-1317, a treasure trove of African drums, Chinese gongs, Tibetan singing bowls, Indian sitars, Native American flutes, Bolivian panpipes, Australian didjeridoos, and other exotic instruments from every corner of the world. The store also offers lessons, workshops, and concerts to promote awareness of world musical culture. Open Mon.–Fri. 11 A.M.–6 P.M., Sat. 9 A.M.–5 P.M.

NORTH BEACH AND VICINITY

For one thing, there isn't any beach in North Beach. In the 1870s, the arm of San Francisco Bay that gave the neighborhood its name was filled in, creating more land for the growing city. And though beatniks and bohemians once brought a measure of fame to this Italian-American quarter of the city, they're all gone now, priced out of the neighborhood.

Quite a number of American poets and writers grubbed out some kind of start here: Gregory Corso, Lawrence Ferlinghetti, Allen Ginsberg, Bob Kaufman, Jack Kerouac, Gary Snyder, Kenneth Rexroth. By the 1940s, North Beach as "New Bohemia" was a local reality. It became a long-running national myth.

Otherwise sound-asleep America of the 1950s secretly loved the idea of the alienated, manic "beat generation," a phrase coined by Jack Kerouac in *On the Road.* The Beats seemed to be everything no one else was allowed to be—mostly, free. Free to drink coffee or cheap wine and talk all day; free to indulge in art, music, poetry, prose, and more sensual thrills just about any time; free to be angry and scruffy and lost in the forbidden fog of marijuana while bopping along to be-bop. But Allen Ginsberg's raging *Howl and Other Poems,* published by Ferlinghetti and City Lights, brought the wolf of censorship—an ungrateful growl that began with the seizure of in-bound books by U.S.

Customs and got louder when city police filed obscenity charges. The national notoriety of an extended trial, and Ginsberg's ultimate literary acquittal, brought busloads of Gray Line tourists. And the Beats moved on, though some of the cultural institutions they founded are still going strong.

Nowadays, North Beach is almost choking on its abundance—of eateries, coffeehouses, tourist traps, and shops. Forget trying to find a parking place; public transit is the best way to get around.

Adding to neighborhood stresses and strains—and to the high costs of surviving—is the influx of Asian business and the monumental increase in Hong Kong-money property investment, both marching into North Beach from Chinatown. Old and new neighborhood residents tend to ignore each other as much as possible, in that great American melting-pot tradition. (Before the Italians called North Beach their home turf, the Irish did. And before the Irish lived here, Chileans did. In all fairness, Fisherman's Wharf was Chinese before the Italians moved in. And of course Native Americans inhabited the entire state before the Spanish, the Mexicans, the Russians, and the Americans.) Like the city itself, life here makes for a fascinating sociology experiment.

What with territorial incursions from Chinatown, the historical boundaries of North Beach increasingly clash with the actual. Basically, the entire valley between Russian Hill and Telegraph Hill is properly considered North Beach. The northern boundary stopped just short of Fisherman's Wharf, now pushed back by rampant commercial development, and Broadway was the southern boundary—a thoroughfare and area sometimes referred to as the "Marco Polo Zone" because it once represented the official end of Chinatown and the beginning of San Francisco's Little Italy. The neighborhood's spine is diagonally running Columbus Ave., which begins at the Transamerica Pyramid at the edge of the Financial District and ends at The Cannery near Fisherman's Wharf. Columbus Avenue between Filbert and Broadway is the still-beating Italian heart of modern North Beach.

History and Museums

Piazza-like **Washington Square,** between Powell and Stockton, Union and Filbert, is the centerpiece of North Beach, though, as the late *San Francisco Chronicle* columnist Herb Caen once pointed out, it "isn't on Washington St., isn't a square (it's five-sided) and doesn't contain a statue of Washington but of Benjamin Franklin." (In terms of cultural consistency, this also explains the statue of Robert Louis Stevenson in Chinatown's Portsmouth Square.) There's a time capsule beneath old Ben; when the original treasures (mostly temperance tracts on the evils of alcohol) were unearthed in 1979, they were replaced with 20th-century cultural values, including a bottle of wine, a pair of Levi's, and a poem by Lawrence Ferlinghetti. In keeping with more modern times Washington Square also features a statue dedicated to the city's firemen, yet another contribution by eccentric little old Lillie Hitchcock Coit, Coit Tower's namesake. **Saints Peter and Paul Catholic Church** fronts the square at 666 Filbert, its twin towers lighting up the whole neighborhood come nightfall. Noted for its rococo interior and accompanying graphic statuary of injured saints and souls burning in hell, the Saints also offers daily mass in Italian and (on Sunday) in Chinese.

Two blocks northeast of Washington Square is the **North Beach Playground,** where bocce ball is still the neighborhood game of choice, just as October's **Columbus Day Parade** and accompanying festivities still make the biggest North Beach party. Just two blocks west of the square are the stairs leading to the top of **Telegraph Hill,** identifiable by **Coit Tower,** Lillie Coit's most heartfelt memorial to the firefighters. (More on that below.)

For an overview of the area's history, stop by the free **North Beach Museum,** 1435 Stockton St. (near Green, on the mezzanine of Bayview Bank), 415/626-7070, open Mon.–Thurs. 9 A.M.–5 P.M. and Friday until 6 P.M., which displays a great collection of old North Beach photos and artifacts in occasionally changing exhibits.

The North Beach "experience" is the neighborhood itself—the coffeehouses, the restaurants, the intriguing and odd little shops. No visit is complete without a stop at Lawrence Ferlinghetti's **City Lights Bookstore,** 261 Columbus (between Broadway and Pacific), 415/362-8193, on the neighborhood's most literary alley. City Lights is the nation's first all-paperback bookstore and a rambling ode to the best of the small presses; its poetry and other literary programs still feed the souls of those who need more nourishment than what commercial bestsellers can offer. A superb small museum, **Lyle Tuttle's Tattoo Museum and Shop,** is a few blocks up the way at 841 Columbus, 415/775-4991.

You can shop till you drop in this part of town. And much of what you'll find has something to do with food. For Italian ceramics, **Biordi Italian Imports,** 412 Columbus (near Vallejo), 415/392-8096, has a fabulous selection of art intended for the table (but almost too beautiful to use). For a price—and just about everything is pricey—the folks here will ship your treasures, too.

While you're wandering, you can easily put together a picnic for a timeout in Washington Square. The landmark Italian delicatessen **Liguria Bakery,** 1700 Stockton (at Filbert), 415/421-3786, which opened in 1911, is the place to stop for traditionally prepared focaccia, and nothing but. Head to **Molinari's,** 373 Columbus (between Broadway and Green), 415/421-2337, for cheeses, sausages, and savory salads, or to the Italian and French **Victoria Pastry Co.,** 1362 Stockton St. (at Vallejo), 415/781-2015, for cookies, cakes, and unbelievable pastries. Other good bakery stops nearby include the **Italian French Baking Co. of San Francisco,** 1501 Grant (at Union), 415/421-3796, known for its French bread. If you didn't load up on reading material at City Lights—for after you stuff yourself but before falling asleep in the square—stop by **Cavalli Italian Book Store,** 1441 Stockton (between Vallejo and Green), 415/421-4219, for Italian newspapers, magazines, and books.

Beats Trail

Caffe Greco, 423 Columbus (between Vallejo and Green), 415/397-6261, is regarded as the most European of the neighborhood's Eurostyle coffeehouses. But for that classic beatnik bonhomie, head to what was once the heart of New Bohemia, the surviving **Caffe Trieste,** 609 Vallejo (at Grant), 415/982-2605. Drop by anytime for opera and Italian folk songs on the jukebox, or come on Saturday afternoon for jazz, opera, or other concerts. Also-been-there-forever **Vesuvio Cafe,** 255 Columbus Ave. (at Broadway), 415/362-3370, across Kerouac Alley from the City Lights bookstore (look for the mural with volcanoes and peace symbols), is most appreciated for its upstairs balcony section, historically a magnet for working and wannabe writers (and everyone else, too). It was a favorite haunt of Ginsberg and Kerouac, as well as an in-town favorite for Welsh poet Dylan Thomas. And Francis Ford Coppola reportedly sat down at a back table to work on *The Godfather.* A painting depicts *Homo beatnikus,* and there's even an advertisement for a do-it-yourself beatnik makeover (kit including sunglasses, a black beret, and poem).

Another righteous place to hide is **Tosca,** 242 Columbus (between Broadway and Pacific), 415/391-1244, a late-night landmark with gaudy walls and comfortable Naugahyde booths where the hissing of the espresso machine competes with Puccini on the jukebox. Writers of all varieties still migrate here, sometimes to play pool in back. But you must behave yourself: Bob Dylan and Allen Ginsberg got thrown out of here for being unruly. **Cafe Malvina,** 1600 Stockton (at Union), 415/391-1290, is a good bet, too, especially for early-morning pastries with your coffee.

Serious social history students should also peek into the **Condor Cafe,** 300 Columbus (at Broadway), 415/781-8222, the onetime Condor Club made famous by stripper Carol Doda and her silicone-enhanced mammaries, now a run-of-the-mill sports bar. Still, the place offers a memory of the neighborhood's sleazier heyday. Other neighborhood perversion palaces, survivors of the same peep-show mentality, are becoming fewer and farther between, and in any event aren't all that interesting.

Nightlife

Opened in 1931, **Bimbo's 365 Club,** 1025 Columbus (between Chestnut and Francisco), 415/474-0365, retains its old-time supper club

POETIC AMUSEMENTS

There's probably only one thing better than reading a good poem in a quiet room by yourself. And that's listening to an impassioned poet reading a poem out loud in a small coffee-scented café full of attentive writers, lawyers, bikers, teachers, computer programmers, divinity students, musicians, secretaries, drug addicts, cooks, and assorted oddball others who all love poetry and are hanging onto every word being juggled by the poet behind the microphone. The only thing better than *that* is to read your own poems at an open-mike poetry reading.

One of the wonderful things about San Francisco and vicinity is that this kind of poetic melee takes place in some café, club, or bookstore almost every night, for those who know where to look. No one revels in the right to free speech like Bay Area denizens, and open poetry readings are as popular as stand-up comedy in many cafés and clubs, with sign-up lists at the door. Bring your own poetry, or just kick back and listen to some amazing musings.

The following suggested venues will get you started. Since schedules for local poetic license programs do change, it's prudent to call or otherwise check it out before setting out. Current open readings and other events are listed in the monthly tabloid *Poetry Flash,* 510/525-5476, www.poetryflash.org, the Bay Area's definitive poetry review and literary calendar, available free at many bookstores and cafés.

—*Ed Aust*

Open-Mike Poetry Readings in San Francisco
Brainwash Cafe and Laundromat, 1122 Folsom St., 415/864-3842
Keane's 3300 Club, 3300 Mission St. (at 29th), 415/826-6886

In the East Bay
Diesel—A Bookstore, 5433 College Ave. (between Lawton and Hudson), Oakland, 510/653-9965
La Val's Pizza and Subterranean Theatre, 1834 Euclid Ave. (at Hearst), Berkeley, 510/843-5617

atmosphere. Bimbo's hosts live music most nights, and if you get there early you can settle into one of the plush red booths lining the stage. The crowd varies according to the band. A fairly inexpensive hot spot, on the site of an old Barbary Coast saloon, is the **San Francisco Brewing Company,** 155 Columbus (between Jackson and Pacific), 415/434-3344, known for its hearty home brews. **The Saloon,** 1232 Grant (at Columbus), 415/989-7666, across from Caffe Trieste at Grant and Fresno Alley, is the city's oldest pub, circa 1861. It's a bit scruffy, but still hosts what's happening after all these years (stiff drinks and blues bands, mostly). **Specs 12 Adler Museum Cafe,** across from Vesuvio at 12 Adler Place (off Columbus, between Broadway and Pacific), 415/421-4112, open daily after 4:30 or 5 P.M., is also a treasure trove-cum-watering hole of eclectic seafaring and literary clutter.

Perhaps destined for a long-lasting run is "Beach Blanket Babylon" at **Club Fugazi,** 678 Green St. (at Powell), 415/421-4222, song-and-dance slapstick of a very contemporary high-camp cabaret style, where even favorite Broadway tunes end up brutally (and hilariously) twisted. Thematic and seasonal changes, like the Christmas revue, make this babbling Babylon worthy of return visits—especially to see what they'll create next in the way of 50-pound decorative headdresses.

ⓜ TELEGRAPH HILL AND COIT TOWER

The best way to get to Telegraph Hill—whether just for the view, to appreciate the city's hanging gardens, or to visit Coit Tower—is to climb the hill yourself, starting up the very steep stairs at Kearny and Filbert or ascending more gradually from the east, via either the Greenwich or Filbert steps. Following Telegraph Hill Blvd. as it winds its way from Lombard, from the west, is troublesome for drivers. Parking up top is scarce; especially on weekends you might sit for hours while you wait—just to park, mind you. A reasonable alternative is taking the #39-Coit bus from Fisherman's Wharf.

Lillie Hitchcock Coit had a fetish for firemen. As a child, she was saved from a fire that claimed two of her playmates. As a teenager, she spent much of her time with members of San Francisco's all-volunteer Knickerbocker Engine Company No. 5, usually tagging along on fire calls and eventually becoming the team's official mascot; she was even allowed to play poker and smoke cigars with the boys. Started in 1929, financed by a Coit bequest, and completed in 1933, Coit Tower was to be a lasting memorial to the firemen. Some people say its shape resembles the nozzle of a firehose, others suggest more sexual symbolism, but the official story is that the design by Arthur Brown was intended to look "equally artistic" from any direction. Coit

SUSAN SNYDER

Whatever its symbolism, Coit Tower offers great views and houses a striking collection of Depression-era frescoes.

Tower was closed to the public for many years, due to damage caused by vandalism and water leakage. After a major interior renovation, the tower is now open in all its original glory, so come decide for yourself what the tower symbolizes. Or just come for the view. From atop the 180-foot tower, which gets extra lift from its site on top of Telegraph Hill, you get a magnificent 360-degree view of the entire Bay Area. Coin-op telescopes allow you to get an even closer look. Coit Tower, 415/362-0808, is open daily 10 A.M.–6 P.M., until 9 P.M. in summer. Admission is free, technically, but there is a charge for the elevator ride to the top: $3.75 adults, $2.50 seniors, $1.50 children ages 6–12.

Another reason to visit Coit Tower is to appreciate the marvelous Depression-era Social Realist interior mural art in the lobby, recently restored and as striking as ever. (At last report, seven of the 27 total frescoes, those on the second floor and along the narrow stairway, weren't available for general public viewing, since quarters are so close that scrapes from handbags and shoes are almost inevitable. You can see these murals on the Saturday guided tour.) Even in liberal San Francisco, many of these murals have been controversial, depicting as they do the drudgery, sometimes despair, behind the idyllic facade of modern California life—particularly as seen in the lives of the state's agricultural and industrial workforce. Financed through Franklin Roosevelt's New Deal-era Public Works Art Project, some 25 local artists set out in 1934 to paint Coit Tower's interior with frescoes, the same year that Diego Rivera's revolutionary renderings of Lenin and other un-American icons created such a scandal at New York's Rockefeller Center that the great Mexican painter's work was destroyed.

In tandem with tensions produced by a serious local dock worker's strike, some in San Francisco almost exploded when it was discovered that the new art in Coit Tower wasn't entirely politically benign, that some of it suggested less than total support for pro-capitalist ideology. In various scenes, one person is carrying *Das Kapital* by Karl Marx, and another is reading a copy of the Communist-party *Daily Worker;* grim-faced "militant unemployed" march forward into the future; women wash clothes by hand within sight of Shasta Dam; slogans oppose both hunger and fascism; and a chauffeured limousine is clearly contrasted with a Model T Ford in Steinbeck's Joad-family style. Even a hammer and sickle made it onto the walls. Unlike New York, even after an outraged vigilante committee threatened to chisel away Coit Tower's artistic offenses, San Francisco ultimately allowed it all to stay—everything, that is, except the hammer and sickle.

Another Telegraph Hill delight: the intimate gardens along the eastern steps. The **Filbert Steps** stairway gardens are lined with trees, ivy, and garden flowers, with a few terraces and benches nearby. Below Montgomery St., the Filbert stairway becomes a bit doddering—unpainted tired wood that leads to enchanting Napier Ln., one of San Francisco's last wooden-plank streets and a Victorian survivor of the city's 1906 devastation. (Below Napier, the stairway continues on to Sansome Street.) The brick-paved **Greenwich Steps** wander down to the cliff-hanging Julius' Castle restaurant, then continue down to the right, appearing to be private stairs to the side yard, weaving past flower gardens and old houses to reach Sansome. If you go up one way, be sure to come down the other.

RUSSIAN HILL

Also one of San Francisco's rarer pleasures is a stroll around Russian Hill, named for the belief that Russian sea otter hunters picked this place to bury their dead. One of the city's early bohemian neighborhoods and a preferred haunt for writers and other connoisseurs of quiet beauty, Russian Hill today is an enclave of the wealthy. But anyone can wander the neighborhood. If you come from North Beach, head up—it's definitely up— Vallejo St., where the sidewalks and the street eventually give way to stairs. Take a break at **Ina Coolbrith Park** at Taylor, named in honor of California's first poet laureate, a woman remarkable for many accomplishments. A member of one of Jim Beckwourth's westward wagon trains, she was the first American child to enter California by wagon. After an unhappy marriage, Coolbrith came to San Francisco, where she

wrote poetry and created California's early literary circle. Many men fell in love with her, the ranks of the hopelessly smitten including Ambrose Bierce, Bret Harte, and Mark Twain. (She refused to marry any of them.) Librarian for both the Bohemian Club and the Oakland Free Library, at the latter Coolbrith took 12-year-old Jack London under her wing; her tutelage and reading suggestions were London's only formal education. Up past the confusion of lanes at Russian Hill's first summit is **Florence Street,** which heads south, and still more stairs, these leading down to Broadway (the original Broadway, which shows why the city eventually burrowed a new Broadway under the hill). Coolbrith's last home on Russian Hill still stands at 1067 Broadway.

To see the second summit—technically the park at Greenwich and Hyde—and some of the reasons why TV and movie chase scenes are frequently filmed here, wander west and climb aboard the Hyde-Powell cable car. Worth exploration on the way up: Green St., Macondray Ln. just north of Jones (which eventually takes you down to Taylor Street), and **Filbert Street,** San Francisco's steepest driveable hill, a 31.5-degree grade. (To test that thesis yourself, go very slowly.) Just over the summit, as you stare straight toward Fisherman's Wharf, is another wonder of road engineering: the one-block stretch of Lombard St. between Hyde and Leavenworth, known as the **Crookedest Street in the World.** People do drive down this snake-shaped cobblestone path, a major tourist draw, but it's much more pleasant as a walk.

FISHERMAN'S WHARF

San Francisco's fishing industry and other port-related businesses were once integral to the city's cultural and economic life. Fisherman's Wharf, which extends from Pier 39 to the municipal pier just past Aquatic Park, was originally the focus of this waterfront commerce. Early on, Chinese fishermen pulled ashore their catch, followed in time by Italian fisherme over the territory. After World War 1 the city's fishing industry declined dr:

San Francisco

the result of both accelerated pollution of San Francisco Bay and decades of overfishing. Today, Fisherman's Wharf has largely become a carnival-style diversion for tourists. Nevertheless, beyond the shopping centers, arcade amusements, and oddball museums, a small fishing fleet struggles to survive.

Pier 39

At Beach St. and Embarcadero, Pier 39 offers schlock par excellence. If you don't mind jostling with the schools of tourists like some sort of biped sardine, you're sure to find *something* here that interests you. But this place really isn't about San Francisco—it's about shopping and otherwise spending your vacation wad. And you could have done that at home.

Unusual stores include the **Disney Store,** selling licensed Disney merchandise; the **Warner Bros. Studio Store,** offering meep-meeps, cwazy wabbits, and the like; the **NFL Shop,** hawking official 49er jerseys and other pigskin paraphernalia; the **College Shop,** selling campus items from schools across the country; and **The Sunken Treasure Museum Store,** displaying artifacts collected by Fisher on his shipwreck dives.

Great fun is the new **San Francisco Carousel,** $2 per ride, handcrafted in Italy and painstakingly hand-painted to depict famous San Francisco landmarks, from the Golden Gate Bridge and Coit Tower to Pier 39's ever-popular California sea lions. At **Turbo Ride Simulation Theatre,** 415/392-8313, you'll be thrown around in your spastic, hydraulically controlled seat in perfect time with what's happening on the big screen before you; think armchair Indiana Jones (and three similar adventure scenarios). Open daily. Summer hours are Sun.–Thurs. 10 A.M.–9:30 P.M., Friday 10 A.M.–11 P.M.; Sat. 10 A.M.–midnight. The rest of the year, it's open Sun.–Thurs. 10:30 A.M.–8:30 P.M., Fri.–Sat. 10 A.M.–10 P.M. Admission is $9 general, $6 seniors/children under 12. And at **Aquarium of the Bay,** 415/623-5300, you can travel through a 300-foot-long acrylic tube on a moving walkway, looking out on schools of glittering anchovies, stingrays, leopard sharks, and other sea creatures swimming through the 700,000-gallon Pier 39 Aquarium. Aquarium of the Bay is open daily 10 A.M.–6 P.M.; extended summer hours. Admission is $12.95 adults, $6.50 seniors, $6.50 children 3–11.

No, you won't lack for attractions to take your money at Pier 39. But for free you can spend time watching the lolling **sea lions** out on the docks, a fairly recent invasion force. The docks once served as a marina full of pleasure boats—until the sea lions started making themselves at home. It turned out to be a futile effort trying to chase them off, so the powers that be decided to abandon the marina idea and let the pinnipeds (up to 600 of them in the peak Jan.–Feb. herring season) have their way, becoming a full-time tourist attraction. Score: Sea Lions 1, Yachties 0.

Most shops at the pier are open daily 10:30 A.M.–8:30 P.M. Hours are longer in summer. For more information, call 415/981-7437, or look up www.pier39.com online. Also here are the **Blue & Gold Fleet** ferries to Alcatraz and elsewhere around the bay.

Pier 45

Don't miss the free **Amusing America** museum exhibit at Pier 45, at the foot of Taylor Street, offered up by San Francisco Museum and Historical Society. This celebration of amusement parks, this "roller coaster ride into history," covers it all, from the 1880s Gilded Age to the 1950s, from dance pavilions, arcades, and "swimming baths" to amusements parks and world's fairs. This exploration of such a democratizing cultural force—bringing together, as it does, people who might otherwise never meet in public—understandably emphasizes San Francisco's playful past. Visitors stroll right through the gap-toothed mouth of Laughing Sal, of the famed Musée Mécanique, formerly at the Cliff House, now at home here.

Along Jefferson Street

A culinary treat on the Wharf, especially in December or at other times during the mid-November-to-June season, is fresh **Dungeness crab.** You can pick out your own, live or already cooked, from the vendor stands, or head for any of the more famous Italian-style seafood restaurants here: **Alioto's, Franciscan Restaurant, Sabella's,** or the excellent and locally favored **Scoma's,** hidden slightly away from the tourist hordes on Pier 47 (near the intersection of Jones and Jefferson), 415/771-4383.

If you're in the mood for still more entertainment, Fisherman's Wharf offers a wacky variety. **Musée Méchanique,** on Pier 45 at Jefferson, 415/346-2000, is a delightful and dusty collection of penny arcade amusements (most cost a quarter)—from nickelodeons and coin-eating music boxes to fortune-telling machines. Open Mon.–Fri. 11 A.M.–7 P.M., Fri.–Sat. 10 A.M.–8 P.M. Admission free. **Ripley's Believe It Or Not! Museum,** 175 Jefferson St. (near Taylor), 415/771-6188, features both bizarre and beautiful items—including a two-headed cow, a shrunken head, and other grotesqueries—collected during Robert L. Ripley's global travels. Open Sun.–Thurs. 10 A.M.–10 P.M., Fri.–Sat. 10 A.M.–midnight. Admission $10.95 adults, $8.95 seniors, and $7.95 children. And the **Wax Museum at Fisherman's Wharf** is back, 145 Jefferson, 800/439-4305, www.waxmuseum.com, open weekdays 10 A.M.–9 P.M. and weekends 9 A.M.–11 P.M., $12.95 adults, $6.95 children. Stars waxing eloquent here include Robin Williams, Keanu Reeves, Ricky Martin, and an all-American Britney Spears.

Around Ghirardelli Square

You can also shop till you drop at elegant **Ghirardelli Square,** 900 North Point (Beach and Larkin), 415/775-5500, a complex of 50-plus shops and restaurants where you can get one of the best hot fudge sundaes anywhere, or **The Cannery,** 2801 Leavenworth (at Beach), 415/771-3112, another huge theme shopping center, this one offering outdoor street artist performances as well as the **Museum of the City of San Francisco,** 415/928-0289; and **Cobb's Comedy Club,** 415/928-4320. Beer and wine lovers will be intoxicated at The Cannery just checking out the offerings of **The Wine Cellar** 415/673-0400, with daily wine-tastings

11 A.M.–7 P.M., and **Jack's Cannery Bar,** 415/931-6400, a restaurant and bar featuring 110 different beers on tap. Time-honored for imports and the occasional bargain is the nearby **Cost Plus,** 2552 Taylor (at North Point).

Quieter, less commercial pleasures are also available along Fisherman's Wharf—a stroll through **Aquatic Park** perhaps, or fishing out on **Municipal Pier.**

San Francisco Maritime National Historical Park

Historic ships and a first-rate maritime museum make up the core of this national park on the west end of Fisherman's Wharf. To get oriented, first stop by the park's **National Maritime Museum of San Francisco** in Aquatic Park at Beach and Polk, 415/561-7100, open daily 10 A.M.–5 P.M., free admission. The double-decker building itself looks like an art deco ocean liner. Washed ashore inside are some excellent displays, from model ships and figureheads to historic photos and exhibits on fishing boats, ferries, and demonstrations of the sailor's arts. The newest permanent exhibit is the interactive *Sparks, Waves & Wizards: Communication at Sea,* which tracks maritime communications history from semaphore to satellite and includes a walk-in re-creation of a radio room on a 1943 Victory ship. The affiliated **J. Porter Shaw Library,** 415/556-9870, housed along with the park's administrative offices west of Fisherman's Wharf in Building E at Fort Mason (a reasonable walk away along a bike/pedestrian path), preserves most of the Bay Area's documented boat history, including oral histories, logbooks, photographs, and shipbuilding plans.

Not easy to miss at the foot of Hyde St. are the **Hyde Street Pier Historic Ships,** 415/561-7100, an always-in-progress collection that is also part of the national park. Admission $5 adults, free for visitors under 17. Here you can clamber across the decks and crawl through the colorfully cluttered holds of some of America's most historic ships.

The Hyde Street fleet's flagship is the three-masted 1886 schooner *Balclutha,* a veteran of twice-annual trips between California and the British Isles via Cape Horn. Others include the sidewheel *Eureka* (the world's largest passenger ferry in her day, built to ferry trains), the 1915 steam schooner *Wapama,* the oceangoing tugboat *Hercules,* the British-built, gold rush-era paddlewheel tug *Eppleton Hall,* the scow schooner *Alma,* and the three-masted lumber schooner *C.A. Thayer.* Also among the collection, but berthed at Pier 45, is the **U.S.S.** *Pampanito,* 415/775-1943, a tight-quarters Balao-class World War II submarine that destroyed or damaged many Japanese vessels and also participated in the tragic sinking of the Japanese *Kachidoki Maru* and *Rayuyo Maru,* which were carrying Australian and British prisoners of war.

Tagging along on a ranger-led tour (complete with "living history" adventures in summer) is the best way to get your feet wet at this national park. Call for tour schedule (guided tours are usually offered daily). But self-guided tours are available anytime the pier is open, which is daily 9:30 A.M.–6 P.M. year-round (until 8 P.M. in summer); open for all major holidays. Special activities give you the chance to sing sea chanteys, raise sails, watch the crews "lay aloft," or participate in the Dead Horse Ceremony—wherein the crowds heave a horse doll overboard and shout "May the sharks have his body, and the devil have his soul!"

SS Jeremiah O'Brien

Berthed at Pier 45, this massive 441-foot-long World War II Liberty Ship made 11 crossings from England to the beaches of Normandy to support the Allied invasion. It even returned to Normandy for the 50th anniversary of D-Day. The ship is still powered by its original engines. In fact, the engine-room scenes in the movie *Titanic* were filmed here.

The historic ship is open for self-guided tours year-round, daily 10 A.M.–5 P.M.; admission is $8 adults, $6 seniors/military, $4 children 6–12, children under 6 free. In addition, the ship makes several day-long cruises each year; rates start at around $100 per person. For more information or for cruise schedule and reservations, call 415/544-0100.

MARINA DISTRICT, COW HOLLOW, AND PACIFIC HEIGHTS

The neat pastel homes of the respectable **Marina District,** tucked in between Fort Mason and the Presidio, disguise the fact that the entire area is essentially unstable. Built on landfill, in an area once largely bay marsh, the Mediterranean-style Marina was previously the 63-acre site of the Panama-Pacific International Exposition of 1915—San Francisco's statement to the world that it had been reborn from the ashes of the 1906 earthquake and fire. So it was ironic, and fitting, that the fireboat *Phoenix* extinguished many of the fires that blazed here following the 1989 earthquake, which caused disproportionately heavy damage in this district.

The Marina's main attractions are those that surround it—primarily the neighborhood stretch of San Francisco's astounding shoreline Golden Gate National Recreation Area, which includes the **Fort Mason** complex of galleries, museums, theaters, and nonprofit cultural and conservation organizations. (For more information on the park and its many facets, see Golden Gate National Recreation Area below.) If you're in the neighborhood and find yourself near the yacht harbor, do wander out to see (and hear) the park's wonderful **Wave Organ** just east of the yacht club on Bay Street. Built of pieces from an old graveyard, the pipes are powered by sea magic. (The siren song is loudest at high tide.) Then wander west toward the Golden Gate Bridge on the **Golden Gate Promenade,** which meanders the three-plus miles from Aquatic Park and along the Marina Green—popular with kite fliers, well-dressed dog walkers, and the area's many exercise freaks—to Civil War-era **Fort Point.** (Be prepared for wind and fog.) The truly ambitious can take a hike across the bridge itself, an awesome experience.

Exhausted by nature, retreat to more sheltered attractions near the Presidio, including the remnants of the spectacular Panama-Pacific International Exhibition of 1915, the Bernard Maybeck-designed **Palace of Fine Arts,** and the indescribable **Exploratorium** inside, fun

SUSAN SNYDER

the Palace of Fine Arts

for children of all ages and a first-rate science museum.

Separating the Marina District from high-flying Pacific Heights is the low-lying neighborhood of **Cow Hollow,** a onetime dairy farm community now noted for its chic **Union Street** shopping district—an almost endless string of bars, cafés, coffeehouses, bookstores, and boutiques stretching between Van Ness and Steiner. Not to be outdone, the Marina boasts its own version: **Chestnut Street.** Other chic areas have included upper **Fillmore Street** near the Heights (and near the still-surviving 1960s icon, the **Fillmore** concert hall, at Geary and Fillmore), and outer **Sacramento Street** near Presidio Avenue. (Who knows where the next trendy block will crop up? The fashion fates are fickle.) **Pacific Heights** proper is the hilltop home pasture for the city's well-shod blue bloods. Its striking streets, Victorian homes, and general architectural wealth are well worth a stroll. Especially noteworthy here is the **Haas-Lilienthal House,** 2007 Franklin (at Jackson), 415/441-3004, a handsome and huge Queen Anne Victorian featured

on A&E's America's Castles' *Castles by the Bay,* a survivor of the 1906 earthquake and the city's only fully furnished Victorian open for regular public tours. Tours are usually conducted Wed., Sat., and Sun.; call for times. Admission is $5 adults, $3 seniors and children.

In the Cow Hollow neighborhood, don't miss the unusual 1861 **Octagon House,** 2645 Gough (at Union), 415/441-7512, owned by the National Society of Colonial Dames of America; it's now restored and fully furnished in colonial and federal period antiques. Open only on the second and fourth Thursday and the second Sunday of each month from noon–3 P.M.(closed in January and on holidays). Call to request special tour times. Donations greatly appreciated.

Exploratorium

Scientific American considers this the "best science museum in the world." Good Housekeeping says it's the "number one science museum in the U.S." It's definitely worth spending some time here. Inside the Palace of Fine Arts, 3601 Lyon St. (at Bay), 415/397-5673, www.exploratorium.edu,

COCKTAIL TIME

Sometimes you just need to cast out those sturdy shoes and the sightseeing parka to join what used to be known as the "jet set" to toast the high life. The following establishments offer a sample of that old San Francisco sparkle.

The revamped classic **Redwood Room**, 495 Geary St. (at Taylor) at the Clift Hotel, 415/775-4700, in the heart of the theater district and just two blocks from bustling Union Square, is something to behold. The Redwood Room is such a sentimental favorite that Save the Redwood Room kept its collective eye on Studio 54 and Royalton hotel king Ian Shrager's renovations, careful that the makeover did not include stripping the walls hewn of 2,000-foot redwood trees. As a concession, the walls remain, and the hunting lodge decor was updated with plasma-screen portraits that move subtly over time, elevating the idea to a highly stylized level of perfection. The crowd of fashion victims occupying chairs and couches ranging from leather numbers to velvet smoking chairs somehow enhances the overall effect, although drinks here are not cheap—a straight shot will set you back $9.

The **Tonga Room** at 950 Mason St. (between California and Sacramento), 415/772-5278, opened its exotic doors in 1945 inside the Fairmont Hotel to bring the Pacific Islander theme to San Francisco. Polynesian decor and thatch-roofed huts surround a deep blue lake, where simulated tropical rainstorms hit every half-hour. The lethal Bora Bora Horror tops the list of intriguing frozen cocktails, combining rum, banana liqueur, and Grand Marnier with a huge slice of pineapple. Rum also features in the Hurricane, Lava Bowl, and the Zombie. Happy hour offers the most economical visit possible. Nor-

---

the Exploratorium is billed as a museum of science, art, and human perception, and is ostensibly designed for children. But this is no mass-marketed media assault on the senses, no mindless theatrical homage to simple fantasy. The truth is, adults also adore the Exploratorium, a wonderfully intelligent playground built around the mysterious natural laws of the universe.

The Exploratorium was founded in 1969 by physicist and educator Dr. Frank Oppenheimer, the original "Explainer" (as opposed to "teacher"), whose research career was abruptly ended during the blacklisting McCarthy era. Brother of J. Robert Oppenheimer (father of the atomic bomb), Frank Oppenheimer's scientific legacy was nonetheless abundant.

"Explaining science and technology without props," said Oppenheimer, "is like attempting to tell what it is like to swim without ever letting a person near the water." The Exploratorium was the original interactive science museum and influenced the establishment of hundreds of other such museums in the U.S. and abroad. Its 650-some three-dimensional exhibits delve into 13 broad subject areas: animal behavior, language, vision, sound and hearing, touch, heat and temperature, electricity, light, color, motion, patterns, waves and resonance, and weather. Everything can be experienced—from a touch-sensitive plant that shrinks from a child's probing hand, to strategically angled mirrors that create infinite reflections of the viewer; from tactile computerized fingerpainting to the wave-activated voice of the San Francisco Bay, as brought to you by the "Wave Organ." The extra special **Tactile Dome**, 415/561-0362 (reservations recommended), provides a pitch-black environment in which your vision is of no use, but your sense of touch gets a real workout.

Stock up on educational toys, games, experiments, and oddities at the Exploratorium Store. Especially worth purchasing, for teachers and brave parents alike, is the Exploratorium Science Snackbook, which includes instructions on building home or classroom versions of more than 100 Exploratorium exhibits.

The Exploratorium is open in summer daily 10 A.M.–6 P.M. (Wednesday until 9 P.M.). The rest of the year, hours are Tues.–Sun. 10 A.M.–5 P.M. (Wednesday until 9 P.M.). On the first Wednesday of each month, admission is free. Otherwise it's $10 adults, $7.50 seniors/students with ID, $6

mally pricey drinks cost $6, and you can graze on a buffet of edible treats (egg rolls, pot stickers, and dim sum) while listening to the house band's forgettable elevator music.

The drinkery at the **Top of the Mark,** 999 California St. (at Mason), 415/392-3434, is the city's most famous view lounge, an ideal place to take friends and dazzle them with the lights of San Francisco. Large windows offer a panorama of San Francisco's landmarks, from the Sutro Tower to the Transamerica Pyramid and the Golden Gate Bridge. There's live music every night, and given the ritzy setting, a $5–10 cover charge doesn't seem all that steep. Classic cocktails—Manhattans, sidecars, and Martinis—are the libations of choice. The bar food is upscale and excellently prepared, with selections ranging from a Mediterranean platter to Beluga caviar.

The word "cocktail" practically whispers from behind the ruby red silk curtains at the glamorous **Starlight Room** at 450 Powell St. (between Post and Sutter), 415/395-8595, perched on the 21st floor of the 1928 Sir Francis Drake Hotel. Polished mahogany fixtures, luxurious furnishings, and a 360-degree view of the city make the Starlight Room one of the nicest cocktail experiences going. The spacious bar, mahogany dance floor, and live music by Harry Denton's Starlight Orchestra, draw an upbeat crowd of young and old couples dressed to the nines for a night out on the town. Light supper options range from pan-roasted crab cakes to oysters on the half-shell. All of this dazzle is surprisingly affordable, with a small evening cover charge and cocktails $7–10.

—*Pat Reilly*

youths 6–17, and children 4 and under free. Admission to the Tactile Dome is $14 per person, which includes museum admission.

THE AVENUES
Richmond District and Vicinity

Originally called San Francisco's Great Sand Waste, then the city's cemetery district (before the bones were dug up and shipped south to Colma in 1914), today the Richmond District is a middle-class ethnic sandwich built upon Golden Gate Park and topped by Lincoln Park and the Presidio. White Russians were the first residents, fleeing Russia after the 1917 revolution, but just about everyone else followed. A stroll down **Clement Street,** past its multiethnic eateries and shops, should bring you up to speed on the subject of cultural diversity.

The area between Arguello and Park Presidio, colloquially called "New Chinatown," is noted for its good, largely untouristed Asian eateries and shops. Russian-Americans still park themselves on the playground benches at pretty **Mountain Lake Park** near the Presidio. And the gold-painted onion domes of the Russian Orthodox

Russian Holy Virgin Cathedral of the Church in Exile, 6210 Geary Blvd., along with the Byzantine-Roman Jewish Reform **Temple Emanu-El** at Arguello and Lake (technically in Pacific Heights), offer inspiring architectural reminders of earlier days.

Highlights of the Richmond District include the **University of San Francisco** atop Lone Mountain, an institution founded by the Jesuits in 1855, complete with spectacular **St. Ignatius** church, and the **Neptune Society Columbarium,** 1 Loraine Ct. (just off Anza near Stanyan), 415/221-1838 or 415/752-7891, the final resting place of old San Francisco families including the newspaper Hearsts and department store Magnins. With its ornate neoclassical and copper-roofed rotunda, the Columbarium offers astounding acoustics, best appreciated from the upper floors. The building is open to the public weekdays 9 A.M.–5 P.M., weekends 10 A.M.–2 P.M.

Seacliff, an exclusive seaside neighborhood nestled between the Presidio and Lincoln Park, is the once-rural community where famed California photographer **Ansel Adams** was raised. West of Seacliff, **Land's End** is the city's most rugged coastline, reached via footpath from Lincoln Park and the Golden Gate National Recreation Area. **China Beach,** just below Seacliff, was probably named for Chinese immigrants trying to evade Angel Island internment by jumping ship, all a result of the Exclusion Act in effect from the 1880s to World War II. During the Civil War, this was the westernmost point of the nation's antislavery "Underground Railroad." You can swim here—facilities include a lifeguard station plus changing rooms, showers, restrooms—but the water's brisk. Northeast is **Baker Beach,** considered the city's best nude beach.

California Palace of the Legion of Honor

The area's main attraction, though, just beyond Lincoln Park's Municipal Golf Course, is the **California Palace of the Legion of Honor,** on Legion of Honor Drive (enter off 34th and Clement), 415/750-3600 (office) or 415/863-3330 (visitor hot line), www.famsf.org. Established by French-born Alma de Bretteville Spreckels, wife of the city's sugar king, this handsome hilltop palace was built in honor of American soldiers killed in France during World War I. It's a 1920 French neoclassic, from the colonnades and triumphal arch to the outdoor equestrian bronzes. Intentionally incongruous, placed out near the parking lot in an otherwise serene setting, is George Segal's testimony to the depths of human terror and terrorism: the barbed wire and barely living bodies of *The Holocaust.* Also here are some original bronze castings from Rodin, including *The Thinker* and *The Shades* outdoors, just part of the Legion's collection of more than 70 Rodin originals. Inside, the permanent collection was originally exclusively French, but now includes the M.H. de Young Museum's European collection—an awesome eight-century sweep from El Greco, Rembrandt, and Rubens to Renoir, Cézanne, Degas, Monet, and Manet. Take a docent-led tour for a deeper appreciation of other features, including the Legion's period rooms.

Special events include films, lectures, and painting and music programs, the latter including Rodin Gallery pipe organ concerts as well as chamber music, jazz, and historical instru-

THE CITYPASS

The money-saving **CityPass** provides admission to six of San Francisco's top attractions—California Academy of Sciences/Steinhart Aquarium, California Palace of the Legion of Honor, the Exploratorium, Museum of Modern Art, Muni and Cable Car 7-Day Passport, and a San Francisco Bay Cruise—for a price, at last report, half of what the individual admissions would cost: $34.95 adults, $25.75 youths 12–17. It's good for seven days and is available at any of the participating attractions, any of the city's visitor information centers, or at www.citypass.com.

ment concerts in the Florence Gould Theater. The Legion of Honor also features a pleasant café and a gift shop. Museum hours are Tues.–Sun. 9:30 A.M.–5 P.M., and until 8:45 P.M. on the first Saturday of every month. Admission is $8 adults, $6 seniors, $5 youths 12–17, free for children under 12 and free for everyone on the second Wednesday of each month. Admission may be higher during some visiting exhibitions.

The fit and fresh-air loving can get here on foot along the meandering **Coastal Trail**—follow it north from the Cliff House or south from the Golden Gate Bridge.

Sunset District

Most of San Francisco's neighborhoods are residential, streets of private retreat that aren't all that exciting except to those who live there. The Sunset District, stretching to the sea from south of Golden Gate Park, is one example, the southern section of the city's "Avenues." In summertime, the fog here at the edge of the continent is usually unrelenting, so visitors often shiver and shuffle off, muttering that in a place called "Sunset" one should be able to see it. (To appreciate the neighborhood name, come anytime *but* summer.) The golden gates, both the city and national parks, offer delights and diversions at the fringe. For beach access and often gray-day seaside recreation, from surfing and surf fishing to cycling, walking, and jogging (there's a paved path), follow the **Great Highway** south from Cliff House and stop anywhere along the way.

Stanyan Street, at the edge of the Haight and east of Golden Gate Park, offers odd and attractive shops, as does the stretch of **Ninth Avenue** near Irving and Judah. Just south of the park at its eastern edge is the **University of California at San Francisco Medical Center** atop Mt. Sutro, the small eucalyptus forest here reached via cobblestone Edgewood Ave. or, for the exercise, the Farnsworth Steps. From here, look down on the colorful Haight or north for a bird's-eye view of the **Richmond District,** the rest of the city's Avenues. **Stern Grove,** at Sloat Blvd. and 19th Ave., is a wooded valley beloved for its Sunday concerts.

Other good stops in the area include large **Lake Merced** just south, accessible via Skyline Blvd. (Hwy. 35) or Lake Merced Blvd., once a tidal lagoon. These days it's a freshwater lake popular for canoeing, kayaking, nonmotorized boating (rent boats at the Boat House on Harding), fishing (largemouth bass and trout), or just getting some fresh air.

The Lake Merced area offers one of the newer sections of the **Bay Area Ridge Trail,** a hiking route (signed with blue markers at major turning points and intersections) that one day will total 400 miles and connect 75 parks on ridgelines surrounding the San Francisco Bay. For more information, contact the **Bay Area Ridge Trail Council,** 1007 General Kennedy Avenue, Suite 3, San Francisco, CA 94129, 415/561-2695, www.ridgetrail.org. Farther south still is **Fort Funston,** a onetime military installation on barren cliffs, a favorite spot for hang gliders and a good place to take Fido for an outing (dogs can be off-leash along most of the beach here). East of Lake Merced are **San Francisco State University,** one of the state university system's best—noted for its **Sutro Library** and **American Poetry Archives**— and the residential **Ingleside,** home to a 26-foot-tall sundial, built as the focal point of the upper-income Ingleside Terraces community in 1913.

San Francisco Zoo

Located between Lake Merced and Ocean Beach, the San Francisco Zoo, 1 Zoo Rd. (Sloat Blvd. At 45th Ave.), 415/753-7061, www.sfzoo.org, isn't considered one of the best zoos in the country, but it has all the animal attractions expected of a major facility, including the Primate Discovery Center and Gorilla World, one of the largest naturalistic gorilla exhibits in the zoo world. The Lion House is home to majestic African lions and highly endangered Siberian and Sumatran tigers (Mealtime for the big cats, 2 P.M. every day except Monday, is quite a viewing treat). Other attractions include The Koala Station, based on an Australian outback station and home to six koalas, the Lemur Forest, which mimics their old-growth forest habitat in Madagascar, and Penguin Island, fashioned after the Patagonian coast of South America, and the setting for a colony of 40 Magellanic penguins. There's also a children's petting zoo, where children can feed the goats, sheep, and Highland cow, and a gorgeous old-fashioned miniature steam train ($2), and nice open spaces for play and picnics. Open daily 10 A.M.–5 P.M.; admission is $10 adults, $7 seniors/youth 12–17, $4 children 3–11, and free on the first Wednesday of every month.

HAIGHT-ASHBURY

Aging hippies, random hipsters, and the hopelessly curious of all ages are still attracted to San Francisco's Haight-Ashbury, once a commercial district for adjacent Golden Gate Park and a solid family neighborhood in the vicinity of Haight Street. The Golden Gate's block-wide Panhandle (which certainly resembles one on a map) was intended as the park's carriage entrance, helped along toward the desired ambience by neighboring Victorian-age Queen Annes. Once abandoned by the middle class, however, Haight-Ashbury declined into the cheap-rent paradise surrounded by parklands that became "Hash-bury," "hippies," and headquarters for the 1967 Summer of Love.

Drawn here by the drum song of the coming-of-age Aquarian Age, some 200,000 young people lived in subdivided Victorian crash pads, on the streets, and in the parks that summer, culturally recognizable by long hair, scruffy jeans, tie-dyed T-shirts, granny glasses, peace signs, beads, and the flowers-in-your-hair style of flowing skirts and velvet dresses. Essential, too, at that time: underground newspapers and unrestrained radio, black-lights and psychedelia, incense, anything that came from India (like gurus), acid and mescaline, hashish, waterpipes, marijuana and multicolored rolling papers, harmonicas, tambourines, guitars, and bongo drums. A Volkswagen van was helpful, too, so loads of people could caravan off to anti–Vietnam War rallies, to wherever it was the Grateful Dead or Jefferson Airplane were playing (for free, usually), or to Fillmore West and Winterland, where Bill Graham staged so many concerts. It was all fairly innocent, at first, an innocence that didn't last. By late 1967, cultural predators had arrived: the tourists, the national media, and serious drug pushers and pimps. Love proved to be fragile. Most true believers headed back to the land, and Haight-Ashbury became increasingly violent and dangerous, especially for the young runaways who arrived (and still arrive) to stake a misguided claim for personal freedom.

"The Haight" today is considerably cleaner, its Victorian neighborhoods spruced up but not exactly gentrified. The classic Haight-Ashbury head shops are long gone, runaway hippies replaced by runaway punks panhandling for quarters (or worse). But Haight St. and vicinity is still hip, still socially and politically aware, still worth a stroll. The parkside Upper Haight stretch has more than its share of funky cafés, coffee shops, oddball bars and clubs, boutiques, and secondhand stores. If this all seems stodgy, amble on down to the Lower Haight in the Western Addition, an area fast becoming the city's new avant-garde district.

Upper Haight

Aside from the commercial versions, there are a few significant countercultural sights in the Upper Haight, like the old Victorian **Dead House** at 710 Ashbury (near Waller), where the Grateful Dead lived and played their still-living music (and possibly where the term "deadheads" first emerged for the Dead's fanatic fans), and the **Jefferson Airplane's** old pad at 2400 Fulton (on the eastern edge of Golden Gate Park at Willard).

Definitely worth a stop, for organic juice and granola, art to meditate by, and New Age computer networking, is **The Red Victorian** at 1665 Haight (near Belvedere), 415/864-1978, www.redvic.com, also a fascinating bed-and-breakfast complex that successfully honors The Haight's original innocence. Do climb on up the steep paths into nearby **Buena Vista Park,** a shocking tangle of anarchistically enchanted forest, just for the through-the-trees views.

Otherwise, the scene here is wherever you can find it. **Bound Together,** 1369 Haight St. (at Masonic), 415/431-8355, is a collective bookstore featuring a somewhat anarchistic collection: books on leftist politics, conspiracy theories, the occult, and sexuality. **Pipe Dreams,** 1376 Haight (at Masonic), 415/431-3553, is one place to go for Grateful Dead memorabilia and quaint drug paraphernalia, like water pipes and "bongs," but **Distractions,** 1552 Haight (between Clayton and Ashbury), 415/252-8751, is truest to the form; in addition to the Dead selection, you can also snoop through head shop supplies, an ample variety of Tarot cards, and Guatemalan clothing imports.

Shops

Style is another Haight St. specialty. Though secondhand clothing stores here tend to feature higher prices than elsewhere, three of the best are **Wasteland,** 1660 Haight (at Belvedere), 415/863-3150; the **Buffalo Exchange,** 1555 Haight (between Clayton and Ashbury), 415/431-7733; and **Aardvarks,** 1501 Haight (at Ashbury), 415/621-3141. For old-style music bargains—and actual albums, including a thousand hard-to-find ones—head to **Recycled Records,** 1377 Haight (at Masonic), 415/626-4075. For thousands of used CDs and tapes, try **Amoeba Music,** housed in a former bowling alley at 1855 Haight (between Stanyan and Shrader), 415/831-1200.

Shops of interest in the Lower Haight include: **Zebra Records,** 475 Haight (near Webster), 415/626-9145, a DJ supply store that's the place to find cutting-edge hip hop, acid jazz, and Latin House; the **Naked Eye,** 533 Haight (between Fillmore and Steiner), 415/864-2985, which specializes in impossible-to-find videos; and **Compound Records,** 597 Haight (at Steiner), 415/626-7855, which specializes in DJ gear and drum and bass records. Well respected in the neighborhood for organic personal decoration is **Love and Haight,** 252 Fillmore (between Haight and Waller), 415/861-9206. Shop the Lower Haight, too, for stylish used clothing stores with good pickings, low prices, and zero crowds.

Nightlife

In the 1980s and '90s, the Haight was known as a rock nightspot, but the Haight's pulse has slowed considerably in the last 20 years. The I-Beam, Kennel Club, and Nightbreak are no more, gone along with the street's ability to attract big talent. In their place, the Haight's comfortable bars make great hideouts from elbow-to-elbow crowds found elsewhere.

A laid-back bar popular with young and old is **The Gold Cane,** 1569 Haight St. (between Ashbury and Clayton), 415/626-1112, serving the cheapest drinks in town. More typical of modern Haight is the **Trophy Room,** 1811 Haight (between Shrader and Stanyan), 415/752-2971, full of self-styled hippies and punks as well as unusual combinations of leather jackets, long hair, and tattoos. **Martin Macks,** 1568 Haight (between Ashbury and Clayton), 415/864-0124, is cleaner, quieter, and a bit more upscale than the usual Haight bar scene, with at least 16imported beers on tap. Retro-swing bars are still quite popular in San Francisco, and **Club Deluxe,** 1511 Haight (at Ashbury), 415/552-6949, is one of the best.

Wilder by far are the bars and clubs in the Lower Haight. No matter what the weather, **Mad Dog in the Fog,** 530 Haight (between Fillmore and Steiner), 415/626-7279, is packed every night, the very mixed clientele attracted by the English pub-style dart boards as much as the live music. Across the street, serious drinking is the main agenda at the loud and boisterous **Toronado,** 547 Haight (between Fillmore and Webster), 415/863-2276. **Nickie's Haight Street BBQ,** 460 Haight (between Fillmore and Webster), 415/621-6508, serves barbecue by day, red-hot DJed dance music by night—everything

from hip-hop and salsa to world beat and the music of Islam. (And the bar jumps, too.) Quieter and perhaps a tad too self-conscious for this very natural neighborhood is the **Noc Noc,** 557 Haight (between Fillmore and Steiner), 415/861-5811, a cavelike, romantically gloomy environment simultaneously inspired by *The Flintstones* cartoons and *Star Trek* reruns. For genuine cultural inspiration, though, that now-gone mural of former president George H. W. Bush shooting up at The Kennel Club was a classic.

MISSION DISTRICT

Vibrant and culturally electric, the Mission District is one of San Francisco's most exciting neighborhoods. The fact that most tourists never discover the area's pleasures is a sad commentary on our times. To the same extent people fear that which seems foreign in America—a nation created by foreigners—they miss out on the experience of life as it is. And the country becomes even more hell-bent on mandating social homogenization despite ideals and rhetoric to the contrary.

On any given day in the Mission District, especially if it's sunny, the neighborhood is busy with the business of life. The largely Hispanic population—Colombian, Guatemalan, Mexican, Nicaraguan, Panamanian, Peruvian, Puerto Rican, Salvadorean—crowds the streets and congregates on corners. Whether Mission residents are out strolling with their children or shopping in the many bakeries, produce stores, and meat markets, the community's cultural energy is unmatched by any other city neighborhood—with the possible exception of Chinatown early in the morning. This remains true now that gentrification has arrived even in the Mission.

Before the arrival of the Spanish, the Bay Area's Ohlone people (they called themselves Ramaytush) established their largest settlement here in the sheltered expanse later known as Mission Valley. Largely uninhabited until the 1860s, the valley attracted a large number of Irish immigrants and became one of the city's first suburbs. Most of the Mission District was spared the total devastation otherwise characteristic in the fiery aftermath of

San Francisco

the 1906 earthquake, so some of San Francisco's finest Victorians are still area standouts.

Even with onrushing gentrification, the Mission's ungentrified modern attitude has created a haven for artists, writers, social activists, and politicos. The Latino arts scene is among the city's most powerful and original. This is one of San Francisco's newest New Bohemias, a cultural crazy quilt where artists and assorted oddballs are not only tolerated but encouraged. Symbolic of this new symbiosis is the **826 Valencia Writing Project** headquartered at McSweeney's literary journal and pirate supply store at 826 Valencia St., a project undertaken by Dave Eggers (author of *A Heartbreaking Work of Staggering Genius*) and other area writers to tutor and otherwise support literacy and constructive risk-taking in the neighborhod's at-risk kids. Businesses catering to this emerging consciousness are also becoming prominent along Valencia St., already considered home by the city's lesbian community.

Technically, the Mission District extends south from near the Civic Center to the vicinity of Cesar Chavez (Army). Dolores or Church St. (or thereabouts) marks the western edge, Alabama St. the eastern. Mission Street, the main thoroughfare (BART stations at 16th and 24th), is lined with discount stores and pawnshops. Main commercial areas include 16th St. between Mission and Dolores, 24th St. between Valencia and York, and Valencia St.—the bohemian center of social life, lined with coffeehouses, bars, bookstores, performance art venues, and establishments serving the lesbian and women's community. For the latest word on feminist and lesbian art shows, readings, performances, and other events, stop by the nonprofit **Women's Building,** 3543 18th St. (just off Valencia), 415/431-1180.

Mission Dolores

With the Mission District's return to a predominantly Hispanic ethnic attitude, a visit to the city's oldest structure seems especially fitting. Completed in 1791, Mission San Francisco de Asis at Dolores and 16th Streets, 415/621-8203, is open daily 9 A.M.–4:30 P.M. A donation of $2

Mission Dolores, the city's oldest structure

SUSAN SNYDER

or more is appreciated. (The best time to arrive, to avoid busloads of tourists and the crush of schoolchildren studying California history, is before 10 A.M.) This is the sixth mission established in California by the Franciscan fathers. Founded earlier, in 1776, the modest chapel and outbuildings came to be known as Mission Dolores, the name derived from a nearby lagoon and creek, Arroyo de Nuestra Señora de los Dolores, or "stream of our lady of sorrows."

And how apt the new shingle proved to be, in many ways. In the peaceful cemetery within the mission's walled compound is the "Grotto of Lourdes," the unmarked grave of more than 5,000 Ohlone and others among the native workforce. Most died of measles and other introduced diseases in the early 1800s, the rest from other varieties of devastation. After California became a state, the first U.S. Indian agent came to town to take a census of the Native American population. It was an easy count, since there was only one, a man named Pedro Alcantara who was still grieving for a missing son. Near the grotto are the vine-entwined tombstones of pioneers and prominent citizens, like California's first governor under Mexican rule, Don Luis Antonio Arguello, and San Francisco's first mayor, Don Francisco de Haro.

The sturdy mission chapel—the small humble structure, not the soaring basilica adjacent—survived the 1906 earthquake due largely to its four-foot-thick adobe walls. Inside, the painted ceilings are an artistic echo of the Ohlone, whose original designs were painted with vegetable dyes. And the simple altar offers stark contrast to the grandeur next door. In a surprise 2004 discovery, an entire wall of original Native American art, religious murals hidden from view since 1796, was discovered in a walled-off crawlspace behind the altar. For a peek at mission artifacts and memorabilia, visit the small museum.

Murals

The entire Mission District is vividly alive, with aromas and sounds competing everywhere with color. And nothing in the Mission District is quite as colorful as its mural art. More than 200 murals dot the neighborhood, ranging from brilliantly colored homages to work, families, and spiritual flight to boldly political attacks on the status quo.

Start with some **"BART art,"** at the 24th St. station, where Michael Rios' columns of humanoids lift up the rails. Another, particularly impressive set, is eight blocks down, off 24th St. on the fences and garage doors along **Balmy Alley,** and also at **Flynn Elementary School** at Precita and Harrison. At 14th and Natoma is a mural honoring Frida Kahlo, artist and wife of Diego Rivera.

Walking tours of the neighborhood murals (with well-informed guides) are led by the **Precita Eyes Mural Arts Center,** a charming gallery at 2981 24th St. (at Harrison), 415/285-2287, www.precita eyes.org. The tours are offered every Saturday and Sunday at 11 A.M. and 1:30 P.M.; $12 general, $5 seniors, $2 youths 18 and under. Call for information on the center's many other tours.

Other good art stops in the area include the nonprofit **Galeria de la Raza,** 2857 24th St. (at Bryant), 415/826-8009, www.galeriadelaraza.org, featuring some exciting, straight-ahead political art attacks; the affiliated **Studio 24** gift shop adjacent, with everything from books and clothing to religious icons and Day of the Dead dolls; and the **Mission Cultural Center for Latino Arts,** 2868 Mission (near BART between 24th and 25th Streets), 415/821-1155, www.mission culturalcenter.org, a community cultural and sociopolitical center that can supply you with more information on area artworks.

Potrero Hill

East of the Mission District proper and southeast of the SoMa scene is the gentrifying (at least on the north side), Noe Valley–like Potrero Hill, known for its roller-coaster road rides (a favorite spot for filming TV and movie chase scenes) and the world-famous **Anchor Brewing Company** microbrewery, 1705 Mariposa St. (at 17th), 415/863-8350, makers of Anchor Steam beer. Join a free weekday tour and see how San Francisco's famous beer is brewed. If you drive to Potrero Hill, detour to the "Poor Man's Lombard" at 20th and Vermont, which has earned the dubious honor of being the city's second most twisty street. This snakelike thoroughfare is not festooned with well-landscaped sidewalks and flowerbeds, but instead an odd assortment of abandoned furniture, beer bottles, and trash. Not yet socially transformed is the south side of the hill, which is close to **Bayview-Hunters Point;** these once-industrialized neighborhoods were left behind when World War II–era shipbuilding ceased and are now ravaged by poverty, drugs, and violence. Railroad buffs, please note: the Hunters Point Naval Shipyard is home to the **Golden Gate Railroad Museum,** 415/822-8728, www.ggrm.org, where (for a fee) you can drive your own full-size steam or diesel locomotive. Museum open weekends 10 A.M.–5 P.M., otherwise by appointment only.

Shops

For the most part Noe Valley's 24th St. is laid-back and boutiquey, a rare combination in San

San Francisco

AN OPEN-MINDED GUIDE TO
NIGHTCLUBBING IN SAN FRANCISCO

First, ask the basic questions: Who am I? What am I doing here? Where do I belong? To go nightclubbing in San Francisco, at least *ask* the questions. The answers don't really matter; your political, social, sexual, and musical preferences will be matched somewhere. Hip-hop, disco, new wave, house, fusion, industrial, world beat—whatever it is you're into, it's out there, just part of the creative carnival world of San Francisco nightclubbing. Everything goes, especially cultural taboos, leaving only freewheeling imaginations and an unadulterated desire to do one thing and only one thing—dance with total abandon. In the city, heteros, gays, lesbians, blacks, whites, Asians, and Latinos all writhe together, unified in a place where all prejudice drops away: the dance floor.

The hottest dance clubs come and go considerably faster than the Muni buses do, so the key to finding the hippest, most happening spot is to ask around. Ask people who look like they should know, such as young fashion junkies working in trendy clothing shops, used-record stores, or other abodes of pretentious cool.

Throbbing together with hundreds of other euphorics, experiencing ecstasy en masse, may be the closest we'll ever really get to living in one united world. Still, San Francisco nightclub virgins tend to avoid their initiation, somehow intimidated by the frenzied cosmic collision of electrifying lights, thumping dance tunes, and sweat-drenched bodies. But be not afraid. There are answers to even the three most common worries:

Worry: I can't dance. *Answer:* It wouldn't matter even if you could. The dance floors are so crowded, at best it's possible only to bounce up and down.

Worry: I'm straight (or gay) and the crowd seems to be predominantly gay (or straight). *Answer:* Since the limits of gender and sexuality are hopelessly blurred in San Francisco, and since nobody would care even if they weren't, just dump your angst and dance.

Worry: I'm afraid I'll look like a fool (feel out of place, be outclassed, fall down, throw up, whatever). *Answer:* As we said, nobody cares. You're totally anonymous, being one of more than 776,733 people in town. And no matter what you do, nobody will notice, since narcissism in San Francisco's clubs is at least as deep as the Grand Canyon.

—Tim Moriarty

Francisco. Finds—and affordable by San Francisco standards—include **A Girl and Her Dog,** 3932 24th St., 415/643-0346, for stylish, comfortable SoMa-style styles; friendly, youthful **Ambiance,** 3985 24th St., 415/647-7144; and been-there-forever **Joshua Simon,** 3915 24th St., 415/821-1068, for quality and comfort. For glorious adornments, peruse the **Gallery of Jewels,** 4089 24th St., 415/285-0626, which offers exquisite jewelry, many pieces by local designers. For the latest retrowear trends, try **Guys and Dolls,** 3789 24th St., 415/285-7174.

Clothes Contact, 473 Valencia (just north of 16th), 415/621-3212, sells fashionable vintage clothing for $8 per pound. (Consumer alert: those big suede jackets in the back weigh more than you might imagine.) Worth poking into, too, is the **Community Thrift Store,** 623-625 Valencia (between 17th and 18th), 415/861-

4910, a fundraising venture for the gay and lesbian Tavern Guild. It's an expansive, inexpensive, and well-organized place, with a book selection rivaling most used bookstores. (The motto here is "out of the closet, into the store.") Cooperatively run **Modern Times Bookstore,** 888 Valencia (between 19th and 20th), 415/282-9246, is the source for progressive, radical, and Third World literature, magazines, and tapes.

If you're down on your luck, head up to **Lady Luck Candle Shop,** 311 Valencia (at 14th), 415/621-0358, a small store selling some pretty big juju, everything from high-test magic candles and religious potions (like St. John the Conqueror Spray) to Lucky Mojo Oil and Hold Your Man essential oil. **Good Vibrations,** 1210 Valencia (at 23rd), 415/974-8980, home of the vibrator museum, is a clean, user-friendly, liberated shop where women (and some men) come for adult toys, and to peruse the selection of in-print erotica, including history and literature.

More common in the Mission District are neighborhood-style antique and secondhand stores of every stripe. Bargains abound, without the inflated prices typical of trendier, more tourist-traveled areas.

Nightlife

The Roxie, 3117 16th St. (at Valencia), 415/863-1087, www.roxie.com, is the neighborhood's renowned repertory film venue, with a full schedule of eclectic and foreign films as well as special programs, including live audience interviews with filmmakers. Most of the Mission's coffeehouses, bars, and clubs are equally entertaining. For good coffee and Ethiopian food (including some vegetarian selections), head to **Cafe Ethiopia,** 878 Valencia St. (at 20th), 415/285-2728.

The Mission District may seem to have a bar on every block, but some are more appealing than others. Scoring high marks on the cool-o-meter is the **Latin-American Club** (aka "the Latin"), 3286 22nd St. (between Mission and Valencia), 415/647-2732. The Latin has a truly neighborhood vibe, funky but comfortable clubhouse atmosphere and good people-watching. Just across the way and favored by local musicians is the **Make-Out Room,** 3225 22nd (between Mission and Valencia), 415/647-2888. Easy to miss from the outside, the small, windowless storefront entrance is painted all black (look for the bar's flickering sign out front). Inside, the dark bar extends back to a pool table and a small stage covered with red velvet curtains.

Shot straight from the glittering heart of NYC (the original site is in Manhattan's East Village), the **Beauty Bar,** 2299 Mission (at 19th), 415/285-0323, offers an odd and intoxicating mix of cocktails and 1950s beauty parlor ambience. The walls are pink, the chrome blow-dryers sparkle, and the crowd is a mix of Mission trendsetters and fashion victims. Specialty drinks are named after beauty products, like the Aqua Net made with blue curaçao and the Prell made with crème de menthe. Come on a weeknight and you may even score a complimentary manicure with your cocktail. A neon sign outside **Doc's**

Clock, 2575 Mission (at 21st), 415/824-3627, announces it's "Cocktail Time," but the vibe down here is more relaxed, and flannel shirts outnumber silver pants 10 to 1.

Up on 16th St., **Doctor Bombay's,** 3192 16th St. (at Guerrero), 415/431-5255, is dim and diminutive, the clientele quite happy to talk the night away while downing the good doctor's award-winning specialty drink, the melon-flavored Pixie Piss. Across the street is **Dalva,** 3121 16th St. (at Valencia), 415/252-7740, another Mission favorite. A handsome mahogany bar and an assortment of wooden tables make this a great place to settle in. Weekday happy "hour" runs from 4 to 7 P.M., and it's best on weekdays as the small room gets packed later in the week. **Esta Noche,** 3079 16th (between Mission and Valencia), 415/861-5757, is the red-hot Latino answer to the almost-all-white gay bars in the Castro.

La Rondalla, 901 Valencia (at 20th), 415/647-7474, is the most festive bar around, what with the year-round Christmas lights, smoke-stained tinsel, and revolving overhead disco ball. (Good traditional Mexican food is served in the restaurant.) Down at the foot of Mission St., hole-in-the wall **El Rio,** 3158 Mission St. (at Cesar Chavez), 415/282-3325, sports a big welcome sign outside announcing this is "Your Dive," and indeed the feeling here is warm yet slightly seedy. The outdoor deck, shuffleboard set-up, and pool tables make it an excellent warm-weather hangout. Next door is **Roccapulco,** 3140 Mission (at Cesar Chavez), 415/648-6611, a supper club where you can dine and dance salsa to live Latino bands.

Live, new theater is the specialty of **The Marsh,** 1062 Valencia St. (near 22nd), 415/826-5750, www.themarsh.com. A neighborhood classic, the Marsh isn't glitzy, fashionable, or expensive (tickets usually cost $7–15). But it has heart. The performers (and audiences) here are serious about art. Experimentation is de rigueur, meaning you're never at risk of encountering formula productions. You won't need your tux here, and your applause will be well-deserved gold to the performers, some of whom may go on to fame and fortune. Definitely check it out.

San Francisco

CASTRO STREET AND VICINITY

The very idea is enough to make America's righteous religious right explode in an apoplectic fit, but the simple truth is that San Francisco's Castro St. is one of the safest neighborhoods in the entire city—and that's not just a reference to sex practices.

This tight-knit, well-established community of lesbian women and gay men represents roughly 15 percent of the city's population and 35 percent of its registered voters. Nationally and internationally, the Castro District epitomizes out-of-the-closet living. (There's nothing in this world like the Castro's Gay Freedom Day Parade—usually headed by hundreds of women on motorcycles, the famous Dykes on Bikes—and no neighborhood throws a better street party.) People here are committed to protecting their own and creating safe neighborhoods. What this means, for visitors straight or gay, is that there is a response—people get out of their cars, or rush out of restaurants, clubs, and apartment buildings—at the slightest sign that something is amiss.

Who ever would have guessed that a serious revival of community values in the U.S. would start in the Castro?

Actually, there have been many indications. And there are many reasons. The developing cultural and political influence of the Castro District became apparent in 1977, when openly gay Harvey Milk was elected to the San Francisco Board of Supervisors. But genuine acceptance seemed distant—never more so than in 1978, when both Milk and Mayor George Moscone were assassinated by conservative political rival Dan White, who had resigned his board seat and wanted it back. (White's "diminished capacity" defense argument, which claimed that his habitual consumption of high-sugar junk food had altered his brain chemistry—the "Twinkie" defense—became a national scandal but ultimately proved successful. He was sentenced to a seven-year prison term.)

The community's tragedies kept on coming, hitting even closer to home. Somewhat notorious in its adolescence as a safe haven for freestyle lifestyles, including casual human relationships

and quickie sex, the Castro District was devastated by the initial impact of the AIDS epidemic. (With younger gays that history seems determined to repeat itself.) The community has been stricken to the center of its soul by the tragic human consequences of an undiscriminating virus. But otherwise meaningless human loss has served only to strengthen the community's humanity. Just as, after Milk's assassination, greater numbers of community activists came forward to serve in positions of political influence, Castro District organizations like the Shanti Project, Open Hand, and the Names Project extended both heart and hand to end the suffering. And fierce, in-your-face activists from groups like Act Up, Queer Nation, and Bad Cop No Donut have taken the message to the nation's streets.

So, while Castro District community values are strong and getting stronger, the ambience is not exactly apple-pie Americana. People with pierced body parts (some easily visible, some not) and dressed in motorcycle jackets still stroll in and out of leather bars. Its shops also can be somewhat unusual, like **Does Your Mother Know,** a seriously homoerotic greeting card shop on 18th St. near Castro.

Museums and Shops

The neighborhood's business district, both avant-garde and gentrified Victorian, is small, stretching for three blocks along Castro St. between Market and 19th, and a short distance in each direction from 18th and Castro. This area is all included, geographically, in what was once recognizable as **Eureka Valley.** (Parking can be a problem, once you've arrived, so take the Muni Metro and climb off at the Castro St. Station.) Some people also include the gentrifying **Noe Valley** (with its upscale 24th St. shopping district) in the general Castro stream of consciousness, but the technical dividing line is near the crest of Castro St. at 22nd. Keep driving on Upper Market St., and you'll wind up into the city's geographic center. Though the ascent is actually easier from Haight-Ashbury (from Twin Peaks Blvd. just off 17th—see a good road map), either way you'll arrive at or near the top of **Twin Peaks,** with its terraced neighborhoods, astounding views, and some of the city's best stairway walks. More challenging is the short but steep hike to the top of Corona Heights Park (at Roosevelt), also noted for the very good **Josephine D. Randall Junior Museum,** 199 Museum Way (at Roosevelt), 415/554-9600, www.randallmuseum.org, a youth-oriented natural sciences, arts, and activities center open Tues.–Sat. 10 A.M.–5 P.M. Admission free; donations welcome.

Down below, **A Different Light,** 489 Castro St. (between Market and 18th Streets), 415/431-0891, is the city's best gay and lesbian bookstore, with literature by and for. Readings and other events are occasionally offered; call for current information. Truly classic and quite traditional is the handsome and authentic art deco **Castro Theater,** 429 Castro (at Market), 415/621-6120, built in 1923. San Francisco's only true movie palace, the Castro is still a favorite city venue for classic movies and film festivals. Another highlight is the massive house Wurlitzer organ, which can make seeing a film at the Castro a truly exhilarating experience. **Cliff's Variety,** 479 Castro (at 18th), 415/431-5365, is another classic, a wonderfully old-fashioned hardware store where you can buy almost anything, from power saws to Play-doh.

Nightlife

Many of San Francisco's 200-plus gay bars are in the Castro District. Those in the know say the best way to find just the scene you're looking for is to wander. **The Cafe,** 2367 Market St. (between 17th and 18th), 415/861-3846, is the Castro's best lesbian bar, also attracting many gay boys and some straights. From its balcony overlooking Market and Castro, you can get a good overview of the whole Castro scene below. Also featured: an indoor patio, pool tables, and a spacious dance floor. DJs spin a loud mix of techno and house with a few '70s and '80s remixes for a crowd that often packs the floor by 11 P.M.

Over at **The Mint,** 1942 Market St. (near Guerrero), 415/626-4726, sing yourself silly with many of the city's top Karaoke singers. Now home to a mixed crowd, including a fair number of office workers letting off steam, this is in fact the oldest gay bar in continuous operation in the Castro, circa 1968. Another neighborhood mainstay, **Twin Peaks Tavern,** at 410 Castro St. (at 17th St.), 415/864-9470, is home away from home for a mainly 40-plus, gay white male crowd. The bar has a light and airy atmosphere, with large windows overlooking the street, good for people-watching and conversation.

Just up the street at 18th and Castro, **Midnight Sun,** 4067 18th St., 415/861-4186, is named for the glow of its TV screens. This is the place for happy-hour renditions of the latest episodes of *Queer As Folk, Will and Grace,* or *Sex and the City.* Hip and unpretentious, **The Pilsner Inn,** 225 Church St. (between Market and 15th St.), 415/621-7058, has a punky soundtrack and barkeeps busy pouring a selection of European ales.

A onetime speakeasy, **Cafe du Nord,** 2170 Market (between Church and Sanchez), 415/861-5016, is underground, quite literally, in the basement of the Swedish American building. Descend the stairs into a nightspot with the look of a classic supper club: deep red walls and mahogany fixtures. Alternative and swing music make this place popular with a diverse crowd, not to mention excellent cocktails, a good dinner menu, and only moderate pretense. DuNord also hosts **Girl66,** a dance club for women, once a month, making this and the Café the only places in the Castro where a significant number of girls regularly congregate.

SOUTH OF MARKET (SOMA)

Known by old-timers as "south of the slot," a reference to a neighborhood sans cable cars, San Francisco's South of Market area was a working- and middle-class residential area—until all its homes were incinerated in the firestorm following the great earthquake of 1906. Rebuilt early in the century with warehouses, factories, train yards, and port businesses at **China Basin,** these days the area has gone trendy. In the style of New York's SoHo (South of Houston), this semi-industrial stretch of the city now goes by the moniker "SoMa."

As is usually the case, the vanguard of gentrification was the artistic community: the dancers, musicians, sculptors, photographers, painters, and graphic designers who require low rents and room to create. Rehabilitating old warehouses and industrial sheds here into studios and performance spaces solved all but strictly creative problems. Then came the attractively inexpensive factory outlet stores, followed by eclectic cafés and nightclubs. The Yerba Buena Gardens redevelopment project sealed the neighborhood's fate, bringing big-time tourist attractions including the **Moscone Convention Center** (newly expanded with the addition of Moscone West at Fourth and Howard), the San Francisco Museum of Modern Art, the Yerba Buena Center for the Arts, and The Rooftop at Yerba Buena Gardens, a multifacility arts and entertainment complex.

Now the city's destination for the young, sleek, and wealthy, the 30-story **W San Francisco,** towers over Third and Howard. Sony's futuristic **Metreon** holds down Fourth and Mission. Even near the once-abandoned waterfront just south of the traditional Financial District boundaries, avant-garde construction like **Number One Market Street,** which incorporates the old Southern Pacific Building, and **Rincon Center,** which encompasses the preserved Depression-era mural art of the Rincon Annex Post Office, have added a new look to once down-and-out areas. More massive highrises are on the way, and land values are shooting up in areas previously dominated by longshoremen's flophouses and garment factories. The starving artists have long since moved on to the Lower Haight and the Mission District, and in SoMa, the strictly eccentric is now becoming more self-consciously so.

San Francisco Museum of Modern Art

SoMa's transformation is largely due to the arrival of the San Francisco Museum of Modern Art (SFMOMA), 151 Third St. (between Mission and Howard), 415/357-4000, www.sfmoma.org, a modern building designed by Swiss architect Mario Botta that many consider to be a work of art in itself. Love it or hate it, you're not likely to miss the soaring cylindrical skylight and assertive red brick of the $60-million structure rising above the gritty streets south of Market.

The museum's heavy hitters include pieces that any museum in the country would kill for: de Kooning's intense *Woman,* and Henri Matisse's masterpiece *Femme au Chapeau.* Also featured in the permanent collection: works by Piet Mondrian, Georgia O'Keeffe, Pablo Picasso, Salvador Dali, Marcel DuChamp, and some outstanding paintings by Jackson Pollock. Mexican painters Frida Kahlo and her husband, Diego Rivera, are represented, as are the works of many Californian artists, including assembler Bruce Connor and sculptor Bruce Arneson. The museum also hosts blockbuster temporary exhibitions showcasing world-renowned individual artists, such as an amazing Paul Klee retrospective in 2002. And if you don't know the difference between a Klee and a Kahlo, fear not; the new **Koret Visitor Education Center** presents exhibits, films, and lectures, often related to the main exhibit. There's a hip little café, the **Cafe Museo,** 415/357-4500, serving fresh, healthful, "artistic" sandwiches, salads and pizzas, and boxed lunches to go, and the **SFMOMA Museum Store,** well stocked with pricey coffee-table books and postcards.

San Francisco Museum of Modern Art

EXEMPLARY DOWNTOWN SCIENCE

The **California Academy of Sciences** is a multifaceted scientific institution and the oldest in the West, founded in 1853 to survey and study the unique natural history of California and vicinity. Long at home in Golden Gate Park and composed of the very distinct Natural History Museum, Steinhart Aquarium, and Morrison Planetarium, in spring 2004 the Academy moved downtown to a temporary home while its former facility is transformed by architect Renzo Piano into a more unified and "sustainable" museum.

The country's only combined aquarium, planetarium, and natural history museum, the Academy is uniquely suited to making dynamic presentations—even in its architecture—about the interconnectedness of the earth, oceans, and space. Boundaries between its elemental institutions will be considerably less distinct in the new building. An example of sustainable architecture, the new Academy will also be "green," or resource efficient. As designed by Piano, the building will harmonize with its surroundings with sustainable features including a "living roof," water reclamation technologies, and the use of renewable energy.

But the new Academy won't open its doors until 2008. Until then, San Francisco's science palace is at home south of Market—and yes, it *was* some feat, transporting those 18 million natural history specimens downtown. The temporary facility features tanks and specimens from the Steinhart Aquarium—sea horses, clown fish, alligator snapping turtles, bat rays, even penguins—plus two floors of natural history and science exhibits, the Academy Store, the Grow Café, and a hands-on Naturalist Center, which offers Children's Story Time every Saturday morning at 11 A.M.

The California Academy of Sciences, 875 Howard St., is open 10 A.M.–5 P.M. daily, all holidays included. Admission is $7 adults, $4.50 seniors, students, and youths, and $2 children ages 4–11. On the first Wednesday of each month, admission is free for everyone. For current Academy information, including events, classes, and lectures, call 415/321-8000 or see www.calacademy.org.

San Francisco

The Museum of Modern Art is open 11 A.M.–6 P.M. daily except Wednesday. Additionally, it's open until 9 P.M. on Thursday, and open 10 A.M.–6 P.M. in summer (Memorial Day through Labor Day). The museum is closed Wednesdays and the following public holidays: Thanksgiving, Christmas, and New Year's Day. Admission is $10 adults, $7 seniors, and $6 students with ID (children under 12 free). Admission is free for everyone on the first Tuesday of each month, and half-price Thursday 6–9 P.M. Admission charge is sometimes higher during special exhibitions.

Yerba Buena Center for the Arts

Opposite the museum on the west side of Third St. is the Yerba Buena Center for the Arts, 701 Mission St. (at Third), 415/978-2700 or 415/978-2787 (ticket office), www.yerbabuena arts.org, a gallery and theater complex devoted to showcasing the works of experimental, marginalized, and emerging artists. The YBC hosts varied exhibitions including pop culture classics such as **Fantastic! The Art of Comics and Illusions,** examining the work of artists showcased in the seminal publication RAW, including Dan Clowes ("Eightball"), Lynda Barry ("Cruddy"), and Art Spiegelman ("Maus"), and screenings of *Surf Trip* and *Star Wars*. A five-acre downtown park surrounds the complex, where a waterfall is dedicated to the memory of Martin Luther King Jr. with the words: "We will not be satisfied until 'justice rolls down like a river and righteousness like a mighty stream.'" Amen. The Center for the Arts galleries are open 11 A.M.–5 P.M. daily except Monday (until 8 P.M. on the first Thursday of each month). Admission is $6 adults, $3 seniors/students; children 12 and under free. Everyone gets in free all day on the first Tuesday of every month.

The Rooftop at Yerba Buena Gardens

Cleverly built atop the Moscone Center along Fourth, Howard, and Folsom Streets, this park-cum-entertainment complex is the youth destination at Yerba Buena Gardens. Rooftop attractions include a 1906 Charles Looff carousel, a full-size indoor ice rink with city-skyline views, a bowling alley, and **Zeum**, 415/820-3349, an interactive art and technology center for children ages 8–18. Hours are Wed.–Sun. 11 A.M.–5 P.M., and admission is $7 adults, $6 seniors and students, $5 youths ages 5–18. The **Ice Skating Center**, 415/777-3727, is open for public skating daily, 1–5 P.M. Admission is $6.50 adults, $4.50 seniors, and $5.00 children ($2.50 skate rental). The **Bowling Alley**, 415/820-3540, is open Sun.–Thurs. 10 A.M.–10 P.M., Fri.–Sat. 10 A.M.–midnight, with Black Lite bowling from 9 P.M.–midnight. Prices are $4 per game for adults, $2.50 per game for children 12 and under.

Metreon

Anchoring the corner of Fourth and Mission Streets like a sleek spacecraft, the block-long, four-story-tall **Metreon** is the latest icon of pop culture to land in San Francisco's SoMa district. The Sony Entertainment-sponsored mall features a 15-screen cinema complex, the biggest IMAX theater in North America (tied with Sony's IMAX theatre in New York), and trendy shopping options including a Sony Style store and Playstation, where you can test drive the latest titles at the videogame bar, or quiz the super user "game tenders" on staff.

Interactive exhibits include **Where the Wild Things Are,** based on Maurice Sendak's magical children's book; **Portal One,** a futuristic gaming area; and **Action Theatre,** a triple-screen theatre dedicated to screening Japanese anime, animated entertainment, and action features. The mall's food court features offshoots of several popular local restaurants: LongLife Noodle Co., Buckhorn, Sanraku, and Firewood Café, gathered under the umbrella "A Taste of San Francisco." For admission prices, hours, and other current information, call Metreon at 415/369-6000, or check www.metreon.com.

Other SoMa Sights

An awesome neighborhood presence is the 1874 granite Greek revival **Old U.S. Mint** building at Fifth and Mission, vacant since 1998 and in

PIONEERING CALIFORNIA

An underappreciated cultural gem in the Yerba Buena neighborhood is the Society of California Pioneers' **Seymour Pioneer Museum,** in Pioneer Hall across from the Moscone Center, 300 Fourth St. (at Folsom), 415/957-1849, www.californiapioneers.org. Recent special exhibits have included Ore to Opulence, capturing the greed, glamour, and glitter of what Mark Twain ironically termed "the Gilded Age"; and Territorial Ambitions: Mapping the Far West, 1772–1872.

Not to be missed, though, is the museum's permanent art collection, including paintings and prints from every significant early California artist, among them Thomas Hill, Ransom G. Holdredge, William Keith, Charles D. Robinson, and Theodore Wores. The museum also boasts an exceptional archive of early California photography. The museum's permanent collection also includes California fashions, including eyeglasses and canes; gold rush artifacts, from gold pans and saddles to musical instruments; and the priceless Vallejo silver collection. Presented to General Mariano Guadalupe Vallejo by Russian government officials sometime between 1833 and 1841, the collection—more than 100 pieces of silver and crystal, from a dinner service for three to combs, tweezers, and boot jacks—fits neatly into mahogany field chest with stacking red Moroccan leather trays.

The museum is typically open Wed.–Sat. 10 A.M.–4 P.M. (closed major holidays), and open late (until 7 P.M.) on the first Saturday of the month. Small admission fee.

The Society of California Pioneers was founded by pioneers who arrived before the gold rush of 1849, and is perpetuated and supported by direct descendants of early California settlers.

need of restoration. At last report the nonprofit **San Francisco Museum and Historical Society** had been given the go-ahead to rehabilitate the building for a new civic museum, retail space, and a new visitor center for the San Francisco Convention & Visitors Bureau—projects dependent on successful financing. The San Francisco Mint was established in 1854 to safeguard gold and silver mined in the West, which may help explain the Old Mint's resemblance to both temple and fortress. The oldest stone building in San Francisco, the Old Mint was also the first and largest federal building in the West when it opened in 1874. The building is listed on the National Register of Historic Places, designed by Architect Alfred B. Mullet, who also designed both the U.S. Treasury building and the Old Executive Office Building in Washington, D.C.

The **Cartoon Art Museum,** 814 Mission (between Fourth and Fifth Streets), 415/227-8666, www.cartoonart.org, chronicles the history of the in-print giggle, from cartoon sketches and finished art to toys and videos. Open Tues.–Sun. 11 A.M.–5 P.M., closed Mondays and major holidays. Admission is $6 adults, $3 seniors/students, $2 children. The first Tuesday of every month is "Pay what you wish day."

The **California Historical Society Museum,** 678 Mission St. (between Second and Third Streets), 415/357-1848, www.californiahistorical society.org, displays rare historical photographs and includes exhibits on early California movers and shakers (both human and geologic), Western art of California, and frontier manuscripts. The museum bookstore features a great selection of books by California authors. The museum and bookstore are open Tues.–Sat. 11 A.M.–5 P.M. Admission is $3 adults, and $1 for seniors and children. Actually closer to the waterfront and Financial District, the **Telephone Pioneers Communications Museum,** 140 New Montgomery (at Natoma), 415/542-0182, offers electronic miscellany and telephone memorabilia dating to the 1870s. Open only Tues.–Thurs. 10 A.M.–2 P.M.

Shops

Shop-and-drop types, please note: Serious bargains are available throughout SoMa's garment

CLEAN UP YOUR ACT AT BRAINWASH

No doubt the cleanest scene among SoMa's hot spots is **BrainWash** at 1122 Folsom, 415/861-FOOD, 415/431-WASH, or www .brainwash.com, a combination café, performance space, nightclub, and Laundromat in a reformed warehouse. The brainchild of UC Berkeley and Free Speech Movement alumna Susan Schindler, BrainWash ain't heavy, just semi-industrial, from the beamed ceilings and neon to the concrete floor. The decor here includes café tables corralled by steel office chairs with original decoupaged artwork on the seats. (Admit it—haven't you always wanted to sit on Albert Einstein's face?) BrainWash also features a small counter/bar area, and bathrooms for either "Readers" (lined with *Dirty Laundry Comics* wallpaper) or "Writers" (with walls and ceiling of green chalkboard, chalk provided for generating brainwashable graffiti). Since literary urges know no boundaries in terms of gender, of course both are open to both basic sexes. And others.

The small café at BrainWash offers quick, simple fare—salads, burgers, pizza, and decent sandwiches (vegetarian and otherwise)—plus pastries and decadent pies, cakes, and cookies. Try a BrainWash Brownie, either double chocolate or double espresso. There's liquid espresso, of course, plus cappuccinos and lattes, fresh unfiltered fruit or carrot juice, teas, beer, and wine.

Behind the café (and glass wall) is the Brain-Wash washhouse, a high-tech herd of washers and dryers ($1.50 per load for a regular wash load, $3.50 for a jumbo washer, and a quarter for 10 minutes of dryer time). Ask about the Laundromat's wash-and-fold and dry-cleaning services. The whole shebang here is open daily 7 A.M.–11 P.M. "Last call" for washers is 9:30 P.M. nightly. Call ahead to make sure, but most nights Brainwash offers free live music, comedy, and spoken word events, television nights available otherwise. BrainWash also sponsors community events, and the place can be rented for private parties.

So come on down, almost anytime, for some Clorox and croissants.

district. The garment industry is the city's largest, doing a wholesale business of $5 billion annually. Most of the manufacturing factories are between Second and 11th Streets, and many have off-price retail outlets for their own wares. But you won't necessarily shop in comfort, since some don't have dressing rooms and others are as jam-packed as the post office at tax time. Major merchandise marts, mostly for wholesalers, are clustered along Kansas and Townsend Streets. Some retail discount outlets for clothing, jewelery, and accessories are here, too, also along Brannan St. between Third and Sixth Streets. If at all possible, come any day but Saturday, and always be careful where you park. The parking cops are serious about ticketing violators. Some of the best places have to be hunted down: **Esprit Direct,** 499 Illinois (at 16th), 415/957-2540, is a warehouse-sized store offering discounts on San Francisco's hippest women's and children's wear. (Try lunch—weekdays only—at **42 Degrees,** tucked behind the outlet at 235 16th St., 415/777-5558.) Anchoring the neighborhood at the border of South Park, **Jeremy's,** 2 South Park (at Second), 415/882-4929, sells hip designer clothes for one-third or more off retail. Consumer alert: because some of the items are returns, be sure to check garments for snags or other signs of wear before buying. **Harper Greer,** 580 Fourth St. (between Bryant and Brannan), 415/543-4066, offers wholesale-priced fashions for women size 14 and larger.

Since shopping outlets open, close, and change names or locations at a remarkable rate, pick up a copy of *Bargain Hunting in the Bay Area* by Sally Socolich, updated annually, or consult the "Style" section of the Sunday *San Francisco Chronicle,* which lists discount centers and factory outlets in SoMa and elsewhere around town.

Nightlife

Many SoMa restaurants do double-duty as bars and club venues. You won't go far before finding something going on. The classic for people who wear ties even after work is **Julie's Supper Club,** 1123 Folsom (at Seventh), 415/861-0707. The **M&M Tavern,** 198 Fifth St. (at Howard), 415/362-6386, is a genuine institution, the place

to find most of the *Chronicle* staff, even during the day.

Catch touring and local rock bands at **Slim's,** 333 11th St. (between Folsom and Harrison), 415/522-0333, the cutting edge for indie rockers; pretty steep cover.

Artistically and genetically expansive, in a punkish sort of way, is the **DNA Lounge,** 375 11th St. (between Harrison and Folsom), 415/626-1409, serving up dancing nightly after 9 P.M., cover on weekends.

Since SoMa in the 1970s was a nighttime playground for the bad-boys-in-black-leather set, the gay bar scene here is still going strong. The original gay bar is **The Stud,** 399 Ninth St. (at Harrison), 415/252-7883, formerly a leather bar, now a dance bar. But the hottest younger-set gay nightclub in the neighborhood, some say in the entire city, is the **Endup** ("you always end up at the Endup"), 401 Sixth St. (at Harrison), 415/357-0827, famous for serious dancing—"hot bodies," too, according to an informed source—and, for cooling down, its large outdoor deck.

Other SoMa clubs to explore (if you dare) include: **Cherry Bar,** 917 Folsom (between Fifth and Sixth), 415/974-1585, a mostly lesbian girl bar with excellent drink specials; **Holy Cow,** 1535 Folsom (between 11th and 12th), 415/621-6087; the **Hotel Utah Saloon,** 500 Fourth St. (at Bryant), 415/546-6300, featuring eclectic live music; and the dance club **1015 Folsom,** 1015 Folsom (at Sixth), 415/431-1200.

GOLDEN GATE NATIONAL RECREATION AREA

One of San Francisco's unexpected treasures, the Golden Gate National Recreation Area (GGNRA) starts in the south along Sweeney Ridge near Pacifica, then jumps north to a narrow coastal strip of land adjacent to Hwy. 1, taking in Thornton Beach, Fort Funston, the Cliff House, and other milestones before it pauses at the pilings of the Golden Gate Bridge. The GGNRA also includes Alcatraz Island, one of the nation's most infamous prison sites, and state-administered Angel Island, "Ellis Island of the West" to the

Chinese and other immigrant groups. In the mid-1990s, the historic Presidio—1,480 acres of forest, coastal bluffs, military outposts, and residences adjacent to the Golden Gate Bridge—was converted from military to domestic purposes and formally included in the GGNRA. Vast tracts of the southern and western Marin County headlands, north of the bridge, are also included within GGNRA boundaries, making this park a true urban wonder. Much of the credit for creating the GGNRA, the world's largest urban park, goes to the late congressman Phillip Burton. Established in 1972, the recreation area as currently envisioned includes more than 36,000 acres in a cooperative patchwork of land holdings exceeding 114 square miles. The GGNRA is also the most popular of the national parks, drawing more than 20 million visitors each year.

One major attraction of the GGNRA is the opportunity for hiking—both **urban hiking** on the San Francisco side, and **wilderness hiking** throughout the Marin Headlands. Get oriented to the recreation area's trails at any visitor center (see below), look up the National Park Service website at www.nps.gov/prsf, or sign on for any of the GGNRA's excellent guided hikes and explorations. The schedule changes constantly, depending upon the season and other factors, but the following outings represent a sample of what's available on the San Francisco end of the Golden Gate Bridge: the Sutro Heights Walk, the Presidio's Mountain Lake to Fort Point Hike and Main Post Historical Walk, and the Point of the Sea Wolves Walk. National Park Service rangers also lead other guided tours through the Presidio, including a Natural History of the Presidio hike. A particularly spectacular section of the GGNRA's trail system is the 2.5-mile trek from the St. Francis Yacht Club to Fort Point and the Golden Gate Bridge. This walk is part of the still-in-progress **San Francisco Bay Trail,** a 450-mile shoreline trail system that will one day ring the entire bay and traverse nine Bay Area counties. Ambitious hikers can follow the GGNRA's **Coastal Trail** from San Francisco to Point Reyes National Seashore in Marin County. Once on the north side of the Golden Gate, possibilities for long hikes and backpacking trips are almost endless.

Special GGNRA events include such worthy offerings as a Story of the Golden Gate Bridge tour, a Family Fun at Muir Woods theater workshop, and presentations at the reserve's several former defense installations, including: Women on Military Posts, and Songs and Sounds of the Civil War (at Fort Point); Seacoast Defense (at Baker Beach); and Rockets to Rangers (at Nike Site 88 on the Marin Headlands).

Ⓜ ALCATRAZ

Visiting Alcatraz is like touring the dark side of the American dream, like peering into democracy's private demon hold. At Alcatraz, freedom is a fantasy. If crime is a universal option—and everyone behind bars at Alcatraz exercised it—then all who once inhabited this desolate island prison were certainly equal. Yet all who once lived on the Rock were also equal in other ways—in their utter isolation, in their human desperation, in their hopelessness.

Former prison guard Frank Heaney, born and raised in Berkeley, is now a consultant for the Blue & Gold Fleet's exclusive Alcatraz tour. When he started work as a correctional officer at age 21, Heaney found himself standing guard over some of America's most notorious felons, including George "Machine Gun" Kelly, Alvin "Creepy" Karpis, and Robert "The Birdman of Alcatraz" Stroud. Heaney soon realized that the terrifying reality of prison life was a far cry from Hollywood's James Cagney version.

The job was psychologically demanding, yet often boring. There was terror in the air, too. Inmates vowed—and attempted—to "break him." But he ignored both death threats and too-friendly comments on his youthful appeal. Guards were prohibited from conversing with the inmates—one more aspect of the criminals' endless isolation—but Heaney eventually got to know Machine Gun Kelly, whom he remembers as articulate and intellectual, "more like a bank president than a bank robber." Creepy Karpis, Ma Barker's right-hand man and the only man ever personally arrested by FBI Director J. Edgar Hoover, was little more than a braggart. And though the Birdman was considered seriously psychotic and spent most of his 54 prison years in solitary confinement, Heaney found him to be "untrustworthy" but rational and extremely intelligent. Many of Heaney's favorite stories are collected in his book *Inside the Walls of Alcatraz,* published by Bull Publishing and available at Pier 39 and the National Park Store gift shop.

Others who remember the Rock, both guards and inmates, are included on the **Alcatraz Cellhouse Tour,** an "inside" audio journey through prison history provided by the Golden Gate National Park Association and offered along with Blue & Gold Fleet tours to Alcatraz.

Among them is Jim Quillen, former inmate, who on the day we visit is here in person. He leans against the rusted iron doors of Cell Block A. His pained eyes scan the pocked walls and empty cells, each barely adequate as an open-air closet. Quillen spent the best years of his life on Alcatraz. "Ten years and one day," he says in a soft voice. "The tourists see the architecture, the history—all I see are ghosts. I can point to the exact spots where my friends have killed themselves, been murdered, gone completely insane."

That's the main reason to visit Alcatraz—to explore this lonely, hard, wind-whipped island of exile. The ghosts here need human companionship.

There is plenty else to do, too, including the ranger-guided walk around the island, courtesy of the Golden Gate National Recreation Area (GGNRA), and poking one's nose into other buildings, other times. National park personnel also offer lectures and occasional special programs. Or take an **Evening on Alcatraz** tour, to see the sun set on the city from the island. For current information, contact the GGNRA at 415/561-4700 or www.nps.gov/goga, stop by the **GGNRA Visitors Center** at Fort Funston in San Francisco, 415/239-2366, or contact the nonprofit, education-oriented Golden Gate National Park Association, 415/561-3000. (For more information about the recreation area in general, see that section elsewhere in this chapter and also Point Reyes National Seashore.)

If you're coming to Alcatraz, contact the **Blue & Gold Fleet,** Pier 41, Fisherman's Wharf, 415/705-8200, www.blueandgoldfleet.com, for general information. To make charge-by-phone ticket reservations—advisable, well in advance, since the tour is quite popular, attracting more than one million people each year—call 415/705-5555, or make reservations through the website. At last report, roundtrip fare with audio was $15.50 per adult, $10.25 per child, plus a $2.25-per-ticket reservation surcharge if you reserve your ticket by phone/Internet; there's also a $1 day-use fee in addition to the ferry price. (Be sure to be there 30 minutes early, since no refunds or exchanges are allowed if you miss the boat.) The entire audio-guided walking tour takes more than two hours, so be sure to allow yourself adequate time. (The audiotape is available in English, Japanese, German, French, Italian, and Spanish.) If at all possible, try to get booked on one of the early tours, so you can see the cellblocks and Alcatraz Island in solitude, before the rest of humanity arrives. Pack a picnic (though snacks and beverages are available), and bring all the camera and video equipment you can carry; no holds barred on photography. Wear good walking shoes, as well as warm clothes (layers best), since it can be brutally cold on Alcatraz in the fog or when the wind whips up.

In the past, the island's ruggedness made it difficult to impossible for those with limited mobility, with moderate to strenuous climbing and limited access for wheelchairs and strollers. Now wheelchair users and others with limited mobility who can't "do" the Alcatraz tour on foot can take SEAT (Sustainable Easy Access Transport) up the 12 percent grade hill one-quarter mile to the prison. Contact the Blue & Gold Fleet information line for details.

If you're not coming to Alcatraz in the immediate future, you can still take a comprehensive virtual tour, on the web at www.nps.gov /alcatraz/tours.

San Francisco–Side Sights

The GGNRA includes the beaches and coastal bluffs along San Francisco's entire western edge (and both south and north), as well as seaside trails and walking and running paths along the new highway and seawall between Sloat Blvd. and the western border of Golden Gate Park.

The original Cliff House near Seal Rocks was one of San Francisco's first tourist lures, its original diversions a bit on the licentious side. That version, converted by Adolph Sutro into a family-style resort, burned to the ground in 1894 and was soon replaced by a splendid Victorian palace and an adjacent bathhouse, also fire victims. Ruins of the old **Sutro Baths** are still visible among the rocks just north. Aptly named **Seal Rocks** offshore attract vocal sea lions.

The current **Cliff House**, across the highway from Sutro Heights Park, dates from 1908 and still attracts locals and tourists alike. The views are spectacular, which explains the success of the building's Cliff House Restaurant, 415/386-3330, as well as the building's Phineas T. Barnacle pub-style deli and the Ben Butler Room bar. The GGNRA **Cliff House Visitor Center,** 415/239-2366, is a good stop for information, free or low-cost publications and maps, and books. Open daily 10 A.M.–5 P.M. A $14 million makeover of Cliff House was completed in 2004, to remove old facades and additions and to add a new building—a modernist north wing—with a grand lobby, two-story "view" dining room, and observation deck. Renovation also added elevators to provide wheelchair access, and repaired the beloved **Camera Obscura & Hologram Gallery** located just below the Cliff House. The Musée Méchanique collection of antique penny arcade amusements has been relocated to Pier 45 at Fisherman's Wharf.

Wandering northward from Cliff House, Point Lobos Ave. and then El Camino del Mar lead to San Francisco's **Point Lobos,** the city's westernmost point. There's an overlook, to take in the view. Nearby is the USS *San Francisco* Memorial, the bridge of the city's namesake ship, lost during WWII, now preserved on a clifftop. Also nearby is **Fort Miley,** 415/556-8371, which features a 4-H "adventure ropes" course. But the most spectacular thing in sight (on a clear day) is the postcard-pretty Golden Gate Bridge. You can even get there from here, on foot, via the **Coastal Trail,** a wonderful city hike that skirts Lincoln Park and the California Palace of the Legion of Honor before passing through the Seacliff neighborhood then flanking the Presidio.

From Fort Point at the foot of the Golden Gate, the truly intrepid can keep on trekking—straight north across the bridge to Marin County, or east past the yacht harbors to Fort Mason and the overwhelming attractions of Fisherman's Wharf.

For some slower sightseeing, backtrack to the Presidio's hiking trails and other attractions. The GGNRA's **Presidio Visitor Center,** 102 Montgomery St. (that's a *different* Montgomery St. than the one downtown), 415/561-4323, can point you in the right direction. It's open year-round, daily 9 A.M.–5 P.M.

Or spend time exploring the coast. At low tide, the fleet of foot can beach walk (and climb) from the Golden Gate Bridge to **Baker Beach** and farther (looking back at the bridge for a seagull's-eye view). Though many flock here precisely because it is a de facto nude beach, the very naked sunbathers at Baker Beach usually hide out in the rock-secluded coves beyond the family-oriented stretch of public sand. Near Baker Beach is the miniature **Battery Lowell A. Chamberlain** "museum," a historic gun hold, home to the six-inch disappearing rifle. Weapons aficionados will want to explore more thoroughly the multitude of gun batteries farther north along the trail, near Fort Point.

Information and Services

For current information about GGNRA features and activities, contact: **Golden Gate National Recreation Area,** Fort Mason, Building 201, 415/556-0560, www.nps.gov/goga. To check on local conditions, events, and programs, you can also call the GGNRA's other visitor centers: **Cliff House,** 415/556-8642; **Fort Point,** 415/556-1693; **Marin Headlands,** 415/331-1540; **Muir Woods,** 415/388-2596; and **Presidio,** 415/561-4323.

To receive a subscription to the quarterly park newsletter and calendar of GGNRA events, join the nonprofit **Golden Gate National Parks Association,** same Fort Mason address, 415/561-3000, an organization that actively supports educational programs as well as park conservation and improvement. Basic annual membership includes five or six members-only events—such as tours of Presidio architecture, moonlight hikes to

San Francisco

the Pt. Bonita Lighthouse, or candlelight after-hours tours of Fort Point.

Useful publications and guidebooks published by the Golden Gate National Parks Association, available at GGNRA visitor center bookstores and elsewhere (such as the National Park Store on Pier 39 at Fisherman's Wharf), include the comprehensive 100-page *Park Guide,* plus *Alcatraz: Island of Change; Fort Point: Sentry at the Golden Gate;* and *Muir Woods: Redwood Refuge.* Also widely available is *The Official Map and Guide to the Presidio,* a detailed multicolored map jam-packed with historical and other information.

For a set of maps of the entire San Francisco Bay Trail ($10.95) or detailed maps of specific trail sections ($1.50 each), contact the **San Francisco Bay Trail Project,** c/o the Association of Bay Area Governments, 510/464-7900, or order the maps online at www.abag.org. About 215 of the Bay Trail's 450 total miles of trails are completed, with planning and/or construction of the rest underway. Call the Association to volunteer trail-building labor or materials, to help with fundraising, or to lead guided walks along sections of the Bay Trail.

Also of interest to area hikers: the **Bay Area Ridge Trail,** a 400-mile ridgetop route that one day will skirt the entire bay, connecting 75 parks. For information, contact the **Bay Area Ridge Trail Council,** 26 O'Farrell St., 415/391-9300, www.ridgetrail.org.

FORT MASON

Headquarters for the Golden Gate National Recreation Area, Fort Mason is also home to **Fort Mason Center,** a surprisingly contemporary complex of onetime military storage buildings at Marina Blvd. and Buchanan St., now hosting a variety of nonprofit arts, humanities, educational, environmental, and recreational organizations and associations.

Since the 1970s, this shoreline wasteland has been transformed into an innovative multicultural community events center—perhaps the country's premier model of the impossible, successfully accomplished. Several pavilions and the Con-

SUSAN SNYDER

Fort Mason: a locus for the arts

ference Center host larger group events, though smaller galleries, theaters, and offices predominate. The variety of rotating art exhibits, independent theater performances, poetry readings, lectures and workshops, and special-interest classes offered here is truly staggering.

Expansion plans include the establishment of a marine ecology center, another theater, more exhibit space, and another good-food-great-view restaurant. All in all, it's not surprising that Fort Mason has been studied by the Presidio's national park transition team, and even by other nations, as a supreme example of how urban eyesores can be transformed into national treasures.

Museums

The **San Francisco African American Historical & Cultural Society,** in Building C, Room 165, 415/441-0640, is a cultural and resource center featuring a library, museum (small admission), speaker's bureau, and monthly lecture series. Open Wed.–Sun. noon–5 P.M.

The **Mexican Museum,** Building D, 415/202-9700 or 415/441-0404, www.mexicanmuseum .org, is devoted exclusively to exhibitions of, and educational programs about, Mexican-American and Mexican art. Its permanent collection includes 9,000 items from five periods, including pre-Hispanic and contemporary Mexican art, and rotating exhibits attract much public attention. The changing exhibits typically focus on one particular artist or on a theme, such as 100 Years of Chroma Art Calendars. Open Wed.–Sun. 11 A.M.–5 P.M.; admission $4 adults, $3 students and seniors.

Exhibits at the **Museo ItaloAmericano,** in Building C, 415/673-2200, foster an appreciation of Italian art and culture. Open Wed.–Sun. noon–5 P.M. Small admission.

Definitely worth a detour is the **San Francisco Craft & Folk Art Museum,** Building A-North, 415/775-0990, www.sfcraftandfolk.org, which features rotating exhibits of American and international folk art. Open Tues.–Fri. and Sun. 11 A.M.–5 P.M.; Sat. 10 A.M.–5 P.M. Free on Saturday, 10 A.M.–noon, otherwise there's a small admission fee.

In addition to any free hours listed above, all of the museums at the center are free (and open until 7 P.M.) on the first Wednesday of every month.

Performing Arts

Fort Mason Center's 440-seat **Cowell Theater,** 415/441-3400, is a performance space that hosts events ranging from the acclaimed Solo Mio Festival and the New Pickle Circus to guest speakers such as Spalding Gray and unusual video, musical, and theatrical presentations. Among its showstoppers is the **Magic Theatre,** Building D, 415/441-8001 (business office) or 415/441-8822 (box office), which is internationally recognized as an outstanding American playwrights' theater, performing original plays by the likes of Sam Shepard and Michael McClure as well as innovative new writers.

Other Fort Mason performing arts groups include the **Performing Arts Workshop,** Building C, 415/673-2634, and the **Young Performers' Theatre,** Building C, 415/346-5550, both for young people. The **Blue Bear School of American Music,** Building D, 415/673-3600, offers lessons and workshops in rock, pop, jazz, blues, and other genres. **Bay Area Theatresports**

(BATS) is an improv comedy group that performs at the **Bayfront Theater,** Building B, 415/474-8935, and **World Arts West,** Building D, 415/474-3914, promotes and produces world music and dance festivals.

Visual Arts

The **Fort Mason Art Campus** of the City College of San Francisco, Building B, 415/561-1840, is the place for instruction in fine arts and crafts. Works of students and faculty are showcased at the **Coffee Gallery,** in the Building B lobby, 415/561-1840. The 10-and-under set should head to the **San Francisco Children's Art Center,** Building C, 415/771-0292. One of the most intriguing galleries here is the **San Francisco Museum of Modern Art Artist's Gallery,** Building A-North, 415/441-4777, representing more than 1,300 artists and offering, in addition to rotating exhibits, the opportunity to rent as well as buy works on display.

Environmental Organizations

The **Endangered Species Project,** Building E, 415/921-3140, works to protect wildlife and habitat and to prevent illegal poaching and trade of endangered animals. The **Fund for Animals,** Building C, 415/474-4020, is an animal-rights organization. The **Oceanic Society,** Building E, 415/441-1106, offers environmental education programs including whale-watching trips, cruises to the Farallon Islands, and coral-reef and rainforest expeditions. The **Resource Renewal Institute,** Building D, 415/928-3774, promotes integrated environmental planning—"Green Plans"—at every level of government, both domestically and internationally. The **Tuolumne River Preservation Trust,** Building C, 415/292-3531, focuses its efforts on protecting and preserving the Tuolumne River watershed.

Greens Restaurant

No one will ever starve here, since one of the country's best vegetarian restaurants, the San Francisco Zen Center's **Greens,** is in Building A-North, 415/771-6222. It's open Tues.–Sat. for lunch, Mon.–Sat. for dinner and late-evening desserts, Sunday for brunch. The restaurant also offers **Greens-To-Go** take-out lunches Tues.–Sun.; call 415/771-6330.

Information and Services

Book Bay Bookstore, Building C-South, 415/771-1076, is run by friends of the San Francisco Public Library. Book sales are regularly held to benefit the city's public-library system.

For more complete information on Fort Mason, including a copy of the monthly *Fort Mason Calendar of Events,* contact the **Fort Mason Foundation,** Building A, Fort Mason Center, 415/441-3400, www.fortmason.org, open daily 9 A.M.–5 P.M. To order tickets for any Fort Mason events, call the **Fort Mason box office** at 415/345-7575.

🅽 PRESIDIO AND FORT POINT

The New Presidio

In 1994 San Francisco's Presidio, both national historic landmark and historic military installation, passed from the Sixth Army Command to the National Park Service, creating a new national park with 1,446 acres and some spectacular features—not the least of which are its wraparound views.

The Presidio lies directly south of the Golden Gate Bridge along the northwest tip of the San Francisco Peninsula, bordered by the Marina and Pacific Heights districts to the east and the Richmond and Presidio Heights districts to the south. To the west and north, a coastal strip of the Golden Gate National Recreation Area frames the Presidio, which boasts some 70 miles of paths and trails of its own winding along cliffs and through eucalyptus groves and coastal flora. The 1,600 buildings here, most of them eclectic blends of Victorian and Spanish-revival styles, housed the U.S. Army beginning in 1847.

Founded by the Spanish in 1776 as one of two original settlements in San Francisco, the Presidio had a militaristic history even then, for the area commands a strategic view of San Francisco Bay and the Pacific Ocean. The Spanish garrison ruled the peninsula for the first 50 years of the city's history, chasing off Russian whalers and trappers by

means of the two cannons now guarding the entrance to the Officer's Club. After 1847, when Americans took over, the Presidio became a staging center for the Indian wars, a never-used outpost during the Civil War, and more recently, headquarters for the Sixth Army Command, which fought in the Pacific during World War II.

Though much of the Presidio looks as it has in the past, change is definitely underway; the park is required to be financially self-sufficient by 2013. To that end, the overall approach is to fill the Presidio's houses, barracks, warehouses, and other buildings with paying customers—tenants whose rents will finance renovations and ongoing maintenance. Limited new construction will be allowed, though open space will increase overall.

Some new construction has enthralled the public, in fact, despite vocal opposition to private use of public lands. A case in point is filmmaker George Lucas's $300 million, 23-acre **Letterman Digital Arts Center,** now being built where the Letterman Hospital and associated research center once stood. The Lucasfilm Ltd. enterprise will house all of Lucas's 2,500 employees and all of his movie production companies, including Industrial Light & Magic. An onsite coffee bar and restaurant, open to the public, are included in development plans.

Most of the Presidio is completely open to the public, however, and visitors may walk, bike, or drive around and admire the neat-as-a-pin streets with their white, two-story wood Victorians and faultless lawns. Get oriented and trace the base's history at the **William Penn Mott Jr. Visitor Center** and gallery in the onetime Officer's Club, Bldg. 50 on Moraga Avenue at the Main Post, 415/561-4323, www.nps.gov/prsf. Pick up a map there showing the Presidio's hiking trails, including a six-mile historic walk and two ecology trails, and ask about scheduled events and activities. Open daily 9 A.M.–5 P.M., closed major holidays, admission free.

Not far from the visitor center is the **San Francisco Film Centre,** Bldg. 39 (39 Mesa St.), providing office, screening, and conference space to film industry tenants in a stunningly renovated Depression-era Mediterranean revival building.

Anyone can stop by the weekdays-only **Desiree Café** here, 415/561-2336, for healthy breakfast and soups, salads, and sandwiches at lunch. Another place for a meal, near the Arguello Boulevard entrance, is the family-friendly **Presidio Café** at the Presidio Golf Course Clubhouse, 300 Finley Rd. (at Arguello), 415/561-4600, open weekdays for lunch (bar menu until 6 P.M.), weekends for brunch, including Sunday Jazz Brunch. For tee times and information about the prestigious public **Presidio Golf Course,** where golfers reserve a month in advance, see www.presidiogolf.com. For those bone-chilling days when the wind and fog flow through the Golden Gate, stop by the welcoming **Warming Hut** on the Golden Gate Promenade, at the western end of Crissy Field and across from Torpedo Wharf, 415/561-3040, a onetime Army warehouse that's been refashioned into a café and bookstore (closed Tuesday and Wednesday). For Crissy Field information, call 415/561-7690 or see www.crissyfield.org.

Among notable nonprofits now calling the Presidio home is famed **Arion Press** and gallery not far from the 15th Avenue entrance at 1802 Hayes St., 415/561-2542, www.arionpress.com, noted for its superb handmade, limited edition books illustrated with original art. Arion is open weekdays, for tours by reservation only on Thursday ($7). Other "new Presidio" highlights include the **Presidio Bowling Center** at 93 Montgomery St., 415/561-2695, and the discount retailer **Sports Basement,** in the onetime commissary at 610 Mason St., 415/437-0100, www.sportsbasement.com.

Ranger-led GGNRA guided tours include the **Bay Area Ridge Trail Hike,** an exploratory lesson in the San Francisco Peninsula's geology, geography, and plant and animal life, which circumnavigates the Presidio; **Presidio Main Post Historical Walks;** and the **Ecological Restoration of the Waterfront** hike along the Crissy Field tidal marsh.

Fort Point

More businesslike in design but in many respects more interesting than the Presidio, Fort Point off Lincoln Boulevard, is nestled directly underneath the southern tip of the Golden Gate Bridge and worth donning a few extra layers to visit. Officially the Fort Point National Historic Site since 1968, the quadrangular redbrick behemoth was modeled after South Carolina's Fort Sumter and completed in 1861 to guard the bay during the Civil War. However, the fort was never given the chance to test its mettle, as a grass-roots plot hatched by Confederate sympathizers in San Francisco to undermine the Yankee cause died for lack of funds and manpower, and the more palpable threat that the Confederate cruiser *Shenandoah* would blast its way into the bay was foiled by the war ending before the ship ever arrived.

Nonetheless, military strategists had the right idea situating the fort on the site of the old Spanish adobe-brick outpost of Castillo de San Joaquin, and through the years the fort-that-could was used as a garrison and general catchall for the Presidio, including a stint during World War I as barracks for unmarried officers. During the 1930s, when the Golden Gate Bridge was in its design phase, the fort narrowly missed being scrapped but was saved by the bridge's chief design engineer, Joseph B. Strauss, who considered the fort's demolition a waste of good masonry and designed the somewhat triumphal arch that now soars above it.

Fort Point these days enjoys a useful retirement as a historical museum, open Fri.–Sun. 10 A.M.–5 P.M., admission free. (Be aware, however, that Fort Point is closed when the nation is on orange or red security alert.) While the wind howls in the girders overhead, park rangers clad in Civil War regalia (many wearing long johns underneath) lead fort history tours through the park's honeycomb of corridors, staircases, and gun ports. Cannon muster is solemnly observed with a Napoleon 12-pounder field cannon. A fairly recent addition is the excellent exhibit and tribute to black American soldiers. At the bookstore, pick up some Confederate money and other military memorabilia. For more information about tours and special events, call Fort Point at 415/556-1693.

San Francisco

⬛ GOLDEN GATE PARK

Yet another of San Francisco's impossible dreams successfully accomplished, Golden Gate Park was once a vast expanse of sand dunes. A wasteland by urban, and urbane, standards, locals got the idea that it could be a park—and a grand park, to rival the Bois de Boulogne in Paris. Frederick Law Olmsted, who designed New York's Central Park, was asked to build it. He took one look and scoffed, saying essentially that it couldn't be done. Olmsted was wrong, as it turned out, and eventually he had the grace to admit it. William Hammond Hall, designer and chief engineer, and Scottish gardener John McLaren, the park's green-thumbed godfather, achieved the unlikely with more than a bit of West Coast ingenuity. Hall constructed a behemoth breakwater on the 1,000-acre park's west end, to block the stinging sea winds and salt spray, and started anchoring the sand by planting barley, then nitrogen-fixing lupine, then grasses. Careful grading and berming, helped along in time by windrows, further deflected the fierceness of ocean-blown storms.

"Uncle John" McLaren, Hall's successor, set about re-creating the land on a deeper level. He trucked in humus and manure to further transform sand into soil, and got busy planting more than one million trees. And that was just the beginning. In and around walkways, benches, and major park features, there were shrubs to plant, flowerbeds to establish, and pristine lawns to nurture. McLaren kept at it for some 55 years, dedicating his life to creating a park for the everlasting enjoyment of the citizenry. He bravely did battle with politicians, often beating them at their own games, to nurture and preserve "his" park for posterity. He fought with groundskeepers who tried to keep people off the lush lawns, and he attempted to hide despised-on-principle statues and other graven images with bushes and shrubs. In the end he lost this last battle; after McLaren died, the city erected a statue in his honor.

McLaren's Legacy

Much of the park's appeal is its astounding array of natural attractions. The botanic diversity alone, much of it exotic, somehow reflects San Francisco's multicultural consciousness—also transplanted from elsewhere, also now as natural as the sun, the moon, the salt winds, and the tides.

The dramatic **Victorian Conservatory of Flowers,** 415/641-7978, www.conservatoryof flowers.org, is a prim and proper presence on John F. Kennedy Drive at the eastern end of the park. Reopened in 2003 after extensive repairs, the conservatory was imported from Europe in crates and originally assembled between 1876 and 1883. It showcases a jungle of tropical plants under its soaring dome, including rare orchids, and also offers seasonal botanic displays.

The 55-acre **San Francisco Botanical Gardens at Strybing Arboretum,** Ninth Ave. at Lincoln Way, 415/661-1316, www.sanfrancisco botanical.org, features more than 7,000 different species, including many exotic and rare plants. Noted here is the collection of Australian and New Zealand plant life, along with exotics from Africa, the Americas, and Asia. Several gardens are landscaped by theme, such as the Mexican Cloud Forest and the California Redwood Grove. The serene Japanese Moon-Viewing Garden is a worthy respite when the Japanese Tea Garden is choked with tourists. The Biblical Garden is a representation of plants mentioned in the Bible or thought to have grown in the eastern Mediterranean Basin during biblical times. Quite a delight, too, is the Fragrance Garden—a collection of culinary and medicinal herbs easily appreciated by aroma and texture, labeled also in Braille. Any plant lover will enjoy time spent in the small store. The arboretum is open weekdays 8 A.M.–4:30 P.M., weekends 10 A.M.–5 P.M.; admission is free, donations appreciated. Guided tours are offered on weekday afternoons and twice a day on weekends; call for tour times and meeting places. Next door is the **San Francisco County Fair Building,** site of the annual "fair"—in San Francisco, it's a flower show only—and home to the **Helen Crocker Russell Library,** 415/661-1316 ext. 303, containing some 18,000 volumes on horticulture and plants.

The **Japanese Tea Garden** on Tea Garden Dr. (just east of Stow Lake, between JFK and Martin Luther King Jr. Drives), 415/752-4227 (admission information) or 415/752-1171 (gift shop), is

The Japanese Tea Garden beckons those in search of serenity.

a striking and enduring attraction, started (and maintained until the family's World War II internment) by full-time Japanese gardener Maokota Hagiwara and his family. Both a lovingly landscaped garden and tea house concession—the Hagiwaras invented the fortune cookie, first served here, though Chinatown later claimed this innovation as an old-country tradition—the Tea Garden is so popular that to enjoy even a few moments of the intended serenity, visitors should arrive early on a weekday morning or come on a rainy day. The large bronze *Buddha Who Sits Through Sun and Rain Without Shelter,* cast in Japan in 1790, will surely welcome an off-day visitor. The Japanese Tea Garden is most enchanting in April, when the cherry trees are in bloom. Open daily Mar.–Dec. 8:30 A.M.–6 P.M., Jan.–Feb. 8:30 A.M.–dusk. The tea house is open 10 A.M.–5:15 P.M. Admission is $3.50 adults, $1.25 seniors and children 6–12.

Also especially notable for spring floral color in Golden Gate Park: the **Queen Wilhelmina Tulip**

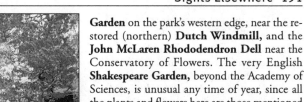

Garden on the park's western edge, near the restored (northern) **Dutch Windmill,** and the **John McLaren Rhododendron Dell** near the Conservatory of Flowers. The very English **Shakespeare Garden,** beyond the Academy of Sciences, is unusual any time of year, since all the plants and flowers here are those mentioned in the Bard's works. Poignant and sobering is the expansive **National AIDS Memorial Grove,** www.aidsmemorial.org, at the east end of the park between Middle Drive East and Bowling Green Drive. Regardless of whether or not you personally know anyone with AIDS, this is a good place to wander among the groves of redwoods and dogwoods, quietly contemplating the fragility of life and your place in it. The grove is maintained by volunteers; to volunteer, or for more information, call 415/750-8340.

The stately **M. H. de Young Memorial Museum,** 75 Tea Garden Dr. (at Ninth Ave.), 415/750-3600, www.thinker.org, built in 1894 for the Midwinter International Exposition in honor of *Chronicle* newspaper publisher M. H. de Young, was seriously damaged in the 1989 earthquake, and a new, $135 million de Young is scheduled to open in 2005. (Until then highlights of the museum's fine collection of American art, including many 20th-century realist paintings, are on display at the Palace of the Legion of Honor.) Designed by Swiss architects Jacques Herzog and Pierre de Meuron, acclaimed for the Tate Modern in London and the Dominus Winery in the Napa Valley, the new de Young will be constructed of light colored natural materials—copper, wood, and glass—and will open to the surrounding park environment thanks to "ribbons" of windows that reflect the landscape, offer panoramic park vistas, and allow park visitors to preview museum art from the outside looking in. The new landscape design by Walter Hood will include a large public plaza with palm trees at the museum's front entrance and a "garden of enchantment" to the east. For an interactive tour of the new de Young, visit the website.

The venerable **California Academy of Sciences,** 415/321-8000, www.calacademy.org, long at home on the Music Concourse, is the oldest scientific institution in the West. The academy

San Francisco

and all its buildings in Golden Gate Park are also undergoing unprecedented reconstruction, with all museums—the Natural History Museum, the Morrison Planetarium, and the Steinhart Aquarium—scheduled to reopen in breathtaking new aspect in 2008. In the meantime, visit a temporary yet nonetheless impressive version downtown at 875 Howard St., open daily.

Events and Information

Kennedy Drive from 19th Ave. to Stanyan is closed to automobile traffic every Sunday; enjoy a walk, bike ride, or rollerblade. Equipment can be rented at **Lincoln Cyclery,** 772 Stanyan St., 415/221-2415, and other businesses on Stanyan, Fulton, and Haight Streets.

Friends of Recreation and Parks, 415/750-5105, www.frp.org, offers free guided tours throughout the park May–Oct. But even more active sports fans won't be disappointed. Golden Gate Park action includes archery, baseball and basketball, boating and rowing, fly-casting, football, horseback riding and horseshoes, lawn bowling, model yacht sailing—there's a special lake for just that purpose—plus polo, roller skating, soccer, and tennis. In addition to the exceptional Children's Playground, there are two other kiddie play areas. Free **Golden Gate Band Concerts** are offered at 2 P.M. on Sunday and holidays at the park's Music Concourse. The **Midsummer Music Festival** in Stern Grove, Sloat Blvd. at 19th Ave., is another fun, and free, park program. Scheduled on consecutive Sundays from mid-June through August, it's quite popular, so come as early as possible. (For exact dates and program information, call the park office, listed below.) A variety of other special events are regularly scheduled in Golden Gate Park, including **A la Carte, a la Park,** San Francisco's "largest outdoor dining event." This gala gourmet fest, with themed pavilions, showcases the wares of Bay Area restaurants and Sonoma County wineries, the talents of celebrity chefs, and a wide variety of entertainment. It's a benefit for the San Francisco Shakespeare Festival, which offers an annual schedule of free public performances in August. A la Carte, a la Park is usually scheduled in late summer, over the

three-day Labor Day weekend. Call 415/458-1988 for information.

To save money on visits to multiple park attractions, purchase a **Culture Pass** for $10 at the park office in ivy-covered **McLaren Lodge,** 501 Stanyan (at Fulton, on the park's east side), 415/831-2700, open weekdays 8 A.M.–5 P.M., which offers free tours of the park, events and activities, and maps. The park's official website is www.parks.sfgov.org.

There's also a park visitor center downstairs in the 1925 Willis Polk–designed **Beach Chalet** at Ocean Beach, 1000 Great Highway, with Depression-era murals, mosaics, and wood carvings commissioned by the Works Progress Administration (WPA). Upstairs is the **Beach Chalet Brewery & Restaurant,** 415/386.8439, www .beachchalet.com. Light meals and snacks are available at other concessions, including the Academy of Sciences and the **Japanese Tea Garden Teahouse** (fortune cookies and tea). There is also great choice in restaurants near the intersection of Ninth Ave. and Irving, or along Haight and Stanyan Streets.

To reach the museums and tea garden via public transportation, board a westbound #5-Fulton bus on Market St., climbing off at Fulton and Eighth Avenue. After 6 P.M. and on Sunday and holidays, take #38-Geary to Geary and Park Presidio. Call 415/673-MUNI or check www.sfmuni.com for other routes and schedule information.

GOLDEN GATE BRIDGE

Nothing is as San Francisco as the astounding Golden Gate Bridge, a bright, red-orange fairy pathway up into the fog, a double-necked lyre plucked by the wind to send its surreal song spiraling skyward. The bridge stands today as testimony to the vision of political madmen and poets, almost always the progenitors of major achievements. San Francisco's own **Emperor Norton**—a gold rush–era British merchant originally known as Joshua A. Norton, who went bankrupt in the land of instant wealth but soon reinvented himself as "Norton I, Emperor of the United States and Protector of Mexico"—was the first lunatic to suggest that the vast, turbulent, and troublesome waters of the Golden Gate could be spanned by a bridge. The poet and engineer **Joseph Baermann Strauss,** a titan of a man barely five feet tall, seconded the insanity, and in 1917 he left Chicago for San Francisco, plans and models in hand, to start the 13-year lobbying campaign.

All practical doubts aside, San Francisco at large was aghast at the idea of defacing the natural majesty of the Golden Gate with a manmade monument; more than 2,000 lawsuits were filed in an effort to stop bridge construction. California's love of progress won out in the end, however, and construction of the graceful bridge, designed by architect Irwin F. Morrow, began in 1933. As Strauss himself remarked later: "It took two decades and 200 million words to convince the people that the bridge was feasible; then only four years and $35 million to put the concrete and steel together."

Building the Golden Gate Bridge was no simple task, rather, an accomplishment akin to a magical feat. Some 80,000 miles of wire were spun into the bridge's suspension cables, a sufficient length to encircle the earth (at the equator) three times, and enough concrete to create a very wide sidewalk between the country's west and east coasts was poured into the anchoring piers. Sinking the southern support pier offshore was a particular challenge, with 60-mile-per-hour tidal surges and 15-foot swells at times threatening to upend the (seasick) workers' floating trestle. Once the art-deco towers were in place, the *real* fun began—those acrobats in overalls, most earning less than $1 an hour, working in empty space to span the gap. Safety was a serious issue with Strauss and his assistant, Clifford Paine. Due to their diligence, 19 men fell but landed in safety nets instead of in the morgue, earning them honorary membership in the "Halfway to Hell Club." But just weeks before construction was completed, a scaffolding collapsed, its jagged edges tearing through the safety net and taking nine men down with it.

When the Golden Gate Bridge was finished in 1937, the world was astonished. Some 200,000 people walked across the virgin roadbed that day,

just to introduce themselves to this gracious steel wonder. At that time, the bridge was the world's longest and tallest suspension structure—with a single-span, between-towers distance of 4,200 feet—and boasted the highest high-rises west of New York's Empire State Building. Its total length was 1.7 miles, and its 746-foot-tall towers were equivalent in total height to 65-story buildings. Even now, the bridge's grace is much more than aesthetic. As a suspension bridge, the Golden Gate moves with the action of the immediate neighborhood. It has rarely been closed for reasons of safety or necessary repairs, though it *was* closed, in 1960, so French President Charles de Gaulle could make a solo crossing. Even in treacherous winds, the bridge can safely sway as much as 28 feet in either direction, though standing on a slightly swinging bridge of such monstrous dimensions is an indescribably odd sensation.

Perhaps the best thing about the Golden Gate Bridge, even after all these years, is that people can still enjoy it, up close and very personally. Though the bridge toll is $5 per car (heading south), for pedestrians it's a free trip either way, although Golden Gate bridge officials hope that the views will inspire visitors to make voluntary contributions to donation boxes on the bridge. Pedestrians may access the sidewalk daily 6 A.M.–6 P.M. (sunrise to sunset, with specific hours adjusted seasonally for daylight savings time). The hike is ambitious, about two miles one-way. For those who don't suffer from vertigo, this is an inspiring and invigorating experience, as close to walking on water as most of us will ever get. (But it's not necessarily a life-enhancing experience for the seriously depressed or suicidal. The lure of the leap has proved too tempting for more than 900 people.) Parking is available at either end of the bridge.

Though the Golden Gate Bridge is the Bay Area's most royal span, credit for San Francisco's propulsion into the modern world of commerce and crazy traffic actually goes to the **Bay Bridge** spanning San Francisco Bay between downtown San Francisco and Oakland. Completed in 1936, and built atop piers sunk into the deepest deeps ever bridged, the Bay Bridge cost $80 million to complete, at that time the most expensive

San Francisco

structure ever built. And in recent history, the Bay Bridge has made front-page and nightly news headlines. The whole world watched in horror when part of the bridge collapsed amid the torqued tensions of the 1989 earthquake, a pre-rush-hour event. There were deaths and injuries, but fewer casualties than if the quake had come during peak commuter traffic. Despite the quake, the bridge still remained structurally sound, and the more critically necessary repairs have been made. Work is already underway on a new eastern span of the Bay Bridge, which is budgeted for $2.6 billion, though in the end it could cost much more. Also in progress is a huge and complex project to demolish the existing double-deck western section of the bridge in San Francisco and replace it with stronger side-by-side roadways.

Entertainment and Events

A selection of entertaining bars, nightclubs, and other worthy diversions is included under sight-seeing sections above, which are organized by neighborhood. To keep abreast of the ever-changing arts and entertainment scene, consult local newspapers, especially the calendar sections of the *Bay Guardian* and other local week-lies, and the pink Datebook section of the Sunday *Chronicle.*

PERFORMING ARTS

San Francisco's performing arts scene offers everything from the classics to the contemporary, kitschy, and downright crazed. Find out what's going on by picking up local publications or calling the San Francisco Convention & Visitors Bureau information hotlines. Tickets for major events and performances are available through the relevant box offices, mentioned below.

Low-income art lovers, or those deciding to "do" the town on a last-minute whim, aren't necessarily out of luck. **TIX Bay Area,** on Stockton St. at Union Square, 415/433-7827, www .theatrebayarea.org, offers day-of-performance tickets to local shows at half price. Payment is cash only, no credit card reservations. Along with being a full-service BASS ticket outlet, TIX also handles advance full-price tickets to many Bay Area events. Open Tues.–Sat. noon–7:30 P.M., closed Mondays. You can get a catalog for ordering advance tickets at half price by calling **TIX by Mail** at 415/430-1140. To charge arts and entertainment tickets by phone or to listen to recorded calendar listings, call Tickets.com 415/478-2277. Another helpful information source: KUSF 90.3 FM's **Alternative Music and Entertainment News (AMEN)** information line, 415/221-2636.

Other ticket box offices include: **City Box Office,** 415/392-4400, **Ticketfinder,** 650/756-1414 or 800/523-1515, or www.ticketfinder .com, and **St. Francis Theatre and Sports Tickets,** a service of the Westin St. Francis Hotel, 415/362-3500, www.premiertickets.com.

Dance and Musical Productions

One of the nation's oldest classical dance companies, the **San Francisco Ballet** has been called "a truly national ballet company" by the *New York Times.* The ballet troupe's regular season, with performances in the Civic Center's War Memorial Opera House, runs Feb.–May, though holiday season performances of the *The Nutcracker* are a long-running San Francisco tradition. For tickets, call 415/865-2000 or order tickets online at www.sfballet.org. The opera house also hosts visiting performances by The Joffrey Ballet and The Kirov Ballet, among others.

The smaller **Herbst Theatre** inside the War Memorial Veteran Building, 401 Van Ness Ave. (at McAllister), 415/621-6600, hosts smaller dance and musical productions, including performances by the San Francisco Chamber Symphony and the San Francisco Early Music Society.

The **San Francisco Opera** season runs Sept.–Dec., offering a total of 10 productions

SAN FRANCISCO ON STAGE

Geary Street near both Mason and Taylor is the official center of the theater district, and the 400 block of Geary serves as the epicenter of the mainstream theater scene. These days the concentration of upscale Union Square hotels roughly demarcates the theater district boundaries. With so many fine theaters scattered throughout the city, it's something of a New York affectation to insist on that designation downtown. But San Francisco, a city that has loved its dramatic song and dance since gold rush days, definitely insists. Poetry readings, lectures, opera, and Shakespeare were integral to the 1800s arts scene. Superstar entertainers of the era made their mark here, from spider-dancer Lola Montez and her child protégé Lotta Crabtree to actress Lillie Langtry, opera star Luisa Tetrazzini, actress Helena Modjeska, and actor Edwin Booth. Today, out-of-towners flock to big spectacular shows like the Andrew Lloyd-Webber musicals and evergreens such as the zany musical revue Beach Blanket Babylon. Luckily, the best shows are often less crowded. Most shows begin at 8 p.m., and the majority of theaters are closed on Monday.

Theater Information

Finding information on what's going on in the theater is not a difficult task. Listings are printed in the *San Francisco Bay Guardian,* the *SF Weekly,* and the Sunday edition of the *San Francisco Chronicle.* Or check out the arts online at **TheatreMania,** www.theatremania.com. And pick up a copy of **Callboard** for its current and comprehensive show schedules.

Getting Tickets

Theater tickets can be purchased in advance or for half price on the day of the performance at **TIX Bay Area,** on Powell St. at Union Square, 415/433-7827, www.theatrebayarea.org. Payment is cash only, no credit card reservations. A full-service Ticketmaster outlet as well, TIX also handles advance full-price tickets to many Bay Area events (open Tues.–Thurs. 11 A.M.–6 P.M., Fri.–Sat. 11 A.M.–7 P.M., Sun. 11 A.M.–3 P.M.). You can get a catalog for ordering advance tickets at half price by calling **TIX by Mail,** at 415/433-1235. Order full-price tickets in advance with a service charge from Ticketmaster, 415/421-8497 or 800/755-4000, www.ticketmaster.com.

Other ticket box offices include: **City Box Office,** 415/392-4400, www.cityboxoffice.com; **Ticketfinder,** 650/756-1414 or 800/523-1515, www.ticketfinder.com; and **Premier Tickets,** 415/346-7222, www.premiertickets.com.

Theater District Venues

For Broadway shows, the **Curran Theatre,** 445 Geary (between Mason and Taylor), 415/551-2000, is the long-running standard. The repertory **American Conservatory Theater** (ACT), 415/834-3200 or 415/749-2228 (box office), performs its big-name-headliner contemporary comedies and dramas in the venerable **Geary Theatre,** 415 Geary (at Mason).

Other neighborhood venues include the **Golden Gate Theatre,** 1 Taylor (at Golden Gate), 415/551-2000, and the **Marines Memorial Theatre,** 609 Sutter (at Mason), 415/551-2000. Both are good bets for off-Broadway shows. Unusual small theaters include the **Plush Room Cabaret,** inside the York Hotel at 940 Sutter (at Leavenworth), 415/885-6800.

Performance Spaces Elsewhere

San Francisco is also home to a number of small, innovative theaters and theater troupes, including the **Magic Theatre, Cowell Theater,** and **Young Performers Theatre** at Fort Mason, and the **Asian American Theatre** in the Richmond District, mentioned in more detail in The Avenues section of this chapter. The **Actors Theatre of San Francisco,** 533 Sutter (between Powell and Mason), 415/296-9179, usually offers unusual plays. **Theatre Rhinoceros,** 2926 16th St. (between Mission and S. Van Ness), 415/861-5079, is America's oldest gay and lesbian theater company, est. 1978.

The long-running **Eureka Theatre Company,** 215 Jackson (between Front and Battery), 415/788-7469, is noted for its provocative, politically astute presentations. **Intersection for the Arts,** 446 Valencia St. (between 15th and 16th), 415/626-2787 (administration) or 415/626-3311 (box office), the city's oldest alternative arts center, presents everything from experimental dramas to performance and visual art and dance. Onetime "new talent" like Robin Williams, Whoopi Goldberg, and Sam Shepard are all Intersection alumni.

San Francisco

with big-name stars. Since this is the heart of the San Francisco social scene, tickets are expensive and hard to come by; call 415/864-3330. Generally more accessible is the **San Francisco Symphony,** which offers a Sept.–June regular season in Louise M. Davies Hall downtown in the Civic Center, plus July pops concerts. For tickets, call 415/864-6000; a limited number of discount tickets go on sale two hours before performances at the box office (cash only). Davies Hall is also a venue for other performances, including some programs of the West's only major independent music conservatory, the **San Francisco Conservatory of Music**—call 415/759-3475 for tickets.

Theater

Wherever you find it, pick up a copy of *Callboard* magazine, for its current and comprehensive show schedules, or check its website at www.theatrebayarea.org For Broadway shows, the **Curran Theatre,** 445 Geary (between Mason and Taylor), 415/551-2000 (information), 415/478-2277 (BASS) for tickets, is the long-running standard. The **Golden Gate Theatre** at Sixth and Market, the **Orpheum** at Eighth and Market, and the **Marines Memorial Theatre** at Sutter and Mason are other popular mainstream venues for comedies, musicals, and revues; call 415/551-2000 for all three theaters. The award-winning **Lamplighters Music Theatre,** 415/227-4797, specializes in Gilbert and Sullivan musicals and schedules three productions a year (in August, October, and January) at the Yerba Buena Center, 415/978-2787, and at other locations around the bay.

The repertory **American Conservatory Theater** (ACT), 415/834-3200 or 415/749-2228 (box office), performs its big-name-headliner contemporary comedies and dramas in the venerable **Geary Theatre,** 415 Geary (at Mason). Union Square's theater district is also where you'll find **Theatre on the Square,** 450 Post (between Powell and Mason), 415/433-9500.

Worth seeing whenever the group is in town is the much-loved, always arresting, and far from silent **San Francisco Mime Troupe,** 855 Treat Ave. (between 21st and 22nd), 415/285-1717, a decades-old institution true to the classic Greek and Roman tradition of theatrical farce—politically sophisticated street theater noted for its complex simplicity. In addition to boasting actor Peter Coyote and the late rock impressario Bill Graham as organizational alumni, and inspiring the establishment of one-time troupe member Luis Valdez's El Teatro Campesino, the Mime Troupe was repeatedly banned and arrested in its formative years. In 1966, the state Senate Un-American Activities Committee charged the group with the crime of making lewd performances, the same year troupe members were arrested in North Beach for singing Christmas carols without a permit. In 1987, the Mime Troupe won a special Tony Award for Excellence in Regional Theater; it has also garnered several Obies and the highly prized San Francisco Bay Area Media Alliance Golden Gadfly Award.

A tad more family-oriented, "the kind of circus parents might want their kids to run away to," according to NPR's Jane Pauley, is the **Pickle Family Circus,** another exceptional city-based theater troupe, which performs at Fort Mason's Cowell Theatre, 415/441-3400.

Bizarre cabaret-style *Beach Blanket Babylon,* playing at **Club Fugazi,** 678 Green St. (between Powell and Columbus) in North Beach, 415/421-4222, is the longest-running musical revue in theatrical history. The story line is always evolving. Snow White, who seems to be seeking love in all the wrong places, encounters characters who strut straight off the front pages of the tabloids.

"Eclectic" is the word used most often to describe the **Audium,** 1616 Bush St. (at Franklin), 415/771-1616 or www.audium.org, perhaps the ultimate performance of sound, certainly the only place like this in the world. Some 169 speakers in the sloping walls, coupled with the suspended ceiling and floating floor, all create an unmatched aural experience. Regular performances are on Friday and Saturday nights at 8:30 P.M.; tickets ($12) go on sale at 8 P.M. at the box office, or buy in advance at Tix in Union Square. Children under age 12 not allowed.

ART GALLERIES AND STUDIOS

The downtown area, especially near Union Square and along lower Grant Ave., is rich with art galleries and arts-related specialty shops. The free *San Francisco Arts Monthly,* www.sfarts.org, available around town and at the visitor information center downtown, includes a complete current listing of special gallery tours, exhibits, and art showrooms. Very useful, too, is *The San Francisco Bay Area Gallery Guide,* 415/921-1600, which details goings-on at galleries large and small, and provides information about current shows at major Bay Area museums.

San Francisco's **Real Food Company** delis and stores—at 3060 Fillmore St., 2140 Polk St., 3939 24th St., and elsewhere in the Bay Area—are the most predictable places to pick up free **San Francisco Open Studios** artists' listings, detailed maps, and resource directories. Or stop by Bay Area bookstores, art supply stores, and selected galleries. The Open Studios concept offers direct-to-you fine arts, plus an opportunity to meet the artists and often see how and where they work. The Bay Area's Open Studios experience, sponsored by local businesses, offers regularly scheduled open-studio days, usually scheduled on consecutive Saturdays and Sundays from October to mid-November. On these days, more than 500 local artists open their studios or personally share their work with the public. You can come just to schmooze, but these working artists will eat better if you buy. For more information, call 415/861-9838 or see www.sfopenstudios.com.

FILM

The **San Francisco International Film Festival,** 415/929-5000 (office) or 415/931-3456 (recorded information), Northern California's longest-running film festival, is scheduled annually, usually from late April into May. This cinematic celebration typically includes 60 or more films from dozens of countries. Call for current program and price information. The city has all sorts of noteworthy festivities focused on film, including the **Lesbian & Gay Film Festival,** usually held at the Castro Theater in late June.

Classic theaters in the neighborhoods, these most likely to host foreign, revival, and other film festivals, include the 1922 **Castro Theater,** 429 Castro St. (near Market), 415/621-6120, where you get live Wurlitzer music during interludes, Hollywood classics, contemporary films, and clever double bills; and the hip **Roxie,** 3117 16th St. (near Valencia), 415/863-1087, www.roxie.com, specializing in independent, oddball, and trendy films, and sometimes showing silent flicks accompanied by organ. At the Haight's **Red Victorian Movie House,** 1727 Haight St., 415/668-3994, count on art films, revivals, interesting foreign fare—and California-casual couch-like benches for comfort.

Hole-in-the-wall **Artists' Television Access (ATA),** 992 Valencia, 415/824-3890, offers truly underground, experimental, and radical political films from unknown, independent filmmakers. Other good movie theater bets: the **Metreon** at 101 Fourth St. (at Mission), 415/369-6000; the **AMC 1000,** 1000 Van Ness Ave., 415/931-9800; and the **Embarcadero Center Cinema** at Embarcadero One, 415/352-8010.

COMEDY AND BILLIARD CLUBS

Bay Area Theatresports (BATS), 415/474-8935, schedules performances in Fort Mason's Bayfront Theater. Their hilarious, improvisational shows are often team efforts, with the "scripts" for instant plays, movies, and musicals created from audience suggestions.

The hottest yuckspot in town, some say, is **Cobb's Comedy Club,** 915 Columbus Avenue, 415/928-4320. Another stand-up venue is **Punchline Comedy Club,** 444 Battery (between Washington and Clay), 415/397-7573.

Located inside the Rincon Center, **Chalkers Billiard Club,** 101 Spear St. (at Mission), 415/512-0450, has the feel of a clubby pub with its dark polished wood, pristine pool tables, and workers unwinding after the 9-to-5 grind at nearby Financial District offices. Also gentrified and comfortable even for absolute beginners is **The Great Entertainer,** 975 Bryant (between Seventh and Eighth), 415/861-8833, once a paint warehouse, now the West Coast's largest pool hall. Most of the tables in the 28,000-square-foot hall are nine feet long. Private suites are available. Also here: snooker, shuffleboard, and Ping-Pong (table tennis) tables.

SPECTATOR AND TEAM SPORTS

The **San Francisco Giants** major-league baseball team plays ball on the bay at the city's 42,000-seat Pacific Bell Park on the Embarcadero, 415/468-3700, www.sfgiants.com. (To betray the city's baseball heritage, zip across the bay to the Oakland Coliseum and the Oakland A's games, 510/430-8020, www.oaklandathletics.com.) Still at home at 3Com Park—once known as Candlestick Park—are the **San Francisco 49ers,** NFL footballers made famous by their numerous Super Bowl victories. For 49er

tickets and information, call 415/656-4900 or check www.sf49ers.com.

San Franciscans are big on participatory sports. Some of the city's most eclectic competitive events reflect this fact, including the famous **Bay to Breakers** race in May, 415/808-5000 or www.baytobreakers.com, which attracts 100,000-plus runners, joggers, and walkers, most wearing quite creative costumes—and occasionally nothing at all. It's a phenomenon that must be experienced to be believed. (Request registration forms well in advance.)

San Francisco's outdoor and other recreational opportunities seem limited only by one's imagination (and income): hot-air ballooning, beachcombing, bicycling, bird-watching, boating, bowling, camping, canoeing, kayaking, hanggliding, hiking, horseshoes, fishing, golf, tennis, sailing, swimming, surfing, parasailing, rowing, rock climbing, running, windsurfing. Golden Gate National Recreational Area and Golden Gate Park are major community recreation resources.

For a current rundown on sports events and recreational opportunities, or for information on specific activities, consult the helpful folks at the San Francisco Convention & Visitors Bureau.

TOURING THE BALLPARK

In one of those surprising twists of San Francisco popular culture, San Francisco Giants baseball fans embraced the corporate moniker Pac Bell Park for its glorious new ballpark but still choke on its replacement, **SBC Park.** No matter what you call it, though, this is one grand ballpark. And you can take the guided tour. Tour guides—baseball fans all, and Giants partisans in particular—lead intrepid explorers through dugouts and batting cages, to nosebleed seats and luxury suites, and on into the stadium's bowels. There's a short video, too, which includes construction footage and coverage of the first regular-season game.

The Giants' SBC Park baseball stadium is located south of Market in China Basin, at Third and King Streets. Guided 90-minute stadium tours are offered almost daily (not on game days) at 10:30 A.M. and 12:30 P.M. Tickets are $10 adults, $8 seniors, and $5 children (12 and under). In conjunction with the Blue & Gold Fleet, the stadium also offers a three-hour **Bay Cruise Doubleheader** or SBC Park & Bay Cruise Tour from May through October, which includes the stadium tour as well as a one-hour ferry cruise of the city's waterfront. Ferry tours depart from and return to Pier 39 as well as SBC Park. For current tour details and reservations, call 415/972-2400 or see http://sanfrancisco.giants.mlb.com.

EVENTS

Even more kaleidoscopic than the city's arts scene, San Francisco events include an almost endless combination of the appropriate, inappropriate, absurd, inspired, and sublime. Well-known among these are the spectacular Chinese New Year Parade, the Gay Pride Parade, the Folsom Street Fair, and the eccentric Bay to Breakers road race. For a fairly complete listing, consult local newspapers or see the San Francisco Convention & Visitor's Bureau website, www.sfvisitor.org. Museums, theaters, neighborhood groups, and other cultural institutions usually offer their own annual events calendars.

January/February

In January or February, Chinatown comes to life with the **Chinese New Year Parade,** 415/982-3000, www.chineseparade.com, when celebratory Asian spirits prevail on the streets of Chinatown. The vibrant nighttime parade features elaborate floats, Chinese acrobats, stilt walkers, lion dancers, capped by the appearance of a 200-foot Golden Dragon ("Gum Lung") festooned with colored lights.

On February 14, let your animal passions run wild at the San Francisco Zoo's **Valentine's Day Sex Tour.** The special narrated Safari Train tour will tell you everything you always wanted to know about sex in the animal kingdom. Horny rhinos? Gay wallabees? Lesbian penguins? Why, it's all true. The tour is followed by a champagne, crepes, and truffles reception where you'll have the chance to get up close and personal with a variety of animals. Reservations required, and, because of the risque subject matter, age 21 and over only. For more information, call 415/753-7165.

March

Expect everything to be Irish and/or green at the United Irish Societies' **St. Patrick's Day Parade,** 415/675-9885, www.uissf.org, celebrated for the last 150 years the Sunday

San Francisco

© ROBERT HOLMES/CALTOUR

celebration of the Chinese New Year

before or after March 17, when it often rains (bring an umbrella). The day starts with a special Mass at St. Patrick's Church, at Fourth and Mission. At noon marching bands, political activists, and Celtic dancers begin winding their way through downtown to the Civic Center; the parade officially ends with a gathering at Justin Herman Plaza. For St. Paddie's Day diehards, the party lasts all weekend at Irish bars around the city.

Later in March, quite the event is the **San Francisco International Asian American Film Festival,** 415/863-7428, www.naatanet.org, a showcase for Asian films from both sides of the Pacific Ocean.

April

Wavy Gravy once walked a plastic fish at the **St. Stupid's Day Parade,** www.saintstupid.com, a day for San Francisco to celebrate its tradition of anything goes, which falls, not coincidentally, on April Fool's Day (April 1). The demonstration/march/celebration starts at the Transamerica Pyramid, the "pointy building" downtown, and weaves its way down Market Street. Prankster participants carry banners like "Do Not Read This Sign," and "I Voted for Bush. (Twice.)"

Health and healing are the focus of the annual **New Living Expo** at the Concourse Exhibition Center, 415/382-8300, www.newageexpo .com, which in previous years featured workshops and lectures by Julia Butterfly Hill, Shakti Gawain, John Gray, and Rodney Yee, as well as a marketplace offering all manner of New Age products and services.

Held over two weekends, Japantown's **Cherry Blossom Festival,** 415/563-2313, showcases traditional Japanese arts with martial arts demonstrations, tea ceremonies, taiko drumming, and other unique cultural festivities. Outdoor life comes back to the bay with a bang as both **baseball season** and **yachting season** start up again. The latter's **Opening Day on the Bay** is quite the sight.

May

In late April or early May, the San Francisco Film

Society presents the two week **San Francisco International Film Festival,** 415/561-5000 or 415/931-3456 (recorded information), www .sfiff.org. The program of approximately 200 new features, documentaries, and shorts offers films from around the world, many of which lack commercial distribution. Past audiences have been the first to see new films by Jean-Luc Godard and Woody Allen. Screenings take place at the Kabuki 8, the Castro, the Pacific Film Archives in Berkeley, and other venues around the Bay Area.

The Mission District hosts two major events in May: the **Cinco de Mayo Parade and Festival,** a two-day party (with plenty of mariachi music and *folklorico* costumes and dancers) scheduled as close to May 5 as possible, and late May's **Carnaval San Francisco,** featuring an uninhibited parade with samba bands, dancers, floats, and hundreds of thousands of revelers. For more information on both, contact the **Mission Economic and Cultural Association,** 415/282-3334, www.medasf.org. In mid-May the whole city turns out for the world's largest footrace, the *San Francisco Examiner* Bay to Breakers, 415/808-5000 or www.baytobreakers.com, when some 100,000 participants, many decked out in hilarious and/or scandalous costumes, hoof it from the Embarcadero out to Ocean Beach. Don't miss this wild, wacky, and wonderfully San Franciscan event.

June

The Haight celebrates its long-gone Summer of Love in June with the **Haight Street Fair,** 415/661-8025. Among the arts, crafts, and other wares, you can probably count on plenty of tie-dyed items, prism-cut glass, and other hippie-style creations. But by summer everyone's in a street-party mood, so June also features the **North Beach Festival,** 415/989-6426, and the **Union Street Art Festival,** 415/441-7055. Also in June are the long-running **Ethnic Dance Festival,** 415/392-4400, www.worldarts west.org, at the Palace of Fine Arts. The **San Francisco International Lesbian and Gay Film Festival,** 415/703-8650, www.frame

line.org, is the longest-running independent gay film festival in the country. Usually also late in June, coinciding with the film festival, is the annual **Lesbian-Gay-Bisexual-Transgender Freedom Day Parade and Celebration,** 415/864-3733 or www.sfpride.org, one huge gay-pride party usually led by Dykes on Bikes and including cross-dressing cowboys (or girls), gay bands and majorettes, cheerleaders, and everyone and everything else. Show up, too, for the start of Golden Gate Park's **Stern Grove Midsummer Music Festival,** 415/252-6253, www.sterngrove.org, which offers concerts in the grove on Sundays at 2 P.M. (The festival ends in late August.)

July

In inimitable American style, **Independence Day** (July 4) is celebrated in San Francisco with costumes—prizes for Most Original Uncle Sam and Best Symbol of America—ethnic food, multicultural entertainment, comics, and nighttime fireworks at Crissy Field. In mid-July, San Francisco's cable car operators compete in the annual **Cable Car Bell-Ringing Championship,** 415/923-6217. Also in July: **Jazz and All That Art on Fillmore,** on Fillmore between Post and Jackson, 415/346-9162, celebrating the cultural and musical heritage of what was once a largely black neighborhood; the **Midsummer Mozart Festival,** 415/292-9620 or www.midsummermozart.org; and the **San Francisco Symphony Pops Concerts,** 415/864-6000. Golden Gate Park's annual **Stern Grove Festival,** www.sterngrove.org, is a free series of R&B, jazz, and world concerts playing through September.

August/September

Hot in August are **Comedy Celebration Day** in Golden Gate Park, 415/777-7120; Fort Mason's **ACC Craft Fair,** 415/896-5060; and the **San Francisco Butoh Festival,** an ethnic dance fest at Fort Mason, 415/441-3687. Or head to Japantown for the **Nihonmachi Street Fair,** 415/771-9861, www.nihonmachistreet fair.org. In late August comes the big **A la Carte, A la Park** food and brewfest to Golden Gate Park, 415/478-2277.

Labor Day weekend brings the popular **San Francisco Shakespeare Festival,** 415/422-2222, www.sfshakes.org, with free performances offered in Golden Gate Park and other parks around the Bay Area through October. In mid-September, look for Chinatown's **Autumn Moon Festival,** 415/982-6306, a large street fair with arts, crafts, lion dances and live music. Also in September: the annual **Bay Area Robot Olympics** at the Exploratorium, 415/563-7337; **Opera in the Park,** 415/864-3330; and the **San Francisco Blues Festival** at Fort Mason, 415/826-6837 or www.sfblues.com, which draws legendary blues artists. Toward the end of the month the **Folsom Street Fair,** 415/861-3247, www.folsomstreetfair.com, unleashes the bondage crowd for an all-day parade of men (and some women) in chaps, biker hats, and restraints.

October

Bless your pet at Grace Cathedral's **St. Francis**

BIG AND BIGGER: THE NEW BLOOMIES

Downtown's oft-discussed Bloomingdale's is finally becoming a reality. Essentially two malls under one roof with a total of 1.5 million square feet, the new shopping center will include the second-largest store in the Bloomingdale's chain as well as the interconnected San Francisco Centre and Nordstrom. When the project opens to the public in 2006, it will be the largest urban shopping center west of the Mississippi River.

The new conjoined shopping center complex will extend from Market to Mission Sts., between Fourth and Fifth—strategically located between Union Square and Yerba Buena Gardens—with interconnecting walkways on five levels. The project will incorporate elements of the historic 19th-century Emporium, particularly its ornate dome—destined to offer more shops as well as charm from yesteryear.

Day service. During **Fleet Week,** the U.S. Navy lowers the plank for the public and also welcomes ships from around the world. A major cultural blowout around Columbus Day is the **Italian Heritage Parade and Festival** on Fisherman's Wharf and in North Beach, 415/989-2220. Also scheduled in October: the **Castro Street Fair,** 415/467-3354 or www.castrostreetfair.org, which attracts large crowds from the gay community; Fort Mason's **San Francisco Fall Antiques Show,** 415/546-6661; and the annual **San Francisco Jazz Festival,** 415/398-5655, www.sfjazz.org, showcasing established and up-and-coming jazz performers. To finish off the month in absolutely absurd style, on a weekend near Halloween head for the **Exotic Erotic Ball,** 415/567-BALL, www.exoticeroticball.com. Alternatively, the best **Halloween** drag and costume show is the Castro's bash, 415/826-1401, actually held in the Civic Center.

November/December

On November 2, the Mission District celebrates the Aztec/Spanish tradition of Dia de los Muertos or **Day of the Dead,** 415/821-1155, www.dayofthedeadsf.org, with a festival of art, music, and dance in honor of dead friends and relatives. Other November events include the **San Francisco International Auto Show** at Moscone Center, 415/331-4406, where auto manufacturers unveil new models and high-tech concept cars to the public; **Tree Lighting** at Pier 39, 415/981-7437, www.pier39.com; and the start of holiday festivities all over town.

Most December events reflect seasonal traditions. The major traditional arts performances are quite popular, so get tickets well in advance. The **San Francisco Ballet** performs *The Nutcracker,* 415/865-2000, and the **American Conservatory Theater** presents *A Christmas Carol,* 415/749-2228, a traditional holiday favorite.

Shopping

Whether the addiction is neighborhood boutique hopping or spending days in major-league malls, San Francisco is a shopper's paradise. To seek something specific, study the visitors bureau's current *San Francisco Book* for mainstream shopping destinations. To pursue shopping as social exploration, wander the city's neighborhood commercial districts. (Be sure to take advantage of museum and arts-venue gift shops, which usually feature an unusual array of merchandise. Secondhand and thrift shops can also be surprising. Some suggestions are included under the neighborhood sightseeing sections of this chapter.) To shop for one's consumer identity—covering as much ground, and as many shops, as possible without having any particular result in mind—visit the city's mall-like marketplaces.

The uptown **Union Square** area is an upscale shoppers delight. Major San Francisco shopping palaces include the nine-story **San Francisco Shopping Centre,** 415/495-5656, a few blocks from Union Square at Fifth and Mar-

ket, astonishing for its marble and granite elegance as well as its spiral escalators and retractable atrium skylight. Also in the neighborhood are **Macy's** overlooking Union Square at 170 O'Farrell St., 415/397-3333; **Neiman-Marcus** across the way at 150 Stockton St., 415/362-3900; and a branch of the New York based retailer **Saks Fifth Avenue** at 384 Post St., 415/986-4300. Another major downtown commercial attraction is the **Embarcadero Center,** 415/772-0500, designed by John C. Portman, Jr., an eight-block complex (between Clay and Sacramento, Drumm and Battery) with three plaza-style levels and four main buildings plus the Hyatt Regency and Park Hyatt hotels, not to mention five office towers.

Blocks from Union Square, Sony's futuristic **Metreon** complex at Fourth and Mission, 415/369-6000, features four levels of entertainment and shopping options, including a PlayStation game store, Moebius comic and action figure shop, MicrosoftSF computer emporium, and Wild Things, with Maurice Sendak books and toys for children.

San Francisco

It's not hard to spot big money when shopping in Union Square.

The three-square-block **Japan Center,** 1625 Post St. (at Laguna), 415/922-6776, in the Western Addition's Japantown, designed by Minoru Yamasaki, adds up to about five acres of galleries, shops, restaurants, theaters, hotels, and convention facilities. **Chinatown** is famous for its ethnic commercial attractions, and adjacent **North Beach** also has its share.

But **Fisherman's Wharf,** along the northeastern waterfront, is becoming shopping central. Most famous of the shopping destinations on the Wharf is 45-acre, carnival-crazy **Pier 39,** 415/981-7437, www.pier39.com, with more than 100 shops and endless family amusements. A close second is onetime chocolate factory **Ghirardelli Square,** 900 North Point (at Beach), 415/775-5500, with stylish shops and restau-

rants, and some great views. **The Cannery,** 2801 Leavenworth (at Beach), 415/771-3112, one block east of the Hyde St. cable car turnaround, is a brick-and-ivy behemoth. Once the world's largest fruit cannery, the building is now home to collected cafés, restaurants, shops, galleries, and a comedy club.

The **Anchorage Shopping Center,** 2800 Leavenworth (bounded by Jefferson, Beach, and Jones), 415/673-7762, is a contemporary, nautical-flavored plaza with daily entertainment and some unusual shops (e.g., Magnet Kingdom and Perfumania). The **Stonestown Galleria,** 415/759-2626, on Hwy. 1 at Winston Dr. near San Francisco State University and Lake Merced, offers all sorts of sophistication—and the luxury, in San Francisco, of free parking.

Accommodations

San Francisco is an expensive city, for the most part. A first-time visitor's first impression might be that no one is welcome here unless they show up in a Rolls Royce. What elsewhere would be considered rather high rent is charged for the "standard" room, two persons, one bed, in peak summer season. (Many hotels offer off-season and weekend deals; always ask about specials before booking.) Most also have higher-priced suites, and if you feel the need to drop $500 or $1,000 (or more) per night on a suite, you'll find plenty of places in town that will be more than happy to accommodate you. If you can afford these prices ("tariffs," actually), you'll not be disappointed. And some of the city's four- and five-star hotels also rank among its most historic, survivors of the great 1906 earthquake and fire.

That said, a little looking uncovers accommodation options suitable for the rest of us. San Francisco offers three hostels affiliated with Hostelling International, in addition to other hostels and inexpensive options. Other than the hostels, some dirt-cheap fleabags can be found, but they're often in seedy areas; budget travelers with city savvy, street smarts, and well-honed self-preservation skills might consider these establishments, but women traveling solo should avoid them. (In the context of truly low-budget accommodations, "European-style" generally means "the bathrooms are in the hallway.")

City-style motels offer another world of possibilities. Some reasonably priced ones are scattered throughout the city, though Lombard St. (west of Van Ness) is the place to go for overwhelming concentrations of motel choice. The city also supports a wide variety of bed-and-breakfast inns, with ambiences ranging from Haight-Ashbury-style funk to very proper Victoriana.

In general, San Francisco offers great choices in the midrange hotel market, including a number of "boutique" hotels. Many of these attractive and intimate hotels—old-timers and aging grand dames now renovated and redecorated for the modern carriage trade—are well located, near visitor attractions and public transit. Lack of convenient off-street parking is rarely a drawback, since most offer some sort of valet parking arrangement. Very good to exceptional restaurants—and room service—are often associated with boutique hotels. When travel is slow, most notably in winter, off-season and package deals can make these small hotels (and others) genuine bargains. Do check around before signing in. Also check at the visitors center on Market St., since some establishments offer special coupons and other seasonal inducements. Many boutique and fine hotels also offer substantial discounts to business travelers and to members of major "travel-interested" groups, including the American Automobile Association (AAA) and the American Association of Retired People (AARP). The visitor center is located at Benjamin Swig Pavilion on the lower level of Hallidie Plaza at Market and Powell Streets. Open weekdays 9 A.M.–5 P.M., Sat. and Sun. until 3 P.M., 415/391-2000. Or see the visitors bureau website, www.sfvisitor.org. You can also call 415/391-2001 24 hours a day for a recorded message listing daily events and activities.

Reservation Services

If you're unable to make an accommodations choice well in advance, or if you'd rather let someone else do the detail work, contact a local reservations service.

San Francisco Reservations, 510/628-4450, or 800/677-1550, www.hotelres.com, offers a no-fee reservations service for more than 200 hotels, most of these in San Francisco, and keeps current on discounts, specials, and packages. The company offers preferred rates for business travelers at some of the city's finest hotels, including many of the boutiques. With one call, you can also take advantage of their free best-deal car rental reservations service. Reservation lines are open daily 7 A.M.–11 P.M.

Places to Stay, 650/392-1705, or 866/826-3850, www.placestostay.com, is a Bay Area-based online reservation service, with over 150 properties in the San Francisco Bay Area and elsewhere. The company is a clearinghouse for hotel bookings, and offers competitive prices on the city's midrange and luxury hotels. The service is free, but prepayment is required at the time of booking, and cancellation fees may apply.

Bed and Breakfast San Francisco, 415/899-0060 or 800/452-8249, www.bbsf.com, offers referrals to a wide range of California bed-and-breakfasts—everything from houseboat and home stays to impressive Victorians and country-style inns—especially in San Francisco, the Napa-Sonoma wine country, and the Monterey Peninsula.

HOSTELS AND OTHER CHEAP SLEEPS: UNDER $50

San Francisco is full of shoestring-priced hostels renting dorm-style bunks for around $18–28 per person per night. Many also have higher-priced private rooms for around $35–48. Some hostels are open to everybody; others, as noted below, are open only to international travelers. Most have group kitchen facilities, laundry facilities, and helpful staff to give you hot tips on seeing the city.

HOSTELS

The Hostelling International **San Francisco City Center Hostel** is the city's newest, opened since late 2002 and centrally located at 685 Ellis St. (between Larkin and Hyde Sts.), 415/474-5721 or 800/909-4776 #62, fax 415/776-0775, www.norcalhostels.org. Just a stroll away from the new Asian Art Museum and Civic Center performance arts venues as well as Union Square, the theater district, and Chinatown, this seven-story 1927 hotel has been beautifully restored. The hostel, once the Atherton Hotel, features 75 rooms, each designed for two to five people, each with a private bathroom. The 12 private rooms feature either a double bed or two twin beds; 62 dormitory-style rooms, both single-gender and coed, feature four or five beds. Linens and towels are provided. A fully stocked shared kitchen, great common areas, 24-hour building

access, on-site Internet kiosks, daily activities and excursions, luggage storage and lockers, bike storage, valet parking, and a full-time housekeeping staff are some of the pluses. Price is another—$22–25 per person for a dorm stay, $66–69 per private room. Make reservations—essential in summer—by mail, phone, fax, or online (at least 48 hours in advance) and confirm with a major credit card (Visa, Mastercard).

Near all the downtown and theater district hubbub is the 285-bed HI-USA **San Francisco Downtown Hostel,** 312 Mason St. (between Geary and O'Farrell), 415/788-5604 or 800/909-4776 #02, fax 415/788-3023, www.norcalhostels.org, another good choice for budget travelers, $22–25 per person for dorm stays. This hotel-style hostel, once the Hotel Virginia, offers double and triple rooms—most share a bathroom—and amenities from kitchen to baggage storage and vending machines. Laundry facilities are nearby. The desk is essentially open for check-in 24 hours; no lockout, no curfew, no chores. Family rooms available. Groups welcome, by reservation only, and reservations for summer stays are essential for everyone and should be made at least 30 days in advance. Reserve online or by mail, phone, or fax with Visa or MasterCard. Rates include linens, but bring your own towel. Ask about the best nearby parking.

The HI-USA **San Francisco Fisherman's Wharf Hostel** is just west of the wharf at Fort Mason, Bldg. 240, 415/771-7277, fax 415/771-1468, www.norcalhostels.org, $21–23 per person. It's a local institution—located on a hill overlooking the bay and occupying part of the city's urban national park, the Golden Gate National Recreation Area. Close to the "Bikecentennial" bike route, Marina Green, and the cultural attractions of the Fort Mason complex, the hostel is within an easy stroll of Fisherman's Wharf and Ghirardelli Square, as well as Chinatown and downtown (you could take the cable car).

The hostel itself is one of HI-USA's largest—and finest—offering a total of 160 beds in clean rooms; one chore a day expected. Popular with all age groups and families, amenities include lots of lounge space, a big kitchen, plenty of food storage, laundry facilities, and pay lockers

San Francisco

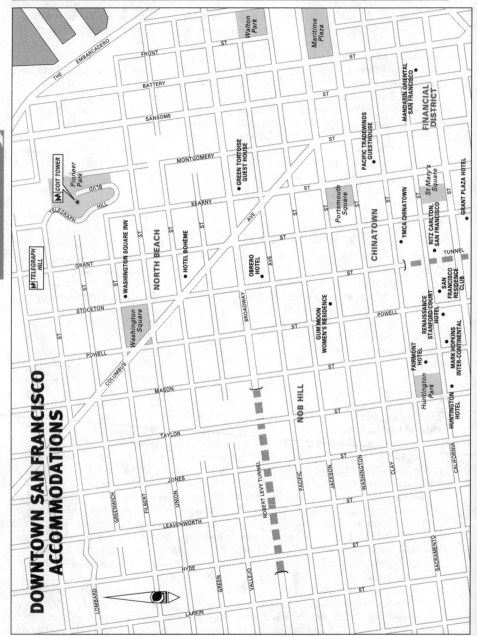

DOWNTOWN SAN FRANCISCO ACCOMMODATIONS

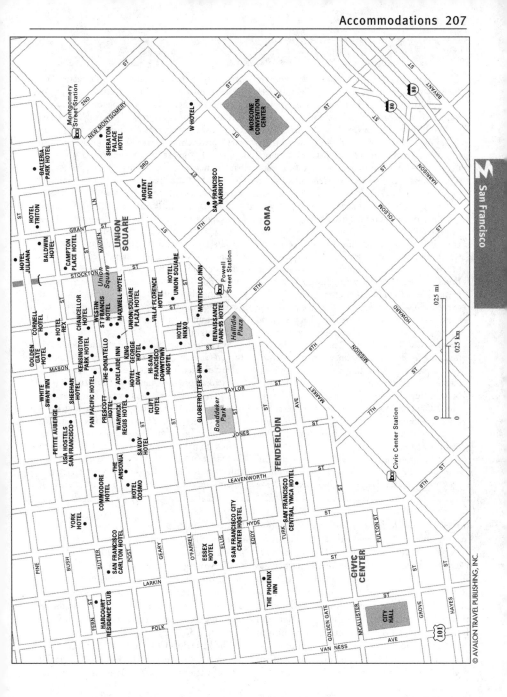

San Francisco

© AVALON TRAVEL PUBLISHING, INC.

SOME HIP SAN FRANCISCO STAYS

Every city has its style, reflected in how things appear, of course, but mostly in how they feel. The following establishments offer just a sample of that inimitable San Francisco attitude.

The Phoenix Inn at 601 Eddy St. (at Larkin), 415/776-1380 or 800/248-9466, www.thephoenixhotel.com, is more than just a 1950s motel resurrected with flamingo pink and turquoise paint. It's a subtle see-and-be-seen art scene, first attracting rock 'n' roll stars and now attracting almost everybody—*the* place in San Francisco to spy on members of the cultural elite. This is, for example, the only place Sonic Youth ever stays in San Francisco. Just-plain-famous folks like Keanu Reaves and Courtney Love can also be spied from time to time. Like the trendy, on-site restaurant, **Buddha,** even the heated swimming pool here is famous, due to its Francis Forlenza mural, "My Fifteen Minutes—Tumbling Waves," the center of a big state-sponsored stink over whether it violated health and safety codes (since public pool bottoms are supposed to be white). "That's how it is up at the corner of Eddy and Larkin, where the limos are always parkin'," according to the inn's complimentary *Phoenix Fun Book,* a cartoon-style coloring book history illustrated by *Bay Guardian* artist Lloyd Dangle. (Also as a service for guests, the Phoenix sporadically publishes its own hippest-of-the-hip guide to San Francisco, *Beyond Fisherman's Wharf.*)

Accommodations at the Phoenix—the inn named for the city's mythic ability to rise from its own ashes, as after the fiery 1906 earthquake—

are glass-fronted, uncluttered, pool-facing '50s motel rooms upscaled to ultramodern, yet not particularly ostentatious, with handmade bamboo furniture, tropical plants, and original local art on the walls. Phoenix services include complimentary continental breakfast (room service also available), a guest library that offers made-in-San Francisco movies (plus a film library with 20 "band on the road" films)—and a complete massage service, including Swedish, Esalen, Shiatsu, even poolside massage. In addition to concierge services, the Phoenix also offers blackout curtains, an on-call voice doctor (for lead vocalists with scratchy throats), and free VIP passes to SoMa's underground dance clubs. Regular rates: $50–100 midweek, $100–150 weekends, and $150–250 for each of the three suites, including the Tour Manager Suites. Ask about deals, including the "special winter rate" for regular customers (subject to availability), with the fourth night free.

Awesomely hip, too, is the playful **Hotel Triton** on Grant, in the heart of the city's downtown gallery district. The onetime Beverly Plaza Hotel just across from the Chinatown Gateway has been reimagined and reinvented by Bill Klimpton, the man who started the boutique hotel trend in town in 1980. The Triton's artsy ambience is startling and entertaining, boldly announcing itself in the lobby with sculpted purple, teal, and gold columns; odd tassle-headed, gold brocade "dervish" chairs; and mythic Neptunian imagery on the walls. Rooms are comfortable and contemporary, with

for baggage. No lockout or curfew. Family rooms are available, as is parking, and it's wheelchair accessible. The ride board here is helpful for travelers without wheels. Guests can also participate in hostel-sponsored hikes, tours, and bike rides. Reservations are essential for groups and advisable for others—especially in summer, when this place is jumping. Rates include linen and free breakfast; 14-day maximum, no minimum stay. Reservations accepted by mail, phone, fax, or online at least 48 hours in advance; confirm with a major credit card (Visa, Mastercard).

Other Hostels

The excellent **Green Tortoise Guest House,** 494 Broadway, 415/834-1000, fax 415/956-4900, www.greentortoise.com, sits on the corner of Broadway and Kearny, where Chinatown runs into North Beach. It offers a kitchen, laundry, sauna, free internet access, and complimentary breakfast. No curfew. Rates: single/double $48, triple $56, and quads $58.

The **Interclub Globe Hostel,** 10 Hallam Place (south of Market near the Greyhound station, just off Folsom), 415/431-0540, is a fairly large,

custom-designed geometric mahogany furniture, sponge-painted or diamond-patterned walls, original artwork by Chris Kidd, and unusual tilework in the bathrooms. Each guest room reflects one of three basic configurations: a king-size bed with camelback upholstered headboards, similar double beds, or oversized daybeds that double as a couch. Imaginative guest suites include the kaleidoscopic J. Garcia suite, furnished with swirls of colorful fabrics and a self-portrait of Jerry next to the bed. All rooms include soundproof windows, same-day valet/laundry service, room service, color TV with remote (also cable and movie channels), in-room fax, voice mail, and two-line phones with long cords and dataports. Basic rates: $150–250 for deluxe rooms and suites. A nice feature of this and other Kimpton-owned hotels, too, is the fully stocked honor bar—unusual in that items are quite reasonably priced. For more information or reservations, contact Hotel Triton, 342 Grant Ave., 415/394-0500 or 800/800-1299, www.hotel-tritonsf.com.

Affordable style is apparent and available at other small San Francisco hotels, including Kimpton's Prescott Hotel, home to Wolfgang Puck's Postrio Restaurant. But there's nothing else in town quite like Haight-Ashbury's **Red Victorian Bed and Breakfast Inn,** a genuine blast from San Francisco's past. This 1904 survivor is red, all right, and it's a bed-and-breakfast—but except for the architecture, it's not very Victorian. The style is early-to-late Summer of Love. Downstairs is the Peace Arts Bazaar, a New Age shopper's paradise.

(Peace Arts also offers a coffee house, computer networking services, meditation room, and gallery of meditative art with calligraphic paintings to help you program yourself, subliminally and otherwise, with proper consciousness.) Everything is casual and *very* cool—just two blocks from Golden Gate Park and its many attractions.

Upstairs, the Red Victorian's 18 guest rooms range from modest to decadent, with sinks in all rooms; some have private baths, others share. (If you stay in a room that shares the Aquarium Bathroom, you'll be able to answer the question: "What happens to the goldfish when you flush the toilet?") The Summer of Love Room features genuine '60s posters on the walls and a tie-dyed canopy over the bed. The Peace Room has an unusual skylight, though the Skylight Room beats the band for exotica. Or get back to nature in the Japanese Tea Garden Room, the Conservatory, or the Redwood Forest Room. Expanded continental breakfast (with granola and fresh bakery selections) and afternoon popcorn hour are included in the rates, which range from $50–100 shared bath and $100–150 private bath to $150–250 for suites (with specials if you stay over three days, two-night minimum on weekends). Spanish, German, and French spoken. No smoking, no TVs, no pets, and leave your angst on the sidewalk. Well-behaved children under parental supervision are welcome. Make reservations for a summer stay well in advance. For more information, contact: The Red Victorian Bed and Breakfast Inn, 1665 Haight St., 415/864-1978, www.redvic.com.

lively place located in the heart of SOMA with clean four-bed hotel rooms, a private sundeck, community lounge, pool table, café, and laundry room. The Globe is specifically for foreign guests, usually students, but these can also include Americans who present passports with stamps verifying their own international travels. Open 24 hours, no curfew. Dorm beds $19 per person, singles/doubles $47. Also in the area and strictly for international travelers ("operated by students for students" and affiliated with the American Association of International Hostels) are two

other SoMa budget outposts: the **European Guest House,** 761 Minna (between Eighth and Ninth Streets), 415/861-6634, with $18-per-person dorm stays and $40 private rooms, and the affiliated **San Francisco International Student Center,** 1188 Folsom (near BrainWash), 415/487-1463 or 415/255-8800, both offering dorm-style accommodations ($15 per person) and basic amenities.

North of Market, the **Globetrotter's Inn,** 225 Ellis St. (at Mason, one block west of Powell), 415/346-5786 (or 415/673-4048 to reach guests), offers $15 dorm beds and $27 private rooms (per person). In the Chinatown area, the lively **Pacific Tradewinds Guest House,** 680 Sacramento St., 415/433-7970 or 800/486-7975, www.sanfranciscohostel.org, is in a prime spot near the Transamerica Pyramid. Widely regarded as the friendliest hostel in the city, the Pacific offers eight-bed rooms or larger dorm rooms for $18–20 per person per night, $108–120 per week; rates include free tea and coffee all day, use of a fully equipped kitchen, Internet access, free maps, laundry service, fax service, and long-term storage. The cozy lounge is a nice place to relax and chat with fellow travelers. No curfew.

Boardinghouses

A good budget bet in the Mission District is the **San Francisco International Guest House,** 2976 23rd St. (at Harrison), 415/641-1411, an un-crowded Victorian popular with Europeans. Accommodations include two- to four-bed dorm rooms, as well as four couples rooms (all $15 per person); five day minimum stay. It's geared toward longer-term stays and usually full. Also a good choice for a longer visit is the **Harcourt Residence Club,** 1105 Larkin, 415/673-7720, where a stay includes two meals a day, Sunday brunch, and access to TV. Unlike most other residence hotels, this one attracts international students—a younger clientele. Weekly rates: $175–275 per person. Inexpensive in Chinatown for women only is the **Gum Moon Women's Residence,** 940 Washington (at Stockton), 415/421-8827. Singles and doubles $22–26, weekly rate for singles and doubles $88/105.

The large **San Francisco Central YMCA Hotel,** 220 Golden Gate Ave. (at Leavenworth), 415/885-0460, www.centralymcasf.org, is in an unappealing area two blocks north of Market at Leavenworth, with adequate rooms for women and men (double locks on all doors), plus a pool, gym, and the city's only indoor track—a plus for runners, since you won't want to run through the neighborhood (for fun, anyway). Room rates include continental breakfast: dorm beds (summer only) $23.50, singles $39, doubles $56, triples $82.50. Hostel beds are also available, for travelers only. Another "Y" option closer to

downtown is the men-only **YMCA Chinatown,** 855 Sacramento St. (between Stockton and Grant), 415/576-9622, singles $35–38.

The **San Francisco Residence Club,** 861 California St. (at Powell), 415/421-2220, www.sfresclub.com, is a European style pension on Nob Hill. Rates include full breakfast and dinner, and there's a comfortable lounge and garden dining area. Daily rates start at $55 per person, weekly rates at $370.

BUDGET HOTELS: $50–100

Perhaps the epitome of San Francisco's casual, low-cost European-style stays is the **Adelaide Inn,** 5 Isadora Duncan Ct. (in the theater district, off Taylor between Geary and Post), 415/441-2261. Reservations are advisable for the 18 rooms with shared baths. Rates include continental breakfast. Also in the area, **The Ansonia,** 711 Post, 415/673-2670, is a real find. This small hotel has a friendly staff, comfortable lobby, nice rooms, a laundry, and breakfast and dinner (except on Sunday). Student monthly rates available.

Close to Union Square, the **Gates Hotel,** 140 Ellis (at Cyril Magnin), 415/781-0430, www .gateshotel.com, features basic rooms. A budget gem in the Chinatown area, the **Obrero Hotel,** 1208 Stockton, 415/989-3960, offers just a dozen cheery bed-and-breakfast rooms with bathrooms down the hall. Full breakfast included. Another best bet is the **Grant Plaza Hotel,** 465 Grant Ave. (between Pine and Bush), 415/434-3883 or 800/472-6899, where amenities include private baths with hair dryers, telephones with voice mail, and color TV. Group rates available. Unpretentious and reasonably priced (private bathrooms) is the **Union Square Plaza Hotel,** 432 Geary (between Powell and Mason), 415/776-7585.

A few blocks north of the Civic Center between Hyde and Larkin, in a borderline bad neighborhood, is the justifiably popular **Essex Hotel,** 684 Ellis St., 415/474-4664 or 800/443-7739 in California, 800/453-7739 from elsewhere in the country. The hotel offers small rooms with private baths and telephones; some have TV. Free coffee. It's especially popular in summer—when rates are slightly higher—with foreign tourists, particularly Germans. Weekly rates, too.

Noteworthy for its comfort, antiques, and fresh flowers is the small **Golden Gate Hotel,** 775 Bush St. (between Powell and Mason), 415/392-3702 or 800/835-1118, www.golden gatehotel.com. Sixteen of the rooms have private bath; the other seven, with shared bath, are less expensive. Rates include complimentary breakfast and afternoon tea.

Located right across from the Chinatown gate just off Union Square, the bright and comfortable **Baldwin Hotel,** 321 Grant Ave. (between Sutter and Bush), 415/781-2220 or 800/622-5394, www.baldwinhotel.com, offers comfortable guest rooms with TV and telephones with modem hookups. Weekly rates available.

BOUTIQUE HOTELS: $100–150

Styled after a 1920s luxury liner, the **Commodore Hotel,** 825 Sutter St., 415/923-6800 or 800/338-6848, www.thecommodorehotel .com, is a fun place to stay downtown. All of the rooms are spacious, with modern bathrooms and data ports on the phones. Downstairs, the **Titanic Café** serves California-style breakfast and lunch, and the Commodore's **Red Room** is a plush cocktail lounge decorated with rich red velvets, pearlized vinyl, and red tile. Other stylish Joie de Vivre hotels near Union Square include the **Hotel Bijou** and the **Andrews Hotel;** for details, see www.jdvhospitality.com.

Between the theater district and Nob Hill is the onetime Amsterdam Hotel, now **USA Hostels San Francisco,** 749 Taylor St. (between Bush and Sutter), 415/673-3277 or 800/637-3444, www.usahostels.com, with clean, comfortable, spacious private rooms, all with queen bed, TV, and private marble-tiled bathrooms. Four-bed dorms also have private baths. The hostel includes a complete kitchen, lounge, two large patios, laundry facilities, Internet access, and complimentary all-you-can-eat pancake and waffle breakfast. (Dinner is $4.) Dorm beds are $14–21, private rooms $35–54.

Near Union Square, the **Sheehan Hotel,** 620 Sutter St. (at Mason), 415/775-6500 or 800/848-1529 in the U.S. and Canada, www .sheehanhotel.com, is a real find—a surprisingly elegant take on economical downtown accommodations. Rooms have cable TV and phones; some have private baths, others have European-style shared baths (these the bargains). Other facilities include an Olympic-size lap pool, a fitness and exercise room, and a downstairs tearoom and wine bar. The hotel is close to shopping, art, BART, and other public transportation. Discount parking is available. Rates include continental breakfast, and children under 12 stay free with parent(s).

Quite charming and quite French, between Union Square and Nob Hill, is the **Cornell Hotel,** 715 Bush St. (at Powell), 415/421-3154 or 800/232-9698, www.cornellhotel.com, where rates include breakfast; all rooms are nonsmoking. Another best bet, and a bargain for the quality, is the **Chancellor Hotel,** 433 Powell (on Union Square), 415/362-2004 or 800/428-4748, www.chancellorhotel.com, offering elegant rooms within walking distance of just about everything. (Or hop the cable car.)

BOUTIQUE HOTELS: $150–250

San Francisco's bouquet of European-style boutique hotels is becoming so large that it's impossible to fit the flowers in any one container. In addition to those mentioned above, the following sampling offers an idea of the wide variety available. Most of the city's intimate and stylish small hotels are included in the annual San Francisco Convention & Visitors Bureau Lodging Guide, listed among all other accommodations options, by area, and not otherwise distinguished from more mainstream hostelries. Two clues to spotting a possible "boutique": the number of rooms (usually 75 to 150, rarely over 200) and prices (for a double room) over $100.

Near Union Square and Nob Hill

The 111-room **M Hotel Diva,** 440 Geary (between Mason and Taylor, right across from the Curran and Geary Theaters), 415/885-0200 or

800/553-1900, www.hoteldiva.com, is a chrome-faced contemporary Italian classic, awarded "Best Hotel Design" honors by *Interiors* magazine. Special features include a complete business center—with computers, wireless Internet, and high-speed access, you name it—daily newspaper, complimentary breakfast delivered to your door, meeting facilities, a 24-hour fitness center, and maid service twice a day.

Cable cars roll right by the six-floor **Hotel Union Square,** 114 Powell St., 415/397-3000 or 800/553-1900, www.hotelunionsquare.com, one of the city's original boutiques, with an art deco lobby and 131 boldly decorated, stylishly contemporary rooms blending with the building's old-brick San Francisco soul. Multiple amenities, including continental breakfast and on-site parking. Wonderful rooftop suites with gardens.

The onetime Elks Lodge #3 is now the 87-room **Kensington Park Hotel,** 450 Post St., 415/788-6400 or 800/553-1900, www .kensingtonparkhotel.com, just steps from Union Square. Its parlor lobby still sports the original handpainted Gothic ceiling and warm Queen Anne floral decor. Guests enjoy all the amenities, including financial district limo service, a fitness center, complimentary continental breakfast, and afternoon tea and sherry. Inquire about hotel/theater packages, since Theatre On The Square is also located here, along with **Farallon** restaurant.

The century-old **King George Hotel,** 334 Mason (at Geary), 415/781-5050 or 800/288-6005, www.kinggeorge.com, is a cozy and charming stop near Geary St. theaters and Union Square. Breakfast and afternoon tea served daily in the traditional English **Windsor Tearoom.**

CITY-STYLE BED-AND-BREAKFASTS

San Francisco's bed-and-breakfast inns can be an intimate alternative to the city's large hotels. Most B&Bs are restored historic houses with eight to 20 rooms, priced in the $150–250 range (for two); a few offer at least some rooms for under $100. Many of the city's bed-and-breakfasts offer standard hotel services—concierge, bellman, valet/laundry, and room service.

The **Chateau Tivoli** townhouse, 1057 Steiner St., 415/776-5462 or 800/228-1647, www.chateau tivoli.com, is an 1892 Queen Anne landmark with an astounding visual presence. "Colorful" just doesn't do justice as a description of this Alamo Square painted lady. The Tivoli's eccentric exterior architectural style is electrified by 18 historic colors of paint, plus gold leaf. Painstaking restoration is apparent inside, too, from the very Victorian, period-furnished parlors to exquisite, individually decorated guest rooms, each reflecting at least a portion of the city's unusual social history. (Imagine, under one roof: Enrico Caruso, Aimee Crocker, Isadora Duncan, Joaquin Miller, Jack London, opera singer Luisa Tettrazini, and Mark Twain. Somehow, it is imaginable, since the mansion was once the residence of the city's pre-earthquake

Tivoli Opera.) Chateau Tivoli offers nine rooms and suites, all but two rooms with private baths, two with fireplaces.

Onetime home to Archbishop Patrick Riordan, the **Archbishop's Mansion,** 1000 Fulton St. (at Steiner), 415/563-7872 or 800/543-5820, www.thearchbishopsmansion.com, is also exquisitely restored, offering comfortable rooms and suites in a French Victorian mood. Some rooms have fireplaces and in-room spas, and all have phones and TVs. Continental breakfast.

Near Alamo Square, the **Grove Inn,** 890 Grove St., 415/929-0780 or 800/829-0780, www.grove inn.com, is a restored Italianate Victorian inn with 19 rooms (some share baths). Off-street parking available for a small fee. Complimentary breakfast.

Close to the Civic Center arts scene is the **Inn San Francisco,** 943 S. Van Ness Ave., 415/641-0188 or 800/359-0913, www.innsf.com, a huge, renovated 1872 Italianate Victorian with 21 guest rooms, double parlors, and a sun deck. The five bargain rooms here share two bathrooms, but most rooms feature private baths. All include TVs, radios, telephones, and refrigerators; some have hot tubs or in-room spa tubs; and two also have fireplaces and balconies.

Ask about seasonal discounts and other specials, with doubles as low as $85.

Fairly reasonable, near the theater scene, and très retro is artsy yet relaxed **N Hotel Cosmo** (formerly the Bedford), 761 Post St., 415/673-6040 or 800/252-7466, www.hotel-cosmo.com, a 17-story 1929 hotel featuring refurbished art deco–style guest rooms as well as more Victorian rooms in florals and pastels. The basics here include in-room coffee, hair dryers, iron, and ironing board. Also appreciate the rotating local art on exhibit. Another good choice in the vicinity is the stylish art deco **Maxwell Hotel**, 386 Geary, 415/986-2000, or 888/734-6299. Specials can go as low as $109 Also close to the theaters is the winderful 1913 **Savoy Hotel**, 580 Geary, 415/441-2700 or 800/227-4223, www.thesavoyhotel.com, a taste of French provincial with period engravings, imported furnishings, and goose down featherbeds and pillows. Amenities include complimentary afternoon sherry and tea.

Closer to Nob Hill and Chinatown is the nine-floor **Hotel Juliana,** 590 Bush St., 415/392-2540 or 866/325-9457, www.julianahotel.com, offering deals in the off-season. The 107 rooms and suites have in-room coffeemakers, hair dryers, and irons and ironing boards. Stylish lobby. Other amenities include complimentary evening wine, morning limo service to the Financial District (just a few blocks away), and the on-site **Malisa** restaurant, serving "nuevo" French-Latin American bistro fare.

Also within an easy stroll of Nob Hill: the elegant art deco **York Hotel,** 940 Sutter St., 415/885-6800 or 800/808-9675 in the U.S. and Canada, www.yorkhotel.com, used as the setting for Alfred Hitchcock's *Vertigo*. The York offers

The **Alamo Square Inn,** 719 Scott St., 415/922-2055 or 800/345-9888, www.alamoinn.com, is another neighborhood possibility, offering rooms and suites in an 1895 Queen Anne and an 1896 Tudor Revival.

Petite Auberge, 863 Bush St. (near Nob Hill and Union Square), 415/928-6000 or 800/365-3004, www.foursisters.com, is an elegant French country inn right downtown, featuring Pierre Deux fabrics, terra-cotta tile, oak furniture, and lace curtains. All 26 guest rooms have private bathrooms; 16 have fireplaces. The "Petite Suite" has its own entrance and deck, a king-size bed, fireplace, and whirlpool tub. Two doors down is the affiliated **White Swan Inn,** 845 Bush, 415/775-1755 or 800/999-9570, www.foursisters.com, with parlor, library, and 26 rooms (private baths, fireplaces, wet bars) decorated with English-style decor, from the mahogany antiques and rich fabrics to floral-print wallpapers. Both inns serve full breakfast (with the morning paper), afternoon tea, and homemade cookies, and provide little amenities like thick terry bathrobes. All rooms have TVs and telephones.

Close to the Presidio and Fort Mason in Cow Hollow is the **Edward II Inn,** 3155 Scott St. (at Lombard), 415/922-3000 or 800/473-2846, www.edwardii.com, an English-style country hotel and pub offering 24 rooms and six suites, all with color TVs and phones, some with shared bathrooms. The suites have in-room whirlpool baths. A complimentary continental breakfast is served.

Peaceful and pleasant amid the hubbub of North Beach is the stylish and artsy 15-room **Hotel Bohème,** 444 Columbus Ave., 415/433-9111, www.hotelboheme.com, offering continental charm all the way to breakfast, which is served either indoors or out on the patio. On-site restaurant, too. Also in North Beach is the French country **Washington Square Inn,** 1660 Stockton St., 415/981-4220 or 800/388-0220, www.wsisf.com, featuring 15 rooms (most with private baths), continental breakfast, and afternoon tea.

Not a B&B per se, but providing as intimate a lodging experience as you'll get, **Dockside Boat & Bed,** Pier 39, 415/392-5526 or 800/436-2574, www.boatandbed.com, contracts a stable of luxury yachts, both motor and sail, on which guests can spend the night and view city lights from the boat deck.

the usual three-star comforts, including limousine service and complimentary breakfast.

The **Villa Florence Hotel,** 225 Powell St., 415/397-7700 or 866/823-4669, www.villa florence.com, features a 16th-century Tuscany/ Italian Renaissance theme, and American-style European ambience. The colorful and comfortable guest rooms feature soundproofed walls and windows—a good idea above the cable cars and so close to Union Square—as well as in-room coffeemakers and all basic amenities. The hotel has a beauty salon and features the adjacent (and outstanding) NorCal-NorItal **Kuleto's Restaurant** and antipasto bar, 415/397-7720.

For an all-American historical theme, consider the **Monticello Inn,** 127 Ellis (between Powell and Cyril Magnin), 415/392-8800 or 866/778-6169, www.monticelloinn.com. Its cool colonial-style lobby features Chippendale reproductions and a wood-burning fireplace. Rooms feature early-American decor, soundproofed walls and windows, refrigerators, honor bars, phones with data ports and voice mail, and other amenities. Complimentary continental breakfast is served in the lobby. The inn's adjacent **Puccini & Pinetti,** 415/392-5500, is a highly regarded Cal-Italian restaurant well patronized by theatergoers.

Between Union Square and Nob Hill is 🏛 **Hotel Rex,** 562 Sutter (between Powell and Mason), 415/433-4434 or 800/433-4434, www.jdvhospitality.com, furnished in 1930s style and "dedicated to the arts and literary world," refurbished and reopened in February 2003. Rates include a complimentary evening glass of wine. Doubles $175–219. Also reasonable by boutique hotel standards is the **San Francisco Carlton Hotel,** 1075 Sutter (at Larkin), 415/673-0242 or 800/922-7586, www.carlton hotel.com, placed on Condé Nast Traveler's 1999 Gold List and offering 165 comfortable rooms with Queen Anne-style chairs and pleasant decor, as well as the on-site Oak Room Grille.

Among other well-regarded small hostelries in the vicinity of Union Square is the wheelchair-accessible, 80-room **Warwick Regis Hotel,** 490 Geary St., 415/928-7900 or 800/203-3232 in the U.S. and Canada, www.warwickregis.com, furnished with French and English Louis XVI

antiques and offering exceptional service. Amenities include hair dryers and small refrigerators in every room, plus cable TV, complimentary morning newspaper, and on-site café and bar. Also exceptional is **The Donatello,** 501 Post St. (at Mason, a block west of Union Square), 415/441-7100 or 800/301-0217 in the U.S. and Canada, www.thedonatello.com, noteworthy for its four-star amenities and its restaurant, **Zingari** (415/885-8850).

Moving into San Francisco's trend-setting strata, the gleeful **Hotel Triton,** 342 Grant Ave., 415/394-0500 or 800/800-1299, www.hotel triton.com, is still the talk of the town—and other towns as well—attracting celebrities galore as well as comparisons to New York's Paramount and Royalton Hotels. For more information, see Some Hip San Francisco Stays.

Other Areas

North of Market at the edge of the Financial District is the **Galleria Park Hotel,** 191 Sutter (between Montgomery and Kearny), 415/781-3060 or 866/756-3036, www.galleriapark.com, its striking art nouveau lobby with crystal skylight still somehow overshadowed by the curvaceous, equally original sculpted fireplace. Amenities include attractive rooms with soundproofed windows and walls, meeting facilities, on-site parking, a rooftop park and jogging track, and athletic club access. Dine at adjacent **Perry's** restaurant.

The Embarcadero YMCA south of Market near the Ferry Building now shares the waterfront building with the **Harbor Court Hotel,** 165 Steuart St. (at Mission), 415/882-1300 or 866/792-6283, www.harborcourthotel.com, a fairly phenomenal transformation at the edge of the financial district and a perfect setup for business travelers. The building's Florentine exterior has been beautifully preserved, as have the building's original arches, columns, and vaulted ceilings. Inside, the theme is oversized, Old World creature comfort. The plush rooms are rich with amenities, including TV, radio, direct-dial phones with extra-long cords, and complimentary beverages. The penthouse features a Louis XVI-style bed and 18-foot ceilings. Business travelers will appreciate the hotel's business center, financial district limo service, and same-day valet laundry service. And to work off the stress of that business meeting, head right next door to the renovated multilevel YMCA, where recreational facilities include basketball courts, aerobics classes, an Olympic-size pool, whirlpool, steam room, dry sauna, and even stationary bicycles with a view. Rates include complimentary continental breakfast and valet parking. Affiliated **Ozumo Restaurant** is a full service Japanese restaurant, with a sushi bar, grill, and sake lounge.

Adjacent and also worthwhile is the **Hotel Griffon**, 155 Steuart St. (at Mission), 415/495-2100 or 800/321-2201 in the U.S. and Canada, www.hotelgriffon.com, with amenities like continental breakfast, complimentary morning newspaper, and a fitness center.

Near Civic Center cultural attractions is the exceptional small **Inn at the Opera**, 333 Fulton, 415/863-8400 or 800/325-2708, www.innathe opera.com, featuring complimentary breakfast and morning newspaper, in-room cookies and apples, free shoeshine service, available limousine service, and an excellent on-site restaurant, **Ovation.** The guest list often includes big-name theater people.

A stylish option in the Marina District is Joie de Vivre's **Hotel Del Sol**, 3100 Webster St., 415/921-5520 or 877/433-5765, www.jdv hospitality.com, a onetime motel redone in the sunny colors of a day at the beach. Abundant amenities, including continental breakfast served out by the pool and free kites, beach balls, and sunglasses for kiddos.

HIGH-END HOTELS: $250 AND UP

In addition to the fine hotels mentioned above, San Francisco offers an impressive selection of

PUTTIN' ON THE RITZ

Serious visiting fans of San Francisco, at least those with serious cash, tend to equate their long-running romance with a stay on Nob Hill, home base for most of the city's ritzier hotels. And what could be ritzier than the Ritz?

The **Ritz-Carlton, San Francisco,** 600 Stockton St. (at California)., 415/296-7465 or 800/241-3333, www.ritzcarlton.com, is a local landmark, San Francisco's finest remaining example of neoclassical architecture. At the Financial District's former western edge, and hailed in 1909 as a "temple of commerce," until 1973 the building served as West Coast headquarters for the Metropolitan Life Insurance Company. Expanded and revised five times since, San Francisco's Ritz has been open for business as a hotel only since 1991. After painstaking restoration (four years and $140 million worth), this nine-story grand dame still offers some odd architectural homage to its past. Witness the terracotta tableau over the entrance: the angelic allegorical figure ("Insurance") is protecting the American family. (Ponder the meaning of the lion's heads and winged hourglasses on your own.)

The Ritz offers a total of 336 rooms and suites, most with grand views. Amenities on the top two floors ("The Ritz-Carlton Club") include private lounge, continuous complimentary meals, and Dom Perignon and Beluga caviar every evening. All rooms, however, feature Italian marble bathrooms, in-room safes, and every modern comfort, plus access to the fitness center (indoor swimming pool, whirlpool, training room, separate men's and women's steam rooms and saunas, massage, and more). Services include the usual long list plus morning newspaper, childcare, video library, car rental, and multilingual staff. Rates run $325–425 for rooms, $525–3,500 for suites. (The Ritz-Carlton's "Summer Escape" package, when available, includes a deluxe guest room, continental breakfast, valet parking, and unlimited use of the fitness center.) The Ritz-Carlton also provides full conference facilities. **The Terrace** restaurant here offers the city's only alfresco dining in a hotel setting—like eating breakfast, lunch, or dinner on someone else's well-tended garden patio. (Come on Sunday for brunch and jazz.) Adjacent, indoors, is the somewhat casual **Lobby Lounge.** More formal, serving neoclassical cuisine, is **The Dining Room.**

large, four- and five-star superdeluxe hotels. The air in these establishments is rarefied indeed. (Sometimes the airs, too.) Many, however, do offer seasonal specials. Business-oriented hotels often feature lower weekend rates.

The Ritz

Peek into **The Ritz-Carlton, San Francisco,** 600 Stockton (between California and Pine), 415/296-7465 or 800/241-3333, www.ritz carlton.com, to see what a great facelift an old lady can get for $140 million. Quite impressive. And many consider the hotel's Dining Room at The Ritz-Carlton among the city's finest eateries. Rooms start at $425. For more information, see Puttin' on the Ritz.

The Palace

Equally awesome—and another popular destination these days for City Guides and other walking tours—is that grande dame of San Francisco hostelries, the renovated and resplendent 1909 **M Sheraton Palace Hotel,** 2 New Montgomery St. (downtown at Market), 415/512-1111 or 800/325-3589, www.sfpalace.com. Wander in, under the metal grillwork awning at the New Montgomery entrance, across the polished marble sunburst on the foyer floor, and sit a spell in the lobby to appreciate the more subtle aspects of the hotel's $150 million renovation. Then mosey into the central **Garden Court** restaurant. The wonderful lighting here is provided, during the day, by the (cleaned and restored) 1800s atrium skylight, one of the world's largest leaded-glass creations; some 70,000 panes of glass arch over the entire room. It's a best bet for Sunday brunch. Note, too, the 10 (yes, 10) 700-pound crystal chandeliers. The **Pied Piper Bar,** with its famous Maxfield Parrish mural, is a Palace fixture, and adjoins **Maxfield's** restaurant. Tours of the hotel are available; call for schedules and information.

In addition to plush accommodations (rooms still have high ceilings), the Palace offers complete conference and meeting facilities, a business center, and a rooftop fitness center. The swimming pool up there, under a modern vaulted skylight, is especially enjoyable at sunset; spa services include a poolside whirlpool and dry sauna. Rooms start at $300.

The St. Francis

Another beloved San Francisco institution is the **Westin St. Francis Hotel,** 335 Powell St. (between Post and Geary, directly across from Union Square), 415/397-7000 or 888/625-5144 in the U.S. and Canada, www.starwood.com/westin, a recently restored landmark recognized by the National Trust for Historic Preservation as one of the Historic Hotels of America. When the first St. Francis opened in 1849 at Clay and Dupont (Grant), it was considered the only hostelry at which ladies were safe, and was also celebrated as the first "to introduce bedsheets to the city." But San Francisco's finest was destroyed by fire four years later. By the early 1900s, reincarnation was imminent when a group of local businessmen declared their intention to rebuild the St. Francis as "a caravansary worthy of standing at the threshold of the Occident, representative of California hospitality." No expense was spared on the stylish 12-story hotel overlooking Union Square—partially opened but still under construction when the April 18, 1906, earthquake and fire hit town. Damaged but not destroyed, the restored St. Francis opened in November 1907; over the entrance was an electrically lighted image of a phoenix rising from the city's ashes. Successfully resurrected, the elegant and innovative hotel attracted royalty, international political and military leaders, theatrical stars, and literati.

But even simpler folk have long been informed, entertained, and welcomed by the St. Francis. People keep an eye on the number of unfurled flags in front of the St. Francis, for example, knowing that these herald the nationalities of visiting dignitaries. And every long-time San Franciscan knows that any shiny old coins in their pockets most likely came from the St. Francis; the hotel's long-standing practice of washing coins—to prevent them from soiling ladies' white gloves—continues to this day. Meeting friends "under the Clock" means the Magneta Clock in the hotel's Powell St. lobby; this "master clock" from Saxony has been a fixture since the early 1900s.

After additions and grand renovations, the St. Francis today offers 1,200 luxury guest rooms and suites (request a suite brochure if you hanker to stay in the General MacArthur suite, the Queen Elizabeth II suite, or the Ron and Nancy Reagan suite), plus fitness and full meeting and conference facilities, a 1,500-square-foot ballroom, five restaurants (including elegant Victor's atop the St. Francis Tower), shopping arcade, and valet parking. The replacement of the time-honored Compass Rose bar and lounge with a swank Michael Mina restaurant in 2004 is a change that's had mixed reviews among the hotel's traditional fans. Rooms start at $249, suites at $650.

Others Downtown

The idea of Ian Schrager, king of New York's Studio 54 and Royalton Hotel, revamping the classic **Clift Hotel** in collaboration with designer Phillippe Stark raised eyebrows among WASPy San Franciscans. Brows furrowed, too, at the thought of renovating the hotel's famous art-deco **Redwood Room** bar, its walls hewn from 2,000-foot redwood trees. Yet the result is an intoxicating combination of old-school luxury and faux-Tinseltown irony. The Redwood Room's walls are intact, now paired with witty modern touches—Ostrich-stamped leather pillows on the chairs, a dramatic curved glass bar, and plasma screen monitors on the walls. The nuevo opulence carries over to the old French Room, now Schraeger's **Asia de Cuba**, a dimly lit Latin restaurant with intimate booths and kitschy artwork. Guest rooms are fairly subdued, featuring lavender walls and orange furnishings. Rooms at the Clift, 495 Geary St. (at Taylor), 415/775-4700 or 800/652-5438, www.clifthotel.com, start at $195, suites at $295.

The city has more classical class, of course. The four-star **N Prescott Hotel,** 545 Post St. (between Taylor and Mason), 415/563-0303 or 866/271-3632, www.prescotthotel.com, elegantly combines uptown style with the feel of a British men's club. Rooms and suites come complete with paisley motif, overstuffed furniture, and every imaginable amenity—from honor bar and terry robes to shoe shines and evening wine and cheeses. Not to mention room service courtesy of Wolfgang Puck's downstairs **Postrio** restaurant, 415/776.7825, where hotel guests also receive preferred dining reservations (if rooms are also reserved well in advance). Services for guests on the Club Level include express check-in (and checkout), continental breakfast, hors d'oeuvres from Postrio, personal concierge service, and even stationary bicycles and rowers delivered to your room on request.

Quite refined, too, with the feel of a fine residential hotel, is **Campton Place Hotel,** 340 Stockton St. (just north of Union Square), 415/781-5555 or 800/235-4300, www.campton place.com, which regularly shows up near the top of U.S. "best of" hotel and restaurant lists. The hotel has all the amenities, including the acclaimed **Campton Place Restaurant,** serving impeccable contemporary American cuisine (415/955-5555). Rooms start at $195, suites at $450.

Also within easy reach of downtown doings is the sleek, modern, four-star **Pan Pacific Hotel,** 500 Post St. (at Mason, one block west of Union Square), 415/771-8600, 800/327-8585 or 800/223-5652, www.panpac.com. The business-oriented Pan Pacific offers three phones with call waiting in each room, personal computers delivered to your room upon request, notary public and business services, and Rolls Royce shuttle service to the Financial District. It's also luxurious; bathrooms, for example, feature floor-to-ceiling Breccia marble, artwork, a mini-screen TV, and a telephone. Specials start at $209, and some include breakfast in your room or at the third-floor **Pacific** restaurant (California-fusion cuisine), 415/929-2087.

Other worthy downtown possibilities include the contemporary Japanese-style **Hotel Nikko,** 222 Mason, 415/394-1111 or 800/645-5687, www.nikkohotels.com, which boasts a glass-enclosed rooftop pool, and the 1,000-room **Renaissance Parc 55 Hotel,** 55 Cyril Magnin St. (Market at Fifth), 415/392-8000 or 800/468-3571, www.renaissancehotels.com. The exquisite **Mandarin Oriental San Francisco,** 222 Sansome, 415/276-9888 or 800/622-0404, www.mandarin-oriental.com, is housed in the top 11 floors of the financial district's California First Interstate Building. The 160 rooms boast great views (even from the bathrooms) and all the amenities. Another plus is **Silks** restaurant, 415/986-2020. The **Hyatt Regency San Francisco,** 5 Embarcadero Center (Market and California), 415/788-1234 or 800/233-1234, www.hyatt.com, is famous for its 17-story lobby, atrium, and rotating rooftop restaurant, **The Equinox,** 415/291-6619. There are Hyatts all over San Francisco, including the nearby **Park Hyatt** on Battery—home of the outstanding **Park Grill,** 415/296-2933—plus those at Union Square, Fisherman's Wharf, and out at the airport in Burlingame; a call can reserve a room at any and all.

Other comfortable hotel choices near the financial district and the booming new media companies south of Market include the super-stylish, granite-faced **W Hotel,** 181 Third St. (at Howard), 415/777-5300 or 877/946-8357 or 888/625-5144 in the U.S. and Canada, www.starwood.com/whotels, which is as sleek as its next-door neighbor, the San Francisco Museum of Modern Art. This business-oriented hotel also offers boutique touches: plush down comforters and Aveda bath products in all rooms. Downstairs, the **XYZ** restaurant and bar, 415/817-7836, serves creative fusion cuisine to a crowd of wannabe supermodels. Also in the area: the **San Francisco Marriott,** 55 Fourth St., 415/896-1600 or 800/228-9290, www.marriott.com, located south of Market and just north of the Moscone Convention Center, and the nearby **Argent Hotel,** 50 Third St. (at Market), 415/974-6400 or 888/238-0302, www.argenthotel.com.

Nob Hill

Some of the city's finest hotels cluster atop Nob Hill. Since judgment always depends upon personal taste, despite official ratings it's all but impossible to say which is "the best." Take your pick.

Across from Grace Cathedral and Huntington Park, the **M Huntington Hotel,** 1075 California St. (at Taylor), 415/474-5400 or 800/227-4683., www.huntingtonhotel.com, is

AHOY, ARGONAUTS

The notably nautical decor of the new Klimpton **Argonaut Hotel,** launched as a new Fisherman's Wharf hotel in August 2003, acknowledges the 1849 argonauts who sailed through the Golden Gate to seek their fortunes in the California goldfields. San Francisco Maritime National Historic Park's 252-room hotel as well as (in the hotel lobby) the park's new visitor center are open daily 9:30 A.M.–7 P.M. Rooms offer all the modern amenities, and some feature the building's venerable brick walls, timbers, steel warehouse doors, or large porthole-style windows. Rates are $200–300, with discounted rates dropping as low as $129. The kid-friendly, pet-friendly, fully accessible Argonaut Hotel is located inside the park, 495 Jefferson St. (at Hyde), 415/563-2800 or 800/790-1415, www.argonauthotel.com. Adjacent is the hotel's **Blue Mermaid Chowder House and Bar.**

the last surviving family-owned fine hotel in the neighborhood. It's a beauty, a destination in and of itself. Every room and suite (onetime residential apartments) has been individually designed and decorated, and every service is a personal gesture. Stop in just to appreciate the elegant lobby. Dark and clubby, and open daily for breakfast, lunch, and dinner, the **Big Four Restaurant** off the lobby pays pleasant homage to the good ol' days of Wild West railroad barons—and often serves wild game entrées along with tamer continental contemporary cuisine. Relax at the **Nob Hill Spa** adjacent to the hotel. Guest rooms start at $315 for two, suites at $490.

Top-of-the-line, too, is the romantic, turn-of-the-20th-century **Fairmont Hotel,** 950 Mason St. (at California), 415/772-5000 or 800/257-7544 for reservations, www.fairmont.com, recognizable to as the setting for the fictional San Francisco hotel the "St. Gregory" in the 1980s TV series *Hotel.* The Fairmont offers 596 rooms (small to large) and suites, all expected amenities, and several on-site restaurants. Locally loved, are the hotel's **Laurel Court,** for steak and seafood (also open for breakfast), and the fantastically kitschy Tiki-inspired **Tonga Room,** which specializes in Chinese and Polynesian cuisine and features a simulated tropical rainstorm every half hour. The Fairmont also offers full conference and business facilities (20 meeting rooms) and the **Club One at Nob Hill Health Club** (extra fee) for fitness enthusiasts. Rooms start at $199, suites at $550. The five-star ⓝ **Renaissance Stanford Court Hotel,** 905 California St. (at Powell), 415/989-3500 or 800/468-3571, www.marriott .com, boasts a 120-foot-long, sepia-toned lobby mural honoring San Francisco's historic diversity. On the west wall, for example, are panels depicting the hotel's predecessor, the original Leland Stanford Mansion, with railroad barons and other wealthy Nob Hill nabobs on one side, Victorian-era African Americans on the other. Other panels depict the long-running economic exploitation of California places and peoples, from Russian whaling and fur trading, redwood logging, and the California gold rush (with Native Americans and the Chinese looking on) to the 1906 earthquake and fire framed by the construction of the transcontinental railroad and California's Latinization, as represented by Mission Dolores. Stop in and see it; this is indeed the story of Northern California, if perhaps a bit romanticized.

The hotel itself is romantic, recognized by the National Trust for Historic Preservation as one of the Historic Hotels of America. The Stanford Court features a decidedly European ambience, from the carriage entrance (with beaux arts fountain and stained-glass dome) to guest rooms decked out in 19th-century artwork, antiques, and reproductions (not to mention modern comforts like heated towel racks in the marble bathrooms and dictionaries on the writing desks). Opulent touches in the lobby include Baccarat chandeliers, Carrara marble floor, oriental carpets, original artwork, and an 1806 antique grandfather clock once owned by Napoleon Bonaparte. Guest services include complimentary stretch limo service, both for business and pleasure. Rooms start at $235, suites at $775. Even if you don't stay, consider a meal (breakfast, lunch,

and dinner daily, plus weekend brunch) at the hotel's Mediterranean-inspired restaurant, **Fournou's Ovens,** 415/989-1910 for reservations, considered one of San Francisco's best.

Don't forget the Mark Hopkins Hotel, now the **Mark Hopkins Inter-Continental,** 1 Nob Hill (California and Mason), 415/392-3434 or 800/327-0200, www.san-francisco.interconti .com, another refined Old California old-timer. Hobnobbing with the best of them atop Nob Hill, the Mark Hopkins features 380 elegant guest rooms and suites (many with great views) and all the amenities, not to mention the fabled **Top of the Mark** sky room, still San Francisco's favorite sky-high romantic bar scene. The French-California **Nob Hill Restaurant** is open daily for breakfast, lunch, and dinner. Rooms start at $290.

Other Areas

Two blocks from Pier 39 at Fisherman's Wharf, the **Tuscan Inn,** 425 North Point, 415/561-1100 or 800/648-4626, www.tuscaninn.com, a Best Western reinvented by hotelier Bill Kimpton. The hotel features an Italianate lobby with fireplace, a central garden court, and 221 rooms and suites with modern amenities. Rates include morning coffee, tea, and biscotti, and a daily wine hour by the lobby fireplace. Rooms start at $249. Just off the lobby is a convenient Italian trattoria, **Cafe Pescatore,** specializing in fresh fish and seafood, pastas, and pizzas (baked in a wood-burning oven) at lunch and dinner. Open for breakfast also.

In Pacific Heights, west of Van Ness and south of Lombard, the **Sherman House,** 2160 Green St. (between Fillmore and Webster), 415/563-3600, www.theshermanhouse.com, is among the city's finest small, exclusive hotels. Once the mansion of Leander Sherman, it now attracts inordinate percentages of celebrities and stars, who come for the privacy and personal service. The ambience here, including the intimate dining room, exudes 19th-century French opulence. Rooms start at $460, suites at $775.

M

San Francisco

Food

San Francisco

San Franciscans love to eat. For a true San Franciscan, eating—and eating well—competes for first place among life's purest pleasures, right up there with the arts, exercising, and earning money. (There may be a few others.) Finding new and novel neighborhood eateries, and knowing which among the many fine dining establishments are currently at the top of the trendsetters' culinary A-list, are points of pride for long-time residents. Fortunately, San Franciscans also enjoy sharing information and opinions—including their restaurant preferences. So the best way to find out where to eat, and why, is simply to ask. The following listings should help fine-food aficionados get started, and will certainly keep everyone else from starving.

UNION SQUARE AND NOB HILL

A well-kept secret, perhaps downtown's best breakfast spot, is **Dottie's True Blue Cafe,** 522 Jones St. (between O'Farrell and Geary), 415/885-2767, a genuine all-American coffee shop serving every imaginable American standard plus new cuisine, such as (at lunch) grilled eggplant sandwiches. Open daily for breakfast and lunch only, 7 A.M.–3 P.M.

Another area classic, if for other reasons, is **John's Grill,** 63 Ellis (just off Powell), 415/986-3274 or 415/986-0069, with a neat neon sign outside and *Maltese Falcon* memorabilia just about everywhere inside. (In the book, this is where Sam Spade ate his lamb chops.) Named a National Literary Landmark by the Friends of Libraries, USA, this informal eatery ode to Dashiell Hammett serves good continental-style American fare, plus large helpings of Hammett hero worship, especially upstairs in Hammett's Den and the Maltese Falcon Room. Open Mon.–Sat. for lunch and dinner; Sunday for dinner only. Live jazz nightly.

For excellent seafood, dive into the French provincial **Brasserie Savoy** at the Savoy Hotel, 580 Geary St. (at Jones), 415/441-2700, open for breakfast (until noon), dinner, and late supper. Gallic stodgy? *Mais, non!* How about a "Lobster Martini?" Or a fish soup described as "haunting" by one local food writer (perhaps she had one too many Lobster Martinis?).

Farallon, 450 Post (near Powell), 415/956-6969, might be *the* place in town for seafood. And the unique Pat Kuleto-designed interior might make you feel like you're under the sea, in an octopus's garden, perhaps. Look for such intriguing specialties as truffled mashed potatoes with crab and sea urchin sauce, or ginger-steamed salmon. Open for lunch Mon.–Sat. and for dinner nightly.

Two blocks from Union Square, **Puccini & Pinetti,** 129 Ellis (at Cyril Magnin), 415/392-5500, is a beautifully designed Cal-Italian restaurant popular with theater crowds. Menu highlights include bruschetta with arugula and roasted garlic, smoked salmon pizzas, and risotto with charred leeks and wild mushrooms. Prices are surprisingly reasonable—most entrées run $10–15. Open for lunch and dinner.

Worth searching for downtown is **Cafe Claude,** 7 Claude Ln. (between Grant and Kearny, Bush and Sutter, just off Bush), 415/392-3505, an uncanny incarnation of a genuine French café, from the paper table covers to the café au lait served in bowls. Good food, plus live jazz four nights a week.

A good choice downtown for pasta is **Kuleto's,** 221 Powell St., 415/397-7720, a comfortable trattoria-style Italian restaurant and bar at the Villa Florence Hotel. It's popular for power lunching and dinner, and it's also open for peaceful, pleasant breakfasts.

Better yet, though, is **Ⓜ Zingari Ristorante,** 501 Post St. (at Mason, in the Donatello hotel), 415/885-8850, justifiably famous for its Northern Italian regional dishes. Dining rooms are small and intimate, and dressing up is de rigueur—putting on a show as good as, or better than, almost anything else in the neighborhood.

People should at least pop into Wolfgang Puck's **M Postrio,** 545 Post St. (at Mason, inside the Prescott Hotel), 415/776-7825, to appreciate the exquisite ribbon-patterned dining room designs by Pat Kuleto. The food here is exceptional, with most entrées representing Puck's interpretations of San Francisco classics. Since the restaurant is open for breakfast, lunch, and dinner, try Hangtown fry and some house-made pastries at breakfast, perhaps a pizza fresh from the wood-burning oven or Dungeness crab with spicy curry risotto at lunch. Dinner is an adventure. Great desserts. Make reservations well in advance, or hope for a cancellation.

Famous among local foodies, not to mention its long-standing national and international fan club, is **Masa's,** 648 Bush St. (at the Hotel Vintage Court), 415/989-7154, one of the city's finest dinner restaurants and considered by many to be the best French restaurant in the United States. Masa's serves French cuisine with a fresh California regional touch and a Spanish aesthetic. Reservations accepted three weeks in advance. Very expensive.

Fleur de Lys, 777 Sutter (between Jones and Taylor), 415/673-7779, is another local legend—a fine French restaurant that also transcends the traditional. Nothing is too heavy or overdone. Expensive. Open Mon.–Sat. for dinner. Reservations.

On Nob Hill, **Charles Nob Hill,** 1250 Jones St. (at Clay), 415/771-5400, is a neighborhood French restaurant featuring specialties like Hudson Valley foie gras and Sonoma duck. Open for dinner Tues.–Sat. Some of the city's finest hotels, on Nob Hill and elsewhere, also serve some of the city's finest food.

FINANCIAL DISTRICT AND EMBARCADERO

Still a haute spot for young refugees from the Financial District is the casual **Gordon Biersch Brewery and Restaurant,** 2 Harrison St., 415/243-8246, along the Embarcadero in the shadow of the Bay Bridge. The German-style lagers here are certainly a draw—three styles (Pilsner to Bavarian dark) are created on the premises—as is the surprisingly good food, which is far from the usual brewpub grub. Open from 11 A.M. daily. (Gordon Biersch also has outposts in Palo Alto, San Jose, Pasadena, San Diego, and elsewhere.)

Also on the Embarcadero, **Boulevard,** 1 Mission St. (at Steuart), 415/543-6084, is a Franco-American bistro serving American classics—ribs, pork chops, mashed 'taters—in an art nouveau atmosphere. Nice views. Open for lunch weekdays and dinner nightly. Also overlooking the Embarcadero is **One Market,** 1 Market St., 415/777-5577, a sleek haven for the expense-account set featuring the best of seasonal fresh California ingredients in its upscale American specialties. Extensive wine list. Open for lunch weekdays and dinner Mon.–Sat.

In the seafood swim of things, **Aqua,** 252 California St.(between Front and Battery), 415/956-9662, is making a global splash among well-heeled foodies. Signature creations include basil-grilled lobster, lobster potato gnocchi, and black-mussel soufflé. Open weekdays for lunch, Mon.–Sat. for dinner. **Jeanty at Jack's,** 615 Sacramento St. (at Montgomery), 415/693-0941, brings Philippe Jeanty's wonderful brasserie fare to one of San Francisco's classic restaurants, 1864-vintage Jack's—from cassoulet to and coq au vin to steak frites.

At **Delancey Street Restaurant,** 600 Embarcadero (at Brannan), 415/512-5179, the restaurant staff is comprised of Delancey's drug, alcohol, and crime rehabilitees. The daily changing menu at this radical chic, sociopolitically progressive place is ethnic American—everything from matzo ball soup to pot roast. And there's a great view of Alcatraz from the outdoor dining area. Open for lunch, afternoon tea, and dinner.

A half-sibling to SoMa's Fringale, homey **Piperade** at 1015 Battery St. (near Green), 415/391-2555, serves a contemporary interpretation of chef Gerald Hirigoyen's Basque roots—everything from pork daube and steamed Pacific snapper to the restaurant's namesake *piperade,* a stew of thin-sliced Serrano ham, bell peppers, tomatoes, and garlic. Wonderful desserts.

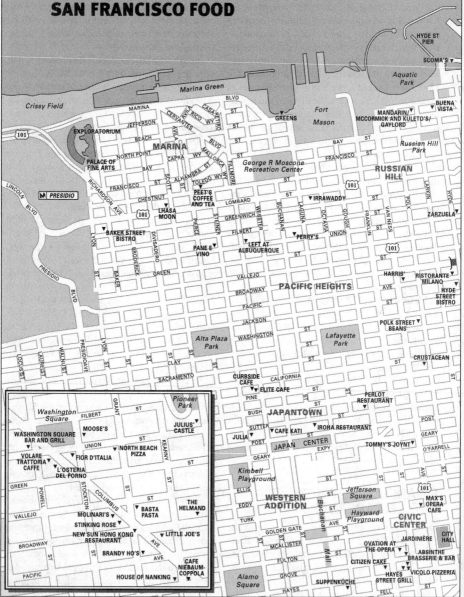

SAN FRANCISCO FOOD

HYDE ST
PIER

SCOMA'S ▼

Aquatic
Park

Marina Green

Crissy Field

BLVD

BUENA
VISTA

MARINA

CASA RETIRO

AVILA

DEL RICO
WY

CERVANTES

CASA

ST

GREENS

Fort
Mason

BAY ST

MANDARIN/ ▼
MCCORMICK AND KULETO'S/
GAYLORD

JEFFERSON

BEACH

NORTH POINT

EXPLORATORIUM

PALACE OF
FINE ARTS

BAY

FRANCISCO

MARINA

CAPRA WY

MALLORCA WY

ALHAMBRA ST

TOLEDO WY

FILLMORE

BLVD

ST

ST

ST

George R Moscone
Recreation Center

FRANCISCO

Russian Hill
Park

RUSSIAN
HILL

101

LINCOLN
BLVD

RICHARDSON AVE

CHESTNUT

SCOTT

ST

PEET'S
COFFEE
AND TEA

ST

IRRAWADDY ▼

ST

LARKIN

HYDE

PRESIDIO

LHASA
MOON

LOMBARD

BUCHANAN

LAGUNA

OCTAVIA

GOUGH

FRANKLIN

VAN NESS

POLK

ZARZUELA ▼

GREENWICH

WEBSTER

BAKER STREET
BISTRO

DIVISADERO

PIERCE

STEINER

FILBERT

GREEN

PANE E ▼
VINO

LEFT AT ▼
ALBUQUERQUE

PERRY'S ▼

UNION

101

LYON ST

BRODERICK

BAKER

VALLEJO

BROADWAY

PACIFIC HEIGHTS

HARRIS' ▼

AVE

RISTORANTE ▼
MILANO

PRESIDIO
BLVD

LYON ST

PACIFIC

JACKSON

ST

HYDE
STREET
BISTRO

PRESIDIO AVE

WALNUT

LOCUST

LAUREL

Alta Plaza
Park

WASHINGTON

ST

Lafayette
Park

POLK STREET ▼
BEANS

CLAY

CRUSTACEAN
▼

SACRAMENTO

CALIFORNIA

CURBSIDE
CAFE

ELITE CAFE ▼▼

ST

ST

Washington
Square

FILBERT

GRANT

ST

Pioneer
Park

PINE

BUSH

JAPANTOWN

PERLOT
RESTAURANT
▼

POST

MOOSE'S

JULIUS' ▼
CASTLE

SUTTER

CAFE KATI ▼

IROHA RESTAURANT ▼

GEARY

WASHINGTON SQUARE
BAR AND GRILL
▼

UNION

NORTH BEACH
PIZZA

KEARNY

JULIA

POST

JAPAN CENTER

TOMMY'S JOYNT ▼

O'FARRELL

VOLARE ▼
TRATTORIA
CAFFE

FIOR D'ITALIA ▼

GEARY

EXPY

L'OSTERIA
DEL FORNO

ST

Kimbell
Playground

ST

AVE

GREEN

STOCKTON

COLUMBUS

ELLIS

Jefferson
Square

101

POWELL

ST

EDDY

WESTERN
ADDITION

BUCHANAN

MAX'S ▼
OPERA
CAFE

VALLEJO

MOLINARI'S ▼

BASTA ▼
PASTA

THE ▼
HELMAND

TURK

Hayward
Playground

CIVIC
CENTER

CITY
HALL

STINKING ROSE ▼

GOLDEN GATE

MALL

JARDINIÈRE ▼

BROADWAY

NEW SUN HONG KONG
RESTAURANT

LITTLE JOE'S ▼

AVE

MCALLISTER

OVATION AT
THE OPERA
▼

ABSINTHE ▼
BRASSERIE & BAR

BRANDY HO'S ▼

AVE

FULTON

CITIZEN CAKE ▼

VICOLO PIZZERIA ▼

PACIFIC

HOUSE OF NANKING ▼

CAFE
NIEBAUM-
COPPOLA
▼

Alamo
Square

GROVE

HAYES

HAYES ▼
STREET GRILL

SUPPENKÜCHE ▼

FELL

PRESIDIO

101

M PRESIDIO

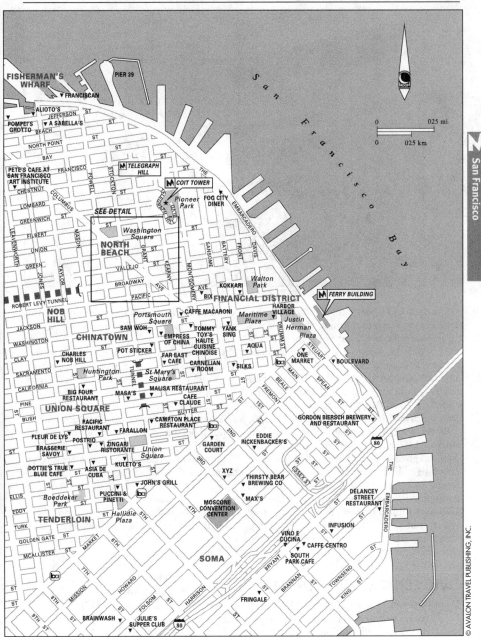

FISHERMAN'S WHARF
PIER 39
▼ FRANCISCAN
▼ ALIOTO'S
JEFFERSON ST
POMPEI'S GROTTO ▼ ▼ A SABELLA'S
BEACH ST
NORTH POINT ST
BAY ST
PETE'S CAFE AT SAN FRANCISCO ART INSTITUTE ▼
FRANCISCO
CHESTNUT
LOMBARD
GREENWICH ST
FILBERT
UNION
GREEN
JONES
LEAVENWORTH
TAYLOR
MASON
COLUMBUS
POWELL
STOCKTON

M TELEGRAPH HILL
M COIT TOWER
★ Pioneer Park
FOG CITY DINER

SEE DETAIL
Washington Square
NORTH BEACH
VALLEJO
BROADWAY
PACIFIC
GRANT
KEARNY
MONTGOMERY
AVE

KOKKARI
Walton Park
▼ BIX
FINANCIAL DISTRICT
M FERRY BUILDING

ROBERT LEVY TUNNEL
NOB HILL
JACKSON ST
WASHINGTON
CLAY
CHARLES NOB HILL
SACRAMENTO
CALIFORNIA
PINE
BUSH ST
CHINATOWN
Portsmouth Square
SAM WOH ▼
EMPRESS OF CHINA
POT STICKER
FAR EAST CAFE ▼
St Mary's Square
Huntington Park
BIG FOUR RESTAURANT
MASA'S ▼
▼ CAFFE MACARONI
TOMMY TOY'S HAUTE CUISINE CHINOISE
CARNELIAN ROOM ▼
MALISA RESTAURANT
CAFE ▼ CLAUDE
Maritime Plaza
YANK SING
AQUA ▼
▼ SILKS
HARBOR VILLAGE
Justin Herman Plaza
ONE MARKET
▼ BOULEVARD
BATTERY
SANSOME
FRONT
DAVIS
DRUMM
STEUART
MAIN
SPEAR
BEALE
FREMONT

UNION SQUARE
PACIFIC RESTAURANT
FLEUR DE LYS ▼ POSTRIO ▼
BRASSERIE SAVOY ▼
CAMPTON PLACE RESTAURANT
▼ FARALLON
▼ ZINGARI RISTORANTE
Union Square
KULETO'S ▼
GORDON BIERSCH BREWERY AND RESTAURANT ▼
1ST ST
2ND ST
GARDEN COURT
EDDIE RICKENBACKER'S
80

DOTTIE'S TRUE BLUE CAFE ▼
ASIA DE CUBA ▼
▼ JOHN'S GRILL
PUCCINI & PINETTI
XYZ
THIRSTY BEAR BREWING CO ▼
MAX'S ▼
3RD ST
4TH ST
DELANCEY STREET RESTAURANT
ESSEX ST

ELLIS
EDDY
TURK
Boeddeker Park
TENDERLOIN
ST Hallidie Plaza
MOSCONE CONVENTION CENTER
INFUSION ▼

GOLDEN GATE ST
MCALLISTER ST
MARKET
5TH ST
6TH
7TH
SOMA
VINO E CUCINA ▼
▼ CAFFE CENTRO
SOUTH PARK CAFE
BRYANT
BRANNAN
TOWNSEND
KING
EMBARCADERO

MISSION ST
HOWARD
FOLSOM ST
HARRISON
8TH
9TH
BRAINWASH ▼
JULIE'S SUPPER CLUB ▼
80
FRINGALE ▼

San Francisco
MOON

0   025 mi
0   025 km

San Francisco

On the 52nd floor of the Bank of America building, the **Carnelian Room,** 555 California St. (between Kearny and Montgomery), 415/433-7500, is the closest you'll get to dining in an airplane above the city. The menu is upscale American, with specialties including Dungeness crab cakes, rack of lamb, and Grand Marnier soufflé. **Yank Sing,** 101 Spear St. (at Mission, inside the Rincon Center), 415/957-9300, is popular with the Financial District crowd and noteworthy for the shrimp dumplings in the shapes of goldfish and rabbits. (There's another Yank Sing at 49 Stevenson St. between First and Second Sts., 415/541-4949.) A good choice for Cantonese food is Hong Kong–style **Harbor Village,** 4 Embarcadero Center (at the corner of Clay and Drumm), 415/781-8833, serving everything from dim sum to Imperial banquets. Open daily for lunch and dinner.

CIVIC CENTER AND VICINITY

Tommy's Joynt, 1101 Geary (at Van Ness), 415/775-4216, is a neighborhood institution—a hofbrau-style bar and grill boasting bright paint, a bizarre bunch of bric-a-brac, beers from just

about everywhere, and a noteworthy pastrami sandwich. Farther north along Polk Gulch (roughly paralleling fairly level Polk St., from Post to Broadway) are abundant cafés, coffeehouses, and avant-garde junque and clothing shops. Worthwhile eateries include **Polk Street Beans,** 1733 Polk (at Clay), 415/776-9292, a funky Eurostyle coffeehouse serving good soups and sandwiches. Pitching itself to the neighborhood's more theatrical standards is **Max's Opera Cafe,** 601 Van Ness (at Golden Gate), 415/771-7300. Like Max's enterprises elsewhere, you can count on being served huge helpings of tantalizing all-American standards. At least at dinner, you can also count on the wait staff bursting into song—maybe opera, maybe a Broadway show tune. Open daily for lunch and dinner, until late (1 A.M.) on Friday and Saturday nights for the post-theater crowds.

Tucked inside the Inn at the Opera, **Ovation at the Opera,** 333 Fulton St. (between Gough and Franklin), 415/305-8842 or 415/553-8100, is a class act noted as much for its romantic charms as its fine French-Continental cuisine—a fitting finale for opera fans who have plenty of cash left to fan (this place is on the expensive side). Open nightly for dinner (until 10:30 or 11 P.M. Fri. and Sat. nights).

Also by the Opera House is the elegant and superlative **Jardinière,** 300 Grove St. (at Franklin), 415/861-5555, a French-Californian restaurant created by the city's top restaurant designer and one of its top chefs, serving very stylish comfort food. Open for lunch weekdays and for dinner nightly (late-night menu available after 10:30 P.M.).

Nearby, in Hayes Valley, are a number of great choices, including the **Hayes Street Grill,** 320 Hayes (at Franklin), 415/863-5545, a busy bistro serving some of the best seafood in town. Open weekdays for lunch, Mon.–Sat. for dinner. For something simpler, also right behind Davies Hall is **Vicolo Pizzeria,** 201 Ivy St. (at Franklin), 415/863-2382, where favorites include the cornmeal-crust pizzas. The **M Absinthe Brasserie & Bar,** 398 Hayes (at Gough), 415/551-1590, is a great little French bistro famous for its weekend brunches. Wonderful for lunch and dinner and absolutely wicked for its cakes, cookies, chocolates, and other sweet treats is **Citizen Cake** café and patisserie, 399 Grove (at Gough), 415/861-2228. A bit farther on but a best bet for gourmet German—really—is casual **Suppenküche,** 601 Hayes (at Laguna), 415/252-9289.

Sometimes more like a moveable feast for fashion, judging from all the suits and suited skirts, the **M Zuni Cafe,** 1658 Market (at Gough), 415/552-2522, is an immensely popular restaurant and watering hole noted for its Italian-French country fare and Southwestern ambience. Expensive.

At Chelsea Square, **Crustacean,** 1475 Polk St. (at California), 415/776-2722, is another one of those cutting-edge eateries enjoyable for ambience as well as actual eats. This place serves exceptional Euro-Asian cuisine (specialty: roast crab) and looks like a fantasy home to those particularly crunchy critters, with underwater murals and giant seahorses, not to mention handblown glass fixtures and a 17-foot wave sculpture. Open for dinners only, nightly after 5 P.M.; valet parking, full bar, extensive wine list. Reservations preferred.

Near Japan Center, **Cafe Kati,** 1963 Sutter (near Fillmore), 415/775-7313, is a well-regarded

neighborhood place serving wonderfully inventive food (expensive). **Iroha Restaurant,** 1728 Buchanan (at Post), 415/922-0321, is a great inexpensive stop for noodles and Japanese standards.

A serious foodie destination, homey, pricey **Julia,** 2101 Sutter (at Steiner), 415/441-2101, offers chef Julia McClaskey and her specialty pot roast, chile verde, king salmon with green curry sauce, and grilled dolmas on couscous salad.

CHINATOWN

To find the best restaurants in Chinatown, go where the Chinese go. Some of these places may look a bit shabby, at least on the outside, and may not take reservations—or credit cards. But since the prices at small family-run enterprises are remarkably low, don't fret about leaving that plastic at home.

Very popular, and always packed, the **House of Nanking,** 919 Kearny (between Jackson and Columbus), 415/421-1429, has a great location at the foot of Chinatown on the North Beach border. At this tiny restaurant, diners often sit elbow to elbow, but the excellent food and reasonable prices make it well worth the wait.

For spicy Mandarin and the best pot stickers in town, try the **Pot Sticker,** 150 Waverly Place, 415/397-9985, open daily for lunch and dinner. Another Hunan hot spot is **Brandy Ho's,** 217 Columbus (at Pacific), 415/788-7527, open daily from noon to midnight.

A great choice for Cantonese, the **Far East Cafe,** 631 Grant Ave. (between Sacramento and California), 415/982-3245, is a dark place lit by Chinese lanterns. Another possibility is the tiny turn-of-the-century **Hang Ah Tea Room,** 1 Pagoda Place (off Sacramento St.), 415/982-5686, specializing in Cantonese entrées and lunchtime dim sum. Inexpensive and locally infamous, due largely to the rude waiter routine of Edsel Ford Wong (now deceased), is three-story **Sam Woh,** 813 Washington St. (at Grant), 415/982-0596, where you can get good noodles, jook (rice gruel), and Chinese-style doughnuts (for dunking in your gruel).

Once one of San Francisco's destination restaurants, the **Empress of China,** 838 Grant Ave.

(between Washington and Clay), 415/434-1345, hasn't changed much since the Nixon administration, though it still attracts large crowds of tourists and young people looking for a campy dining experience. The ground floor lobby is worth a look for its forgotten celebrities; Eric Estrada, Jerry Hall, Englebert Humperdink, and Raymond "Perry Mason" Burr all beam from the walls. The top floor dining room is splendid, with peacock feathers curling up against beautifully ornate furnishings, and amazing views of Coit Tower and Telegraph Hill. It's been a long time since anyone came here for the food, a relic of old-style Chinese-American cuisine featuring chow mein, fried won tons, and egg rolls. Stick to the basic menu items, and this place is a kick for the atmosphere.

Great Eastern Restaurant, 649 Jackson (between Grant and Kearny), 415/986-2500, is a relaxed family-style place serving good food at great prices. A best bet here is the fixed-price seafood banquet.

JACKSON SQUARE, NORTH BEACH, AND RUSSIAN HILL

Jackson Square

Seductively combining upscale American cuisine with an exotic 1940s-style film noir atmosphere, **Bix,** 56 Gold St., 415/433-6300, is a high-toned supper club complete with richly detailed fixtures and a dramatic mahogany bar, hidden away in a narrow alley between Jackson and Pacific, Montgomery and Sansome. Traditional dishes such as grilled pork chops and buttery mashed potatoes are prepared with fresh local ingredients. You'll want to get dolled up and bring a date; classic cocktails are de riguer, of course. At Kearny and Columbus, you'll find movie-magnate-turned-winemaker Francis Ford Coppola's **Cafe Niebaum-Coppola,** 916 Kearny St., 415/291-1700, which offers an Italian menu and a good wine bar (serving, among other selections, Coppola's own vintages). At last report, contemporary American **Moose's,** 1652 Stockton St. (near Filbert), 415/989-7800, boasted chef Jeffrey Amber, previously of XYZ, and served impressive entrées such as lobster with globe squash, pork chops with cabbage and figs, and pan-seared duck breast with quinoa pilaf.

One of the country's best Greek restaurants is **Kokkari,** 200 Jackson St. (at Front), 415/981-0983. Open weekdays for lunch and Mon.–Sat. for dinner. While in the Montgomery-Washington Tower, **Tommy Toy's Haute Cuisine Chinoise,** 655 Montgomery St. (between Washington and Clay), 415/397-4888, serves up classical Chinese cuisine with traditional French touches, called "Frenchinoise" by Tommy Toy himself. The restaurant itself is impressive enough; it's patterned after the reading room of the Empress Dowager of the Ching Dynasty, and the rich decor includes priceless Asian art and antiques. Open for dinner nightly and for lunch on weekdays; reservations always advisable.

North Beach

Farther north in North Beach proper, you'll find an almost endless selection of cafés and restaurants. Historically, this is the perfect out-of-the-way area to eat, drink good coffee, or just while away the hours. These days, North Beach is a somewhat odd blend of San Francisco's Beat-era bohemian nostalgia, new-world Asian attitudes, and other ethnic culinary accents. An example of the "new" North Beach: the **New Sun Hong Kong Restaurant,** 606 Broadway (at thecultural convergence of Grant, Broadway, and Columbus), 415/956-3338. Outside, marking the building, is a three-story-tall mural depicting the North Beach jazz tradition. But this is a very Chinatown eatery, open from early morning to late at night and specializing in hot pots and earthy, homey, San Francisco–style Chinese fare.

Also here are some of old San Francisco's most traditional traditions. The **Washington Square Bar and Grill,** also affectionately known as "The Washbag," is back at 1707 Powell St. (at Union), 415/982-8123, following a brief flirtation with its dot-com identity as the Cobalt Tavern. The Washbag, one of Herb Caen's haunts, may once again become a social stopoff for the city's cognoscenti. The venerable **Fior D'Italia,** 601 Union St. (at Stockton), 415/986-1886, established in 1886, is legendary for its ambience—including the Tony Bennett Room and the Godfather Room—and its historic ability to attract highbrow Italians from around the globe.

"Follow your nose" to the **Stinking Rose,** 325 Columbus (between Broadway and Vallejo), 415/781-7673, an exceptionally popular Italian restaurant where all the food is heavily doused in garlic. For exceptional food with a more elevated perspective, a dress-up restaurant on Telegraph Hill is appropriately romantic: **Julius' Castle,** 1541 Montgomery St. (north of Union), 415/392-2222, for French and Italian, and beautiful views of the city. Not that far away (along the Embarcadero), renowned for its fine food and flair, is the one and only **Fog City Diner,** 1300 Battery St. (at Lombard), 415/982-2000. Though this is the original gourmet grazing pasture, Fog City has its imitators around the world.

But the real North Beach is elsewhere. For genuine neighborhood tradition, head to standup **Molinari's,** 373 Columbus (between Broadway and Green), 415/421-2337, a fixture since 1907. It's a good deli stop for fresh pastas, homemade sauces, hearty sandwiches, and tasty sweet treats. Or stop off for a meatball sandwich or cappuccino at landmark **Mario's Bohemian Cigar Store Cafe,** 566 Columbus (near Washington Square), 415/362-0536. The inexpensive sandwiches, frittata, and cannelloni here are the main menu attraction, but folks also come to sip cappuccino or Campari while watching the world whirl by, or while watching each other watching. Sorry, they don't sell cigars.

"Rain or shine, there's always a line" at very–San Francisco **Little Joe's,** 523 Broadway (between Kearny and Columbus), 415/433-4343, a boisterous bistro where the Italian food is authentic, the atmosphere happy, and everyone hale and hearty. The open kitchen is another main attraction. For faster service, belly up to a counter stool and watch the chefs at work. Classic, too, especially with the lots-of-food-for-little-money set, is the casual **Basta Pasta,** 1268 Grant Ave., 415/434-2248, featuring veal, fresh fish, and perfect calzones fresh out of the wood-burning oven.

Volare Trattoria Caffe, 561 Columbus (between Union and Green), 415/362-2774, offers superb Sicilian cuisine—try the exceptional cal-imari in tomato-garlic sauce. Owner Giovanni Zocca plants himself outside on Friday and Saturday nights and sings the restaurant's theme tune, "Volare, volare, volare, ho ho ho." Just up the street is **L'Osteria del Forno,** 519 Columbus, 415/982-1124, a tiny storefront trattoria with six tables. This place is a great budget bet for its wonderful Italian flatbread sandwiches.

For pizza, the place to go is **North Beach Pizza,** 1499 Grant (at Union), 415/433-2444, where there's always a line, and it's always worth standing in. Heading down toward the Financial District, **Caffe Macaroni,** 59 Columbus (between Washington and Jackson), 415/956-9737, is also a true blue—well, red, white, and green—pasta house in the Tuscany tradition: intimate, aromatic, and friendly.

Exceptional for Afghan fare is **The Helmand,** 430 Broadway (between Keany and Montgomery), 415/362-0641. Here linguistics majors can enjoy ordering such dishes as *dwopiaza, bowlani,* and *sabzi challow.* Most entrées are oriented around lamb and beef, but vegetarian entrées are available and are separated out on the menu, making for easy selection.

A CUPPA AT CAFÉ COPPOLA

Try something downright cinematic for your next cuppa—**Café Niebaum-Coppola** in North Beach, 916 Kearny St. (at Columbus Ave.), 415/291-1700, www.cafecoppola.com, movie director Francis Ford Coppola's latest commercial venture. This one, a European style bistro conveniently located on the ground floor of Coppola's American Zoetrope film production company, extends his wine-and-food empire into fairly sophisticated yet rustic culinary territory. The very Italian wood-fired pizzas are the main attraction, some named after various family members. The wine bar features Niebaum-Coppola wines from Coppola's Napa Valley winery. Here as there, sample an exuberant supply of merchandise. There's another Café Niebaum-Coppola in Palo Alto at 473 University Ave. (at Cowper St.), 650/752-0350.

San Francisco

Russian Hill

Zarzuela, 2000 Hyde St. (at Union, right on the Hyde/Powell cable-car route), 415/346-0800, offers its eponymous signature dish—a seafood stew—and other Spanish delicacies, including paella and assorted tapas. Open for dinner Tues.–Sat. Another neighborhood possibility is the **Hyde Street Bistro,** 1521 Hyde St. (between Jackson and Pacific), 415/292-4415, one of those sophisticated little places where San Franciscans hide out during tourist season. It's quiet, not too trendy, and serves good French cuisine. Appreciate the breadsticks.

Ristorante Milano, 1448 Pacific Ave. (between Hyde and Larkin), 415/673-2961, is a happy, hopping little Italian restaurant with pastas—do try the lasagna—fresh fish, and sometimes surprising specials.

Not far away and a real deal for foodies who don't care one whit about the frills is **Pete's Cafe at San Francisco Art Institute,** 800 Chestnut St. (at Jones), 415/749-4567, where you can get a great lunch for $5 or less, along with one of the city's best bay views. The atmosphere is arty and existential, with paper plates and plastic utensils just to remind you that this is for students. Everything is fresh and wholesome: Southwestern black bean/vegetable stew, white bean and escarole soup, even house-roasted turkey sandwiches. Good breakfasts, too. Open in summer Mon.–Fri.

9 A.M.–4 P.M., and during the school year Mon.–Fri. 8 A.M.–9 P.M., Sat. 9 A.M.–2 P.M. (hours can vary; it's best to call ahead).

FISHERMAN'S WHARF AND GHIRARDELLI SQUARE

Fisherman's Wharf is both tourist central and seafood central. Most locals wouldn't be caught dead eating at one of the Wharf's many seafood restaurants—but that doesn't mean the food isn't good here. Pick of the litter is probably **Scoma's,** on Pier 47 (walk down the pier from the intersection of Jefferson and Jones Streets), 415/771-4383. It's just off the beaten path (on the lightly pummeled path) and therefore a tad quieter and more relaxing than the others—or at least it seems so. The others would include: **A. Sabella's,** 2766 Taylor St. (at Jefferson), 415/771-4416; **Alioto's,** 8 Fisherman's Wharf (at Jefferson), 415/673-0183; the **Franciscan,** Pier 43, The Embarcadero, 415/362-7733; **Pompei's Grotto,** 340 Jefferson St. (near Jones), 415/776-9265; and a large number of places at Pier 39. You can get a decent bowl of clam chowder and a slab of sourdough bread at any of them.

Ghirardelli Square, 900 North Point (at Larkin), though technically part of the same Fisherman's Wharf tourist area, houses some fine restaurants patronized by locals even in broad

THE SAN FRANCISCO FOOD? SOURDOUGH BREAD

As mentioned elsewhere, if only in passing, San Francisco has a long roster of culinary inventions—from the all-American Chinese fortune cookie (invented in the Japanese Tea Garden) and Italian fish stew, or cioppino, to hangtown fry and peach melba. But nothing is more San Francisco in the food department than sourdough French bread, a much-loved local specialty. Dating from gold rush days, when yeasts and shortenings were scarce, breads were leavened by fermented "starters" of flour, water, and other live ingredients, this bacteria-enhanced souring ingredient was then added in small amounts to bread dough. With each new batch of bread, some dough was pinched and put aside as the next generation of leavening. And on and on, down through time. Since sourdough-bread connoisseurs believe that a good starter, and the bread line it creates, can only improve with age, a bakery's most prized asset is its own unique variety. It's no surprise, then, that during the great San Francisco earthquake and fire of 1906, many of the city's bakers risked their lives to rescue their starters. Such heroic acts are directly responsible for the time-honored tastes of the city's best breads.

daylight. The fourth floor **Mandarin,** 415/673-8812, was the city's first truly palatial Chinese restaurant and the first to serve up spicy Szechuan and Hunan dishes. The food here is still great. Stop by at lunch for off-the-menu dim sum (including green onion pie, spring rolls with yellow chives, and sesame shrimp rolls), served 11:30 A.M.–3:30 P.M. daily, or come later for dinner. You won't go wrong for seafood at second floor **McCormick and Kuleto's,** 415/929-1730, which features its own Crab Cake Lounge and 30 to 50 fresh specialties every day. Another much-loved Ghirardelli Square eatery is the third floor **Gaylord,** 415/771-8822, serving astounding Northern Indian specialties with a side of East Indies decor.

Elsewhere in the area, the Victorian-style **Buena Vista,** 2675 Hyde St. (at Beach), 415/474-5044, is notorious as the tourist bar that introduced Irish coffee. It's a great spot to share a table for breakfast or light lunch, and the waterfront views are almost free.

PACIFIC HEIGHTS, FILLMORE, AND MARINA

Perhaps San Francisco's most famous, most fabulous vegetarian restaurant is **N Greens,** at Building A, Fort Mason (enter at Buchanan and Marina), 415/771-6222, where the hearty fare proves for all time that meat is an unnecessary ingredient for fine dining—and where the views are plenty appetizing, too. Open for lunch and dinner Tues.–Sat., and for brunch on Sunday; reservations always advised. The bakery counter is open Tues.–Sun. from 10 A.M.–mid- or late afternoon.

Left at Albuquerque, 2140 Union St. (at Fillmore in Cow Hollow), 415/749-6700, offers Southwestern ambience and an energetic, dining-and-drinking clientele. Modern-day Malcolm Lowrys could spend the rest of their tormented days here, sampling from among 100-plus types of tequila. (Stick with the 100 percent blue-agave reposados.) Good food, too. Open daily for lunch and dinner.

For coffee and tasty pastries, an outpost of that Berkeley intellectual original **Peet's Coffee and Tea** is at 2156 Chestnut (between Pierce

and Steiner), 415/931-8302. **Pane e Vino,** 3011 Steiner St. (at Union), 415/346-2111, is a justifiably popular neighborhood trattoria that's unpretentious and unwavering in its dedication to serving up grand, deceptively simple pastas. If you tire of privacy, head over to **Perry's,** 1944 Union (between Buchanan and Laguna), 415/922-9022, one of the city's ultimate see-and-be-seen scenes and a great burger stop.

Named for the winding river that irrigates Burma's fertile plains, **Irrawaddy,** 1769 Lombard St. (between Octavia and Laguna), 415/931-2830, is well-regarded for its Burmese cuisine. **Curbside Cafe,** 2417 California, 415/929-9030, specializes in flavorful delights from all over—France, Morocco, Mexico, and the Caribbean (the crab cakes are justifiably famous). **Lhasa Moon,** 2420 Lombard (at Scott), 415/674-9898, offers excellent, authentic Tibetan cuisine Thurs.–Fri. for lunch, and Tues.–Sun. for dinner.

Elite Cafe, 2049 Fillmore (between Pine and California), 415/346-8668, is a clubby pub serving Cajun and Creole food in a dark, handsome room. It's somehow appropriate to the neighborhood. **Baker Street Bistro,** 2953 Baker St., 415/931-1475, is on the quiet end of Baker near Lombard. Warm atmosphere and hearty fare are what make this a popular local's place. Tasty meals are classic Paris bistro: Sonoma rabbit in a light Dijon sauce, steak frites, and crispy chicken. The prix-fixe menu is a bargain at $15.

Close to Japantown and adjacent to the Majestic Hotel (a onetime family mansion), the **Perlot Restaurant,** 1500 Sutter St. (at Gough), 415/441-1100, is a perfect place to go for a romantic tête-a- tête. The setting radiates old-world charm: ornate Edwardian decor, pale green and apricot decor with potted palms. It's sedate, yet far from stuffy, serving plentiful breakfasts on weekdays and brunch on weekends. Listen to a live classical pianist Fri.–Sat. nights and at Sunday brunch. Lunch is served Tues.–Fri., dinner nightly. Reservations are wise.

East of Pacific Heights, where Hwy. 101 surface-streets its way through the city en route to the Golden Gate Bridge, is **Harris',** 2100 Van Ness Ave. (at Pacific), 415/673-1888, the city's best steakhouse, and unabashedly so. This is the place to come for a martini and a steak: T-bones, ribeyes, and filet mignon all star on a beefy menu. Open for dinner daily.

THE RICHMOND, SEACLIFF, AND THE SUNSET

A fixture in the midst of the Golden Gate National Recreation Area and a favorite hangout at the edge of the continent, the current incarnation of the **Cliff House,** 1090 Point Lobos Ave. (at Upper Great Hwy.), 415/386-3330, is also a decent place to eat. Sunsets are superb, the seafood sublime. As close to fancy as it gets here is **Upstairs at the Cliff House,** an Old San Francisco-style dining room. Decidedly more casual at this cliff-hanging complex are both the **Seafood and Beverage Company** and the **Phineas T. Barnacle** pub. Come to the **Terrace Room** for Sunday brunch.

Heading south down the beachfront, on the opposite side of Great Hwy. is the **Beach Chalet Brewery and Restaurant,** 1000 Great Hwy. (between Fulton and Lincoln), 415/386-8439. This delightful renovation, upstairs (above the Golden Gate Park visitor center) in the old 1925 Willis Polk–designed building, features wall-to-wall windows looking out on the surf (a great spot to watch the sunset) as well as creative California cuisine and a long list of house-made microbrews. The atmosphere is casual—don't come in your bathing suit, but you won't need the dinner jacket—and the service is friendly. Open daily for lunch and dinner.

Moving inland, exceptional ethnic fare is a specialty of Richmond District restaurants. The 100-plus eateries lining Clement St.—among them Asian, South American, Mexican, Italian, and even Russian restaurants and delis—are representative of the district's culinary and cultural mix.

Notable in the city's "new Chinatown," the modern **Fountain Court,** 354 Clement St. (at Fifth Ave.), 415/668-1100, is a wonderful, inexpensive stop for northern-style dim sum and other Shanghai specialties. One of the few San Francisco restaurants serving spicy, sweet Singapore-style fare is **Straits Cafe,** 3300 Geary (at Parker), 415/668-1783, a light, airy, white-walled rendition complete with interior palm trees. For delicious (and cheap) Taiwanese food, head to the **Taiwan Restaurant,** 445 Clement (at Sixth), 415/387-1789, which serves great dumplings.

Good for Indonesian fare is **Jakarta,** 615 Balboa St. (between Seventh and Eighth Avenues), 415/387-5225, another airy and bright place featuring an extensive menu of unusually well-done dishes, plus an eye-catching array of artifacts, musical instruments, and shadow puppets. Some say that the romantic **Khan Toke Thai House,** 5937 Geary (at 23rd Ave.), 415/668-6654, is San Francisco's best Southeast Asian restaurant (and a good deal). Open daily for dinner only, reservations accepted. Another reliable neighborhood choice is **Bangkok Cafe,** 2845 Geary (at Collins), 415/346-8821.

For the whole Moroccan experience, including a belly dancer on some nights, try **El Mansour,** 3121 Clement (near 32nd Ave.), 415/751-2312. A bit more grand, **Kasra Persian & Mediterranean Cuisine,** 349 Clement (at Fifth Ave.), 415/752-1101, is a very good choice for all kinds of shish kabobs.

Unpretentious, welcoming **Café Riggio,** 4112 Geary (between Fifth and Sixth Aves.), 415/221-2114, is much appreciated for its antipasti, world-class calamari, and homemade cannoli for dessert.

Clement Street Bar & Grill, 708 Clement (at Eighth Ave.), 415/386-2200, serves a mostly American menu featuring vegetarian fare, grilled seafood, and California-style pastas. Farther up Geary toward the beach, **Bill's Place,** 2315 Clement (between 24th and 25th Aves.), 415/221-5262, is an eclectic burger joint with presidential portraits on the walls and a Japanese-style garden. The culinary creations here are named in honor of local celebrities. Guess what you get when you order a Carol Doda burger: two beefy patties with an olive sticking out smack dab in the middle of each. **Tia Margarita,** 300 19th Ave. (at Clement), 415/752-9274, is a long-running family café serving American-style Mexican food.

Things are more than a bit gentrified in Presidio Heights. Just a few blocks south of the Presidio is the **Magic Flute Garden Ristorante,** 3673 Sacramento (between Locust and Spruce),

415/922-1225, which offers Italian and other continental specialties in a sunny French country atmosphere.

Out at the edge of the Sunset District, assemble everything for a memorable picnic from the delis and shops along Taraval. Or check out the diverse ethnic neighborhood eateries. People from all over travel out to the Sunset for **Thanh Long,** 4101 Judah (at 46th Ave.), 415/665-1146, for its signature whole roasted crabs. Thanh Long shares owners with popular Crustacean restaurant, and their French, Vietnamese and Chinese influenced menu also features wonderful garlic noodles and seafood soup. **Brother's Pizza,** 3627 Taraval (near 46th Ave.), 415/753-6004, isn't much to look at, but the pizzas (try the pesto special), pastas, and calzone overcome that first impression in a big hurry. **El Toreador Fonda Mejicana,** 50 W. Portal (between Ulloa and Vicente), 415/566-2673, is a homey place serving traditional Central and Southern Mexican food. Just down the way on the buzzing West Portal retail strip, **Cafe for All Seasons,** 150 W. Portal (between Vicente and 14th Ave.), 415/665-0900, is a popular stop for hungry shoppers. The California-American menu emphasizes light pastas, grilled fish, and big salads.

HAIGHT-ASHBURY AND VICINITY

On any afternoon, most of the restaurants and cafés lining the Haight will be filled to the gills with young hipsters chowing down on brunch specials or self-medicating with food to cure party-related hangovers.

Campy as all get out, what with those murals and all, **Cha Cha Cha,** 1805 Haight St. (at Shrader), 415/386-5758, is just a hop or skip from Golden Gate Park. A hip Caribbean restaurant, it features unforgettable entrées such as grilled chicken paillard in mustard sauce, shrimp in spicy Cajun sauce, and New Zealand mussels in marinara. It's one of the most popular places around, so it's sometimes hard to find a place to park yourself.

Love the Haight: you can fill up at hippie-ish prices (cheap!) at several places that serve all-day

breakfasts or pizza by the slice. For monstrously generous omelettes and a hearty side of potatoes, slide on into **All You Knead,** 1466 Haight (between Ashbury and Masonic), 415/552-4550. You'll get just that. The Haight is always popular for pizza, try **Fat Slice** at 1535 Haight St. (at Ashbury), 415/552-4200, and **Cybelle's,** 203 Parnassus (at Stanyan), 415/665-8088. When East Coast transplants get homesick, they escape to **Escape from New York Pizza,** 1737 Haight (between Cole and Shrader), 415/668-5577. (There's another Escape at 508 Castro, at 18th, 415/252-1515.)

In the Haight's heyday, **Magnolia Pub & Brewery,** 1398 Haight (at Masonic), 415/864-7468, was occupied by the Drugstore Café and later by Magnolia Thunderpussy's, a way-cool dessert-delivery business. The place has retained much of its bohemian charm with colorful murals and sweeping psychedelic signs out front. The menu offers a twist on traditional pub fare— mussels steamed in India Pale Ale, mushroom risotto cakes, along with regular old burgers and house-cut fries. The formidable house-made beer list includes Pale Ales, Porters, and more offbeat selections like the Old Thunderpussy Barleywine, a tribute to the brewpub's most famous tenant.

The strip referred to as "the lower Haight" is an avant-garde enclave sandwiched between the Western Addition and Market Street, with nary a tourist attraction in sight. Without the homeless, runaways, and drug dealers notable in the upper Haight, this several-block area bounded by Webster and Divisadero has become a fairly happy haven for artists and low-end wannabes, as well as the cafés, bars, and restaurants they inhabit. (Great people-watching.) **Kate's Kitchen,** 471 Haight (at Fillmore) 415/626-3984, is a small storefront diner where the emphasis is on down-home American food like buttermilk pancakes and scallion-cheese biscuits. A bit more boisterous, with sunny-day sidewalk tables, is the **Horse Shoe Coffee House,** 566 Haight (between Fillmore and Steiner), 415/626-8852, which also offers high-octane coffee and Internet access.

Most of the neighborhood's bars serve fairly decent food during the day and into the evening; try

Mad Dog in the Fog, 530 Haight (between Steiner and Fillmore), 415/626-7279, a rowdy English-style pub, or just across the street, painfully hip **Noc Noc,** 557 Haight, 415/861-5811. In the spirit of the neighborhood, customers at the **Toronado,** 547 Haight, 415/863-2276, often duck next door to **Rosamunde Sausage Grill,** 545 Haight, 415/437-6851, for a German sausage-stuffed bun to accompany their beer (the Toronado has more than 40 on tap).

MISSION DISTRICT AND THE CASTRO

The Mission District is known for its open-air markets. One of the best is **La Victoria Mexican Bakery & Grocery,** 2937 24th St. (at Alabama), 415/642-7120. Buy some homemade tamales, fruit, and a few *churros* (Mexican sugar-dipped doughnuts) and have a feast at the children's park (between Bryant and York on 24th) while studying the murals. Other ethnic bakeries worth poking into for impromptu picnic fixings include **Pan Lido Salvadoreno,** 3147 22nd St. (at Capp), 415/282-3350, and **Pan Lido Bakery,** 5216 Mission (at Niagra), 415/333-2140. An ethnic change-up, serving great sandwiches, is **Lucca Ravioli Company,** 1100 Valencia (at 22nd St.), 415/647-5581. For superb bread and French-inspired pastries—from perfect croissants to cookies and lemon tarts—the place is **Tartine,** 600 Guerrero St. (near 18th St.), 415/487-2600.

Among the Mission's inexpensive neighborhood joints is the justifiably famous **Taqueria Can-Cun,** 2288 Mission (at 19th), 415/252-9560, which serves jumbo-size veggie burritos, handmade tortilla chips, and scorching salsa. There are two other locations: 10 blocks south at 3211 Mission (nearCesar Chavez), 415/550-1414, and at Sixth and Market, 415/864-6773. **Fina Estampa,** 2374 Mission St. (between 19th and 20th), 415/824-4437, is a nondescript Peruvian outpost featuring exceptional seafood, chicken, and beef entrées (humongous portions) and good service (there's another one at 1100 Van Ness (at Geary), 415/440-6364). At **La Rondalla,** 901 Valencia (at 20th), 415/647-7474,

mariachi bands play while you eat. At **Pancho Villa Taqueria,** 3071 16th (between Mission and Valencia), 415/864-8840, you'll be hard-pressed to find anything over seven bucks. And the portions are huge, including the grand dinner plates of grilled shrimp. Across the street from the murals at the Mission Cultural Center, **La Taqueria,** 2889 Mission (at 25th), 415/285-7117, is one of the most popular taquerias in the neighborhood. The staff don't use rice in the burritos, so you get more meat for your buck—their carne asada and carnitas rate among the city's best. At **Los Jarritos,** 901 S. Van Ness Ave. (at 20th), 415/648-8383, the "little jars" add color to an already colorful menu of Jalisco specialties.

The line between the Mission and Castro Districts, like distinct geographical and sociopolitical divisions elsewhere in the city, is often blurred. Yet the Mission is becoming *the* foodie destination, despite the fact that parking is such a challenge. **Destino,** 1815 Market St. (between Valencia and Guerrero), 415/552-4451, has an almost religious South American feel what with all the candles, wood-and-amber walls, and heavy oak chairs. The food here measures up to the cultural interpretation: the ceviche and empanadas pair nicely with wines from Chile, Argentina, Spain, and California. The place for inspired Peruvian is modest, citrus-splashed **Limon,** 524 Valencia St., 415/252-0918, serving some 20 flavorful selections—everything from bouillabaisse and *tamal criollo* to exceptional pork chops. **Platanos,** 598 Guerrero (at 18th St.), 415/252-9281, is another understated hotspot, serving excellent *pupusas* and enchiladas Centro Americana as appetizers and entrées including mole *poblano,* chiles rellenos, and a paella made with coconut milk.

Popular with young foodies is casual, festive **M Luna Park,** 694 Valencia (at 18th St.), 415/553-8584, where people's favorites range from hunter's pie and grilled chicken to house-made Graham crackers for the make-your-own S'mores. Superchic **Foreign Cinema,** 2534 Mission St. (between 21st and 22nd Sts.), 415/648-7600, keeps an internationally intellectual atmosphere by beaming foreign films on a wall in the outdoor courtyard. The restaurant is a happy marriage between Berkeley's Chez Panisse and Zuni Café, with a distinct Mission district spin. People flock from all over the city, so make a reservation or be prepared to wait.

One more stop along the Mission's restaurant row (Valencia between 16th and 24th Streets) is the lively and colorful tapas bar **Ramblas,** 557 Valencia (at 16th), 415/565-0207, the place to go for a social evening of grazing on small plates of Paella Las Ramblas and classic tortilla espanola while knocking back the fruity house sangria. A few blocks down, a no less pleasant Vietnamese alternative is **Saigon Saigon,** 1132 Valencia (at 22nd), 415/206-9635, serving an astounding array of authentic dishes, from majestic rolls and barbecued quail to Buddha's delight (vegetarian). Open for lunch on weekdays, for dinner nightly.

In a neighborhood saturated with tapas bars, **Esperpento,** 3295 22nd St. (at Valencia), 415/282-8867, stands out as a great place for delectable Catalonian entrées, as well as tasty and sophisticated Spanish finger foods. Fairly inexpensive. Open Mon.–Sat. for lunch and dinner.

A neighborhood classic in the retro diner genre is **Boogaloos,** 3296 22nd St. (at Valencia), 415/824-4088, famous for huge breakfasts, slacker crowds, and its signature dish, the Temple o' Spuds. **Cafe Ethiopia,** 878 Valencia (at 20th), 415/285-2728, offers all the usual espresso drinks plus Ethiopian cuisine, including poultry, beef, and vegetarian dishes from mild to spicy hot. Hugely popular and excellent value for the money, **Ti Couz,** 3108 16th St. (at Valencia), 415/252-7373, specializes in crepes—stuffed with everything from spinach to salmon to berries. Meanwhile, denizens of the Mission have discovered that the filling Indian and Pakistani food at **Pakwan,** 3182 16th St. (between Valencia and Guerrero), 415/255-2440, is perfectly suited for sustenance between bars. Flavorful curries, tandooris and daals are the main attractions. There's no table service (you order at a counter), and no alcohol.

For real cheap eats in the Castro, head to **Hot 'n' Hunky,** 4039 18th St.(at Castro), 415/621-6365, for locally famous burgers and renowned French fries, not to mention excessive neon and Marilyn Monroe memorabilia. Very Castro is **Cafe Flore,** 2298 Market St. (at Noe), 415/621-8579, a popular gay hangout and café serving up omelettes and crepes, salads and good sandwiches, and current information about what's going on in the neighborhood. (Great for people-watching, especially out on the plant-populated patio.)

Missed by most tourists but popular for brunch is the **Bagdad Cafe,** 2295 Market St. (at 16th), 415/621-4434, offering a healthy take on American-style fare, plus great salads. Nearby, and wonderful for succulent seafood, is the **Anchor Oyster Bar,** 579 Castro (between 18th and 19th), 415/431-3990.

It's Tops, 1801 Market (at McCoppin), 415/431-6395, looks like a classic American greasy spoon—the decor hasn't changed since 1945—but the surprise is just how good the pancakes and other breakfast selections are. **Sparky's 24-Hour Diner,** 242 Church St. (between Market and 15th), 415/626-8666, got lost somewhere in the 1950s, style-wise, but the breakfast omelettes, burgers, and salads are certainly up to modern expectations.

The atmosphere at suave, contemporary **2223 Market** (at Noe), 415/431-0692, is cozy, and the food is down-home American. Excellent garlic mashed potatoes and onion rings.

Beyond the Mission and Castro—but not that far—is upstairs-downstairs **Chenery Park** in Glen Park/Noe Valley, 683 Chenery St. (near Diamond), 415/337-8537, a restaurant that draws foodies from all over and specializes in homey yet stylish Americana. Chenery Park's changing menu of comfort foods includes such things as pot roast with root vegetables; baked macaroni and cheese; seafood gumbo with scallops, shrimp, and catfish; and braised lamb shank with red wine and polenta.

SOUTH OF MARKET (SOMA)

San Francisco's answer to New York City's SoHo, the South of Market area, or SoMa, is geographically a large neighborhood, extending from Market Street to China Basin, and Hwy. 101 to the Bay. The new money is here, and new businesses spring up every month, though many areas of the neighborhood are still considered unsafe, especially after dark. Reality here ranges from street-people chic to chichi restaurants and clubs. The row of nightclubs around 11th Street has survived since the 1980s, but business owners have done their demographic homework, so SoMa has seen a steady growth of trendy new restaurants.

The burgers at **Eddie Rickenbacker's,** 133 Second St.(between Mission and Minna), 415/543-3498, are considered by connoisseurs to be close to the best, though other good bets at Eddie's include the salads, soups, and fish dishes.

Head toward the bay down second to reach the delightful South Park neighborhood, home to photo studios and shops serving the multimedia and advertising industries, as well as trendy coffeehouses, restaurants, and the block-square greensward of South Park itself (bordered by Bryant and Brannan, Second and Third). A crowd that appears to have walked off the pages of *Dwell* magazine is energized by South Park's **Infusion,** 555 Second St. (at Brannan), 415/543-2282, a busy, chic restaurant beloved for its innovative, spicy menu and fruit-infused vodka drinks. Inside leafy South Park, crowded and noisy **Caffe Centro,** 102 South Park, 415/882-1500, packs in a lively multimedia crowd for breakfast and lunch. The lures: excellent coffee, panini sandwiches, and soup, along with consistently good Franco-style salads (including a classic Nicoise). On sunny days order at the To-Go window and dine alfresco in the park on one of the benches, or better yet, on the lawn. Straight across the park is the smart and locally-favored **South Park Cafe,** 108 South Park, 415/495-7275, a little pocket of Paris in the city, with a zinc-topped bar, sidewalk seating, and an international selection of newspapers hanging from wooden rods. The menu features bistro classics such as grilled steak with frites, mussels in white wine sauce, or leg of lamb with couscous, and wonderful desserts.

After exploring Moscone Center and Yerba Buena Gardens, drop in for a cold one at **Thirsty Bear Brewing Co.,** 661 Howard (between Second and Third), 415/974-0905, where you can enjoy one of the seven house-made microbrews and outstanding Spanish and Catalan dishes. Marked by the huge tomato hanging outside, no-fuss **Vino e Cucina,** 489 Third St. (at Bryant), 415/543-6962, offers fine Italian cuisine, including pastas, pizzas, and unusual specials. Down two blocks, **Max's,** 311 Third St. (between Folsom and Howard), 415/546-6297, has a lighthearted New-York diner atmosphere and heavyweight portions of deli sandwiches, burgers, and gigantic breakfasts. The décor and food remain true to diner tradition, with a few "Californian" concessions (salads). Exceptional **M Fringale,** 570 Fourth St. (between Bryant and Brannan), 415/543-0573, is a bright and contemporary French/American bistro serving excellent food at remarkably reasonable prices—a place well worth looking for.

Continuing southwest through the district, you'll find good and pretty cheap, fast-as-your-laundry-cycle fare at **BrainWash,** 1122 Folsom (between Seventh and Eighth), 415/861-3663 (see Clean Up Your Act at BrainWash). It's by one of the area's sociocultural flagships, **Julie's Supper Club,** 1123 Folsom (between Seventh and Eighth), 415/861-0707, a restaurant and nightclub/bar known for its combination of space-age-meets-the-1950s supper-club style and Old West saloon atmosphere. Not to mention the famous martinis. For spice and great atmosphere, **India Garden,** 1261 Folsom (at Ninth), 415/626-2798, is well worth poking into for wonderful nans (flatbreads) and *kulchas* baked in a tandoor oven.

It's another trendy Asian-Californian fusion restaurant. Or maybe its not. What's certain is that **Asia SF,** 201 Ninth St. (at Howard), 415/255-2742, is as much a nightclub as a restaurant. There's a DJ every night of the week, and the cocktails are as famous as the waitstaff of beautiful and talented gender illusionists. And, surprisingly, the kitchen staff take their job seriously—turning out well-respected fusion cuisine (try the noodle dishes). At the bar, the girls command your attention on the half-hour; they climb atop the colossal structure then kick it up to pop hits. This is one of the most "San Francisco" places going. Bring an open mind and your go-go boots.

If you're on a tight budget, you won't go wrong at **Manora's Thai Cuisine,** 1600 Folsom (at 12th), 415/861-6224, which serves deliciously spicy Thai food at bargain prices. The menu features well-prepared seafood and curries. Night owls like to come here before hitting the nearby clubs.

Over in China Basin the industrial-chic hotspot (great view of the railroad tracks) is **42 Degrees,** 235 16th St. (behind the Esprit Outlet at Illinois, along the waterfront in China Basin), 415/777-5558, serving "nouvelle Mediterranean" food. The menu offers cuisine from southern France, Italy, Spain, and Greece—all regions at 42° north latitude. This is still one of the trendiest spots around, so sometimes you wait awhile.

Information and Services

The clearinghouse for current visitor information is the **San Francisco Convention & Visitors Bureau,** 900 Market St. (at Powell, downstairs—below street level—outside the BART station at Hallidie Plaza), P.O. Box 429097, San Francisco, CA 94142-9097, 415/391-2000, www.sfvisitor .org. Here you can pick up official visitor pamphlets, maps, booklets, and brochures about local businesses, including current accommodations bargains and various coupon offers. Multilingual staffers are available to answer questions. The Visitor Information Center is open for walk-ins weekdays 9 A.M.–5 P.M., Sat.–Sun. 9 A.M.– 3 P.M.; closed major holidays.

If you can't make it to the Visitor Information Center or are planning your trip in advance and need information, you have a couple of options. To find out what's going on in town, from entertainment and arts attractions to major professional sports events, you can call the city's free, 24-hour visitor hot line, available in five languages. To get the news in English, call 415/391-2001; in French, 415/391-2003; in German, 415/391-2004; in Japanese, 415/391-2101; and in Spanish, 415/391-2122. The information is updated weekly. You can also write to the SFCVB to request current information on accommodations, events, and other travel planning particulars. For $3 postage and handling, you can get a copy of the SFCVB's semiannual *The San Francisco Book,* which contains thorough information about sights, activities, arts, entertainment, recreation, shopping venues, and restaurants, as well as a detailed map. (And then some.) If you'll be in town awhile, it's worth the money to request in advance.

The state of California operates the **California Welcome Center & Internet Café @ Pier 39** in the Pier 39 shopping center at Fisherman's Wharf, 415/956-3491, www.weblightningcafe.com, open daily 9 A.M.–8 P.M. The center offers a number of travel-related services for the greater San Francisco Bay Area and California's northern coast—from free tourist information, itinerary planning, hotel reservations, and special discounts tostamps and phone cards. The Internet Café features 30 high-speed, dedicated T-1 stations with email access, low cost Internet phones, and digital camera rentals. Espresso and coffee drinks, teas, deli sandwiches, salads, and pastries are served daily. The Café also has a great view overlooking the Marina.

PUBLICATIONS

Available free at hotels, restaurants, and some shops around town is the small, magazine-style *Key: This Week San Francisco,* which is chock-full of the usual information and has a thorough and current arts, entertainment, and events section. Though focused primarily for permanent Bay Area residents, *San Francisco Focus* magazine also offers regular food and entertainment columns, plus in-depth feature articles about the real world of San Francisco and environs.

Where: San Francisco is a slick, free magazine full of useful information on accommodations, dining, shopping, and nightlife. It's available at the Hallidie Square visitor center and elsewhere around town. You can also order a subscription by contacting: Where Magazine, 74 New Montgomery

St., Ste. 320, San Francisco, CA 94105, 415/546-6101, or online at www.wheremagazine.com.

Even more real: the *San Francisco Bay Guardian,* www.sfbg.com, and *SF Weekly,* www.sfweekly.com, popular tabloid newspapers available free almost everywhere around town. The Guardian's motto (with a hat tip to Wilbur Storey and the 1861 *Chicago Times,* as interpreted by Editor/Publisher Bruce Brugmann), "It is a newspaper's duty to print the news and raise hell," is certainly comforting in these times and also generates some decent news/feature reading, along with comprehensive arts, entertainment, and events listings. The Guardian also publishes insider guides to the city with some of the same punchy, irreverent writing. The *Weekly* also offers what's-happening coverage and—to its everlasting credit—Rob Brezsny's *Free Will Astrology* column. Way to go. Excellent for alternative media info online is the **San Francisco Bay Artea Independent Media Center,** sf.indymedia.org.

While roaming the city, look for other special-interest and neighborhood-scope publications. The *San Francisco Bay Times* is a fairly substantive gay and lesbian biweekly. For comprehensive events information, pick up a copy of the *Bay Area Reporter.* Widely read throughout the Sunset and Richmond Districts is *The Beacon.* Other popular papers include the award-winning, hell-raising, *Street Sheet,* published by the Coalition on Homelessness in San Francisco and distributed by the homeless on San Francisco's streets; the *New Mission News;* and the *Noe Valley Voice.*

The city's major daily, *San Francisco Chronicle,* www.sfgate.com, is universally available at newsstands and in coin-op vending racks. The *San Francisco Examiner,* www.examiner.com, formerly the city's scrappy afternoon/evening paper, continues (at least for a while) only as a free daily paper available at city newsstands and retail stores. In 2000 the Hearst Corporation purchased the *Chronicle,* and planned to sell or close the city's competing daily *Examiner* if no buyer could be found. The purchase was complicated by antitrust concerns. The two papers had been linked in a federally regulated operating agreement since the 1960s, and any deal that led to a one-paper town would have been blocked. The sale was finally approved when the well-connected Fang family purchased the *Examiner,* in a deal that included a three-year, $66 million subsidy from Hearst. Yet the new owners laid off almost its entire staff in 2003, creating, finally, a one-newspaper town. The *Chronicle* was never considered a top major-city newspaper, but after being sold to Hearst it has shown an increased interest in publishing better, tougher coverage of local politics—perhaps because all of the *Examiner's* reporters and editors immediately went to work for the *Chronicle.* The *Chronicle's* humongous Sunday newspaper, once published in conjunction with the *Examiner,* is still popular for its *Datebook* section, sometimes called The Pink, packed with readable reviews, letters from sometimes demanding or demented Bay Area readers, and the most comprehensive listings of everything going on.

San Francisco's major non-English and ethnic newspapers include *Asian Week,* the *Irish Herald,* and the African-American community's *Sun Reporter.*

Bookstores and Libraries

San Francisco is a well-read city, judging solely from the number of booksellers here. Perhaps most famous is that bohemian bookshop of lore in North Beach, **City Lights,** 261 Columbus Ave. (at Broadway), 415/362-8193, founded in 1953 by Lawrence Ferlinghetti and Peter Martin. The small press and poetry sections here are especially impressive. Also well worth a stop is **A Clean, Well Lighted Place for Books,** 601 Van Ness Ave. (between Golden Gate and Turk), 415/441-6670.

For European books and magazines, head over to the **European Book Company,** 925 Larkin (between Geary and Post), 415/474-0626, offering a selection of books in French, German, and Spanish, as well as a good travel section including English-language titles.

At Union Square, you'll find a four-story outpost of **Borders Books and Music,** 400 Post (at Powell), 415/399-1633 (books) or 415/399-0522 (music). The store stocks more than 200,000 titles, and has its own coffee shop on the second floor, and the fourth floor is devoted to

CDs. Open Mon.–Thurs. 9 A.M.–11 P.M., Fri.–Sat. 9 A.M.–midnight, Sunday 9 A.M.–9 P.M.

Probably the best downtown San Francisco stop for travel and maps is the Financial District's **Rand McNally Map and Travel Store,** 595 Market St. (at Second), 415/777-3131. Worthwhile elsewhere is **Get Lost—Travel Books, Maps, and Gear,** 1825 Market St. (at Guerrero), 415/437-0529, www.getlostbooks.com, which offers travel guides, travel literature, luggage and travel accessories, maps, atlases, and author events. It's open Mon.–Fri. 10 A.M.–7 P.M., Sat. 10 A.M.–6 P.M., Sun. 11 A.M.–5 P.M.

Just off Union Square, **Brick Row Bookshop,** 49 Geary, 415/398-0414, specializes in antiquarian books, with a wide assortment of 18th- and 19th-century British and American literature.

Some unusual specialty or neighborhood bookstores include pulp-fiction bookseller **Kayo Books,** downtown at 814 Post (between Hyde and Leavenworth), 415/749-0554; the **San Francisco Mystery Book Store,** 4175 24th St. (between Castro and Diamond, in Noe Valley), 415/282-7444; and **Marcus Book Store,** 1712 Fillmore St. (at Post, in the Western Addition),

415/346-4222, specializing in African-American books. Foreign-language book specialists include: **Kinokuniya,** 1581 Webster St. (at Fillmore in the Japan Center), 415/567-7625; **Russian Books,** 332 Balboa (Richmond District), 415/668-4723; and **Znanie Bookstore,** 5237 Geary (at 11th Ave.), 415/752-7555, also in the Richmond and also specializing in Russian titles.

If you don't feel obliged to buy what you need to read, the controversial yet technologically state-of-the-art **San Francisco Main Library,** downtown at 100 Larkin (at Grove), 415/557-4400, is a good place to start becoming familiar with the local library system.

Weather

San Francisco's weather can upset even the best-laid plans for a frolic in the summertime California sun. For one thing, there may not be any sun. In summer, when most visitors arrive, San Francisco is enjoying its citywide natural air-conditioning system, called "fog." When California's inland areas are basting in blast-furnace heat, people here might be wearing a down jacket to go walking on the beach. (Sometimes it does

© SUSAN SNYDER

Don't miss a visit to City Lights bookstore.

San Francisco

get hot—and "hot" by San Francisco standards refers to anything above 80° F.) Especially during the summer, weather extremes even in the course of a single day are normal, so pack accordingly. Bring warm clothing (at least one sweater or jacket for cool mornings and evenings), in addition to the optimist's choice of shorts and sandals, and plan to dress in layers so you'll be prepared for anything. The weather in late spring and early autumn is usually sublime—balmy, often fog-free—so at those times you should bring two pairs of shorts (but don't forget that sweater, just in case). It rarely rains May–Oct.; raingear is prudent at other times.

For current **weather information** or to find out when the next fog bank is rolling in, call the free TellMe interactive phone service, 800/555-8355, for a summary of San Francisco weather, news, travel, sports, stock news, and entertainment happenings.

Access and Other Services

Modern buildings in San Francisco and most public-transit facilities are required by law to provide access to people in wheelchairs and those with other physical limitations; hotels, restaurants, and entertainment venues housed in historic facilities have a staff member who can help with access to their building and events.

An invaluable regional resource for visitors in wheelchairs and those who are otherwise physically challenged is **Access Northern California,** 1427 Grant St., Berkeley, CA 94703, 510/524-2026, www.accessnca.com, which describes its work as "ramping the way to accessible travel." Their *Access San Francisco* travel guide is available through the Convention & Visitors Bureau. For special assistance and information on the city's disabled services, contact San Francisco's disability coordinator at the **Mayor's Office of Community Development,** 25 Van Ness Ave., Ste. 700, 415/252-3100, and the helpful local **Easter Seals Bay Area,** 180 Grand Ave., Ste. 300, 510/835-2131, www.esba.org. For the ins and outs of disabled access to local public transit, request a copy of the *Muni Access Guide* from Muni Accessible Services Program, 415/923-6142 weekdays or 415/673-6864 anytime, or

visit the Rider Information section of Muni's website, www.sfmuni.com.

All of San Francisco's (and California's) public buildings and restaurants are nonsmoking. Most motels and hotels have nonsmoking rooms, and many have entire floors of nonsmoking rooms and suites.

Unless otherwise stated on a restaurant menu, restaurants do not include a gratuity in the bill. The standard tip for the wait staff is 15 percent to 20 percent of the total tab, and the average tip for taxi drivers is 15 percent. It's customary to tip airport baggage handlers and hotel porters ($1 or more per bag, one way), parking valets, and other service staff. When in doubt about how much to tip, just ask someone.

SAFETY

San Francisco is a reasonably safe city. Definitely unsafe areas, especially at night, include The Tenderloin, some areas south of Market St. (Sixth and Seventh Sts.), parts of the Western Addition, and parts of the Mission District (including, at night, BART stops). For the most part, drug-related gang violence is confined to severely impoverished areas. The increased number of homeless people and panhandlers, particularly notable downtown, is distressing, certainly, but most of these people are harmless lost souls.

If you're driving, be observant and look around before entering and returning to parking lots. When you get in your car, be sure to lock the doors immediately. Though rare, over the years there have been highly publicized cases involving carjacking.

If your own vehicle isn't safe, keep in mind that no place is absolutely safe. Sadly, in general it still holds true that female travelers are safest if they confine themselves to main thoroughfares. As elsewhere in America, women are particularly vulnerable to assaults of every kind. At night, women traveling solo, or even with a friend or two, should stick to bustling, yuppie-happy areas like Fisherman's Wharf and Union Street. The definitely street-savvy, though, can get around fairly well in SoMa and other nightlife areas, especially in groups or by keeping to streets with plenty of benign human traffic. (You can usually tell by looking.)

Transportation

GETTING THERE

At least on pleasure trips, Californians and other Westerners typically drive into San Francisco. The city is reached from the north via Hwy. 101 across the fabled Golden Gate Bridge ($5 toll to get into the city, no cost to get out); from the east via I-80 from Oakland/Berkeley across the increasingly choked-with-traffic Bay Bridge ($3 toll to get into the city, no cost to get out); and from the south (from the coast or from San Jose and other South Bay/peninsula communities) via Hwy. 1, Hwy. 101, or I-280/19th Avenue. Whichever way you come and go, avoid peak morning (7–9 A.M.) and afternoon/evening (4–6 P.M.) rush hours, unless you qualify for the carpool lane (driver plus two or more passengers, or driver plus one passenger in a two-seat vehicle). Carpools don't have to pay tolls during commute hours, and you'll be able to whiz through the backup at the bridge. The Bay Area's traffic congestion is truly horrendous.

Airports

About 15 miles south of the city via Hwy. 101, **San Francisco International Airport** (SFO), 650/876-2377 (general information) or 650/877-0227 (parking information), www.flysfo.com, perches on a point of land at the edge of the bay. (That's one of the thrills here: taking off and landing just above the water.) Travel time from downtown is 40 minutes during peak commute hours, and 20 to 25 minutes at other times. Each of the terminals—Terminal 1, Terminal 2, and Terminal 3—has two levels, the lower for arrivals, the upper for departures. San Francisco's state-of-the-art International Terminal, built in 2000, is the largest international terminal in the U.S. More than 40 major scheduled carriers (and smaller ones, including air charters) serve SFO. Big news in 2004 was news that British entrepreneur Richard Branson will establish operational headquarters for **Virgin USA,** expected to begin operations here in 2005.

San Francisco International has its quirks. For one thing, its odd horseshoe shape often makes for a long walk for transferring passengers; the "people movers" help somewhat, but people seem to avoid the second-floor intraterminal bus. (In all fairness, though, since SFO is primarily an origin/destination airport, for most travelers this isn't a problem.) For another, with such a high volume of air traffic—an average of 1,000 flights per day—delays are all too common, especially when fog rolls in and stays.

People complain, too, that facilities always seems to be under major construction, as the airport continues with a multi-billion-dollar expansion. And in the wake of the 2001 terrorist attacks, increased security measures have made for a lengthier check-in process and possible delays. Airlines and governments have added their own new regulations, so check directly with your travel agent or airline for specifics. The following general tips may help expedite the process: Plan on arriving two hours prior to your scheduled flight, bring proper identification and a printout of your E-ticket, and limit carry-on baggage to two pieces—one personal bag (briefcase or purse) and one carry-on. Again, check with your airline before departure, as some carriers seem to take perverse pleasure in making regulations increasingly complicated.

Information booths are located in the lower (arrivals) level of all terminals, open daily 8 A.M.–midnight. Traveler's Aid Society booths can be found on the upper (departures) level and are open daily 9 A.M.–9 P.M. ATMs are located in all terminals. Weary travelers can take a shower after a long-haul flight Mon.–Sat. 8 A.M.–5 P.M. at **Hairport,** in the International Terminal to right of the security checkpoint for G gates. Hairport offers valet services, a hair salon, and massage. There is a medical clinic on the lower floor of Terminal 2. Other airport facilities include outposts of popular San Francisco restaurants (Harry Denton's in the International Terminal, the North Beach Deli in Terminal 1, among others), and shops including

San Francisco

the California Product Shop (where you can get some wine and smoked fish or crab to go with that sourdough bread you're packing) and several bookstores, which prominently features titles by Bay Area and California writers.

Due to its excellent service record and relatively lower volume, many travelers prefer flying into and out of efficient, well-run **Oakland International Airport** just across the bay, 510/577-4000, www.oaklandairport.com. It's fairly easy to reach from downtown San Francisco. Travel time by car or shuttle is 30 minutes (depending on traffic), or take BART from downtown to the airport.

Airport Taxi and Shuttles

If flying into and out of SFO, avoid driving if at all possible; parking and curbside access are limited. Airport shuttles abound, however, and are fairly inexpensive and generally reliable. The airport offers a hot line, 800/736-2008, for information on ground transportation. Operators are available weekdays 7:30 A.M.–5 P.M. Most companies offer at-your-door pick-up service if you're heading to the airport (advance reservations usually required) and—coming from the airport—both taxis and shuttles take you right where you're going. **Taxis** operate on the airport's lower level. A taxi from the airport to downtown San Francisco will cost $30 to $35, plus tip. The usual one-way fare for shuttles, depending upon the company, is around $15 per person for most SFO/San Francisco hotel service. Inquire about prices for other shuttle destinations.

The blue-and-gold **SuperShuttle** fleet has some 100 vans coming and going all the time, 415/558-8500, www.supershuttle.com. When you arrive at SFO, the company's shuttle vans to the city (no reservation needed) are available at the outer island on the upper level of all terminals. To arrange a trip to the airport, call and make your pick-up reservation at least a day in advance. (And be ready when the shuttle arrives—they're usually on time.) Group, convention, and charter shuttles are also available, and you can pay on board with a major credit card. (Exact fare depends on where you start and end.)

SFO Airporter, 650/624-0500, www.sfairporter.com, offers nonstop runs every 20 minutes between the airport and the Financial District or Union Square. No reservations are required in either direction. **City Express Shuttle** in Oakland, 510/638-8830, offers daily shuttle service between the city of San Francisco and Oakland International Airport. **Bayporter Express, Inc.,** 415/656-2929 or 415/467-1800, or 800/287-6783 (from inside the airport), specializes in shuttle service between most Bay Area suburban communities and SFO, and offers hourly door-to-door service between any location in San Francisco and the Oakland Airport. **Marin Airporter** in Larkspur, 415/461-4222, provides service every half hour from various Marin communities to SFO daily, 4:30 A.M.–11 P.M., and from SFO to Marin County daily, 5:30 A.M.–midnight.

BART and Trains

The ride to the airport will surely get easier. The **Bay Area Rapid Transit (BART),** 650/992-2278, www.bart.gov, extension to SFO was launched in June 2003, connecting travelers to a network of stations around the bay, including several along Market Street in San Francisco near Union Square and the Financial District. The extension adds 8.7 miles of track to the existing system and new stations in San Francisco, San Bruno, Millbrae, plus a station at the International Terminal inside the airport. The one-way fare from SFO to the Powell Street near Union Square will cost around $5, and take just 30 minutes, making it an attractive alternative to the shuttles.

Of course BART is more than just a fancy airport shuttle; primarily, it's a high-speed train and subway system connecting San Francisco to the East Bay. Yet BART can also take passengers across the bay (actually, *under* the bay) to and from the **Amtrak** station at Oakland's Jack London Square for train connections both north and south. For details call Amtrak, 510/238-4306 or 800/USA-RAIL, or see www.amtrak.com. Amtrak does have a ticket office/waiting room in San Francisco, inside The Agricultural Building at the foot of Market St., 101 Embarcadero (at

Mission), Ste. 118, open daily 5:45 A.M.–10 P.M. The only staffed station in San Francisco, Amtrak services include ticket sales, checked baggage, and package express. Buses carry passengers between San Francisco Amtrak stops and trains departing and arriving across the bay at the Emeryville Station, located at 5855 Landgegan St., just off Powell.

Primarily a regional commuter service, **Cal-Train,** 800/660-4287 within Northern California, www.caltrain.com, runs south from downtown to Palo Alto, Stanford, Mountain View, Sunnyvale, Santa Clara, San Jose, Morgan Hill, and Gilroy, among other stops. The San Francisco CalTrain depot is at Fourth and Townsend Streets. A $64.5-million expansion is underway, to accommodate CalTrain's "baby bullet" express commuter trains.

Buses

San Mateo County Transit (SamTrans), 800/660-4287, www.samtrans.com, offers extensive peninsula public transit, including express and regular buses from SFO to San Francisco. It's cheap, too ($2.20 to $3). Buses leave the airport every 30 minutes from very early morning to just after midnight; call for exact schedule. The express buses takes just 35 minutes to reach the Transbay Terminal near downtown San Francisco but limit passengers to carry-on luggage only, so heavily laden travelers will have to take one of the regular buses—a 55-minute ride to the city.

The **Transbay Terminal,** 425 Mission St. (just south of Market St. between First and Fremont), 800/231-2222, is the city's regional transportation hub. An information center on the second floor has displays, maps, and fee-free phone lines for relevant transit systems. Bus companies based here include **Greyhound,** 415/495-1569, www.greyhound.com, with buses coming and going at all hours; **Golden Gate Transit,** 415/455-2000, www.goldengatetransit.org, offering buses to and from Marin County and vicinity; **AC Transit,** 415/817-1717, www.actransit.org, which serves the East Bay; and **San Mateo County Transit** (SamTrans), 800/660-4287, www.samtrans.org, which runs as far south as Palo Alto.

Ferries

Since the city is surrounded on three sides by water, ferry travel is an unusual (and unusually practical) San Francisco travel option. Before the construction of the Golden Gate Bridge in 1937, it was the only way to travel to the city from the North and East Bay areas. Nowadays, the ferries function both as viable commuter and tourist transit services.

The **Blue & Gold Fleet,** 415/773-1188 (recorded schedule) or 415/705-5555 (reservations and information), www.blueandgoldfleet.com, based at Fisherman's Wharf, Piers 39 and 41, offers roundtrip service daily between San Francisco (either the Ferry Building or Pier 41) and Oakland (Jack London Square), Alameda (Gateway Center), Sausalito, Tiburon, Angel Island, and Vallejo (via high-speed catamaran). During baseball season, Blue & Gold also offers ferry service from Oakland and Sausalito to a launch near Pac Bell Park. Return ferries depart about 20 minutes after the end of the game. The company also offers bay cruises, tours of Alcatraz, an "Island Hop" tour to both Alcatraz and Angel Island, and various land tours (Muir Woods, Yosemite, Monterey/Carmel, Wine Country).

Golden Gate Transit Ferries, headquartered in the Ferry Building at the foot of Market St., 415/923-2000, www.goldengateferry.org, specializes in runs to and from Sausalito (adults $5) and more frequent large-ferry (725-passenger capacity) trips to and from Larkspur. Family rates available, and disabled pasengers and seniors (over age 65) travel at half fare.

Red & White Fleet at Fisherman's Wharf, Pier 43, 415/673-2900or 877/855-5506, www.redandwhite.com, offers bay cruises and various land tours, as well as a commuter run to Richmond.

GETTING AROUND

San Francisco drivers are among the craziest in California. Whether they're actually demented, just distracted, insanely rude, or perhaps intentionally driving to a different drummer, walkers beware. The white lines of a pedestrian crosswalk seem to serve as sights, making people easier targets. Even drivers must adopt a heads-up attitude. In many areas, streets are narrow and/or incredibly steep; if you're driving a stick (manual) transmission, make sure you're well versed in hill-starts. Finding a parking place requires psychic skills. So, while many people drive into and out of the Bay Area's big little city, if at all possible many use public transit to get around town.

But some people really want to drive in San Francisco. Others don't want to, but need to, due to the demands of their schedules. A possible compromise: if you have a car but can't stand the thought of driving it through the urban jungle yourself, hire a driver. You can hire a chauffeur, and even arrange private sightseeing tours and other outings, through companies like **WeDriveU, Inc.,** 60 E. Third Ave. in San Mateo, 650/579-5800 or 800/773-7483. Other local limousine companies may be willing to hire-out just a city-savvy driver; call and ask.

Though those maniacal bicycle delivery folks somehow manage to daredevil their way through downtown traffic—note their bandages, despite protective armor—for normal people, cycling is a no-go proposition downtown and along heavy-traffic thoroughfares. Bring a bike to enjoy the Golden Gate National Recreation Area and other local parks, though it may be easier to rent one. Rental outlets around Golden Gate Park include **Avenue Cyclery,** 756 Stanyan, 415/387-3155, and other businesses on Stanyan, Fulton and Haight Streets. In Golden Gate Park, you can rent a bike, Rollerblades, or a pedal-powered surrey at **Golden Gate Park Bike & Skate,** 3038 Fulton (between Sixth and Seventh Aves.), 415/668-1117.

Car Rental

Some of the least expensive car rental agencies have the most imaginative names. Near the airport in South San Francisco, **Bob Leech's Auto Rental** 435 S. Airport Blvd., 650/583-3844, specializes in new Toyotas, from $30 per day with 150 fee-free miles. (You must carry a valid major credit card and be at least 23 years old; call for a ride from the airport.) Downtown, family-owned **Reliable Rent-A-Car,** 349 Mason,

415/928-4414, rents new cars with free pick-up and return for a starting rate of $29 per day ("any car, any time"). That all-American innovation, **Rent-A-Wreck,** 2955 Third St., 415/282-6293, rents out midsize used cars for around $29 per day with 150 free miles, or $159 per week with 700 free miles.

The more well-known national car rental agencies have desks at the airport, as well as at other locations. Their rates are usually higher than those of the independents and vary by vehicle make and model, length of rental, day of the week (sometimes season), and total mileage. Special coupon savings or substantial discounts through credit card company or other group affiliations can lower the cost considerably. If price really matters, check around. Consult the telephone book for all local locations of the companies listed below.

Agencies with offices downtown include: **Avis Rent-A-Car,** 675 Post St., 415/885-5011 or 800/831-2847; **Budget Rent-A-Car,** 321 Mason, 415/928-7864, or 800/763-2999; **Dollar Rent-A-Car,** 364 O'Farrell (opposite the Hilton Hotel), 415/771-5301 or 800/800-4000; **Enterprise,** 1133 Van Ness Ave., 415/441-3369 or 800/736-8222; **Hertz,** 433 Mason, 415/771-2200 or 800/654-3131; and **Thrifty Rent-A-Car,** 520 Mason (at Post), 415/788-8111 or 800/367-2277.

For a transportation thrill, all you wannabe easy riders can rent a BMW or Harley-Davidson motorcycle from **Dubbelju Tours & Service,** 271 Clara St., 415/495-2774. Rates start at $99 a day and include insurance, 100 free miles, and road service. Weekly and winter rates available. Open Mon.–Fri. 9 A.M.–noon and 4–6 P.M., Sat. 9 A.M.–noon, or by appointment. German spoken.

Driving

Curbing your wheels is the law when parking on San Francisco's hilly streets. What this means: turn your wheels toward the street when parked facing uphill (so your car will roll into the curb if your brakes and/or transmission don't hold), and turn them toward the curb when facing downhill.

Also, pay close attention to painted curb colors; the city parking cops take violations seriously.

Red curbs mean absolutely no stopping or parking. Yellow means loading zone (for vehicles with commercial plates only), half-hour time limit; yellow-and-black means loading zone for trucks with commercial plates only from 7 A.M.–6 P.M., half-hour limit; and green-yellow-and-black means taxi zone. Green indicates a 10-minute parking limit for any vehicle from 9 A.M.–6 P.M., and white means five minutes only, effective during the operating hours of the adjacent business. As elsewhere in the state, blue indicates parking reserved for vehicles with a California disabled placard or plate displayed. Pay attention, too, to posted street-cleaning parking limits, to time-limited parking lanes (open at rush hour to commuter traffic), and avoid even a quick-park at bus stops or in front of fire hydrants. Any violation will cost $25 to $275 (fire lane), and the police can tow your car—which will cost you $140 or so (plus daily impound fees) to retrieve.

Parking

If you're driving, you'll need to park. You also need to find parking, all but impossible in North Beach, the Haight, and other popular neighborhoods. San Franciscans have their pet parking theories and other wily tricks. Some even consider the challenge of finding parking a sport, or at least a game of chance. But it's not so fun for visitors, who usually find it challenging enough just to find their way around. It's wise to park your car (and leave it parked, to the extent possible), then get around by public transit. Valet parking is available (for a price, usually at least $15 per day) at major and midsize hotels, and at or near major attractions, including shopping districts.

Call ahead to inquire about availability, rates, and hours at major public parking garages, which include: **Fisherman's Wharf,** 665 Beach (at Hyde), 415/673-5197; **Fifth and Mission Garage,** 833 Mission St. (between Fourth and Fifth Sts.), 415/982-8522; **Downtown,** Mason and Ellis, 415/771-1400 (ask for the garage); **Moscone Center,** 255 Third St. (at Howard), 415/777-2782; **Chinatown,** 733 Kearny (underground, near Portsmith Square), 415/982-6353; and **Union Street,** 1550 Union, 415/

673-5728. For general information on city-owned garages, call 415/554-9805.

And good luck.

Muni

The city's multifaceted San Francisco Municipal Railway, or Muni, 415/673-MUNI weekdays 7 A.M.–5 P.M., Sat.–Sun. 9 A.M.–5 P.M., www.sfmuni.com, is still the locals' public transit mainstay. One of the nation's oldest publicly owned transportation systems, Muni is far from feeble, managing to move almost 250 million people each year. Yet even small glitches can wreak havoc when so many people depend on the system; heated criticism regularly crops up on local talk-radio shows and in the Letters to the Editor sections of local newspapers.

The city's buses, light-rail electric subway-and-surface streetcars, electric trolleys, and world-renowned cable cars are all provided by Muni. It costs $3 to ride the cable car. (It's odd that people stand in long lines at the Powell and Market turnaround, since it actually makes much more sense—no waiting, unless there's absolutely no space available—to grab on at Union Square or other spots en route.) Otherwise, regular Muni fare is $1.25 ($0.35 for seniors and youths, children under 5 free), exact coins required, and includes free transfers valid for two changes of vehicle in any direction within a two-hour period. If you'll be making lots of trips around town, pick up a multitrip discount Muni Passport (which includes cable

TAKING A TAXI

Taxis from SFO to San Francisco cost around $30–35 (plus tip, usually 15 percent). Standard San Francisco taxi fare, which also applies to around-town trips, was at press time $2.85 for the first mile, $2.25 per additional mile. Among the 24-hour taxi companies available, these are recommended.

DeSoto Cab Co., 415/970-1300
Luxor Cab, 415/282-4141
Veteran's Taxicab Company, 415/552-1300
Yellow Cab, 415/626-2345

San Francisco

car transit), available for sale at the Muni office, the Convention & Visitors Bureau information center downtown, Union Square's TIX box office, the City Hall information booth, and the Cable Car Museum. A one-day pass costs $6, a three-day pass $10, a seven-day pass $15, and a monthly pass $45.

Muni route information is published in the local telephone book yellow pages, or call for route verification (phone number listed above). Better yet, for a thorough orientation, check out one of the various Muni publications, most of which are available online or wherever Muni Passports are sold (and usually at the Transbay Terminal). A good overview and introduction is provided (free) by the *Muni Access Guide* pamphlet and the useful, seasonally updated *TimeTables,* which list current route and time information for all Muni transit. Especially useful for travelers is Muni's *Tours of Discovery* brochure, which lists popular destinations and possible tours with suggested transit routes (including travel time) and optional transfers and side trips. But the best all-around guide, easy to carry in pocket or purse, is the official annual *Muni Street & Transit Map* ($2), available at bookstores and grocery stores in addition to the usual outlets. The Muni map explains and illustrates major routes, access points, frequency of service, and also shows BART and Muni Metro subway stops, along with the CalTrain route into San Francisco. As a city map, it's a good investment, too.

San Francisco's Muni buses are powered by internal-combustion engines, and each is identified by a number and an area or street name (such as #7 Haight or #29 Sunset). Similarly numbered local trolleys or streetcars are actually electrically operated buses, drawing power from overhead lines, and are most notable downtown and along the steepest routes. The Muni Metro refers to this five-line system of streetcars, often strung together into trains of up to four cars, that run underground along Market St. and radiate out into the neighborhoods. Metro routes are identified by letters in conjunction with point of destination (J-Church, K-Ingleside, L-Taraval, M-Oceanview, and N-Judah). Muni Metro's

streetcars also include an international fleet of vintage streetcars, the F-Market Line, which starts at the Embarcadero and runs along Market St. to and from Castro St.; the F-Line also runs to Fisherman's Wharf. Another landmark line of historic streetcars, the E-Embarcadero, which will run from Mission Bay to Fort Mason, is coming one day soon. For more info, call 415/956-0472 or see www.streetcar.org.

Cable Cars

With or without those Rice-a-Roni ads, Muni's cable cars are a genuine San Francisco treat. (Don't allow yourself to be herded onto one of those rubber-tired motorized facsimiles that tend to cluster at Union Square, Fisherman's Wharf, and elsewhere. They are not cable cars, just lures for confused tourists.) San Francisco's cable cars are a national historic landmark, a system called "Hallidie's Folly" in honor of inventor Andrew S. Hallidie when these antiques made their debut on August 2, 1873. The only vehicles of their kind in the world, cable cars were created with the city's challenging vertical grades in mind. They are "powered" by an underground cable in perpetual motion, and by each car's grip-and-release mechanism. Even though maximum speed is about nine mph, that can seem plenty fast when the car snaps around an S-curve. (They aren't kidding when they advise riders to hold onto their seats.) After a complete system overhaul in the early 1980s, 26 "single-enders" now moan and groan along the two Powell St. routes, and 11 "double-enders" make the "swoop loop" along California Street. (New cars are occasionally added to the city's collection.) To get a vivid education in how cable cars work, visit the reconstructed Cable Car Barn and Museum.

BART

The Bay Area's 104-mile **Bay Area Rapid Transit** (BART) system, headquartered in Oakland, 510/464-6000 or 650/992-2278 (transit information), www.bart.gov, calls itself "the tourist attraction that gets people to the other tourist attractions." Fair enough. Heck, it is pretty thrilling to zip across to Oakland and Berkeley *underwater* in the Transbay Tube. An idea seem-

SUSAN SNYDER

San Francisco

one of the more traditional ways to climb—and descend—the city's steep streets

ingly sprung from Jules Verne, the concept had been proposed at various times since 1911—and emerged once again in 1947, when a joint U.S. Army-Navy review board proposed such a transit link to prevent traffic congestion on the Bay Bridge. The rest, as they say, is transportation history. And as far as it goes—which is not nearly far enough—BART is a good get-around alternative for people who would rather not drive. In San Francisco it's a convenient link from downtown to the Mission District. (When the BART-SFO extension is completed, travelers will be able to board BART inside the International Terminal at the San Francisco Airport for a fast and convenient ride to downtown San Francisco and other stops around the bay.) From Oakland/Berkeley, lines extend north to Richmond, south to Fremont, and east to Pittsburg or

Pleasanton. BART Express buses extend transit service to other East Bay communities

Helpful publications include the annual *All About BART* (with fares, travel times, and other details), and the *BART & Buses* BART guide to connections with the bus system. BART trains operate Mon.–Fri. 4 A.M.–midnight, Sat. 6 A.M.–midnight, and Sun. 8 A.M.–midnight. Exact fare depends upon your destination, but one-way fares vary from $1.15 to the maximum fare for the longest trip (about 53 miles) of $6.90. Tickets are dispensed at machines based at each station. (Change machines, for coins or dollar bills, are nearby.) Various discounts are available, for students and seniors as well as the disabled. If you don't have a current BART map, you can get your bearings at each station's color-keyed wall maps, which show destinations and routes.

South from San Francisco

The unstable wave-whipped coast south of San Francisco is all buff-colored bluffs and sandy beaches faced with rough rocks. Often foggy in summer, the coastline in winter is crowded with bird- and whalewatchers. But from late summer into autumn, the weather is usually good and the crowds mimimal, making this the perfect time for a superb escape. Wetsuit-clad surfers brave the snarling swells even in gale-force winds, yet swimming is dangerous even on serene sunny days due to treacherous undertows. Many of the region's beaches are officially accessible as state beaches or local beach parks; others are state-owned and undeveloped, or privately owned. Almost 20 miles of this 51-mile-long coastline are included as part of the San Mateo Coast State Beaches, starting with Daly City's **Thornton Beach** (popular for fishing and picnicking) in the north and ending with tiny **Bean Hollow State Beach** just north of Año Nuevo in the south. Though campgrounds are available inland, seaside public camping is possible only at Half Moon Bay State Beach, 650/726-8820. For more information, call **San Mateo State Beaches,** 650/726-8819. For more information on public-transit access to the San Mateo coast, call Sam-Trans at 650/508-6219 or 800/660-4287 or see www.samtrans.org.

PACIFICA

The self-proclaimed Fog Capital of California, Pacifica is sometimes a dreary place. But the locals make up for the opaque skies with *attitude.* Come here in late September for the annual **Pacific Coast Fog Fest,** which features a Fog Calling Contest (almost everyone's a winner), the Phileas Fogg Balloon Races, high-octane alcoholic "fog-cutters" (if drinking, *don't* drive off into the fog), plus a fog fashion show. When the weather's sunny, the town offers superb coastal views. And good food abounds here—fog or shine. For more information on the town or the Fog Fest, call the **Pacifica Chamber of Commerce** at 650/355-4122 or see www.pacificachamber.com/.

At **Sharp Park State Beach** along Beach Blvd. (reached from Hwy. 1 via Paloma Ave., Clarendon Rd., or streets in between) is the **Pacifica Pier,** popular for fishing and winter whale-watching. Migrating gray whales are attracted to the abundant plankton at the end of the community's sewage outfall pipe (the treatment plant is the building with the Spanish arches). Some old salts here say the great grays swim so close to the pier you can smell the fish on their breath.

Farther south is sort-of-secluded **Rockaway Beach,** a striking black-sand beach in a small rectangular cove where the coast has backed away from the rocky bluffs. Hotels and restaurants cluster beyond the rock-reinforced parking lot.

South from Pacifica

Long and narrow **Montara State Beach** offers hiking and rock-and-sand beachcombing. The state's tiny **Gray Whale Cove Beach** (a.k.a. Devil's Slide) here is a concession-operated clothing-optional beach, open for all-over tans only to those 18 and over; for information, call 650/726-8819. Just south of Montara proper is the cypress-strewn **Moss Beach** area, named for the delicate sea mosses that drape shoreline rocks at low tide.

Best for exploration Nov.–Jan. are the 30 acres of tidepools at the **James V. Fitzgerald Marine Reserve** (open daily from sunrise to sunset), which stretches south from Montara Point to Pillar Point and Princeton-by-the-Sea. At high tide, the Fitzgerald Reserve looks like any old sandy beach with a low shelf of black rocks emerging along the shore, but when the ocean rolls back, these broad rock terraces and their impressive tidepools are exposed. For area state park information, call 415/330-6300; for information on low-tide prime time at the Fitzgerald Reserve, call 650/728-3584; for more about docent-led guided tours of the reserve, call Coyote Point Museum, 650/342-7755, or see www.coyoteptmuseum.org.

Nearby, along Hwy. 1 in Montara, are **McNee Ranch State Park** and Montara Mountain, with hiking trails and great views of the Pacific. Next south is **El Granada,** an unremarkable town except for the remarkable music showcased by the **Bach Dancing & Dynamite Society,** 311 Mirada Rd. (technically in Miramar), 650/726-4143, www.bachddsoc.org, the longest-running venue for jazz greats in the Bay Area. Begun in 1958 when jazz fanatic Pete Douglas started letting jazz musicians hang out at his house and jam, public concerts blast off every Sunday (except around Christmas and New Year's) in a baroque beatnik beachhouse. The family lives downstairs; upstairs at "the Bach" is the concert hall and deck, though guests are free to amble down to the beach and back at all times. Admission isn't charged, but a contribution of $20–25 or so is the usual going rate for Sunday concerts. The Dancing & Dynamite Society has become so popular that Friday night candlelight dinner concerts cosponsored by local businesses or other supporters are also offered (reservations and advance payment required). For a fee, anyone can join the society and receive a newsletter and calendar of coming attractions.

Practicalities

If price is the primary issue, stay at the Montara hostel. Otherwise, the English-style **Seal Cove Inn,** 221 Cypress Ave. in Moss Beach, 650/728-4114 or 800/995-9987, www.sealcoveinn.com, is quite the find—an elegant and romantic country inn overlooking the Fitzgerald Marine Reserve, operated by Rick and Karen Brown Herbert, she the publisher of the popular Karen Brown guidebook series. The 10 guest rooms here each feature a wood-burning fireplace, refrigerator, TV, and ocean views; some have a private deck. For small group meetings, there's even a conference room. Rooms are $200–250, suites $300.

Traditional for a meal in Moss Beach is the old **Moss Beach Distillery** in Moss Beach, 140 Beach Way (at Ocean), 650/728-5595, now a romantic cliffside restaurant, very good for seafood, ribs, lamb, and veal. Open for lunch and dinner. **Barbara's Fish Trap,** 281 Capistrano Rd. in Princeton-by-the-Sea, 650/728-7049, open daily for lunch and dinner, offers great Half Moon Bay views, fishnet kitsch decor,

and fish selections that are a cut above the usual. Try the garlic prawns. Head for **Mezza Luna,** 459 Prospect Way, 650/728-8108, for authentic, relaxed Italian. **Café Gibraltar** at 425 Alhambra Ave. in El Granada, 650/560-9039, is just about everyone's favorite Mediterranean, serving everything from flatbread pizzas to polenta with mushrooms and lamb shank slow-braised with North African spices.

HALF MOON BAY

Known until the turn of the 20th century as Spanishtown, Half Moon Bay was a farm community settled by Italians and Portuguese, specializing in artichokes and Brussels sprouts. Down and out during the early 1900s, things picked up during Prohibition when the area became a safe harbor for Canadian rumrunners. Fast becoming a fashionable Bay Area residential suburb, Half Moon Bay is famous for its pumpkins and offers a rustic Main Street with shops, restaurants, and inns, plus pseudo-Cape Cod cluster developments along Hwy. 1. In 1999, Half Moon Bay's commercial ship-to-shore radiotelegraph station, the nation's last, tapped out its final Morse code transmission.

Just a few miles south of Half Moon Bay off Pillar Point and legendary among extreme surfers is **Mavericks,** home of the world's baddest wave. When surf's up here, during wild winter storms, Mavericks creates mean and icy 35-foot waves—mean enough to break bones and boards. Near Half Moon Bay is **Burleigh H. Murray Ranch,** 650/726-8819, state park property and still largely undeveloped, though the former 1,300-acre dairy ranch is now open to the public for day use (bring your own water). You can take a hike up the old ranch road, which winds up through sycamores and alders along Mill Creek. About a mile from the trailhead is the ranch's most notable feature, the only known example of an English bank barn in California. This century-old structure relied on simple but ingenious design, utilizing slope ("bank") and gravity to feed livestock most efficiently. Especially for those who can't remember even the basics of farm life, other outbuildings also deserve a peek. To get here,

San Francisco

a contender in the Great Pumpkin Weigh-Off

© ROBERT HOLMES/CALTOUR

turn east on Higgins-Purisima Rd. from Hwy. 1 just south of Half Moon Bay. It's about two miles to the parking area (marked, on the left).

A Portuguese **Chamarita** parade and barbecue are held in Half Moon Bay seven weeks after Easter. Over the July 4th weekend, the community's **Coastside County Fair and Rodeo** takes place. Half Moon Bay's **Great Pumpkin Weigh-Off** in early October awards the prize to the largest pumpkins grown on the West Coast, an event followed by the annual **Art & Pumpkin Festival,** featuring everything from pumpkin-carving and pie-eating contests to haunted house. For a complete list of area events and other information, contact the **Half Moon Bay/Coastside Chamber of Commerce,** 520 Kelly Ave., 650/726-8380, www.halfmoonbaychamber.org.

Accommodations

At **Half Moon Bay State Beach,** 650/726-8819, actually four separate beaches, the Francis Campground is first-come, first-camped. Group campsites are reservable. Call the park for more information.

The in thing in Half Moon Bay is inns, many of which offer reduced midweek rates. Much loved is the **Mill Rose Inn** bed-and-breakfast,

615 Mill St. in "old town," 650/726-8750, or 800/900-7673, a romantic Victorian with frills like fireplaces, a spa, English gardens, and excellent breakfasts. Midweek room rates $150–250, weekend room rates and suites $250 and up. Another local favorite is the restored **San Benito House** country inn, 356 Main St., 650/726-3425, www.sanbenitohouse.com, with 12 rooms on the upper floor (three share a divided bath), plus a sauna, redwood deck with flowers and firepit, and a downstairs restaurant and saloon. Street and deck side rooms $100–150. The **Old Thyme Inn,** 779 Main St., 650/726-1616 or 800/720-4277, www.oldthymeinn.com, has some rooms with two-person whirlpools. For special occasions or extra privacy, book the Garden Suite, which features a private entrance. The atmosphere here is very English, in a casually elegant style. Rooms are individually decorated, and some feature fireplaces and/or in-room whirlpool tubs. Especially delightful for gardeners is the herb garden here, boasting more than 80 varieties (true aficionados are allowed to take cuttings). Expect such treats as homemade scones and marmalade, or possibly even French cherry flan. Standard rooms $150–250, deluxe rooms and suites $250 and up.

Another historic local favorite is the **Zaballa House,** 324 Main St. (right next door to the San Benito House), 650/726-9123. It's Half Moon Bay's oldest surviving building (circa 1859) and now features nine standard guest rooms and three private-entrance suites, all with private bath. Several rooms have two-person whirlpool tubs and/or fireplaces. Ask about the "resident ghost" in Room 6. Rates $100–150.

The contemporary **Cypress Inn,** 407 Mirada Rd. (three miles north of Hwy. 92, just off Hwy. 1; exit at Medio Ave.), Miramar, 650/726-6002 or 800/832-3224, www.cypressinn.com, is right on the beach and just a few doors down from the Bach Dynamite & Dancing Society. The inn's motto is "in celebration of nature and folk art," and the distinctive rooms—each with an ocean view and private deck, fireplace, and luxurious private bath—do live up to it, whether you stay in the Rain, Wind, Sea, Sky, Star, Sun, or Moon rooms. For a special treat, head up into the Clouds (the penthouse). Gourmet breakfasts, afternoon tea, wine-tasting, and hors d'oeuvres included. Massage is available by appointment. $250 and up. North of Half Moon Bay, **Pillar Point Inn** 380 Capistrano Rd. in El Granada, 650/728-7377 or 800/400-8281, www.pillarpoint.com, overlooks the harbor in Princeton-by-the-Sea. All rooms have fireplaces and other modern amenities. Rates $150–250.

A lot of people are still plenty upset by the hugeness of its presence on this low-key stretch of coastline—don't the rich people already have everything else?—yet the **Ritz Carlton Half Moon Bay Resort** arrived in 2001. What you get is what you expect from Ritz Carlton, starting with accommodations inspired by swank 19th-century seaside resorts—only these rooms and suites include every imaginable luxury, down to the laptop-compatible in-room safes. The resort also features the fine-dining **Navio** restaurant, the more casual **Conservatory** restaurant/bar, complete with telescopes for spying on the ocean; the stylish **Salon** tearoom; full fitness and spa facilities; and 36 holes of "view" golf. And if you have to ask how much all that costs, you definitely can't afford it. For more information, contact the resort at 650/712-7000, www.ritzcarlton.com.

Food

The **Half Moon Bay Bakery,** 514 Main St., 650/726-4841, is also a stop on the local historic walking tour. The bakery still uses its original 19th-century brick oven and offers sandwiches, salads, and pastries over the counter. Other popular eateries include wonderful **Pasta Moon** café, 315 Main St., 650/726-5125; and the **San Benito House** restaurant inside the hotel, 356 Main (at Mill), 650/726-3425, noted for its French and Northern Italian country cuisine at dinner. Open Thurs.–Sun. for dinner only. Call for reservations. Simpler but excellent lunches (including sandwich selections on homemade breads) also served at the hotel's Garden Deli Café.

FROM SAN GREGORIO SOUTH

On the coast just west of tiny San Gregorio is **San Gregorio State Beach,** with the area's characteristic bluffs, a mile-long sandy beach, and a sandbar at the mouth of San Gregorio Creek. San Gregorio proper is little more than a spot in the road, but the back-roads route via Stage Road from here to Pescadero is pastoral and peaceful.

Inland Pescadero ("Fishing Place") was named for the creek's once-teeming trout, not for any fishing traditions on the part of the town's Portuguese settlers. (For more area information, contact the **Pescadero Village Association,** www.pescaderovillage.com.) Both **Pomponio** and **Pescadero State Beaches** offer small estuaries for same-named creeks. The 584-acre **Pescadero Marsh Natural Preserve** is a successful blue heron rookery, as well as a feeding and nesting area for more than 200 other bird species. (To birdwatch—best in winter—park at **Pescadero State Beach** near the bridge and walk via the Sequoia Audubon Trail, which starts below the bridge.) Rocky-shored **Bean Hollow State Beach,** a half-mile hike in, is better for tidepooling than beachcombing, though it has picnic tables and a short stretch of sand.

For a longer coast walk, head south to the **Año Nuevo** reserve. (Año Nuevo Point was named by Vizcaíno and crew shortly after New

Year's Day in 1602.) The rare northern elephant seals who clamber ashore here are an item only in winter and spring, but stop here any time of year for a picnic and a stroll along Año Nuevo's three-mile-long beach.

Accommodations

Affordable—and quite appealing in a back-to-basics style—are the two lighthouse hostels offered in California by Hostelling International (HI-USA), both located on the coast north of Santa Cruz.

If the hostels are full, the campground at **Butano State Park,** 650/879-2040, probably will be too—at least on Fridays, Saturdays, and holidays May–September. Campsites do not have showers or running water. Reached from Pescadero via

Cloverdale Rd. (or from near Gazos Beach via Gazos Creek Rd.), the park offers 21 family camp-sites, 19 walk-in sites, and a handful of backcountry trail camps. During the high season, reserve main campsites through **ReserveAmerica,** 800/444-7275, www.reserveamerica.com. The rest of the year, it's usually first-come, first-camped.

Unusual in the nature getaway category is **Costanoa Coastal Lodge and Camp** on the coast near Pescadero. In addition to its sophisticated 40-room lodge, deluxe traditional cabins, luxurious "camp bathroom" comfort stations, and gourmet-grub General Store, Costanoa also offers the nation's first "boutique camping resort." Though some RV and pitch-your-own-tent campsites are available, most of the camping provided is tent camping—in 1930s-style canvas

HOSTELS

Two spectacular lighthouse hostels, both affiliated with Hostelling International (HI-USA), are finds for travelers—including families—looking for cheap sleeps along the San Mateo coastline. And with online reservations available as of summer 2004, planning a stay in hostel territory is easier than ever.

Closest to Santa Cruz is the **Pigeon Point Lighthouse Hostel,** 210 Pigeon Point Rd. (at Hwy. 1) in Pescadero, 650/879-0633 (for phone-tree reservations, call 800/909-4776 #73), www.norcalhostels.org—*the* inexpensive place to stay while visiting the elephant seals. Named after the clipper ship *Carrier Pigeon,* one of many notorious shipwrecks off the coastal shoals here, the 1872 lighthouse is now automated but still impressive with its Fresnel lens and distinctive 10-second flash pattern. Lighthouse tours (40 minutes) are offered by state park staff every weekend year-round, and also on Fridays in summer; rain cancels. Small fee. For tour reservations, call 650/879-2120.

The hostel itself is made up of four former family residences for the U.S. Coast Guard—basic male or female bunkrooms, plus some spartan couples' and family rooms. The old Fog Signal Building is now a rec room; there's also a hot tub perched on rocky cliffs above surging surf. Fabulous sunset views, wonderful tidepools. Bunk-bed rates are

well under $50, at $18–25 adult, $13–18 child/youth. Private rooms, for up to two adults and two children, were $47–57 at last report. Extra charge for linen rental (if you don't bring your own sleep sack or sleeping bag). Get groceries in Pescadero and prepare meals in the well-equipped communal kitchens, or ask for local restaurant suggestions. For information and/or to check in, the hostel office is open 7:30–10 A.M. and 4:30–11 P.M. only. Photo ID required. Very popular, so reserve well in advance.

Farther north, beyond Half Moon Bay between Montara and Moss Beach, is picturesque **Point Montara Lighthouse Hostel,** 16th St. at Hwy. 1 in Montara, 650/728-7177 (for phone-tree reservations, call 800/909-4776 #64), www.norcalhostels.org. Point Montara is popular with bicyclists, and it's also accessible via bus from the Bay Area. The 1875 lighthouse itself is no longer in operation, and the Fog Signal Building here is now a roomy woodstove-heated community room. Hostel facilities include kitchens, dining rooms, laundry, bunkrooms, and couples' and family quarters. Volleyball court, outdoor hot tub, and bicycle rentals are also available. Open to travelers of all ages. Popular, so reserve in advance. Bunk-bed rates are well under $50, $18–21 adults, and $12 children. The five private rooms, ideal for couples or families, are $51–78.

"safari tents," complete with skylights, that range from economy to luxury. Deluxe canvas cabins feature queen-size beds, heated mattress pads, nightstands with reading lamps, and Adirondack chairs for taking in the great outdoors. Pitch-your-own-tent camping is under $50. RV camping and most canvas cabins: $50–100. Deluxe canvas cabins: $100–150. Regular cabins and lodge rooms: $150–250. For more information, contact: Costanoa, 2001 Rossi Rd. (at Hwy. 1) in Pescadero, 650/879-1100 or 800/738-7477 for reservations, www.costanoa.com.

Hard to beat for an overnight in Pescadero are the six cottages at **Estancia del Mar**, 460 Pigeon Point Rd., 650/879-1500, estanciadm @aol.com. Located on a working Peruvian Paso horse ranch and situated 500 yards from the surf, each attractive cottage sleeps four and includes custom-tiled bathroom, fully equipped kitchen, wood-burning stove, and stereo/CD player/radio and VCR. Linens and towels are provided. Kids and pets welcome. Rates $150–250, with multinight discounts.

Another option is the Spanish-style **Rancho San Gregorio** bed-and-breakfast, 5086 La Honda Rd. in San Gregorio, 650/747-0810, a best bet featuring just four attractive rooms (three have woodstoves; all have private baths). Many of the veggies and fruits served at breakfast are home-grown. Great hiking nearby. Rates: $100–150. Or head south along the coast. About nine miles north of Santa Cruz, the **New Davenport Bed and Breakfast Inn,** 31 Davenport Ave. (Hwy. 1), 831/425-1818 or 800/870-1817, www.daven portinn.com, is a colorful ocean-view hideaway (rooms above the restaurant) with artist owners and beach access. Rates: $100–150.

Food

In Pescadero, down-home **Duarte's Tavern,** 202 Stage Rd., 650/879-0464, open since 1894, is most noted for its artichoke soup and delicious olallieberry pie, not to mention the ever-changing fresh fish specials scrawled across the menu chalkboard. Open daily for breakfast, lunch, and dinner; reservations wise (especially in summer) for dinner and Sunday brunch. Stop by the **Arcangeli Grocery Company** nearby, 650/879-0147, www.arcangeligrocery.com, for artichoke bread and other surprises. Near Pescadero is **Phipps Country Store & Farm,** 2700 Pescadero Rd., 650/879-0787, www.phippscountry.com,

San Francisco

GOING COASTAL

From south of Half Moon Bay to Santa Cruz, people will be able to go coastal in perpetuity, thanks in large part to ongoing land acquisition efforts of the **Peninsula Open Space Trust (POST)**, 650/854-7696 www.openspacetrust.org. Thousands and thousands of acres on and near the coast are now protected from the possibility of development; some parcels are under the jurisdiction of the California Department of Parks and Recreation or other agencies, and many are open to the public (or soon will be) for day use.

Among these is **Cowell Ranch Beach** just south of Half Moon Bay, 650/726-8819, where a half-mile trail leads out to the point, and stairs trail down to a well-protected sandy beach.

Gazos Creek Beach, 650/879-2025, with its abundant tidepools, is now included within Año Nuevo State Reserve. The reserve also includes the 2,914 acres of **Cascade Ranch,** which adjoins Big Basin and Butano State Parks. Only a dream in years past, it's now possible to hike from the redwoods to the sea via the associated **Whitehouse Ridge Trail.** The result of one of the largest land deals ever negotiated by POST, one day the hiking and equestrian trails within the 5,638-acre Cloverdale Coastal Ranch south of Half Moon Bay will also be included in the new coastal parks landscape.

Just north of Santa Cruz, the 2,305-acre **Gray Whale Ranch** now part of **Wilder Ranch State Park,** 650/426-0505, was donated by the Save-the-Redwoods League and the Packard Foundation. A key wildlife corridor, the new ranch lands offer hiking and mountain-biking trails.

For all its successes, one-third of the lands targeted by POST for preservation remain to be acquired. Donations are appreciated.

where berries, dried beans, baby lettuce, squash, and other local produce are available in season. San Mateo County's *Coastside Harvest Trails* map lists other regional produce stands.

Down the coast toward Santa Cruz, the **New Davenport Cash Store & Restaurant,** 831/426-4122, is a store, arts and crafts gallery, and inexpensive eatery serving decent, healthy food (whole grains, salads, soups) and great desserts. Bed-and-breakfast rooms upstairs.

 AÑO NUEVO STATE RESERVE

About 20 miles north of Santa Cruz and just across the county line is the 4,000-acre Año Nuevo State Reserve, breeding ground and rookery for sea lions and seals—particularly the unusual (and once nearly extinct) northern elephant seal. The pendulous proboscis of a "smiling" two- to three-ton alpha bull dangles down like a fire hose, so the name is apt.

At first glance, the windswept and cold seaward stretch of Año Nuevo seems almost desolate, inhospitable to life. This is far from the truth,

however. Año Nuevo is the only place in the world where people can get off their bikes or the bus or get out of their cars and walk out among aggressive, wild northern elephant seals in their natural habitat. Especially impressive is that first glimpse of hundreds of these huge seals nestled like World War II torpedoes among the sand dunes. A large number of other animal and plant species also consider this area home; to better appreciate the ecologically fascinating animal and plant life of the entire area, read *The Natural History of Año Nuevo,* by Burney J. Le Boeuf and Stephanie Kaza.

The Northern Elephant Seal

Hunted almost to extinction for their oil-rich blubber, northern elephant seals numbered only 20 to 100 at the turn of the 20th century. All these survivors lived on Isla de Guadalupe off the west coast of Baja California. Their descendants eventually began migrating north to California. In the 1950s, a few arrived at Año Nuevo Island, attracted to its rocky safety. The first pup was born on the island in the 1960s. By 1975 the mainland dunes had been colonized by seals crowded off the island rookery, and the first pup

MELISSA SHEROWSKI

Año Nuevo State Reserve

was born onshore. By 1988, 800 northern elephant seals were born on the mainland, part of a total known population of more than 80,000 and an apparent ecological success story. (Only time will tell, though, since the species' genetic diversity has been eliminated by the swim at the brink of extinction.) Though Año Nuevo was the first northern elephant seal rookery established on the California mainland, northern elephant seals are now establishing colonies elsewhere along the state coastline.

Mating Season

Male northern elephant seals start arriving in December. Who arrives first and who remains dominant among the males during the long mating season is important because the alpha bull gets to breed with most of the females. Since the males are biologically committed to conserving their energy for sex, they spend much of their time lying about as if dead, in or out of the water, often not even breathing for stretches of up to a half hour. Not too exciting for spectators. But when two males battle each other for the "alpha" title, the loud, often bloody nose-to-nose battles are something to see. Arching up with heads back and canine teeth ready to tear flesh, the males bellow and bark and bang their chests together.

In January the females start to arrive, ready to bear offspring conceived the previous year. They give birth to their pups within the first few days of their arrival. The males continue to wage war, the successful alpha bull now frantically trying to protect his harem of 50 or so females from marauders. For every two pounds in body weight a pup gains, its mother loses a pound. Within 28 days, she loses about half her weight, then, almost shriveled, she leaves. Her pup, about 60 pounds at birth, weighs 300 to 500 pounds a month later. Although inseminated by the bull before leaving the rookery, the emaciated female is in no condition for another pregnancy, so conception is delayed for several months, allowing the female to feed and regain her strength. Then, after an eight-month gestation period, the cycle starts all over again.

Etiquette

The Marine Mammal Act of 1972 prohibits people from harassing or otherwise disturbing these magnificent sea mammals, so be respectful. While walking among the elephant seals, remember that the seemingly sluglike creatures *are* wild beasts and can move as fast as any human across the sand, though for shorter distances. For this reason, keeping a 20-foot minimum distance between you and the seals (especially during the macho mating season) is important. No food or drinks are allowed on the reserve, and nothing in the reserve may be disturbed. The first males often begin to arrive in November, before the official docent-led tours begin, so it's possible to tour the area unsupervised. Visit the dunes without a tour guide in spring and summer also, when many elephant seals return here to molt.

The reserve's "equal access boardwalk" across the sand makes it possible for physically challenged individuals to see the seals.

Information and Tours

No pets are allowed, not even if left in your vehicle. Official 2.5-hour guided tours of Año Nuevo begin in mid-December and continue through March, rain or shine, though January and February are the prime months, and reservations are necessary. The reserve is open 8 A.M.–sunset; the day-use parking fee is $6 (hike-ins and bike-ins are free, but you still must pick up a free day-use permit). Tour tickets ($4–8 plus surcharge for credit card reservations) are available only through ReserveAmerica's Año Nuevo and Hearst Castle reservations line, 800/444-4445. For international reservations, call 916/638-5883. Reservations cannot be made before November 1. To take a chance on no-shows, arrive at Año Nuevo before scheduled tours and get on the waiting list. The reserve offers a 1,700-foot-long wheelchair accessible boardwalk for seal viewing. There's also a van equipped with a wheelchair lift, to transport visitors from the parking lot to the boardwalk; accessible restrooms; and guided walks offered in American Sign Language (by advance reservation). For wheelchair access reservations,

December 15 through March 15, call 650/879-2033, 1 to 4 P.M. only on Monday, Wednesday, and Friday.

Organized bus excursions, which include walking tour tickets, are available through **San Mateo County Transit,** 800/660-4287 or 650/508-6441 (call after November 1 for reservations), www.samtrans.com, and **Santa Cruz Metro.** The HI-USA Pigeon Point Hostel, near Año Nuevo, sometimes has extra tickets for hostelers. For more information, contact the Año Nuevo State Reserve office, New Year's Creek Rd. in Pescadero, 650/879-0227 (recorded information) or 650/879-2025.

OTHER SAN MATEO PARKS

Five miles inland from Año Nuevo State Reserve is **Butano State Park,** 650/879-2040, which offers 30 miles of excellent if strenuous hikes among redwoods, plus picnicking, camping, and summer campfire programs. Another worthy redwoods destination is **San Mateo Memorial County Park,** 9500 Pescadero Rd. (eight miles east of Pescadero), 650/879-0238, which features a nature museum, 200-foot-tall virgin trees, creek swimming, camping, and trails connecting with surrounding local and state parks. Adjacent **Pescadero Creek County Park** (same address and phone) includes the steelhead trout stream's upper watersheds—6,000 acres of excellent hiking. (The Old Haul Rd. and Pomponio Trails link Pescadero to nearby Memorial and Portola Parks.)

Just to the north outside La Honda (though the entrance is off Pescadero Road) is 867-acre **Sam McDonald County Park** (same address and phone as San Mateo Memorial and Pescadero Creek Parks), offering rolling grasslands and redwoods, trails interconnecting with Pescadero Park, and a Sierra Club hiker's hut for overnights (to reserve, call the Loma Prieta chapter of the Sierra Club at 650/390-8411). To the southeast via Alpine Rd. and Portola State Park Rd. is La Honda's **Portola State Park,** 650/948-9098, comprised of rugged redwood terrain between Butano and Skyline Ridges. Here you'll find backcountry hiking, a short nature trail, a museum and visitor center, picnicking, and year-round camping. Campsite reservations are usually necessary Apr.–Sept.; call **ReserveAmerica** at 800/444-7275 (reserve the trail camp through park headquarters).

The **Midpeninsula Regional Open Space District,** 330 Distel Circle, Los Altos, 650/691-1200, administers other parkland in San Mateo and Santa Clara Counties—primarily preserves and limited-use areas perfect for hikers seeking even more seclusion. Among these: Purisima Creek Redwoods, southeast of Half Moon Bay; Mount El Sereno, south of Saratoga; the Long Ridge Preserve near Big Basin; and the rugged chaparral Sierra Azul-Limekiln Canyon Area near Lexington Reservoir. Contact the district's office for more information and maps.

Monterey Bay

The only remembered line of the long-lost Ohlone people's song of world renewal, "dancing on the brink of the world," has a particularly haunting resonance around Monterey Bay. Here, in the unfriendly fog and ghostly cypress along the untamed coast, the native "coast people" once danced. Like the area's vanished dancers, Monterey Bay is a mystery: everything seen, heard, tasted, and touched only hints at what remains hidden.

The first mystery is magnificent Monterey Bay itself, almost 60 miles long and 13 miles wide. Its offshore canyons, grander than Arizona's Grand Canyon, are the area's most impressive (if unseen) feature: the bay's largest submarine valley dips to 10,000 feet, and the adjacent tidal mudflats teem with life.

A second mystery is how cities as different as Carmel, Monterey, and Santa Cruz could take root and thrive near Monterey Bay.

The monied Monterey Peninsula is fringed by shifting sand dunes and some of the state's most ruggedly wild coastline. Carmel, or Carmel-by-the-Sea, is where Clint Eastwood once made everybody's day as mayor. (Inland is Carmel Valley, a tennis pro playground complete with shopping centers. The Carmel Highlands hug the coast on the way south to Big Sur.) Noted for its storybook cottages and spectacular crescent beach, Carmel was first populated by artists,

Must-Sees

Look for ⋈ to find the sights and activities you
can't miss and ⋈ for the best dining and lodging.

⋈ Santa Cruz Beach Boardwalk: This is the West Coast's answer to Atlantic City, an authentic amusement park complete with a classic wooden roller coaster (page 266).

⋈ Big Basin Redwoods State Park: California's first state park, about 24 miles up canyon from Santa Cruz, Big Basin is a stunning haven for coast redwoods and hikers alike (page 291).

⋈ Elkhorn Slough Reserve: Among California's largest remaining coastal estuaries, Elkhorn Slough was once the mouth of the Salinas River. Now it's a protected estuarine wildlife sanctuary, prime for birding, kayaking, and nature walks (page 297).

⋈ Monterey Bay Aquarium: The fish are back on Cannery Row. This world-class fish tanks built into the Row's converted Hovden Cannery is now the number-one aquarium in the U.S. (page 301).

⋈ Monterey State Historic Park: This "pathway of history" in California's first capital city preserves a variety of fine historic adobes, many of which exemplify the Monterey colonial style (page 310).

⋈ National Steinbeck Center: The first American to win both the Pulitzer and Nobel Prizes for literature, John Steinbeck wasn't always appreciated in his hometown of Salinas. This high-tech museum is changing all that (page 335).

⋈ Steinbeck House: A must-see for Steinbeck fans, this jewel-box Victorian just two blocks from the National Steinbeck Center is also a delicious destination for lunch (page 336).

⋈ Pinnacles National Monument: Exploring these barren 24,000 acres of volcanic spires and ravines atop the San Andreas Fault is a little like rock climbing on the moon (page 338).

⋈ Carmel Mission: California's second mission features an evocative 1797 baroque stone church, one of the state's most graceful buildings, complete with a four-bell Moorish tower, arched roof, and star-shaped central window (page 355).

⋈ Robinson Jeffers's Tor House: Now a national historic landmark, this medieval-looking granite retreat presides over Carmel Bay. Tor House was built by the famed California poet Robinson Jeffers, who helped haul the huge stones up from the beach below with horse teams (page 355).

⋈ Point Lobos: A jewel in the crown of California's state parks, Point Lobos just south of Carmel offers miles of pounding surf and a dramatic, cypress-fringed rocky coastline (page 359).

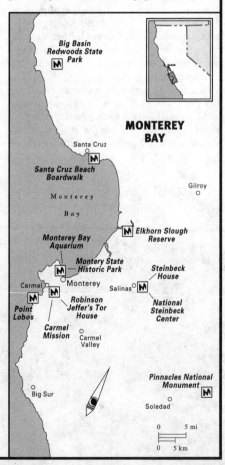

MONTEREY BAY

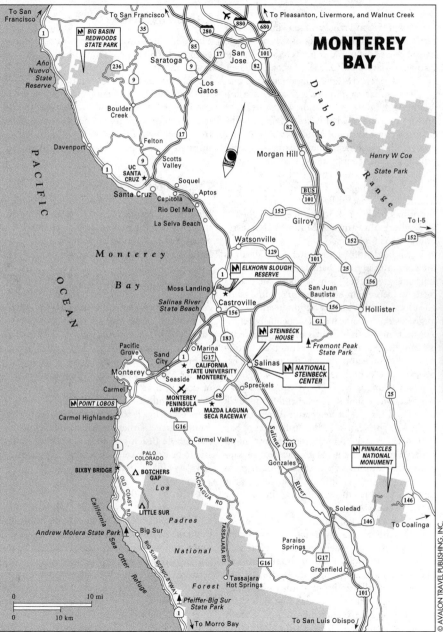

writers, and other assorted bohemians who were shaken out of San Francisco following the 1906 earthquake. Yet the founding of Carmel would have to be credited to Father Junípero Serra and the Carmelite friars of the Carmel Mission, built here in 1771, the second Spanish mission in California.

The original version of the Carmel mission was built the previous year, however, near the Spanish presidio in what is now Monterey. The cultured community of Monterey would later boast California's first capital, first government building, first federal court, first newspaper, and—though other towns also claim the honor—first theater. Between Carmel and Monterey is peaceful Pacific Grove, where alcohol has been legal only since the 1960s—and where the annual Monarch butterfly migration is big news.

Just inland from the Monterey Peninsula is the agriculturally rich Salinas Valley, boyhood stomping grounds of John Steinbeck. Steinbeck's focus on Depression-era farm workers unleashed great local wrath—all but forgotten and almost forgiven since his fame has subsequently benefited area tourism. South of Salinas and east of Soledad is Pinnacles National Monument, a fascinating volcanic jumble and almost "the peak" for experienced rock climbers. Not far north, right on the San Andreas Fault, is Mission San Juan Bautista, where Jimmy Stewart and Kim Novak conquered his fear of heights in Alfred Hitchcock's *Vertigo*. Nearby are the headwaters of San Benito Creek, where lucky rockhounds might stumble upon some gem-quality, clear or sapphire-blue samples of the state's official gemstone, benitoite, found only here. Also in the neighborhood is Gilroy, self-proclaimed garlic capital of the world.

Once working-class Santa Cruz has the slightly seedy Boardwalk, sandy beaches, good swimming, surfers, and—helped along by the presence of UC Santa Cruz—an intelligent and open-minded social scene. Nearby are the redwoods, waterfalls, and mountain-to-sea hiking trails of Big Basin, California's first state park, plus the Año Nuevo coastal area, until recently the world's only mainland mating ground for the two-ton northern elephant seal.

LAND AND SEA

Much of the redwood country from San Francisco to Big Sur resembles the boulder-strewn, rough-and-tumble coast of far Northern California. Here the Pacific Ocean is far from peaceful; posted warnings about dangerous swimming conditions and undertows are no joke. Inland, the San Andreas Fault menaces, veering inland from the eastern side of the Coast Ranges through the Salinas Valley and on to the San Francisco Bay Area.

The Monterey Peninsula

Steinbeck captured the mood of the Monterey Peninsula in *Tortilla Flats*—"The wind. . . drove the fog across the pale moon like a thin wash of watercolor. . . . The treetops in the wind talked huskily, told fortunes and foretold deaths." The peninsula juts into the ocean 115 miles south of San Francisco and forms the southern border of Monterey Bay. The north shore sweeps in a crescent toward Santa Cruz and the Santa Cruz Mountains; east is the oak- and pine-covered Santa Lucia Range, rising in front of the barren Gabilan ("Sparrow Hawk") Mountains beloved by Steinbeck. Northward are the ecologically delicate Monterey Bay Dunes, now threatened by off-road vehicles and development. To the south, the piney hills near Point Pinos and Asilomar overlook rocky crags and coves dotted with wind-sculpted trees; farther south, beyond Carmel and the Pebble Beach golf mecca, is Point Lobos, said to be Robert Louis Stevenson's inspiration for Spyglass Hill in *Treasure Island*.

Monterey "Canyon"

Discovered in 1890 by George Davidson, Monterey Bay's submerged valley teems with sealife: bioluminescent fish glowing vivid blue to red, squid, tiny rare octopi, tentacle-shedding jellyfish, and myriad microscopic plants and animals. This is one of the most biologically prolific spots on the planet. Swaying with the ocean's motion, dense kelp thickets are home to sea lions, seals, sea otters, and giant Garibaldi "goldfish." Opal-eyed perch in schools of hundreds swim by leopard sharks and bottom fish. In the understory near

SEA OTTERS DECLINING AGAIN

Sea otters range north along the coast to Jenner in Sonoma County, and south to Cambria (and beyond). Watching otters eat is quite entertaining; to really see the show, binoculars are usually necessary. Carrying softball-sized rocks in their paws, sea otters dive deep to dislodge abalone, mussels, and other shellfish, then return to the surface and leisurely smash the shells and dine while floating on their backs, "rafting" at anchor in forests of seaweed. They feed heartily, each otter consuming about two and a half tons of seafood per year—much to the dismay of commercial shellfish interests.

Such scenes are still fairly common, yet the California sea otter, listed as a threatened species under the federal Endangered Species Act, is declining again. In 1995, the U.S. Fish and Wildlife Service counted 2,377 sea otters. By 1998, the population had dropped to 1,937—and some 200 dead otters washed ashore on area beaches, for reasons unknown. The average spring-count population declined at a rate of about four percent per year between 1985 and 1994, but since the mid-1990s the annual decline has averaged eight percent. Scientists are still figuring out why.

Obvious ongoing hazards include coastal pollution, infectious disease, natural toxins (such as red tide algae), entrapment in fishing nets or wire fishing pots, even occasional shark attacks. Yet recent research suggests parasitic disease is the primary culprit, causing fatal disase in the brains and nervous systens of sea otters and other animals. Two primary parasites have been discovered—*Toxoplasma gondii*, its spores introduced by cat feces flushed into sewage systems, and *Sarcocystis neurona*, spread through opossum feces.

In centuries past, an estimated population of almost 16,000 sea otters along the California coast was decimated by eager fur hunters. A single otter pelt was worth upward of $1,700 by 1910, when it was generally believed that sea otters were extinct here. But a small pod survived off the coast near Carmel, a secret well guarded by biologists until the Big Sur Highway opened in 1938.

Until the 1990s, the sea otters seemed to be making a comeback; their range had expanded widely up and down the coast. Much to the chagrin of the south coast commercial shellfish industry, sea otters had even started moving south past Point Conception into shellfish waters.

the rocky ocean floor live abalones, anemones, crabs, sea urchins, and starfish.

Students of Monterey Canyon geology quibble over the origins of this unusual underwater valley. Computer-generated models of canyon creation suggest that the land once used to be near Bakersfield and was carved out by the Colorado River; later it shifted westward due to plate tectonics. More conventional speculation focuses on the creative forces of both the Sacramento and San Joaquin Rivers, which perhaps once emptied at Elkhorn Slough, Monterey Canyon's principal "head."

However Monterey Canyon came to be, it is now centerpiece of the 5,312-square-mile **Monterey Bay National Marine Sanctuary** which extends some 400 miles along the coast, from San Francisco's Golden Gate in the north to San Simeon in the south. Established in 1992 after a 15-year political struggle, this federally sanc-

tioned preserve is now protected from offshore oil drilling, dumping of hazardous materials, the killing of marine mammals or birds, jet skis, and aircraft flying lower than 1,000 feet. As an indirect result of its federal protection, Monterey Bay now boasts a total of 18 marine research facilities.

Climate

The legendary California beach scene is almost a fantasy here—almost but not quite. Surfers can be seen here year-round, though often in wetsuits. Sunshine warms the sands (between storms) from fall to early spring, but count on fog from late spring well into summer. Throughout the Monterey Bay area it's often foggy and damp, though clear summer afternoons can get hot; the warmest months along the coast are August, September, and October. (Sunglasses, suntan lotion, and hats are prudent, but always bring a sweater.) Inland, expect hotter weather in summer, colder in winter. Rain is possible as early as October, though big storms don't usually roll in until December.

FLORA AND FAUNA

Flora

California's central coast region, particularly near Monterey, exhibits tremendous botanic diversity. Among the varied vascular plant species found regionally is the unusually fast-growing Monterey pine, an endemic tree surviving in native groves only on hills and slopes near Monterey, Cambria, and Año Nuevo, as well as on Guadalupe and Cedros Islands off the coast of Baja, Mexico. It's now a common landscaping tree—and the world's most widely cultivated tree, grown commercially for its wood and pulp throughout the world. The unusual Monterey cypress is a relict, a specialized tree that can't survive beyond the Monterey Peninsula. The soft green Sargent cypress is more common, ranging south to Santa Barbara along the coast and inland. The Macnab cypress is found only on poor serpentine soil, as are Bishop pines, which favor swamps and the slopes from "Huckleberry Hill" near Monterey south to the San Luis Range near Point Buchon and Santa Barbara County.

Coastal redwoods thrive near Santa Cruz and south through Big Sur. Not as lusty as those on the north coast, these redwoods often keep company with Douglas fir, pines, and a dense understory of shade-loving shrubs. Other central coast trees include the Sitka spruce and beach pines. A fairly common inland tree is the chaparral-loving knobcone pine, with its tenaciously closed "fire-climax" cones. Other regional trees include the California wax myrtle, the aromatic California laurel or "bay" tree, the California

Monterey Bay

FIGHTING OAK FUNGUS AMONG US

California's newest plant plague is sudden oak death, or *Phytophthora ramorum,* a shockingly sudden, fast-moving funguslike primitive brown alga that afflicts native California oak, madrone, and bay trees, as well as rhododendrons, camellias, and other ornamental plants. First identified in the mid-1990s near Mt. Tamalpais in Marin County and now found as far south as Big Sur, as far north as southern Oregon, and in 13 other states, the disease is most prevalent along California's central coast regions.

Trees in their death throes have large, weeping cankers that "bleed" dark red viscous fluid; they also host swarms of beetles and the *Hypoxylon* fungus, evidence that tree tissues are dying. (There was some confusion about this fungal infection when sudden oak death was first identified. It's now believed that the fungus is a symptom rather than cause—already present in trees, harmlessly, breaking out and growing rapidly only where sapwood is dying.) Sudden oak death is similar to a pathogen that has afflicted forests in the Pacific Northwest since the 1960s. Perhaps ominously, it has also been found in redwood trees. There is no known cure, though in 2003 a breakthrough phosphite product proved successful in protecting oak trees from infection, and in helping infected oaks fight off the disease. In 2004 the disease's genome was mapped, raising hopes that a universal cure will be developed. So far sudden oak death has been spreading within the coastal "fog belt." The disease spreads through soil and root systems, and probably also through water. The cooperation of hikers, mountain bikers, and even casual visitors is required to avoid spreading sudden oak death. Preventive steps include thoroughly washing one's shoes and tires before leaving infected areas, as well as prohibiting the export of wood products and plants. Complicating the problem further is the fact that a variety of other plants serve as "hosts" and spreaders of sudden oak death. These include coffeeberry, huckleberry, and California buckeye, though the two dominant sources of ongoing infection are rhododendrons and California bay laurels.

For current information about sudden oak death, including quarantines and preventive measures, see the California Oak Mortality website: www.suddenoakdeath.org.

nutmeg, the tan oak (and many other oaks), plus alders, big-leaf maples, and occasional madrones. Eucalyptus trees thrive in the coastal locales where they've been introduced.

Whales and Sharks

The annual migration of the California gray whale, the state's official mammal, is big news all along the coast. From late October to January, these magnificent 20- to 40-ton creatures head south from Arctic seas toward Baja (pregnant females first). Once the mating season ends, males, newly pregnant females, and juveniles start their northward journey from February to June. Females with calves, often traveling close to shore, return later in the year, between March and July. Once in a blue moon, when the krill population mushrooms in winter, rare blue whales will feed in and around Monterey Bay and north to the Farallon Islands.

A wide variety of harmless sharks are common in Monterey Bay. Occasionally, 20-foot-long great white sharks congregate here to feed on sea otters, seals, and sea lions. Unprovoked attacks on humans do occur (to surfers more often than scuba divers) but are very rare. The best protection is avoiding ocean areas where great whites are common, such as Año Nuevo Island at the north end of the bay; don't go into the water alone and never where these sharks have been recently sighted.

Seals and Sea Lions

Common in these parts is the California sea lion; the females are the barking "seals" popular in aquatic amusement parks. True seals don't have external ears, and the gregarious, fearless creatures swimming in shallow ocean waters or lolling on rocky jetties and docks usually do. Also here are northern or Steller's sea lions—which roar instead of bark and are usually lighter in color. Chunky harbor seals (no ear flaps, usually with spotted coats) more commonly haul out on sandy beaches, since they're awkward on land. Less common but rapidly increasing in numbers along the California coast—viewable at the Año Nuevo rookery during the winter mating and birthing season—are the massive northern elephant seals,

the largest pinnipeds (fin-footed mammals) in the Western Hemisphere. One look at the two- or three-ton, 18-foot-long males explains the creatures' common name: their long, trunklike noses serve no real purpose beyond sexual identification, as far as humans can tell.

Pelicans and Other Seabirds

The ungainly looking, web-footed brown pelicans—most noticeable perched on pilings or near piers in and around harbors—are actually incredibly graceful when diving for their dinners. A squadron of 25 or more pelicans "gone fishin'" first glide above the water then, one by one, plunge dramatically to the sea. Brown pelicans are another back-from-the-brink success story, their numbers increasing dramatically since DDT (highly concentrated in fish) was banned. California's pelican platoons are often accompanied by greedy gulls, somehow convinced they can snatch fish from the fleshy pelican pouches if they just try harder.

Seabirds are the most obvious seashore fauna; besides brown pelicans you'll see long-billed curlews, ashy petrels nesting on cliffs, surf divers like grebes and scooters, and various gulls. Pure white California gulls are seen only in winter here (they nest inland), but yellow-billed western gulls and the scarlet-billed, white-headed Heermann's gulls are common seaside scavengers. Look for the hyperactive, self-important sandpipers along the shore, along with dowitchers, plovers, godwits, and avocets. Killdeers—so named for their "ki-dee" cry—lure people and other potential predators away from their clutches of eggs by feigning serious injury.

Tidepool Life

The twice-daily ebb of ocean tides reveals an otherwise hidden world. Tidepools below rocky headlands are nature's aquariums, sheltering abalone, anemones, barnacles, mussels, hermit crabs, starfish, sea snails, sea slugs, and tiny fish. Distinct zones of marine life are defined by the tides. The highest, or "splash," zone is friendly to creatures naturally protected by shells from desiccation, including black turban snails and hermit crabs. The intertidal zones (high and low) protect spiny sea urchins and the harmless sea anemone. The "minus tide" or surf zone—farthest from shore and almost always underwater—is home to hazardous-to-human-health stingrays (particularly in late summer, watch where you step) and jellyfish.

HISTORY

Cabrillo spotted Point Piños and Monterey Bay in 1542. Sixty years later, Vizcaíno sailed into the bay and named it for the viceroy of Mexico, the count of Monte-Rey. A century later came Portolá and Father Crespi, who, later joined by Father Junípero Serra, founded both Monterey's presidio and the mission at Carmel.

The quiet redwood groves near Santa Cruz remained undisturbed by civilization until the arrival of Portolá's expedition in 1769. The sickly Spaniards made camp in the Rancho de Osos section of what is now Big Basin, experiencing an almost miraculous recovery in the valley they

BEACHCOMBING BY THE BAY

Beachcombing is finest in February and March after winter storms—especially if searching for driftwood, agates, jasper, and jade—and best near the mouths of creeks and rivers. While exploring tidepools, refrain from taking or turning over rocks, which provide protective habitat for sea critters (like the Monarch butterfly, other animals don't like being molested, either). Since low tide is the time to "do" the coast, coastwalkers, beachcombers, and clammers need a current tide table (useful for a range of about 100 coastal miles), available at local sporting goods stores and dive shops. Also buy a California fishing license, since a permit is necessary for taking mussels, clams, and other sealife. But know the rules: many regulations are enforced to protect threatened species, and others are for *human* well-being. There's an annual quarantine on mussels, for example, usually from May through October, to protect omnivores from nerve paralysis caused by the seasonal "red tide."

called Cañada de Salud (Canyon of Health). A Spanish garrison and mission were soon established on the north end of Monterey Bay.

By the end of the 1700s, the entire central California coast was solidly Spanish, with missions, pueblos, and military bases or presidios holding the territory for the king of Spain. With the Mexican revolution, Californio loyalty went with the new administration closer to home. But the people here carried on their Spanish cultural heritage despite the secularization of the missions, the increasing influence of cattle ranches, and the foreign flood (primarily American) that threatened existing California tradition. Along the rugged central coast just south of the boisterous and booming gold rush port of San Francisco, the influence of this new wave of "outsiders" was felt only later and locally, primarily near Monterey and Salinas.

Monterey

In addition to being the main port city for both Alta and Baja California, from 1775 to 1845 Monterey was the capital of Alta California—and naturally enough, the center of much political intrigue and scheming. Spared the devastating earthquakes that plagued other areas, Monterey had its own bad times, which included being burned and ransacked by the Argentinean revolutionary privateer Hippolyte Bouchard in 1818. In 1822, Spanish rule ended in California, and Mexico took over. In 1845, Monterey lost part of its political prestige when Los Angeles temporarily became the territory's capital city. When the rancheros surrendered to Commodore Sloat in July 1846, the area became officially American, though the town's distinctive Spanish tranquility remained relatively undisturbed until the arrival of farmers, fishing fleets, fish canneries, and whalers. California's first constitution was drawn up in Monterey, at Colton Hall, in 1849, during the state's constitutional convention.

Santa Cruz

Santa Cruz, the site of Misión Exaltación de la Santa Cruz and a military garrison on the north

© ROBERT HOLMES/CALTOUR

Artists are still alive and well in Monterey.

end of Monterey Bay, got its start in 1791. But the 1797 establishment of Branciforte—a "model colony" financed by the Spanish government just across the San Lorenzo River—made life hard for the mission fathers. The rowdy, quasi-criminal culture of Branciforte so intrigued the native peoples that Santa Cruz men of the cloth had to use leg irons to keep the Ohlone home. And things just got worse. In 1818, the threat of pirates at nearby Monterey sent the mission folk into the hills, with the understanding that Branciforte's bad boys would pack up the mission's valuables and cart them inland for safekeeping. Instead, they looted the place and drank all the sacramental wine. The mission was eventually abandoned, then demolished by an earthquake in 1857. A small port city grew up around the plaza and borrowed the mission's name—Santa Cruz—while Branciforte, a smuggler's haven, continued to flourish until the late 1800s.

Carmel

Carmel-by-the-Sea was established in 1903 by real estate developers who vowed to create a cultured community along the sandy beaches of Carmel Bay. To do this they offered to "creative people" such incentives as building lots for as little as $50. As the result of such irresistible inducements Carmel was soon alive with an assortment of tents and shacks, these eventually giving way to cottages and mansions.

Tourism grew right along with the art colony; the public had a passion for travel during those early days of automobile adventuring. Quaint Carmel, home to "real Bohemians," also offered tourists the chance to view (and buy) artworks—a prospect cheered by the artists themselves. Carmel's commitment to the arts and artists was formalized with the establishment of the Carmel Art Association in 1927. Still going strong, with strict jury selection, this artists' cooperative is a cultural focal point in contemporary Carmel.

Santa Cruz

Still in tune with its gracefully aging Boardwalk, Santa Cruz is a middle-class tourist town enlightened and enlivened by retirees and the local University of California campus. It's possible to live here without a lot of money, though that's getting harder, with the advent of Silicon Valley commuters. Still, Santa Cruz is quite a different world from the affluent and staid Monterey Peninsula.

The Santa Cruz attitude has little to do with its name, taken from a nearby stream called Arroyo de Santa Cruz ("Holy Cross Creek") by Portolá. No, the town's relaxed good cheer must be karmic compensation for the morose mission days and the brutishness of nearby Branciforte. The Gay Nineties—the 1890s, that is—were happier here than anywhere else in

Northern California, with trainloads of Bay Area vacationers in their finest summer whites stepping out to enjoy the Santa Cruz waterfront, the Sea Beach Hotel, and the landmark Boardwalk and amusement park. The young and young at heart headed straight for the Victorian amusement park, with its fine merry-go-round, classic wooden roller coaster, pleasure pier, natatorium (indoor pool), and dancehall casino. More decadent fun lovers visited the ships anchored offshore to gamble or engage the services of prostitutes.

Santa Cruz still welcomes millions of visitors each year, yet it somehow manages to retain its dignity—except when embroiled in hot local political debates or when inundated by college students during the annual rites of spring. A

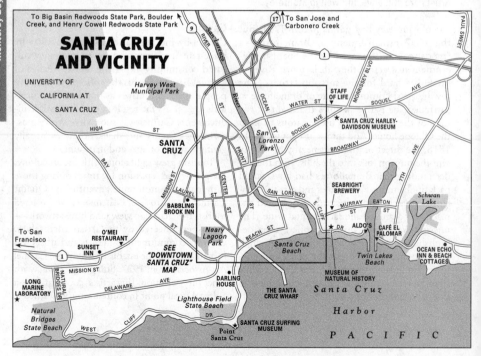

tourist town it may be, but some of the best things to do here are free: watching the sun set from East or West Cliff Drive, beachcombing, bike riding (excellent local bike lanes), swimming, surfing, and sunbathing.

Old-timers weren't ready for the changes in community consciousness that arrived in Santa Cruz along with the idyllic UC Santa Cruz campus in the 1960s. More outsiders came when back-to-the-landers fled San Francisco's Haight Ashbury for the hills near here, and when Silicon Valley electronics wizards started moving in. The city's boardwalk-and-beach hedonism may be legendary, but so are the Santa Cruz City Council's foreign policy decisions opposing contra aid, proclaiming the city a "free port" for Nicaragua, and calling for divestiture of South African investments. In October 2000 Santa Cruz passed its own "living wage" law, mandating a minimum pay rate of $11 per hour ($12 without benefits) for city workers and companies that contract with the city.

Though there's always some argument, the city's progressive politics are now firmly entrenched, as are other "dancing-on-the-brink" attitudes. The "People's Republic of Santa Cruz" is also a way station for the spiritually weary, with its own unique evangelical crusade for higher consciousness. Dreams and dreamers run the show.

HISTORY

The charming Santa Cruz blend of innocence and sleaze has roots in local history. The area's earliest residents were the Ohlone people, who avoided the sacred redwood forests and subsisted on seafood, small game, acorns, and foods gathered in woodland areas. Then came the mission and missionaries, a Spanish military garrison, and the den-of-thieves culture of Branciforte; the latter community posed an active threat to the holy fathers' attempted good works among the heathens. Misión Exaltación de la Santa Cruz declined, was abandoned, then collapsed following an earthquake in 1857.

A small trading town, borrowing the mission's name, grew up around the old mission plaza in the 1840s. The town supplied whalers with fruits and vegetables. Nearby Branciforte became a smugglers' haven, hosting bullfight festivals and illicit activities until 1867. The "education" and excitement imported by foreigners proved to be too much for the Ohlone; the only traces of their culture today are burial grounds. Branciforte disappeared, too, absorbed as a suburb when loggers and "bark strippers" (those who extracted tannin from tan oaks for processing leather) arrived to harvest the forests during the gold rush.

By the late 1800s, Santa Cruz was well established as a resort town. Logging continued, however, in the early 20th century, the local lumber industry was ready to log even majestic Big Basin. But those plans were thwarted by the active intervention of the Sempervirens Club, which successfully established California's first state park.

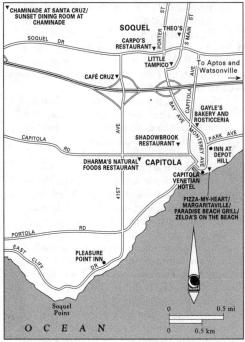

Monterey Bay

GREATER SANTA CRUZ

Just east of Santa Cruz, along the south-facing coast here, are the towns of Soquel, Capitola, and Aptos—the Santa Cruz burbs. High-rent **Soquel,** once a booming lumber town and the place where Portolá and his men were all but stricken by their first sight of coastal redwoods, is now noted for antiques and oaks.

The wharf in **Capitola** has stood since 1857, when the area was known as Soquel Landing. The name "Camp Capitola" was an expression of Soquel locals' desire to be the state capital—the closest they ever came. The city was, however, the state's first seaside resort. Nowadays, Capitola is big on art galleries and fine craft shops—take a stroll along Capitola Avenue from the trestle to the creek—but it's still most famous for its begonias. The year's big event is the **Begonia Festival,** usually held early in September. Stop by

Antonelli Bros. Begonia Gardens, 2545 Capitola Rd., 831/475-5222, to see a 10,000-square-foot greenhouse display of begonias, best in August and September.

Aptos, on the other side of the freeway, is more or less the same community as Capitola but home to Cabrillo College and the **World's Shortest Parade,** usually held on the July 4th weekend and sponsored by the Aptos Ladies' Tuesday Evening Society.

Heading north on Hwy. 9 from Santa Cruz will take you through the Santa Cruz Mountains and the towns of Felton, Ben Lomond, and Boulder Creek before winding down the other side of the mountains into Saratoga on the flank of Silicon Valley. This route is the gateway to several beautiful redwood state parks, including Henry Cowell, Fall Creek, Big Basin, and Castle Rock.

SIGHTS

◼ Santa Cruz Beach Boardwalk

The Santa Cruz Beach Boardwalk may be old, but it's certainly lively, with a million visitors per year. This is the West Coast's answer to Atlantic City. The original wood planking is now paved over with asphalt, stretching from 400 Beach Street for a half mile along one of Northern California's finest swimming beaches. A relatively recent multimillion-dollar facelift didn't diminish the Boardwalk's charms one iota. Open daily from Memorial Day to Labor Day and on weekends the rest of the year, the Boardwalk is an authentic amusement park, with dozens of carnival rides, odd shops and eateries, good-time arcades, even a big-band ballroom. Ride the **Sky Glider** to get a good aerial view of the Boardwalk and beach scene—and, across the street, the **Boardwalk Bowl** bowling alley at 115 Cliff St. (at Beach), 831/426-3324.

None other than *The New York Times* has declared the 1924 **Giant Dipper** roller coaster here one of the nation's 10 best. A gleaming white wooden rocker 'n' roller, the Dipper is quite a sight anytime, but it's truly impressive when lit up

at night. The 1911 **Charles Looff carousel,** one of a handful of Looff creations still operating in the United States, has 70 handcrafted horses, two chariots, and a circa-1894 Ruth Band pipe organ—all lovingly restored to their original glory. (Both the Dipper and the carousel are national historic landmarks.)

Newer rides feature more terror, of course. The **Cliff Hanger** offers spins and hang gliding–likethrills, and the pendulum-like **Fireball** serves up fiery upside-down spins. The bright lights and unusual views offered by the Italian-made **Typhoon** are just part of the joys of being suspended upside down in midair. The **Hurricane** is the Boardwalk's modern high-tech roller coaster, providing a two-minute thrill ride with a maximum gravitational force of 4.7 Gs and a banking angle of 80 degrees. Also state of the art in adrenaline inducement at the Boardwalk is the **Wave Jammer**—not to mention **Chaos, Crazy Surf, Tsunami,** and **Whirl Wind.** For a scary change-up, try the new **Fright Walk** dungeon (separate admission).

The antique devices in the penny arcades at the Boardwalk's west end cost a bit more these days, but it's worth it to Measure the Thrill of Your Kisses or

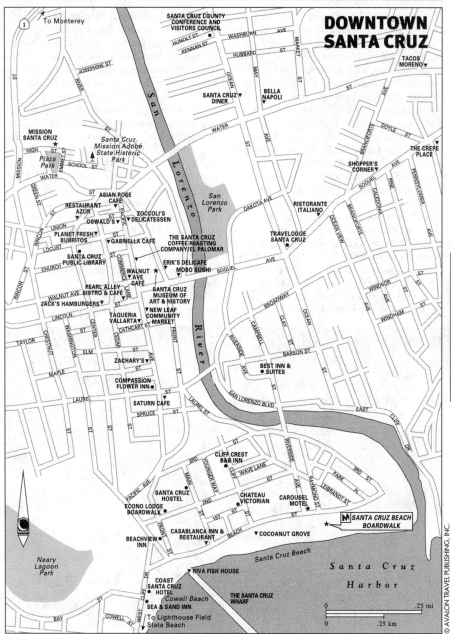

DOWNTOWN SANTA CRUZ

To Monterey

SANTA CRUZ COUNTY CONFERENCE AND VISITORS COUNCIL

TACOS MORENO▼

JOSEPHINE ST

WASHBURN AVE

HUNOLT ST
KENNAN ST
HUBBARD ST

SANTA CRUZ▼ DINER

BELLA NAPOLI▼

THE CREPE PLACE▼

MISSION SANTA CRUZ ★

Santa Cruz Mission Adobe State Historic Park

WATER

SHOPPER'S CORNER▼

Plaza Park

SCHOOL ST

San Lorenzo Park

WATER

ASIAN ROSE CAFE

DAKOTA AVE

RISTORANTE ITALIANO▼

RESTAURANT AZUR▼
OSWALD'S▼

ZOCCOLI'S ▼DELICATESSEN

PLANET FRESH▼ BURRITOS

TRAVELODGE SANTA CRUZ

▼GABRIELLA CAFE

THE SANTA CRUZ COFFEE ROASTING COMPANY/EL PALOMAR

SANTA CRUZ PUBLIC LIBRARY

ERIK'S DELICAFE
▼MOBO SUSHI

SOQUEL

WALNUT ▼AVE CAFE

PEARL ALLEY BISTRO & CAFE▼

SANTA CRUZ MUSEUM OF ART & HISTORY

JACK'S HAMBURGERS▼

▼NEW LEAF COMMUNITY MARKET

TAQUERIA VALLARTA▼

CATHCART ST

ZACHARY'S▼

BEST INN & ● SUITES

COMPASSION FLOWER INN ●

SATURN CAFE

SPRUCE ST

SAN LORENZO BLVD

EAST CLIFF

CLIFF CREST B&B INN
● ▼WAVE LANE

SANTA CRUZ HOSTEL

CHATEAU VICTORIAN

CAROUSEL MOTEL

ECONO LODGE BOARDWALK●

Ⓜ SANTA CRUZ BEACH BOARDWALK

CASABLANCA INN & RESTAURANT▼

BEACHVIEW INN●

▼COCOANUT GROVE

Santa Cruz Beach

Neary Lagoon Park

Santa Cruz Harbor

COAST SANTA CRUZ ● HOTEL

▼RIVA FISH HOUSE

Cowell Beach
SEA & SAND INN●

THE SANTA CRUZ WHARF

To Lighthouse Field State Beach

0 .25 mi
0 .25 km

Monterey Bay

Find Your Ideal Mate. Playing miniature golf at the **Neptune's Kingdom** amusement center—housed in the Boardwalk's original "plunge" building, or natatorium—is a nautical-themed adventure in special effects, with an erupting volcano, firing cannons, and talking pirates. It's the perfect diversion for the video-game generation and their awestruck parents. Though the rest of the Boardwalk's attractions are seasonal, Neptune's Kingdom and the arcade are open daily year-round. Nearby is the esteemed **Cocoanut Grove** casino and ballroom, a dignified old dancehall that still swings with nostalgic tunes from the 1930s and '40s at special shindigs. Sunday brunch in the Grove's Sun Room, with its Victorian-modern decor and galleria-style retracting glass roof, is a big event.

To fully appreciate the Boardwalk then and now, pick up the *Walking Tour of the Historical Santa Cruz Boardwalk* brochure, as well as a current attractions listing/map. Both will help you locate yourself, then and now. Annual events held at the Boardwalk include the **Clam Chowder Cook-Off and Festival** in late February; the **Central Coast Home & Garden Expo** in early April; the **Santa Cruz Band Review** in October, a fundraiser for local high school bands; and the **Santa Cruz Christmas Craft and Gift Festival** held at the Cocoanut Grove during Thanksgiving weekend. On Friday nights in summer, starting in June, come for free concerts.

Admission to the Boardwalk is free, though enjoying its amusements is not. If you'll be staying all day, the best deal is usually the all-day ride ticket, $25.95 at last report, or Unlimited Rides Plus, $29.95, which offers unlimited rides plus two other attractions. During **65 Cent Nights,** on certain Monday and Tuesday evenings in summer, ride prices revert to olden-days equivalents—$.65 per ride, and also $.65 for hot dogs, cotton candy, and Pepsis. Season passes are available. Height, age, and chaperone requirements are enforced. For current complete information, contact the **Santa Cruz Seaside Company,** 400 Beach St. in Santa Cruz, 831/423-5590, www.beachboardwalk.com. While you're at it, inquire about special vacation packages.

Santa Cruz Beach Boardwalk

For current Boardwalk hours, call 831/426-7433. For information on special Boardwalk activities, call 831/423-5590. To find out what's happening at the Cocoanut Grove, call 831/423-2053.

The Wharf

The pier at the western end of Santa Cruz Beach, once a good place to buy cheap, fresh fish, did booming business during the state's steamship heyday. Today, the place is packed instead with tourists, and most fish markets, restaurants, and shops here charge a pretty penny. Still, the wharf's worth a sunset stroll. (Peer down into the fenced-off "holes" to watch the sea lions.) A few commercial fishing boats still haul their catches of salmon and cod ashore in summer, doubling as whale-watching tour boats in winter. Worth a look, too, are the kiosk displays on wharf and fishing history.

OTHER SIGHTS

If you're over- or underwhelmed by the Boardwalk, take the Santa Cruz **walking tour.** This expedition is a lot quicker than it used to be—since many of the city's unusual Victorians—with frilly wedding-cake furbelows and "witch's hat" towers on the Queen Annes—departed to that great Historical Register in the Sky during the 1989 earthquake. But some grande dames remain. To find them, stop by the visitors center and pick up the *Historic Santa Cruz Walking Tours and Museum Guide* brochure. Most houses are private homes or businesses, so don't trespass. **Ocean View Avenue** is so perfect in terms of period authenticity that it took only a few loads of topsoil (to cover the asphalt street with dirt) to successfully transform the neighborhood into the cinematic setting for John Steinbeck's *East of Eden.* A good example of the Colonial Revival style is **Villa Perla** at the head of Ocean View. Near the Santa Cruz Mission are other notables, including the **Stick Villa** at 207 Mission Street; the **Schwartz Mansion** at 222 Mission; and the saltbox-style **Willey House** on the corner of Mission and Sylvar.

To find out more about area history, stop by the Santa Cruz Museum of Art and History. In particular, the museum staff can fill you in on regional historical sites under their care, including the Davenport Jail (1917), up the coast in Davenport, though no longer open to the public, and the Evergreen Cemetery (established 1850) at Evergreen and Coral Streets, one of the oldest Protestant cemeteries in California. Next door to the museum is the visitors center.

Santa Cruz Museum of Art and History

A sure sign that downtown Santa Cruz is almost done digging out from the rubble of the devastating 1989 earthquake is the Museum of Art and History at the McPherson Center, 705 Front St. (Front and Cooper), 831/429-1964, www .santacruzmah.org. Traveling exhibits and local artists get prominent play. Memorable shows have included 2001's **Art Undercover: Tom Killion, Gay Schy, Peter and Donna Thomas,** an examination of "small press art," 2002's **Simply Scene: The California Paintings of Herman Struck (1887-1954),** and 2003's **El Rio/The River: Artists Impressions.** Up on the roof is the new **Mary and Harry Blanchard Sculpture Garden,** showcase for intriguing works from the museum's permanent collection. The museum is open Tues.–Sun. 11 A.M.–5 P.M. A small admission fee ($5 general) is charged, though admission is free on the first Friday of the month. Or come for **After Hours** ($1) on the first Thursday evening of the month, 5–7 P.M., for wine, appetizers, live music, and a lesiurely look at current exhibits. Adjacent to the museum is The Octagon, an eight-sided 1882 brick building relocated here, now the museum store. Inside is an intriguing collection of gift and art items, including—at least sometimes—the marvelously whimsical work (including greeting cards) of Santa Cruz artist James Carl Aschbacher.

Santa Cruz Mission Adobe State Historic Park

Restored and open to the public is the Santa Cruz Mission Adobe, a state historical park just off Mission Plaza at 144 School St., 831/425-5849 or 831/429-2850. This is one of the county's last remaining original adobes, built by and for Native Americans "employed" at Mission Santa Cruz. It was later a 17-unit "home for new citizens." Only seven units remain, these now comprising a California history museum circa the 1840s. Restored rooms illustrate how Native American, Californio, and Irish American families once lived. Call for current information about guided tours and "living history" demonstrations (usually offered on Sundays, the latter just in March). School groups are welcome on Thursdays and Fridays—by advance reservation only. Come in September for **Mission Adobe Day.** Plan a picnic here anytime (bring your own water). The park is open Thurs.–Sun. 10 A.M.–4 P.M. A small admission fee is charged.

Mission Santa Cruz

Nearby, at 126 High St., is what's left of the original mission: just a memory, really. The original site of the **Misión de Exaltación de la Santa Cruz** was at High and Emmet Streets, too close to the San Lorenzo River, as it turned out. The move to higher ground left only the garden at the lower level. The original Santa Cruz mission complex was finished in 1794 but was completely destroyed by earthquakes in the mid-19th century. The replica church, scaled down by half and built in 1931 on the upper level, seems to have lost more than just stature. It's open Tues.–Sat. 10 A.M.–4 P.M., Sun. 10 A.M.–2 P.M.; call 831/426-5686 for more information.

Santa Cruz City Museum of Natural History

At least for now, the city's natural history museum is at home in Tyrell Park above Seabright/Castle Beach, east of the Boardwalk at 1305 E. Cliff Drive. The onetime 1915 Carnegie Library that anchors the park's southern edge, overlooking Monterey Bay, features exhibits and displays on the Santa Cruz area's natural and cultural history. There's a Tidepool Touch Tank and a Fossil Sand Dollar Dig—and the kids also dig that big cement gray whale on the lawn. The museum is open Tues.–Sun. 10 A.M.–5 P.M. A small admission fee is charged. The mu-

seum also sponsors a year-round schedule of classes and events. For more information, call 831/420-6115 or see www.santacruz museums.org.

Santa Cruz Harley-Davidson Museum

The local Harley-Davidson shop, 1148 Soquel Ave., 831/421-9600, www.santacruzharley.com, is something of a "destination dealership." Among the exquisitely restored Harleys on display are an H-D bicycle, first introduced in 1917, a 1929 JDH two-cam twin, and a stylish 1930 VL. Historical photos, posters, and memorabilia round out the collection, which is available for public viewing Tues.–Sunday. The website offers a grand tour, too.

Santa Cruz Mystery Spot

The much bumper-sticker ballyhooed Mystery Spot is a place where "every law of gravitation has gone haywire." Or has it? Trees, people, even the Spot's rustic shack and furnishings seem spellbound by "the force"—though people wearing slick-soled shoes seem to have the hardest time staying with the mysterious program. Hardcore tourists tend to love this place—Mom, Dad, and the kids can *literally* climb the walls—but others leave wondering why they spent the $5 to get in.

The Mystery Spot is located at 465 Mystery Spot Rd., 831/423-8897, www.mysteryspot.com. To get there, follow Market Street north from Water Street for a few miles. Market becomes Branciforte; Mystery Spot Road branches left off Branciforte—you can't miss it. Open daily 9 A.M.–7 P.M. (last tour at 7) in summer, 9 A.M.–5 P.M. (last tour at 5) the rest of the year.

Santa Cruz Surfing Museum

Cowabunga! Instead of cutting a ribbon, they snipped a hot pink surfer's leash when they opened the world's first surfing museum here at **Lighthouse Field State Beach** in May 1986. This historical exhibit reaches back to the 1930s, with displays on the evolution of surfboards and equipment—including the Model T of boards, a 15-foot redwood plank weighing 100 pounds, and an experimental Jack O'Neill wetsuit made of nylon and foam, the forerunner to the Neoprene "short john." Some say two Polynesian princes introduced surfing to Santa Cruz in 1885. True or not, by 1912 local posters announced the surfing exploits of Olympic swimmer and "Father of Surfing" Duke Kahanamoku. Come at Christmas for the popular **Caroling under the Stars** annual event.

The museum's location on the ground floor of the brick lighthouse on West Cliff Drive, northwest of town near Steamer's Lane—prime surf turf—seems the most fitting place for official homage to life in pursuit of the perfect wave. The lighthouse was built by the family of Mark Abbott, a surfer killed nearby. The museum's gift shop is a great place to get one-of-a-kind T-shirts and other emblems of California cool. The surfing

SURF'S UP AT O'NEILL'S

A Santa Cruz phenomenon with considerable worldwide renown is **O'Neill Surf Shop,** the legendary business legacy of Jack O'Neill, a local surfer who in the 1950s created a wetsuit that protected surfers from Northern California's chilling waters. The business grew and flourished, becoming the world's number-one wetsuit manufacturer. O'Neill also sells popular surfing-styled sportswear. There are four O'Neill shops in Santa Cruz County, including one at the beach, 222 E. Cliff Dr.; one at the Boardwalk, 400 Beach St.; and one downtown at 110 Cooper St., Ste. 100-D. The fourth is in Capitola at 1115 41st Ave. For more information, call the company at 831/475-4151 or see the website: www.oneill.com.

O'Neill's legacy is broader and deeper, however, especially the O'Neill children are now fully involved in the company's enterprises. The slogan "It's always summer on the inside" is not just a marketing slogan but a life philosophy. Come to Santa Cruz in February for a literal test of the summer-inside lifestyle at the famed **O'Neill Cold Water Classic,** a contest that attracts top surfers from around the world. The **O'Neill Sea Odyssey,** www.oneillseaodyssey.org, is an ocean-going environmental education program offered free for grammar school children onboard the 65-foot Team O'Neill catamaran.

museum is open noon–4 P.M. Wed.–Mon. in summer, Thurs.–Mon. in winter; requested donation $1. For more information, call 831/420-6289 or see www.santacruzsurfing museum.org. For beach information, call 831/420-5270.

Santa Cruz now has two functioning lighthouses. The **Santa Cruz Harbor Light** on the rock jetty at the entrance to the Santa Cruz harbor, also known as Walton's Lighthouse in honor of Derek Walton, was officially dedicated in June 2002.

Spiritual/Supernatural Attractions

Perhaps more interesting even than the Mystery Spot are two other oddball attractions, located at the **Santa Cruz Memorial Park & Funeral Home,** 3301 Paul Sweet Rd., 831/426-1601. Here you'll find a wax interpretation of *The Last Supper,* plus displays attempting to rekindle the controversy over the **Shroud of Turin**—that renowned piece of linen purported to show Christ's after-death visage—by challenging the conclusions of carbon tests declaring the shroud a fake.

An interpretation of Da Vinci's famous painting in life-sized wax figures, *The Last Supper* is the original work of two Katherine Struberghs (mother and daughter) from Los Angeles. The women spared themselves no trial or trouble in this endeavor. (Each hair on every wax head was implanted by hand—that task alone requiring eight months.) But after some 40 years' residence at the Santa Cruz Art League, Jesus and his disciples were in a sad state of disrepair. That was before the funeral home and local Oddfellows Lodge took on the task of financing something of a resurrection. The job involved patching the cracks in the figures' heads, washing and setting their hair and beards, replacing fingers (and fingernails and toenails), and polishing their glass eyeballs.

Visitors can see both attractions Mon.–Fri. by appointment. Contributions are appreciated.

University of California at Santa Cruz

The city on the hill just beyond town is the UC Santa Cruz campus, planned by architect John Carl Warnecke and landscape architect Thomas

Monterey Bay

ALL HAIL THE SANTA CRUZ SLUGS

Refreshingly out of step with the period's hyperactive corporate careerism, the UC Santa Cruz student body convinced then-Chancellor Robert Sinsheimer in 1986 to declare as their school mascot the noble banana slug—a common on-campus companion—instead of the more socially acceptable sea lion, after a hard-fought, five-year campaign. When the chancellor declared the Santa Cruz Sea Lions the official choice in 1981, students protested that the banana slug would more appropriately be "a statement about the ideology of Santa Cruz," a philosophy with no room for football teams, cheerleaders, fraternities, and sororities.

Finally acceding to the students' preference for a slimy, spineless, sluggish, yellow gastropod—defended as "flexible, golden, and deliberate" by one professor—Sinsheimer said that students should have a school mascot "with which they can empathize." He also proposed genetic engineering research on slugs to "improve the breed" because "the potential seems endless."

Church—a total of 10 clustered colleges and associated buildings overlooking the Pacific Ocean. Campus buildings were designed by noted architects including Charles Moore, William Wurster, Joseph Esherick, Ernest Kump, Antoine Predock, Hugh Stubbins, Ralph Rapson, William Turnbull, and Kathy Simon. When the doors of UC Santa Cruz opened in the 1960s, few California students could gain admission to the close-knit, redwood-cloistered campus. The selection process (complete with essay) was weighted in favor of students with unusual abilities, aptitudes, and attitudes—those not likely to thrive within the traditional university structure. So many children of movie stars and other members of California's moneyed upper classes have attended UC Santa Cruz that it has been playfully dubbed "California's public finishing school." The university's student body has so far remained relatively small (more than 12,000 currently), though growth is on the agenda. A sign that the times they are a-changin' at Santa Cruz came in February 2000, when the faculty voted overwhelmingly to eliminate the university's founding "no required grading" policy.

The University of California regents set about transforming the redwood-forested rangeland here, once the Henry Cowell Ranch, into California's educational Camelot in 1961. Designs ranged from modern Mediterranean to "Italian hill village" (Kresge College). The official explanation for the Santa Cruz "college cluster" concept was to avoid the depersonalization common to large UC campuses, but another reason was alluded to when then-Governor Ronald Reagan declared the campus "riot-proof."

To truly appreciate this place, wander the campus hiking trails and paths (but not alone). Some of the old converted ranch buildings are worth noting: the lime kilns, blacksmith's shop, cookhouse, horse barn, bull barn, slaughterhouse, cookhouse, workers' cabins, and cooperage. On a clear day, the view of Monterey Bay (and of whales passing offshore in winter and spring) from the top of the hill on the 2,000-acre campus is marvelous. For information and guided campus tours, stop by the wood-and-stone Cook House near the entrance. You can also contact Cook House at 831/459-4008 or slugvisits@Gats .ucsc.edu. For other campus information, see www.ucsc.edu.

Long Marine Laboratory

Well worth a stop for nature lovers, the Joseph M. Long Marine Laboratory is just off Delaware Avenue near Natural Bridges State Beach on the western edge of town. A university research and education facility, the lab is affiliated with the on-campus Institute of Marine Sciences, established in 1972. Research conducted here ranges from marine biology and marine geophysics to paleooceanography and coastal processes—from plankton to blue whales, from cold water ecology to tropical coral reefs. Associated facilities include an 18,000-square-foot California Department of Fish and Game Marine Wildlife Veterinary Care and Research Center, the nation's largest and most advanced, and a state-of-the-art National Marine Fisheries Service laboratory, which conducts fisheries research and houses the nation's first National Science Center for Marine Protected Areas. Under construction, at last report: the UC Santa Cruz Center for Ocean Health and a seabird/raptor facility.

To help interpret the lab's work and to educate future generations of marine biologists, the new **Seymour Marine Discovery Center** is open to the public Tues.–Sat. 10 A.M.–5 P.M., Sunday noon to 5 P.M. Admission is $5 adults; $3 students, seniors, and youths 6 to 16; free for children 5 and under. Docent-led tours of the lab's other marine research facilities are available. For information contact 831/459-3800 or www2.ucsc.edu/seymourcenter. Lab tours are offered at 1, 2, and 3 P.M., on a first-come, first-escorted-around basis (sign up an hour in advance). For additional information about Long Marine Lab programs and facilities, see www.natsci.ucsc.edu.

To get here from Santa Cruz, take Hwy. 1 (Mission Street) north, turn left on Swift Street, then right on Delaware Avenue. Continue on Delaware to the Long Marine Lab entrance at the end of the road.

RECREATION

Most of the outdoor action in Santa Cruz proper happens at local beaches; swimming, surfing, and fishing are all big, as are tamer pastimes like beachcombing, sandcastle building, and sunbathing. The in-town **Santa Cruz Beach** at the Boardwalk, with fine white sand and towel-to-towel baking bodies in summer, is "the scene"— especially for outsiders from San Jose, locals say. For more privacy, head east to the mouth of the San Lorenzo River. Southwest of the pier, **Cowell Beach** is a surfing beach, where Huey Lewis and the News filmed one of their music videos. Just before **Lighthouse Field State Beach** on West Cliff is the Santa Cruz Surfing Museum, an eclectic lighthouse collection of surf's-up memorabilia keeping watch over the hotdoggers in churning Steamer Lane.

Natural Bridges State Beach

Located farther southwest, at the end of West Cliff Drive, Natural Bridges attracts the mythic monarch butterflies each year from October to May. Though Pacific Grove near Monterey proudly proclaims itself the destination of choice for these regal insects, Santa Cruz claims to get the most monarchs. This is the only state-owned monarch butterfly preserve in California. One of the sandstone "natural bridges" here collapsed in 1980, under assault from a winter storm. The other still stands, though. To the north are some great tidepools, available for exploration (don't touch) at low tide. Leathery green fields of brussels sprouts fringe the fragile sandy cliffs.

Monarch butterfly tours (wheelchair accessible) are offered on weekends from mid-October through February. For information on guided butterfly walks and tidepool tours, stop by the visitors center or call 831/423-4609. For additional parks information, see www.santacruzstateparks.org and www.scparkfriends.org. Come in October for **Welcome Back Monarchs Day** and again in February for the annual **Migration Festival** sendoff, a park fundraiser cosponsored by Friends of Santa Cruz State Parks. (The monarchs may be leaving, but the gray whales offshore are just arriving in February; migrants come and go all year.) The parking fee at Natural Bridges is $6 per car; walk-ins and bike-ins are free. Natural Bridges is open daily 8 A.M.–sunset.

Beaches and Surfing

Along East Cliff Drive are **Tyrell Park** and more inaccessible sandy beaches. **Twin Lakes State Beach,** near the Santa Cruz Yacht Harbor on the eastern extension of East Cliff before it becomes Portolá, is a popular locals' beach, usually quite warm. Beyond the Santa Cruz Yacht Harbor, various small, locally popular beaches line East Cliff Drive. The unofficially named **26th Street Beach** (at the end of 26th Street, naturally enough) is probably tops among them. Hot for local surfing is the **Pleasure Point,** East Cliff at Pleasure Point Drive.

Davenport Beach, at Davenport Landing up the coast toward Año Nuevo, is a hot spot for sailboarders and is often relatively uncrowded.

Santa Cruz is one of the most popular surfing spots in Northern California.

Red White and Blue Beach, at the red, white, and blue mailbox, 5021 Coast Rd., just south of Davenport, 831/423-6332, is a popular, privately operated nude beach (too popular, some say; women shouldn't go alone). It costs $10 per day for an all-over tan ($1 children). Camping ($15) is also available. Nearby is **Bonny Doon Beach,** up the coast from Santa Cruz at the intersection of Hwy. 1 and Bonny Doon Road south of Davenport. It's free, and even wilder for sunbathing sans swimsuit. It's also popular with surfers.

About six miles down the coast from Santa Cruz City Beach and just south of the Capitola suburbs is immensely popular **New Brighton State Beach,** 1500 Park Ave., 831/464-6330. Its 93 often-sunny acres are protected by wooded headlands that offer a great family campground (campsites $20–35), nature trails, good bird-watching, and a dazzling nighttime view of Monterey Bay. The day-use fee is $6. A coming attraction at New Bright, once adequate funding is secured, will be the snazzy new **Pacific Migrations** visitor center.

Several miles farther south, two-mile-long **Seacliff State Beach,** on Park Drive in Aptos, 831/685-6500 or 831/685-6442 (recorded information), or 831/685-6444 (visitors center), is so popular you may not be able to stop. It's nice for hiking, pelican-watching, fossil spotting, swimming, and sunbathing. The wheelchair-accessible pier reaches out to the concrete carcass of the doomed World War I–vintage *Palo Alto,* sunk here after seeing no wartime action and now a long-abandoned amusement pier (not open to the public). Birds live in the prow these days. People enjoy the adjacent pier's more mundane pleasures: people-watching, fishing (no license required), and strolling. Guided walks are occasionally offered; call the visitors center for schedules and reservations. The day use fee is $6. Campsites here are for RVs only, $35.

As the name suggests, **Rio del Mar State Beach** is where Aptos Creek meets the sea. Here you'll find restrooms, miles of sand, and limited parking. It's free.

To reserve state beach campsites—absolutely essential in summer—contact **ReserveAmerica,**

CIRCLE OF ENCHANTMENT TRAIL

Tour the eclectic scenery of Santa Cruz greenbelt areas on the area's Circle of Enchantment Trail, also known as the Circle Trail. The 23-mile trail is actually two separate loops; each segment can be hiked in a half day. Begin either loop in downtown Santa Cruz at the San Lorenzo River pedestrian bridge, just off Front Street.

The circle's western loop, about a 12-mile hike, follows the river down to the Boardwalk. It then climbs to the bayside recreation trail along W. Cliff Drive and continues on to Natural Bridges State Park and the Long Marine Lab before angling in-

land. The route then follows Delaware Avenue into wooded Arroyo Seco Canyon, then up the hill to the UC Santa Cruz campus—redwoods and fabulous views—and the Pogonip grasslands before circling back to the river levee.

The eastern loop is more urban, yet it eventually leads to the "Top of the World" lookout, Arana City Park, Santa Cruz Yacht Harbor, and along E. Cliff Drive and the Pleasure Point area before returning to Lorenzo Park downtown.

A general route map and detailed directions are available at www.ecotopia.org.

800/444-7275, www.reserveamerica.com. For more information on regional state beaches and parks, see www.santacruzstateparks.org and www.scparkfriends.org.

Sailing

For an unusual view of the Boardwalk and the bay, take a boat ride. One of the best going—definitely not just any boat—is the *Chardonnay II*, a 70-foot ultralight sailing yacht offering special-emphasis cruises. Choose from astronomy, fireworks, "gourmet on the bay," marine ecology, wine-tasting, and whale-watching (winter and spring) cruises. There's even a Wednesday night Boat Race Cruise in the company of almost every other boat from the Santa Cruz Yacht Harbor. At last report, per-person fare for most scheduled trips was $39.50. This sleek albino seal of a sailboat can hold up to 49 passengers and features every imaginable amenity, including a CD player, TV/VCR, built-in bar, cellular phones, and plenty of below-deck space, making it fun as a private group charter for personally designed adventures. There's a two-hour minimum rental for departures from Santa Cruz, a three-hour minimum from Monterey. Private charter rates are $550–800 per hour. For more information and to make reservations (required), call **Chardonnay Sailing Charters** at 831/423-1213 or inquire online at www.chardonnay.com.

Other boat and charter companies at or near the city's yacht harbor include **Pacific Yachting,**

790 Mariner Park Way, 831/423-7245 or 800/374-2626, www.pacificsail.com, which offers similar boat rides on smaller yachts as well as sailing lessons and a six-day seagoing instruction vacation. Probably the best deal going, though, is through the University of California at Santa Cruz Boating Club. In summer, UCSC sailing and boating courses are open to the public. For information, call 831/425-1164, ucscboat@Gats .ucsc.edu, or see www.ucsc.edu/opers/boating. If you qualify for membership—as a student or alumnus—you can use the boats all year. The local **Coast Guard Auxiliary,** 432 Oxford Way, 831/423-7119, also offers sailing, boating skills, seamanship, and coastal navigation courses.

Other Water Sports

For more traditional boat tours, whale-watching trips (winter and summer), and fishing charters, contact **Stagnaro's Sportfishing** at the municipal wharf, 831/427-2334, www.stagnaros .com, or **Scurfield's Landing/Shamrock Charters** at the yacht harbor, 831/476-2648, www .scurfslanding.com.

Kayaking is great sport in these parts. **Venture Quest,** 125 Beach St., 831/427-2267, and at the municipal wharf, 831/425-8445, www.kayak santacruz.com, sells kayaks and accessories and offers lessons and guided tours. **Kayak Connection** at the Santa Cruz Yacht Harbor, 413 Lake Ave., 831/479-1121, and also at Elkhorn Slough (2370 Hwy. 1 in Moss Landing), 831/724-5692,

Monterey Bay

www.kayakconnection.com, also rents and sells equipment, in addition to offering guided bird-watching, fishing, and moonlight tours.

Several full-service dive shops in town can provide complete information on local diving conditions, as well as instruction, rentals, and sales. Try **Aqua Safaris Scuba Center,** 6896-A Soquel Ave., 831/479-4386, www.aquasafaris .com, or **Adventure Sports Unlimited,** 303 Potrero St., 831/458-3648 or 888/839-4286, www.asudoit.com.

Club Ed, on Cowell Beach (on the right side of Santa Cruz Wharf, in front of the WestCoast Santa Cruz Hotel), 831/464-0177 or 800/287-7873, rents surfboards, boogie boards, skim boards, and sailboards, and offers lessons in riding all of the above. Find out more about Ed's surf camps on the Web at www.club-ed.com.

ENTERTAINMENT AND EVENTS

For an introduction to local galleries, at the visitors council request the self-guided **Gallery Walk** tour map of downtown Santa Cruz, which will also guide you to coffeehouses and unusual shops. (Come on the first Friday of each month

for the Gallery Walk as evening event.) Santa Cruz has more than its fair share of good movie theaters and film series. The historic 1936 **Del Mar Theatre,** 1124 Pacific Ave., 831/469-3220, has been lovingly renovated and now shows great art house and independent films. (Come to the Del Mar for the annual **Santa Cruz Film Festival,** www.santacruzfilmfestival.com, where Bernard Shakey—Neil Young—showed up for the benefit debut of his film *Greendale.*) If it's not playing at the Del Mar, then it's probably at the associated **Nickelodeon Theatre,** 210 Lincoln St., 831/426-7500. For what's playing at both, see www.thenick.com. Pretty darned hip for flicks too is the **Rio Theatre for the Performing Arts,** 1205 Soquel Ave., 831/423-8209, www .riotheatre.com, which also stages live performances. For what's playing where at a glance, scan local entertainment papers.

Nightlife

If you're into big-band swing, check out **Cocoanut Grove** dances (see www.beachboard walk.com or call 831/423-5590 for information); tickets run $15 and up. **The Kuumbwa Jazz Center,** 320-2 Cedar St. #2, 831/427-2227,

---

SANTA CRUZ WINERIES

The coastal mountains near Santa Cruz are well known for their redwoods. But since the late 1800s, they have also been known for their vineyards. Regional winemaking is back, helped along since 1981 by the official federal recognition of the Santa Cruz Mountain appellation for wine grapes grown in the region defined by Half Moon Bay in the north and Mount Madonna in the south. More than 40 wineries now produce Santa Cruz Mountain wines.

The eclectic **Bonny Doon Vineyard,** north of Santa Cruz at 10 Pine Flat Rd., 831/425-4518, www.bonnydoonvineyard.com, specializes in Rhône and Italian varietals, though wine lovers and critics are also smitten with the winery's worldly, witty, and wildly footnoted newsletter (also available online). Open 11 A.M.–5 P.M. daily for tastings, except major holidays.

Nearby in Felton is the award-winning and historic **Hallcrest Vineyards,** 379 Felton Empire Rd. (call for directions), 831/335-4441, noted for its cabernet sauvignon, chardonnay, merlot, and zinfandel. Hallcrest is also home to **The Organic Wine Works,** 800/699-9463, producing the nation's first certified organic wines. Made from certified organically grown grapes, the winemaking process is also organic, without the use of sulfites. Open daily 11 A.M.–5:30 P.M. Also in Felton and open only by appointment is the small **Zayante Vineyards,** 420 Old Mount Rd., 831/335-7992.

There are dozens more. For more information about area wineries, including a current wineries map and upcoming events, contact: **Santa Cruz Mountains Winegrowers Association,** 7605 Old Dominion Ct., Ste. A, in Aptos, 831/479-9463, www.wines.com/santa_cruz_mountains.

www.kuumbwajazz.com, is a no-booze, no-cigarettes, under-21-welcome place with great jazz (often big names), and it's rarely packed. Most shows are Monday and Friday at 8 P.M.; ticket prices vary and are often low. The **Catalyst,** 1011 Pacific Ave., 831/423-1336, is legendary for its Friday afternoon happy hour in the Atrium—seems like *everybody's* here from 4:30 to 7 P.M., drinking beer, making the scene, and sometimes tapping their toes to the house band, Wally's Swing World, or groups like REO Haywagon. The 700-seat theater (massive dance floor) hosts good local bands or national acts nightly (cover charge). Wednesday is Dollar Night, and a buck will get you three new bands in the main-stage back room plus DJed dancing in the Atrium out front. Other area clubs, hot spots for younger unknown bands especially, include the **Aptos Club,** 7941 Soquel Dr. in Aptos, 831/688-9888, and the **Mediterranean Club,** near Seacliff Beach at 265 Center Ave., 831/688-9840. Local coffeehouses from Santa Cruz to Capitola also offer casual, relaxed, and sometimes highbrow entertainment. Like poetry readings.

MELISSA SHEROWSKI

the performing arts complex at UC Santa Cruz

Performing Arts

On a smaller scale, local performing arts are always an adventure. The **Santa Cruz Chamber Players** specialize in both traditional and modern chamber music, with an emphasis on the unusual. For a performance schedule, call 831/425-3149. The **Santa Cruz County Symphony,** 200 Seventh Ave., Ste. 225, 831/462-0553, schedules performances year-round at both the Santa Cruz Civic Auditorium and Watsonville's Mello Center.

The noted **Tandy Beal & Company** dance troupe, 740 Front St., Ste. 300-B, 831/429-1324, performs locally when not touring internationally. The **Santa Cruz Ballet Theatre,** 2800 S. Rodeo Gulch Rd. in Soquel, 831/479-1600, is a good bet for a year-end production of *The Nutcracker.* **Santa Cruz County Actors' Theatre,** 1001 Center St., 831/425-1003, www.sccat .org, schedules live stage productions year-round. In Capitola, the Quonset hut–housed Capitola Theater at 120 Monterey Avenue is now the **Bay Shore Lyric Opera Company and Theater for the Performing Arts,** 831/462-3131, www.bslopera.com.

For information on what's going on at UCSC, pick up a copy of the quarterly **UCSC Performing Arts Calendar,** available around town, or call 831/459-2787 (459-ARTS). Other useful campus numbers include Arts and Lectures, 831/459-2826; Theatre Arts, 831/459-2974; and the Music Department, 831/459-2292. Or, for other current on-campus performance information, see http://arts.ucsc.edu. To order tickets by phone (small service charge), call the UCSC Ticket Office at 831/459-2159.

Events

For an up-to-date quarterly calendar of city and county events, contact the local visitors council. Bike races have prominent local appeal, and professional volleyball competitions are also held year-round. Whale-watching in winter is another popular draw.

For wine lovers, mid-January features the countywide **Wineries Passport Program,** offering tours, tastings, and open houses at Santa Cruz Mountains wineries (also held in mid-April, mid-July, and mid-November); for details, see www.scmwa.com. Mid-month, Santa Cruz celebrates its **Fungus Fair,** always fun for mushroom lovers.

Cold and very cool in February is the **O'Neill Cold Water Classic** surfing competition, sponsored by Santa Cruz–based O'Neill, Inc. and its legendary founder, Jack O'Neill, inventor of the wetsuit. Also in February, the **Migration Festival** at Natural Bridges State Beach celebrates many migrants, from monarch butterflies and the gray whale to salmon, salamanders, elephant seals, and shorebirds. The decades-long tradition of the **Santa Cruz Baroque Festival** starts in February and continues until May, offering concerts of early music masterworks. For information, call 831/457-9693 or see www.scbaroque.org. Head for the Boardwalk in late February for the annual **Clam Chowder Cook-Off.**

Come in March for the free annual **Jazz on the Wharf** festival, which serenades Monterey Bay from the Santa Cruz Municipal Wharf and its restaurants, and for the **Santa Cruz Kayak Surf Festival,** the world's largest. In mid- to late March, Felton holds its **Great Train Robberies** festival, followed by the **Amazing Egg Hunt** in April (usually). Memorial Day weekend brings the annual **Civil War Reenactment** at Roaring Camp.

May is big for art, wine, and music, starting with **Celebrate Santa Cruz Art, Wine & Jazz** in downtown Santa Cruz and continuing with the **Boulder Creek Art, Wine & Music Festival.** Also fun in May: **Bug Day** at Henry Cowell Redwoods State Park in Felton. Come in June for the **We Carnival Street Parade and World Music Festival.** Come on July 4 for Aptos's **World's Shortest Parade.**

The acclaimed and innovative **Shakespeare Santa Cruz** festival runs mid-July through August in an outdoor theater in the redwoods at UCSC. For information call 831/459-2121, for tickets 831/459-2159, or see www.shakespeare santacruz.org. The very fast **Santa Cruz to Capitola Wharf-to-Wharf Race** in late July is a major event for runners, with more than half the applicants turned away due to the event's immense popularity—a popularity fueled by the $12,000 total prize purse. For information, call the race hotline, 831/475-2196 or see www.wharftowharf.com.

After 20-some years, the famed August **Cabrillo Music Festival** (described by *The New Yorker* as one of the most adventurous and attractive in America) is still going strong, with performances at UC Santa Cruz, Mission San Juan Bautista, and Watsonville. For information—and do make your plans well in advance—contact the Cabrillo Music Festival, 831/426-6966, www.cabrillomusic.org. To reserve tickets, call 831/420-5260, beginning in late June. Another possibility in August is the **Musical Saw Festival** at Roaring Camp in Felton—not classical but definitely a gas.

The first couple of weeks in September, Capitola's **Begonia Festival,** www.begoniafestival .com, includes several big events, including a sandcastle contest and nautical parade. It's followed (and nearly overshadowed) in mid-September by the city's annual **Art & Wine Festival,** which has become incredibly popular. On three weekends in October, come for the countywide artists' **Open Studios,** with open-house art shows held everywhere, from private homes and studios to galleries and museums. It's wonderful exposure for artists and great pleasure for aficionados. At last report the first Open Studios weekend emphasized north-county artists; the second weekend, south-county artists; and the final weekend was an encore. For more information—each year's program/artist guide is available in September—call the Cultural Council of Santa Cruz County at 831/475-9600 or see www.ccscc.org/openstudios.htm

In late November, look for Felton's **Mountain Man Rendezvous** and the **Christmas Craft and Gift Festival** at the Boardwalk's Cocoanut Grove. In December, Felton sponsors its **Holiday Lights Train** Christmas festivities.

For more information on many of the above festivals, contact **Santa Cruz County Conference and Visitors Council,** downtown at 1211 Ocean St., 831/425-1234 or 800/833-3494, www.santacruzca.org.

SHOPPING

Clothing shops abound along Pacific Avenue, places such as **The Vault** at 1339 Pacific Ave., 831/426-3349, noted for unique jewelry and clothing, and **Eco Goods** at 1130 Pacific Ave., 831/429-5758, "an alternative general store offering organic, recycled, and non-toxic products at affordable prices"—everything from organic cotton underwear and hemp backpacks to handcrafted maple bedroom sets. **Madame Sidecar** at 907 Cedar St., 831/458-1606, offers distinctive style in quality women's clothing, lingerie, jewelry, and accessories—inspired by flattering 1930s and 1940s fashions. Downtown also boasts thrift and vintage clothing shops. **Cognito Clothing,** 821 Pacific, 831/426-5414, offers such things as swing dance fashions, two-toned panel shirts, and Hawaiian shirts. Other best bets include **The Wardrobe,** 113 Locust St., 831/429-6363.

There are plenty of bookstores, too, including the classic **Bookshop Santa Cruz,** 1520 Pacific Ave., 831/423-0900, www.bookshopsantacruz .com, a community institution that offers a full calendar of author and reader events. Downtown also draws music fans, to **Rhythm Fusion,** 1541 Pacific, 831/423-2048, and **Union Grove Music,** 1003 Pacific, 831/427-0670.

Santa Cruz County is marvelous for locally made wares—some almost affordable. Barbra Streisand and Oprah Winfrey are among the national fans of Santa Cruz's **Annieglass,** which has a shop downtown at 109 Cooper St., 831/427-4260, www.annieglass.com. Translucent sculptural glass dinnerware with fused metal rims, Annieglass comes in various styles, including Roman antique gold or platinum. For a large selection of strictly local wares, including **Strini Art Glass,** head for the Santa Cruz Wharf and **Made in Santa Cruz,** 831/426-2257 or 800/982-2367, www.madeinsantacruz.com. Here you'll find everything from art glass, ceramics, and sculpture—check out the struttin' teapots—to soap, salsa, and jewelry.

For a truly unique housewarming gift, head for **West Coast Weather Vanes** in Bonny Doon, 831/425-5505 or (U.S.) 800/762-8736, a company whose artisans carefully craft—without molds—copper and brass weather vanes in the Victorian tradition. Visitors are welcome by appointment.

For more shopping ideas, contact the **Downtown Association of Santa Cruz,** 831/429-1512, www.downtownsantacruz.com, and the **Santa Cruz County Conference & Visitors Council,** 831/425-1234 or 800/833-3494, www.santacruzca.org.

MADE IN SANTA CRUZ

It should surprise no one that the Santa Cruz area's creativity is also expressed in fine arts and crafts. **Lundberg Studios** in Davenport is noted for its luminescent blue "worldweights"— globe-styled paperweights that have been presented to various luminaries. Another star is **Annieglass** handcrafted sculptural glass dinnerware designed by artist Ann Morhauser—everyday, dishwasher-safe "art for the table" sought out by celebrities including Barbra Streisand and Oprah Winfrey. **West Coast Weather Vanes** is famed for its custom handcrafted American folk art copper and brass weather vanes. The **Santa Cruz Guitar Co.** is at the forefront of modern guitar making, famous for its acoustic guitars.

ACCOMMODATIONS

Beach Camping

Best for nearby tent camping is **New Brighton State Beach,** 1500 Park Ave. in Capitola, 831/464-6330 or 831/464-6329. "New Bright" features 115 developed campsites (especially nice ones on the cliffs), some sheltered picnic tables, and a small beach. It's a good base camp for the entire Santa Cruz area. You can get here via local bus—take number 58 or the Park Avenue route. This area was once called China Beach or China Cove, after the Chinese fishermen who built a village here in the 1870s. Developed family campsites cost $20–35. The campground is popular, so reserve (see below) for summer at least six months ahead.

Monterey Bay

Near Aptos, **Seacliff State Beach,** 831/685-6500 or 831/685-6444, has a better beach than New Brighton, but camping is a disappointment. Strictly an RV setup, the park has 26 sites (with hookups) that cost $35 (less for overflow campsites).

For more information about the area's beach parks, contact the state parks office in Santa Cruz, 600 Ocean St., 831/429-2850, www.santacruzstateparks.org. For state campground reservations, contact ReserveAmerica at 800/444-7275 or www.reserveamerica.com.

Redwoods Camping

Big Basin Redwoods State Park, 21600 Big Basin Hwy. in Boulder Creek, 831/338-8860, www.bigbasin.org, offers 146 family campsites, group camps, and horse camps. Family campsites are $20–24. Tents-only trail campsites are $15–20; hiker/biker campsites $3 per person. The park also boasts 41 year-round "tent cabins," each with two double beds, a camp lamp, and a woodstove. Tent cabins sleep four comfortably but can house up to eight. Rates are $50, two-night minimum on weekends, three-night minimum on holidays. (Add $10 for linen and blanket rental in lieu of sleeping bags.) You can also arrange "hassle-free" tent camping—all you have to pack is kids and clothes. For cabin reservations, call 800/874-8368 1–6 P.M. on weekdays or reserve online at www.bigbasintentcabins.com. To reserve trail camps, call Big Basin headquarters, 831/338-8860 (see website for more details).

Henry Cowell Redwoods State Park, just north of the UC campus on Hwy. 9 in Felton, 831/335-4598 (administration) or 831/438-2396 (campground), offers 150 sites, 105 of them developed ($20–24). Sites in the developed areas are quite civilized, with amenities including hot showers, flush toilets, tables, barbecues, and cupboards. Primitive hike-in and family backpacking campsites are available at Castle Rock State Park, 15000 Skyline Blvd. in Los Gatos. For more information about Castle Rock, call the park at 408/867-2952 or Big Basin at 831/338-8861.

Family and group campsites at both Big Basin and Henry Cowell Redwoods State Park are sometimes available at the last minute, even in summer and on warm-season weekends. But make reservations—up to seven months in advance—to guarantee a space. Reserve through ReserveAmerica, 800/444-7275, www.reserveamerica.com.

Private campgrounds and trailer parks are always a possibility; a fairly complete current listing is available at the local chamber of commerce, or see Tom Stienstra's *California Camping* (Avalon). Area possibilities include **Cotillion Gardens,** 300 Old Big Trees Rd. in Felton, 831/335-7669; **Carbonero Creek,** 917 Disc Dr. in Scotts Valley, 831/438-1288 or 800/546-1288; and the **Santa Cruz KOA,** 1186 San Andreas Rd. in Watsonville, 831/722-0551 or 800/562-7701, www.koa.com.

Hostels

The **HI-USA Santa Cruz Hostel** downtown on Beach Hill, 321 Main St. between Second and Third Streets, 831/423-8304, www.hi-santacruz.org, occupies the historic 1870s Carmelita Cottages. The hostel is open year-round, is wheelchair accessible, and features an on-site cyclery, fireplace, barbecue, lockers, and rose and herb gardens. Family rooms and limited parking available (extra fee for both). Reservations strongly suggested. Under $50.

In additional to the Hostelling International hostel in downtown Santa Cruz, the region boasts other exceptional budget choices—including the **Pigeon Point** and **Point Montara Lighthouse Hostels** up the coast toward San Francisco, both unique and incredibly cheap for on-the-beach lodgings—if you don't mind bunk beds or spartan couples' rooms. Or try the **Sanborn Park** hostel just over the hills in Saratoga, 408/741-0166 or 408/741-9555, www.sanbornparkhostel.org. If you're heading south, another best bet is the new **Carpenter's Hall Hostel** in Monterey (see that chapter for details). Rates at all are under $50.

Motels and Hotels

As a general rule, motels closer to the freeway are cheaper, while those on the river are seedier. There are some fairly inexpensive motels near the beach (some with kitchens, whirlpool tubs, pools, cable TV, etc.). Off-season rates in Santa Cruz are usually quite reasonable, but prices can sometimes mysteriously increase in summer and on weekends and holidays—so verify prices before you sign in.

All of the following have rates starting at $50–100. The **Beachview Inn,** less than a block from the beach at 50 Front St., 831/426-3575 or 800/946-0614, features all the essentials plus air-conditioning and direct-dial phones, with rooms $90 and up in the high season. The **Econo Lodge Santa Cruz,** just a block from the Boardwalk and the Wharf at 550 Second St., 831/426-3626 or 800/553-2666, offers rooms for $75 and up. Close to downtown, **Travelodge Santa Cruz,** 525 Ocean St., 831/426-2300 or 800/578-7878, offers high-season rates of $89 and up.

Most rates at the following start at $100–150. Between Santa Cruz and Aptos and quite close to the beach is the renovated 1930s-vintage **Ocean Echo Inn & Beach Cottages,** 401 Johans Beach Dr., 831/462-4192, www.oceanecho.com. Cottages, including a two-story water tower, accommodate two to six guests. Many have fully equipped kitchens or kitchenettes, and some offer ocean views. In the off season, some rates dip below $100. Endlessly convenient for Boardwalkers is the Boardwalk's own **Carousel Motel,** 110 Riverside Ave., 831/425-7090 or 800/214-7400, www.santacruz motels.com. Also a best bet is the attractive **Best Inn & Suites,** 600 Riverside Ave., 831/458-9660 or 800/527-3833, www.bestinnssantacruz.com, where standard rooms include two queen beds. Other options are available—including two-story suites and "evergreen" rooms with air, water, and shower filtration. The inn also features a heated pool and hot tubs, a pleasant garden courtyard, and a picnic area with barbecues, plus complimentary expanded continental breakfast. Some rooms at the pleasant **Sunset Inn,** close to UC Santa Cruz and Natural Bridges at 2424 Mission St., 831/423-7500, also fit this price category. Amenities include microwaves, refrigerators, some in-room whirlpool tubs, free local phone calls, breakfast, a hot tub, and a sauna.

Close to the wharf and overlooking the bay is the small but immensely popular **Sea & Sand Inn,** 201 W. Cliff Dr., 831/427-3400, www .santacruzmotels.com. All 20 rooms boast an ocean view; suites have abundant amenities. Rates are $150–250, though off-season rates go as low as $99.

All of the following have rates of $250 and up. Adjacent to the wharf and across from the Santa Cruz Beach Boardwalk, the imposing **Coast Santa Cruz Hotel,** 175 W. Cliff Dr., 831/426-4330 or 800/716-6199, www.coast hotels.com, is right on the beach—the only beachfront hotel in Santa Cruz—and not far from the lighthouse. It features 163 rooms and suites with balconies and patios, in-room coffeemakers and refrigerators, modern extras including terry robes and iron/ironing board, wireless high-speed Internet access, satellite TV and in-room movies, Sony Playstation, a heated pool, and a whirlpool.

Even more romantic is the **Casa Blanca Inn** at Beach and Main, at the beach and right across from the Boardwalk, 831/423-1570 or 800/644-1570, www.casablanca-santacruz.com. The historic Cerf Mansion has been remade into a stylish hotel with 39 rooms—some with fireplaces, terraces or balconies, and full kitchens—and all feature cable TV, phones with data ports, and in-room refrigerators, microwaves, coffeemakers, and safes. Elegant onsite restaurant, too.

For value and views, nothing beats **Chaminade at Santa Cruz,** up on the hill and overlooking Monterey Bay at 1 Chaminade Lane (just off Paul Sweet Rd.), 831/475-5600 or 800/283-6569, www.chaminade.com. Occupying the old Chaminade Brothers Seminary and Monastery, this quiet resort and conference center offers a wealth of business amenities—but also personal perks such as a health club (with massage and men's and women's therapy pools), jogging track, lighted tennis courts, heated pool, saunas, and whirlpools. There are full spa services, too. Rooms and suites are scattered around the 80-acre grounds in 11 "villas" that include shared parlors with refrigerators, wet bars, and conference tables. Rooms feature king or queen beds, in-room coffeemakers, irons and ironing boards, and two direct-line phones. Valet parking and airport transportation are available. Chaminade also

Monterey Bay

boasts two good restaurants and a bar (with meal service), all open to the general public.

Bed-and-Breakfasts

One of the loveliest newer B&Bs in Santa Cruz is actually the nation's first "BB&B"—Bed, Bud, and Breakfast. The **M** **Compassion Flower Inn,** 216 Laurel St., 831/466-0420, www.compassionflowerinn.com, opened in March 2000 with the express purpose of being a hemp- and medical marijuana–friendly bed-and-breakfast. The establishment is "named for both the beauty of the passionflower and the compassion of the medical marijuana movement" to which the owners have dedicated themselves. If you come, don't expect to find some tie-dyed, weed-happy scene reminiscent of San Francisco's Haight-Ashbury district during the Summer of Love. The proprietors have impeccably restored this gothic revival Victorian, at a cost of a half-million dollars. Tastefully and creatively decorated with antiques, hand-painted furniture, and custom tilework, the Compassion Flower Inn instead harks back to its historical roots as the onetime home of Judge Edgar Spalsbury, who made regular trips to a pharmacy downtown to buy opium as a pain medication for his tuberculosis. Rooms range from the fairly simple **Hemp Room** and **Passionflower Room,** "twin" accommodations tucked under the eaves (these two share a bath), to the first-floor, fully wheelchair accessible **Canabliss Room** and the elegant **Lovers' Suite.** Particularly striking in the suite is its bathroom, where exquisite tiled hemp designs wrap the two-person sunken tub. Rates, $100–200, include full organic breakfast, with fair-trade coffee and fresh-baked bread (two-night minimum stay).

Other Santa Cruz inns tend to cluster near the ocean. The stylishly renovated oceanfront **Pleasure Point Inn** at 2-3665 E. Cliff Dr. (at 37th Avenue), 831/469-6161 (voice mail) or 831/475-4657, www.pleasurepointinn.com, is indeed a pleasure. The adults-only inn offers four fresh, uniquely decorated rooms, each with abundant amenities—from in-room refrigerator, microwave, coffeemaker, and digital safe to gas-burning fireplace and private patio. Fresh fruit platter and continental breakfast every

morning, and a "welcome basket" on arrival. And, oh, those views—especially from the hot tub and the rooftop deck. Most rooms are $200–250; the second-story Coral Room is $265. Ask about specials and packages.

Tastefully decorated is the **Cliff Crest Bed and Breakfast Inn,** just blocks from both downtown and Main Beach at 407 Cliff St., 831/427-2609, www.cliffcrestinn.com, a Queen Anne by the beach and Boardwalk. Full breakfast is served in the solarium. Rates fall in the $200–250 range. The **Chateau Victorian,** 118 First St., 831/458-9458, www.chateauvictorian.com, offers seven rooms a bit more on the frilly side, with queen-sized beds, private tiled bathrooms, and wood-burning fireplaces. Local Santa Cruz Mountains wines are served, as are generous continental breakfasts. Most rates run $100–150; two rooms are $155.

For something more formal, the 1910 **Darling House** seaside mansion at 314 W. Cliff Dr., 831/458-1958 or 800/458-1988, www.darlinghouse.com, is an elegant 1910 Spanish Revival mansion designed by architect William Weeks. In addition to spectacular ocean views, Darling House offers eight rooms (two with private baths, two with fireplaces), telephones, and TV on request. There's a hot tub in the backyard; robes are provided. If you loved *The Ghost and Mrs. Muir,* you'll particularly enjoy the Pacific Ocean Room here—complete with telescope. Rates, including breakfast and evening beverages, are $100–300.

Legendary is the been-there-forever local landmark, the **Babbling Brook Inn,** 1025 Laurel St., 831/427-2437 or 800/866-1131, www.babblingbrookinn.com. Once a log cabin, this place was added to and otherwise spruced up by the Countess Florenzo de Chandler. All 13 rooms and suites are quite romantic, with private bathrooms, phones, and TVs. Most are decorated to suggest the works of Old World artists and poets, from Cézanne and Monet to Tennyson. Most also feature a fireplace, private deck, and outside entrance. Two have whirlpool bathtubs. Full breakfast and afternoon wine and cheese (or tea and cookies) are included. Also here: a babbling brook, waterfalls, and a garden gazebo. Rates run $150–300.

Davenport

If you're heading up the coast from Santa Cruz, consider a meal stop or a room with a view at the **Davenport Bed and Breakfast Inn,** 31 Davenport Ave. (Hwy. 1), 831/425-1818 or 800/870-1817, www.davenportinn.com, located in the midst of a vast coastal preserve. The 12 comfortable rooms are located in an adjacent cottage and upstairs, above the New Davenport Cash Store and Restaurant, where the food is very good at breakfast, lunch, and dinner. Rates, including full breakfast at the restaurant, are $100–150. Some of the pastries served here are made just up the road at **Whale City Bakery Bar & Grill,** 831/423-9803 or 831/429-6209, where the wide variety of homemade treats and very good coffee are always worth a stop.

Ben Lomond and Felton

Nothing fancy, but fine for pine-paneled cabin ambience just five miles north of Santa Cruz, the **Fern River Resort Motel,** 5250 Hwy. 9 in Felton, 831/335-4412, www.fernriver.com, offers 14 cabins with kitchens or kitchenettes, fireplaces, cable TV, and a private beach on the river. Rates are $50–150, starting at $80 in summer.

For a bed-and-breakfast stay in Ben Lomond, consider the lovely and woodsy **Fairview Manor,** 245 Fairview Ave., 831/336-3355, www.fairviewmanor.com, which features five rooms with private baths as well as a big deck overlooking the San Lorenzo River. Rates run $100–150. For a super-stylish (and expensive) stay, there's the elegant **Inn at Felton Crest,** 780 El Solyo Heights Dr. in Felton, 831/335-4011 (also fax) or 800/474-4011, www.feltoncrest.com, featuring just four guest rooms, each with in-room whirlpool tubs, cable TVs and VCRs, and private baths. Rates start around $400.

Capitola

A long-standing Capitola jewel is the **Capitola Venetian Hotel,** 1500 Wharf Rd., 831/476-6471 or 800/332-2780, www.capitolavenetian.com, California's first condominium complex, built in the 1920s. These clustered, Mediterranean-style stucco apartments are relaxed and relaxing, and close to the beach. In various combinations, rooms have kitchens with stoves and refrigerators, in-room coffeemakers, color TV with cable, and telephones with voicemail and data ports; some have separate living rooms, balconies, ocean views, and fireplaces. High-season ates are $150–250, with real deals available in the off-season.

Almost legendary almost overnight, Capitola's ℕ **Inn at Depot Hill,** 250 Monterey Ave., 831/462-3376 or 800/572-2632, www.innatdepothill.com, is a luxurious bed-and-breakfast (essentially a small luxury hotel) housed in the onetime railroad depot. Each of the eight rooms features its own unique design motif, inspired by international locales (the Delft Room, Stratford-on-Avon, the Paris Room, and Portofino, for example), as well as a private garden and entrance, fireplace, telephone with modem/fax capability, and state-of-the-art TV/VCR and stereo system. The private white-marble bathrooms feature bathrobes, hair dryers, and other little luxuries. Bathrooms have double showers, so two isn't necessarily a crowd. The pure linen bed sheets are hand washed and hand ironed daily. Rates include full breakfast, afternoon tea or wine, and after-dinner dessert. Off-street parking is provided. Rates are $250 and up, once you factor in all taxes, though inquiire about specials and modest off-season discounts. A very special place, for very special getaways.

Aptos

The apartment-style **Rio Sands Motel,** 116 Aptos Beach Dr., 831/688-3207 or 800/826-2077, www.riosands.com, has a heated pool, spa, and decent rooms not far from the beach. The "kitchen suites" feature full kitchens and a separate sitting room and sleep up to four. "Super rooms" sleep up to six and include a refrigerator and microwave. All rooms have two TVs. Extras include the large heated pool, spa, picnic area with barbecue pits, and expanded continental breakfast. Peak-season rates are $150–250, with real deals ($70–150) available in winter.

Also a pleasant surprise is the **Best Western Seacliff Inn,** just off the highway at 7500 Old Dominion Court, 831/688-7300 or 800/367-2003, www.seacliffinn.com. It's a cut or two above the usual motel and an easy stroll to the

Monterey Bay

beach. Rooms are large and comfortable, with private balconies. They cluster village-style around a large outdoor pool and whirlpool tub area. Suites have in-room spas. But the best surprise of all is the restaurant, **Severino's**, 831/688-8987, which serves good food both inside the dining room and outside by the koi pond. Great "sunset dinner" specials are served Sun.–Thurs. 5–6:30 P.M. Rates are $150–250.

On the coast just north of Manresa State Beach is the luxurious condo-style **Seascape Resort Monterey Bay,** 1 Seascape Resort Dr., 831/688-6800 or 800/929-7727,www.seascape resort.com. Choices here include tasteful studios and one- and two-bedroom villas. You'll also find a restaurant, golf course, tennis courts, and on-site fitness and spa facilities. Two-night minimum stay, late May through September. Rates are $250 and up.

For a bed-and-breakfast stay, the historic **Sand Rock Farm** at 6901 Freedom Blvd., 831/688-8005, www.sandrockfarm.com, offers a huge, exquisitely restored, turn-of-the-20th-century Craftsman-style home—complete with original push-button light switches. The 10-acre setting includes country gardens, walking trails, and the ruins of the old Liliencrantz family winery. Open since fall 2000, Sand Rock features five guest rooms and suites with in-room whirlpool tubs, cable TV, VCRs, and private baths, plus a lounge, fireplace, hot tub, and room service. Well-informed foodies will make a beeline to Sand Rock strictly for the wondrous breakfasts and winemaker dinners created by famed Chef Lynn Sheehan. Rates are $150–250.

Historic Victoriana in Aptos includes the **Apple Lane Inn,** 6265 Soquel Dr., 831/475-6868 or 800/649-8988, www.applelaneinn.com. Rates are $100–250. Also quite nice, and near Forest of Nisene Marks State Park, is the newly restored and redecorated **Bayview Hotel Bed and Breakfast Inn,** 8041 Soquel Dr., 831/688-8654 or 800/422-9843, www.bayviewhotel.com, an 1878 Italianate Victorian hotel with new owners and 12 elegant guest rooms, all with private baths and some with fireplaces and two-person tubs. Rooms also feature TVs, telephones, and modem hookups. Rates are $100–150.

FOOD

Farm Trails and Markets

To do Santa Cruz area farm trails, pick up a copy of the *Country Crossroads* map and brochure, a joint venture with Santa Clara County row-crop farmers and orchardists. It's the essential guide for hunting down strawberries, raspberries, apples, and homegrown veggies of all kinds. Or head for the local farmers' markets. The **Santa Cruz Community Certified Farmers Market,** 831/454-0566, is held downtown at Lincoln and Cedar every Wednesday from 2:30 to 6:30 P.M. There are many other markets in the area; inquire at the visitors center for a current listing.

Everyone's favorite family-run grocery since 1938 is **Shopper's Corner,** 622 Soquel Ave., 831/423-1398, where you can get regular and special grocery items, including fresh local produce (even organic fruits and vegetables), 150 kinds of cheeses, and locally baked breads and pastries. There's an old-time butcher shop, fresh fish and seafood, and a huge selection of wines, too, including just about every Santa Cruz Mountain wine you can imagine. For natural foods specifically, try **Staff of Life,** 1305 Water St., 831/423-8632, or the **New Leaf Community Market,** 1134 Pacific Ave., 831/425-1793.

A vegetarian visit to Santa Cruz wouldn't be complete without feasting at the **Whole Earth Restaurant** on the UC Santa Cruz campus (Redwood Blvd. next to the library), 831/426-8255. But for "natural fast foods," don't miss **Dharma's Natural Foods Restaurant,** in Capitola at 4250 Capitola Rd., 831/462-1717, where you can savor a Brahma Burger, Dharma Dog, or Nuclear Sub sandwich—baked tofu, guacamole, cheese, lettuce, olives, pickle, and secret sauce on a roll.

Inexpensive Fare Downtown

Absolutely wonderful is **Zoccoli's Delicatessen,** 1534 Pacific Ave., 831/423-1711, where it's common to see people lining up for sandwiches, salads, fresh homemade pastas, and genuine "good deal" lunch specials, usually under $5 or $6.

Open Mon.–Sat. 9 A.M.–5:30 P.M. Legendary for breakfast, nearby **Zachary's,** 819 Pacific Ave., 831/427-0646, serves sourdough pancakes with real maple syrup, whole-grain cereals, plus massive omelettes and scrambles. Mike's Mess will overwhelm even the heartiest of collegiate appetites. Weekend tip: Get here very early for breakfast, 7–8 A.M., or be prepared for a wait. Open daily for breakfast and lunch.

Another great local breakfast place is cozy, coffee shop-style **Walnut Avenue Café** at 106 Walnut Ave. (between Pacific and Cedar), 831/457.2307 where you get a mountain of fresh, wholesome food for a reasonable price—everything from fluffy nine-grain pancakes to eggs Benedict, omelettes, and tofu scrambles. Grand lattes, too. Open daily for breakfast and lunch. Particularly great at breakfast, too, **Café Brasil,** 116 Kalkar Dr. (north of High Street, east of the university campus), 831/429-1855, serves the real deal from way south of the border—from the Brazilian (chicken and creamed corn) omelette to the feijoada and Orfeu negro. Great chai, too. But try to bike it if you can, since parking nearby is next to impossible.

A great choice for fast-food Mexican is **Taqueria Vallarta,** inside the UC Extension building at 1101 Pacific Ave., 831/471-2655, complete with neo-Aztec murals. It's all good, from the fresh snapper or roasted pork tacos to the red beans and burritos. Open until midnight. Another great cheap-eats stop is **Tacos Moreno,** 1053 Water St., 831/429-6095, a Santa Cruz favorite for two decades and counting, beloved for its *al pastor* barbecued pork and cabbage burritos, chile verde tacos, vegetarian favorites, quesadillas, and more. You can't miss it at lunch time, what with the line of eager customers snaking down the street. **Planet Fresh Burritos,** 1003 Cedar St., 831/423-9799, is another possibility.

The **Santa Cruz Coffee Roasting Company** at the Palomar Inn, 1330 Pacific Ave., 831/459-0100, serves excellent free-trade coffee and a bistro-style café lunch. The **Saturn Cafe,** downtown at 145 Laurel St., 831/429-8505, has inexpensive ($8 or less) and wonderful vegetarian and vegan meals for lunch, dinner, and beyond. If you're low on cash but really hungry, come mid-day (11:30 A.M.–5 P.M.) for the Cheap Eats Menu—lots of substantial, healthy choices for

NEWMAN'S OWN SANTA CRUZ

Not Paul Newman, but the other one—Nell Newman, Cool Hand Luke's daughter—is the farm-loving Santa Cruz resident posing with the famed actor on all those tongue-in-cheek, stylized *American Gothic* Newman's Own Organics product labels. And how appropiate, since it was a father and daughter so stoically represented in the original *American Gothic.*

Formerly a biologist with the Ventana Wilderness Sanctuary Research and Education Center down the coast in Big Sur, Nell Newman is an accomplished cook who in 1993 was inspired by the Santa Cruz area's love affair with whole food to add an organics division to her father's popular company, Newman's Own.

The point of Newman's Own Organics is producing "good tasting food that just happens to be organic." Early on the brand has focused on what might be considered the inessentials—snack foods including chocolate bars, tortilla chips, pretzels, Pop's Corn, and several cookie varieties, from Fig Newmans to Oreo-like Newman-O's. Look for organic premium pet foods, too, and fair-trade coffee.

Like the first generation of Newman's Own, Newman's Own Organics—the second generation—donates 100 percent of after-tax profits to charitable causes. These have included the University of California Santa Cruz Farm and Garden Project, the Organic Farming Research Foundation, the Henry A. Wallace Institute for Alternative Agriculture, and the Western Environmental Law Center in Taos, New Mexico. For more information, see www.newmansownorganics.com.

MELISSA SHEROWSKI

Zoccoli's sidewalk seating

$5 or so. Open daily for lunch and dinner, until late for desserts and coffee. Themes days here can be a scream. During Monday Madness, the decadent favorite Chocolate Madness sells at two for the price of one. Random Tuesdays (on random Tuesdays) showcase live local music. On Wig Out Wednesday, just wear a wig and you'll get 20 percent off your tab. Such a deal. Also good for a quick vegetarian bite downtown is the Sri Lankan **Asian Rose Café,** 1547 Pacific Ave., 831/458-3023 (the main restaurant is on Soquel Avenue). **Erik's DeliCafe,** 712 Front St., is a local favorite for fresh, house-made soups and other good food—veggie choices, too—which explains why there are so many Erik's outlets in the greater Santa Cruz area.

Unforgettable for breakfast or lunch is funky **Aldo's,** also Aldo's Bait & Tackle, 616 Atlantic Ave. (at the west end of the yacht harbor), 831/426-3736. The breakfast menu features various egg and omelette combinations. Best of all, though, is the raisin toast, made with Aldo's homemade focaccia bread. Eat outdoors on the old picnic tables covered with checkered plastic tablecloths

and enjoy the sun, sea air, and seagulls. At lunch and dinner, look for homemade pastas and fresh fish. The place for peoples's seafood is laid-back **Riva Fish House** at the wharf, 831/429-1223.

Santa Cruz's classic **Jack's Hamburgers,** downtown at 202 Lincoln St., 831/423-4421, serves good 'n' juicy ones, not to mention great chocolate shakes and surprisingly good chocolate cake. Open daily for lunch and dinner. A good late-night stop is the **Santa Cruz Diner,** 909 Ocean St., 831/426-7151.

The Crepe Place, 1134 Soquel Ave. (west of Seabright), 831/429-6994, offers inexpensive breakfasts, dessert crêpes (and every other kind), good but unpretentious lunches, and dinners into the wee hours—a great place for late-night dining. Great garden patio, too. Open daily for lunch and dinner, on weekends for brunch. The **Seabright Brewery** brewpub, 519 Seabright Ave., Ste. 107, 831/426-2739, is popular for its Seabright Amber and Pelican Pale—not to mention casual dining out on the patio. If you're heading toward Boulder Creek, beer fans, stop by the **Boulder Creek Brewery and Cafe,** 13040 Hwy. 9, 831/338-7882.

High-End Dining Downtown

Downtown Santa Cruz is getting pretty uptown these days. **⚡ Gabriella Café,** 910 Cedar St., 831/457-1677, made famous by Chef Jim Denevan's Outstanding in the Field organic farm tours and dinners, is a long-running romantic favorite. The seasonally changing menu is a cornucopia of dishes made from locally grown organic fruits and vegetables, other area farm products, and the freshest fish and seafood—from corn fritters with Nova smoked salmon crab cakes to the truffle gnocchi. Desserts are the stuff of local legend, too. Double chocolate torte, anyone? Great wine list. Open daily for lunch (brunch on weekends) and dinner.

Intimate **Oswald's,** 1547 Pacific Ave. (near Cedar), 831/423-7427, is another stylish local favorite, serving innovative California cuisine crafted from the freshest seafood, meats, and local produce. Fashionable yet eclectic is the fun **Pearl Alley Bistro,** 110 Pearl Alley (at Cedar, between Lincoln and Walnut)), 831/429-8070, where the monthly changing menu might include zucchini Parmeggiana and Mongolian barbecue, with your choice of fresh meats and veggies, or corned beef pasties, chicken and buttermilk-biscuit pie, or Smithfield ham. Open daily for dinner. Full bar. Everybody's favorite for sophisticated Chinese is **O'mei**, 2316 Mission St. (at King), 831/425-8458, whether it's the apricot-almond chicken, lichee pork, or gan pung chicken. And don't miss the toasted coconut ice cream. Sushi lovers, locals say *the* place is **Mobo Sushi**, 105 S. River St. (east of Front), 831/429-8070.

El Palomar at the Pacific Garden Mall, 1336 Pacific Ave., 831/425-7575, is a winner for sit-down Mexican meals, and especially good for seafood. It's been just about everybody's top choice for south-of-the-border fare, starting with oysters on the half shell topped with salsa fresca or the seafood appetizer plate and continuing through entrées such as prawn burritos and enchiladas, charbroiled red snapper with guacamole and tomatillo salsa, and tostadas de ceviche. Open daily for breakfast, lunch, and dinner. Full bar. (At the yacht harbor, you'll find **Café El Palomar**, 2222 E. Cliff Dr., 831/462-4248, open 7 A.M.–5 P.M. daily.)

Charming for patio dining, thanks to that three-story "old world" mural, is **Ristorante Italiano**, in the Branciforte Plaza at 555 Soquel Ave., 831/458-2321, everyone's favorite Italian, for both traditional and more innovative selections. Surprises include cacciuco, or Italian seafood and fish stew in marinara sauce, and prawns Parma. Open daily for lunch and dinner; "light and early" dinners are served 5–6:30 P.M. Everyone's favorite trattoria is **Caffé Bella Napoli**, 503 Water St., 831/426-7401, open for lunch and dinner daily.

For romantic Bavarian cuisine, the place is **Casablanca Restaurant**, 101 Main St. (at Beach), 831/426-9063, open for dinner nightly and brunch on Sunday. For fine dining farther afield: The historic 1929 **Hollins House** at Pasatiempo Golf Club—where the renowned course was designed by Alister MacKenzie—is a destination in its own right, just the place for exquisitely prepared dinner in a clubby atmosphere. Hollins House is at 20 Clubhouse Dr., 831/459-9177, open for

dinner Wed.–Sat. 5:30–8:30 P.M. For something simpler, consider breakfast or lunch at the **MacKenzie Bar & Grill** next to the pro shop, 831/459-9162, open daily dawn to dusk.

Felton, Ben Lomond, and Boulder Creek

The **White Raven** bookshop in Felton, 6253 Hwy. 9, 831/335-3611, is also a cool coffee and pastry stop. At the charmingly retro **La Bruschetta** Italian roadhouse, in the Felton Guild hall at 5447 Hwy 9, 831/335-3337, specialty pastas such as nicchi in pomodoro sauce and agnolotti alla ragusana are the stars. Open daily for breakfast, lunch, and dinner. The been-there-forever **Trout Farm Inn**, 7701 E. Zayante Rd., 831/335-4317, is serving good, solid surf and turf these days, such as trout almondine and sea scallops with artichoke heart. Open Tues.–Sun. for lunch and dinner. Best bet for wholesome, hearty sit-down breakfast and lunch is the **Blue Sun Café** down the road in Boulder Creek, 13070 Hwy. 9, 831/338-2105. Ben Lomond's **Tyrolean Inn**, 9600 Hwy. 9, 831/336-5188, serves good traditional German fare.

Soquel

Quite reasonable for impressive quantities of very good, very fresh fast food, kid-friendly ⋈ **Carpo's** diner in Soquel at 2400 Porter St., 831/476-6260, is beloved for such things as shrimp and crab sandwiches, great burgers and fries (or onion rings), seafood and bell pepper kebabs, and broiled salmon. For dessert, try the ollallieberry piue. The way it works here: Place your order at the counter, and they'll give you a vibrating buzzer. When your food's up, you'll get the message. Carpo's is immensely popular, so come at off times if at all possible. Also a pretty good deal for families is **Little Tampico**, 2605 Main St., 831/475-4700, which offers a daily lunch special and an all-you-can-eat taco and tostada bar at lunch for $5–6. A good value at dinner is the specialty Otila's Plate, a mini-taco, enchilada, tostada, and taquito, plus rice and beans for just over $10. Another good choice: nachos with everything. If you miss this one, various Tampico restaurant relatives dot the county.

A tad fancier is lively **Café Cruz** rosticceria and bar, 2621 41st Ave. in Soquel, 831/476-3801, which also emphasizes fresh food, including local produce. At lunch sandwiches include such things as a grilled prawn club sandwich and the Cruz burger, made with Bradley Ranch natural beef. At dinner expect the grilled gulf prawns, arugula, and strawberry salad, baby spinach and three cheese ravioli, honey-cured smoked rotisseried chicken, and Harris Ranch New York steak. Children's menu, too.

Top of the food chain in these parts is **Theo's**, 3101 N. Main St., 831/462-3657, where you might start with boar sausage-stuffed cabbage and sail on through Maine lobster pot pie, house-smoked wild salmon, or slow-roasted Sonoma duckling. Spectacular desserts, good wine list. Great winemakers' dinners, too. Open for dinner Tues.–Sat. from 5:30 P.M.

Capitola

Dharma's Natural Foods Restaurant, a Santa Cruz institution at 4250 Capitola Rd., 831/462-1717, is purported to be the oldest completely vegetarian restaurant in the country. Open daily for breakfast, lunch, and dinner. Also classic in Capitola is **Pizza-My-Heart,** 209-A Esplanade, 831/475-5714.

Casual, in more upscale style, and unbeatable for pastries and decadent desserts is **▧ Gayle's Bakery and Rosticceria,** 504 Bay Ave., 831/462-1200. The rosticceria has a wonderful selection of salads and homemade pastas, soups, sandwiches, pizza, spit-roasted meats—even dinners-to-go and heat-and-serve casseroles. But the aromas drifting in from Gayle's Bakery are the real draw. The bakery's breakfast pastries include various cheese Danishes, croissants, chocolatine, lemon tea bread, muffins, pecan rolls, apple nut turnovers, and such specialties as a schnecken ring smothered in walnuts. The apple crumb and ollalieberry pies are unforgettable, not to mention the praline cheesecake and the two dozen other cakes—chocolate mousse, hasselnuss, raspberry, poppy seed, mocha. . . (All pies and cakes are also served by the slice.) For decadence-to-go, try Grand Marnier truffles, florentines, éclairs, or Napoleons. Gayle's also sells more than two dozen types of fresh-baked bread. The Capitola sourdough bread and sour baguette would be good for picnics, as would the two-pound loaf of the excellent Pain de Compagne. Gayle's is open daily 7 A.M.–7 P.M. (If you're heading toward the bay or San Jose the back way via Corralitos, stop by the **Corralitos Market and Sausage Co.,** 569 Corralitos Rd., 831/722-2633, for homemade sausages, smoke-cured ham and turkey breast, or other specialty meats—all great with Gayle's breads.)

Near the beach, on or near the Esplanade, you'll find an endless variety of eateries. **Margaritaville,** 312 Esplanade, 831/476-2263, serves appetizers and sandwiches and all kinds of Mexican along with its margaritas. Open for lunch and dinner daily and for brunch on weekends. The **Paradise Beach Grill,** 215 Esplanade,

OUTSTANDING IN THE FIELD

Outstanding in the field of foodie tourism is Outstanding in the Field, a hugely popular food, wine, and farm experience originally served up by chef Jim Denevan of the Gabriella Café in Santa Cruz. Local organic farmers and winemakers get together with visiting chefs to create unique regional dining events that combine a personal farm tour with a spectacular multicourse meal. The inviting, well-laden tables—yes, the tables are out standing in the farmer's field—become the "meeting place between the sky and the soil." The family-style, four- to six-course meal, complete with a wine selected to accompany each course, salutes the land from which the bounty comes. Just for fun, dinner guest are encouraged to bring their own plates, especially plates that come with their own stories, as an icebreaker. All dinnerware will be washed and returned by meal's end.

Some of Northern and Central California's most honored chefs and winemakers joyfully participate in Outstanding in the Field dinners. For an upcoming Outstanding schedule and other information, see www.outstandinginthefield.com. For reservations, call 877/886-7409.

831/476-4900, offers California cuisine as well as a variety of international dishes. Great views. Open for lunch and dinner daily. Also serving California cuisine is **Zelda's on the Beach,** 203 Esplanade, 831/475-4900, which features an affordable lobster special on Thursday night.

The most famous restaurant in Capitola is the **Shadowbrook Restaurant,** 1750 Wharf Rd. (at Capitola Rd.), 831/475-1511, known for its romantic garden setting—ferns, roses, ivy outside, a Monterey pine and plants inside—and the tram ride down the hill to Soquel Creek. The Shadowbrook is open for "continental-flavored American" dinners nightly. The wine list is extensive. Brunch, with choices like apple and cheddar omelettes, is served on weekends. Reservations recommended.

Aptos

For stylish and fresh Mexican food, the place is **Palapas** at Seascape Village on Seascape Boulevard, 831/662-9000, open daily for lunch and dinner, brunch on Sunday. For stylish all-American comfort food—meat loaf, house-made chicken soup, boysenberry cobler—the place is the **Bleu Spoon** bistro, 207 Sea Ridge Rd., 831/685-8654. If you're out to dent your pocketbook, the **Bittersweet Bistro,** 787 Rio Del Mar Blvd., 831/662-9799, offers Mediterranean-inspired bistro fare featuring fresh local and organic produce—everything from Greek pizzettas and seafood puttanesca to garlic chicken and grilled Monterey Bay king salmon.

INFORMATION AND SERVICES

The best all-around source for city and county information is the **Santa Cruz County Conference and Visitors Council,** downtown at 1211 Ocean St., 831/425-1234 or 800/833-3494, www.santa cruzca.org, open Mon.–Sat. 9 A.M.–5 P.M., Sun. 10 A.M.–4 P.M. Definitely request the current accommodations, dining, and visitor guides. If you've got time to roam farther afield, also pick up a current copy of the *County Crossroads* farm trails map and ask about area wineries. Cyclists, request the *Santa Cruz County Bikeway Map.* Antiquers, ask for the current *Antiques,*

Arts, & Collectibles directory for Santa Cruz and Monterey Counties, published every June— not a complete listing, by far, but certainly a good start. If you once were familiar with Santa Cruz and—post-1989 earthquake—now find yourself lost, pick up the *Downtown Santa Cruz Directory* brochure.

A valuable source of performing arts information, focused on the university, is the *UCSC Performing Arts Calendar,* published quarterly and available all around town. The excellent UC Santa Cruz paper, *City on a Hill,* http://slugwire .ucsc.edu, is published only during the regular school year. *Metroactive Santa Cruz,* www .metroactive.com/cruz, is the noteworthy local alternative newspaper, and a good source for local goings-on. *Santa Cruz Good Times* www.gdtimes .com, is a good, long-running free weekly with an entertainment guide and sometimes entertaining political features. The free *Student Guide* comes out seasonally, offering lots of ads and some entertaining reading about Santa Cruz. The *Santa Cruz County Sentinel,* www.santacruzsentinel .com, and the *Watsonville Register-Pajaronian,* www.register-pajaronian.com, are the traditional area papers. The **Santa Cruz Parks and Recreation Department** 831/420-5270, usually publishes a *Summer Activity Guide* especially useful for advance planning.

The Santa Cruz post office is at 850 Front St., 831/426-5200, and is open weekdays 8 A.M.– 5 P.M. The **Santa Cruz Public Library** is at 224 Church St., 831/420-5700. If you want to hobnob with the people on the hill, visit the **Dean McHenry Library** on campus, 831/459-4000.

TRANSPORTATION

Getting There

If you're driving from the San Francisco Bay Area, the preferred local route to Santa Cruz (and the only main alternative to Hwy. 1) is I-280 or 880 south to San Jose, then hop over the hills on the congested and treacherously twisting Hwy. 17.

The **Greyhound** bus terminal is at 425 Front St. in Santa Cruz, 831/423-1800. Greyhound provides service from San Francisco to Santa Cruz (also Monterey), as well as connections south to

Monterey Bay

ROARING CAMP AND BIG TREES RAILROAD

F. Norman Clark, the self-described "professional at oddities" who also owns the narrow-gauge railroad in Felton, bought the Southern Pacific rails connecting Santa Cruz and nearby Olympia, to make it possible for visitors to get to Henry Cowell Redwoods State Park and Felton (*almost* to Big Basin) by train. During logging's commercial heyday here in the 1900s, 20 or more trains passed over these tracks every day.

Today you can still visit Roaring Camp and ride the rails on one of two different trips. Hop aboard a 100-year-old steam engine and make an hour-and-fifteen-minute loop around a virgin redwood forest ($18 general, $12 kids 3–12), or take a 1940s-vintage passenger train from Felton down to Santa Cruz (round-trip fare $20

general, $15 kids 3–12). Parking is $6. The year-round calendar of special events includes October's Harvest Faire and the Halloween Ghost Train, the Mountain Man Rendezvous living history encampment in November, and December's Holiday Lights Train.

The railroad offers daily runs (usually just one train a day on nonsummer weekdays) from spring through November and operates only on weekends and major holidays in winter. For more information, contact: Roaring Camp and Big Trees Narrow-Gauge Railroad, 831/335-4484, www.roaringcamp.com. For advance tickets to the popular Ghost Train and the Holiday Lights Train, call the Blue & Gold Fleet's TeleSails at 415/705-5555 or 888/253-83687.

L.A. via Salinas or San Jose. From the East Bay and South Bay, take Amtrak, now also offering bus connections from San Jose and from Salinas. You can get *close* to Santa Cruz by plane. The **San Jose International Airport,** 408/501-7600, www.sjc.org, the closest major airport in the north and not far from Santa Cruz, is served by commuter and major airlines. Or fly into Monterey.

Getting Around

Bicyclists will be in hog heaven in Santa Cruz, with everything from excellent bike lanes to locking bike racks at bus stops. But drivers be warned: Parking can be impossible, especially in summer, especially at the beach. There's a charge for parking at the Boardwalk (in lots with attendants) and metered parking elsewhere. Best bet: Drive to the beach, unload passengers and beach paraphernalia, then park a mile or so away. By the time you walk back, your companions should be done battling for beach towel space. You can usually find free parking on weekends in the public garage at the county government center at 701 Ocean Street.

The **Santa Cruz Metro,** 230 Walnut Ave., 831/425-8600, www.scmtd.com, provides superb public transit throughout the northern Monterey Bay area, including bus service to the beach, mission, lighthouse, university, even

nearby burgs including Bonny Doon. The Metro has a "bike and ride" service for bicyclists who want to hitch a bus ride partway (bike racks onboard). Call for current route information or pick up a free copy of the excellent *Headways* (which includes Spanish translations). Buses will get you anywhere you want to go in town and considerably beyond for $1.50 ($4.50 for an all-day pass)—exact change only.

You can rent a car from **Enterprise Rent-A-Car,** 1025-B Water St., 831/426-7799 or 800/325-8007; **Avis,** 630 Ocean St., 831/423-1244 or 800/831-2847; or **Budget,** 919 Ocean St., 831/429-6612 or 800/527-0700. **Yellow Cab** is at 131 Front St., 831/423-1234, also home to the **Santa Cruz Airporter,** 831/423-1214 or in California 800/497-4997, which provides shuttle van service to both the San Francisco and San Jose Airports, as well as to Caltrain and the Amtrak station in San Jose.

Getting Away

Santa Cruz Metro buses can get you to Boulder Creek, Big Basin, Ben Lomond, Felton, north coast beaches, and *almost* all the way to Año Nuevo State Reserve just across the San Mateo County Line.

Another way to get out of town is via Metro's **Hwy. 17 Express** buses to the San Jose train station—more than 10 trips daily on weekdays (fewer on weekends and holidays)—which directly connect with **Caltrain** (to San Francisco) and **Amtrak** (to Oakland, Berkeley, and Sacramento). The fare is just $4 one way, $8 for a full-day pass. For information, call 831/425-8600 or see www.scmtd.com. For **Caltrain** fares and schedules, call 650/508-6200 or 800/660-4287 (in the service area) or see www.cal train.com. For Amtrak, contact 800/872-7245 or see www.amtrak.com.

Amtrak's Coast Starlight runs from Los Angeles to Seattle with central coast stops in Oxnard, Santa Barbara, San Luis Obispo, Salinas, and Oakland. If you'll be heading to the San Francisco Bay Area from the Monterey Peninsula, keep in mind that Amtrak also connects in San Jose with the San Francisco–San Jose **Caltrain,** 650/817-1717 or 800/660-4287 (in the service area), www.cal train.com. For help in figuring out the way to San Jose—and how to get around the entire Bay Area by rapid transit—see www.transit.511.org.

North of Santa Cruz

Travelers heading north toward San Francisco via Hwy. 1 will discover Año Nuevo State Reserve, breeding ground for the northern elephant seal—quite popular, so don't expect to just drop by—and two delightful hostels housed in former lighthouses. Not far from Año Nuevo, as the crow flies, is spectacular Big Basin Redwoods State Park, California's first state park, and other spectacular redwood parks.

ⓜ BIG BASIN REDWOODS STATE PARK

California's first state park was established here, about 24 miles up canyon from Santa Cruz on Hwy. 9. To save Big Basin's towering *Sequoia sempervirens* coast redwoods from loggers, 60-some conservationists led by Andrew P. Hill camped at the base of Slippery Rock on May 15, 1900, and formed the Sempervirens Club. Just two years later, in September 1902, 3,800 acres of primeval forest were deeded to the state, the beginning of California's state park system.

Flora and Fauna

Today, Big Basin Redwoods State Park includes more than 18,000 acres on the ocean-facing slopes of the Santa Cruz Mountains, and efforts to protect (and expand) the park still continue under the auspices of the Sempervirens Fund and the Save-the-Redwoods League. (Donations are always welcome.) Tall coast redwoods and Douglas fir predominate. Wild ginger, violets,

and milkmaids are common in spring, also a few rare orchids grow here. Native azaleas bloom in early summer, and by late summer huckleberries are ready for picking. In the fall and winter rainy season, mushrooms and other forest fungi "blossom."

At one time, the coast grizzly (one of seven bear species that roamed the state's lower regions) thrived between San Francisco and San Luis Obispo. The last grizzly was spotted here in 1878. Common are black-tailed deer, raccoons, skunks, and gray squirrels. Rare are mountain lions, bobcats, coyotes, foxes, and opossums. Among the fascinating reptiles in Big Basin is the endangered western skink. Predictably, rattlers are fairly common in chaparral areas, but other snakes are shy. Squawking Steller's jays are ever-present, and acorn woodpeckers, dark-eyed juncos, owls, and hummingbirds—altogether about 250 bird species—also haunt Big Basin. Spotting marbled murrelets (shorebirds that nest 200 feet up in the redwoods) is a birding challenge.

Sights and Recreation

The best time to be in Big Basin is in the fall, when the weather is perfect and most tourists have gone home. Winter and spring are also prime times, though usually rainier. Road cuts into the park offer a peek into local geology—tilted, folded, twisted layers of thick marine sediments. Big Basin's **Nature Lodge** museum features good natural history exhibits and many fine books, including *Short Historic Tours of*

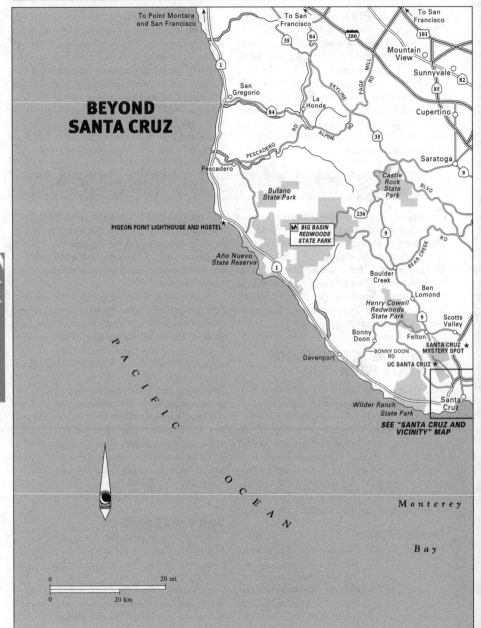

To Point Montara
and San Francisco

To San
Francisco

To San
Francisco

**BEYOND
SANTA CRUZ**

San
Gregorio

La
Honda

Mountain
View

Sunnyvale

Cupertino

Saratoga

Pescadero

Butano
State Park

Castle
Rock
State
Park

PIGEON POINT LIGHTHOUSE AND HOSTEL ★

BIG BASIN
REDWOODS
STATE PARK

Año Nuevo
State Reserve

Boulder
Creek

Ben
Lomond

Henry Cowell
Redwoods
State Park

Scotts
Valley

Bonny
Doon

Felton

Davenport

SANTA CRUZ ★
MYSTERY SPOT

UC SANTA CRUZ ★

Wilder Ranch
State Park

Santa
Cruz

SEE "SANTA CRUZ AND
VICINITY" MAP

P A C I F I C

O C E A N

M o n t e r e y

B a y

0   20 mi

0   20 km

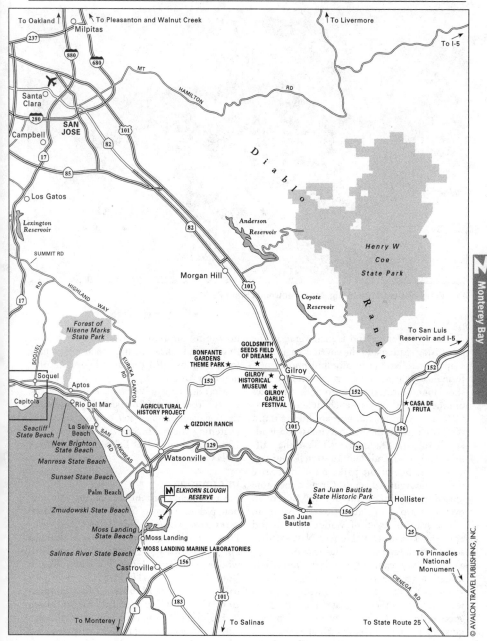

MELISSA SHEROWSKI

the Highway 1 entrance to Big Basin Redwoods State Park

Big Basin by Jennie and Denzil Verado. The carved-log seating and the covered stage at the amphitheater attract impromptu human performances (harmonica concerts, freestyle softshoe, joke routines) when no park campfires or other official events are scheduled.

Also here: miles and miles of hiking trails. (Get oriented in the Sempervirens Room adjacent to park headquarters.) Take the half-mile **Redwood Trail** loop to stretch your legs and to see one of the park's most impressive stands of virgin redwoods. Or hike the more ambitious **Skyline-to-the-Sea** trail, at least an overnight trip. It's 11 miles from the basin rim to the seabird haven of Waddell Beach and adjacent **Theodore J. Hoover Natural Preserve,** a freshwater marsh. There are trail camps along the way (camping and fires allowed only in designated areas). Hikers, bring food and water, as Waddell Creek flows with reclaimed wastewater. Another popular route is the **Pine Mountain Trail.** Thanks to recent land acquisitions along the coast north of Santa Cruz, the new 1.5-mile **Whitehouse Ridge Trail**

now joins Big Basin with Año Nuevo State Reserve; call ahead or inquire at either park for directions. Also ask about hiking in other new area park lands.

Most dramatic in Big Basin are the waterfalls. **Berry Creek Falls** is a particularly pleasant destination, with rushing water, redwood mists, and glistening rocks fringed with delicate ferns. Nearby are both **Silver Falls** and the **Golden Falls Cascade.**

Information

For reasonably current area hiking information, pick up a copy of *The Santa Cruz Mountains Trail Book* by Tom Taber (Oak Valley Press), which also offers coastal access details. For park information, contact Big Basin Redwoods State Park, 21600 Big Basin Way in Boulder Creek, 831/338-8860, www.bigbasin.org, and the **Mountain Parks Foundation,** 525 North Big Trees Park Rd. in Felton, 831/335-3174, www.mountainparks.org, which offers educational and interpretive activies at Big Basin and also at Henry Cowell

WILDER RANCH STATE PARK

Open to the public since mid-1989, Wilder Ranch State Park is best summed up as "a California coastal dairy-farm museum," a remnant of the days when dairies were more important to the local economy than tourists. Before it was a dairy farm, this was the main rancho supplying Mission Santa Cruz. Though damaged by the 1989 earthquake, the old Victorian ranch house is open again, decked out in period furnishings. The grounds also include an elaborate 1890s stable, a dairy barn, and a bunkhouse/workshop with water-driven machinery. Seasoned vehicles and farm equipment, from a 1916 Dodge touring sedan to seed spreaders and road graders, are scattered throughout the grounds.

Almost more appealing, though, are the park's miles of coastline and thousands of acres of forest, creeks, and canyons (not to mention the Brussels sprouts). To help visitors take in the landscape, 7,000-acre Wilder Ranch features 34 miles of hiking, biking, and equestrian trails. Restoration of these coastal wetlands is ongoing.

General ranch tours, led by docents dressed in period attire, are offered every Saturday and Sunday, usually at 1 P.M. Historical games are played on the lawn—hoop 'n' stick, bubbles, stilts—on weekends as well. A variety of other history- and natural history-oriented events are sponsored throughout the year, from demonstrations on making corn-husk dolls or quilts to mastering cowboy-style roping, plus guided hikes and bird walks. Usually on the first Saturday in May is the park's annual open house, a full day of old-fashioned family fun (and fundraising, for future park restoration work).

The main entrance to Wilder Ranch is two miles north of Santa Cruz on the west side of Hwy. 1 at 1401 Coast Rd., about a mile past the stoplight at Western Drive. For more information, call 831/423-9703 or 831/426-0505, or see www.santacruzstateparks.org and www.scparkfriends.org. The ranch is open for day-use ($6 per car) and for equestrian camping (call for details). No dogs are allowed. The park's new interpretive center is open daily in summer, at last report only Fri.–Sat. 10 A.M.–4 P.M. in winter. To get here by bus, take Santa Cruz Metro No. 40 and ask the driver to drop you at the ranch.

Monterey Bay

State Park, including the Fall Creek area. To get oriented to the town, pick up a copy of the Boulder Creek Historical Walking Tour, available at most area merchants and at the **San Lorenzo Valley Historical Museum,** now at home in a onetime church built with local old-growth redwood at 12547 Hwy. 9, 831/338-8382, at last report open on Wednesday, Saturday, and Sunday afternoons. Call for current details. To get oriented to the coastal side of Big Basin Redwoods, head for Rancho Del Oso State Park near Davenport and contact the **Rancho Del Oso Nature and History Center** some 16 miles north of Santra Cruz via Hwy. 1, 831/427-2288. To reserve backpackers' trail camps at Rancho Del Oso, call 831/338-8861. To reserve equestrian trail camps, call 831/425-1218.

Big Basin has reservable family campsites ($20–24) plus five group camps. Make reservations through ReserveAmerica, 800/444-7275, www.reserveamerica.com, up to seven months in advance. An unusual "outdoor" option: the park's tent cabins. To reserve backpacker campsites at the park's six trail camps, contact park headquarters for details. Hiker-biker campsites are $3. Big Basin's day-use fee is $6 per vehicle (walk-ins and bike-ins are free), and a small fee is charged for the map/brochure showing all trails and major park features.

Henry Cowell Redwoods State Park

The Redwood Grove in the dark San Lorenzo Canyon here is the park's hub and one of the most impressive redwood groves along the central coast, with the Neckbreaker, the Giant, and the Fremont Tree all standouts; the self-guided nature path is wheel chair- and stroller-accessible. And check out the state of the art nature center. You can camp at Graham Hill, picnic near the grove, or head out on the vast web of hiking and horseback trails. The park's northern **Fall Creek** section takes in most of the creek's watershed, known for its limestone deposits; ruins of lime kilns are scattered among the more natural trailside attractions. New in the summer of 1999 was the **U-Con Trail** connecting Henry Cowell to Wilder Ranch State Park on the coast—making it possible to hike, bike, or horseback ride from the redwoods to the ocean on an established trail.

The fine family campground at Henry Cowell was recently named one of the nation's top 100 by ReserveAmerica. For information about Henry Cowell Redwoods State Park, off Hwy. 9 in Felton, call 831/335-4598 or 831/438-2396 (campground). Henry Cowell has 150 campsites; reserve through ReserveAmerica, 800/444-7275 or www.reserveamerica.com.

Other Parks off Hwy. 9

Between Big Basin and Saratoga is **Castle Rock State Park,** 15300 Skyline Blvd., Los Gatos, 408/867-2952, an essentially undeveloped park and a hiker's paradise offering some primitive camping. **Highlands County Park,** 8500 Hwy. 9 in Ben Lomond, is open daily 9 A.M.–dusk. This old estate, transformed into a park with picnic tables and nature trails, also has a sandy beach along the river. Another swimming spot is at **Ben Lomond County Park** on Mill Street, which also offers shaded picnic tables and barbecue facilities. Free, open daily in summer. Closer to Big Basin is **Boulder Creek Park** on Middleton Avenue east of Hwy. 9 in Boulder Creek, also free. The swimming hole here has both shallows and deeps, plus there's a sandy beach. Other facilities include shaded picnic tables and barbecue pits.

South of Santa Cruz

MOSS LANDING AND VICINITY

Near the mouth of Elkhorn Slough on the coast, Moss Landing is a crazy quilt of weird shops and roadside knickknack stands, watched over by both a towering steam power plant—built circa 1948, the second largest in the world, formerly under PG&E (Pacific Gas & Electric) control and now owned and recently expanded by Duke Energy—and a Kaiser firebrick-making plant. All of which makes for an odd-looking community. First a Salinas Valley produce port, then a whaling harbor until 1930, Moss Landing is now surrounded by artichoke and broccoli fields. The busy fishing harbor and adjoining slough are home to hundreds of bird and plant species, making this an important center for marinelife studies.

These days the area is also noted for its indoor recreational opportunities, with more than two-dozen antique and junk shops along Moss Landing Road. Show up on the last Sunday in July for the annual **Antique Street Fair,** which draws more than 350 antiques dealers and at least 12,000 civilian antiquers.

For more information about the area, contact the **Moss Landing Chamber of Commerce,** 831/633-4501, www.monterey-bay.net/ml.

Moss Landing Marine Laboratories

The laboratories here, at 895 Blanco Circle, 831/755-8650, are operated by San Jose State Univeresity and shared by other researchers, including the Monterey Bay Aquarium Research Institute. Students and faculty study local marinelife, birds, and tidepools, but particularly Monterey Bay's spectacular underwater submarine canyons, which start where Elkhorn Slough enters the bay at Moss Landing. Stop for a visit and quick look around, but don't disturb classes or research projects. Better yet, come in spring— usually the first Sunday after Easter—for the big open house, when you can take a complete tour; explore the "touch tank" full of starfish, sea cucumbers, sponges, snails, and anemones; and see slide shows, movies, and marinelife dioramas.

MELISSA SHEROWSKI

Monterey Bay

Moss Landing: marina and refinery

New at the marine lab, expected to be completed by the end of 2005, is a $4 million, 500-foot-long concrete **research pier,** which replaces the 1870s-vintage wooden pier damaged in the 1989 Loma Prieta earthquake and later demolished. The new pier will allow scientists studying everything from global warming to whales to more efficiently load research ships, and also allow large research ships—like the 209-foot *Melville*—to tie up at Moss Landing. Though locals would have liked pier access, including the chance to fish, public access is limited to a small, informational public viewing area at the foot of the pier. Guided pier tours are also offered.

Elkhorn Slough Reserve

Most people come here to hike and bird-watch, but the fishlife in this coastal estuary, the second largest in California, is also phenomenal. No wonder the Ohlone people built villages here some 5,000 years ago. Wetlands like these, oozing with life and nourished by rich bay sediments, are among those natural environments most threatened by "progress." Thanks to the Nature Conservancy, the Elkhorn Slough (originally the mouth of the Salinas River until a 1908 diver-

sion) is now protected as a federal and state estuarine sanctuary and recognized as a National Estuarine Research Reserve—California's first. Elkhorn Slough is managed by the California Department of Fish and Game.

These meandering channels along a seven-mile river are thick with marshy grasses and wildflowers beneath a plateau of oaks and eucalyptus. In winter an incredible variety of shorebirds (not counting migrating waterfowl) call this area home. Endangered and threatened birds, including the brown pelican, the California clapper rail, and the California least tern, also thrive here at Elkhorn, desinated a Globally Important Bird Area by the American Bird Conservancy. The tule elk once hunted by the Ohlone are long gone, but harbor seals bask on the mudflats, and bobcats, gray foxes, muskrats, otters, and black-tailed deer are still here.

Though this is a private nature sanctuary, not a park, the public can visit. Some 4.5 miles of trails pass by tidal mudflats, salt marshes, and an old abandoned dairy. The reserve and visitors center, which offers a bird-watchers map/guide to the Pajaro Valley, are open Wed.–Sun. 9 A.M.–5 P.M. There's a small day-use fee to use the trails. Docent-led walks are offered year-round on Saturday and Sunday at 10 A.M. and 1 P.M. On the first Saturday of the month, there's also an Early Bird Walk at 8:30 A.M. Still, there's no better way to see the slough than from the seat of a kayak. Stop by the visitors center at the entrance to arrange a guided tour or contact the **Elkhorn Slough Foundation,** 1700 Elkhorn Rd. in Moss Landing, 831/728-2822 or 831/728-5939, www.elkhornslough.org. Arrange kayak tours through **Monterey Bay Kayaks,** 693 Del Monte Ave. in Monterey, 831/373-5357 or 800/649-5357, www.montereybaykayaks.com, or **Kayak Connection,** 831/724-5692, www.kayakconnection.com. For a guided tour aboard a 27-foot pontoon boat, contact **Elkhorn Slough Safari** in Moss Landing, 831/633-5555, www.elkhornslough.com.

Practicalities

A big plus in Moss Landing is the 1906-vintage **M Captain's Inn B&B,** 831/633-5550, www.captainsinn.com, once home to the Pacific Coast Steamship Company, now meticulously, creatively, nautically restored and expanded—from the cozy library and game area in the historic building to the classic "boat beds" in the newer boat house. A stay here offers style as well as a terrific location and good value. All rooms have private baths, antiques or creative furnishings, and refreshing décor; many have fireplaces and "romance showers" or two-person tubs. Boathouse rooms face the river, with large windows for wildlife-watching. The boat beds are the real deal, be they fishing boats or catamarans. The four rooms in the main building are $100–200, the six rooms in the boat house $150–250, big breakfasts and other goodies included. Go ahead. Sail away. Determined landlubbers, at last report "en route camping" for self-contained RVs was still possible at **Moss Landing State Beach** on Jetty Road, 831/649-2836, a beach area popular for picnics and bird-watching.

Time-honored people's eateries abound in Moss Landing, particularly near the harbor. Most serve chowders and seafood and/or ethnic specials. Quite good, right on the highway, is **The Whole Enchilada,** 831/633-3038, open for lunch and din-

ner daily and specializing in Mexican seafood entrées. (The "whole enchilada," by the way, is filet of red snapper wrapped in a corn tortilla and smothered in enchilada sauce and melted cheese.) The Enchilada's associated **Moss Landing Inn and Jazz Club** adjacent, 831/633-9990, is a bar featuring live jazz on Sunday 4:30–8:30 P.M. Hit **Haute Enchilada Art Cafe,** 7902-A Sandholdt Rd., 831/633-5843, for some folk art along with your food. Everyone's favorite for fish is **M Phil's Fresh Fish Market and Eatery** on Sandholdt, 831/633-2152, www.philsfishmarket.com. Monday and Thursday are bluegrass nights. (To get there from Moss Landing Road, take the first and only right-hand turn and cross the one-lane bridge; it's the wooden warehouse just past the research institute.) Stop for fresh fruit smoothies and generous deli sandwiches at the associated **Phil's Snack Shack & Deli,** 7921 Moss Landing Rd., 831/633-1775. Head for the shack in mid-May for the annual **Bluegrass on the Slough** festival.

Castroville

The heart of Castroville is Swiss-Italian, which hardly explains the artichokes all over the place. Calling itself "Artichoke Center of the World," Castroville grows 75 percent of California's artichokes—real artichokes, the globe variety—though that delicious leathery thistle grows throughout Santa Cruz and Monterey Counties. Come for the annual **Artichoke Festival** and parade every May; call 831/633-6545 or see www.artichoke-festival.org for information. It's some party, too, replete with artichokes fried, baked, mashed, boiled, and added as colorful ingredients to cookies and cakes. Nibble on french-fried artichokes with mayo dip and artichoke nut cake, sip artichoke soup, and sample steamed artichokes. Sometimes Hollywood gets in on the action: In 1947 Marilyn Monroe reigned as California's Artichoke Queen. If you miss the festival there are other artichoke options, including **Giant Artichoke Fruits and Vegetables** at 11241 Merritt St., 831/633-2778831/633-3501—wine and cheese shop adjacent—and the **Thistle Hut,** just off Hwy. 1, 2047 Watsonville Rd. (at Cooper-Molera Road), 831/633-4888. Best place around for barbecue is

FOREST OF NISENE MARKS STATE PARK

Forest of Nisene Marks is definitely a hiker's park. Named for the Danish immigrant who hiked here until the age of 96 and whose family donated the land for public use, Nisene Marks is an oasis of solitude. (This was also the epicenter of the 1989 earthquake that brought down much of Santa Cruz.) You'll have lots to see here but less to hear, little more than birdsong, rustling leaves, and babbling brooks. The park encompasses 10,000 acres of hefty second-growth redwoods on the steep southern range of the Santa Cruz Mountains, six creeks, lovely Maple Falls, alders, maples, and more rugged trails than anyone can hike in a day. Also here are an old mill site, abandoned trestles and railroad tracks, and logging cabins.

To get here from the coast, take the Aptos-Seacliff exit north from Hwy. 1 and turn right on Soquel Drive. At the first left after the stop sign, drive north on Aptos Creek Rd. and across the railroad tracks. (Bring water and food for day trips. No fires allowed.) The park is open daily 6 A.M.–sunset. Day use is $6. Dogs, on short leashes, are allowed only on fire roads. For more information and a trail map, contact: Forest of Nisene Marks State Park on Aptos Creek Road (at Soquel Drive) in Aptos, 831/763-7062 (recorded) or 831/763-7063 (campsite reservations), www.santacruzstateparks.org. Call to reserve the trailside campsites at least one week in advance. For $3 per person per night you get glorious solitude but not much else— a six-mile one-way hike, just six primitive sites to choose from, no water (BYO), no fires allowed, pit toilet only.

Castroville's **The Central Texan BBQ**, 10500 Merritt, 831/633-2285. The Italian **Ristorante La Scuola** is housed in Castroville's first schoolhouse, 10700 Merritt, 831/633-3200.

WATSONVILLE AND VICINITY

Watsonville, an agriculturally rich city of about 50,000, is the mushroom capital of the United States, though the town calls this lovely section of the Pajaro Valley the Strawberry Capital of the World and Apple City of the Ives. Farming got off to a brisk clod-busting start during the gold rush, when produce grown here was in great demand. Among the early settlers were Chinese, Germans, Yugoslavs, and immigrants from the Sandwich Islands and the Azores. None gained as much notoriety as Watsonville stage driver Charley Parkhurst, one of the roughest, toughest, most daring muleskinners in the state—a "man" later unveiled as a woman, the first to ever vote in California.

Watsonville made history still earlier. Nothing remains today to commemorate the site of the 1820s Casa Materna or "Mother House" of California's Vallejo clan, yet the **House of Glass**

once stood about 2.5 miles southeast of Watsonville near Hwy. 1. (The precise location was at the edge of the bluff 1,000 feet north of the intersection of Hillcrest and Salinas Roads.) General Mariano Guadalupe Vallejo was one of five sons and eight daughters born to his parents there, in a house with 20-inch-thick walls and hand-hewn redwood window frames and joists. It was called the House of Glass for its completely glassed-in second story veranda. Legend has it the veranda got its unique fishbowl design when Don Ignacio Vincente Ferrer Vallejo mistakenly received a shipment of 12 dozen windows instead of one dozen. It was from the Vallejo ranch that Jose Castro, Juan Bautista Alvarado, and their rebel troops launched their 1835 attack on Monterey to create the free state of Alta California. The victorious single shot (fired by a lawyer who consulted a book to figure out how to work the cannon) hit the governor's house, and he surrendered immediately.

Sights

Watsonville itself is mushrooming these days, with plans for a new, four-story downtown civic center and higher density downtown residential development saving space for mushrooms and other agricultural production. Other outposts of the new Watsonville include the **Green Valley Grill,** upstairs at 40 Penny Ln. (at Green Valley Road), 831/728-0644, open weekdays for lunch and Mon.–Sat. for dinner. It's all here—tortilla lime soup, tender green salads and local produce in many other guises, oakwood-grilled duck breast or prawns wrapped in pancetta, even Gizdich Ranch olallieberry pie for dessert. For the local *Country Crossroads* farm trails map and other visitor information, contact the **Pajaro Valley Chamber of Commerce,** 444 Main St. in Watsonville, 831/724-3900, www.pajarovalley-chamber.com. Or stop by Country Crossroads headquarters at the farm bureau office, 141 Monte Vista Ave., 831/724-1356. Get up to speed on local agricultural history at the **Agricultural History Project** at the Santa Cruz County Fairgrounds, 2601 E. Lake Ave., 831/724-5898. Museum exhibits and demonstrations are open to the public on Fri. and Sat. noon–4 P.M. An almost mandatory stop, from May through January, is **Gizdich Ranch,** 55 Peckham Rd., 831/722-1056, www.gizdich ranch.com, fabulous from late summer through fall for its fresh apples, homemade apple pies, and fresh-squeezed natural apple juices. Earlier in the season, this is a "Pik-Yor-Sef" berry farm, with raspberries, olallieberries, and strawberries (usually also available in pies, fritters, and pastries). Another best bet is **Emile Agaccio Farms,** 4 Casserly Rd., 831/728-2009, known for its you-pick raspberries and chesterberries (a blackberry variety). Also worth seeking in Watsonville are Mexican and Filipino eateries, many quite good, most inexpensive. Watsonville has its share of motels, too, in addition to camping at Pinto Lake (see below) and at the Santa Cruz KOA.

Beaches

At **Manresa State Beach,** 400 San Andreas Rd., 831/724-3750, stairways lead to the surf from the main parking lot and Sand Dollar Drive; there are restrooms and an outdoor shower. No camping here, but walk-in camping is available one mile south at Manresa Uplands Campground ($20). Rural San Andreas Road also takes you to **Sunset**

State Beach, 201 Sunset Beach Rd., 831/763-7062 or 831/763-7063, four miles west of Watsonville in the Pajaro Dunes (take Bus No. 54B from Santa Cruz). Sunset offers 3.5 miles of nice sandy beaches and tall dunes, with the historic Van Laanan farm as backdrop. Sunset also features a wooded campground with 90 campsites (tents and RVs, but way too many RVs and not much privacy), group campsites, and 60 picnic sites. After sunset the beach is open only to campers. Day use at both is $6, camping $20–35. For more on area state parks, see www.santa cruzstateparks.org and www.scparkfriends.org. To reserve family campsites at all state beaches and parks, contact ReserveAmerica, 800/444-7275, www.reserveamerica.com.

Parking for pretty **Palm Beach** near Pajaro Dunes—a great place to find sand dollars—is near the end of Beach Street. Also here are picnic facilities, a par course, and restrooms. **Zmudowski State Beach** is near where the Pajaro River reaches the sea. You'll find good hiking and surf fishing. The beach is rarely crowded. Next, near Moss Landing, are **Salinas River State Beach** on Potrero Road, 831/384-7695, and **Jetty State Beach.**

Recreation

Just a few miles northwest of Watsonville is tiny **Pinto Lake City Park,** 451 Green Valley Rd., 831/722-8129, www.pintolake.com, where you can go swimming, sailing, pedal-boating, sailboarding, fishing, or RV camping (28 sites with full hookups, $25, tent trailers OK).

The **Ellicott Slough National Wildlife Refuge,** a 180-acre ecological reserve of coastal uplands for the Santa Cruz long-toed salamander, is four miles west along San Andreas Road. To get there, turn west off Hwy. 1 at the Larkin Valley Road exit and continue west on San Andreas Road to the refuge, next to the Santa Cruz KOA. For information about the reserve, generally closed to the public, call 510/792-0222.

Events

The area also offers unusual diversions. The biggest event here is the annual **West Coast Fly In & Air Show** in May (Memorial Day weekend), when more than 50,000 people show up to appreciate hundreds of classic, antique, and home-built airplanes on the ground and in the air. Originally held over Memorial Day week-

end but now usually scheduled for early August is the annual **Monterey Bay Strawberry Festival,** www.mbsf.com. Come in mid-September for the **Santa Cruz County Fair.**

Monterey

In his novel by the same name, local boy John Steinbeck described Monterey's Cannery Row as "a poem, a stink, a grating noise, a quality of light, a tune, a habit, a nostalgia, a dream," and also as a corrugated collection of sardine canneries, restaurants, honky-tonks, whorehouses, and waterfront laboratories. The street, he said, groaned under the weight of "silver rivers of fish." People here liked his description so much that they eventually put it on a plaque and planted it in today's touristy Cannery Row, among the few Steinbeck-era buildings still standing.

Local promoters claim that the legendary writer would be proud of what the tourist dollar has wrought here, but this seems unlikely. When Steinbeck returned in 1961 from his self-imposed exile, he noted the clean beaches, "where once they festered with fish guts and flies. The canneries that once put up a sickening stench are gone, their places filled with restaurants, antique shops, and the like. They fish for tourists now, not pilchards, and that species they are not likely to wipe out."

An early port for California immigrants—California's first pier was built here—and now a bustling tourist mecca, Monterey (literally, "the King's Wood") is trying hard to hang onto its once-cloistered charm. The justifiably popular Monterey Bay Aquarium is often blamed for the hopeless summer traffic snarls, though tourism throughout the Monterey Peninsula is the actual culprit. *Creative States Quarterly* editor Raymond Mungo once described Monterey as a city "under siege," asking rhetorically: "How do you describe the difference a tornado makes in a small town, or the arrival of sudden prosperity in a sleepy backwater?" How indeed?

During peak summer months you can avoid feeling under siege yourself—and worrying that you're contributing unduly to the city's siege

state—by using Monterey's public WAVE trolleys whenever possible.

MONTEREY BAY AQUARIUM

The fish are back on Cannery Row, at least at the west end. Doc's Western Biological Laboratory and the canneries immortalized by Steinbeck may be long gone, but Monterey now has an aquarium that the bohemian biologist would love.

Just down the street from Doc's legendary marine lab, the Monterey Bay Aquarium on Cannery Row is a world-class cluster of fish tanks built into the converted Hovden Cannery. Luring 2.35 million visitors in 1984, its first year, Monterey's best attraction is the brainchild of marine biologist Nancy Packard and her sister, aquarium director Julie Packard. Much help came from Hewlett-Packard computer magnate David Packard and wife, Lucile, who supported this nonprofit, public-education endeavor with a $55 million donation to their daughters' cause. Not coincidentally, Packard also personally designed many of the unique technological features of the major exhibits here. Through the aquarium's foundation, the facility also conducts its own research and environmental education and wildlife rescue programs. The aquarium's trustees, for example, have allocated $10 million for a five-year unmanned underwater exploration and research project in the bay's Monterey Canyon.

The philosophy of the folks at the Monterey Bay Aquarium, most simply summarized as "endorsing human interaction" with the natural world, is everywhere apparent. From a multi-level view of kelp forests in perpetual motion to face-to-face encounters with sharks and wolf eels, from petting velvety bat rays and starfish in

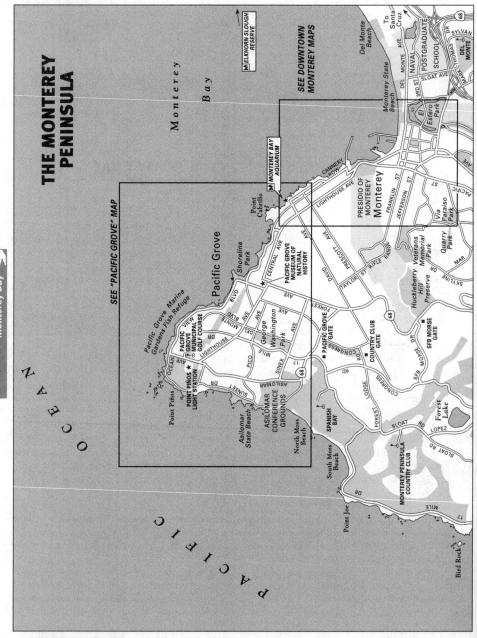

THE MONTEREY PENINSULA

SEE "PACIFIC GROVE" MAP

SEE DOWNTOWN
MONTEREY MAPS

M ELKHORN SLOUGH
RESERVE

To Santa-Cruz

68

POSTGRADUATE
SCHOOL

SYLVAN DR

THOMAS AVE

DEL MONTE

NAVAL

3RD ST

DEL MONTE AVE

SLOAT AVE

Del Monte
Beach

Monterey State
Beach

El Estero Park

Via Paraiso Park

Monterey Bay

M o n t e r e y   B a y

M MONTEREY BAY
AQUARIUM

CANNERY ROW

Point
Cabrillo

LIGHTHOUSE AVE

PRESIDIO OF
Monterey

FRANKLIN ST

JEFFERSON ST

PACIFIC ST

Quarry Park

MAR

SKYLINE DR

Pacific Grove

Shoreline Park

CENTRAL AVE

PACIFIC GROVE
MUSEUM OF
NATURAL HISTORY

PRESCOTT AVE

DAVID

TAYLOR ST

RIFLE RANGE

Huckleberry
Hill
Preserve

Veterans
Memorial
Park

Pacific Grove Marine
Gardens Fish Refuge

PACIFIC
GROVE
MUNICIPAL
GOLF COURSE

PACIFIC VIEW

DEL MONTE BLVD

LIGHTHOUSE

AVE

AVE

AVE

George
Washington
Park

FOREST

AVE

PACIFIC GROVE
GATE

68

COUNTRY CLUB
GATE

SFB MORSE
GATE

PICO

SINEX

17 MILE

ASILOMAR

CONGRESS

RD

SFB MORSE DR

Point Piños

POINT PIÑOS
LIGHT STATION

OCEAN

SUNSET DR

ASILOMAR
CONFERENCE
GROUNDS

69

SPANISH
BAY

LODGE RD

FOREST

CONGRESS

Forest
Lake

Asilomar
State Beach

North Moss
Beach

SLOAT RD

LOPEZ

SOUTH Moss
Beach

MONTEREY PENINSULA
COUNTRY CLUB

SLOAT RD

17 MILE DR

Point Joe

P A C I F I C

O C E A N

Bird Rock

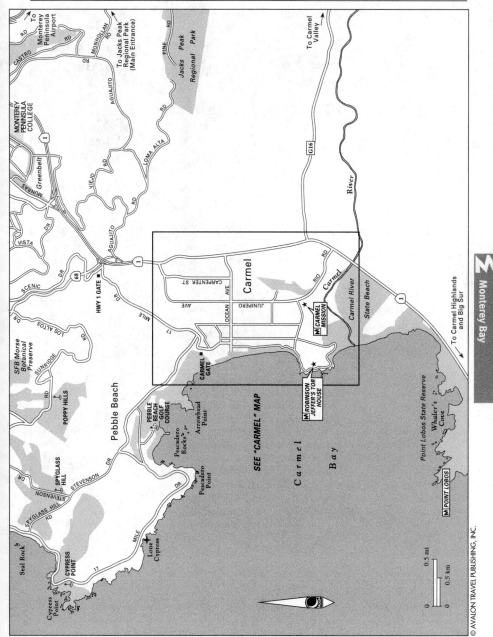

SEE "CARMEL" MAP

Monterey Bay

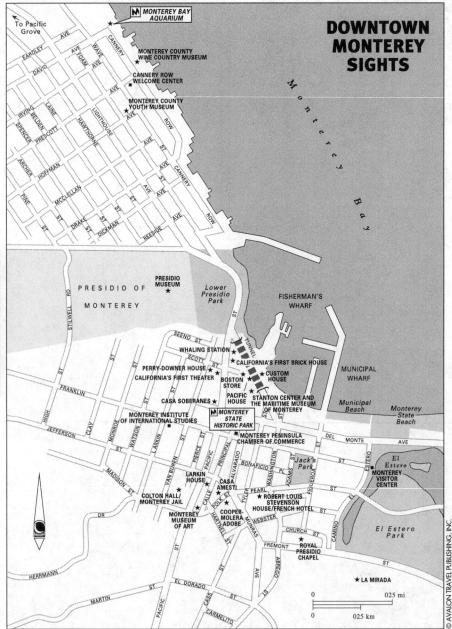

DOWNTOWN MONTEREY SIGHTS

To Pacific Grove

M MONTEREY BAY AQUARIUM

MONTEREY COUNTY WINE COUNTRY MUSEUM

CANNERY ROW WELCOME CENTER

MONTEREY COUNTY YOUTH MUSEUM

EARDLEY AVE
DAVID AVE
IRVING
SPENCER
BELDEN
LAINE
PRESCOTT
ARCHER
HOFFMAN
PINE
McCLELLAN
DRAKE
DICKMAN
WAVE AVE
FOAM AVE
HAWTHORNE
LIGHTHOUSE
CANNERY
AVE
ROW ST
CANNERY ROW
REESIDE
STILWELL RD

Monterey Bay

PRESIDIO OF MONTEREY

PRESIDIO MUSEUM

Lower Presidio Park

FISHERMAN'S WHARF

SEENO ST
WHALING STATION
SCOTT
PERRY-DOWNER HOUSE
CALIFORNIA'S FIRST THEATER
CASA SOBERANES
MONTEREY INSTITUTE OF INTERNATIONAL STUDIES

CALIFORNIA'S FIRST BRICK HOUSE
CUSTOM HOUSE
BOSTON STORE
PACIFIC HOUSE
STANTON CENTER AND THE MARITIME MUSEUM OF MONTEREY

M MONTEREY STATE HISTORIC PARK

TUNNEL

MUNICIPAL WHARF

Municipal Beach

Monterey State Beach

MONTEREY PENINSULA CHAMBER OF COMMERCE

FRANKLIN
JEFFERSON
HIGH
CLAY
MONROE
WATSON
LARKIN
PIERCE
PACIFIC
PRINCIPAL
ALVARADO
BONAFICIO
WASHINGTON
ADAMS
FIGUEROA
TYLER
DEL MONTE AVE
ESTERO
CAMINO
Jack's Park

El Estero

MONTEREY VISITOR CENTER

LARKIN HOUSE
CASA AMESTI
PEARL
COOPER-MOLERA ADOBE
VAN BUREN
CALLE
POLK
HARTNELL ST
MUNRAS
WEBSTER
MADISON ST
COLTON HALL/ MONTEREY JAIL
MONTEREY MUSEUM OF ART

ROBERT LOUIS STEVENSON HOUSE/FRENCH HOTEL

CHURCH ST
FREMONT
ROYAL PRESIDIO CHAPEL

El Estero Park

HERRMANN
MARTIN
PACIFIC
EL DORADO
CASS
CARMELITO
ABREGO
AVE

★ LA MIRADA

N MOON

0 _____ 025 mi
0 _____ 025 km

© AVALON TRAVEL PUBLISHING, INC.

Monterey Bay

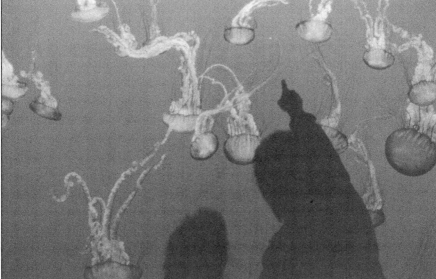

Sea nettles capture the fancy of visitors in the Outer Bay galleries at the Monterey Bay Aquarium.

"touch pools" to watching sea otters feed and frolic, here people can observe the native marine plants and wildlife of Monterey Bay up close and personal. More than 300,000 animals and plants representing 571 species—including fish, invertebrates, mammals, reptiles, birds, and plant life—can be seen here in environments closely approximating their natural communities. Volunteer guides, dressed in rust-colored jackets, are available throughout the aquarium and are only too happy to share their knowledge about the natural history of Monterey Bay.

The engineering feats shoring up the amazingly "natural" exhibits in the Monterey Aquarium are themselves impressive. Most remarkable are the aquatic displays, concrete tanks with unbreakable one-ton acrylic windows more than seven inches thick. The exhibits' "wave action" is simulated by a computer-controlled surge machine and hidden water jets. In the Nearshore Galleries, more than a half-million gallons of fresh seawater are pumped through the various aquarium tanks daily to keep these habitats healthy. During the day, six huge "organic" water filters screen out microorganisms that would otherwise cloud the water. At night, filtration shuts down and raw, unfiltered seawater flows through the exhibits—nourishing filter-feeders and also carrying in plant spores and animal larvae that settle and grow, just as they would in nature. The Outer Bay Galleries operate as a "semi-closed" system, with water from the main intake pipes heated to 68° F and recirculated through the exhibits. Wastes are removed by biological filters and ozone treatment, and a heat-recovery system recaptures energy from the water (cools it) before it is discharged into the bay.

In the event of an oil spill or other oceanic disaster, the aquarium's 16-inch intake pipes can be shut down on a moment's notice and the aquarium can operate as a "closed system" for up to two weeks.

Just in time for the aquarium's 20th anniversary in 2004 came the blockbuster **Sharks: Myth** and **Mystery** exhibit. In addition to a variety of other improvements, from the appealing new ticket lobby and glass-roofed atrium to the second-story gallery skywalk, more new exhibits have arrived—including the new giant Pacific octopus exhibit in the Ocean's Edge gallery—and just about all aquarium exhibits have had a celebratory spruce-up.

Just inside the aquarium's entrance, serving as an introduction to the **Nearshore Galleries,** is the 55,000-gallon, split-level **Sea Otter Tank.** These sleek aquatic clowns consume 25 percent of their body weight in seafood daily. If they're not eating or playing with toys, they're grooming themselves—and with 600,000 hairs per square inch on their pelts, it's easy to understand why otters were so prized by furriers (and hunted almost to extinction). To spot an occasional otter or two slipping into the aquarium over the seawall, or to watch for whales, head for the outdoor observation decks, which include telescopes for bay watching. The **Outdoor Tidepool** is surrounded by the aquarium itself on three sides, on the fourth by artificial rock. It is home to sea stars, anemones, small fish—and visiting sea otters and harbor seals that occasionally shimmy up the stairs for a better look at the people. Also here are telescopes for bay watching.

The Nearshore Galleries are being transformed into the **Ocean's Edge: Coastal Habitats of Monterey Bay,** scheduled to open in mid-2005, though many of the original features remain, presented in new confidurations. The three-story-tall **Giant Kelp Forest** exhibit, the aquarium's centerpiece and the first underwater forest ever successfully established as a display, offers a diver's-eye view of the undersea world. "Dazzling" is the only word for the nearby **Anchovies** exhibit, a cylindrical tank full of darting silver shapes demonstrating the "safety in numbers" group-mind philosophy. The 90-foot-long hourglass-shaped **Monterey Bay Habitats** display is a simulated underwater slice of sealife. Sharks roam the deep among colorful anemones and sea slugs, bat rays glide under the pier with the salmon and mackerel, accompanied by octopi and wolf eels. The craggy-shored, indoor-outdoor **Coastal Stream** exhibit has a steady rhythm all its own

and provides a small spawning ground for salmon and steelhead. In the huge **Marine Mammals Gallery,** you'll see models of a 43-foot-long barnacled gray whale and her calf, plus killer whales, dolphins, sea lions, and seals.

Unusual among the predominantly bay-related exhibits, but popular, is the live chambered nautilus in the **Octopus and Kin** exhibit. Also exciting here, in a spine-tingling way, is watching an octopus suction its way across the window. But to really get "in touch" with native underwater life, visit the **Bat Ray Petting Pool,** the **Touch Tidepool** of starfish and anemones, and the **Kelp Lab.** Visitors can stroll through the **Sandy Shore** outdoor aviary to observe shorebirds.

New exhibits are continually added to the Monterey Bay Aquarium. The stunning $57 million **Outer Bay Galleries** nearly doubled the aquarium's exhibit space when it opened in early 1996. Devoted to marine life "at the edge," where Monterey Bay meets the open ocean, the centerpiece exhibit is a million-gallon "indoor sea," housing a seven-foot sunfish, sharks, barracudas, stingrays, green sea turtles, and schooling bonito—all seen through the largest aquarium window yet built, an acrylic panel some 15 feet high, 54 feet wide, and 78,000 pounds. Quite visually arresting in the **Drifters Gallery** is the orange and deep-blue **Sea Nettles** jellyfish exhibit, where one might stand and watch the show—something like a giant, pulsing lava lamp—for hours. Equally mesmerizing, on the way into the Outer Bay, is the swirling, endlessly circling stream of silvery mackerel directly overhead. The best way to watch—you'll notice that young children, not yet socially self-conscious, figure this out immediately—is by lying flat on your back. The **Mysteries of the Deep** exhibit studies the often-bizarre creatures that inhabit the murky depths. Seldom seen in an aquarium environment, the deep-dwelling species in this exhibit include mushroom soft coral, the predatory tunicate, the spiny king crab, and many others—a total of 40 to 60 species at any one time. In addition, daily video programs present live broadcasts from a remote submersible vehicle exploring the depths of Monterey Bay.

Other fairly recent exhibits have included the **Splash Zone: Rock and Reef Homes** exhibit, designed particularly for families with small children, an interactive tour through two different shoreline habitats; **Saving Seahorses,** exploring the survival challenges of unique fish so popular in traditional Asian medicine; and **Mysteries of the Deep,** an exhibit of more than 40 species of animals collected from the depths of submarine Monterey Canyon just offshore. **Jellies: Living Art** was a blockbuster on the scale of the new sharks exhibit. Throughout the aquarium, also expect several rotating special exhibits each year. Anytime—or at least anytime from 7 A.M. to 7 P.M.—you can get online and see what's happening via the aquarium's Live Monterey Bay Cam. And don't miss the Shark Cam.

According to the *Zagat Survey's* 2004 **U.S. Family Travel Guide,** the Monterey Bay Aquarium is the number one aquarium in the United States, and the nation's number three family attraction. So do plan ahead. Advance tickets are highly recommended, especially in summer. Call 831/648-4937 or, from within California, 800/756-3737. You can also order tickets via Ticketweb. If you purchase tickets more than 10 days in advance, they can be mailed to you. Otherwise, you can order tickets online as late as 7 A.M. on the day you arrive (assuming they're available); at the aquarium, you won't need to wait in line. Simply present your email confirmation receipt at the will call/group entrance window and walk on in. You also can come on a just-show-up-and-take-your-chances basis—not advisable in summer.

The aquarium is open daily except Christmas, 10 A.M.–6 P.M. (from 9:30 A.M. in summer). At last report, admission was $19.95 for adults; $17.95 seniors, $15.95 youths age 13 to 17, students with college ID, and active-duty military; $8.95 for children ages 3 to 12 and disabled visitors; and free for tots under 3.

Free self-guided tour scripts with maps, also available in Spanish, French, German, and Japanese, are available at the aquarium's information desk, along with current "special event" details, including the exhibit feeding schedule. All aquarium facilities and exhibits are accessible to the disabled; an explanatory brochure is available at the information desk. At last report taped audio tours Had been suspended, though docent-guided aquarium tours and tours of the aquarium's research and operations facilities are available, for a fee. Guided tours for school groups are free, however. For group tour information and reservations, call 831/648-4860. The steadily expanding

Monterey Bay

SEAFOOD WATCH

Much of the work done by the Monterey Bay Aquarium is not necessarily visible to visitors. Since the mission of the aquarium is to "inspire conservation of the oceans," public education and scientific research are high priorities.

Particularly useful for seafood fans, and accessible via the aquarium's website, www.mbayaq.org, is its *Seafood Watch—A Guide for Consumers,* a regularly updated listing designed to help us all make enlightened choices about the fish and seafood we eat. On the aquarium's "avoid" list at last report, for example, were bluefin tuna from the Atlantic and the Pacific; Chilean seabass; Atlantic cod; lingcod; orange roughy; Pacific snapper, red snapper, and other rockfish; all sharks; all swordfish; all farmed salmon; and all imported shrimp. Consumer guidance in support of sustainable fisheries worldwide is available as a wallet-sized card, which can easily beprinted from the website.

Specific research initiatives sponsored by the Monterey Bay Aquarium include the Sea Otter Research and Conservation Program (SORAC) and the Tuna Research and Conservation Center (TRCC), the latter in conjunction with Stanford University's Hopkins Marine Station. The Monterey Bay Aquarium Research Institute (MBARI) at Moss Landing initiates dozens of bay-related projects each year and is also a full research partner in the Monterey Bay National Marine Sanctuary's Research Program. More information on all of these is available via the website.

Aquarium Adventures program offers behind-the-scenes fun like scuba for kids and feeding tours as well as educational kayaking and sailing trips on Monterey Bay with museum naturalists. In summer, two-hour guided **Fishing for History Walking Tours** are offered in conjunction with the Maritime Museum of Monterey.

The aquarium's restaurant and gift/bookstores are worthwhile. The **Portola Café and Restaurant** has very good food and an oyster bar—the very idea surely a shock to the aquarium's permanent residents—and is fine for a glass of wine at sunset (open 10 A.M.–5 P.M.). Along with good books, educational toys, and nature art, the aquarium gift shops have some touristy bric-a-brac and forgettable edibles like chocolate sardines.

For additional information, contact Monterey Bay Aquarium, 886 Cannery Row, in Monterey, 831/648-4800 or 831/648-4888 (24-hour recorded information). For recorded information in Spanish, call 800/555-3656. Or visit the "E-Quarium" anytime for virtual tours and information, www.mbayaq.org. For more information about the bay, the **Monterey Bay National Marine Sanctuary** headquarters and information center is near the aquarium at 299 Foam St. (at D St.), 831/647-4201, www.mbnms.nos.noaa.gov.

Avoid the worst of the human crush and come in the off-season (weekdays if at all possible). If you do come in summer, avoid the traffic jams by riding Monterey's WAVE trolleys, which operate from late May into September.

CANNERY ROW

Today the strip is reminiscent of Steinbeck's Cannery Row only when you consider how tourists are packed in here come summertime: like sardines.

Of all the places the Nobel Prize–winning author immortalized, only "Doc's" marine lab at 800 Cannery Row still stands unchanged—a humble brown shack almost as unassuming as it was in 1948, the year marine biologist Ed Ricketts met his end quite suddenly, his car smashed by the Del Monte Express train just a few blocks away. Today the lab is owned and

preserved as a historic site by the city and is open for guided public tours from time to time.

Wing Chong Market, Steinbecked as "Lee Chong's Heavenly Flower Grocery," is across the street at 835 Cannery Row and now holds a variety of shops. The fictional "La Ida Cafe" cathouse still survives, too, in actuality the most famous saloon on the Monterey Peninsula, **Kalisa's**, at 851 Cannery Row, 831/644-9316. Billed as "A Cosmopolitan Gourmet Place," Kalisa's, since the 1950s, has really been an eclectic people's eatery. Steinbeck personally preferred the beer milkshake.

Nowadays along Cannery Row, food and wine are becoming attractions in their own right. The new, 10,000-square-foot **Culinary Center of Monterey,** 625 Cannery Row, Ste. 200, 831/333-2133, www.culinarycenterofmonterey.com, bills itself as a "Fantasy Land for Foodies." Here food lovers will find a complete food and wine center offering classes in just about everything—from classes for kids and cooking fundamentals to the latest trends, from Low Carb Recipes, Artisan Breads, Chocolate Desserts, and Cooking with Beer to Heart Healthy Cuisine and Sushi Party. The latter might be particularly inspiring after a tour through the Monterey Bay Aquarium. (Or maybe not.) You can also dine here, at Mary's Restaurant. Gourmet takeout is also available, the choices including an in-house bakery, appetizer bar (including local wines and microbrews), and cheese market. Inside the old Monterey Canning Company cannery, 700 Cannery Row, wine enthusiasts can enjoy **A Taste of Monterey,** 831/646-5446, www.tastemonterey.com, which offers tastings of regional wines as well as local produce (there's another located in downtown Salinas); **Bargetto Winery's** tasting room downstairs, 831/373-4053, www.bargetto.com, or **Baywood Cellars** across from the Monterey Plaza Hotel, 831/645-9035, www.baywood-cellars.com.

Wine-tasting or no, adults might escort the kids to the nearby **Monterey County Youth Museum** (M.Y. Museum), 601 Wave St., 831/649-6444 or 831/649-6446, www.mymuseum.org, a hands-on adventure full of interactive exhibits on science, art, and more. The mu-

ABOUT DOC RICKETTS

Marine biologist **Edward F. Ricketts** (Steinbeck's character "Doc") was, according to Richard Astro, the writer's "closest friend and his collaborator on *Sea of Cortez*—his most important work of nonfiction, a volume which contains the core of Steinbeck's worldview, his philosophy of life, and the essence of a relationship between a novelists and a scientist. . . . " Much of the novelist's success, he says, is due to Ricketts's influence on Steinbeck's thinking.

According to Steinbeck himself: "He was a great teacher and a great lecher—an immortal who loved women. . . . He was gentle but capable of ferocity, small and slight but strong as an ox, loyal and yet untrustworthy, generous but gave little and received much. His thinking was as paradoxical as his life. He thought in mystical terms and hated and mistrusted mysticism."

To explore the world according to both Steinbeck and Ricketts, pick up a copy of *The Log from the* **Sea of Cortez**, published in a paperback edition by Penguin Books.

seum is open Mon.–Sat. 10 A.M.–5 P.M. (closed Wednesday) and Sunday noon–5 P.M. Admission is $5.50 (under 2 free). Older kids probably won't let you dodge the **Edgewater Packing Company Family Fun Center,** 640 Wave St., 831/647-1769, full of high-tech and classic amusements—from the NASCAR simulator, virtual-reality batting cage, and Dance Dance Revolution Extreme video game to air hockey and pool. Just empty out those pockets and play along.

For more information about Cannery Row, or to seriously trace Steinbeck's steps through the local landscape, check in at the Cannery Row Foundation's **Cannery Row Welcome Center** in the green railroad car at 65 Prescott Ave., 831/372-8512, www.canneryrow.org. Guided tours of Cannery Row can also be arranged there. The free and widely available *Official Cannery Row Visitors Guide* is well done, historically, and quite helpful. For other information, including shopping and dining options, see www.canneryrow.com.

FISHERMAN'S WHARF

Tacky and tawdry, built up and beat up, Fisherman's Wharf is no longer a working wharf by any account. Still, a randy ramshackle charm more honest than Cannery Row surrounds this 1846 pier, full of cheap shops, food stalls, decent restaurants, and stand-up bars indiscriminately frosted with gull guano and putrid fish scraps (the latter presumably leftovers from the 50-cent bags tourists buy to feed the sea lions). Built of stone by enslaved natives, convicts, and military deserters when Monterey was Alta California's capital, Fisherman's Wharf was originally a pier for cargo schooners. Later used by whalers and Italian American fishing crews to unload their catches, the wharf today is bright and bustling, full of eateries and eaters. Come early in the morning to beat the crowds, then launch yourself on a summer sightseeing tour of Monterey Bay or a winter whale-watching cruise.

MARITIME MUSEUM OF MONTEREY

A good place to start any historic exploration is the colossal Stanton Center at 5 Custom House Plaza. Inside you'll find the Monterey History and Art Association's impressive Maritime Museum of Monterey, 831/372-2608, www.montereyhistory.org. The lobby **theater** screens a 17-minute state park-produced film about area history—a good way to quickly grasp the area's cultural context. The museum itself is an ever-expanding local maritime artifact collection—compasses, bells, ship models, the original Fresnel lens from the Point Sur lighthouse, and much more—as well as the association's maritime research library, an acclaimed ship photography collection, and a scrimshaw collection. The museum's permanent exhibits, many interactive, cover local maritime history, from the first explorers and cannery days to the present. Special exhibits in 2004 included A Tale of Two Adobes, curated in conjunction with the Santa Cruz Museum of Art and History.

The museum is open daily 10 A.M.–5 P.M., closed Thanksgiving, Christmas, and New Year's

Day. Admission is $8 adults, $5 seniors and youth, free for children under 12. Guided group tours are available by reservation. The Monterey History and Art Association also preserves for posterity a number of significant homes, additional outposts of local history. For more information, see the website.

MONTEREY STATE HISTORIC PARK

Monterey State Historic Park, with headquarters at 20 Custom House Plaza, 831/649-7118, www.parks.ca.gov, protects and preserves some fine historic adobes, most of which were surrounded at one time by enclosed gardens and walls draped with bougainvillea vines. Definitely worth seeing are the Cooper-Molera, Stevenson, and Larkin homes, as well as Casa Soberanes. If you have time, see them all.

Most of the park's homes and museums are open 10 A.M.–3 P.M.—though not all buildings are open on the same days—and closed Christmas, Thanksgiving, and New Year's Day. Admission to all buildings open to visitors is free. Also free are guided tours of particular homes (see below), as are general guided walking tours. Walking tours of Old Monterey begin at the Pacific House Museum and are offered on Tuesday, Wednesday, and Friday as well as "holiday Mondays" at 10:30 A.M.; tours last about 45 minutes. Wear comfortable walking shoes. Schedules for all tours can change, for various reasons, so be sure to call to verify current tour times on the day you plan to tour the park. Historic garden tours are offered for groups only, and are scheduled well in advance; call 831/649-7109 for current fee information (usually $8–10 per person) and to schedule garden tour appointments. To poke around on your own, pick up the free self-guided walking tour map before setting out. Available at most of the buildings and elsewhere around town, the brochure details the park's adobes as well as dozens of other historic sights near the bay and downtown. Also stop by the Stanton Center (see above) for the short introductory Monterey history film.

Custom House and Pacific House Museums

On July 7, 1846, Commodore John Drake Sloat raised the Stars and Stripes here at Alvarado and Waterfront Streets, commemorating California's passage into American rule. The Custom House Building is the oldest government building on the West Coast—and quite multinational, since it has flown at one time or another the flags of Spain, Mexico, and the United States. Until 1867, customs duties from foreign ships were collected here. Stop by to inspect typical 19th-century cargo.

Once a hotel, then a military supply depot, the building at Scott and Calle Principal was called Pacific House when it housed a public tavern in 1850. Later came law offices, a newspaper, a ballroom for "dashaway" temperance dances, and various small shops. Today the recently renovated Pacific House includes an excellent museum of Native American artifacts (with special attention given to the Ohlone people) upstairs and interactive historical exhibits covering the city's Spanish whaling industry, pioneer/logging periods, California statehood, and more. The Pacific House museum is wheelchair accessible, with Braille interpretive materials and video and audio recordings available. The museum's Memory Garden connects, via wheelchair accessible gate and pathway, to the city's Sensory Garden.

Both museums are open 10 A.M.–3 P.M. Custom House is closed Tuesday and Wednesday. Pacific House is closed Monday and Thursday.

Larkin House and Others

Built of adobe and wood in 1835 by Yankee merchant Thomas Oliver Larkin, later the only U.S. consul in the territory during Mexican rule, this home at Jefferson and Calle Principal became the American consulate, then later military headquarters for Kearny, Mason, and Sherman. A fine pink Monterey adobe and the model for the local Colonial style, Larkin House is furnished with more than $6 million in antiques and period furnishings. Larkin House is open daily. For 45-minute guided tours, meet the guide here on Wednesday, Saturday, or Sunday at 2 P.M.

The tiny adobe home and headquarters of William Tecumseh Sherman is next door; it's now a museum focusing on both Larkin and Sherman. Around the corner at 540 Calle Principal, another Larkin building, the **House of the Four Winds,** is a small adobe built in the 1830s and named for its weathervane. The **Gutierrez Adobe,** a typical middle-class Monterey "double adobe" home at 580 and 590 Calle Principal, was built in 1841 and later donated to the state by the Monterey Foundation.

Cooper-Molera Adobe
The *casa grande* (big house) at 508 Munras Avenue, a long, two-story, Monterey Colonial adobe, was finished in pinkish plaster when constructed in 1829 by Captain John Bautista Rogers Cooper for his young bride, Encarnación (of California's influential Vallejo clan). The 2.5-acre complex, which includes a neighboring home, two barns, gardens, farm animals, and visitor center, has been restored to its 19th-century authenticity. Downstairs rooms in all buildings are wheelchair accessible, as are restrooms and the Victorian garden picnic area. Stop by the **Cooper Store** here, run by the nonprofit Old Monterey Preservation Society, to sample the wares—unique books, antique reproductions, and other specialty items representing the mid-1800s. The Cooper-Molera Adobe is open daily. For 45-minute guided tours, meet the guide here on Wednesday, Friday, Saturday, or Sunday at 1 P.M.

Robert Louis Stevenson House/French Hotel
Stevenson House was scheduled to open in 2005, following renovation, but call for current details. The sickly Scottish storyteller and poet lived here at the French Hotel adobe boardinghouse at 530 Houston Street for several months in 1879 while courting his American love (and later wife) Fanny Osbourne. In a sunny upstairs room is the small portable desk at which he reputedly wrote *Treasure Island.* While in Monterey, Stevenson collected *Treasure* material on his convalescing coast walks and worked on "Amateur Immigrant," "The Old Pacific," "Capital," and "Vendetta of

the West." He also worked as a reporter for the local newspaper—a job engineered by his friends, who, in order to keep the flat-broke Stevenson going, secretly paid the paper $2 a week to cover his wages. The downstairs is stuffed with period furniture. Several upstairs rooms are dedicated to Stevenson's memorabilia, paintings, and first editions. Local rumor has it that a 19th-century ghost—Stevenson's spirit, according to a previous caretaker—lives upstairs in the children's room.

Casa Soberanes
Also known as the House of the Blue Gate, this is an 1830 Mediterranean-style adobe with a tile roof and cantilevered balcony, hidden by thick hedges at 336 Pacific St. (at Del Monte Avenue). Home to the Soberanes family from 1860 to 1922, it was later donated to the state. Take the tour—the furnishings here are an intriguing combination of Mexican folk art and period pieces from China and New England—or just stop to appreciate the garden and its whalebone-and-abalone-bordered flowerbeds, some encircled by century-old wine bottles buried bottoms up. Tours of Casa Soberanes, lasting about 30 minutes, are offered Tuesday at 1 P.M. and Friday at 11:30 A.M.

California's First Theater
First a sailors' saloon and lodging house, this small 1844 weathered wood and adobe building at Scott and Pacific was built by the English sailor Jack Swan. It was commandeered by soldiers in 1848 for a makeshift theater, and it later—with a lookout station added to the roof—became a whaling station. Wander through the place and take a trip into the bawdy past, complete with the requisite painting of a reclining nude over the bar, brass bar rail and cuspidor, oil lamps, ancient booze bottles, and old theatrical props and paraphernalia. A modern postscript is the garden out back. Now being restored, the building is sometimes open for tours. Call the park for current details.

Boston Store
Built by Thomas Larkin at the corner of Scott and Olivier as part of his business empire, this

two-story chalk and adobe building once known as Casa del Oro (House of Gold) served a number of purposes. At one time or another it was a barracks for American troops, a general store (Joseph Boston & Co.), a saloon, and a private residence. Rumor has it that this "house of gold" was also once a mint or, when it functioned as a saloon, that it accepted gold dust in payment for drinks—thus the name. Since the store boasted Monterey's first safe (still here), more likely is that during the California gold rush miners stored their wealth here. These days it's the Boston Store once more, operated by the nonprofit Historic Garden League and themed as if in the 1850s. Antiques and reproductions, including handcrafted Russian toys and games, are on sale here. The garden league also operates the **Picket Fence** shop. For more information, call 831/649-3364.

Whaling Station

The old two-story adobe Whaling Station at 391 Decatur Street near the Custom House, now maintained and operated by the Junior League of Monterey County, was a flophouse for Portuguese whalers in the 1850s. Tours are sometimes available (call the main state park number for information) and include access to the walled garden. The junior league also makes the house and gardens available for weddings and other special events; call 831/375-5356 for details. Whale lovers, walk softly—the sidewalk in front of the house is made of whalebone, once a common sight in the U.S. and now quite rare.

Historic Homes

This building nearby at 351 Decatur was started by Gallant Duncan Dickenson in 1847, built with bricks fashioned and fired in Monterey. The builder left for the goldfields before the house was finished, so the home—the first brick house in California—and 60,000 bricks were auctioned off by the sheriff in 1851 for just over $1,000. Open daily.

Notable historic Monterey homes now preserved for posterity and ongoing public education include a number of homes in the care of the Monterey History & Art Association, 831/372-2608, www.montereyhistory.org. The showcase **Casa Serrano** at 412 Pacific St. was the home of Don Florencio Serrano, a Spaniard who became Monterey's second alcade (mayor) under American rule. Open for docent-led tours 2–4 P.M. on weekends, Casa Serrano features intact 20-inch-thick adobe walls and redwood beams, ceilings, and shingled roofs—and inside, a wealth of early California art and antiques. The 1860 **Perry-Downer Costume House**, 201 Van Buren St., 831/375-9182, is another of Monterey's great historic homes, a Victorian woodframe house

MONTEREY'S DISTINCTIVE ARCHITECTURE

Monterey State Historic Park's **Larkin House,** a two-story redwood frame with low shingled roof, adobe walls, and wooden balconies skirting the second floor, and the **Cooper-Molera Adobe** are both good examples of the "Monterey colonial" architectural style—a marriage of Yankee woodwork and Mexican adobe—that evolved here. Most traditional Monterey adobes have south-facing patios to absorb sun in winter and a northern veranda to catch cool summer breezes. On the first floor were the kitchen, storerooms, dining room, living room, and sometimes even a ballroom. The bedrooms on the second floor were entered from outside stairways, a tradition subsequently abandoned.

Also distinctive in Monterey are the "swept gardens"—dirt courtyards surrounded by colorful flowers under pine canopies—which were an adaptation to the originally barren home sites.

That so many fine adobes remain in Monterey today is mostly due to a long local run of genteel poverty; until recently, few developers with grandiose plans came knocking on the door. For an even better look at traditional local adobes and their gardens, come to the Monterey **Historic Adobe** and **Historic Garden Tours** in late April and/or early May, when Monterey State Historic Park and also many private adobes and gardens are open for special public tours.

built by whaling captain Manuel Perry and his wife Mary de Mello Silva of Boston. The house, originally one story, has been significantly remodeled over the years. The two-story house now shows changing fashion exhibits, such as Crazy for Paisley. At last report Perry House was open Tuesday 10 A.M.–3 P.M. and Sarturday 1–4 P.M. Adjacent to the Perry House, the restored **Carriage House,** complete with stained glass ceiling, is available for private events. Californiacs, the **Mayo Hayes O'Donnell Library** at 155 Van Buren St. an impressive historical library emphasizing Monterey and early California history, was originally the 1876 Saint James Episcopal Church, built at Franklin and High Streets and later moved here for salvation from the wrecking ball of progress. The nearby 1860s **Doud House,** 177 Van Buren, was built by Francis Doud, an Irish-born American soldier who helped arrange California's Constitutional Convention in Monterey. The association's small two-story adobe **Frémont House,** was long been thought to be headquarters for John C. Frémont, when he and his "heavily armed topographers"

came to Monterey in July of 1846. Now it's believed that Frémont and his wife Jessie stayed here in 1849, when he served as a delegate to the new state's constitutional convention.

Colton Hall

The Reverend Walter Colton, Monterey's first American alcalde, or local magistrate, built this impressive, pillared "Carmel Stone" structure at 351 Pacific (between Madison and Jefferson), as a schoolhouse and public hall. Colton and Robert Semple published the first American newspaper in California here, cranking up the presses on August 15, 1846. California's constitutional convention took place here during September and October of 1849, and the state constitution was drafted upstairs in Colton Hall. Now a city museum, Colton Hall is open daily 10 A.M.–noon and 1–5 P.M. Closed Thanksgiving, Christmas, and New Year's Day. For more information, call 831/646-5640 or see www.monterey.org/museum.

Next door is the 1854 **Monterey jail** (entrance on Dutra Street), a dreary, slot-windowed prison once home to gentleman-bandit Tiburcio

Colton Hall

Vasquez and killer Anastacio Garcia, who "went to God on a rope" pulled by his buddies.

Monterey Museum of Art

The fine Monterey Museum of Art at the Civic Center, across the street from Colton Hall at 559 Pacific, 831/372-5477, www.montereyart.org, offers an excellent collection of California and regional art—and Western art, including bronze cowboy-and-horse statues by Charles M. Russell. The Fine Arts collection includes folk art, high-concept graphics, photography, paintings, sculpture, and other contemporary art in changing exhibits. Open Wed.–Sat. 11 A.M.–5 P.M., Sun. 1–4 P.M., closed holidays. Admission $5, which also gets you into La Mirada.

An impressive Monterey-style adobe, the amazing **La Mirada,** the onetime Castro Adobe and Frank Work Estate at 720 Via Mirada, 831/372-5477, is now home to the museum's Asian art and artifacts collection. The home itself is exquisite, located in one of Monterey's oldest neighborhoods. The original adobe portion was the residence of Jose Castro, one of the most prominent citizens in California during the Mexican period. Purchased in 1919 by Gouverneur Morris—author/playwright and descendant of the same-named Revolutionary War figure—the adobe was restored and expanded, with the addition of a two-story wing and huge drawing room, to host artists and Hollywood stars. The Dart Wing, added in 1993, was designed by architect Charles Moore.

These days, the 2.5-acre estate overlooking El Estero still reflects the sensibilities of bygone eras. The house itself is furnished in antiques and early California art, and the gardens are perhaps even more elegant, at least in season, with a walled rose garden (old and new varieties), traditional herb garden (medicinal, culinary, fragrant, and "beautifying"), and a rhododendron garden with more than 300 camellias, azaleas, rhododendrons, and other flowering perennials and trees. Changing exhibits are displayed in four contemporary galleries that complement the original estate. La Mirada is open Wed.–Sat. 11 A.M.–5 P.M., Sun. 1–4 P.M. Admission is $5, which also gets you into the civic center museum (see above). Come 1:30–3:30 P.M. on the first Sunday of each month for **First Sunday at La Mirada,** offering light refreshments (wine available) and free admission to the gardens and art galleries.

Monterey Institute of International Studies

This prestigious, private, and nonprofit graduate-level college, headquartered at 425 Van Buren, 831/647-4100, www.miis.edu, specializes in foreign-language instruction. Students here prepare for careers in international business and government, and in language translation and interpretation. Fascinating and unique is the school's 200-seat auditorium, set up for simultaneous translations of up to four languages. Visitors are welcome Mon.–Fri. 8:30 A.M.–5 P.M., and most of the institute's programs—including guest lectures—are open to the public.

Presidio of Monterey

One of the nation's oldest military posts, the Presidio of Monterey is the physical focal point of most early local history. The original complex, now gone, was founded by Portolá in 1770 to protect the Spanish mission (later moved Carmel) and was located in the area defined these days by Webster, Fremont, Abrego, and El Estero Streets. History buffs, head for 26-acre **Lower Presidio Historic Park** and note the commemorative monuments to Portolá, Junípero Serra, Vizcaíno, and Commodore Sloat, plus late-in-the-game acknowledgement of native peoples. (When Lighthouse Avenue was widened through here, most of what remained of a 2,000-year-old Rumsen village was destroyed, leaving only a ceremonial rain rock, a rock mortar for grinding acorns, and an ancient burial ground marked by a tall wooden cross.) The 31-foot-tall granite Sloat Monument sits at the base of the Civil War-era Fort Mervine, a diamond-shaped fortress. The fort's forward ravelin is all that remains. Also here: incredible panoramic views of Monterey Bay.

The new **Presidio Museum,** at the base of the bluff beneath the Sloat Monument in Building 113, Cpl. Ewing Rd. (just off Artillery Street),

PITCHING THE MONTEREY PINE

Eons ago, Monterey pines blanketed much of California's coastline. Today, only a few native stands remain in California—and within a decade at least 80 percent of these trees will be gone, done in by a fungus. That fungus, known as **pine pitch canker,** was first discovered in Alameda and Santa Cruz Counties in the mid-1980s. Since then, it has spread throughout California, via contaminated lumber and firewood, Christmas trees, infected seedlings, pruning tools, insects, birds, and wind; there is no known cure. Afflicted trees first turn brown at the tips of their branches, then erupt in pitchy spots; within the tree, water, and nutrients are choked off. The open infections attract bark beetles, which bore into tree trunks and lay eggs, an invasion that hastens tree death. Usually within four years, an infected tree is completely brown and lifeless. The United Nations has declared the Monterey pine an endangered species.

Enjoy the majestic groves of Monterey pine near Monterey while they still stand, endangered as they are both by disease and further development plans. Also take care to avoid being an unwitting "carrier" for the disease; don't cart home any forest products as souvenirs. Pine pitch canker has been found in at least eight other species, including the Ponderosa pine, sugar pine, and Douglas fir, though it appears the Monterey pine is most susceptible. The California Department of Forestry is justifiably concerned that the disease will soon spread—or is already spreading—into the Sierra Nevada and California's far northern mountains.

831/646-3456, www.monterey.org/museum /pom, was once a tack house. So it seems appropriate that it's now filled with cavalry artifacts, uniforms, pistols, cannons, photos, posters, and dioramas about the U.S. Cavalry and local history, beginning with Native Americans and the arrival of the Spanish and continuing into Monterey's Mexican then American periods. The museum is open Monday 10 A.M.–1 P.M., Thurs.–Sat. 10 A.M.–4 P.M., and Sunday 1–4 P.M. Call for driving directions. To reach the museum it's not necessary to pass through a security checkpoint.

The Presidio's main gate at Pacific and Artillery Streets leads to the **Defense Language Institute Foreign Language Center,** 831/242-5000, http://pom-www.army.mil, top drawer for foreign language education.

Royal Presidio Chapel

Originally established as a mission by Father Junípero Serra in June 1770, this building at 550 Church Street near Figueroa became the Royal Presidio Chapel of San Carlos Borromeo when the mission was relocated to Carmel. A national historic landmark, the chapel was originally wood but rebuilt with stone and adobe, this version 1791–95, and after secularization in 1835 it became the San Carlos Cathedral, a parish church. The cathedral's interior walls are decorated with Native American and Mexican folk art. Above, the upper gable facade is the first European art made in California, a chalk-carved Virgin of Guadalupe tucked into a shell niche. To get here, turn onto Church Street just after Camino El Estero ends at Fremont—a district once known as Washerwoman's Gulch.

SAND DUNE CITIES

The sand-dune city of **Marina** was once the service center supporting Fort Ord. The U.S. Army base is now closed, replaced by the fledgling campus of California State University at Monterey Bay. So Marina, the peninsula's most recently incorporated city (1975), is also being transformed. Marina now boasts a new municipal airport, sports arena, and state beach popular for hang-gliding and surfing. On the ground, explore the nearby dunes; they're serene in a simple, stark way, with fragile shrubs and wildflowers. Some are quite rare, so don't pick. The new **Fort Ord Dunes State Park,** 831/649-2836, once part of Fort Ord, features a four-mile stretch of beachfront, though not yet open to the public at last report.

The University of California at Santa Cruz is beginning to have a notable local presence, too, starting with UCSC's **Monterey Bay Education,**

Monterey Bay

SUCH A DEAL: SEASIDE AND MARINA

The secret may no longer be much of a secret, but just in case: People who live on the Monterey Peninsula know that prices for both food and lodging can be considerably lower in the "sand dune cities" of Seaside and Marina.

Ethnic eateries abound, most of them quite good. In Seaside, the wonderful **Fishwife Seafood Cafe,** 789 Trinity (at Fremont), 831/394-2027, is everyone's favorite for seafood. The Fishwife offers quick and interesting seafood, pastas, and other California cuisine standards with a Caribbean accent, fresh Salinas Valley produce, and house-made desserts. (There's another Fishwife in Pacific Grove near Asilomar.) For more exceptional seafood, consider the Salvadoran **El Migueleño,** also in Seaside at 1066 Broadway, 831/899-2199. The house specialty, Playa Azul, combines six different kinds of seafood with ranchera sauce, white wine, and mushrooms, served with white rice and beans. Yum. Seaside's **La Tortuga Torteria** at 1257 Fremont, 831/394-8320, is known for intriguing *tortas* like the *nopalitos con huevo,* an egg sandwiched between cactus paddles. But do try at least one of the *licuados,* milk, sugar, and cinnamon blended with fruit—banana, papaya, mango, peach, strawberry, or cantaloupe. Yum again. But there are more nationalities to sample in Seaside. For Chinese food, there's the excellent **Chef Lee's Mandarin House,** 2031 N. Fremont St., 831/375-9551. Or head for University Plaza at 1760 N. Fremont, not all that aesthetic but something of a haven for ethnic eateries. Best bets include **Fuji Japanese Restaurant and Sushi Bar,** 831/899-9988, with good lunch specials; **Orient Restaurant,** 831/394-2223, for Chinese and Vietnamese specialties, notably an abundance of soup and noodle dishes; and **Barn Thai,** 831/394-2996, where a great lunch goes for about $5.

Science & Technology Center (MBEST) near the airport, just off Reservation Road east of the city at 3180 Imjin Rd., 831/582-1020, www.ucmbest.org, a 500-acre research and development technology park. Off to a slow start, given the doldrums even in Silicon Valley these days, the center offers extension classes, showcases various community collaborations, and supports "technology transfer"—such as the onsite **Swords to Plowshares** program, developed in conjunction with UCSC's Center for Agroecology and Sustainable Food Systems, in which Dynasty Farms is cultivating a large-scale organic farm on former military lands. Artistic highlights include the **Monterey Sculpture Center,** 711 Neeson Rd., 831/384-2100, a bronze sculpture foundry that offers the Sculpture Habitat at Marina, a collection of original sculptures by both local and world-renowned artists scattered throughout the grasslands, live oaks, and chaparral shrubs. Handicapped accessible.

Likewise locals laud the new **California State University Monterey** campus—the school's mascot is the sea otter—which has to date taken over some 2,000 acres at Fort Ord (of the 13,065 set aside for it) and is expected to grow to a student population of 13,000 to 15,000 by 2015. The emphasis at California's 21st state university campus is fairly unconventional. The focus here is on mastering subjects, rather than simply amassing course credits. Students are expected to become fluent in a second language as well as fully computer literate and to engage in community service work, along with mastering more than a dozen other essential skills. For information about and reservations (required) for 45-minute guided tours of campus, usually offered Mon.–Fri. at 10 A.M. and 2 P.M. and Saturday at 10 A.M., call 831/582-3518 at least two weeks in advance. For other information, see www.csumb.edu. Also worth exploring are some 50 miles of trails open to the public—now known as **Fort Ord Public Lands.** The 16,000 acres, administered by the U.S. Bureau of Land Management, are just about the last truly wild areas remaining on the Monterey Peninsula. Two fishable lakes and picnic areas are also available. As fun as it is to be out and about in these wide-open spaces, hikers, bikers, and horseback riders should take care to stick only to authorized trails; military explosives and other hazards are found in still-restricted areas, and habitat

Marina offers great possibilities, too—starting with the new **Marina Everyone's Harvest Certified Farmers' Market,** held 10 A.M.–P.M. every Sunday, just west of Hwy. 1 at the Marina Transit Station, 280 Reservation Rd.; for details, call 831/384-6961. Great for quickie authentic Mexican and all the essential ingredients is **El Rancho Market** at 346 Reservation Rd., 831/384-5151. Then there's **Café Pronto! Italian Grill,** 330-H Reservation Rd., 831/883-1207, where pastas, pizzas, and seafood specialties star. For Korean, head for **Nak Won,** also in the 330 Reservation complex, 831/883-2302.

In accommodations, less expensive choices in Seaside include the **Thunderbird Motel,** 1933 Fremont Blvd., 831/394-6797, with some rates under $50. Good rooms are available for $50–100 at the **Best Western Magic Carpet Lodge,** 1875 Fremont Blvd., 831/899-4221; the **Pacific Best**

Inn, 1141 Fremont, 831/899-1881; the **Seaside Inn,** 1986 Del Monte Blvd., 831/394-4041; and the **Sand Castle Motel,** 1101 La Salle Ave., 831/394-6556.

The newest resort on the Monterey Peninsula is in Marina—the plush 30-room **Marina Dunes Resort** in the dunes just west of Hwy. 1 at 3295 Dunes Dr., 831/883-9478 or 877/944-3863, www.marinadunes.com. Rooms and suites in these beachfront bungalows feature California King beds, oversized furnishings, gas fireplaces, fully tiled baths with pedestal sinks, and either a private patio or balcony. Extras include heated pool, lap pool, hydrotherapy, and complete spa services—plus the opportunity to stroll on the beach, for miles in either direction. Rates are $100 and up. The lodge building offers meeting facilities and the **A.J. Spurs** restaurant and tapas bar.

restoration is underway. Some 35 rare and endangered species inhabit Fort Ord Public Lands. For current trail information, contact the BLM field office in Hollister, 831/630-5000, www.ca.blm.gov/hollister.

Seaside and **Sand City,** to Marina's north, share "ownership" of former Fort Ord and the new CSU Monterey campus—and all three cities, the peninsula's traditionally low-rent neighborhoods, are still feuding with more affluent Monterey, Pacific Grove, and Carmel over future development plans. Opponents contend that proposed new hotels, golf courses, conference and shopping centers, and housing developments in these northern towns will adversely affect limited area water supplies, roads and other public infrastructure, and the environment.

Head inland on Canyon del Rey Road to **Work Memorial Park** and the nearby **Frog Pond Natural Area** (entrance in the willows near the Del Rey Oaks City Hall), a seasonal freshwater marsh home to birds and the elusive inch-long Pacific tree frog. Or take Del Monte Avenue off Hwy. 1 to **Del Monte Beach,** one of the least-bothered beaches of Monterey Bay (no facilities).

Del Monte Avenue also takes you past the **U.S. Naval Post-Graduate School,** 831/656-2441, www.nps.edu or www.nps.navy.mil, a navy preflight training school during World War II and now a military university offering doctorates. It's housed on the grounds of the stately 1880 Spanish-style **Del Monte Hotel.** The state's oldest large resort and once queen of American watering holes for California's nouveau riche, the Del Monte was built by Charles Crocker and the rest of the railroading Big Four. You can tour the university grounds from 8 A.M.–4:30 P.M. daily. Downstairs in the old hotel is the school's **museum,** with memorabilia from the Del Monte's heyday (open Mon.–Fri. 11 A.M.–2 P.M., closed on major holidays).

Worth stopping for in Seaside is the tranquil **Monterey Peninsula Buddhist Temple,** 1155 Noche Buena, 831/394-0119, surrounded by beautiful Asian-style gardens and carp-filled ponds. Come in May for the bonsai show.

For the present at least, accommodations are considerably less expensive here than elsewhere on the Monterey Peninsula. For example, RVers can hole up at the spiffed-up **Marina Dunes RV Park,** 3330 Dunes Dr. in Marina, 831/384-6914,

MONTEREY PENINSULA GOLFING

Golfers from around the globe make a point of arriving on the Monterey Peninsula, clubs in tow, at some time in their lives. The undisputed golf capital of the world, the Pebble Beach area between Carmel and Pacific Grove is the most famous, largely due to "The Crosby," which is now the AT&T Pebble Beach National Pro-Am Golf Tournament, www.attpbgolf.com. Making headlines in 1999 was news that the Pebble Beach Company and its four world-class courses had been bought by a high-powered American investor group—Clint Eastwood, Richard Ferris, Arnold Palmer, and Peter Ueberroth—for $820 million. Just previously, Clint Eastwood's debuted his superb **Tehama** golf club, 25000 Via Malpaso in Carmel Valley, 831/622-2200, a private course with a by-invitation-only membership of 300. Heady days at the head of the food chain.

It may cost a pretty penny—the greens fee at Pebble Beach Golf Links, for example, is more than $350—but the public is welcome at private **Pebble Beach Golf Links,** ranked the number one public course in America by *Golf Digest* in 2003-04. Other options include the **Links at Spanish Bay, Spyglass Hill Golf Course,** the **Peter Hay Par 3,** and the 1897 **Del Monte Golf Course** in Monterey, the oldest course in continuous operation west of the Mississippi. All are associated with Pebble Beach Resorts, headquartered at The Lodge at Pebble Beach on 17 Mile Drive. For more information on any of these courses and to make reservations, see www.pebblebeach.com or call 800/654-9300.

There is affordable golf around too, however, the best thing going being the unpretentious **Pacific Grove Municipal Golf Links,** 77 Asilomar Ave.,

---

www.marinadunesrv.com, which has sites with full hookups (including cable TV) as well as tent sites. It's just nine miles from Monterey, making this a good potential base of operations. And the new **Marina Dunes Resort,** 831/883-9478, www.marinadunes.com, is the first new resort hotel built in the greater Monterey area in 20 years.

For more information about the sand dune cities, contact the **Marina Chamber of Commerce,** 211 Hillcrest, 831/384-9155, www.marinachamber.com, and the **Seaside/Sand City Chamber of Commerce,** 505 Broadway in Seaside, 831/394-6501, www.seaside-sandcity.com.

RECREATION

The 18-mile **Monterey Peninsula Recreation Trail** is a spectacular local feature—a walking and cycling path that stretches from Asilomar State Beach in Pacific Grove to Castroville. Scenic bay views are offered all along the way, as the trail saunters past landmarks including Point Pinos Lighthouse, Lovers Point, the Monterey Bay Aquarium, Cannery Row, Fisherman's Wharf, Custom House Plaza, and Del Monte Beach. The 14-acre **Monterey Beach** is not very impressive (day use only), but you can stroll the

rocky headlands on the peninsula's north side without interruption, traveling the Monterey Peninsula Recreation Trail past the **Pacific Grove Marine Gardens Fish Refuge** and **Asilomar State Beach,** with tidepools, rugged shorelines, and thick carpets of brightly flowered (but nonnative) ice plants.

For ocean swimming, head south to **Carmel River State Beach,** which includes a lagoon and bird sanctuary, or to **China Cove** at Point Lobos. **El Estero Park** in town—bounded by Del Monte Avenue, Fremont Boulevard, and Camino El Estero—has a small horseshoe-shaped lagoon with ducks, pedal boat rentals, picnic tables, a par course, hiking and biking trails, and the **Dennis the Menace Playground,** designed by cartoonist Hank Ketcham. (Particularly fun here is the hedge maze.) Also at El Estero is the area's first **French Consulate,** built in 1830, moved here in 1931, and now the local visitor information center. The **Don Dahvee Park** on Munras Avenue (one leg of local motel row) is a secret oasis of picnic tables with a hiking/biking trail.

For information on local parks and beaches—including the new **Palo Corona Ranch Regional Park,** gateway to Big Sur, set to open to the public in spring 2005—contact the **Monterey Penin-**

831/648-5777, serving up Pebble Beach views at a fraction of the cost. The first nine holes were designed by Chandler Egan, in classic rural-England style, the back nine by Jack Neville, the original designer of the Pebble Beach Golf Links. Fees for 18 holes are $32 on weekdays, $38 in weekends. Great for beginners. Reservations can be made no more than seven days in advance.

Also open to the public are the **Poppy Hills Golf Course,** 3200 Lopez Rd. (just off 17 Mile Dr.), 831/624-2035, designed by Robert Trent Jones, Jr.; the **Bayonet** and **Black Horse Golf Courses** on North-South at former Fort Ord, 831/899-7271; and the Robert Trent Jones (Sr. and Jr.) **Laguna Seca Golf Club** on York Road between Monterey and Salinas, 831/373-3701 or 888/524-8629.

Though Pebble Beach is world-renowned for its golf courses and golf events, Carmel Valley and vicinity has nearly as many courses—most of them private in the country-club model, most recognizing reciprocal access agreements with other clubs. The **Rancho Cañada Golf Club,** about a mile east of Hwy. 1 via Carmel Valley Rd., 831/624-0111 or 800/536-9459, is open to the public, however. As part of accommodations packages, nonmembers can golf at **Quail Lodge Resort & Golf Club,** 8000 Valley Greens Dr., 831/624 2888, and at **Carmel Valley Ranch,** 1 Old Ranch Rd. in Carmel, 831/625-9500, which features an 18-hole Pete Dye course. And you can always try to find someone who knows someone who knows someone who's a member of Clint's club, Tehama, to see if they can get you in.

sula Regional Park District, 831/372-3196, www.mprpd.org.

Jacks Peak County Park

The highest point on the peninsula (but not *that* high, at only 1,068 feet) and the focal point of a 525-acre regional park, Jacks Peak offers great views, good hiking and horseback trails, and picnicking, plus fascinating flora and wildlife. Named after the land's former owner—Scottish immigrant and entrepreneur David Jacks, best known for his local dairies and their "Monterey Jack" cheese—the park features marked trails, including the self-guided **Skyline Nature Trail.** Almost 8.5 miles of riding and hiking trails wind through Monterey pine forests to breathtaking ridge-top views. From Jacks Peak amid the Monterey pines, you'll have spectacular views of both Monterey Bay and Carmel Valley—and possibly the pleasure of spotting American kestrels or red-shouldered hawks soaring on the currents. The park's first 55 acres were purchased by the Nature Conservancy, and the rest were bought up with county, federal, and private funds.

The park is located at 25020 Jacks Peak Park Rd.; to get here, take Olmstead County Road (from Hwy. 68 near the Monterey Air-

port) for two miles. The park is open daily at least 10 A.M.–5 P.M. Call 888/588-2267 for more park information.

Golf and Biking

Monterey and vicinity is most famous, of course, as an elite golfing oasis. For information on public access to area courses, which are primarily private—including Clint Eastwood's course—see Monterey Peninsula Golfing.

Otherwise, get some fresh air and see the sights by bicycle. Either bring your own or rent one at any of several local outfits. Bike rentals and pedal-powered surreys are the specialties of **Wheel Fun Rentals @ Bay Bikes,** on the bike path at 585 Cannery Row and also at 99 Pacific St. just above Fisherman's Wharf, 831/655-2453, www.bay bikes.com. Or tool around on a moped, available for rent through **Monterey Moped Adventures,** 1250 Del Monte Ave., 831/373-2696, which also rents bikes.

Water Sports

Coolest place to get ready to hang five or ten is **On the Beach Surf Shop,** 693 Lighthouse Ave. in New Monterey, 831/646-9283. Another way to "see" Monterey Bay is by getting right in it is by kayak. **Monterey Bay Kayaks,** 693 Del Monte Ave., 831/649-5357 or 800/649-5357, www.montereybaykayaks.com, offers tours—bay tours and sunset tours and full-moon tours, even trips into Elkhorn Slough and along the Salinas River—as well as classes and rentals of both open and closed kayaks. Wetsuits, paddling jackets, life jackets, water shoes, and a half-hour of on-land instruction are included in the basic all-day rental pric. **AB Seas Kayaks,** 32 Cannery Row #5, 831/647-0147 or 866/824-2337, www.montereykayak .com, offers similar services at similar prices, including guided wildlife and birding tours. **Adventures by the Sea** also offers kayak rentals and tours—in addition to bike rentalsand bike trips, in-line skate rentals, and custom beach parties. Offices are located at 299 Cannery Row. For information and reervations call 831/372-1807 or 831/648-7236, or see www .adventuresbythesea.com.

Carrera Sailing, 66 Fisherman's Wharf (at Randy's Fishing Trips), 831/375-0648, www .sailmontereybay.com, offers the comfortable 32-foot sloop *Carrera* for nature tours, sunset cruises, and chartered sails. **Scenic Bay Sailing School and Yacht Charters,** 831/372-6603, www .montereysailingcharters.com, offers sailing lessons and is also willing to sail off into the sunset. Another possibility, for photo and nature outings, dinner cruises, even extreme sailing, is **Monterey Bay Sailing & Diving** on Cannery Row, 831/372-7245, www.montereysailing.com.

Other boating companies also offer bay tours (including cocktail cruises), winter—and year-round—whale-watching, and fishing trips. Discount coupons are often available at local visitor information centers. Recommended for whale-watching by the Monterey Bay Aquarium, **Sanctuary Cruises** (now located at Moss Landing Harbor), 831/917-1042, www.sanctuarycruises .com, offers weekend and some weekday whale-watching aboard the *Princess of Whales,* a double-decked power catamaran that holds up to 149 people. And BTW: the Princess fuels up on biodiesel—and even features an ADA-compliant restroom, along with full onboard galley serving organic free-trade coffee and other goodies, plus full bar. Some weekday trips are offered on-board the *Sanctuary.*

Other good choices include **Monterey Whale Watching Cruises,** 96 Fisherman's Wharf No. 1, 831/372-2203 or 800/200-2203, www .montereywhalewatching.com; **Randy's Fishing Trips,** 66 Fisherman's Wharf #1, 831/372-7440 or 800/251-7440, www.randysfishingtrips.com, which also offers Point Sur fishing charters; and **Chris' Fishing Trips,** 48 Fisherman's Wharf #1, 831/375-5951, www.chrissfishing.com, which offers a fleet of four big boats, including the 70-foot *New Holiday.*

Another way to see the bay is to get a fish-eye view. The **Aquarius Dive Shop,** at home here since 1970, located at 2040 Del Monte Ave., 831/375-1933, www.aquariusdivers.com, is a best bet for rentals, instruction, equipment, and repairs. Aquarius also offers guided underwater tours (specializing in photography and video) and can provide tips on worthwhile dives worldwide. Another possibility is the **Monterey Bay Dive Center,** 225 Cannery Row, 831/656-0454 or 800/607-2822, www.montereyscuba diving.com, which offers rentals and lessons, chartered dive trips, guided dives and snorkeling, and night dives.

Adrenaline junkies can get a bird's-eye view of the bay by throwing themselves out of an airplane with **Skydive Monterey Bay,** 3261 Imjin Rd. in Marina, 831/384-3483 or 888/229-5867, www.skydivemontereybay.com. No experience is necessary; after a bit of instruction, you'll make a tandem jump harnessed to a veteran skydiver. The cost is $199. The company is open daily, year-round.

ENTERTAINMENT AND EVENTS

Still a fairly new pleasure in Monterey are the cool **New Osio 6 Cinemas,** next to the Crown & Anchor at 350 Alvarado St., 831/644-8171, www.osiocinemas.com, screening five or more indie and foreign films every week.

Viva Monterey at 414 Alvarado St., 831/646-1415, is the favorite for rockin' out, though Viva is branching out into blues, funk, and reggae too. **Sly McFly's** at 700 Cannery Row, 831/649-

8050, is the best blues club, though you might also catch hot salsa bands some nights. For jazz, head for **Cibo Ristorante Italiano,** 301 Alvarado St., 831/649-8151. Locals say the best local dance club is **Club Octane,** 321 Alvarado, 831/646-9244.

The Monterey Peninsula also offers an impressive year-round calendar of theater, arts, lectures, museum and gallery exhibits, and other cultural events. See local newspapers for current listings.

Events

Visitors have a whale of a time at January's free **Whalefest** weekend, held at Fisherman's Wharf. Come in February for **A Day of Romance in Old Monterey**—"living history" storytelling, with 19th-century Monterey characters holding forth from the Cooper-Molera and Diaz Adobes, Larkin House, and Sherman Quarters—and the Valentine's Day **Love at the Aquarium.** In late February come for the **Steinbeck Cannery Row Birthday Celebration** (there's another bash in Salinas). In early March, **Dixieland Monterey** brings three days of Dixie and swing to various venues around town. Later in March, come for the waterfront's **Clam Chowder Festival.** April brings the **Sea Otter Classic,** one of the world's best cycling parties, designed for both mountain bike and road racers, and the **Monterey Wine Festival,** when more than 200 California wineries strut their stuff. Traditionally, though, April is adobe month in Monterey, with the popular **Adobe Tour** through public and private historic buildings toward the end of the month. In late April or early May begin Monterey's **Historic Garden Tours,** beginning at the Cooper-Molera Adobe and including the Stevenson and (usually) Larkin Houses, which continue into September. At least tangentially related is the Earth Day-focused **Elkhorn Slough Mud Stomp** just north of town in Moss Landing, organized to create nesting holes for endangered snowy plovers in the slough's salt flats. The **Old Monterey Plein Air Painting and Art Promenade** is also in April.

Come in May for the **Marina International Festival of the Winds,** which includes the annual **Tour de Ford Ord** bike ride, and for the free Memorial Day weekend **Red, White & a Little Blues** music festival, staged at Custom House Plaza and along Alvarado Street in Monterey. Also in May: the **Ed "Doc" Ricketts Birthday Party** and the once-a-year **Ed "Doc" Ricketts Lab Tours** on Cannery Row, plus the **Block Party on Cannery Row.** In late May, the Kiwanis-sponsored **Great Monterey Squid Festival** is a chic culinary indulgence for those with calamari cravings, plus arts, crafts, and entertainment.

June brings the acclaimed **Monterey Bay Blues Festival,** and also the **Monterey Bay TheatreFest** at Custom House Plaza, which includes an arts and crafts festival, a family-oriented theatre festival, historical reenactments, and the "Human Chess Game" on the waterfront. The **Fourth of July** celebration here is fun, with fireworks off the Coast Guard Pier, music in historic Colton Hall, and living history in Old Monterey. Neighboring Seaside starts a day early, with its community-wide **Festival of Patriots** block party on July 3. Come mid-month for the **Rock & Art Festival** at the Monterey Fairground, a celebration of rock-n-roll. There's almost always something going on at nearby Mazda Racetrack Laguna Seca, too, including July's **Honda International Superbike Classic** and August's **Rolex Monterey Historic Automobile Races.** In August, the **Monterey County Fair** comes to the fairgrounds, bringing amusement rides, livestock shows, and young faces sticky with cotton-candy residue. Also come in August for **Otter Days** at the Monterey Bay Aquarium and the annual **Winemaker's Celebration** in Custom House Plaza.

Come in September for the fastest weekend of them all, the **Grand Prix of Monterey** at Mazda Raceway Laguna Seca. Come mid-September, it's time for the city's most famous event of all: the **Monterey Jazz Festival,** the oldest continuous jazz fest in the nation. Not as daring as others, it nonetheless hosts legendary greats and up-and-coming talent. This is the biggest party of the year here, so get tickets and reserve rooms well in advance (four to six months). Another big deal in September is artist Equity's annual three-day **Artists Studio Tour,** a self-guided exploration of more than 70 Monterey County studios.

October possibilities include the annual **Old Monterey Seafood & Music Festival** and the **California Constitution Day** reenactment of California's 1849 constitutional convention. In mid-November come the **Great Wine Escape Weekend**, when area wineries all hold open houses, and the **Cannery Row Christmas Tree Lighting.** The **Christmas in the Adobes** yuletide tour in mid-December is another big event, with luminaria-lit tours of 15 adobes, each dressed up in period holiday decorations. Festivities are accompanied by music and carolers. Also come in December for the **Brighten The Harbor** boating parade of lights and the annual **Cowboy Poetry & Music Festival.** Celebrate New Year's Eve through the arts at **First Night Monterey,** immensely popular here.

SHOPPING

Cannery Row is the obvious starting point for most visiting shoppers. Wander the Row's shops on the way to and from the aquarium. Don't overlook the gift and book shop at the nonprofit **Monterey Bay Aquarium** itself, 886 Cannery Row, 831/648-4800, which offers good books and a wonderful selection of educational and "eco" items. Proceeds support the aquarium and its educational and research mission. The **Monterey Soap & Candle Works,** 685 Cannery Row Ste. 109, 831/644-9425, offers natural, handmade coconut, glycerin, and specialty soaps as well as beeswax candles. Great for antiques is the **Cannery Row Antique Mall,** 471 Wave St., 831/655-0264.

Shopping is good in adjacent Pacific Grove, too—starting right next to Cannery Row at the **American Tin Cannery Premium Outlet** mall, 125 Ocean Ave., 831/372-1442, where shops include Carole Little, Carter's Children's Wear, Nine West, and Woolrich, not to mention specialty shops like Windborne Kites. **The First Noel,** 562 Lighthouse Ave., 831/648-1250, specializes in all things Christmas, with other holidays thrown in for good measure. The best boutique around for women's clothing is **The Clothing Store,** 510 Lighthouse Ave., 831/649-8866.

The Monterey area boasts its fair share of antique and "heritage" shops. But consider actively supporting the preservation of local history. A few shops within downtown's Monterey State Historic Park actually operate out of park buildings—to help generate funds for historic preservation, garden development, and other improvements. Worth a look along Monterey's Path of History is the **Cooper Shop** in the Cooper-Molera Adobe at Polk and Munras Sts., 831/649-7111, operated by the nonprofit Old Monterey Preservation Society, which offers quality 1800s-vintage reproductions, from toys to furniture. The **Boston Store** or Casa del Oro at the corner of Scott and Olivier, 831/649-3364, is run by the nonprofit Historic Garden League and offers antiques, collectibles, and reproductions. The garden league also operates the **Picket Fence,** an upscale garden shop.

There are many great shops downtown, and just wandering around is an enjoyable way to find them. Great for second-hand and vintage clothing, accessories, and other treasures is eclectic **Blue Moon Trading Company,** 75 Bonifacio Plaza (east of Alvarado), 831/641-0616. Another possibility for previously loved clothing is **Nice Twice,** 397 Calle Principal, 831/373-5665. The unique **California Views Historical Photo Collection,** 469 Pacific St., 831/373-3811, offers more than 80,000 historical photographs of California and Monterey.

A first stop for books and magazines is **Bay Books,** 316 Alvarado St., 831/375-1855, with a nice selection of Steinbeck and titles of local or regional emphasis. Used-book possibilities include **Book End,** 245 Pearl St., 831/373-4046; **The Book Haven,** 559 Tyler St., 831/333-0383; and the **Cannery Row Old Book Company,** 471 Wave St., 831/656-9264. **Carpe Diem Fine Books** at 502 Pierce St., 831/643-2754, specializes in rare and out-of-print books and is open only by appointment. A destination in its own right for used-book aficionados is Pacific Grove's **Lighthouse Avenue** in New Monterey. The unique used bookeries here include **Books & Things,** 224 Lighthouse Ave., 831/655-8784; the **Book Worm,** 600 Lighthouse, 831/375-4208; **Old Capitol Books,** 639 Lighthouse, Ste.

A, 831/375-2665; **Basset Books,** 800 Lighthouse Ave., Ste. C, 831/655-3433; and **Lighthouse Books,** 801 Lighthouse, 831/372-0653.

In addition to gathering up fresh produce and bakery items, head for downtown's Tuesday **Old Monterey Market Place** on Alvarado Street and Bonafacio Place (4 to 7 or 8 P.M.) for quality crafts.

The best all-purpose shopping center just happens to be conveniently installed astride motel row, Munras Avenue—the **Del Monte Shopping Center,** 1410 Del Monte Center, 831/373-2705, where you'll find coffee, food, boutiques, books, and furniture plus Macy's and Mervyn's. The center's **Avalon Beads,** 831/643-1847, www.avalonbeads.com, features beads from around the globe as well as imported jewelry.

For more shopping ideas and other visitor information, contact the **Monterey County Convention & Visitors Bureau** (see below), 831/648-5373, 831/626-1426, or 888/221-1010, www.montereyinfo.org, and the **Old Monterey Business Association,** 321 Alvarado St. Ste. G, 831/655-8070, www.oldmonterey.org.

ACCOMMODATIONS

Camping

Right in downtown Monterey, RV campers can plug in at **Cypress Tree Inn,** 2227 N. Fremont St., 831/372-7586 or 800/446-8303 (in California), www.cypresstreeinn.com. Otherwise a pleasant motel, the Cypress Tree features concrete for RVers too, plus amenities including water and electric hookups, showers, restrooms, a waher and dryer, and use of the motel's hot tub and sauna. Rates are under $50. Also in Monterey, if you're feeling lucky—or desperate—try pitching a tent in year-round **Veterans Memorial Park** on Via del Rey adjacent to the presidio, 831/646-3865, $20 per night. First-come, first-camped; 30 of the 40 sites can accommodate trailers. Hiker/biker sites available too. Facilities include restrooms and hot showers. No hookups. (Best bet: Arrive before 3 P.M. and get a permit from the attendant.) Three-day maximum stay.

Outside town on the way to Salinas is **the Laguna Seca Recreation Area,** at the **Mazda Raceway at Laguna Seca** just off Hwy. 68, with some 93 tent sites and 102 spots for RVs. The various campgrounds, aome offering private, oak-shaded sites, look down on the track. The park is not recommended for light sleepers when the races are on. For information and reservations during non-race times, contact Laguna Seca County Recreation Area in Salinas, 831/422-6138 (information), 831/755-4899 (reservations), or 888/588-2267, www.co.monterey.ca.us/parks. When races aren't scheduled, the day-use fee is $6 per day. RV camping is $30 per night, and Tent sites are $22 per night (each plus $5 reservation fee). To reserve camping during race periods, call the ticket office at 800/327-7322. Premier and Reserved sites are reservable in advance; others are first-come, first-camped. For other track and campground particulars, see www.laguna-seca.com.

For other camping options, head south to Carmel.

Hostels

It's happened at last: Monterey's onetime Carpenter's Union Hall, now the town's long-awaited 45-bed hostel, is finally open. Thanks to the Monterey Hostel Society, travelers can now bunk in separate women's and men's dorms (shared bathrooms) just four blocks from Cannery Row. Among its other features, the HI-USA **Carpenter's Hall Hostel** offers the latest in water conservation technology—token-operated showers, metered faucets, ultra-low-flow half-gallon Microphor toilets, and water-saving appliances. Rates are under $50. The price includes a pillow, sheets, and a blanket; bring your own sleep sack for $1 discount (no sleeping bags allowed). Family rooms and private "group rooms" (for up to 35) are available. For groups, discounts on overnight fees are available for youths and children. Given the area's popularity, advance reservations are usually essential. (Call, email the hostel at info@montereyhostel.org, or see the website for reservation details.) Reserve with personal check or Visa/MasterCard. Free onsite parking. To avoid adding to local traffic woes, leave your vehicle here and take public transportation. For more hostel information contact

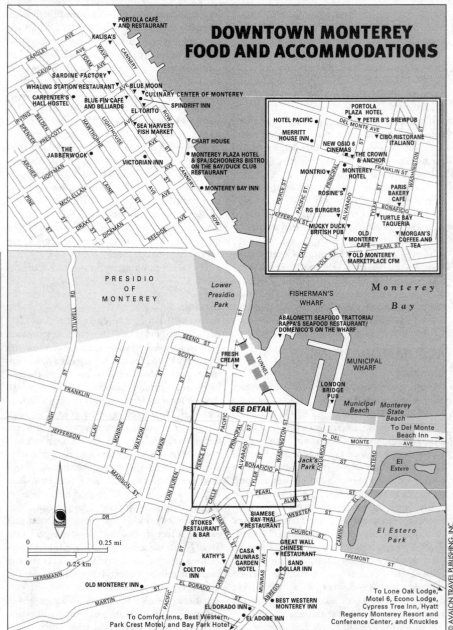

DOWNTOWN MONTEREY FOOD AND ACCOMMODATIONS

PORTOLA CAFÉ AND RESTAURANT
KALISA'S
EARDLEY AVE
FOAM AVE
WAVE AVE
DAVID AVE
CANNERY
SARDINE FACTORY
WHALING STATION RESTAURANT
BLUE MOON
CARPENTER'S HALL HOSTEL
BLUE FIN CAFE AND BILLIARDS
CULINARY CENTER OF MONTEREY
EL TORITO
FOAM ROW
SPINDRIFT INN
IRVING
BELDEN
SPENCER
PRESCOTT
HAWTHORNE
LIGHTHOUSE AVE
SEA HARVEST FISH MARKET
THE JABBERWOCK
VICTORIAN INN
CHART HOUSE
MONTEREY PLAZA HOTEL & SPA/SCHOONERS BISTRO ON THE BAY/DUCK CLUB RESTAURANT
ARCHER
HOFFMAN
LAINE
AVE
AVE
AVE
MONTEREY BAY INN
PINE
MCCLELLAN
ROW
DRAKE
DICKMAN
RESSIDE
CANNERY ROW

DETAIL
HOTEL PACIFIC
PORTOLA PLAZA HOTEL
DEL MONTE AVE
PETER B'S BREWPUB
MERRITT HOUSE INN
NEW OSIO 6 CINEMAS
CIBO RISTORANE ITALIANO
THE CROWN & ANCHOR
MONTRIO
MONTEREY HOTEL
FRANKLIN ST
PIERCE ST
PACIFIC ST
PRINCIPAL ST
ROSINE'S
ALVARADO
WASHINGTON ST
TYLER ST
PARIS BAKERY CAFÉ
BONAFICIO PL
RG BURGERS
JEFFERSON ST
TURTLE BAY TAQUERIA
MUCKY DUCK BRITISH PUB
CALLE
OLD MONTEREY CAFE
PEARL ST
MORGAN'S COFFEE AND TEA
POLK ST
OLD MONTEREY MARKETPLACE CFM

PRESIDIO OF MONTEREY
Lower Presidio Park
FISHERMAN'S WHARF
Monterey Bay
STILWELL RD
ST
ABALONETTI SEAFOOD TRATTORIA/ RAPPA'S SEAFOOD RESTAURANT/ DOMENICO'S ON THE WHARF
SEENO ST
SCOTT ST
FRESH CREAM
TUNNEL
MUNICIPAL WHARF
FRANKLIN
HIGH ST
LONDON BRIDGE PUB
Municipal Beach
Monterey State Beach
JEFFERSON
CLAY
MONROE
WATSON
ST
SEE DETAIL
PACIFIC ST
PRINCIPAL ST
ALVARADO
WASHINGTON ST
DEL MONTE AVE
To Del Monte Beach Inn
VAN BUREN
MADISON ST
PIERCE ST
CALLE
BONAFICIO PL
TYLER ST
FIGUEROA ST
Jack's Park
ESTERO ST
El Estero
PEARL ST
ALMA ST
MOON
DR
SIAMESE BAY THAI RESTAURANT
WEBSTER ST
CAMINO
El Estero Park
0   0.25 mi
0   0.25 km
STOKES RESTAURANT & BAR
CHURCH ST
KATHY'S
CASA MUNRAS GARDEN HOTEL
GREAT WALL CHINESE RESTAURANT
SAND DOLLAR INN
FREMONT ST
HERRMANN
OLD MONTEREY INN
COLTON INN
CASS ST
MUNRAS AVE
ABREGO ST
HARTNELL ST
EL DORADO ST
BEST WESTERN MONTEREY INN
MARTIN
PACIFIC ST
EL DORADO INN
EL ADOBE INN
To Comfort Inns, Best Western, Park Crest Motel, and Bay Park Hotel

To Lone Oak Lodge, Motel 6, Econo Lodge, Cypress Tree Inn, Hyatt Regency Monterey Resort and Conference Center, and Knuckles

Monterey Bay

Carpenter's Hall Hostel, 778 Hawthorne St., 831/649-0375, www.montereyhostel.org. The office is open 8–10 A.M. and 5–10 P.M.

Now that there is genuinely affordable accommodation available in Monterey, there are debts to be paid. Please express your gratitude by sending an extra contribution to the Monterey Hostel Fund, in care of the hostel.

If you'll be continuing on, excellent HI-USA hostels are available in Santa Cruz, just north, and also farther north along the San Mateo County coastline. If you're heading south, there's also a great hostel in San Luis Obispo. For current details on these and other hostels in California, see http://hostelweb.com/california.htm.

Motels and Hotels

Current complete listings of accommodations (including prices) and restaurants in Monterey proper are available free from the convention and visitors bureau. Discounts of 50 percent or more are available at many inns, hotels, and motels during off-season promotions.

Monterey has a reasonable supply of decent motels, with most rooms in the $100 to $150 range, but many much higher. Most offer all modern amenities, and many establishments provide complimentary breakfast and other extra services. If you're here for the Jazz Festival, plan to stay at a motel in Marina or Seaside and vicinity, or on Fremont Street (motel and fast-food row) just a block from the fairgrounds. Motels on Munras are generally pricier. Be on the lookout, especially during high season, for "floating" motel rates, wherein the price may double or triple long *after* you've made your reservation. When in doubt, request written reservation and price confirmation.

For assistance in booking midrange to high-end accommodations in and around Monterey, contact **Resort II Me Room Finders,** 800/757-5646, www.resort2me.com, a firm with a good track record in matching peninsula visitors with appropriate local lodgings.

$50–100: Motels with at least some lower-priced rooms include the **Lone Oak Lodge,** 2221 N. Fremont St., 831/372-4924 or 800/283-5663,

www.loneoaklodge.com, pleasant **El Adobe Inn,** 936 Munras Ave., 831/372-5409, www.El-Adobe-Inn.com; amenities include in-room coffeemakers and refrigerators. Another possibility is the **Motel 6,** 2124 N. Fremont, 831/646-8585, which is clean, has a pool, and isn't far from the downtown action—reachable on any eastbound bus (take number 1). It's popular, so make reservations six months or more in advance or stop by at 11 A.M. or so to check for cancellations. There's another Motel 6 in the same price range (a bit less expensive) just outside Monterey proper, at 100 Reservation Rd. in Marina, 831/384-1000. For reservations at any Motel 6, call 800/466-8356 or try www.motel6.com.

Quite nice, quite reasonably priced, and surprisingly homey are the locally owned Comfort Inns on Munras Avenue. **Comfort Inn—Carmel Hill,** 1252 Munras Ave., 831/372-2908, features 30 cheery rooms with the usual amenities and electronic door locks. Adjacent is the **Comfort Inn-Munras,** 1262 Munras, 831/372-8088. (For reservations at either, call 888/970-7666; for online info, see www.stayatmonterey.com.) Both are close enough—but not too close—to local attractions, especially if you look forward to some vigorous walking. The best thing about the location, which is quite close to Hwy. 1 and the Del Monte Shopping Center, is its walkability. Directly across the way, flanking Munras all the way back downtown to its junction with Abrego, is long, narrow **Dan Dahvee Park,** with its pleasant trees, flowers, birds—and walking paths.

Other motels with at least some lower-priced rooms include the 15-room **El Dorado Inn,** 900 Munras Ave., 831/373-2921, and the very nice **Best Western Park Crest Motel,** 1100 Munras, 831/372-4576 or 888/829-0092, www.bestwesterncalifornia.com, where rooms include in-room coffeemakers and refrigerators, and extras include TVs with free HBO, a pool, a hot tub, and free continental breakfast. There are also a number of good motels off Fremont.

$100–150: Most of the area's less expensive motels, including those listed above, also offer pricier rooms. Centrally located, near Hwy. 1

and within easy reach of all area towns, is the **Bay Park Hotel,** 1425 Munras Ave., 831/649-1020 or 800/338-3564, www.bayparkhotel.com, featuring in-room coffeemakers, refrigerators, and hair dryers, plus onsite extras including fitness faciliuties and a restaurant, pool, and hot tub. Rates for family-friendly rooms with two double beds can drop to $79. The nonsmoking **Best Western Monterey Inn,** downtown at 825 Abrego, 831/373-5345 or 877/373-5345, www.montereyinnca.com, is quite pleasant, with 80 spacious rooms—some with fireplaces, all with in-room coffeemakers and refrigerators. The motel also has a heated pool and hot tub. Another best bet is the nearby **Sand Dollar Inn,** 755 Abrego St., 831/372-7551 or 800/982-1986, www.sanddollarinn.com, with pool, hot tub, and some fireplace rooms.

$150–250: Set to debut in September 2005 following an $8 million renovation and expansion, downtown's historic **Ⓜ Monterey Hotel,** 831/375-3184 or 800/966-6490 (reservations), www.montereyhotel.com, now boasts a main entrance on Calle Principal in addition to its previous address at 406 Alvarado St., and is otherwise set for a spiff centennial. The new Monterey Hotel shows off much of its original 1904 Victorian bone structure yet now includes a total of 69 rooms (an increase of 24), a 1,200-square-foot fitness facility, additional meeting space, and extra parking. There's also a new pedestrian walkway, linking Alvarado and Calle Principal. Rooms feature custom-made armoires (with TV sets), hand-carved furnishings, plantation shutters, ceiling fans, telephones, private marble baths with tub showers, and tasteful yet subtle decorating touches, all individualized. Every floor features an outdoor landing and deck area, and the third-floor interior landing boasts an intimate atrium parlor lit by a skylight. See the website for renovation news.

Offering good value in comfortable accommodations on acres of lovely landscape is the **Casa Munras Garden Hotel,** 700 Munras, 831/375-2411 or 800/222-2446 in California, 800/222-2558 nationwide, www.casamunras-hotel.com, conveniently located close to historic downtown. A restaurant is onsite.

Another good deal, right downtown, is the attractive and accommodating **Colton Inn,** 707 Pacific, 831/649-6500 or 800/848-7007, www.coltoninn.com, where the basics include VCrs with free videos and phones with dataports, and extras include a sauna and sundeck. Some rooms have real fireplaces and whirlpool tubs. The comfortable **Portola Plaza Hotel** (formerly the Doubletree Hotel) at 2 Portola Plaza, adjacent to the Convention Center downtown at Pacific and Del Monte, 831/649-4511 or 888/222-5851 (reservations), www.portolaplazahotel.com, and boasts an onsite brewpub, restaurant, bar, full-service fitness center, 370 rooms, and 10 suites—all brightly redecorated in fall 2002. Plus it's convenient to just about everything, especially if you prefer walking to the sights. Some great specials and packages, too.

$250 and Up: For definite bayside luxury, head for the 290-room, Craftsman-style **Monterey Plaza Hotel & Spa,** 400 Cannery Row, 831/646-1700 or 800/368-2468, www.woodsidehotels.com. The Monterey Plaza's fine accommodations include Italian Empire and 18th-century Chinese furnishings, every convenience (even a complete fitness center with six Nautilus stations), and exceptional food service, including the Duck Club, one of the area's finer restaurants. The 15 Grand Suites feature grand pianos. Great onsite restaurants; rental bikes and kayaks are available. Recently, the Monterey Plaza added a $6 million, 10,000-square-foot, Eurostyle rooftop full-service spa and three spa-level suites. Coming soon to the neighborhood is a new IMAX theater.

Also deluxe and downtown is the contemporary, faux-adobe-style **Hotel Pacific,** 300 Pacific, 831/373-5700 or 800/554-5542, www.hotelpacific.com. All rooms are suites and feature hardwood floors, separate sitting areas, balconies or decks, fireplaces, wet bars, honor bars, in-room coffeemakers, irons, ironing boards, two TVs, two phones, and terrycloth bathrobes. The tiled bathrooms have a separate shower and tub. Some rooms have a view. Continental breakfast, afternoon tea, and free underground parking.

Surprisingly appealing is the **Spindrift Inn,** a onetime bordello at 652 Cannery Row (at

Hawthorne), 831/646-8900 or 800/841-1879, www.spindriftinn.com. Rooms feature hardwood floors, wood-burning fireplaces, TVs with VCRs, second telephones in the tiled bathrooms, marble tubs, featherbeds (many canopied) and goose-down comforters, all-cotton linens, and terry bathrobes. In the morning, continental breakfast and the newspaper of your choice is delivered to your room. With a rooftop garden and sky-high atrium, the Spindrift also offers a luxurious lobby with Oriental rugs and antiques.

The huge (575-room) **Hyatt Regency Monterey Resort and Conference Center,** 1 Old Golf Course Rd., 831/372-1234 or 800/824-2196 (in California), or 800/233-1234 (central reservations), www.monterey.hyatt.com, is definitely a resort, and a newly renovated one. The spacious grounds here include the 18-hole Del Monte Golf Course, six tennis courts (extra fee for both), two pools, whirlpools, and a fitness center—the works. In summer there's even a jazz festival. The sports bar here, **Knuckles,** offers 200 satellite channels, 11 TV monitors, and entire lifetimes of sports memorabilia. There's also quieter **Café Monterey** lobby bar and the **Peninsula Restaurant,** for steaks and seafood.

Other upscale stays in town include the **Monterey Bay Inn,** 242 Cannery Row, 831/373-6242 or 800/424-6242, www.montereybayinn.com, offering contemporary accommodations right on the bay (many view rooms with balconies). Near the Row is the 68-room **Best Western Victorian Inn,** 487 Foam St., 831/373-8000 or 800/232-4141, www.victorianinn.com, where gas fireplaces, complimentary continental breakfast, and afternoon wine and cheese are among the amenities. Concierge-level rooms include featherbeds and robes; some feature whirlpool tubs. Two family suites are available.

Bed-and-Breakfasts

Monterey's showcase country inn is the gorgeous ivy-covered 1929 English Tudor **N Old Monterey Inn,** 500 Martin St., 831/375-8284 or 800/350-2344, www.oldmontereyinn.com, featuring 10 elegant rooms and suites, most with fireplaces. All have sitting areas, featherbeds, CD players, a whirlpool tub for two, and special touches such as skylights and stained glass. Not to mention an abundance of amenities—making this a destination of choice for special-event getaways. As if the inn itself isn't appealing enough, it is shaded by a specimen oak amid stunning gardens. You'll also enjoy marvelous full breakfasts and a sunset wine hour. Rates are $250 and up.

The Jabberwock, 598 Laine St., 831/372-4777 or 888/428-7253, www.jabberwockinn.com, is a seven-room "post-Victorian" with a Victorian name and an Alice-through-the-looking-glass sensibility. Some rooms share baths. Rates include full breakfast (imaginative and good) plus cookies and milk at night. Rates are $100–250.

A classic in inimitable Monterey style is the historic **Merritt House Inn,** downtown at 386 Pacific St., 831/646-9686 or 800/541-5599, www.merritthouseinn.com. The original adobe, built in 1830, features three suites with 19th-century sensibility and modern bathrooms. Rates are $250 and up. The 22 surrounding motel-style rooms are more contemporary, with rates are $150–250.

At the European-style **Del Monte Beach Inn,** close to Monterey Bay at 1110 Del Monte Ave., 831/649-4410, rooms share baths—there are one or two clean, individual bathrooms per floor—which means this place is quite appealing and affordable for people who don't normally do B&Bs. Rates, including continental breakfast, are $50 to $100.

FOOD

In Monterey, eating well *and* fairly inexpensively is easier than finding low-cost lodgings. Hard to beat is picnicking at the beaches or local parks. Happy hour—at the wharf, on the Row, and elsewhere—is a big deal in the area. In addition to cheap drinks, many bars serve good (free) food from 4 to 7 P.M. Due to an abundance of reasonably priced (and generous) breakfast places, an inexpensive alternative to three meals a day is skipping lunch (or packing simple picnic fare), then shopping around for early-bird dinners, a mainstay at many local restaurants. Do-it-yourselfers can pick up whatever suits their culinary fancy at the open-air **Old Monterey**

© KIM WEIR

haggling over fresh strawberries at the farmers market on Alvarado Street

Marketplace Certified Farmers Market on Alvarado Street at Pearl, held every Tuesday 4–8 P.M. year-round (until 7 P.M. in winter). Great food, great fun. For more information, call 831/665-8070. On Thursday, head for the Monterey Bay Peninsula College CFM, 831/728-5060, held 2:30–6 P.M. year-round at 980 Fremont St. (Fremont and Phisher). For fresh seafood the place is Sea Harvest Fish Market, 598 Foam St., 831/646-0547 (also located on the highway in Moss Landing, 831/633-8300). Best bet for gourmet ingredients and organic produce—though there is a Trader Joe's in adjacent Pacific Grove—is probably the Whole Foods Market in the Del Monte Shopping Center, 831/333-1600.

No doubt helped along by the abundance of fresh regional produce, seafood, cheese and other dairy products, poultry, and meats, the Monterey Peninsula has also become a sophisticated dining destination. Some of the area's great restaurants are listed below (in various categories). But to get a true "taste" of the Monterey Peninsula, consider dining as well in nearby Pacific Grove and Carmel.

Standards

By "standard," we mean places people can happily—and affordably—frequent. The Old Mon-

terey Cafe, 489 Alvarado, 831/646-1021, serves all kinds of omelettes at breakfast—try the chile verde—plus unusual choices like calamari and eggs, lingüiça and eggs, and pigs in a blanket. Just about everything is good at lunch, too, from homemade soups, hearty shrimp Louie, and the Athenian Greek salad (with feta cheese, Greek olives, shrimp, and veggies) to the three-quarter-pound burgers and steak or calamari sandwiches. Fresh-squeezed juices and espresso and cappuccino are featured beverages. Open daily for breakfast and lunch, 7 A.M.–2:30 P.M.; breakfast served until closing.

Rosine's, nearby at 434 Alvarado (near Bonifacio), 831/375-1400, is locally loved at breakfast, lunch, and dinner. In addition to good pancakes, waffles, and other standards, at breakfast here you can get veggie Benedict (with avocado, sautéed mushrooms, and tomatoes instead of Canadian bacon). Lunch features homemade soups, salads, sandwiches, and burgers. Pasta, chicken, seafood, and steak appear on the menu at dinner, with prime rib available on Friday and Saturday nights. Wonderful desserts.

Great for burgers and fries is kid-friendly RG Burgers, 470 Alvarado St., 831/647-3100 (also at 201 Crossroads Blvd. in Carmel, 831/626-8054), where you can get all kinds, from the biggest and beefiest to the turkey guacamole burger and lemon pepper falafel. Still reasonable (and delicious) for all-American fare is Kathy's, amid the warren of oddball downtown streets at 700 Cass St. (south of Webster, west of Munras), 831/647-9540. Pick any three items for a fluffy omelette. Your meal includes home fries, cheese sauce, bran muffins, and homemade strawberry jam for around $5. Sandwiches, similarly priced, are best when eaten on the patio.

Turtle Bay Taqueria, 431 Tyler St. (at Bonifacio), 831/333-1500, is sibling to the region's hot Fishwife restaurants, and serves fast, good, very reasonably priced coastal Mexican fare, from grilled meat and seafood to flautas and tacos. Great selection of salsas, too. (There's another Turtle Bay in Seaside at 1301 Fremont, 831/899-1010.) Thai food fanatics should try Siamese Bay Thai Restaurant, 131 Webster St., 831/373-1550. You can make a meal of the appetizers—such things as veggie tempura with plum sauce and crushed peanuts. The **Great Wall Chinese Restaurant,** 724 Abrego St., 831/372-3637, has wonderful soups and an extensive vegetarian menu.

Stop in at **Morgan's Coffee and Tea,** 498 Washington, 831/373-5601, a pretty darned hip coffeehouse serving superb coffees as well as organic green, black, and herb teas—not to mention sweets like mixed nut cake and pear tarts. Unusual sandwiches and a great $4.95 pizza are available at lunch. You can get your wi-fi fix here, too. Morgan's offers pleasant outdoor street seating, complete with tables, chairs, and umbrellas. One block away, at 271 Bonifacio Place, is another reasonable breakfast or lunch stop, **Paris Bakery Café,** 831/646-1620. The lunch menu includes sandwiches, salads, and soups, and the breads and pastries are wonderful.

Pubs

A notable beer lovers' destination is the fairly new **English Ales Brewery & Pub** in Marina at 223 Reindollar Ave., 831/883-3000, which serves some impressive British-style homebrew, such as Ramsay's Fat Lip Ale—grand stuff, already served on tap in the Bay Area and at other sophisticated locales.

With a logo depicting a one-eyed jack doing the proverbial 12-ounce curl, **Peter B's Brewpub,** 2 Portola Plaza (in the alley behind the Doubletree Hotel), 831/649-4511, is a real find in Monterey proper, offering great microbrews on tap and good pub grub. The Brit-style pub in Monterey is **The Crown & Anchor,** across from the Marriott at 150 W. Franklin St., 831/649-6496, dark and inviting with a brassy seagoing air. The full bar features 20 beers on tap, and the food is pretty darn good and reasonably priced—from the fish and chips or bangers and mash to spicy meatloaf, curries, cottage pie, and steak and mushroom pie. You'll also find salads and sandwiches and a special menu for the "powder monkeys" (Brit sailor slang for kids). Open for lunch and dinner daily, with the full menu available until midnight. Or consider the **London Bridge Pub,** Municipal Wharf (north of Fisherman's Wharf, at Del Monte and Figueroa),

831/655-2879, which specializes in authentic British cuisine and pours more than 60 different beers (the "Hall of Foam") to wash it down.

At the Wharf

Named for tender squid breaded and then sautéed in butter, TV chef John Pisto's **Abalonetti Seafood Trattoria,** 57 Fisherman's Wharf, 831/373-1851, offers relaxed lunch and dinner—primarily seafood (especially calamari) and standard Italian fare. The restaurant is fairly inexpensive with a nice view. Out on the end of the secondary pier at the wharf is very good **Rappa's Seafood Restaurant,** Fisherman's Wharf #1, 831/372-7562, an ocean-side oasis with outdoor dining, reasonable prices, good food, and early-bird dinners. Equally good **Domenico's on the Wharf,** another Pisto outpost, 50 Fisherman's Wharf #1, 831/372-3655, has a Southern Italian accent. The menu features fresh seafood, homemade pasta, chicken, steak, and veal dishes and an award-winning, very California wine list. Full bar. The oyster bar is open from 10 A.M. daily.

Cannery Row

If you're spending most of the day at the Monterey Aquarium, try the **Portola Café and Restaurant** there. Or head out onto the Row. Many of the places along Cannery Row offer early-bird dinners, so if price matters, go deal shopping before you get hungry.

Get your margarita fix and decent Mexican fare at **El Torito,** 600 Cannery Row, 831/373-0611. Jose Cuervo flaming fajitas, anyone? For something simple, an interesting choice for "views, brews, and cues" is the **Blue Fin Café and Billiards,** 685 Cannery Row, 831/375-7000. In addition to salads, sandwiches, and full dinners, the Blue Fin boasts a full bar emphasizing bourbons and scotches and also serves some 40 beers, including 22 ales and lagers on tap. There's plenty to do besides eat and drink, too, thanks to 18 pool tables, snooker, foosball, darts, and shuffleboard. Live music and DJs, too. No cover.

Naturally enough, seafood is the predominant dinner theme along the Row. The **Chart House,** 444 Cannery Row, 831/372-3362, brings its trademark casually elegant, nautical-themed decor to the Row, serving primarily seafood, steaks, and prime rib—predictably tasty. A bit inland but still looking to the sea for inspiration is TV chef John Pisto's casual **Whaling Station Restaurant,** 763 Wave, 831/373-3778, another locally popular dinner house offering everything from seafood and house-made pastas to mesquite-grilled Black Angus steaks. Open daily. Pisto's Paradiso Trattoria has been replaced by the elegant, Far East-themed **Blue Moon,** 654 Cannery Row, 831/375-4155, which still includes seafood and Italian specialties like cioppino and crab risotto.

The exceptional and expensive **Sardine Factory,** 701 Wave St., 831/373-3775, serves New American regional fare, from seafood and steaks to pasta and other specialties, in an elegant setting. Seafood served here, by the way, is included on the Monterey Bay Aquarium's approved "sustainable fisheries" list. Full bar. Open daily for dinner.

Another upscale Row restaurant going for the nautical theme is much more casual **Schooners Bistro on the Bay,** 400 Cannery Row (at the Monterey Plaza Hotel), 831/372-2628, specializing in California cuisine at lunch and dinner. Another possibility is the hotel's renowned but still casual **Duck Club Restaurant,** 831/646-1706, which serves outstanding bay views and superb American regional cuisine for breakfast and dinner daily.

Stylish Dining

N Fresh Cream, across from Fisherman's Wharf and upstairs at 100-C Heritage Harbor, 99 Pacific St., 831/375-9798, features wonderful French country cuisine lightened a bit by a fresh California sensibility. Fresh Cream has won so many awards people can't keep track of them all—not even all those consecutive years of the *Wine Spectator's* Award of Excellence. Everything is worthy of a recommendation, from the mushroom bisque, duckling in black-currant sauce, and Holland Dover sole Meuniere to the Grand Marnier soufflé. Great views of Monterey Bay are served, too. One of the Monterey Peninsula's best restaurants, Fresh Cream is also dressier than most. Meals are expensive, but even travelers light in the pocketbook can afford dessert and coffee. Open

for dinner only; menu changes daily. Call for information and reservations.

Still popular is the relaxed, kid-friendly all-American bistro **Montrio,** 414 Calle Principal (at Franklin), 831/648-8880, another of Monterey's favorite restaurants, this one at home in a onetime firehouse. You might start with fire-roasted artichokes, terrine of eggplant, or Dungeness crab cakes, then continue with grilled gulf prawns, lamb tenderloins, or Black Angus New York steak. Vegetarians can dig into the oven-roasted portobello mushroom over polenta and veggie ragout. At last report, Monday was still cioppino night. You'll also enjoy marvelous sandwiches at lunch, exquisite desserts, a full bar (good bar menu), and a great wine list. Open Mon.–Sat. for lunch, daily for dinner.

Equally stylish is the historic 1833 **N Stokes Restaurant & Bar,** 500 Hartnell St. (at Madison), 831/373-1110, its exteriors—including the gardens—preserving that Monterey Colonial style, its impressive interiors suggesting the Old World. But the excellent food is the thing. On the menu here is rustic, refined, and reasonably affordable California-style country Northern Mediterranean made from the freshest available local ingredients, from savory soups, salads, and tapas to seafood, chicken, lamb, and beef. Small plates might feature choices such as house-made mozzarella and ciabatta bread served with herbed olive oil and oven-roasted spinach gratin with mussels and herbed breadcrumbs. Large plates might include pasta tubes with house-made fennel sausage, manila clams, and spinach aioli; seared hanger steak with spinach cheese tart; or perhaps grilled lavender pork chops with leek-lemon bread pudding. Full bar, good wines. Open for lunch Mon.–Sat., for dinner daily.

Other Mediterranean possibilities include relaxed, kid-friendly **Cibo Ristorante Italiano,** 301 Alvarado, 831/649-8151, serving rustic but stylish Sicilian fare—plenty of pizzas and pastas—including the specialty bay shrimp in pesto, vodka, and cream sauce—and good house-made desserts. A three-course fixed-price menu is served nightly from 5 to 7 P.M.

Serving up stylish "American country" fare, **Tarpy's Roadhouse,** inside the historic stone

Ryan Ranch homestead three miles off Hwy. 1 on Hwy. 68 (at Canyon del Rey), 831/647-1444, is not to be confused with some cheap-eats-and-beer joint. The point here is reinterpreting American classics—and that's no cheap-eats tale. Dinner includes such things as Indiana duck, Dijon-crusted lamb loin, baby back ribs, and grilled vegetables with succotash. Great desserts; salads and sandwiches at lunch; full bar. Open for lunch and dinner daily; brunch on Sunday.

For other fine dining in Monterey, head for the **Duck Club** on Cannery Row (see above) or consider some of the great possibilities in nearby cities.

INFORMATION

The **Monterey Visitor Center,** Camino El Estero at Franklin, 831/648-5373, is staffed by the Monterey County Convention & Visitors Bureau and offers personal expertise as well as reams of flyers on just about everything in and around the region. It's open April–Oct., Mon.–Sat. 9 A.M.–6 P.M., Sun. 9 A.M.–5 P.M.; Nov.–March, Mon.–Sat. 9 A.M.–5 P.M., Sun. 10 A.M.–4 P.M. You can also stop by the "mini-center" at the Visitor & Convention Bureau's main office, downtown at 150 Oliver St., 831/626-1426, open weekdays 10 A.M.–5:30 P.M. (There are also CVB satellite centers in Salinas and King City.) For additional area information, including a current visitor guide, call 888/221-1010 or see www.montereyinfo.org. Via the website you can also book a room at more than 100 area motels and hotels; request a meeting planner; send an e-postcard; and get up to speed on attractions, arts, and events. Other resources include the **Monterey Peninsula Chamber of Commerce,** 380 Alvarado St. in Monterey, 831/648-5360, www.mpcc.com, and the **Old Monterey Business Association,** 321 Alvarado St. Ste. G, 831/655-8070, www.oldmonterey.org.

The *Monterey County Herald,* www.montereyherald.com, is the mainline community news source. For an alternative view of things, pick up the free *Monterey County Weekly,* www.coastweekly.com, also offering entertainment (including clubs) and events information.

TRANSPORTATION

You can come bus, either by Greyhound or local transit (see below, and also see the Santa Cruz section) **Greyhound** is at 1042 Del Monte Ave., 831/373-4735 or 800/231-2222 (system-wide

ON MONTEREY FOG

I t is the Pacific that exercises the most direct and obvious power upon the climate. At sunset, for months together, vast, wet, melancholy fogs arise and come shoreward from the ocean. From the hilltop above Monterey the scene is often noble, although it is always sad. The upper air is still bright with sunlight; a glow still rests upon the Gabelano Peak; but the fogs are in possession of the lower levels; they crawl in scarves among the sand-hills; they float, a little higher, in clouds of a gigantic size and often of a wild configuration; to the south, where they have struck the seaward shoulder of the mountains of Santa Lucia, they double back and spire up skyward like smoke. Where their shadow touches, color dies out of the world. The air grows chill and deadly as they advance. The trade-wind freshens, the trees begin to sigh, and all the windmills in Monterey are whirling and creaking and filling their cistern with the brackish water of the sands. It takes but a little while till the invasion is complete. The sea, in its lighter order, has submerged the earth. Monterey is curtained in for the night in thick, wet, salt, and frigid clouds; so to remain till day returns; and before the sun's rays they slowly disperse and retreat in broken squadrons to the bosom of the sea. And yet often when the fog is thickest and most chill, a few steps out of town and up the slope the night will be dry and warm and full of inland perfume.

Excerpted from Robert Louis Stevenson's "The Old Pacific Capital," Fraser's Magazine, 1880

information and reservations), www.grey
hound.com. Or you can come by train. Amtrak's
Coast Starlight runs from Los Angeles to Seattle
with central coast stops in Oxnard, Santa Barbara,
San Luis Obispo, Salinas, and Oakland. If you'll
be heading to the San Francisco Bay Area from
the Monterey Peninsula, keep in mind that Amtrak also connects in San Jose with the San Fran-
cisco-San Jose **Caltrain,** 650/817-1717 or
800/660-4287 (in the service area), www.cal
train.com. For help in figuring out the way to San
Jose—and how to get around the entire Bay Area
by rapid transit—see www.transitinfo.org.

Monterey-Salinas Transit buses can get you
to and from the **Amtrak** station in Salinas, 11
Station Place. Contact 831/422-7458 (depot),
800/872-7245, or website: www.amtrak.com for
reservations and schedule information, including
information on Amtrak's Thruway bus connections from Monterey and vicinity, a service included in some fares.

By Air

Not far from Santa Cruz, the **San Jose International Airport,** 408/501-7600, www.sjc.org, is
the closest major airport served by commuter
and major airlines. To get to Monterey from the
airports in San Jose or San Francisco—or vice
versa—you can take **Monterey-Salinas Airbus,**
based at Marina Municipal Airport, 791 Neeson Rd., Marina, 831/883-2871. The buses shuttle back and forth up to 10 times daily.

You can fly directly into the Monterey Peninsula area. The **Monterey Peninsula Airport,** 200
Fred Kane Dr. #200, 831/648-7000, www.mon
tereyairport.com, offers direct and connecting
flights from all domestic and foreign locales—
primarily connecting flights, because this is a
fairly small airport. **United Airlines/United Express,** 800/241-6522; **American/American Eagle
Airlines,** 800/433-7300; and **America West Air-
lines/America West Express,** 800/235-9292, are
all allied with major domestic and/or international carriers. You can fly directly into Monterey
from San Francisco, Los Angeles, or Phoenix.

The newest peninsula airport is the **Marina
Municipal Airport,** north of Monterey proper
on Neeson Road in Marina, 831/582-0102,

www.airnav.com/airport/OAR. Another possibility is the **Salinas Municipal Airport,** 831/758-
7214, www.salinasairport.com, a mecca for
private pilots and charters, helicopter tours, and
flight training companies.

By Car

Getting around by car can be a problem; even
finding streets is confusing due to missing signs,
complex intersections and traffic signals, and
one-way routes. Local traffic jams can be horrendous. So save yourself some headaches and
avail yourself of local public transportation (see
below). Drivers, park at the 12-hour meters near
Fisherman's Wharf—the cheapest lots are downtown—and walk (or bike) elsewhere. Or take
the shutle or bus. For more specific parking advice, pick up the free *Smart Parking in Monterey:
How to Find Affordable Legal Public Parking*
brochure at area visitors centers.

By Bicycle

Bicycling is another way to go. The local roads are
narrow and bike paths are few, but you can get
just about everywhere by bike if you're careful.
Rent bikes at **Wheel Fun Rentals @ Bay Bikes,**
640 Wave St. (on Cannery Row), 831/646-
9090, www.baybikes.com, where you can opt
for mountain bikes, touring bikes, or four-wheel
covered surreys known as pedalinas. You can
also rent bikes at **Adventures by the Sea,** 299
Cannery Row, 831/372-1807, www.adventures
bythesea.com, which offers guided bike tours
as well as rental mountain bikes, bikes built for
two, and pedalinas, and **A B Seas Kayaks,** 32
Cannery Row, Ste. 5, 888/371-6035, www
.montereykayak.com.

By Shuttle and Bus

Once parked, from Memorial Day through Labor
Day you can ride Monterey-Salinas Transit's
MST Trolley—a free rubber-tired trolley system connecting the Tin Cannery shopping center (at the edge of Pacific Grove), the Monterey
Bay Aquarium, Cannery Row, Fisherman's
Wharf, and the town's historic downtown adobes
with the downtown conference center, nearby
motels and hotels, and parking garages. The free

COURTESY OF THE MINETA SAN JOSE INTERNATIONAL AIRPORT

San José International Airport

trolleys run daily 10 A.M.–7 P.M. See a Monterey-Salinas Transit guide—or MST's website—for a route map (MST trolley) and schedule. A separate MST trolley route serves adjacent Pacific Grove Tues.–Sat. 10 A.M.–7 P.M.

To get around on public buses otherwise, contact **Monterey-Salinas Transit,** headquartered at 1 Ryan Ranch Rd., 831/899-2555 or 831/424-7695 (from Salinas), www.mst.org, though most buses roll out from the downtown transit center. "The Bus" serves the entire area, including Pacific Grove, Carmel, and Carmel Valley, from Watsonville south to Salinas. Local buses can get you just about anywhere, but some run sporadically. Pick up the free Rider's Guide schedule at the downtown **Transit Plaza** (where most buses stop and where Alvarado, Polk, Munras, Pearl, and Tyler Streets converge) or at motels, the chamber of commerce, and the library. The standard single-trip fare (one zone) is $1.75; exact change required; free transfers. Some longer routes traverse multiple zones and cost more. Seniors, the disabled, and children can ride for $.85 with the transit system's courtesy card. Children under age 5 ride free. A regular adult day pass costs $3.50, and a super day pass (valid on all routes and all zones) is $7; seniors and students pay half price. In April, for the Big Sur Marathon—

and for other special events—and otherwise from late May through early September, bus 22 runs south to famous Nepenthe in Big Sur (two buses per day in each direction; $3.50 one way).

Keep in mind that Monterey-Salinas Transit buses can get you to and from the **Amtrak** station in Salinas, 11 Station Place. Call 831/422-7458 (depot) or 800/872-7245, or see www.amtrak.com for reservations and schedule information, including information on Amtrak's Thruway bus connections from Monterey and vicinity, a service included in some fares.

Tours

An unusual thrill: cruising town in a facsimile Model A or Phaeton from **Rent-A-Roadster,** 229 Cannery Row, 831/647-1929, www.rent-a-roadster.com. The basic rate is about $30–40 an hour (with weekday deals) but you can arrange half-day and full-day tours, too—and head south to Big Sur and San Simeon in style.

Ag Venture Tours in Monterey, 831/643-9463 or 888/643-9463, www.whps.com/agtours, specializes in winery tours in the Monterey Wine Country, Carmel Valley, Salinas Valley, and Santa Cruz Mountains. A typical daylong tour includes tasting at three different wineries, a vineyard walk, and a picnic lunch.

Salinas and Vicinity

The sometimes bone-dry Salinas River starts in the mountains above San Luis Obispo and flows north through the Salinas Valley, much of the time underground, unseen. Named for the salt marshes, or salinas, near the river's mouth, the Salinas River is the longest underground waterway in the United States. The 100-mile-long Salinas Valley, with its *fertile* soil and lush lettuce fields, is sometimes referred to as the nation's Salad Bowl. To the west is the Santa Lucia Range; to the east are the Gabilan and Diablo Mountains. Cattle graze in the hills.

No longer such a small town—suddenly and surprisingly at least somewhat hip—Salinas was long the blue-collar birthplace of novelist John Steinbeck, who chronicled the lives and hard times of California's down-and-out. Some things don't change much. More than 60 years after the 1939 publication of Steinbeck's Pulitzer Prize–winning *The Grapes of Wrath,* the United Farm Workers (UFW) are still attempting to organize the primarily Hispanic farm laborers and migrant workers here. The idea of a unionized agricultural labor force has never been popular in the United States, and certainly not with Salinas Valley growers. In 1936, during a lettuce workers' strike, Salinas was at the center of national attention. Reports to the California Highway Patrol that communists were advancing on the town—an event "proven" by red flags planted along the highway, some of which were sent as evidence to politicians in Sacramento—led to tear gas and tussling between officers, growers, and strikers. The state highway commission later insisted that the construction warning banners be returned to the area's roadsides.

SIGHTS

A Salinas tradition (since 1911) is the four-day **California Rodeo,** held on the third weekend in July. It is one of the world's largest rodeos, with bronco busting and bull riding, roping and tying, barrel racing, kiddie parade, cowboy poetry, and a big western dance on Saturday night. The rowdiness here—cowboy-style, of course—rivals Mardi Gras. For information, contact the California Rodeo, 1034 N. Main St. in Salinas, 831/775-3100 or 800/771-8807 (office) or 800/549-4989 (advance ticket sales), www.carodeo.com. There's western high art, too. See the massive triptych sculpture by Claes Oldenberg, titled *Hat in Three Stages of Landing,* on the lawn of the nearby Salinas Community Center, 940 N. Main Street. The series of 3,500-pound yellow hats appear to have been tossed from the nearby rodeo grounds. Art lovers, also note the **John Cerney agriculture-related art,** colossal cut-out displays out standing in the fields surrounding Salinas.

The **Boronda Adobe,** 333 Boronda Rd. (at W. Laurel), 831/757-8085, headquarters for the Monterey County Historical Society, www.mchsmuseum.com, is an outstanding example of a Mexican-era Monterey Colonial adobe. Built between 1844 and 1848 by Jose Eusebio Boronda and virtually unaltered since, the tiny structure has been refurbished and now features museum displays and exhibits, including a few handsome original furnishings. Note the wood shingles, a considerable departure from traditional red-clay tiles. Open Mon.–Fri. 10 A.M.–2 P.M. and Sun. 1–4 P.M. for tours (donation requested). Also here is the one-room 1897 **Old Lagunita School House** that starred in the John Steinbeck story "The Red Pony," and a turn-of-the-20th-century home designed by architect William H. Weeks, currently being restored for use as a museum.

Toro Park, six miles out of town on the way to Monterey at 501 Monterey-Saliunas Hwy. (Hwy. 68), is a good picnic stop, a pleasant 4,756-acre regional park with good hiking, biking, and horseback trails. For an invigorating walk and views of both Monterey Bay and Salinas Valley, take the 2.5-mile trail to Eagle Peak. The park is open daily 8 A.M.–dusk. The day-use fee is $4 on weekdays, $6 on weekends and holidays. For information and group picnicking call 831/755-4899 or 888/588-2267.

Forget all those cowpoke jokes. These days Salinas is cowtown cool, continuing to find new ways to blend the old and the new. The arrival downtown of the National Steinbeck Center started something of a Salinas Valley cultural renaissance. Now Old Town boasts some stylish coffee stops and restaurants—sometimes with a happy tip of the Stetson to Western heritage, as at Hullaballoo on Main and Smalley's (see below for details). And shops, such as **Rooms in Bloom,** 246 Main St., 831/753-7080; **This Or Die** next door at 248 Main, 831/751-6777; and **Lush,** 345 Main, 831/771-9002. In summer 2004 the 16-screen **Maya Cinemas** complex was under construction—thanks to movie producer Moctesuma Esparza, of *The Milagro Beanfield Wars* and *Selena* fame—creating yet another reason to come downtown. There are intriguing events, too, including **Vino, Vittles and Verse,** a Cowboy Poetry Wine Supper associated with A Taste of Monterey, staged in July in Old Town Salinas. In September comes **Taste of the Valley,** a food and wine festival serving as centerpiece for the annual local Salute to Agriculture. Also part of the same general party is the **Farm Workers Challenge** at The Farm, an afternoon "inter-farm challenge" in which farm workers race to lay sprinkler pipes, back up an outhouse, and pack fresh lettuces. Afterward, there's complimentary corn on the cob all around.

◪ National Steinbeck Center

The Grapes of Wrath didn't do much for John Steinbeck's local popularity. Started as a photojournalism project chronicling the "Okie" Dust Bowl migrations to California during the Depression, Steinbeck's *Grapes* instead became fiction. The entire book was a whirlwind, written between June and October 1938. After publication, it became a bestseller and remained one through 1940. Steinbeck was unhappy about the book's incredible commercial success; he believed there was something wrong with books that became so popular.

Vilified here as a left-winger and Salinas Valley traitor during his lifetime, Steinbeck never came back to Salinas. (The only way the town would ever take him back, he once said, was in a six-foot

wooden box. And that's basically how it happened. His remains are at home at the local Garden of Memories Cemetery.) Most folks here have long ago forgiven their local literary light for his political views, so now you'll find his name and book titles at least mentioned, if not prominently displayed, all around town.

Some people have long been trying to make it up to Steinbeck. After all, he was the first American to win both the Pulitzer and Nobel Prizes for literature. Efforts to establish a permanent local Steinbeck center finally succeeded, and in summer 1998 the doors of the $10.3 million National Steinbeck Center opened to the public. Billed as a "multimedia experience of literature, history, and art," the Steinbeck Center provides at least one answer to the question of how to present literary accomplishment to an increasingly nonliterary culture. And that answer is—ta da—high-tech interactivity. In addition to changing exhibits, seven themed permanent galleries—incorporating sights, sounds, and scents—introduce Steinbeck's life, work, and times, in settings ranging from Doc Rickett's lab on Cannery Row and the replica boxcar of "ice-packed" lettuce to the (climbable) red pony in the barn. Seven theaters show clips from films derived from Steinbeck's writings. But some appreciations are strictly literal, including John Steinbeck's trusty green truck and camper Rocinante (named after Don Quixote's horse), in which the writer sojourned while researching *Travels with Charley.* The **Art of Writing Room,** with literary exhibits and all kinds of technical interactivity, explores the themes of Steinbeck's art and life. The 30,000-piece **Steinbeck Archives** here, open only to researchers by appointment, was originally housed in the local John Steinbeck Library on Lincoln Avenue. The archival collection includes original letters, first editions, movie posters, and taped interviews with local people who remember Steinbeck. Some of the barbed remarks, made decades after the publication of *The Grapes of Wrath,* make it clear that local wrath runs at least as deep as the Salinas River. The relatively new, highly interactive **Valley of the World Gallery** showcases local agriculture, on its own terms more so than those Steinbeck represented. It's a valuable contribution to public awareness

Monterey Bay

nonetheless, given the California's increasing distance from its agricultural roots.

Other attractions include the sunny **One Main Street Café** and the **museum store,** which features a good selection of books in addition to gift items. To visit some of the actual places Steinbeck immortalized in his fiction, be sure to pick up the 24-page *Steinbeck Country: A Guide to Exploring John Steinbeck's Monterey County.* Also see if you can find a used copy of *The John Steinbeck Map of America,* now out of print.

The center is open daily 10 A.M.–5 P.M., but is closed on Easter, Thanksgiving, Christmas, and New Year's Day. Admission is $10.95 adults, $8.95 seniors (over age 62) and students with ID, $7.95 youths (ages 13 to 17), $5.95 children (age 6 to 12), free for age 5 and under. For more information about the center and its events and activities, contact National Steinbeck Center, 1 Main St. in Salinas, 831/775-7240 or 831/796-3833, www.steinbeck.org.

Steinbeck House

Steinbeck described the family home—a jewel-box Victorian, located just two blocks from the National Steinbeck Center—as "an immaculate and friendly house, grand enough, but not pretentious." And so it still is, as both a dining and historic destination—a must-see for Steinbeck fans. The Salinas Valley Guild serves up gourmet lunches for Steinbeck fans and literary ghosts alike, featuring Salinas Valley produce and Monterey County wines and beer, at Steinbeck House, the author's birthplace and "a living museum" at 132 Central St., open Mon.–Sat. 11 A.M.–2:30 P.M. The menu changes weekly, served by volunteers dressed in period Victorian costumes. Call 831/424-2735 for information and reservations (suggested but not required). The house is also open for guided tours (call for current information), and there's a "Best Cellar" book and gift shop in the basement, 831/757-0508. All proceeds maintain and support the Steinbeck House and local charities.

Other Steinbeck Attractions

On the first weekend in August, come for the annual **Steinbeck Festival**—four days of films, lectures, tours, and social mixers. And in late February or early March, the town throws a Piscean **Steinbeck Birthday Party.** For information and tickets for these and other events, call 831/775-4721 or 831/796-3833. **The Western Stage** performs occasional Steinbeck works, other dramatic productions, and popular concerts on the Hartnell College campus, 156 Homestead Avenue. For information and reservations call 831/755-6816 or see www.westernstage.com.

ACCOMMODATIONS

Camp at the **Mazda Raceway Laguna Seca** facility near Monterey. **Fremont Peak State Park,** on San Juan Canyon Road (southeast from San Juan Bautista), 831/623-4255, has some first-come, first-camped primitive campsites, though that only makes sense if you're heading that way anyway.

In the Soledad and King City areas, **Arroyo Seco** features several U.S. Forest Service campgrounds; take Arroyo Seco Road west off Hwy. 101, just south of Soledad, or take Carmel Valley Road south to its end and turn right. Or camp at **Los Coches Wayside Camp,** just south of Soledad, or **Paraiso Hot Springs,** nearby on Paraiso Springs Road, 831/678-2882. **San Lorenzo County Park,** on the Salinas River near King City, 831/385-5964, boasts some 200 campsites with hot showers and picnic tables; call 831/385-1484 for information and reservations. The **Monterey County Agricultural & Rural Life Museum** in San Lorenzo Park at 1160 Broadway, 831/385-8020, features Spreckels farmhouse, a barn with antique farm equipment, a cook wagon, a schoolhouse, and a historic railroad depot. Continuing south toward San Luis Obispo, both **Lake San Antonio** (north and south shore, call 831/385-8399 for information) and **Lake Nacimiento** have abundant campsites. All camping options are under $50.

Budget travelers, Salinas has a nice array of inexpensive motels, these including the usual Days Inn, Econo Lodge, Motel 6, and Super 8. Most other motels lining Hwy. 101 are a bit more upscale. Rooms at the **Comfort Inn,** just off the freeway at 144 Kern St., 831/758-8850 or

800/888-3839, feature in-room coffeemakers; some have microwaves and refrigerators. Rates are $100–$150. The fairly new, three-story **Best Western Hanns Inn** across the way at 175 Kern, 831/784-0176 or 888/829-0092 (central reservations), www.bestwesterncalifornia.com, has all the modern comforts and similar rates.

For something more rural, head for **Barlocker's Rustling Oaks Ranch Bed & Breakfast,** off River Road at 25252 Limekiln Rd., 831/675-9121. There are five guest rooms. Extras include horseback rides and trails, swimming pool (in season), a pool table, and a genuine country breakfast. Rates are $100–250.

SUGAR TOWN AND A STAGE STOP

A satellite community southeast of Salinas, the town of **Spreckels** was developed by Claus Spreckels in the late 1890s to house employees of his sugar beet factory. This is a genuine "company town," down to the sugar-beet architectural motifs in the roof gables of many historic homes. **Natividad** is a onetime stage station about seven miles north of Salinas and the site of the 1846 Battle of Natividad, where Californios attacked Yankee invaders herding 300 horses to Frémont's troops in Monterey.

FOOD

Get up to speed on the local politics of food production, then sample that famed Salinas Valley produce. The **Alisal Certified Farmers Market** is held at E. Alisal and Pearl every Thursday 9 A.M.–6 P.M. (until 8 P.M. in summer). Call 831/757-1819 for details. If you're here on the weekend, head for the **Salinas Sunday Certified Farmers Market** at the Northridge Mall, 796 Main St., 831/728-5060, held on Sunday from 8 A.M.–noon. Another possibile stop, any day, is **The Farm,** on Hwy. 68 just west of Salinas off the Spreckels exit, 831/455-2575—just look for the giant, mural-like sculptures by John Cerney—featuring certified organic fruits and vegetables, specialty products, agricultural memorabilia, and the opportunity to get out in the fields and commune with the vegetables. Open Mon.–Sat. 10 A.M.–6 P.M. Farm tours are available by reservation. There's a little farm-animal zoo here, too. For more information, see www.thefarm-salinasvalley.com.

A wonderful coffee stop just a couple blocks from the Steinbeck Center is the **Cherry Bean Gourmet Coffee House & Roastery,** 332 Main St., 831/424-1989. (And if you're really in a hurry—just passin' through—Salinas has an **In-N-Out Burger,** at 151 Kern Street.) For breakfast downtown, try the breakfast specialists at **First Awakenings,** 171 Main, 831/784-1125, where the pancakes are reputedly the best in the county. Open daily 7 A.M.–2:30 P.M. Cheap and good is

the locally popular **Rosita's Armory Café,** 231 Salinas St., 831/424-7039. Best bet for burgers and a long-running Salinas tradition is the unassuming **Toro Place Café** at 665 Monterey-Salinas Hwy., 831/484-1333. Weather permitting, take your burger out to the patio. And yes, that's a real bull's head on the wall.

The new Salinas hot spot, at last report, was unpretentious all-American **Hullaballoo** at 228 S. Main St., 831/757-3663, where you can covet the cheeseburgers and country-fried chicken, savor the backyard salmon, or go bonkers over the blackened prime rib. **Smalley's Roundup,** 700 W. Market, 831/758-0511, is an icon, though, locally famous for its oak-wood barbecue and other cowboy-style fine dining. (Reservations advised at dinner.) Open Tues.–Fri. for lunch, Tues.–Sun. for dinner. Always a best bet for literary lunch, especially for Steinbeck fans, is the historic **Steinbeck House,** just two blocks from the National Steinbeck Center at 132 Center St., open Mon.–Sat. 11 A.M.–2:30 P.M., 831/424-2735 (see listing above for more information).The **Salinas Valley Fish House,** 172 Main St., 831/775-0175, offers various "fresh catches" plus an oyster bar

INFORMATION AND SERVICES

The **Salinas Valley Chamber of Commerce,** 119 E. Alisal, 831/424-7611, www.salinaschamber .com, offers information on accommodations and sights, as well as a great little brochure: *Steinbeck*

Monterey Bay

Country Starts in Salinas. The Salinas chamber is also an official Monterey County Convention & Visitor Bureau outpost—and headquarters for the **Old Town Salinas Association,** 831/758-0725, www.oldtownsalinas.com—so stop here for any downtown event and business information or general Monterey County visitor information. Open 8:30 A.M.–5 P.M. Mon.– Fri., 9 A.M.–3 P.M. on Sat. (closed Sunday). There's another in King City, the **King City Visitors Center** in San Lorenzo Park, 1160 Broadway in King City, 831/385-1484, open daily 10 A.M.–4 P.M.

Amtrak is at 11 Station Place; call 831/422-7458 or 800/872-7245 or see www.amtrak.com for fare and schedule information. There's no train station in Monterey, but you can connect from here to there via **Monterey-Salinas Transit** bus 20 or 21 (or via the Amtrak Thruway bus as part of your train fare). For more information, contact Monterey-Salinas Transit, 1 Ryan Ranch Rd., Monterey, 831/424-7695 or 831/899-2555, www.mst.org. **Greyhound** is at 19 W. Gabilan St., 831/424-4418 or 800/231-2222, www.greyhound.com. The **Salinas Municipal Airport** is on Airport Boulevard, 831/758-7214.

SOLEDAD

Soledad, a sleepy town where no one hurries, is the oldest settlement in the Salinas Valley. Stop by the local bakery *(panadería)* on Front Street for fresh Mexican pastries and hot tortillas. **Misión Nuestra Señora de la Soledad** was founded here in 1791 to minister to the Salinas Valley natives. Our Lady of Solitude Mission three miles southwest of town was quite prosperous until 1825. But this, the 13th in California's mission chain, was beset by problems ranging from raging Salinas River floods to disease epidemics before it crumbled into ruin. The chapel was reconstructed and rededicated, and another wing has since been restored. The original 1799 mission bell still hangs in the courtyard of this active parish church. Outside is a lovely garden. The mission, 831/678-2586, which also offers a museum and gift shop, is open daily 10 A.M.–4 P.M. Just three miles south of Soledad (west at the Arroyo Seco interchange from Hwy. 101) is another historic

survivor, the 1843 **Richardson Adobe,** at Los Coches Rancho Wayside Campground. For more information about the area, contact **Soledad Mission Chamber of Commerce,** 635 Front St., 831/678-2278.

Paraiso Hot Springs

Nestled in a grove of lovely palm trees, with a sweeping valley view, this 240-acre old resort a few miles southwest of Soledad has an indoor hot mineral bath (suits required), outdoor pools, picnic tables and barbecues, campgrounds, and Victorian cabins—all rarely crowded. Weekly and monthly rates are available. Most people fancy day use, a bit pricey at $35. For more information and reservations, contact Paraiso Hot Springs, 34358 Paraiso Springs Rd. west of Soledad, 831/678-2882.

PINNACLES NATIONAL MONUMENT

Exploring these barren 24,000 acres of volcanic spires and ravines is a little like rock climbing on the moon. The weird dark-red rocks are bizarrely eroded, unlike anywhere else in North America, forming gaping gorges, crumbling caverns, terrifying terraces. Rock climbers' heaven (not for beginners), this stunning old volcano offers excellent trails, too, with pebbles the size of houses to stumble over. Visitors afraid of earthquakes should know that the Pinnacles sit atop an active section of the San Andreas Fault. Spring is the best time to visit, when wildflowers brighten up the chaparral, but sunlight on the rocks creates rainbows of color year-round. Rock climbing is the major attraction, for obvious reasons. Climbers come during the cool weather. But you can also hike, and in winter watch the raptors: golden eagles, red-shouldered hawks, kestrels, and prairie falcons.

Though it was Teddy Roosevelt who first utilized presidential decree on behalf on the Pinnacles—protecting it as a national monument in 1906—in early 2000 President Bill Clinton announced plans to expand the park by some 5,000 acres. Some of that acreage, when acquired, may encourage gentler, more family-oriented recreation.

Hiking

Of Pinnacles' existing (pre-expansion) 24,000-plus acres, nearly 16,000 are protected as wilderness. Only hiking trails connect the park's east and west sides. Some trails are fairly easy, while others are rugged. Pinnacles has four self-guided nature trails; the **Geology Hike** and **Balconies Trail** are quite fascinating. The short **Moses Spring Trail** is one of the best. Longest is the trek up the **Chalone Peak Trail,** 11 miles round-trip, passing fantastic rock formations (quite a view of Salinas once you get to the top of North Chalone Peak). Less ambitious is the **Condor Gulch Trail,** an easy two-mile hike into Balconies Caves from the Chalone Creek picnic area. Various interconnecting trails encourage creativity on foot. The best caves, as well as the most fascinating rock formations and visitors center displays, are on the park's east side. The fit, fast, and willing can hike east to west and back in one (long) day. Easiest return trip is via the Old Pinnacles Trail, rather than the steep Juniper Canyon Trail. Pack plenty of water.

Practicalities

As lasting testament to the land's rugged nature, there are two districts in the Pinnacles—west and east—and it's not possible to get from one to the other by road. Within the monument, bicycles and cars may only be used on paved roads. If coming from the west, get visitor information at the **Chaparral Ranger Station,** reached via Hwy. 146 heading east (exit Hwy. 101 just south of Soledad). For most visitors, Pinnacles is most accessible from this route, but it's a narrow road, not recommended for campers and trailers. If coming from the east, stop by the **Bear Gulch Visitor Center,** reached via Hwy. 25, then Hwy. 146 heading west. From Hollister, it's about 34 miles south, then about five miles west to the park entrance. Pinnacles is open for day use only; the vehicle entry fee is $5, the walk-in fee is $2; valid for seven days. An annual pass costs $15. Within the monument, bicycles and cars may only be used on paved roads. For additional information, contact Pinnacles National Monument, 5000 Hwy. 146 in Paicines, 831/389-4485, www.nps.gov/pinn.

Good rules of thumb in the Pinnacles: Carry water at all times and watch out for poison oak, stinging nettles, and rattlesnakes. Spelunkers should bring good flashlights and helmets. Pick up guides to the area's plantlife and natural history at the visitors centers, and also topo maps. Rock climbers can thumb through old guides there for climbing routes.

No camping is offered (or allowed) within the park. The closest private camping is **Pinnacles Campground, Inc.,** near the park's entrance on the east side, 2400 Hwy. 146, 831/389-4462, www.pinncamp.com. The campground is quite nice, featuring flush toilets, hot showers, fire rings, picnic tables, a swimming pool, some RV hookups, and group facilities. Under $50. Basic supplies and some food are available at the campground's store. But you can also stay in considerable style, thanks to the **Inn at the Pinnacles** just a few miles west of the park's west entrance, 831/678-2400, www.innatthepinnacles.com. Rates are $200–250.

Pinnacles National Monument

Monterey Bay

SAN JUAN BAUTISTA AND VICINITY

The tiny town of San Juan Bautista is charming and charmed, as friendly as it is sunny. (People here say the weather in this pastoral valley is "salubrious." Take their word for it.) Named for John the Baptist, the 1797 Spanish mission of San Juan Bautista is central to this serene community at the foot of the Gabilan Mountains. But the historic plaza, still bordered by old adobes and now a state historic park, is the true center of San Juan—rallying point for two revolutions, onetime home of famed bandit Tiburcio Vasquez, and the theatrical setting for David Belasco's *Rose of the Rancho.* Movie fans may remember Jimmy Stewart and Kim Novak in the mission scenes from Alfred Hitchcock's *Vertigo,* which were filmed here.

One of the most colorful characters ever to stumble off the stage in San Juan Bautista was one-eyed stagecoach driver Charley Parkhurst, a truculent, swaggering, tobacco-chewing tough. "He," however, was a woman, born Charlotte Parkhurst in New Hampshire. (Charley voted in Santa Cruz in 1866, more than 50 years before American women won the right to vote.)

In addition to history, San Juan Bautista has galleries, antiques and craft shops, and an incredible local theater troupe. To get oriented, pick up a walking tour brochure around town or at the **San Juan Bautista Chamber of Commerce,** 1 Polk St., 831/623-2454, www.sanjuan bautista.com, open weekdays only. In June experience mid-1800s mission days at **Early Days in San Juan Bautista,** a traditional celebration complete with horse-drawn carriages, period dress, music, and fandango. The barroom at the Plaza Hotel is even open for card games. Also fun in June is the **Peddler's Faire and Street Rod Classic Car Show,** one of the biggest street fairs anywhere, the chamber's annual fund raiser. The **Flea Market** here in August, with more than 200 vendors, is one of the country's best. Later in the month, **San Juan Fiesta Day** is the most popular venue of the wandering **Cabrillo Music Festival.** But the event of the year is *La Virgen del Tepeyac* or *La Pastorela* (they alter-nate yearly), traditional Christmas musicals that attract visitors from around the world—if they're still on. For more details and current information, contact El Teatro Campesino (see below). Christmas chorale music is also offered at the mission.

History

Partly destroyed by earthquakes in 1800 and 1906 (the San Andreas Fault is just 40 feet away), **Mission San Juan Bautista** has been restored many times. The 15th and largest of the Franciscan settlements in California, the mission here is not as architecturally spectacular as others in the Catholic chain. Visitors can tour sections of the mission—which still features an active parish church—though it's not really part of the adjacent state historic park. After visiting the small museum and gardens, note the old dirt road beyond the wall of the mission cemetery. This is an unspoiled, unchanged section of the 650-mile El Camino Real, the "royal road" that once connected all the California missions. Archaeological excavations at the mission by CSU Monterey, Hartnell College, and Cabrillo College students unearthed the foundations of the mission's original quadrangle, tower, well, and convent wing (which many historians previously believed had never existed). Students also cleared the 1799 Indian Chapel of debris and restored it; inside is an ornate altar built in the 1560s and moved to the chapel for the Pope's visit in 1987. Many of the students' other discoveries are on display in the mission's museum.

San Juan Bautista's oldest building is the **Plaza Hotel** at Second and Mariposa Streets on the west side of the plaza, originally barracks built in 1813 for Spanish soldiers. In horse and buggy days, San Juan Bautista was a major stage stop between San Francisco and Los Angeles, and the hotel was famous statewide. (Note the two-story outhouse out back.) Also fascinating are the stable—with its herd of fine old horse-drawn vehicles and the Instructions for Stagecoach Passengers plaque out front—and the restored blacksmith shop. Also worth a peek: the jail, washhouse, and cabin. The park day-use fee is $2.

Above the town of San Juan Bautista is **Pagan Hill.** Today a giant concrete cross stands where mission fathers once put up a wooden one, intended to ward off evil spirits supposedly summoned by Indian neophytes secretly practicing their traditional earth religion. The park is open daily 10 A.M.–4:30 P.M., in summer until 5 P.M. For information, contact San Juan Bautista State Historic Park, 19 Franklin St., 831/623-4881.

El Teatro Campesino

Don't pass through San Juan Bautista without trying to attend a performance by San Juan Bautista's El Teatro Campesino. Chicano playwright Luis Valdez founded this small theater group as guerrilla theater on the United Farm Workers' picket lines more than two decades ago. But Valdez's smash hits *Zoot Suit* and *Corridos* have since brought highly acclaimed nationwide tours and the birth of other Chicano *teatros* throughout the American Southwest. El Teatro's Christmas-season *La Pastorella,* the shepherd's story that alternates with the miracle play *La Virgen del Tepeyac,* is a hilarious and deeply poetic spectacle, a musical folk pageant about shepherds trying to get past comic yet terrifying devils to reach the Christ child. Besides Spanish-language plays, concerts, and film festivals, the company also presents contemporary and traditional theater in English. El Teatro Campesino's permanent playhouse is at 705 Fourth St., 831/623-2444. For a current calendar of events, call or see the website: www.elteatrocampesino.com.

Practicalities

A few tent sites and 165 RV hookups are available at the private **Mission Farm Campground and RV Park,** in a walnut orchard at 400 San Juan–Hollister Rd., 831/623-4456. Or, for fishing and tent/RV camping, try private (stocked) **McAlpine Lake,** 900 Anzar Rd., 831/623-4263, www.mcalpinelake.com. Under $50. There are also a few cabins. Accommodations with the right ambience are available at the mission-style **Posada de San Juan Hotel,** 310 Fourth St., 831/623-4030, with fireplace and whirlpool tubs in almost every room. Rates are $100–150.

For farm-fresh produce, pick up a copy of the free guide to nearby family farms and ranches. Fresh cherries are available in June; apricots in July; and apples, walnuts, and kiwis in the fall. For good bread—at least 35 kinds—plus pastries and picnic fixings, stop by **San Juan Bakery & Grocery,** 319 Third, 831/623-4570.

The **Mission Cafe,** 300 Third St., 831/623-2635, is good for families at breakfast and lunch. Try **Felipe's,** 313 Third St., 831/623-2161, for Mexican and Salvadoran food. **Doña Esther,** 25 Franklin, 831/623-2518, serves Mexican fare—and the best margaritas in town. More upscale is **Jardines de San Juan,** 115 Third St., 831/623-4466, where you can get *pollos borachos* (drunken chickens) at lunch and dinner daily. Nice garden setting. For Italian, try either **Don Ciccio's,** 107 The Alameda, 831/623-4667, or the **Inn at Tres Pinos** south of Hollister in Tres Pinos at 6991 Hwy. 25, 831/628-3320.

For steaks with plenty of giddyup, locals single out the very Western, dinner-only **The Cutting Horse** at 307 Third St., 831/623-4549. People say this is the best steakhouse around. Despite the ominously accurate name, well worth a stop for continental-style lunch and dinner (and the view of the San Juan Valley) is the **Fault Line Restaurant** nearby at 11 Franklin, 831/623-2117.

Fremont Peak State Park

In March 1846, Gen. John C. Frémont and Kit Carson built a "fort" here in defiance of the Mexican government, unfurled their flags on Gabilan Peak (now Fremont Peak), and waited for the supposedly imminent attack of Californio troops. When no battle came, they broke camp and took off for Oregon. Fremont Peak State Park, a long, narrow, isolated strip in the Gabilan Mountains northeast of Salinas, has rolling hills with oaks, madrones, Coulter pines, and spring wildflowers that attract hundreds of hummingbirds. The park offers good hiking in spring and good views from the top of Fremont Peak. Another attraction at Fremont Peak is an observatory with a 30-inch Challenger reflecting telescope, open to the public at least twice monthly for free programs including lectures and observation; call 831/623-2465 for details (recorded) or see www.fpoa.net.

Camping is available in about 25 primitive campsites (some in the picnic area) and a group camp. To get to the park from Hwy. 156, head 11 miles south on San Juan Canyon Road (County Road G1)—paved but very steep and winding (trailers definitely not recommended). Campsites are $11–15. For reservations, contact **ReserveAmerica,** 800/444-7275, www.reserve america.com. Park day use is $4. For more park information, contact Fremont Peak State Park, 831/623-4255, www.parks.ca.gov.

Hollister

If Gilroy is the garlic capital of the world, then Hollister is the earthquake capital. Because of the region's heavy faulting, some say this San Benito County town moves every day, however imperceptibly. (A small 1985 quake shook loose a 20,000-gallon oak wine cask and flooded the Almaden Winery just south of town.) Agricultural Hollister is as historic as San Juan Bautista, but the "feel" here is straight out of the Old West. Stop by the **San Benito County Historical Society Museum,** 498 Fifth St. (at West), 831/635-0335 (open Saturday and Sunday 1–3 P.M.; other times by appointment), then wander through Old Town (particularly along Fifth) to appreciate Hollister's old Victorians.

Traditional cowboy events and some unique competitions are the name of the game during June's **San Benito County Rodeo,** an event dedicated to the vaquero. The **Fiesta-Rodeo** in July dates back to 1907, when it was first held to raise funds for rebuilding Mission San Juan Bautista after the big quake in 1906. The most memorable event here is the big **Hollister Independence Rally,** a motorcyclists' gathering on the **Fourth of July** weekend made famous by Marlon Brando in the movie *The Wild Ones.*

GILROY AND VICINITY

Will Rogers supposedly described Gilroy as "the only town in America where you can marinate a steak just by hanging it out on the clothesline." But Gilroy, the "undisputed garlic capital of the world," dedicates very few acres to growing the stinking rose these days. The legendary local garlic farms have been declining due to soil disease since 1979—ironically, the first year of the now-famous and phenomenally successful Gilroy Gar-

lic Festival. Gilroy now grows housing subdivisions—former *San Francisco Chronicle* columnist Herb Caen defined modern Gilroy as the place "where the carpet ends and the linoleum begins"—and the San Joaquin Valley grows most of California's garlic. Nonetheless, that unmistakable oily aroma still permeates the air in summer, since more than 90 percent of the world's garlic is processed or packaged here.

Other attractions in Gilroy include Goldsmith Seeds' seasonal six-acre **Field of Dreams** experimental flower seed garden. Call 408/847-7333 for tour information. Downtown Gilroy has its historic attractions, too. The best place to start exploring is the **Gilroy Historical Museum** at Fifth and Church, 408/848-0470, open weekdays 9 A.M.–5 P.M.

For more information about what's cookin' in and around Gilroy, contact the **Gilroy Visitor Bureau,** 7780 Monterey St., 408/842-6436, www.gilroyvisitor.org, and the **Gilroy Chamber of Commerce,** 7471 Monterey, 408/842-6437, www.gilroy.org.

Gilroy Garlic Festival

It's chic to reek in Gilroy. On the last full weekend in July, 150,000 or more garlic lovers descend on the town for several dusty days of sampling garlic perfume, garlic chocolate, and all-you-can-eat garlic ice cream (for some reason, just a few gallons of the stuff takes care of the entire crowd). Who wouldn't pay the $10 admission for belly dancing, big bands, and the crowning of the Garlic Queen? For more information, contact the **Gilroy Garlic Festival Association,** 7473 Monterey, 408/842-1625, www.gilroygarlic festival.com. If you're looking for garlic gifts and accessories at other times, Gilroy boasts a number of garlic-themed shops; get a current listing from the city's website, www.gilroy.org.

Wineries

Besides sniffing out local Italian scallions, tour the Gilroy "wine country." Most of the area's wineries are tucked into the Santa Cruz Mountain foothills west of the city, seven of these along Hwy. 152's Hecker Pass—just beyond Goldsmith Seeds and the Bonfante Gardens theme

MELISSA SHEROWSKI

Gilroy celebrates garlic-ness

park (see below). At the mountain's summit is 3,688-acre **Mt. Madonna County Park,** 7850 Pole Line Rd., 408/842-2341 ($5 day use, reservable campsites available), where 20 miles of hiking trails wind through redwoods and oak woodlands. Stop for a picnic, or a bite at the venerable **Mt. Madonna Inn Restaurant,** 831/724-2275. The hearty, full-flavored red wines produced here are still made by hand. **Solis Winery,** 3920 Hecker Pass Rd., 408/847-6306 or 888/411-6457, www.soliswinery.com, offers tastings of its chardonnay, Sangiovese, merlot, cabernet sauvignon, and syrah 11 A.M.–5 P.M. daily (tours by appointment), closed for major holidays. Come by **Sarah's Vineyard,** 4005 Hecker Pass Rd., 408/842-4278, http://sarahs-vineyard.com, for tasting its estate-grown chardonnays and pinot noirs on Friday noon–5 P.M. and weekends 11 A.M.–5 P.M. The **Fortino Winery,** 4525 Hecker Pass Rd., 408/842-3305, www.fortinowinery.com, is run by the Fortino family, and specializes in hearty old-country red wines. Other Gilroy area wineries include the **Thomas Kruse Winery,** 3200 Dryden Ave.,

408/842-7016, with its eclectic collection of antique equipment, presided over by philosopher-winemaker Thomas Kruse. His Gilroy Red and other wines sport handwritten, offbeat labels.

Bonfante Gardens

The region's most amazing new visitor attraction, Gilroy's glorious, $100 million Bonfante Gardens Theme Park is an inspired horticultural feat. That's right—*horticultural.* Trees and shrubs, in particular. Some 23 years were spent planning and developing the 75-acre park's unique landscape before Bonfante Gardens finally opened its gates in June 2001. Botanical oddities abound, from the five themed gardens to the 25 wonderful "circus trees" created by the late Axel Erlandson—wonders created by grafting and pleaching, feats that have never been successfully duplicated. Kids are equally impressed by the Monarch Garden's immense greenhouse with a monorail, train, and river running through it.

Though the pace here is relaxed and the thrills understated, traditional theme park attractions haven't been neglected. Bonfante Gardens includes

40 family-friendly rides and attractions, from the cheerful 1927 Illions Supreme Carousel and the Quicksilver Express roller coaster to the very cool antique car ride. The latter allows you to "tour" either the 1920s or 1950s—dig those old gas stations—depending on where you climb on. Still, encouraging people to appreciate trees is the main point of Bonfante Gardens. All attractions are literally woven into the landscape. New in 2004: the **Wild Bird Adventure,** a 1,500-square-foot aviary where kids can feed and interact with the birds.

At last report, park admission was $31.99 adults, $22.99 seniors and children ages 3–6 (age 2 and under free); parking, $7 per vehicle. Advance ticket prices on the website can go as low as $19.99 adults, however, and at various times there may be other specials—such as Bring A Friend For Free. The park is open daily in summer, weekends only during much of the rest of year. For current hours and days of operation, admission prices, special events, and other details, contact Bonfante Gardens, 3050 Hecker Pass Hwy. (west of Gilroy on Hwy. 152), 408/840-7100, www.bonfantegardens.com.

Casa de Fruta and Coyote Reservoir

Unforgettable is one word for Casa de Fruta on Pacheco Pass Highway, 831/637-0051, www

.casadefruta.com. The sprawl of neon-lit, truck stop–type buildings is complete with trailer park and swimming pool, motel, petting zoo, merry-go-round, and miniature train and tunnel. Stop off at the Casa de Fruta Coffee Shop (open 24 hours) and read about the Casa de Fruta Country Store, Casa de Fruta Gift Shop, Casa de Fruta Fruit Stand, Casa de Burger, Casa de Sweets Bakery and Candy Factory, Casa de Choo-Choo, and Casa de Merry-Go-Round on the "mail me" souvenir paper placemats. (This being California, there's a Casa de Wine, too.) To see the coffee cups "flip," ask the coffee shop staff for a show.

Coyote Reservoir, eight miles north of Gilroy, is great for sailboarding, sailing, and fishing. Open year-round 8 A.M.–sunset for day use ($5); 75 campsites ($9–18). For information, contact **Coyote Lake County Park,** 10840 Coyote Lake Rd. in Gilroy, 408/842-7800, www .parkhere.org. Reserve campsites at www .gooutsideandplay.org. To get to Coyote Lake, take the Leavesley Road/Hwy. 152 exit east from Hwy. 101; after two to three miles, head north on New Avenue then east on Roop Road to Gilroy Hot Springs Road. The Coyote Reservoir Road turnoff is about a mile farther, the campground two miles more.

Pacific Grove

Pacific Grove began in 1875 as a prim, proper tent city founded by Methodists who, Robert Louis Stevenson observed, "come to enjoy a life of teetotalism, religion, and flirtation." No boozing, waltzing, zither playing, or reading Sunday newspapers was allowed. Dedicated inebriate John Steinbeck lived here for many years, in the next century, but had to leave town to get drunk. Pacific Grove was the last dry town in California: Alcohol has been legal here only since 1969. The first Chautauqua in the western states was held here—bringing "moral attractions" to heathen Californians—and the hall where the summer meeting tents were stored still stands at 16th and Central Avenues.

Nicknamed Butterfly City U.S.A. in honor of migrating monarchs—there's a big fine and/or six months in jail for "molesting" one—Pacific Grove dazzles with its rocky shoreline with wonderful tidepools and sparkles with Victorians and modest seacoast cottages, community pride, and an absolutely noncommercial Butterfly Parade in October. Also here is Asilomar, a well-known retreat—now a state-owned conference center—with its own beautiful beach. In addition to impressive accommodations and restaurants, the town also offers some great bargains—especially for secondhand shoppers. Trendy **Time After Time,** 301 Grand Ave., 831/643-2747, and **Encore Boutique,** 125

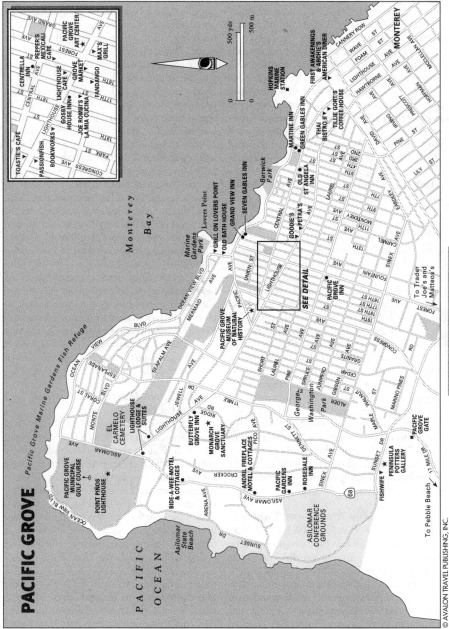

PACIFIC GROVE

Monterey Bay

Monterey Bay

MONTEREY

Pacific Grove Marine Gardens Fish Refuge

PACIFIC OCEAN

PACIFIC GROVE MUNICIPAL GOLF COURSE

POINT PIÑOS LIGHTHOUSE

EL CARMELO CEMETERY

LIGHTHOUSE LODGE & SUITES

BIDE-A-WEE MOTEL & COTTAGES

BUTTERFLY GROVE INN

MONARCH GROVE SANCTUARY

ANDRIL FIREPLACE COTTAGES

ROSEDALE INN

PACIFIC GARDENS INN

FISHWIFE

PENINSULA POTTERS GALLERY

PACIFIC GROVE GATE

ASILOMAR CONFERENCE GROUNDS

Asilomar State Beach

To Pebble Beach

To 17 Mile Dr

SEE DETAIL

PACIFIC GROVE MUSEUM OF NATURAL HISTORY

Lovers Point

Marine Gardens Park

GRILL ON LOVERS POINT
OLD BATH HOUSE
GRAND VIEW INN
SEVEN GABLES INN

Berwick Park

MARTINE INN
GREEN GABLES INN

THAI BISTRO II

OLD ST. ANGELA INN

GOODIE'S
PETRA'S

TILLIE GORT'S COFFEE HOUSE

PACIFIC GROVE INN

HOPKINS MARINE STATION

FIRST AWAKENINGS & ARCHIE'S AMERICAN DINER

CANNERY ROW

Washington Park

To Trader Joe's and Matteo's

500 yds
500 m

© AVALON TRAVEL PUBLISHING, INC.

Detail inset

GRAND AVE

PACIFIC GROVE ART CENTER

PEPPER'S MEXICAL CAFE

MAX'S GRILL

CENTRELLA INN

GROVE MARKET

FANDANGO

LIGHTHOUSE INN

BOOKWORKS

GOSBY HOUSE INN

JOE ROMBI'S
LA MIA CUCINA

TOASTIE'S CAFE

PASSIONFISH

Central Ave., 831/375-1700, are good places to start. And don't miss all those usd bookstores along Lighthouse Avenue.

Pacific Grove is well served by Monterey-Salinas Transit buses (see Monterey section). For events, accommodations, restaurants, and other current information, stop by the **Pacific Grove Information Center** at Forest and Central, or contact the **Pacific Grove Chamber of Commerce,** 831/373-3304 or 800/656-6650, www .pacificgrove.org. Another interesting web portal is www.93950.com. The **Pacific Grove Public Library,** 550 Central (at Fountain), 831/648-3160, is open Mon.–Thurs. 10 A.M.–8 P.M., Fri.–Sat. 10 A.M.–5 P.M.

SIGHTS

From Pacific Grove, embark on the too-famous 17-Mile Drive in adjacent Pebble Beach. But better (and free), tour the surf-pounded peninsula as a populist. The city of Pacific Grove is one of few in California owning its own beaches and shores, all dedicated to public use. Less crowded and hoity-toity than 17-Mile Drive, just as spectacular, and absolutely free, is a walk, bike ride, or drive along Ocean View Boulevard. Or take the Monterey Peninsula Recreation Trail as far as you want; this path for walkers, joggers, bicyclists, skaters, and baby-stroller-pushers runs all the way from Marina to Pebble Beach. It's paved in places (right through downtown Monterey, for example), dirt in others. Or cycle from here to Carmel on the Del Monte Forest ridge via Hwy. 68 (the Holman Highway) for a spectacular view of the bay, surrounding mountains, and 17-Mile coastline to the south.

The "Three-Mile Drive"—or Walk
Along the Ocean View route are Berwick Park, Lovers Point, and Perkins Park; altogether, Pacific Grove boasts 13 community parks. These areas (and points in between) offer spectacular sunsets, crashing surf, craggy shorelines, swimming, sunbathing, and picnicking, plus whale-watching in season, sea otters, sea lions, seals, shorebirds, and autumn flurries of monarch butterflies. Stanford University's **Hopkins Marine Station** on Point

Cabrillo (China Point) is also along the way, the crystal offshore waters and abundant marinelife attracting scientists and students from around the world. This is the first marine laboratory on the Pacific coast. (An aside for Steinbeck fans: This was the location of Chin Kee's Squid Yard in *Sweet Thursday.*) As for **Lovers Point,** the granite headland near Ocean View Boulevard and 17th Street, there is considerable disagreement over whether Pacific Grove could have been *sexual* in Methodist days, when it was named. The popular local opinion, still, is that the name was originally Lovers of Jesus Point. But conscientious researchers have established that the reference is to romance—and was, at least as far back as 1890. (For help in divining other arcane area details, pick up a copy of *Monterey County Place Names: A Geographical Dictionary* by Donald Thomas Clark, and its companion *Santa Cruz County Place Names.* If you can find them.) Trysting place or no, Lovers Point is not a safe place to be during heavy weather; entirely too many people have been swept away to their deaths. Picnic at **Perkins Point** instead, or wade or swim there (safe beach). **Marine Gardens Park,** an aquatic park stretching along Ocean View, with wonderful tidepools, is usually a good spot for watching sea otters frolic in the seaweed just offshore.

Pacific Grove Museum of Natural History
Pacific Grove's Museum of Natural History at Forest and Central showcases *local* wonders of nature, including sea otters, seabirds (a huge collection with more than 400 specimens), rare insects, and native plants. A fine array of Native American artifacts is on rotating display. Particularly impressive is the relief map of Monterey Bay, though youngsters will probably vote for *Sandy,* the gray whale sculpture right out front. Besides the facsimile butterfly tree, the blazing feathery dried seaweed exhibit is a must-see. Many traveling exhibits visit this museum throughout the year, such as 2004's *Portraits of the Great Apes, by Robert Cooper.* The museum's annual **Wildflower Show** on the third weekend in April is excellent. For information, contact the museum at 165 Forest Ave., 831/

648-5716, www.pgmuseum.org. Open Tues.–Sun. 10 A.M.–5 P.M. Admission is free (donations greatly appreciated).

Point Piños Lighthouse

Built of local granite and rebuilt in 1906, this is the oldest continuously operating lighthouse on the Pacific coast, listed on the National Register of Historic Places. The beacon here and the mournful foghorn have been warning seagoing vessels away from the point since February 1, 1855. The original French Fresnel lenses and prisms are still in use, though the lighthouse is now powered by electricity and a 1,000-watt lamp instead of whale oil. The lighthouse and the **U.S. Coast Guard Museum** inside are free and open Thurs.–Sun. 1–4 P.M. **Doc's Great Tidepool,** yet another Steinbeck-era footnote, is near the foot of the lighthouse. The lighthouse and associated museum, two blocks north of Lighthouse Avenue on Asilomar Boulevard, are regularly open to the public 1–4 P.M. Thurs.–Mon., in summer 11:30 A.M.–5 P.M. daily. Small

MELISSA SHEROWSKI

Point Piños lighthouse

donation. For information, contact the Pacific Grove Museum (see above).

Across from the lighthouse parking lot is fascinating **El Carmelo Cemetery,** a de facto nature preserve for deer and birds. For more bird-watching, amble down to freshwater **Crespi Pond** near the golf course at Ocean View and Asilomar Boulevards.

Asilomar

The Young Women's Christian Association's national board of directors coined this Spanish-sounding non-word from the Greek *asilo* ("refuge") and the Spanish *mar* ("sea") when they established this facility as a YWCA retreat in 1913. **Asilomar State Beach** has tidepools and wonderful white-sand beaches, shifting sand dunes, wind-sculpted forests, spectacular sunsets, and sea otters and gray whales offshore. Not to mention all those surfers. Inland, many of Asilomar's original buildings—designed by architect Julia Morgan, best known for Hearst's San Simeon estate—are now historical landmarks. Primarily a conference center offering meeting rooms and accommodations for groups, Asilomar is now a nonprofit unit of the California state park system; subject to room availability, the general public can also stay here. Guest or not, anyone can fly kites or build sandcastles at the beach, stop to appreciate the forest of Monterey pine and cypress, and watch for deer, raccoons, gray ground squirrels, hawks, and owls.

For current information, contact: Asilomar Conference Center, 800 Asilomar Blvd. in Pacific Grove, 831/372-8016 or 831/642-4242 (reservations for leisure travelers), www.visitasilomar.com. You can book online. To stay here, make reservations up to 90 days in advance, or call—not more than a week in advance—to inquire about cancellations. Rates are $100–150—full country-style breakfast included. Children ages 3–12 can stay (in the same room with an adult) for $5 more.

The 17-Mile Drive

The best place to start off on the famed 17-Mile Drive—technically in Pebble Beach—is in Pacific Grove or, alternatively, the Carmel Hill

MONARCH BUTTERFLIES

Pacific Grove is the best known of the 20 or so places where monarch butterflies winter. Once partial to Monterey pine or cypress trees for perching, monarchs these days prefer eucalyptus introduced from Australia. Adults arrive in late October and early November, their distinctive orange-and-black Halloweenish wings sometimes tattered and torn after migrating thousands of miles. But they still have that urge to merge, first alighting on low shrubs, then meeting at certain local trees to socialize and sun themselves during the temperate Monterey Peninsula winter before heading north to Canada to mate in the spring and then die. Their offspring metamorphose into adult butterflies the following summer or fall and—mysteriously—make their way back to the California coast without ever having been here. Milkweed eaters, the monarchs somehow figured out this diet made them toxic to bug-loving birds, who subsequently learned to leave them alone.

MELISSA SHEROWSKI

Pacific Grove loves its monarch butterflies.

Even when massed in hundreds, the butterflies may be hard to spot: with wings folded, their undersides provide neutral camouflage. But if fog-damp, monarchs will spread their wings to dry in the sun and "flash"—a priceless sight for any nature mystic.

---

gate off Hwy. 1. Not even 17 miles long anymore, since it no longer loops up to the old Del Monte Hotel, the drive still skirts plenty of ritzy digs in the 5,300-acre, privately owned Del Monte Forest in the four-gated "town" of Pebble Beach. Note the Byzantine castle of the banking/railroading Crocker family. Believe it or not, the estate's private beach is heated with underground pipes.

From **Shepherd's Knoll,** there's a great panoramic view of both Monterey Bay and the Santa Cruz Mountains. **Huckleberry Hill** does have huckleberries, but botanically more fascinating is the unusual coexistence of Monterey pines, Bishop pines, and Gowen and Monterey cypress. Sadly, these days pitch canker disease is taking its toll in the forest, killing off even venerable specimen trees. **Spanish Bay,** a nice place to picnic, is named for Portolá's confused land expedition from Baja in 1769; Portolá was looking

for Monterey Bay, but he didn't find it until his second trip. **Point Joe** is a treacherous, turbulent convergence of conflicting ocean currents, wet and wild even on calm days. ("Joe" has been commonly mistaken by mariners as the entrance to Monterey Bay, so countless ships have gone down on these rocks.) Both **Seal Rock** and **Bird Rock** are aptly named. **Fanshell Beach** is a secluded spot good for picnics and fishing, but swimming is dangerous.

Most famous of all is the landmark **Lone Cypress**—the official (trademarked) emblem of the Monterey Peninsula—at the route's midpoint. No longer lonely, this craggy old-timer is visited by millions each year; it's now "posed" with supporting guy wires, fed and watered in summer, and recovering well from a recent termite attack. At **Pescadero Point,** note the cypress bleached ashen and ghostlike by sun, salt spray, and wind.

From Pacific Grove by car, the tour costs $8, map included. The drive is open for touring from sunrise to 30 minutes before sunset year-round. For more information, call 831/647-5235 and ask for concierge.

Pebble Beach

Very private Pebble Beach has seven world-class golf courses made famous by Bing Crosby's namesake tournament. The Crosby, now called the **AT&T Pebble Beach National Pro Am Golf Tournament,** is held each year in late January or early February. For golfing information or reservations, contact 800/654-9300 or see www.pebble beach.com. Only guests at the ultra-upscale resort accommodations can reserve more than 24 hours in advance. (And some guests book their stays one to two years in advance.) Other facilities are open to the public, including jogging paths and beautiful horse trails. Just about everything else—country clubs, yacht clubs, tennis courts, swimming pools— is private (and well guarded), though the public is welcome to stay here and play here, for a price. If you're here in August, join in the **Scottish Highland Games** or take in the **Concours d'élégance** classic car fest at The Lodge.

Events

Pacific Grove boasts more than 75 local art galleries, enough to keep anyone busy. The **Peninsula Potters Gallery,** 2078 Sunset Dr., 831/372-8867, is the place to appreciate the potter's art; open Mon.–Sat. 10 A.M.–4 P.M. Also worth a stop is the excellent **Pacific Grove Art Center,** 568 Lighthouse, 831/375-2208.

There are hometown-style events year-round. The renowned Pacific Grove **Wildflower Show** is held on the third week in April, an exhibit of more than 600 native species (150 outdoors) in bloom at the Pacific Grove Museum of Natural History. Also come in April for the **Pacific Grove Poetry Festival.** In March or April, the **Good Old Days** celebration brings a parade, Victorian home tours, and arts and crafts galore. In late July, come for the annual **Feast of Lanterns,** a traditional boat parade and fireworks ceremony that started when Chinese fishermen lived at China Point (their village was torched in 1906).

Pacific Grove's biggest party comes in October with **Welcome Back Monarch Day.** This native, naturalistic, and noncommercial community bash heralds the return of the migrating monarchs and includes the **Butterfly Parade,** carnival, and bazaar, all to benefit the PTA. Not coincidentally, from October to February the most popular destination in town is the **Monarch Grove Sanctuary** on Ridge Road (just off Lighthouse), where docent-led tours are offered daily; for reservations, call 831/375-0982 or 888/746-6627. Otherwise, come in October for the **Pacific Grove Victorian Home Tour** or in November for the **State Championship High School Marching Band Festival.** In December, check out **Christmas at the Inns,** when several local B&Bs, decorated for the holidays, hold an open house and serve refreshments. Here as in Monterey, **First Night** is everyone's favorite kick-off for the new year.

ACCOMMODATIONS

To maintain its "hometown America" aura, Pacific Grove has limited its motel development. The local chamber of commerce provides accommodations listings. Bed-and-breakfast inns are popular in Pacific Grove—see separate listings, below—and these comfortable, often luxurious home lodgings compare in price to much less pleasant alternatives elsewhere on the peninsula.

Hotels and Inns: $100–150

The state-owned **M Asilomar Conference Center,** 800 Asilomar Ave. in Pacific Grove, 831/372-8016 or 831/642-4242 (reservations for leisure travelers), fax 831/372-7227, www.asilomarcen ter.com, enjoys an incredible 60-acre setting on the Pacific Ocean, complete with swimming pool, volleyball nets, horseshoe pits, and miles of beaches to stroll. When it's not completely booked with businesspeople, conferences, and other groups, it can be a reasonably priced choice for leisure travelers. Adding to the earthy appeal: architect Julia Morgan designed many of the resort's pine lodges. Generally less expensive are the older, rustic cottages, though all have private bathrooms. Some units have kitchens and fireplaces. Call ahead for reservations, up to 90 days in advance, or hope for last-minute cancellations. Rates are $100–150, full country breakfast included. Children ages 3–12 stay (in same room with adult) for $5 more. Asilomar now offers T-1 high-speed Internet access, so guests can check their email in the lobby, and a new patio with bonfire ring—s'mores, anyone?—and regulation sand volleyball court.

Otherwise, closest to the beach are the 1930s-style cottages at **Bide-a-Wee-Motel & Cottages,** near Asilomar at 221 Asilomar Blvd., 831/372-2330, www.bideaweemotel.com. Some of the cottages have kitchenettes; in the off-season some rooms are under $100. Also across from Asilomar and family-owned is comfortable, woodsy **Andril Fireplace Motel & Cottages,** 569 Asilomar Blvd., 831/375-0994, www.andrilcottages .com, which feature all the comforts. Outdoor whirlpool tub, too. Cottages have full kitchens, fireplaces (wood provided), free DVDs, even private decks. Some of the larger cottage configurations—such as two bedroom with a separate living room—are more than $150 but still a good deal for families or couples traveling together.

Near Asilomar is the **Pacific Gardens Inn,** 701 Asilomar Blvd., 831/646-9414 or 800/262-1566 in California, www.pacificgardensinn.com, where the contemporary rooms feature wood-burning fireplaces, refrigerators, TVs, and phones—even popcorn poppers and coffeemakers. Suites feature full kitchens and living rooms. Complimentary continental breakfast and evening wine and cheese are offered. Very nice. Right across from Asilomar is the recently renocated, all-suites **Rosedale Inn,** 775 Asilomar Blvd., 831/655-1000 or 800/822-5606, www .rosedaleinn.com, where all rooms have a ceiling fan, fireplace, large whirlpool tub, wet bar, refrigerator, microwave oven, in-room coffeemaker, remote-control color TV and VCR, even a hair dryer. Some suites have two or three TVs and/or a private patio. Especially if the monarchs are in town, consider a stay at the **Butterfly Grove Inn,** 1073 Lighthouse Ave., 831/373-4921 or 800/337-9244, www.butterflygroveinn.com. Butterflies are partial to some of the trees here. The inn is quiet, with a pool, a spa, some

kitchens, and fireplaces. Choose rooms in a comfy old house or motel units. Some are under $100.

Hotels and Inns: $150 and Up

The **Lighthouse Lodge and Suites,** 1150 and 1259 Lighthouse Ave., 831/655-2111 or 800/ 858-1249, www.lhls.com, are two adjoining properties. The 31 Cape Cod–style suites feature abundant amenities—king beds, large whirlpool tubs, plush robes, mini-kitchens with stocked honor bars—and are the most expensive. The 64 lodge rooms feature abundant comforts, too, and are family friendly, with extras including large-screen TV with cable, refrigerator, microwave, in-room coffee, even breakfast and a complimentary poolside barbecue in the afternoon (weather permitting). Lower rates in the off-season; two-night minimum on summer weekends.

Those super-swank choices in adjacent Pebble Beach are definitely beyond the reach of most people's pocketbooks. But if you win the lottery, check 'em out. At **The Inn at Spanish Bay,** 2700 17 Mile Dr. (at the Scottish Links Golf Course), 831/647-7500, rooms are ultra-deluxe, with gas-burning fireplaces, patios, and balconies with views. Amenities include the usual luxuries plus beach access, a pool, saunas, whirlpools, a health club, tennis courts, and a putting green. (BTW, the Inn at Spanish Bay's hotel lobby is a swell place to lounge around and at least pretend you're a swell, what with the spectacular views, gorgeous interiors, inviting couches in front of the fireplace, and open-air patio. That bagpiper playing at sunset is an unexpected bonus.)

Also an unlikely choice for most travelers is **The Lodge at Pebble Beach,** another outpost of luxury on 17 Mile Drive, 831/624-3811. (If you don't stay, peek into the exclusive shops here.) A recent addition are the elegant, estate-style cottages at the 24-room **Casa Palmero,** near both The Lodge and the first fairway of the Pebble Beach Golf Links. For still more pampering, the **Spa at Pebble Beach** is a full-service spa facility. For reservations at any of these Pebble Beach Resort facilities, contact 800/654-9300 or website: www.pebblebeach.com.

Bed-and-Breakfasts

Victoriana is particularly popular in Pacific Grove. The most famous Victorian inn in town is the elegant **Seven Gables Inn,** 555 Ocean View Blvd., 831/372-4341, www.pginns.com, which offers ocean views from all 14 rooms and an abundance of European antiques and Victorian finery. Rates include fabulous full breakfast and afternoon tea. Sharing the garden and offering equally exceptional, if more relaxed, Victorian style is the sibling **Grand View Inn** next door, 557 Ocean View Blvd., 831/372-4341. The view from all 11 rooms, with their antique furnishings and luxurious marble bathrooms, is indeed grand. Full breakfast, afternoon tea. Rates at both are $150 and up.

The lovely **Green Gables Inn,** 104 Fifth St., 831/375-2095 or 800/722-1774, www.four sisters.com, is a romantic gabled Queen Anne. The seaside "summer house" offers marvelous views, five rooms upstairs, a suite downstairs, and five rooms in the carriage house. Of these, seven feature private bathrooms. Rates include continental breakfast. Rates are $100–300. The **Gosby House Inn,** 643 Lighthouse Ave., 831/375-1287 or 800/527-8828, is another of the Four Sisters—this one a charming (and huge) Queen Anne serving up fine antiques, a restful garden, homemade food, and fresh flowers. All 22 rooms boast great bayside views, and most feature private bathrooms. Some have fireplaces, whirlpool tubs, and TVs. Rates are $100 and up.

The 1889 **Centrella Inn,** 612 Central Ave., 831/372-3372 or 800/233-3372, www.centrel lainn.com, a national historic landmark, offers 20 rooms plus a whirlpool tub–equipped garden suite and five cottages with wood-burning fireplaces and wet bars. The cottage-style gardens are quite appealing, especially in summer. Rates include complimentary morning newspaper, full buffet breakfast, and a social hour in the afternoon (wine and hors d'oeuvres). Rates are $150–300.

The Cape Cod–style **Old St. Angela Inn,** 321 Central Ave., 831/372-3246 or 800/748-6306, www.sueandlewinns.com, is a converted 1910 country cottage featuring eight guest rooms decorated with antiques, quilts, and other homey

touches. Amenities include a garden hot tub, solarium, living room with fireplace, complimentary breakfast, and afternoon wine or tea and hors d'oeuvres. Rates are $100–250. The historic three-story (no elevator) **Pacific Grove Inn** is at 581 Pine (at Forest), 831/375-2825 or 800/732-2825, www.pacificgrove-inn.com. Some rooms and suites in this 1904 Queen Anne have ocean views, most have fireplaces, and all have private baths and modern amenities like color TVs, radios, and telephones. Breakfast buffet every morning. Rates are $150–250.

FOOD

A good Pacific Grove grocery stop is **Grove Market,** 242 Forest Ave., 831/375-9581. For edible eclectica—the usual impressive selection—plus affordable wine, PG has a **Trader Joe's,** 1170 Forest Ave., 831/656-0180, though if you want to "go local," consider **Tillie Gort's** on Central (see below), a very popular natural foods restaurant that opened an associated market in 2004. The best place around for a deli sandwich is **Goodie's,** at home in what served as Red Williams' gas station in John Steinbeck's novel *Cannery Row,* sharing space with a produce market at 518 Lighthouse Ave., 831/655-3663. Ham and baked brie, anyone?

Breakfast

A local favorite for breakfast, just a stroll from the Monterey Bay Aquarium, is **First Awakenings** in the American Tin Cannery at 125 Oceanview Blvd., 831/372-1125, where you can fill up on "bluegerm pancakes" (blueberry with wheat germ), omelettes, and crêpes. Sandwiches such as the "chicado"—grilled chicken, avocado, and cheese—star at lunch. Eat inside or out. Open daily for breakfast and lunch.

You can get marvelous crêpes for breakfast or lunch, as well as good waffles and homemade soups, at **Toastie's Cafe,** 702 Lighthouse Ave., 831/373-7543, open daily 7 A.M.–2 P.M. Also good for breakfast is the **Lighthouse Café** inside the onetime Winston Hotel at 602 Lighthouse, 831/372-7006. Or try the vegetarian and vegan dishes at **Tillie Gort's Coffee House** and art gallery, just a stroll from Cannery Row at 111 Central, 831/373-0335. The Mediterranean frittata, cinnamon raisin French toast, and tofu and various other scrambles shine at breakfast, though sides of chicken apple sausage, bacon, and Canadian bacon are available. If the Summer of Love is just a vague memory, one you'd like to revisit, you'll love this place. Tillie Gort's is locally famous for those decadent black bottom cupcakes, too, though try to hold off on those until lunch or dinner. Live music sometimes, too. Plus now there's a natural foods market.

For lattes, cappuccinos, espressos or just a good cuppa joe, head to the dual-purpose **Bookworks,** 667 Lighthouse Ave., 831/372-2242, where you can sample the wares in the bookstore as well as the coffeehouse. **Patisserie Bechler,** 1225 Forest Ave., 831/375-0846, is the place for French bakery goods.

Lunch and Dinner

Already revered is **M Matteo's** trattoria, an authentic and welcoming Sicilian cafè tucked into a little shopping center at 1180 Forest, 831/333-1035, the creation of Matteo Enea and his wife Cheryl. Enjoying Southern Italian comfort food is the whole point here. Everything is housemade, from the panini and flavorful sauces to the eggplant Parmigiana.

Thai Bistro II, 159 Central Ave., 831/372-8700, is the place to go for outstanding Thai food. Those with a fireproof palate will love the restaurant's spicy dishes, and vegetarians will appreciate the large number of meatless entrées. Open for lunch and dinner daily. (There's another Thai Bistro in Carmel Valley at 55 W. Carmel Valley Rd., 831/659-5900.) The locals' favorite for white-tablecloth Italian is **Joe Rombi's La Mia Cucina,** 208 17th St., 831/373-2416; for Mediterranean, **Petra's,** 477 Lighthouse Ave., 831/649-2530.

Locals say the homemade *chiles rellenos* at immensely popular **Peppers MexiCali Cafe,** 170 Forest Ave., 831/373-6892, are the best on the peninsula, but you won't go wrong with any of the Mexican and seafood specialties here, including tamales, seafood tacos, or spicy prawns. Beer and wine are served. Closed Tuesday, but

otherwise open weekdays and Saturday for lunch, nightly for dinner. Excellent for seafood, here with a Caribbean flair, is the relaxed, reasonably priced, and family-friendly **Fishwife** in the Beachcomber Inn, 1996-1/2 Sunset Dr. (at Asilomar), 831/375-7107, where such things as Boston clam chowder and grilled Cajun snapper fill out the menu. Full bar. Open daily for lunch and dinner.

A popular burger option is the Tin Cannery's **Archie's American Diner,** 831/375-6939, just the place to load up on Monterey burgers and garlic fries. Another good bet for burgers, not to mention that view, is the fast-food **Grill on Lovers Point,** 618 Oceanview Blvd., 831/649-6859.

Dinner-only **Passionfish,** 701 Lighthouse Ave., 831/655-3311, is another seafood hot spot, this one serving only seafood from fisheries currently considered sustainable. Meals are quite reasonable priced at $20 or less for most entrées, from wild Monterey Bay salmon to tilapia in sweet roasted red pepper vinaigrette over veggie risotto. Save room for some house-made dessert. Wine is an adventure here, too, especially since they're priced at retail. You can also order by the glass—even dessert wines—from an ever-changing international selection.

Stylish Dining

Among the Monterey Peninsula's hottest new restaurants, at last report, was casually dressy **M Max's Grill,** 209 Forest Ave., 831/375-7997, where most of the produce and other main ingredients are regional and fresh, and just about everything else, down to the breads and pastas, is house-made. Chef Hisayuki "Max" Muramatsu was most recently executive chef at Carmel's Anton & Michel; before that he was an award-winning chef in Tokyo, cooking at Maxim's of Paris. The menu changes regularly, yet house specialties such as grilled farm-fresh baby abalone with citrus capers in white wine sauce and Max's oen "surf and turf," coconut encrusted prawns plus broiled filet mignon in red wine sauce with potatoes Maxim's, are always on the menu. Quite reasonable prices, too, nice wine list. A truly great deal, especially for smaller appetites, is Max's fixed-price Sunset Menu, served 5–6 P.M. For

$13.95 you get soup or salad and your choice of a handful of entrées, these including blackened salmon, grilled calamari, and chicken piccata. Max's is open Tues.–Sun. 5–9:30 P.M. (closed Mondays), reservations essential on Friday and Saturday nights.

For boisterous Basque food, try **Fandango,** in the stone house at 223 17th St. off Lighthouse Ave., 831/372-3456. Still one of the best restaurants around, Fandango serves wonderful Mediterranean country fare—from mesquite-grilled seafood, steak, and rack of lamb to tapas, pastas, and paella—in several separate dining rooms warmed by fireplaces. Try the chocolate nougatine pie or *vacherin* for dessert. Sunday brunch here is superb. Dressy attire prevails at dinner in the smaller dining rooms, but everything is casual in the Terrace Room. Open for lunch (brunch on Sunday) and dinner daily.

Still a local favorite for that special night out is romantic, welcoming, and fairly expensive **N The Old Bath House** at Lovers Point, 620 Ocean View Blvd., 813/375-5195, beloved for its lively Northern Italian and French fare, exceptional desserts, and appetizing views. Full bar, venerable Scotch list, extensive wine list. Early Dinner and Children's Menus, too. Open nightly for dinner.

Carmel

Vizcaíno named the river here after Palestine's Mount Carmel, probably with the encouragement of several Carmelite friars accompanying his expedition. The name Carmel-by-the-Sea distinguishes this postcard-pretty coastal village of almost 5,000 souls from affluent Carmel Valley 10 miles inland and Carmel Highlands just south of Point Lobos on the way to Big Sur. Everything about all the Carmels, though, says one thing quite clearly: money. Despite its bohemian beginnings, these days Carmel tends to crankily guard its quaintness while cranking up the commercialism. (Shopping is the town's major draw.) Still free at last report are the beautiful city beaches and visits to the elegant old Carmel Mission. Almost free: tours of Robinson Jeffers's **Tor House** and fabulous **Point Lobos** just south of town.

Carmel hasn't always been so crowded or so crotchety. Open-minded artists, poets, writers, and other oddballs were the community's original movers and shakers—most of them shaken up and out of San Francisco after the 1906 earthquake. Upton Sinclair, Sinclair Lewis, Robinson Jeffers, and Jack London were some of the literary lights who once twinkled in this town. Master photographers Ansel Adams and Edward Weston were more recent residents. But, as often happens in California, land values shot up and the original bohemians were priced right out of the neighborhood. Still, the arts are still proud local residents.

In summer and on most warm-weather weekends, traffic on Hwy. 1 can back up for a mile or more in either direction due to the Carmel "crunch." At such times parking is usually nonexistent. (Even if you do find a parking spot in downtown Carmel, don't dawdle; parking is limited to one hour, and you risk a steep fine if you're late getting back.) Sane people take the bus, ride bikes, or walk. Better yet, come for the weekend and pretend you live here. That's really the only way to appreciate the town's unique characteristics—including the absence of streetlights, traffic signals, street signs, sidewalks, house numbers, mailboxes, neon signs, and jukeboxes.

Another thing about Carmel: It's gone to the dogs. For one thing, dogs can run free on Carmel Beach. For another, dogs are not only welcome but pampered at many hostelries and eateries around town, and many shopkeepers pass out doggie treats with no prompting. There's even a dogs-only drinking fountain in town, the **Fountain of Woof** at Carmel Plaza. And don't miss the doggie boutiques.

SIGHTS

To get oriented, take a walk. Carmel has a few tiny parks hidden here and there, including one

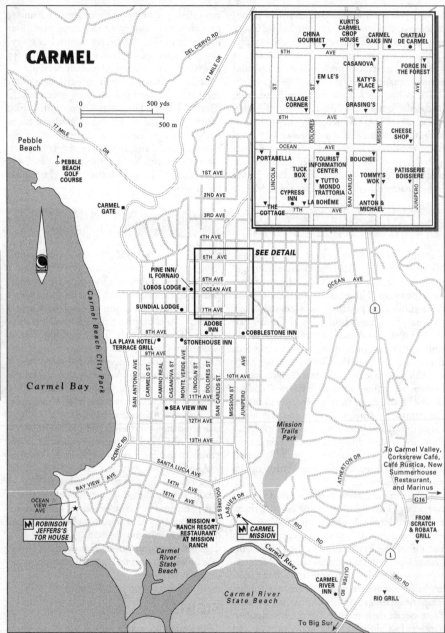

CARMEL

Pebble
Beach

PEBBLE
BEACH
GOLF
COURSE

CARMEL
GATE

Carmel Beach City Park

Carmel Bay

OCEAN
VIEW
AVE

ROBINSON
JEFFERS'S
TOR HOUSE

DEL CIERVO RD

17 MILE DR

1ST AVE

2ND AVE

3RD AVE

4TH AVE

5TH AVE

SEE DETAIL

PINE INN/
IL FORNAIO

6TH AVE

LOBOS LODGE

OCEAN AVE

OCEAN   AVE

7TH AVE

SUNDIAL LODGE

ADOBE
INN

8TH AVE

COBBLESTONE INN

LA PLAYA HOTEL/
TERRACE GRILL

STONEHOUSE INN

9TH AVE

SAN ANTONIO AVE

CARMELO ST

CAMINO REAL

CASANOVA ST

MONTE VERDE AVE

LINCOLN ST

DOLORES ST

SAN CARLOS ST

MISSION ST

JUNIPERO

10TH AVE

11TH AVE

SEA VIEW INN

12TH AVE

13TH AVE

Mission
Trails
Park

SANTA LUCIA AVE

BAY VIEW   AVE

14TH
AVE

15TH   AVE

DOLORES ST

LASUEN DR

SCENIC RD

MISSION
RANCH RESORT/
RESTAURANT
AT MISSION
RANCH

CARMEL
MISSION

Carmel
River
State
Beach

Carmel River
State Beach

ATHERTON DR

To Carmel Valley,
Corkscrew Café,
Café Rustica, New
Summerhouse
Restaurant,
and Marinus

G16

FROM
SCRATCH
& ROBATA
GRILL

RIO

OLIVER RD

RIO RD

Carmel River

CARMEL
RIVER
INN

RIO GRILL

To Big Sur

0   500 yds

0   500 m

Detail

5TH

AVE

CHINA
GOURMET

KURT'S
CARMEL
CHOP
HOUSE

CARMEL
OAKS INN

CHATEAU
DE CARMEL

CASANOVA

FORGE IN
THE FOREST

EM LE'S

KATY'S
PLACE

ST

ST

ST

ST

AVE

VILLAGE
CORNER

GRASING'S

6TH

AVE

DOLORES

MISSION

CHEESE
SHOP

OCEAN

AVE

PORTABELLA

TOURIST
INFORMATION
CENTER

BOUCHEE

LINCOLN

TUCK
BOX

TUTTO
MONDO
TRATTORIA

TOMMY'S
WOK

SAN CARLOS

PATISSERIE
BOISSIERE

JUNIPERO

CYPRESS
INN

LA BOHÈME

ANTON &
MICHAEL

THE
COTTAGE

7TH

AVE

MOON

17 MILE DR

Carmel Beach City Park

© AVALON TRAVEL PUBLISHING, INC.

Monterey Bay

especially for walkers—**Mission Trails Park,** featuring about five miles of trails winding through redwoods, willows, and wildflowers (in season). Finding it is challenging since Carmel doesn't believe in signs. To do the walk the easy way, start at the park's cleverly concealed Flanders Drive entrance off Hatton Road (appreciate the **Lester Rowntree Memorial Arboretum** just inside) before strolling downhill to the Rio Road trailhead near the mission. Then visit the mission or head downtown. Carmel's shops and galleries alone are an easy daylong distraction for true shoppers, but local architecture is also intriguing. The area between Fifth and Eighth Streets and Junipero and the city beach is packed with seacoast cottages, Carmel gingerbread "dollhouses," and adobe-and-post homes typical of the area.

Carmel Walks

For a great two-hour guided walk, Carmel Walks, 831/642-2700, www.carmelwalks.com, tours walkers past the town's original fairytale cottages, architecture by Bernard Maybeck and Charles S. Greene, onetime homes of bohemians, the local doings of photographers Edward Weston and Ansel Adams, and oddities such as a house made entirely of doors and the another built from pieces of old ships. The tour also visits Doris Day's pet-friendly hotel, includes tales of locally famous dogs, and notes local restaurants where dogs are permitted to dine with the family out on the patio. At last report, walks—$20 per person—were offered Tues.–Fri. at 10 A.M. and Sat. at 10 A.M. and 2 P.M. Reservations required.

Carmel Mission

The Carmel Mission, properly called Mission Basilica San Carlos Borroméo del Rio Carmelo, is wonderful and well worth a visit. California's second mission, it was originally established at the Monterey Presidio in 1770, then moved here the following year. It is the onetime headquarters and favorite foreign home of Father Junípero Serra, whose remains are buried at the foot of the altar in the sanctuary. The mission's magnificent vine-draped cathedral is the first thing to catch the eye. The romantic Baroque stone church, one of the state's most graceful buildings, complete with a four-bell Moorish tower, arched roof, and star-shaped central window, was completed in 1797.

Most of the buildings here are reconstructions, however, since the Carmel Mission fell to ruins in the 1800s. But these "new" old buildings, painstakingly rebuilt and restored in the 1930s under the direction of Sir Harry Downie, fail to suggest the size and complexity of the original bustling mission complex: an odd-shaped quadrangle with a central fountain, gardens, kitchen, carpenter and blacksmith shops, soldiers' housing, and priests' quarters. The native peoples attached to the mission—a labor force of 4,000 Christian converts—lived separately in a nearby village. More than 3,000 "mission Indians" are buried in the silent, simple cemetery. Most graves in these gardens are unmarked, but some are decorated with abalone shells. The gardens themselves, started by Downie, are fabulous, with old-fashioned plant varieties, from bougainvillea to bird of paradise, fuchsias, and "tower of jewels."

The Carmel Mission has three museums. The "book museum" holds California's first unofficial library—the 600 volumes Padre Serra brought to California in 1769. The silver altar furnishings are also originals, as are the ornate vestments, Spanish and native artifacts, and other mission memorabilia. Serra's simple priest's cell is a lesson by contrast in modern materialism.

The mission is just a few blocks west of Hwy. 1 at 3080 Rio Rd., 831/624-3600 (gift shop) or 831/624-1271 (rectory), and is open for self-guided tours on weekdays 9:30 A.M.–4:30 P.M., weekends 10:30 A.M.–4:15 P.M. Admission is $4 adults and seniors, $1 children 5–17 (under 5 free), but additional donations are appreciated. For current mission and parish information, see www.carmelmission.org.

Robinson Jeffers's Tor House

A medieval-looking granite retreat on a rocky knoll above Carmel Bay, Tor House was built by family-man poet Robinson Jeffers, who hauled the huge stones up from the beach below with horse teams. The manual labor, he said, cleared

poet Robinson Jeffers

his mind, and "my fingers had the art to make stone love stone." California's dark prince of poetry, Jeffers was generally aloof from the peninsula's other "seacoast bohemians." On the day he died here, January 20, 1962, it snowed—a rare event along any stretch of California's coast. James Karman's literary biography, **Robinson Jeffers: Poet of California** (Story Line Press, 1995), offers wonderful insight into Jeffers's life and work.

You can only begin to appreciate Tor House from the outside (it's just a short walk up from Carmel River Beach, on Ocean View Avenue between Scenic Road and Stewart Way). Jeffers built the three-story Hawk Tower, complete with secret passageway, for his wife, Una. The mellow redwood paneling, warm oriental rugs, and lovely gardens here soften the impact of the home's bleak tawny exterior—the overall effect somehow symbolizing Jeffers's hearth-centered life, seemingly far removed from the world's insanity. Almost whimsical is the collection of 100-

plus unicorns the poet gathered. Now a national historic landmark—don't go snooping around on your own—Tor House is open for small-group guided tours on Friday and Saturday, advance reservations required. Adults pay $7, full-time college students $4, high school students $2. The first tour begins at 10 A.M. and the final tour at 3 P.M. Tours are limited to six people; no children under 12 are allowed. For more information and reservations contact Tor House, 26304 Ocean View Ave. in Carmel, 831/624-1813, www.torhouse.org. Make reservations by phone or via email (see the website for details).

The Tor House Foundation also offers a full schedule of events, from its annual poetry prize, readings, and sunset garden parties to the Robinson Jeffers Seminars, Jeffers Country Bus Tour (of Big Sur), and Jeffers Poetry Walk.

Carmel Valley

The sunny (and warmer) sprawling "village" of Carmel Valley stretches some 14 miles inland via Carmel Valley Road, a well-designed but hellacious highway, at least between Carmel and these affluent suburbs and golf and tennis farms (including John Gardiner's Tennis Ranch). Locals curse tourists and others who drive the speed limit.

The village area has definite diversion value for the wealthy and the wannabes—note the shopping centers—but the valley has always been the one Carmel's just plain folks were most likely to inhabit. In 1939 Rosie's Cracker Barrel on Equiline Road became the valley's general store and soon the unofficial community center. Though Rosie's was always the place to pick up picnic supplies and whatnot, there was also a bar out back where locals held forth—definitely not a tourist joint. Rosie's is closed now; plans to reopen it as a museum are in the works. Still, some notable before-the-wealthy Carmel Valley traditions remain—like wide-open spaces. Outdoorsy types will appreciate **Garland Ranch Regional Park,** north of town at 700 W. Carmel Valley Rd., 831/659-4488. The park offers hiking trails on 4,500 hilly acres; you'll get an astounding view from the top of Snively's Ridge.

Monterey Bay

For more information about Carmel Valley and vicinity, contact the **Carmel Valley Chamber of Commerce,** 91 W. Carmel Valley Rd., 831/659-4000, www.carmelvalleychamber.com.

Tassajara Zen Mountain Center

Tassajara Hot Springs, beyond Carmel Valley Road, was long a respected area resort, established in 1869. (The Tassajara Road turnoff is off Cachagua Road near the southward intersection with Tularcitos.) According to Native American legend, these curative springs first flowed from the eyes of a young chief seeking help for his dying sister. Offering himself as a sacrifice to the sun, he turned to stone, and his tears became the hot springs.

Now the monastic Tassajara Zen Mountain Center, affiliated with the **San Francisco Zen Center,** Tassajara is the first Soto Zen monastery outside of Asia, open to the general public from April or May until early September. Guest stays require "a commitment to explore Zen practice," and summer work stays can also be arranged. Otherwise people can apply to come here as day guests, for the hot

ROBINSON JEFFERS MEETS UNA

I f William Hamilton Jeffers [his father] was the archetypal wise old man in Robinson's life, then Una Call Kuster was, in Jungian terms, his anima ideal. Robinson met Una the first year he attended USC [the University of Southern California], in 1906. They were in Advanced German together, reading *Faust.* Una was strikingly beautiful and very intelligent. She was also three years older than Robinson and married. Nevertheless, a friendship developed that was nurtured by a mutual love for literature and ideas. She gave him Arthur Symons' *Wordsworth and Shelley* to read, and the two spent many hours discussing this and other essays, books, and poems.

When Jeffers left USC for the University of Zurich, he sent her an occasional note. When he returned to begin medical studies, the friendship resumed and deepened.

At this time in her life, Una was struggling to define her own identity. Several years before, at eighteen, she had left Mason, Michigan, in order to enter the University of California at Berkeley. She met a young attorney there, Edward ("Teddie") Kuster, whom she promptly married. When they moved to the Los Angeles area, she lived the life of a successful lawyer's wife—with golf at the San Gabriel Country Club, social events, even road races in big, expensive cars taking up most of her time. But something was missing. . . .

Inevitably, her marriage fell apart. Her husband, trying to explain to an interested public what had happened, blamed the breakdown on Una's unconventional ideas. As he says in an interview that appeared in the February 28, 1913, edition of the *Los Angeles Times,* "my wife seemed to find no solace in the ordinary affairs of life; she was without social ambition, and social functions seemed a bore to her. Her accomplishments are many, and she sought constantly for a wider scope for her intelligence. She turned to philosophy and the school of modern decadents, and she talked of things beyond the ken of those of us who dwelt upon the lower levels."

Though Teddie could not understand his wife, he knew there was someone who could—a "vile poetaster" named Robinson Jeffers.

From the first time they met, Robinson had listened to Una and shared her enthusiasms. His own extensive background in languages, philosophy, religion, and literature made him a perfect conversation partner. Moreover, he was a handsome man, rugged, poetic, melancholy, and intense.

And Una listened to Robinson. She was perhaps the only person he had ever known who could understand and appreciate the complex thoughts he brooded on. Moreover, she was unconventional and passionate. While the fashionable women wore their hair in high pompadours topped by large hats, Una often wore hers in a braid that fell loose down her back.

In time, their casual friendship grew more rich. "Without the wish of either of us," says Una, "our life was one of those fatal attractions that happen unplanned and undesired."

Excerpted with permission from the literary biography Robinson Jeffers: Poet of California *by James Karman (Ashland, OR: Story Line Press, 1995)*

Monterey Bay

CROWN OF CARMEL HIKING

Now that the Monterey Peninsula Regional Park District has acquired a portion of the vast Palo Corona Ranch, a spectacular community park offers public access to property known locally as the Old Fish Ranch. The new **Palo Corona Ranch Regional Park,** accessible from the foothills near Carmel and scheduled for a spring 2005 debut, starts with the ranch's stunning northern slopes, some 680 acres. Ultimately the Palo Corona park will total 4,300 acres and offer access for hiking, biking, dog walking, and horseback riding.

Ranging from near sea level to more than 3,000 feet in elevation, the property offers outstanding views of Santa Cruz, both Carmel and Monterey Bays, Pebble Beach, Point Lobos, and the Big Sur coastline as well as Fremont Peak and the Pinnacles Range.

The entire Palo Corona Ranch, nearly 10,000 acres, was purchased in 2002 by The Nature Conservancy and The Big Sur Land Trust. Still serving as gateway to Big Sur, the ranch connects 13 previously conserved lands, protects 20 rivers, and preserves a 70-mile wildlife corridor between Carmel and Hearst Ranch near San Simeon.

Since Palo Corona Ranch Regional Park is new and public access in its infancy, get current details before setting out. For information, contact the Monterey Peninsula Regional Park District, 831/372-3196, www.mprpd.org.

---

springs (bathing suits required), fabulous wilderness access, and marvelous vegetarian meals. With confirmed reservations, the center will send a map and directions. For current details, see the Zen Center's website, www.sfzc.com. There is no phone at Tassajara—and no cell phones, radios, tape players, TVs, or cars are allowed.

Not far from Tassajara, on Cachagua Road, is the onetime site of the 10-story, 34-ton AT&T **Jamesburg Earth Station,**—an impressive parabolic COMSAT dish antenna which once transmitted (via satellite) more than half the phone calls between the U.S. and Asia. Long a popular stop for space technology fans, the station was unplugged in October 2003 by AT&T, since the transmission task had been taken over by fiber optic cables laid down on the ocean's floor.

For an exursion, take Tularcitos Road until it joins Arroyo Seco Road then jog southwest toward the backside of Big Sur and the Arroyo Seco River canyon. There you can enjoy camping, picnicking, and hiking. Backpackers can head west on a long but rewarding trek to remote, undeveloped **Sykes Hot Springs,** near Horse Bridge Camp.

MIRA Observatory

If for some reason you decide to drive the last six miles of unpaved Tassajara Road, this is where you'll end up. Not officially open to the public, the MIRA Observatory, built atop Chews Ridge by the Monterey Institute for Research in Astronomy (MIRA), is a barrel-shaped, roll-top professional observatory 12 miles inland from Big Sur. MIRA's earth-tone, two-story corrugated Oliver Observing Station—named after a retired Hewlett-Packard vice president who kicked in some cash, some advanced electronics, and a 36-inch telescope—includes office and living space. It has earned design awards from the American Institute of Architects. Monthly summer and early fall tours of the observing station and occasional guest lectures are offered. For current information, call MIRA at 831/883-1000 or see www.mira.org. The institute is now developing the **Richard W. Hamming Astronomy Center** on the old site of Fort Ord, near the new CSU Monterey Bay campus.

Beaches

The downtown crescent of **Carmel Beach City Park** is beautiful—steeply sloping, blinding-white sands and aquamarine waters—but too cold and dangerous for swimming. It's also a tourist zoo in summer. (A winter sunset stroll is wonderful, though.) A better alternative is to take Scenic Road (or Carmelo Street) south from Santa Lucia off Rio Road to **Carmel River**

COURTESY OF MONTEREY COUNTY CONVENTION AND
VISITORS BUREAU/ MONTEREY AQUARIUM, RANDY WILDER

Visitors and locals enjoy the sandy shore and dramatic coastline at Carmel Beach.

State Beach, 831/649-2836, fringed with eucalyptus and cypress and often uncrowded (quite dangerous in high surf). This is where locals go to get away. The nearby marsh is a bird sanctuary providing habitat for hawks, kingfishers, cormorants, herons, pelicans, sandpipers, snowy egrets, and sometimes flocks of migrating ducks and geese. Still part of the park, just beyond, yet almost a secret, are **Middle Beach,** a curving sandy crescent on the south side of the Carmel River, and **Monastery Beach** at San Jose Creek, just south. Middle is accessible year-round by taking Ribera Road from Hwy. 1; in summer or fall you can also get there by walking across the dry riverbed and following the trail. Safety note: Middle Beach is hazardous for swimming and sometimes even for walking, due to freak 10-foot waves. Monastery Beach is popular for scuba diving, but its surf conditions are equally treacherous.

Ⓝ POINT LOBOS

One of the crown jewels of California's state parks, Point Lobos State Reserve is a 1,250-acre coastal wonderland about four miles south of Carmel. Pack a picnic; this is the best the Monterey area has to offer. The relentless surf and wild winds have pounded these reddish shores for millennia, sculpting six miles of shallow aquamarine coves, wonderful tidepools, aptly named Bird Island, and jutting points: Granite, Coal, Chute, China, Cannery, Pinnacle, Pelican, and Lobos itself. From here, look to the sea, as Santa Cruz poet William Everson has, "standing in cypress and surrounded by cypress, watching through its witchery as the surf explodes in unbelievable beauty on the granite below." Local lore has it that Point Lobos inspired Robert Louis Stevenson's Spyglass Hill in *Treasure Island.* The muse for Robinson Jeffers's somber "Tamar" definitely lived (and lives) here.

Sights and Recreation

From the dramatic headlands, watch for whales in winter. Many other marine mammals are year-round residents. Brown pelicans and cormorants preen themselves on offshore rocks. Here, the sea otters aren't shy: They boldly crack open abalone and dine in front of visitors. (The entire central coast area, from San Francisco south to beyond Big Sur, is protected as part of the **Monterey Bay National Marine Sanctuary.** And by order of former President Bill Clinton, the state's entire coastline is now protected as the California Coastal National Monument.) If you're heading south into Big Sur country, watch offshore otter antics—best with binoculars—from highway turnouts. Harbor seals hide in the coves. The languorous, loudly barking sea lions gave rise to the original Spanish name Punta de los Lobos Marinos ("Point of the Sea Wolves"). Follow the crisscrossing reserve trails for a morning walk through groves of bonsai Monterey cypress and pine, accented by colorful seasonal wildflowers (300 species, best in April). Watch for poison oak, which thrives here, too. Whalers Cove near the picnic and parking area was once a granite quarry, then a whaler's cove—the cabin and cast-iron rendering pot are still there—and an abalone cannery. It's something of a miracle that the Point Lobos headland exists almost unscarred, as cattle grazed here for decades. Fortunately for us all, turn-of-the-20th-century subdivision plans for Point Lobos were scuttled.

Head for Whalers Cove to bone up on local history. **Whalers Cabin Museum,** "the shack" overlooking Whalers Cove, built by Chinese fishermen, tells the story of Point Lobos and vicinity. The adjacent **Whaling Station Museum,** once a garage, features displays about shore whaling along California's central coast—everything from harpoons and whale-oil barrels to historic Monterey Peninsula whaling photos. Both museums are open as staffing allows, usually 11 A.M.–3 P.M. Guided hikes are also offered at Point Lobos; see the monthly schedule posted at the park's entrance. Curious students of history and natural history can also get an impressive area introduction via the park's website, below.

Safety

Point Lobos is considered one of the state's "underwater parks," in recognition of its aquatic beauty. Scuba and free diving are popular but allowed by permit only; call 831/624-8413 for reservations or see the website. Diver safety is a major concern of park staff. Get permits and current information about what to expect down below before easing into the water. People aren't kidding when they mention "treacherous cliff and surf conditions" here, so think first before scrambling off in search of bigger and better tidepools. Particularly dangerous even in serene surf is the Monastery Beach area, near San Jose Creek just beyond the reserve's northern border; there's a steep offshore drop-off into submarine Carmel Canyon and unstable sand underfoot. Children should be carefully supervised, and even experienced divers and swimmers might think twice before going into the water.

Practicalities

Point Lobos is beautiful—and popular. It can be crowded in summer and sometimes on spring and fall weekends. Since only 450 people are allowed into the park at one time, plan your trip accordingly and come early in the day (or wait in long lines along Hwy. 1—not fun). Open for day use only (sunrise till sunset in summer; until 5 P.M. in winter); admission (parking) is $8 per car, a fee waived for walk-ins and bike-ins. Small fee for trail brochures. Bikes must stay on pavement in the park—no trail riding.

You can also get to Point Lobos on Monterey-Salinas Transit's bus 22 (to Big Sur). From Carmel, it's a fairly easy bike ride. The weather can be cold, damp, and windy even in summer, so bring a sweater or jacket in addition to good walking shoes (and, if you have them, binoculars). The park's informative brochure is printed in five languages. Guided tours are offered daily. To better appreciate local flora and the 200-plus species of birds spotted at Point Lobos, pick up the plant and bird lists at the ranger station. In May, the Department of Fish and Game's **Marine Resources and Marine Pollution Studies Laboratory** at Granite Canyon sponsors an open house. For more information, call Point Lobos State Reserve at 831/624-4909, email ptlobos@mbay.net, or see http://pt-lobos.parks.state.ca.us.

ENTERTAINMENT AND EVENTS

Sunsets from the beach or from craggy Point Lobos are entertainment enough. But the **Sierra Club** folks above the shoe store, on Ocean near Dolores, 831/624-8032, provide helpful information on hikes, sights, and occasional bike rides. Open Mon.–Sat. 12:30–4:30 P.M., at last report.

For live drama, the outdoor **Forest Theater,** on the north side of Mountain View between Santa Rita and Guadalupe, 831/626-1681, hosts light drama and musicals, Shakespeare, and concerts staged by the Pacific Repertory Theatre (see below). General seating, so come early. Come from mid-May through July for the theatre's **Films in the Forest,** screened every Wednesday night. There's also an *indoor* **Forest Theater,** at the corner of Mountain View Avenue and Santa Rita Street, 831/624-1531, www.cetstaffplayers.org, with performances staged by the **Children's Experimental Theatre & Staff Players Repertory Company.** The **Pacific Repertory Theatre Company,** 831/622-0700, http://pacrep.org, presents a variety of live stage productions in the outdoor Forest Theater; at the **Golden Bough Theatre,** on Monte Verde between Eighth and Ninth; and at the **Circle Theatre of the Golden Bough,** located on the east side of Cassanova between Eighth and Ninth. Pacific Rep also sponsors the annual **Carmel Shakespeare Festival.** For current information, call or see the website; to reserve tickets online, see http://ticketguys.com/pacrep.

Carmel proper has laws prohibiting live music and leg-shaking inside the city limits. **Mission Ranch Resort,** in the county 11 blocks out of town at 26270 Dolores, 831/625-9040, has a piano bar. Otherwise, you'll have to head into rowdy Monterey for dancing and prancing. But you can always go bar-hopping locally.

Wine-Tasting

Not surprising in such a moderate Mediterranean climate, vineyards do well near Monterey and Carmel—particularly with chardonnay and pinot noir yet also cabernet sauvignon, merlot, syrah, and sauvignon blanc. Wineries and wines, quickly rising in stature, are recognized as eight distinct appellations. To keep up with them all, pick up the free *Monterey Wine Country* brochure and map at area visitor centers, or contact the **Monterey County Vintners & Growers Association,** 831/375-9400, www.montereywines.org. Wine-related events well worth showing up for include the **Annual Winemakers' Celebration** in August and the **Great Wine Escape Weekend** in November. If you're short on touring time this trip, many Monterey County wines are available for tasting at **A Taste of Monterey,** 700 Cannery Row in Monterey, 831/646-5446, www.taste monterey.com, open daily 11 A.M.–6 P.M.

The very small **Chateau Julien Winery,** 8940 Carmel Valley Rd., 831/624-2600, www.chateau julien.com, is housed in a French-style chateau and is open daily for tasting, for tours by reservation. The winery's chardonnay and merlot have both been honored as the best in the United States at the American Wine Championships in New York. Southwest of Carmel Valley and bordering Los Padres National Forest is the remote spring-fed "boutique" **Heller Estate Vineyards,** originally owned by the late William Durney and his wife, screenwriter Dorothy Kingsley, and still noted for its award-winning organic wines. The winery is not open to the public, but the organic wines—chenin blanc, chardonnay, pinot noir, cabernet sauvignon, and merlot—are available for tasting in Carmel Valley Village at 69 W. Carmel Valley Rd., and also widely available in Carmel, Monterey, and vicinity. For more information call 831/659-6220 or 800/625-8466, www.hellerestate.com.

At posh **Bernardus Winery,** 5 W. Carmel Valley Rd., 831/659-1900 or 800/223-2533, www.bernardus.com, centerpiece of the notable foodie empire, wine is an art. You can sample that art, traditionally aged Bordeaux varietals, at the tasting room, open 11 A.M.–5 P.M. daily. Also look around for other premium, small-production wineries, such as **Joullian Vineyards,** 831/659-8100 or 866/659-8101, www.joullian.com, with cabernet sauvignon, sauvignon blanc, merlot, zinfandel, and chardonnay. Joullian's new tasting room in Carmel Valley at 2 Village Dr., Ste. A, is open for tasting and sales daily 11 A.M.–5 P.M., excluding holidays. The winery is occasionally open for special Saturday open house or members-only events; call for details.

Between Greenfield and Soledad along the inland Hwy. 101 corridor are a handful of good wineries. The 1978 private reserve cabernet sauvignon of **Jekel Vineyards,** 40155 Walnut Ave. in Greenfield, 831/674-5522, washed out Lafite-Rothschild and other international competitors in France in 1982. Tastings daily 11 A.M.–4 P.M., tours by appointment. **Hahn Estates/Smith & Hook Winery,** 37700 Foothill Rd. in Soledad, 831/678-2132, www.hahnestates.com, is known for its cabernet sauvignon—also for the amazing view across the Salinas Valley to the Gabilan Mountains. Open daily 11 A.M.–4 P.M.; tours by appointment. Also in the area: **Chalone Vineyard** on Stonewall Canyon Road (at Hwy. 146 E.), 831/678-1717, www.chalonewinegroup.com, the county's oldest vineyard and winery, known for its estate-bottled varietals; and noted **Paraiso Vineyards,** 38060 Paraiso Springs Rd., 831/678-0300, www.paraisovineyards.com.

Not open to the public (no tasting room) but well worth visiting during special events is **Morgan Winery** in Salinas, 831/751-7777, www .morganwinery.com, which has garnered a glut of gold medals and other recognition for its chardonnays. Winners here, too, are the syrah, pinot noir, and sauvignon blanc.

True wine fanatics must make one more stop—at America's most award-winning vineyard, **Ventana Vineyards/Meador Estate,** 2999 Monterey-Salinas Hwy. (near the Monterey Airport just outside Monterey on Hwy. 68), 831/372-7415, www.ventanawines.com. Open daily 11 A.M.–5 P.M., until 6 P.M. in summer.

Events

Come on New Year's Day for the annual **Rio Grill Resolution Run** and in February for the annual **Masters of Food & Wine** at the Highlands Inn. Come in May for the **Jeffers Tor House Garden Party,** the annual fundraiser, and June for the Carmel Valley **California Cowboy Show,** where you can put your boots up and enjoy cowboy music, cowboy poetry, and a cowboy-friendly glass of wine. June also kicks off the theater season in Carmel. Right around the first of the month (or slightly before), the Pacific Repertory Theatre troupe opens its performance season, part of which is devoted to the **Carmel Shakespeare Festival,** with plays presented from August into October. Plays are presented at the outdoor Forest Theater, the Golden Bough Playhouse, and other venues. The summer **Films in the Forest** at the outdoor Forest Theater begins in mid-May.

Johann Sebastian Bach never knew a place like Carmel, but his spirit lives here nonetheless. From mid-July to early August, Carmel sponsors its traditionally understated **Bach Festival,** 831/624-2046 for tickets, www.bachfestival.org, honoring J. S. and other composers of his era, with daily concerts, recitals, and lectures at the mission and elsewhere, sometimes including the Hotel Del Monte at the Naval Postgraduate School in Monterey. If you're going, get your tickets *early.* Otherwise, closer to actual performance dates stop by the festival office at the Sunset Cultural Center, San Carlos at Ninth, to check on ticket availability.

At Carmel Beach, usually on a Sunday in late September or early October, the **Great Sandcastle Building Contest** gets underway. Events include Novice and Advanced Sandbox. (Get the date from the Monterey Chamber of Commerce, as Carmel locals generally "don't know," just to keep the tourists away.) Also in October, the **Tor House Festival,** the annual **Carmel Performing Arts Festival,** and both the annual **Taste of Carmel** and the **Carmel Valley Wine Festival.** In December, the **Music for Christmas** series at the Carmel Mission is quite nice.

SHOPPING

For something different to tote home as a souvenir, **It's Cactus** on Mission between Ocean & Seventh, 831/626-4213, www.itscactus.com, offers colorful indigenous folk art from Guatemala, Indonesia, and other places around the globe. For candles, candlesticks, and oil lamps, try **Wicks & Wax** in the Doud Arcade, Ocean at San Carlos, 831/624-6044. For fine soaps, other bath products, and home scents, head for the **Rainbow Scent Company,** on Lincoln between Ocean and Seventh, 831/624-6506.

Locals say the best home furnishings store around is **Homescapes,** on the southeast corner of Seventh and Dolores in Carmel proper, 831/624-6499, www.homescapescarmel.com, offering an impressive import selection, including many personally selected antiques from China, Korea, Japan, England, and Europe. (There's also a Homescapes outlet in Carmel Valley Village, 13766 Center St., 831/659-9990, open just Friday and Saturday 11 A.M.– 5 P.M. and by appointment.)

You'll find plenty of antique shops in and around Carmel. For old toys and memorable memorabilia try **Life In The Past Lane,** San Carlos and Fifth, 831/625-2121. **Sabine Adamson Antiques & Interiors,** on Dolores between Fifth and Sixth, 831/626-7464, specializes in fine European antiques and accessories. **Conway of Asia,** Seventh and Dolores, 831/624-3643, offers antiques and oriental rugs from Myanmar (Burma), India, Tibet, and Thailand. **Vermillion** in the Crossroads Shopping Center

(Rio Road and Hwy. 1), 831/620-1502, www .vermillionasianarts.com, emphasizes museum-quality Japanese items, both antique and contemporary.

For all its antique finery, Carmel has even more art galleries—dozens of them. A great place to start is the **Carmel Art Association Gallery** on Dolores between Fifth and Sixth, 831/624-6176, founded here in 1927. The art association features more than 120 local artists and regularly presents an impressive selection of their painting, sculpture, and graphic arts. The **Weston Gallery, Inc.,** on Sixth between Dolores and Lincoln, 831/624-4453, www.westongallery.com, offers 19th- and 20th-century photographs by namesake local photographers Edward Weston and Brett Weston as well as Ansel Adams, Michael Kenna, Jeffrey Becom, and Jerry Uelsmann.

Wonderful for local art is **Savage Stephens Contemporary Fine Art** at Su Vecino, Dolores between Fifth and Sixth, 831/626-0800. The bronze and stone sculptures by Sharon Spencer are standouts. The impressive **Highlands Sculpture Gallery,** on Dolores between Fifth and Sixth, 831/624-0535, is Carmel's oldest contemporary art gallery.

Carmel's also no slouch when it comes to personal fashion, most of it on the pricey side. Definitely upscale is **Girl Boy Girl** at the Court of the Fountains, Mission and Seventh, 831/626-3368, featuring contemporary women's fashions from more than 50 designers. Worth exploring at Carmel Plaza, Ocean and Mission, is classic **Ann Taylor,** 831/626-9565. Always fun for something more exotic is **Exotica** at the Crossroads Shopping Center, 831/622-0757, where you'll find handpainted and batiked natural fiber fashions along with Laurel Burch, other interesting jewelry, and folk art.

Carmel being a pet-pampering town, Fido generally fares well here. **Diggidy Dog** at Mission and Ocean across from the Carmel Plaza, 831/625-1585, offers all the essential mutt merchandise, from toys and treats to well-stuffed beds. (Token cat items available too.) At more upscale **Mackie's Parlour** at Ocean and Monte Verde (formerly another dog store, Fideaux), 831/626-0600, you can even get doggie feather beds. To help less fortunate creatures, buy gently used clothing, jewelry, art, books, collectibles, and antiques at the **SPCA Benefit Shop** (Society for the Prevention of Cruelty to Animals), Su Vecino Court between Fifth and Sixth, 831/624-4211.

For current shopping information and more suggestions, contact the **Carmel Chamber of Commerce** on San Carlos between Fifth and Sixth, 831/624-2522 or 800/550-4333, www .carmelcalifornia.org.

ACCOMMODATIONS

Camping and Hostel

Mary Austin's observation that "beauty is cheap here" may apply to the views, but little else in the greater Carmel area—with the exception of camping and the fine local elderhostel.

Carmel by the River RV Park, 27680 Schulte Rd. (off Carmel Valley Road), 831/624-9329, www.carmelrv.com, is well away from it all. Some 35 attractively landscaped sites sit right on the Carmel River, with full hookups, cable TV, laundry facilities, a rec room, and other amenities. Nearby **Saddle Mountain Recreation Park,** also at the end of Schulte Road, 831/624-1617, offers both tent and RV sites (reservations accepted for weekends only), restrooms, showers, picnic tables, a swimming pool, a playground, and other recreational possibilities—including nearby hiking trails. Another option is **Veterans Memorial Park.**

In the primitive-and-distant category, you can camp southeast of Carmel Valley at the U.S. Forest Service **White Oaks Campground** at Chews Ridge, which has seven sites, or nearby **China Camp,** with six sites; both are free, first-come, first-camped, and best suited for wilderness trekkers. Farther on you'll find **Tassajara Zen Mountain Center,** often offering camping (and other accommodations) in summer by advance reservation—call 415/865-1899 after April 1, or try www.sfzc.com. The nearby Forest Service **Arroyo Seco Campground** has 46 sites. Camping is also plentiful to the south in Big Sur (see below). The Forest Service sites require purchase of a daily (or annual) Adventure Pass, available at Forest

Service ranger stations and many sporting goods stores and other vendors. For more information on local Forest Service campgrounds, contact the Monterey District of Los Padres National Forest at 831/385-5434, www.fs.fed.us/r5/lospadres.

Those who qualify as elders can sign on for a very affordable, very educational Carmel stay, thanks to **Elderhostel at Hidden Valley,** a program of Carmel Valley's Hidden Valley Music Center, 831/659-3115, www.hiddenvalley music.org. The five-night stays include room, board, and programs such as *The Eden Steinbeck Was East Of* or *Birding at Monterey Bay* or *Wine, Wonderful Wine* all for less than $100 per day. Such a deal. For current program details or to register, see www.elderhostel.org.

Hotels and Inns: $100–150

Classic is the only word for the historic **Pine Inn,** downtown on Ocean between Monte Verde and Lincoln, 831/624-3851 or 800/228-3851, www.pine-inn.com. This small hotel offers comfortable "Carmel Victorian" accommodations and fine dining at the onsite **Il Fornaio** restaurant and bakery; there's even a gazebo with a rollback roof for eating alfresco, fog permitting. Even if you don't stay, sit on the terrace, act affluent, and sip Ramos fizzes.

The **Carmel River Inn,** 26600 Oliver Rd. (south of town on Hwy. 1 at the Carmel River Bridge), 831/624-1575 or 800/882-8142, www.carmelriverinn.com, is a pleasant riverside spread with a heated pool, 24 cozy, family-friendly cottages and duplexes (some with wood-burning fireplaces and kitchens), and 19 motel rooms. Some cottages go for as low as $85. Two-night minimum stay on weekends. Pets welcome for a $25-per-pet fee.

Other above-average Carmel accommodations—and there are plenty to choose from—include the **Carmel Oaks Inn,** Fifth and Mission, 831/624-5547 or 800/266-5547, www.carmel oaksinn.com, attractive and convenient and a bargain by local standards, and the **Lobos Lodge,** Monte Verde and Ocean, 831/624-3874, www .loboslodge.com. Another option is the recently

Carmel Valley

© ROBERT HOLMES/CALTOUR

upgraded, 20-room Victorian-style **Chateau de Carmel** at Fifth and Junipero, 831/624-1900 or 800/325-8515, www.chateaudecarmel.com, a restyled two-story motel offering some lower-priced rooms.

Hotels and Inns: $150–250

The **Sundial Lodge,** Monte Verde and Seventh, 831/624-8578, www.sundiallodge.com, is a cross between a small hotel and a bed-and-breakfast. Each of the 19 antique-furnished rooms has a private bath, TV, and telephone. Other amenities include lovely English gardens and a courtyard, continental breakfast, and afternoon tea.

The landmark 1929 **Cypress Inn,** downtown at Lincoln and Seventh, 831/624-3871 or 800/443-7443, www.cypress-inn.com, is a charming, gracious, and intimate place—another small hotel with a bed-and-breakfast sensibility, recently updated. Pets are allowed—invited, actually—since actress-owner Doris Day is an animal-rights activist. (Dog beds provided.) And when hotel staff place a mint on your pillow at turn-down, they'll also leave a treat for your dog or cat. How's *that* for service? Rates start at $125 and top out at $425, continental breakfast included.

Très Carmel, and a historic treasure, is the Mediterranean-style 1904 **Ⅳ La Playa Hotel,** Camino Real and Eighth, 831/624-6476 or 800/582-8900, www.laplayahotel.com, where lush gardens surround guest rooms and cottages on the terraced hillside. Recently remodeled, rooms at La Playa feature evocative Spanish-style furnishings; rates start at $175. The five cottages (starting at $335) feature fireplaces, ocean-view decks, and separate living areas. Especially enjoyable when the gardens are in their glory is the onsite **Terrace Grill.**

Bed-and-Breakfasts

Local inns offer an almost overwhelming amount of choice, though that "inn" in Carmel may be a revamped motel. Local bed-and-breakfast inns are comparable in price to most Carmel area motels, and they're usually much homier. Two-night stays are usually required on weekends.

A notable value is the relaxed yet stylish **Ⅳ Carmel Country Inn** on Dolores at Third,

831/625-3263 or 800/215-6343, www.carmelcountryinn.com, where the well-tended gardens are also an attraction. All rooms feature private bathrooms (some with whirlpool tubs) and come with quilted bedcoverings, down comforters, country-pine furniture, gas fireplaces, color TV with cable, in-room coffeemakers, and refrigerators. Continentral breakfast included. Pets and well-behaved children welcome. Rates start at $150.

The **Cobblestone Inn,** on Junipero near Eighth, 831/625-5222 or 800/833-8836, www.foursisters.com, is a traditional Carmel home now transformed into a Four Sisters inn—complete with a cobblestone courtyard, gas fireplaces in the guest rooms, and English country-house antiques. Rates start at $125 and include a full breakfast buffet, complimentary tea, and hors d'oeuvres. A Carmel classic is the ivy-draped **Stonehouse Inn,** Eighth and Monte Verde, 831/624-4569 or 877/748-6618, www.carmelstonehouse.com, constructed by local Indians. All six rooms here are named after historical local luminaries, including writers, and all but two share bathrooms. Rates include full Southern-style breakfast, wine and sherry, and hors d'oeuvres. Rates are $100–250.

The **Adobe Inn,** downtown at Dolores and Eighth, 831/624-3933 or 800/388-3933, www.adobeinn.com, features just about every inn-style comfort. Large rooms feature elegant furnishings and include gas fireplaces, wet bars with refrigerators, patios or decks, color TVs, phones, data ports; some have ocean views. Other amenities include a sauna and heated pool, complimentary newspaper, and continental breakfast—delivered to your room.

Mission Ranch Resort

Long the traditional place to stay, just outside town, is the Mission Ranch, 26270 Dolores (at 15th), 831/624-6436 or 800/538-8221, www.missionranchcarmel.com. Once a pastoral dairy farm and now a quiet, small ranch owned by Clint Eastwood, relaxed Mission Ranch overlooks the Carmel River and features views of the Carmel River wetlands and Point Lobos. And the mission *is* nearby. With Eastwood ownership, the

Victorian farmhouse and its outbuildings have had an expensive makeover and together now resemble a Western village. The 31 guest rooms are decorated here and there with props from Eastwood movies. Lodgings are available in the historic main house, the Hayloft, the Bunkhouse (which has its own living room and kitchen), and the Barn. The newer Meadow View Rooms feature, well, meadow views. Rates for most rooms are $100–250; some suites are $265. Another attraction, inside the former creamery, is the casually Western yet sophisticated **Restaurant at Mission Ranch**, 831/625-9040, which serves make-my-day American fare at dinner—steaks, chops, fresh local salmon and such—complete with checkered tablecloths and a wood-burning stove that starred in *The Unforgiven*. There's an outdoor patio, too, grand cove views, even a children's menu. Best yet, local jazz artists often perform in the piano bar here. Sunday champagne brunch, another live jazz event, is legendary.

Carmel Highlands

The swank and well-known 1916 **M Highlands Inn,** along Hwy. 1 four miles south of Carmel, 831/620-1234 or 800/233-1234 (Hyatt central reservations), www.hyatt.com, is indeed beautiful, though most people would have to default on their house payment to stay long. That the Highlands Inn is now beginning to sell off its luxurious rooms and suites as timeshares—a reality not too popular with long-time guests—makes rooms that much more precious. Offering some of the world's most spectacular views, some Highlands Inn suites feature wood-burning fireplaces, double spa baths, fully equipped kitchens, and all the comforts—down to the handmade local soaps. Rates are $250 and up. Even those of more plebeian means can enjoy a stroll through the Grand Lodge to appreciate the oak woodwork, twin yellow granite fireplaces, gorgeous earthtoned carpet, leather sofas and chairs, and granite tables. Or stay for a meal—the exceptional **Pacific's Edge** features stunning sunset views and is locally beloved, not to mention a consistent award-winner. Open for lunch, dinner, and Sunday brunch. The more casual **California Market** is open daily 7 A.M.–10 P.M.

The nearby **Tickle Pink Inn,** just south of the Highlands Inn at 155 Highlands Dr., 831/624-1244 or 800/635-4774, www.ticklepink.com, offers equally spectacular views and 35 inviting rooms and suites, an ocean-view hot tub, continental breakfast, and wine and cheese at sunset. Two-night minimum stay on weekends. Rates are $250 and up.

Carmel Valley

The historic **Los Laureles Country Inn,** 313 W. Carmel Valley Rd., 831/659-2233, www.loslaureles.com, was once part of the Boronda Spanish land grant, later a Del Monte ranch. Rooms here once stabled Muriel Vanderbilt's well-bred thoroughbreds. The inn has an excellent restaurant (American regional), saloon, pool, and conference facilities. Golf packages are available. Room rates are $100–200 (as low as $75 in the off season). Suites are $150 and up. And if it ever opens again—recent word is, expect a reopening by late 2005—another intriguing local tradition is the 1928 **Robles del Rio Lodge,** 200 Punta Del Monte, www.roblesdelriolodge.com. Perched atop a hill overlooking Carmel Valley and reached via winding back roads, Robles del Rio has been closed since 1999 yet at last report was still destined to become a 59-room "luxury boutique spa."

Dog-friendly **Carmel Valley Lodge** on Carmel Valley Road at Ford, 831/659-2261 or 800/641-4646 (reservations only), www.valleylodge.com, offers nice little extras, like Barista French roast coffee, phone with data ports, cable TV with VCR (free video library), and original art on the walls. The lodge features rooms fronting the lovely gardens plus one- and two-bedroom cottages with wood-burning fireplaces, kitchens, and private patios or decks. Other amenities include a pool, sauna, hot tub, and fitness center. Rates are $150–250. Two-bedroom, two-bath cottages are $250 and up.

To see how the other 1 percent lives, head for the five-star **Quail Lodge Resort & Golf Club** at the Carmel Valley Golf and Country Club, 8205 Valley Greens Dr., 831/624-2888, www.quaillodge.com, The lodge features elegant contemporary rooms and suites, some with fireplaces, plus access to private tennis and golf facilities and fine dining at **The Covey** restaurant. Rates are $250 and up. Pricey, too, in the same vein is Wyndham Hotels's **Carmel Valley Ranch Resort,** 1 Old Ranch Rd. (off Robinson Canyon Rd.), 831/625-9500, www.wyndham.com, a gated resort with 100 suites, all individually decorated, with wood-burning fireplaces and private decks. Some suites feature a private outdoor hot tub. Recreation facilities include a private golf course, 12 tennis courts, pools, saunas, and whirlpools. Rates are $250 and up.

Luxurious but still something of a new concept in Carmel Valley accommodations is the **Bernardus Lodge,** 831/659-3247 or 888/648-9463, www.bernardus.com, a luxury resort affiliated with the Bernardus Winery and open since August 1999. Crafted from limestone, logs, ceramic tiles, and rich interior woods, the nine village-style buildings feature 57 suites for "discriminating travelers" and offer endless luxury amenities, including a different wine-and-cheese tasting every night at turn-down and a full-service spa. Definitely unique are special educational forums on gardening, the culinary arts, and viticulture, not to mention the onsite ballroom, celebrated **Marinus** restaurant, and more casual **Wickets** bistro. Outdoor recreation options include tennis and bocce ball, croquet, swimming, hiking and horse-

back riding on adjacent mountain trails, and golfing at neighboring resorts. Rates are $250 and up.

For a super-luxury stay—and to avoid the country clubs and other "too new" places—the choice is the 330-acre **Stonepine Estate Resort,** 150 E. Carmel Valley Rd., 831/659-2245, www.stonepinecalifornia.com, once the Crocker family's summer estate, now a thoroughbred horse ranch complete with polo grounds, hunter and cross-country jumper courses, sulky track, and dressage arenas. Rates are truly astronomical.

FOOD

Breakfast

For a perfect omelette with home fries and homemade valley pork sausage, try **The Cottage,** on Lincoln between Ocean and Seventh, 831/625-6260. Another good choice for breakfast is **Katy's Place,** on the west side of Mission between Fifth and Sixth, 831/624-0199, another quaint cottage, this one boasting the largest breakfast and lunch menu on the West Coast. Great eggs Benedict—10 different varieties to choose from! Open daily. Also cozy and crowded is **Em Le's,** Dolores and Fifth, 831/625-6780. Try the buttermilk waffles, available for lunch or dinner. The **Tuck Box** tearoom, on Dolores near

Monterey Bay

EARTHBOUND AND ROADSIDE

Remember the days when roadside family-farm fruit and vegetable stands were everywhere, popping up along country roads like so many mushrooms after a good rain? Those days are gone. But here and there in California local U-pick farms and fresh produce stands—including **Gizdich Ranch** in Watsonville and **The Farm** in Salinas—still proudly serve forth their bounty.

Another prominent area fresh-produce destination is **Earthbound Farm,** an impressively successful, fairly large organic produce company that supports a 60-acre showcase farm and produce stand in Carmel Valley. The Earthbound bounty includes just-picked local organic produce, organic greens and produce farmed in other prime locales,

organic flowers, ready-to-eat and ready-to-cook meals from The Organic Kitchen, and a great selection of picnic-basket gourmet goodies, including cheeses and fresh-baked breads. Personal garden adventures are possible, too, in the Kids' Garden and Cut-Your-Own Herb Garden as well as the Aromatherapy Labyrinth. In autumn there's an immensely popular Corn Maze, too, and some 30 varieties of pumpkins to pick. Come for special Saturday events, including Chef Walks, Harvest Walks, Bug Walks, and Flower Walks.

Earthbound Farm is just a few miles east of Hwy. 1 in Carmel Valley, at 7250 Carmel Valley Rd. For more information, call 831/625-6219 or see www.ebfarm.com.

Seventh, 831/624-6365, inspires you to stop just to take a photograph. It was once famous for its pecan pie, shepherd's pie, and Welsh rarebit, as well as great cheap breakfasts. New owners have changed the menu—and prices.

For good value and elegant ambience at breakfast, not to mention abundant Sunday brunch, try the **Terrace Grill** at the historic La Playa Hotel, Camino Real at Eighth, 831/624-6476. A local classic, open daily for breakfast, lunch, and dinner daily, is the landmark **Village Corner** California-Mediterranean bistro at Sixth and Dolores, 831/624-3588, beloved for its heated patio dining and pastas, seafood, fish, and all-Monterey wine list. Kid-friendly but on the expensive side.

Dog- and Kid-Friendly

Ready to get down with the dogs? A Carmel pooch pleaser is eclectic, employee-owned **The Forge in the Forest,** a onetime blacksmith shop at Fifth and Junipero, 831/624-2233, where eight tables are reserved for dogs and their people. Favorites here include Reuben egg rolls with Russian dressing (really, they're good), baked onion soup, and, for dessert, the chocolate chip cookie dream. For Fido or Fifi, ask for the Dog Pound Menu, which includes the Quarter Hounder. Open for lunch and dinner daily, for brunch on Sunday. Also notably dog-friendly is the charming, quintessentially Carmel **PortaBella** on Ocean Avenue between Lincoln and Monte Verde, 831/624-4395, serving wonderful Mediterranean—such things as fresh goat cheese ravioli, porcini-crusted dayboat scallops, Dungeness crab cakes, and the signature roasted corn and Dungeness crab bisque. Very reasonable. Open for lunch and dinner daily. And if you're traveling with the kids (and/or canine kid), they can all sit with you out on the flagstone patio. Canine kiddos get the white-linen water dish treatment.

The equally kid-friendly **Rio Grill,** in the Crossroads Shopping Village, 101 Crossroads Blvd. (Hwy. 1 at Rio Road), 831/625-5436, is a long-running favorite for innovative southwestern-style American fare. Everything is fresh, or made from scratch; many entrées are served straight from the oak wood smoker, like the chipotle chicken. Don't miss the Rio's famous ice-cream sandwich. Open for lunch and dinner daily, great Sunday brunch.

Inexpensive **From Scratch** restaurant at The Barnyard Shopping Center, 831/625-2448, is a casual and eclectic place with local art on the walls. From Scratch serves up an abundant, ambitious, and very "local" breakfast menu, from fresh-squeezed orange and grapefruit juice to smoothies and pancakes and huevos rancheros. Look for soups, salads, pastas, and sandwiches at lunch, and such things as seafood pasta with shrimp, crab, and scallops or pork chops glazed in honey-mustard sauce at dinner. Open for breakfast and lunch daily, for dinner Tues.–Sat., and for brunch on Sunday. A best bet in Carmel for sushi is The Barnyard's been-there-forever, family-friendly **Robata Grill & Sake Bar,** 831/624-2643, open weekdays for lunch, nightly for dinner.

Popular Carmel Valley newcomer is the new-American **The New Summer House,** 6 Pilot Rd., 831/659-5020, specializing in new renditions of comfort-food classics—from Chinese chicken salad, meatloaf, and chicken pot pie to prawns risotto and "every day, all day, turkey dinner." Open for lunch and dinner daily in summer, and for brunch too—for Monterey omelettes, blueberry pancakes, even vegetarian eggs Benedict—from 9 A.M. on weekends. Closed on Tuesdays in winter. Dogs welcome on the patio.

Lunch and Dinner

A local's favorite in Carmel Valley is friendly, quite reasonable **Café Rustica,** 10 Delfino Place, 831/659-4444, brought to you by the same people who launched the Taste Café & Bistro in Pacific Grove. The fare here covers vast continental territory, so at lunch you can enjoy an egg salad sandwich on a baguette, a small pizza, or a grilled vegetable salad with creamy balsamic vinaigrette. Try the Pasta Rustica at dinner. Also beloved in Carmel Valley is the **Corkscrew Café,** sibling to Carmel's Casanova, at 55 W. Carmel Valley Rd., 831/659-8888, serving up local wines, the café's own organic garden produce, and great things at lunch—from the grilled portabella mushroom sandwich and black-bean chicken and cheese enchiladas to salmon niçoise salad. And check out the Corkscrew Museum.

Back in Carmel proper, For rustic yet romantic Italian the place is **Tutto Mondo Trattoria** on Dolores between Ocean and Seventh, 831/624-8977, where the bruschettas, soups, and salads could make a meal though pastas, pizzas, and other heftier fare is available. Woinderful desserts, plus Italian, French, and California wines. Open daily for both lunch and dinner.

Great for Chinese at lunch and dinner—even takeout—in Carmel is **Tommy's Wok** on Mission between Ocean and Seventh, 831/624-8518, beloved for its potstickers, pinenut or paper-wrapped chicken, and pu pu platter. Organic veggie choices, too. Fine for takeout pastries and desserts or a light French-country lunch is **Patisserie Boissiere,** also on Mission between Ocean and Seventh, 831/624-5008. If excellent cheese and an apple would suffice for lunch, head for **The Cheese Shop** at Carmel Plaza, Ocean and Junipero, 831/625-2272, which features an awesome selection, foreign and domestic. If you're not packing your own two-buck Chuck, for wine stop into sophisticated **Bouchee** on Mission (near Ocean), 831/626-7880, a wine shop by day and an impressive wine bar and French restaurant by night.

Fine Dining

Sophisticated yet simple is excellent **N La Bohême,** Dolores and Seventh, 831/624-7500, www.laboheme.com, a tiny, family-style place serving French country cuisine at dinner. The three-course, prix-fixe meal is served family-style—starting with salad and soups, continuing through the evening's entrée, and finishing with house-made dessert. No reservations; call for the day's menu, see the website, or pick up the monthly calendar when you get to town. Open daily for dinner.

N Casanova, on Fifth between Mission and San Carlos, 831/625-0501, is a Carmel classic, from its renowned, hand-dug wine cellar to its romantic Old World-cottage dining rooms and stellar food. Casanova serves both Southern French and Northern Italian cuisine in a land-mark Mediterranean-style house featuring several provincial-style dining rooms, plus a heated garden for temperature-sensitive romantics. Housemade pastas here are exceptional, as are the desserts. Open daily for lunch and dinner.

Immensely popular **Grasing's** in the Jordan Center at the corner of Sixth and Mission, 831/624-6562, serves colorful "coastal cuisine." At lunch this translates into some coastal options yet also sandwiches—grilled eggplant with roasted peppers, onions, and mushrooms, perhaps, or the "bistro burger" with apple-wood smoked bacon, avocado, and cheddar cheese. At dinner, fish and seafood star, starting with the crab risotto. Or try the paella; dig into bronzed salmon with portabella mushrooms, roasted garlic, and Yukon golds; or choose the petite filet mignon with shallot marmalade, baby carrots, asparagus, and potato cakes. Vegetarians won't starve, with choices such as lasagna with artichokes, tomatoes, spinach, Asiago cheese, and lemon vinaigrette. Somewhat less "fishy" is Kurt Grasing's upbeat **Carmel Chop House,** Fifth and San Carlos, 831/625-1199, a true steak house featuring the Chop House Caesar salad and corn-fed meat—beef and lamb—and Maine lobster. Every entrée is served with potatoes and veggies.

Even if you can't afford to stay there, you can probably afford to eat at the Highlands Inn, on Hwy. 1 south of Carmel. The inn's **California Market** restaurant, 831/622-5450, serves California regional dishes with fresh local ingredients. You'll enjoy ocean-view and deck dining, plus fabulous scenery. Open for breakfast, lunch, and dinner daily. Yet the locals' favorite for fine dining is the innovative **Pacific's Edge Restaurant,** at the Highlands Inn, 831/622-5445, which showcases local ingredients. If you can't swing an exquisite five-course meal, how about a smashing cocktail with a still more smashing view?

More marvelous hotel dining is offered at the resort-casual, California-French **Marinus** at Bernardus Lodge, 415 Carmel Valley Rd., 831/658-3400, a well-heeled foodie destination, worthy recipient of *Wine Spectator*'s Grand Award, and at **Covey** at Quail Lodge Resort, 8205 Valley Greens Dr., 831/620-8860.

INFORMATION AND SERVICES

The weekly *Carmel Pine Cone* newspaper, www.carmelpinecone.com, covers local events and politics. The **Carmel Chamber of Commerce** and visitor center is in the Eastwood Building on San Carlos between Fifth and Sixth, 831/624-2522 or 800/550-4333, www.carmel california.org. Its annual *Guide to Carmel* includes information on just about everything—from shopping hot spots to accommodations and eateries. The **Carmel Valley Chamber of Commerce** is in the Oak Building at 71 W. Carmel Valley Rd. in Carmel Valley, 831/659-4000, www.carmelvalleychamber.com.

To get to Carmel from Monterey without car or bike, take Monterey-Salinas Transit bus 52 (24 hours), 831/899-2555, www.mst.org.

The Central Coast

Note: See color maps in the front of this book

Along this swath of coastline where north becomes south, something in the air eventually transforms people into curmudgeons. The prevailing attitude is quite straightforward: *go away.* Henry Miller, one of the coast's crustiest and lustiest curmudgeons, believed the source of this sentiment was the land itself, speaking through its inhabitants. "And so it happens," he wrote from his home in Big Sur, "that whoever settles in this region tries to keep others from coming here. Something about the land makes one long to keep it intact—and strictly for oneself." And so it happens, like children denied candy or toys or the latest fashion fad, we want it all the more. In many ways the central coast's aloofness is its greatest appeal. Yet there are other attractions, particularly farther south.

CALIFORNIA 1

Must-Sees

Look for **M** to find the sights and activities you can't miss and **M** for the best dining and lodging.

M Big Sur Scenic Byway: Hwy. 1 slips around the prominent ribs of the Santa Lucia Mountains, snakes through dark wooded canyons, and soars across graceful bridges spanning the void (page 377).

M Hearst San Simeon State Historic Monument: Architect Julia Morgan built this grand mountaintop palace for media magnate William Randolph Hearst (page 389).

M San Luis Obispo Wineries: The southern San Luis Obispo County wineries include the appellations of Edna Valley and Arroyo Grande (page 406).

M La Purísima Mission State Historic Park: The 11th and largest mission complex in the state, originally built in 1787, is now situated on 1,000 unspoiled acres (page 417).

M Solvang: This cheery, authentically Danish town just north of Santa Barbara was founded in 1911—and is still just the place for *frikadeller*, pickled herring, and farm-style breakfast (page 418).

M Mission Santa Barbara: The Queen of the Missions is distinguished by its two massive squared towers, arcades, domed belfries, dignified Ionic columns, arched entrance, and double-paneled doors (page 427).

M Downtown Santa Barbara History Walk: Guided or self-guided tours lead visitors to the Santa Barbara Historical Society Museum, the Carriage and Western Arts Museum, the famed Santa Barbara County Courthouse, the Santa Barbara Public Library, and the reconstruction of El Presidio de Santa Barbara State Historic Park (page 427).

M Santa Barbara Museum of Natural History: The best of natural Santa Barbara is on display here, a Spanish-style cluster of buildings featuring excellent exhibits on the Chumash and other indigenous peoples, fossil collections, geology displays, nature exhibits (including a busy beehive), even some original Audubon lithographs. The John

and Peggy Maximus Gallery exhibits some of its 1,100 natural history prints. Kids love the 72-foot-long skeleton of a blue whale (page 430).

M Channel Islands National Park: Biologists describe the Channel Islands as North America's Galápagos. Many are inhabited by rare, endangered, and endemic animals and plant species. The five northernmost Channel Islands are now included in 250,000-acre Channel Islands National Park (page 462).

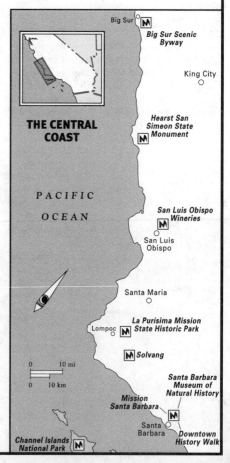

THE CENTRAL COAST

PACIFIC OCEAN

THE LAND

The land itself is unfriendly, at least from the human perspective. Especially in the north, the indomitable unstable terrain—with its habit of sliding out from under whole hillsides, houses, highways, and hiking trails at the slightest provocation—has made the area hard to inhabit. Despite its contrariness, the central coast, that unmistakable pivotal point between California's north and south, successfully blends both.

Though the collective Coast Ranges continue south through the region, here the terrain takes on a new look. The redwoods thin out, limiting themselves to a few large groves in Big Sur country and otherwise straggling south a short distance beyond San Simeon, tucked into hidden folds in the rounded coastal mountains. Where redwood country ends, either the grasslands of the dominant coastal oak woodlands begin or the chaparral takes over, in places almost impenetrable. Even the coastline reflects the transition—the rocky rough-and-tumble shores along the Big Sur coast transform into tamer beaches and bluffs near San Simeon and points south.

Los Padres National Forest inland from the coast is similarly divided into two distinct sections. The northernmost (and largest) Monterey County section includes most of the rugged 100-mile-long Santa Lucia Range and its Ventana Wilderness. The southern stretch of Los Padres, essentially the San Luis Obispo and Santa Barbara backcountry, is often closed to hikers and backpackers during the summer due to high fire danger. This area includes the southern extension of the Santa Lucias, the La Panza Range, the Sierra Madre Mountains, also the San Rafael Wilderness and a portion of the San Rafael Mountains. Farther south but still in Los Padres National Forest are the Santa Ynez Mountains east of Santa Barbara, angling northwest to Point Arguello near Lompoc, and part of the unusual east-west Transverse Ranges that create the geographic boundary between north-central and Southern California.

Another clue that the north-south transition occurs here is water or, moving southward, the increasingly obvious lack of it. Though both the North and South Forks of the Little Sur River, the Big Sur River a few miles to the south, and other northern waterways flow to the sea throughout the year, as does the Cuyama River in the south (known as the Santa Maria River as it nears the ocean), most of the area's streams are seasonal. But off-season hikers, beware: even inland streams with a six-month flow are not to be dismissed during winter and spring, when deceptively dinky creekbeds can become death-dealing torrents overnight.

Major lakes throughout California's central coast region are actually water-capturing reservoirs, including Lake San Antonio, known for its winter bald eagle population, Lake Nacimiento on the other side of the mountains from San Simeon, and Santa Margarita Lake east of San Luis Obispo near the headwaters of the Salinas River. Other popular regional reservoirs include Lopez Lake southeast of San Luis Obispo and Lake Cachuma near Santa Barbara.

Big Sur

The poet Robinson Jeffers described this redwood and rock coast as "that jagged country which nothing but a falling meteor will ever plow." It's only fitting, then, that this area was called Jeffers Country long before it became known as Big Sur. Sienna-colored sandstone and granite, surly waves, and the sundown sea come together in a never-ending dance of creation and destruction. Writer Henry Miller said Big Sur was "the face of the earth as the creator intended it to look," a point hard to argue. Still, Big Sur as a specific *place* is difficult to locate. It's not only a town, a valley, and a river, but the entire coastline from just south of Carmel Highlands to somewhere north of San Simeon (some suggest the southern limit is the Monterey County line) is considered Big Sur country.

Once "in" Big Sur, wherever that might be, visitors notice some genuine oddities—odd at least by California standards. Until recently, most people here didn't have much money and didn't seem to care. (This situation is changing as the truly wealthy move in.) They built simple or unusual dwellings—redwood cabins, glass tepees, geodesic domes, even round redwood houses with the look of wine barrels ready to roll into the sea—both to fit the limited space available and to express that elusive Big Sur sense of *style*.

Because the terrain itself is so tormented and twisted, broadcast signals rarely arrive in Big Sur. In the days before satellite dishes, there was virtually no TV; electricity and telephones with dial service have been available in Big Sur only since the 1950s, and some people along the south coast and in more remote areas still have neither.

Social life in Big Sur consists of bowling at the naval station, attending a poetry reading or the annual Big Sur Potluck Revue at the Grange Hall in the valley, driving into "town" (Monterey) for a few movie cassettes, or—for a really wild night—drinks on the deck at sunset and dancing cheek to cheek at Nepenthe. Big Sur is a very *different* California, where even the chamber of commerce urges visitors "to slow down, meditate," and "catch up with your soul."

It's almost impossible to catch up with your soul, however, when traffic is bumper-to-bumper. Appreciating Big Sur while driving or, only for the brave, bicycling in a mile-long coastline convoy is akin to honeymooning in Hades—a universal impulse but entirely the wrong ambience. As it snakes through Big Sur, California's Coast Highway (Hwy. 1), the state's first scenic highway and one of the world's most spectacular roadways, slips around the prominent ribs of the Santa Lucia Mountains, slides into dark wooded canyons, and soars across graceful bridges spanning the void. Though its existence means that a trip into Monterey no longer takes an entire day, people here nonetheless resent the highway that brings the flamed out and frantic.

To show some respect, come to Big Sur during the week, in balmy April or early May, when wildflowers burst forth, or in late September or October to avoid the thick summer fog. Though winter is generally rainy, weeks of sparkling warm weather aren't uncommon. In April, Big Sur hosts the annual **Big Sur International Marathon**, with 1,600 or more runners hugging the highway curves from the village to Carmel.

HISTORY

The earliest Big Sur inhabitants, the Esselen people, once occupied a 25-mile-long and 10-mile-wide stretch of coast from Point Sur to near Lucia in the south. A small group of Ohlone, the Sargenta-Ruc, lived from south of the Palo Colorado Canyon to the Big Sur River's mouth. Though most of the area's Salinan peoples lived inland in the Salinas Valley near what is now Fort Hunter-Liggett, villages were also scattered along the Big Sur coast south of Lucia. Little is known about area natives, since mission-forced intertribal marriages and introduced diseases soon obliterated them. It is known, though, that the number of Esselens in Big Sur was estimated between 900 and 1,300 after the Spanish arrived in 1770 and that the Esselen people lived in the Big Sur valley at least 3,000 years ago.

The Esselen people were long gone by the time the first area settlers arrived. Grizzly bears were the greatest 18th-century threat to settlement, since the terrain discouraged any type of travel and the usual wildlife predation that came with it. The name Big Sur ("Big South" in Spanish, a reference point from the Monterey perspective) comes from Rio Grande del Sur, or the Big Sur River, which flows to the sea at Point Sur. The river itself was the focal point of the

1834 Mexican land grant and the Cooper family's Rancho El Sur until 1965.

In the early 1900s came the highway, a hazardous 15-year construction project between Big Sur proper and San Simeon. Hardworking Chinese laborers were recruited for the job along with less willing workers from the state's prisons. The highway was completed in 1937, though many lives and much equipment were lost to the sea. Maintaining this remote ribbon of highway and its 29 bridges is still a treacherous year-round task. Following the wild winter storms of 1982–83, for example, 42 landslides blocked

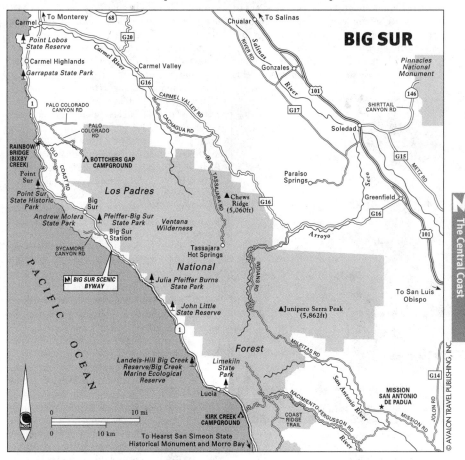

The Central Coast

the highway; the "big one" near Julia Pfeiffer Burns State Park took 19 bulldozers and more than a year to clear.

"Big Surbanization"

Today only 1,300 people live in Big Sur country—just 300 more than in the early 1900s. Yet "Big Surbanization" is underway. Land not included in Los Padres National Forest and the Ventana Wilderness is largely privately owned. Plans for more hotels, restaurants, and civilized comforts for frazzled travelers continue to come up, and the eternal, wild peace Robinson Jeffers predicted would reign here forever has at last been touched by ripples of civilization. Nobody wants the character of Big Sur to change, but people can't agree on how best to save it.

As elsewhere in California, some Big Sur landowners believe that private property rights

© KIM WEIR

"That same prehistoric look. The look of always," Henry Miller said of Big Sur. "Nature smiling at herself in the mirror of eternity."

are sacrosanct, beyond the regulation of God or the government. Others argue that state and local land-use controls are adequate. Still others contend that federal intervention is necessary, possibly granting the region scenic area or national park status—an idea fought sawtooth and nail by most residents. The reason Big Sur is still ruggedly beautiful, they say, is because local people have kept it that way. A favorite response to the suggestion of more government involvement: "Don't Yosemitecate Big Sur." In March 1986, both of California's senators proposed that the U.S. Forest Service take primary responsibility for safeguarding Big Sur's scenic beauty—with no new logging, mining claims, or grazing privileges allowed. The final plan, which limits but doesn't eliminate new development, seems to please almost everyone—except when new controversies arise.

Some proposed changes create no controversy, such as the late 2000 acquisition by Los Padres National Forest of 784 acres along San Carpoforo Creek and the 2001 purchase of the 1,226-acre Bixby Ocean Ranch by the Trust for Public Land for eventual inclusion in the national forest. The Bixby Ranch, once owned by the late Allen Funt, host of TV's *Candid Camera,* was prime Big Sur property otherwise slated for development. In May 2002, The Nature Conservancy and The Big Sur Land Trust bought the 10,000-acre Palo Corona Ranch, the "gateway to Big Sur" beginning a block south of Carmel. That property, most of which will be managed as state park land and accessible to the public, connects 13 other parks and preserves. And in late 2002 the Big Sur Wilderness and Conservation Act was signed into law, extending wilderness protections to some 55,000 acres of federal lands, most of these previousuly unprotected sections of Los Padres National Forest.

Yet some "preserves" raise eyebrows, such as the private, 20,000-acre **Santa Lucia Preserve,** which preserves some 18,000 acres for the private use of 300 estate owners inhabiting the rest of the property as a "sustainable development." Others raise quite a ruckus, such as the Hearst Corporation's plans to build a luxury golf result just south of Big Sur near San Simeon and the famed Hearst Castle. Secret negotiations to establish conservation easements and development rights for the corporation's 83,000-acre Piedras Blancas Ranch, which surrounds Hearst's castle, were continuing, at last report.

SIGHTS

M Big Sur Scenic Byway

One of the world's truly spectacular coastal drives, both a California Scenic Highway and National Scenic Byway, driving Hwy. 1 through Big Sur mean gliding around tight turns, sliding across graceful arched bridges, and trying to keep those eyes on the road despite the fact that some of the most breathtaking scenery anywhere is calling your name. Beautiful though the highway is, it's also one of the state's most dangerous roadways. To live to tell about your Big Sur adventure, drive defensively, given the countless blind curves and corners. Go slow; the official speed limit is 55 miles per hour, but the number of 25- to 35-mile-per-hour turns is so high a sane driver will rarely go the speed limit. Buckle up, because seatbelts are required in California. Keep your eyes on the road at all times; if you must look at the scenery, pull over and park first (there are few pullouts, so watch for them). When pulling over, avoid quick stops on the unpaved pull outs and shoulders *Do not* pass on the double yellow line—head-on collisions due to unsafe passing are all too common. Respect the landscape, which means don't litter—and don't throw cigarette butts out of your vehicle, which creates an extreme fire danger.

Garrapata State Park

Garrapata State Park stretches north along the coast for more than four miles from Soberanes Point, where the Santa Lucia Mountains first dive into the sea. Southward, the at-first unimpressive **Point Sur** and its lighthouse beacon stand out beyond 2,879-acre Garrapata State Park and beach, the latter named after the noble wood tick and featuring a crescent of creek-veined white sand, granite arches, caves and grottos, and sea otters. Ticks or no ticks, the unofficial nude beach here is one of the best in Northern

California. Winter whale-watching is usually good from high ground. On weekends in January, ranger-led whale-watch programs are held at Granite Canyon. Or, if it's not foggy, take the two-mile loop trail from the turnout for the view.

For more information about the park, call 831/624-4909, or call the **Big Sur Station** joint State Parks/U.S. Forest Service office at 831/667-2315.

South of Garrapata and inland is private **Palo Colorado Canyon,** reached via the road of the same name. Dark and secluded even in summer, the canyon is often cut off from the rest of the world when winter storms stomp through. The name itself is Spanish for "tall redwood." About eight miles in at the end of the road is isolated **Bottchers Gap Campground,** complete with restrooms, picnic tables, and multiple trailheads into the Ventana Wilderness. A few miles farther south on the highway is the famous **Rainbow Bridge** (now called Bixby Creek Bridge), 260 feet high and 700 feet long, the highest single-arch bridge in the world when constructed in 1932 and still the most photographed of all Big Sur bridges.

Point Sur State Historic Park

Up atop Point Sur stands the Point Sur Lightstation, an 1889 sandstone affair still standing guard at this shipwreck site once known as the Graveyard of the Pacific. In the days when the only way to get here was on horseback, 395 wooden steps led to the lighthouse, originally a giant multi-wick kerosene lantern surrounded by a Fresnel lens with a 16-panel prism. The Point Sur Lightstation is now computer-operated and features an electrical aero-beacon, radio-beacon, and fog "diaphone." This 34-acre area and its central rocky mound (good views and whale-watching) is now a state park, though the Coast Guard still maintains the lighthouse. Guided three-hour lighthouse walking tours are offered five or six times a week in summer, three times weekly in winter. Full moon tours are also offered monthly, spring through fall. Tours are $5 adults, $3 teens, $2 children. Current tour information is posted throughout Big Sur. For details, contact the park at 831/625-4419. For

The Central Coast

© CALIFORNIA DEPARTMENT OF PARKS AND RECREATION

Andrew Molera State Park

information about winter whale-watching programs here and at both Garrapata and Julia Pfeiffer Burns State Parks, call 831/667-2315.

Andrew Molera State Park

Inland and up, past what remains of the pioneering Molera Ranch (part of the original Rancho El Sur), is marvelous Andrew Molera State Park, 2,100 acres first donated to the Nature Conservancy by Frances Molera in honor of her brother, then deeded to the state for management. There's no pavement here, just the pioneer family's home, now the Molera Cultural and Natural History Center; a dirt parking lot; and a short trail winding through sycamores, maples, and a few redwoods along the east fork of the Big Sur River to the two-mile beach and adjacent seabird sanctuary-lagoon below. (The big breakers cresting along the coast here are created by the Sur Breakers Reef.) The trail north of the river's mouth leads up a steep promontory to Garnet Beach, noted for its colorful pebbles.

The new, improved Andrew Molera Trail Camp opened in April 2003—a primitive yet peaceful walk-in campground with 24 environmental campsites, first-come, first-camped, three-night limit, no RVs, four people maximum per site (call for current prices, most likely less than $10). New restrooms. Dogs allowed only with a leash and proof of current rabies vaccination—and not beyond beyond the picnic area. At last report day use at Andrew Molera, open daily from just before sunrise to just after sunset, was $6–7. For more park information call 831/667-2315.

Also at the park: **Molera Horseback Tours,** 831/625-5486 or 800/942-5486, www.molera horsebacktours.com, which offers regularly scheduled one- to three-hour rides along the beach and through meadows and redwood groves. Guides explain the history, flora, and fauna of the area. Private rides are also available by appointment. Scheduled rides are $25–60; custom rides are $36 per hour.

Pfeiffer–Big Sur State Park

Inland, on the other side of the ridge from Andrew Molera State Park, is protected, sunny Big Sur Valley, a visitor-oriented settlement adjoining the Ventana Wilderness and surrounding picnic, camping, and lodge facilities at 821-acre Pfeiffer–Big Sur State Park. Take the one-mile nature trail or meander up through the redwoods to **Pfeiffer Falls,** a verdant, fern-lined canyon at its best in spring and early summer, then to **Valley View** for a look at the precipitous Big Sur River gorge below. Redwoods, sycamores, big-leaf maples, cottonwoods, and willows hug the river, giving way to oaks, chaparral, and Santa Lucia bristlecone fir at higher elevations. There's abundant poison oak, and raccoons can be particularly pesky here, like the begging birds, so keep food out of harm's way.

To hike within the Ventana Wilderness, head south on the highway one-half mile to the U.S. Forest Service office, 831/667-2315, for a permit and current information (trails begin here). About a mile south of the entrance to Pfeiffer-Big Sur is the road to Los Padres National Forest's **Pfeiffer Beach** (take the second right-hand turnoff after the park) and its cypresses, craggy caves, and mauve and white sands streaked with black. It's heaven here on a clear, calm day, but the hissing sand stings mercilessly when the weather is up. On any day, forget the idea of an ocean swim. The water's cold, the surf capricious, and the currents tricky; even expert divers need to register with rangers before jumping in. Pfeiffer Beach is open to the public from 6 A.M.–sunset (day-use fee charged).

The outdoor amphitheater at Pfeiffer-Big Sur State Park (which hosts many of the park's educational summer campfires and interpretive programs) and lagoons were built by the Civilian Conservation Corps during the depression. The large developed year-round campground features 214 family campsites with picnic tables and hot showers; ratesare $15–20 and $25–30 (premium) per night. Group campsites also available. To make camping reservations—essential in summer, when the park is particularly crowded, and on good-weather weekends—contact ReserveAmerica, 800/444-7275, www.reserve america.com. At last report the day-use fee, required for short park hikes and picnicking, was $6–7. For more information, contact Pfeiffer–Big Sur State Park, 831/667-2315.

Urban Big Sur

Nowhere in Big Sur country are visitors really diverted from the land, because there are no big-time boutiques, gaudy gift shops, or even movie theaters. But urban Big Sur starts at Big Sur Valley and stretches south past the post office and U.S. Forest Service office to the vicinity of Deetjen's Big Sur Inn. This "big city" part of Big Sur includes the area's most famous and fabulous inns and restaurants: the Ventana Inn, the Post Ranch Inn, Nepenthe, and Deetjen's.

Fascinating about Nepenthe is that although cinematographer Orson Welles was persona non grata just down the coast at San Simeon (for his too-faithful portrayal of William Randolph Hearst in *Citizen Kane*), when he bought what was then the Trails Club Log Cabin in Big Sur for his wife Rita Hayworth in 1944, he was able to haunt Hearst from the north. Welles's place became Nepenthe ("surcease from sorrows" in the *Odyssey*) shortly after he sold it in 1947. More or less across the street from Nepenthe is the **Hawthorne Gallery,** 48485 Hwy. 1, 831/667-3200, www.hawthornegallery.com, something of a Hawthorne family enterprise also offering Albert Paley forged metal sculptures, Max DeMoss bronze castings, Jesus Bautista Moroles granite sculptures, and the landscape creations of Frederick L. Gregory, among others.

North of Deetjen's is the **Henry Miller Memorial Library,** a collection of friendly clutter about the writer and his life's work, located on the highway about one mile south of the Ventana Inn but almost hidden behind redwoods and an unassuming redwood double gate. Henry Miller lived, wrote, and painted in Big Sur from 1944 to 1962. The library is housed not in Henry Miller's former home but in that of the late Emil White. A good friend of Miller's, White said he started the library "because I missed him." Now a community cultural arts center, the library sponsors exhibits, poetry readings, concerts, and special events throughout the year. Original art and prints, posters, and postcards are available in the gallery. Miller's books, including rare editions, are also available. In summer the library is often open daily, but year-round it is typically open Wed.–Sun. 11 A.M.–6 P.M. and for special events.

The Central Coast

For current information, contact the Henry Miller Library, 831/667-2574, www.henry miller.org.

South of Deetjen's is the noted **Coast Gallery** at Lafler Canyon (named for editor Henry Lafler, a friend of Jack London), 831/667-2301, www.coastgalleries.com, open daily 9 A.M.–5 P.M. Rebuilt from redwood water tanks in 1973, the Coast Gallery offers fine local arts and crafts, from jewelry and pottery to paintings—including watercolors by Henry Miller—plus sculpture and woodcarvings.

Julia Pfeiffer Burns State Park

Partington Cove is about one mile south of Partington Ridge, the impressive northern boundary of Julia Pfeiffer Burns State Park. To get to the cove, park on the east side of the highway and head down the steep trail that starts near the fence (by the black mailbox) on the west side of the road. The branching trail leads back into the redwoods to the tiny beach at the stream's mouth, or across a wooden footbridge, through a rock tunnel hewn in the 1880s by pioneer John Partington, and on to the old dock where tan bark was once loaded onto seagoing freighters. A fine place for a smidgen of inspirational solitude.

There's a stone marker farther south at the park's official entrance, about seven miles south of Nepenthe. These spectacular 4,000 acres straddling the highway also include a large underwater park offshore. (Only experienced scuba divers, by permit, are allowed to dive offshore.) Picnic in the coast redwoods by McWay Creek, almost the southern limit of the tee's range. Or hike up into the chaparral and the Los Padres National Forest. After picnicking, take the short walk along McWay Creek (watch for poison oak), then through the tunnel under the road to **Saddle Rock** and the cliffs above **Waterfall Cove,** where you'll see the only California waterfall that plunges directly into the sea. The cliffs are rugged here at the overlook; it's a good place to view whales and otters.

The park also features limited year-round camping at walk-in environmental sites and group campgrounds. The two hike-in environmental campsites (up to eight people each) offer

spectacular views. For more information about the park, including day-use fees, camping fees, and winter whale-watching programs, call 831/667-2315.

The still-raw, 1,400-foot-wide slash of earth just north of Julia Pfeiffer Burns State Park, which stopped traffic through Big Sur for more than a year, has earned the area's landslide-of-all-time award (so far). Heading south from the park, the highway crosses Anderson Creek and rugged Anderson Canyon, where an old collection of highway construction cabins for convicts sheltered such bohemians as Henry Miller and his friend Emil White in the 1940s. A few human residents and a new population of bald eagles now call Anderson Canyon home.

Esalen Institute

The Esselen and Salinan peoples frequented the hot springs here, supposedly called *tok-i-tok,* "hot healing water." In 1939, Dr. H. C. Murphy (who officiated at John Steinbeck's birth in Salinas) opened Slate's Hot Springs resort on the site. The hot springs were transformed by grandson Michael Murphy into the famed Esalen Institute, where human-potential practitioners and participants including Joan Baez, Gregory Bateson, the Beatles, Jerry Brown, Carlos Castaneda, Buckminster Fuller, Aldous Huxley, Linus Pauling, B.F. Skinner, Hunter S. Thompson, and Alan Watts taught or learned in residential workshops.

Esalen is the Cadillac of New Age retreats, according to absurdist/comedian/editor Paul Krassner. Even writer Alice Kahn who, before arriving at Esalen, considered herself the "last psycho-virgin in California" and "hard-core unevolved," eventually admitted that there was something about the Esalen Institute that defied all cynicism.

Esalen's magic doesn't necessarily come cheap. The introductory "Experiencing Esalen" weekend workshop runs $455–595 or so, including simple but pleasant accommodations and wonderful meals. Five- to seven-day workshops are substantially more, $795 and up. Esalen tries to accommodate the less affluent with scholarships, a work-study program, senior citizen discounts, family rates, and sleeping bag options. Membership discounts, too. You can also arrange a personal retreat, assuming space is available.

Esalen offers more than 400 workshops each year, these "relating to our greater human capacity." Topics cover everything from the arts and creative expression to "intellectual play," from dreams to spiritual healing, from martial arts to shamanism. Moving in a more intellectual and philosophical direction these days, Esalen increasingly offers programs such as *Psyche and Cosmos in the 21st Century: The Return of Soul to the World* and *Sure Enough: Getting Comfortable with Irreducible Uncertainty.* Not to mention *Applied Wisdom: Enduring Truths of the World's Wisdom Traditions.*

Equally elevated are Esalen's baths. In February 1998 a mudslide roared down the hill to demolish the previous bathhouse facilities. The new, improved Esalen baths now open, include a geothermally heated swimming pool and a handicapped-accessible hot tub and massage area—at a cost of $5.3 million. Designed by architect Mickey Muennig, the new baths "float" above the ocean, thanks to an engineering feat that required driving 34 piers and horizontal anchors into 25 feet of rock. Note the outdoor massage deck, tile work, fountain, and the "living roof," planted in native coastal grasses. Esalen satisfies the California Coastal Commission's public access requirement by allowing the general public access to the hot tubs (at the fairly unappealing hours of 1–3 A.M. daily). Call for details. The massages at Esalen are world-renowned, from $50 an hour. Nudity is big at Esalen, particularly in the hot tubs, swimming pool, and massage area, though not required.

Entrance to Esalen and its facilities is strictly by reservation only. For information on workshops and lodgings and to request a copy of Esalen's current catalog, contact: Esalen Institute, 831/667-3000, www.esalen.org. The website's online *In the Air* magazine offers a good sense of what Esalen is all about and also includes a complete current workshop catalog (which you can download). To make workshop reservations, call 831/667-3005 or fax completed registration forms to 831/667-2724.

Nature Reserves

Just south of the Esalen Institute is the **John Little State Reserve,** 21 acres of coast open to the public for day use (frequently foggy). For current information call 831/667-2315. About five miles south of Esalen, beyond the Dolan Creek and dramatic Big Creek bridges, is the entrance to **Landels-Hill Big Creek Reserve,** more than 4,200 acres owned by the University of California. Adjacent is the 1,200-acre **Big Creek Marine Ecological Reserve.** The two are co-managed as the Big Creek Reserve. Safe behind these rusted cast-iron gates are 11 different plant communities, at least 350 plant species, 100 varieties of birds, and 50 types of mammals. A 10-acre area is open as a public educational center; groups are welcome. For more information, contact **Big Creek Reserve,** 831/667-2543, www.redshift.com/-bigcreek.

Lucia and the New Camaldoli Hermitage

The tiny "town" of Lucia is privately owned, with a gas station and a good down-home restaurant, open from 7 A.M. until dark, when they shut off the generator. Try the homemade split pea soup. Different, too, is a stay in one of the 10 rustic coastal cabins at **Lucia Lodge,** a tiny 1930s-vintage lodge chiseled into a cliff overlooking the ocean. High-season rates are $175–$250, as low as $125 in the winter. Lunch and dinner available, "view" deck. A simple yet spectacular spot. Call 831/667-2391 or 866/424-4787 and see www.lucialodge.com for current information and reservations.

South of Lucia (at the white cross), the road to the left leads to the New Camaldoli Hermitage, a small Benedictine monastery at the former Lucia Ranch. The sign says that the monks "regret we cannot invite you to camp, hunt, or enjoy a walk on our property" due to their customary solitude and avoidance of "unnecessary speaking." But visitors *can* come to buy crafts and homemade fruitcake and to attend daily mass. In addition, the hermitage is available for very serene retreats of up to two weeks, though few outsiders can stand the no-talk rules for much longer than a few days. Simple meals are included. The suggested offering is $60 per day for the retreat rooms, $70 per day for trailer hermitages. For more information, contact the New Camaldoli Hermitage in Big Sur, 831/667-2456, www.con templation.com.

Limekiln State Park

About two miles south of Lucia is the newest Big Sur state park, open since 1995. It encompasses 716 acres in an isolated and steep coastal canyon, preserving some of the oldest, largest, and most vigorous redwoods in Monterey County. Named for the towering wood-fired kilns that smelted quarried limestone into powdered lime—essential for mixing cement—here in the late 1800s, Limekiln State Park offers a steep one-mile round-trip, creekside hike through redwoods to the four kilns, passing a waterfall (to the right at the first fork), pools, and cascades along the way. The park includes a day-use area for picnicking plus a very appealing family campground with minimal amenities but abundant ambience. Campsites are $15–20; extras include hot showers and laundry facilities. To get there, take the signed turnoff (on the inland or landward side of the highway) just south of the Limekiln Canyon Bridge. For more information, contact Limekiln State Park, 63025 Hwy. 1 in Big Sur, 831/667-2403.

RECREATION

The ultimate activity in Big Sur is just bumming around, scrambling down to beaches to hunt for jade, peer into tidepools, or scuba dive or surf where it's possible. Cycling, sightseeing, and watching the sunset are other entertainments. Along the coastline proper there are few long hiking trails, since much of the terrain is treacherous, and most of the rest privately owned, but the Big Sur backcountry offers good hiking and backpacking.

Ventana Wilderness

Local lore has it that a natural land bridge once connected two mountain peaks at Bottchers Gap, creating a window (or *ventana* in Spanish) until the 1906 San Francisco earthquake brought it all tumbling down. The Big Sur, Little Sur, Arroyo Seco, and Carmel Rivers all cut through this 161,000-acre area, creating dramatic gorges and wildland well worth exploring. Steep, sharp-crested ridges and serrated V-shaped valleys are clothed mostly in oaks, madrones, and dense chaparral. Redwoods grow on north-facing slopes near the fog-cooled coast; pines at higher elevations. The gnarly spiral-shaped bristlecone firs found only here are in the rockiest, most remote areas, their total range only about 12 miles wide and 55 miles long.

Most of all, the Ventana Wilderness provides a great escape from the creeping coastal traffic (a free visitor permit is required to enter) and offers great backpacking and hiking when the Sierra Nevada, Klamath Mountains, and Cascades are still snowbound—though roads here are sometimes impassible during the rainy season. Hunting, fishing, and horseback riding are also permitted. Crisscrossing Ventana Wilderness are nearly 400 miles of backcountry trails and 82 vehicle-accessible campgrounds (trailside camping possible with a permit).

The wilderness trailheads are at Big Sur Station, Carmel River, China Camp, Arroyo Seco, Memorial Park, Bottchers Gap, and Cone Peak Road. The Ventana Wilderness recreation map, available for $4 from ranger district offices, shows all roads, trails, and campgrounds. Fire-hazardous areas, routinely closed to the public after July 1 (or earlier), are coded yellow on maps.

Trail and campground traffic fluctuates from year to year, so solitude seekers should ask rangers about more remote routes and destinations. Since the devastating Marble Cone fire of 1978 (and other more recent fires), much of what once was forest is now chaparral and brush. As natural succession progresses, dense undergrowth obliterates trails not already erased by erosion. Despite dedicated volunteer trail work, lack of federal trail maintenance has also taken its toll.

Backcountry travelers should also heed fire regulations. Because of the high fire danger in peak tourist season, using a camp stove or building a fire outside designated campgrounds requires a fire permit. Also, bring water—but think twice before bringing Fido, since flea-transmitted plague is a possibility. Other bothersome realities include ticks (especially in winter and early spring), rattlesnakes, poison oak, and fast-rising rivers and streams following rainstorms.

For more Ventana Wilderness information, contact the Big Sur Station office (see above) or **Los Padres National Forest** headquarters, 6755 Hollister Ave., Ste. 150 in Goleta, 805/968-6640, www.r5.fs.fed.us/lospadres. Additional information is available from the **Ventana Wilderness Society,** 831/455-9514, www.ventanaws.org, and the **Ventana Wilderness Alliance,** 831/423-3191, www.ventanawild.org. For guided trips on horseback, contact **Ventana Wilderness Guides and Expeditions,** 38655 Tassajara Rd. in Carmel Valley, 831/659-2153, www.nativeguides.com, operated by members of the Esselen tribe.

Hiking

The grandest views of Big Sur come from the ridges just back from the coast. A great companion is *Hiking the Big Sur Country* by Jeffrey P. Schaffer (Wilderness Press). The short but steep **Valley View Trail** from Pfeiffer-Big Sur State Park is usually uncrowded, especially midweek; there are benches up top for sitting and staring off the edge of the world. Those *serious* about coastal hiking should walk all the way from Pfeiffer-Big Sur to Salmon Creek near the southern Monterey County line. The trip from Bottchers Gap to Ventana Double Cone via **Skinner Ridge Trail** is about 16 miles one way and challenging, with a variety of possible campsites, dazzling spring wildflowers, and oak and pine forests.

Otherwise, take either the nine-mile **Pine Ridge Trail** from Big Sur or the 15-mile trail from China Camp on Chews Ridge to undeveloped Sykes Hot Springs, just 400 yards from Sykes Camp (very popular these days). Another good, fairly short *visual* hike is the trip to nearby Mount Manuel, a nine-mile round trip. The two-mile walk to **Pfeiffer Beach** is also worth it—miles from the highway, fringed by forest, with a wading cove and meditative monolith.

Back-roads

For an unforgettable dry-season side trip and a true joy ride, take the **Old Coast Road** from

just north of the Bixby Bridge inland to the Big Sur Valley. You'll encounter barren granite, a thickly forested gorge, and good views of sea and sky before the road loops back to Hwy. 1 south of Point Sur near the entrance to Andrew Molera State Park. **Palo Colorado Road,** mostly unpaved and narrow, winds through a canyon of redwoods, ferns, and summer homes, up onto hot and dry Las Piedras Ridge, then down into the Little Sur watershed.

Marvelous for the sense of adventure and the views is a drive along the **Nacimiento-Fergusson Road** from the coast inland to what's left of old Jolon and the fabulous nearby mission, both included within the Fort Hunter-Liggett Military Reservation. (Taking this route is always somewhat risky, particularly on weekends, since all roads through Hunter-Liggett are closed when military exercises are underway.) Even more thrilling is driving rough-and-ready **Los Burros Road** farther south, an unmarked turnoff just

Bixby Bridge

The Central Coast

south of Willow Creek and Cape San Martin that leads to the long-gone town of Manchester in the Los Burros gold mining district. An indestructible vehicle and plenty of time are required for this route, and it's often closed to traffic after winter storms.

Big Sur back-roads leading to the sea are rarer and easy to miss. About one mile south of the entrance to Pfeiffer-Big Sur State Park is **Sycamore Canyon Road,** which winds its way downhill for two exciting miles before the parking lot near Pfeiffer Beach. At Willow Creek there's a road curling down from the vista point to the rocky beach below, and just south of Willow Creek a dirt road leads to Cape San Martin (good for views any day but especially fine for whale-watching).

ACCOMMODATIONS

Public Camping

In the accommodations category, nothing but camping is truly inexpensive in Big Sur, so to travel on the cheap, make campground reservations *early* (where applicable) and stock up on groceries and sundries in Monterey up north or in San Luis Obispo to the south. All the following options are Under $50. The U.S. Forest Service **Bottchers Gap Campground** on Palo Colorado Canyon Road has primitive, walk-in tent sites (first-come, first-camped, $12). Rough road, no drinking water. The Forest Service **Kirk Creek Campground** is far south of urban Big Sur and just north of the intersection with Nacimiento-Fergusson Road. It consists of 33 first-come, first-camped sites ($18), picnic tables, and grills, all situated on a grassy seaside bluff, plus some walk-in/bike-in tent sites ($5). Inland, halfway to Jolon, are two small creekside campgrounds managed by Los Padres National Forest. They are free, since there's no reliable drinking water, and are popular with deer hunters. Also run by the Forest Service and even farther south, north of Gorda, is the 43-site **Plaskett Creek Campground,** $18 (walk-in/bike-in site $5), first-come, first-camped.

For more information on the area's national forest campgrounds and for free visitor permits, fire permits, maps, and other information about Los Padres National Forest and the Ventana Wilderness, stop by the **Big Sur Station** State Parks/U.S. Forest Service office at Pfeiffer-Big Sur State Park, open daily 8 A.M.–4:30 P.M., 831/667-2315, www.fs.fed.us/r5/lospadres, or the **Monterey Ranger District** office at 406 S. Mildred Ave. in King City, 831/385-5434.

At state park facilities, for secluded camping try **Andrew Molera State Park,** with walk-in tent sites not far from the dusty parking lot, three-night maximum; or **Julia Pfeiffer Burns State Park,** with two separate environmental campsites (far from RVs). More comforts (including flush toilets and hot showers) are available at the attractive family campground at **Pfeiffer–Big Sur State Park.** It has 214 family campsites, group campgrounds, plus a regular summer schedule of educational and informational programs. There are no hookups. Another possibility, just south of Lucia, is the postcard-pretty **Limekiln State Park,** 63025 Hwy. 1, 831/667-2403, which takes up most of the steep canyon and offers some good hiking in addition to attractive tent and RV sites (no hookups, but water, hot showers, and flush toilets are available). For information about any of the area's state park campgrounds, stop by the office at Pfeiffer-Big Sur State Park or call 831/667-2315. For ReserveAmerica reservations (usually necessary May through early September and on warm-weather weekends) at Pfeiffer–Big Sur and Limekiln, call 800/444-7275 or reserve online at www.reserveamerica.com.

Private Camping

Not far from the state campgrounds at Pfeiffer–Big Sur State Park is the private riverside **Big Sur Campground,** Hwy. 1, 831/667-2322, with tent sites and RV sites including hookups. Tent cabins and cabins are also available, as well as hot showers, laundry facilities, a store, telephone access, and a playground. Also on the Big Sur River, with similar facilities and prices, is the **Riverside Campground,** Hwy. 1, 831/667-2414, with tent or RV sites plus cabins. The private **Ventana Campgrounds,** managed by the Ventana Inn, Hwy. 1, 831/667-2712, www.ventanabigsur.com, has 80 very private, pretty sites in a scenic 40-acre redwood setting along Post Creek. There are some RV hookups, hot showers (three bathhouses), fireplaces, and picnic tables. Rates for all the above are under $50.

Cabins and Motels

Always a best bet for cabins and affordable for just plain folks is the charming **Ripplewood Resort,** about a mile north of Pfeiffer-Big Sur, 831/667-2242, www.ripplewoodresort.com. The primo units, most with fireplaces and kitchens (bring your own cookware), are down by the Big Sur River (and booked months in advance for summer). Rates are $100–150. Convenient on-site café, too; open for breakfast and lunch. At last report there were still several nice, private cabins at **Mill Creek Ranch,** 64955 Hwy. 1 (at Nacimiento Road), 831/667-2757, website: bigsurmillcreek.com, set up for weekly or monthly rentals (call for other possibilities). The one-bedroom Kiwi Cabin is $600/week; the two-bedroom, two-story Bay Tree House is $800/week; and the striking, redwood and stone Wisteria House is $1,250/week. Winter weekend rates are quite reasonable.

Other Big Sur options include the adobe **Glen Oaks Motel,** 831/667-2105, www.glenoaksbigsur.com, and the **Fernwood Resort,** 831/667-2422, both on Hwy. 1 and both with rates of $50–150. The **Big Sur River Inn,** on Hwy. 1 in Big Sur Valley, 831/625-5255 or 800/548-3610, is a motel-restaurant-bar popular with locals and featuring views of the river and live music most weekends. The 61-room **Big Sur Lodge** nearby, just inside the park's entrance at 47225 Hwy. 1, 831/667-3100 or 800/424-4787, www.bigsurlodge.com, is quiet, with a pool, sauna, restaurant, and circle of comfy cabins, each with its own porch or deck. Some rooms feature wood-burning fireplaces or fully stocked kitchens. Rates start at $50. A lodge stay includes a complimentary pass to all area state parks.

Deetjen's Big Sur Inn

Just south of the noted Nepenthe restaurant and the Henry Miller Library is the landward Norwegian-style Deetjen's Big Sur Inn in Castro Canyon, 831/667-2377, a rambling, ever-blooming inn with redwood rooms—now listed on the National Register of Historic Places. *Very* Big Sur. The 20 eccentric, rustic rooms and cabins—one's named Chateau Fiasco, after the Bay of Pigs invasion—are chock-full of bric-a-brac and feature thin walls, front doors that don't lock, fireplaces, books, and reasonably functional plumbing. No TVs, no telephones. Forget about trendy creature comforts. People love this place—and have ever since it opened in the 1930s—because it has *soul.* Private or shared baths. Reservations advised because rooms are usually booked up many months in advance. Rooms are $100 and up. Eating at Deetjen's is as big a treat as an overnight. Wonderfully hearty, wholesome breakfasts are served 8 to 11:30 A.M., and dinner starts at 6:15 P.M. Reservations are also taken for meals.

Ventana Inn & Spa

Perhaps tuned into the same philosophical frequency as Henry Miller—"There being nothing to improve on in the surroundings, the tendency is to set about improving oneself"—the Ventana Inn didn't provide distractions like TV or tennis courts when writer Lawrence A. Spector first built the place in 1975. Though it's still a hip, high-priced resort, and there are still no tennis courts, things have changed. Now the desperately undiverted *can* phone home, if need be, or watch in-room TV or videos. But the woodsy, world-class Ventana high up on the hill in Big Sur, 831/667-2331 or 800/628-6500, www.ventanainn.com, still offers luxurious and relaxed contemporary lodgings on 240 acres overlooking the sea, outdoor Japanese hot baths, and heated pools, and a full-service spa. Family travelers, please note: Children are discouraged at Ventana, which is not set up to entertain or otherwise look after them. Rates are $250 and up; reservations usually essential; two-night minimum stay on weekends.

This rough-hewn and hand-built hostelry comprises 12 separate buildings with rooms featuring unfinished cedar interiors, parquet floors, and down-home luxuries like queen- or king-sized beds with hand-painted headboards, handmade quilted spreads, and lots of pillows. All

NEPENTHE

Nepenthe, about a mile south of the Ventana Inn, was built almost exactly on the site of the cabin Orson Welles bought for Rita Hayworth. So it's not too surprising that the restaurant is almost as legendary as Big Sur itself. A striking multilevel structure complete with an arts and crafts center, the restaurant was named for an ancient drug mentioned in Homer's *The Odyssey*, taken to help people forget their grief. Naturally enough, the bar here does a brisk business.

As is traditional at Nepenthe, relax on the upper deck (the "gay pavilion," presided over by a sculpted bronze and redwood phoenix) with drink in hand to salute the sea and setting sun—surreal views. The open-beamed restaurant and its outdoor above-ocean terrace isn't nearly as rowdy as all those bohemian celebrity stories would suggest. Nonetheless, thrill-seekers insist on sitting on the top deck, though there's often more room available downstairs at the Café Kevah health food deli and deck, open Mar.–Dec. for brunch and lunch. The fare at Nepenthe is good, but not as spectacular (on a clear day) as the views. Try the homemade soups, the hefty chef's salad, any of the vegetarian selections, or the world-famous Ambrosia burger (an excellent cheeseburger on French roll with pickles and a salad, for a hefty price) accompanied by a Basket o' Fries. Good pies and cakes for dessert.

To avoid the worst of the tourist traffic and to appreciate Nepenthe at its best, come later in September or October. And although Nepenthe is casual any time of year, it's not *that* casual. Local lore has it that John F. Kennedy was once turned away because he showed up barefoot. Nepenthe is open for lunch and dinner daily, with music and dancing around the hearth at night. For more information or reservations, call 831/667-2345. To reach Café Kevah, call 831/667-2344.

And if at the moment you can't be here in person, you can be here in spirit—much easier now that Nepenthe has an online weather camera pointing south over the back deck. To "see" what's happening along Nepenthe's coastline, try www.nepenthebigsur.com.

rooms are reasonably large and have in-room refrigerators; most have fireplaces. Rooms and suites with both fireplaces and hot tubs are at the top of the inn's price range. The Ventana Inn also has a library, not to mention hiking trails and hammocks. Complimentary group classes—so very *California*—include Native American tai chi, Chi Gong, guided meditation, yoga, and hiking. Complimentary continental breakfast is served (delivered to your room by request), and in the afternoon from 4 to 5:30 P.M. you can enjoy the complimentary wine and cheese buffet in the main lodge. The full-service spa offers world-class massage, wraps, facials, scrubs, and other body therapies.

If a stay here or a self-pampering spa session seems just *too rich,* try drinks with a view or a bite of enticing California cuisine served in the inn's lovely two-tiered **Cielo** restaurant overlooking the ocean, a pleasant stroll through the woods. The Ventana Inn is located 0.8 miles south of Pfeiffer–Big Sur State Park; look for the sign on the left.

Post Ranch Inn

For good reason, new Big Sur commercial development was rare in the 1990s. If further coastal development must come, the environmentally conscious Post Ranch Inn offers the style—if not the price range—most Californians would cheer. All the upscale travel mags rave about the place, open since 1992, calling it "one of the best places to stay in the world" *(Condé Nast Traveler)* and "the most spectacular hotel on the Pacific Coast" *(Travel & Leisure).* This place is something special. Developer Myles Williams, of New Christy Minstrels folksinging fame, and architect Mickey Muennig took the Big Sur region's rugged love of the land to heart when they built the very contemporary Post Ranch Inn. They also acknowledged the community's increasing economic stratification and took other real-world problems into account, adding 24 housing units for workers (affordable housing is now scarce in these parts) and donating land for Big Sur's first fire station.

Perched on a ridge overlooking the grand Pacific Ocean, the Post Ranch Inn is a carefully executed aesthetic study in nature awareness. The 30 redwood-and-glass "guest houses" are designed and built to harmonize with—almost disappear into—the hilltop landscape. The triangular "tree houses" are built on stilts, to avoid damaging the roots of the oaks with which they intertwine; the spectacular sod-roofed "ocean houses" literally blend into the ocean views; and the gracious "coast house" duplexes impersonate stand-tall coastal redwoods. Absolute privacy and understated, earth-toned luxury are the main points here. Each house includes a wood-burning fireplace, a two-person spa tub in the stunning slate bathroom, a good sound system, in-room refrigerators stocked with complimentary snacks, a private deck, a king-sized bed—and views. Extra amenities include plush robes, in-room coffeemakers and hair dryers, even walking sticks. Priced for Hollywood entertainment execs and Silicon Valley survivors, rates are $250 and up—emphasis on "up"—continental breakfast included.

Guests can also enjoy the **Post Ranch Spa**—offering massage, wraps, and facials—and the exceptional California-style **Sierra Mar** restaurant, where the views are every bit as inviting as the daily changing menu. Full bar. Open for lunch and dinner.

The Post Ranch Inn is 30 miles south of Carmel on Hwy. 1, on the west (seaward) side of the road. As at Ventana, children are discouraged here. For more information, contact Post Ranch Inn in Big Sur, 831/667-2200, www.postranchinn.com. For inn reservations, call 800/527-2200. For restaurant reservations, call 831/667-2800.

FOOD

Look for fairly inexpensive fare in and around the Big Sur Valley. Good for breakfast is the **Ripplewood Resort** just north of Pfeiffer-Big Sur near the tiny Big Sur Library, 831/667-2242, where favorites include homemade baked goods and French toast. Another local find is the **Big Sur Bakery & Restaurant** near the post office,

831/667-0520. **Deetjen's**, 831/667-2377, is special for breakfast—wholesome and hearty fare served in the open-beamed, hobbit-style dining rooms. Dinner is more formal (fireplace blazing to ward off the chill mist, classical music, and two seatings, by reservation only), with entrées including steaks, fish, California country cuisine, and vegetarian dishes. Tasty home-baked pies are an after-meal specialty at the casual and cheery **Big Sur Lodge Restaurant** at the Big Sur Lodge, 831/667-3111, overlooking the river and also known for red snapper and California-style fare. Beer and wine. Another draw is the lodge's **Espresso House**, perfect for coffee, tea, or a quick snack.

Everyone should sample the view from famed **Nepenthe**, 831/667-2345, at least once in a lifetime; just below Nepenthe is **Café Kevah**, 831/667-2344, open March through December for brunch and lunch. A culinary hot spot is the locally popular **Bonito Roadhouse** (previously the Glen Oaks Restaurant) at the Glen Oaks Motel, next door to the Ripplewood Resort, 831/667-2264. It is diverse, low-key, and likable à la Big Sur. Entrées emphasize what's local and fresh and include crêpes, good vegetarian dishes, seafood gumbo, and chicken pot pie. Open for dinner Wed.–Mon. nights. The roadhouse also serves a fine Sunday brunch, with omelettes, eggs Benedict, and cornmeal hotcakes. A quarter-mile north of Palo Colorado Rd. on Hwy. 1 is the **Rocky Point Restaurant**, 831/624-2933, a reasonably well-heeled steak and seafood place overlooking the ocean. Open for lunch, dinner, and cocktails daily.

The finest of local fine dining is served at the area's luxury-hotel restaurants—at **Cielo** at the Ventana Inn & Spa and **Sierra Mar** at the Post Ranch Inn—which both serve lunch and dinner daily. For information, see listings above.

INFORMATION AND SERVICES

For general information about the area, contact the **Big Sur Chamber of Commerce**, 831/667-2100, www.bigsurcalifornia.org. (Send a stamped, self-addressed legal-sized envelope for a free guide to Big Sur, or download it from the website.)

The Central Coast

EYEING E-SEALS

E veryone knows that massive northern elephant seals lumber ashore every winter at Año Nuevo, north of Santa Cruz, much as the swallows come back to Capistrano. Yet most people don't know that if you can't get reservations to see the "e-seals" at the Año Nuevo preserve, you can come observe them from a vista point just south of Piedra Blancas, about 4.5 miles north of Hearst Castle.

The northern elephant seal colony here began in November 1990, when a handful of seals hauled ashore at the small cove just south of the Piedras Blancas lighthouse; the following spring, almost 400 seals came ashore to molt; and in 1992 the first pup was born. By 2002, the total Piedras Blancas population of northern elephant seals was estimated at 8,500, including 2,150 new pups. More than 2,600 pups were born during the 2002–2003 pupping season. The seals' breeding and pupping season begins in December and lasts into March. (Keep your distance at all times, and never come between an e-seal and the ocean, their natural escape route. These are wild animals that will react to provocation and perceived threats.) From April to August the e-seals molt, a natural phenomenon that looks like an outbreak of disease as old fur is shed and shiny new skin emerges. Docents at the designated viewing area explain the natural history and habits and life cycles of the northern elephant seal. Tours can be arranged.

For more information, stop by the **Friends of the Elephant Seals** office in the Plaza del Cavalier in San Simeon, 250 San Simeon Ave., Ste. 3B (next door to the San Simeon Chamber of Commerce), or contact the Friends at 805/924-1628, www.elephantseal.org.

Combined headquarters for area state parks and the U.S. Forest Service is **Big Sur Station** on the south side of Pfeiffer-Big Sur on Hwy. 1, 831/667-2315. Open daily 8 A.M.–4:30 P.M., this is the place to go in search of forest and wilderness maps, permits, and backcountry camping and recreation information. There's a **laundromat** at Pfeiffer-Big Sur State Park in the Big Sur Lodge complex.

Bicycling Big Sur can be marvelous, except when you're fighting RVs and weekend speedsters for road space. Forewarned, fearless cyclists should plan to ride from north to south to take advantage of the tailwind. (Driving south makes sense, too, since most vistas and turnouts are seaward.) It takes *at least* five hours by car to drive the 150 miles of Hwy. 1 between Monterey and San Luis Obispo.

Hitchhiking is almost as difficult as safely riding a bicycle along this stretch of road, so don't count on thumbs for transportation. More reliable is **Monterey-Salinas Transit** Bus 22, which runs to and from Big Sur daily mid-April to October, stopping at Point Lobos, Garrapata State Park, the Bixby Creek Bridge, Point Sur Lightstation, Pfeiffer-Big Sur and the River Inn, Pfeiffer Beach, the Ventana Inn, and Nepenthe; call 831/899-2555 for information.

San Simeon and Vicinity

Hearst San Simeon State Historic Monument

The Hearst San Simeon State Historic Monument just south of Big Sur ranks right up there with Disneyland as one of California's premier tourist attractions. Somehow that fact alone puts the place into proper perspective. Media magnate William Randolph Hearst's castle is a rich man's playground filled to overflowing with artistic diversions and other expensive toys, a monument to one man's monumental ego and equally impressive poor taste.

In real life, of course, Hearst was quite wealthy and powerful, the man many people still believe was the subject of the greatest American movie ever made, Orson Welles's 1941 *Citizen Kane*. (These days even Welles's biographers say the movie was about the filmmaker himself.) Yet there's something to be said for popular opinion. "Pleasure," Hearst once wrote, "is worth what you can afford to pay for it." And that attitude showed itself quite early; for his 10th birthday little William asked for the Louvre as a present. One scene in the movie, in which Charles Foster Kane shouts across the cavernous living room at Xanadu to attract the attention of his bored young mistress, endlessly working jigsaw puzzles while she sits before a fireplace as big as the mouth of Jonah's whale, won't seem so surreal once you see San Simeon.

Designed by Berkeley architect Julia Morgan, the buildings themselves are odd yet handsome hallmarks of Spanish Renaissance architecture. The centerpiece La Casa Grande alone has 100 rooms (including a movie theater, a billiards room, two libraries, and 31 bathrooms) adorned with silk banners, fine Belgian and French tapestries, Norman fireplaces, European choir stalls, and ornately carved ceilings virtually stolen from continental monasteries. The furnishings and art Hearst collected from around the world

© ROBERT HOLMES/CALTOUR

The Central Coast

the Neptune Pool at Hearst Castle

complete the picture, one that includes everything but humor, grace, warmth, and understanding.

The notably self-negating nature of this rich but richly disappointed man's life is somehow fully expressed here in the country's most ostentatious and theatrical temple to obscene wealth. In contrast to Orson Welles's authentic artistic interpretation of either his own or Hearst's life, William Randolph's idea of hearth, home, and humanity was full-flown fantasy sadly separated from heart and vision.

The Cast of Characters

Orson Welles, his brilliant film career essentially destroyed by William Randolph Hearst, was probably never invited to the famous celebrity encounters staged at La Cuesta Encantada, The Enchanted Hill. Hearst's wife, who refused to divorce him despite his insistence, never socialized here either (though she did come to the castle on occasion when summoned to preside over meetings with presidents and such). But those attending Hearst's flamboyant parties, carefully orchestrated by the lord of the manor and his lady and mistress, Ziegfeld Follies showgirl Marion Davies, included characters such as Charlie Chaplin, Greta Garbo, Clark Gable, Vivien Leigh, Laurence Olivier, Shirley Temple, Mary Pickford, and Rudolph Valentino. Even Hollywood moguls like Louis B. Mayer, Jack Warner, and Darryl Zanuck got through the gates, as did garrulous professional gossips including Hedda Hopper and Louella Parsons. Celebrities from farther afield, including Winston Churchill, President Calvin Coolidge, Charles Lindbergh, and George Bernard Shaw, also helped Hearst stave off the inevitable loneliness at the top. Cary Grant, a regular at "the ranch," said it was "a great place to spend the Depression."

Among Hearst's numerous house rules—informal dress only, no dirty jokes, no drinking in excess, and (ironically) no accompaniment by anyone other than one's spouse—perhaps his most revealing was: "Never mention death." But in the movie, only on his deathbed does Charles Foster Kane finally recognize the true worth and wreckage of his life. The word he whispers at the end—remembering the only thing he had ever really loved, his little sled—almost echoes through the great halls of San Simeon: *Rosebud. . . .*

Citizen Hearst

The name San Simeon was originally given to three Mexican land grants—40,000 acres bought by mining scion George Hearst in 1865. The first millionaire Hearst owned Nevada's Comstock Lode silver mine, Ophir silver mine, and the rich Homestake gold mine in South Dakota, and staked-out territory in California's goldfields. George Hearst later expanded the family holdings to 250,000 acres (including 50 miles of coastline) for the family's "Camp Hill" Victorian retreat and cattle ranch. With his substantial wealth, he was even able to buy himself a U.S. Senate seat.

But young William Randolph had even more ambitious plans—personally and for the property. The only son of the senator and San Francisco schoolteacher, socialite, and philanthropist Phoebe Apperson, the high-rolling junior Hearst took a fraction of the family wealth and his daddy's failing *San Francisco Examiner* and created a successful yellow-journalism chain, eventually adding radio stations and movie production companies.

Putting his newfound power of propaganda to work in the political arena, Hearst (primarily for the headlines) goaded Congress into launching the Spanish-American War in 1898. But unlike his father, William Randolph was unable to buy much personal political power. Though he aspired to the presidency, he had to settle for two terms as a congressmember from New York.

Following his parents' death, Hearst decided to build a house at "the ranch," partly as a place to store his already burgeoning art collection. Architect Julia Morgan, a family favorite, signed on for the project in 1919—for her, the beginning of a 28-year architectural collaboration. Morgan and Hearst planned the ever-evolving Enchanted Hill as a Mediterranean hill town, with La Casa Grande, the main house, as the "cathedral" facing the sea. Three additional palaces were clustered in front, the whole town surrounded by lavish terraced gardens. Hearst's obsession was never satisfied and the project never technically finished, but most of La Casa Grande and adjacent buildings, pools, and grand gardens graced La Cuesta Encantada by the time major construction ceased in 1947, the year Hearst became ill and moved away. He died four years later.

Though the family, through the Hearst Corporation, gave the white elephant San Simeon to the state in 1958, in memory of Phoebe Apperson Hearst, descendants still own or control most of the surrounding land, proposed for development but with any luck at all destined for land-trust preservation. They also own Hearst's art, much of it on display in the castle.

Julia Morgan

As San Simeon's architect, Julia Morgan supervised the execution of almost every detail of Hearst's rambling 165-room pleasure palace. This 95-pound, teetotaling, workaholic woman was UC Berkeley's first female engineering graduate (at a time when a total of two-dozen women were enrolled there) and the first woman to graduate from the École des Beaux-Arts in Paris. Her eccentric mentor, Bernard Maybeck, whose California redwood homes characteristically "climb the hill" on steep lots to blend into the landscape, encouraged her career, as did John Galen Howard of New York.

Though credited only after her death for her accomplishments, Morgan deserved at least as much recognition for her work as Edith Wharton in American literature and Mary Cassatt in painting, irate architecture and art historians have pointed out. But if acclaim came late for Morgan, it was partly her preference. She loathed publicity, disdained the very idea of celebrity, and believed that architects should be like anonymous medieval masters and let the work speak for itself.

Morgan's work with Hearst departed dramatically from her belief that buildings should be unobtrusive, the cornerstone of her brilliant but unobtrusive career. "My style," she said to those who seemed bewildered by the contradiction, "is to please my client." Pleasing her client in this case was quite a task. Hearst arbitrarily and habitually changed his mind, all the while complaining about slow progress and high costs. And she certainly didn't do the job for money, though

Hearst and her other clients paid her well. Morgan divided her substantial earnings among her staff, keeping only about $10,000 annually to cover office overhead and personal expenses.

The perennially private Morgan, who never allowed her name to be posted at construction sites, designed almost 800 buildings in California and the West, among them the original Asilomar, the Berkeley City Club, the Oakland YWCA, and the bell tower, library, social hall, and gym at Oakland's Mills College. She also designed and supervised the reconstruction of San Francisco's Fairmont Hotel following its devastation in the 1906 earthquake. Other Hearst commissions included the family's Wyntoon retreat near Mount Shasta as well as the *Los Angeles Herald-Examiner* building.

Castle Tours

In spring when the hills are emerald green, from the faraway highway Hearst Castle appears as if by magic up on the hill. (Before the place opened for public tours in the 1950s, the closest view commoners could get was from the road, with the assistance of coin-operated telescopes.) One thing visitors *don't* see on the tour shuttle up to the enchanted hill is William Randolph Hearst's 2,000-acre zoo—"the largest private zoo since Noah," as Charles Foster Kane would put it— once the country's largest. The inmates have long since been dispersed, though survivors of Hearst's exotic elk, zebra, Barbary sheep, and Himalayan goat herds still roam the grounds.

The four separate tours of the Hearst San Simeon State Historic Monument take approximately two hours each. Theoretically you could take all the San Simeon tours in a day, but don't try it. So much Hearst in the short span of a day could be detrimental to one's well-being. A dosage of two tours per day makes the trip here worthwhile yet not overwhelming. Visitors obsessed with seeing it all should plan a two-day stay in the area or come back again some other time. Whichever tour, or combination of tours, you select, be sure to wear comfortable walking shoes. Lots of stairs.

The **Experience Tour,** or Tour One, is the recommended first-time visit, taking in the castle's main floor, one guesthouse, and some of the gardens—a total of 150 steps and a half mile of walking. Included on the tour is a short showing in the theater of some of Hearst's "home movies." Particularly impressive in a gloomy Gothic way is the dining room, where silk Siennese banners hang over the lord's table. The poolroom and mammoth great hall, with Canova's *Venus*, are also unforgettable. All the tours include both the Greco-Roman Neptune Pool and statuary and the indoor Roman Pool with its mosaics of lapis lazuli and gold leaf. It's hard to imagine Churchill, cigar in mouth, cavorting here in an inner tube. The Experience Tour also includes the National Geographic movie, *Hearst Castle—Building the Dream.*

Tour Two requires more walking, covering the mansion's upper floors, the kitchen, the libraries, and Hearst's Gothic Suite, with its frescoes and rose-tinted Venetian glass windows (he ran his 94 separate business enterprises from here). The delightfully lit Celestial Suite was the nonetheless depressing extramarital playground of Hearst and Marion Davies. **Tour Three** covers one of the guesthouses plus the "new wing," with 36 luxurious bedrooms, sitting rooms, and marble bathrooms furnished with fine art.

Gardeners will be moved to tears by **Tour Four** (offered April–Aug. only), which includes a long stroll through the San Simeon grounds but does not go inside the castle itself. Realizing that all the rich topsoil here had to be manually carried up the hill makes the array of exotic plantlife, including unusual camellias and about 6,000 rosebushes, all the more impressive for the fact that gardeners at San Simeon worked only at night because Hearst couldn't stand watching them. Also included on the fourth tour is the lower level of the elegant, 17-room Casa del Mar guesthouse (where Hearst spent much of his time), the recently redone underground Neptune Pool dressing rooms, the never-finished bowling alley, and Hearst's wine cellar. David Niven once remarked that, with Hearst as host, the wine flowed "like glue." Subsequently, Niven was the only guest allowed free access to the castle's wine cellar.

Fairly new at San Simeon are the **Hearst Castle Evening Tours,** two-hour adventures featuring the highlights of other tours—with the added benefit of allowing you to pretend to be some Hollywood celebrity, just arrived and in need of orientation. (Hearst himself handed out tour maps, since newcomers often got lost.) Guides dress in period costume and show you around. It's worth it just to see the castle in lights. At last report, evening tours were offered on Friday and Saturday nights March–May and Sept.–Dec., but call for current details. December **Christmas at the Castle** tours are particularly festive.

Wheelchair-accessible tours, which explore the ground floor only, take about two hours and are offered at least three times daily. Wheelchairs are available for lending, at no extra charge. Chairs brought by visitors need to be able to get through doorways 28 inches wide. Someone strong enough to maneuver an occupied chair up and down narrow ramps and steep inclines must accompany visitors requiring wheelchairs.

Accessible Tours

The monument's visitor facilities include fully accessible parking, visitor center, exhibit areas, restrooms, and gift shops. For visually impaired and blind guests, various "touchable" artifacts are available on all tours. With prior notification, assistive listening devices and American Sign Language interpreters are also available on all tours; a narrative Braille tour is also available.

A special tour of Hearst Castle is offered for the physically challenged. (Tour reservations must be made at least 10 days in advance.) A lift-equipped bus is provided for the trip to and from Casa Grande, and a tram is used on the castle grounds. Wheelchairs are provided free of charge; visitors bringing their own chairs are advised that personal chairs must be capable of entering doorways 28 inches wide. Visitors must also be accompanied by a person strong enough to move an in-use wheelchair up and down narrow ramps and long, steep inclines. The modified tour, which is available at least three times daily and takes just under two hours to complete, includes the mansion's ground floor only, due to the many flights of stairs required to explore upper floors. Indoors, the tour includes the main floor of Casa Grande, including the

Roman Pool, and outdoors includes the gardens, a glimpse of the Neptune Pool, and views of the guest cottages.

To make reservations for **physically challenged/wheelchair-accessible tours,** call Hearst Castle directly at 805/927-2070, 10 days or more in advance.

Practicalities

San Simeon is open daily except Thanksgiving, Christmas, and New Year's Day, with the regular two-hour tours leaving the visitor center area on the hour from early morning until around dusk. Tour schedules change by season and day of the week. Reservations aren't required, but the chance of getting tickets on a drop-in, last-minute basis is small. For current schedule information and reservations, call ReserveAmerica at 800/444-4445 and have that credit card handy. You can also book online via the website: www.hearst castle.org. For cancellations and refunds, in the U.S. call 800/695-2269. (To make ticket reservations from outside the U.S., call 916/414-8400 ext. 4100.) Wheelchair-access tours of San Simeon are offered on a different schedule; call 805/927-2070 for reservations and information. The TDD number is 800/274-7275.

Admission to the Experience Tour (Tour One) is $24 adult and $12 youth (ages 6–17) in season ($20/$10 off season). Recommended for first-time visitors, the Experience Tour includes the movie *Hearst Castle—Building the Dream.* Each of the other three San Simeon day tours is $20 adults and $10 youth in season ($16/$8 off season). Evening tour rates are $30 adults and $15 youth. A special brochure for international travelers (printed in Japanese, Korean, French, German, Hebrew, Italian, and Spanish) is available. With a little forethought—head for Cambria or the town of San Simeon—visitors can avoid eating the concession-style food here.

Adjacent to the visitor center is the Hearst Castle's giant-screened **National Geographic Theater,** 805/927-6811, where at last report the larger-than-life *Hearst Castle—Building the Dream* and *Everest* were showing on the 70-foot by 52-foot screen. Call for current times and details (no reservations required).

For other information, contact: Hearst San Simeon State Historic Monument, 750 Hearst Castle Rd. in San Simeon, 805/927-2020 (recorded) or 805/927-2000, www.hearstcastle.org. You can purchase tour tickets via the website—up to an hour before a same-day tour time, a major recent advance—or (in the U.S.) by calling 800/444-4445; for cancellations or refunds, call 800/695-2269. To make reservations from outside the U.S., see the website or call 916/414-8400 ext. 4100. Camp, find a motel, and get meals nearby (see below), or plan your castle tour(s) as part of a Morro Bay or San Luis Obispo stay, since both are within reasonable driving distance.

SAN SIMEON

Done with the display of pompous circumstance on the hill, head for the serene sandy beaches nearby for a long coast walk. Good ocean swimming. Nude sunbathers sometimes congregate at the north end of **William Randolph Hearst Memorial State Beach,** 805/927-2020, across the highway from Hearst Castle, indulging in a healthy hedonism Hearst would absolutely hate. Otherwise this is a family-style stop with good picnicking (tables and barbecues), restrooms, a public pier popular for fishing, plus kayak and boogie board rentals (California Kayaks Company, 805/927-1744). No beach day-use fee.

Another picnicking possibility is **Piedras Blancas Light Station** just up the coast, an area quite popular with whalewatchers. The lighthouse, built in 1874, is now automated and (since 2003) open for monthly tours ($10 adults, $5 children ages 6-16). For current information call 888/804-8608. For a nice lighthouse history, see www.lighthouse friends.com. Wonderful tidepools and good abalone diving are characteristics of the coast near here, at **Twin Creeks Beach,** but public access may be restricted, as the area has become seasonal home for a northern elephant seal colony. Docent-guided "e-seal" tours are available. For current details call 805/924-1628, stop by the Friends of the Elephant Seals office next to the chamber office (see below), or see www.elephantseal.org.

The beaches at **San Simeon State Park** farther south near Cambria (no day-use fee) are larger

The Central Coast

and rockier. The park features three separate areas popular for fishing and picnicking plus 70 primitive campsites and 134 developed campsites near San Simeon Creek off San Simeon Creek Rd. (five miles south of San Simeon on Hwy. 1). Washburn campsites are $11-15 (higher in summer) and San Simeon Creek campsites are $15-20. If you need to stretch your legs, take the pleasant three-mile **San Simeon Creek Trail,** starting from the Washburn Day Use Area. For physically challenged nature lovers, there is also a short access trail and boardwalk through the wetlands. For park information, call 805/927-2035 or 805/927-2020. For campground reservations (March 15 through September), contact ReserveAmerica at 800/444-7275.

The "town" of San Simeon is actually two tiny towns: the original Spanish-style, red-tile-roofed village built for Hearst employees, and "San Simeon Acres," the highway's motel row. The old **Sebastian's General Store,** 805/927-4217, in the real San Simeon is a state historic monument and a great picnic supply stop with old-time post office and more modern garden café. Quite casual and comfortable, with whaling implements on the wall. Party boats powered by **Virg's Fish'n,** 805/927-4676 or (805/927-4677, set out from the harbor March-Oct. for fishing. Ask about whale-watching tours.

For more information about the area, including events, accommodations, and restaurants, contact the **San Simeon Chamber of Commerce,** on the highway just south of the Sands Motel in the Cavalier Plaza, 9255 Hearst Dr., 805/927-3500.

CAMBRIA

Its borders blending into San Simeon about eight miles south of Hearst Castle, the artsy coastal town of Cambria now bears the Roman name for ancient Wales but was previously called Rosaville, San Simeon, and (seriously) Slabtown. In some ways Cambria is becoming the Carmel of southern Big Sur, with galleries and come-hither shops but usually without the overwhelming crowds. Several of the area's historic buildings remain, including the 1877 Squibb-

Darke home, the Brambles restaurant on Burton Drive in Old Town to the east, and the restored Santa Rosa Catholic Church on Bridge Street (across Main, past the library and post office). **Moonstone Beach** offers a boardwalk, miles of walking (in search of smooth, translucent jasper, or moonstones), tidepools, sea otters, sunsets, and good surfing. **East-West Ranch,** 430 acres coastal acres tucked into a residential neighborhood, offers a mile-long Bluff Trail, five other trails, and benches and chairs fashioned from driftwood. South of Harmony and north of Cayucos are the **Estero Bluffs,** with 3.5 miles of coastline threaded with trails.

Just outside Cambria in Cambria Pines is Arthur Beal's beautifully bizarre **Nit Wit Ridge,** an eccentric middle-class San Simeon and a state historical monument since 1981. This multi-level, sandcastle-like cement structure was lovingly built by local garbage man Art Beal (also known as Captain Nit Wit and Dr. Tinkerpaw). Construction started in 1928 with a one-room shack architecturally enhanced with cement, abalone shells, glass, discarded car parts, toilet seats, and beer cans, with later additions of bones, driftwood, feathers, and rock. Art Beal died in 1992 but his three-story masterpiece still stands and is open for private tours ($10 adults, $5 children). For current details, call 805/927-2690. To get to Nit Wit Ridge, in Cambria head south on Main Street, turn left on Sheffield, left again on Cornwall, then right on Hillcrest and head uphill.

Something of a tragedy for Cambria, and for everyone who loves this lovely town, is news that its breathtaking stands of Monterey pines are doomed, victims of a virulent fungus known as pine pitch canker, expected to wipe out 80% of the trees here over the next few decades. Cambria's native forest of Monterey pines is one of only three in California, five in the world. Worried foresters fear further spread of the disease elsewhere along the coast, perhaps eventually into the Sierra Nevada, so do *not* pick up pine cones or other forest souvenirs to take home, since you may also transport this plague.

Come in September for the **Cambria Hoot Indian Summer Acoustic Music Festival** and, over Labor Day weekend, for the long-running Lion's Club **Pinedorado Days**—three full days of follies, feasts, and parading, not to mention bingo, arts, and entertainment. Fully restored and enthroned in its own "lantern room" on the Pinedorado grounds (on Main), thanks to local Friends of the Piedras Blancas Lighthouse, is the restored original Fresnel lens from the local light station.

For more information on the area, including events, accommodations, restaurants, and details on **Otter Trolley** routes and schedules, contact the **Cambria Chamber of Commerce,** 767 Main St., 805/927-3624, www.cambriachamber.org.

ACCOMMODATIONS

Campers, head for **San Simeon State Park** (see above). From October or November into midspring, even the more expensive motels in San Simeon proper feature cheaper rates. A good choice in San Simeon proper, sometimes offering great bargains in the off-season, is the pet-friendly **Silver Surf Motel,** 9390 Castillo Dr. (the frontage road parallel to the highway), 805/927-4661 or 800/621-3999 (reservations only), www.silversurfmotel.com. Some rooms feature ocean views, balconies, and fireplaces; all have phones, TV, and complimentary coffee and tea. Indoor heated pool and spa, rooftop sundeck. Sheltered courtyard garden area with picnic areas. Summer rates are $50–100. Quite nice and the only oceanfront motel around is the **Best Western Cavalier Oceanfront Resort,** 9415 Hearst Dr., 805/927-4688 or 800/826-8168, www.cavalierresort.com, offering everything from family-friendly rooms (two double beds to romantic oceanfront rooms with wood-burning fireplaces). Fully wheelchair-accessible rooms too. All rooms feature a refrigerator, coffeemaker, hair dryer, honor bar, TV with cable and VCR, voice mail, and computer port. All kinds of other little extras, too, from s'mores at bluff bonfires to whale-watching telescopes. Rates are $100–300.

Cambria offers a wider accommodations selection. For warm, welcoming, and affordable European-style guest lodgings (shared bathrooms), head for the charming **Bridge Street Inn,** a historic onetime parsonage at 4314 Bridge St., 805/927-7653, www.bridgestreetinncambria.com. This small, homey hostel offers private bedrooms ($40-70) plus bunkbeds (about $20 each) in a shared bunkroom. Some bedrooms are well-configured for families, with a larger bed plus one or two bunkbeds. All guests share two bathrooms upstairs and a half-bath downstairs. Quite popular, sometimes closed in winter, so be sure to reserve before you come. Prices go up during high-demand periods.

The bluebird of happiness has also been known to alight downtown at the **Bluebird Motel** at 1880 Main St., 805/927-4634 or 800/552-5434, www.bluebirdmotel.com, where standard rooms are $70 and up, deluxe rooms and suites $120–200. Another local classic is the recently updated **Cambria Pines Lodge,** tucked into 25 acres of pines and gardens up the hill at 2905 Burton Dr., 805/927-4200 or 800-445-6868, www.cambriapineslodge.com, offering everything from 1920s-vintage cabins to two-bedroom suites. Most rooms have wood-burning fireplaces. Grand heated Olympic-size pool. Full breakfast buffet included, served in the warm and welcoming main lodge. Nice onsite restaurant, featuring organic produce from the lodge's own gardens. Rates are $100 and up. Cambria Pines is also headquarters for **Moonstone Hotel Properties,** www.moonstonehotels.com, a small boutique chain offering many other good choices here and elsewhere.

Cambria offers some fine selections for the bed-and-breakfast set. The top-drawer **Blue Whale Inn,** 6736 Moonstone Beach Dr., 805/927-4647 or 800/753-9000, www.bluewhaleinn.com, features six striking European country-style "mini-suites" with ocean views and separate entrances, not to mention canopy beds, gas fireplaces, whirlpool tubs, and in-room refrigerators. Full breakfast, afternoon refreshments. Rates are $200–300, with a two-night minimum stay on weekends.

The two-story early American **J. Patrick House** at 2990 Burton Dr., 805/927-3812 or 800/341-5258, www.jpatrickhouse.com, is Cambria's first B&B, an intriguing log home and guest house. All eight guest rooms (seven in the guesthouse) are named after Ireland and feature

HEARST RANCH ACQUIRED

Thanks to $34.5 million in California parks funds, in September 2004 the state acquired development rights for the 13 miles of coastline and portions of 83,000-acre Piedra Blanca Ranch, the Hearst Corp. lands surrounding Hearst San Simeon State Historical Monument—guaranteeing the land's protection. Other portions of the ranch were purchased for $95 million. Cattle ranching is still allowed on part of the historic ranch, and the company may yet build a 100-room hotel, 27 homes, and employee housing. A prod to the public land acquisition came in 1998, when the Hearst Corp. announced plans to build a 650-room hotel, 18-hole golf course, and luxury home development.

As a result of the 2004 acquisition, the public gained access to lands, which were previously off limits. For current access information, contact area state parks and visitor bureaus.

private baths; most have a wood-burning fireplace. Comfortable garden room, where delectable breakfast and veggie hors d'oeuvres are served. Chocolate chip cookies too. Rates are $150-200. Furnished with Victorian florals, lace, and turn-of-the-last-century antiques is the charming two-story 1870s Greek revival **Olallieberry Inn** and cottage on the banks of Santa Rosa Creek at 2476 Main, 805/927-3222 or 888/927-3222, www.olallieberry.com. Just look for that spectacular redwood tree. The nine guest rooms, each with private bath (some down the hall), offer unique charms. Great breakfast, afternoon wine and hors d'oeuvres. And such a deal, with room rates as low as $115. Rooms are $100–200, the Creekside Suite slightly more.

FOOD

Stop at **Sebastian's General Store** downhill from the castle in San Simeon proper, 805/927-4217, to stock up on picnic supplies or enjoy burgers and such in the outdoor café. If you're here in winter, keep an eye out for the migrating monarch butterflies that flutter to these cypress and eucalyptus trees. For "view dining," consider the **Ragged Point Inn** about 15 miles north of Hearst Castle, 805/927-4502.

Most restaurants are in Cambria. **Linn's Main Bin Restaurant & Gifts** at 2277 Main, 805/927-0371, is a best bet for specialty pot pies, soups, salads, and sandwiches. Did we mention the house-made olallieberry pie? Open daily (except Christmas) for breakfast, lunch, and dinner. Otherwise, to sample Linn's jams, jellies, and gift baskets try **Linn's Fruit Bin Farmstore** just east of town on Santa Rosa Creek Road or see www.linnsfruitbin.com. There's another Linn's restaurant in downtown San Luis Obispo, at Marsh and Chorro. Great for lunch or dinner is warm, welcoming **Robin's** at 4095 Burton Dr., 805/927-5007, where you can settle in near the fireplace and contemplate the possibilities. Tasty vegetarian entrées include grilled eggplant sandwiches, avocado croissant melt, Marsala mushrooms, and Black Bean Surprise, but you can also get a hefty burger here along with curried chicken salad, salmon fettuccine, and Tandori prawns. For dessert, how 'bout some fresh fruit cobbler or Belgian dark chocolate mousse? (For pastries and cakes, try **Robin's French Corner Bakery.**) Outdoor patio dining too. Reservations suggested on weekends, or call ahead for takeout. Try **Mustache Pete's** sports bar across the street, 4090 Burton Dr., 805/927-8589, for Italian, particularly calzones and pizzas (takeout and early-bird dinners).

Relaxed and quite good for American fare, famous for its fresh-baked breads and pastries, is small, dinner–only **Sow's Ear** restaurant at 2248 Main, 805/927-4865, serving up peppercorn pasta, fresh salmon in parchment, even chicken and dumplings. Open nightly from 5 P.M.; early dinners (5–6 P.M.) are such a deal. Don't feel bad about being a pig, either. The place is full of 'em.

Diners *can* get a good hamburger for dinner at the English-style **Brambles Dinner House,** 4005 Burton Dr. in Cambria, 805/927-4716, but even better are the homemade soups, breads, and oakwood-broiled salmon. The Brambles is famous for its prime rib with Yorkshire pudding, excellent roast rack of lamb, and brandy ice cream for dessert. Reservations essential, even at Sunday brunch.

Morro Bay and Vicinity

The first thing visitors notice is the Rock, spotted by Cabrillo in 1542. Morro Reef has been a significant navigational landfall for mariners for more than three centuries and was noted in the diaries of Portolá, Crespi, and Costanso. That wouldn't impress the native peoples, though; Chumash artifacts found here date to 4700 B.C. Morro Rock is the last visible volcanic peak in the 21-million-year-old series of nine cones that stretch to San Luis Obispo; the chain has long been known locally as the Seven Sisters but it's actually the **Nine Sisters,** since one sis is submerged and one is out of line. Before extensive quarrying, this "Gibraltar of the Pacific" stood much higher than its current 576 feet and, until the 1930s, was an island at high tide. The height of the Rock seems reduced even more by the proximity of the three 450-foot-tall power plant smokestacks jutting from the edge of the bay like giant gun barrels, part of the scenery since 1953.

Until the rise of tourism, commercial fishing, especially for abalone and albacore, was Morro Bay's major industry. But intrepid amateurs can try clam digging for geoducks (Washington clams) or some barehanded grunion snatching during full-moon high tides from March through August. Pier fishing is also good here on the city's three T-piers, north of the Embarcadero and opposite the Rock. Morro Bay also boasts a thriving nature-oriented tourism industry—and a kitsch- and gift-shop-oriented tourism industry, perfect for shopaholics. Head out in a kayak with **Kayak Horizons,** 551 Embarcadero, 805/772-6444, www.kayakhorizons.com. Or watch the boats in the bay from **Tidelands Park,** at the south end of the Embarcadero. Or take a ride on the *Tiger's Folly II* replica river boat.

Thanks to a few local bars and the Morro Bay Chess Club, Morro Bay also has *culture.* The star in that department is the chess club's **giant outdoor chessboard,** especially eye-catching when demonstration tournaments are under way after noon on Saturday along the Embarcadero. With each of the game's carved redwood pieces weighing between 18 and 30 pounds, playing chess here offers more than a mere mental workout. Anyone can play, by reservation, either on the giant board or on punier standard-sized chess tables along the perimeter. During the town's **Harbor Days Celebration** in October, local drama buffs in full costume *become* chess pieces. Another major event is the **Morro Bay Winter Bird Festival.** And come to Morro Bay in December for the **Christmas Parade** of lighted boats on the bay's waters.

Laid-back, two-block-long **Baywood Park** on the south side of the bay, a few miles from the burg of Morro Bay, is a better choice for those determined to avoid the crowds. **El Moro Elfin Forest,** pygmy coast live oaks and other native vegetation, can be reached from the town's boardwalk; park at the end of 16th Street off Santa Ysabel Avenue (tours offered). Just a stroll from downtown, near Fourth Street on the north side of Ramona Avenue, is the Audubon Society's **Sweet Springs Nature Preserve,** salt- and freshwater wetlands and forest—a window onto the neighborhood's natural world, including migrating waterfowl and monarch butterflies in winter.

For more information about local attractions, events, and practicalities, contact the **Morro Bay Chamber of Commerce,** 880 Main St., 805/772-4467 or 800/231-0592, www.morrobay.org, and the **Los Osos/Baywood Park Chamber of Commerce,** 781 Palisades Ave. (at Los Osos Valley Road), 805/528-4884, www.losososbaywoodpark.org. For information about what's up just north along the coast, contact the **Cayucos Chamber of Commerce,** 158 N. Ocean Ave. in Cayucos, 805/995-1200 or 800/563-1878, www.cayucoschamber.com.

SIGHTS

The entire town of Morro Bay, including Morro Rock, is a bird sanctuary and nature preserve in deference to the endangered peregrine falcons, great blue herons, and other bird species that have selected the Rock and vicinity

The Central Coast

as a rookery. The bay and adjacent mudflats create a fertile wetland, one of the most significant along the California coast for sheer number of resident bird species and one of the top 10 national bird-watching spots. Guns are banned throughout Morro Bay—the rock, the town, and the state park.

Morro Bay State Park

A multifaceted park dominating the entire bay area, Morro Bay State Park includes the mudflats, sand dunes on the spit, dual Morro Strand State Beach farther north, a natural history museum, adjacent golf course, and the Los Osos Oaks State Reserve just inland from the bay on Los Osos Valley Road. The park's campgrounds and picnic areas are value-added bonuses.

Eucalyptus trees shade the bay near park headquarters and attract monarch butterflies after the October bloom. The eucalyptus grove also serves as a heron rookery. A good first stop for the kiddos is the park's excellent **Museum of Natural History** on Country Club Drive, 805/772-2694, www.mbspmuseum.org, which enjoyed a $3 million facelift in 2002. The museum's cartoony guide Rocky the Rock is still here, though, still of-

fering a kid-friendly natural history introduction. Exhibits emphasize the local landscape and wildlife by land and by sea, including hands-on touch pools. Good bookshop, too, and great views of Morro Bay below. It's open daily 10 A.M.–5 P.M., closed Thanksgiving, Christmas, and New Year's Day; free for campers, otherwise small admission.

Next, explore the mouth of **Los Osos Creek,** one of the largest natural coastal marshlands remaining in California. Wildflowers on adjacent grassy hills are most striking in spring, but their blooms, seeds, and vegetation attract birds year-round. Rent a canoe or kayak for some unforgettable eyeball-to-eyeball encounters. (Get an area bird checklist and other local bird-watching information at the museum.) Take a boat to reach the **Sand Spit Wild Area,** the pristine peninsula separating Morro Bay from the ocean (protected shell mounds, good birding), or come the long way from Montaña de Oro State Park to the south. For the adventurous: Hike the entire Morro Bay sand spit, an eight-mile roundtrip from the Sunset Terrace golf course around the inlet and over the sand dunes toward Morro Rock.

ALL SHOOK UP: PASO ROBLES AND VICINITY

All Paso Robles really wanted for Christmas in 2003 was some reassurance that the ground would stop moving and shaking. A December 22 earthquake killed two people, destroyed or seriously damaged 82 unretrofitted and historic brick buildings, and created a sulfurous sinkhole—The Hole From Hell, a natural hot spring—in the parking lot at city hall. Local wineries also suffered substantial losses.

But this historic central coast town, once famous for its healing mineral-spring resorts and cattle ranches, is back in the saddle again, hard at the work of rebuilding. The town has faced challenges before, after all. Evidence of previous trying times is on display at the **Estrella Warbird Museum** at the airport, a onetime Army Air Corps base at 4251 Dry Creek Rd., 805/227-0440 (recorded) or 805/238-9317, www.ewarbirds.org,

open weekends. The **Paso Robles Pioneer Museum,** 2010 Riverside Ave., 805 239-4556, www.prpioneermuseum.org, shares the story of Paso Robles, everything from antique dolls and horse-drawn carriages to Depression-era memorabilia (open Thurs.–Sun. 1–4 P.M.). Another place to round up some local heritage is the **Work Family Guest Ranch** on Ranchita Canyon Road in nearby San Miguel, 805/467-3362, www.work ranch.com, where you can sign on for a trail ride, a farm stay, or a family vacation.

Still, present-day Paso Robles has plenty to offer, including up-and-coming wineries (see Touring the County's Wineries) and great restaurants. Charming **Villa Creek,** 1144 Pine St., 805/238-3000, specializes in organic, "ecologically sound" produce and other ingredients, served Early Californian/Mexican style—from

Once known separately as Morro Strand and Atascadero state beaches, the two sections of **Morro Strand State Beach** north of Morro Bay feature several broad miles of sandy strand with small naked dunes along Estero Bay and adjacent to residential areas; the beach is popular for surfing, skin diving, surf fishing, swimming, and sunning (clam digging prohibited). Another spot of state beach, with picnic tables, pier, and playground, is in family-friendly **Cayucos** just north.

Los Osos Oaks State Reserve, southeast of the bay at the end of Los Osos Valley Road, is a 90-acre grove acquired in 1972 to preserve one of the few old stands of coast oaks remaining in the area. These gnarled oldsters, coast live oaks, scrub oaks, and various hybrids, create an eerie impression on early morning hikes. Stay on the trail: the understory here is mostly poison oak. The park is open for day use sunrise to sunset daily.

There is currently no day-use or parking fee charged for any of the area's state parks or beaches. For camping information, see below. For other park information, contact the natural history museum (above) or call 805/772-2560.

Montaña de Oro State Park

Just south of the sand spit is Montaña de Oro State Park ("Mountain of Gold"), its name particularly apt in spring when the hills are ablaze with yellow and orange wildflowers, from California poppies and yellow mustard to goldfields and fiddleneck. Any time of year, 8,400-acre Montaña de Oro is a hiker's park. The seclusion here also means abundant wildlife: sea lions, harbor seals, and sea otters at sea; gray foxes, mule deer, bobcats, and sometimes even mountain lions on land. From near **Point Buchon** (private property), the whale-watching is superb, but you can find other good vantage points along the Bluff Trail.

The area's wild beauty stretches from the seven-mile shoreline of 50-foot bluffs and tidepools, surging surf, and sandy beaches inland to Valencia Peak (great ocean views looking north to Piedras Blancas, south to Point Sal) and up Islay Creek to the waterfalls. More than 50 miles of multiuse trails connect the sights. The best tidepools are at **Corallina Cove,** though **Quarry Cove** comes in a close second. There's good tidepooling after the five-minute creekside scramble down from Hazard Canyon, also access to the entire sand spit and silent beaches. South of

traditional paella and stuffed poblano chiles to slow-braised short ribs with polenta and mole sauce. The unpretentious French **Bistro Laurent,** usually serving forth from 1202 Pine St. (at 12th), 805/226-8191, was still rebuilding at last report, yet open for dinner nightly at J. Lohr winery on Airport Road (805/610-2038). Call for current details. The three- and four-course fixed-price dinners, with or without the paired wines, are great deals. If the bistro is downtown again by the time you arrive, perhaps its **Le Petit Marcel** lunchtime patio will also be back in business, serving very reasonable lunches (under $10), from seafood specials and little pizzas to house-made pastas. For grand Italian—from baked eggplant and grilled seafood salad to lobster and linguine—try **Buona Tavola,** 943 Spring St. (near 9th), 805/237-0600. And if you're heading

north from the area, **McPhee's Grill** at 416 Main St. in Templeton, 805/434-3204, is known for its imaginative American. Wine is a real deal here, too, so you'll sample local wares. For genuine Mexican seafood and more, the place is **Salsitas,** 8783 El Camino Real in Atascadero, 805/461-5500.

Come to Paso Robles in early August for the **California Mid-State Fair,** in May for the **Paso Robles Wine Festival.** Come to Templeton in June for the annual **Wine & Roses Bike Ride** and BBQ, a community benefit. For more information about the area, contact the **Paso Robles Visitor & Conference Bureau,** 1225 Park St., 805/238-0506 or 800/406-4040, www.pasorobles chamber.com, and the **Templeton Chamber of Commerce,** 805/434-1789, www.templeton chamber.com.

the **Spooner's Cove** visitor center, part of the old ranch, is an old Chumash campsite.

To get to Montaña de Oro, head west on Los Osos Valley Road from San Luis Obispo back roads or Hwy. 101, and then follow Pecho Valley Road south to the end. For basic information and to get oriented, stop by the natural history museum at Morro Bay State Park (see above) or call 805/528-0513 or 805/772-7434. Montaña de Oro's facilities are appropriately limited but picnic tables overlook the cove. Nearby is the valley **Islay Creek Campground,** 50 primitive, environmental, and hiker/biker sites, with pit toilets.

ACCOMMODATIONS

Other than camping, the best place around for a truly cheap sleep is the great little HI-USA hostel in nearby San Luis Obispo (see below). Basic beach camping is the set-up at **Morro Strand State Beach** north of the bay, 104 barren beachfront RV parking lot sites (no hookups) featuring some tent camping sites. Campsites ($15–20) include tables, stoves, restrooms, and cold outdoor showers. Considerably more comfortable is camping at **Morro Bay State Park** near park headquarters, 135 tree-shaded campsites with tables, stoves, hot showers, restrooms, and laundry tubs ($15–20) also 20 RV sites with hookups and sanitation station ($24–29). Campers please note: The state plans to close the Morro Bay campground for thorough renovation; at that point the campground will be closed to the public (and off the reservations system) for a year or so. Call for current details. **Montaña de Oro State Park** also offers camping at its Islay Creek Campground—50 wooded primitive (tents and RVs) and environmental sites, pit toilets only ($11–15). To reserve campsites—Islay Creek primitive sites are reservable only in summer—contact **ReserveAmerica,** 800/444-7275 or www.reserveamerica.com. For other information, call each park directly.

There are a number of quite reasonably priced motels in Morro Bay, including small, freshly remodeled **Ascot Inn** motel, 845 Morro Ave., 805/772-4437 or 800/887-6454, www.ascotinn .com, with both queen (standard) and king rooms

(four-poster beds) with in-room coffee, TV with HBO, and other basic comforts. Rates are $50–200 (discounts and specials available), though off-season promotional rates can drop to $39. Next door is the affiliated **Ascot Suites** (same phone and website for information and reservations), for quite swank hotel accommodations.

A definite winner in these parts is the Cape Cod-style **Inn at Morro Bay** a mile south of town just outside the entrance to Morro Bay State Park, 805/772-5651 or 800/321-9566 (reservations), www.innatmorrobay.com. Attractive, comfortable, contemporary rooms go as low as $100–110. Even smaller rooms have blond woods and all the comforts. Bay views come at a premium, of course, especially on summer weekends, though discounts and specials are possible year-round. There's a waterfront cottage, too. Less expensive rooms overlook the pool and golf course. Great onsite restaurant plus extras including cruiser bikes and golf course. High-season rates are $150–350.

From the outside it looks like something you'd find in any business park, yet the unique, themed suites are welcoming and romantic at the **Baywood Inn Bed & Breakfast,** 1370 Second St. in Baywood Park, 805/528-8888, www.baywood inn.com, with high-season rates $100 and up. The basics for each room here include a separate entrance, fireplace, in-room coffee, microwave, and stocked small refrigerator. Full breakfast and afternoon wine and cheese included. At least report eight new units were being added, along with the affiliated 10-room **Baywood Village Inn.**

FOOD

A local tradition is grand-view **Dorn's Original Breakers Cafe,** 801 Market St., 805/772-4415, with wonderful pecan waffles, buttermilk and blueberry pancakes, pigs-in-a-blanket, and veggie omelettes for breakfast, an impressive Boston clam chowder plus marinated seafood salads and various sandwiches at lunch. Generous seafood dinners.

People could drown in the aquatic ambience around Morro Bay. For more fresh fish, stop off at **Giovanni's Fish Market** right in front of the boat docks at 1001 Front St., 805/772-2123, open 9 A.M.–6 P.M. Seafood places leap out all along the Embarcadero, many of them open for lunch and dinner and many featuring early-bird dinner specials. Fish and chips is a neighborhood specialty. The place for sushi and such is **Harada,** 630 Embarcadero, 805/772-1410.

For dinner to write home about, one choice is romantic **Windows On the Water** at Marina Square, overlooking the bay at 699 Embarcadero, 805/772-0677, which serves exquisite Californian with French and Asian accents—from the

smoked salmon pizza and clam chowder to oak-fired ribeye steak and cilantro grilled shrimp. California and French wines, full bar. Or head for the **Dining Room,** an excellent continental–Pacific Californian at the Inn at Morro Bay at Morro Bay State Park, 805/772-2743. Start with the curried fried shrimp with banana tamarind salsa, panko-crusted abalone with black bean mango salsa, or whatever seems freshest and best on the menu. Entrées might include vegetarian vol-au-vent, crab-crusted halibut, and lobster brûlée. Don't miss Sunday brunch.

JAMES DEAN DIED HERE

Rebels otherwise without a cause might spend a few minutes in **Cholame** (sho-LAMB), 27 miles east of Paso Robles on the way to Lost Hills via hustle-bustle Hwy. 46. At the onetime intersection of Hwys. 41 and 46 (the exact routing of the roads has since changed), actor James Dean met death at the age of 24. The star of only three movies—*East of Eden,* his trademark *Rebel Without a Cause,* and *Giant,* all in the same calendar year—Dean, heading west into the blinding sun, died instantly when his speeding silver Porsche Spyder slammed head-on into a Ford at 5:59 P.M. on September 30, 1955.

And every September 30th since 1979, members of a Southern California car club trace the route of Dean's last road trip, starting in Van Nuys, during the annual en masse migration to Cholame on the James Dean Memorial Run. Arriving at the James Dean Memorial Junction is just about the ultimate experience for 1950s car enthusiasts.

In front of Cholame's postage stamp-sized post office and the Jack Ranch Café a half mile from the actual place Dean died, there's an oddly evocative stainless-steel obelisk in his memory, paid for by a businessman from Japan. The memorial is wrapped around a lone tree and landscaped with 9,000 pounds of imported Japanese gravel, a concrete bench, and engraved bronze tablets—a pilgrimage site for fans from around the world. (Inside, Dean fans can buy memorial T-shirts, sun visors, posters, and postcards. The proceeds go toward maintaining the monument.)

Seita Ohnishi's explanation etched on the tablets reads:

This monument stands as a small token of my appreciation for the people of America. It also stands for James Dean and other American Rebels. . . . In Japan, we say his death came as suddenly as it does to cherry blossoms. The petals of early spring always fall at the height of their ephemeral brilliance. Death in youth is life that glows eternal.

But in keeping with James Dean's own favorite words—from Antoine de Saint-Exupery, "What is essential is invisible to the eye"—what was important about Dean's life is not necessarily here.

Some distance north of Cholame is spot-in-the-road **Parkfield,** self-proclaimed Earthquake Capital of the World and ground zero for ongoing earthquake-prediction experiments. The famous San Andreas Fault mosies right down Parkfield's Main Street. Since 1857 a quake of at least magnitude 6 on the Richter scale has been measured here roughly every 22 years. (The 6.5 and 6.0-magnitude quakes that hit the area so hard in 2003 and 2004 were over a decade late.) Despite the local earthquake photo gallery inside the Parkfield Café, some of the signs on the wall suggest a certain nonchalance, such as: If You Feel a Shake or a Quake, Get Under Your Table and Eat Your Steak.

The Central Coast

Hoppe's Hip Pocket Bistro on the Embarcadero is no more, alas, but a renowned relative dazzles locals and visitors alike in nearby Cayucos. **Hoppe's Garden Bistro & Wine Shop** at the Historical Way Station, 78 N. Ocean Ave., 805/995-1006, serves exquisite, wholesome food, starting with such things as curried cauliflower soup, sand dab tempura, and smoked pheasant ravioli. How 'bout the goat cheese and red pepper omelette or portabella burger for lunch? The seasonally changing dinner menu might include hand-made fettucine with smoked chicken, sauteed Cayucos red abalone in hazelnut–mango butter, even vegan selections such as roasted butternut squash with wild mushroom and carmelized shallots. And then there's dessert. Chocolate hazelnut terrine with raspberry coulis, anyone? The spectacular sparkling-wine brunch is $20 adults, $10 kids. Open Wed.–Sun. for lunch and dinner. Special events include cooking classes and winemaker dinners.

San Luis Obispo and Vicinity

Before freeway arteries pulsed with California car traffic, when trips between San Francisco and Los Angeles took at least two days, north–south travelers naturally appreciated San Luis Obispo as the most reasonable midpoint stopover. So it's not surprising that San Luis Obispo gave birth to both the concept and the word "motel," a contraction of "motor hotel." In 1925 when the Spanish colonial **Milestone Mo-tel** (later the Motel Inn) opened in San Luis Obispo, it was the first roadside hostelry to call itself a motel. A sign at the entrance told travelers how to pronounce the new word, and Pasadena architect Arthur Heineman, who designed the place, even copyrighted it.

Playwright Sam Shepard uses motels as symbols of all that is déclassé, desolate, and depressing in the United States. Vladimir Nabokov vilified motels from a continental perspective in *Lolita:* "We held in contempt the plain whitewashed clapboard Kabins, with their faint sewerish smell or some other gloomy self-conscious stench and nothing to boast of. . . ." J. Edgar Hoover, former FBI director and self-styled arbiter of the nation's personal and political morality, attacked motels in 1940 as "assignation camps" and "crime camps" contributing to the downfall of America. From that perspective, then, seemingly innocent San Luis Obispo is where the downfall of America began.

Hoover's opinions aside, San Luis Obispo is a peaceful and pretty college town that has so far escaped the head-on collision with urban and suburban traffic under way in places such as Monterey and Ventura. **California State Polytechnic University** (Cal Poly) here is a major jewel in the community's crown, though the college is still snidely referred to as "Cow Poly" or "Cow Tech" in some circles. The Beef Pavilion, crops, swine, and poultry units do collectively clamor for center-stage attention on the campus just northeast of town, but the college is not just an agricultural school anymore. Cal Poly's architectural school is excellent, the largest in the country, as are the engineering and computer science departments. And since students here "learn by doing," there's almost always something fascinating doing on campus—particularly now that the impressive $30 million **Performing Arts Center** has opened its opera house-style doors.

San Luis Obispo as a mission fortress was established in 1772 and named for the 13th-century Saint Louis, bishop of Toulouse, who also inadvertently lent his name to this California city and county in 1850. But San Luis Obispo's saintly antecedents have been overshadowed, politically speaking, by PG&E's Diablo Canyon Nuclear Power Plant. (Diablo, in Spanish, means "the devil.") Though some claim Diablo Canyon has tarnished the town's halo of rural serenity, most of the forward-looking folks of San Luis Obispo don't seem bothered. They assume, like the rest of us, that the devil's due won't come due anytime soon.

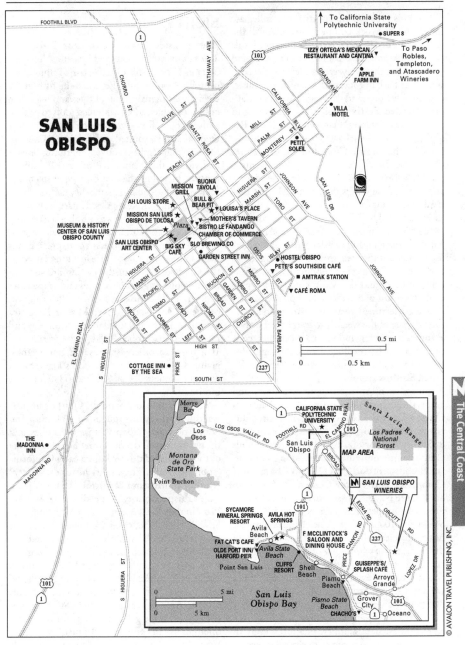

FOOTHILL BLVD

1

To California State
Polytechnic University

● SUPER 8

HATHAWAY AVE

101

IZZY ORTEGA'S MEXICAN
RESTAURANT AND CANTINA ▼

To Paso
Robles,
Templeton,
and Atascadero
Wineries

CHORRO ST

CALIFORNIA BLVD

GRAND AVE

● APPLE
FARM INN

● VILLA
MOTEL

SAN LUIS
OBISPO

OLIVE ST

SANTA ROSA ST

MILL ST

PALM ST

MONTEREY ST

● PETIT
SOLEIL

PEACH ST

HIGUERA ST

MARSH ST

JOHNSON AVE

SAN LUIS DR

MOON

BUONA
TAVOLA
MISSION
GRILL

BULL &
BEAR PIT

LOUISA'S PLACE ▼

TORO ST

AH LOUIS STORE ★

MISSION SAN LUIS
OBISPO DE TOLOSA ★

MOTHER'S TAVERN ▼
BISTRO LE FANDANGO ▼

MUSEUM & HISTORY
CENTER OF SAN LUIS
OBISPO COUNTY

Plaza

CHAMBER OF COMMERCE

SAN LUIS OBISPO
ART CENTER

BIG SKY
CAFÉ

SLO BREWING CO ●

ISLAY ST

GARDEN STREET INN

HOSTEL OBISPO

OSOS ST

PETE'S SOUTHSIDE CAFÉ

JOHNSON AVE

HIGUERA ST

MARSH ST

■ AMTRAK STATION

▼ CAFÉ ROMA

PACIFIC ST

BUCHON ST

MORRO ST

CHORRO ST

PISMO ST

BEACH ST

GARDEN ST

BROAD ST

ARCHER ST

CARMEL ST

NIPOMO ST

CHURCH ST

SANTA BARBARA ST

EL CAMINO REAL

S HIGUERA ST

LEFF ST

HIGH ST

0   0.5 mi

0   0.5 km

COTTAGE INN ●
BY THE SEA

PRICE ST

227

SOUTH ST

Morro
Bay

CALIFORNIA STATE
POLYTECHNIC
UNIVERSITY ★

1

Santa Lucia Range

THE
MADONNA ●
INN

MADONNA RD

Los
Osos

LOS OSOS VALLEY RD

FOOTHILL RD

EL CAMINO REAL

101

San Luis
Obispo

BROAD

MAP AREA

Los Padres
National
Forest

Montana
de Oro
State Park

Point Buchon

SAN LUIS OBISPO
WINERIES

1

EDNA RD

ORCUTT RD

SYCAMORE
MINERAL SPRINGS
RESORT

AVILA HOT
SPRINGS

101

Avila
Beach

F MCCLINTOCK'S
SALOON AND
DINING HOUSE ★

PRICE CANYON RD

227

LOPEZ DR

FAT CAT'S CAFÉ
OLDE PORT INN/
HARFORD PIER ▼

Avila State
Beach

GUISEPPE'S/
SPLASH CAFÉ ▼

Point San Luis

CLIFFS
RESORT

Shell
Beach

1

S HIGUERA ST

101

1

0   5 mi

0   5 km

San Luis
Obispo Bay

Pismo
Beach

Pismo State
Beach

CHACHO'S ▼

Grover
City

Arroyo
Grande

1 ○ Oceano

The Central Coast

© AVALON TRAVEL PUBLISHING, INC.

San Luis Obispo's rip-snortin' intercollegiate rodeo and livestock competitions in April, the notorious **Poly Royale,** is no more, since locals got a bit tired of the out-of-control crowds and partying. But there's always **La Fiesta** at the Mission Plaza Park in May, with Spanish-era music, costumes, feasting, and dancing, as well as the annual **Garden Festival** held by Friends of San Luis Obispo Botanical Garden at El Chorro Regional Park on Hwy. 1 (www.slobg.org). In July, come for the **Central Coast Renaissance Faire.** One of the West Coast's finest cycling events is the **SLO Criterium,** also in July. The biggest arts event of the year is the annual **Mozart Festival** (www.mozartfestival.com) in late July and early August. The 20 or more intimate concerts are held at the on-campus Performing Arts Center, at the mission, and in cafés, parks, and wineries throughout the area, from Arroyo Grande to San Miguel. Composers, conductors, and musicians from around the world come to town to evoke the spirit of Amadeus. Free public Mozart Akademie lectures by various distinguished visitors are part of the week's program; the **Festival Fringe** activities include free art exhibits, concerts, and poetry readings. Come in August for the **Central Coast Wine Festival,** October for **Open Studios** art tours.

For more information about attractions and events throughout the county, contact: **San Luis Obispo County Visitors and Conference Bureau,** 1041 Chorro St., Ste. E downtown, 805/541-8000 or 800/634-1414, www.sanluis obispocounty.com. Alternatively, stop by or contact the adjacent **San Luis Obispo Chamber of Commerce and Visitor Center,** 1039 Chorro St., 805/781-2777, www.visitslo.com. The visitor center is open Tues.–Fri. 8 A.M.–5 P.M. and Sat.–Mon. 10 A.M.–5 P.M. The chamber also sells tickets for Hearst Castle tours at San Simeon up the coast, if you're thinking of heading that way and don't have reservations. For information about area arts events, contact the **San Luis Obispo County Arts Council,** 570 Higuera St., 805/544-9251, www.sloartscouncil.org. For whatever else is happening here and in northern Santa Barbara County, pick up a copy of *New Times* magazine, www.newtimes-slo.com.

SIGHTS

The creekside **Mission San Luis Obispo de Tolosa** downtown, founded by Father Junípero Serra in 1772, is still an active parish church and central to community life. This, the fifth in the chain, was originally built of tules and logs, then of five-foot-thick adobe with tiled roofs to prevent native peoples from torching the place. Recently renovated and repainted with original 1820s motifs—golden seashells, olives, charming flowers and vines—the mission has other truly unique features, including the stars on the parish church ceiling and the combination belfry and vestibule. The museum, once the priest's quarters, is worth a short stop for the arrowheads, baskets, Father Serra's vestments, and tangential trivia: books, portraits of mission workers, a winepress, handmade knives, and 1880s office furniture carved by the Cherokee. Out in the garden are some of the mission's original olive trees and grape vines still thrive. The mission itself, at 751 Palm St. on the edge of the downtown Mission Plaza area between Chorro and Garden and Monterey and Higuera Streets, is open 9 A.M.–5 P.M. in summer, 10 A.M.–4 P.M. otherwise (closed Easter, Thanksgiving, Christmas, and New Year's Day). Small donation requested. Call 805/543-6850 for more information.

From the mission, San Luis Obispo's historic walking tour leads through parts of a hip and homey downtown, past Victorians, adobes, and the old-time train depot. **Court Street** is the site of the old Bull and Bear Pit, an early California "sporting" arena. The county historical society's refurbished **Museum & History Center of San Luis Obispo County** at the far end of Mission Plaza in the old Carnegie library, 696 Monterey St., 805/543-0638, open Wed.–Sun. 10 A.M.–4 P.M., houses a collection of local memorabilia, including Chumash artifacts and settlers' glassware, antique clothes, even hair wreaths, also an extensive historical photo archive and public research room. Just across the street is the **San Luis Obispo Art Center,** 1010 Broad St., 805/543-8562, with three galleries of California artists, open daily in July and August, otherwise Wed.–Mon. 11 A.M.–5 P.M. On the other side

THE CARRIZO PLAIN: CALIFORNIA'S SERENGETI

Remote **Carrizo Plain National Monument,** sometimes referred to as California's Serengeti, was established in 2001 to protect the 250,000-acre plain, the largest remaining tract of virtually untouched San Joaquin Valley grassland prairie. The monument provides habitat for many endangered, threatened, and rare plant and animals species—the latter including the San Joaquin kit fox, the blunt-nosed leopard lizard, the San Joaquin antelope squirrel, and the giant kangaroo rat. The Carrizo Plain is "critical habitat" for endangered California condors, and was the first region in California to reintroduce both pronghorn antelope and tule elk, native ungulates that had been hunted to the brink of extinction by the late 1800s. Winter birding is fine. Raptors thrive here, along with wintering sandhill cranes and mountain plovers. To the east of the Carrizo Plain is the Temblor Range—and the best aerial view of the famed San Andreas Fault, which resembles the long-buried spinal column and scraggly skeleton of some giant dragon or other ancient beast. To the west are the rolling hills of the Caliente Range, velvet green and embroidered with wildflowers in spring but sparse and spare in the searing summer heat. Yet the rains make their mark here as well; roads maybe impassable in winter.

Centerpiece of the Carrizo Plain, is **Soda Lake,** a 3,000-acre seasonal alkali lake that fills with rainwater in winter then disappears in the sere summer, its receding shoreline marked by crunchy white carbonate and sulfate crusts. **Painted Rock,** a sacred site to native Chumash people, features abstract pictographs of humans and animals between 200 and 2,000 years old. Visits to Painted Rock are restricted (see below), and dogs are not allowed.

Serving as Carrizo's de facto visitor center is the **Guy L. Goodwin Education Center,** 805/475-2131, located a half-mile west of the junction of Painted Rock and Soda Lake Roads. Exhibits explain the uniqueness of the Carrizo and adjoining Elkhorn Plain landscapes, where "the closer you look, the more you see." The center is typically open December through May, Thurs.–Sun. 9 A.M.–5 P.M., though maps and brochures are available at the front door when it's closed. The Goodwin Center also boasts an expanded native plant garden, a convenient "classroom" for studying Carrizo Plain botany.

Come to Carrizo in spring for docent-guided tours, available on weekends by reservation. (Special group tours can also be scheduled for weekdays.) Free docent-led Painted Rock tours are offered on Saturdays—in spring the area is accessible by tour only, and access may be restricted at other times—and guided Wallace Creek (San Andreas fault) walks are scheduled for Sundays. You can also visit Wallace Creek without a guide; there's a new interpretive trail along the creek and a portion of the San Andreas Fault. Self-guiding brochures are available at the trailhead or at the Goodwin Center. To explore Carrizo Plain geology on your own, a booklet featuring two self-guided auto tours is available for purchase at the Goodwin Center or through the BLM Bakersfield Field Office.

Before you come, keep in mind that this is a remote area with minimal facilities; start out with a full tank of gasoline. There is no drinking water available, so bring your own. Handicapped-accessible restrooms are located at the Goodwin Center and at Painted Rock; portable toilets are available in several locales. The nearest public phone is in California Valley, 15 miles north of the Goodwin Center on Soda Lake Road. (Forget cell phones on the Carrizo Plain.) Emergency services are also available in California Valley, at the California Division of Forestry fire station.

Originally protected as a Nature Conservancy preserve, the Carrizo Plain is now jointly managed by the U.S. Bureau of Land Management, the California Department of Fish and Game, and The Nature Conservancy. For more information, contact the **BLM Bakersfield Field Office,** 3801 Pegasus Dr. in Bakersfield, 661/391-6000, www.ca.blm.gov/bakersfield, or the Goodwin Education Center, 805/475-2131, from December through May.

The Central Coast

of the public bathrooms is the historic **Murray Adobe.** The **Ah Louis Store,** 800 Palm St., is all that remains of San Luis Obispo's once-thriving Chinatown. Established in 1874, Ah Louis's store was the county's first Chinese general store and the bank, counting house, and post office for the many Chinese employed by the Southern Pacific Railroad between 1884 and 1894 to dig eight train tunnels through the Cuesta Mountains. A noteworthy contemporary landmark is **Bubblegum Alley**—yes, the used kind, stuck on the walls reaching up to 20 feet high—in an alley between Higuera and Marsh Streets.

Visitors can tour downtown, its sights, shops, and galleries, onboard the **Old SLO Trolley** ($.25), which circulates downtown on Thursday evenings, Friday and Saturday noon–9 P.M., more limited hours on Sunday. And Friday night is **Art Night** downtown. Most galleries are open late (until 9 P.M.) on the first Friday of the month, but many are open every Friday night. Or catch a movie at the art deco **Fremont Theater,** blazing forth in all its neon glory downtown at 1025 Monterey St., 805/541-2141.

Farm Trails

The "Ag's My Bag" bumper stickers on cars and pickup trucks you'll see throughout San Luis Obispo don't lie; agriculture seems to be everybody's bag here. In San Luis Obispo County, local produce *is* local and remarkably diverse because of the mild and varied climate. Bring bags and boxes along and take home seasonal produce, everything from almonds to zucchini. To find the best of the county's bounty, pick up pamphlets at the visitor bureau or chamber offices—or attend any of the eight weekly area farmers markets.

The biggest and some say the best of these, a cross between a no-bargains-barred shopping spree and a street party, is San Luis Obispo's main event. The **San Luis Obispo Higuera Street Certified Farmers' Market,** 805/544-9570, is held in downtown San Luis Obispo every Thursday 6–9 P.M., weather permitting, along the 700-900 blocks of Higuera (between Osos and Broad Streets). Show up early to find a parking place, since the whole county comes to the city on

Thursday evenings—the main reason area shops and restaurants are open late on this particular weeknight. On tap Thursday evenings: live entertainment, arts, crafts, and good food in addition to fine fresh fruits, vegetables, and flowers. There are other area markets, too; the visitor bureau can fill you in.

Particularly worth it, too, from late summer into early November, is the 13-mile **See Canyon apple tour** of the half-dozen 1900s-vintage orchards in the narrow canyon southwest of town. Apples grown here are not the kind usually found in supermarkets: old-time Arkansas Blacks, Missouri Pippins, Winter Bananas, Splendors from Tasmania, and Gravensteins plus more modern "Jonalicious," New Zealand Galas, and the very tart Tohuku variety so popular in France. To take the See Canyon tour: Head south from San Luis Obispo on Hwy. 101 and then west on San Luis Bay Drive; after a mile or so turn right onto See Canyon Road, which eventually becomes Prefumo Canyon Road—great views of Morro Bay—and connects farther north with Los Osos Valley Road. A left turn here leads to Morro Bay, a right back to Hwy. 101 just south of San Luis.

ⓜ Wineries

When you're done with apples, try some fruit of the vine. The region's wine history reaches back more than 200 years, though the earliest wines were produced at the missions for sacramental use. Southern San Luis Obispo County wineries shine in both the **Edna Valley** and **Arroyo Grande** appellations just inland from the California coast; the small wineries here were first successful with chardonnay and pinot noir grapes. **Edna Valley Vineyard,** for example, specializes in both, while **Meridian** features an exceptional Edna Valley chardonnay. Many of these regional wineries lie between San Luis Obispo and Arroyo Grande, on small agricultural holdings and hillsides east of Hwy. 227. Come the first weekend in May for the annual **Roll Out the Barrels** winery barrel tasting and "passport" event, and in November for the annual **Harvest Celebration.** Progressive food and wine pairings are scheduled from time to time in downtown San Luis Obispo, too. A current wine-tasting map is available on the website. For more information, contact: **San Luis Obispo Vintners and Growers Association,** 5825 Orcutt Rd., 805/541-5868, www.slowine.com.

North county wineries are also well worth exploring. Another of California's newer small winery regions is the Paso Robles appellation, in the general vicinity of **Paso Robles, Templeton,** and **Atascadero,** throughout the hills and valleys both east and west of Hwy. 101. In this region cabernet, chardonnay, merlot, syrah, and zinfandel grapes do well. As in Edna Valley and Arroyo Grande, most wineries here are small, family-run operations producing 5,000 or fewer bottles per year—unassuming, casual, and "country," as different from the now-big-business Napa and Sonoma county wine industries as well-broke cowboy boots are from Bruno Maglis. Many offer tours only with reservations, especially during the hectic autumn harvest season. Yet as the awards and accolades stack up, Brunos, upscale B&Bs, and big-time production are more common all the time. Some recent vintages may be in short supply, since the December 2003 earthquake caused substantial losses.

A remnant of old-timey regional style is **York Mountain Winery,** west of Hwy. 101 outside Templeton at 7505 York Mountain Rd., 805/238-3925 (tasting room), www.yorkmountainwinery.com, a tiny winery founded in 1882—the oldest regional winery still in operation—and now owned by the Martin & Weyrich Winery people. York Mountain, known for its award-winning muscat, black muscat, viognier, pinot noir, and Roussanne, has its own appellation. Its tasting room tucked into a charming 1886 schoolhouse, **Peachy Canyon Winery,** 480 N. Bethel Rd., 805/239-1918, www.peachycanyon.com, is known for its zinfandels. Lauded for its pinot noir, syrah, zin, viognier, and heirloom varietals, **Wild Horse Winery & Vineyards** is east of Hwy. 101 (off Templeton Road) at 1437 Wild Horse Winery Court, 805/434-254, www.wildhorsewinery.com.

Among top stops closer to Paso Robles is **Justin Vineyards and Winery** west of Hwy. 101 at 11680 Chimney Rock Rd., 805/238.6932, www.justinwine.com, specializing in barrel-fermented chardonnays and known for its Isosceles, a blend of cabernet franc, cabernet sauvignon, and merlot. Tasting daily, tours by appointment only. The onsite **Just Inn,** 805/237-4149, offers three stunning B&B suites, weekend patio lunches (reservations advised), and exclusive dinners at tiny **Deborah's Room** restaurant. Among wineries east of 101 is the **Martin & Weyrich's Winery** on Buena Vista Road, 805/238-2520, www.martinweyrich.com, known for its "Cal-Italia" varietals. Try the Tuscan-style Etrusco cabernet sauvignon, a blend of sangiovese and cabernet grapes. In fact, a great many aspects of the winery are designed with Tuscany in mind, including the tasting room and the appealing onsite **Villa Toscana** B&B, 805/238-5600, www.myvillatoscana.com. For something a little bit cowboy, head for Old West-style **Tobin James Cellars,** about eight miles east of Paso Robles via Hwy. 46 at 8950 Union Rd., 805/239-2204, www.tobinjames.com, where the saloon-style tasting room boasts an 1860s-vintage Brunswick mahogany bar originally from Blue Eye, Missouri. Not only that, the wine club here is known as the James Gang. The gang here enjoys some spectacular zinfandels, including Charisma and Late Harvest dessert zinfandels.

Come to Paso Robles and vicinity in March for the annual **Celebration of Zinfandel,** mid-May for the huge **Paso Robles Wine Festival Weekend,** and October for the **Harvest Wine Tour.** For current regional wineries information, contact the **Paso Robles Vintners and Growers Association,** 622 12th St. in Paso Robles, 805/239-8463, www.pasowine.com, as well as the local visitors bureau.

Avila Beach Area

Gentler than Big Sur's, the coastline near San Luis Obispo offers rocky terraces, sandy dunes, and a big-picture view of seven of the Nine Sisters, volcanic peaks that saunter seaward from San Luis Obispo to "the rock" at Morro Bay. By car the coastal communities of Morro Bay, Avila Beach, and Pismo Beach are all less than 15 minutes away from San Luis Obispo.

The pier at **Port San Luis,** old Port Hartford and once a regular steamship stop, is now a

The Central Coast

favorite fishing spot. **Avila Beach** just east along the bay is a favorite surfers' beach town on the way to becoming trendy, its protected beaches tucked into the cove. (Try to ignore the oil tanks looming overhead.) These days Avila Beach as a community is still recovering from Unocal Corp.'s massive "oil change" on the beach, a multi-million-dollar project that involved excavating then replacing tons of soil and sand soaked with some 420,000 gallons of petroleum. Many of the area's famously funky Front Street beach-shack businesses and other buildings were relocated or demolished then replaced. Stop by and see how clean a cleaned-up beach town can get. Less appealing but definitely private is clothing-optional **Pirate's Cove** beaches a mile south of Avila Beach (weirdos possible, so bring a friend).

But before leaving Avila Beach, do the hot springs. Relaxed, funky, and family-friendly **Avila Hot Springs,** 250 Avila Beach Dr., 805/595-2359, www.avilahotsprings.com, features a large freshwater swimming pool in addition to private step-down tiled hot mineral tubs in the original 1930s bathhouse and the hot outdoor pools. (Rent inner tubes and float in the warm pool.) Spa services are also available. Or sample the healing waters at **Sycamore Mineral Springs Resort,** 1215 Avila Beach Dr., 805/595-7302 or 800/234-5831, www.sycamoresprings.com, an inviting collection of secluded, private redwood hot tubs (for two to six people) tucked into the oak woodlands. The Oasis "rock spa," with a cascading tropical waterfall, is available for groups. At last report rates were $20/first person per hour, $10/additional person per hour. Call for reservations, available from 7 A.M. to 1 A.M. You can also sign on for massage and spa services or the yoga institute. Or get a good meal or stay overnight.

NOT TOURING DIABLO CANYON

Since guards at the two-unit Diablo Canyon Nuclear Power Plant control the traffic flow here near Port San Luis, don't plan on walking in for a casual look-see. Years of anti-nuclear protest and more recent concerns about terrorism have made security a serious priority. Visitor bus tours have been discontinued.

Trouble was Diablo's middle name for 20 years, thanks to relentless anti-nuclear energy protesters. Critics of the plant, which was built just a few miles from the offshore Hosgri earthquake fault, have consistently attempted to shut down construction—then, later, the online plants—with lawsuits and civil disobedience. In 1997 Pacific Gas & Electric (PG&E) agreed to pay $14 million to settle charges it had deliberately underreported damage to sealife at Diablo Canyon, the indirect result of the 2.5 billion gallons of seawater sucked into the plant each day. A more recent lawsuit, filed against the Bush administration in early 2004, contends that risks posed by the plant due to potential terrorism haven't been adequately addressed—especially now that PG&E is storing nuclear wastes onsite. California Attorney General Bill Lockyer, along with his counterparts in three other states, have joined in the suit.

Despite naysayers, PG&E promotes the plant as "solid as the Rock of Gibraltar," a good neighbor until the end of time; PG&E also hopes its rock is a rock-solid investment, with its total $5.8 billion construction price tag financed through Northern California customers' utility bills. Though both nuclear reactors are now online, Diablo's reactor set a nationwide performance record during its first year of operation, producing more than eight billion kilowatt-hours of electricity while operating at capacity 93 percent of the time.

How do local people feel about Diablo Canyon? You'll find both gung-ho support and absolute opposition but primarily, in the typically apolitical American tradition, a "let's-wait-and-see" attitude prevails.

The utility's pretty, Spanish-looking **PG&E Community Center** about 12 miles south of San Luis Obispo via Hwy. 101 at 6588 Ontario Rd. (exit at San Luis Bay Drive) in Avila Beach, 805/546-5280, www.pge.com, open Mon.–Sat. 9 A.M.–1 P.M., no longer offers its popular overlook tours. But you can guide yourself through the simple, flashy presentations on fission nuclear energy.

Shell Beach south of Pirate's Cove and north of Pismo Beach is a marine-terrace town with lots of antique shops and two wooden staircases leading to the rocky coast below. Primo is shoving off from Shell Beach for ocean kayaking, an adventure easily undertaken with help from **Central Coast Kayaks** on Shell Beach Road, 805/773-3500, www.centralcoastkayaks.com.

Pismo Beach Area

Shell Beach segues into **Pismo Beach** proper, once a haute destination for 1930s celebrities, now a cleaned-up, family-friendly, and fairly affordable beach community. Pismo Beach was first famous for its pismo clams, a population now nearly decimated. The Spanish *pismo* means "a place to fish," but the Chumash *pismu* means "a place where blobs of tar wash up on the beach." Since good fishing is a historical fact and, in the absence of major coastal oil spills, beach tar from here to Santa Barbara is a nat-

© ROBERT HOLMES/CALTOUR

Pismo Beach

ural phenomenon, pick your own derivation. For more information about the area and its attractions, contact: **Pismo Beach Chamber of Commerce & Visitors Center,** 581 Dolliver, 805/773-4382, www.pismochamber.com.

The six miles of shoreline from Pismo Beach to Oceano is primarily **Pismo State Beach,** 805/489-2684, with a small dunes preserve tacked on to the southern end. Dominated by the **Oceano Dunes State Vehicular Recreation Area** dune buggy heaven, Pismo features two campgrounds (some hookups available; see below) but typically offers little for solitude-seeking beach and dune lovers beyond pier fishing. Significant stretches of beach are closed to even dune buggy enthusiasts, however, during the March–Sept. nesting season for the Western snowy plover. Discover more about local natural history at the **Pismo Nature Center** at the Oceano Campground on Pier Avenue. Solitude seekers will feel considerably more comfortable at the Nature Conservancy's now extensive **Guadalupe-Nipomo Dunes Preserve** farther south (see Santa Maria section below) or at isolated **Point Sal State Beach,** reached from Hwy. 101 south of Santa Maria via Betteravia and Brown Roads.

Oceano and vicinity, just south of Pismo Beach, have seen wilder days. Sneaky sand dunes advanced on the town's famous dance pavilion, cottages, and wharf years ago, destroying them all. The dunes here are the highest and whitest in the state, blocked from straying farther south by the Point Sal cliffs. Inland are marshes and shallow lagoons, resting areas for mallards and teal and home during the Depression to the "Dunites," an eclectic group of artists, astrologers, loners, nudists, and writers. These days Oceano's most notable attraction is **The Great American Melodrama & Vaudeville,** 805/489-2499, www.americanmelodrama.com, an impressive local theater where the old-fashioned entertainment comes with dinner.

Inland from Oceano and the Pismo Beach area is **Arroyo Grande,** nothing but a stage stop in 1877, now an attractive village with Old West-style antique and other shops, some bed and breakfasts, and surrounding flower seed farms. At the Village Green near city hall, you'll see a small

The Central Coast

park and a 71-foot-long swinging bridge built in 1875. For more information, contact: **Arroyo Grande Chamber of Commerce & Visitors Center,** 800 W. Branch, 805/489-1488, www .arroyograndecc.com.

ACCOMMODATIONS

Camping

Camp at Lopez Lake about 11 miles northeast of Arroyo Grande, a pretty little reservoir also good for year-round fishing, swimming (water-slides, too), sailing, windsurfing, and hiking. Primitive tent campsites, shaded by oaks, are $15, sites with hookups $19–24. Marina and store, too. For general information, call **Lopez Lake Recreation Area** at 805/788-2381 or see www.slocountyparks.com. Make reservations up to one year in advance on the website, or call 805/781-5930.

Camping near the ocean is also a good bet. State park campsites are available at Morro Bay, with the best developed ones at **Morro Bay State Park** and primitive ones at **Montaña de Oro.** For details, see Morro Bay and Vicinity, above. **Pismo State Beach** offers both **North Beach Campground** ($15–20) and **Ocean Campground** ($15–20 and $24–29), sites reservable through ReserveAmerica, 800/444-7275, www .reserveamerica.com. There's also first-come, first-camped county **Oceano Memorial Park and Campground** (RV or tent sites) and private fishing lagoon near Pismo State Beach, $21–25. Full hook-ups, showers; for information, call 805/781-5930. Adjacent to the beach—and the new beach boardwalk—in Pismo Beach is the very nice **Pismo Coast Village RV Resort,** 165 S. Dolliver St., 805/773-1811 or 888/782-3224, www.rvbeach.com. Little extras include laundromat, large heated pool, miniature golf, bike rentals, and satellite TV. Rates are $31–42.

Hostels and Motels

San Luis Obispo has a great HI-USA hostel—**Hostel Obispo,** housed in a pleasant two-story Victorian at 1617 Santa Rosa St., 805/544-4678, www.hostelobispo.com, with a per-bed rate of $18–20 for dorm beds, $40–60 for couples rooms, $50–70 for family rooms (3–5 people). Call to make reservations; credit cards accepted. Extras here include laundry, bike rentals, onsite parking, and a garden and patio with barbecue. No curfew.

Most San Luis Obispo motels are on or near Monterey Street. Particularly inviting is whimsical, blue-shuttered **Petit Soleil** just blocks from downtown at 1473 Monterey St., 805/549-0321 or 800/676-1588, www.petitsoleilslo.com, a one-time motel redone as a Provençal inn—from the cobblestone courtyard and sunny European décor to delectable breakfast quiche. The inn's 15 "themed" rooms—Le Chantecleer, Herbes de Provence, Van Gogh, Chocolat, La Cage aux Folles, and more—feature private bathrooms, TVs tucked away in armoires, radio/CD players, and phones (free local calls). Better yet, they are configured for maximum traveler flexibility, from king, queen, and double queen rooms to a queen with trundle bed. Rates are $100–200, starting at $129; two-night minimum often required on weekends. Full breakfast, evening wine and appetizers included, served in the cheery dining room or out on the garden patio.

The Milestone Motel (later known as the Motel Inn), Luis Obispo's first and original "mo-tel," closed some years back for historic renovation and eventual expansion. In the meantime a mod-

HIKING THE DIABLO COAST

The 10 miles of coast north of Port San Luis is pristine and rugged, home to sea lions, pelicans, and cormorants. The presence of the Diablo Canyon Nuclear Plant means this entire area has long been off-limits to coastwalkers for security reasons. But now the **Pecho Coast Trail** traverses several miles of this once-lost coast, from just north of Avila Beach to Point San Luis Lighthouse and the marine terrace just beyond. Before you strap on those hiking boots, though, pick up the phone and call 805/541-8735; the area is accessible on naturalist-guided hikes only, and only by reservation. Half-day and full-day trips are available.

ern variation on the motel theme is right next door—the **Apple Farm Inn** 2015 Monterey St., 805/544-2040 or 800/255-2040, www.apple farm.com. Behind homey, locally famous **Apple Farm Restaurant** is the rest of the ranch—in this case, a quaint yet contemporary three-story, country-style motel. Rooms feature fireplaces, four-poster beds, and other period furnishings, even armoires, yet all the modern comforts. Equally pleasant but less expensive are the more motel-like rooms in the **Apple Farm Trellis Court,** adjacent. Inn rooms are $200–400 in the high season, $200–300 in winter. Motel rooms start at $129 in summer, $99 at other times.

The Cliffs Resort, 2757 Shell Beach Rd. in Pismo Beach, 805/773-5000, or 800/826-7827 (reservations in California), www.cliffsresort.com, once offered the only seaside-resort accommodations in the San Luis Obispo area. It's still just about the best. The Cliffs sits right on the beach—actually, the cliffs above the beach—and its recently refurbished (2003) rooms are spacious and attractive, done in earthy day-at-the-beach colors. Each features the usual modern amenities plus in-room coffeemaker, hair dryer, ironing board/iron, and a big TV with HBO, pay movies, and PlayStation. Most have private patios and ocean views. (Even the spectacular swimming pool here has a view.) The suites are something special, complete with Italian marble bathrooms and in-room whirlpool tubs. High-season rates are $150–350, but ask about discounts, off-season specials, and packages. To get here from Hwy. 101: If coming from the north, exit at Shell Beach Road; from the south, exit at Spyglass Road.

For something to really write home about, consider **The Madonna Inn,** 100 Madonna Rd., 805/543-3000 or 800/543-9666, www.madonna inn.com. One of the most unusual motels anywhere, the Madonna is noted for its 109 quirky "theme" rooms and suites, some with waterfalls and other dramatic elements, each one of the 109 rooms here unique. Some sample themes: the Daisy Mae Room, the Caveman Room, the Cloud Nine Suite, the Love Nest. You get the idea—over the top and immensely popular with newlyweds and couples tired of the same old an-

niversary celebration. Some parts of this Madonna are getting a bit tired, but a stay here is *different.* Do check it out. Rooms are $150–200 for two, suites $200–350. Those who don't stay are welcome to satisfy their curiosity by wandering the halls and peeking into open rooms. Men—and undaunted women—should also check out the men's bathroom off the lobby, most notable for its free-flowing white flagstone waterfall urinal and seashell washbasins. Other attractions include a very good steakhouse, everything upholstered in pink leather; bar; café; onsite bakery; and shops.

Bed-and-Breakfasts

Fun for bed-and-breakfast fans: the 13-room **Garden Street Inn,** just a block from the mission at 1212 Garden St., 805/545-9802 or 800/488-2045, www.gardenstreetinn.com. This 1887 Italianate Queen Anne Victorian was originally centerpiece of the local Mission Vineyard. Rooms and suites are individually decorated; Valley of the Moon commemorates the life and times of Jack London, Walden is a Thoreau tribute, and Amadeus remembers Mozart. No phone, no TVs, and a well-stocked library so prepare to truly relax. Suites include extras such as whirlpool tub bath/showers, private decks, separate bedrooms. Full breakfast is served every morning, wine and cheese every evening. Rates are $100–200; rooms start at $140, suites at $180, with a two-night minimum stay on weekends.

Quite relaxing in an actively therapeutic way is **Sycamore Mineral Springs Resort** in Avila Beach at 1215 Avila Beach Rd., 805/595-7302 or 800/234-5831, www.sycamoresprings.com. Spa services include acupressure, reflexology, polarity therapy, shiatsu, facials, and Swedish massage are. Motel-style rooms here, each with a private hot tub outside on the patio or deck, are $150–200. The resort's suites, with four-poster beds, fine wood furnishings, and wet bars, marble fireplaces, and sofas, are $250 and up, starting at $260. A stay here also includes a credit toward breakfast at very good, very reasonably priced California-style **The Gardens of Avila** restaurant here, which also serves lunch and dinner daily and Sunday brunch.

The Central Coast

FOOD

A fun family-style place convenient to motel row is **Izzy Ortega's Mexican Restaurant and Cantina** next to the Holiday Inn at 1850 Monterey St., 805/543-3333, open daily 11:30 A.M. until at least 9 P.M. (bar open later). Colorful and cheerful with a party-hearty American attitude, Izzy's is one of San Luis Obispo's most popular restaurants. The food's quite good, and considerably more authentic than most Americanized Mexican. Try the shrimp or fish tacos, for example, the pork tamales, or the tasty bean soup. Entrées get more ambitious, including steak ranchero and broiled garlic shrimp. Children's menu available.

San Luis Obispo boasts more than 60 eateries, so look around—especially downtown, where delis, small cafés, and restaurants surround the plaza area. Good for classic breakfast is **Louisa's Place,** 964 Higuera St., 805/541-0227, a countertop-style café locally popular for its buckwheat pancakes and lunch specials. **Pete's Southside Café,** 1815 Osos St., 805/549-8133, is an outpost of the original Avila Beach Pete's all gussied up for more stylish times. But the fresh seafood is still fresh, the Mexican selections still good, and the atmosphere still bright and bustling. It's open for lunch and dinner, on Sunday for dinner only. The cool destination for the weekday "Happy Hour and a Half" is the old-brick **SLO Brewpub & Restaurant** downtown at 1119 Garden St. (between Higuera and Marsh), 805/543-1843, open for lunch and dinner daily (just noon–5 P.M. on Sunday). Great fish and chips on Friday. Brewpub fans believe the main attractions here are the Amber Ale, Pale Ale, and Porter—and at least one seasonal brew, on tap. Pool's on tap, too, along with live entertainment (later) most nights.

Right across from the mission is the **Mission Grill,** 1023 Chorro St., 805/547-5544, serving stylish Southwestern fare such as piñon-crusted salmon, slow-roasted prime rib, pasta Provençal, and Conquistador Newburgh. Sunday brunch here is grand, offering everything from Paradise Island French Toast (with five different Puerto Rican rums) to crab and avocado omelettes.

The **Big Sky Café,** 1121 Broad St., 805/545-5401, serves "analog food for a digital world." And if you're not clear on what that means, here's a clue: great Southwestern and eclectic New American fare at breakfast, lunch, and dinner. How 'bout a Portobello mushroom scramble, scrambled eggs with charbroiled chicken and cherry sausage, or red flannel turkey hash? Vegan mushroom burger, charbroiled eggplant sandwich, or classic BLT with double-thick bacon? Lemongrass shrimp, Gulf Coast seafood tacos, or Caribbean adobo steak? However you slice it, there's something here for everyone—including the fresh fruit cobbler and mango-lime pie. Justifiably popular, too, is award-winning **Mother's Tavern,** 725 Higuera St., 805/541-8733, where the specialty is "California tavern food"—everything from burgers and steaks to pastas, salads, and sandwiches. Another hit at Mother's is the tavern's house band, the jump blues and swing band Sugar Daddy Swing Kings. (So cool.) Lots of other great talent takes the stage here too. A world away yet right next door is **Bistro le Fandango,** 717 Higuera St., 805/544-5515, serving French with some Basque accents, like shrimp and scallops with garlic and Basque chiles.

Stylin' it in San Luis Obispo might also include lunch or dinner at **Cafe Roma,** in a new location at Railroad Square near the train station, 1020 Railroad Ave., 805/541-6800, open Tues.–Fri. for lunch and Tues.–Sun. for dinner. Noted for its authentic northern Italian fare, Cafe Roma is one of San Luis Obispo's most popular fine food destinations. The pastas are always good, and you probably won't go wrong with the Tuscan chicken or filet mignon. The wine list is also a treat, a mix of classy regional Californians and classic Italians. Also quite good, downtown next to the Fremont Theater, is **Buona Tavola,** 1037 Monterey St., 805/545-8000, beloved for its numerous salads and handmade pastas, such as tortelloni stuffed with pumpkin and ricotta cheese in a sage–mascarpone cheese sauce with toasted walnuts. Open for lunch and dinner.

Outside San Luis Obispo

A great place to take the kids, especially if you can get them to pay: the original **F. McClintocks**

Saloon and Dining House, 750 Mattie Rd. in Pismo Beach, 805/773-1892, open daily (after 3 or 4 P.M.) for dinner, and on Sunday at 9:30–9 A.M., for "ranch breakfast," early supper, and dinner (closed some major holidays). Beef— aged, "hand-cut," and then barbecued over oak wood—is the secret to the success of this kicky outpost of commercialized mom-and-pop cowboy kitsch. (The gift shop overfloweth.) Everything here is pretty good, however. The machismo challenge, typically issued by men to men, is eating the oddest menu item—fried turkey nuts—without squawking. And if you like that sort of thing, come in mid-July for the Annual Mountain Oyster Feed, held out back. But kids are more impressed by the wait staff,

who pour water by holding the pitcher at least two feet above the table—and never spill a drop. And don't miss the Birthday Picture Gallery. Or mosey on over to the other area F. McClintocks locations; there's one in SLO at 686 Higuera St., 805/541-0686, and others in Paso Robles and Arroyo Grande.

For huevos rancheros and good burgers, head for Port San Luis and the patio at **Fat Cat's Café,** 805/595-2204. Stylish and quite good for seafood—Greek-style calamari and scallops, anyone?—is the **Olde Port Inn,** in Avila Beach at Port San Luis's Pier #3, 805/595-2515. The classic surfers' fuel center in Pismo Beach is the **Splash Café,** just a block from the pier at 197 Pomeroy Ave., 805/773-4653, where you can

WORTHWHILE NORTH OF SAN LUIS OBISPO

North of San Luis Obispo proper, Santa Margarita was once a small outpost of the mission, with a chapel, grain storage, and lodging rooms. Stop by the **Round Up Café,** 22412 El Camino Real, 805/438-3828, for breakfast, or the **Margarita Merchantile,** 22304 G St., 805/438-5714, for deli sandwiches. The biggest thing around today, though, is tiny **Santa Margarita Lake,** which offers camping, picnicking, and fishing (no swimming, though there's a pool). For info and camping reservations, call 805/788-2397 or see www.slocountyparks.com. Continue east via Pozo Road to spot-in-the-road Pozo and the classic Wild West **Pozo Saloon,** 805/438-4225, just the place for some pool and 'cue and the annual spring Pozo Whisky Games.

East via Hwy. 58 is the fascinating **Carrizo Plain National Monument,** sometimes referred to as "California's Serengeti." The Carrizo Plain somehow missed out on the march of progress. The San Andreas Fault is on the plain's eastern edge, and the region is hot in summer and cold in winter. Yet the plain, once a prehistoric lake, was sacred to the Chumash, whose Great Spirits lived here— and shook the earth when angered. Eight miles wide and 50 miles long, the Carrizo Plain preserves the last large remnant of the San Joaquin Valley's natural terrain, where sandhill cranes winter and pronghorn still roam.

North via Hwy. 101 are **Atascadero** and **Paso Robles,** center of another notable California wine country. Still farther north on the main highway is sleepy little **San Miguel** with its fine old mission (closed in late 2003 due to earthquake damage) and, to the west, **Lake Nacimiento.** As the highway hums northward through the Salinas Valley, to the west lies **Lake San Antonio,** popular for bald eagle watching in winter.

Beyond Jolon, smack in the midst of Fort Hunter-Liggett, is **Mission San Antonio de Padua,** 831/385-4478, not the biggest nor most ravishingly restored mission, certainly not the most popular, but somehow the most evocative of Spanish California—well worth the detour. For a simple yet special stay less than a half-mile away, consider the **Hacienda Guest Lodge,** 831/386-2900, the original ranch house designed for William Randolph Hearst by Julia Morgan and built in 1922. Later an officers club, the Hacienda is now a combination hotel, restaurant, bar, bowling alley with snack bar, and campground. Nothing fancy, but a tremendous value. A steak dinner is $10 or so. Rooms and suites are $50–150. Not to mention the chance to appreciate a nearly pristine Julia Morgan building. Weather and road conditions permitting, from Fort Hunter-Liggett it's possible to take the back-roads route, Nacimiento-Fergusson Rd., over the mountains to Big Sur.

The Central Coast

get a bread bowl full of wonderful New England-style clam chowder for under $5. Also loved by locals is **Giuseppe's** at 891 Price St., 805/773-2870, which serves up superb wood-fired pizzas and delightful pastas. (No reservations, so feel free to call ahead for takeout—or go walk on the beach while you wait.) For genuine Mexican without much ambience, head for **Chacho's,** 1911 Cienaga St. in Oceano, 805/489-5136. Well worth looking for in nearby Arroyo Grande is **Massimo's,** 840 Oak Park Blvd., 805/474-9211, where northern Italian is the specialty.

SANTA MARIA

This onetime ranch-country hitching post on the northern fringe of Santa Barbara County is quickly growing out into its flower fields, thanks in part to the proximity of Vandenberg Air Force Base. Skyrocketing housing prices in and around Santa Barbara have also accelerated local development. Built on sand flats, Santa Maria has one of the West's best repertory theater programs, an abundance of trees, and unusually broad streets— at least in the older parts of town—since very wide streets were necessary to reverse eight-mule wagon rigs.

Come in April for the annual **Santa Maria Valley Strawberry Festival** at the county fairgrounds. The "West's Best Rodeo," Santa Maria's **Elks Rodeo and Parade,** is the big event in late May or early June. The **Santa Barbara County Fair** in late July is old-fashioned family fun complete with carnival, exhibits, entertainment, and horse show. But good times anytime are almost guaranteed by the fine **Pacific Conservatory of the Performing Arts,** which offers Shakespeare, musicals such as *Narnia* and *I Do, I Do,* Moss Hart's *Light Up the Sky* and other comedies, and dramas such as *Amadeus* and Eugene O'Neill's *Long Day's Journey Into Night.* Performances are also held in Solvang (June through October only), but the troupe's year-round headquarters are at the local Allan Hancock College, 800 S. College Drive. For information and tickets call 805/922-8313 or see www.pcpa.org.

Impressive in the neighborhood is the two-hangar **Santa Maria Museum of Flight,** 3015 Airpark Dr., 805/922-8758, www.smmof.org, open Fri.–Sun. 10 A.M.–4 P.M., which documents general flight history with both antique and model planes, with an emphasis on local contributions to aviation history. (Santa Maria was a basing station during World War II.) The once-secret Norden bombsight, a Bowers Flybaby, a 1929 Fleet Model 2, and the Stinson V77-Reliant are among the treasures on display. The Early Aviation Hangar houses aircraft, memorabilia, models, and photos chronicling the years stretching between the Wright Brothers' first flights to World War II. Come in September for the annual fly-in, the **Classic Aircraft and Vintage Auto Roundup.** For broader local historical perspective, the **Santa Maria Valley Historical Museum** is downtown (adjacent to the visitor bureau) at 616 S. Broadway, 805/922-3130, open Tues.–Sat. noon–5 P.M. A fascination here: the Barbecue Hall of Fame.

For more information about Santa Maria and vicinity, contact the **Santa Maria Visitor and Convention Bureau,** 614 S. Broadway, 805/925-2403 or 800/331-3779, www.santamaria.com, which offers accommodations, food, and regional wine-tour information. Also pick up a copy of the *Walk Through History* local walking tour guide. To find out what's going on otherwise, pick up a copy of the free weekly *Santa Maria Sun.* For area camping and regional recreation information, contact the **Santa Lucia Ranger District** office of the Los Padres National Forest at 1616 N. Carlotti Dr. in Santa Maria, 805/925-9538, www.fs.fed.us/r5/lospadres.

Practicalities

If you need to spoil yourself but don't have big enough bucks to do that in places like Carmel or Santa Barbara, consider the **Santa Maria Inn,** a half-mile south of Main Street at 801 S. Broadway, 805/928-7777 or 800/447-3529 (reservations), www.santamariainn.com. This historic English Tudor-style hostelry, built in 1917, is Santa Maria's pride and joy—a grande dame that once hosted California luminaries such as William Randolph Hearst and actress Marion Davies on their way to and from San Simeon and Hollywood stars including Charlie Chaplin,

IN SEARCH OF THE TEN COMMANDMENTS

The coastal dunes due west of Santa Maria provide habitat for California brown pelicans and the endangered least terns, though Cecil B. DeMille probably didn't think much about such things in 1923 when he built, and then buried, a dozen four-ton plaster sphinxes, four statues of Ramses the Magnificent, and an entire pharaonic city here—the original movie set for *The Ten Commandments*. Referred to as the dune that never moves, Ten Commandment Hill is now part of the **Guadalupe-Nipomo Dunes Preserve** and the first thing visitors see at the Guadalupe entrance.

This large coastal dunes preserve is part of the seemingly simple yet quite complicated and fragile Nipomo Dunes ecosystem, 18 miles of coastline stretching from Pismo Beach south to Vandenberg. Created by howling wind and enormous offshore swells, the seaward dunes are sizable parabola-shaped mounds of sharp-grained sand in almost perpetual motion. The more stable back dunes stand 200 feet tall and offer more hospitable habitat for the 18 endangered and rare endemic coastal scrub species counted to date by members of the California Native Plant Society. Among the most instantly impressive is the yellow-flowered giant coreopsis, which grows only on the Channel Islands and on the California coast from Los Angeles north to the Nipomo Dunes. More than 1,400 species of plants and animals have been identified in the Guadalupe-Nipomo Dunes.

Oso Flaco Lake to the north of Guadalupe is a surprising sparkling blue coastal oasis, actually a group of small lakes fringed by shrubs and surrounded by sand dunes (and the din from dune buggyists penned up just northward at the Oceano Dunes State Vehicular Recreation Area). To the south is **Mussel Rock,** actually a 500-foot-tall sand dune. Sit and watch the sunset while the surf spits and sputters across the sand. Or hike to Point Sal and **Point Sal State Beach,** a wonderfully remote stretch of headlands, rocky outcroppings, and sand (just north of Vandenberg. (The treacherous surf is unsafe for swimming.) Good whale-watching. To get there, head west on the Brown Road turnoff three miles south of Guadalupe, and then take Point Sal Road.

Though the preserve holdings started with 3,400 acres, including the critical central section relinquished by Mobil Oil Corporation, the preserve now embraces a total of 20,000 acres owned by the Nature Conservancy and various public agencies. The San Luis Obispo-based People for Nipomo Dunes led the dunes preservation effort with the idea of creating a Nipomo Dunes National Seashore, protected federally like Point Reyes to the north. The dunes are now recognized as a National Natural Landmark.

The preserve is accessible from Hwy. 101 in Santa Maria (via Hwy. 166) or from Hwy. 1 farther west near Guadalupe. There are two preserve entrances. To reach the Guadalupe entrance, from Guadalupe continue to the west end of Main Street. To reach the Oso Flaco Lake entrance, from Hwy. 1 about three miles north of Guadalupe turn left onto Oso Flaco Lake Road. The Oso Flaco Lake area is handicapped accessible, with a mile-long boardwalk. The preserve is open dawn to dusk 365 days each year. No overnight camping, dogs, or four-wheel drive vehicles are allowed. Docent-guided walks and bird walks, as well as various educational programs, are offered

For a natural history introduction and other information, stop by the **Dunes Visitor Center,** in its new location in a lovingly restored Craftsman at 1055 Guadalupe St. (Hwy. 1) in downtown Guadalupe, 805/343-2455, or see www.dunescenter.org. The center is open Tues.–Sun. 10 A.M.–4 P.M.; the center's main entrance is from the parking lot out back. Of particular interest in **Nipomo** proper is the **Dana Adobe,** 671 S. Oak Glen Ave., 805/929-5679, the county's oldest surviving residence and a state historic landmark. Open Sunday noon–4 P.M. and at other times by appointment.

The Central Coast

Mary Pickford, Douglas Fairbanks, Rudolph Valentino, Marlene Dietrich, Marilyn Monroe, John Wayne, and Jimmy Stewart. More recently, even Demi Moore. The Santa Maria Inn, renovated and redecorated in Old English style, now includes full fitness facilities in addition to the swimming pool. Rooms in the older hotel section are smaller yet more "historic"; more spacious accommodations are situated in the hotel's newer Tower. All accommodations feature abundant amenities, from color TVs with video players and hair dryers to in-room coffeemakers and refrigerators. Rooms are $100–150, suites are $150–300, with various discounts, specials, and packages also available. The inn's restaurant and lounge are also local stars. Come on Sunday for the hotel's famous brunch, usually including Santa Maria-style barbecue.

Since the area boasts agricultural abundance, you can usually count on good pickin's at local farmers' markets. The **Santa Maria Certified Farmers' Market** is held Wednesday noon–4 P.M. in the Mervyn's parking lot, Broadway and Main. For more information, call 805/709-6740.

Otherwise, Santa Maria is a difficult place for vegetarians to avoid feeling deprived. But there are compensations—like the great Cajun/Mexican fare at **M Chef Rick's Ultimately Fine Foods,** in the Lucky Shopping Center at 4869 S. Bradley Rd., 805/937-9512, where the motto is: "Everything I do from now on gonna be funky." Funky here, of course, is quite fine, ultimately, with favorites such as Yucatan chicken soup, jambalaya, and seafood salads. Good wines, too, everything reasonably priced. Closed Sunday. (There's another Rick's in Santa Ynez.) Otherwise carnivores might want to track down some world-famous **Santa Maria-style barbecue.** A tradition passed down from the days of the vaqueros, real local 'cue includes delectable slabs of prime sirloin beef barbecued over a slow red-oak fire, then sliced as thin as paper—and served with the chunky *salsa cruda* people drown it in—pinquito beans (grown only in Santa Maria Valley), salad, toasted garlic bread, and dessert, unquestionably the ultimate in California cowboy fare. Especially on Saturday, barbecue is the easiest meal to find in and around Santa Maria. The

most authentic local version is served on weekends at local charity affairs of one sort or another, but several steakhouses serve it anytime.

The best of the Santa Maria barbecue bunch is the **Hitching Post,** open 5–9:30 P.M. at 3325 Point Sal Rd., 805/937-6151, in Casmalia, a tiny town southeast of Santa Maria more recently famous as the state's Class I toxic waste landfill. (For years the big sign at the landfill read: Casmalia Toxic Dump—It's A Resource.) Back at the Hitching Post, you can watch the meat being barbecued over the oak fire from the other side of the glass wall. Though the wine selection is good—full bar, too—they say it's okay to drink the water here because it's pumped in from the Santa Maria Valley. Another best bet, just north of Santa Maria, is **Jocko's,** 125 N. Thompson St. in Nipomo, 805/929-3686, a Santa Maria-style steakhouse also known for its spicy beans, open daily. West of Santa Maria is tiny Guadalupe, a Latino-Italian-Swiss-Filipino-Chinese colony also famous for its small and authentic ethnic eateries. Locals say the **Far Western Tavern,** 899 Guadalupe, 805/343-2226, serves the best filet mignon around. Other people like this place for its inimitable ambience, from the ever-vigilant critter heads on the walls to the genuine cowhide drapes.

LOMPOC

Probably Chumash for "shell mound," Lompoc (pronounced LOM-poke) these days is a bustling military town amid blooming flower fields, a commercial crazy-quilt patchwork of fragrant sweet peas, larkspurs, asters, poppies, marigolds, zinnias, and petunias adding vivid bloom to the city's cheeks from June through August. The local flower seed business is under pressure from housing developments and foreign agricultural production, but the bloom boom is still 1,500 acres or so, healthy enough to make the tourists smile. At **Vandenberg Air Force Base** just west of town—home of the 30th Space Wing, and the only U.S. military installation that launches unmanned government and commercial satellites in addition to intercontinental ballistic missiles (ICBMs)—evening launches create colorful sky trails at sunset. Free tours of Vandenberg, which might include a former space shuttle launch site, an underground missile silo, and a shipwrecked 1923 naval destroyer, are offered the second and fourth Wednesday at 10 A.M. (security conditions and pending missions permitting). For details and reservations, call 805/606-3595.

Another significant but subtler local presence is the area's medium security prison—until recently also a comfortable minimum security prison camp known fondly as Club Fed, historic home away from home for white-collar criminals, including Nixon-era Watergate scandal alumni Dwight Chapin, John Dean, H.R. Haldeman, and Donald Segretti. Inside trader Ivan Boesky, former San Diego Chargers running back Chuck Muncie, and convicted Soviet spy Christopher Boyce (of *The Falcon and the Snowman* fame) did some time here, too.

Mission La Purísima Concepción (see below) is the area's main attraction, but stop by the **Lompoc Museum**, in the old Carnegie library at 200 S. H St., 805/736-3888, open afternoons Tues.–Sun., to review the city's pioneering Prohibitionist history. And poke around town to appreciate the **Lompoc Valley Mural Project** (more than 60 and counting) and the city's unique Italian stone pines. Beach hikers can head south for miles from **Ocean Beach County Park** at Vandenberg Air Force Base, reached from Lompoc via Hwy. 246 (heading west) and then Ocean Beach Road; often windy, so come prepared. Locally famous for beach walks, good picnics, fishing, and fabulous sunsets is isolated, windswept, and wicked-waved **Jalama Beach County Park** about five miles south of Lompoc via Hwy. 1 and Jalama Road. Also on Jalama Road is the 310-acre **Return to Freedom American Wild Horse Sanctuary,** 805/737-9246, www.returntofreedom.org, dedicated to humane management of wild horses in natural habitats, in family groups and herds. Sign on for a look-see, up close and personal, on a wild horse walking adventure. Come to town in late June for the annual **Lompoc Flower Festival** and associated **Valley of the Flowers Half-Marathon.**

For more information about the area, contact the **Lompoc Valley Chamber of Commerce,** 111 S. I St., 805/736-4567, www.lompoc.com, which offers a "flower drive" brochure/map, events, and practical information.

La Purísima Mission State Historic Park

The largest mission complex in the state, now situated on 1,000 unspoiled acres about four miles east of Lompoc on Hwy. 246, Misión de la Concepción Purísima de María Santísima ("Mission of the Immaculate Conception of Most Holy Mary") was the 11th in California's chain of coastal missions when it was built in what is now downtown Lompoc in 1787. Almost all of the original Mission La Purísima was destroyed just before Christmas Day in 1812 by a devastating earthquake and deluge. Another traumatic year was 1824, when rebellious Chumash, angry at their exploitation by soldiers, captured the mission and held it for a month. Ten years later, the mission was essentially abandoned.

Now an impressive state historic park and California's only complete mission complex, the new La Purísima (built between 1813 and 1818) is unusual in its layout. All buildings line up like ducks in a row along El Camino Real, rather than occupying more traditional positions surrounding an interior courtyard. Also unique here is the fine Depression-era restoration work accomplished primarily by the Civilian Conservation Corps under state and national parks supervision. Completely rebuilt from the ground up with handmade adobe bricks, tiles, and dyes essentially identical to the originals, the mission's handhewn redwood timbers, doors, and furniture, even the artwork and decorative designs, also come as close to authenticity as well-disciplined architectural imagination allows.

At La Purísima, secular existence has been emphasized over the religious life. Workshops and living quarters, the soldiers' quarters, and simple cells of the padres offer a sense of the unromantic and less-than-luxurious life in mission times. More interesting, though, are the shops where the mission's work went on: the bakery, the soap and tallow factory, weaving rooms, olive press, and grain mill. The mission's museum includes an excellent collection of artifacts and historical displays. Wander along remnants of El Camino Real, past the livestock corrals, the cemetery, and the long, narrow church. (Inside, notice the abalone shells for holding holy water and the absence of benches; worshippers knelt on the adobe brick floor.)

Mission gardens, at one time irrigated by an ingenious water system, include scarecrow-guarded vegetables mixed with flowers and herbs, native plant gardens, even Castilian roses. The old pear orchards and vineyards have been replanted though a few ancient specimens remain.

Main mission events include the **Fiesta** in mid-May, spring and summer demonstrations of mission arts, crafts, and daily life—Purísima's **People's Days**—and the luminaria-lit **Founding Day** celebration in December (very popular, so plan; advance tickets required). The mission is open daily 9 A.M.–5 P.M. (closed Thanksgiving, Christmas, and New Year's Day) for self-guided tours, though come later in the day to avoid school groups. Free guided tours are offered daily (except during Living History Days and other special events), weekends and holidays at 11 A.M. and 2 P.M., weekdays at 2 P.M. only. The day-use fee for private vehicles was still $4, at last report, substantially more for commercial vans and buses. A new exhibit building was completed in 2004; fundraising for other new visitor buildings and facilities continues, so feel free to contribute. For more park information, contact **La Purísima Mission State Historic Park,** 2295 Purisima Rd., 805/733-3713, www.lapurisimamission.org.

Point Conception

Just below Vandenberg Air Force Base is the place California turns on itself. Point Conception, an almost inaccessible elbow of land stabbing the sea some 40 miles north of Santa Barbara, is the spot where California's coastal "direction" swings from north-south to east-west, the geographical pivotal point separating temperature and climate zones, northstate from southstate. A lone wind-whipped lighthouse, complete with forlorn foghorn, teeters at the edge of every mariner's nightmare, California's Cape Horn.

Inaccessible by car, Point Conception can be reached by hikers from **Jalama Beach County Park** just south of Vandenberg (from south of Lompoc, take Jalama Road west from Hwy. 1). Some hike along the railroad right-of-way on the plateau—illegal, of course, so you've been warned—but with equal caution one can take the more adventurous route along the beach and cliffs to commune with startled deer, seals, sea lions, and whales offshore.

Practicalities

For absolutely budget travelers, the best bet is camping. Near Lompoc, camp south of Vandenberg at **Jalama Beach County Park,** once the site of a Chumash village, where campsites are first-come, first-camped; for more information call 805/736-6316 (recorded) or 805/736-3504. Other possibilities include **Lopez Lake** to the north and state park campsites near Morro Bay (for area information, see above). Motels in Lompoc are fairly inexpensive, most of them along H Street.

Most of the year the **Lompoc Certified Farmers' Market** is held Friday 2–6 P.M. on the corner of I Street and Ocean Avenue, but in summer—June through October—it's 2–7 P.M. and located at Cypress and H Streets. For more information, call 805/709-6740. **Tom's** in Lompoc at 115 E. Cottage Ave., 805/736-9996, is everybody's favorite burger joint. For burgers fresh off the oak-fired barbecue pit, the place is the **Outpost,** 118 S. H St., 805/735-1130. But, for café society, head for the **South Side Coffee Company,** 105 S. H St., 805/737-3730. As unlikely as it may seem to find a good Japanese restaurant in these parts, don't pass up **Oki Sushi,** 1206 W. Ocean Ave., 805/735-7170.

⋈ SOLVANG AND VICINITY

Solvang, "sunny meadow" or "sunny valley" in Danish, was founded in 1911 by immigrants from Denmark who sought a pastoral spot to establish a folk school. This attractive representation of Denmark is now a well-trod tourist destination in Santa Ynez Valley, complete with Scandinavian-style motels, restaurants, shops, even windmills. Recent history has also had its impact here. Though national media always put

COURTESY OF THE SOLVANG CONFERENCE & VISITORS BUREAU/ THE SANTA BARBARA CONFERENCE & VISITORS BUREAU

Solvang

former President Ronald Reagan's Western White House in Santa Barbara, it was actually closer to Solvang, off Refugio Road. The Reagans don't live at the ranch any more. But when they did, they made quite an impression. When Ron and Nancy arrived at the Solvang polls to vote, for example, SWAT teams took over the town.

In summer and on many weekends, tourists take over the town. To appreciate the authentic taste of Denmark here—and, surprisingly, the experience is largely authentic—come some other time, in winter, spring, or fall. Come in February for the **Flying Leap Storytellers Festival,** in March for **A Taste of Solvang.** Roll into town in late April for the **Gourmet Century Bike Ride,** 805/688-6385, a 100-mile bike ride through the scenic Santa Ynez Valley wine country that serves everyone a prize, at race's end—an exquisite dinner. Return in May for the **Vintners Festival.** And in September Solvang hosts **Danish Days,** a colorful community celebration honoring the

old country since 1936, with authentic dress, outdoor dancing and feasts, roving entertainers, and theater. Yet there is a special compensation for those who do come in summer: **Summer Theaterfest** performances by the **Pacific Conservatory of the Performing Arts** in Solvang's 700-seat outdoor Solvang Festival Theatre. For current information, call the theatre at 805/922-8313 or try the website, www.pcpa.org. And about four miles from the onetime Reagan ranch, the **Circle Bar B Guest Ranch** at 1800 Refugio Rd., 805/968-1113, www.circlebarb.com, stages dinner theater productions in an old barn (now a 100-seat theater) from May into November; call 805/967-1962 for current details and reservations.

For more information on attractions and events in and around Solvang, contact: **Solvang Conference and Visitors Bureau,** 1639 Copenhagen Dr., 805/688-6144 or 800/468-6765, www.solvangusa.com, or the **Solvang Chamber of Commerce,** 1595 Mission Dr., 805/688-0701, www.solvangcc.com.

Sights

A wander through Solvang offers thatched-roofed buildings with wooden roof storks, almost endless bakeries and gift shops, and surprises such as the **wind harp** near the **Bethania Lutheran Church** (church services are still conducted in Danish once each month). For the total two-mile experience, pick up a copy of the free *Self-Guided Walking Tour of Historic Solvang* wherever you find it around town. The **Wulff Windmill** on Fredensborg Canyon Road northwest of town is a historic landmark, once used to grind grain and pump water. For an appreciation of Danish culture, stop by the **Elverhøj Danish Heritage and Fine Arts Museum** on Elverjoy Way, 805/686-1211, an accurate representation of an 18th-century Danish farmhouse open Wed.–Sun. 1–4 P.M. The **Hans Christian Andersen Museum** upstairs in the Book Loft building, 1680 Mission Dr., 805/688-2052, is surprisingly engaging, with first-edition Andersen works, manuscripts, sketches, letters, and more. Perfect for picnics: **Hans Christian Andersen Park** off Atterdag Road, three blocks north of Mission Drive, complete with children's playground.

The Central Coast

But Solvang also serves up some surprises, like its **Solvang Vintage Motorcycle Museum,** just around the corner from the mission inside the onetime Brooks Brothers shop at 320 Alisal Rd., 805/686-9522, www.motosolvang.com, open weekends 11 A.M.–5 P.M. or by appointment, $5 admission (under 10 free). Displayed here is a selection of rare vintage cycles from the larger private collection of Virgil Elings. These might include a 1910 FN, a 1918 Thor, a 1926 Sunbeam, a 1946 Indian Chief, and one of the four Vincent Grey Flashes entered in 1950's Isle of Man TT race. Open for tours by reservation only, the free **Western Wear Museum,** 435 First St., 805/693-5000 or 805/688-3388, boasts 10 rooms of silver-screen cowboy regalia and other western wear themes; most fun for the kiddos is the "cowkids" room.

Mission Santa Inés just east of Solvang off Hwy. 246 (on Mission Drive), 805/688-4815, www.missionsantaines.com, was established in 1804, the 19th of the state's 21 missions and the last in the region. Get a more complete story on the tour of this rosy-tan mission with its copper roof tiles, attractive bell tower, original murals, and decent museum. It's open daily; small donation requested. Bingo and such are the main attractions at the otherwise almost invisible **Santa Ynez Indian Reservation,** on the highway in Santa Ynez. Also of interest is the **Santa Ynez Valley Historical Society Museum** on Sagunto Street in Santa Ynez, 805/688-7889, open Tues.–Sun. noon–4 P.M., a respectful look at local tradition. Also stop by the affiliated **Parks-Janeway Carriage House,** with its exceptional collection of horse-drawn buggies, carriages, carts, stagecoaches, vintage harnesses, and saddles.

Santa Ynez Valley

Horse ranches, whether specializing in Arabians, American paints, quarterhorses, thoroughbreds, Peruvian *paso finos* or other breeds, are big business in these parts. Monty Roberts of *The Man Who Listens to Horses* fame, is headquartered in the valley at 110-acre **Flag is Up Farms,** a thoroughbred racing and training ranch and event center.

Most Santa Ynez Valley back roads offer wonderful cycling, increasing numbers of small wineries, and sublime pastoral scenery. **Santa Barbara County wineries**—a cornucopia—are becoming big business, and a major regional attraction. For more on area wineries, see elsewhere in this chapter.

Nojoqui Falls County Park, www.sbparks .com, is about six miles south of Solvang on Alisal Road, a beautiful bike ride from town but more easily accessible from Nojoqui Pass on Hwy. 101. Some say the Chumash word *nojoqui* (nah-HO-wee) means "honeymoon," a possible reference to a tragic love story staged here in Chumash mythology. The park itself includes 84 acres of oaks, limestone cliffs, and a sparkling 168-foot vernal (spring only) waterfall, in addition to hiking trails and picnic and playground facilities.

Los Olivos, once a stage stop at the end of a narrow-gauge railroad rolling down from the north, is now a tiny Western revival town seemingly transplanted from the Mother Lode. If Los Olivos looks familiar, it may be because its main street served as a set for the TV series *Mayberry RFD.* Nowadays, the county's booming boutique wine trade is quite visible from here. Well worth a stop for wine aficionados is the **Los Olivos Wine & Spirits Emporium** on Grand Avenue south of town, 805/688-4409 or 888/729-4637, www.sbwines.com, which definitely purveys some of the area's finest. Also check out the **Wildling Museum—America's Wilderness in Art,** in town across from St. Mark's, 805/688-1082. The main attraction in nearby **Ballard** is the Ballard School, a classic little red schoolhouse still used for kindergarten classes. **Los Alamos** off Hwy. 101 northwest of Buellton is another spot in the road experiencing a Western-style wine country renaissance. From Los Alamos, take a spin through the Solomon Hills, hideout for the notorious anti-gringo *bandito* Salomon Pico, Pio Pico's cousin, a native Northern Californian and inspiration for the mythical Zorro of comic book and movie fame. Head south on Hwy. 101, and then turn left on little-traveled Alisos Canyon Road to Foxen Canyon Road, which leads past the granite **Frémont-Foxen Monument** commemorating John C. Frémont's bloodless December 1846 capture of Santa Barbara (with the help of local guide Benjamin Foxen). To take in more of the area's charms, try an alternate route to Hwy. 101 between Santa Barbara and the Solvang area—the beautiful but bustling backroads route (via Hwy. 154 just beyond Santa Ynez) over San Marcos Pass to Lake Cachuma.

Accommodations

Solvang has a number of nice hotels and motels; local visitor bureaus can offer suggestions. For just the basics (and a tip o' the cap to everyone's favorite prince of Denmark) head for the 15-room **Hamlet Motel,** 1532 Mission Dr., 805/688-4413 or 800/253-5033. Rates start at $60 for two. Surprisingly nice is the **Solvang Gardens Lodge,** 293 Alisal Rd., 805/688-4404, www.solvanggardens.com, Solvang's first motel, overlooking Alisal Ranch at the edge of town yet close to everything. Most rooms have recently been restyled; some feature full kitchens and/or living room. Rates are $50–150, with higher summer and weekend prices; a few rooms approach $200. Backyard gardens and "billiard cottage," too. For a storybook bed-and-breakfast stay right in town, try the nine-room **Storybook Inn,** 409 First St., 805/688-1703 or 800/786-7925, www.solvangstorybook.com. Each room is unique, named after a Hans Christian Andersen tale—Emperor's New Clothes, Ugly Duckling, The Nightingale—has a private bathroom and is furnished with attractive antiques and feather comforters. All have cable TV and VCRs, most have fireplaces. Two suites feature two-person whirlpool tubs. Rates, considerably higher on weekends, are $100–250, full breakfast and afternoon wine and cheese included. For Old World style with all the modern comforts, try the **Petersen Village Inn,** 1576 Mission Dr., 805/688-3121 or 800/321-8985, www.peterseninn.com, where rooms are $200–300 and suites (with fireplace and whirlpool tub) are $340.

Since 1946 the Solvang area's 10,000-acre cattle ranch, **The Alisal Guest Ranch,** has been one of California's premier resorts—this one offering absolute peace and simple luxury, with no phones, no television sets, and no radios. Though

the "cottages" here are quite comfortable, the real appeal is out of doors: long hikes, wrangler-led horseback rides, tennis, horseshoes, shuffleboard, croquet, badminton, volleyball, pool, table tennis, swimming, and just lounging around the pool. The Alisal even has its own lake. But some come just for the exceptional 18-hole golf course. Others, just to loaf in the mild climate—bestirring themselves only to head for the excellent ranch-house restaurant (breakfast and dinner are included; lunch is also available). The Alisal provides a children's program in summer. For summer, book well in advance. Rates aren't affordable for most real cowpokes, though, starting at $410 for a studio. Two-night minimum. For more information, contact The Alisal Ranch and Resort, 1054 Alisal Rd., 805/688-6411 or 800/425-4725 for reservations, www.alisal.com.

Other Solvang-area stays include the historic Western-French **Fess Parker's Wine Country Inn** in Los Olivos, formerly the Los Olivos Grand Hotel. The hotel's elegant but casual **Vintage Room** restaurant is open for lunch and dinner daily, breakfast on weekends. Rooms, with gas fireplaces, are $250–400, but ask about discounts and off-season specials. For more information and reservations, contact Fess Parker's Wine Country Inn, 2860 Grand Ave., 805/688-7788 or 800/446-2455, www.fessparker.com.

Quite special and also smack dab in the middle of Santa Barbara County wine country, is **The Ballard Inn** in Ballard, 2436 Baseline Ave., 805/688-7770 or 800/638-2466 for reservations, www.ballardinn.com, a contemporary two-story country inn with 15 rooms and all the amenities. Rates are $200–250. Breakfast is cooked to order, but don't forget the afternoon hors d'oeuvres and wine-tasting. The inn's dinner-only **Cafe Chardonnay** serves well-prepared fish, chicken, chops and other wine-enhancing possibilities.

The newest upscale wine country retreat is in Santa Ynez—the Victorian-styled yet very elegant, very contemporary **Santa Ynez Inn,** 3627 Sagunto St., 805/688-5588 or 800/643-5774, www.santaynezinn.com. The inn's 14 rooms offer all the luxuries, from fireplaces and Frette linens to whirlpool tubs and double steam showers. Complete fitness center includes a sauna and spa services—or take a soak in the outdoor heated whirlpool, sundeck and gardens. Rates start at $315, including full breakfast, afternoon tea, and evening wine and hors d'oeuvres.

Food

Solvang's Danish bakeries are legendary, and many visitors manage to eat reasonably well without going much farther. The **Solvang Bakery,** 460 Alisal Rd., 805/688-4939, is one good choice. There are lots of possibilities for the Danish smorgasbord experience, none better than **Bit o' Denmark,** 473 Alisal Rd., 805/688-5426, a Solvang classic—from the roast pork and sauerbraten to *frikadeller* (Danish meatballs) and pickled herring. Farm-style breakfast places and pancake houses are also big around town. **Paula's Pancake House,** 1531 Mission Dr. (at Fourth Place), 805/688-2867, serves breakfast all day— and all kinds of breakfast, from sourdough French toast and buttermilk or whole-wheat pancakes to three-egg and Egg Beaters omelettes.

Grand for gourmet sandwiches—the bread is fresh-baked daily—along with house-made soups and tasty salads is **Panino,** 475 First St., 805/688-0608, a sidewalk-café descendant of the original shop in Los Olivos (see below). Beer and wine. Open daily for lunch and dinner. Or try **New Frontiers Natural Foods** deli and juice bar, 1984 Old Mission Dr., 805/639-1746.

Another alternative to Danish tradition is the Cal-Ital **Café Angelica** bistro, 490 First St., 805/686-9970, where the menu might include salmon primavera, spicy grilled prawns, and filet mignon stuffed with mushrooms and bleu cheese. Nice local wine list. Open daily for lunch and dinner. And hey, Elmer Dills and *Gourmet* fans: **Cabernet Bistro,** 478 Fourth Pl., 805/693-1152, is a favorite Dills destination, for the roast duckling in particular, though there are many impressive "French comfort food" selections. Open Tues.–Sun. for dinner only. Reservations definitely advised.

The general consensus is that it's not as good as it once was, now that it's become a restaurant chain, but the original **Andersen's Pea Soup** split-pea soup palace is in nearby Buellton (you can't miss it on Hwy. 246), complete with its own Best Western motel. Buellton has other possibilities, though, including a best bet for breakfast: **Ellen's Danish Pancake House,** 272 Avenue of the Flags, 805/688-5312. Buellton also boasts the sibling of the original Hitching Post barbecue palace and steakhouse in Casmalia (see above), the unbelievably good, dinner-only **Hitching Post II,** 406 E. Hwy. 246, 805/688-0676, where the main course—steaks, chops, chicken, and more—is grilled over a red-oak fire, and the French fries are world-class. Be sure to appreciate the Hitching Post wines.

Some grand food destinations are scattered throughout surrounding vineyard country. The casual French country-style **Ballard Store** restaurant in block-long Ballard closed in late 1999, alas. But there are other neighborhood possibilities, including the small **Cafe Chardonnay** in the Ballard Inn, 2436 Baseline Rd., 805/688-7770, open for dinner Wed.–Sun. nights. Reservations are advisable. Or head to Los Olivos.

About five miles north of Solvang on Hwy. 154 in Los Olivos is historic Mattei's Tavern, once a train depot and stage stop. Though brothers Matt and Jeff Nichols got their start in Solvang, they finally arrived when in 2002 they reopened as relaxed, California steakhouse-style **M Brothers Restaurant at Mattei's Tavern** at 2350 Railway Ave., 805/688-4820, the best restaurant for many miles around. The changing menu offers what's best and freshest but usually includes grilled salmon and prime rib. Full bar. Open Tues.–Sun. for dinner. Reservations are a must. Another possibility is the elegant **Vintage Room** at Fess Parker's Wine Country Inn, 2860 Grand Ave., 805/688-7788, open for breakfast, lunch, and dinner. The relaxed Mediterranean-style **Los Olivos Café & Wine Merchant,** 2798 Grand Ave., 805/688-7265, at lunch serves delectable sandwiches, at dinner a selection of pizzas, pastas—such as chicken and portobello ravioli in white-wine cream sauce—and chicken dishes. Open daily for lunch and dinner. If the café's too crowded at lunch, swing by **Panino,** 2900 Grand Ave., 805/688-9304, for any one of the 30-something sandwiches, picnic supplies, and smoothies.

As elsewhere in the Santa Ynez Valley, in Santa Ynez proper the tried-and-true bumps up against the new, though wine-country sensibilities are fast outpacing cowboy-style steak and eggs. Still going strong, though, for basic 1950s breakfast and great burgers and fries is the **Longhorn Cof-** **fee Shop & Bakery,** 3687 Sagunto St., 805/688-5912. The very good **Trattoria Grappolo** in the same complex, 805/688-6899, is famous for its homemade pastas and wood-fired pizza.

Santa Barbara and Vicinity

Santa Barbara is beautiful, rich, and proud of it. Though her past is somewhat mysterious (she goes by the name "Santa Teresa" in the works of mystery writers Ross MacDonald and Sue Grafton), her presence hints at natural luck almost as incredible as her beauty, cosmic beneficence only briefly perturbed by unavoidable misfortune. If she were a flesh-and-blood woman, she would sway down the brick sidewalks, nose pointed upward, a satisfied smile on her face.

But such easy grace is no accident; Santa Barbara's beauty regimen is strict. She insists that the facades of all buildings (including McDonald's) reflect the Spanish style she favors. Death, decay, or other disarray in her environment displeases her; the only time she curses is when she spits out the words "developer," "development," and "oil companies," these latter responsible for the 1969 oil spill that fouled 20 miles of her pristine beaches. Her most peculiar personality quirk is that she secretly believes she lives in Northern California, despite social intercourse with everything Southern Californian.

Santa Barbara is generous with her gifts, and she has everything: beautiful beaches and understated, stark chaparral slopes, colleges and universities, a celebrated arts and entertainment scene, fine restaurants (more restaurants per capita than any other U.S. city, in fact) and luxury resorts, trendy boutiques, antique shops. Though her sun shines brightest on the area's celebrity residents—among them, in recent history, Jeff Bridges, Carole Burnett, Julia Child, Michael Douglas, Steve Martin, Priscilla Presley, and John Travolta—she magnanimously allows the middle class to bask in her glow. Still, there are so many celebrities, so many extremely wealthy people here that in 2001, when Oprah Winfrey wrote a personal check for $50 million

to buy a 40-acre estate in Montecito, hardly anyone raised an eyebrow.

Yet the shadow side to Santa Barbara's radiance is the basically ugly belief that she must shun any and all things unsightly. Poverty is unsightly and Santa Barbara doesn't want to see it. Thus local laws prohibit the homeless from sleeping on public sidewalks, though that certainly hasn't made the problem disappear.

THE LAND

The city itself faces south, spreading back toward the dry but dignified Santa Ynes Mountains like a Spanish fan. The Channel Islands offshore protect Santa Barbara's sublime coastal bay and unruffled beaches. Despite the genuine devastation of the 1969 oil spill here, the gooey blobs of tar on shoreline rocks and white sand are primarily natural, from Monterey shale petroleum deposits hundreds of feet thick in some areas. Near Santa Barbara, earthquake fault lines run east-west, like the mountains whose deformed rock formations hint at the intensity of underground earth movement.

The palms and eucalyptus trees—in fact *most* of the plants commonly growing along Santa Barbara streets and beaches—are introduced species. Native plants in and around Santa Barbara today include live oaks, pines, and California bay trees, also toyon, greasewood, manzanita, and other chaparral shrubs. Shadier valleys and grassy hillsides are dazzling with wildflowers in spring. About 400 species of birds are found in the Santa Barbara region. The most common "city birds" include the western mockingbird, California jays, house finches, sparrows, and hummingbirds. At the beach, sandpipers, terns, gulls, and other seabirds are common. Migrating ducks, geese, and other waterfowl visit the city's lake refuge.

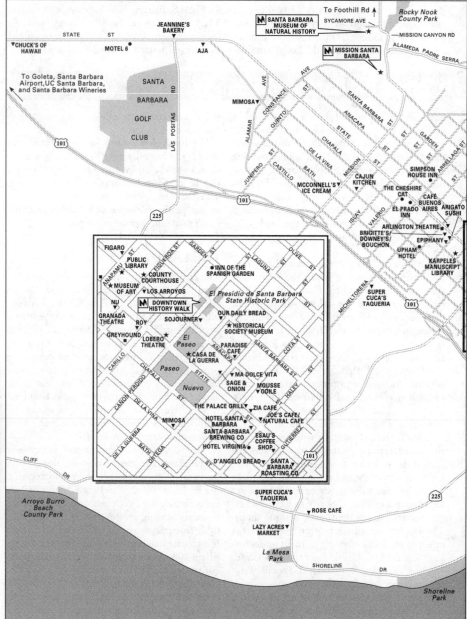

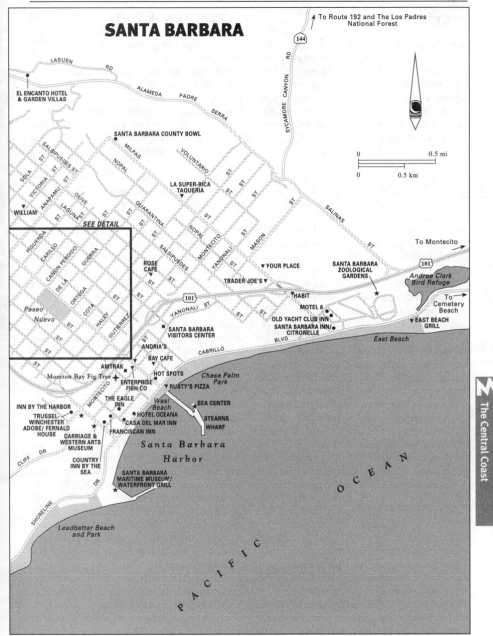

SANTA BARBARA

To Route 192 and The Los Padres
National Forest

144

LASUEN RD

EL ENCANTO HOTEL
& GARDEN VILLAS

ALAMEDA

PADRE

SERRA

SYCAMORE CANYON RD

SANTA BARBARA COUNTY BOWL

MILPAS

VOLUNTARIO

NOPAL

LA SUPER-RICA
TAQUERIA

0   0.5 mi

0   0.5 km

SALSIPUEDES ST

SOLA ST

VICTORIA ST

ANAPAMU ST

OLIVE ST

LAGUNA ST

WILLIAM

QUARANTINA ST

SALINAS ST

To Montecito

SEE DETAIL

FIGUEROA

CARILLO

CANON PERDIDO

DE LA GUERRA

ORTEGA

COTA

HALEY

GUTIERREZ

Paseo
Nuevo

ROSE
CAFE

SALSIPUEDES ST

MONTECITO ST

YANONALI ST

MASON

YOUR PLACE

SANTA BARBARA
ZOOLOGICAL
GARDENS

Andree Clark
Bird Refuge

TRADER JOE'S

HABIT

MOTEL 6

101

YANONALI ST

OLD YACHT CLUB INN

SANTA BARBARA INN/
CITRONELLE

CABRILLO

BLVD

To
Cemetery
Beach

EAST BEACH
GRILL

East Beach

101

SANTA BARBARA
VISITORS CENTER

ANDRIA'S

BAY CAFE

AMTRAK

Moreton Bay Fig Tree

ENTERPRISE
FISH CO

HOT SPOTS

RUSTY'S PIZZA

Chase Palm
Park

MONTECITO

THE EAGLE
INN

West
Beach

SEA CENTER

INN BY THE HARBOR

TRUSSEL-
WINCHESTER
ADOBE/ FERNALD
HOUSE

HOTEL OCEANA

CASA DEL MAR INN

FRANCISCAN INN

CARRIAGE &
WESTERN ARTS
MUSEUM

CLIFF DR

COUNTRY
INN BY THE
SEA

STEARNS
WHARF

Santa Barbara

Harbor

SANTA BARBARA
MARITIME MUSEUM/
WATERFRONT GRILL

SHORELINE

Leadbetter Beach
and Park

PACIFIC

OCEAN

The Central Coast

© AVALON TRAVEL PUBLISHING, INC.

HISTORY

Before there even was a Santa Barbara, before the Bronze Age, an ancient Oak Grove people lived here. Then later, equally mysterious Hunting People arrived with improved technology: arrows, clubs, spearheads, and tools used for digging shellfish. These hunters and gatherers slowly merged their society with still later arrivals to become the industrious Chumash, whose few descendants today live inland and along nearby coasts.

As with many native California peoples the central focus of the Chumash was spiritual, though they nonetheless found time for their industries: boat-making, fishing, and trading with island residents across the channel. Only remnants of the rich ancient Chumash culture remain—baskets, beads, charms, and money—many of these items now in museums. Forced into Christianity by zealous Spanish missionaries, the Chumash near Santa Barbara were all but wiped out by foreign diseases, their own social and spiritual decline, and alcoholism.

Despite its aura of established comfort, Santa Barbara has suffered two major earthquakes (the first flattened the original mission), a tidal wave, direct enemy attack during World War II, an ecologically devastating offshore oil spill, and fires—many, many fires. Vizcaíno was the first to Europeanize the place. He named the channel after Saint Barbara in 1602, though the name "Santa Barbara Virgin and Martyr" didn't have much to stick to until it was later applied to the presidio in 1782 and the mission four years later.

For many years, aristocratic Spanish families basked in their own gentility here, making Santa Barbara the social capital of Alta California even if Monterey was designated the political capital. With mission secularization, Santa Barbara high society became landed gentry—but only briefly. The grand ranchos all but dried up, littered with cattle bones picked clean by condors and vultures during the devastating drought of the 1860s. Upstart Americans then snatched up the land and with it, local political power. In the late 1880s the industrialists arrived along with old money, banks, brokerage houses, and the South-

ern Pacific Railroad. When oil was discovered offshore in the 1890s and the first offshore oil well started pumping near Summerland in 1896, they kept coming.

No sooner had the Montecito mansions and Santa Barbara power palaces settled onto their new foundations than they were removed from those foundations—suddenly, shockingly. From the present-day perspective the earthquake of June 1925, which left the city in ruins, was the best thing that ever happened to Santa Barbara. During the city's reconstruction, a quickly formed architectural review board declared that new buildings in Santa Barbara would henceforth be Mediterranean in design and style, appropriate to the area's balmy climate and sympathetic to its Hispanic cultural heritage. The town's trademark old Spanish California adobe look—cream-colored stucco, sloping red-tile roofs, and wrought-iron grillwork—is a unified effect of fairly recent origin.

Santa Barbara had barely rebuilt itself when a Japanese submarine surfaced offshore in 1942 to attack an oil refinery nearby. Oil was the issue again in 1969, when a massive spill from an offshore oil rig blackened 20 miles of beaches in and around Santa Barbara, killing thousands of birds and destroying the local marine ecology. That event fired up ocean lovers all over California and helped launch the successful 1972 California Coastal Protection Initiative, which created the California Coastal Commission to protect the coast as well as the public's access. Starting in the 1980s, a seven-year drought forced Santa Barbara residents to drain their swimming pools and paint their dried-up lawns green. (Water conservation is a serious concern in these parts.) Then, in 1990, the devastating Painted Cave arson fire killed one person and torched 4,900 acres, racing through the chaparral near San Marcos Pass and then seaward, down into the residential canyons of Goleta and northern Santa Barbara. Sometimes change is a challenge to survival.

Yet even change-wary Santa Barbara welcomes innovation, as it did in the early 1990s when CalTrans coughed up $58 million to widen U.S. Hwy. 101 through the city to six lanes, remove all four freeway stoplights, and route crosstown traffic either over or under the freeway instead of across it—thus eliminating one of California's most complicated and nightmarish traffic bottlenecks. Innovation is also a byword in the local business community, increasingly high-tech, increasingly cutting-edge. The neighborhood is also increasingly inaccessible for just plain folks, with average homes going for well over $1 million.

SIGHTS DOWNTOWN

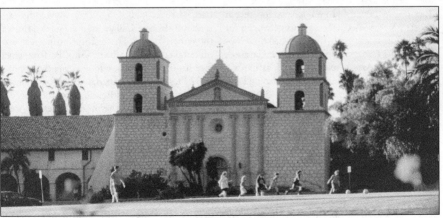M Mission Santa Barbara

Since the founding of Mission Santa Barbara in 1786 at the upper end of what is now Laguna Street, the altar light has never been extinguished—and that's saying something. Originally a collection of simple adobes, Santa Barbara's "Queen of the Missions" and California's 10th was named for a Roman virgin beheaded by her pagan father. The mission was subsequently all but flattened by the 1812 earthquake, the same year the town on the coastal plain below was all but swept away by a huge tidal wave. Another earthquake, in 1925, did its best to bring the mission down.

The Queen of the Missions still stands—indeed queenly, presiding over the city and sea below with two massive squared towers, arcades, and domed belfries. The dignified Ionic columns, arched entrance, and double-paneled doors add to the mission's grace. The genesis of the city's original water system is also here, an impressive network of aqueducts, filter house, and Spanish gristmill. The larger of the mission's two reservoirs, circa 1806, is still in use by the city, and the 1807 mission dam is now part of the Santa Barbara Botanic Garden just up the canyon. The **museum** tells the mission's story with history displays, photographs, and a reconstructed kitchen. Self-guided tours are offered daily 9 A.M.–5 P.M., $4 (children under age 12 free). For details or more information, stop by the mission at 2201 Laguna St., call 805/682-4149 or see www.sbmission.org/history.

Downtown History Walk

Most remnants of Santa Barbara history are downtown. Many surviving adobes, now private residences or office buildings, are included on downtown's self-guided **Red Tile Walking Tour,** outlined in the visitor guide and also available on the website. For something more, sign on with the Architectural Foundation of Santa Barbara's "Sabado y Domingo" **Historic Downtown Walking Tours,** docent-led strolls ($5) through downtown. The Saturday tour meets at 10 A.M. in De La Guerra Plaza, at the steps of City Hall, and explores historic adobes, the Lobero Theater, Meridian Studios, and more. The Sunday tour meets at 10 A.M. at the downtown public library (see below), and examines the art and architecture of downtown Santa Barbara

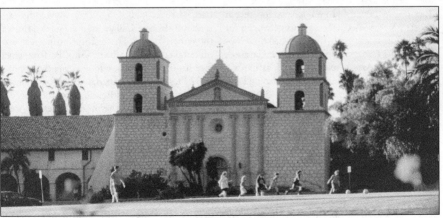

BILL ZELDIS/THE SANTA BARBARA CONFERENCE & VISITORS BUREAU

Queen of the Missions

as the city rebuilt itself following the devastating 1925 earthquake. For more information (recorded) on either tour, call 805/965-6307.

Downtown visitors, please note: Santa Barbara is quite generous with its downtown parking, thanks to area merchants. Park in any of 12 downtown lots (also the lot at the Amtrak depot) and the first 75 minutes is free, $1 per hour after that. The incorrigibly cheap could, conceivably, move their cars from lot to lot at precise intervals and stay downtown all day for free. But considering neighborhood generosity, who wants to be a cheapskate?

Get oriented at the **Santa Barbara Historical Society Museum,** 136 E. De La Guerra, 805/966-1601, www.santabarbaramuseum.com, an impressive regional history museum featuring everything from antique toys to vaquero-style saddles within its collection of period costumes, documents, and Santa Barbara memorabilia. The museum is open Tues.–Sat. 10 A.M.–5 P.M., Sunday noon–5 P.M. Guided tours are offered; call for details. Admission is free, though nonmembers must pay for use of the historical society's associated **Gledhill Library,** which includes 50,000 historic photos; library tours are offered on the first Saturday of every month. The museum's adjacent 19th-century **Casa Covarrubias** and **Historic Adobe** also offer a peek into the past. (Museum docents can also tell you about the society's restored **Trussell-Winchester Adobe** and the 1862 Queen Anne **Fernald House,** located together at 412-414 W. Montecito St. and usually open for guided tours on Saturday, 1–3 P.M. Call 805/966-1601 for information. Nearby is the **Carriage and Western Arts Museum,** 129 Castillo St., 805/962-2353, at the north end of Pershing Park, open by donation Mon.–Sat. 8 A.M.–3 P.M. and Sunday 1–4 P.M.)

The walking tour's traditional starting point is the 1929 **Santa Barbara County Courthouse,** a must-see destination one block from State Street at Anapamu and Anacapa, 805/962-6464. Designed by William Mooser III as an L-shaped Spanish-Moorish castle, its spacious interiors decorated with murals, mosaics, ceramic Tunisian tile, and handcarved wood, this is quite possibly the most beautiful public building anywhere

in California. County supervisors meet in the Assembly Room, with its romantic four-wall historic mural created by a Cecil B. DeMille set designer, and sit in comfortable leather-covered, brass-studded benches and chairs under handmade iron chandeliers. The spectacular views of the city from the clock tower or the *mirador* balcony alone are worth the trip. The courthouse is open 8 A.M.–5 P.M. on weekdays, 9–5 on weekends and holidays, with free guided tours offered at 2 P.M. Mon.–Sat., also at 10:30 A.M. on Monday, Tuesday, and Friday.

Across the street at 40 E. Anapamu St. sits the stunning Spanish-style **Santa Barbara Public Library,** 805/962-7653, with its grand Peake-Warshaw murals and both the Faulkner Gallery and Townley Room art displays. It's open Mon.–Thurs. 10 A.M.–9 P.M., Friday and Saturday 10 A.M.–5:30 P.M., and Sunday 1–5 P.M. Well worth a stop in the other direction is the Santa Barbara outpost of the unusual private **Karpeles Manuscript Library,** 21 W. Anapamu, 805/962-5322, a free museum featuring an extensive collection of both original and facsimile manuscripts—music, letters, maps, illustrations, books, treaties, and such—including the original draft of the U.S. Constitution's Bill of Rights. It's open daily 10 A.M.–4 P.M., closed on Christmas.

An ambitious reconstruction of **El Presidio de Santa Barbara State Historic Park,** 123 E. Cañon Perdido St. (between Anacapa and Santa Barbara Streets), 805/965-0093, www.sbthp.org, is now under way. Call to arrange a guided tour of the entire "park." The restoration project was undertaken by the private Santa Barbara Trust for Historic Preservation to re-create the original 1782 Presidio Real, imperial Spain's last military outpost in California. Before restoration began, all that remained of the original presidio were two crumbling adobe buildings; one, El Cuartel, is Santa Barbara's oldest building and the second oldest in the state. Started in 1961, to date the project has restored two buildings and reconstructed five. Exploration and restoration are ongoing. Stop by the **La Casa de la Guerra Museum,** 11–19 E. De la Guerra, the onetime home of the Presidio's fifth commander, open Thurs.–Sun. noon–4 P.M.

Downtown Art Walk

Along with history, downtown offers it own perspectives on the history of art at the **Santa Barbara Museum of Art,** 1130 State St. (between Anapamu and Figueroa), 805/963-4364, www.sbmuseart.org, an outstanding regional museum that also attracts impressive traveling exhibits. The permanent collection here boasts 19th-century Impressionists including Chagall, Matisse, and Monet; O'Keeffe, Eakins, Hooper, and other major American artists; and an eclectic assortment of classical antiquities, Asian art, photography, prints, and drawings. But don't miss the 1932 David Alfaro Siqueiros mural *Portrait of Mexico Today.* Good bookstore and onsite café. The museum is open Tues.–Sat. 11 A.M.–5 P.M. (until 9 P.M. on Friday) and Sunday noon–5 P.M. Docents guide free gallery tours at 1 P.M. Tours of special exhibitions are offered Wednesday and Saturday only, at noon. Admissions is $7 adults, $5 seniors, $4 students with ID and children ages 6–17. The museum is free to everyone, though, every Thursday and on the first Sunday of every month (under age 6 always free).

Confusing the line between real and faux history are downtown's many stylish shops—art galleries galore and **Brinkerhoff Avenue,** famous for its antiques—and, now, two shopping centers. **El Paseo,** California's first shopping center and the originator of the city's distinctive architectural "look," is a clustered two-story collection of Spanish colonial revival shops built in the early 1920s around courtyards, fountains, and gardens (enter from State Street, near De La Guerra). The stylish new **Paseo Nuevo** mission-style mall, anchored by Nordstrom and The Broadway between State and Chapala Streets and Ortega and Cañon Perdido, offers upscale shops and shopping. Particularly worthwhile here is the 4,500-square-foot **Contemporary Arts Forum,** 653 Paseo Nuevo, 805/966-5373, www.sbcaf.org, an adventurous contemporary arts gallery and exhibition space often sponsoring traveling shows, special exhibits, and lectures.

OTHER SIGHTS

The **Moreton Bay Fig Tree** at Chapala and Montecito Streets (where Hwy. 101 rolls by) is considered the nation's largest. Affectionately called "the old rubber tree" by some, though it produces neither rubber nor figs, this Australian

NIK WHEELER/SANTA BARBARA CONFERENCE & VISITORS BUREAU

Stearns Wharf

The Central Coast

native is large enough (they say) to shelter 10,000 people from the noonday sun. Nearby is the Santa Barbara harbor area, though the city's "bay" is little more than a curvaceous beach front. One of the best ways to tour the area is by bike, following the three-mile paved, stunningly scenic **Cabrillo Bike Path,** which stretches from the harbor to the zoo then on to the Andree Clark Bird Refuge. Rent bikes (built for one or two), three-wheelers, and pedalinas at **Cycles-4-Rent,** a block from the wharf at 101 State St., 888/405-2453, www.cycles4rent.com.

Stearns Wharf at the foot of State Street, 805/564-5518, www.stearnswharf.org, is the longest and oldest working wood wharf in California, offering pier fishing as well as shops, restaurants. Particularly worthwhile here when it reopens following a $6.5 million expansion (late 2004, at last report) is the new, improved **Sea Center,** a branch of the Santa Barbara Museum of Natural History, www.sbnature.org. The new center will still emphasize the marine life of the Santa Barbara Channel, just offshore, but in a hands-on facility twice its original size, designed to look, feel, and function like a working marine biology and ocean science laboratory.

To the east of the pier is pleasant **East Beach,** buffered from busy Cabrillo Boulevard by the manicured lawns, footpaths, and bike trails of expanded **Chase Palm Park,** which stretches along the north side of Cabrillo from Garden Street to Calle César Chávez. At the east end of East Beach is **Cemetery Beach,** a popular nude beach (one of four in the area). Also reasonably secluded is Montecito's **Butterfly Beach,** below the Four Seasons Biltmore Hotel. West of Stearns Wharf is the municipal harbor, protected by a long stone breakwater, and **West Beach.**

Santa Barbara Museum of Natural History

The best of natural Santa Barbara and vicinity is on display at the exceptional Santa Barbara Museum of Natural History, two blocks north of the mission at 2559 Puesta Del Sol Rd., 805/682-4711, www.sbnature.org. This Spanish-style cluster of buildings and courtyards includes excellent exhibits on the Chumash and other indigenous peoples, collections of fossils, geology displays, nature exhibits (including a busy beehive), even some original Audubon lithographs. In addition to the museum's classes on every natural history topic under the sun, there's a planetarium and observatory here, too, offering a popular Sunday afternoon program. But don't forget the art of nature. The John and Peggy Maximus Gallery, a fairly recent addition, collects some 1,100 natural history prints, the work of American and European artists and illustrators from the 17th to 19th centuries. The museum also sponsors a year-round schedule of films and special events—including monarch butterfly tours in January (by reservation) and the Wine Festival in August. On the way in or out, stop outside near the parking lot to appreciate the 72-foot-long skeleton of a blue whale, recently restored. The natural history museum is open 10 A.M.–5 P.M. daily. Closed Thanksgiving, Christmas, New Year's Day; the museum also closes early on Christmas Eve, and on the first Friday in August (noon) for Fiesta. Admission is $6 adults, $5 seniors and students (ages 13–17), and $4 children age 12 and under. Free for everyone on the first Sunday of every month. Nearby and perfect for an almost-country picnic is Rocky Nook County Park.

Santa Barbara Maritime Museum

Then there's the promising new Santa Barbara Maritime Museum, 805/962-8404, www.sbmm.org, situated at the harbor entrance, in the Waterfront Center (the Old Naval Reserve Center). Main floor exhibits explore navigation history and technology of the seafaring native Chumash people, including a 23-foot hand-made wooden tomol, or canoe, as well as European explorers, otter and seal hunting, whaling, the hides, tallow, and early shipping trades, and impressive ship models. Histories of the offshore Channel Islands and regional oil drilling are also depicted. Upstairs is the state-of-the-art Munger Theater, disguised as a ship's hull, and many more displays, from the shipwreck exhibit and the story of the Loughead F-1 Flying Boat to signal flags, local military history (complete with operating periscope), and sailing and yachting exhibits.

Open Thurs.–Tues. 11 A.M.–5 P.M. (until 6 P.M. in summer). General admission is $5. Farther west are **Leadbetter Beach** and **Shoreline Park,** also tiny **La Mesa Park** and **Arroyo Burro Beach,** popular for swimming and surfing.

Santa Barbara Botanic Garden

The 65-acre Santa Barbara Botanic Garden, 1212 Mission Canyon Rd., 805/682-4726, www.santa barbarabotanicgarden.org, is "dedicated to the study of California's native plants." Too many people miss this natural Santa Barbara treasure. Plants native to Santa Barbara and vicinity are the main event (don't miss the spectacular spring wildflowers) but cacti, other succulents, even redwoods are at home in the gardens here. Good gift shop—particularly popular with gardeners and plant lovers. Lectures, classes, trips, and special events are often scheduled, and docent-guided tours are offered daily at 2 P.M., also on Thursday, Saturday, and Sunday at 10:30 A.M. Best, though, is showing up when nothing's going on and just wandering the grounds—a stroll that can easily become a brisk five-mile hike. The botanic garden is open daily 9 A.M.–sunset (until 4 P.M. in winter, 5 P.M. in summer), an hour later on weekends. Admission is $6 adults, $4 seniors, $3 teens, $1 children (under age 5 free). Donations and membership support are always appreciated.

Other Gardens and Sanctuaries

Overlooking West Beach is the **Santa Barbara Zoological Gardens,** a onetime estate at 500 Niños Dr. (off E. Cabrillo Boulevard), 805/962-6310 (recorded) or 805/962-5339, www.santa barbarazoo.org, with more than 600 exotic animals in almost natural habitats—one of the best smaller zoos anywhere. Santa Barbara's zoo has an outstanding walk-through "aquatic aviary," a portholed Sealarium, and islands for squirrel monkeys and gibbons. Nocturnal Hall, a walk-in tropical aviary on the outside, houses nocturnal animals within. Also here: a peaceful picnic area, small botanic garden, farmyard, Wild West playground, and zany mini-trains. The zoo is open daily 10 A.M.–5 P.M. (closed Thanksgiving and Christmas), adults $9, children and seniors $7 (under age 2 free), parking $3. The **Andree Clark**

Bird Refuge is a landscaped 50-acre preserve of reclaimed marshland at the east end of E. Cabrillo Boulevard adjoining the zoo, with freshwater fowl, also bike trails and footpaths. Guided refuge tours are sometimes offered by the local Audubon Society chapter.

UC AND GOLETA

Just up the coast from Santa Barbara proper on a beautiful stretch of beachfront property in Goleta is the **University of California at Santa Barbara** campus, 805/893-8000, www.ucsb.edu. Bordered on two sides by the Pacific Ocean, miles of white-sand beaches, and a natural lagoon, the campus itself is a beauty. Noted for its comprehensive environmental studies program—one of the first of its kind in the nation—and its engineering, education, and scientific instrumentation programs, the university gained national attention in the late 1960s and early '70s for anti–Vietnam War activities in the adjacent "student ghetto" of **Isla Vista,** still jam-packed with stucco apartment buildings and bustling with student-oriented businesses and activities. The university is also known for its surfers, always a substantial presence on campus.

Diversions in nearby **Goleta** include the free **South Coast Railroad Museum,** 300 N. Los Carneros Rd., 805/964-3540, www.goleta depot.org, featuring a restored 1901 Southern Pacific depot, antiques and artifacts, a 300-square-foot model railroad, miniature train rides, and handcar rides (small fee for both rides). Open Wed.–Sun. 1–4 P.M. Next door is the historic Victorian **Stow House** and associated Sexton Museum, 805/964-4407, open weekends only 2–4 P.M. (museum closed in January, on rainy days, and on Thanksgiving and Christmas), though the grounds are open year-round. Popular local events staged at Stow House include the annual **California Lemon Festival** in October. Another area attraction is the two-acre **Santa Barbara Orchid Estate,** 1250 Orchid Dr., 805/967-1284, www.sborchid.com, with more than 100 varieties on display (plants and cut flowers available for sale), an entire acre of them under glass.

MONTECITO

The balmy beaches, yacht harbor, and exclusive wooded estates of unincorporated Montecito, just east of Santa Barbara, seem tailor-made for the people behind commercial trademarks such as DuPont, Fleischmann, Pillsbury, and Stetson— and they were.

Especially worth seeing in Montecito is surreal 37-acre **Lotusland,** created by the flamboyant Madame Ganna Walska, thwarted opera singer and compulsive marrier of millionaires. Here you'll find the world's finest private collection of cycads (relatives of pine trees that look like palms), also cacti and succulents, a luxuriant fern garden lacking only prehistoric dinosaurs, an eccentric "Japanese" garden, a fantastic aloe-and-abalone-shell "forest," weeping euphorbias, 20-foot-tall elephant's feet, lily and lotus ponds, bromeliads, orchids, and roses. Casual or drop-in garden tours are not possible, but the gardens are open by reservation to those interested in horticulture or botany. Make reservations for the two-hour guided toursby contacting the Ganna Walska Lotusland Foundation, 695 Ashley Rd., 805/969-3767, www.lotusland.org. Because the house and gardens are in a residential area, there is an annual limit on visitors (no drive-by lookie-loos, please; such voyeurism upsets the neighbors, and you can't see anything anyway). Regular tours are offered mid-February through mid-November, Wed.–Sat. at 10 A.M. and 1:30 P.M. Beginning on or about November 15, reservations are taken for the following year—and the entire year's tours are often booked by January 15, though later in the year you can always hope for a cancellation. Tours are $15 for adults and older children. Special, abbreviated tours, on which younger children are welcome, are offered every Thursday and also on the second Saturday of every month. Special admission is $8 for children ages 2–9, free under age 2.

If you somehow miss Lotusland, don't miss the 1925 Spanish colonial revival **Casa del Herrero,** rich with Italian and Spanish antiquities. George Fox Steedman's onetime estate, Casa del Herrero is open for guided 90-minute tours of the house, workshop, and gardens on Wednesday (or Thursday) and Saturday at 10 A.M. and 2 P.M., by advance reservation only. The fee is $10 per person, children under 10 not permitted. For more details and reservations, call 805/565-5653 or see www.casadelherrero.com.

SUMMERLAND AND CARPINTERIA

Summerland and Carpinteria just south along the coast are still great beach towns—undiscovered, almost, though it's almost impossible to say that about any locale in California these days. Summerland is the site of California's first offshore oil drilling in the 1890s. The Spiritualists, a sect known for its séances and merriment, settled on former mission lands here in 1888— thus the locals' derogatory nickname, "Spookville." Most architectural evidence of Summerland's past was bulldozed during the 1925 construction of Hwy. 101 and 15 years later, when the highway became a freeway. Summerland offers a county park, a nice beach, and a boom in antique shops, restaurants, and bed-and-breakfast inns, but the town's most entertaining feature somehow disappeared in the last decade—the sign reading: Population 3,001, Feet Above Sea Level 280, Established 1870, Total: 5,151. Following Lillie Avenue east (it becomes Villa Real) leads to the **Santa Barbara Polo and Racquet Club,** where exhibitions and tournaments are scheduled on Sunday, sometimes on Saturday, spring through fall.

Carpinteria farther south was once a Chumash village. Cabrillo stumbled upon it in August of 1542, and Portolá later called it Carpinteria or "carpenter shop" because of the natives' industrious canoe-making. People say **Carpinteria State Beach,** a onetime bean field now complete with large campground and hiker/biker campsites, is the "safest beach in the world" because the surf breaks 2,000 feet out from shore, beyond the reef, and there's no undertow. The day-use fee is $8. Rincon Point is renowned among surfers. Other local attractions include the free **Carpinteria Valley Museum of History,** 956 Maple Ave., 805/684-3112 (free, but donations appreciated). Carpinteria's main streets also boast an abundance of antique shops. Come in early October for the town's huge **California Avocado Festival,** www.avofest.com.

For more information about Summerland and Carpinteria, contact the **Carpinteria Valley Chamber of Commerce,** 5285 Carpinteria Ave., 805/684-5479 or 800/563-6900, www.carpcofc.com.

From south of Carpinteria, Hwy. 150 leads to Lake Casitas and to Ojai, made famous as a setting for Shangri-La in the movie *Lost Horizon.*

RECREATION

If it's remotely related to sky, sea, sand, or sand-trap, Santa Barbara has it. Popular local recreational pursuits vary from in-line skating, strolling, and cycling to sailing and scuba diving, from kayaking to lawn bowling, hiking and horseback riding to polo. Winter whale-watching tours, windsurfing, golf—a major regional pastime, judging from the number of world-class courses scattered throughout Santa Barbara County—and tennis also keep people out and about.

For a complete listing of boat and charter rentals, also organized tours in and around Santa Barbara, stop by local visitor centers—or consult the current phone book. An official concessionaire for trips to offshore Channel Islands National Park is Santa Barbara's own **Truth Aquatics,** 301 W. Cabrillo Blvd., 805/962-1127 or 800/927-4688, www.truthaquatics.com, an award-winning scuba diving fleet that also offers island hiking, camping, and natural history tours. If you'd rather shove off from Ventura, connect with **Island Packer Cruises** in Ventura (see Channel Islands National Park, below). The **Santa Barbara Museum of Natural History,** 805/682-4711, www.sbnature.org, also offers whale-watching tours, along with **Condor Cruises,** 805/882-0088 or 888/779-4253, www.condorcruises.com, and **Captain Don's Harbor Tours,** 805/969-5217, www.captdon.com.

CARPINTERIA.COM PHOTO GALLERY/SANTA BARBARA CONFERENCE & VISITORS BUREAU

The Central Coast

Carpinteria Beach

Beaches

Attractions along the coast north of Santa Barbara and Goleta include three spectacular state "beach" parks. Farthest north is **Gaviota State Park,** about 22 miles north of Goleta, a small beach area that also includes 3,000 associated acres of chaparral, campsites, picnic areas, hiking trails, and hike-in hot springs. Surf fishing is popular here, and there's a small pier on the beach's west end. Day-use parking is beyond the Southern Pacific railroad trestle. Family campsites are available, too, most of the year. The next beach downcoast and perhaps loveliest of all, just 12 miles north of Goleta, is breathtaking **Refugio State Beach,** a white-sand cove fringed by palm trees near Refugio Creek and protected from the pounding surf by a rocky point. Refugio offers more picnic tables, and more campsites—just five facing the beach—plus a glorious group camp. Two miles east, connected by paved bike path to Refugio, is **El Capitan State Beach,** with sandy beach, tidepools, picnicking, tree-shaded El Capitan Creek, and both en-route and family campsites. From the bluffs, stairs lead down to the beach. All three beaches are open daily from dusk until dark for day use ($8 per vehicle). For current information on all three beaches, call 805/968-1033. Make camping reservations—essential in summer and on weekends—call ReserveAmerica at 800/444-7275 or see www.reserveamerica.com.

Wildlife

About 18 miles northwest of Santa Barbara, on the way to Solvang and Santa Ynez via Hwy. 154, is **Cachuma Lake,** the largest manmade lake in Southern California, a 3,200-acre, trout-stocked, oak woodland reservoir open for day use 6 A.M.–10 P.M. daily. Stop by the **Cachuma Nature Center** to get oriented. Also a county park, Cachuma is ripe for year-round recreation: boating, sailing, hiking, and swimming in pools (Memorial Day through Labor Day only). No "body contact" with the lake is allowed, since this is the city of Santa Barbara's primary water supply. Fishing is a year-round draw, as is bird-watching; more than 275 bird species have been spotted here. A major attraction here is the two-hour **Eagle Cruise** led by the park's naturalist, of-

fered only November to March when the bald eagles arrive for their own winter respite ($15 adults, $7 children, by reservation only). The rest of the year cruises emphasize wildflower, wildlife, and birds. The lake has pleasant picnic areas and developed campsites for both tents and RVs, also group camps. Day use is $6 per vehicle ($3 per dog, proof of rabies vaccination required). Camping and yurt stays available. And a quarter will get you a three-minute hot shower. For more information, contact: Cachuma Lake Recreation Area, HC 58–Hwy. 154, 805/686-5054 (recorded) or 805/686-5050 for information, weekend events, and Fish Watch, www.sbparks.com. Remote **Gibraltar Reservoir** off Paradise and Camuesa Roads farther south is open for long-weekend trout fishing January through March, but reservations and permits from the city of Santa Barbara are necessary.

Also worth seeing, for dedicated back-roaders, is **Chumash Painted Cave State Historic Park** off Painted Cave Road, with its characteristic black, red, and yellow pictographs, Chumash religious drawings and depictions of fishing dating back to the 1600s. Gaze in through the iron grating now in place to discourage vandals, and call 805/733-3713 for further information. Parking on the road's narrow shoulder accommodates only one or two cars (definitely no trailers or RVs).

ENTERTAINMENT AND EVENTS

Local bookstores, cafés, and college campuses boast their fair share of poetry readings and other literary events. The **Santa Barbara Writers' Conference,** www.sbwc.org, which in the past has attracted popular scribes including Ray Bradbury, Christopher Buckley, Amy Tan, and Neil Simon, convenes in June. Traditionally held at Miramar, currently closed, the conference is held at Westmont College in the hills of Montecito. Come in late September for the **Santa Barbara Book & Author Festival,** www.sbbookfestival.org, highlighting everything from mystery and suspense to poetry and children's literature.

Public concerts have a long history in Santa Barbara. Native peoples greeted Portolá and com-

NIK WHEELER/SANTA BARBARA CONFERENCE & VISITORS BUREAU

I Madonnari Italian Street Painting Festival

pany not with arrows, after all, but with "weird noises" on bowl flutes and whistles. Such tradition is perhaps why the small city of Santa Barbara offers an astounding array of arts events—including more concerts per capita than anyplace else in the country, from the classics and jazz to rock and pop.

Performances by the **Santa Barbara Symphony,** 805/898-9626, www.thesymphony.org, and Montecito's **Music Academy of the West,** 805/969-4726, www.musicacademy.org, are held throughout the year, throughout the community. The symphony holds its summer concerts at the Santa Barbara County Bowl, its regular series performances at the spectacular Arlington Center for the Performing Arts (for more on these venues, see below). The academy's eight-week summer music festival, held at various venues in Santa Barbara and at a private estate in Montecito, is one of the world's most acclaimed. The **Los Angeles Philharmonic** also performs fairly

regularly in Santa Barbara, along with an ever-changing roster of world-class and regional performers. The **UC Santa Barbara Arts and Lectures** program, 805/893-2080 or 805/893-3535 (tickets), www.artsandlectures.ucsb.edu, sponsors a lengthy calendar of special events, including readings and lectures, ballet, modern dance, and chamber music. If you're in the Goleta area, stop by to appreciate changing exhibits at the fine **University Art Museum,** 805/961-2951, www.uam.ucsb.edu. **Santa Barbara City College** in Santa Barbara proper has a modern performing arts complex, the **Garvin Theatre,** 805/965-5935, www.sbcc.cc.ca.us, which stages dozens of performances each year.

Santa Barbara's **Lobero Theatre,** 33 E. Cañon Perdido St., 805/963-0761, www.lobero.com, the city's first fashionable theatrical venue, was first established in 1873 in an old adobe schoolhouse. Headquartered here are the **Contemporary Music Theatre,** the **Santa Barbara Grand Opera Association,** and the **Santa Barbara Chamber Orchestra,** though various other groups and series also call the Lobero home. To arrange a backstage tour, call 805/966-4946, e xt. 613. The **Santa Barbara Civic Light Opera,** 805/962-1922, performs at the **Granada Theatre,** 805/966-2324. Another popular local venue is the sylvan **Santa Barbara County Bowl** outdoor amphitheater—cut-stone seating, revolving stage, great visibility and acoustics—which hosts a wide variety of contemporary and classical acts, usually from May through September. To see what's up, see www.sbbowl.com.

But Santa Barbara's cultural gem is the Alhambra-like Arlington Theatre, also known as the **Arlington Center for the Performing Arts,** built on the site of the old Arlington Hotel at 1317 State St., 805/963-9503 or 805/963-4408 (tickets), a onetime 1930s movie palace where the domed ceiling still sparkles with electric stars; in its heyday there was even a cloud-making machine here. An arched passageway leads into the lobby, and the stage is flanked by two Spanish "villages," part of its architectural allure. In addition to regular Santa Barbara Symphony performances, the Arlington also hosts guest speakers and touring symphonies and other classical acts

The Central Coast

SANTA BARBARA WINE COUNTRY

Santa Barbara County is premium wine country. The county's winemaking history reaches back more than 200 years, though small vineyards and wineries established since the 1970s and 1980s are responsible for the area's regional viticultural revival. The unusual east-west orientation of the Santa Ynez Mountains and associated valleys allows fog-laden ocean air to flow inland—creating dry summers with cool nights and warm days. Cabernet sauvignon, sauvignon blanc, pinot noir, chardonnay, and riesling are among the wine grapes that thrive here, though Rhône varietals are a new trend.

Yet when does a good thing become too much of a good thing?

That question is asked more frequently here and elsewhere in California, given the pressure to expand vineyards—often at the cost of native oak woodlands, an increasing threat to ecosystem diversity. Large native oaks were bulldozed in the Los Alamos Valley in such great numbers in the late 1990s that a severely restrictive 1998 land-use ballot initiative almost passed—just the motivation necessary to get grape growers, environmentalists, and county planning officials to come up with a collaborative solution.

Even at that time, though, many vineyardists had already started to preserve native oaks, by planting around them. One example is the award-winning **Gainey Vineyard,** 3950 E. Hwy. 246 in Santa Ynez, 805/688-0558 or 888/424-6398, www.gaineyvineyard.com, noted for its sauvignon blanc, chardonnay, riesling, and merlot.

The contemporary 12,000-foot winery and tasting room and adjacent picnic area are open daily 10 A.M.–5 P.M. for tasting and very informative tours. The vineyard also sponsors a variety of evening concerts—popular regional jazz bands and the likes of Randy Newman and Tower of Power—which sell out fast. Tickets for the famous late September crush party also go quickly. Also notably conscientious—early on—with its oak trees is **Firestone Vineyard,** 5000 Zaca Station Rd. in Los Olivos, 805/688-3940, www.firestonewine.com, open daily 10 A.M.–5 P.M. for tasting (closed major holidays). "Hands-on" tours are also offered, at a quarter past each hour from 10:15 A.M. to 3:15 P.M. Tastings and tours are free, but a fee is charged for groups of 15 or more. Firestone was the first in the country to produce estate-grown wines. People go out of their way to pick up Firestone's award-winning cabernet sauvignon, though the winery is actually best known for Johannesburg riesling—and its 2002 vintage won the gold medal and was designated Best Riesling of California at the 2003 California State Fair. Shows staged in Firestone Meadow for the Valley Music Festival really rock—like Neil Young and David Crosby in 2003. Picnicking here is a pleasure anytime, or walk "Brooks' Trail" to nearby Curtis Winery.

A popular stop along the Foxen Canyon Wine Trail is the **Fess Parker Winery,** 6200 Foxen Canyon Rd. in Los Olivos, 805/688-1545 or 800/841-1104, www.fessparker.com, open for tast-

sponsored by the **Community Arts Music Association,** 805/966-4324, www.camasb.org.

For advance tickets for most local arts performances, call **State of the Arts,** 800/398-0722 or **Ticketmaster,** 805/583-8700 or 800/765-6255.

After touring the **Santa Barbara Museum of Art,** 1130 State St., 805/963-4364, www.sbmuseart.org, and poking into nearby galleries—including the **Contemporary Arts Forum** at the Paseo Nuevo mall downtown, 805/966-5373, www.sbcaf.org, which exhibits both established and up-and-coming artists. To dabble in more

artsy-craftsy fare, every sunny Sunday there's a **Beach Arts and Crafts Show** in Santa Barbara at Palm Park along Cabrillo Boulevard, just east of Stearns Wharf, from 10 A.M. to dusk.

Santa Barbara hosts an amazing number of arts and crafts fairs, benefits, cat, dog, and horse shows, community festivals, and other events throughout the year. To find out what's going on while you're in town—and what might be hip or happening in local nightlife—pick up a current issue of the free *Santa Barbara Independent,* www.independent.com, published on Thursday each week and offering local news coving and sales daily 11 A.M.–5 P.M. (from 10 A.M. on weekends), closed Thanksgiving, Christmas, and New Year's Day. Group tours by arrangement. Most popular here is syrah, which tends to sell out almost instantaneously every year, and a very good chardonnay. And anyone with a yen for the good ol' days of 1950s television will have fun in the gift shop, featuring *Davy Crockett* "coonskin" caps and wine toppers and other Fess Parker TV-star memorabilia. On most weekends Parker is available in person to autograph wine bottles. (Tours and admission to the gift shop are free, but there is a fee for tastings.) At least with locals, Parker is a lot less popular since he announced plans to team up with the local Chumash Nation to achieve his development plans for some 745 acres of land destined for luxury homes, golf courses, and a resort hotel. Since the Chumash are a sovereign nation, his detractors—including many Chumash—contend that Parker has entered into this agreement with the tribal leadership in order to circumvent the land-use planning process (which might have rejected his development). Wine boycotts have been underway, locally, since early in 2004.

Zaca Mesa Winery, 6905 Foxen Canyon Rd., 805/688-9339, www.zacamesa.com, specializes in estate-grown Rhône-style varietals. Open to the public 10 A.M.–4 P.M. daily, until 5 P.M. on summer weekends. Lovely grounds, picnic areas, tours and tasting by appointment. Not far away is **Rancho Sisquoc Winery,** 6600 Foxen Canyon Rd., 805/934-4332, www.ranchosisquoc.com, where winning

wines include the Cellar Select meritage and the syrah, and **Foxen Winery**'s rustic roadside wine shed, 7200 Foxen Canyon Rd., 805/937-4251, serving up some great cabernets and syrahs. Southeast of Santa Maria is another Foxen Canyon stop, the prestigious **Byron Vineyard and Winery,** now owned by Robert Mondavi and located at 5230 Tepusquet Rd., 888/303-7288, www.byronwines.com, noted for its estate-grown chardonnays and pinot noirs. Tours and tastings are offered only with advance reservations, Mon.–Fri. 10 A.M.–3 P.M.

The area's newest appellation is Santa Rita Hills, just a handful of wineries between Buellton and Lompoc, including the small, very well-regarded **Babcock Winery & Vineyards,** 5175 E. Hwy. 246, 805/736-1455, www.babcockwinery.com, noted for its winning Fathom red blend, syrah, sangiovese, pinot noir, chardonnay, and Cuvee Sublime gewürztraminer. The "value" wines here are the Troc varietals. Babcock is open Fri.–Sun. 10:30 A.M.–4 P.M. for tasting, midweek only by appointment.

Still, with 80 or so member wineries in the local vintners' association—and major events such as the spring **Santa Barbara County Vintners' Festival,** the fall **Celebration of Harvest,** and other galas to help introduce them—it takes more than a few stops to fully appreciate the region. For a current winery map and guide, and for current events information, contact the **Santa Barbara County Vintners' Association,** 805/688-0881 or toll-free 800/218-0881, www.sbcountywines.com.

erage and excellent arts and entertainment features, reviews, and calendar listings. The daily *Santa Barbara News-Press,* www.newspress .com, also features calendar listings and a special Friday *Scene* magazine insert.

Events

Come in late January/early February for the **Santa Barbara International Film Festival,** www.sb filmfestival.org, quite the bash by any measure, with premieres and screenings of both international and U.S. films, film maker events, and more. Come in March for the **Santa Barbara**

Kite Festival and the similarly family-friendly **Whale Festival & Week of the Whale.** Also in March, Santa Barbara hosts the annual **International Orchid Show,** a major flower fest. (The Santa Barbara Orchid Fair comes in July.) Come in April for the three-day multiethnic **Presidio Days,** Santa Barbara's annual birthday party.

In May wine aficionados and foodies come to town for the annual **Santa Barbara County Vintners' Festival.** Another main event in May—there are many, including **Cinco de Mayo**—is the *I Madonnari* **Italian Street Painting Festival,** a chalk art festival, the first in the nation, named for the 16th-century Italian street painters and held at the Santa Barbara Mission courtyard. June brings the **Summer Solstice Parade,** a sometimes sunny longest-day-of-the-year lunacy including wacky floats, giant puppets, fantasy costumes and masks, dance, mime, and a festive street fair. Also in late June: **Semana Nautica,** a two-week summer sports festival featuring air, sea, land, pool, and adaptive sports.

Santa Barbara's **Fourth of July** includes a parade downtown, fireworks along the waterfront, and festivities all over town—including the Santa Barbara Symphony's free pops concert at the Santa Barbara Courthouse sunken gardens. The Santa Barbara **National Horse Show** in July is one of the top equine events in the U.S., followed by the black-tie **Charity Hunt Ball.** Also in July: the **Chinese Festival** in Oak Park, the annual **California Outrigger Championships,** and the annual **Santa Barbara County Fair** in Santa Maria. August's **Old Spanish Days Fiesta** is a classy five-day celebration of the city's heritage with parades, carnival, rodeo, herds of horses, performances, other special events, and two colorful marketplaces—festive but dignified, a festival featuring plentiful freebies. Also come in August for the annual **Mariachi Festival.**

The prestigious **Pacific Coast Open Polo Tournament** is held on three consecutive weekends in August. In late September or early October comes the **Santa Barbara International Jazz Festival and World Music Beach Party** at Stearns Wharf. In October comes the Santa Barbara Vintners' Association **Celebration of Harvest,** another foodie and wine festival, this one also featuring dancing, exhibits, and storytelling, and the **Santa Barbara Art Walk** fine arts show and sale. Also in October is the **Santa Barbara Harbor and Seafood Festival** (formerly the Fishermen's Festival). **Santa Barbara's National Amateur Horse Show** in November has a few days of Western events and a week of English-style riding competition in the largest amateur show in the nation. In December the **Yuletide Boat Parade** lights up Stearns Wharf. Also show up for **Winterfest** at the Santa Barbara Botanic Garden and various other venues.

ACCOMMODATIONS

Santa Barbara is a popular destination year-round. It's a wonderful winter getaway when the rest of the nation is snowbound, but the "high season" is July and August, balmy days that extend into fall, when coastal fog all but disappears. Most accommodation rates, fairly high any time, are highest in the summer, on weekends, and during special events. If you come in summer and are particular about where you'll be staying—an issue for budget travelers and families as well as the affluent—book your reservations many months, even a year, in advance. Increasingly not just B&Bs but motels and hotels require a two-night minimum stay on weekends (three-night minimum on holiday weekends).

For help in sorting out the possibilities, try local no-fee booking agencies, including **Coastal Escapes,** 123 Arboleta Rd., 800/292-2222, www.coastalescapes.com, and **Santa Barbara Hot Spots,** 36 State St., 805/564-1637 or 800/793-7666, www.hotspotsusa.com.

Camping

Nearby **Los Padres National Forest** offers plenty of campgrounds. Get complete campground information from the national forest headquarters in Goleta, 6755 Hollister Ave., Ste. 150, 805/968-6640, www.fs.fed.us/r5/lospadres, or at the **Santa Barbara Ranger District** office, 3505 Paradise Rd. in Santa Barbara, 805/967-3481. Primitive campsites ($5) are first-come, first-camped. Developed campsites are $14–15 ($20 for horse sites), reservable by calling **ReserveUSA,** 877/444-6777, www.reserveusa.com. All sites in the immediate area are managed by a concessionaire; for current campsite information, call 805/967-8766.

Closer to the ocean are the three developed state beach campgrounds northwest of Santa Barbara—**Gaviota, Refugio,** and **El Capitan.** All are popular and quite nice, even for sunny winter camping (popular with snowbirds), seven-night maximum stay. Dogs (six-foot leash) are permitted at all of these state campgrounds, but are not allowed on beaches or trails. The campground at reclusive Gaviota is tiny, just 36 short

RV sites (no hookups) and 18 tent sites, first-come, first-camped; the campground here is sometimes open restricted days, so call for current details. Family campsites are $15, hike/bike sites $5. Refugio is loveliest, a refuge of golden sand in a sheltered cove with palm trees—something right out of the movies—complete with playground and horseshoe pits. The 85 campsites here have running water, flush toilets, and hot, coin-op showers. Family sites are $21, hike/bike sites $5. Jam-packed El Capitan, connected to Refugio at the other end of the cove via 2.5-mile bikepath, offers 140 family campsites—tent and RV sites, but no hookups—plus picnic area and parcourse. Family sites are $30, hike/bike sites $5. Group camps, too. Also within reasonable range is huge—262 total campsites, 126 with RV hookups—**Carpinteria State Beach** 12 miles southeast of Santa Barbara and just off Hwy. 101. Family campsites are $21–39, hike/bike sites $5. For general information on all these parks, call 805/968-1033 (recorded). Reserve campsites at Refugio, El Capitan, and Carpinteria through ReserveAmerica, 800/444-7275, www.reserveamerica.com.

For more luxurious camping not far from the beach, private **El Capitan Ranch** has it all. The ranch offers 100 luxurious cedar cabins with electricity, full bathrooms (some have whirlpool tubs) and kitchenettes, telephones, and quality linens and towels. Also inviting are the 26 spacious safari tents, built on raised wooden decks and furnished with comfortable willow-framed queen beds and down comforters, tables, trunks, and chairs. Shared bathroom facilities with showers are located nearby. Both cabins and tents have outdoor firepits and picnic tables. Five yurts are available for retreats and special events. Onsite market and deli, too. Equestrians can stable their horses at the ranch, too, and take advantage of area trails. Other special events and activities include live Saturday night bluegrass or jazz in summer, hiking, biking, and kayaking. But all this camping comfort will cost you. Safari tents are $100–150, starting at $115 (highest in summer), and cedar cabins are $100–250, starting at $135 (suites to $305). For information and reservations, contact El Capitan Canyon, 11560 Calle Real, 805/685-3887 or 866/352-2729, www.elcapitancanyon.com.

The biggest campground around is a bit farther away and inland via Hwy. 154: the county's very pleasant **Cachuma Lake Recreation Area,** which offers tent, yurt, and RV camping with a total of almost 600 family campsites available on either a first-come or reservation basis, $16–25. Hookups—full electrical, water, and sewer or just water and electrical—are available. The fabric-covered yurts feature platform beds, electric lights and heating, lockable doors, and wood-framed screened windows, $45–65 per night, two-night stay on weekends. General camping amenities include hot showers, restrooms, fireplaces with grills, picnic tables, swimming pools (summer only), and nonswimming lake recreation opportunities. Primitive and hiker/biker campsites are less expensive. For current reservation information and other specifics, call 805/686-5054 or 686-5055, www.sbparks.org.

Hostels and Retreats

Santa Barbara offers the **Santa Barbara Tourist Hostel,** just two blocks from the beach at 134 Chapala St., 805/963-0154 or 800/346-7835, www.sbhostel.com, right across from the train station and an easy walk to the bus station. Laundry room, internet access, bike and surfboard rentals, too. Dorm beds are $21, private rooms $45 and up; private cottage rooms are available in summer.

For a peaceful retreat, consider the mountaintop **Mount Calvary Guest House** at 2500 Gilbraltar Rd., 805/962-9855, www.mount-calvary.org, a palatial 1940s Spanish-style villa with incredible vistas, great hiking access, plenty of comfortable spare bedrooms, and Benedictine monks happy to serve you. In addition to the non-refundable $50 deposit, weekend rates (suggested donations) are $75 per person (weekday, $70), all meals included, with both single and double rooms available (singles share an adjoining bath). Individuals—no partiers, please—are welcome for personal retreats; study and working retreats are also offered.

A yoga stay, anyone? In addition to the yurts available at Lake Cachuma, there's also the **White**

The Central Coast

Lotus Foundation, 2500 San Marcos Pass, 805/964-1944, www.whitelotus.org, a yoga teaching institute that makes their yurts available for personal retreats Mon.–Thurs. for $75 per person per night, $140 per couple.

Discover your inner dude or dudette at the **Circle Bar B Guest Ranch** at 1800 Refugio Rd. beyond Goleta, 805/968-1113, www.circle barb.com, a genuine ranch dedicated to horseback rides (extra) and all kinds of family-appropriate fun—hiking, picnicking, even diving into the neighborhood swimming hole. The dinner theater does drama down at the barn, spring through fall. Accommodations, some cabin-style, are Western-themed and quite comfortable. Rates are $200–300 for two, all meals included (two-night minimum on weekends, three nights on holiday weekends). In summer, plan to book at least six weeks in advance on weekends, four weeks otherwise. The ranch is about three and a half miles inland from Refugio State Beach, via Refugio Road, 20 miles from Santa Barbara via Hwy. 101.

Motels and Hotels

Beyond camping or a hostel stay, finding bargain accommodations in Santa Barbara is a challenge. There's always Motel 6, yet here it isn't all that inexpensive. The **Motel 6 Santa Barbara,** 443 Corona Del Mar, 805/564-1392 or 800/466-8356 (nationwide), www.motel6.com, was the first Motel 6 in the nation, though, and it's still a good stop. Close to East Beach and the zoo, this small Motel 6 features the usual just-the-basics furnishings plus color TV, HBO, phone (free local calls), and outdoor pool. Very popular, so book well in advance—at least three to six months out. High-season rates are $92 for two (weekends in summer and fall are highest). If there's no room here, there's another Motel 6 downtown, 3505 State St., 805/687-5400, still another north of town near Goleta, and two more south of town near Carpinteria.

The attractive 53-room **Franciscan Inn,** 109 Bath St. (just south of Hwy. 101), 805/963-8845 or 800/663-5288, www.franciscaninn.com, is close to the wharf, marina, and downtown, and offers tasteful, homey decor and all the comforts

plus big TVs with HBO and VCRs, video and book library, data ports, swimming pool, and whirlpool. Almost half the rooms here have kitchenettes. High-season rates are $100–250, with off-season rates as low as $85.

Another find is **The Eagle Inn,** 232 Natoma Ave. (three blocks south of Hwy. 101, at Bath), 805/965-3586 or 800/767-0030, www.theea gleinn.com. Most rooms at this very attractive Spanish-style motel, a onetime apartment complex, are more like apartments, with full-stocked kitchens and the homey, well-kept kind of comfort that makes you want to stay longer than you'd planned. Even better is the fact that the Eagle Inn is only a block and a half from the beach. On-site laundry, cable TV, and free movies (no air conditioning). Rates are $100–200, with high-season rates starting at $125. Off-season and weekday rates can be a real deal. For summer, book rooms by mid-May. Also a best bet is nearby **Casa Del Mar Inn,** 18 Bath St. (near Cabrillo), 805/963-4418 or 800/433-3097, www.casadelmar.com.

The sprawling beachfront **Miramar Hotel** in Montecito has long been everybody's favorite affordable getaway, though those days are probably gone for good. The charmingly creaky resort was bought by upscale New York hotelier Ian Schrager some years back, and at last report progress in its $100 million "redo" had been halted by permit problems. But if Schrager and the city ever work it out, do swing by to see whether the gracious old dame has somehow managed to survive all the speculation.

Boutique Hotels

The "boutiquing" of downtown Santa Barbara has meant fewer of the stately older hotels are available as inexpensive residence hotels—accelerating the cycle of homelessness. Appealing and fairly affordable among the burgeoning boutique population is the 1926-vintage **Hotel Santa Barbara,** 533 State St. (at Cota), 805/957-9300 or 800/549-9869, www.hotelsantabarbara.com. Rooms are light, airy, and attractively decorated, with modern necessities including data ports and voice mail. An abundance of great restaurants are just a stroll away from the welcoming lobby.

Rooms and suites are $100–250, starting at $129—rates are lowest on weekdays—but look for seasonal specials.

The very stylish Holiday Inn Express **N** **Hotel Virginia,** just a hop and skip from the beach at 17 W. Haley St. (east of State Street), 805/963-9757 or 800/549-1700, www.hotelvirginia.com, is listed on the National Register of Historic Places. Décor in this 1916-vintage, 61-room hotel emphasizes the spectacular Malibu and Catalina tilework now preserved and restored here—including the striking mosaic fountain in the lobby—and also showcases local art and artists. Rooms, decked out in a contemporary take on classic art-deco style, feature all the modern comforts, from state-of-the-art phones and data ports to hair dryers and in-room irons and ironing boards; some have balconies with wrought-iron railings and French windows. A stay includes expanded continental breakfast, with good coffee, fresh juices and fruit, locally baked goods, cereals, and yogurt. Regular rates are $150–300, though off-season specials can drop the tab to as low as $119.

Not all the downtown boutiques are oldtimers, however. Some just look like it, notably the swank, red tile-roofed **Inn of the Spanish Garden,** 915 Garden St. (between Cañon Perdido and Carrillo), 805/564-4700 or 866/564-4700, www.spanishgardeninn.com, a tasteful contemporary take on sunny Spanish California style. Expect every comfort, from fireplaces and Frette linens to lap pool, fitness facilities, even complimentary espresso bar and continental breakfast. Rooms start at $225, suites at $325.

Though it's really just a spiffed-up Santa Barbara beach motel, dedicated foodies are drawn to the 71-room **Santa Barbara Inn,** 901 E. Cabrillo Blvd., 805/966-2285 or 800/231-0431, www.santabarbarainn.com. That's because after filling up on the fine California-French fare at Citronelle, chef Michel Richard's onsite restaurant, guests can just waddle right over to their rooms—or across the street to the beach—and rest until mealtime comes around again. Rooms here are spacious and attractive, with refrigerators, coffeemakers, and color TV with cable; some have kitchens, some have air

conditioning. In addition to the heated pool and whirlpool, there's a sundeck on the third floor. Rack rates are $250 and up—continental breakfast at Citronelle included—though discounts and off-season specials can drop the tab considerably.

What do you get when you reconfigure four vintage Spanish-style beach motels as a single compound, connecting them with palm trees, exuberant bougainvillea vines, hidden gardens with classic tiled fountains, and swimming pools? The stylish yet relaxed **Hotel Oceana,** 202 W. Cabrillo Blvd. (between State and Castillo), 805/965-4577 or 800/965-9776, www.hoteloceana.com, slightly lower-rent kissing cousin to Santa Monica's Oceana. It's clear that these were once motel rooms, but all the snazzy touches make it easy to forget—from the in-room data ports, CD players, and Internet access to the kicky custom furnishings, duvets, and fresh Frette linens. Regular rates are $230 and up, but even in high season AAA and other discounts can bring that down to $200. But specials and packages can be great deals, such as the two-night midweek Wine Country Sampler, $280 for two. And talk about nostalgia: Right next door is the original Sambo's restaurant.

In 1928 the little tramp himself, Charlie Chaplin, and his later scandal-plagued partner Fatty Arbuckle established the **Montecito Inn,** 1295 Coast Village Rd., 805/969-7854 or 800/843-2017, www.montecitoinn.com, as a Hollywood hideout. These days an attractive and trendy small hotel with Mediterranean provincial style, the Montecito Inn features somewhat small rooms with all the usual amenities—no air conditioning, but there are ceiling fans—plus an attractive pool and spa area out back. Seven spacious new Mediterranean-style luxury suites feature bathrooms of Italian marble plus whirlpool tubs; some suites have fireplaces. The inn sits close to the freeway, right in town—an easy stroll to most of Montecito's action. Luxury, with rates $200–300, though look for $100 off-season weekday discounts.

Bed-and-Breakfasts

Santa Barbara is a B&B bonanza, that phenomenon otherwise quite rare in and around

Southern California. Many local bed-and-breakfasts and B&B-style inns are as reasonably priced as local motels, if not more so, and most offer reduced rates, specials, or packages for off-season and/or weekday stays. Many require a two-night minimum stay on weekends and/or a three-night stay over longer holiday weekends. Here as elsewhere, most bed and breakfasts are smoke-free—though you may be allowed to smoke on a terrace or patio, or on a nearby street corner. Contact the visitor bureau for a more comprehensive current listing.

For anyone uncomfortable with the forced social intimacy of most bed-and-breakfast inns, the historic **M Upham Hotel,** 1404 De La Vina St., 805/962-0058 or 800/727-0876, www.uphamhotel.com, offers a friendly alternative. Built in 1871 by Amasa Lincoln, a Boston banker who set sail for California to build himself a New England-style inn, these days the Upham is still more hotel than bed-and-breakfast. This Victorian hotel features 50 rooms and garden cottages, furnished with period antiques yet stylishly updated—all on an acre of land in the heart of town, just a stroll from State Street. The Upham's primary eccentricity is in its guest register—an incongruous celebrity collection including Richard Nixon, Aldous Huxley, and Agatha Christie. Rooms in the main building are smallish but comfortable, with nice antique touches; more contemporary, more expensive rooms and suites are situated in various outbuildings and garden cottages. The cozy lobby (with fireplace) resembles an English parlor. The buffet breakfast can be taken indoors, out on the wraparound veranda, or out in the garden in an Adirondack chair. Wine and cheese are served in the evening. The onsite **Louie's** restaurant is quite good. Rates for rooms and suites are $150–300.

Near the beach is the award-winning **Old Yacht Club Inn,** 431 Corona Del Mar Dr., 805/962-1277 or 800/549-1676 (California), or 800/676-1676 (U.S.), www.oldyachtclubinn.com, actually once a yacht club, though this homey 1912 stucco craftsman was built as a private home. Santa Barbara's first bed-and-breakfast, open since 1980, the Yacht Club boasts yachting memorabilia and guestrooms—both in the main

house and in Hitchcock House next door—decorated in period furnishings of various moods. Just a stroll from winning East Beach, the Yacht Club also offers neighborhood bike tours. Fabulous breakfasts and famous, five-course Saturday night dinners (extra, by reservation). Most rooms and suites are $150–250, highest in summer, lowest in winter.

For a B&B stay in Laura Ashley style, the place is **The Cheshire Cat,** 36 W. Valerio St. (at Chapala), 805/569-1610, www.cheshirecat.com, a collection of houses and cottages with most rooms and suites named after characters in Alice's adventures in *Through the Looking Glass.* Many have whirlpool tubs and TV, some have a frig, fireplace, or deck/patio. Most rooms are $150–250, suites and cottages higher.

Truly exceptional among Santa Barbara's—and the nation's—bed-and-breakfasts is the landmark **M Simpson House Inn,** 121 E. Arrellaga St., 805/963-7067 or 800/676-1280 (U.S.), www.simpsonhouseinn.com. Centerpiece is the uncluttered 1874 Eastlake Italianate Victorian, exquisitely restored with period furnishings, oriental rugs, and English lace. Other rooms are in a onetime barn—the 19th-century "barn suites," complete with authentic interior walls—and three separate garden cottages with stone fireplaces and English charm. Amenities are endless, from Egyptian cotton towels, robes, and down comforters to whirlpool tubs (some rooms), TVs and VCRs (free video lending library), and phones with voice mail and modem hookup. The lush English gardens, an entire acre of century-old trees, fountains, and flowers sculpted into various semi-private "outdoor rooms," are most charming of all. (Croquet, anyone?) Full gourmet breakfast is served in your room, on the veranda, or in the formal dining room, along with afternoon or evening hors d'oeuvres (including Santa Barbara County wines). Rates start at $225.

Quite nice is the 16-room English country-style **Inn on Summerhill** south of Montecito at 2520 Lillie Ave. south of town in Summerland, 805/969-9998 or 800/845-5566, www.innonsummerhill.com, another winning bed-and-breakfast. This one boasts suite-style rooms with canopied beds and all the contemporary comforts—in-room refrigerators, whirlpool tubs, color TV with cable and VCRs—plus full home-made breakfast and, come evening, hors d'oeuvres and dessert. Most rooms are $200–250.

If you're pushing farther on down the coast, a bed-and-breakfast gem along the way—particularly for fans of T.S. Eliot—is **Prufrock's Garden Inn**, 600 Linden Ave. in Carpinteria, 805/566-9696 or 877/837-6257, www.prufrocks.com. Go and make your visit in any of the welcoming rooms, most furnished with quilts and other charms; two upstairs rooms share a bath. Rooms are $150–300, with two-for-one weekday and three-for-two weekend specials available.

Resorts

If money is no object—if this is your honeymoon or otherwise a once-in-a-lifetime visit and you want something close to guaranteed bliss—the place is the **W Four Seasons Biltmore Hotel** in the Montecito area at 1260 Channel Dr., 805/969-2261 or 805/565-8299 (local reservations), 800/332-3442 (U.S.), or 800/268-6282 (Canada), www.fourseasons.com, one of the finest resorts in the nation. The vast but intimate tile-roofed 1927 resort, designed in "Spanish ecclesiastical" style with endless other Mediterranean details by architect Reginald Johnson, just oozes luxurious old-money charm. Visitors could spend an entire stay just appreciating the craftsmanship, from the hand-made decorative Mexican tiles and the irregular mission-style *ladrillos* (tile floors) to the massive oak doors at the hotel's entrance. Endless archways, stairways, low towers, fountains, loggias, and bougainvillea-draped walkways threaded through the lush 21-acre grounds make just finding your room an architectural adventure. Yet for all its understated elegance and luxury—and its pool, lighted tennis courts, full fitness and spa facilities, kids program, excellent restaurants, multilingual staff, full conference and business services—a stay can be almost reasonable. For sheer extravagance, nobody beats the Biltmore's Sunday brunch. Rates are $250 and up, starting at $490, with larger ocean-view rooms, suites, and cottages more expensive; check for special packages and off-season specials.

The newest resort in the region and already on the *Condé Nast Traveler* Gold List is huge **Bacara** north of town in Goleta, www.bacararesort.com a more contemporary Mediterranean village with lush gardens, 311 villa-style rooms and suites, and endless accommodating spa services. On-site restaurants include dramatic French-California Miró, fabulous for seafood, as well as The Bistro and The Spa Café. Rooms start at $425 and climb precipitously.

Or head to exclusive **San Ysidro Ranch,** in Montecito at 900 San Ysidro Ln. (at Mountain Dr.), 805/969-5046 or 800/368-6788, www .sanysidroranch.com, also on the gold list. Actor Ronald Colman owned the ranch in the 1930s, and in those rowdier years it was a popular Hollywood trysting place. One can still see why. These romantic cottages—the ultimate rooms with a view, scattered throughout some of Santa Barbara's most stunning gardens—are prized for their seclusion as well as their understated luxury. John and Jackie Kennedy honeymooned here, Laurence Olivier and Vivien Leigh were married here, and ink-stained scribes including Somerset Maugham, Sinclair Lewis hid, even Winston Churchill (at work on his memoirs) hid out here to write. Individually decorated rooms feature wood-burning fireplaces and endless little luxuries—such as in-room massage and other spa and beauty services (extra)—and the grounds include a swimming pool, wading pool, tennis courts, and stables. Horseback riding is immensely popular here. You can also golf, with privileges at the nearby Montecito Country Club. If you can't afford to stay here, a special meal at the excellent California-style American **Stonehouse Restaurant**—known for its grilled lobster sandwich—or the **Plow & Angel Bistro** at least gets you a look around (reservations highly recommended). Rooms are $400–500, cottages and suites $600 and up (way up), two-night minimum stay on weekends, a three- or four-night minimum on holiday weekends.

Just as enchanting in its own way, and a tad less expensive, is the 10-acre hilltop **W El Encanto**

Hotel & Garden Villas, 1900 Lasuen Rd. (at Alameda Padre Serra), 805/687-5000 or 800/346-7039, www.elencantohotel.com. This sprawling country inn, just a half-mile from the Santa Barbara Mission, once served as student and faculty housing for the original University of California at Santa Barbara campus; when the university headed north to Goleta in 1915, El Encanto was born. A charter member of the National Trust for Historic Preservation's Historic Hotels of America, El Encanto is a maze of tile-roofed Spanish colonial revival-style *casitas* and craftsman-style cottages tucked in among the oaks and luxuriant hillside gardens. (Don't lose the map the staff give you when you check in; you'll definitely need it to find your way around.) Over the years El Encanto has welcomed endless celebrities and dignitaries, including Franklin Delano Roosevelt. But just about anyone will feel at home in these understated yet very pleasant lodgings, decorated in French country style. Many rooms feature wood-burning fireplaces, quite cheering on rain- or fog-chilled evenings; hotel staff regularly replenish the wood supply on the porch. Some have refrigerators and kitchens. "View" rooms are higher on the hillside, some distance from the main building. A private, reclusive resort, El Encanto's amenities include a year-round solar- and gas-heated swimming pool, tennis courts and full-time tennis pro, library, and lounge. Views from the excellent onsite restaurant—open daily for breakfast, lunch, and dinner—and the hotel lobby overlook the city and the vast Pacific Ocean, a dazzling sight at sunset. Rooms are $250 and up.

FOOD

The **Santa Barbara Downtown Certified Farmers' Market,** 805/962-5354, is the place to load up on premium fresh flowers, herbs, vegetables, fruits, nuts, honey, eggs, and other farm-fresh local produce. The market is held on the corner of Santa Barbara and Cota Streets every Saturday 8:30 A.M.–12:30 P.M. The **Santa Barbara Old Town Certified Farmers' Market** (same phone) convenes along the 500–600 blocks of State Street on Tuesday, 4–7:30 P.M. in summer and 3–6:30 P.M. in winter. There's another certified

market, at La Cumbre Plaza, on Weds. afternoon; other area markets are held in Goleta and Carpinteria on Thursday afternoon, and in Montecito on Friday morning; call for locations, current hours, and other details.

Lazy Acres Market, 302 Meigs Rd. (at Cliff Drive), 805/564-4410, www.lazyacres.com, has fresh and organic produce and just about everything else—bulk foods, fresh seafood and meats, juice and smoothie bar, and full-service deli. The **Italian and Greek Deli,** 636 State St., 805/962-6815, is also full of grand possibilities for a picnic. (If you stop for a sandwich, dogs are allowed at the outdoor tables.) There's a **Trader Joe's,** too, 29 S. Milpas St. (at Hwy. 101), 805/564-7878. Great local bakeries include **Our Daily Bread,** 831 Santa Barbara St., 805/966-3894, and **D'Angelo Bread,** 25 W. Gutierrez, 805/962-5466. Find Santa Barbara's best scones and other surprises at **Jeannine's American Bakery,** with two State Street locations—3607 State, 805/687-8701, and 3305 State, 805/569-3222.

For locally roasted coffee, try **Santa Barbara Roasting Company,** 321 Motor Way (near State and Gutierrez), 805/962-0320, definitely a jazzy place. Since 1949 Santa Barbara's favorite homegrown ice cream has been **McConnell's,** still served up from the original shop at 201 W. Mission (State and Mission Streets), 805/569-2323, where winning super premium flavors include French vanilla, chocolate burnt almond, island coconut, and red raspberry sorbet.

Inexpensive

Santa Barbara is a great restaurant town. Even people who can't afford to sleep here can usually find a good meal. For "gourmet tacos," Santa Barbara's most famous dining destination is **La Super-Rica Taqueria,** 622 N. Milpas, 805/963-4940, an unassuming hole-in-the-wall and long-running favorite of chef Julia Child and appreciative fellow foodies. This mom-and-pop place serves the best soft tacos around—fresh house-made corn tortillas topped with chorizo, chicken, beef, or pork—and unforgettable seafood tamales. Any of the tamales are worth writing home about. For Santa Barbara at its best, grab a tamale or taco and a cold beer and adjourn to the patio—or get it all to go then head for the beach and a sunset picnic. Also worth a stop: **Los Arroyos**, 18 W. Figueroa St., 805/962-5541, where fish tacos star and even the salsa is made fresh daily, and **Super Cuca's Taqueria**, near the city college at 2030 Cliff Dr., 805/966-3863 (also at 626 W. Micheltorena, 805/962-4028), serving Santa Barbara's best burritos. Everybody's favorite sit-down Mexican restaurant is the **Rose Café**, on the mesa at 1816 Cliff Dr., 805/965-5513. Don't miss the enchiladas verdes. All-day breakfast, too, from huevos rancheros to breakfast burritos. The original Rose is downtown at 424 E. Haley.

Santa Barbara is a health-conscious city; people from all walks of life tend to appreciate foods that'll do their bodies good. A local's favorite is the **Natural Café**, 508 State St., 805/962-9494, almost as good for people-watching as it is for the healthy fare—veggie burgers, sandwiches, salads, house-made pastas, fresh fish, grilled chicken, juice and coffee bars, regional wines, microbrews, and more. (There's another Natch in Goleta at 5892 Hollister Ave., 805/692-2363.) Best bet for Indian specialties—lots of veggie choices—is the **Taj Café**, 905 State St., 805/564-8280. Been-there-forever **Sojourner**, 134 E. Cañon Perdido St., 805/965-7922, serves inexpensive vegetarian and vegan fare, from vegetable-rich home-made soups and black-bean stew to veggie lasagna. Some of the best desserts in town, too. Grand for smoothies, wherever you find it—they're all over town—is **Blenders in the Grass**, downtown at 720 State St., 805/962-5715.

But what about all-American eats, healthy and otherwise? Super for inexpensive breakfast is the people's favorite **Esau's Coffee Shop**, 403 State St., 805/965-4416, where everything is home-made, right down to the biscuits and home fries. It's open until 1 P.M. for breakfast and lunch (most people do breakfast). Also a favorite for breakfast—pancakes and omelettes and such—or for a burger and beer at the beach is the **East Beach Grill**, beyond the Cabrillo Pavilion at 1118 E. Cabrillo Blvd. (at Milpas), 805/965-8805. Otherwise, locally loved for burgers is **The Habit**, 216 S. Milpas, 805/962-7472; there's another at 628 State St., still another at 1019 Chapala. If sampling local microbrews is item one, the place is the boisterous **Santa Barbara Brewing Company**, 501 State St., 805/730-1040, a sports bar serving surprising good food. Order a bleu cheese chicken wrap, Cajun-spiced grilled halibut sandwich, or baby-back ribs to go with your tall, crisp Santa Barbara Blonde. Santa Barbara's favorite pizza place since just about forever is **Rusty's** at the lighthouse, 15 E. Cabrillo Blvd., 805/564-1111; Rusty's is everywhere, including 3731 State St. and 414 N. Milpas.

Almost the most venerable place in town (that honor goes to the classic Casa de Sevilla), down-home **Joe's Cafe** and bar, 536 State St. (near Cota), 805/966-4638, is reasonably inexpensive. Appreciate the history on the walls while you enjoy ravioli, all-American steaks, fried chicken, rainbow trout, and Santa Maria-style barbecue. *Big* meals, no desserts, and notoriously potent drinks. Open for lunch and dinner daily. Since Joe's is often mobbed, come at an off hour.

Locals' Favorites

The city's better restaurants also tend to cluster downtown, making many city blocks irresistible for foodies. Besieged as they are by the tourist hordes, Santa Barbarans tend to distinguish between good locals' restaurants and the too hip, too hyped places angling for the attention of visiting food snobs. Good, reasonably priced restaurants—establishments favored by actual Santa Barbarans—are sprinkled among the high-priced spreads.

Fun at breakfast, lunch, and dinner is the other-era **Paradise Cafe**, 702 Anacapa St., 805/962-4416, specializing in new renditions of predominantly all-American fare—eggs and omelettes, beefy burgers, and woodfire-grilled chicken, chops, fish, and steaks. But the Paradise Cafe is most famous for its steamed mussels—fresh from the Santa Barbara Channel, scraped off the legs of offshore oil rigs—and for the fact that it serves an exceptional selection of Santa Barbara County wines. Lively bar scene, open late for dining. Half the town shows up on Sunday (starting at 9 A.M.) for the Paradise Café's killer breakfast/brunch. Breakfast is served only on Sunday.

Locally beloved for Cajun is the original **Cajun Kitchen**, 1924 De la Vina, Ste. A (near Mission

The Central Coast

Street), 805/965-1004. Those in the know say to show up early on Saturday morning—before everyone else gets there—for the unforgettable chile verde. There are Cajun Kitchens all over, elsewhere in town at 901 Chapala St., 805/965-1004, and also in Goleta and Carpinteria (and there are lines there, too). **The Palace Grill,** 8 E. Cota St. (at State), 805/966-3133, is Santa Barbara's other New Orleans niche, serving imaginative and exceptionally well-prepared fish, crawfish, "Cajun popcorn," and other Cajun-Creole and Caribbean fare, though you'll find pastas too. For dessert, how 'bout Key lime pie or Louisiana bread pudding? Open for lunch and dinner, daily changing menu.

Brigitte's eclectic California-style bistro at 1325 State St., 805/966-9676, serves everything one would expect—wood fire-baked pizzas with pizzazz (smoked chicken with red onion), refined pastas (basil fettuccine with prawns, red peppers and smoked mozzarella sauce), grill specialties, grand salads—along with an impressive California wine list. For something simpler, stop by the associated bakery and deli adjacent for sandwiches, takeout salads, fresh-baked breads, and other bakery items.

A new local favorite is **Figaro** bistro and bakery, across from the courthouse at 129 E. Anapamu St., 805/884-9218, open daily for breakfast, lunch, and dinner (until 11 P.M. on weekends). Patio dining, great weekend brunch. The uplifting courtyard **Arts & Letters Café,** behind Sullivan Goss Books & Prints at 7 E. Anapamu St. (at State), 805/730-1463, is another best bet for weekend brunch—served well into the afternoon—otherwise open at lunch and on pre-theater evenings. Particularly artistic here are such things as pumpkin soup, roasted lamb panini, and grilled salmon salad. **William,** 230 E. Victoria St. (at Santa Barbara), 805/966-7759, is a welcoming neighborhood bistro serving such things as buckwheat crepes, mixed mushroom and gruyere cheese omelettes, and sautéed sand dabs. Reasonably priced wine list. Perennially cool **M Roy,** 7 W. Carillo, 805/966-5636, serves local art on its walls and California-style American at astonishingly low prices—try three-course dinner for $20—plus

it's everybody's favorite for late-night dining, live music. Lots of great veggie selections, organic bread, plus entrées such as sliced pork tenderloin with apple-raisin wine sauce.

If you're careful what you order, even **Chad's** is reasonable. Housed in the charming Sherman House at 625 Chapala St. (between Cota and Ortega), 805/568-1876, Chad's makes you feel like you've come home—if either of your parents could cook like this! American comfort-food favorites include chicken brie pasta, Montana pork chops, Jack Daniel's caramelized ribeye steak, and "downtown meatloaf" made from prime rib and Cajun spices. Good happy hour specials. Patio dining, too, with smoking permitted. Otherwise everybody's favorite steakhouse is still **Chuck's of Hawaii,** home of California's first salad bar, at 3888 State St., 805/687-4417.

If the adjacent Wine Cask is too steep yet you're looking for something unmistakably upscale, the Cask's comfy sibling **Intermezzo,** 813 Anacapa St. (at Cañon Perdido), 805/966-9463, might be just the ticket. Lunch or dinner can be less than $10—try the great BLT, cooked up with Niman Ranch bacon on whole wheat bread, or the braised pork torta—plus Intermezzo is open late, until 11 P.M. for its regular menu, until midnight for pizzas and pastas and such. Great place for cocktails or a glass of wine.

Deliciously exotic **Café Buenos Aires** bistro, 1316 State St., 805/963-0242, serves up tasty tidbits from all over the map—tapas, arroz con pollo (rice with chicken) from Cuba, pollo relleno, low-cholesterol Argentinian beef, and Brazilian *feijoada*. It's hard to beat a simple lunch of empañada (Argentinian pastry pie) with soup or salad—under $10. Most dinner entrées top $20, but there are some sweet exceptions, such as the three-mushroom ravioli and the *pastel de choclo,* a "pie" layered with ground sirloin, olives, raisins, sweet corn, tomato, and basil.

For Southwestern, seek out the blue-corn tortillas and marvelous cheese *chiles rellenos* at the **Zia Cafe,** 532 State St., 805/962-5391, open daily for both lunch and dinner. Still everybody's favorite for Thai is **Your Place,** 22 N. Milpas St., 805/966-5151, serving such classics as cashew nut chicken, barbecued chicken, and satay. Hungry for some mini crab tacos, or maybe some Kahlua pork? Then the place is the very reasonable Pan-Asian **Aja,** 3132 State St., 805/563-2007, an intimate local's favorite also serving firecracker salmon, mixed-grill satay, baby-back ribs, and chicken ravioli. Nice wine list. Reservations advised. A good stop for pizza or pastas is **Ma Dolce Vita,** 700 State St., 805/965-3535, a place also perfect for people-watching in warmer months.

Fish, fish, fish—the ocean around here is still full of them, even after the Bay Cafe has had its way. The **Bay Cafe,** 131 Anacapa St., 805/963-2215, open for lunch and dinner daily, serves all kinds of charbroiled fish at dinner, from salmon to swordfish, plus the Bay's rendition of surf 'n' turf, paellas, and shrimp and other seafood pastas. At lunch, expect some of the same but also fish and chips, tostadas, crab melts, and seafood salad. Just about everything tastes better if you're sitting out on the patio. The Bay Cafe is open for lunch and dinner daily.

Most everyone loves **Enterprise Fish Co.,** too, downtown at 25 State St., 805/962-3313, where fresh fish—usually at least six selections each days—is mesquite-grilled to order in the central grilling area. Lunch and dinner menus are similar, though lunch is the better deal—house-made clam chowder, say, and a generous serving of grilled halibut plus Romano mashed potatoes for under $15. Also popular for seafood and just a stroll farther up State, is **Andria's,** 214 State St. (at Yanonali), 805/966-3000.

Quite reasonable for lunch or appetizers and drinks on the patio at sunset is the **Waterfront Grill,** another resident of the old Naval Reserve building now home to the maritime musuem, 113 Harbor Way (at Cabrillo), 805/564-1200. Killer Kahuna burgers, the abalone-style calamari sandwich, beer-battered fish and chips, seafood pozole or Baja fish stew in a sourdough bread bowl—there are lots of good choices under $10. More sophisticated dinner entrées might include clam linguini with pesto and light cream, lightly breaded Pacific sand dabs on fresh basil sauce, sesame- and black pepper-crusted halibut, also steaks and filet mignon. Oysters on the half shell and the fish are fresh off the harbor boats, too.

Superb for sushi is **Arigato,** 11 W. Victoria St., 805/965-6074, though **Piranha** at 714 State St. (near De la Guerra), 805/965-2980, has some impressive specialties too.

Fine Dining

In Santa Barbara, perennially laid-back, even fine dining is often a reasonably casual affair. Jackets are required in some dining rooms; if you're concerned about being too dressed up or down, call ahead.

Santa Barbarans love warm, inviting 🄼 **Mimosa** at 2700 De La Vina, 805/682-2272, among the best in town for French—classical and Alsatian country-style—and reasonably priced, especially the fixed-price dinners. Mimosa's menu usually features bouillabaisse, coq au vin, rack of lamb, sautéed trout niçoise, and specialties such as Alsatian onion tart—plus surprising nightly specials.

Santa Barbara's still abuzz about Michel Richard's California-French **Citronelle** restaurant at the Santa Barbara Inn, 901 Cabrillo Blvd., 805/963-0111, coastal sibling to the famous Citrus in Los Angeles and one of the country's best restaurants, thanks to the tireless efforts of Chef Isabelle Alexandre. Starters at this attractive, upbeat, and airy oceanside bistro might include porcupine shrimp, a smoked salmon–onion tart with créme fraiche, hominy corn soup, or broiled eel carpaccio with light ginger dressing. Among seasonally changing entrées ($20–35): double pork chop with potato-fennel gratin, roasted monkfish with black bean chile and avocado, and potato-crusted chicken. Children's menu, winemaker dinners, cooking classes too. Exceptional California wine list, and unforgettable desserts—such as the famed chocolate hazelnut bar. It's open daily for dinner, for brunch on special occasions.

For nouvelle California-French, the local favorite is **Downey's,** 1305 State St. (at Victoria), 805/966-5006, close to the Arlington and a favorite pre-theater dining room. The daily changing menu might feature anything from Santa Barbara shellfish, seabass, or steelhead to organic chicken and Ojai squab. Rich regional wine list. And try to make at least some of the "seasonal dinners."

NIK WHEELER/SANTA BARBARA CONFERENCE & VISITORS BUREAU

There is no lack of fine dining in Santa Barbara.

Still a relative newcomer, **Bouchon** at 9 W. Victoria St. (at State), 805/730-1160, is gathering up acclaim along with the region's freshest fish, local produce, and farm-reared rabbits, poultry, ostrich, and venison. Favorites include bourbon and maple glazed duck, honey mustard-marinated venison with toasted hazelnuts, and roasted white seabass. Great wine list starring regional chardonnays, pinot noir, and syrah—more than 50 available by the glass—and dozens of microbrews, too. Open nightly for dinner.

The Patio at the Four Seasons Biltmore, 1260 Channel Dr., 805/969-2261, is open daily for breakfast, lunch, and dinner. Even if a stay at Santa Barbara's venerable Biltmore is impossible, almost anyone can swing a meal here—at least at The Patio, reasonably relaxed and quite good. A wonderful French, Mediterranean, or Italian buffet is served every evening. If money's no object, of course, the ultimate is dress-up dinner in the Biltmore's ocean-view **La Marina**

restaurant. Seafood typically stars on the menu but roasted pheasant, chicken, steaks, even delectable vegetarian selections are also available. Either choice offers an excuse to appreciate the lobby and explore the grounds of this stunning 1927 Spanish-Mediterranean hotel, exquisitely restored in 1987.

Also exceptional is the **Stonehouse** restaurant at the San Ysidro Ranch in Montecito, 900 San Ysidro Ln., 805/969-5046, open daily for breakfast, lunch, and dinner, also serving wonderful Sunday brunch. Another, more casual possibility at the ranch is the **Plow & Angel Bistro.**

Actor Kevin Kostner is a Santa Barbara resident and also part-owner of the romantic New American **Epiphany,** 21 W. Victoria St. (at State), 805/564-7100. The monthly changing menu includes entrées such as paella, grilled ribeye with cabernet sauce and bleu cheese gratin, and oxtail pot pie. Nice local wine list, full bar—and bar menu, too (until midnight on weekends). And chocoholics, do try the Fire &Ice for dessert.

Nu, 1129 State St. (at Anapamu), 805/965-1500, is another stylish dining destination, this one particularly adept at seafood—pan-seared grouper and seared ahi with wasabi mashed potatoes—and classics including double-cut pork chops and filet mignon. Largely European and Santa Barbaran wine list.

Definitely different is **Sage & Onion,** a block off State Street at 34 E. Ortega (at Anacapa), 805/963-1012, serving British-style Euro-American—but don't expect anything like bangers and mash. The seasonally changing menu features starters such as Asian duck dumplings, crispy sweet corn spoon bread, wild game pot pie, and veggie potstickers in lemongrass, coconut, and ginger broth.

Out of Town

Everybody's favorite for seafood and sunsets north of town is the **Beachside Bar & Café** at Goleta Beach Park next to the airport, 5905 Sandspit Rd., 805/964-7881, where the signature dish is Alaskan halibut stuffed with Dungeness crab and goat cheese. Great appetizers, rawbar, lots of local wines. For something different on the San Marcos Pass route between Santa Barbara

The Central Coast

and the Solvang area, stop at **Cold Spring Tavern,** an old stagecoach stop at 5995 Stagecoach Rd. off Hwy. 154, 805/967-0066. The evocative Old West ambience here comes with some fairly sophisticated fare—such things as charbroiled quail, grilled pheasant, and kangaroo—along with more traditional meat, potatoes, and biscuits with gravy. It's open daily for lunch and dinner, on weekends only for breakfast.

Beyond the Santa Ynez Valley, prime for fine dining is Montecito. This downcoast suburb has its share of snazzy restaurants, many of them strung out along Coast Village Road, the main drag—also home to the Friday morning farmers' market—and many of them reasonably priced. Celebrities are no surprise—no one in Montecito gawks at celebs—even at unpretentious **Tom's Montecito Coffee Shop,** 1498 E. Valley Rd., 805/969-6250, where everyone goes for breakfast, especially the eggs Benedict. Across the street is **Pierre Lafond** market, bakery, and deli, 516 San Ysidro Rd., 805/565-1505. Always a best bet is the California-style **Montecito Cafe** at the Montecito Inn, 1295 Coast Village Rd., 805/969-3392, open daily for lunch and dinner, serving perfect pastas and grilled fish. Casual, sunny **Montecito Wine Bistro,** 1280 Coast Village Rd., 805/969-3955, serves up such things as crab and rock shrimp cakes with fennel slaw, potato-crusted salmon, and pan-roasted chicken. Julia Child—and just about everyone else in town—is a huge fan of **Lucky's,** across the way at 1279 Coast Village Rd. (at Olive Mill), 805/565-7540, a snazzy steakhouse with celebs on the walls (and often in the seats), and with exquisite comfort food served forth from the kitchen—chops and Maine lobster to rack of lamb. Everybody's favorite Italian and another notable celebrity magnet is Ⓜ **Pane e Vino,** in the Upper Village minimall at 1482 E. Valley Rd. (at San Ysidro), 805/969-9274, featuring house-made pastas, fresh grilled fish, and specialty desserts.

Farther downcoast in Carpinteria, restaurants cluster near the state beach. **The Palms,** 701 Linden Ave., 805/684-3811, is a long-running local favorite, serving cook-your-own seafood selections and steaks. New in 2004, **Siam Elephant** just above the railroad tracks at 509 Linden Ave., 805/684-2391, is the place for Thai—great panang, roasted duck, and other curries, fish dishes, even fresh mango for dessert. Open daily for lunch and dinner. Irresistible among Linden's shops is **Robitaille's Fine Candies,** 900 Linden, 805/684-9340, famous for producing the mints for President Ronald Reagan's second inauguration.

INFORMATION

To request information before your trip, contact the **Santa Barbara Conference and Visitors Bureau,** 510 State St., 805/966-9222 or 800/549-5133, www.santabarbaraca.com. For a copy of its comprehensive current visitor guide, call 800/927-4688, order one from the website—or download a PDF version. (There's also a downtown parking map on the web.) Or stop in for visitor information when you arrive.

The visitor bureau sponsors a walk-in visitor center at the harbor, too—the **Outdoor Santa Barbara Visitor Center,** 113 Harbor Way (fourth floor of the Waterfront Center), 805/884-1475, open weekdays 11 A.M.–6 P.M., Saturday 9 A.M.–7 P.M., Sunday from 10 A.M. The local chamber of commerce sponsors another, at **Hot Spots,** 36 State St., 805/564-1637, www.sbcham ber.org, staffed Mon.–Sat. 9 A.M.–9 P.M., Sunday until 4 P.M. The lobby is open 24 hours, however, so you can pick up maps and brochures; there's also an ATM here, and a coffee machine.

The **main post office** is at 836 Anacapa, 805/564-2266 or 800/275-8777, and the attractive **Santa Barbara Central Library** is at 40 E. Anapamu, 805/962-7653. For current entertainment and events information, pick up current copies of the weekly *Santa Barbara Independent,* www.independent.com, and the daily *Santa Barbara News-Press,* www.news press.com. You'll find other publications around town, too.

TRANSPORTATION

Many of the region's finest pleasures, including the Santa Barbara wine country and the lovely state beaches 20-plus miles north of town, can't be reached by public transit. Look in the telephone yellow pages or contact the local chamber of commerce or visitor bureau for car rental agencies.

To get around town without a car, **Santa Barbara Metropolitan Transit District** buses offer mainly commuter services but connect with most nearby destinations, including Goleta and Carpinteria. The transit center, 1020 Chapala St. at Cabrillo, is behind Greyhound. Call 805/683-3702 for current route and fare information, or see www.sbmtd.gov. But for many people the transit district's electric **Downtown–Waterfront Shuttles,** which run along State Street between Cabrillo Boulevard (at Stearns Wharf) and Sola Street, and along the Waterfront (Cabrillo Blvd.); at last report the all-day fare was still just 25 cents. The less frequent morning and early evening service (times vary depending on the day) runs between the zoo on the east and the Arlington Theatre on the west. Also convenient in some cases is the **Santa Barbara Trolley Tour,** 805/965-0353, www.sbtrolley.com, which connects downtown's sights with destinations as far-flung as Santa Barbara Mission and the nearby botanic gardens with the waterfront, the zoo,

and downtown Montecito. All routes start and end at Stearns Wharf. Tickets are good for all day, and you can get off and get back on all along the route—but be sure you have a schedule in hand. At last report all-day trolley fare was $14 adults, $7 children, with a $5 discount coupon available on the website.

Greyhound, 34 W. Carrillo, 805/965-7551, www.greyhound.com, offers good bus connections to and from L.A. and San Francisco. Even better than buses, though, is the opportunity Santa Barbara provides for traveling by train. The **Amtrak** station is downtown at 209 State St., with trains rolling south to Los Angeles and north to San Francisco; for current schedule and fare information, call 800/872-7245 or try the websites, www.amtrak.com or www.amtrakwest.com.

Limited commercial air transport is available at the **Santa Barbara Municipal Airport** just north in Goleta at 601 Firestone Rd., 805/967-7111, www.flysba.com. But you can also arrange a ride to or from LAX with **Santa Barbara Airbus,** 805/964-7759 or 800/423-1618, www.santabaraairbus.com, $40 one-way, at last report. Prepaid online reservations are lower.

South from Santa Barbara

Here's a thought to ponder while fueling that gas hog for a cruise from Santa Barbara to Ventura County, Los Angeles, and beyond. Scientists from USC now predict that rising sea levels caused by global warming will create havoc along much of the Ventura County coastline in the coming 50 years, with coastal military bases, power plants, harbors, hotels, businesses, and residential areas increasingly battered by major storms and associated floods. Because the coastal Oxnard Plain is so level, and so near sea level, the effects of global warming will be felt there sooner than elsewhere along the California coastline. By the year 2040, they say, sea level here will be permanently two feet higher than it is today. A 10-foot increase in sea level is "highly unlikely"—except during serious storms.

Roadtrippers not yet running on empty because of fossil-fuel guilt will find much to enjoy here along the coast north of Los Angeles.

The scenic route into Los Angeles County from the north is via the Pacific Coast Highway (PCH) to Malibu, though most people take the Ventura Freeway through the San Fernando Valley—one of L.A.'s most congested freeways. A more serene if roundabout inland alternative is Hwy. 126 through Piru, Fillmore, and Santa Paula; or take the Ronald Reagan Freeway, Hwy. 118, through Simi Valley.

Ventura County highlights include artsy Ojai, home to the annual Ojai Music Festival, and very Victorian Santa Paula, inland, home to the Santa Paula Union Oil Museum. Quite appealing along the coast is Ventura, with its San Buenaventura Mission and welcoming old-fashioned downtown, state beach, and pleasant boat harbor—headquarters for Channel Islands National Park and point of departure for most park visitors. Fun for harbor hounds, too, is nearby Oxnard, with its downtown Heritage Square and historical museums.

OJAI

To the native Chumash peoples, Ojai (OH-hi) was the spiritual center of the world. Plenty of later arrivals shared similar beliefs, which is why the Krishnamurti Foundation and Library, the Krotona Institute of Theosophy and Library, Aldous Huxley's Happy Valley School, and so many other philosophical and religious icons have centered themselves in this lovely valley.

The Ojai Valley and its avocado and citrus groves nest in the shadows of the dramatic Topa Topa Mountains. According to local lore, Ojai means "the nest" in Chumash, though linguists say "moon" is the word's actual meaning; some residents now interpret the name of their spiritual nesting place as "valley of the nesting moon." Also according to local lore, Frank Capra set up his cameras at Dennison Grade east of town to shoot Ronald Coleman's first impressions of lush Shangri-La, the valley of eternal youth, for his 1937 film *Lost Horizons*—a film fact still in some dispute, since most of Capra's filming actually took place near Palm Springs.

But no one disputes the truth of Ojai's fabled "pink moment," that magical time close to sunset when the entire valley glows pink in the light of the waning sun—the community's most unifying spiritual event.

For more information about the area, contact: **Ojai Valley Chamber of Commerce and Visitors Bureau,** 150 W. Ojai Ave., 805/646-8126, www.the-ojai.org. For area hiking, camping, and other national forest information, stop by the **Ojai Ranger District Office** of Los Padres National Forest, 1190 E. Ojai Ave., 805/646-4348, www.fs.fed.us/r5/lospadres.

Sights

Artsy, laid-back downtown Ojai is nonetheless striking, architecturally distinguished by its mission revival architecture, particularly the clock tower atop the downtown post office and the pergola fronting Libbey Park. Much of town was conceived by wealthy glass manufacturer Edward Drummond Libbey, part of a 1917 master plan adopted when locals decided to leave behind the town's previous identity of Nordhoff. For a brief community introduction, stop by the

The Central Coast

Ojai Valley Museum, 130 E. Ojai Ave., 805/646-1390. Or explore the various antique shops, art and pottery galleries, boutiques, and bookstores. A local institution is **Bart's Corner,** 302 W. Matilija, 805/646-3755, an open-air used bookstore not known so much for bargains as for its inimitable ambience (closed Monday).

Ojai's 8,000 inhabitants seem to share a striking love of the land. Bicyclists love the 16-mile **Ojai Valley Trail** to Ventura, a rails-to-trails conversion designed for walkers, runners, and bikers, joined to an equestrian trail. (If you need a bike, look around town and borrow one, thanks to Ojai's free yellow bike program.) People here also love the arts. Find out what's going on, artistically speaking, at the **Ojai Center for the Arts,** 113 S. Montgomery St., 805/646-0117, www.ojai artcenter.org, which sponsors monthly art shows, community theater, weekly poetry readings, and more. Except in July, August, and December, the **Ojai Film Society,** www.filmfestival.ojai.net, presents fine films every Sunday at 4:30 P.M. at the Ojai Playhouse. The society also sponsors the annual **Ojai International Film Festival** in October.

As famous as The Pink Moment is Ojai's three-day **Ojai Music Festival,** "the class act of all California music festivals" since the 1940s, held either on the last weekend in May or in early June under the oaks at the Libbey Park Bowl. Along with the classics, the Ojai festival distinguishes itself by showcasing post-World War II works, including progressive and avant-garde compositions. Single-performance ticket prices are $15–65, depending on where you sit, and series tickets are $70–290. Hard wooden benches are the "good seats" (bring a cushion, or buy one); cheap-seaters get to sprawl out on the lawn behind the bowl. For current schedule information, call 805/646-2094 or see www.ojaifestival.org. Order tickets online or call the box office at 805/646-2094.

Listen to music free in summer at the **summer band concerts** held in Libbey Park every Wednesday in July and August, starting at 8 P.M. Other worthwhile local events include the big-deal **Ojai Valley Tennis Tournament** in late April, the oldest junior tournament in the U.S.; the **Ojai Valley Garden Tour** in May; the **Bowl-**

ful of Blues festival in August; and the **Ojai Valley Mexican Fiesta** in September.

Lake Casitas

Central to outdoor Ojai life is lovely Lake Casitas to the west off Hwy. 150, a 6,200-acre regional recreation area and reservoir most famous for its trout and bass fishing. The 1984 Olympics rowing and canoeing events were held here. Prime for camping and fun for picnicking and letting the kids let off a little steam—there are many playgrounds here—Lake Casitas has never been open for public swimming, but officials are at least considering changing that policy, much to the dismay of fisherfolk. Campgrounds and group camps here are quite nice, featuring both basic tent camping sites and full hookups for RVs. Two- or three-night minimum stays are required on weekends. Camping fees begin at $16–18 per campsite per day (up to six people) and climb to $22–44 for hookups. Hiker/biker campsites are $2 per person. Other facilities include boat launch and docking facilities, a full-service marina, snack bar, store, and coin-operated showers. Boat rentals are available. No swimming is allowed in the lake, but there is a water park, open weekends only.

The lake's day-use fee is $6.50 per vehicle, $2.50 extra for pets (on leashes). For general park information, call 805/649-2233 or see www.casitaswater.org. For camping reservations, call 805/649-1122. You can reserve campsites up to several days, but no more than six months, in advance of your arrival.

Accommodations

If you're not camping at Lake Casitas, consider the national forest's shaded **Wheeler Gorge Campground** on Matilija Creek, about eight miles north of Ojai on Hwy. 33, near Wheeler Springs, $12–15 for a single site, $24–30 double. For campground information call the Ojai Ranger District, 805/646-4348. For reservations, call 800/280-2267 or see www.reserveamerica.com. Another possibility is Ventura County's woodsy **Camp Comfort** on San Antonio Creek two miles south of town at 11969 N. Creek Rd., 805/646-2314 or 805/654-3951 for reservations. With

CAROLE TOPALIAN

Lake Casitas

tent sites and some RV hookups, extras here include hot showers, laundry, and a small store.

Good choices among midrange area motels include the **Hummingbird Inn,** 1208 E. Ojai Ave., 805/646-4365 or 800/228-3744, www .hummingbirdinnofojai.com, with clean rooms, a pool, and on-site spa; pets are allowed on approval. Regular high-season (April–Oct.) rates are $100–150 double for rooms and bungalows, with off-season and AAA discounts. The associated **Rose Garden Inn of Ojai,** adjacent to the Ojai Valley Trail at 615 W. Ojai Ave., 805/646-1434 or 800/799-1881, www.rosegardeninn ofojai.com, features 16 knotty-cedar rooms plus two attractive cottages with fireplaces; all are spacious, with vaulted ceilings. All have an alcove area, with microwave and refrigerator or, in some, kitchenettes (bring your own pots, pans, and utensils). Ceramic tile-floored bathrooms, hair dryers, cable TV, direct-dial phones, gas wall heaters, and air conditioning are all standard. Also onsite are two rose gardens, shaded lawns

with hammocks and bench swings, plus pool, whirlpool tub, and sauna. No pets. Room rates are $50–150 (starting at $80). Cottage rates are $100–200, two-night minimum required for three-day weekends. All prices drop in winter.

For a sublime bed-and-breakfast stay, the place is **The Moon's Nest Inn,** 210 E. Matilija St., 805/646-6635, www.moonsnestinn.com, an 1874 schoolhouse later transformed into the Ojai Manor Hotel. Completely restored and transformed once again, Moon's Nest décor is a delightful blend of antique fundamentals and contemporary whimsy, creating an easy, feel-right-at-home atmosphere. Five of the seven rooms feature private baths. Rates are $100–200, starting at $115 for a room with two antique twin beds (shared bath), including expanded continental breakfast and evening wine and cheese.

Just about the hippest place around, though, is a onetime motor court south of town, restyled into the artsy ⓝ **Blue Iguana Inn,** 11794 N. Ventura Ave. (Hwy. 33 at Loma Drive),

The Central Coast

805/646-5277, www.blueiguanainn.com, where you can meet Iggy the iguana yourself at the tiled mosaic fountain in the courtyard. The inn, carefully crafted in old mission style—arched designs, terra cotta tile roofs, handmade Ojai tilework—showcases the work of local artists and craftspeople. Lovely pool and garden areas, too. Rooms are $100–150, one-bedroom suites with kitchens are $150–200. There's also a two-bedroom suite with half kitchen, and a separate house with full kitchen, $150–250.

The same idea only a bit more swank is what you'll find at the associated **Emerald Iguana Inn** downtown at the end of Blanche Street, 805/646-5277, www.emeraldiguana.com. There are five custom designed one-bedroom cottages ($150–250) with fully equipped kitchens, and three two-bedroom cottages ($200–400), all tucked into verdant grounds with large trees, surrounding an appealing kidney-shaped pool with spa. Several cottages have rooms that can be "added on," too, for a larger configuration. Many cottages have a private patio or decks, woodstoves, and either a clawfoot or whirlpool tub. Weekly rates are available.

For peeling away the pounds and inches, one place is **The Oaks at Ojai,** "the affordable spa" at 122 E. Ojai Ave., 805/646-5573 or 800/753-6257, www.oaksspa.com, where the total fitness and stress management program comes with all meals—1,000 calories per day—and rates of $150–300 per person per night.

For the most luxurious local spa stay, just west of town is the historic 800-acre **Ojai Valley Inn,** appropriately situated on Country Club Road, 805/646-5511 or 888/697-8780 (hotel), 888/772-6524 (spa), www.ojairesort.com. In 1923 the wealthy glass manufacturer Edward Drummond Libbey, whose name crops up frequently in these parts, commissioned architect Walter Neff to design the stylish Spanish colonial golf course clubhouse here. The rest of the Ojai Valley Inn grew up around it, from the 18-hole golf course (now featured on the Senior PGA Tour) and putting green, tennis center, riding stables and "ranch," Camp Ojai for kids, and complete health spa, exercise (with lap pool), business, and conference facilities. Completely renovated and restyled in the 1980s, until its radical 2004 expansion this Spanish-style grande dame featured 207 rooms and suites, two swimming pools, two restaurants, The new, improved inn, with 305 more rooms andsuites, three additional restaurants, and a pub—everything designed to continue the Spanish colonial terracotta-tile mood—was scheduled to be unveiled in summer 2004. Even during guests continue to enjoy 24-hour room service, bike rentals, and hiking and jogging trails. Rooms start at $300, though discounts and off-season specials can drop the tab considerably.

Food

The weekly **Ojai Certified Farmers' Market,** with local baked goods and pastries in addition to the usual cornucopia of fresh produce and flowers, convenes every Sunday morning 9 A.M.–1 P.M. downtown behind the Arcade, 300 E. Matilija, 805/698-5555. Great for authentic Mexican is **Los Caporales,** 307 E. Ojai Ave. (at Signal), 805/646-5452. Poke around town for pizza places and café-style possibilities. French-influenced California-style **Suzanne's Cuisine,** 502 W. Ojai Ave., 805/640-1961, is a best bet at lunch and dinner (closed on Tuesday). Another long-standing local favorite is **Boccali's,** 3277 E. Ojai Ave., 805/646-6116, where the vegetables accompanying the pizza and traditional Italian come from the restaurant garden.

For natural food elevated to fine dining *experience,* the place is the **Ranch House** restaurant on S. Lomita Ave. (near Besant Road), 805/646-2360. Founder Alan Hooker first came to Ojai in 1946 to hear Krishnamurti speak, and within a few years he was catering the event—and thus the original Ranch House was born. Since it moved to a spot closer to the highway, the restaurant still serves the finest, freshest natural foods anywhere, here often accompanied by rich sauces and—gasp!—real creamery butter. (Herbs still come from the restaurant's herb garden.) The Ranch House is open for dinner only Wed.–Sat., for lunch and dinner on Sunday, closed Monday and Tuesday. To take this place home with you, pick up a copy of *California Herb Cookery: From the Ranch House Restaurant.*

From Ojai

It's a quick trip from Ojai back to Santa Barbara via Hwy. 50 and then either Hwy. 192 or Hwy. 101 along the coast—the usual route, for daytrippers. For a much longer alternative road trip to Santa Barbara, head north past Wheeler Springs on Hwy. 33, up the switchbacks to Pine Mountain Summit, then drop down into Cuyama Valley; follow Hwy. 166 past the badlands burg of New Cuyama into Santa Maria. From there, dabble in Santa Barbara County's boutique wine country around Los Alamos and Los Olivos before cruising past Cachuma Lake and into Santa Barbara via Hwy. 154.

SANTA PAULA

Like nearby Fillmore, Santa Paula is most famous for its delightful 19th-century downtown, both in its architecture and ambience. The Victorian-era buildings along well-manicured Main Street, in other respects representing an antiquers' holiday, are constructed, uniquely, of weathered red brick and Sespe sandstone. Queen Anne and Victorian homes line nearby streets, blending here and there with Mediterranean and craftsman styles. Yet Santa Paula offers its historic eccentricities; on the four-sided clock tower downtown, notice the bullet holes on the clock's north face, a distinguishing feature. Even the privately owned airport here is a surprise, a relic from the heyday of open-cockpit aviation; planes in the air on any weekend here comprise an ever-changing antique plane museum.

Still surrounded by orange and lemon groves and occasional oil derricks—and so far spared the indignities of suburban sprawl—Santa Paula was built from the wealth generated by the California oil boom of the late 1800s and the subsequent success of area agriculture. The free **Santa Paula Union Oil Museum,** 1001 E. Main St. (10th and Main), 805/933-0076, open Wed.–Sun. 10 A.M.–4 P.M., tells part of the story. The museum store sells copies of the Santa Paula Historical Society's *Neighborhoods and Neighbors of the Past,* which tells some of the rest by guiding visitors through historic residential neighborhoods. A drive through Santa Paula's surrounding

FILLMORE'S SPAGHETTI WESTERNS

Family-style fun in Fillmore includes rides on the **Fillmore & Western Railway,** 250 Central Ave. (red caboose on the north side of city hall), 805/524-2546 or 800/773-8724, www.fwry.com, where special-event trains include Friday Night, Saturday Night, Sunday Brunch, Summer Sunset BBQ, "Spaghetti Western," and Murder Mystery dinner trains, as well as special Mother's Day, Father's Day, Pumpkin Liners, and Christmas Tree excursions. Easter lunch was $43 adult and $23 children, at last report, but Murder Mystery dinner was $89; call for current prices. Come in late March for the annual **Fillmore Spring Railfest,** a celebration of railroading and Western heritage, offering vintage train rides, gunslingers, antique farm implements, and other family fun. The 19th-century locomotives, passenger cars, and freight cars that "star" here were largely acquired from MGM, Paramount, and 20th Century Fox movie studios, who have long used the area in Hollywood TV and film production. Fairly recent shoots have included *Seabiscuit, O Brother, Where Art Thou,* and *Nixon.*

citrus groves completes the tale. Ventura County is still California's largest lemon producer (California is the largest producer in the U.S.), and Santa Paula is the industry star. Come in mid-July for the annual **Santa Paula Citrus Festival.** Santa Paula's Limoneira Co. is the county's largest lemon grower, with 40 percent of its crop—the most perfect oval fruit—exported to Hong Kong and elsewhere in Asia, where the lemons can fetch a price of $2 each. Airplane buffs, make time for the 1930-vintage **Santa Paula Airport,** 805/933-1155, one of the largest antique aircraft collections in the world. Show up on the first Saturday of the month, 10 A.M.–3 P.M., for the best show. The airport's **Aviation Museum of Santa Paula,** 805/525-1109, tells the story.

For more information about the area, stop by the **Santa Paula Chamber of Commerce** at the historic train depot, 200 N. 10th St. (10th and Santa Barbara Streets), 805/525-5561.

The Central Coast

Near Santa Paula

Two-lane Hwy. 126 between Hwy. 101 and I-5 is one of the few remaining "citrus scapes" in all of Southern California, groves of Valencia and navel oranges and lemons. Here the sweet perfume of citrus blossoms, once common throughout the southstate, is intoxicating. Just roll down the windows and drink it in. Driving east is the best way to tour the citrus groves, since most of the mom-and-pop fruit stands are on the south side of the busy highway. (In winter there are navels, in June Valencias.) For a more leisurely tour, take South Mountain Road south then east from Santa Paula then meander east; pick up Guiberson Road on the other side of Hwy. 23 (south of Fillmore) and wander all the way into Piru. Or vice versa.

Another of Southern California's "last best small towns" is historic **Fillmore** between Santa Paula and Piru, also noted for its intriguing brick-and-masonry downtown. But Fillmore sits astride the Oak Ridge earthquake fault. Right after a costly downtown spruce-up campaign, in early 1994 came the devastating Northridge earthquake. About $250 million in structural damage later—much of it to downtown buildings—Fillmore has put itself back together again, and is looking good. Stop to appreciate the reopened art deco Fillmore Towne Theater. Family-style fun here includes rides on the **Fillmore & Western Railway.** For more information about the area, contact the **Heritage Valley Tourism Bureau,** 275 Central Ave. in Fillmore, 800/700-1251, www.her itagevalley.net.

Directly south of Fillmore via Hwy. 23 is the affluent suburb of **Moorpark,** most famous as the first town in the U.S. to be completely powered by nuclear energy—a 1957 event that actually lasted only about an hour but which 20 million people watched on TV two weeks later, thanks to newsman Edward R. Murrow. Moorpark's nuclear adventure was an early Southern California Edison experiment. A small nuclear plant in the Simi Hills supplied only a part of the city's energy during most of the experiment, which lasted just a couple of years.

VENTURA

Travelers on Hwy. 101 are typically in such a hurry to get either to or from Santa Barbara that they miss Ventura, still one of the most pleasant surprises along the coast north of Los Angeles. Its surrounding farmlands are fast being lost to the usual California housing developments and shopping centers, but historic downtown Ventura retains both its dignity and serenity. Stopping here is like visiting an old friend's oft-described hometown, since you'll feel like you've been here before.

Fun local events include the annual **Fourth of July Street Faire** and the children's **Pushem Pullem Parade** downtown as well as the August **Summer ArtWalk** and the **Ventura County Fair.** If you're here in September, don't miss Southern California's own **Kinetic Sculpture Race at Ventura,** www.kineticrace.com, a people-powered artistic event to benefit the local homeless. Come in December for the **Parade of Lights** at Ventura Harbor.

For more information, contact: **Ventura Visitors and Convention Bureau,** 89 S. California St., Ste. C, 805/648-2075 or 800/333-2989, www.ventura-usa.com. Among available information: local guides to antique shops and art galleries, and listings of sportfishing and whale-watching tour companies, shopping centers, local golf courses, and parks and other area recreational facilities.

Sights

Pick up the self-guided downtown walking tour at the visitor bureau, or sign on for a guided downtown heritage tour, $8–12; call 805/658-4726 on weekdays for information and reservations. The centerpiece of Ventura's homey downtown Main Street business district is **Mission San Buenaventura,** 211 E. Main St., 805/643-4318, the ninth mission established in California and the last founded by Father Junípero Serra. Nearby is the very enjoyable **Ventura County Museum of History and Art,** 100 E. Main, 805/653-0323, www.vcmha.org, open Tues.–Sun. 10 A.M.–5 P.M. (closed major holidays). Beyond the excellent exhibits—the

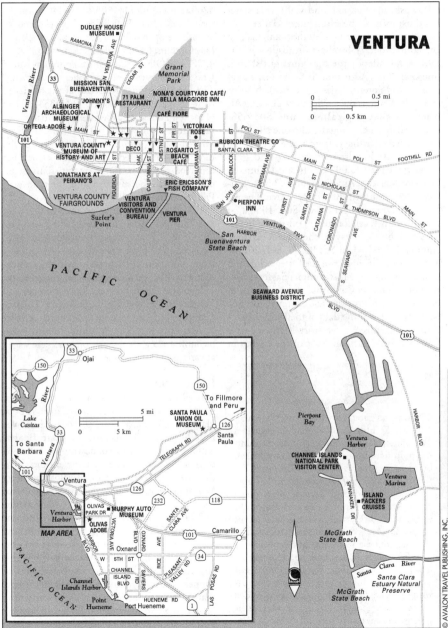

VENTURA

DUDLEY HOUSE MUSEUM ■
RAMONA ST
Grant Memorial Park
33
MISSION SAN BUENAVENTURA
JOHNNY'S ▼
71 PALM RESTAURANT
NONA'S COURTYARD CAFÉ/ BELLA MAGGIORE INN
ALBINGER ARCHAEOLOGICAL MUSEUM
CAFÉ FIORE
ORTEGA ADOBE ★ MAIN ST
VICTORIAN ROSE
POLI ST
101
VENTURA COUNTY MUSEUM OF HISTORY AND ART
DECO
RUBICON THEATRE CO
SANTA CLARA ST
ROSARITO BEACH CAFÉ
MAIN ST
POLI ST
FOOTHILL RD
JONATHAN'S AT PEIRANO'S
ERIC ERICSSON'S FISH COMPANY
NICHOLAS ST
VENTURA COUNTY FAIRGROUNDS
VENTURA VISITORS AND CONVENTION BUREAU
PIERPONT INN
E. THOMPSON BLVD
Surfer's Point
VENTURA PIER
101
VENTURA FWY
San Buenaventura State Beach
HARBOR
PACIFIC OCEAN
SEAWARD AVENUE BUSINESS DISTRICT ■
S. SEAWARD AVE
BLVD
101

0   0.5 mi
0   0.5 km

33
150
Ojai
River
150
To Fillmore and Peru
Lake Casitas
SANTA PAULA UNION OIL MUSEUM ★
126
Santa Paula
33
To Santa Barbara
0   5 mi
0   5 km
TELEGRAPH RD
101
Ventura
126
232
118
OLIVAS PARK DR
MURPHY AUTO MUSEUM ■
SANTA CLARA AVE
Camarillo
Ventura Harbor
OLIVAS ADOBE
VICTORIA AVE
HARBOR BLVD
OXNARD AVE
RICE AVE
101
34
MAP AREA
PACIFIC OCEAN
Oxnard
W 5TH ST
CHANNEL ISLAND BLVD
SAVIERS RD
PLEASANT VALLEY RD
LAS POSAS RD
Channel Islands Harbor
HUENEME RD
1
Point Hueneme
Port Hueneme

Pierpont Bay
Ventura Harbor
Ventura Marina
CHANNEL ISLANDS NATIONAL PARK VISITOR CENTER ■
SPINNAKER DR
ISLAND PACKERS CRUISES ■
HARBOR BLVD
McGrath State Beach
Santa Clara River
Santa Clara Estuary Natural Preserve
McGrath State Beach
Moon

N The Central Coast

Chumash, mission-era, and California statehood exhibits of the Huntsinger Gallery, the "three-dimension portraits" of the Smith Gallery, the contemporary local art on display in the Hoffman Gallery—the museum's gift shop is unusually fine. Admission is $4 adults, $3 seniors, $1 children (under age 6 free). Nearby, at 113 E. Main, is the small but fascinating **Albinger Archaeological Museum,** 805/658-4728, where an ongoing dig into one city block has unearthed artifacts from more than 3,500 years of coastal civilization; in 1974 and 1975 alone, more than 30,000 prehistoric, Chumash, Spanish, Mexican, American, and Chinese artifacts were unearthed. Admission is free. The Albinger museum is open Wed.–Sun. 10 A.M.–4 P.M. in summer; call for current off-season hours.

A few blocks away is the simple **Ortega Adobe,** 215 W. Main St., 805/658-4726, the 19th-century birthplace of the Ortega chile and salsa company—the first commercial food concern of its kind in California and originator of both the chile fire-roasting and canning processes. More evocative of the days of the Mexican ranchos, however, is the two-story Monterey-style **Olivas Adobe** hacienda east of the harbor at 4200 Olivas Park Dr., 805/644-4346, once the main house of vast Rancho San Miguel. Grounds at both are open daily 10 A.M.–4 P.M., weekends only for tours; for tour information, call 805/658-4728. The Olivas Adobe hosts courtyard Music Under the Stars concerts and other special events. The **Dudley House Museum** at the corner of Ashwood and Loma Vista, 805/642-3345, is one of the few authentically restored Victorian house in Ventura County open to the public. Tours are offered Jan.–Nov. on the first Sunday of the month, 1–4 P.M. Dudley House is open at other times for special whodunnit mystery dinners and other events. You can also tour the renovated Pierpont Inn (see below).

Classic car buffs, drive on over to the fairly new **Murphy Auto Museum,** 2340 Palma Dr., 805/654-0731, www.murphyautomuseum.com, a collection of more than 60 cars—including a large collection of Packards—owned by many collectors. It's open on weekends for limited hours.

If you get the chance, take in a performance of Ventura's excellent Equity **Rubicon Theatre Company,** housed in a onetime church at 1006 E. Main St., Ste. 300, 805/667-2900 www.rubicontheatre.org, though performances are staged at various other venues as well.

A PERRY MASON MYSTERY

During his career, Perry Mason mystery author Erle Stanley Gardner sold an estimated 325 million books worldwide. Author of countless pulp-fiction stories and the Perry Mason books—*The Case of the Terrified Typist* and *The Case of the Stuttering Bishop* among his 127 novels—Gardner was himself a case of lawyer turned writer. As an attorney in the Ventura firm of Orr and Gardner, Erle Stanley Gardner was famous for his dramatic courtroom presentations. But it wasn't until the 1920s that he began to write pulp-fiction short stories, and the 1930s that the first Perry Mason novel, *The Case of the Velvet Claws,* was published. Some of the writer's favorite Ventura haunts are included on guided Ventura walking tours. For information, reservations, and advance tickets, call 805/658-4726.

Recreation

Not all of Ventura's pleasures are downtown, however—at least not right downtown. A popular surfing locale, Ventura also boasts fine two-mile-long **San Buenaventura State Beach,** within strolling distance of downtown, extended by miles and miles of beach access up and down the coast. The recently restored 1,958-foot-long **Ventura Pier,** just south of downtown and east of California Street off Harbor Boulevard, reopened in 1993 after a seven-year renovation and unveiled anew in 2000 with a new octagonal extension, is the state's oldest and longest wooden pier. Still popular for fishing, the pier boasts a large restaurant, snack bar, the blowhole-like copper kinetic sculpture *Wavespout,* and lights that illuminate the beach after dark. West of the pier, at the end of Figueroa Street, is **Surfer's Point,** one of the state's premiere point breaks—a good place to watch longboard surfing. Two miles west of Ventura, at the end of Main Street, is **Emma Wood State Beach,** 805/968-1033, popular for swimming, surfing, and fishing. First-come, first-camped RV sites.

South along the coast, past the beach-scene **Seaward Avenue Business District,** is relaxed **Ventura Harbor,** just off Harbor Boulevard. For information on the Channel Islands and permitted recreational activities, see below. Immediately south of San Buenaventura, the harbor, and various local beaches is **McGrath State Beach,** 2211 Harbor Blvd., 805/968-1033, where scenes from Rudolph Valentino's romantic *The Sheik* were filmed. So beautiful was the beach, in fact, that Valentino eventually bought a house on the beach near Oxnard (see below), as did many of his friends—a neighborhood that became known as Hollywood Beach. McGrath is famous these days as one of the best bird-watching areas in California, thanks to the lush riverbanks of the Santa Clara River and sand dunes along the shore. A nature trail leads to the Santa Clara Estuary Natural Preserve. Two miles of beach provide surfing and fishing opportunities, however, swimmers are urged to use caution because of strong currents and riptides. The park offers great campsites right by the beach, $16–21, so you can go to sleep listening to the waves wash ashore. To reserve campsites call ReserveAmerica, 800/444-7275, or see www.reserveamerica.com.

Accommodations

Stylish downtown is the historic **Bella Maggiore Inn,** 67 S. California St. (on the west side of California between Main and Santa Clara), 805/652-0277 or 800/523-8479 (reservations). This three-story bed-and-breakfast hotel, built in 1924, has a breezy Mediterranean style—with fireplace, potted palms, and Italian chandeliers in the lobby, and shuttered windows, Capuan beds, ceiling fans, and fresh flowers in the graceful guest rooms. Rates are $75–200. Weather permitting—and it usually is—breakfast is served outside, in the lovely interior courtyard. In fact **Nona's Courtyard Cafe** here, a snazzy little Californian with a Northern Italian accent, is reason enough to stay. Breakfast can be a simple matter of coffee, pastries, and fresh fruit, or, for hearty appetites, omelettes

Bella Maggiore Inn

and egg dishes. Expect good salads, sandwiches, and pastas at lunch, and chicken, fresh fish, and seafood at dinner (menu changes weekly). Nona's is open daily for breakfast, Mon.–Sat. for lunch, and Friday, Saturday, and Sunday for dinner. Ventura's **Victorian Rose** B&B, 896 E. Main St., 805/641-1888, www.victorian-rose.com, a very Gothic onetime church where the five gorgeous guest rooms all feature private baths. Full breakfast included. Rates are $100–175.

The restored 1910 Craftsman **Ⓜ Pierpont Inn & Racquet Club** is a class act overlooking the ocean (and the freeway) from 550 San Jon Rd., 805/643-6144 or 800/285-4667, www.pierpont inn.com. The inn's East Wing was built in the 1950s and has been thoroughly remodeled, maintaining the Pierpont's Craftsman heritage with Stickley reproduction furniture. Money from a lawsuit against the state of California, which built a freeway rather than a state park on family land deeded to the state, financed construction of the

The Central Coast

three-story West Wing in the 1960s. Rooms and suites, many of them understated and "period," have been thoroughly updated, so visitors get a king-sized bed and hair dryers, irons, ironing boards, and DSL lines along with dovetail joints. Most intriguing are the Pierpont's unique accommodations. The Austen Pierpont Suite, offering classical Craftsman style and spectacular ocean views, is the inn's first step in restoring and reopening its original second-story guest rooms. The 1925 English Tudor-style cottages designed by Austen Pierpont, are charming, as is the three-bedroom Spanish revival Vickers' Estate. Totally cool: the 1950s' futurism on display in the 1950s' Flat, a one-bedroom apartment also known as the Jetsons' House. Rooms are $150–200. Suites, cottages, and Vickers' rooms are $200–350. The Jetsons' House is $350–400. A stay includes privileges at the adjacent racquet club—tennis, swimming, exercise equipment, classes, whirlpools, saunas, even kid's programs with childcare. Inn guests can also enjoy the very good onsite Austen's restaurant, serving healthy and good New American at breakfast, lunch dinner, and Sunday brunch. How about quiche du jour for lunch, or warm poached salmon tostadas?

Food

Johnny's, 176 N. Ventura Ave., 805/648-2021, is famous for its burritos. People come from miles around just to sink their teeth into *chile verde* burritos, *chile relleno* burritos, and other intriguing possibilities. Another local draw is the **Rosarito Beach Café,** 692 E. Main St., 805/653-7343, where fresh fish is a main attraction but even the regional Mexican specialties are quite good. Patio dining, too. For a boatload of seafood at lunch or dinner, head to the pier and **Eric Ericsson's Fish Company,** 668 Harbor Blvd., 805/643-4783.

Back downtown, appealing **Nona's Courtyard Café** at the historic Bella Maggiore Inn, 67 S. California St. (see above), is just the casual California-style Italian antidote for too much freeway-flying. Across the street is the stylish **Café Fiore,** 66 California, 805/653-1266, which offers traditional regional and nouvelle Italian served up with live jazz several nights each week. The charming **71 Palm Restaurant,** at home in a Craftsman at 71 N. Palm St., 805/653-7222, specializes in French country classics. Already a local classic is uptown, gallery-style **Deco,** 394 E. Main St., 805/667-2120, where dinner might start with coconut curried prawns or a Deco crab cake and continue with organic venison or New Zealand lamb. Full bar, good wine list.

OXNARD AND VICINITY

Recent and continuing growth, subdivisions and commercial developments, have all but consumed the county's once sleepy, agricultural past. Oxnard, still known for its annual May **California Strawberry Festival** and increasingly for produce-related events such as October's **Salsa Festival,** was once famous for its sugar beet, bean, and strawberry fields, along with mile after mile of citrus orchards and packing sheds. The vanishing fruit industry is memorialized at the stylized Oxnard Factory Outlet mall at Rice Avenue off Gonzales Road.

Sights

The center of civic pride downtown is impressive **Heritage Square,** a collection of immaculately restored, landmark historic local buildings and replicas now home to shops, law offices and such. In summer, come for the square's free summer concert series—from big band and doo wop to Latin jazz—every Friday from mid-June through August starting at 6 P.M. A stroll away is the neoclassical **Carnegie Art Museum,** 424 S. C St., 805/385-8157, which showcases local arts and artists (open Thurs.–Sun. 10 A.M.–5 P.M. and Sunday 1–5 P.M., small admission), and the **Ventura County Gull Wings Children's Museum,** 414 W. Fourth St., 805/483-3005 (open Wed.–Sun. 1–5 P.M., small admission). Or head for the waterfront and Oxnard's surprisingly tony **Channel Islands Harbor,** where the engrossing **Ventura County Maritime Museum** at Fisherman's Wharf, 2731 S. Victoria Ave., 805/984-6260, open daily 11 A.M.–5 P.M., offers an overview of maritime history, ship models, and ocean-themed artwork. Among the treasures collected here: a copy of the map of Anacapa Island drawn by James Whistler. The ship models are astonishing too, especially the detailed work by "master modeler" Edward Marple. Don't miss the *Genealogy of the Ship*, 36 ship models that trace the development of water transportation from 4000 BC to the present day.

Car enthusiasts, make every effort to visit the 45,000-square-foot **Vintage Museum of Transportation**, 1421 Emerson Ave., 805/486-5929, www.chandlerwheels.com, Otis Chandler's extraordinary collection of muscle cars, rare antique vehicles, milestone motorcycles, big game trophies, and fine art depicting automotive and wildlife themes. Ever seen a 1934 Packard 12-cylinder boattail speedster, a Duesenberg Derham Tourster, or a Porsche 959? Chandler and his collection are widely admired among fellow aficionados. Chandler's museum is open to the public only for limited "open house" events, however, about four or five dates per year, 10 A.M.–2 P.M., $7 per person (no children under age 10). Call or see the website for the upcoming schedule. P.S.: If the name "Otis Chandler" sounds vaguely familiar, it should. In 1960, when he was 32 and a Southern California surfer, Chandler became publisher of the family newspaper, the *Los Angeles Times*—and transformed it a legendary, widely respected paper. A fascinating read is *Privileged Son: Otis Chandler and the Rise and Fall of the L.A. Times Dynasty*, by Dennis McDougal.

Still, what can compete with nature? Most appealing of all in Oxnard is the beach—here a long series of lovely, uncrowded beaches strung together like so many pearls on a necklace, starting in the north with McGrath State Beach (see Ventura listing) and continuing south to Mandalay County Park, Oxnard Shores Beach, **Oxnard State Beach**—broad and sandy, backed by dunes and comfortably weathered beach bungalows—Hollywood Beach, Silver Strand Beach, and Port Hueneme Beach Park. Regulations about dogs, campfires, and everything else vary considerably, depending on the jurisdiction, so contact the visitor bureau for guidance.

For more information about the area, contact: **Oxnard Convention & Visitors Bureau** inside Connelly House at Heritage Square, 200 W. Seventh St., 805/385-7545 or 800/269-6273, www.oxnardtourism.com. For harbor information, contact: **Channel Islands Harbor Visitor Center,** 3810 W. Channel Islands Blvd., Ste. G, Oxnard, CA 93035, 805/985-4852, www.channel islandsharbor.com.

Port Hueneme

The area's military-industrial development is most notable just south of Oxnard in and around Port Hueneme (wy-NEE-mee), about 60 miles north of L.A. and 40 miles south of Santa Barbara. A Chumash word meaning "halfway" or "resting place" and previously spelled Y-nee-ma,

EXCURSION INLAND: COMMEMORATIVE CAMARILLO

Big news in nearby Camarillo these days is the new 670-acre **CSU Channel Islands** campus, www.csuci.edu, the 23rd campus in the California State University system and a gorgeous Spanish revival complex that was once Camarillo State Hospital. There are other fascinations in Camarillo, including the Southern California Branch of the all-volunteer **Commemorative Air Force Museum,** at home in two new large hangers at the Camarillo Airport. Previously known as the Confederate Air Force, the CAF collects, restores to flyable condition, and offers tours of vintage World War II-era aircraft including a Japanese "Zero" fighter, a Grumman F8F-2 "Bearcat" Fighter, and a North American B-25 Mitchell Bomber. A recent arrival is a fully restored and flyable 1954 Convair C-131 D Transport. The museum, library, and gift shop, 455 Aviation Dr. (corner of Eubanks) at the Camarillo Airport, 805/482-0064, are open daily 10 A.M.–4 P.M. Also a worthy destination is the spectacular 17-room **Camarillo Ranch** Victorian, 201 Camarillo Ranch Rd., 805/389-8182, centerpiece of the onetime 10,000-acre ranch where Adolfo Camarillo, California's "last Don," developed the Camarillo White Horse breed. Docent-guided tours of the 4.5-acre site ($3) also visit a large barn, stables, and tack room. Open Wednesday and Sunday noon–4 P.M. and Saturday 10 A.M.–2 P.M.

The Central Coast

Wyneema, and, officially, Wynema until 1940, when the U.S. Post Office altered it, Hueneme is still sometimes pronounced "way-NAY-ma" by old-timers here. A major military and civilian port—the only deep water port between San Francisco and Los Angeles—Hueneme is most noted for its **Point Mugu Naval Air Weapons Station,** at last report still a survivor of U.S. defense budget cuts. The **Naval Construction Battalion Center,** "Home of the Pacific Seabees," has been at home here since 1942. If naval history fans first stop at the Ventura Road gate for a visitor pass, the free **U.S. Navy Civil Engineer Corps/Seabee Museum** on the base at Ventura Road and Sunkist Avenue, 805/982-5165, is well worth a visit—one of the finest military museums around. Open Mon.–Sat. 9 A.M.–4 P.M., Sunday 12:30–4:30 P.M. Free. Port Hueneme also boasts a small city history museum downtown next to the chamber of commerce. The 1874 **Port Hueneme Lighthouse** is unique in the use of a Fresnel lens—exquisitely beveled, brass-encased glass prisms—on the main light.

Accommodations and Food

Oxnard is quite reasonable, compared to other coastal locales, offering a number of affordable hotels and motels; contact the visitors bureau for suggestions. To splurge, stay at the superbly situated Embassy Suites **Mandalay Beach Resort,** off Channel Islands Boulevard at 2101 Mandalay Beach Rd., 805/984-2500, www.mandalaybeach.embsuites.com, an all-suites hotel right on the beach—lovely tropical grounds with pool and spa, generous complimentary breakfast. There's a surprisingly good onsite restaurant, too—**Capistrano's.** Regular room rates are $200 and up, but ask about weekday and off-season specials

If you don't have time to drive area back roads in search of fresh produce—the visitors bureau has a great brochure, if you do—the **Oxnard Certified Farmers' Market,** 805/483-7960, held in Downtown Plaza Park at Fifth and C Streets on Thursday, 9:30 A.M.–1 P.M. The **Oxnard-Channel Islands Harbor CFM,** 805/643-6458, is held on Sunday 10 A.M.–2 P.M. along the water at 3350 Harbor Boulevard. Otherwise, almost

anyone will tell you that **The Whale's Tail** in the harbor at 3950 Blue Fin Circle, 805/985-2511, is the best place around. Also quite good is **SeaFresh Restaurant** upstairs in the Marine Emporium at 3600 S. Harbor, 805/815-4661, open for breakfast, lunch, and dinner.

CHANNEL ISLANDS NATIONAL PARK

Privately owned **Santa Catalina Island** is the only truly populated island among Southern California's eight Channel Islands. Populated by humans, that is. Many of the rest are inhabited by, or surrounded by, such rare, endangered, and endemic animals and plants—various whale and seal species, the island fox, the giant coreopsis "tree" (tree sunflowers), and the Santa Cruz Island ironweed among them—that biologists describe the Channel Islands, collectively, as North America's Galápagos.

San Miguel, Anacapa, Santa Cruz, and Santa Rosa Islands are seaward extensions of the east-west-trending Transverse Ranges (Santa Monica Mountains), and Santa Barbara, San Clemente, and San Nicolas are the visible ocean outposts of the Peninsular Range. Out-there **San Nicolas** and **San Clemente Islands,** property of the U.S. Navy, have rarely been visited. San Clemente has the unfortunate history of being used for bombing runs and military target practice. In the 1950s San Nicolas, inspiration for the book *Island of the Blue Dolphins,* was a top-secret post for monitoring submarines from the U.S.S.R. Since San Nicolas still contains ancient petroglyphs of dolphins, sharks, and whales, it's entirely appropriate that this same Cold War technology is now used to track the movements of migrating whales. An archaeologist working on San Nicolas has uncovered relics of an ancient island society, the Nicoleño Indians, people who lived in shelters built of whale bone and braided ropes from seaweed, traveled by boat, traded with the mainland, and disappeared in the 19th century.

Channel Islands preservation efforts first succeeded in 1938, when President Franklin D. Roosevelt protected Anacapa and Santa Barbara

COURTESY OF THE NATIONAL PARK SERVICE

Channel Islands National Park

Islands as a national monument. The five northernmost Channel Islands are now included in Channel Islands National Park, 250,000 acres of isolated Southern California real estate set aside in 1980 by President Jimmy Carter for federal preservation. (Odd, by national park standards, is the fact that half these acres are below the ocean's surface.) With some planning, visitors can set out for the park's **San Miguel, Santa Rosa, Santa Cruz, Anacapa,** and **Santa Barbara Islands.** Primitive camping is allowed on all five islands.

Islands in Time

The Channel Islands discovery of a complete fossilized skeleton of a pygmy or "dwarf" mammoth generated major excitement in the summer of 1994. Scientists speculate that this unusual miniature species, standing only four to six feet tall, was descended from woolly mammoths who swam here from the Southern California mainland during the Pleistocene, when the islands were "one" and just a few miles off the coast.

These islands in time reveal more surprises. For one thing, they are still on the move. Satellite measurements in the early 1990s showed that Santa Catalina, San Clemente, and San Nicolas Islands are moving northwest about one-half inch per year, and that a section of California's coastline is slowly converging with Santa Cruz and Santa Rosa islands—narrowing the Santa Barbara Channel by the same one-half inch each year.

For another, the Channel Islands provide some of the earliest North American evidence of human habitation. Prehistoric cooking pits found in conjunction with mammoth bones on Santa Rosa Island point to a neighborhood barbecue bash about 30,000-40,000 years ago.

Humans, other animals, and plant species have been introduced to the islands over the vast expanse of time; some failed, and some evolved into unique species as geographical isolation created genetic isolation—145 species of Channel Islands plants and animals are found nowhere else on earth.

The Central Coast

Unusual animals found on the islands today include the docile Channel Islands fox—a distant relative of the mainland's gray fox and about the size of a cat—which in 2004 was added to the federal endangered species list, decimated by newly arrived golden eagles and by disease spread by dogs. Other unique species include various rodents, bats, and feral goats and pigs. (Of the islands' endemic mammals, the deer mouse is known to carry hantavirus.) More than 260 bird species have been spotted on and around Santa Cruz Island alone. Brown pelican rookeries and the largest U.S. colony of Xantus's murrelet and black petrels are Channel Islands highlights.

Channel Islands National Park is also a national marine sanctuary and an international biosphere preserve, an ecosystem protectorate including all five islands and a six-mile area surrounding each one. In 2001 the Channel Islands were declared one of the 100 Globally Important Bird Areas by the nonprofit American Bird Conservancy. In 2002 the California Fish and Game Commission banned fishing in 175 square miles surrounding the islands, creating one of the largest marine reserves in U.S. waters.

During its annual migration south to Baja, Mexico, between January and March, the California gray whale appears in large numbers throughout the Channel Islands. In recent years a fairly large population of the rare and endangered blue whale, the world's largest creature, has tarried here as well. Dozens of species of marine mammals—27 whale species, more than 30 species of shark, dolphins and porpoises, various seal and sea lion species, sea otters—inhabit these waters during at least part of the year. Because of "upwelling" along California's coast and the Pacific Ocean's rich nutrient levels, vast kelp and other marine "forests" provide food and shelter for vast numbers of animals. Island tidepools also teem with sealife.

San Miguel Island

The most westerly of the Channel Islands, 9,325-acre San Miguel in the north is most famous for the thousands and thousands of seals and sea lions—up to 30,000 in summer, the population including the once-rare northern elephant seal—

that bask in the sun at Bennett Point. Also notable for hikers are its giant coreopsis "trees" and ghostly caliche forests, the latter an odd moonscape of calcified plant fossils—a natural variation on sandcasting—of up to 14,000 years old. Local landmarks include a modest memorial to Cabrillo, believed to have died here in 1583, and the ruins of the Lester Ranch of caretaker Herbert Lester, "King of San Miguel," who committed suicide here in 1942 rather than be forcibly evicted by the military. The weather can be wicked—always windy, foggy, often rainy—so come prepared. Primitive camping—it's a mile hike uphill from th beach, just nine campsites—hiking, beach exploration, and ranger-led hikes are the main attractions. Whatever else you do here, be sure to stick to established trails. San Miguel was once used for bombing practice, and live ordnance is constantly being discovered beneath the island's shifting sands.

Santa Rosa Island

The national park system has owned 52,794-acre Santa Rosa since 1986. The island's main attractions aren't the usual tourist trappings, but are rather along the lines of some 2,000 archaeology sites (strictly off-limits) related to Chumash Indian and Chinese abalone fishing settlements. Ruthlessly wind-whipped, Santa Rosa nonetheless protects rare and endangered plants, including one of only two surviving natural stands of Torrey pines (the other is near La Jolla). In addition to kayak beach camping and primitive camping inland—there are 15 campsites, with windbreaks and a shower, in Water Canyon—hiking, ranger-guided hikes, and vehicle tours are Santa Rosa's main attractions.

Santa Cruz Island

In 1997, preservationists finally took complete possession of 24-mile-long, 60,645-acre Santa Cruz Island, the largest of the eight Channel Islands. Island Adventures, a private firm that had offered private bow-hunting trips and bed-and-breakfast overnights on the east end of Santa Cruz, was evicted and the National Park Service bought its part of the island. The Nature Conservancy owns 76 percent of the island, the western sections, and manages it as the **Santa Cruz Island Preserve,** to date a noticeably healthier ecosystem. But park officials are restoring damaged east-end habitats, long overgrazed by sheep, goats, and feral pigs, and the historic Gherini Ranch. The ranch will eventually become the human-oriented hub of the park's five islands.

Already the park's primary draw, Santa Cruz is the most luxuriant of the Channel Islands. Two mountain ranges traverse Santa Cruz, one red, one white, and the island's picturesque Central Valley is an active earthquake zone. (According to local lore, terror created by the great California earthquake of 1812 finally convinced the native Chumash to leave Santa Cruz for life in the mainland's Franciscan missions.) This slice of the French Mediterranean right off the coast of California is the onetime ranching empire of Justinian Caire. Caire's winery here, finally closed during Prohibition, was at that time one of Southern California's largest. The Caire family's chapel and other buildings of the subsequent Santa Cruz Island Company ranch were preserved by subsequent owners, members of the Stanton family, and by The Nature Conservancy.

The island's curvaceous coastline boasts many natural harbors, bays, and popular dive spots, along with some spectacular sea caves. The landscape features 10 distinct plant communities, about 650 plant species scattered from pine forests, oak woodlands, and riparian streams and springs to meadows, sandy beaches, and dunes. The seascape features many more plant and animal communities, which makes Santa Cruz paradise for divers, kayakers, snorkelers, and tidepoolers. (Look, but don't touch.) More than 260 bird species have been spotted on and around the island, including the endemic Santa Cruz Island scrub jay, bigger and bluer than its mainland cousins. Hike, camp, and explore on the park's property. Access to the Nature Conservancy preserve is available only on guided Island Packers outings (see below). Private boaters, see the California Nature Conservancy website, www.tnccalifornia.org, to request permission to land on the west side of Santa Cruz (complete a landing permit).

Santa Cruz Island is immensely popular for camping. The 40 shaded **Scorpion Valley** camp-

sites are scattered throughout the valley. All supplies—including "enclosed" campstoves, during high-risk fire periods—must be carried in, though there is potable water. Four new **Del Norte** backcountry coastal-view campsites are clustered together in an oak grove some 11 miles west from Scorpion Valley, and about 3.5 miles from Prisoners Landing.

Anacapa Island

Wind-whipped Anacapa Island is most accessible from the mainland, just 11 miles from Oxnard. Quite popular for daytrippers, 699-acre Anacapa is actually three distinct islands divided by narrow channels. **East Anacapa,** with seven campsites, is the usual human destination. On the way to Landing Cove is 80-foot-tall **Arch Rock,** an immense eroded volcanic "bridge" with a 50-foot arch, unofficial emblem of the Channel Islands since James Whistler sketched it during his stint in the U.S. Coast Guard. Once ashore it's a quick 154 steps straight up to the blufftops, where the meandering nature trail begins. Beyond the visitor center, standing vigil at the entrance to the Santa Barbara Channel, is the U.S. Coast Guard's restored, solar-powered **East End Lighthouse** and associated museum, open for public tours. (Inquire at the park's mainland visitor center for details.) If time, weather, and water conditions permit, **Landing Cove** and **Frenchy's Cove** are popular for snorkeling and swimming. Guided **kayak tours** are also popular here.

On **Middle Anacapa** the stands of giant coreopsis ("tree sunflowers") are stunning when in bloom—on a clear day, their vibrant color is visible from the mainland. Craggy **West Anacapa,** the largest of the three, is off-limits to the public, protected as a brown pelican rookery and reserve.

Santa Barbara Island

Ever fantasized about being stranded on a desert island? Want to play *Survivor?* Here's a possible destination. Unlike the lushly landscaped, socially sophisticated mainland city of the same name, 639-acre Santa Barbara Island is a piece of California in the raw. Smallest of the park's five islands, Santa Barbara has no trees, no natural beaches, and no fresh water. Its sheer cliffs rise abruptly from the sea. It's often windy and foggy in quick succession; in winter Santa Barbara's thin thatch of grass and scrub is green. Most popular with birders, divers, and kayakers, in warm weather Santa Barbara also attracts pinniped peerers, hikers, and campers. (Bring *everything*, including water.) A lonely 25 miles west of Catalina, a long, often choppy three hours from Ventura Harbor, Santa Barbara is most appreciated by avid island and/or wildlife aficionados. There are eight campsites here, a half-mile uphill from the boat dock, and five miles of hiking trails.

Tours

Unless you have your own boat, if you're shoving off from Ventura you'll be going via **Island Packer Cruises,** which offers the rare opportunity to get up close and personal with Channel Islands National Park, an area otherwise all but inaccessible for the average traveler. Since island access is limited, extra benefits of an Island Packer trip—some trips, anyway—include the chance to hike, snorkel, or kayak. Camping dropoffs can also be arranged. Whale-watching (January through March) is particularly popular, especially since whales, dolphins, seals, and sea lions favor the protected waters and abundant food supplies near the Channel Islands. But every season has its unique pleasures. Spring, for example, offers the chance to see wildflowers and rare endemic plants in bloom. For a quicker trip to Santa Cruz, Island Packers launched the faster new 64-foot catamaran powerboat *Islander* in 2003-cutting the one-way trip time in half, to just one hour.

For current information, contact Island Packer Tours, 1867 Spinnaker Dr. in Ventura, 805/642-7688 (recorded) or 805/642-1393, www.island packers.com. The company's office is adjacent to the park's visitor center in Ventura Harbor (closed Thanksgiving and Christmas). Reservations are required for all trips, but are subject to last-minute cancellation in case of big waves or bad weather. For popular weekend outings, reserve well in advance. In spring and summer, Island Packer operates tours to—or around—all five islands. See the website or call for specific information about "transport" services for backpackers and long-term campers.

If you're departing from Santa Barbara, the official Channel Islands trip concessionaire there is **Truth Aquatics,** 301 W. Cabrillo Blvd. in Santa Barbara, 805/962-1127, www.truthaquat ics.com.

Channel Islands Aviation offers daytrip transportation, tours, and "dropoffs" to and from Santa Rosa Island (and Santa Catalina Island). For current information, contact: Channel Islands Aviation, 305 Durley Ave. in Camarillo, 805/987-1301.

A variety of area outfitters offer guided kayaking excursions, including **Adventours Outdoor Excursions,** 726 Reddick Ave. in Santa Barbara, 805/899-2929, www.adventours.com; **Channel Islands Kayak Center** in Oxnard, 805/984-5995; and the **Southwind Kayak Center** in Irvine, 17855 Skypark Circle #A, 949/261-0200 or 800/768-8494, www.southwindkayaks.com.

Practicalities

For more information on the islands and permitted recreational activities, contact: **Channel Islands National Park Visitors Center,** 1901 Spinnaker Dr. in Ventura, 805/658-5730 (recorded), www.nps.gov/chis. To reach park headquarters call 805/658-5700 (recorded) or 805/658-5711. Or sign on for an island tour (see below). The visitor center in Ventura Harbor is *the* stop for relevant books, maps, and a good general introduction to the history and natural history of the islands. For hiking permits for San Miguel Island—to travel unescorted beyond the ranger station—call 805/658-5711.

Primitive campgrounds are available on all five islands (see individual islands, above, for more details). If you're planning to camp or hike (permits required), come prepared for anything—wind, in particular—because the weather can change abruptly. For current information, inquire at the park's visitor center. Camping reservations—$12.35 per day, at last report—are available by contacting **National Park Service Reservations,** 800/365-2267, http://reservations.nps.gov. For beach camping permits for Santa Rosa Island, call park headquarters at 805/658-5711.

Los Angeles Coast

Scribes and small-screen prognosticators love to announce the death of Los Angeles. With every new disaster they do it again. Most recently L.A. was dead because of its raging wildfires and devastating earthquakes. Before that, L.A.'s demise was due to the decline of California's defense industry, overwhelming freeway traffic, police brutality, race riots, illegal immigration, and gang warfare. Not to mention the smog.

The apocalyptic tendencies of Los Angeles—more accurately, our need to place Los Angeles at the center of our fascinations with disaster and futuristic despair—are as well-represented in literature as in real life. Consider the nuclear holocaust in Thomas Pynchon's *Gravity's Rainbow.* The earthquake in *The Last Tycoon.* The riot in *The Day of the Locust.* And little-known classics such as Marie Corelli's strange 1921 romance *Secret Power,* in which L.A. is decimated by an atomic explosion. Then there's Ward Moore's hilarious 1947 *Greener Than You Think,* in which the city is done in by bermuda grass. Movies have also made their contribution to the cult of L.A. apocalypse, of course, *Blade Runner* most memorably.

4

Must-Sees

Look for **M** to find the sights and activities you can't miss and **N** for the best dining and lodging.

M **Santa Monica Pier and Pacific Park:** Now fully restored, the pier features the two-story landmark **Hippodrome** and 1916 Looff carousel, original arcades, and bumper cars. The new pier extension includes a five-story, ocean-view roller coaster and giant ferris wheel, the **Pacific Wheel** (page 478).

M **South Bay Bicycle Trail:** This wide paved bike path, accessible at many points, connects Will Rogers State Beach with beaches and beach attractions all the way south to Torrance (page 479).

M **Third Street Promenade:** The Third Street Promenade is one of L.A.'s hot "destination streets," a shopping and entertainment district just blocks from the beach (page 483).

M **Ocean Front Walk and Venice Beach:** Here's the L.A. that amazes the rest of the world—the rollerskating swamis, fire-eaters, palmists, tarot card readers, and bikini-clad babes on in-line skates blithely dodge bicyclists, baby strollers, and bug-eyed tourists (page 488).

M **Malibu Lagoon and Adamson House:** Adjoining the pier and state beach, tiny Malibu Lagoon offers impromptu nature appreciation. The grand 1929 Spanish-Moorish Adamson House, is a showcase for the Malibu Tile Company's exceptional craftsmanship—down to the tiled outdoor dog shower (page 511).

M *Lane Victory* **Cruise:** Cruise to Catalina Island and back onboard the SS *Lane Victory,* a national historic landmark manned by an impressive, well-informed volunteer crew that reenacts the World War II experience—complete with aerial dogfight (page 526).

M **Long Beach Aquarium of the Pacific:** With 550 species of aquatic life in three major galleries, the aquarium represents the ocean's three regions—Southern California/Baja, the Tropical Pacific, and the Northern Pacific (page 531).

M RMS *Queen Mary:* With its sleek streamline-modern interiors this is one of the largest passenger ships ever built (page 532).

M **Avalon:** Fringed with palms, olive trees, and tourists, Avalon looks like a Mediterranean hill town (page 537).

M **Two Harbors:** Two Harbors is "the other Catalina," the one where you really can get away from it all (page 538).

LOS ANGELES COAST

Malibu

Malibu Lagoon State Beach/ Adamson House

South Bay Bicycle Trail

Santa Monica Pier/Pacific Park

Santa Monica

Third Street Promenade

Venice

Venice Beach/Ocean Front Walk

Santa Monica Bay

Manhattan Beach

Redondo Beach

PACIFIC OCEAN

Lane Victory

Long Beach Aquarium of the Pacific

San Pedro

Two Harbors

Long Beach

RMS Queen Mary

Santa Catalina Island

Avalon

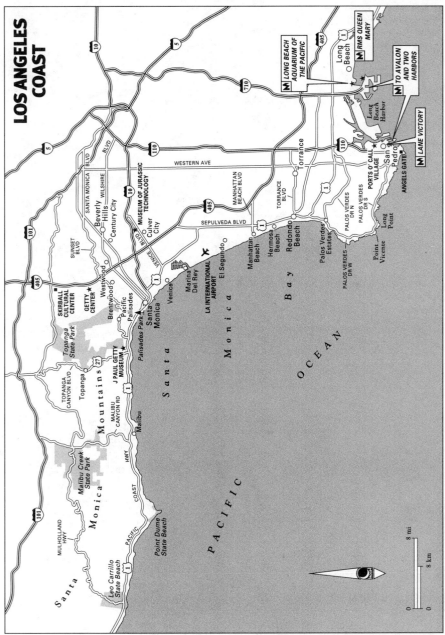

LOS ANGELES
COAST

Los Angeles Coast

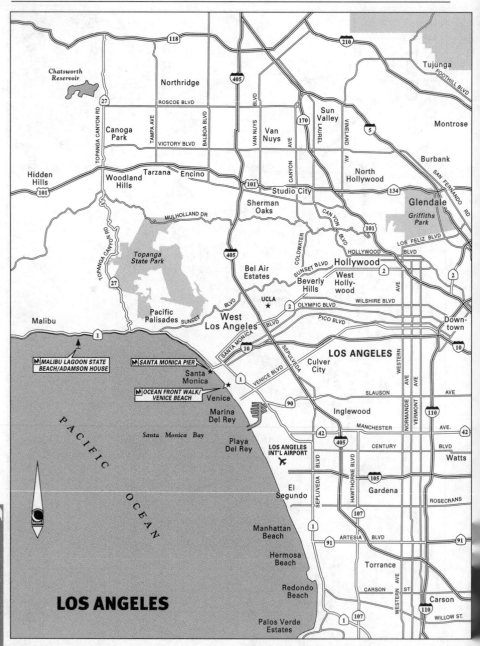

118
210
Tujunga
FOOTHILL BLVD
Chatsworth
Reservoir
Northridge
405
Sun
Valley
Montrose
27
ROSCOE BLVD
170
5
Burbank
TOPANGA CANYON RD
Canoga
Park
TAMPA AVE
BALBOA BLVD
VAN NUYS
VINELAND
LAUREL
CANYON
AV.
North
Holly-
wood
SAN FERNANDO RD
VICTORY BLVD
Van
Nuys
AVE
Hidden
Hills
Tarzana Encino
Woodland
Hills
101
Studio City
134
Glendale
101
MULHOLLAND DR
Sherman
Oaks
CAN YON
Griffiths
Park
LOS FELIZ BLVD
TOPANGA CANYON RD
405
BLVD
COLDWATER
HOLLYWOOD
BLVD
Topanga
State Park
Bel Air
Estates
SUNSET BLVD
Hollywood
2
2
27
West
Holly-
wood
AVE
Pacific
Palisades
SUNSET
BLVD
UCLA
2
OLYMPIC BLVD
WILSHIRE BLVD
Beverly
Hills
Malibu
1
West
Los Angeles
BLVD
PICO BLVD
Down-
town
SANTA MONICA
10
SEPULVEDA
LOS ANGELES
10
MALIBU LAGOON STATE
BEACH/ADAMSON HOUSE
SANTA MONICA PIER
Santa
Monica
Culver
City
WESTERN
NORMANDIE
VERMONT
AVE
AVE
OCEAN FRONT WALK/
VENICE BEACH
Venice
VENICE BLVD
1
SLAUSON
AVE
90
Marina
Del Rey
Inglewood
110
PACIFIC
Santa Monica Bay
Playa
Del Rey
42
405
MANCHESTER
CENTURY
AVE.
BLVD
42
Watts
LOS ANGELES
INT'L AIRPORT
SEPULVEDA
HAWTHORNE BLVD
105
OCEAN
El
Segundo
Gardena
ROSECRANS
MOON
107
Manhattan
Beach
1
ARTESIA
BLVD
91
91
Hermosa
Beach
Torrance
WESTERN AVE
ST
LOS ANGELES
Redondo
Beach
CARSON
Carson
110
WILLOW ST.
Palos Verde
Estates
1
107

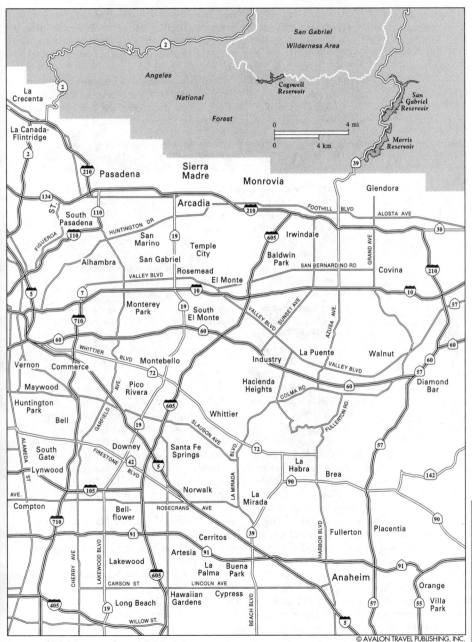

Even so, in recent years L.A. has suffered from entirely too much dystopia, entirely too much rumination on the subject of utopia gone wrong. Entirely too much *reality*. And reality has never been the point here. Los Angeles, after all, is both the world's foremost fantasy factory and psychic playground for America's most childlike narcissisms.

The lesson of Los Angeles is the lesson of the movies. Big faces on the big screen reassure us that "individual lives have scope and grandeur," in the words of California writer Richard Rodriguez. "The attention L.A. lavishes on a single face is as generous a metaphor as I can find for the love of God."

From a strictly secular point of view, the sun is also generous. In Los Angeles the sun always shines, on the degenerate and deserving alike. At last report this was still true.

Santa Monica

Is there a sunnier place anywhere? Santa Monica is the quintessential L.A. beach town, a distinction held since the early 1900s when the original Looff "pleasure pier" was the bayside beacon for long days of Southern California-style fun in the sun. Unlike other popular L.A. tourist destinations, Santa Monica is much more than just a pretty face and a good time on the weekends—despite its place in L.A. literature as the barely disguised 1930s' "Bay City" in Raymond Chandler's *Farewell My Lovely*. These days the city is considered politically progressive, a rarity in Southern California. That tendency has translated into rent control and a trend toward liberal politicians that's still going strong. Santa Monica's state senator is Sheila Kuehl—better known in some circles as the character Zelda Gilroy from *The Many Lives of Dobie Gillis* 1960s TV series—California's first openly gay legislator, a Harvard Law School grad who was elected to the Assembly in 1994, and the first woman in California history to be named as speaker pro tem. The city's political tendencies have spawned, particularly among local landlords, the disparaging nickname of People's Republic of Santa Monica—not nearly as marketable as Zenith City by the Sunset Sea of the late 19th century, or the contemporary Real Life Alternative. By Southern California standards the community is also atypical socially. Here, movie stars and the just plain wealthy blend with a large expatriate British population, senior citizens, middle-class and low-income families, and poverty-stricken activists, artists, and street people. As odd as it seems in these days of escalating public intolerance, most everyone here gets along most of the time. Pressure to rein-in rampant homelessness is increasing, however.

Most of Santa Monica's initial attractions are front and center, along or near the edge of Santa Monica Bay—the bay that's served as a backdrop for a number of movies, including *Funny Girl, The Net* and *Beverly Hills Cop III*. The city's own strand of sand is Santa Monica State Beach. On weekends and in summer an equal draw is the associated Santa Monica Pier—now including a 1922 carousel (the one Paul Newman operated in *The Sting*) and a carnival of fun rides. But Santa Monica offers much, much more, including the nearby pleasures of Malibu, Venice, the Santa Monica Mountains National Recreation Area, and Will Rogers State Historic Park, wacky and world-class art galleries, imaginative shopping, and an unusual range of good accommodations and great restaurants—in every price category. Beach town or no, Santa Monica has it all.

Most people arrive via the Santa Monica Freeway (I-10), though one of the city's claims to fame is its location at the Pacific Ocean end of the original Route 66. Once here, it's easy to get around via the city's Big Blue Bus. (If you're driving, bring pockets full of quarters. Local parking meters, particularly near the beach, have voracious appetites.) For current information about "Bay City," contact: **Santa Monica Visitor Center,** in a little kiosk at 1400 Ocean Ave. in Palisades Park, 310/393-7593, www.santamonica .com, and open for drop-in assistance daily 10 A.M.–4 P.M. (until 5 P.M. in summer). Watch L.A.-area newspapers for Santa Monica special events, major ones scheduled on weekends and/or summer evenings, or visit the Santa Monica visitor bureau's "calendar" section on the website, with searchable events listings.

HISTORY

Gaspar de Portolá claimed what is now Santa Monica for Spain in 1769. According to local legend, Franciscan Father Juan Crespi selected the name—choosing St. Monica because the area's natural springs reminded him of the tears she shed when her son Augustine, destined to become a saint himself, turned to Christianity. But the grassy mesa was still unoccupied in 1822, when nascent Mexico rousted the Spanish. A three-way tussle over its ownership because of conflicting land-grant titles was resolved only in 1851, after California statehood: Don Francisco Sepulveda received 30,000-acre Rancho San Vicente y Santa Monica, while Ysidro Reyes and Francisco Marquez jointly gained the 6,600-acre Boca de Santa Monica, which included Santa Monica Canyon and much of the bayside coastline.

In 1872 cattleman Colonel R.S. Baker bought the Sepulveda spread and much of the Reyes-Marquez property. Just two years later Baker sold three-fourths of his land wealth to the British-born millionaire John P. Jones, the junior U.S. senator from Nevada. Jones had big ideas. Together he and Baker planned the new town of Santa Monica, which would include a wharf and interconnected trans-California railroad—to serve Jones's Nevada silver mines and other future industry. Some in Los Angeles detected a threat to their own potential prosperity and attacked the planned city of Santa Monica as an intended rival. But others lined up eagerly in 1885 to buy the city's first lots. Within months Santa Monica was booming, boasting more than 150 homes, 75 or so "tent" or temporary homes, and 1,000 citizens. With the wharf open for business and the railroad under construction, a prosperous future seemed assured.

In 1877 the city's first resort, the Santa Monica Bath House, opened for business. A full day's stagecoach ride from downtown Los Angeles, Santa Monica nonetheless beckoned as a balmy respite while the rest of L.A. scorched in the summer heat. Vacationers could enjoy the cool ocean breezes from tents pitched in Santa Monica Canyon. Hotels, restaurants, and shops soon followed; summer residents began to stay year-round. In 1887 Santa Monica voted to incorporate and become an independent city.

Yet Santa Monica's success would be some time coming. Jones lost most of his fortune—and his railroad—when silver prices plummeted. His wharf was condemned and quickly demolished.

The Pier

The earliest incarnation of Santa Monica's pier was known in the early 1870s as "Shoo-Fly Landing," the point of departure for asphalt tar from Hancock Park's La Brea Ranch that was destined to become paved streets in San Francisco. Then came John Jones's 1875 Los Angeles and Independence railroad, its wharf and depot allowing steamers to deliver goods destined for Los Angeles via railway.

In the late 1880s the Los Angeles "port war" began. Collis Huntington, owner of Southern Pacific Railroad, wanted L.A.'s official harbor to be in Santa Monica—where he, coincidentally, owned most everything. Those who feared Huntington's monopoly in the Santa Monica area and elsewhere fought hard against his plans. Nonetheless determined that the Port of Los Angeles would be in Santa Monica, Huntington upped the ante by building California's most massive pier; his finished Santa Monica Pier measured 4,720 feet long and 130 feet wide when it opened for business in 1902. Yet Huntington lost the war, and San Pedro to the south became L.A.'s primary port city. All Santa Monica shipping stopped by 1910, and raging surf ravaged Huntington's grand pier.

But if Santa Monica failed as a center of commerce and trade, it succeeded as one of the region's preferred recreation destinations. Santa Monica's grand Arcadia Hotel, the North Beach Bath House, and the Deauville Beach Club soon signaled the city's arrival among L.A.'s monied minions. And the city's final incarnation of its earlier dreams, the Santa Monica Municipal Pier,

Los Angeles Coast

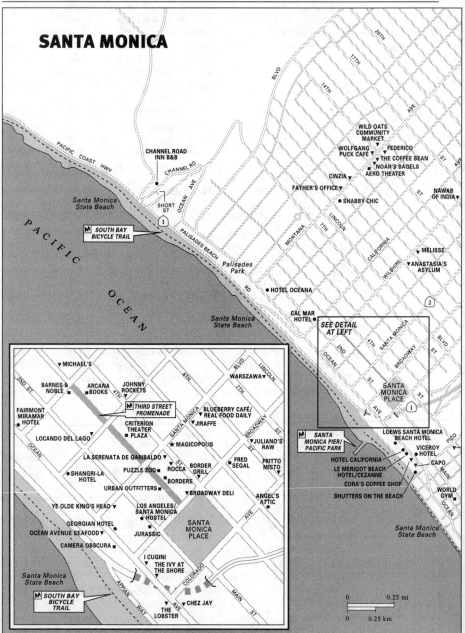

SANTA MONICA

CHANNEL ROAD
INN B&B

*Santa Monica
State Beach*

SOUTH BAY
BICYCLE TRAIL

PACIFIC COAST HWY

PACIFIC
OCEAN

CHANNEL RD

OCEAN AVE

SHORT ST

PALISADES BEACH

*Palisades
Park*

PALISADES BEACH RD

*Santa Monica
State Beach*

WILD OATS
COMMUNITY
MARKET
WOLFGANG
PUCK CAFÉ ▼ FEDERICO ▼
▼ THE COFFEE BEAN
▼ NOAH'S BAGELS
AERO THEATER
CINZIA ▼
FATHER'S OFFICE ▼
■ SHABBY CHIC

MONTANA
7TH
LINCOLN
CALIFORNIA
WILSHIRE

MÉLISSE ▼
▼ ANASTASIA'S
ASYLUM

NAWAB
OF INDIA ▼

● HOTEL OCEANA

CAL MAR
HOTEL ●

SEE DETAIL
AT LEFT

2ND ST
OCEAN
4TH
SANTA MONICA
BROADWAY
2
BLVD

SANTA
MONICA
PLACE

1

SANTA
MONICA PIER/
PACIFIC PARK

LOEWS SANTA MONICA
BEACH HOTEL
HOTEL CALIFORNIA ● VICEROY ●
HOTEL
LE MERIGOT BEACH ● ● CAPO
HOTEL/CEZANNE
CORA'S COFFEE SHOP ●
SHUTTERS ON THE BEACH ●
WORLD
GYM ■

PICO
MAIN
OCEAN

*Santa Monica
State Beach*

Detail map

▼ MICHAEL'S

2ND ST
BARNES &
NOBLE ■
ARCANA
■ BOOKS
4TH
JOHNNY
ROCKETS
FAIRMONT
MIRAMAR
HOTEL ●

THIRD STREET
PROMENADE
CRITERION
THEATER
■ PLAZA

8TH
7TH
BLVD
LINCOLN

WARSZAWA ▼

SANTA MONICA
BLUEBERRY CAFÉ/
REAL FOOD DAILY
▼ JIRAFFE

LOCANDO DEL LAGO ▼

★ MAGICOPOLIS

BROADWAY

▼ JULIANO'S
RAW

OCEAN

LA SERENATA DE GARIBALDO ▼
● SHANGRI-LA
HOTEL
PUZZLE ZOO ▼
URBAN OUTFITTERS ■
★ ROCCA
BORDER
GRILL
■ BORDERS

FRED
SEGAL

FRITTO
MISTO

▼ BROADWAY DELI

YE OLDE KING'S HEAD ▼
GEORGIAN HOTEL ●
OCEAN AVENUE SEAFOOD ▼
CAMERA OBSCURA ■

LOS ANGELES/
SANTA MONICA
● HOSTEL
■ JURASSIC

SANTA
MONICA
PLACE

AVE

ANGEL'S
ATTIC

SOUTH BAY
BICYCLE
TRAIL

APPIAN WAY

*Santa Monica
State Beach*

■ I CUGINI
THE IVY AT
THE SHORE

▼ CHEZ JAY
THE
LOBSTER

AVE
COLORADO
MAIN ST

SANTA MONICA PLACE

SANTA
MONICA
PLACE

0   0.25 mi
0   0.25 km

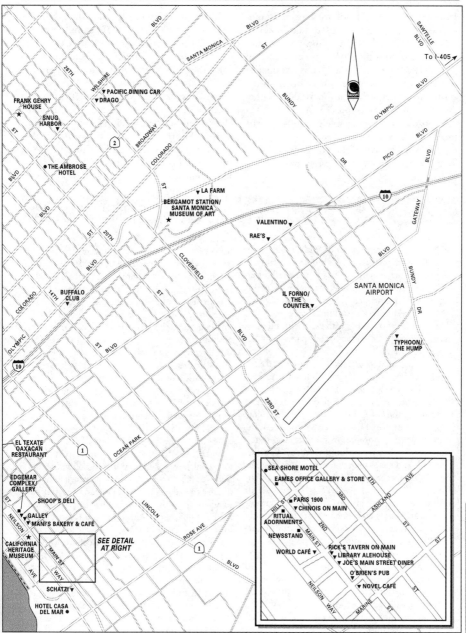

To I-405

FRANK GEHRY HOUSE

PACIFIC DINING CAR
DRAGO
SNUG HARBOR

THE AMBROSE HOTEL

LA FARM
BERGAMOT STATION/ SANTA MONICA MUSEUM OF ART

VALENTINO
RAE'S

BUFFALO CLUB

IL FORNO/ THE COUNTER

SANTA MONICA AIRPORT

TYPHOON/ THE HUMP

EL TEXATE OAXACAN RESTAURANT

EDGEMAR COMPLEX/ GALLERY

SHOOP'S DELI

GALLEY
MANI'S BAKERY & CAFÉ

CALIFORNIA HERITAGE MUSEUM

SEE DETAIL AT RIGHT

SCHATZI

HOTEL CASA DEL MAR

SEA SHORE MOTEL
EAMES OFFICE GALLERY & STORE

PARIS 1900
CHINOIS ON MAIN
RITUAL ADORNMENTS
NEWSSTAND
WORLD CAFÉ
RICK'S TAVERN ON MAIN
LIBRARY ALEHOUSE
JOE'S MAIN STREET DINER
O'BRIEN'S PUB
NOVEL CAFÉ

Los Angeles Coast

© AVALON TRAVEL PUBLISHING, INC.

arrived in 1912, quickly followed by the adjoining Looff "pleasure pier" in 1916. The Looff pier featured a trademark carousel, other amusements, and the enormous Blue Streak roller coaster. In July of 1924 the La Monica Ballroom opened at pier's end; it was the largest ballroom in the world, host to crowds of up to 10,000. Rather than a rough industrial port, Santa Monica became instead a sleepy seaside retreat—a serene small town largely unperturbed by progress until the 1960s and the completion of the Santa Monica Freeway, when it became easier for the world to get here.

Yet illicit entertainment did arrive, symbolized in the 1920s by offshore gambling ships. These 24-hour floating casinos were careful to remain at least three miles from shore, just beyond the state's legal jurisdiction. Water taxis ferried customers from the pier to the *Tango, Texas, Showboat,* and *Rex,* ships that could host up to 1,900 guests at a time. Offshore gambling flourished here until 1939, when the California Supreme Court declared the area between Point Dume and Point Vicente as "bay," not open sea, and therefore subject to state regulation.

LIFE'S A BEACH

Along with the cult of celebrity, palm trees, and fancy freeways lined with bright shiny cars, the beach is among L.A.'s most universal symbols. The beach—as in The Beach, the youthful social creation of 1950s Los Angeles—is all about sun-bleached attitude, arcane sports, superficial sexuality, and saltwater-scented steel guitar. And The Beach lives on today, with each youthful summer's new toast-brown crop happily packed into the stucco sameness of beachfront sardine cans. Pale imitations turn up in places such as Florida and Australia, but Los Angeles invented The Beach.

So the slang phrase Life's a Beach takes on genuine meaning in Los Angeles County, where the sunny sands of L.A. lore now suffer a relentless assault of urban ills, all related to the southstate's relentless population growth. Too much traffic and too little parking. Garbage. Graffiti. Alcohol- and gang-related violence. Water pollution. Still a localized problem, ocean water pollution levels are generally decreasing because of improved sewage treatment facilities and greater citizen awareness about the effects of dumping toxic substances into sewers and storm drains. Yet if pollution is disappearing, in some places so is the sand—in a natural southward drift exacerbated by the construction of breakwaters and harbors and, inland, by damming the rivers, streams, and associated sediment flow that would otherwise replenish the sand supply. These days, maintaining the bay's wide white beaches is additional engineering work.

Fun in the Sun

Santa Monica Bay, the shallow white sand-fringed coastal indentation harboring most of L.A. County's beaches, was once one of the world's richest fishing areas. Those days are long gone, after a half-century's relentless flow of industrial chemicals and other toxic wastes from land to sea. But the bay is slowly getting cleaner—clean enough that even porpoises have returned. According to L.A.'s **Heal the Bay,** to swim safely avoid obvious pollution "problem areas" (usually posted as no-swim areas), steer clear of all storm drains (most of which are *not* signed or otherwise identified, so heads up), and don't swim for at least three days after a rainstorm. For the latest information on the environmental health of Santa Monica Bay's beaches, contact: Heal the Bay, 3220 Nebraska Ave. in Santa Monica, 310/453-0395 or 800/HEAL BAY (California only), www.healthebay.org. A nonprofit coalition working to achieve fishable, swimmable, and surfable coastal waters—with pollution levels within standards set by the federal Clean Water Act—Heal the Bay publishes an **Annual Beach Report Card** for L.A. County's beaches, also available on the website, complete with maps and charts of both dry (summer) and wet weather pollution measurements. To support its work, Heal the Bay sponsors occasional fundraisers and community events and also sells T-shirts, sweatshirts, and other items. Go ahead and buy one. It's a very good cause.

But if alcohol—even beer or wine—is a central cause in your life, forget about enjoying it at the

The beachfront running south of the Santa Monica Pier to Venice Beach was Chandler's mythic if slightly sleazy Bay City. Stretching along the pearly sand north of the pier was early L.A.'s notorious Gold Coast, where sumptuous spreads included the fabulous beach homes of Marion Davies (mistress of William Randolph Hearst) and others of Hollywood's party-hearty set. Almost all that remains of that era is the Sand and Sea Club at 415 PCH, once servants' quarters for the Davies mansion, and most notable recently as a location for the TV show *Beverly Hills 90210*. A few surviving Gold Coast-era mansions have been similarly reincarnated, or walled off from public view. Other old-timers hang on, or try to. Santa Monica's landmark 1926 Breakers Beach Club hosted stars Greta Garbo, Frank Sinatra and Jean Harlow in its heyday—more recently reborn as the SeaCastle Apartments, luxury apartments with some custom "beach suites" available for long-term stays.

SIGHTS

Chances are good that you'll recognize **Palisades Park,** recently refurbished, even if you've never

beach. It is illegal to drink alcohol on public beaches (and at city and county parks), a zero-tolerance policy that can get you booted off the beach and fined on the spot. The get-tough beach booze policy is in response to astronomical increases in alcohol-related assaults, drownings, and post-beach car wrecks. (And what lifeguards say is law at the beach. Unless you want to leave the beach earlier than planned, think twice before defying them.)

You can sunbathe, though. And swim, fairly safely where lifeguards are on duty. And surf, body surf, and boogie-board. And play very competitive beach volleyball. And picnic. Particularly north of Malibu and near the Palos Verdes Peninsula you can tidepool. Pier and surf fishing are permitted at most piers and many public beaches. Catches include spotfin and yellowfin croakers, corbina, and barred and walleyed perch. And you can run with the grunion, which come ashore to spawn on certain nights in March, June, July, and August. When the annual grunion runs are announced in local media, hundreds of people suddenly arrive after dark, flashlights in hand, ready to gather the slippery silver fish by hand—or try to. Or you can watch sunsets, often spectacularly colorful given L.A.'s polluted air.

Deep-sea fishing expeditions—in search of barracuda, kelp bass, bonito, halibut, mackerel, rockfish, and sheepshead—and winter whale-watching excursions depart from Paradise Cove, Santa Monica, Marina del Rey, Redondo Beach, San Pedro, Long Beach and other spots along the coast. Contact local visitor bureaus and chambers of commerce for excursion boat suggestions.

Beach Practicalities

Beach curfews are fairly standard, with beaches usually closed to the public midnight–6 A.M.; some parking lots also close at midnight, though others close at sunset. No parking is allowed on most stretches of Pacific Coast Hwy. (PCH) 10 P.M.–6 A.M.; PCH parking is free, where you can find it. For public parking lots, available at many beaches, weekday rates range from $4 to $8 per day (rates usually higher on weekends). *Pay close attention to signs regarding parking restrictions* to avoid the unhappy experience of returning from a blissful day at the beach only to find that your car has been locked up for the night or, worse yet, towed and impounded. It'll be mighty expensive to get it out of car jail.

For general beach information, stop by or call the **Los Angeles County Department of Beaches and Harbors Visitor Information Center,** 4701 Admiralty Way in Marina del Rey, 310/305-9545 or 310/305-9546, http://beaches.co.la.ca.us. For questions about specific beaches, call **L.A. County Lifeguard Headquarters** at 310/577-5700. (Be patient if you're put on hold; rescues and other beach emergencies take precedence. And these folks do get busy, particularly in summer and on balmy weekends.) For general beach weather and tides (recorded), call 310/457-9701. Make reservations for state park and beach campgrounds along the L.A. County coast, mentioned elsewhere in this chapter, through ReserveAmerica, 800/444-7275, www.reserveamerica.com.

been there. Most people have seen it hundreds of times on TV and in the movies—the classic leisurely-L.A.-at-the-beach setting, where lovers stroll at sunset against a backdrop of swaying palms and rustling eucalyptus, and everybody's grandparents walk the poodle or gather on park benches to gossip and play friendly games of chess. This popular film location, a narrow 14-block-long strip of lawn, benches, and trees perched atop steep, eroding bluffs overlooking the Santa Monica Pier, the beach, and the Pacific Ocean, is often visitors' first stop, given the convenient location of the Santa Monica Visitor Center here. Nearby, one of Santa Monica's oldest attractions is the **Camera Obscura,** inside the Senior Recreation Center at 1450 Ocean Ave., 310/458-8644, a tourist attraction more popular in the 18th- and 19th-century U.S. than today. Perhaps the optical "illusion" created by a camera obscura—rendering reality so clearly—is simply too real in these days of virtual reality. (Ask for the key and see for yourself. Small fee.) An oddity that dates to Leonardo da Vinci's notebooks and 11th-century Arab scholarship, the Camera Obscura is composed of prisms, lenses, and mirrors installed in a darkened chamber that allows light in through an opening no larger than a pinhole. The camera then projects a reversed (upside-down) image of the outside world (in this case, a swath of the coastline) onto a white circular disk along the chamber's opposite wall.

Once reality has been virtually established, head for the beach. The good news is, the wide strand of dazzling white sand at **Santa Monica State Beach** is one of the busiest beaches around in summer—which is bad news if you're looking for privacy. It's also bad news if the ocean is temporarily off-limits because of pollution, an ongoing storm-drain and urban-waste disposal problem generated throughout L.A. and an issue that raises the ire of residents around Santa Monica Bay. (For the possibility of wide open spaces at the beach, head north beyond Malibu or south to the world-famous weirdness of Venice Beach, where most of the action is along the Boardwalk.) A day at the beach includes the usual seeing-and-being-seen scene, sometimes a rousing round of beach volleyball, a serious game of chess

at the International Chess Park nearby, and performance artists—California clowns. Not to mention those overgrown lifeguard chairs-cum-musical instruments—let's call them "wind" instruments—installed as public art projects between the pier and Pico Boulevard. On a breezy day the aluminum pipes atop artist Douglas Hollis's 18-foot-tall *Singing Beach Chairs* catch the wind and make odd tunes.

There's plenty more fun in the sun. You and the kiddos can learn to surf from various local surf schools, including **BlueRider Surf,** 310/709-1955, www.blueridersurf.com (reservations required). Or take a lesson from Olympic figure skating medalist Debbie Merrill's **Skate Great USA** open-air in-line skating school, 888/866-6121, www.skategreat.com.

ⓜ Santa Monica Pier and Pacific Park

Santa Monica's mild-mannered municipal pier and pleasure pier survived the usual ups and downs of tourist-town life largely unscathed until the 1970s, when civic warfare raged over the fate of the dilapidated piers, then slated for demolition by the Santa Monica City Council. But after being abandoned for several years and battered by severe storms, the slow work of rebuilding the past began. Work on the municipal pier was completed in the 1990s, including restoration of the two-story landmark **Hippodrome** (with its 1916 Looff carousel), the original arcades, and the old bumper cars. Much of the rest of the pier is lined with restaurants, fast fooderies, and curio shops. Fishing, once a favorite recreational activity at the pier, is no longer recommended because of bay pollution. In summer, the pier comes to life with special events such as *Drive in at the Pier* film presentations and Thursday night free *Twilight Dance Series* concerts, featuring musicians such as the "King of Surf Guitar" Dick Dale, Grateful Dead tribute band Dark Star Orchestra, and lounge band Los Amigos Invisibles. Some performers attract over 10,000 people, so plan to arrive early to stake out your spot on the boardwalk.

At the foot of the rebuilt and expanded pier complex is the **children's playground** designed

© LACVB

Santa Monica Pier

by Moore, Rubell, and Yudell, featuring an assortment of kiddie-style carnival rides and a huge dragon's head carved from river-washed granite that "snorts" a soothing, safe mist (water).

Santa Monica's new pier extension is Pacific Park, 310/260-8744, www.pacpark.com. Pacific Park harks back to the good ol' days of California amusement piers, until now an extinct species on the West Coast. Major new attractions here include an ocean-view roller coaster—the five-story-tall **Santa Monica West Coaster**—and California's only giant ferris wheel, the **Pacific Wheel.** In addition to more pedestrian rides for the kids, a thrill for adults is the **Sig Alert** bumper-car adventure.

Other pier attractions include the **Santa Monica Pier Aquarium,** (formerly known as the UCLA Ocean Discovery Center), 310/393-6149, actually located *underneath* the pier at 1600 Ocean Front Walk. Operated by Heal the Bay, the interactive aquarium-style education center features a tidepool and marine life exhibits where visitors can interact with underwater sealife in "wet labs" that focus on the delicate ecology of the

Pacific Ocean. Summer hours are Mon.–Fri. 2–6 P.M., Sat.–Sun. 12:30–6:30 P.M. From Labor Day to Memorial Day, hours are Mon.–Fri. 2–5 P.M., Sat.–Sun. 11 A.M.–6 P.M.

Admission to both the municipal pier and Pacific Park is free, but there is a charge for various attractions. Prices for most of the Pacific Park amusement rides are in the $1–3 range; unlimited ride wristbands are $19.95 for adults, $10.95 for children under 42 inches tall. The amusement park is open daily 11 A.M.–11 P.M. in summer, with an abbreviated schedule in winter.

South Bay Bicycle Trail

What better way to see the beach, and the Los Angeles beach scene, than by bike? Accessible at any point along the route, the rebuilt and widened South Bay Bicycle Trail weaves south from the white sand of Will Rogers State Beach through local beaches to Torrance, with a strategic inland detour only to bypass the harbor at Marina del Rey. Highlights along the way include the dazzling Santa Monica beach scene, wild and wacky Venice Beach, complete with

Los Angeles Coast

rollerbladers run amok and muscle-bound Muscle Beach, and the tony trendiness of Marina del Rey's boating brigade. And the swaying palms, sun, sand, and fresh ocean air. Oh sure, a few ecstasy-assassinating intrusions await along the way, especially toward the South Bay, where the L.A. Department of Water and Power's power plant smokestacks and incessant LAX jet traffic detract from an otherwise postcard-perfect setting. But you can pull over to rest your angst at municipal piers and other key attractions, including Marina del Rey's boat harbor and the shop-happy King Harbor at the north end of Redondo Beach.

Since most people in greater Los Angeles don't make it to the beach until close to noon, early morning is a great time for a bike ride. (This being the beach side of a very urban area, avoid being on the bike path after dark.) The paved bike path runs a total distance of about 22 miles; even a biking beginner can make the one-way trip in two hours or less. Start early and stop for breakfast before heading back. Bike, rollerskate, and rollerblade rental establishments are available all along the beachfront bike path.

Museum of Flying

Airplane fans and fanatics will enjoy this colorful museum, at last report still starring the *New Orleans* (on loan from the Natural History Museum of Los Angeles), the first plane to fly around the world—one of two open-cockpit Douglas World Cruisers that made the trip in 1924. Douglas Aircraft Company memorabilia is well-represented throughout, in fact—which is only fitting since the original museum occupied the site of the original Douglas Aircraft Company, precursor to McDonnell Douglas. But all planes have been meticulously restored. Other favorites have included the red-and-yellow checkerboard *Harvard II* T-6 trainer and the *Dago Red* P-51 Mustang, the world-record speeder clocked at 570 miles per hour in 1983.

Located for a number of years at 2772 Donald Douglas Loop N, on the north side of the Santa Monica Airport (one block south of Ocean Park Blvd. via 28th Street), the Museum of Flying was on the move at last report—though not moving far. The museum is scheduled to open in 2005 in a new northside hangar, and the history of the airport and Douglas Aircraft Company will be key themes. (Immensely popular at the museum's first location was the original Donald Douglas boardroom—a fabulous 22-seat round table with a built-in illuminated globe as its centerpiece.) Other Southern California aviation and aerospace companies will be represented, along with vintage aircraft. To encourage visitors to observe the action on airport runways, visitor viewing areas are included in the new museum layout.

At last report the Museum of Flying was open Saturday and Sunday 10 A.M.–5 P.M., with admission of $8 adults, $6 seniors and students with ID, and $4 for children ages 3–17. For current information—including precisely where to find the museum—call 310/392-8822 or see www.museumofflying.org.

While you're in the general neighborhood, tour architect Gregory Ain's **Mar Vista** futuristic housing subdivisions, built for Douglas Aircraft workers in the late 1940s, on the 3500 blocks of Meier, Moore, and Beethoven Streets. Like Douglas aircraft, some houses have survived in near-original condition.

And you can eat well at the airport, too. Adjacent to the original museum site at 2800 Donald Douglas Loop N. is very good **DC3 Restaurant,** 310/399-2323, open for lunch and dinner and serving soups, salads, seafood wontons, and entrées such as blackened swordfish or Napoleon of salmon filet.

Santa Monica Museum of Art

The high price of real estate has just about run artists out of this part of town, yet some remain. Santa Monica cool extends to its arts scene, which succeeds in being as cutting edge—or just "edge," as they say in these parts—as any in L.A. To start your personal search for edge art, try the Santa Monica Museum of Art, 310/586-6488, www.smmoa.org, at home among various local edge galleries at Bergamot Station, 2525 Michigan Ave., Bldg. G-1. Also surrounded by architect's offices and working artists' studios, the museum exhibits modern and contemporary

EXPLORING GREATER LOS ANGELES

If you set off to explore the vast mystery that is greater Los Angeles—L.A. County is larger than 4,000 square miles—take along some information. To receive a comprehensive and current visitors guide, the glossy *Essential LA,* and other information before coming to Los Angeles, see the **Los Angeles Convention and Visitors Bureau (LACVB)** www.lacvb.com; call 213/689-8822 or the 24-hour information line, 800/228-2452 (U.S. and Canada only); or write the bureau at 333 S. Hope St., 18th Floor, Los Angeles, CA 90071. Other publications include a variety of popular "pocket guides" and the annual magazine-style *Festivals of Los Angeles* guide. To find out what else is going on around town, call the bureau's 24-hour events hot line at 213/689-8822; with a touch-tone phone, dial up current events information in English, French, German, Japanese, and Spanish. Visitors can also make hotel and rental car reservations through the LACVB.

Los Angeles also sponsors two separate walk-in visitor centers, both of which provide regionwide information—maps, brochures, calendars, information on foreign-language tours, shopping, dining, even listings of upcoming television tapings—much

of it available in six languages, as well as multilingual personal assistance. The LACVB's **Downtown Visitor Information Center,** 685 S. Figueroa St. (between Wilshire Blvd. and Seventh P.M. The satellite **Hollywood Visitor Information Center** 6801 Hollywood Blvd. (at Highland), 323/467-6412, is open Mon.–Sat 10 A.M.–11 P.M., Sun. 10 A.M.–9 P.M. For visitor assistance by phone, call the LACVB at 213/689-8822.

Other local publications can be particularly helpful in introducing oneself to the wonders of Los Angeles. The local newspaper of record—California's newspaper of record, really—is the *Los Angeles Times,* www.latimes.com, distributed everywhere. But to find out what's really hip and happenin', pick up alternative publications such as the *L.A. Weekly,* www.laweekly.com, not to mention countless 'zines that come and go faster than freeway traffic, available in coffeehouses, neighborhood restaurants, bookstores, and other popular hangouts. Particularly good, wherever you might find them: *Poetry Flash,* www.poetryflash.org, *Citizenrobot,* www.citizenrobot.com, and *Art Commotion,* 213/689-8822, www.artcommotion.com, is open Mon.–Fri. 8 A.M.–5 P.M., and Sat. 8:30 A.M.–5

---

sculpture and painting by relatively unknown artists and also presents performance and video art. Call for information on current shows and events. At last report the museum was open Tues.–Sat. 11 A.M.–6 P.M. and for Friday night "salons," closed Sunday and Monday and all legal holidays. But call to verify hours, as well as current exhibit information, because the schedule is somewhat fluid. Admission is by suggested donation—$3 for most folks, $1 for artists.

Other Museums

Extremely hip Santa Monica claims its share of attractions from yesteryear, including the **Angel's Attic** museum of antique dollhouse miniatures, toys, trains, and dolls housed in a beautifully restored 19th-century Victorian at 516 Colorado Ave. (at Fifth Street), 310/394-8331, open Thurs.–Sun. 12:30–4:30 P.M. Admission is $6.50 adults, $4 seniors, and $3.50 children under

age 12. With reservations and an extra fee, you can enjoy tea, lemonade, and cookies on the veranda. Angel's Attic supports the Julia Ann Singer Center and its efforts to elevate the quality of life for autistic children and adults. The **California Heritage Museum,** 2612 Main St., 310/392-8537, open Wed.–Sat. 11 A.M.–4 P.M., Sunday noon–4 P.M., is housed in an 1894 American colonial revival mansion designed by Sumner P. Hunt and later moved to the unlikely intersection of Ocean Park Avenue and Main. The home once belonged to Roy Jones, son of city founder John Jones. The first floor has been restored and furnished in typical Santa Monica style of three eras: the 1890s, the 1910s, and the 1920s. The second floor serves as a gallery for historical exhibits and shows by contemporary local artists. The city's archives are also housed here. General admission is $3, students and seniors $2.

CITIES ON A HILL

Two "cities" recently risen on the hills overlooking Sepulveda Pass, just off the San Diego Freeway north of Brentwood and Bel-Air, are among L.A.'s most striking cultural attractions. The $800 million Getty Center, one of the world's most remarkable arts facilities, also offers panoramic views of the city, the sea, and surrounding mountains. Originally envisioned as a second location for the renowned J. Paul Getty Museum in Malibu, since it opened in 1997 "the Getty" has become considerably more—starting with six huge stone building complexes and gorgeous central garden on 110 terraced acres. The complex includes a restaurant and two cafés; a 450-seat auditorium; a 750,000-volume library; education classrooms, programs, and interactive technologies; and sophisticated art conservation and restoration facilities. Not far north of the Getty is the impressive $65 million Skirball Cultural Center, a three-winged modernist monument of pink granite, green slate, and curving stainless steel with visitor-friendly facilities, including the extraordinary Skirball Museum of Jewish History and a children's Discovery Center.

Getty Center

"The Getty" is L.A.'s latest astonishment—architect Richard Meier's contemporary yet classic arts enclave, a 25-acre complex built of imported Italian travertine marble rising like a medieval castle above both city and sea. "If God had the money," observed L.A. design critic Sam Hall Kaplan years before the Getty Center even opened its doors, "this is perhaps what he would do." The architectural statement, in his view, is that "this is a cultural institution here for the ages, not a passing indulgence, not a deconstructionist exercise by yet another narcissistic architect."

Whatever else the Getty Center accomplishes, it has successfully created facility space—lots of it, nearly one million square feet—to make art appreciation more central to L.A. life. The Getty Center's centerpiece is its museum. Surrounding the central garden courtyard are the five museum pavilions—vast galleries that allow display of much more of the J. Paul Getty Museum's collection, including European sculptures, illuminated manuscripts from the Middles Ages and the Renaissance, and previously unseen photographs from its collection of more than 60,000. Galleries are also highly interactive, with audio guides, multimedia computer stations, and expanded special-audience educational programs.

Prominently on display, in the sophisticated natural light of second-floor galleries, are stars of the Getty's growing Impressionist and post-Impressionist painting galaxy, including Vincent van Gogh's *Irises* and Claude Monet's *Rouen Cathedral*

Bergamot Station

Bergamot Station, named for the old Red Car trolley station that stood here until the 1950s, at 2525 Michigan Ave., Bldg. G-2 (near the freeway and the intersection of 26th Street and Olympic Boulevard), 310/586-6488, www.bergamotstation.com, is an industrial-cum-arts zone that's been the epicenter of L.A.'s visual arts scene since it opened in 1994. The corrugated-steel covered buildings house a contemporary but still fairly low-rent conglomeration of over 30 fine-arts galleries featuring almost six acres of arts space—this is the place to browse works best described as "eclectic"—political posters, "subverted" advertising billboards, or lifesize soap-on-a-rope nudes. Located in a former water heater factory, the

center's Bergamot Café, 310/828-4001, is good for lunchtime sandwiches and salads.

Bergamot Station is typically open Mon. 9 A.M.–4 P.M., Tues.–Fri. 9 A.M.–5 P.M., Sat. 10 A.M.–5 P.M., closed Sunday, but various galleries may schedule events at other times.

For a more comprehensive listing of local galleries, inquire at the visitor center—and pick up a current copy of the *LA Weekly*.

Frank Gehry House and Other Architecture

Speaking of art and artists: In what sort of home would an acclaimed local architect live? Take a drive by 1002 22nd St. (at Washington) and see for yourself. Noted for his innovative designs,

and *Wheatstacks.* Visitors may also see fairly new Renaissance acquisitions—including Michelangelo's 1530 chalk-and-ink drawing *The Holy Family with the Infant Baptist on the Rest on the Flight into Egypt,* and Fra Bartolommeo's *Flight Into Egypt,* painted in 1509. The museum's 15-room decorative arts section is a study in opulence. Here, exquisitely tarted-up rooms—with damask walls, faux marble, mirrors, and elaborately carved and painted panels—authentically exhibit the Getty's French furniture, tapestries, and other elegant domestic wares from baroque, neoclassical, Régence, rococo, and other stylistic periods.

Another Getty Center attraction is the 134,000-square-foot Central Garden near the museum, designed by Robert Irwin as an intentionally self-conscious human-crafted garden reflecting upon the natural world as humanity has made it. Like a sculptor using both geometric and photosynthetic elements as "clay," Irwin has created a garden shaped like a huge handheld mirror. Take a look.

Plan to spend the day, and either pack a picnic or sample any of several good restaurants. You'll be in company. About 1.5 million visitors commune with the Old Masters and other elements of the Getty's art world here each year. They all arrive at the hilltop palace after a five-minute electric monorail-style tram ride up the hill from the six-story underground parking garage at the west end of Getty Center Dr. just off the San Diego Freeway (the 405) and N. Sepulveda Blvd. The Getty is open to the public Tues.–Thurs. 10 A.M.–6 P.M., Fri. and Sat. 10 A.M.–9 P.M., and Sun. 10 A.M.–6 P.M. Closed on Monday and on major holidays. Admission is free, though there is a $5 parking fee. Parking reservations are no longer required.

For current information on special programs, current exhibits, and reservations, contact the Getty Center, 1200 Getty Center Dr. 310/440-7300, www.getty.edu.

Skirball Cultural Center

About two miles north of the Getty Center is the splendidly simple four-story Skirball Cultural Center, designed by Boston-based architect Moshe Safdie. Various other museums and cultural monuments document the Jewish experience, but this one celebrates Jewish life—and Jewish-American life. Yet the Skirball center is dedicated to full participation in L.A.'s efforts to "create a new paradigm for its cultural institutions." Part of the point here is interpreting the American-Jewish experience as it translates to the experience of all immigrants, to strengthen the fabric of American society and its institutions.

The 15,000-square-foot museum covers 4,000 years of Jewish history throughout the world, (continued on next page)

Santa Monica's own Frank O. Gehry transformed this house, once a small Dutch-style cottage, into a highly unusual example of the architectural arts. Using low-cost materials such as sheet metal and chain-link fencing for which Gehry has become famous, his domestic creation was included in a *Los Angeles Magazine* article titled "Nightmare Neighbors." The Gehry House so enraged one local architecture critic that he encouraged his dog to do his "duty" on Gehry's lawn, making his own symbolic statement.

For a traditionally pleasing local architectural tour, take a look at local **John Byers** homes. A prolific architect of the late 1920s, Byers built an enclave of attractive Spanish colonial houses on lovely La Mesa Drive, just off San Vicente, in the shade of gigantic Moreton Bay fig trees planted by Santa Monica's earliest residents. Look for some of Byers's homes at 2021, 2034, 2101, 2153 and 2210 La Mesa Dr., and for his onetime office nearby at 246 26th Street.

⛰ Third Street Promenade

When you're done with the public parade on and around the pier, try this one. Santa Monica's Third Street Promenade has become one of L.A.'s hottest "destination streets," an easygoing shopping and entertainment district just blocks from the beach. A pedestrian-only adventure, Third Street between Wilshire and Broadway is an intriguing mix of old and new Santa Monica, of kitsch and chic and chain stores, all decked

Los Angeles Coast

CITIES ON A HILL (Cont'd)

celebrating in particular the American-Jewish experience. (An earlier, much smaller incarnation of the museum was housed at Hebrew Union College just south of downtown L.A.) The core permanent exhibit—Visions and Values: Jewish Life from Antiquity to America—includes artifacts and art from ancient Israel and around the world, an ancient mosaic from Tiberias, re-created ruins of a sixth-century synagogue, and gallery exhibits on beliefs and celebrations. Then visitors "cross the big ocean," accompanied by sounds of the sea, beginning the American Jewish experience. Particularly evocative here: the huge replica of the Statue of Liberty's torch and original benches from Ellis Island. After more American Jewish history—including a reminder of the first Jewish arrivals in North America, who came from Brazil in the mid-1600s—ex-

hibits integrate American Jewish accomplishments and experience with the Holocaust and the rise of present-day Israel.

The Skirball Cultural Center is on N. Sepulveda Blvd., on the west side of the San Diego Freeway just south of Mulholland Dr.; from the 405, exit at Sepulveda and follow the signs. The museum is open Tues.–Sat. noon–5 P.M., and Sun. 11 A.M.–5 P.M. Facilities include a great on-site restaurant and gift shop. Call or see the website for current information on changing exhibits. The Skirball is closed on Monday and on Thanksgiving, Christmas, and New Year's Day; call for other holiday closings. Admission is $8 adults, $6 seniors and students, free for children under age 12. For more information, contact: Skirball Cultural Center, 2701 N. Sepulveda Blvd., 310/440-4500 www.skirball.com.

---

out with palm trees, topiary sculpture, pushcart vendors, and street entertainers. Beyond the boutiques and funky stores here, diversions and entertainment along these three blocks include great bookstores, galleries, multiplex movie theaters, coffeehouses, and good restaurants.

Start with the bookstores, though the indies in the vicinity are under pressure, a reality symbolized by the summer 2004 closure of long-running **Midnight Special.** (See www.msbooks.com, to see if the store successfully relocated.) **Arcana,** 1229 Third, 310/458-1499, stocks high-quality glossy photo books along with rare and out-of-print books and publications on architecture, art, design and photography. The chains are here, too. The neighborhood boasts a **Barnes & Noble,** 1201 Third (at Wilshire), 310/260-9110, and a **Borders** bookshop, music store, and café at 1415 Third (between Santa Monica and Broadway), 310/393-9290.

Equally fun, though, are the eccentricities of some of the trendy shops—assuming they haven't been displaced by the chain-sponsored commerce rapidly increasing here. The usual out-of-towner outlets—Banana Republic, Anthropologie, and a Z Gallery—are all represented. Always entertaining: the **Urban Outfitters** warehouse at 1440 Third,

310/394-1404, stark in its ersatz post-Apocalypse decor and specializing in consumer goods for nonconsumers and **Jurassic**'s museum-grade fossils located a block away from the promenade at 131 Broadway (at Second), 310/899-2992. One of the most intriguing toy stores around is **Puzzle Zoo,** 1413 Third, 310/393-9201, www.puzzlezoo.com, where you might find the limited edition Nascar Official #94 Barbie and the Excalibur Saber IV electronic chess board.

Then try the eateries—**Johnny Rockets** 310/394-6362, for burgers; the more uptown **Broadway Deli** on the promenade 310/451-0616; and quintessential California restaurant **Michael's,** 310/451-0843, with open-air dining on the garden patio outfitted with comfortable armchairs. And if those don't appeal, there's a California collection of takeout along the promenade—everything from hot dogs to tandoori chicken to Korean BBQ.

A fascination quite near the promenade is **Magicopolis,** 1418 Fourth St., 310/451-2241, www.macicopolis.com, a theater devoted entirely to live magic acts. On weekends the family-friendly show is staged in the 150-seat Abracadabra Theater, and on weekdays you'll settle in for a show at the 40-seat Hocus Pocus Room.

© LACVB

Third Street Promenade

At the south end of the promenade, just across Broadway, is **Santa Monica Place,** for still more shopping. This three-story enclosed mall was designed by influential modern architect Frank Gehry, who lives nearby; it has an open, breezy feel, thanks to its ocean-facing windows and skylights. Among other claims to fame—including **Ann Taylor**'s classic women's clothing, **Williams-Sonoma** housewares, and **The Body Shop**'s soaps and lotions—Santa Monica Place starred in Arnold Schwarzenegger's *Terminator 2.*

Just north of the Third Street action is **Fred Segal,** 500 Broadway (at Fifth), 310/451-7139, the hippest of hip department stores, companion to the original store on Melrose. Divided into a series of stylish boutiques for men, women, and children, this is a great people-watching place even if you'll never afford the freight. Fred Segal seems to attract affluent and hip teens and people who look like recording artists (and may well be). Look for the spectacular half-price sales each

September—though even then Fred Segal is quite expensive.

Best for Third Street Promenade parking, by the way, are the various public lots along Fourth, reasonably inexpensive. But if you're just here for a quick stroll, the parking lot at Santa Monica Place is free for a stay under three hours (small flat fee in the evening).

Montana Avenue

Long considered one of Santa Monica's most stylish shopping streets, Montana Avenue between Lincoln Boulevard and 17th Street (near Brentwood north of Wilshire) is *very* Westside, an expensive blend of chic shops and nosh stops located away from the beach and the crowds (locals joke that Montana is named after the state because its about that far from anything else in Santa Monica). Stores mainly sell women's wear and items for the home. **Federico,** 1522 Montana, 310/458-4134, is a long-running local favorite, selling Native American, Mexican, and silver jewelry. **Cinzia,** 1129 Montana, 310/393-7751, specializes in hand-painted garden accessories. One of the country's few **Shabby Chic,** stores is here, too, at 1013 Montana, 310/394-1975, selling its trademark poufy slipcovered sofas and flea market furniture. Stop at **The Coffee Bean** at 1426 Montana, 310/453-2093, for delicious coffee and baked goods. Or try the casual **Wolfgang Puck Café** at 1323 Montana Ave. (at 14th), 310/393-0290. And while you're in the neighborhood, see what's playing at the independent **Aero** theatre, 1328 Montana, 310/395-4990, which starred in the movie *Get Shorty.*

Main Street

A stroll along Main always affords an intriguing introduction to the real Santa Monica and its unique cultural combination of chi-chi and cheap. Main connects Santa Monica and Venice, stretching south from Pico Boulevard on the north to Rose Avenue in Venice Beach. Particularly popular for shopping and dining is the area between Ocean Park and Rose, where the classic old-brick buildings attract both the trendy and the traditional. You'll know you've gone too far,

Los Angeles Coast

and drifted south into eccentric Venice, once you see sculptor Jonathan Borofsky's clownish three-story-tall "ballerino" looming above Main like the crazed stage creation of some mad puppeteer—a huge ballerina's body, en pointe, crowned by a sad clown face complete with five-o'clock shadow.

Most often noted along Main are some of Santa Monica's most famous restaurants, including **Schatzi**, 3100 Main St., 310/399-4800, once owned by Arnold Schwarzenegger, and Wolfgang Puck's **Chinois on Main**, 2709 Main St., 310/392-9025. But the many other main attractions include Joe Gold's **World Gym**, 2210 Main, 310/450-0080, where Arnold Schwarzenegger got serious about working out (he still drops by occasionally) and where the clients include a list of big and bulky world champs as long as your arm.

There are less star-struck attractions, however, including **Newsstand**, 2726 Main St., 310/396-7722, boasting L.A.'s best selection of magazines and newspapers. Another hit is **Ritual Adornments**, 2708 Main, 310/452-4044, a treasure trove of beautiful trinkets: African-inspired masks, primitive folk-art religious statues, sterling silver charms, and beads for making jewelry. **Paris 1900**, 2703 Main St., 310/396-0405, recycles the glad rags of the rich circa 1900-1930. Fans of the 1950s and 1960s won't want to miss the family-run **Eames Office Gallery**, 2665 Main, Ste. E, 310/396-5991, www.eamesoffice.com, which is both archive/museum and gift shop/showroom celebrating the architecture, furniture, and other contemporary designs of Charles and Ray Eames. (See the website for current information about touring the Eames House.) A great rest stop is **Novel Cafe** 212 Pier Ave (Main and Pier), 310/396-8566, where local literary types come to kick-start the afternoon with some espresso. The café has plenty of comfy chairs and over 2,000 books on its shelves.

Formerly home to the Santa Monica Museum of Art, the **Edgemar** complex at 2415–2449 Main St., was designed by Santa Monica architect Frank O. Gehry, a new creation constructed in part from previous buildings, including the old Edgemar Egg Company. The complex houses the latest incarnation of famed **Röckenwagner**, 310/399-6504, Hans Röckenwagner's long-running Santa Monica eatery, now a California-casual brasserie enclosing a more intimate, fixed-price dining room. Also at Edgemar: an annex of the **The Museum of Contemporary Art Store** and the first **Ben & Jerry's** outlet west of Chicago. The **Edgemar Center for the Arts**, 310/399-3666, www.edgemar.com, at home since 1994 in Edgemar's original 1908 Imperial Ice Company warehouse, was founded by acting teachers Michelle Danner and Larry Moss. Live performances of new and classical theater, dance, and music plus a yearly film festival are staged in the 99-seat main theatre and smaller 65-seat theatre. Tickets are usually $20–30.

VENICE

Tobacco magnate Abbot Kinney had a dream. That dream became a vision, a utopian plan, then an obsession. What was Abbot Kinney's dream? He built an exotic seaside resort here, patterned after the great Italian city (complete with canals), and he expected the grandeur of his creation to spark an early 20th-century American cultural renaissance and create an international image of Los Angeles as sophisticated Mediterranean city. Kinney's plans never quite succeeded. In recent decades his vision has been revisited, as Venice has become one of L.A.'s avant-garde outposts of the arts and architecture. Yet, as in Kinney's day, the hedonistic eccentricities of Venice Beach and along its two-mile Ocean Front Walk are still the community's main attractions.

For some local events and referral information, call the **Venice Area Chamber of Commerce** at 310/396-7016 or visit www.venice.net. For other current visitor information, contact the L.A. visitor bureau at 213/689-8822, www.lacvb.com.

History

After making his millions selling Sweet Caporal cigarettes, Abbot Kinney came to California to build his personal Venice. In 1904 Kinney bought 160 acres of marshland just south of

Santa Monica for his "Venice of America" seaside resort. He drained the marsh, recreating it as a canal-laced landscape, and then hired architect Norman F. Marsh to design Venice, patterned after its namesake Italian city. The first phase of Kinney's dream included an elaborate Italianate business district, its first first-class hotel—the St. Mark Hotel, patterned after St. Mark's Cathedral in Venice, Italy—and a grand 2,500-seat public auditorium out on the new pier.

The city's three-day opening gala, a veritable circus of enthusiasms, began on July 4, 1905. More than 40,000 potential buyers toured Venice's 19 miles of 40-foot-wide canals in gondolas imported for the occasion, like their gondoliers, from Italy. Others paraded down city streets on the backs of camels. In the auditorium out on the pier, Sarah Bernhardt performed *Camille* during a black-tie performance, backed by the Chicago Symphony Orchestra. Enthralled tourists came and went, and many bought property. Hundreds of lots at the beach along Venice's new canals were sold, some for the then-astronomical price of $2,700 each— twice the going price of Beverly Hills real estate. Yet construction was slow. A number of modest craftsman-style homes were built along Venice's canals, but not the grand rococo palaces that Kinney had envisioned.

Abbot Kinney soon concluded that most people were more interested in the pleasures of sun and surf than in high culture, and in 1907 he built a grand casino. Buoyed by that success, Venice soon featured the world's largest amusement park, with 10-cent camel rides, two roller coasters—including the famous Race through the Clouds—and a dance pavilion. He imported the Ferris wheel from Chicago's 1893 Columbian Exposition. He built an Arabian-style bathhouse with hot salt water, and a bowling alley, a skating rink, a shooting gallery, and an aquacade. Abbot Kinney's Venice became a metaphor for what L.A. would become—a unique combination of popular and classical cultures.

Yet for all its successes, large and small, Abbot Kinney's dream seemed to depend on him, personally, for its continuing existence. After he died in 1920, Venice soon hit the skids—largely

because of the demise of L.A.'s electric trolley system and the increasing popularity of the automobile. (Venice's location, far from a major thoroughfare, put the resort at a competitive disadvantage for the tourist trade.) Then small oil wells and derricks dotted the landscape throughout Venice, petroleum-based goo blackened the canals and beaches, and the remaining tourists left town. Kinney's dream became a nightmare. Soon plagued by storms, fires, and political scandals, Venice residents voted in the 1920s to annex themselves to the city of Los Angeles. Most of the city's increasingly murky canals were filled in because of public health concerns. Abbot Kinney's dream died.

In a style Abbot Kinney could never have imagined, the dream of Venice as cultural mecca did revive. Drawn to the community's relatively low rents and unique, vaguely European style— including the arched bridges over the canals—in the 1950s beatniks and other bohemians arrived to establish L.A.'s latest avant-garde enclave, quickly followed in the 1960s by Summer of Love devotees. Musician Jim Morrison of The Doors lived here, and the cultural renaissance continued in the 1970s with the arrival of working artists. Many well-known L.A. artists have studios in Venice, lured by the (once) affordable rents, eccentric ambience, and proximity to the beach. In the 1980s Venice—certain parts of Venice—became a chi-chi address for cool-conscious Westsiders. The latter turn of events has spawned some interesting architectural styles as well. Since building codes here are more lenient than in adjacent beach towns, architects solved the problem of postage stamp-size lots by building multilevel structures—and then sometimes finishing them with intentionally shabby exteriors to discourage burglars. Though beset in recent years by seemingly uncontrollable gang violence and other urban ills, Venice still proudly parades its eccentricities. A community where million-dollar homes stand next to run-down shanties, Venice has even cleaned up its canals.

Venice has had its share of troubles in recent years. In the mid-1990s, Black vs. Latino gang wars over the crack-cocaine trade broke out throughout the region—in Oakwood, Santa

Los Angeles Coast

Monica, Mar Vista, and Culver City. Outraged Venetians pushed for a greater L.A. police presence and protection—and got it, at least during the day, when tourists were afoot. But chaos still reigned at night.

Despite Venice's considerable bad press, most neighborhoods here are vital, with genuine and genuinely strong cross-cultural community connections. Most of the community is united against gangster violence, and the Boardwalk has undergone a major renovation and cleanup, adding new palm trees, a beachside sculpture park, and improved lighting. For haven't-got-a-clue visitors and tourists, however, local history suggests due caution. If at all in doubt about one's street savvy, stick to the well-trodden tourist path along the Venice Boardwalk—and plan to blow this pop stand well before nightfall. The after-dark scene can get mighty unsavory, not just here but elsewhere along the L.A. coast where major boulevards or freeway exit/on-ramp routes dead-end at the beach. Such strategic spots tend to attract gangsters with an eye to making a quick getaway, as necessary.

Ocean Front Walk and Venice Beach

Abbot Kinney's gaudy amusement park, the Coney Island of the West for two decades, is long gone. But its spirit lives on. Unless the kids have led a truly sheltered suburban life—or perhaps especially if they have—they'll probably enjoy the human zoo that Venice's Ocean Front Walk, known locally as the Venice Boardwalk, has exhibited in recent years. Watch 'em watch Rastafarians and bikini-clad babes on in-line skates blithely dodge bicyclists, baby strollers, and bug-eyed tourists, rollerskating swamis, fire-eaters, palmists, and tarot card readers along with dancers, singers, and comedians. Sidewalk merchants sell T-shirts, sunglasses, hats, clothing, jewelry, crystals, and posters along the Venice Boardwalk, which stretches for two miles along Ocean Front Walk between Ozone Avenue and Washington Street.

Once the kids are satiated with the street performance, nudge them on to recently expanded and revamped Muscle Beach, "the pit" where muscle people get pumped on open-air weight-

Venice Beach

© ROBERT HOLMES/CALTOUR

Los Angeles Coast

lifting. (This Muscle Beach is no real relation to the original Muscle Beach of Jack LaLanne fame, just south of the Santa Monica Pier; old-timers say it was originally known as Mussel Beach—after those well-muscled bivalves.) Among the endless snack stands, best bet for meat lovers is **Jody Maroni's Sausage Kingdom,** 2011 Ocean Walk (between Venice Beach Boardwalk and Venice Boulevard), 310/822-5639, famous throughout L.A. for its fabulous all-natural links—from sweet Italian to Yucatán chicken. But if the Boardwalk's crowded sidewalk cafés seem just too crowded, beat a retreat to the **Rose Cafe,** 220 Rose Ave. (at Main Street), 310/399-0711, Venice's coolest coffeehouse, bakery, deli, and neighborhood café since almost forever. While in the neighborhood, die-hard shoppers should stop by **DNA Clothing Company,** 411 Rose (at Fourth Avenue), 310/399-0341, one of L.A.'s best outlet shopping spots, featuring top-drawer clothing and jeans for women and men at bargain-basement prices.

Then do the beach, which doesn't get nearly the attention—or crowds—as do the Venice Boardwalk or Santa Monica State Beach just north. Venice Beach is a *beautiful* beach, a broad belt of palm-dotted white sand stretching up coast and down and out into the surf. The redone concrete **Venice Pier** at the foot of Washington Boulevard, reopened in 2000, is quite popular with skaters and pier fishers and open daily 5 A.M.–10 P.M.

Other Sights

Like Abbot Kinney, start with the canals and then move on to the arts. A grid of six **Venice Canals** survive just minutes east of the busy beach scene, in a fairly upscale neighborhood bordered on the south by Washington Street, on the north by S. Venice Boulevard, on the west by Pacific Avenue, and on the east by Ocean Avenue. After decades of political battles, the surviving canals underwent a six million dollar restoration in the 1990s. **Grand** and **Eastern** Canals run north-south, and **Carroll, Linnie, Howland,** and **Sherman** Canals run east-west. Since the neighborhood's transportation system is largely dependent on canal and footpath, only

the Grand Canal—along Pacific Avenue—can be reached by road.

The Grand Lagoon, or where it once was, can be found at Windward Avenue and Main Street. Now a concrete traffic circle, this originally was where all of the canals met. A few of the original **Venice arcades,** patterned after those surrounding the Piazza San Marco in Venice, Italy, remain at St. Mark's Place, 67–71 Windward.

Yet don't wander too far. Not many blocks from the canals is the now-notorious neighborhood known as **Oakwood.** Plagued with drug and gang activity, Oakwood is known locally as the Demilitarized Zone or DMZ. While living in this neighborhood, according to L.A. artistic lore, actor Dennis Hopper was inspired to direct the film *Colors.*

More inspiring for most people are local arts venues. The **Beyond Baroque Literary Arts Center** is housed in Venice's onetime city hall, 681 Venice Blvd., 310/822-3006 or www.beyond baroque.org. Both small press-oriented bookstore and library, this is also the place for poetry readings and other local literary events. Next door, in the 1923 art-deco old Venice Police Station, is the **Social and Public Art Resource Center (SPARC),** 685 Venice Blvd., 310/822-9560, www.sparcmu rals.com, where a block of jail cells has been converted into an art gallery. Yet SPARC is considerably more famous for its work in preserving and promoting mural art projects throughout Los Angeles. Stop by for some local suggestions—SPARC knows everything about public murals, and there are endless people's-art displays throughout the area, some dating to the 1960s.

Come in May and meet local artists during the popular annual **Venice Art Walk,** an open studios-style arts event and silent auction that's also a primary fundraiser for the Venice Family Clinic. The Venice Art Walk is usually scheduled in mid-May. Or shop for art anytime. Long-running local galleries include **L.A. Louver,** 45 N. Venice Blvd., 310/822-4955, www.lalouver .com, famous for its representation of artists Wallace Berman, David Hockney, and Edward Kienholz, among many others.

More affordable for most folks are the arts, crafts, and antique shops along the 1200–1600

MUSEUM OF JURASSIC TECHNOLOGY

If you bring the kids, prepare for possible whining. Prepare for the fact that they'll think you tricked them. They'll think you offered an afternoon in Jurassic Park (as in Jurassic Park—The Ride) when instead, you offered them something equally amazing from "real life"—a view of the world as seen from the edge of science.

The motto of West L.A.'s strange Museum of Jurassic Technology is "nature as metaphor." This particular metaphorical interpretation of the natural world is most intriguing. Half the exhibits are real—or seem to be—and the others are highly unlikely, from the mounted horns, spore-eating ants, and fruit-stone carvings to the superstitions exhibit. And enormous hits such as the exhibit of "microminiature" creations by Soviet-Armenian violinist Hagop Sandaldjian, including likenesses of Disney's Goofy and Snow White and the Seven Dwarfs, even Pope John Paul II, all mounted on sewing needles and visible only through microscopes explore obscure areas of the natural sciences. Some of Sandaldjian's works are still on display in the Churchy Marrin Annex, where at last report the main exhibit was **Garden of Eden**

on Wheels: Selected Collections from Los Angeles Area Mobile Home and Trailer Parks. On exhibit in the Coolidge Pavilion is **The World is Bound with Secret Knots: The Life and Works of Athanasius Kircher, S.J., 1602–1680.**

In the opinion of Lawrence Weschler, author of *Mr. Wilson's Cabinet of Wonder,* the Jurassic rekindles one's sense of wonder while undermining "the sense of the authoritative" normally extended to museums. But the museum's curator suggests you leave even that preconception at home. Wonder is as wonder does—metaphorically speaking.

The Museum of Jurassic Technology, in a nondescript storefront in Culver City's historic Palms District, on Venice Blvd. four blocks west of Robertson Blvd. (directly across from Bagley), is open Thurs. 2–8 P.M. (sometimes from noon) and Fri.–Sun. noon–6 P.M. (closed major holidays and the first Thursday in May). Suggested donation is $5 adults, $3 children (under age 12 free), students, seniors, and the unemployed. For more information, contact: Museum of Jurassic Technology, 9341 Venice Blvd. in Culver City, 310/836-6131, www.mjt.org.

---

blocks of **Abbot Kinney Boulevard**—one of L.A.'s "destination" streets. Here, the art-deco splendor hasn't been bulldozed as it has elsewhere in L.A. Also noteworthy here, shops catering to out-of-towners haven't wiped out smaller, "local" businesses. To get started, try **Scentiments,** 1331 Abbot Kinney Blvd., 310/399-4110, a florist shop where you can also purchase a beautiful collection of tableware. Furniture stores are a specialty here. Three of the best are **Double Vision,** 1225 Abbot Kinney, 310/314-2679, for elegant modern furniture; **Bountiful,** 1335 Abbot Kinney, 310/450-3620, for reproduction furniture and antiques; and **French 50's–60's,** 1427 Abbot Kinney, 310/392-9905, for modernist designs straight from the Paris flea-markets. **Surfing Cowboys,** 1624 Abbot Kinney, 310/450-4891, features a somewhat anarchic collection of items: vintage surfboards, Hawaiian Hula Man figures, and Vespa scooters. For pizza, stop by **Abbot's Pizza Company,**

1407 Abbot Kinney Blvd., 310/396-7334, famous for its funky atmosphere and killer pizzas. Abbot's even offers breakfast and dessert pizzas. Right next door is **Abbot's Habit** coffeehouse, 310/399-1171, serving the real thing by the mug or by the pound, along with bakery items.

MARINA DEL REY AND VICINITY

Undeveloped coastal wetlands until 1968, when the county of Los Angeles set about the business of draining one of the coast's last remaining wetlands and building the largest man-made smallcraft harbor in the world, Marina del Rey is largely boat harbor—and boats, boats, boats. When row after row of life-at-the-beach-themed apartment houses and condominiums were built here in the late 1960s and early '70s it was only natural, given the area's proximity to LAX, that planeloads of stewardesses, stewards, and other

© LACVB

Marina del Rey

unattached airline employees would move in to share the neighborhood with the retirees and yachties—which won Marina del Rey its reputation as preferred port for swinging singles. Redevelopment plans—allowing 22-story high-rise "residential towers," apartment buildings, and hotels while ignoring the need for new parks and other genuine public access—will likely change the character of the neighborhood yet again.

Marina del Rey offers few attractions beyond upscale hotels (including a Ritz-Carlton) and fairly corporate entertainments. For tourist kitsch there's always **Fisherman's Village,** 13755 Fiji Way, 310/823-5411, an odd replication of a New England fishing village featuring gift shops, restaurants, South Seas foliage, and a view of the Marina channel. From here, you can sign on for a dinner cruise with **Hornblower Dining Yachts,** 310/301-6000, or sportfishing and winter whale-watching tours with **Marina del Rey Sportfishing,** 310/822-3625.

According to the annual "beach pollution report card" issued by Heal the Bay, always-popular **Mother's Beach** on Palawan Way within the marina is not recommended for swimming—especially for kids—because of continuing harbor pollution. A better bet by far is **Dockweiler State Beach,** sometimes known locally as Playa del Rey, below the bluffs along the harbor's face, with little at-the-beach clutter but clean restrooms, lifeguards, and some grassy picnic areas. Dockweiler stretches from Venice south to the mouth of the harbor and beyond, on the harbor's south side. Water quality is generally good at Dockweiler, except near storm drain outlets and, south of the harbor, near the outfall for the Hyperion sewage treatment plant.

For more information about the area, contact: **Los Angeles County Dept. of Beaches and Harbors,** Visitor Information Center, 4701 Admiralty Way, Marina del Rey, 310/305-9546 or http://beaches.co.la.ca.us.

Just south of Marina del Rey and east of the beach, surrounding the intersection of Lincoln and Jefferson Boulevards, is a surviving 1,087-acre section of the once-wildlife-rich **Ballona Wetlands,** owned at one time by eccentric billionaire Howard Hughes, who built his famous *Spruce Goose* here. The fate of the Ballona Wetlands—how much should be preserved or restored, how, and where—is the battleground in one of L.A.'s latest development wars. The wetlands, which look like a desolate wasteland to the uneducated eye, are home to numerous bird species, including brown pelicans, snowy egrets and the great blue heron. Now Ballona is becoming a vast development, **Playa Vista,** (Spanish for "beach view"), one that will preserve a large sections of the wetlands as parks and open space due to a court-ordered compromise with environmentalists. The development will ultimately include homes for more than 25,000 residents, commercial office space, and 750 hotel rooms—sufficient presence to merit its own zip code, Playa Vista 90094.

ACCOMMODATIONS

Santa Monica and other coastal enclaves are typically well-booked and most expensive on

Los Angeles Coast

weekends, though midweek and seasonal specials are possible. More significant, for true budget travelers and families, is the fact that in addition to the ubiquitous luxury options, Santa Monica and other coastal communities feature a variety of hostels and other inexpensive and midrange motel options.

Hostels and Motels

The best bargain around is the 235-bed Hostelling International USA **Los Angeles/Santa Monica Hostel,** 1436 Second St. (between Santa Monica Boulevard and Broadway) in Santa Monica, 310/393-9913 or 800/909-4776 #137 (from the U.S. only), www.hilosangeles.org. This is a budget traveler's bonanza, even though prices here are a bit higher than in other area hostels. What you get for the difference is an exceptional value, just two blocks from the beach and pier and, in the other direction, one block from the lively Third Street Promenade. The Santa Monica International is at home in the four-story onetime town hall, an aged brick and dark wood building complete with historic common room (once a saloon), full-service travel store, laundry and kitchen, library, TV room, large open-air courtyard, bicycle storage, and lockers. Most of the rooms are dormitory style with two or four beds per room (linen rental, small extra fee), though private rooms are available for couples. Bathrooms are shared. Discount airport shuttle service and organized area tours (extra) are also offered. This hostel is understandably popular, so make reservations (online or by phone, fax, or mail, with credit card confirmation) well in advance. Dorm beds are under $50 ($27 members, $30 nonmembers at last report), and private rooms $50–100.

As elsewhere along the coast, midrange accommodations seem impossible to find in summer, abundant at other times. Some of Santa Monica's "classic" and high-rent stays (see listings below) can become quite affordable for a winter mid-week stay. It often pays to ask. A notable deal even in summer and perfect for families, in a nice residential neighborhood just one block away from the Third Street Promenade and an easy stroll to the beach, is the all-suite **Cal Mar Hotel,** 220 California Ave., 310/395-5555 or 800/776-6007, www.calmar hotel.com, actually a 1950s-vintage apartment complex reconceived as a motel. Here you get a full kitchen and dining area, one bedroom with either a king or two double beds plus a pull-out sofa in the living room (rollaways and cribs available). Nothing stylish or high-tech, but all the essentials (including laundry facilities) plus a courtyard kidney-shaped pool. Rates are $150–200. Free onsite parking. Not so quiet but otherwise a deal is small, family-run **Sea Shore Motel** 2637 Main St., 310/392-2787 or www.seashoremotel.com. A good bet for the budget-conscious bound for the beach, just two blocks away, the Sea Shore is also located in the middle of Santa Monica's Main Street action, with a full slate of shops, galleries, and restaurants a jump away. Guest rooms feature refrigerators, cable TV, voicemail, and data-jack ports on the telephones. Onsite deli and a laundromat next door. Standard singles and doubles are $50–100.

And yes, there really is a **⚀ Hotel California**—more than one, actually—but at least one of them is right here in Santa Monica—more precisely, at 1670 Ocean Avenue. For information or reservations, call 310/393-2363 or see www.hotelca.com. (If you saunter up to the front desk with some version of the Eagles' lyrics, such as "I can check out any time I like but I guess I can never leave, heh heh," *trust* these people: they've heard it before.) Relatively affordable, recently renovated, down to the hardwood and tile floors, and perfectly located—just a stroll from both the beach and the Third Street Promenade—the Hotel California offers abundant comforts, from 100 percent Egyptian cotton sheets and Beautyrest mattresses to mini-refrigerators, satellite TV, VCRs, and free local phone calls and voice mail. Original ceiling murals and California-themed are particularly nice touches. Some suites have surfboard headboards and whirlpool tubs. There's one handi-capped-accessible suite, too. Rooms are $150–200, suites are $200–300, but check the website for specials. Beach cottages are available for longer stays.

Surprisingly reasonable, at last for some rooms, is Santa Monica's stunning new take on Craftsman style, **⚠ The Ambrose Hotel,** nowhere near the beach but across from St. John's Health Center at 1255 20th St. (at Arizona), 310/315-1555 or 877/262-7673, www.ambrosehotel.com. Rooms feature all the comforts, from Italian linens and towels, Aveda natural bath products, and surround-sound TV with VCR, DVD, and AM/FM radio, with little extras like organic Starbucks coffee, herbal elixirs, and on-call Pilates. Unique "spaces" here—designed to feel more like home than a hotel—include the living room-style lobby, the study, the library looking out onto the Asian-style garden, and the well-appointed rec room. Rooms start at $150–250.

Shangri-La Hotel

Santa Monica's 1939 Shangri-La Hotel, 1301 Ocean Ave. (at Arizona Avenue), 310/394-2791 or 800/345-7829, www.shangrila-hotel.com, is a local favorite, an art-deco ocean liner of a building looming large from a corner berth. Popular with writers and more eccentric movie stars, the Shangri-La has no pool and no bar, but this small 55-room hotel does offer evocative elegance overlooking Palisades Park, a nice continental breakfast and free morning newspaper, and afternoon tea. Free parking. Most of the tasteful rooms—successfully restored to their original deco glory, but with color TVs and cable—feature full kitchens and sundecks; most have ocean views. Studio suites $150–250, deluxe/penthouse suites $250 and up.

Georgian Hotel

Another art-deco gem, the historic eight-story Georgian near the pier at 1415 Ocean Ave., 310/395-9945 or 800/538-8147, www.georgian hotel.com, was lovingly restored to a contemporary take on a 1933 ambience in 2000. Most of the 84 rooms and suites offer ocean views, along with contemporary comforts including coffeemakers, honor bars, and cable TV (free movies); some have microwaves. Other basics include wireless Internet, phone with data port and voice mail, iron and ironing board, hair dryer, and laptop-sized in-room safe. No air con-

ditioning, though, since that's usually unnecessary here. Breakfast is served in the dining room every morning, afternoon tea and cocktails on the veranda. Lunch and dinner are also available. Rooms $150–250, suites $250 and up.

Hotel Oceana

Another likely spot to spot the occasional off-duty celebrity is the very cool, all-suites Hotel Oceana a few blocks north of Wilshire at 849 Ocean Ave. (between Montana and Idaho Avenues), 310/393-0486 or 800/777-0758, www.hoteloceana.com. Tasteful rooms overlook the courtyard pool; others offer ocean views. Basic amenities include kitchens, in-room coffeemakers, microwaves, cable TV (free movies). Air conditioning is rarely needed so close to the ocean, so the Oceana doesn't have it. Though technically this is a pretty high-rent class act, if you opt for one of the few studio apartments—and if you come in the dead of the off season, say, February—a stay here might be almost affordable, about half the usual tab; rates are higher but still more reasonable in spring and fall. Continental breakfast included. All-suites hotel, $250 and up.

Viceroy Hotel

Built at the corner of Ocean Avenue and Pico Boulevard as the Pacific Shores Hotel in 1969, the 168-room Viceroy Hotel near both the beach and Main Street at 1819 Ocean Ave., 310/451-8711 or 800/622-8711, www.viceroysantamonica.com, was completely revamped and reopened in 2002. This playful ode to England in the heart of Santa Monica boasts classic furnishings—from cameos on the walls to Staffordshire china dogs flanking the elevators—and a sophisticated green, dark gray, black, and bright white palette, The plush, eclectic décor could star in *Interior Design,* from custom beds with down comforters and Italian Frette linens to plush sleeper sofas and all those techie extras. Some rooms have ocean views. Other attractions include the retro *Cameo* bar and Viceroy's *Whist* restaurant, named after an old English card game. And dig those poolside cabanas. Rooms and suites $250 and up, starting at around $300.

SOME RULES OF THE ROAD

People in Los Angeles measure distance not in miles but in minutes—meaning minutes by freeway, or drive time. Angelenos also chronically underestimate drive times. This peculiar form of bragging rights ultimately implies that a *true* Angeleno could actually get from Pasadena to Santa Monica in 15 minutes, though you'll soon realize that you won't. (Angelenos also typically blame traffic when they're late—an excuse almost everyone will accept.) When taking directions from locals, then, visitors would be wise to generously pad the alleged drive time—or to double-check it, with the aid of a good map.

In keeping with their underestimation of average drive times, Los Angeles drivers also grossly underestimate their travel speed. If the posted speed limit is 65 miles per hour, most Angelenos will drive 80 or 85—and actually believe themselves when they tell the California Highway Patrol officer they were only going 60.

Angelenos typically refer to local freeways by name, not number—which can be mighty confusing for neophytes, since the Hollywood Freeway 101/is also the Ventura Freeway, the Santa Monica Freeway (I-10) is also the San Bernardino Freeway, the Golden State Freeway (I-5) is also the Santa Ana Freeway, and the faithful north-south San Diego Freeway never actually arrives in San Diego (not until after it's become I-5). When Angelenos *do* mention freeway numbers instead of names they use "the" as a fairly pointless modifier, as in "the 405" and "the 110," so when you hear such phrases you'll at least know that the topic of freeways is under discussion. Fortunately for visitors, most maps list both freeway names and numbers.

Then there are those unique L.A. words or phrases that make no sense whatsoever to inno-

Hotel Casa Del Mar

If you have money to burn, go ahead and ignite some here. During Santa Monica's gleaming Gold Coast days, the beachfront Club Casa Del Mar opened in 1926 as a beach club and hotel—the most opulent of them all. The grandly refurbished Hotel Casa Del Mar continues that theme, thanks to the grande dame's $60 million facelift. Open as a hotel since 1999, the Casa Del Mar features guest rooms and suites with panoramic views and plush, day-at-the-beach attitude, from the breezy white draperies, chaise lounge, fruitwood furniture, and stylized bamboo headboard to the luxurious bathrooms with rubber duckies in the whirlpool tub and white Italian Calacata marble walls and floors. And there's more, from the full spa and health club to the New American **Oceanfront** "view" restaurant. Rooms start at around $300, but having that beach just outside the door—priceless. For more information about Hotel Case Del Mar, located at 1910 Ocean Way, call 310/581-5533 or 800/898-6999 and see www.hotelcasadelmar.com.

Channel Road Inn Bed and Breakfast

A real find for B&B fans, the Channel Road Inn just east of Pacific Coast Highway is just a mile or two north of the Santa Monica Pier and Third Street Promenade. The inn is an inviting shingle-sided 1910 colonial revival period piece moved to this site in the 1960s and then transformed into a 14-room inn in the late 1980s. Most rooms and suites offer ocean views, some feature fireplaces, and all have private baths. Just a block from the beach, technically just beyond Santa Monica city limits, the inn also offers a friendly introduction to neighborhood life. Bikes are available if you feel like exploring, or soak up the ambience from the bayview hot tub. A good deal including full breakfast with home-baked muffins. For more information or reservations, contact: Channel Road Inn, 219 W. Channel Rd., 310/459-1920, www.channelroadinn.com. Standard rooms $150–250, view rooms and suites $250 and up.

Fairmont Miramar Hotel

Santa Monica's classic classy hotel is downtown's historic Miramar, "where Wilshire meets the sea," now a Fairmont, 101 Wilshire Blvd., 310/576-7777 or 800/325-3535, www.fairmont.com. Onetime private mansion and Santa Monica playground for Hollywood stars including Humphrey Bogart, Greta Garbo, and Betty Grable, the Mira-

cent tourists, such as "Sigalert," even if they are listed in the *Oxford English Dictionary.* A Sigalert, according to the *OED,* is "a message broadcast on the radio giving warning of traffic congestion; a traffic jam," though technically Sigalerts apply only to tie-ups of 30 minutes or more. The word itself pays homage to L.A. radio broadcaster Loyd Sigmon, whose breaking traffic-jam bulletins of the 1950s are the stuff of local legend.

More important than local lingo, however, is a clear understanding of the local rules of the road. Los Angeles drivers never signal their intention to change lanes on the freeway, for example—a sure mark of a tourist—because doing so only allows others an opportunity to fill that particular spot of road first. Yet if someone honks, rudely cuts you off—which probably wouldn't have happened if you hadn't signaled—or tailgates for revenge, do

remain calm. Don't allow that middle finger to leave the steering wheel, either, since no amount of rude driving is worth getting rammed at 70 miles per hour (or worse).

Also, never drive in front of a BMW or behind a Volvo.

Be particularly generous to L.A. drivers—give them a wide berth—if it's "pouring down rain" (as measured in actual precipitation, a tenth of an inch or less) because most Angelenos have never seen rain. Those who have tend to use wet roadways as yet another technique to increase their overall speed, through the miracle of hydroplaning. Most L.A. drivers don't know the difference between headlight high beams and low beams, either, so don't bother trying to explain the concept. In Los Angeles, headlights are either on or off. Be grateful, when it's dark outside, if the car coming toward you has them on.

mar still requires an entrance; visitors drive in through impressive wrought-iron gates and circle the huge Moreton Bay fig. Time and a $33 million restoration continue to transform the Miramar. The once-palatial grounds have been subdivided by progress, and the hotel's fabled courtyard bungalows, surrounding the lush jungle, pool, and patio just beyond the bright and spacious lobby, have been replaced with 31 snazzy new ones. Yet the Miramar abides, with a sophisticated international atmosphere both rarified and relaxed. The hotel's historic charms are most apparent in the older brick Palisades wing, overlooking Palisades Park, yet rooms in the more contemporary Ocean Tower come with almost aerial views. Amenities abound, including in-room safes, coffeemakers, and honor bars, color TVs with cable (free movies), countless little luxuries, a wonderful on-site restaurant, and full fitness facilities. Rates $250 and up, but promotions and off-season deals can be bring the price into the $150–250 range.

Le Merigot Beach Hotel

A stunner located just a block from the beach at 1740 Ocean Ave., Le Merigot is a contempo

rary take on the city's art deco sensibilities, from the potted palms, blond woods, and day-on-the-Gold-Coast colors in the lobby to the artfully furnished guest rooms—chic yet casual, some with views. The attitude here is European—so L.A.—and extends to the hotel's exceptional **Cézanne** restaurant, 24-hour room service, and **Le Troquet** bar. Not to mention the spa, one of L.A.'s best. For more information or reservations, call 310/395-9700 or 888/539-7899, www.lemerigotbeachhotel.com. Luxurious, with rates $250 and up.

Loews Santa Monica Beach Hotel

Before Shutters opened its shutters onto the Santa Monica sands (and before Casa del Mar), the Loews Santa Monica Beach Hotel, 1700 Ocean Ave. (between Pico and Colorado), 310/458-6700 or 800/235-6397 (central reservations), www.loewshotels.com, was L.A.'s only beachfront hotel. Though this hotel isn't exactly *on* the beach, it's certainly close enough. The stunning contemporary lobby, colored in soft tones of sea-grass green, peach, and sand and accented by potted palms and bold wrought-iron grillwork and glass, somehow evokes L.A.'s most intriguing Victorian-era architecture, downtown L.A.'s famed Bradbury Building. The same general idea—inspiring skylit enclosures—carries over to the indoor-outdoor pool area overlooking the beach. Many of the hotel's 350 rooms and 35 one- and two-bedroom suites, luxuriantly decked out and featuring the usual amenities, overlook the beach. Other attractions include complete fitness facilities (personal trainers available), the adult-supervised Splash Club for vacationing families, the sophisticated French Provincial **Lavande** restaurant, 310/576-3181, and the casual **Papillon** lounge serving tapas-style dishes, aperitifs, and afternoon tea. Rates $250 and up.

Shutters on the Beach

Definitely on the beach, Shutters on the Beach, 1 Pico Blvd. (just off Ocean Avenue), 310/458-0030 or 800/334-9000, www.shuttersonthe beach.com, looms over the sand like an overgrown Cape Cod beachhouse—shutters and all—by design. Shutters, with its 198 rooms and suites right on the beach, was designed in the spirit of Southern California beach homes and resorts of the 1920s and 1930s. Otherwise, everything is cutting-edge contemporary, light, open, and vaguely reminiscent of plein-air watercolors. Rooms are small but attractive—note that some "partial view" rooms barely spy the sea—with the usual luxury amenities, marble bathrooms, and large whirlpool tubs. Sliding shutter doors open onto private patios or balconies, providing the "shutters" of the hotel's name. Other pluses include two good on-site restaurants, the outstanding **One Pico,** 310/587-1717, and the casual café **Pedals,** both the **HandleBar** and an attractive lobby lounge, large pool and patio areas, spa, full fitness facilities—even a rental service for Santa Monica essentials, from bikes, in-line skates, and volleyball nets to swim fins and children's beach toys. Unfortunately for determined ocean swimmers, the hotel's beach sits at the mouth of the Pico-Kenter storm drain, with its attendant bacterial "danger" signs from time to time—so heads up if you actually brave the waters. Rates $250 and up.

Venice

The **Cadillac Hotel,** 8 Dudley Ave. (at Ocean Front Walk), 310/399-8876, www.thecadillac hotel.com, isn't the Cadillac of hotels. Venice isn't the Cadillac of beach towns, for that matter, and not a totally comfortable area after dark. But if the wild and wacky rush of Southern California humanity is your scene—people-watching from sidewalk cafés, dodging the in-line skaters and cheap trinket stalls on the way to the wide, wide expanse of white sand—then the restored art-deco Cadillac Hotel is one place to park yourself come nightfall. Most rooms are $100–150, with onsite extras including sundeck, sauna, gym, laundry, and storage facilities, even a pool table. Free airport shuttle service.

The **M Venice Beach House** is an L.A. rarity—a bed-and-breakfast. This one is a rarity among rarities, however, since this lovely, early 20th-century home also happens to be a graceful, ivy-covered Craftsman bungalow just steps from the beach and a block from the Venice Canals. North of Washington Boulevard and west of Pacific Boulevard on one of Venice's "walk streets" (onetime canals, long since filled in), the Venice Beach House features nine well-appointed period rooms with antiques and wicker. The Pier Suite comes with a sitting room, fireplace, king-size bed, and ocean view. Doubles with private bath are $150–250; smaller, less expensive garden-view rooms share bathrooms ($100–150). For reservations, contact Venice Beach House, 15 30th Ave. in Venice, 310/823-1966 or visit www.venicebeachhouse.com.

For a motel stay, one with space and attractive rooms, good value in Venice is the Best Western **Marina Pacific Hotel and Suites** just a block from the beach and otherwise smack-dab in the middle of everything at 1697 Pacific Ave., 310/452-1111 or 800/421-8151, www.mp hotel.com. Rooms are $100–150, suites are $150–300.

Marina del Ray

Reigning monarch of the South Bay hotel scene is **The Ritz-Carlton, Marina del Rey,** 4375 Admiralty Way, Marina del Rey, 310/823-1700 or 800/241-3333, www.ritzcarlton.com, which here

LOS ANGELES AS DIVERSION

Unless one refuses to participate in the ongoing circus that is Los Angeles, it's almost impossible to avoid diversion here—starting with the family-focused theme parks scattered throughout Southern California. But L.A. offers much more to see and do, from exceptional museums to classic movie theaters, from live theater and concert performances to endlessly cool dance clubs. And the impressive Los Angeles parade of festivals and special community events could keep anyone entertained for a lifetime.

There are two primary approaches for experiencing Los Angeles arts and entertainment. The first is placing a major arts or entertainment performance (or community event) at the center of one's travel plans, and then planning everything else—where you'll stay and eat, what else you'll see and do—accordingly. The other is to grab a local newspaper—the *L.A. Weekly*, www.laweekly.com, say, or the Thursday or Sunday calendar sections of the *Los Angeles Times*, www.latimes.com—and see what strikes your fancy at the moment, a style of "planning" most Angelenos exercise frequently. The *Times* also maintains a comprehensive entertainment website, www.calendarlive.com, with up-to-the-minute information on LA's restaurants, nightlife, movies and live music. Or, at least for major goings-on, contact the **Los Angeles Convention and Visitors Bureau** at 213/689-8822 or www.lacvb.com.

serves as scenic backdrop for yachts and yachters. The usual ritzy amenities abound, thick terrycloth robes and every other imaginable comfort, plus full fitness and business facilities. The crisp, classic decor includes French doors in most rooms, opening out onto balconies overlooking the boat harbor. Dining options include the excellent fusion restaurant **Jer-né** (a play on words for "journey") and the less formal **Wave Café** poolside restaurant (seasonal). Rooms and suites $250 and up.

More fun and much more affordable for most people, though, is the **Best Western Jamaica Bay Inn** on Mother's Beach at 4175 Admiralty Way, 310/823-5333 or 888/823-5333, www .bestwestern-jamaicabay.com, the only place around actually *on* the beach. (Because of harbor pollution, however, ocean swimming here is not advisable.) Rooms are large, with either terraces or balconies, and bathrooms are a bit small. Pleasant beachfront café. High-season room rates $150–250, $100–150 otherwise.

FOOD

Farmers' Markets

If you time things right, load up on fresh fruits, vegetables, fabulous flowers, and other essentials at the big-deal **Santa Monica Certified Farmers'**

Market, held year-round at Arizona Avenue between Second and Third Streets on Wednesday 9 A.M.–2 P.M. (bring quarters for area parking meters) and—for a completely organic experience— on Saturday 8:30 A.M.–1 P.M. Also on Saturday, there's an open-air Certified Farmers' Market at the intersection of **Pico Boulevard and Cloverfield,** 8 A.M.–1 P.M. On Sunday there's still another, at **Victorian Heritage Square** at Ocean Park Boulevard and Main Street, scheduled 9:30 A.M.–1 P.M., the fun here including pony rides and other kid's stuff. For more information on area markets, call 310/458-8712 or see www .farmersmarket.santa-monica.org.

Otherwise, for natural foods, cosmetics, and such, there's always the **Wild Oats Community Market,** 1425 Montana Ave. (at 15th Street), 310/576-4707, a link in the chain that genuine co-ops tend to disdain.

Inexpensive Fare at the Promenade

Start searching for possibilities where almost everyone else does, along the Third Street Promenade. Prime for people-watching—one of those only-in-L.A. places—is the spacious, light, and airy **Broadway Deli,** 1457 Third St. (at Broadway), 310/451-0616, where the proprietors don't do a particularly good job with traditional New York deli standards. (But hey, this is California.)

The Broadway does just about everything else, though, from superb French bistro fare to reinvented American comfort food, including macaroni and cheese and killer burgers. (Not necessarily impressive: the blintzes, pastrami sandwiches, lox, and other Jewish deli standards, though they are served here.) Put together an unforgettable picnic lunch or dinner by ordering takeout from the deli counter. Or settle into a booth, and order just about anything your heart desires—from blueberry pancakes and French toast to Caesar salad, beef stew, chicken pot pie, pizza, mushroom barley soup, and tapioca crème brûlée. This is a fairly pricey place, but if you order judiciously you'll still be able to afford the gas—or plane fare—to get home. Espresso bar, fresh-baked breads and bagels, delightful desserts. Astonishing foodie shop, too, which you'll get to know well while you wait (no reservations). The Broadway Deli is open daily 7 A.M.–midnight, 8 A.M. until 1 A.M. on Friday and Saturday nights. One of the best places for an uptown burger is the old-brick **Broadway Bar & Grill** at 1460 Third St. (near Broadway), 310/393-4211, where it comes topped with applewood-smoked bacon.

One block east of the Promenade and well worth the detour is the flamboyant 🅼 **Border Grill**, 1444 Fourth St. (near Broadway), 310/451-1655. The bizarre and bright faux folk art-splashed walls serve as apt accompaniment to the stunning food served here—everything the creation of chefs Mary Sue Milliken and Susan Feniger of the Food Network TV show *Too Hot Tamales*, who apply their formal training in classical French cooking to the bold flavors of coastal Mexico and Central America. You can make a meal of the appetizers, the green corn tamales, the *panuchos* and *platano empañadas* stuffed with cheese and black beans, thereby keeping the total tab almost reasonable. Then again, you'd miss the entrées—such things as grilled skirt steak marinated with garlic, cilantro and cracked pepper, served with moros, avocado-corn relish and Roma tomatoes, sautéed rock shrimp with toasted *ancho* chiles, and marinated breast of chicken served with onion-orange salsa. And for dessert, how about a slice of Oaxacan chocolate cake? Full bar. The Border Grill is open daily for lunch

and dinner, with a late night menu available Friday and Saturday (closed major holidays).

Or consider the Santa Monica outpost of East L.A.'s authentic Mexican **La Serenata de Garibaldi,** 1416 Fourth St. (at Santa Monica Boulevard), 310/656-7017, not exactly inexpensive yet beloved for its seafood and fish specialties—shrimp tacos, anyone?—and serene Mexican colonial style. For something grandly rustic and imaginative at dinner, try white-linen **Rocca,** 1432 Fourth St., 310/395-6765, grand for pastas and surprises like wild boar sausages with green-apple mustard. Another possibility is excellent **Locando del Lago,** 231 Arizona Ave. (between Second and Third Streets), 310/451-3525, noted for dishes from Lombardy, Italy. The patio is also a plus.

For something distinctly different, **Juliano's Raw** at 609 Broadway (at Sixth Street), 310/587-1552, which serves the "gourmet living cuisine" of Juliano Brotman, often acknowledged as a founder of the raw food movement. Raw the food here is, and also certified organic and stylish, from vegetable pad thai and sun-baked pizzas to meat-free cheeseburgers and smoothies.

Inexpensive Fare at the Pier

Tucked in among the high-priced hotels is **Cora's Coffee Shoppe** at 1802 Ocean Ave. (at Vicente Terrace), 310/451-9562, a 1920s-vintage diner and onetime haunt of surfers and other traditionally low-rent types, now in the hands of celebrity chef Bruce Marder and in step with tonier, more organic times. OK, it's a tad pricey for a coffee shop but the food's quite good, from the fresh-squeezed juices, organic coffees, and intriguing omelettes and huevos rancheros to sublime panini.

For an extreme stylistic alternative, a good bet for families, head for **Ye Olde King's Head Restaurant and Pub,** 116 Santa Monica Blvd. (between Ocean and Second Street), 310/451-1402, which has been serving forth English specialties for just about forever—everything from fish and chips and bangers and mash to royal tea. Entertainment provided by warm beer and darts. It's open for lunch and dinner daily, for high tea Saturdays only.

Numerous people's possibilities lie along the Third Street Promenade, an easy stroll from the beach. For an array of dining options, check out the food court at the **Criterion Theater Plaza,** 1315 Third St., where nothing on any menu is more than $12 (most choices are much less). Among the stars here is **Wolfgang Puck Express,** 310/576-4770, for fast reasonably priced pastas, pizzas, and salads. This and other fast fooderies here are open daily 11 A.M.–10 P.M.

A real deal for authentic Mexican is colorful **El Texate Oaxacan Restaurant,** 316 Pico Blvd. (at Fourth Street), 310/399-1115, which at first glance looks something like a surfer bar. The treasure here is the wide selection of rich mole sauces, blends of roasted chiles, seeds, nuts, and spices so perfect with chicken (start with the *coloradito,* or "little red"). Entrées include enchiladas, *chiles rellenos, empañadas,* and pizzalike *clayudas* and *memelas.* If you're not in the mood for margaritas or beer, wash everything down with *tejate*—the traditional summer drink created from cornmeal, chocolate, and walnuts. El Texate is open daily 9 A.M.–11:30 P.M.

Blueberry lovers may find the bluebird of happiness at the **Blueberry Café,** 510 Santa Monica Blvd. (at Fifth), 310/394-7766, where all day long you can get blueberry ice cream and blueberry pancakes with blueberry syrup. You can opt for an omelette waffle or egg dishes at breakfast, salads and sandwiches at lunch. For organic and vegetarian food, a best bet is **Real Food Daily,** 514 Santa Monica Blvd., 310/451-7544, fresh and unusually good, from *seitan* fajitas to vegetable sushi and eggless Caesar and Peruvian quinoa salads. Good desserts, too. It's open Mon.–Sat. for lunch and dinner.

Inexpensive Fare on Main Street

Given the endless possibilities along Main, one of the better choices is among the least expensive—attractive **Rick's Tavern on Main,** 2907 Main St. (at Ashland Avenue), 310/392-2772, serving contemporary takes on all-American standards in nouveau 1930s style. Great patio, too. Come on Tuesday or Thursday night for the burger madness special. A good stop for pub grub is **O'Brien's Irish Pub & Restaurant,** 2941 Main

St. (near Pier Street), 310/396-4725, also serving live music. For some after-dinner cheer, the **Library Alehouse,** 2911 Main, 310/314-4855, is a veritable library of Pacific Northwest microbrews on tap, where the various "taster specials" allow you to sample five three-ounce samples. (You can also "read" on the patio.) Some might prefer splurging on a Salty Dog—grapefruit juice and vodka served margarita style in a salt-rimmed glass. The place to get 'em is the **Galley,** 2442 Main, 310/452-1934, Santa Monica's oldest surviving dark bar and surf and turf restaurant.

Another classic on Main is **Shoop's Delicatessen** at 2400 Main St. (at Hollister), 310/452-1019, a tiny European grocery and deli—a great stop for packing that extraordinary picnic basket. There's something for everyone at the **World Café,** 2820 Main (near Ashland), 310/392-1661, from fat-free and lo-cal specials to vegetarian quesadillas and seafood potstickers. And dig those decadent desserts. **Joe's Main Street Diner,** nearby at 2917 Main St., 310/392-5804, is a good neighborhood diner, just the place for substantial breakfasts and burgers.

If you've been frugal while wandering Main, blow a few bucks at local sweets and dessert shops, including **Mäni's Bakery,** 2507 Main St. (between Ocean and Park), 310/396-7700, famous for creating organic desserts, including sugar free and vegan options.

Inexpensive Fare Elsewhere in Town

A best bet for vegetarians, with the kitchen open into the wee hours seven days a week, is **Anastasia's Asylum,** 1028 Wilshire Blvd. (at 11th Street), 310/394-7113, a fun and funky art gallery/coffeehouse/restaurant serving such things as tofu lasagna along with music every night. Exceptional vegetarian fare is available at **Nawab of India,** 1621 Wilshire Blvd. (at 17th Street), 310/829-1106, noted for its homestyle Northern Indian lunch buffets (brunch buffet on weekends).

One of the best for all-American breakfast is **Rae's,** 2901 Pico Blvd. (at 29th Street), 310/828-7937, a real-deal 1950s diner where, most weekends, people are only too happy to line up and wait. (No credit cards.) Rae's is open daily for

Los Angeles Coast

breakfast, lunch, and dinner. Or head to break-fast-anytime **M̃ Snug Harbor,** 2323 Wilshire Blvd. (between 23rd and 24th Streets), 310/828-2991, where diner standards, including the dinner salad, are more sophisticated than you'd expect. Omelettes star at breakfast—available anytime—along with fresh-squeezed orange and grapefruit juices. Snug Harbor is open daily for breakfast and lunch.

Still looking for burger love? Some say the place to put together the perfect burger is **The Counter,** 2901 Ocean Park Blvd. (at 29th Street), 310/399-8383, where the choices are almost endless. First you choose a type of meat (or meat alternative) and burger size (up to a shocking full pound) then select from all those toppings—various cheeses, mayos, salsas, green chiles, pineapple, even peanut sauce. If carbs are out of the question, there's even a burger in a bowl.

A bit fancy for cheap-eats freaks but quite affordable for the genre is Italian **Il Forno,** 2901 Ocean Park Blvd. (between 29th and 30th Streets), 310/450-1241, a best bet for antipasti, pastas, and pizza. It's noisy, friendly, reliable, and open weekdays only for lunch, daily for dinner.

And there's another fabulous Italian in town— **Fritto Misto,** 601 Colorado Ave. (at Sixth Street), 310/458-2829, busy, unbelievably reasonable, and well worth the long waits. Owner Robert Kerr makes his own pasta, ravioli, and sausages fresh daily. House specialties include such things as "atomic" pasta—two seared Cajun-seasoned chicken breasts served on a bed of chile linguine and tossed with peppers and onions in a chipotle cream sauce. Not to mention some marvelous vegetarian selections. Here, you can also create your own specialty by selecting pasta, sauce, and favorite add-ins. The wine list includes boutique

"REAL" LOS ANGELES

Outsiders' interpretations of Los Angeles—what everyone thinks they know about the place—are often seriously mistaken. For all its casual friendliness, Los Angeles is actually an aloof city, self-protective. One certainly experiences that truth on the freeways—so many millions of people, so oblivious to each other, every person moving through life in his own freewheeling, independent world. For all its fabled flamboyance and sometimes shameless public shenanigans, Los Angeles is in real life a very private place. "Real" L.A. is a private, not a public, domain—which is why finding it can be such a challenge for visitors. When L.A. isn't performing on its varied public stages—and L.A. in all its guises works long, hard hours—the city stays home with family and friends, or goes out to play, privately. Los Angeles tolerates its tourists as revenue enhancements—"tourist" a term that was invented here—but rarely invites them home or out on the town. Traditionally, the supremacy of individuality and the need for privacy follow Angelenos everywhere.

For all its vastness, or perhaps because of it, L.A. is also parochial and self-absorbed. "Family values" matter here because immediate family is almost all there is to anchor people in such a fast-paced,

unrooted society. Even political battles in Los Angeles are largely fought on the neighborhood level. Yet such self-absorption has its price. While Southern California can't muster the political will to properly finance its public schools, libraries, and health-care services, Los Angeles is number one in the nation for plastic surgery: breast enhancements, liposuction, facelifts, nose and eyelid jobs. Fitness centers are also central to Southern California culture, as are psychiatrists and psychologists and sometimes out-there spiritual advisers.

For all its vast wealth, Los Angeles largely lacks the memorable monuments to grand ideas and idealism so typical of European and other American cities, be they cathedrals, museums, or public libraries. While exceptions to this rule can still be found downtown and in affluent communities including Beverly Hills and Pasadena, the most striking architecture in Los Angeles is private, not public. Rather than invest its billions in old-fashioned public betterment and enlightenment, L.A. spends its money on private pleasures—on great walled mansions and estates and, on a more modest scale out in the suburbs, on backyard barbecues, swimming pools, and all the other accoutrements of middle-class family living.

wines listed at half the price other restaurants charge. Such a deal! Don't miss the delectable desserts. Open daily for lunch and dinner.

Fine Dining on Wilshire

According to *Wine Spectator* magazine, L.A.'s own **N Pacific Dining Car,** the 1921-vintage original in downtown L.A. and the newer Santa Monica outpost at 2700 Wilshire Blvd. (at 27th Street), 310/453-4000, is among the nation's top five steakhouses. The corn-fed USDA prime beef served here, from the spectacular T-bone to filet mignon and ribeye, is dry aged and hand cut on the premises then ultimately grilled over mesquite. Lunch might be a smaller steak, or filet mignon Caesar salad, or a perfect prime rib sandwich. For breakfast—the Dining Car's most affordable meal—try the avocado or asparagus scramble, the Louisiana blue crab omelette, or ba-nana-pecan pancakes with applewood-smoked bacon. Open 6 A.M.–2 A.M. for breakfast, lunch, afternoon tea, dinner, late-night dinner, and early breakfast.

Josiah Citrin's elegant **Mélisse** at 1104 Wilshire Blvd. (at 11th Street), 310/395-0881, serves New American with classical French accents, meals that begin with the freshest produce and products from regional farms. The seasonally changing menu might include white asparagus soup, sweet white corn ravioli, farmers market vegetable terrine, roasted wild king salmon, diver scallops with apple-vanilla purée, or roasted Bobo Farms squab with endive and date compote. It may be impossible to choose from the lengthy list of exquisite desserts, from chocolate soufflé and crepes Suzette "a l'American" to brown butter pear tart.

Known for its fine contemporary French, casual **JiRaffe,** 502 Santa Monica Blvd. (at Fifth

---

Parochial Los Angeles does seem improbable, given the city's social and cultural perch at the edge of both Mexico and the Pacific Rim. Yet even L.A.'s recent arrivals tend to settle into particular neighborhoods. Because of its insularity, until quite recently Los Angeles could imagine itself untouched by the multiethnic chaos that now defines it.

Rather than a melting pot, L.A. is a multicultural anthology in which every recent ethnic arrival has its own page, if not an entire separate chapter. Immigrants from more than 140 different nations live within Los Angeles County, including the largest populations of Armenians, Filipinos, and Koreans outside their respective nations and the largest U.S. populations of Cambodians, Iranians, and Japanese. Latin American immigrants—Guatemalans, Mexicans, and Salvadorans—dominate many chapters, as do third- and fourth-generation migrants from the U.S. Midwest. Still, the story lines rarely intersect.

This, says writer Richard Rodriguez, is as it has always been in Los Angeles—and in America. Thanks to Protestantism, he says, the 19th-century U.S. with its waves of new immigrants "became a country of tribes and neighborhoods more truly than a nation of solitary individuals. Then, as today, Amer-icans trusted diversity, not uniformity." Yet, according to Rodriguez, "any immigrant kid could tell you that America exists. There *is* a culture. There is a shared accent, a shared defiance of authority, a shared skepticism about community." By extension, there is also a shared culture in Los Angeles.

A strikingly tolerant city, Los Angeles is also quite lively. National trendsetter in popular entertainment, lifestyle, style, and vocabulary, Los Angeles boasts more university graduates per capita than any other U.S. city. There are more colleges and universities here, a total of 176 at last count, than in the entire state of Massachusetts. But culture here doesn't always come with a university degree. Los Angeles is also the mural capital of the world, with a "collection" of more than 1,500 outdoor wall paintings displayed on storefronts (and sides), street corners, and alleyways throughout the county. Long characterized as culturally and intellectually vapid, Los Angeles is home to more actors, artists, dancers, filmmakers, musicians, and writers than any other city—at any time in the history of civilization.

After taking a good look around, even visitors soon realize that Los Angeles is not just a trip to Universal Studios or Disneyland anymore.

Street), 310/917-6671, is one of the Westside's most innovative and popular restaurants—and refreshingly free of foodie pretensions. The creation of talented L.A. chef Raphael Lunetta, formerly of Jackson's in West Hollywood, JiRaffe serves such things as grilled smoked pork chops with wild rice, smoked bacon, apple chutney, and cider sauce, and whitefish with zucchini and artichokes, fava beans, and sugar snap peas. Open Tues.–Fri. for lunch, nightly for dinner.

Though there's plenty of competition these days, **Chinois on Main,** 2709 Main St. (between Hill and Ashland), 310/392-9025, is still one of L.A.'s best, and most popular, restaurants. One of the oldest L.A. offspring of celebrity chef Wolfgang Puck and interior designer Barbara Lazaroff (Puck's wife), Chinois as environment reflects the China of Lazaroff's childhood imagination as painted in celadon green, fuschia, and black, with chinoiserie cranes and dragon on the walls. Carved window frames open onto an orchid garden. Chinois as eatery was originally invented by Puck in partnership with chef Kazuto Matsusaka; most of the "Chinois Classics" are still here, including the fried catfish with ginger, the tuna tempura sashimi with uni sauce, and the Szechuan pancakes with stir-fried duck, mushrooms, and cilantro. But the menu has also evolved under the guidance of new chef Luis Diaz into something simpler and lighter, with lovely warm sweet curried oysters with cucumber sauce and salmon pearls and seared scallops with a sauce of red onions, red wine, cream, and butter. Chinois is noisy, expensive, and sometimes a challenge for reservations—if it's important, try weeks in advance—but it's still one of the best shows in town.

If you can't get reservations at Chinois then try **Ⓜ Valentino,** 3115 W. Pico Blvd. (four blocks west of Bundy Drive), 310/829-4313, the best Italian restaurant in L.A.; respectable restaurant critics say it's the best in the entire country. This chic dining destination (jackets required) stars lobster cannelloni and other surprising pastas, osso buco, and fish, lamb, rabbit, and veal entrées. As important as the spectacular food is Valentino's wine list, "the greatest cellar in the U.S." according to *Wine Spectator* magazine. The 3,800-label cellar was painstakingly assembled over 30 years

in business, though it did suffer something of a setback when about 20,000 bottles of wine shattered in the 1994 Northridge earthquake. Valentino is open for dinner only, Mon.–Saturday. Very expensive; reservations mandatory.

Drago, 2628 Wilshire Blvd. (at 26th Street), 310/828-1585, is Santa Monica's other dashing, elegant Italian, showcasing variations on Sicilian country fare—pastas and risottos, grilled fish and roasted quail. Excellent wine list. It's open for lunch on weekdays, for dinner every night. Reservations required.

Michael's, 1147 Third St. (just beyond the Promenade), 310/451-0843, was Santa Monica's—and one of L.A.'s—original California cuisine scenes. Owner Michael McCarty, a Cordon Bleu chef, opened his restaurant here in 1979 at the brash age of 26—quickly "blowing L.A.'s mind" with his modern American cuisine. Many of L.A.'s great chefs and restaurant owners-Nancy Silverton, Ken Frank, Roy Yamaguchi, Mark Peel and Jonathan Waxman—worked here at one time or another. While California cuisine may not be as revolutionary and popular as it was when it opened, especially in L.A., you can pretend its the go-go eighties again and slap some plastic (prices are astronomical). But the patio still beckons as one of the prettiest dining destinations in the city, and McCarty's personal contemporary art collection still enlivens the restaurant's walls. Michael's is open Mon.–Fri. for lunch, Mon.–Sat. for dinner. Reservations wise. There's another **Michael's** in New York City.

Fine Dining at the Pier

The Lobster at the entrance to the Santa Monica Pier, 1602 Ocean Ave. (at Colorado), 310/458-9294, once a 1920s-vintage fish market-style café, is back—quite sophisticated this time, with aquarium, grand views, and delectable seafood, from lobster chowder and crab cakes to roasted bass.

Santa Monica's legendary high-class diner and sawdust-floored dive is **Chez Jay,** just steps from the pier's entrance at 1657 Ocean Ave. (between Pico and Colorado), 310/395-1741, once a favorite coastal hangout for regulars Ava Gardner, Vivien Leigh, Frank Sinatra, and Willie Shoemaker. The private booth in back is sometimes called the Kissinger Room, because Henry Kissinger often hid out there with his dates. According to local lore, this is also the place Daniel Ellsburg—working next door at the Rand Corporation think tank—passed the Vietnam War-era *Pentagon Papers* to a reporter. Things are a bit less exciting these days. Continental Chez Jay, the name alone an uncanny spoof on L.A. food snobbery, serves such things as exceptional steaks, lobster thermidor, steamed clams, and shrimp curry, most everything accompanied by the restaurant's famous side dish—baked potatoes, bananas, and sour cream. Dessert is "nonfattening homemade organic cheesecake." Chez Jay is open for lunch on weekdays, dinner nightly.

Always worth the dent in the pocketbook: **Ocean Avenue Seafood,** 1401 Ocean Ave. (at Santa Monica), 310/394-5669, a stylish yet classic oyster bar and seafood restaurant featuring modern art, pastel walls, dark wood paneling, and an indoor-outdoor bar. Classics such as the New England clam chowder, crab cakes, and blackened catfish are always available—but the ever-changing list of fish and fish dishes, usually offering more than two dozen choices on any given day, keeps everyone surprised. It's open daily for lunch and dinner (brunch on Sunday). Another good seafood choice—dig those fish-shaped fountains—is Ocean Avenue's Italian sibling **i Cugini,** 1501 Ocean Ave. (at Broadway), 310/451-4595, where you can get a great Italian seafood stew, shrimp and pesto pizza, and breaded calamari steaks.

Substantially more expensive is **The Ivy at the Shore,** almost facing the pier from 1541 Ocean Ave. (at Colorado), 310/393-3113. This fashionable faux beach shack, complete with bamboo, breezy patio seating (glassed-in and heated on nippy evenings), and tropical-themed bar, is notable along palm-lined Ocean. Like its stylish older sibling near West Hollywood, this Ivy specializes in California-style adaptations of no-nonsense regional Americana—crab cakes, shrimp, and other seafood specialties, Cajun prime rib, Louisiana meatloaf, pizzas, and pastas. Simpler at lunch are the sandwiches and salads (don't forget the Maui onion rings). The Ivy's Caesar salad is famous throughout Los Angeles.

Almost equally famous: delectable desserts. Ivy's is open daily for lunch and dinner (brunch on Sunday); closed major holidays.

Money burning a hole in your pocket? In the mood for some delicious Italian scallions? Then Bruce Marder's **Capo,** 1810 Ocean Ave. (at Pico), 310/394-5550, is the place, serving up sizzling steaks as well as four-cheese ravioli and lobster risotto. Absolutely excellent and not necessarily all that expensive is **Cézanne** at Le Merigot, 1740 Ocean Ave., 310/395-9700, where you'll be tempted by the Santa Barbara prawns stuffed with Dungeness crab or prime rib in horseradish sauce.

Fine Dining Elsewhere in Town

According to *Esquire,* seriously stylish **Father's Office** bar and grill at 1018 Montana Ave., 310/393-2337, offers one of nation's best burgers. There's also a great bar menu, little plates, and nice wine and beer selections.

Farms in Los Angeles are few and far between, but **L.A. Farm** at 3000 Olympic Blvd. (at Centinela), 310/449-4000, at least offers farm animals in the décor as well as the "farm" selections—from the pricey Farmburger and chicken pot pie to steaks—and seafood and veggie selections. French and Californian wines. For a pricey taste of "the bizz," toss on your Hollywood glad rags and mosey on down to this semi-industrial neighborhood and the retro, speakeasy-style **Buffalo Club,** 1520 Olympic Blvd. (at 14th Street), 310/450-8600, owned by *Miami Vice* creator Tony Yerkovich. All-American comfort food makes the menu here, from killer mac and cheese and chicken pot pies to the signature Maine lobster with asparagus and morel mushrooms to banana cream pie. The patio, with its arboreal canopy and Chinese lanterns, is prime for people-watching.

In the mood for Provence? A visit to **Chez Mimi,** 246 26th St. (near San Vicente), 310/393-0558, might just take you there. With multiple dining rooms and patios there's romance to spare. And the food is equally inviting, from the onion and chilled cucumber soups to lemon-rosemary roasted chicken, fresh trout with almonds, and steak with pommes frites. Always a good choice among the delectable desserts is Chez Mimi's a award-winning Tart tatin with vanilla ice cream.

Culinary stars at the Santa Monica Airport include the stylish Pacific Rim-style **Typhoon,** upstairs in the administration building at 3221 Donald Douglas Loop S. (at Airport Avenue), 310/390-6565, where the "pilot's pillar" showcases the pilot's licenses of some of the famous and infamous who have flown in for the pan-Asian fare. Universal favorites include Thai coconut chicken curry, Indonesian stir fry, and fried catfish. Upstairs, on the third floor along with the Skydeck viewing platform, is stylish sibling and excellent sushi bar **The Hump,** 310/313-0977, named for the route over the Himalayas the Flying Tigers took during World War II.

Warszawa, 1414 Lincoln Blvd. (between Santa Monica Boulevard and Broadway), 310/393-8831, is the only Polish restaurant in town—and a very good one. In a onetime private home, Warszawa serves hearty dinners in four cozy lace-curtained rooms. Favorite dishes here include the thick pea soup with smoked ham, roast duckling stuffed with herbs, and hunter's stew with sausage, sauerkraut, beef, bacon, and dumplings. For dessert, try the cheesecake with brown sugar crust, the rum torte, or the chocolate cream walnut cake. Warszawa is open Tues–Sun. for dinner.

Venice

For all practical purposes the unincorporated Venice district of L.A. is the southern extension of Santa Monica—quite convenient if you've got wheels and typically safe to explore if you stick to the main drags and don't hang out too late after nightfall.

If you're in or around Venice, the premier local people's place is the **Rose Cafe,** 220 Rose Ave. (at Main Street), 310/399-0711. Not the best restaurant in town and not one of the trendy beachfront venues, in many ways the Rose Cafe *is* Venice. This is where true Venetians hang out, along with an inordinate number of movie people at times and young execs. The style here is beach bohemian, coffee and pastries being the staff of life. For lunch and dinner, consider a salad or simple sandwich. The patio is the place to be. Great for Mexican seafood is **Casablanca** at

220 Lincoln Blvd. (near Rose Avenue), 310/392-5751, a setting both Bogie and Bergman would love. Or head to **La Cabaña** nearby at 738 Rose Ave., 310/392-6161, for the handmade tortillas, fish tacos, and memorable margaritas.

Figtree's Cafe, right on the Venice Boardwalk at 429 Ocean Front Walk, 310/392-4937, is another locals' favorite for breakfast. (Get there early on weekends, by 9 A.M., and expect slow service; regulars are liable to nurse their cappuccinos and read the Sunday paper for hours.) Vegetarian dishes are a specialty. Try the wonderful polenta, the hearty French toast on thick-sliced raisin nut bread, or the satisfying Santa Fe omelette. Lunch and dinner fare includes pastas, burritos, tostadas, veggie stir fry, and fresh fish. Figtree's is open daily for breakfast, lunch, and dinner. Technically in Marina del Rey, **26 Beach Café** at the foot of Venice Pier, 26 Washington Blvd., 310/821-8129, is the place for big, buff burgers. A onetime railroad bunkhouse is now the **New American Amuse Café,** 796 Main St. (at Thornton Avenue), 310/450-1956, great for breakfast—from maple oat pancakes with strawberries and macadamia nuts to the smoked salmon frittata—just about any time. For lunch, try the shrimp salad sandwich. Now that Amuse has its liquor license, dinners are a hot ticket too.

A best bet among more expensive Venetian venues lives with Jonathan Borofsky's Emmett Kelly-faced dancer, the sad *Ballerina Clown en pointe* above the intersection of Rose and Main. Trendy **Chaya Venice,** 110 Navy St. (at Main), 310/396-1179, stars art-deco Asian decor, eclectic Franco-Japanese-style Californian, and seafood—curried crab soup, spring rolls, even a sushi bar (with happy-hour sushi specials). It's open weekdays for lunch, Sunday for brunch, nightly for dinner.

The onetime West Beach Café is now stylish and energetic **James' Beach,** 60 N. Venice Blvd. (near Pacific Avenue), 310/823-5396, serving impressive New American comfort food, such as chicken pot pie and meat loaf, and a pleasing patio. Across the street is the equally hip sibling **Canal Club,** 2025 Pacific Ave., 310/823-3878, serving sushi and wood-grilled Pacific Rim specialties such as satay and moo shu tofu. Fairly inexpensive and quite good for Thai is romantic **Siamese Garden** right on Venice's Grand Canal at 301 Washington Blvd. (near Strongs Drive), 310/821-0098, open for lunch daily (except Monday), for dinner nightly.

At **ℕ Joe's Restaurant** at 1023 Abbot Kinney Blvd. (between Westminster and Broadway), 310/399-5811, a real find for frugal foodies, seafood often stars on the California-French menu. Lunch and weekend brunch are such a deal; $10–15 will buy you such things as grilled shrimp on saffron risotto; chicken, spinach, and ricotta cheese ravioli salad; green chili and turkey chorizo breakfast burritos; and autumn French toast with caramelized quince, persimmons, white raisins, and nutty Tahitian vanilla mousse. The prix fixe menu is substantially more, $52–62. One of L.A.'s best restaurants, serving one of L.A.'s best Sunday brunches. Reservations strongly recommended.

Abbot Kinney has become an in-your-face foodie boulevard, starting with relaxed places like **Abbot's Habit** café and coffee stop, 1401 Abbot Kinney, 310/399-1171. For stylish picnic fixings and good sandwiches, head for **Stroh's Gourmet,** 1239 Abbot Kinney, 310/450-5119. The grand **French Market Café** at 2321 Abbot Kinney Blvd. (near Venice Boulevard), 310/577-9775, open for breakfast and lunch, serves good coffee, croissants, smoked salmon omelettes, and French-country specialties. Italian **Massimo's** at 1029 Abbot Kinney, 310/581-2485, serves great sandwiches and salads—and grand house-made gelato.

A seriously cool and stylish Venetian, open for dinner and lunch or brunch daily, **ℕ Hal's Bar & Grill,** 1349 Abbot Kinney Blvd. (near California), 310/396-3105, serves zany cocktails—dig that cantaloupe martini—local art on the walls, and impressive live jazz every Sunday and Monday night. Specialties here include the grilled half-chicken, burger with fries, Caesar salad, bread pudding, and ice cream sundae. *Bon Appetit* named Hal's one of the nation's top 10 neighborhood restaurants. So there you have it.

Marina del Rey

Aunt Kizzy's Back Porch in the Villa Marina Shopping Center at 4325 Glencoe Ave. (between Washington Boulevard and Mindanao Way), 310/578-1005, is not exactly what you'd expect in a Marina del Rey minimall. Aunt Kizzy's is a fantastic country-style soul food café serving hefty portions of crispy fried chicken, catfish, ribs, pork chops, and jambalaya, along with rice and red beans and Southern-style vegetables. Everything here is so good that people are willing to wait and wait to get in—and they do, with nary a complaint. Aunt Kizzy's is open daily for lunch 11 A.M.–4 P.M. with an all-you-can-eat Sunday brunch 11 A.M.–3 P.M., for dinner 4–10 P.M. (closed Thanksgiving and Christmas).

If you just can't wait, another possibility is **Benny's Barbecue,** 4077 Lincoln Blvd. (near Washington), 310/821-6939, a takeout stand in the marina that's locally famous for dishing out fiery barbecued ribs, lamb shanks, L.A.'s best hot links, beans, and excellent coleslaw. Also beloved in these parts: **Killer Shrimp,** 523 Washington St. (at Ocean), 310/578-2293. You like the name? You'll like the place. An unassuming storefront in an ugly minimall that serves one item only: killer shrimp, flown in fresh daily from Louisiana, prepared in a lively sauce of beer, butter, garlic, secret herbs and spices, and served with crusty French bread just made for dipping.

Considerably more stylish and expensive is the California-style **Cafe del Rey,** 4551 Admiralty Way (at Bali Way), 310/823-6395, where the eclectic international fare runs from the very simple—pizzas, tasty burgers, niçoise salad—to the surprisingly imaginative. The café is open daily for lunch and dinner, also a good choice for Sunday brunch. Another fine-dining choice, especially if you're en route to LAX, is dinner-only **The Library** at the Los Angeles Renaissance Hotel, 9620 Airport Blvd. in Inglewood, 310/337-2800, famous for its exceptionally well-prepared steaks and seafood. For a dining *experience,* the place is contemporary fusion restaurant **Jer-ne** at the Ritz-Carlton, 4375 Admiralty Way, 310/823-1700.

North of Santa Monica

Heading north from Santa Monica via the Pacific Coast Highway (PCH, or Hwy. 1) leads to the pleasures of Ventura, Santa Barbara, and San Luis Obispo Counties and, eventually, the famous Big Sur coast. Well worth exploring on this side of the L.A. County line are some of L.A.'s favorite residential hideouts—Pacific Palisades, Topanga Canyon, and Malibu—and some of its best beaches. Seeming almost as vast as the Pacific Ocean it looms above, the Santa Monica Mountains National Recreation Area is a crazy quilt of wilderness areas and preserves interspersed with outposts of suburbia.

PACIFIC PALISADES

Like sections of Santa Monica and Malibu, Pacific Palisades perches atop high cliffs (palisades) overlooking the Pacific Ocean. The cliffs are famous for giving way during heavy rains, encouraging expensive homes to slip off their moorings and entire hillsides to slide away to sea—mudslides that inconveniently block the Pacific Coast Highway below. Otherwise the main event in this amazingly upmarket neighborhood just north of Santa Monica is the annual **Fourth of July parade**—an event in which members of the community's longrunning **Optimist Club** march down the street, in close-order drill, in their underwear. The existence of the Optimists is still central to community life, as is Swarthmore Avenue, center of the low-key local business district. But Will Rogers State Historic Park is usually more celebrated—as are Gelson's grocery, a best bet for spotting local celebrities, and Mort's deli, *the* place to eat (celebs primarily hang on the wall). Celebrities are legion in Pacific Palisades. Ron and Nancy Reagan lived here before they moved to the White House in 1984, for example, and past mayors of Pacific Palisades include Chevy Chase, Dom DeLuise, Ted Knight, and Rita Moreno.

For current information on the area, contact: **Pacific Palisades Chamber of Commerce,** 15330 Antioch St., Pacific Palisades, 310/459-7963 or www.palisadeschamber.com.

History

Pacific Palisades began its official community life as a movie studio back lot built by Thomas Ince at the end of Sunset Boulevard in the early 1900s. The area was more thoroughly settled in the 1920s by members of the Methodist Episcopal Church who hoped to establish a western Chautauqua here. The Chautauqua was a cultural, educational, moral, and philosophical program with communal overtones, a social movement started in New York in the late 1870s. Summer Chautauqua events featuring artists, writers, and other philosophers were held in Pacific Palisades during these early years—which helps explain why local streets are largely named for former Methodist bishops, religious schools, and scholars. But interest in the Chautauqua movement soon faded, and the Methodist movers and shakers here lost their land grant in 1928.

Artists, writers, and movie stars soon arrived in their stead, a trend that lasted for two solid decades. Some of them, including Aldous Huxley, Elsa Lancaster, Charles Laughton, and Thomas Mann, emigrated to escape the threat of Nazi Germany. (Pacific Palisades reminded them of the French Riviera, it was said.) By the 1940s the community was well-established as an L.A. center for art and architecture, though affluence is the primary criterion for residence nowadays.

Harry Haldeman—grandfather of H. R. (Bob) Haldeman, a key player in ex-President Richard Nixon's infamous Watergate debacle—was a jovial plumbing supply businessman originally from Chicago, a man as passionate about hard liquor and Cuban cigars as conservative politics. Inspired by the example of San Francisco's exclusive Bohemian Club, in 1913 Haldeman and like-minded revelers recruited from the still-prestigious Los Angeles Athletic Club established the Uplifters Club—the name "The Lofty and Exalted Order of Uplifters" contributed by *The Wizard of Oz* author L. Frank Baum. Though the group's official motto was "to uplift art and promote good fellowship," the ability to lift up one's glass was also crucial. After Prohibition's nationwide alcohol ban went into effect in 1919, the group bought 120 acres of redwoods and eucalyptus groves in Rustic Canyon (below what would later become the Will Rogers ranch) and founded the Uplifters Ranch—a private retreat where captains of industry and a select group of talented friends could protect their sybaritic revelry from the long arm of the law.

The Uplifters' social centerpiece was its clubhouse, now part of the eight-acre **Rustic Canyon Recreation Center** and park on Latimer Road, 310/454-5734, open to the public. In its hard-drinking heyday the Spanish colonial revival clubhouse featured drinking halls, a grand ballroom, and a "library" (actually a poker parlor). Uplifting the grounds were tennis courts, a swimming pool, polo field, trapshooting range, outdoor amphitheater, and dormitories, all part of the wooded playground enjoyed by Walt Disney, Busby Berkeley, Harold Lloyd, Daryl F. Zanuck, and others among L.A.'s most privileged ranks. In 1922 members began to build rustic weekend and summer cabins on land leased from the Uplifters; many of these structures remain. The Uplifters Club dissolved more than 50 years ago but artists, writers, and actual and spiritual descendants of the Uplifters continue to live here.

To reach Rustic Canyon Recreation Center—and to take a respectful peek at this part of the Pacific Palisades past—head south from Sunset Boulevard via Brooktree Road, which follows a tree-lined brook, to the old clubhouse at 600-700 Latimer Road. (Allow plenty of time to get lost. Both Latimer and Haldeman Roads, the Uplifters' main thoroughfares, are narrow, with no curbs or gutters, and largely unlighted at night.) A handful of cabins and lodges—all private residences, so don't trespass or otherwise be obnoxious—still stand, among them 31, 32, 34, 35, and 38 Haldeman and 1, 3, and 8 Latimer. The Marco Hellman cabin at 38 Haldeman was transplanted from *The Courtship of Miles Standish* 1923 movie set. Earl Warren, former California governor and U.S. Supreme Court justice, summered here during the 1940s and '50s.

Sights

The most popular local attraction lies well east along Sunset, near Brentwood—**Will Rogers State Historic Park,** 1501 Will Rogers State Park Rd. (just north of Sunset Boulevard), 310/454-8212. This 187-acre ranch estate is where noted cowboy humorist and philosopher Will Rogers lived from 1924 until his death in 1935. Rogers's ranch-style home, open daily for public tours, is also a museum; don't fail to appreciate the wraparound shower on the second floor. (For more information on the Rogers park and the adjacent Topanga State Park wilderness, see The Santa Monica Mountains.) The lush lawns and landscaped grounds, where the horsey set still plays polo matches on weekends, are also perfect for picnics, Frisbee, and sunbathing.

Near the ocean end of Sunset is the **Self-Realization Fellowship Lake Shrine,** 17190 Sunset Blvd., 310/454-4114, which was used as a movie location before Paramahansa Yogananda, author of *Autobiography of a Yogi,* bought the 10-acre site in 1950. At the center of the shrine, dedicated to the universality of all religions and the exaltation of nature, is the picturesque, luxuriantly landscaped spring-fed lake. A small chapel shaped like a Dutch windmill, a golden-domed archway, a houseboat, and gazebos frame lake views and provide good photo ops. The shrine is open to the public for peaceful walks and meditation. The grounds are open Tues.–Sat. 9–4:30 P.M., Sunday 12:30–4:30 P.M.; admission and parking are free.

Other Pacific Palisades sights are architectural. Most of the significant area architecture was influenced by John Entenza, editor and publisher of the trendsetting *Arts and Architecture* magazine, and his **Case Study House Project,** which encouraged prominent Southern California architects to experiment with new materials and styles. Noted "case study" houses include the landmark international-style **Eames House and Studio,** 203 Chautauqua Blvd., something like a three-dimensional Mondrian painting set in a meadow, designed by Charles Eames in 1947–49; the similar **Entenza House,** 205 Chautauqua Blvd., designed by Charles Eames and Eero Saarinen in 1949; and the international redwood-and-brick

Bailey House, 219 Chautauqua, designed by Richard J. Neutra in 1946–48. Pacific Palisades features many other architectural gems, most of which are not visible from public streets.

Quite accessible, however, are the **Castellammare Stairways,** (Castellammare is Italian for "Castle on the Sea") reached from Sunset Boulevard via Castellammare Drive, which leads up to this enclave of million-dollar homes overlooking the Pacific Ocean. Among the vertical hiking possibilities here (near Castellammare): the stairway just off Posetano Road that climbs to Revello Drive, and the stairway from Breve Way to Porto Marina. For sheer popularity, however, stop on the way back into Santa Monica for a run up the 200-step **Adelaide Stairway** (promoted as L.A.'s Ultimate Stairway in myriad magazine "lifestyle" articles), which starts, on the uphill end, at Fourth Street and Adelaide Drive and winds down to E. Channel Road. Come during the week to avoid the hordes of fitness fanatics who turn the stairway into a human freeway on weekends.

Topanga Canyon

The equally indefinable inland and upland neighbor to Malibu is the laid-back burg of Topanga in mountainous Topanga Canyon, reached from PCH via Topanga Canyon Boulevard (Hwy. 27), increasingly a high-speed commuter thoroughfare. (The tailgaters' apparent message: Pull over or die.) Beyond the highway, the artsy community sprawls off in all directions—up tortured hillsides, down one-lane roads—within the canyon's watershed. Famous for its mudslides, Topanga Canyon does shed water after heavy winter rains—which certainly explains the Chumash name, Topanga, roughly translated as "Mountains that Run into the Sea." Here, they often do. When hillsides aren't preoccupied with slip-sliding away, rustic cabins, lodges, standard-brand ranch homes, and more ambitious architectural adventures provide both physical and spiritual home for Topanga's people, predominantly actors, artists, musicians, poets, writers, and screenwriters. Topanga thrives on its artistic ambience and its community eccentricities—the roadside crystal stands and such—many of which hark back to the earliest inklings of the Age of Aquarius. Yet given the region's increasing suburban popularity, back-to-the-landers without 30-year-old roots would be financially challenged to plant themselves here today.

Most of Topanga the town is strung out along the highway about halfway between the San Fernando Valley and the Pacific Ocean. A popular stop for lunch is **Abuelita's,** 137 S. Topanga Canyon Blvd., 310/455-8788. You can also stop locally for supplies and deli sandwiches at places such as **Fernwood Market,** 446 S. Topanga Canyon Blvd., 310/455-2412, and **Froggy's Topanga Fresh Fish Market** (also a good restaurant), 1105 N. Topanga Canyon Blvd., 310/455-1728.

Some classic Topanga neighborhoods and destinations, including the **Inn of the Seventh Ray** natural-foods restaurant, 310/455-1311, are tucked in among the creekside oaks and sycamores alongside Old Topanga Canyon Road, which eventually intersects scenic Mulholland Highway. For books about the area and basic New Age supplies, stop by **The Spiral Staircase** next to the Inn of the Seventh Ray at 128 Old Topanga Canyon, 310/455-3370.

Another wonder in Topanga is **The Will Geer Theatricum Botanicum,** 1419 N. Topanga Canyon Blvd., 310/455-3723, www.theatricum .com, a small, woodsy outdoor theater that remains part of the legacy of actor/philosopher Will Geer. The classically trained Geer eventually became one of the world's most beloved actors—baby boomers will remember him as Grandpa Walton on *The Waltons* TV series—yet his professional and personal lives were all but undone in the 1950s by his refusal to cooperate with the communist-hunting House Committee on Un-American Activities. "Blacklisted," or barred from working in Hollywood, Geer moved his family to Topanga Canyon and established a Shakespearean theater to showcase the talents of other blacklisted Hollywood talent. Along with theater tickets, he and his family also sold their home-grown vegetables. Call for current program information or see the website.

Easily accessible from Topanga is **Topanga State Park,** prime for hiking—in the absence of major storms and mudslides—especially in "the green months" of winter and early spring.

MALIBU

Aside from an appreciation for clean beaches, good surf, and aquamarine waters, the one thing that unites Malibu residents is the Pacific Coast Highway, which here is a tenuous lifeline. Celebrated for its surfing, its celebrities, and its chic coastal cachet, Malibu most often makes it into the news as a disaster area for its almost predictable "natural" disasters, created by human incursions into an unstable, fire-adapted ecosystem. Whether or not wildfires have finished their occasional summer and fall windsprints to the sea, the rains begin—and the mudslides, which may carry houses, carports, landscaped yards, sometimes streets and entire hillsides with them. If the Pacific Coast Highway is closed for days at a time, be it from behemoth bouncing boulders or mudslides, people here take it in stride. Building more houses here—and continually rebuilding them—is not particularly intelligent.

Yet try telling that to people in Malibu, who moved here to get away from it all. The fact that "it" had already arrived, in the forms of crushing urban crowds and nightmarish traffic, was a prime motivating factor for Malibu's incorporation in 1990. During his one-year term as the city's "honorary mayor," actor Martin Sheen declared Malibu a nuclear-free zone and a refuge for the homeless. But since incorporation residents have drawn battle lines over growth-related issues.

Despite the definitive dot on most maps, Malibu as place has always been difficult to find. Though the star-studded Malibu Colony, the Malibu Pier, and several Malibu beaches have served as unofficial community signposts, in most people's minds "Malibu" was a rather vague regional appellation taking in the 20-plus miles of Los Angeles County coastline between Topanga Canyon and Ventura County. But now Malibu has definite city limits, and an official 20-square-mile territory, stretching north from Topanga Canyon to Leo Carrillo State Beach at the Ventura County line.

The main attractions are Malibu's beaches—more than 20 miles of them. The beaches along the Malibu coastline are still reasonably clean, despite heavy recreational use and some local pollution problems, and provide some of the best surfing and ocean swimming in Southern California. Traffic on a summer day along the Pacific Coast Highway can be brutal and parking nearly impossible, however. Plan to arrive before the noontime "rush hour"—say, by 11 A.M., if not earlier—while parking places are still available. A second highway rush usually occurs between 4 and 5 P.M., when most people head home for dinner. If you're well supplied and willing to while away some time, the good news is that sunsets are fairly unpopulated and peaceful. Better yet, come in the off season—spring, fall, and winter—when beaches can be quite balmy and pleasant yet much less crowded. The weather is moderate year-round. Barring the occasional storm, some of the finest beach days come in winter—though some spots are crowded on weekends during whale-watching season.

For current information about the area, contact: **Malibu Chamber of Commerce,** 23805 Stuart Ranch Rd., Ste. 100, 310/456-9025, www.malibu.org.

History

Though the ocean here draws the soul, the land is more highly valued. After the native Chumash people were dispatched to nearby Franciscan missions, Malibu's history became an endless tangle of land and road-building disputes.

José Bartólome Tapía traveled to California from Sonora, Mexico, in 1775 with the de Anza expedition. In 1805 Spain granted Tapía, a farmer and the eldest of nine children, the Topanga Malibu Sequit ranch, named for three area Indian villages. The ranch thrived until Tapía died in 1824, though his wife, Doña Maria, kept it until 1848. After the death of her eldest son Doña Maria sold the ranch, for 400 pesos, to a granddaughter's husband, Leon Victor Prudhomme, a 26-year-old Frenchman. But in the transition from Mexican to American rule in 1850, records detailing the early Spanish land grant to Tapía were lost. After a long legal dispute with the California Land Commission, Prudhomme sold the ranch in 1857 to Matthew Keller, an Irishman who took advantage of the defective title and the Panic of 1857 to buy it for the outrageously low price of 10 cents per acre, or a total of less than $1,400. Keller gained undisputed legal title in 1863 and presided over the ranch's 13,300-plus acres, which produced some of California's first wines, until his death in 1881. Son Henry Keller sold the land in 1887 for $10 an acre.

Frederick Hastings Rindge, son of a Massachusetts wool merchant, inherited a $2 million estate in 1883 at the age of 26. A Harvard graduate, Rindge established a city hall, public library, a boys' school, and children's sanitarium in Cambridge before he and his wife, May, bought the Malibu rancho and moved to California. The change, Rindge believed, would improve his health. The family built a home on Ocean Avenue in Santa Monica—a day's journey by wagon from Malibu, where the primitive dirt road could be crossed only at low tide—and began to improve the isolated ranch. As detailed in Rindge's book, *Happy Days in Southern California*, published in 1898, the family built a lovely, landscaped home east of Malibu Creek, added a barn, corrals, and bunkhouses, and planted grain and lemon groves. Most of the land was set aside for cattle grazing, though. The Rindge family eventually owned the entire 24-mile stretch of coastline north of Las Flores Canyon.

The happiest days ended in 1903 thanks to the worst fire in Malibu's recorded history, probably started by squatters. Fanned by hot Santa Ana winds, the wildfire rapidly torched the entire ranch. Along with most everything else the family home was destroyed, which forced the Rindges to move into Los Angeles. Two years later Frederick Rindge died.

When Frederick Rindge died in 1905, his widow, May, began fighting what became an endless series of turf battles to protect the land from trespasses large and small—from homesteaders, squatters, railroads, and the state of California's highway-building plans. When armed guards, high fences, and dynamiting her own roads failed to stop progress, May Rindge resorted to the courts. She appealed California's plan to condemn part of her property, to build the Pacific Coast Highway, all the way to the U.S. Supreme Court—and lost.

In the midst of the daunting financial problems generated by her war against the Pacific Coast Highway, the "Queen of Malibu" May Rindge decided to lease out beachfront property, at Malibu La Costa and between Carbon Canyon and the Malibu Pier. Actress Anna Q. Nilsson signed the first lease, and the area was quickly established as a residential colony for publicity-shunning movie people. Among Malibu's first wave of celluloid celebrities were Clara Bow, Ronald Colman, Dolores Del Rio, John Gilbert, Barbara Stanwyck, and Jack Warner. Later, Escondido, Trancas, and Zuma Beaches were opened to development, and still more movie stars moved to the area. The celebs have been coming ever since, their presence now central to the Malibu mystique. (Less celebrated citizens try not to stare but still get a thrill from spotting movie stars stopping for basic supplies at Trancas Market and other local shopping hot spots.) Luminaries of current or recent history include Johnny Carson, Ted Danson, Barbara Streisand, Dustin Hoffman, Madonna, Mel Gibson, Whoopi Goldberg, Robert Redford, Steven Spielberg, and Sylvester Stallone. Not to mention David Geffen, Leonardo DiCaprio, and the Arquettes (David and Courtney Cox). And not counting the colony's large numbers of artists, writers, and other talented citizens.

Malibu is also famous for its surfers, who cherish access to the coast's best breaks and beaches as much as Malibu's movie stars cherish absolute privacy—a continuing source of social tension that somehow adds to the peculiar ambience. Here, throughout the Malibu Colony, megamillion-dollar beachfront bungalows and baronial estates adopt a sober streetside decorum that rarely hints of the glass-walled glories on the private side. Building such exclusive homes in the style of townhouses—with little or no space in between to discourage both snooping and beach access—somehow just encourages public curiosity, making people ever more determined to find the few available access walkways (follow the surfers). Malibu Road along the waterfront is a classic example.

Malibu Pier

Start exploring Malibu at the 700-foot Malibu Pier, opened to the public with great fanfare and fireworks on July 4, 1945. The present-day pier was damaged by storms and closed for a number of years until the state of California and the community restored and reopened the landmark in 2004. The pier area is particularly popular for fishing (tackle and bait available) and watching both surfers and sunsets. Surrounding the pier is Malibu Lagoon State Beach, which includes the Malibu estuary, the historic Adamson House and associated museum, and **Malibu Surfrider Beach,** one of the West Coast's most famous surfing beaches. Largely east of the pier (it feels "south") though the best breaks are to the west ("north"), Malibu Surfrider Beach has been celebrated in countless Frankie Avalon, Annette Funicello, and *Gidget* movies. More significantly, according to local lore, Surfrider is California's 1926 surfing birthplace. In summer perfect waves roll to shore at Surfrider day after day—an accident of ocean currents, upwellings, and winds that creates heaven for surfers, kayakers, and windsurfers but hell for those who dislike overcrowded beaches. Swimming and surfing aren't recommended here, since Heal the Bay regularly "flunks" Surfrider and adjacent beaches in its annual water quality survey. But surfers still come, since they have to go where the waves are. If you want to watch, the pier offers ringside railings for surfing voyeurs.

If you hunger for a bracing after-beach breakfast, head for the **PierView Cafe and Cantina,** 310/456-6962, on the beach just east of the pier. Or head for local shopping malls. Best bets for breakfast or weekend brunch—and later meals—include **Marmalade** in the Cross Creek Plaza, 310/317-4242, and, at Malibu Colony Plaza (W. Malibu Road at Webb Way), both casual **Coogie's,** 310/317-1444, and uptown **Granita,** 310/456-0488, the latter sea-themed culinary adventure established by Wolfgang Puck and Barbara Lazaroff.

Malibu Lagoon State Beach and Adamson House

Malibu Lagoon offers an opportunity for impromptu bird-watching and nature appreciation, right off the highway. One of only two estuaries remaining within the boundaries of Santa Monica Mountains National Recreation Area, this small patch of marsh at the mouth of Malibu Creek serves as a natural fish nursery—and bountiful buffet for neighborhood and migrating shorebirds. (While visiting, stay on the boardwalks.) More than 200 species of birds use Malibu Lagoon as a migratory stopover. Nearby beach areas are popular for swimming, though water at the mouth of Malibu Creek is polluted—twice monthly, the lagoon is drained—and swimming is not recommended on those days. With its offshore reefs and kelp beds, the area is also popular with skin and scuba divers.

Also well worth exploring: the adjoining **Malibu Lagoon Museum** and the grand **Adamson House.** Chances are you'll never see the inside of local movie stars' homes, so amuse yourself, while touring Adamson House, with the knowledge that most celebrities would kill to own a place like this. Former home of Rhoda and Merritt Adamson—daughter and son-in law of Frederick and May Rindge, who owned the vast Malibu Ranch in the early 1900s—this 1929 Spanish-Moorish beach house was designed by architect Stiles O. Clements, who took full advantage of the Rindge-owned Malibu Tile Company's exceptional craftsmanship. The stunning Adamson House, listed on the National Register of Historic Places, is rich with handcrafted teak, graceful wrought-iron work, and leaded-glass windows. But, inside and out, it is primarily a tile-setter's fantasy—a real-life museum-quality display of 1920s' California tilework, richly colored geometric and animal-motif patterns worked into the walkways, walls, and lavish fountains. There's even a tiled outdoor dog shower. The museum adjacent, at home in the home's seven-car garage, chronicles area history with memorabilia, art, artifacts, and photographs.

Malibu Lagoon State Beach adjoins the Malibu Pier and includes famous Malibu Surfrider Beach (see above). Adamson House and the Malibu Lagoon Museum, 23200 Pacific Coast Hwy. (Hwy. 1), are one-quarter mile west of the Malibu Pier and 13 miles west of Santa Monica. The lagoon and Adamson House grounds are technically open 24 hours, though the adjacent county parking lot, shared with Surfrider Beach, is open daily 8 A.M.–5 P.M. only (side-street parking available early morning and evening). Another parking lot is one block north at Cross Creek Road. Beach, lagoon, and museum access are free. Adamson House tours are $5 adults, $2 free for youths 6–17. The Adamson House is open only for tours (one hour), usually offered Wed.–Sat. 11 A.M.–3 P.M. (last tour at 2 P.M.); the museum is open during the same hours. Reservations are required for groups of 12 or more and the museum closes on days with moderate to heavy rain—call ahead. No interior photography allowed. For more information, call 310/456-8432 or see www.adamsonhouse.org.

J. Paul Getty Museum

Beyond the surf and the stars, the community's most famous attraction is now the second location for the renowned J. Paul Getty Museum, 17985 Pacific Coast Hwy. (between Sunset and Topanga Canyon Boulevards), Malibu, www.getty.edu—still closed at last report, the expansion project delayed when neighbors challenged it in court, though after a settlement the museum was expected to reopen in fall 2005 as the Getty Center's classical antiquities exhibit and restoration center. Call first, though, because completion dates have been rather fluid for some time. (If you can't wait, head to Brentwood and the glorious Getty Center, 310/440-7300.) The museum's collection of European paintings and drawings—Goya, Cézanne, van Gogh, Rembrandt, Renoir—along with illuminated manuscripts, American and European photography, home furnishings fit for French royalty, and European sculpture, bronzes, ceramics, and glass, are now installed at the Getty Center.

The Getty Villa is, and will be, perfect for the Getty classics, one of the finest U.S. collections of ancient Greek and Roman art and artifacts—sculptures and figurines, vases, mosaics, and paintings. When the museum reopens, expect special exhibits of ancient Asian and Eastern European art, and a 450-seat amphitheater. The Villa will also be home to the nation's first master's degree program in archaeological and ethnographic conservation, thanks to a partnership between the Cotsen Institute of Archaeology at UCLA and the Getty Conservation Institute.

The Getty Villa is also a classic—a re-creation of the Villa dei Papiri, an ancient Roman country house with a view of the Bay of Naples. Even the Getty gardens, the trees, shrubs, and flowers, the statuary and outdoor wall paintings, represent those at the original villa of 2,000 years ago. Villa dei Papiri, thought to have belonged to Julius Caesar's father-in-law, was buried by the volcanic rubble of Mt. Vesuvius when the mountain erupted in A.D. 79. Discovered by treasure hunters and excavated during the 18th century, the reborn villa inspired Getty; the Getty Villa, completed in 1974, was constructed from excavation drawings.

Other Sights

Other attractions include the prestigious private **Pepperdine University** campus, 24255 Pacific Coast Hwy., 310/506-4000, a nondenominational Christian four-year liberal arts college established in 1973 by George Pepperdine, founder of Western Auto Supply. The attractive 819-acre campus, on a hill overlooking the ocean, was designed by architect William Pereira. These days Pepperdine is particularly noted for its postgraduate law and business schools. The men's volleyball team is typically one of the best in the country—which isn't that surprising, given the number of beach volleyball nets strung up all along the Malibu coast. Pepperdine's popularity among Southern California surfers was lampooned in Garry Trudeau's *Doonesbury* cartoon strip in the late '90s, when it was announced that Whitewater special prosecutor Kenneth Starr would soon join the faculty here. Bigger news in most years: summer's **Malibu Strawberry Creek Music Festival** and other special performances and events held here.

Then there's the vast expanse of **Santa Monica Mountains National Recreation Area,** which dips its chaparral-covered toes into the sea all along the Malibu coastline.

Charmlee Regional County Park is a little-known but charming park overlooking the Pacific—460 acres of meadows, oak woodlands, and chaparral on bluffs up to 1,300 feet above sea level. Charmlee is stunning for spring wildflowers and a perfect spot for watching the winter

NEON, L.A.'S SIGNATURE FLASH

If imitation is the sincerest form of flattery, just imagine how flattered Los Angeles is by the existence of Las Vegas and all that flashy neon.

The **Museum of Neon Art (MONA)** in downtown L.A. celebrates the city's love affair with neon lighting—a commercial art form that once decorated countless L.A. storefronts, theater marquees, and roof lines. The original fuel for L.A.'s signature flash was neon itself, a colorless, odorless gas that glows orangey-red when zapped by electricity, a fact of nature first discovered in France in 1898. (Other colors are created by other gases.) America's first neon signs, manufactured in France, were installed in 1923 at an L.A. Packard dealership.

Some of L.A.'s original tubular light show still shines, lighting up **Broadway** downtown, sections of **Wilshire Boulevard, Western Avenue** between Wilshire and Third St., **Alvarado Street** flanking MacArthur Park, and countless other streets. Other areas, such as **Melrose Avenue,** are at the forefront of the city's neo-neon renaissance, thanks in large part to citywide consciousness-raising credited to MONA and its founding artist Lili Lakich.

Downtown on the first floor of the Renaissance Tower, in Grand Hope Park on W. Olympic, the MONA is the only permanent neon museum in the world. A stunning and electrically enigmatic likeness of the Mona Lisa—the museum's logo, designed by Lakich—marks the spot. The permanent collection at MONA includes an impressive array of classic L.A. neon and electric signs, dating from the 1920s. Changing exhibits—such as the museum's opening exhibition, Electric Muse: A Spectrum of Neon, Electric, and Kinetic Sculpture (1996)—emphasize neon as a contemporary art form. Head to **CityWalk** outside Universal Studios to appreciate more of the MONA collection, which includes the Richfield Eagle and the Melrose Theater sign.

For a still flashier appreciation of local lights, sign on for the museum's after-dark "Neon Cruise" L.A. bus tour, offered at least monthly, $45 per person. In addition to its neon tours, the museum offers introductory classes in neon design and technique four times each year.

The Museum of Neon Art is open Wed.–Sat. 11 A.M.–5 P.M. and Sun. noon–5 P.M. (closed Mon., Tues., and major holidays). On the second Thursday of every month, the museum is also open 5–8 P.M.—and at that time admission is free to all. Otherwise admission is $5 adults, $3.50 seniors and students (children age 12 and under free). Call for current information on docent-led tours, current exhibits, neon art classes, and "Neon Cruise" tours. The museum's entrance is on Hope (at Olympic); during regular museum hours, free parking is available in the Renaissance Tower's garage on Grand just south of Ninth Street.

For current exhibit and other information, and to make reservations for MONA's Neon Tours, contact: Museum of Neon Art (MONA), Renaissance Tower, 501 W. Olympic Blvd., 213/489-9918, www.neonmona.org.

---

migration of the gray whales, just offshore. The undeveloped park is also ideal for a simple get-off-the-highway picnic, or for hiking on trails and fire roads. It's open during daylight hours, year-round. To get here, take Encinal Canyon Road from Pacific Coast Highway north of Malibu.

Recreation

Last stop before the Ventura County line in the north is **Leo Carrillo State Park,** typically much less crowded than the "city beaches" closer to Malibu Colony, Santa Monica, and urban points south. Named for the actor who played Pancho in the early 1950's *Cisco Kid* TV series, later known as "Mr. California" due to his impressive public service, 1,600-acre Leo Carrillo features 1.5 miles of stupendous craggy coastline and both rocky and sandy beaches—the totality perfect for surfing, sailboarding, swimming, and, at low tide, tidepooling. A popular whale-watching spot in winter, Leo Carrillo is also good for scuba diving. (Riptides are a danger occasionally.) Inland, ranger-guided hikes are regularly scheduled, and, in summer, campfire programs. Pleasant picnicking, too. A pretty campground, across the highway, is set among the sycamores back from the beach, and there's another nearby at North Beach. For a spectacular ocean view with minimal effort, take the short trail up the hill from near the booth at the campground entrance. Leo Carrillo State Park, 35000 Pacific Coast Hwy. (Hwy. 1), is 25 miles west of Santa Monica and about 15 miles from "downtown" Malibu. Leo Carrillo's main entrance is just east of Mulholland Highway's intersection with the highway—a great drive, if you're out exploring. Camping is $15–20 for family sites (including self-contained RV sites), $3 for hike/bike sites. The beach is open daily 8 A.M.–midnight. The visitor center is open daily in summer. For more information, call 818/880-0350. For camping reservations, a must in summer and on most weekends, call ReserveAmerica at 800/444-7275 or visit www.reserveamerica.com.

Next east is one of L.A.'s best-kept secrets, rumored to be the preferred beach escape for L.A.'s lifeguards on their days off—picturesque, pristine, and remote **Nicholas Canyon County Beach,** 34000 Pacific Coast Highway. Nicholas, a graceful quarter moon of sand curving around a small bay, is well-protected from highway noise and has no skate rentals, no snack stands—none of the usual L.A. beach chaos and clutter. Just peace, quiet, and a few kayakers and surfers. (And lifeguards and restrooms.) The **Robert H. Meyer Memorial State Beach,** next east at 33000 Pacific Coast Hwy., is actually a string of smaller state beaches tucked into a residential area: **El Pescador, La Piedra,** and **El Matador,** the lovely latter beach the most popular. As many as 10 episodes of *Baywatch* were once filmed here each year, but most people come for the dramatic cliffs, rock formations, and caves along the sandy beach. (No lifeguards, but picnic tables and portable toilets. Parking lot open 8 A.M.–sunset, fee.) Nearby is **El Sol State Beach,** difficult to find.

Trancas Beach at PCH and Guernsey Avenue is another residential-area beach, most accessible by walking from **Zuma Beach.** Zuma, 30000 Pacific Coast Hwy., was the location for a multitude of 1950s and 1960s surfing movies—the likes of *Deadman's Curve, Beach Blanket Bingo,* and *Back to the Beach*—but gathered even more fame in the 1970s, thanks to singer/songwriter Neil Young's album *Zuma.* Postcard-pretty if hardly private, Zuma's appeal is as fundamental as its endless expanse of white sand, rowdy beach volleyball, and children's playground. Popular with the rowdy surfing set. For all the fun and frolic, though, think safety. Riptides here have been known to drag up to 20 people at a time straight out to sea—keeping the lifeguards plenty busy. Access to the beach, open sunrise to sunset, is free but there is a fee to park in the *huge* lot. Locals avoid even that by jockeying for highway and street parking. Full services are available (lifeguards, restrooms, snack bars, and rental shops). Just below often-packed Zuma is clean, sandy, and equally popular **Westward Beach,** reached from Pacific Coast Highway via Westward Beach Road (limited free parking along the beach road). Or, park at Zuma and walk along the beach.

Continue on Westward Beach Road to reach the parking lot for busy **Point Dume State Beach,** whose sand neatly segues into Westward's. Point Dume once featured a vertical "point"—a rocky peak—in addition to its seaward point, until the former was flattened for a housing development. Reaching Point Dume's secluded series of sandy pocket beaches and rocky shores, scattered below impressive cliffs, requires a little walking. Small caves and tidepools abound throughout the 35-acre **Point Dume Natural Preserve,** where the rocky west face is popular with technical climbers. A stairway and hiking trail start at Westward Beach and climb to the headlands and the **Point Dume Whale Watch,** popular series of sites for watching the midwinter migration of California gray whales—good for views any time. Look for California brown pelicans, California sea lions, and harbor seals on offshore rocks. Though it's not condoned as a nude beach officially (deputies have been known to cite suitless sunbathers), historically beach-in-the-buff enthusiasts have always hiked around the point or down the stairway from the headlands to the rocky north end of **Pirate's Cove** and its stunning beach, but winter storms often block access. Point Dume is a good swimming, sunbathing, and diving beach (for experienced divers), only fair for surfing; lifeguards, very clean restrooms, outdoor showers, and a soft drink vending machine provided.

Point Dume adjoins pretty, private **Paradise Cove Beach.** But unless you're absolutely desperate to find a place to toss down the beach towel, the parking fee alone—$25—is enough to discourage most people from trying this tiny beach near the pier on Paradise Cove Road. (If you park on PCH and walk in, it'll cost you only $5. And the restaurant validates parking.) But it is a quiet, family-friendly beach with rocky bluffs, caves, and tidepools to explore. At Pacific Coast Highway and Escondido Road is coastal access (highway parking only) for residential-area **Escondido Beach,** narrow, sandy, and empty, indeed fairly well hidden. Look for the Coastal Access signs. Actual "access" begins at a gate on the ocean side of the highway, which is unlocked 6:30 A.M.–6:30 P.M. daily, just north of Geoffrey's Restaurant in the 27400 "block" of the Pacific Coast Highway; the beach path starts at a stairwell between two houses. No lifeguard, no services.

Then there's very narrow **Dan Blocker State Beach,** named for the big, brawny actor better known as affable Hoss Cartwright on TV's long-running *Bonanza.* Dan Blocker extends from Malibu Road (at Pacific Coast Highway) to Corral Canyon Road. Most people head for the sandier southeast end, which can be packed; beach fans can find more privacy toward the less accessible, rockier end near the mouth of Corral Creek. Highway parking only, easy beach access. Popular for surf fishing and swimmers; lifeguards in summer and on busy weekends.

For those willing to brave the movie-star-beachhouse obstacles along Malibu Road, back in Malibu Colony both **Puerco Beach** and **Amarillo Beach** beckon (no lifeguards, bathrooms, or other services). Park on the north end of Malibu Road, where it meets the highway, or from the highway take Webb Way south to Malibu Road, praying all the while for a parking spot. To reach Amarillo and points east, it's easiest to walk from Puerco.

Along the coast are a few decent stops for a meal with a view, including the **Paradise Cove Beach Café** at Paradise Cove, 310/457-2503, and **Geoffrey's** near Point Dume, 310/457-1519. If your beach explorations lead you far afield,

don't forget the ever-popular **Neptune's Net** on PCH about a mile north of the Ventura County line, 310/457-3095, beloved for its downhome, no-frills funk. Best bet at lunch or dinner is the steamed shellfish. Pick your own lobsters or crabs right out of the fish tanks.

Beyond Malibu Lagoon State Beach and Malibu Surfrider Beach near the pier (see Malibu Pier and Malibu Lagoon listings above) is a string of difficult-to-reach residential-area sandy spots: **Carbon Beach,** 22200 Pacific Coast Hwy., just west of Carbon Canyon Road; **La Costa Beach,** 21400 PCH; **Las Flores Beach,** 20900 PCH; and **Big Rock Beach** (look for the big rock), 20600 PCH, just north of Carbon Canyon Road. The best way to reach all of these beaches—and watch the tides, so you don't get stranded—is by walking east from Malibu Surfrider Beach or west from Las Tunas. By contrast, rocky **Las Tunas Beach** next east, right on the highway, is very easy to reach but not all that pleasant because of the din of traffic. It's most popular with surf fishers and scuba divers; lifeguards in season, portable toilets. Bring water.

Topanga State Beach, easy to find along the 18700 "block" of Pacific Coast Highway, a quarter-mile west of the J. Paul Getty Museum and a quarter-mile east of Topanga Canyon Boulevard, is popular for swimming (if you don't mind dodging a few ocean rocks) and sunny picnics. On a clear day, from the bluffs here you can see Catalina Island. Sometimes you can also see dolphins just offshore, or passing whales. Mostly what you'll see at Topanga, though, are surfers and sailboats. The swells here are second only to those at Malibu Surfrider. The water quality is usually good, too, so in summer the beach can be quite crowded. The small parking lot is usually full by 11 A.M., or try to find a spot along the highway. Lifeguards, full services. Another good possibility is **Castle Rock Beach** across the highway from the Getty Museum, a pleasant sandy beach with easy access, parking lot, portable toilets, lifeguards.

Will Rogers State Beach seems to stretch forever beneath the unstable palisades of Pacific Palisades—and this strand of sand does go on some distance, since from here to Redondo Beach it is interrupted only by the boat harbor at Marina del Rey. An excellent swimming beach—particularly toward the north, where water quality is usually best—Will Rogers is uncrowded, at least compared to teeming Santa Monica State Beach just south, because of limited parking. Surfing is fair. Facilities include playgrounds, picnic tables, volleyball nets, lifeguards, restrooms, the works.

SANTA MONICA MOUNTAINS

One of the few east-west-trending mountain ranges in the United States, the Santa Monica Mountains extend upward from the sea as part of the Channel Islands and then eastward from Pacific Ocean beaches and tidepools to Mt. Hollywood in Griffith Park on the mainland, creating the geographical divide between the Los Angeles Basin and the San Fernando Valley.

The Santa Monica Mountains National Recreation Area, a 150,000 acre-plus parkland pastiche created by Congress in 1978, protects much of the remaining open space in the Santa Monica Mountains—city, county, state, federal, private, and once-private lands and beaches—within a unified identity. Yet within that unity is great diversity. Maintaining separate boundaries are parks of long standing, including Malibu Creek State Park, Topanga State Park, and Will Rogers State Historic Park, various public beaches, and attractions such as Paramount Ranch, Peter Strauss Ranch, and Ramirez Canyon Park, former residence of Barbara Streisand. Thanks to the Santa Monica Mountains Conservancy and other groups and individuals, land acquisitions continue to expand this national park—and the boundaries of individual parks within it—while extending the recreation area's trail system, popular with hikers, mountain bikers, and horseback riders. At last report, hikers, bikers, and equestrians were still battling over the issue of increasing mountain bike access to back-country trails—to some an issue of overuse and abuse of trails as well as "machine-age encroachment," to others a question of equal rights for cyclists.

At the beaches summer is prime time, but the off seasons offer at least the opportunity for solitude (and better beachcombing). Winter and spring, when the sky is blue and the hills are green, are the best seasons for exploring the mountains, which boast about 860 species of flowering plants in environments varying from grasslands, oak woodlands, and riparian sycamore and fern glades to coastal chaparral and craggy red-rock canyons. The only Mediterranean ecosystem protected by the National Park Service, the Santa Monicas have posed for TV and movie crews as Greece, Italy, France, Korea, the Wild West, and the antebellum South. Some areas are absolutely otherworldly; interplanetary film possibilities have yet to be fully explored here.

But because so much of the area is urban, surrounded by millions of people and bordered by two of the world's busiest freeways, and its attractions far-flung, finding one's way around in the Santa Monica Mountains can get complicated. To get oriented, stop by or contact the national park's visitor center and associated bookstore (open daily 9 A.M.–5 P.M., closed Thanksgiving, Christmas, and New Year's Day). Along with maps and other helpful publications, the office offers a wonderful quarterly calendar of guided walks and other events, *Outdoors in the Santa Monica Mountains National Recreation Area.*

For more information, contact: **Santa Monica Mountains National Recreation Area Visitor Center,** 401 W. Hillcrest Dr. in Thousand Oaks, 805/370-2301, www.nps.gov/samo. To get there from the Ventura Freeway (Hwy. 101), exit at Lynn Rd. and continue north; turn east on Hillcrest; then turn left onto McCloud. The visitor center is the first driveway on the right. For information on area state parks, contact **California State Parks,** 1925 Las Virgenes Rd. in Calabasas, 818/880-0350. Though associated state parks and beaches charge at least a nominal day-use fee, general access to national parks land is free. Access hours also vary. Wildfires are a major threat to the park and its urban and suburban neighbors, so no fires are allowed within most park areas. Permission to explore environmentally sensitive areas, including **Cold Creek Canyon Preserve** near Topanga State Park, is by permit only, so docent-led hikes are usually the best way to go.

Highlights of Santa Monica Mountains National Recreation Area include:

Will Rogers State Historic Park

"The more you read about politics," laureate Will Rogers once observed, "you got to admit that each party is worse than the other." America's favorite cowboy commentator, originally a rodeo trick roper, was still making a name for himself in 1928 when he and his family settled at this ranch in then-rural Pacific Palisades, just north of Santa Monica.

The unassuming 31-room home features mission-style furniture, eclectic Western decor, and some eye-catching oddities—including a stuffed calf Rogers regularly used for indoor roping practice. Museum exhibits tell the Will Rogers story, up to and including his tragic death in 1935. To make a day of it, enjoy the picnic grounds and the national park's hiking trails—including very popular Backbone Trail, now open to mountain bikers. Otherwise, the big weekend draw is the equestrian action—polo matches, a continuation of the tradition started by Rogers himself, open to the public. There's also a roping and training area for horses.

For more information, contact: Will Rogers State Historic Park, 1501 Will Rogers State Park Rd. in Pacific Palisades, 310/454-8212. The park is open daily 8 A.M.–7 P.M. in summer, 8 A.M.–6 P.M. in other seasons. The Rogers home/museum has been closed for renovations but normally it is open 10:30 A.M.–5 P.M. daily for tours (closed Thanksgiving, Christmas, and New Year's Day). Tours run every hour on the half-hour, starting at 10:30 A.M., with the last tour at 4:30 P.M. Weather permitting, polo matches are scheduled here on the weekends, which is the only outdoor polo field in Los Angeles county. Park admission is free, technically, but there is a fee for parking.

Topanga State Park

Native peoples called this canyon "Topanga," meaning "the place where the mountains meet the sea." And so it is. One of the world's largest urban wildlands, Topanga State Park's 11,000-plus acres, preserved as open space, are almost all within L.A.'s city limits. Topanga is a hiker's and equestrian's park, with most fire roads now

also open to mountain bikers. Most trailheads start at the old Trippet Ranch at the park's official entrance, with pleasant picnic area and self-guided nature trail. The eastern section of the aptly named Backbone Trail ambles along ridgetops and then down toward the sea, ending at Will Rogers State Historic Park—and offering, en route, some dazzling views of the Pacific Ocean and Santa Monica Bay.

To reach the park entrance, head south from the Ventura Freeway (the 101) or north from Pacific Coast Highway (Hwy. 1), exit at Topanga Canyon Blvd. and turn east onto Entrada Road. Hikers can also reach the park from Will Rogers State Historic Park. The park is open daily 8 A.M.–sunset (parking lot hours), but Topanga is actually never closed except during extreme fire danger or other emergency. Technically, park admission is free, but there is a parking fee. No dogs allowed. For more information, contact: Topanga State Park, 20825 Entrada Rd. in Topanga, 310/454-8212 or 818/880-0350.

Malibu Creek State Park

Fans of the *M*A*S*H* television series, filmed at Malibu Creek State Park, will recognize the scenery—and enjoy posing for impromptu photos inside the junked jeep and ambulance parked in weeds along the Crags Road trail route. Much of the land now included in the park was owned by Twentieth Century Fox until the mid-1970s, so, naturally, many TV shows and movies have been filmed here over the years—and at adjacent Paramount Ranch. Free and technical rock-climbing are also popular here.

Yet trails are the real draw. The short one-mile hike to Century Lake is an easy trek for the kids. (The old *M*A*S*H* set is one mile farther.) Starting at the parking lot, head west on Crags Road to Malibu Creek. Head right at the fork to reach the visitor center, for basic information and orientation. Cross the bridge here and continue up the road; at the crest, descend to the left. Man-made Century Lake, now something of a freshwater marsh, is quite inviting to ducks and other waterfowl. If the kids are still willing, backtrack toward the bridge and then take the Gorge Trail south to Rock Pool—yet another one of those

SANTA ANA WINDS

Wherever you find yourself in the Los Angeles universe, things change when the Santa Ana winds blow from the northeast off the desert, typically between November and January. The atmosphere here becomes hot and dry and unbelievably irritating. The way Raymond Chandler described it in his short story "Red Wind," the dusty, desiccating Santa Ana winds "come down through the mountain passes and curl your hair and make your nerves jump and your skin itch. On nights like that every booze party ends in a fight. Meek little wives feel the edge of the carving knife and study the backs of their husbands' necks." This notable Southern California weather phenomenon, which reverses the usual cool west-to-east air flow off the ocean, also increases the danger of late fall wildfires and plays havoc with people's allergies. But don't let a blustery Santa Ana season put you off. Desert winds do have the beneficial effect of scrubbing the air clean throughout the entire Los Angeles Basin—which is why a December or January day can offer the most glorious scenic vistas in Southern California.

Southern California sights that seems vaguely familiar since you may have seen it before—in movies such as *Swiss Family Robinson*.

Six miles of the Backbone Trail also traverse the park. For inveterate hikers, Malibu Creek State Park also offers trail access to the city of Calabasas's **Lost Hills Park.** Other visitor draws include pleasant picnicking, a large campground, and the regional state park headquarters. The land's main claim to fame, however, is as the southernmost natural habitat of California's valley oak.

Parking lot hours (parking fee) are 8 A.M.-sunset, though the park itself is open 24 hours except in extreme fire danger or other emergency. The visitor center is open limited hours, on weekends only. Call for information on nature walks and special activities. To get here: From the Ventura Freeway (the 101) in Calabasas, head south on Las Virgenes Road three miles to the Mulholland Hwy. intersection. Continue south on Las Virgenes/Malibu Canyon Rd. another quar-

ter-mile to the park's entrance. From Pacific Coast Highway (Hwy. 1), head north almost six miles on Malibu Canyon Road to the park entrance. For more information, contact: Malibu Creek State Park, 1925 Las Virgenes Rd. in Calabasas, 818/880-0367 or 818/880-0350.

Paramount Ranch

The primary set for filming the popular television series *Dr. Quinn, Medicine Woman,* Western Town at Paramount Ranch boasts an illustrious Hollywood-western history. A remnant of 2,700 acres of Rancho Las Virgenes bought by Paramount Studios in 1927, the ranch also served as studio set for *The Rifleman* and *Have Gun Will Travel* episodes, not to mention *Bat Masterson* and *The Cisco Kid.*

When the kids are done poking through the facades of Western Town, why not take a hike? Just behind Western Town is half-mile Coyote Canyon Trail. In early spring the route leads up through the wildflowers and oak woodlands to some possible picnic sites—and a good eagle's-eye view of Western Town below—before circling back down. For a more ambitious hike, set out on the park's Run Trail. A recent 320-acre addition to Paramount Ranch adds still more trail.

On weekdays, Western Town is often used for film shoots. During filming the public is welcome to observe but not to wander through the sets. The Old West sets are open to the public every weekend and on weekdays when no filming is under way. Filming or no, the ranch is open to the public daily for picnicking and hiking, 8 A.M.–sunset. Most educational, however, are the monthly Saturday-morning guided hikes (free, call for scheduled dates).

To get here: From the Ventura Freeway (the 101), exit at Kanan Road and continue south for about three-fourths of a mile. Turn left at the "Cornell Way" sign and then go to the right (Cornell Way becomes Cornell Road). The ranch entrance is another two-and-a-half miles on the right.

Celebrity Spreads: Streisand and Strauss

Wonderful as a respite from San Fernando Valley gridlock is the **Peter Strauss Ranch** near Agoura, where you can picnic on the lawn or stretch your legs on a mile-long stroll. Among newer park acquisitions is **Ramirez Canyon Park,** formerly the Barbara Streisand Center for Conservancy Studies, and even more formerly the Streisand Malibu estate, an exclusive 22.5-acre, $15 million Malibu spread donated to the state by actress, songstress, and movie producer Barbra Streisand. Tours are offered only on Wednesdays, and carpooling is required (local regulations allow only 40 trips a day on the winding roads leading to the site). Visitors tour the center's architectural, botanical, and historical features, including four homes here; the fee of $30 includes a very nice afternoon tea. Call 310/589-2850 ext. 301 for tour reservations. For more information on Peter Strauss Ranch call the national park office at 818/597-1036.

Point Mugu State Park

Here, about 10 miles south of Oxnard in Ventura County, the Santa Monica Mountains meet the sea. Many hillside areas were seriously burned in Southern California's raging 1993 wildfires, as was much of Malibu's mountainous backdrop, but the coastal chaparral and woodlands are rapidly regenerating. The rugged Boney Mountain Wilderness, a section of the Backbone Trail, and the ocean-view La Jolla Canyon Loop Trail are hiking highlights of this 13,300-acre park. To enjoy the beach, try Sycamore Cove or Thornhill Broome (the latter backed by campsites). Inquire about swimming safety. Adjacent to Point Mugu, in the north, is the national park's Rancho Sierra Vista and Satwiwa Native American Natural Area. Adjoining on the southeast is the recreation area's Circle X Ranch.

Visitor facilities include developed woodland campsites (less wooded now) at Big Sycamore Creek Campground and primitive campsites at the beach, picnic areas, restrooms, dump station, and trails for horses, hikers, and mountain bikers. For campsite reservations, especially during the peak April–Sept. season (and weekends), contact ReserveAmerica, 800/444-7275, www .reserveamerica.com. For other visitor information, contact: Point Mugu State Park, 9000 W. Pacific Coast Hwy. in Malibu, 818/880-0350 or 805/488-5223 (recorded), or 805/488-1827.

Palo Comado Canyon and Other Acquisitions

In the 1990s the Santa Monica Mountains Conservancy acquired about 1,600 acres owned by entertainer Bob Hope in Palo Comado Canyon next to the Ventura County line; the deal was part of a complicated land transaction involving the Ahmanson Ranch development in the works northeast of Calabasas in nearby Las Virgenes Canyon. (Runkle Ranch, more than 4,000 acres near Simi Valley, and 339-acre Corral Canyon near Malibu are also set for acquisition.) The hiking high point of Palo Comado is 750 acres of oaks, meadows, and old movie sets at **China Flat.**

Another long-standing park priority was acquiring parcels to extend popular **Backbone Trail** the entire 70-mile distance between Will Rogers State Historic Park and Point Mugu State Park. New sections of trail include **Fossil Ridge** and **Hondo Canyon,** both accessible from Mulholland Highway.

The Santa Monica Mountains Conservancy and the recreation area are in the process of acquiring other new acreage. For current information on new areas open to the public, contact the national parks office.

ACCOMMODATIONS

Malibu offers the main accommodations action north of Santa Monica. And Malibu is a bit short on inexpensive places to stay—on places to stay, period—which is just the way Malibu likes it. Beyond the area's state park campsites, the 30 fairly quaint but clean 1920s-vintage cabins of the historic **Topanga Ranch Motel** south of central Malibu, right across from the beach at 18711 Pacific Coast Hwy. (PCH), 310/456-5486, once housing for workers building the Pacific Coast Highway. These clean, quaint cabins are among the area's more affordable options—though for how long is uncertain, since the motel sits on land recently acquired by the state park system. Some units have kitchens; a few boast two bedrooms. Basic rates are $50–100. The attractive 21-room **Ⓝ Casa Malibu Inn** right on the beach in "downtown" Malibu, 22752 PCH, 310/456-2219, features an inviting central courtyard, some rooms with kitchens and balconies. Good value: $100–150 for basic garden view rooms, $150–250 for deluxe/beachfront rooms, $250 and up for suites. Another possibility is the remodeled 16-room **Malibu Country Inn** motel north of Malibu proper, overlooking Zuma Beach at 6506 Westward Beach Rd. (at PCH), 310/457-9622, www.malibucountryinn.com, with a small swimming pool, in-room refrigerators and coffeemakers. Rates are $150–250, but somewhat less expensive in the off season. The great little California-Mediterranean **Hideaway Café** here offers sweeping views along with its tasty fish sampler.

The seriously stylish **Malibu Beach Inn,** sits right on the beach, snuggled in near the pier at 22878 Pacific Coast Hwy., 310/456-6444 or 800/462-5428, www.malibubeachinn.com. Space here is too tight for so much as a swimming pool—but who needs a pool when the wide blue Pacific Ocean is in your front yard? Rooms are reasonably spacious, feature tilework and berber carpets, and have the usual luxury amenities, small private balconies, and gas fireplaces (most rooms). Perfect for just hanging out: the motel's friendly Mediterranean-style terra-cotta-tiled patio hanging out over the rocky shore. Two-night minimum stay on weekends from May through October. Rates are $250 and up.

For a still quieter, still more serene weekend stay, room to retreat is often available for individuals at the Franciscan **Serra Retreat Center,** 3401 Serra Rd. in Malibu, 310/456-6631, or www.serraretreat.org, which offers regular group retreats at this scenic remnant of the original Topanga Malibu Sequit ranch, the spot where "Queen of Malibu" May Rindge started but never completed her hilltop mansion. Suggested per-day donation is $100–150, which includes three substantial meals.

FOOD

Pacific Palisades

Just north of Santa Monica in Pacific Palisades, **Gladstone's 4 Fish,** 17300 Pacific Coast Hwy. (at Sunset Boulevard), 310/454-3474, has always been one of the most popular restaurants on the Westside—not because the food was so great but because, for singles, it was such a terrific place for trolling. The wait is always long, the crowd is always noisy. But even if you eat elsewhere, have a tropical drink on the patio at sunset just to experience the scene.

Dinner-only **Modo Mio,** 15200 Sunset Blvd. (enter on La Cruz), 310/459-0979, is the place for dinner, a stylish yet cozy neighborhood favorite serving rustic Tuscan fare. The incredible selection of specials keeps everyone surprised. For less expensive reservations-required fare, closer to Santa Monica, *the* place is the popular Italian **Caffe Delfini,** 147 W. Channel Rd. (at Pacific Coast Highway), 310/459-8823, where seafood and pastas star, along with Delfini's famous seafood soup and such things as broiled shrimp with fresh tomato and basil and homemade ravioli. The restaurant also has a regular celebrity clientele. Everybody's favorite in Pacific Palisades for house-made ravioli is **Il Ristorante di Giorgio Baldi,** 114 W. Channel Rd. (at PCH), 310/573-1660. Tiny Mediterranean **Sam's by the Beach,** 108 W. Channel Rd., 310/230-9100, is famous for its fresh seafood. Inexpensive just off Pacific Coast Highway is **Marix Tex Mex Playa,** 118 Entrada Dr., 310/459-8596, the coastal cousin of West Hollywood's happiest Tex-Mex joint, famous for its fajitas. This place is open daily for breakfast, lunch, and dinner.

Not to be missed in Topanga Canyon: **Froggy's Topanga Fresh Fish Market,** 1105 N. Topanga Canyon Blvd. (Hwy. 27), 310/455-1728. Malibu's chichi crowd may do fish at some swank place near the beach, but everybody else comes here. This fun and funky fish palace, a Topanga Canyon classic, doesn't get by on looks or general eccentricity. The fish is the thing, and here it's done quite well. Open for dinners, Froggy's is noteworthy for its rotisserie chicken and salads but famous for chowder, shrimp, lobster, and just about anything else that's fresh and on the menu. It's open 5 P.M.–9:30 P.M., until 10 P.M. on Friday and Saturday nights, closed Thanksgiving and Christmas. This place is easiest to find when navigating by local landmarks. With that proviso, Froggy's is on Topanga

Canyon Boulevard (Hwy. 27) on the San Fernando Valley side of the post office but on the Pacific Coast Highway side of Theatricum Botanicum, the very cool community theater. Also locally famous, for vegetarian and some meatier entrées: the hip **Inn of the Seventh Ray** in Topanga Canyon at 128 Old Topanga Rd., 310/455-1311, famous for its homemade bread and Sunday brunch. The inn is open daily for lunch and dinner.

Malibu

The place for crab and avocado tostadas and a pitcher of microbrew is the **Coral Beach Cantina,** 29350 Pacific Coast Hwy. (near Heathercliff), 310/457-5503. The people's place for fresh seafood and sunsets is seriously casual, seriously affordable **Malibu Seafood,** 25653 Pacific Coast Hwy. (near Coral Canyon Road), 310/456-3430. For fish tacos and such, surfers and like-minded souls roll in to the fun and funky **Reel Inn,** 18661 Pacific Coast Hwy. (at Topanga Canyon Boulevard), 310/456-8221. More sophisticated and stylish, quite good for simpler fare and take-out, is **Marmalade,** 3894 S. Cross Creek Rd. (at PCH), 310/317-4242, a simple deli café featuring fresh bakery items (with or without marmalade), good salads, soups, and such things as chicken pot pie. (There's another Marmalade in Santa Monica, on Montana Avenue, and one in Westlake Village.) Pricier but unpretentious is Italian **Allegria,** 22821 Pacific Coast Hwy. (just south of Cross Creek Road), 310/456-3132, a lively trattoria serving authentic Venetian-style pastas and thin-crusted pizza. Another celeb-watching hotspot, open daily for lunch and dinner. To linger over a homey Italian meal, the place is **Tra di Noi,** 3835 Cross Creek Rd. (at PCH), 310/456-0169.

Top of the food chain in Malibu proper, at least in terms of interior design, is gloriously garish **Granita** in the Malibu Colony Plaza mall at 23725 W. Malibu Rd., 310/456-0488, another of Wolfgang Puck and Barbara Lazaroff's progeny, sometimes puckishly referred to as Spago-by-the-Sea. The interior, with the trademark open kitchen and equally typical high decibel levels, was designed to resemble an underwater sea cave inhabited by eclectic fishlike creatures—no wilder than the imaginative California-style Mediterranean fare. Yet it almost seems barbaric to dive into so much fish and seafood, no matter how delectable, while they're watching. Reservations optional, especially if you come during the week. It's very expensive. Open for brunch on Saturday and Sunday, for dinner every night.

Best place for fine dining with views is **Geoffrey's** up on the hill at 27400 Pacific Coast Hwy. (near Malibu Canyon Road), 310/457-1519, reservations essential. The menu runs from Geoffrey's eggs Faberge with caviar to spiced shrimp in sweet Vermouth butter sauce, coconut curry prawns, and filet mignon. Also impressive for food with a view is romantic **Beau Rivage,** 26025 Pacific Coast Hwy. (near Malibu Canyon Road), 310/456-5733, serving classical Mediterranean with French accents—from the 20-ounce bistecca alla Fiorentina to herb-crusted New Zealand rack of lamb. A still more spectacular fine-dining destination—if you find yourself in the vicinity of Malibu and in the mood for a drive—is exquisite **Saddle Peak Lodge,** a one-time hunting lodge in the Santa Monica Mountains near Calabasas, 818/222-3888.

The South Bay

The strands of sand and beach towns south of Los Angeles International Airport (LAX) comprise L.A.'s "South Bay," the southern Santa Monica Bay. This is where the Beach Boys came of age—in Manhattan Beach—and where, in nearby Hermosa Beach and Redondo Beach, Southern California's middle-American surf culture got its biggest sendoff in the 1950s and '60s. But it all started in 1907 when George Freeth, billed as "the man who could walk on water," was imported to Redondo Beach by that ceaseless land-sales promoter Henry Huntington for a special "prove it" performance. Walking the offshore waves with the help of an eight-foot, 200-pound wooden surfboard, Freeth introduced the ancient Polynesian sport of kings to the neighborhood. You can tour the entire area from a bicycle seat, thanks to the 22-mile **South Bay Bike Trail** that runs from Will Rogers State Beach (north of Santa Monica) to Torrance Beach in the south. Or you can drive. Huge public parking lots abound along the South Bay's beaches.

Rising above the southernmost reach of Santa Monica Bay is the Palos Verdes Peninsula, a collection of affluent residential enclaves that separate L.A.'s surf cities and their semi-industrial inland neighbors from San Pedro and the Port of Los Angeles, next south, and Long Beach, home port of the RMS *Queen Mary*, the new Long Beach Aquarium of the Pacific, and other attractions. Next stop south of Long Beach is Orange County.

EL SEGUNDO AND MANHATTAN BEACH

El Segundo is sometimes also described as L.A.'s own Mayberry, U.S.A., for its insular Midwestern mores. Before the end of the Cold War and the rapid decline of Southern California's defense industry, no one much minded comments about "El Stinko," a reference to Playa del Rey's 144-acre Hyperion Waste Treatment Plant and its downwind influence here. And no one complained about the huge circa-1911 Chevron oil refinery just south. (The town was named for it. El Segundo means "The Second [One]" in Spanish, since Standard Oil's first refinery—this plant was Standard before it was Chevron—opened in Richmond, near San Francisco.) And no one seemed to hear the ear-rending racket from LAX jet traffic overhead. Everyone was too busy working—at Aerospace Corp., Hughes Aircraft, Northrop, Rockwell, and TRW. Not to mention Mattel Toys. Some of those jobs have disappeared, in L.A.'s new post-defense economy, but others have taken their place.

These days El Segundo—conveniently near LAX, after all—is getting serious about attracting new industry and, closer to the beach, trendier and tourism-related businesses. Thanks to the Surfrider Foundation, El Segundo is also trying to recreate good surf breaks lost when Chevron built a rock jetty at Dockweiler State Beach to protect its plant. **Pratte's Reef,** created from submerged sandbags, has produced mixed results to date; Surfriders consistently point out that it's better to protect the coast than try to re-create what's been lost.

Chic Manhattan Beach, just south, already riding the latter wave, doesn't have such problems—which is why restaurants and businesses along the El Segundo side of the bustling, increasingly chi-chi Rosecrans Avenue corridor shamelessly advertise their address as "Manhattan Beach." At the beach—Manhattan State Beach, a continuation of the nearly seamless broad bay strand that starts north of Santa Monica—you'll find excellent swimming, lifeguards, both clean water and sand, the works. If you're driving, you'll find free parking along Vista del Mar to Highland, metered parking along most streets, and public lots close to attractive "downtown," at both 11th and 13th Streets. There's also a metered lot at 43rd Street. For fishing, try 900-foot **Manhattan Beach Pier** at the foot of Manhattan Beach Boulevard. A small building at the tip of the pier is home to the **Roundhouse Marine Studies Lab & Aquarium,** 310/379-8117, where you can get a close up look at a variety of fishes found in the Santa Monica Bay—including baby sea animals such as the horn shark, moray eels, and sea urchins. Admission is free, but a $2 donation is suggested. You can also stroll **The Strand,** which here wanders past beachfront homes as it meanders south to Hermosa Beach. Not to be missed in the neighborhood is the independent **Nations! Travelstore,** 1590 Rosecrans Ave. (between Sepulveda and Aviation), 310/318-9915 or 800/546-8060, www.nationstravelmall.com, a combination bookstore, map and supply stop, and travel agency beloved for its exceptional product selection and customer service.

For more information about the area, contact the **City of El Segundo,** 310/524-2300, www.elsegundo.org, and the **City of Manhattan Beach,** 310/802-5000, www.ci.manhattan -beach.ca.us.

REDONDO BEACH AND HERMOSA BEACH

Redondo State Beach is the hot-weather hot spot in these parts, though nothing like this old resort town's turn-of-the-century heyday. Still, at times it's almost as difficult to park your beach towel as it is your car. As elsewhere along L.A.'s South Bay, the two miles of beach here are wide and sandy. The **Redondo Beach Pier,** at the foot of Torrance Boulevard, marks the beach's northern reaches. In 1988 storms and subsequent fires ravaged the 60-year-old wooden horseshoe-shaped pier, and the most recent of many local pier incarnations—and the city rebuilt in grand style. Designed by Edward Beall, the new, nautically themed $11 million Redondo Beach Pier—complete with sail-like awnings—is a sturdy yet wondrous concrete creation, complete with 1,800 life-size etchings of marine life, including sharks, scuba divers, and whales. (Water quality near the pier is less than perfect, though.) **King Harbor** just north, along Harbor Drive between Horondo and Beryl Streets, is the result of a massive redevelopment that cost Redondo Beach its historic downtown, replacing it with 50 acres of high-rise apartment buildings. King Harbor has its own piers, with restaurants, shops, and such, and also offers harbor cruises, sportfishing and

winter whale-watching charters, and bike and other sports equipment rentals. Not to take a back seat to Long Beach, Redondo Beach even offers gondola rides at King Harbor, through **Gondola Amore,** 310/376-6977. The best surfing is just north, at Hermosa Beach, and well south of Redondo at Torrance Beach. Be that as it may, come to Redondo in August for the annual **Surf Festival.**

Head north from Redondo to Hermosa Beach, most famous as L.A.'s best for beach volleyball, site of numerous competitions and championship matches. Hermosa Beach also features row upon row of at-the-beach apartments and the **Hermosa Beach Pier,** historically a fishing pier. The pier and downtown around Pier Avenue underwent major renovations about seven years ago, resulting in a pleasant pedestrian zone with plenty of boutiques, coffeehouses, restaurants and bars. **The Strand** oceanfront walkway here is also quite pleasant, passing beach homes, restaurants, and shops and continuing on to Manhattan Beach.

Head south from Redondo to Torrance Beach and then, for top-notch surfing, stroll to Malaga Cove below the bluffs. It's easier to get to the cove from the Palos Verdes Peninsula (see below).

For more information about the area, contact: **Redondo Beach Chamber and Visitors Bureau,** 200 N. Pacific Coast Hwy., 310/376-6911, www.redondochamber.org, and the **Torrance Visitors Bureau,** 3400 Torrance Blvd., 310/.540-5858, or see www.visittorrance.com.

PALOS VERDES PENINSULA

If you lived in paradise, wouldn't you want to keep it that way? The upper-middle-class communities atop Palos Verdes Peninsula are removed from the fray and largely proud of it—a sense of entitlement that, unfortunately, sometimes extends to local beaches. Demonstrating an international surfing phenomenon known as "localism," the feared Bay Boys of Palos Verdes—"trust-fund babies," according to a *Surfer* magazine editor—have made it their business to keep nonlocals out of primo surf spots such as Lunada Bay. Legal or not, no one here wants the now-common California beach overcrowding problems and related

Los Angeles Coast

traumas—trash, graffiti, violence—that are increasing all along the coast, particularly at the best surfing beaches.

Few such troubles perturb the Palos Verdes Peninsula, which eons ago was one of the Channel Islands. Serious social problems here include the challenge of dodging horses and riders on public streets (equestrians have the right-of-way) and coping with the noise and effluence of the wild peacock flocks in Rolling Hills Estates and Palos Verdes Estates. The peninsula is home to several of L.A.'s most affluent communities—Rolling Hills is, officially, one of the wealthiest towns in America, and its neighbors are also at the top of the list—and what its people value most is their privacy. Yet despite ongoing surf-turf wars the peninsula's parks, other public facilities, and businesses generally welcome visitors.

Though you must meander the peninsula's winding interior roads to get a close-up view of life here, most people are satisfied with a leisurely coastal drive. And, on a clear day, the views are spectacular. Starting in the north, from Pacific Coast Highway (Hwy. 1) head southwest on Palos Verdes Boulevard, which soon becomes Palos Verdes Drive W, then, at Hawthorne Boulevard, Palos Verdes Drive S; heading north on Palos Verdes Drive E eventually leads to east-west Palos Verdes Drive N, completing the blufftop "perimeter" drive. But a true coastal tour would continue east along 25th Street into San Pedro, perhaps jogging south to Paseo del Mar and then east again to the Cabrillo Marine Aquarium.

Sights

First stop along the peninsula coast tour is in town, actually, in Palos Verdes Estates. The **Neptune Fountain** at the **Malaga Cove Plaza** was inspired by the architecture of Italy's Sorrentine Peninsula. (When in the 1960s King Neptune's anatomy was somehow dismembered, locals rallied and replaced the notable lost part with a strategic fig leaf.) Elsewhere throughout this area are architectural reminders of what the Palos Verdes Peninsula might have been, if plans made in the 1920s by banker Frank A. Vanderlip, architect Myron Hunt, and the similarly talented sons

of landscape architect Frederick Law Olmsted had been fully realized. Olmsteds's local heritage can be seen at national landmark **La Venta Inn,** 796 Via del Monte, 310/373-0123, now used mainly for private events, then it's off to **Malaga Cove** proper, accessible from Paseo del Mar (east of Via Arroyo), an inspiring sidetrip in its own right. Also known as **RAT Beach** (short for "Right After Torrance" Beach, not an urban wildlife reference), this top-notch surfing beach is equally popular for rock and shell collecting and tidepool exploration.

From Malaga Cove the truly adventurous can scrabble south over the rocks to the shale-cliffed scenery of **Bluff Cove,** also popular with surfers, and on to the famous surf-turf battleground of **Lunada Bay,** a six-mile roundtrip. This adventure is recommended only during pacific surf—and only at low tide, when the tide's heading out. Notable near Lunada is the 1961 wreckage of the Greek freighter *Dominator,* which failed to dominate these treacherous shores.

Back on the main road, continue south to one of L.A.'s premier winter whale-watching sights—the **Point Vicente Interpretive Center** at 31501 Palos Verdes Dr. W, 310/377-5370, where the second-floor gallery is packed with California gray whale voyeurs from mid-December into March each year. Any time—at least on a clear day—the center offers an impressive view of Santa Catalina Island and a worthwhile introduction to area natural history. Open daily 10 A.M.–5 P.M., except major holidays. Small fee.

The historic 1926 **Point Vicente Lighthouse** perches on a cliff farther down the coast at 31550 Palos Verdes Dr. W, 310/541-0334. The 67-foot-tall lighthouse is powered by a two-million-candlepower bulb, and visitors can climb the 74 steps to the top to check out the handcrafted Fresnel lens that produces the long light beam. Tours are held every second Saturday 10 A.M.–4 P.M. and by appointment for groups. Free admission.

Next south is the peninsula's rather notorious **Portuguese Bend** area, where in the 1950s massive landslides doomed more than 100 homes. Things are still plenty unstable today. One of this neighborhood's most popular attractions is the small but stunning **Wayfarers Chapel,** 5755 Palos Verdes Dr. S, 310/377-1650, designed by Lloyd Wright (son of Frank Lloyd Wright) and built of glass, redwood, and Palos Verdes stone. Except during special events—weddings are understandably popular here, typically scheduled on weekends between 1 and 3 P.M.—this Swedenborgian Church chapel and lovely grounds are open daily for meditation.

For some prime-time picnicking, try nearby **Abalone Cove Shoreline Park and Ecological Preserve,** a federal reserve near Portuguese Point at 5970 Palos Verdes Dr. S., 310/377-1222, where the grassy lawn offers easy access to the rocky beach below—and to tidepools teeming with these precious, and protected, ocean creatures. Best time for abalone voyeurism is in December and January. Parking $5. Nearby **Smuggler's Cove** is a long-popular nude beach, unofficially, so a subject of local conflict.

If you're making a day of it, the best bet in Southern California for dahlia and fuchsia displays is the **South Coast Botanic Garden,** a onetime landfill at 26300 Crenshaw Blvd., 310/544-6815, where the peak dahlia bloom comes in mid-August. Also here: plant collections representing every continent except Antarctica (organized by color), some 1,600 roses, and the "Garden of the Senses."

To explore local features and natural history in more detail, sign on for one of the monthly guided hikes offered through the **Palos Verdes Peninsula Land Conservancy,** 310/541-7613, www.pvplc.org. For more information about the area, contact: **Palos Verdes Peninsula Chamber of Commerce,** 707 Silver Spur Rd., Ste. 100 in Rolling Hills Estates, 310/377-8111, www.palosverdes.com/pvpcc.

SAN PEDRO

Some local wags suggest that San Pedro, with its hilly streets, ocean fog, views, and military installations, is L.A.'s own little San Francisco—complete with a miniature, but much friendlier, Mission District, along Pacific Street. (It's san PEE-dro, by the way, despite California's occasional preference for correct Spanish pronuncia-

tion.) That perspective is a hard sell in this semi-industrial port city, however.

If people find themselves in San Pedro, most head to the shops, restaurants, and other tourist diversions of **Ports O' Call Village** at the end of Sixth Street, an aging shopping mall in the style of a New England seaside village. But San Pedro has more intriguing features—including the **Port of Los Angeles** itself, which was created at a cost of $60 million between 1920 and 1940. The best way to get the big picture is on guided boat tours ($8–12) with **Spirit Cruises,** 310/548-8080, which depart from Ports O' Call. From the **World Cruise Terminal** and **Catalina Express Terminal** here, travelers depart on sea journeys near and far. A particularly impressive sight is soaring **Vincent Thomas Bridge,** which from the Harbor Fwy. (the 110) connects San Pedro (via Hwy. 47) to Terminal Island. Since it's the closest suspension bridge to Hollywood, the Vincent Thomas has starred in many movies, including *Gone in 60 Seconds, Charlie's Angels* and *To Live and Die in L.A.* **Terminal Island,** once known as Rattlesnake Island, was a vibrant resort destination earlier in this century, L.A.'s own Brighton Beach, complete with pleasure pier. Starting in 1906, it was also home to a close-knit village of Japanese-American fishermen and their families—an idyllic life ended forever with World War II-era Japanese internment in 1942. Terminal Island today, an uninviting diesel-scented jungle of canneries, loading cranes, and old warships, also includes a federal penitentiary.

Significant San Pedro attractions include two seaworthy museums: the **Los Angeles Maritime Museum** at Berth 84 (at the foot of Sixth Street), 310/548-7618, and the **SS** *Lane Victory* **Ship Museum** at Berth 94 (near the World Cruise Terminal), 310/519-9545, a onetime ammunition carrier, now a national historic landmark. Wander the rest of Old Town San Pedro—some of it rather new—to discover delights like **Williams Book Store,** 443 West Sixth St., 310/832-3631, www.williamsbookstore.com, oldest book store in Los Angeles, and **Pirate Leathers,** 405 West Sixth, 310/519-8833, with some great used leather jackets. There are galleries galore, too. The **Angels Gate Cultural**

Center arts enclave, housed in onetime barracks at 3601 S. Gaffey St., 310/519-0936, www. angelsgateart.org, sponsors the area's First Thursday open studios gallery tour.

Definitely worth a stop, especially with tots in tow, is the **Cabrillo Marine Aquarium and Museum,** 3720 Stephen White Dr., 310/548-7562, www.cabrilloaq.org, open Tues.–Fri. noon–5 P.M. and on weekends 10 A.M.–5 P.M. (open on some "holiday" Mondays, closed Thanksgiving, Christmas). Fresh from a $10 million renovation and expansion, changes that debuted in October 2004, the Cabrillo aquarium now includes a new wing designed by Barton Phelps and Associates—including an Aquatic Nursery (visit baby sea animals), a hands-on Exploration Center showcasing the habitats and organisms of the Cabrillo Beach Coastal Park; the Virginia Reid Moore Marine Research Library; and the S. Mark Taper Courtyard. Technically the aquarium is free—suggested donation is $5 adults, $1 children and seniors, and parking is $7—and it's also full of educational opportunity, thus quite popular with school groups. But anyone can be a kid here. The main aquarium, housed in a contemporary Frank Gehry–designed building, features 38 tanks now home to an abundance of Southern California sealife. Among the most popular exhibits: the "tidal tank," a veritable room with a view of a wave, and the shark tank. Other exhibits include a "touch tank" filled with sea anemones and starfish, and a whalebone graveyard. The aquarium also offers seasonal whalewatching tours and "grunion run" programs; call for current information. From here, set out for both **Cabrillo Beach** and 1,200-foot **Cabrillo Pier,** just inside the breakwater. The Romanesque **Angels Gate Lighthouse** at the end of the breakwater has been shining forth here since 1913.

Angels Gate Park, back toward the Palos Verdes Peninsula on S. Paseo del Mar, includes the historic 1874 Victorian **Point Fermin Lighthouse,** now the park superintendent's residence. Lighthouse tours are offered every Sunday 1–4 P.M., the last tour beginning at 3:30 P.M. Also in the neighborhood is the **Fort MacArthur Military Museum** 310/548-2631, www.ftmac.org, housed at Battery Osgood-Farley at the onetime

Fort MacArthur, the U.S. Army post that guarded L.A.'s harbor until 1974. Not to mention the HI-USA **Los Angeles/South Bay Hostel,** 310/831-8109. Next to Point Fermin is San Pedro's own "sunken city." In 1929 an entire neighborhood of exclusive homes started slipping to sea here—at the rate of 12 inches per day—and was quickly relocated to more solid ground. But the ground kept slipping, and keeps slipping. The jumble of old pavement and palm trees is a slightly surreal sight. If you get hungry and enjoy biker bars, *the* place locally is **Walker's Cafe,** almost on the sunken-city spot at 700 S. Paseo Del Mar, 310/833-3623.

The best beach around for scuba diving and pleasant scenery is San Pedro's rocky **Royal Palms State Beach** on the Palos Verdes Peninsula at the south end of Western Avenue.

Well worth a stop inland from the port in nearby **Wilmington** are the **Banning Residence Museum,** 401 E. M St., 310/548-7777, the restored 1864 Greek revival mansion of General Phineas Banning and a major interpretive center for 19th-century L.A. history, and the **Drum Barracks Civil War Museum,** 1052 Banning Blvd., 310/548-7509, the only remaining structure from the Civil War-era Camp Drum, where 7,000 troops were based. Both museums are open only for guided tours (call for times); donations greatly appreciated.

For more information about the area, contact: **San Pedro Peninsula Chamber of Commerce,** 390 W. Seventh St., 310/832-7272 or 888/447-3376, www.sanpedrochamber.com.

Lane Victory Cruise

The ranks of the Greatest Generation are thinning fast—so for hands-on instruction in just how World War II was done, hurry on down to San Pedro for a cruise to Catalina Island and back onboard the SS *Lane Victory.* A fully operational cargo ship, the *Lane Victory* is a national historic landmark, one now manned by an impressive, well-informed volunteer crew capable of entertaining and enlightening some 800 passengers.

The cruise to Catalina Island and back starts with continental breakfast after boarding, between

7:30 and 8 A.M. At 9 A.M. the tugs make fast and the *Victory* steams down the main channel, across the outer harbor, through the Queens Gate, and out to the sea. Following an onboard memorial service for the hundreds of merchant ships lost during WWII, the engine room tours begin.

But hark—is that General McArthur over there? And is that really Patton? If you don't encounter celebrity warriors in the wheel house, radio room, either of the two onboard museums, or gift shop, maybe they'll show up for lunch, an impressive all-you-can-eat buffet.

Just when you start scoping out nooks and crannies apt for an afternoon nap, suddenly all heck breaks loose on deck. The crew has captured a spy! The despicable character is ceremoniously paraded around deck, in irons, but not before he somehow manages to radio his position to the enemy. The general alarm is sounded, and the armed guard and crew man the guns. Sure enough, here come the enemy attackers—but here, too, come the American flyboys, and the dogfight is on. After victory, and as the *Lane Victory* approaches Angels Gate for the return to port, colorful Stearman bi-planes approach from the south and make celebratory passes, to the vicarious delight of all.

Lane Victory cruises are offered on a very limited number of days, on weekends in July, August, and September. At last report cruise tickets were $100 adults and $60 youths (15 and under). For more information, call 310/519-9545 or see www.lanevictory.org.

ACCOMMODATIONS

Options south of Santa Monica range from very inexpensive at-the-beach hostels to midrange motels and five-star luxury hotels. In addition to the excellent hostel in San Pedro—see the Long Beach section below—there's also a hostel at the beach. The **Surf City Hostel** in Hermosa Beach, 26 Pier Ave., 310/798-2323 or 800/305-2901, www.lasurfcityhostel.com, is right on the beach and close to everything. Amenities for budget travelers are abundant—from free breakfast, tea, and coffee as well as blankets, pillows, and baggage storage to a fully equipped kitchen and loaner body boards. Rates are $19 for a bed in a shared dorm and $48 per night for a couple's room (two people). For a tad more privacy **The Beach House** in Hermosa Beach, 1300 The Strand, 310/374-3001 or 888/895-4559, www.beach-house.com, is ever-popular. Right on the beach, loft suites start at $250.

Close to both beach and LAX in Manhattan Beach is ever-popular **Barnabey's Hotel,** 3501 Sepulveda Blvd. (a half block south of Rosecrans), 310/750-0300 or 888/296-6836. Three-story Barnabey's is a real surprise—an ersatz 19th-century English inn with four-poster beds and an antique-rich ambience yet all the modern conveniences, including in-room coffeemakers and data ports, on-site pub, pool, and whirlpool tub. Rates are $100–150 and include a big breakfast buffet.

FOOD

The motto at **Good Stuff,** 1300 Highland Ave. (at 13th Street) in Man Beach, 310/545-4775 (also at 1286 The Strand in Hermosa Beach, 310/374-2334), is "You are what you eat—so eat good stuff." It's hard to argue with that philosophy, especially when in the company of one of GoodStuff's famous avocado bacon cheeseburgers or, at breakfast, those marvelous whole-wheat pancakes. Come for GoodStuff's special Get-Stuffed Dinners, too—on Tuesday for tacos, Friday for fish and chips, Saturday for Gulf of Mexico stew. For fancier fare near the pier try **Rockn' Fish** at 120 Manhattan Beach Blvd., 310/379-9900, specializing in oak wood-grilled seafood, chops, and steaks plus specialties including New Orleans barbecued shrimp. Nice wine list. There is a busy bar here, too, definitely part of the scene after 10 P.M., where everyone's favorite is the potent Navy Grog.

Samba (previously the Blue Moon Saloon) in Redondo at 207 N. Harbor Dr., 310/374-3411, is *the* place for Brazilian barbecue and, on weekends, Samba dancers. Best bet for bistro fare is stylish **Aimee's,** 800 S. Pacific Coast Hwy., 310/316-1081. A foodie favorite is **Zazou** in Redondo at 1810 S. Catalina St., 310/540-4884.

Quite good in Torrance for eclectic California

cuisine is **Christine,** open for weekday lunches and dinner daily at the Hillside Village, 24530 Hawthorne Blvd., 310/373-1952, but **Aioli,** 1261 Cabrillo Ave. (at Torrance Boulevard), 310/320-9200, offers options beyond the sit-down dining room—including the **Breadstix Bakery** and tapas. Aioli is open for dinner Mon.–Sat., for lunch on weekdays only, and closed on Sunday.

Locally beloved for seafood in Rancho Palos Verdes is **The Admiral Risty** at 31250 Palos Verdes Dr., 310/377-0050. Uniquely creative in these parts and expensive, **Bistro 767** at 767 Deep Valley Dr. (near Roxcove) in Rolling Hills Estates, 310/265-0882, serves eclectic variations on the California cuisine theme, from salmon with pineapple-cilantro chile sauce to lamb loin in a balsamic vinegar reduction with bleu cheese.

And who ever would have thought San Pedro would become such a hot arts and restaurant town? For fresh seafood with absolutely no frills

head for the **San Pedro Fish Market & Restaurant** next to Ports O'Call Village, 1190 Nagoya Way (at Sixth), 310/832-4251, where you pick what you want from the tanks and they cook it right up. Belly up to the beach towel-draped tables at the **Beach City Grill,** 376 W. Sixth St., 310/833-6345, and sample a world of good food, from blackened salmon tacos and black bean soup to jambalaya. Decadent desserts, too. Or sit down to lunch with Rodin's *The Thinker* at Ⓜ **Think Café,** 302 W. Fifth St., 310/519-3662. Make a meal of the appetizers—warm crab dip with toasted bread, smoked salmon quesadillas—or try a pizza, salad, or those Cajun shrimp tacos. (There's also a thoughty sibling, **Think Bistro,** 1420 W. 25th St., near Western Avenue, 310/548-4797.) Among more romantic choices in Old Saint Pete is the **Sixth Street Bistro,** 354 W. Sixth St. (near Mesa), 310/521-8818, where you can sample some excellent wines by the glass, try entrées such as fire shrimp, and savor the signature chocolate ravioli for dessert.

Redondo Beach

COURTESY OF REDONDO BEACH VISITORS BUREAU

Los Angeles Coast

Long Beach

Long Beach is the second-largest city in Los Angeles County, dwarfed only by L.A. itself, and the fifth-largest in the state. The city's history follows the fairly predictable Southern California course, from coastal wilderness and rangeland suburb of Spain and Mexico to extensive Midwestern settlement. The population of transplants from Iowa was once so dominant, in fact, that "Iowa picnics" became the most memorable community social gatherings during the Great Depression. Then came turn-of-the-20th-century seaside resort and booming port, regional oil development, and the monumental Long Beach earthquake that flattened downtown in 1933— the indirect impetus for downtown's then-new art deco style. Howard Hughes, the aviator and engineer later famous as the world's most eccentric billionaire, made history here in 1947 when he took his *Spruce Goose*—the world's largest airplane—for its first and only flight.

During and since World War II, but before the post-Cold War era of military downsizing, the U.S. Navy was central to Long Beach life, given the presence of the Long Beach Naval Station, Long Beach Naval Ship Yard, and Boeing, McDonnell Douglas, and other aviation and defense-related industry. Symbol of that past was the Iowa-class USS *Missouri*, America's last active battleship, host to Japan's formal surrender at the end of World War II and later recruit for offshore duty in the Persian Gulf during Operation Desert Storm. When "Mighty Mo" was finally decommissioned here in 1992, thousands and thousands turned out for the event. Both the naval station and shipyard have since been shut down. Yet the city is determined to recover from its defense-related economic losses. The Port of Long Beach is the busiest cargo port on the West Coast, doing a brisk Pacific Rim trade, and promoting downtown and port-side tourism is also a major priority.

Long Beach is an astonishingly diverse community with large immigrant populations, recently gaining national notoriety as the first California city to adopt a uniforms-only public school dress code. Despite the city's pressing social problems, people visit Long Beach primarily because it's still apple-pie appealing, unassuming, and affordable, with clean air and coastal diversions, a spruced-up downtown, and a lively cultural scene. (Many also show up here on business; both the Long Beach Convention and Entertainment Center and the World Trade Center are downtown.) And some say there are more worthy breakfast, burger, and pie shops in Long Beach than anywhere else in L.A. County.

Though bad press from occasional outbreaks of gang warfare is a bane of Long Beach existence, visitors don't need to be overly concerned. (One area at high risk for violent crime is north of downtown, straddling the 710 between Hwy. 47 and Temple Avenue, south of Pacific Coast Highway and north of Seventh Street; another, well north of downtown, stretches between Long Beach Boulevard and Orange Avenue, south of South Street and north of Del Amo Boulevard.) Reasonable precautions are prudent, of course, as in any urban area.

Special annual events well worth the trip include the **Toyota Grand Prix of Long Beach** in April—an event that transforms Shoreline Drive, Seaside Way, and other downtown streets into an international raceway—the **Long Beach Bayou Festival** Cajun, Zydeco, blues, and jazz festival in June, and the long-running **Long Beach Blues Festival** over Labor Day Weekend (late August/September) outdoors at CSU Long Beach.

The **Long Beach Freeway,** the 710, a major shipping corridor, delivers residents, visitors, and truckers alike right into downtown and/or the port district. Newcomers, heads up: Should you see a spectacular crash on six-lane **Shoreline Drive** in Long Beach, it's not always necessary to call 911. One of Hollywood's favorite filming sites for "freeway" disasters, Shoreline is regularly shut down for film shoots—20 or more times in an average year. (Don't worry. Actual traffic is routed around the action.) But in Long Beach, it's uniquely possible to get out—and stay out—of your car altogether. Excellent public transportation includes L.A. Metrorail's **Blue Line** mass transit system, 213/626-4455 (schedules) or 213/922-6235 (information), which runs 22 miles between Long Beach and downtown L.A. At downtown's **Long Beach Transit Mall** at First Street and the Promenade, riders can connect to 36 different local bus routes and interconnect with other bus systems. For detailed regional bus route and schedule information, stop by the **Long Beach Transit Information Center,** 223 E. First St., or contact Long Beach Transit, 562/591-2301, www.lb transit.com.

Best yet for visitors are those big red—and largely free—**Passport** downtown shuttles, which ferry folks around downtown Ocean Boulevard and to and from the *Queen Mary,* Shoreline Village, the convention center, hotels, restaurants, and shopping districts. (Fee charged beyond Atlantic Avenue.) If you'd prefer to get around by water but left the yacht back home, the 40-foot Catalina Express **Passport Aquabus** water taxi, 800/995-4386, connects the aquarium with Shoreline Village, the *Queen Mary,* and with the Catalina Express terminal (for the trip to Catalina Island) for a $1 one-way fare. The Express' 60-foot **Aqualink** water taxi connects Rainbow Harbor, the Queen Mary, and the Alamitos Boat Landing near Seal Beach for a $2 round-trip fare.

For more information about Long Beach and its attractions, contact the **Long Beach Convention and Visitors Bureau,** One World Trade Center, Ste. 300 in Long Beach, 562/436-3645 or 800/452-7829, or www.visitlongbeach.com.

SIGHTS

The visitor action in Long Beach is downtown and nearby, on the waterfront. The famed **Pike Amusement Park**—where Southern California once entertained itself on the roller coaster and boardwalk, and where W.C. Fields, Buster Keaton, and other early film-industry icons made movies—once stood near the current site of the huge Long Beach Convention and Entertainment Center. Though Hollywood subsequently stole the moviemaking spotlight, later Long

Beach films have included *The Creature from the Black Lagoon, Corrina Corrina, Speed,* and the opening scenes to *Lethal Weapon.* And until quite recently TV's *Baywatch* was filmed here, too, at least in part.

Though the new **Long Beach Aquarium of the Pacific** (see below) is the city's newest big attraction, surrounding **Rainbow Harbor** and **Shoreline Village** are home port for arcades and restaurants sure to please the whole family. For more boating, take a Venetian-style gondola ride through the Naples Island neighborhood with **Gondola Getaway,** 562/433-9595, www.gon dolagetawayinc.com, where the crackers and cheese are provided—along with the *O Sole Mio*—but you'll have to bring your own vino. Still most famous in Long Beach, though, is the RMS *Queen Mary* (see below), a floating cruise ship-cum-museum moored on the other side of Queensway Bridge featuring hotel rooms, restaurants, and shops. The gigantic golf ball-like geodesic dome nearby is the Queen Mary Seaport Dome, onetime home of Howard Hughes's *Spruce Goose,* now a popular movie-making soundstage.

Looking out onto the Queen, from the downtown side of the bay, is the **Shoreline Village** shopping complex at 407 Shoreline Village Dr., 562/435-2668, www.shorelinevillage.com, complete with a 1906 **Charles Looff carousel** for the kiddos.

Or head for the wide white sandy beach. Or take a beachfront bike ride. Well worth a stop at the beach is the **Long Beach Museum of Art,** 2300 E. Ocean Blvd., 562/439-2119, www .lbma.org, where you get artistic beach views in addition to an eyeful of contemporary art, photography, and sculpture. The 1912 Craftsman was recently renovated and expanded with a 12,500-square-foot addition showcasing Arts and Crafts-era and more contemporary decorative arts. The museum is open Tues.–Sun. 11 A.M.–5 P.M. Admission is $5 adults, $4 students/seniors.

Beaches and Piers

The paved **Shoreline Path** introduces bicyclists to Long Beach as both port and "pleasure place," weaving its way from the Los Angeles River and

Shoreline Village on the west to Belmont Shore on the east, paralleling Ocean Boulevard—and the beach—for much of the way. The route starts at the port, near Shoreline Village and within view of the venerable RMS *Queen Mary.* The path heads east along the broad, sandy beach—and those enticing semitropical "islands" offshore, actually dressed-up oil drilling platforms—while sashaying past some stately historic buildings along Ocean Boulevard, including one mansion now home to the **Long Beach Museum of Art.** End of the line is the remarkably congested **Belmont Shore** area, where the "elite retreat" cachet still holds. (A popular respite is the Belmont Brewing Company at the foot of tiny **Belmont Pier,** beloved locally for fishing.) Beyond the beachfront homes the bike path becomes a boardwalk, for pedestrians only. Only locals get to the beach early, which makes mornings the best time for a bike ride. As is always prudent in L.A., avoid being on the bike trail after dark.

Long Beach is also as good a place as any to begin a more ambitious tour of L.A.'s **Port of Los Angeles** commercial and industrial development, a trek not advisable by bike. San Pedro is L.A.'s cruise ship central as well as departure point for many Catalina ferries and other pleasure craft. Farther west are the placid coastal pleasures of Palos Verdes and vicinity; continue north to explore a few South Bay beach towns. To explore south of Long Beach, follow Second Street in Belmont Shore to Pacific Coast Highway (PCH) and then continue southeast across the San Gabriel River to arrive in Orange County and Seal Beach, Huntington Beach, and Newport Beach along the coast.

Long Beach Aquarium of the Pacific

The latest star—shall we say sea star?—brightening the Long Beach waterfront is the $100 million, 120,000-square-foot Long Beach Aquarium of the Pacific. At least indirectly inspired by the phenomenal success of the Monterey Bay Aquarium, which was the first to examine local ocean ecology in such exquisite, intimate, and technologically enhanced detail, the emphasis here is on the entire Pacific Ocean, the largest body of water on earth.

The Aquarium of the Pacific features 550 species of aquatic life in three major galleries, these corresponding to the ocean's three regions: **Southern California/Baja,** the **Tropical Pacific,** and the **Northern Pacific.** The Great Hall of the Pacific—the size of a football field, to represent the Pacific's vastness—offers an overview and a preview. New habitats, such as 2002's **Shark Lagoon,** are added regularly. Also look for special changing exhibits, such as 2004's Weird, Wild & Wonderful.

The aquarium first dips into the offshore waters of Southern California and the Baja Peninsula, from underwater kelp forests to bird's- and otter's-eye views of seals and sea lions frolicking in a facsimile Catalina Island environment. The interactive Kids' Cove here teaches the kiddos about other families' habits and habitats—in this case, those of marine animal families—and allows them to hike through whale bones, "hatch" bird eggs, and hide out with the hermit crabs. Then it's a quick splash south to Baja's Sea of Cortez and its sea turtles, skates, and rays. The Northern Pacific exhibits begin in the icy Bering Sea, where puffins nest near playful sea

BIKE IT OR NOT

The first of its species in the U.S., **Bikestation Long Beach** is a freestanding bicycle parking and support facility strategically located on the First Street Transit Mall, also a nexus for light rail, bus, pedestrian, and local shuttle traffic. Nearby are more than 30 miles of shoreline and river bicycle paths, as well as bike paths connecting to other parts of the city. In addition to secure, covered valet bike parking, Bikestation Long Beach offers bike repairs and rentals, a bike accessories shop, a refreshment stand with outdoor seating, and—for commuters—a changing room/restroom. Members can rent electric bikes and scooters, too, reasonable rates, and also participate in Flexcar car-sharing. For more information, call 562/733-0106 or see www.bikestation.org.

Los Angeles Coast

COURTESY OF THE LONG BEACH CONVENTION AND VISITORS BUREAU

Long Beach's new Aquarium of the Pacific

otters. This frigid sea shares other aquatic wealth, from schooling fish to giant octopuses and Japanese spider crabs. First stop in the Tropical Pacific is a peaceful lagoon in Micronesia, which sets the stage for the stunning 35,000-gallon Deep Reef exhibit—the aquarium's largest—with its vivid panorama of tropical sealife. If you time it right, you can watch divers feed the fish. Should you need feeding yourself, dive into the aquarium's **Café Scuba,** overlooking Rainbow Harbor. And to take home some specific memento of the Pacific Ocean, see what's on sale at the **Pacific Collections** gift shop.

The Long Beach Aquarium of the Pacific is centerpiece of the $650-million Queensbay Bay redevelopment project. The largest waterfront development in California history, Queensway Bay also encompasses the Rainbow Harbor resort complex.

Just off Shoreline Drive at 100 Aquarium Way (follow the signs), the Aquarium of the Pacific is open daily 9 A.M.–6 P.M. (closed Christmas). At last report admission was $18.95 adults, $14.95 seniors (age 60 and older), and $10.95 children (ages 3–11). Group rates (for 20 or more) are available with advance reservations. For more information or to purchase advance tickets, call the aquarium at 562/590-3100 or check the website at www.aquariumofpacific.org. The 40-foot Catalina Express **Passport Aquabus** water taxi, 800/995-4386, connects the aquarium with Shoreline Village, the *Queen Mary,* and the Catalina Express terminal (for the trip to Catalina Island).

RMS Queen Mary

If the kids have never been on an ocean liner, a setting right out of old romantic movies, they might enjoy exploring this one. Who knows? If they loved *Titanic* the movie, they might just love this ship. The RMS *Queen Mary,* with its sleek streamline-modern interiors, was first launched in 1936. At 1,019 feet long, this is one of the largest passenger ships ever built. More details—and some insight into luxury travel standards of yesteryear—are revealed in stateroom and other exhibits. The engine room and the bridge offer hands-on perspective on the mechanics of this massive ship. Also onboard: hotel rooms, restaurants, and shops. New **Ghost En-**

counters tours, with renowned paranormal investigator Peter James, are offered daily and included in the regular admission price. The adjacent **Queen Mary Seaport** offers more of Southern California's ubiquitous shopping.

At last report *Queen Mary* general admission was $23 adults, $20 seniors (age 55 and older) and active members of the military (with ID), $12 children ages 4–11. With a special behind-the-scenes guided tour, guided World War II tour, and admission to the *Scorpion* (see below), the cost is an additional $5 adults, $3 children. The Haunted Encounters Passport is also $28 for adults. Parking is $8 per day. For more information and hotel and restaurant reservations, call 562/435-3511, or 800/437-2934 (hotel reservations), or check www.queenmary.com. The *Queen Mary* is open daily 10 A.M.–6 P.M.; last admission is 30 minutes before closing on Saturday, otherwise 90 minutes before closing. The *Queen Mary* is directly across the harbor from the Aquarium of the Pacific at 1126 Queen's Hwy., Pier J. From the end of the Long Beach Freeway (the 710), follow the signs. From downtown, get here via Shoreline Drive and Queensway Bridge.

A new companion for the *Queen* is a retired Soviet submarine once capable of firing low-grade nuclear torpedoes. Commissioned in 1973 by the Soviet government, Podvodnaya Lodka B-427, also known by the code name *Scorpion,* was decommissioned in 1994. Tours of the *Scorpion,* berthed at the bow of the *Queen Mary,* are $10 adults and $9 seniors, military with I.D. and children ages 4–11. Hours are 10 A.M.–6 P.M. daily, but last admission is 30–90 minutes before closing (depending on the day). Call 562/435-3511 for current details.

Other Sights

The new **Museum of Latin American Art** close to downtown at 628 Alamitos Ave. (the northern extension of Shoreline Drive, south of Seventh Street), 562/437-1689, www.molaa.com, is the only U.S. museum with this exclusive artistic focus. This 1920-vintage 20,000-square-foot building houses the Robert Gumbiner Foundation collection of Latin American art, rotating contemporary exhibits, "La Galeria" gallery and

store, and both performance area and research library. The museum is open Tues.–Sat. 11:30 A.M.–7:30 P.M., Sunday 11 A.M.–6 P.M. Admission is $5 adults, $3 students and seniors, free for children 12 and under. Call for current exhibit information or check the museum website.

Other Long Beach museums include the free **Lifeguard Museum** at the historic Long Beach **Marine Stadium,** 5255 Appian Way, built for the 1932 Olympics, 562/570-1360, open only 10 A.M.–2 P.M. on the second Saturday of each month. (But call first. Sometimes the lifeguard business gets too busy to indulge even such a small amount of history, especially during summer.) For an introduction to local history, stop by the **Historical Society of Long Beach Gallery and Research Center,** in the Breakers Building, 210 E. Ocean Blvd., 562/495-1210, open Tues.–Fri 1 –5 P.M., Thursdays until 7 P.M.

Amateur historians should also explore two small outposts of early Southern California still at home in Long Beach. The seven-acre remnant of **Rancho Los Alamitos,** 6400 E. Bixby Hill Rd., 562/431-3541, offers tours of the 1800-vintage adobe, later farm buildings, and lovely gardens Wed.–Sun. 1–5 P.M. (last tour starts at 4 P.M.). **Rancho Los Cerritos,** 4600 Virginia Rd., 562/570-1755, www.rancholoscerritos.org, offers weekend-only guided tours of this 1844 Monterey-style adobe home and surrounding gardens—once the center of a 27,000-acre sheep ranch—open to the public Wed.–Sun. 1–5 P.M., guided tours offered weekends only, at 1, 2, 3, and 4 P.M. Admission to both homes is free, donations are welcome. Closed on holidays.

Historians of California's future should visit **Little Cambodia** along Anaheim Street, the largest Cambodian settlement outside Phnom Penh. For business, restaurant, and other information, call the **Cambodian Association of America,** 562/424-0138, or the **United Cambodian Community,** 562/438-3932.

Book lovers, don't miss family-run **Acres of Books,** 240 Long Beach Blvd. (at Maple), 562/437-6980, www.acresofbooks.com, the nation's largest selection of used books, open here since 1934 and reported to be one of writer Ray Bradbury's favorites. Prime-time for shopping is a

COURTESY OF THE LONG BEACH CONVENTION AND VISITORS BUREAU

RMS *Queen Mary*

15-block stretch of Second Street in Belmont Shore and downtown's Pine Avenue/Broadway district.

ACCOMMODATIONS

In the absence of a major downtown convention, and particularly in the off-season, Long Beach-area accommodations can be a relative bargain for families and budget travelers. The best bargain otherwise, complete with panoramic ocean views and surrounding sports fields, park, and picnic areas, is the nearby 60-bed HI-USA **Los Angeles/South Bay Hostel** in Angels Gate Park in San Pedro at 3601 S. Gaffey St., Bldg. 613, 310/831-8109, www.hostelweb.com, primarily dorm-style accommodations (groups welcome) though private rooms are available. The hostel features onsite kitchen and laundry, library, TV and VCR, and barbecue—and from here it's just a stroll to the beach. Dorm beds under $25 members/non-members; private rooms under $50 members/non-members. Reservations essential in summer.

Other fairly inexpensive accommodations abound in Long Beach along or near Pacific Coast Highway. Here, though, the highway runs through some rough neighborhoods and—if you were expecting oceanfront views—doesn't get close to the coast until it reaches the Orange County line. There are other decent choices closer to the beach and just a few blocks from the convention center along Atlantic Avenue. The city's major hotels are also in that general area, including the **Hyatt Regency Long Beach** at Two World Trade Center (Ocean Avenue and Golden Shore Street), 562/491-1234 or 800/633-7313 in the U.S. and Canada (800/532-1496 for AAA members), www.hyatt.com, with rates $100–250; the **Renaissance Long Beach Hotel,** 111 E. Ocean Blvd. (at Pine), 562/437-5900 or 888/236-2427, www.marriott.com, with rates $100–250; and the **Westin Long Beach,** 333 E. Ocean Blvd., 562/436-3000 or 800/228-3000, www.starwood.com, with rates $150–250. Contact the visitors bureau for current accommodations listings.

For something definitely different, consider an onboard overnight at the RMS *Queen Mary,* at 1126 Queen's Hwy., Pier J, 562/435-3511, www.queenmary.com, and sleep in a 1936-vintage oceanliner cabin. Special package deals include the Catalina Getaway, Bed and Brunch

Los Angeles Coast

Package, and the Royal Romance Package. Rates are $100–150 for basic cabins, $150–250 deluxe cabins, $250 and up suites. For more ship information, see the general travel listing for the *Queen Mary,* above.

Long Beach also offers bed-and-breakfast choices, including the inviting 1913 Craftsman **Beachrunners' Inn,** 231 Kennebec Ave. in Belmont Heights, 866/221-0001, www.beachrun nersinn.com. The five charming rooms feature comfy beds, TV with cable, private baths, and there are other nice touches—including the backyard whirlpool tub and the hooked-up laptop in the living room, so you can check email. Rates are $100–150.

FOOD

Downtown

Increasingly stylish dining and shopping star downtown on and near Pine Avenue and along Belmont Shore's Second Street. Popular and good for fresh fish and seafood downtown is **King's Fish House Pine Avenue,** 100 W. Broadway (at Pine), 562/432-7463, open for lunch and dinner daily, for breakfast on weekends. Very good value. Among the many other choices in the neighborhood: the see-and-be-seen **Alegria Cocina Latina,** 115 Pine (at First), 562/436-3388, where tapas star but gazpacho, sandwiches, salads, and substantial dinners are also on tap (the deli opens in the morning, too, for pastries and coffee). Live music nightly, and don't miss the Flamenco show. Open daily for lunch and dinner. Next door is the classy Northern Italian sibling **L'Opera,** 101 Pine (at First Street), 562/491-0066, open nightly for dinner, weekdays for lunch.

At the top end of the Long Beach stylish dining scene, seductively combining continental cuisine with modern art-deco ambience, **The Sky Room,** 40 S. Locust Ave. (near Ocean Boulevard, on the 15th floor of the historic Breakers Building), 562/983-2703, is a high-toned statement of supper club style serving superb, expensive fare. Polished mahogany furnishings, luxurious fixtures, and a panorama view of L.A. and Catalina Island make this one of the nicest dining experi-

ences in town. There's live jazz and dancing to big-band swing music on the weekends.

After dinner downtown, there's entertainment. Among downtown's most popular nightclubs and bars are the **Blue Cafe,** 210 Promenade North (at Broadway), 562/983-7111, famous for its blues acts, billiards, and low ($5–10) cover charge; **Cohiba Club,** 144 Pine (at Broadway, above Mum's restaurant), 562/491-5220, for dancing to DJs and live bands; and the **Yard House,** 401 Shoreline Village Dr. (near the Marina), 562/628-0455, a boisterous pub where some 250 beers are served on tap in glasses that extend to a yard high (for serious drinkers). But nothing could be better than the **Cotton Club West** jazz and blues club, 730 E. Broadway Ave., 562/437-8355, www.cottonclub west.com, brought to you by Roscoe's House of Chicken 'n Waffles.

If making the scene isn't your scene, the mellowest coffeehouse around is **The Library,** 3418 E. Broadway (at Redondo Avenue), 562/433-2393, where for the price of a cappuccino you can settle in to one of the plush couches and pull a paperback off the shelf. Also here: banana-flavored cheesecake and baseball-sized blueberry muffins. And you can always go to the movies, at the large selection of screens downtown provided by AMC's **Pine Square 16,** 243 Pine Ave., 562/435-4262, one of Southern California's largest cinema complexes.

Near Belmont Shore

The classic vegetarian hot spot in Belmont Shore is inexpensive **Belmont Heritage Natural Market & Cafe,** 5000 E. Second St. (at Argonne Avenue), 562/439-1059, serving a great TLT—tofu, lettuce, and tomato sandwich—as well as broccoli sesame pasta, vegetable shepherd's pie, spinach lasagne, and veggie and tempeh burgers. The classic Long Beach all-American burger joint is **Hof's Hut,** 6257 E. Second St. (at PCH), 562/598-4070, where the Hofburger is the main attraction—not counting the snorkeler's fin dangling from the stuffed shark's mouth.

For fine American regional fare at dinner, from seafood gumbo and chicken-fried steak to blackened fish, the place is **M Shenandoah Cafe,** 4722 E. Second (at Park), 562/434-3469. Finish your meal with bananas Foster or chocolate pecan pie. Best for Italian is genuinely friendly **Christy's Italian Cafe,** 3937 E. Broadway (at Termino Avenue), 562/433-7133, owned by Christy Bono, daughter of the late Sonny B. (If you're one of those cigar-sucking trendoids, the **Havana Cigar Club** is right next door, 562/433-8053.) Other good choices include **Babette's Feast** café and bakery, 4621 E. Second St., 562/987-4536; always-packed **La Crêperie Café,** 5110 E. Second St. (Granada Ave.), 562/434-8499; and

Frenchy's Bistro & Wine Bar, 4137 E. Anaheim St. (near Belmont), 562/494-8787. For fabulous Indian food, the place is **Natraj,** 5262 E. Second St. (near La Verne Avenue), 562/930-0930, where the Mon.–Sat. lunch buffet and the all-you-can-eat Sunday brunch are particularly great deals. For big-time beefeaters, pricey **555 East** at 555 E. Ocean Blvd. (near Atlantic), 562/437-0626, bills itself as an American steakhouse and is generally considered the best in Long Beach.

Catalina

Thanks to one of those schmaltzy old songs, Santa Catalina Island's original location in the American imagination as "island of romance" was "twenty-six miles across the sea," though it's actually only 22 miles from San Pedro on the mainland. But romantic it was—first famous as the private fiefdom of William Wrigley Jr., of chewing gum fame, and as onetime spring training camp for his Chicago Cubs. The western pulp writer Zane Grey, whose "pueblo" now serves as a hotel, also loved Catalina. And the roster of movie stars and celebrities who have been here at one time or another, for one reason or another, would practically fill a book. Catalina even has its own movable movie memorabilia—a herd of buffalo, woolly chocolate-colored descendants of beasts originally imported in 1924 for the filming of *The Vanishing American.*

Yet all is not nostalgic. In its own way, quaint Catalina also walks the cutting edge. To solve its ongoing water supply problems, for example, Catalina started up its own desalination plant to transform seawater into drinking water. Because unrestrained automobile traffic would clearly ruin the town, perhaps even sink the island, few cars are allowed on Catalina. Instead, if not on foot most people get around greater Avalon by golf cart—an appropriate local transportation. And most of the island is owned, and protected, by private trusts—which means that all but the most innocuous activities, such as eating and shopping, are strictly regulated. Hiking and biking are by permit

only, for example, and camping in the interior is by reservation only.

Present-day Catalina, second largest of the Channel Islands at 48,438 acres, otherwise retains its charms—fresh air and mild climate, rugged open space, a healthy ocean environment—because the island is relatively unpopulated. Avalon, the island's only town, boasts barely 3,000 souls. Southern California's version of a whitewashed Mediterranean hillside village perched above a balmy bay, Avalon is brushed with bright colors and stunning tiles—the most concentrated public and private displays of 1930s' California tile work anywhere. Anchoring Avalon Bay on the north, just beyond the town's tiny bayside commercial district, is the spectacular Moorish Casino, the art-deco masterpiece built by William Wrigley Jr., to house the first theater specifically designed for movies. Beyond Avalon the island's other primary visitor destination is remote Two Harbors, snuggled into the isthmus to the northwest.

The official island population may be miniscule but the unofficial head count can be astronomical in summer and on "event" weekends. (Avoid the crazy crowds by coming in spring or in October—on a weekday if at all possible.) If you're a people person, annual events well worth the trip over include the **Silent Film Festival** at the Casino's Avalon Theatre in June, a benefit for the Catalina Island Museum Society; the **Fourth of July** gala, including golf cart parade and spectacular fireworks over Avalon Bay; the

© ROBERT HOLMES/CALTOUR

Avalon Casino on Catalina Island

Catalina Festival of Art in September; the three-weekend Catalina Jazz Trax Festival in October; and the glitzy big-band New Year's Eve Celebration at the Casino Ballroom.

Crowds or no crowds, most folks manage only a daytrip—taking in the ocean wind and waves on the way and then sampling the shops and the island's main "urban" sights before climbing back on the ferry to head home. (For daytrips avoid Tuesday and Wednesday, when the cruise ships dock.) One of California's small tragedies is the fact that so few visitors realize that on a longer stay Catalina offers *solitude,* a very rare Southern California commodity, and a wealth of other worthwhile pursuits.

SIGHTS
M Avalon

Avalon is fringed with palms, olive trees, and tourists. Most of the latter spend most of their time clustered along bayside Crescent Avenue, the city's main commercial strip. While you're still figuring out where else to go, the moment you step off the ferry start your impromptu Avalon "tile tour." The city's eccentric beach-

front plaza is one huge outdoor installation of decorated geometric tiles. All along the waterfront, watch for Catalina's unique building facades, fountains, and decorative planters. Don't miss El Encanto Market Place and, along the beach, the Serpentine Wall. If a brisk but brief walk fits the agenda, head uphill to the recently restored Wrigley Memorial. The granddaddy of all tile destinations, though, is on the other end of town—Wrigley's Casino at the north end of the bay. Included in the Casino's small museum collection are dishware, pottery, and inlaid tables. Along with other interior and exterior tile work, the Casino's patio is paved with classic Catalina tiles.

Catalina Island's grand Casino was originally William J. Wrigley, Jr.'s Casino, a circular Moorish palace built for dancing (he forbade drinking and gambling) and sedately presiding over the bay since 1929. Wrigley was a stickler for detail. So perfect were the acoustics of the movie theater here—the first designed specifically for "talking pictures"—that in 1931 engineers for New York's Radio City Music Hall came to Catalina for a lesson. But the theater's glories don't stop with the sound. The art-deco murals and spectacular tile

Los Angeles Coast

SUPREME RIDER OF THE PURPLE SAGE

The bestselling Western yarnspinner of all time—the author of *Riders of the Purple Sage, The Buffalo Hunter,* and *The Last of the Plainsmen* among his 60-some Westerns—the pulp writer **Zane Grey** was born in 1872 in the Ohio Valley, a son of pioneers. After his breakthrough 1910 novel *Heritage of the Desert,* Grey and his family moved to California and bought a house in Altadena.

Of all the landscapes he came to love in California, Zane Grey was particularly smitten with Santa Catalina Island. An avid fisherman, Grey was attracted by the island's superb deep-sea fishing. Among his local legacies is Catalina's healthy herd of bison, descendants of the 14 left behind after the 1924 filming of *The Vanishing American.* His former home is another. A rambling adobe on a hill overlooking Avalon, Grey's house is now the historic 1926 Hopi Indian–style Zane Grey Pueblo Hotel, which offers the town's best view of Avalon Harbor. For voluminous information about the author and his works, try the Zane Grey's West Society website at www.zanegreysws.com.

work are both by John Gabriel Beckman, one-time art director for Columbia Studios, who also painted Grauman's Chinese Theater in Hollywood. Completely refurbished, the Casino harbors other attractions—including its original **Page pipe organ,** small **art gallery,** the **Catalina Island Museum** (open daily, small donation), and a grand second-floor **ballroom.** And its view of the bay. Sadly, for impromptu types, the only way to see the entire Casino is on a guided walking tour (see below). Otherwise you can visit the museum and art gallery separately, the ballroom only during special events. For information on the weekly movie—usually well worth it, and one of the few ways to appreciate the fabulous interior of the Casino's **Avalon Theatre**—call 310/510-0179.

If time permits, and if Avalon proper loses its appeal, head for the ocean—or the island's interior. Swimming, sunbathing, snorkeling, skin-diving, sportfishing, kayaking, golfing, para-sailing, sailing, bicycling, hiking, and camping are a few possible diversions. Various tours, by land or by sea, are also quite worthwhile.

Ⓜ Two Harbors

Welcome to The Other Catalina—the one where you really can get away from it all, especially in the winter. The most protected of Two Harbors' "two" is **Catalina Harbor,** on the island's ocean side; **Isthmus Cove,** the other, faces into the channel on Catalina's north side. Once called Union Harbor, this unassuming half-mile-wide isthmus bore witness to much of Catalina's most colorful history, starting with the mysterious temple and rites of the native Gabrieleño Indians reported by the 1602 Vizcaíno expedition. From the island's own fur trader, smuggler, bootlegger, and gold rush days through late 19th-century tourism, Two Harbors has maintained both its solitude and serenity, a dirt-road refuge remaining the getaway "mooring" of choice for both boaters and campers—and filmmakers. Movies filmed in and around Two Harbors include *Mutiny on the Bounty, Treasure Island, Sea Hawk, The Ten Commandments, The King of Kings, McHale's Navy,* and *MacArthur.*

The sweeping seascape is the main attraction at Two Harbors, about six miles from Catalina's western tip, whether one enjoys it on the beach, on foot, or onboard a kayak. By way of general introduction, take the short hike from the village at Isthmus Cove—where the ferries and shuttles dock—across the isthmus to Catalina Harbor. (Beware of buffalo.) In addition, from Two Harbors hikers can set out on Catalina's most westerly trails. West island campsites, camping tepees, tent cabins, rustic cabins (available mid-October to mid-April only), boat-accessible yurts, the Banning House bed-and-breakfast, kayak and "safari" tours, and scuba and snorkeling trips are all available through a single concessionaire—the SCI Company at Two Harbors, 888/510-7979, www.visittwoharbors.com. Also here is the **Wrigley Marine Science Center** operated at Big Fisherman's Cove (near Isthmus Cove) by the University of Southern California's Institute for Environmental Studies, available for group tours by reservation.

RECREATION

It's possible to tour Catalina Island's hilly back-country terrain by bus, but, if at all possible, hiking or biking is the better way to go. The sights, sounds, and scents offered by Catalina's unique sea-bound ecosystem, including unusual plant and animal life and some astonishing 360-degree vistas, are so much more savory when discovered in solitude. You can combine almost two dozen trails—some long, some short, some scenic, some less so—to turn an island trip into a trek. Make it an overnight or multiday trip by camping at Little Harbor Campground and/or Two Harbors Cove Campground—and more remote campsites beyond. But unless you're willing to literally carry the kids, a trans-island trek may be too challenging for youngsters.

The most ambitious island bike ride starts from Avalon and traverses the entire island's hilly terrain, by road, to Two Harbors. You can bring your own bicycles across from the mainland, by arrangement with Catalina's Express, or rent bikes on the island. Again, the trek is typically too tough for the kiddos; bike rides in and around Avalon are a fun family alternative.

Hiking or biking into Catalina's interior is by permit only; bike permits ($50 per person or $75 per family per year) are required for treks beyond Avalon and vicinity. To obtain permits and other current information, contact the **Santa Catalina Island Conservancy** at 310/510-2595.

Guided hikes and other outdoor adventures are available through **Spa at Catalina/Catalina Fitness Company,** 310/510-9255, and other local concerns.

Tours

If hiking and biking seem too *vigorous* and you're without golf cart, consider taking one of Catalina's popular guided tours. Discovery Tours, 800/626-1496, operated by the island's Santa Catalina Island (SCI) Company, www.scico.com, dominates the market—and has since 1894. For a trip to the isthmus for a picnic dinner take the **Sundown Isthmus Tour,** offered only in the warmer months. Also exciting, also seasonal, are the **Flying Fish** and **Seal Rocks** tours onboard searchlight equipped open boats. Among the newest tours Discovery offers is the **Undersea Tour.** If you're not a scuba diver or snorkeler, the best way to see the sea—and under the sea—surrounding Catalina Island is from onboard a semi-submersible boat. Both the *Starlight* and *Emerald* cruise the swaying fronds of the offshore kelp forest. Passengers get up close and personal with the fish, crustaceans, and other sea creatures through the large underwater windows. As on glass bottom boat tours, on a night cruise you may also see a live ocean light show—the phenomenon of phosphorescence.

Discovery Tours for landlubbers, 800/626-1496, include the very worthwhile **Casino Walking Tour,** which pokes into the Casino Ballroom, the Avalon Theatre, and almost every other cranny of William Wrigley, Jr.'s masterpiece. To see the rest of Avalon without walking up and down all those hills, sign on for the **Avalon Scenic Tour** or the **Avalon Scenic & Botanical Garden Tour.** The **Skyline Drive** tour offers an inland "overview," between Avalon and the Catalina Nature Center at the airport. The 28-mile, half-day **Inland Motor Tour** includes a refreshment stop at William Wrigley, Jr.'s **El Rancho Escondido** Arabian horse ranch. Tour prices start at about $10 and range to $50 per person, at last report, with lower rates for children and seniors. "Combo" tours can save a few dollars. For more information or reservations, contact the SCI Company's **Discovery Tours,** 310/510-8687 or 800/626-1496 (reservations); once on the island, stop by the Discovery Tours center across from the Green Pleasure Pier. For something more adventurous on land, the Santa Catalina Island Conservancy offers **Jeep Eco-Tours,** 310/510-2595.

Other individuals and groups also offer tours and activity-oriented attractions—including ocean rafting, scuba and "shark" diving, sportfishing, and golfing and miniature golfing. For a current list of suggestions, contact the visitor bureau (see below) or, once arrived, poke around the Green Pleasure Pier in Avalon and elsewhere along the waterfront. Or head for Two Harbors (see above), which offers its own diversions.

ACCOMMODATIONS

Camping

If you'll be here longer than a day, you'll need a place to stay. The most inexpensive option is camping. Avalon's only campground is **Hermit Gulch** just over a mile outside town, 310/510-8368, which features flush toilets and lighted restrooms, coin showers, and both tent cabins and tepees in addition to standard campsites. The most popular place "on the other side" is the large **Two Harbors Campground** at the isthmus, with flush toilets and cold showers. Teepee camping—definitely something different—is also available at Two Harbors, as are rustic cabins (off-season only) and fairly uptown "yurts" at Goat Harbor. Other "out there" developed campgrounds include palm-fringed and protected **Little Harbors Campground,** the only option along the island's south (windward) side; **Black Jack** in the pines atop Mt. Black Jack, the only inland choice; and on-the-beach **Parson's Landing** north of Two Harbors. Call 310/510-8368 for reservations at any of these campgrounds. Reservations for and various Catalina Island Conservancy primitive boat-in "cove" campsites—including **Starlight Beach** and **Frog Rock Cove,** on the island's leeward side—are available through Two Harbors, 310/510-2800. **Descanso Beach Ocean Sports,** 310/510-1226, www .kayakcatalinaisland.com, offers camping trips—by kayak—to remote island locales.

Hotels and Inns

With the exception of campgrounds, most accommodation options are in Avalon. The local visitor bureau (see below) is quite helpful in arranging hotels and bed-and-breakfast inn reservations—mandatory during the island's summer season—or, request current visitor information well in advance of your trip and go it on your own. (Prices can be "fluid," especially at peak visitor times, so get a firm commitment when you reserve. Two- or three-night minimum stays on weekends, especially in summer, are the rule.) For bargain rates, come in the off-season—the best time to come anyway, in many respects—which generally runs from mid-October through mid-April. Ask about other specials and packages. The visitor bureau can also recommend local home and condominium rental agencies.

"Uptown" in Two Harbors is the **M Banning House Lodge,** 310/510-2800 or 800/785-8425, www.scico.com, a most comfortable base camp for backcountry Catalina exploration. This comfortably rustic turn-of-the-century hunting lodge, now an 11-room bed-and-breakfast overlooking both harbors, has hosted Hollywood celebrities on location and, during World War II, U.S. Coast guard officers. Each room has a view and a historic theme. Warm yourself by the living room fireplace in the evenings, in the company of fellow explorers and the vacant stares of animal-head trophies. Summer room rates start at $179; winter rates go as low as $89. In winter cabins are also available.

Most elegant in Avalon is the **M The Inn on Mt. Ada,** overlooking Avalon Bay from Wrigley Rd., 310/510-2030 or 800/608-7669, www .catalina.com/mtada. One of California's most elegant bed-and-breakfast inns, this onetime summer estate of chewing gum magnate William Wrigley Jr. and family is a graceful Georgian colonial mansion built in 1921. Now included on the National Register of Historic Places, this six-room bed-and-breakfast still boasts many of its original furnishings and all the accoutrements of upper-class ease. Yet the friendliness of its new identity makes it Southern California's getaway of choice for celebrating very special events. (For weddings, anniversary celebrations, and other occasions, you can rent the entire inn.) A stay here is much less expensive—and the island itself is much less crowded—on winter weekdays. High-season rates are $250 and up (two-night minimum on weekends), starting at $320 in the off season. All meals included.

Intriguing choices in town, for different reasons, include the pretty pink **Hotel St. Lauren** on Beacon Street, 310/510-2299 or 800/645-2496, www.stlauren.com, a "modern Victorian" with ample motel-style amenities, rooftop patio, and high-season rates of $150–250 (as low as $85 in the off season), and the actually historic **Zane Grey Pueblo Hotel** at 199 Chimes Tower Rd., 310/510-0966 or 800/378-3256. Zane Grey,

American master of the romantic cowboy adventure novel, started his romance with Catalina Island in the 1920s. The island's healthy herd of bison is one Zane Grey legacy—descendants of the 14 left behind after the 1924 filming of *The Vanishing American.* Avalon's Zane Grey Pueblo is another. A rambling adobe on a hill overlooking Avalon, Grey's former home is now a bed-and-breakfast-style hotel with modern plumbing and private baths but few other concessions to modern times. The Pueblo features rooms named after Zane Grey novels, striking 1920s-style Southwestern decor, even an arrowhead-shaped swimming pool. Rates are $150–250.

Across from the beach and fairly affordable is the SCI Company's stylishly renovated **Pavilion Lodge,** 800/626-1496, www.scico.com, with high-season rates $150–250. But check for packages and off-season specials; in the winter, prices drop to $100–150. Popular high-end hotels (motels without cars or parking) along bustling Crescent Avenue that sometimes offer affordable rooms in the off-season or midweek include the romantic Mediterranean-style **Hotel Villa Portofino,** 310/510-0555 or 800/346-2326, www.hotelvilla portofino.com, and the beautifully renovated **Hotel Metropole,** 310/510-1884 or 800/300-8528 (in California), or 800/541-8528 (U.S. and Canada), www.hotel-metropole.com.

For cheaper rates—and a better workout—plan to climb Avalon's hills and/or stay in older small hotels. The diver-friendly **Catalina Beach House,** 310/510-1078 or 800/974-6835, offers high-season weekend rates as low as $100–150, with discounts during the week and in the off-season. Charming and quaint, also usually best bets for low weekday rates, are the old-Catalina-style housekeeping cottages at **La Paloma,** 310/510-1505 or 800/310-1505. High season rates are $100–150, and $50–100 at other times.

FOOD

Thanks to its "destination" setting, Avalon's restaurants are pricey (with a few exceptions). Snack shacks and restaurants cluster along Avalon's waterfront. For pizza and Italian-style sandwiches in an eclectic college-kid atmosphere,

the place is **Antonio's Pizzeria** at 230 Crescent Ave. (at Metropol), 310/510-0008. **Cafe Prego** at 603 Crescent (near Clarissa), 310/510-1218, is friendly and comfortable, a neighborhood bistro facing the bay along Avalon's main drag—just about perfect for escaping the madding crowds at dinner (in summer, lunch too). You won't go wrong with the seafood pastas or the lasagna, but you can also "go American" and get a good steak. Or head for all-American steak and fish at **Steve's Steakhouse** at 417 Crescent (at the green pier), 310/510-0333. Catalina's classic local breakfast café, also open for lunch, is the **Pancake Cottage** up the street from the Green Pier at 118 Catalina St., 310/510-0726

The time-honored choice for fresh fish at lunch or dinner is **Armstrong's Fish Market and Seafood Landing** at 306 Crescent Ave., 310/510-0113, also serving great views and a deck. Eclectic **The Landing Bar and Grill,** at El Encanto Marketplace, 310/510-1474, serves "island" fare, from seafood and steaks to tacos, pizzas, and exotic drinks. **Ristorante Villa Portofino,** next to the Hotel Portofino at 101 Crescent Ave., 310/510-0508, is the place for cioppino, seafood ravioli, and rack of lamb. For romantic classics, the place is **The Channel House** at the Metropole Marketplace, 205 Crescent Ave., 310/510-1617.

INFORMATION AND SERVICES

For an unforgettable trip over to Catalina, take the helicopter—a 15-minute ride over via **Island Express,** 310/510-2525 or 800/2AVALON, www.islandexpress.com. Though Catalina boasts a small airport and yacht harbors, most people get here via commercial ferry. **Catalina Express** ferries, 310/519-1212 or 800/360-1212, www .catalinaexpress.com, depart from San Pedro Harbor and Long Beach, as well as Dana Point in Orange County. From June into September, the Express also offers a 45-minute coastal shuttle between Avalon and Two Harbors. Express options include the *Catalina Jet* 499-seat catamaran, which makes the one-way trip in just an hour. Another possibility by sea is **Catalina Passenger Service,** 949/673-5245, www.catalinainfo.com, which sets

Los Angeles Coast

© MICHELLE AND TOM GRIMM/LOS ANGELES CONVENTION AND VISITORS BUREAU

helicopter view of Catalina Island

sail from Newport Beach at the Balboa Pavilion. You can also come from Marina del Rey by catamaran—the 149-seat **Catalina–Marina Del Rel Flyer** catamaran based at Fisherman's Village, 310/310-7250, www.catalinaferries.com, which makes the trip over in just 1.5 hours.

For current details on transportation options, tours, special events, accommodations options and packages, and other practical information, contact: **Catalina Island Chamber of Commerce and Visitors Bureau,** 310/510-1520, www.catalina.com.

Orange County Coast

Sun-kissed Southern California rivals, Orange County and Los Angeles argue endlessly about whose neighborhood is most blessed—a full-blown feud evolved into advanced social sport, sometimes nasty, sometimes hilarious.

The differences between the two are difficult to grasp for those just passing through, though. Both feature sunny neighborhoods strung together by shopping centers and stressful freeways. Both have sped through the Southern California boom-bust cycles of agriculture, oil, land development, and aerospace. Both steal their water from elsewhere. Both have sandy beaches, bad neighborhoods, good neighborhoods, all of it high-priced. Both embrace an idealized self-image, disregarding uglier truths. And both believe the other is missing the best of all possible worlds.

Some say the spat started in the late 1800s, when Los Angeles County was almost as large as Ohio. Tired of taxation without representation, and bitter about their second-class status,

Must-Sees

Look for **M** to find the sights and activities you can't miss and **M** for the best dining and lodging.

M Bolsa Chica State Beach and Reserve: One of the Orange County's few remaining wetland tracts, it provides seasonal habitat for many species of waterfowl and shorebirds, including the endangered California least tern (page 549).

M Orange County Museum of Art: Marooned in a business park near Fashion Island is the Orange County Museum of Art, known for its cutting-edge special exhibits (page 558).

M Newport Pier: Most historic here is the **Newport Dory Fishing Fleet,** the only surviving dory fleet on the West Coast (page 560).

M Balboa Pier: Notable in Balboa is the Balboa Fun Zone, with genuine arcade gamesand rides, plus the striking Balboa Pavilion, once a big-band bandstand (page 560).

M Upper Newport Bay Ecological Reserve: Once known as Frog Swamp, this brackish salt- and freshwater marsh is the largest remaining unengineered estuary in Southern California (page 564).

M Crystal Cove State Park: Crystal Cove is the largest remaining patch of coastal land still open to the general public—with tidepools and sandy coves

along more than three miles of reasonably lonely beach (page 574).

M Pageant of the Masters/Festival of the Arts: Staged together in July and August, the Festival of Arts features fine arts and crafts—all strictly local—and the Pageant of the Masters exhibits *tableaux vivants,* or living pictures, that superbly imitate well-known works of art and other scenes (page 575).

M Laguna Art Museum: Scores of American artists arrived in Laguna Beach determined to paint in the open air *(en plein air)* like the French impressionists. Much of that legacy lives in here, at the only Southern California art museum to focus exclusively on American art (page 578).

M Mission San Juan Capistrano: The schmaltzy 1939 Leon Rene tune *When the Swallows Come Back to Capistrano* is responsible for the excited flutter here every year on March 19, when tourists flock to town to welcome the return of the cliff swallows to the mission (page 589).

M San Clemente State Beach: Backed by craggy white sandstone bluffs and coastal chaparral, mile-long San Clemente State Beach is one of the best around (page 590).

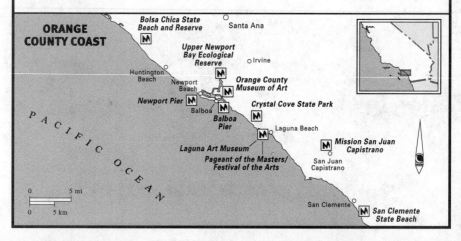

residents of the Santa Ana Valley—modern-day Orange County—staged their first anti-tax rebellion by seceding from L.A. Though often amicable, the post-break-up bickering continues to this day.

Urbane Angelenos point out that orange trees in Orange County are about as abundant as the seals at Seal Beach. (There are no seals at Seal Beach.) That high culture in Orange County is best represented by the John Wayne statue at the airport. That the entire county, in fact, is more G-rated than a Disney cartoon. That only Orange County could produce the likes of ex-President Richard Nixon, not to mention local politicians prone to stating publicly that men who support abortion rights are "women trapped in men's bodies. . . who are looking for an easy lay" as Rep. Robert K. "B-1 Bob" Dornan of Garden Grove once said. (Dornan since lost his congressional seat to a Latina, Loretta Sanchez, a subject that still rankles in some circles.) That at its best Orange County exhibits a standard-brand and superficial beauty, at its worst, vapid nouveau-riche snobbery. That the FBI has identified Orange County as the capital of white-collar crime, and that when Orange County filed for bankruptcy in 1994, it entered the record books with the biggest municipal bankruptcy in U.S. history. That, all things considered, Orange County is little more than an emergency gasoline stop on the road to San Diego.

Indignant Orange County residents counter that people from Los Angeles are self-absorbed cultural elitists who live only to consume the latest fads in food, clothing, and thought. Behind all that anti-Orange posturing, they say, Angelenos are just jealous—because Orange County, not L.A., now represents the quintessential Southern California lifestyle. (Thus *The OC* on TV, and *USA Today*'s declaration in 2003 that Orange County is the "new capital of cool.") Orange County has no smog. People in Orange County can still drop the tops on their convertibles and surf the freeways fast enough to get speeding tickets. They can go to the beach without getting caught in gang crossfire. And they aren't social hypocrites. People in Orange County, where beach-bleached blondes are the societal ideal,

don't congratulate themselves on multiculturalism in the light of day and then retreat at night, in the L.A. style, to economically and ethnically segregated neighborhoods.

But according to T. Jefferson Parker in his entertaining essay "Behind the Orange Curtain," only one fundamental difference separates Los Angeles citizens from those who inhabit the Big Orange:

L.A. people all want to be someone else. Look at them, and, as Jim Harrison has written, "see the folly whirling in their eyes." The waiters all want to be novelists; the novelists all want to be screenwriters; the screenwriters all want to direct; the directors all want to produce; the producers all want to keep the other guys relegated to net participation and guild minimums.

Now take Orange Countians. We know who we are. The blandly handsome, heavily mortgaged, marathon-running, aerospace department manager, driving to work in his Taurus, does not entertain dreams of movie making. He has weapons to build, a

Cruising out of Newport Harbor

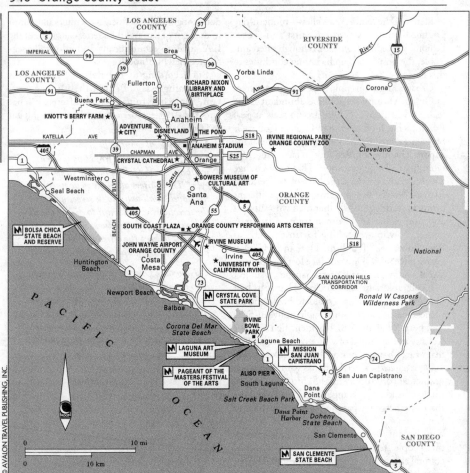

country to defend, a family to provide for. Or take the blond mall rat, age 16, eyes aflame with consumer fever. She doesn't secretly wish to be Michelle Pfeiffer. She actually has never heard of Michelle Pfeiffer. The loose-jawed surfer dude in Huntington Beach entertains not a single thought besides the next south swell, south being to his left, he's pretty sure, if he's facing the gnarlical tubes of the Pacific, which he usually is.

People in L.A., Parker explains, "want to be someone else because they're miserable; people in Orange County are content to be who they are because they're happy. It's clear. People in L.A. can't face reality. We can."

Reality is complicated, of course. Orange County is whiter and wealthier than Los Angeles, still, but in 1999, for the first time in 15 years, fewer than half of registered Orange County voters were Republicans. Besides, L.A. voters were also eager to send Richard Nixon and Ronald Reagan to the White House. Orange County voters are more likely than Angelenos to oppose offshore oil-drilling and to support environmental action, but these days both regions are

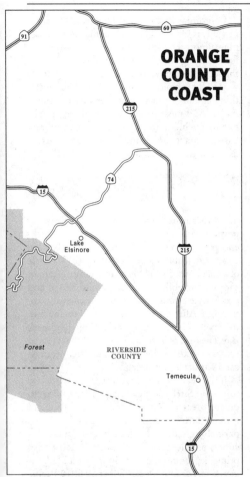

ORANGE COUNTY COAST

youth, the City of Angels seems more willing to acknowledge the shadow side of the sunny Southern California dream and to struggle to make peace with it.

ORIENTATION

Orange County's 42-mile coastline arches to the southeast like a sliver of moon, from the San Gabriel River and Seal Beach in the north to San Clemente and San Diego County in the south. Seal Beach suns itself on the ocean edge of what once were vast coastal wetlands, spongy salt-grass marshes that provided prime bird habitat. Then came the discovery of oil; the region's oil and housing industries devised new and better land uses. Small oil derricks still dot the landscape, as they have for some time. The major 1920s community celebration in Huntington Beach just to the south, for example, was the Black Gold Days Festival, held over Labor Day weekend. In these times, though, Huntington Beach worships the ocean—specifically, spectacular surf, the draw for international surf competitions and associated tourist trade.

Just south of the Santa Ana River begins Newport Beach, premier yachting port for Southern California since the 1920s. Not so staid these days, now the symbolic center of Orange County's high-rolling, high-living lifestyle, the Newport Beach area embraces an upscale collection of bayside communities including Balboa Island, Lido Isle, and Corona del Mar. The next major city down coast is Laguna Beach, a low-key artists' enclave in the early 1900s but renowned today for its high-rent real estate and highly unusual ode to the arts, the Pageant of the Masters. The coast saunters south past Laguna Niguel, one of Orange County's newest cities, then Dana Point, the small yacht-harbor community named for Richard Henry Dana, Jr., author of *Two Years Before The Mast*. Taking leave of Harvard University in the 1830s, in hopes that the sea air might improve his health, Dana and shipmates came ashore here strictly for commerce—to load tanned cattle hides from the nearby mission at San Juan Capistrano. Famous for the expectation that swallows will return (as the song goes)

equally lathered over the issue of illegal immigration. And, all denial aside, Orange County does have smog, as well as nightmarish freeway congestion. But it also has culture with a capital "C," symbolized by the spectacular Performing Arts Center adjacent (you guessed it) to its most famous shopping mall.

Born into endless summer, freed from community by freeways, and taught to believe that here, life can be all things to all people, Orange County and Los Angeles are actually very much alike. But Los Angeles is older, more experienced. Like a village elder trying to atone for the folly of

every year on March 19th, the mission is a worth-while destination any day of the year.

Last stop along the Orange County coast is San Clemente, where the onetime Western White House compound of ex-President Richard M. Nixon is visible from the state beach. For the details of Nixon's astonishing journey from Orange County homeboy to national and international leader, head for northeastern Orange County and the town of Yorba Linda, site of the Richard Nixon Library and Birthplace.

California's Pacific Coast Highway (PCH), or Hwy. 1, is Orange County's scenic route—running almost the entire length of the coastline before merging with I-5 just east of Dana Point in the south county. A multilane route most of the way, PCH is typically a slog—slowed like everything else in Southern California by too much traffic. And most people here do drive, usually one to a vehicle. To join them on a temporary basis, contact the visitor bureau for a current listing of area car rental agencies.

Seal Beach to Huntington Beach

SEAL BEACH

Enticed by more famous Orange County beach towns, tourists tend to miss Seal Beach—a neat-as-a-pin neighborhood with a 1950s' bohemian feel, an attractive downtown, and plenty of pom-pom palms. The beach itself is wide and sandy and refreshingly noncommercial, offering views of both ocean and the man-made offshore island featuring California's first offshore oil well, drilled in 1954.

At the end of Main Street is the **Seal Beach Pier,** one of the longest along the coast (1,865 feet) and a focal point of local life since its original construction in 1906. Crown jewel of the "Jewel City" amusement complex, the pier once sported 50 giant rainbow-making "scintillator" lamps to enhance night-time ocean swimming. Jewel City itself featured a roller coaster shipped down from San Francisco after the 1915 World's Fair. Movie stars and special events, such as stunt fliers, also happily attracted the crowds. Eventually the Depression dragged everything down into a local variation of Sin City—a moral dive that righted itself during World War II.

Enjoy Main Street. The **Red Car Museum,** with a Pacific Electric red car as its focal point, offers a peek into area history at the corner of Electric and Main. Open 1–4 P.M. on the second and fourth Saturday of each month. Particularly inspiring among the shops and galleries is an outpost of **Heifer International,** upstairs at 330 Main, 562/431-4849, www.heifer.org, one of *Forbes* magazine's 10 "gold star" charities, this

one dedicated to lifting the world's people out of poverty with donations of goats, sheep, chickens, pigs, and cows—livestock wealth that can create sustainable family economies. (FYI, a share of a goat is just $10.) Stop nearby for ice cream or cappuccino; bikini and surfboard shops and beach-style boutiques offer more expensive distractions. After the beach and a stroll on the pier, to stay longer take in a movie at the landmark **Bay Theatre,** 340 Main, 562/431-9988, beloved for its eclectic art-house films and its magnificent Wurlitzer pipe organ.

If the beach scene here gets too crowded, just south are **Surfside Beach** and **Sunset Beach,** quieter areas with public beaches and lifeguard towers. (Stroll. Bike it. Take the bus. If driving, park along either North or South Pacific Avenues, parallel to PCH.) Sunset Beach is also prime departure point for Huntington Harbour kayakers. **Malibu Ocean Sports,** 16910 Pacific Coast Hwy., 562/592-0800, http://malibuoceansports.com, rents (and sells) its own Malibu Kayaks, singles starting as low as $8 an hour, $25 per day.

For a fine bike ride, the **bikeway** at Bolsa Chica State Beach, just south, begins at Warner and runs south all the way to Huntington State Beach, about five miles. Heading north by bike is not much fun, with cyclists competing with cars on PCH all the way to Belmont Shores (Long Beach).

For more information about the area, contact the **Seal Beach Chamber of Commerce,** located next to city hall at 201 Eighth St., Ste. 120, 562/799-0179, www.sealbeachchamber.com, open 10 A.M.–4 P.M. on weekdays.

Accommodations and Food

If you think this laid-back, blast-from-the-past beach town is the perfect place to park yourself permanently, think again. At last report Seal Beach had Orange County's highest rents. You also won't find much here in the way of budget accommodations. Still, if the 1850s are more your style than the 1950s, consider a stay at the two-story **₪ Seal Beach Inn and Gardens**, a stylish and secluded 23-room bed-and-breakfast close to the beach at 212 Fifth St., 562/493-2416 or 800/443-3292, www.sealbeachinn.com. Guest rooms and suites, some with kitchens, refrigerators, and whirlpool baths, are furnished with antiques and named after flowers—many of which you'll find here, part of the riot of color blooming forth from every container, cranny, and nook. There's a small swimming pool, too. Rates are $150–250, depending upon type of room; there's also a penthouse suite.

Head to the pier for bomber-size burgers and a view of the oil wells. *The* place forever—or at least since the Seal Beach Grand Old Opry House gave up the ghost—is flashy diner-style **Ruby's** at the end of the pier, 562/431-7829, where you'll find all kinds of patties, including chicken, turkey, and veggie, plus great shakes and other tasty pleasures from the past. Breakfast is good, too. (And if you miss it here, Ruby's is almost an institution along the coast and elsewhere in Orange County.) **Nick's Deli** at 223 Main, 562/598-5072, is a kosher deli famous for its breakfast burritos. Also locally popular for breakfast is the homey, long-running **Harbor House Cafe** on PCH (at Anderson) just south of town in unincorporated Sunset Beach, 562/592-5404, open 24 hours, famous for its omelettes, almost as famous for the gallery of movie stars on knotty-pine walls.

The most popular all-around hangout in Seal Beach is **Hennessey's Tavern**, 140 Main, 562/598-4419, one of a small chain of Irish-style pubs serving breakfast, lunch, and dinner in addition to beer, here overflowing with surfers, hippies, country music, and the scent of suntan lotion.

If seafood is your passion, though, head for **₪ Walt's Wharf,** 201 Main, 562/598-4433, where the motto is: "If it's fresher, it's still swimming." Walt's offers great creativity with whatever's in season—the daily-changing menu includes such things as oak-grilled Pacific snapper—but is equally talented with surprises like oak-grilled artichokes and quesadillas. There's an oyster bar here, too, plus a good selection of imported beers. (Full bar, wide-ranging wine list.) Open daily for lunch and dinner. Try to come at an off time, though; no reservations are taken, and it can be a wait.

₪ BOLSA CHICA STATE BEACH AND RESERVE

Stretching south three miles from Seal Beach in the north to the Huntington Beach Pier, broad, sandy Bolsa Chica State Beach is in one sense an extension of what you'll find farther south at Huntington State Beach—thousands of paved parking places, restrooms with showers, fire rings, snack stands, and all. The primary differences? This is a better bet for beginning surfers than Huntington Beach. Also, Bolsa Chica offers 50 RV campsites ($25–39, depending on location and season). The main parking lot entrance is on PCH about 1.5 miles south of Warner Avenue. Due to recent fee increases, day use (parking fee) is around $10. For more information about Bolsa Chica, call 714/377-5691. To reserve a campsite, call ReserveAmerica at 800/444-7275 or see www.reserveamerica.com.

In many ways more fascinating than the beach is 1100-acre **Bolsa Chica Ecological Reserve** across PCH. Not exactly pristine, Bolsa Chica is an ongoing oilfield restoration project; some areas are not open to the public. Bolsa Chica, one of the county's few remaining wetland tracts, provides seasonal habitat for many species of waterfowl and shorebirds, including the endangered California least tern. In fact, in the past decade an official 321 out of Orange County's 420 bird species were spied here. Amigos de Bolsa Chica, a local citizens' group, is responsible for preventing the total loss of Bolsa Chica to another marina and housing development after a decades-long fight. Yet aggressive new restoration plans, which involve digging a new outlet to the ocean through the state beach to re-create true tidal wetlands, are generating considerable local controversy—beyond the $63 million price tag. Other environmental groups worry that restoring species diversity at Bolsa Chica will damage beach and ocean ecology. This conundrum suggests the real lesson of Bolsa Chica is that the cost of habitat destruction truly is endless, and incalculable.

While you're here, shake that sand out of your shoes and stroll the loop trail. Free guided walks are offered on the first Saturday of the month; just show up between 9 and 10:30 A.M. Group tours are also offered, on weekdays and weekends, by advance reservation. For current information, contact **Amigos de Bolsa Chica** headquarters at 16531 Bolsa Chica St., Ste. 312, 714/840-1575, www.amigosdebolsachica.org. Come in October for Amigos' **Running is for the Birds** 5K and 10K run, an annual fundraiser. The **Bolsa Chica Land Trust,** 714/964-8170, offers its free Wetlands Table and Mesa Tour on the third Sunday of each month, 10 A.M. to noon. The **Bolsa Chica Conservancy** operates the wetlands interpretive center at 3842 Warner Ave. (near PCH), across from the fire station, 714/846-1114, www.bolsachica.org.

HUNTINGTON BEACH

If you've tried to find Surf City on a California map, put an "X" right here, on the once-grungy blue-collar oil town of Huntington Beach. The city has long called itself "Surfing Capital of the World" and "Surf City," the latter inspired by Jan and Dean's *Surf City USA* which was inspired by Huntington Beach. But now it's official. After some public skirmishes with Santa Cruz, that scrappy little surf city up north, Huntington Beach ended up with the Surf City trademark.

Surfers have dominated the local fauna since the 1920s. But surfing didn't become a social phenomenon even in Huntington Beach until the 1960s, when Bruce Brown of nearby Dana Point was knighted the "Fellini of foam" for *End-*

less Summer, his classic surfing film, and Dick Dale, "King of the Surf Guitar," rode the same wave to the top of the pop music charts. (Dale's sound was a total Orange County creation, since even his guitar—a Fender Stratocaster—was a local invention, thanks to Leo Fender of Fullerton.) Then came the Beach Boys, who captured the national teenage imagination and catapulted surfing into the category of popular sport. But who could foresee the Beatles? Almost overnight everyone—everyone except serious surfers—tuned into another wavelength, an entirely different cultural wave.

According to local lore, surfing was imported to Huntington Beach from Hawaii in 1907. In those days surfers were all but alone in the Orange County surf, riding 100-pound homemade redwood boards. Wood has long since given way to polyurethane, plain canvas swim trunks to neoprene wetsuits. And "mellow" has lost out to "aggro" (aggressive attitude, in the lingo) now that conditions are crowded and surfing is a multibillion-dollar international sports and fashion industry.

For current information about Surf City, contact the **Huntington Beach Conference and Visitors Bureau,** located at 301 Main St., Ste. 208, 714/969-3492 or 800/729-6232 (SAY-OCEAN), www.hbvisit.com.

Sights

Mandatory for any serious study of local history is a visit to Huntington Beach's **International Surfing Museum,** 411 Olive Ave., 714/960-3483. The spruced-up 1930s' building itself offers hidden cultural history as the onetime location of Sam Lanni's acclaimed Safari Sam's nightclub—*the* local club scene until 1985, when Sam sauntered off to hunt new challenges. Among the oldies but goodies collected inside are vintage surfboards, of course, including Batman's board from the original movie. Also here: the cornerstone from the original 1903 pier, and the bust of Duke Kahanamoku once on display at the foot of the pier. Famed Hawaiian swimmer and four-time Olympic winner, Kahanamoku was 20 years old in 1911 when he and his friend George Freeth surfed local beaches—introducing the sport to California, according to local lore—on the way to the 1912 Olympic games. The museum is open (small fee) noon–5 P.M., daily in summer and Wed.–Sun. in winter. From March through October, show up on Sundays 1–2 P.M. for the free Surfin' Sundays authentic surf band concert series.

Yet there *was* life before surfing, even in Huntington Beach. The best place to explore that life is the **Newland House** at 19820 Beach Blvd. (at Adams Avenue), 714/962-5777, a Victorian farmhouse included on the National Register of Historic Places. The house and gardens have been meticulously refurbished; many of the 19th-century furnishings are original family pieces. If you think recorded music began with compact discs, check out the working Victrola here. The Newland House is open Wednesday and Thursday 2–4:30 P.M., and on weekends noon–4 P.M. Friendly, informative guides are available for tours. Small admission.

Also worth a stop, if something special's going on, is the cultural focal point of local redevelopment—the **Huntington Beach Art Center,** 538 Main, 714/374-1650, which offers gallery shows, traveling exhibitions, and studio space for artists-in-residence programs, plus sponsors a multitude of community arts education programs.

Surfing

More than 14 million people do Huntington Beach every year, most just day-tripping. It's tough to find the skurfy surf-rat bar scenes and seedy low-rent storefronts of yore, though. They're all but gone—replaced in the 1980s and '90s by a strategically redeveloped business and tourism district with a crisp California-Mediterranean style. Huntington Beach figured that spiffing up the neighborhood might attract a different crowd—people inclined to spend more money than surfers typically do, thereby increasing sales tax revenues. Subsequent downtown redevelopment involved razing seven of nine city blocks and ponying up large public subsidies for developers—investments that haven't entirely paid off yet.

From the point of view of history-minded surfers, there went the neighborhood.

But even with redevelopment, surfing is still the main event in Huntington Beach. Annual competitions include the famed late July/August **U.S. Open of Surfing,** sponsored by Honda and O'Neill and also featuring Soul Bowl skateboarding and BMX bike competitions. In September comes the long-running annual freestyle **Summer Surf Contest.** Come in late May for the **AVP Pro Beach Volleyball Tournament.** If battling the sun-crazed crowds during big-time competition is unappealing, you'll find many smaller, more neighborly events staged throughout the year. Particularly invigorating every January 1 is the annual **Huntington Beach Polar Bear Plunge,** sponsored by the local Rotary Club. Comparatively tame adventures include the February **Kite Festival,** the late March **A Taste of Huntington Beach** wine and food fest, and June's annual **Huntington Beach Pier Swim.** If you like crowds—up to 250,000 people—come for the huge **Fourth of July Parade,** the largest parade west of the Mississippi River. Also quite popular is October's famed **Huntington Beach Sand Castle Festival.** Come in December to see decorated boats cruise Huntington Harbour during the **Cruise of Lights.**

Beaches

The city beach or **Main Beach** starts in the north at Goldenwest, saunters past the Huntington Beach Pier—itself a seaward extension of Main Street—and then meanders south, merging at Beach Boulevard (south of Main) with **Huntington State Beach.** The state beach stretches south another two miles to just beyond Brookhurst, at the Santa Ana River and Newport Beach border. Dogs aren't allowed on local beaches except—on a leash—at **Dog Beach,** an area just west of Goldenwest at Pacific Coast Highway.

The pier area is Huntington's most famous and challenging surfing zone, but the state beach is the stuff of surfing movies—one of the widest, whitest expanses of sand you'll see this side of the Colorado Desert. In summer, and on almost any hot-weather weekend, plan to arrive quite early to stake out territory for your beach towel. Aside from sunbathing, swimming, surfing, and

GRUNION RUN FREE, SO WHY CAN'T WE?

It's a live sex show, yet almost innocent, even wholesome—and certainly educational. This particular procreation education usually begins after midnight. Sometimes shining small flashlights to show the way, people suddenly dash onto the beach, giggling and grabbing—for grunion, those silvery Southern California sexpots of the smelt persuasion.

Human voyeurs come down to the beach not only to watch the frenzied fish but also to catch them—literally—in the act. The hunt seems unsporting, since the grunion are, after all, deeply distracted. Without the aid of nets, window screens, kitchen sieves, and other illegal devices, however, grabbing grunion is actually a challenge. Grunion fisherfolk, optimistically armed with buckets as well as flashlights, can use only their bare hands. And grunion are slippery, like long, wriggling bars of soap. They're also rather sly. No matter what tide charts may say, grunion never show up exactly when and where they're predicted, sometimes skipping the days, hours, and locales people expect. Sometimes just a few roll in with the surf, sometimes thousands. Grunion seem to be more patient even than surfers, content to flip and flop around in the water as long as necessary, waiting for the right wave.

For many years the "grunion run," strictly a Southern California phenomenon, was thought to be some form of moonstruck romance. Much to the delight of local romantics, it was commonly believed that the fish swam ashore during spring and summer simply to fin-dance in the moonlight.

Scientists established in 1919, however, that nature was quite purposeful. The way it really works is this: After dark, near both the new and full moons but after high tide has started to recede, wave after wave of grunion surf onto local beaches. Each wave's "dance" takes 30 seconds or less. Females burrow into the sand, dorsal fin-deep, to lay their eggs (about 2,000 each) while the males circle seductively, fertilizing the roe. All parental responsibility thus discharged, the grunion catch the next wave and head back out to sea. About two weeks later, at the next moon-heightened high tide, the young 'n' grunion hatch and are washed out into the big, big watery world.

Fairly remote beaches all along the coast, from Santa Barbara south, are good bets for the grunion grab. Prime possibilities in Orange County include dark stretches of beaches at or near Bolsa Chica, Huntington Beach, Laguna Beach, Dana Point, and San Clemente.

March through August are peak grunion-running periods. Grabbing grunion is against the law in April and May, however, to allow the species some spawning success. And anyone over age 16 must have a California fishing license—available at most local bait and sporting goods shops, along with tide charts, tall tales, and free advice.

---

just bummin' around, beaches around here are known for very serious volleyball. They're also popular for picnicking and the peaceable pursuit of surf fishing and cycling. Facilities include countless paved parking spaces, wheelchair access, restrooms with cold showers and dressing rooms, picnic tables, stores and snack stands, even fire rings for after-dark beach parties—the happening scene, especially near the pier. And the lifeguards mean it when they tell you to quit doing whatever you're doing.

For beach parties, be aware that the curfew is 10 P.M. (strictly enforced). No camping is allowed. At last report all-day parking for the city beach (at Beach Boulevard) was $9 (lower in winter), and $12 for the state beach, thanks to recent state parks fee increases. Or bring lots of quarters and try metered parking on the north side of the pier, $1.50 per hour. Of course if you park elsewhere and walk, the beach is free. Parking lots are accessible from PCH at Magnolia, Newland, Huntington, and Main. For current information about the state beach, call 714/536-1454; for city beach info, call 714/536-5281.

Huntington Beach Pier

In 1904 the city was officially christened Huntington Beach after Henry Huntington, the fellow responsible for extending the Pacific Electric Railroad out this way. But the first pier here was built in 1903, when Huntington Beach was still called Pacific City and still hoping to become the West Coast rival to Atlantic City. In 1914 the original was replaced with a concrete pier, the first ever built in the U.S.—bearing some resemblance to the brand-new pier you'll see today, opened to great public fanfare in 1992. The new, improved, pedestrian-friendly Huntington Beach Pier, 12 feet taller than the original and 1,856 feet long, is still the place for watching sunsets and daring surfers. Open daily 5 A.M. to midnight, the pier's fishing is a strong local tradition. Another link in the Ruby's dining chain anchors the pier's ocean end. For other dining and diversions, there are good choices at the foot of the pier, like Duke's and Chimayo. Or head across PCH to Main Street. Unveiled in 1998, **Pier Plaza** amphitheater at the foot of the pier hosts community, cultural, and sporting events—including Orange County's only regular outdoor music series, held on weekends May through October.

Dwight's, 714/536-8083, on the beach just south of the pier, is the place to go for almost any kind of rental, including beach chairs, boogie boards, bikes, and in-line skates. (For rentals, bring a driver's license.) Just north of the pier is the **Kite Connection,** 407 PCH, 714/536-3630, which sells and rents "sport kites" (lessons are free) and also offers yo-yos.

For surfing lessons, contact local surf shops. Most offer beginner and intermediate lessons, if not advanced. **Corky Carroll's Surf School,** headquartered at 624 20th St., 714/969-3959, www.surfschool.net, is open for lessons (at Bolsa Chica State Beach) from May through October. One-hour group lessons (one hour of instruction plus an hour of in-the-water practice) start at $35 per person per day. A week of half-day lessons is $125, full-day lessons, $250—plus weekly students get a photo op with Corky Carroll, celebrated surfing icon who also writes a column for the *Orange County Register* and often entertains the crowds at Duke's Surf City when he's in town. (Sing along with *Tan Punks on Boards,* anyone?) Inquire about surfing summer camp and private lessons. And if you're looking for an excuse to head south, Corky has another school in Costa Rica.

Accommodations

Best bet for budget travelers (especially surfers) is the **Colonial Inn Youth Hostel,** just blocks from the beach, housed in a circa-1903 three-story colonial at 421 Eighth St., 714/536-3315, www.huntingtonbeachhostel.com. Opt for a bed in one of several communal rooms or more private accommodations. Spacious guest kitchen, TV room, laundry facilities. Rates start at $20 per bed; private rooms (doubles) are $46. Extras include backyard barbecues and sunbathing decks. Curfew here is 11 P.M., but you can rent a late key.

Huntington Beach offers more reasonably priced choices than most beach towns—contact the visitor bureau for a broad listing—but most of the better motel deals are inland along Beach Boulevard. Comfortable, reasonable, and right across the highway from the beach is the small **Sun 'n' Sands Motel,** 1102 PCH (five blocks north of the pier, between Main and Goldenwest), 714/536-2543, www.sunnsands.com, with all the basics plus pool and free movies, cable TV. Rates are $100–150.

New star in the galaxy of upscale Orange County coastal hotels is the four-story, villa-style **Hyatt Regency Huntington Beach Resort & Spa,** practically on the beach at 21500 Pacific Coast Highway. The Hyatt boasts 517 guest rooms, 57 suites, three onsite restaurants, two bars, retail shops, pool, and the 20,000-square-foot Pacific Waters Spa. There's even a pedestrian bridge arching over PCH, leading right to the beach. Summer rates start at $200–250, but ask about off-season specials and packages. For more information and reservations call 714/698-1234 or 800/633-7313 (U.S. and Canada) or see www.huntingtonbeach.hyatt.com. Another pillar of downtown redevelopment is the stylish **Hilton Waterfront Beach Resort,** scraping the sky and otherwise looming over Main Beach at 21000 PCH, 714/845-8000 or 800/822-7873, www.hilton.com. Beyond the stunning lobby, with its waterfalls and tropical plants, the Waterfront offers 12 stories of ocean-view rooms across from the beach, balmy palm landscaping, pretty pool area, tennis courts, fitness center, and the Palm Court and Surf Hero restaurants. Summer rates are $200 and up in summer.

Scheduled to open downtown in 2004 is **The Strand** on Fifth Street near Main—more shops and a Residence Inn. Also in the pipeline: the **Pacific City** development, with still more hotel rooms and shops.

Food

The **Huntington Beach Certified Farmers' Market,** 714/573-0374, the place to pick up farm-fresh produce, herbs, and flowers, runs 1 P.M.–dusk at Pier Plaza, PCH at Main Street.

Some of the traditional surf scene's most beloved hangouts survive, much to everyone's post-redevelopment relief. **The Sugar Shack,** 714/536-0355, still stands, for example, a funky little café at 213 Main, the place *everybody* goes, for more than 25 years. The Shack serves surfer-sized breakfast starting at 5 A.M., juicy burgers and such at lunch and early dinner. Open until 4 P.M. most days, until 8 P.M. on Wednesdays. Or try **Dwight's at the Beach,** a beach beacon since 1932 one block south of the pier on the board-walk, 714/536-8083, famous for burgers and those cheese strips with secret hot sauce. Also everybody's favorite, wherever you find it in Orange County, along the southern L.A. coast, and elsewhere, is **Wahoo's Fish Tacos,** 120 Main St., 714/536-2050. A Wahoo's Fish of the Day or Banzai Burrito will fill you up just fine—and deliciously—for under $5. Fun **Duke's,** upstairs from Chimayo at the foot of the pier, Main and PCH, 714/374-6446, is named not for John Wayne but for Hawaii's four-time Olympic champion and "father of surfing" Duke Kahanamoku. Starters include crab and macadamia nut wontons, Sharky's Seafood Bowl ("fresh fish and anything else left in the net"), and panko dipped calamari. What's on the entrée menu depends on what's freshest but count on fish and chips, fish tacos, coconut shrimp, and sesame glazed salmon. Open for lunch, dinner, and Sunday brunch.

For healthy vegetarian, the place is **Mother's Market and Kitchen** next to the Newland House at 19770 Beach Blvd., 714/963-6667, where breakfast, lunch, and dinner are served daily, 9 A.M.-9:30 The market here is well worth a wander, too, selling fresh produce, kitchen gadgets, and natural cosmetics.

A popular locals' choice is the **Park Bench Cafe** in Huntington Central Park, 17732 Goldenwest (at Slater), 714/842-0775, especially enjoyable on a glorious sunny day—and most famous recently for the addition of its special Canine Cuisine menu, a bone tossed to patrons also visiting the neighborhood "bark park." Doggie selections include the Hot Diggity Dog (hot dog on a bun) and the Wrangler Roundup (ground turkey patty). Humans shouldn't fear that the place has gone to the dogs, however. Dogs and their people dine only on the perimeter of the patio, on the lawn. Breakfast and lunch are served daily except Monday (closed).

But don't miss **Tosh's Mediterranean Cuisine and Bakery,** 16871 Beach Blvd., 714/842-3315, where you can pack a special picnic basket or sit down for marvelous Greek and Turkish fare at either lunch or dinner (seafood and vegetarian selections also available). Very good value if you're ravenous, since bread, soup, and salad are served with meals. For good sushi and such, try **Matsu Japanese Restaurant, Steakhouse, and Sushi Bar** across from the Friendship Inn at 18035 Beach Blvd. (at Talbert), 714/848-4404.

The casual yet glamorous 1940s Shanghai-style **Red Pearl Kitchen,** 412 Walnut Ave. 714/969-0224, is the esteemed sibling of Aubergine in Newport Beach and Costa Mesa's Troquet. Rather than exquisite French, the Pearl serves up a tasty Californian take on Southeast Asian fare—such things as hot chili crusted calamari, black-pepper jumbo prawns, and Korean charbroiled pork. Do try the jasmine rice. Live music, too, at least some nights; call for current details. BTW: To stay in the mood, court the retro after-dinner muse at the **Martini Blues** supper club in the Vons shopping center, 5874 Edinger Ave. (near Springfield), 714/840-2129, www.martiniblues.com. The Martini serves up 1940s "elegance without arrogance," and live blues to boot, in both the Legends Room and Celebrity Room. So come on—dress up and get down! Karaoke and comedy, too. Call or see the website for the current calendar.

Immensely popular for stylish seafood, from seafood cocktails and King Crab legs to surf and turf, David Wilhelm's **Chimayo at the Beach,**

315 Pacific Coast Hwy., 714/374-7273, also serves up some primo outdoor dining at the foot of the pier. The exotic cocktails alone are enough to make your head spin. Open for lunch, dinner, and Sunday brunch.

Airy, inviting, dinner-only **Baci,** 18748 Beach Blvd. (at Ellis), 714/965-1194, is quite good—some say the best, locally—for Italian, and reasonably priced as well. Choices include an impressive variety of risotto, pasta, fish, chicken, and meat selections. Chateaubriand and a six-sauce beef fondue are house specialties. The very good continental **Palm Court** restaurant at the Waterfront Hilton, 714/960-7873, is also quite popular—casual during the day but dress-up dining with a view come nightfall. Top of the food chain at the Hyatt is **The Californian,** 714/698-1234.

Newport Beach and Vicinity

Postsuburbia assumes the supremacy of the new. In most parts of Southern California, for example, tradition dictates that at the first sign of aging either a bulldozer or cosmetic surgeon be called in. That said, even Orange County has history. And Newport Beach is a good place to start looking for it.

After native peoples were safely corralled at the missions, the land now known as Newport Beach was originally included in the Rancho Santiago de Santa Ana, granted by the Spanish government in 1810 to Juan Peralta and Jose Antonio Yorba. In 1837 the Mexican government gave the land to Jose Sepulveda as part of his 47,000-acre Rancho San Joaquin. On early maps the upper reaches of what is now Newport Bay were identified as Bolsa de San Joaquin (Pocket or Bay of San Joaquin) or Bolsa de Guigara (Bay with High Banks). The as-yet-unformed harbor area was poetically described as Cienega de los Ranos (Frog Swamp) and Cienega de San Joaquin (San Joaquin Swamp). The modern name, La Puerta Nueva (The New Port) came in the 1870s, with the construction of a livestock/supply loading chute, wharf, and warehouse.

Now a nouveau-riche niche with a nautical theme, in the 1920s and '30s Newport Beach

accessible Corona del Mar State Beach

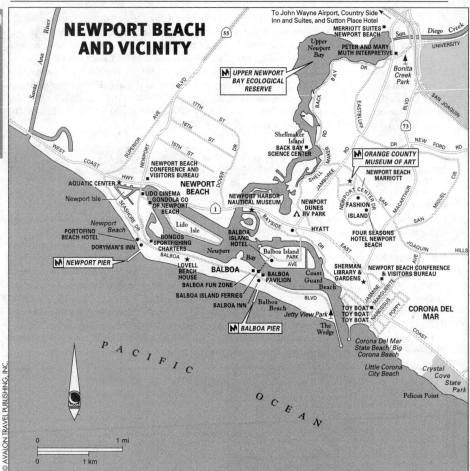

was the preferred seaside escape for the old-money minions from Los Angeles. (In California "old money," like all other things, is relative.) Henry E. Huntington made it all possible with the extension of the Pacific Electric Railroad to Newport Bay. And close-to-home adventure continued outward from Newport, the cat's meow being the ferryboat daytrip to Catalina Island. Once the shallow harbor was dredged, landfill islands, yachting marinas, and summer homes starting popping up all over the place.

Famous former residents include John Wayne, Shirley Temple, George Burns and Gracie Allen,

even Roy Rogers and Dale Evans. Celebrities come and go, though. In the end the truly astounding thing about Newport Beach is the price paid here for social status, reflected most obviously in the value of both real estate and boat slips. A few million will buy little more than a modest beach bungalow with no yard, no parking, and no rest from the daily summer struggle against nightmarish tourist traffic. Some of the luxury yachts on display in Newport Harbor carry equally phenomenal price tags. And some people would sell their very souls just for the chance to drop anchor in one of the 10,000 slips

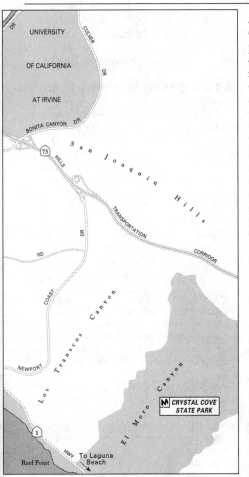

here, *the* high-price, high-prestige California yacht harbor.

Go figure.

Of course the *weather* is quite nice, year-round. For those who track the ever-changing local identity of California's Hwy. 1, or Pacific Coast Highway, as it slides south along the coast, here it's called West Coast Highway until it crosses the channel on the west side of the harbor at lower Newport Bay, and East Coast Highway on the east side. For more information on the area, contact the **Newport Beach Conference and Visitors Bureau,** 110 Newport Center Dr.,

Ste. 120, 949/719-6100 or 800/942-6278 (94-COAST) in the U.S. and Canada, www.new portbeach-cvb.com. For information on adjacent Costa Mesa, contact the **Costa Mesa Conference and Visitor Bureau,** P.O. Box 5071, Costa Mesa, CA 92628, 714/384-0493 or 800/399-5499, www.costamesa-ca.com.

SIGHTS AND RECREATION

Despite its high-priced harbor and hotels, keep in mind that Newport Beach is still more residential area than tourist destination. The unmistakable aroma of money, money, money is often aloft on the sea breeze, but just plain folks still find plenty to do here. Newport Beach is just so darned *pleasant.*

Hold that thought when you're trapped in traffic on Pacific Coast Highway or desperately trying to snare a parking place.

Parking is such a nightmare, particularly near the college-student scene at Newport Pier, that touring the area on foot is truly a stress-reducing alternative. If hiking long urban distances isn't feasible, cycling might be—so bring bikes if you've got them, or plan to rent.

Exploring Newport Harbor from its watery underside isn't all that pleasurable, given the sheer numbers of boats and people. The exception to the rule is Corona del Mar State Beach, with offshore reefs worth exploring. Even better is Crystal Cove State Park between Newport and Laguna Beach, an underwater marine sanctuary with good diving. Laguna Beach is actually closer to Crystal Cove, but if you're based in Newport rent snorkeling or scuba gear (certification required for divers) at the **Aquatic Center,** 4537 W. Coast Hwy. (at Balboa), 949/650-5440, www .aquaticcenter.net, a well-established enterprise that also offers lessons.

The best way to tour Newport Harbor is by boat. Unusual is a one-hour evening gondola tour with **Gondola Company of Newport,** headquarters at Lido Marina Village, 3400 Via Oporto, Suite 102B, 714/675-1212, www .gondolas.com. Rates start at $75. (Dress warmly.) **Watts on the Harbor,** 949/291-1953, www.wattsontheharbor.com, offers two-hour

Duffy electric boat tours (lunch, brunch, dessert, and hors d'eouvre options) for $75. For the classic harbor cruise—during which you'll find out just which celebrities lived where, et cetera—try **Catalina Passenger Service** and its *Pavilion Paddy*, a two-story Mississippi-style river boat docked at the Balboa Pavilion. In addition, CPS offers trips to and from Catalina Island as well as whale-watching tours. For current information call 949/673-5245 or 800/830-7744.

Most whale-watching and sportfishing tours also shove off from the pavilion. **Bongos Sportfishing Charters,** 2140 Newport Blvd., 949/673-2810, offers whale trips from December through March and sportfishing year-round, as does **Davy's Locker,** 400 Main in Balboa, 949/673-1434, and **Newport Landing Sportfishing,** 309

Palm St., 949/675-0550. For information on private exclusive yacht charters, for total privacy and/or to accommodate large groups, contact the visitors bureau for referrals.

Orange County Museum of Art

Marooned in a business park near Fashion Island is the Orange County Museum of Art, originally known as the Newport Harbor Art Museum, 850 San Clemente Dr., 949/759-1122, www.ocma.net, nationally acclaimed by the late 1980s for its contemporary California art collection and cutting-edge special exhibits.

Particularly striking outside are this museum's red "gem," a sculpture by Jonathan Borofsky, a rusting six-foot iron cube protruding from the building, and the outdoor sculptures. Particu-

THE BOWERS MUSEUM OF CULTURAL ART

That the largest museum in Orange County is dedicated to preserving the art and artifacts of the world's indigenous peoples is quite fitting, given the county's increasing cultural diversity.

Easily accessible from Newport Beach, the Bowers Museum of Cultural Art in Santa Ana is as expansive in scope as it is small in size. The appealing 1932 Spanish mission–style building downtown, complete with courtyard, was not only recently renovated but expanded, tripling exhibit space to more than 19,000 square feet. Still, the territory is too tight for permanent display of the museum's 85,000-piece collection. So the Bowers Museum is known for its imaginative special shows, such as Tibet: Treasures from the Roof of the World, African Icons of Power, Perú Before the Inca, Art of the Himalayas; and River of Gold: Pre-Columbian Treasures from Sitio Conte. There's always a reason to come back.

Among permanent exhibits are Arts of Native America—art and artifacts from various North American cultures, including intricate beadwork from Plains cultures and exquisite Pomo basketry from Northern California—and Realm of the Ancestors, representations of the argonaut cultures of Southeast Asia and Pacific Oceania. Ancient stone art and ceramics of pre-Columbian Mexico

and Central America are collected in Vision of the Shaman, Song of the Priest.

Also permanent is California Legacies, both tribute to Orange County's diverse cultural heritage and homage to the museum's humble beginnings as an odd collection of local memorabilia. (The museum's first show—recently repeated—was a collection of dolls donated by children.) Starting in the 1970s the Bowers Museum began to supplement its collection of regional ceramics and orange crate labels in an aggressive acquisitions program emphasizing pre-Columbian and Native American culture.

The museum's special evening and weekend events, such as Spirits of the Rainforest and California Folk Art, are usually well worth the trip.

Family fun at the Bowers Museum centers around is 11,000-square-foot **Kidseum,** an adjunct facility to "promote cultural understanding among the peoples of Africa, the Americas, and the Pacific Rim." Among the Kidseum's unique attractions: the storytelling room, the theater, the art laboratory, and exhibit space for children's art from around the world.

The Bowers Museum "partnership"—the institution is owned by the city of Santa Ana, managed and governed by a private, nonprofit Board of

larly striking inside are the rotating exhibits—and here, even the impressive permanent collection rotates. Recent exhibits have included Girls' Night Out, showcasing women in photography and video, Views and Visions: Exploring the California Landscape, the Zine Scene, and Light Screens: The Leaded Glass of Frank Lloyd Wright. Docents offer free tours of the permanent collection and current exhibitions daily at 1 P.M., on weekends at noon and 2 P.M., and at other times during major exhibits. The museum is open Tues.–Sun. 10 A.M.–5 P.M. (closed Monday). Admission is $7 adults, $5 students/seniors, free for children under 12. Admission to rare exhibits, such as 2004's *Picasso to Pollock,* may be substantially more. Don't miss the onsite café and great museum shop—just the place to find that elusive art book or oddball gift. There's a second, free, mini-outpost of OCMA at South Coast Plaza, at the Bristol Street Entrance, near the Carousel Court.

Depending on your artistic leanings, folks at OCMA may be able to guide you to the most likely area art galleries.

ON THE BALBOA PENINSULA

First and often last stop on a people's tour is the Balboa Peninsula, a long, arthritic finger of sand pointing south from **Newport Boulevard,** the seaward end of the line for the Costa Mesa (55) Freeway. You can also get here from the Coast Highway and **Balboa Boulevard.** Humanity is so well-established here, the entire harbor so sheltered

Governors, and financed with contributions from the private sector—also sponsors an impressive community education program. Unusual, too, is the Bowers's international cultural art travel program (members only).

Plan a stop at the museum shop for its unusually thoughtful array of books, jewelry, and one-of-a-kind art from around the world. Proceeds support the museum and its programs.

Do enjoy the Bowers Museum international culinary offerings. New at the Bowers since late 2000, replacing David Wilhelm's Southwesternesque Topaz Café as the museum's social centerpiece, is **Tangata** ("mankind" in Maori), owned and operated by renowned L.A.-area restaurateurs Joachim and Christine Splichal, of Patina and Pinot fame. Exceptional meals and memorable desserts—from pulled Caribbean spiced pork with mango barbecue sauce, tropical sambal, and sweet potato fries to fettuccini with eggplant and smoked mozzarella marinara or perhaps grilled chateau steak medallions—are not all that expensive. The indoor-outdoor Tangata is open for lunch Tues.–Sat. 11 A.M.–3 P.M. and for buffet brunch on Sunday (same hours)—the latter very popular and highly recommended. Brunch reservations are wise.

The Bowers Museum of Cultural Art, 2002 N. Main St. in Santa Ana (on Main at 20th), has free parking available in the adjacent lot (between 19th and 20th). Museum galleries are open Tues.–Sun. 11 A.M.–5 P.M. The Kidseum galleries, 1802 N. Main, are open Sat. and Sun. 10 A.M.–4 P.M. and also Thurs. 3–5 P.M. Museum admission is $14 adults, $8 seniors, and $6 for children ages 5–11 (under 5 free). For general information call the Bowers Museum at 714/567-3600 or see www.bowers.org. For tours, 714/567-3680; for museum store information, 714/567-3643. To reach the Kidseum, call 714/480-1520. For schedule information and reservations at Tangata, call 714/550-0906.

Though the Orange, Garden Grove, and Costa Mesa Freeways converge quite close to downtown Santa Ana, the easiest way to get to the Bowers Museum from the coast is via the 55 (the Costa Mesa Freeway) then the Santa Ana Freeway (I-5). From I-5 northbound, exit at 17th St. and head west four blocks to Main and turn north (right). If for some reason you're on I-5 southbound, exit at Main and turn right. (Call to verify directions; the details may change once freeway construction in the area is completed.) By bus, OCTA route 53 will get you to the Bowers.

from sea-driven storms, it's a surprise to discover that the peninsula is a geological newborn. The Balboa Peninsula didn't begin to exist until after 1825, a year of massive flooding that caused the Santa Ana River to suddenly change course and deposit sand and sediments in the harbor.

Newport Pier

The Newport Pier—about a half-mile past the highway at the ocean end of McFadden Place, between 20th and 21st Streets—was originally McFadden's Wharf, built in 1888 to accommodate the train from Santa Ana delivering produce and steamship passengers. **Newport Beach**—the actual beach by that name—stretches both west and east from the pier (this one constructed in the 1940s), which serves as madding-crowd central in summer and on most weekends.

The most historic attraction at the Newport Pier is the **Newport Dory Fishing Fleet** adjacent. Hard at it since 1891, this is the only surviving dory fleet on the West Coast. Arrive by 10 A.M. to scoop up some of the day's catch, marketed in open-air stalls. For more information on the fleet and other aspects of Newport's harbor history, stop by the **Newport Harbor Nautical Museum** at its new location in the *Reuben E. Lee* "river barge," 151 E. Coast Hwy., 949/675-8915, www.nhnm.org, open Tues.–Sun. 10 A.M.–5 P.M. In addition to the permanent displays, from impressive ship models to nautical art, expect changing exhibits such as Hooked! The Lure and Lore of Sportfishing. Free admission.

Balboa Pier

A stroll to the Balboa Pier, which juts into the ocean from Balboa's Main Street, two miles to the east, takes considerably longer—especially if you dawdle along the concrete boardwalk. Accompanied by landscaped lawn, bandstand, and palm trees, the Balboa Pier is the focal point for more placid pursuits. On most days **Balboa Beach** is relatively lonely and quiet, especially on the stretch toward the jetty. Even the ocean is quieter here, since the sandy beach falls away steeply and the waves seem to arrive from nowhere.

Downcoast is the jetty, a rocky chin protecting the harbor mouth as it inhales and exhales sail-

boats. The angle formed between Balboa Beach and the jetty is known as **The Wedge,** internationally famous for its stupendous shore breaks, locally infamous for bone-breaking bodysurfing, surfing, and swimming. (It's dangerous. No joke.) To get the big picture, head out to **Jetty View Park** at the tip of the peninsula.

Balboa

Both the pier and the **Balboa Pavilion** at 400 Main St.—originally a bathhouse cum boathouse, now de facto loading dock for boat tours—were built in 1905 by Southern California developers working overtime to attract home buyers to this otherwise desolate sandspit. (Encouraged by a generous cash donation and free railroad right-of-way, Henry E. Huntington aided their cause on July 4, 1906, when the first of his electric trolleys to Newport Beach delivered potential buyers from Los Angeles.) In the 1940s the pavilion was a big-band bandstand—home of the "Balboa" dance craze—though the nearby Rendezvous Ballroom, long gone, was the more famous venue.

Not to be missed amid the surrounding shops and schlock is the reconstructed **Balboa Fun Zone** promenade along the bay, 600 E. Bay Ave., 949/673-0408, www.thebalboafunzone.com, one of the few places left anywhere with genuine arcade-era pinball machines, skee ball, and such. For electronics addicts, video games are available. But dig that ferris wheel, those bumper cars, that merry-go-round—not to mention the Scary Dark Ride.

Adjacent to the pavilion is the three-car **Balboa Ferry,** for making the very short trip to and from Balboa Island.

Also worth appreciating is the lovely 1930 Spanish colonial **Balboa Inn** at the foot of the pier, a hotel designed by architect Walter Hagedohn, more famous for his Union Station in Los Angeles.

A still grander presence presides at W. Ocean Front and 13th Street, back toward the Newport Pier—the concrete **Lovell Beach House.** Considered one of the finest American examples of early modern architecture, it was designed in 1926 by Rudolph M. Schindler for health enthusiast Dr. Lovell. The house is suspended above the beach by columns and cantilevers, actually five poured-concrete frames. The ground level is an outdoor living area combining a fireplace with the necessities of parking, play, and washing up. The main living area above (two stories) ponders the Pacific. Sleeping balconies, once al fresco, are now enclosed—surely in recognition of the fog-chill factor—and the roof features a sunken sunbathing deck. But Bauhaus is not *your* house, so don't bother the residents.

OFF THE BALBOA PENINSULA

Not to be confused with Balboa Peninsula is **Balboa Island** just off the mainland, a buffed neighborhood of beach bungalows reached by car from W. Coast Highway and Marine Avenue. If you drive, though, you won't see much, because you'll never find a place to park. A better option—and much more fun—is coming over as a pedestrian on the nearly perpetual **Balboa Island Ferries,** 949/673-1070, a service shuttling people and automobiles (maximum capacity, three cars at a time) back and forth daily since the early 1900s. The ferries ($1.25 fare for vehicles, 50 cents per pedestrian adult) run daily—from 6:30 A.M. to midnight Sun.–Thurs., until 2 A.M. on Friday and Saturday nights—between Palm Avenue on the peninsula and Agate Avenue on the island.

"Agate," by the way, indicates another island oddity. Most cross streets are named for gems and stones—Jade, Topaz, Garnet, and Emerald.

Marine Avenue is the village boutiquery and business district, where one can also pursue simple pleasures—such as a world-famous "Balboa bar" (vanilla ice cream bars dipped in chocolate and your favorite topping) from **Dad's,** or a frozen chocolate-dipped banana from **Sugar 'n' Spice.** *The* restaurant on Balboa Island is **Amelia's,** 311 Marine Ave., 949/673-6580, known for seafood, Italian specialties, and family-run atmosphere.

Ask locals to point out the spaceship-style, copper-roofed dome home (officially named Chemosphere but locally known as Jaws) designed by famed California Modern architect

John Lautner and completed in 1980. To eyeball James Cagney's onetime island estate, head west. That's it, just offshore at the end of Park— **Collins Isle,** sticking out from the west side of Balboa Island like a sandy little toe. Like other private landfill islands scattered around the bay, **Lido Isle** to the harbor's far west—reached from the peninsula via Newport Boulevard and Via Lido—is an elite and elegant residential enclave where potentially public lawn areas are designated "private" community parks.

Corona del Mar

Gardeners enjoy the **Sherman Library and Gardens** in Corona del Mar. Here they get a thorough education in just what will grow, and grow well, in the onetime desert of Southern California. Just south of the harbor on the mainland at 2647 E. Coast Hwy. (at MacArthur Boulevard), the Sherman honors the "Pacific Southwest" in its specialized library and two-acre garden of desert and tropical plants. More tropicals, and a koi pond, are in the modern conservatory. Also here: a wheelchair-accessible "discovery garden" for the seeing-impaired. The gardens and gift shop are open 10:30 A.M.–4 P.M. daily except major holidays, the library 9 A.M.–4:30 P.M. on weekdays only (Tues.–Thurs. in winter). Small admission (free on Monday). The onsite Cáfe Jardin, 949/673-0033, serving up a nice view of the central gardens and fabulous garden-fresh French, thanks to Chef Pascal Olhats (of Pascal restaurant fame); open weekdays 11:30 A.M.–2 P.M. for lunch and (spring through fall) Sunday 10:30 A.M.–2:30 P.M. for brunch. For more information call 949/673-1880 (library), 949/673-0920 (gift shop), and 949/673-2261 (gardens), or see www.slgardens.org.

If you've been wondering Where the Toys Are, you'll find most of them at **Toy Boat Toy Boat Toy Boat,** 3331 E. Coast Hwy., 949/673-3791, www.tbtbtb.com, a classic toy store featuring everything from great horned owl hand puppets and Bling Bling Bead Kits to talking microscopes. Old-time candy counter, too.

Aside from gardens and shopping, the star attraction of Corona del Mar is half-mile-long **Corona del Mar State Beach** at the mouth of

CONSUMERISM AS CULTURE

Think of it as a theme park for consumerism, this one attracting more than 20 million visitors each year and, raking in an estimated $12.4 billion. The most notable diversion at Orange County's **South Coast Plaza** mega-mall in Costa Mesa is the mall itself. Unique in the neighborhood, though, are the sociocultural segues between art, commerce, entertainment, finance, and fine dining—Orange County's foremost foray into the culture of consumerism and consumerism as culture.

This being one of the largest-grossing retail centers in the U.S., going to South Coast Plaza typically involves spending money. But rest assured that here commerce is not crass. The preferred promotional etiquette at South Coast Plaza is to refer the mall itself as a "retail center," its shoppers as "guests."

All in all, it's hard to imagine the landscape a few short decades ago, when it was just another Orange County lima bean field.

As in other theme parks, the territory here is geographically subdivided. The center is three-story **South Coast Plaza at Bristol,** 3333 Bristol St. (between the 405 and Sunflower), with its multistory atriums and elegant decor and a surprising variety of shops anchored by Bullock's, Nordstrom, Macy's, Sears, and Robinsons-May. On the west end is **Jewel Court,** Orange County's version of Rodeo Drive, with upscale shops including Tiffany & Co., Emporio Armani, Louis Vuitton, Cartier, and Chanel. Centerpiece of **Carousel Court** on the mall's east end is—you guessed it—a turn-of-the-20th-century carousel, a fitting enticement for the Sesame Street General Store, Disney Store, Gap-Kids, and other attractions aimed at the younger set.

Then there's the single-level **South Coast Plaza Village** just east of the main mall at Sunflower and Bear Streets, and **South Coast Plaza at Bear,** north of the main mall at 3333 Bear Street, with its own eclectic array, from Abercrombie & Fitch to Adrienne Vittadini. Fairly new anchors include a huge Crate & Barrel Home Store, the chain's West Coast flagship, and a Macy's Home store. Also new is an elevated pedestrian walkway to connect the Bear and Bristol malls.

South of South Coast Plaza and Bristol is the **South Coast Plaza Town Center,** sometimes referred to as The Offices, an area bisected by Anton Blvd. and Town Center Dr.—a shimmering 96-acre orchard of bank and business office towers, visual and performing-arts venues, multiplex movie theaters, and inviting eateries.

California Scenario

The neighborhood's main action may be trafficking in commerce and consumer goods, but the main attraction is art—most of it in Town Center.

Almost perfectly hidden, wedged into the courtyard created by two black-glass business towers and the adjacent public parking lot, is an understated yet powerful exploration of the California myth—*California Scenario* by the late Isamu Noguchi, tucked away behind the Great Western Bank Building, 3200 Park Center Drive (off Anton Boulevard); parking is available in the adjacent public lot. This expansive "sculpture garden" offers much more than the term typically implies, staging separate but unified California themes with stunning directness and native-son humor. *Land Use,* for example, is a long, narrow chunk of concrete-colored granite dominating the crest of a landscaped knoll. A meandering stream flows from the tall *Water Source,* past *Desert Land,* to squat, stylized *Water Use.* Funniest of all, though, is *Spirit of the Lima Bean,* 15 dignified desert-colored boulders of decomposed granite piled up to honor South Coast Plaza's primary developers and benefactors, the Segerstrom family—perhaps only incidentally paying homage to the land's previous purpose.

Various other public sculptures—by **Henry Moore, Joan Miró, Alexander Calder, Claire Falkenstein,** and others—are scattered throughout the Town Center area, indoors and out. If you're too rushed to see them all after doing the mall, walk over to the performing arts center on Town Center Drive—take the pedestrian bridge that spans Bristol—for the stunning first-time impact of Richard Lippold's 60-foot-tall *Fire Bird,* a spectacular vision any time but especially after dark.

Also worthwhile in the arts department is the gallery inside **Bank of America,** 555 Anton. At South Coast Plaza proper, the **Laguna Art Museum** hosts a satellite gallery inside its shop at the mall's east end. Both are free.

Performing Arts

The striking, contemporary **Orange County Performing Arts Center** counts among its artistic partners the Pacific Symphony Orchestra, the Philharmonic Society of Orange County, Opera Pacific, Pacific Chorale, and the William Hall Master Chorale. The center also hosts the Los Angeles Philharmonic and touring companies, including the American Ballet Theatre, the Joffrey Ballet, and the New York City Ballet, though classical music, jazz, cabaret, and Broadway musicals predominate. Near-perfect acoustics are the hallmark of the center's 3,000-seat Segerstrom Hall. Incidentally, the center's $74 million construction tab was picked up entirely through private donations—a trend that continues with the current capital campaign for the larger **Segerstrom Center for the Arts,** which will include, across the street, the spectacular 2,000-seat **Renée and Henry Segerstrom Concert Hall** and 500-seat **Samueli Theater.** The Orange County Performing Arts Center is on Town Center Drive at Avenue of the Arts. Call 714/556-2787 for current performance and ticket information (recorded) or 714/556-2122

(administration), or see the website, www.ocpac.org. Buy tickets for most performances in advance online or through Ticketmaster, 714/740-7878, though day-of-performance seats are often available.

Destined for inclusion as part of the Segerstrom Center for the Arts is the Tony award-winning **South Coast Repertory Theater,** 655 Town Center Dr., 714/708-5500 or 714/708-5555 (tickets) or see www.scr.org. Started decades ago as a seat-of-the-pants repertory troupe, critical acclaim came along for South Coast Repertory with the brave decision to produce works by new playwrights, though not everything presented is avant-garde. The main **Segerstrom Stage** seats 507. The new, 336-seat **Julianne Argyros Stage** proscenium theater, designed by renowned architect Cesar Pelli, is part of a major recent expansion resulting in the building's sweeping new façade as well as new dressing rooms and office space. Call well in advance for current show schedule and reservations; last-minute tickets are scarce. Best bet for spur-of-the-moment attendance: matinees and midweek performances.

not a lima bean field any more!

Newport Harbor, operated by the city and framed by cliffs and the rocky jetty at the eastern harbor entrance. Offshore is crystal-clear azure ocean; underfoot, warm white sand; everywhere around, lush landscaping—the classic California postcard. It would be wonderful, too, if everyone else in Southern California weren't so determined to be here. To reach the parking lot and day-use facilities for the main beach, from the Coast Highway take Jasmine Street to Ocean Boulevard. Day use (parking) is about $10, but for the privilege of paying it, be sure to get here early. For more information, call 949/644-3151. Also hardly a secret is **Big Corona Beach** off Marguerite Avenue, where one can just sit and watch the boats pass. The secluded cove at **Little Corona Beach,** with its **tidepool reserve** (visit at low tide), is reached via Ocean Boulevard (at Poppy).

Other Newport Beaches

Back in Newport is the only "secret" beach around, the small **Coast Guard Beach** at the Harbor Master Coast Guard Station. Here you'll find a relatively peaceful stretch of sand, safe swimming, volleyball nets (bring your own ball), and picnic tables. Park on the street. The Coast Guard Beach is off the 1900 block of Bayside Drive. To get here from the highway, take Jamboree toward Balboa Island and then turn left onto Bayside.

"Bay beaches" include just about any accessible patches of sand fringing Newport Bay. One with lifeguards, volleyball nets, restrooms, showers, and some wind protection is on the peninsula's Bay Avenue between 18th and 19th Streets. Look for others at Montero and 10th Streets, and at the end of every street on Balboa Island.

UPPER NEWPORT BAY ECOLOGICAL RESERVE

Visitors quickly appreciate why the Spanish called this place "Frog Swamp," since the Upper Newport Bay Ecological Reserve or "Back Bay" is a brackish salt- and fresh-water marsh complete with cattails, pickleweed, and aromatic mudflats. The most frightening fact is that this very small preserve is the largest remaining unengineered estuary in Southern California.

The Back Bay may be small but it is a marvel—an ecologically rich Pacific Flyway sanctuary that provides shelter to about 200 bird species and 20,000-30,000 birds during the year. Two endangered species, the light-footed clapper rail and Belding's savanna sparrow (found only in Southern California), can be spotted here, along with the California brown pelican, the California least tern, and the peregrine falcon. Waterfowl abound during the Pacific Flyway migrations.

Cut off by the Coast Highway on the west and otherwise surrounded by view homes perched high on the earthy diatomaceous cliffs, the Back Bay is best appreciated on foot or by bike—bike trails span the northern stretches and follow San Diego Creek—though you can see most of it by car. Auto tour access (one-way only) is off lower Jamboree Road; turn onto Backbay Drive at the Hyatt Newporter and keep going. Parking areas are scattered along the route—so even if you're driving, pick a spot, park, and get out to see the sights in person.

From October through March, Newport Bay Friends offer free walking tours on the second Saturday of the month. Naturalist-guided walks are scheduled on the first or third Saturday of the month. Evening "marsh prowls" are also offered monthly. To appreciate the Back Bay from the water, sign up for a kayak, canoe, or solar-powered Duffy electric boat tour. You can also sign on for some serious science study. The **Back Bay Science Center,** a hands-on marine ecology education center, is at home on Shellbaker Island, open to the public only for scheduled classes and events.

The Back Bay is also accessible from the north. The heavily eroded, star-thistly perimeter is less aesthetic—this is, after all, primarily a judiciously preserved wetlands area—but otherwise wonderful for a meditative stroll up and down the bluffs.

For more Back Bay information, visit the fascinating **Peter and Mary Muth Interpretive Center,** built of recyclables—plastic bottles, scrap lumber, and such—and tucked into the bluff (on the north side) at 2301 University Dr. (corner of University and Irvine), 714/973 6820. The Muth center, open Tues.–Sun. 10 A.M.–4 P.M., isn't visible from the road, though it's an easy stroll from the parking lot. For current information about hikes, special events, and other programs, contact **Newport Bay Naturalists & Friends,** headquartered here; call 949/640-6746 or 949/923-2269, or see www.newportbay.org. For a pleasant picnic after a Back Bay adventure, head to **Bonita Creek Park** on University Drive, just one block east of the Jamboree-Eastcliff intersection.

To get here from the 405, the 55, then Hwy. 73: Exit at Irvine Avenue and head west about one mile, then turn left onto University Drive. If coming from the south via the Hwy. 73 toll road, exit the 73 at Birch then go two traffic lights to Irvine.

ENTERTAINMENT AND EVENTS

For art-house and limited-run films, the place is the Laemmle **Lido Cinema,** 3459 Via Lido, 949/673-8350, a classic and cozy one-screen theatre with comfortable seating. Pop into the Lido Diner next door for a taste of nostalgia.

To avoid the making-the-scene scene, a comfortable alternative is a coffeehouse. Something of

a surprise on the peninsula is the **Alta Cafe Warehouse and Roasting Co.,** 506 31st St. (off Newport Boulevard), 949/675-0233. The fare is simple but wholesome at breakfast, lunch, and dinner, the atmosphere relaxed and moody, the coffee blends strong and witty. (The Frank Sumatra, for example, is distinguished by its "good personality.") For entertainment, blues, jazz, and folk music are on the menu. Alta Cafe is typically open 7 A.M.-11:30 P.M. P.M., until 12:30 A.M. on Friday and Saturday nights.

Best bet for jazz, though, is the **Studio Cafe** near the Balboa Pier, 100 Main St. (at Balboa), 949/675-7760, with top-flight blues or jazz on tap nightly. It also offers a dining room and full bar, so you could do worse than to just park yourself here once the sun sets. The Sunday afternoon jam is worth a special trip. Other possibilities include David Wilhelm's romantic Paris-style **Chat Noir Jazz Lounge** and patio, not far inland in Costa Mesa at 655 Anton Blvd., 714/557-6647, serving live and house-mix jazz along with the champagne cocktails and martinis.

The seriously cool **Kitsch Bar,** in a funky strip mall at 891 Baker St. in Costa Mesa,

Christmas on Newport Harbor

714/546-8580, offers retro atmosphere (all the way back to the 1980s: basic black with accessories) and organic DJed house—yet not so loud you can't also hold a conversation. How rare is that? But there's plenty of loud, sharky action around. Get in the swim at the **Shark Club** nearby at 841 Baker, 714/751-6428, where the décor includes a 2,000-gallon shark tank, mahogany and rosewood pool tables, fireplaces, and beautiful trendoids on Thursday, Friday, and Saturday night dance nights. For more of the same go trolling through local entertainment calendars.

There are tamer diversions. If you find yourself washed ashore with the kids (or grandkids) anywhere near Fashion Island, for example, rocking out in the mall's parking lot is Orange County's outpost of the **Hard Rock Cafe**, 451 Newport Center Dr. (at San Miguel), 949/640-8844. Just look for the 40-foot-tall Fender Stratocaster—so Orange County. The usual burgers and such are served, along with hygienic exposure to rock 'n' surf memorabilia, as suitable for young rockers as for aging hipsters. Also stop by to collect T-shirts and the local version of Hard Rock's glam-rock guitar lapel pin.

Events

The most famous local event is the annual **Newport Harbor Christmas Boat Parade** wherein more sporting members of the local yachting crowd decorate their boats in lights and sometimes outlandish decorations and then cruise the harbor. During the week before Christmas, typically, the parade circumnavigates the harbor from 6:30–8:30 P.M.—beginning and ending at Collins Island—putting on quite a show for the folks assembled in restaurants and along public beaches. (Also fun at Christmas: the outrageously beautiful—and outrageously expensive—Christmas decorations at **Roger's Gardens**, 2301 San Joaquin Hills Rd., 949/640-5800.) Expect similar silliness at the theme-oriented **Character Boat Parade**, usually held in mid- to late July. Come in April for the annual **Newport Beach Film Festival**, in June for the **Newport Beach Food & Wine Festival**. The 10-day **Newport Seafest**, which includes seafaring fun as well as **A Taste of Newport**, usually begins in mid-September. Con-

tact the visitor bureau at 949/719-6100 or 800/942-6278, www.newportbeach-cvb.com, for a more complete events calendar.

ACCOMMODATIONS

In Newport Beach and elsewhere along the coast, you'll pay a premium for seaside location and ocean views. Still, most ritzier hotels cluster near the airport and area malls. It's certainly no crime to seek more modest accommodation in Costa Mesa, just inland from Newport. Contact area visitor bureaus for suggestions.

Camping

It's not cheap except by comparison. Still, the **Newport Dunes Resort** RV encampment just off Jamboree Road at 1131 Back Bay Dr., 949/729-3863, www.newportdunes.com, is exquisitely close to the harbor action. It's also practically in the Back Bay, if you're hankering for a hike or aquatic adventure. But this is more than just an RV park. It's a community—one with a "waveless" swimming lagoon, spa, pavilions, cabanas, barbecues, tiled restrooms, a rec room with large-screen TV and laundry, even a giant movie screen on the beach for family movie nights. And do try the seafood chowder at the onsite Back Bay Café. The resort even has a small marina (rental boats available) and children's playground. Bikes and in-line skates are available for rent, too. But if you're going to play here, you'll pay: Most RVers and intrepid tent campers unpack themselves onto small concrete slabs—like sardines into a can—and pay $43 and up in summer. (Camping alternatives include state park campgrounds up and down the coast.) Another possibility here is a cottage. Studio and one-bedroom beachfront cottages are $100–300 in summer, $50–150 in winter. Cottage lofts also available.

Hotels and Resorts

Big news in Newport Beach is the **M Balboa Bay Club & Resort,** a ritzy new public resort right on the water, associated with a long-running and exclusive private club. Rising up next to the bay like an Italian Renaissance palace, the Balboa nonetheless exudes tropical luxury, down to the rattan furniture and plantation shutters. Guest rooms have it all, from in-room safes, refrigerators, and coffee/tea to plush robes, satellite TV, and highspeed Internet connections. Other pluses include full spa and fitness facilities, a 150-slip marina, the first-cabin **First Cabin** restaurant, and **Dukes' Place** lounge for live jazz, named after former club member John Wayne. Rooms start at $225, suites at $750. For information and reservations, contact the Balboa Bay Resort at 1221 W. Coast Hwy., 949/645-5000 or 888/445-7153, www.balboabayclub.com.

Many of the area's up-market and luxury hotels generally do double-duty as both business and pleasure destinations, thus their locations—within easy reach of corporate business parks, major malls, and John Wayne Airport. Official rates are high; ask about specials and packages, especially for off-season weekends.

Otherwise top of the mark is the 19-story **Four Seasons Hotel Newport Beach** near Fashion Island, 690 Newport Center, 949/759-0808 or 800/819-5053 (U.S. and Canada), www.fourseasons.com, a world-class yet relaxed hotel. From the outside it looks like yet another too-tall, bewindowed box. Inside, though, it's elegant yet airy, all sand-beige and pastels. And those windows let in some grand views. Along with luxury in-room amenities and comforts, facilities here include tennis courts, a huge pool (complete with cabanas), complete fitness center, and guaranteed tee times and weekend golf packages at nearby courses. The Four Seasons even offers free mountain bikes—the better to explore the Bay. Among the several restaurants here is **Pavilion,** where people dress up for the California-style American. The Four Seasons also boasts a complete business center, not to mention full conference facilities. Rates are $250 and up.

From the outside the **Sutton Place Hotel** (formerly Le Meridien Newport Beach), 4500 MacArthur Blvd., 949/476-2001 or 800/243-4141, www.suttonplace.com, looks something like a squared-off cruise ship, this one with big windows on every deck. Inside, it's very contemporary, very Southern California, with all the expected amenities, including tennis courts, pool, and business center. Beloved at Sutton Place is the classy California-French restaurant **Accents,** where the Sunday brunch is unbelievably good. Rates are $100–200, starting at $130. Take advantage of special packages.

More convenient to Newport Harbor is the **Hyatt Newporter,** 1107 Jamboree Rd., 949/729-1234 or 800/233-1234, http://newporter.hyatt.com, with spacious resort-style grounds and an amazing array of sports and fitness facilities—including access to the John Wayne Tennis Club. The annual summer jazz series here is immensely popular too. Rates are $160 and up.

A good deal just off the 405 Freeway in Costa Mesa is the Ayres **Country Inn and Suites** 325 S. Bristol St. in Costa Mesa (on South Bristol at Red Hill Avenue, on the west side of the street), 714/549-0300 or 800/454-1692, www.countrysuites.com. This well-appointed hotel, within easy reach of the coast and all other major Orange County attractions, has country French bed-and-breakfast style. Amenities include in-room refrigerators and color TV with videocassette players. Some rooms and studio suites feature microwaves and whirlpools. Extras include full buffet breakfast and morning newspapers, plus two swimming pools, whirlpools, exercise facilities, coin laundry. Since the hotel does substantial "business" business, weekend rates are often lower—a real boon for pleasure travelers. Rates are $200–250, weekly and monthly rates available.

Bed-and-Breakfasts

Newport Beach bed-and-breakfast inns deliver the most ocean ambience. Probably the best bet for romance—and not really all that pricey, considering the neighborhood—is the two-story **Portofino Beach Hotel** on Balboa Peninsula just north of the pier, 2306 W. Ocean Front (at 23rd Street), 949/673-7030 or 800/571-8749, www.portofinobeachhotel.com, with 15 rooms, four villas, and a "casa" that sleeps 10. The style here is upscale European, with décor running to antiques, armoires, and brass beds. Some rooms and three villas look out over the ocean; some feature skylights, fireplaces, and in-room whirlpool tubs. Rates are $179 and up (higher on weekends), and children 16 and under can stay free. Breakfast is included; there's also a restaurant on the premises. Vacation apartments available.

For Victorian romance with frills, flounces, and French and American antiques, try the **M Doryman's Inn** nearby, a dignified 1891 brick beauty across from the Newport Pier at 2102 W. Ocean Front, 949/675-7300, www.dory mansinn.com. Every room or suite is unique, though each features a fireplace and marble sunken marble whirlpool tub. Besides breakfast, other goodies include a bottle of wine or champagne upon arrival, butter cookies and chocolates in the evening, a patio with a view, even a rooftop sundeck. Rates are $200 and up, but check for specials. The onsite 21 Oceanfront restaurant is another boon, serving up Old World serenity and spectacular seafood.

FOOD

You'll find no shortage of coffee-and-pastry stops in and around Newport Beach. For atmosphere à la Berkeley on Balboa Peninsula, try the **Alta Coffee Warehouse and Roasting Co.,** in Cannery Village, 506 31st St. (off Newport Boulevard), 949/675-0233. As beloved in Orange County as Peet's is in Berkeley, **Diedrich Coffee** is the native java hot spot. The closest Newport location for most folks is actually in Costa Mesa at 474 E. 17th St. (the extension of Westcliff Drive, near Irvine Avenue), 949/646-0323. There's another in Newport Beach proper, at 3601 Jamboree Rd., 949/833-9143, more convenient to the Back Bay. If you're prepared to wait, for homey and wholesome breakfast—omelettes to banana pancakes—head for immensely popular **Side Street Café,** 1799 Newport Blvd. (at 18th Street) in Costa Mesa, 949/650-1986. Another excellent hearty-breakfast possibility is stylish **Plums,** 369 E. 17th St. (between Santa Ana and Raymond Avenues), 949/548-7586, which, except for the lack of rain, will soon have you convinced you're actually in the Pacific Northwest.

Food snobs pooh-pooh the place, but for inexpensive and tasty seafood *everybody* goes to **M The Crab Cooker** restaurant and fish market, a lobster-red presence on the peninsula at 2200 Newport Blvd., 949/673-0100. Lunch and dinner specialties include Manhattan-style clam chowder, mesquite-grilled seafood and, yes, crab. As you can tell from a glance at the shuffling crowd on the sidewalk outside, no reservations are taken here (no credit cards either); add your name to the list and then join the line. Once you land a table, do appreciate the ambience. A shark chained to the ceiling presides over the close-quarters decor: formica tables with quaint plastic breadstick and condiment containers, paper plates and placemats, even disposable silverware. At last report copies of the proprietor's 45 rpm single, *I Know Why The Fishes Cry,* were still available for $1. There's another Crab Cooker in Tustin, 17260 E. 17th St., 714/573-1077.

Virtually immune to tourist traffic is **M Sabatino's Lido Shipyard Sausage Company,** 949/723-0645, tucked in among the boat shops and warehouses at 251 Shipyard Way, Cabin D on the Lido Peninsula—itself an opposable thumb on Balboa Peninsula, accessible via Lido Park Drive just off Lafayette Avenue in Newport Beach. (Call for directions.) Eat café-style outdoors, weather permitting, to fully appreciate the semi-industrial shipyard ambience, or indoors, where the atmosphere is also relaxed. Sandwiches and salads dominate the lunch menu; you can't go wrong with any Sabatino's sausage sandwich or a Caesar salad, but the Sizzling Sausage Platter is a star attraction, served with pasta and bread (best with the giardinera, or Italian-style olive relish). The wonderful Sicilian sausages here date from an 1864 Sabatino family innovation, in which fat is removed from the meat and special goat's-milk cheese added in its stead. The result? Sausages, either mild or spicy, that are quite moist and incredibly tasty. Especially at dinner Sabatino's is also popular for its pasta specialties and other traditional Italian dishes—chicken, fresh fish, and veal selections, not to mention a superb rack of lamb. But unless you're religious about vegetarianism, do *not* leave this place without taking along at least one selection from the sausage counter. Sabatino's is open daily for lunch and dinner.

The 1940s-style **Ruby's** out on Balboa Pier, 949/675-7829, is the first and original in this popular chain of boogying burger joints done in red, white, and polished chrome. Sitting on the roof for al fresco breakfast is a real treat at this one. Best bet for *fast* fast food—fresh burgers sans ambience—is **In-N-Out Burger,** closest here at 594 19th St. in Costa Mesa, 800/786-1000, where snap-to service comes with the employee profit-sharing plan.

Lunch and Dinner

Jack Shrimp, 2400 W. Coast Hwy. (near Tustin Avenue), 949/650-5577, is hot stuff, a jammin' jambalaya joint serving secret-recipe jambalaya and Louisiana-style shrimp specialties in a very casual atmosphere. Lunch is served only on Friday, dinner nightly.

Fabulous for delicious, affordable Mexican, is the **Taco Mesa** stand just north of Newport Boulevard at, 647 W. 19th St., between Harbor Boulevard and Placentia Avenue, 949/642-0629. Specialties include carnitas or blackened calamari tacos, quesadillas *rajas,* overstuffed *tortas,* and *pollo negro en pasta* Also appreciate the well-cooked beans (not refried), fluffy rice, and the thick fresh-fruit milkshakes and "fruit waters" served here. Yumm. You can't miss the place—the only orange-and-blue brick building across from the DMV. (Parking can be a challenge.) Also good for healthy Mexican is **La Fogata** near the Port Theater in Corona del Mar, 3025 E. Coast Hwy., 949/673-2211.

One of the area's best bets for Chinese is in Costa Mesa—the long-running **Mandarin Gourmet,** 1500 Adams Ave., 714/540-1937, beloved for its traditional Peking duck, seafood dishes, and almost endless menu. For impressive California-style sushi in a less inspiring setting, try the Japanese **Abe** restaurant, 2900 Newport Blvd., 949/675-1739, open for lunch and dinner. Watch what you order to keep the tab reasonable at the relaxed yet sumptuous Indian **Mayur,** 2931 E. Coast Hwy., 949/675-6622, featuring seafood and other specialties, such as shrimp Vindaloo, shrimp Tandoori, and chicken tikka Masala. For exceptional French picnic fixings and light breakfast, lunch, and takout dinner, try the **N Pascal Èpicerie,** 949/261-9041, adjacent to the famed restau-

rant of the same name on Bristol Street. For more information, see below.

To dent the bankroll on behalf of the beefeater tradition, hoof it over to **Five Crowns,** 3801 E. Coast Hwy. (at Poppy) in Corona del Mar, 949/760-0331. This ersatz English manor is beloved by tourists and locals alike for its serving wenches and humongous portions of prime rib and other specialties. The filet mignon is excellent, tender enough to slice with a spoon.

Fine Dining

Genuine gastronomic adventure awaits in Newport Beach. Head to the south of France, for example, via one of Orange County's best restaurants. Serving Provençal in a rose garden of a bistro, **N Pascal** in a shopping center just off the Del Mar Freeway at 1000 N. Bristol Ave. (near Jamboree), 949/752-0107, is just about everyone's favorite unstuffy French restaurant. Specialties include seared salmon filet with watercress sauce and baby lamb rack with sweet garlic. Reservations definitely advised. Men: jacket required. You can also try Pascal to go—thanks to the dandy little breakfast, lunch, and takeout épicerie adjacent, 949/261-9041, which offers baguette sandwiches and such things as eggplant caviar, unusual salads, whole cooked chickens, and French ham and cheeses.

Another contender for favorite French restaurant is **Aubergine** on the Balboa Peninsula at 508 29th St., 949/723-4150, open Tues.–Sat. from 6 P.M. (reservations a must). Fine dining doesn't get finer than this, at a Cal-French restaurant still one of the brightest stars on the south-state's dining scene. Set in a beachside cottage, the restaurant features stylishly understated décor.

The Golden Truffle, 1767 Newport Blvd. (between 17th and 18th, just before the 55 Freeway begins in Costa Mesa), 949/645-9858, is as unassuming as it is exceptional, a French-Caribbean bistro serving specialties such as Chianti braised lamb shank with noodles, Caribbean prime Angus skirt steak with "soul slaw" and fries, and Jamaican jerk chicken salad. Lots of vegetarian choices, too. The menu changes seasonally, featuring 15–20 specials every night. It's open Tues.–Sat. for lunch and dinner. Also fabulous for more French is **Pescadou Bistro** across from city hall at 3325 Newport Blvd., 949/675-6990, with a surprisingly reasonable fixed-price menu.

The sleek, shiny New American **Bayside,** coastal kin of Bistango, is located at 900 Bayside Dr. (near PCH), 949/721-1222, and dedicated to "dining as art, the art of dining." On the lower end of this changing menu, this art might mean griddle crab cakes, tiger prawns wrapped in applewood-smoked bacon, or exotic mushrooms and pine nuts on fusilli pasta with light Alfredo sauce. Come on Sunday for champagne brunch.

Tasty **Sage,** in the Eastbluff Center at 2531 Eastbluff Dr. (near Vista del Oro), 949/718-9650, is a study in shades of sage—and might cost you some green, too. Yet a meal here isn't so expensive if you sample appetizers—the tortilla soup, say, and perhaps also the Sage salad, a symphony of root veggies—or stick with the great little pizzas, from seafood and pesto to Cajun barbecue chicken. Open daily for lunch (Brunch on Sunday) and dinner. At last report a new Sage was scheduled to open along the coast.

Quite special for Sunday brunch—any meal, actually—is the **Pavilion** at the Four Seasons Hotel near Fashion Island at 690 Newport Center Dr. (at Santa Cruz), 949/760-4920. It's all good—from the peekytoe crab omelette or smoked trout eggs Benedict at breakfast to peppered swordfish steak with jasmine rice or wild mushroom and spinach cannelloni.

EXCURSION INLAND: DISNEYLAND

Anyone who has been a child or had a child since Walt Disney first opened his Magic Kingdom in 1955 already knows most everything of import about Disneyland.

In Disneyland, stories have happy endings. And every performer on the 76-acre Disney stage—from Mickey Mouse and Donald Duck to the latest batch of lovable audio-animatronic cre-

the granddaddy of amusement parks, Disneyland

ations—smiles, waves, and then smiles some more, as a matter of company policy. They don't call this "The Happiest Place On Earth" for nothing. In Disneyland, if the hero doesn't do it single-handedly, then whiz-bang technological wizardry will save the day. In Disneyland, democracy equals capitalism. And capitalism automatically creates social justice. In other words, Disneyland isn't real, though corporate America desperately wants to believe it is. Still, real or not, Disneyland is as good as it gets in Southern California, if what you're looking for is a clean, well-lighted, life-sized fantasy theater showcasing Mom, Pop, apple pie, and the American flag. It's also one of the few public places in socially subdivided Southern California where families go out and play in public.

Disneyland proper offers eight distinct lands. Once "shoppe"ed out on **Main Street, U.S.A.,** from the Central Plaza wander straight ahead—through Sleeping Beauty's castle—into **Fantasyland** and then to **Mickey's Toontown,** both of these latter destinations mandatory for younger youngsters. Turn left to reach **Adventureland** (where the *Indiana Jones Adventure* still draws rave reviews and big crowds) and **Frontierland/Rivers of America, Critter Country** (home of **The Many Adventures of Winnie the Pooh** ride), and **New Orleans Square.** Turn right and you'll land in **Tomorrowland,** where Walt Disney's original 1950s futurism has been transformed by new technological wonders including the new *Astro Orbitor* and the *Rocket Rods*.

COME TAKE A TRIP IN MY AIRSHIP

Ever thought what a gas it would be to float over Disneyland in an airship, looking down on the madding crowds? Well, it's no Fantasyland fantasy—especially if you can cough up the $300 per person for a one-hour ride. And fear not, this blimp won't catch on fire and fall from the sky, as in the *Hindenburg* disaster, because non-flammable helium is the "lifting gas." For more information, contact **Anaheim Blimp,** 949/637-7198, www.anaheimblimp.com.

Yet there's so much more playground now that Disneyland has been expanded into the **Disneyland Resort,** which also includes the **Downtown Disney** shopping, dining, and entertainment district and 55-acre **Disney's California Adventure**—a separate theme park featuring everything from the kid-sized **A Bug's Land** and the new **Twilight Zone Tower of Terror,** to a reincarnation of Disneyland's beloved **Electrical Parade.**

Practicalities

Though hours are subject to change, in summer the park is open 9 A.M.–midnight Sunday through Friday, until 1 A.M. on Saturday night. Otherwise, Disneyland is typically open 10 A.M. to 6 or 8 P.M. on weekdays and 9 A.M. to midnight on weekends. Disney's California Adventure usually closes earlier; contact the resort for current details.

Bring plenty of money—what you'd like to spend and then some. At last report a one-day ticket to either Disneyland or Disney's California Adventure (not both), covering park admission plus all attractions and rides, was $47 adult, $37 child (ages 3 to 9), kids under 3 free. Two-day "park hopper" passes allow admission to both parks and at last report were $98 adults (three- and five-day passes also available). All prices typically increase at least slightly every year. Guided Disneyland tours—including *Walk in Walt's Footsteps*—as well as annual passes, and special packages are available. Members of AAA, AARP, and other organizations may also receive special discounts.

But the price of admission is only the beginning. There's parking, too, and Disneyland doesn't allow you to pack in food or beverages, so expect to spend at least $25–35 per person for two meals and snacks. (If you're a chowhound, the food tab can go higher.) The total cost of Mickey Mouse ears, miscellaneous T-shirts, and other Disney memorabilia may floor otherwise frugal fun lovers. Also, park your car and keep it parked. (Parking's extra, too.) The new **Anaheim Resort Transit (ART)** trolleys provide easy on-off transport throughout the Disneyland/convention center area, running every 10 minutes in summer and at other peak times, at least every

SPORTING ORANGE COUNTY

Some sort of sports-franchise virus has been afflicting Southern California in recent years. Foreshadowing the Los Angeles loss—or, more appropriately, *return*—of the L.A. Raiders football team to Oakland, in 1995 Orange County lost its **Los Angeles Rams** pro football team to St. Louis. The **Angel Stadium of Anaheim**, once known as Edison Field, still hosts **Anaheim Angels** baseball games, however. For information, call 714/634-2000 or see www.angelsbaseball.com. For almost any stadium event, by the way, a popular pre- and post-game stop is **The Catch** restaurant right across the street, 714/935-0101, where fresh fish and Angus steaks are served in lively sports-bar style.

Also notable is the Disney Company's **Mighty Ducks of Anaheim** National Hockey League expansion team, 714/704-2500, part of the NHL Pacific Division and the 2002-03 Western Conference champions. Though some wags refer to the endeavor as the "Mighty Bucks," the Ducks nest at the area's newest sports stadium, the impressive **Arrowhead Pond of Anaheim** ("The Pond") across the street from the Anaheim Stadium. The Ducks' season begins in early October and runs through April. Also stirring up The Pond on weekends from February into April is the **Anaheim Storm,** the newest National Lacrosse League team. Occasional **Disney on Ice** presentations are also staged at The Pond.

half hour otherwise. (Small fee.) For route and other information in both English and Spanish, call 888/364-2787.

Devil-may-care types arrive in Disneyland on a whim, but most people (certainly most people with small children) *plan,* and plan carefully. Considering the investment of time, money, and emotional energy a trip to Disneyland requires—and since it matters what you'll see and do, and whether you'll enjoy it—it pays to make appropriate plans, including hotel or motel reservations, well in advance. A two- or three-day stay will allow you to see and do just about everything, much less stressfully than a whiz-bang one-day whirlwind tour. But if your family can't afford the extra time or expense, do Disneyland in a day by accepting in advance that you won't accomplish everything—then set priorities. The **FastPass** service allows you to bypass long lines for more popular attractions; the new **colored wristband** system lets parents know right away which rides their kids are tall enough to ride.

For current information, contact the **Disneyland Resort,** 1313 Harbor Blvd. in Anaheim, 714/781-4565, www.disneyland.com.

Other Amusements Parks

Just minutes from Disneyland in Buena Park is **Knott's Southern California Resort,** originally Knott's Berry Farm, the nation's first theme park.

First famous for Cordelia Knott's fried chicken dinners and for its fresh berries—in particular Orange County's own boysenberries, a delectable cross between blackberries, raspberries, and loganberries that Walter Knott helped develop during the Depression—Knott's slowly evolved into a family-run, family-friendly monument to America's pioneering spirit. It was only in 1968 that the family decided to fence the park and charge admission. Nowadays millions of people drop by each year to share the original Knott family homestead. From attractions like **Ghost Town**—Walter Knott's first and original outpost of wholesome, old-fashioned Old West fun—and other themed areas to radical rides like **HammerHead,** Knott's offers family fun for all ages. A major attraction, come October, is Knott's **Halloween Haunt**—the best adult Halloween party *anywhere*—and **Knott's Scary Farm,** for the kids. Very popular, so get your tickets early. At last report park admission was $43 adults, $38 seniors, and $13 children. For more information, contact Knott's Berry Farm, 8039 Beach Blvd., 714/220-5200, www.knotts.com.

Family-style amusement is a major industry in Buena Park, with other diversions strung along Beach Boulevard like Christmas lights. One of the best is **Medieval Times,** an ersatz trip into the days of sword fights and knights in armor jousting on horseback. Show times at Medieval Times,

THE RICHARD NIXON LIBRARY & BIRTHPLACE FOUNDATION

Orange County Coast

The Richard Nixon Library reflection pond serves as a perfect centerpiece to the gardens.

7662 Beach Blvd., 714/523-1100 or 888/935-6878, www.medievaltimes.com, vary depending on the day, so call for details. Reservations and an early arrival are advisable, too, since tour groups can pack the place. For current area information, contact: **Buena Park Convention & Visitors Office,** 6601 Beach Blvd., Ste. 200, 714/562-3560 or 800/541-3953, www.buena park.com/cvo.

EXCURSION INLAND: RICHARD NIXON LIBRARY

After his death in 1994, ex-President Richard Milhous Nixon finally came home—to the **Richard Nixon Library and Birthplace** in Yorba Linda, first opened on July 19, 1990, and recently expanded with a new wing. Unlike other presidential museums, funded at least in part by the government and subject to some degree of federal review, Nixon's is entirely self-supporting—a fact that threatened, early on, to embroil the institution in as much controversy as the ex-president himself. Before the Nixon Library even

opened its doors, critics charged that Nixon and his employees would offer only a flattering spin on his life and times.

It's true that the Nixon Library—more accurately, museum—serves primarily to glorify its namesake rather than explain, let alone criticize. (With or without federal funding, the same can be said of all post-presidency memorials, however.) It's also true that the displays here are exceptionally well done, conceptually and technically. Exploring the place for yourself is well worth the side trip into Orange County's suburban hinterlands. Galleries positively spin Nixon's life and times, from his early years as a Red-baiting congressman to the Watergate scandal that led to his fall. The museum's newest permanent gallery, Area 37: Richard Nixon and the History of America in Space, begins with the creation of NASA and includes a tape recording of the conversation between Nixon and the Apollo 11 astronauts. There are other recordings here, too, including—in the perhaps intentionally obfuscated Watergate Gallery—the so-called "smoking gun" conversation between Nixon and

John Dean. Nixon's presidential limo is a fairly recent addition to the Domestic Affairs Gallery. And don't miss the gift shop.

No matter how humbling his end—Nixon was the only American president ever forced by impending impeachment to resign from office—his beginnings were humble indeed. He was born on January 9, 1913, in a tiny farmhouse built from a Sears Roebuck kit by his father, Frank. His mother, Hannah, named him after the English king Richard Plantagenet, "Richard the Lionhearted," though all the Nixon boys were named after English kings. Restored to its original simplicity at a cost of $400,000, the Nixon birthplace is definitely worth a stop after the museum tour.

A major expansion, doubling the library's size, includes the country's only replica of the White House's East Room.

The Nixon Library and Birthplace is at the corner of Yorba Linda Boulevard and Eureka Avenue. For information (pre-recorded), including special exhibits and events, call 714/993-5075 or see www.nixonfoundation.org. The museum is open Mon.–Sat. 10 A.M.–5 P.M., Sunday 11 A.M.–5 P.M. Admission is $5.95 adults, $4.95 active military, $3.95 seniors, and $2 children ages 8–11 (7 and under free). Free parking.

If you're coming by car, both Hwy. 57 (the Orange Freeway) and Hwy. 91 (the Riverside Freeway) will get you here; both are also accessible from I-5. From Newport Beach and nearby coastal areas, the best option is heading inland via Hwy. 55, which merges into Hwy. 91 (then go east.) From Hwy. 91, exit at Hwy. 90 (the Imperial Highway) and head north, exiting at Yorba Linda Boulevard and then heading west. From Hwy. 57, exit at Yorba Linda Boulevard and head east.

M CRYSTAL COVE STATE PARK

South along the coast toward Laguna Beach is one of Orange County's genuine gems, Crystal Cove State Park, the largest remaining patch of coastal land still open to the general public. And what a patch it is—tidepools and sandy coves along more than three miles of shoreline, plus, on the other side of the highway, once-wooded

El Moro Canyon in the San Joaquin Hills, a total of 2,791 acres owned until 1979 by the Irvine Company.

The beach here, open daily from 6 A.M. to sunset, is usually one of the loneliest around—a real draw when you've had enough of Orange County crowds. Offshore, to a depth of 120 feet, is one of the state's official "underwater parks," a prime scuba- and skin-diving locale. For more pedestrian aquatic explorations, study local tide tables and head for the tidepools. This low-tide adventure (don't touch) is usually better in winter, when the tides are more extreme because of the gravitational pull of both sun and moon. Access points to beach parking and facilities are at El Moro Canyon, Reef Point, Los Trancos, and Pelican Point.

Inland, some 23 miles of trails wind through the hills of El Moro Canyon, which is heaven for mountain bikers, hikers, and pikers on horseback. Climb on up, at least for the ocean views, or come along on park-sponsored interpretive walks, tours, and backcountry hikes—the latter often to places not otherwise open to the public.

Also fascinating is the *town* of **Crystal Cove,** seemingly unchanged since the 1920s and now included on the National Register of Historic Places. On weekends, stop by the neighborhood's "blue bungalow" visitor center to get the story, along with trail maps and other park information. At least some of the 46 beachfront bungalows, built to house Irvine Company ranch hands, are scheduled to be spiffed up to "habitable rustic" standards and made available as reasonably priced vacation rentals by the end of 2005. A new developed campground is planned for south of town. (Call the park for details on both.) Other facilities are available, including fairly unobtrusive picnic areas, restrooms with showers, and inland backpack trailside campsites. Sign up for docent-guided hikes and tours, and call the parks office for information about horseback rides.

The day-use fee at Crystal Cove is $10. Trailside camping (it's a several-mile hike in) is $15 per night from March through November, $10 per night in winter. For other park information, contact Crystal Cove State Park, 8471 Pacific Coast Hwy., 949/494-3539 or 492-0802, www.crystalcovestatepark.com.

Laguna Beach

Unlike most beach towns, laid-back Laguna Beach has tried to put a lid on the booming business of T-shirteries and other standards of the tourism trade—to little avail. It's hard to believe that this village of just under 30,000 attracts about three million tourists each year. Why do they come? Because Laguna Beach is lovely, for one thing, with a woodsy, small-town feel, white-sand beaches, and craggy coastal coves and outcroppings vaguely reminiscent of Big Sur. For another, because this artsy onetime artists colony has a quirky creative character.

Built on land never included within a land-grant rancho, since the days of early settlement Laguna Beach has gone its own way. And the town still cultivates its eccentricities. Chief among them is the odd and oddly compelling annual Pageant of the Masters presentation of *tableaux vivants*, "living pictures" allowing life to imitate art imitating life. Other oddities persist. Even in this uncharitable bottom-line age, for example, affluent Laguna Beach still tries to find room for artists, oddballs, and assorted others who don't fit the mass-produced American mold. Nonetheless, having money is almost a necessity here. Worthy civic intentions notwithstanding, bohemians have all but been replaced by BMWs and beach resorts.

Even this latest Laguna Beach lifestyle is threatened by success. The city's population has more than doubled in the past 10 years. With the arrival of tourist season every summer, the population doubles again. On summer weekends in particular, traffic can become hopelessly snarled—in town, and up and down the highway—with parking spaces nearly as precious as local real estate. And more people are on the way. Like waves from an inland sea, new residential developments roll toward Laguna Beach from the north, south, and east.

For more information about the area and its attractions, contact the **Laguna Beach Visitor Bureau and Chamber of Commerce,** 252 Broadway, Laguna Beach, 949/497-9229 or 800/877-1115 (pre-recorded), www.lagunabeachinfo.org.

SIGHTS

By the 1920s half the population of Laguna Beach were artists, drawn by the area's undisturbed beauty. The town soon became one of the West's most important arts communities, and a center for California impressionism. By the 1930s Laguna Beach was still hardly the typical California tourist destination, its real appeal the possibility of escaping Los Angeles. Big-screen stars fleeing their own celebrity, including Charlie Chaplin and Bette Davis, joined a galaxy of lesser-known artists to populate little Laguna Beach—a place close enough to L.A. for convenience yet far enough away to avoid public curiosity and scrutiny. That trend continued over the years, even as cultural celebs became more beat, then countercultural. In the 1960s, for example, Timothy Leary was a common local sighting. These days the Laguna Beach arts scene is populated in part by members of the city's large gay and lesbian community, responsible for obtaining new public housing and other support for AIDS patients. Financial pressures for local artists—those still here—are immense, however, since most are quickly being priced out of the market for both living and studio space.

Pageant of the Masters / Festival of the Arts

Especially on a first-time trip to Laguna Beach, seeing the sights should be synonymous with attending the town's simultaneous Festival of the Arts and Pageant of the Masters, held together during July and August. The fine arts and crafts on display for the festival—all strictly local, displayed by artists and craftspeople from up and down the Orange County coast—*are* fine, the variety great: hand-made musical instruments, furniture, sculpture, and scrimshaw. There's even a "junior art" division. But the pageant is unlike anything you're likely to encounter anywhere else on earth—a living, breathing tribute to the art world's old masters and ancient treasures, a carefully staged two-hour magic show that's been tickling everyone's fancy since the 1930s.

The pageant's *tableaux vivants,* or living pictures, are large-scale sleight of hand or trompe l'oeil, literally, "fooling the eye." Whether the oversized artwork on display is Leonardo da Vinci's *Last Supper* (a pageant favorite), Renoir's *Grape Pickers at Lunch,* or Monet's *Women in the Garden,* on cue the costumed participants come on stage and freeze into the background frieze. Then—after the house goes dark and the stage lights come on—the entire audience gasps. Because there on stage, 50 times larger than life, is an uncanny reproduction of the real thing. So there's really no need to traipse across the country to the Metropolitan, or cross oceans to the Louvre or Uffizi, when you can come to Laguna Beach.

It's not all high art, though. In the process of dazzling the crowds with impersonations of two- and three-dimensional reality, pageanteers have been known to pose as sculptures, California or-ange-crate labels, hair combs and other jewelry, even postage stamps.

It takes endless volunteer effort—not to mention 100 gallons of makeup, 75 gallons of paint, 1000 yards of fabric, and an unbelievable budget to pull off this elaborate charade. Annual pageant proceeds support scholarships for high school and college students.

The annual arts festival and pageant take place at Irvine Bowl Park, also known as the Festival of the Arts Pageant Grounds, 650 Laguna Canyon Road. The theater is the Irvine Bowl itself, a 2,500-seat theater nestled into the canyon hillside.

More than 250,000 people typically attend these events, so also plan for lodgings. If you're staying in town, walk to the festival; it's only a few blocks from Main Beach. If you're here just for the day and driving, once parked, stay parked—then, if you're also heading downtown, walk. To find a parking place, arrive very early in the day.

placing the figure at the Pageant of the Masters

A shuttle bus service (small fee) runs between the area's summer festivals and the parking lots along Laguna Canyon Road.

Pageant tickets are $15–300 each and are generally sold out months in advance, but if you're lucky there may be cancellations on an appropriate performance night. Without a pageant ticket there is a separate $5 festival admission. For general information and to order tickets contact **Festival of the Arts/Pageant of the Masters,** 650 Laguna Canyon Rd., 949/494-1145 (main office), 949/497-6582 or 800/487-3378 (box office), www.foapom.com.

The Sawdust Festival and Art-A-Fair

Since the 1960s the Sawdust Festival has been the "alternative" Laguna Beach arts celebration, now a major-league crafts fair held more or less concurrently with the Festival of the Arts but across the road at 935 Laguna Canyon Rd., 949/494-3030, www.sawdustartfestival.org. These days it's an "Auld Tyme Faire," in the ever-popular Renaissance style, with mimes, strolling minstrels, and plenty of ale. Come also for pre-Christmas art shopping, winter art classes, and the spring art studio tour. Also going on every summer are the juried Art-A-Fair festivities at 777 Laguna Canyon Rd., 949/494-4514, or check www.art-a-fair.com, with hundreds of artists and endless variety.

Arts and Crafts Fairs

If slogging through the summer crowds seems unappealing, come some other time. Arts and crafts fairs of some sort are scheduled year-round, including the April **Art Walk Lunch** at the festival grounds (eat, then meet the artists) and the Sawdust Festival's **Winter Fantasy** from mid-November into December. During the rest of the year, crafts fairs are typically scheduled at least twice each month; contact the visitors bureau for details. Come any time for the local art scene's **First Thursdays Art Walk** evening, 6–9 P.M.—definitely a happening, starting at the Laguna Art Museum. Shuttles run between galleries, which serve wine, goodies, and sometimes good art advice. For current info, see www.first thursdaysartwalk.com. Or plan to come during

GETTING HERE, GETTING ORIENTED, GETTING PARKED

Those famous Laguna Beach arts festivals make the sun-loving summer beach scene that much more congested and crazed. Anyone phobic about personal space (and parking space) might consider coming for the arts festivals as a daytrip—staying elsewhere—and returning at some other time for more thorough exploration. Daytrip or otherwise, if you plan to come or go from the east via Laguna Canyon Road (Hwy. 133), which connects Laguna Beach to the 405 inland—*be extra cautious.* This narrow two-lane highway has become Orange County's blood alley, its high accident rate attributed to too many people in too much of a hurry. The same caution holds for the alternative route inland, Laguna Canyon Road to El Toro Road to I-5. Aside from the coast highway, there are no other routes into Laguna Beach.

Once here, you'll need to orient yourself to Pacific Coast Highway. Laguna Beach highway addresses north of Broadway are designated "North Coast Highway"; those south of town to Crown Valley Parkway, "South Coast Highway."

Unless your vehicle is safely stored at a local motel or hotel, parking is a challenge. Metered parking (the rate is $1 per hour so bring *lots* of quarters) is available on many streets. There are also various lots (try Ocean) where all-day parking runs $8–10. If you're coming just for the Pageant of the Masters and associated arts festivals, *come early,* park in the large lots along Laguna Canyon Road, and shuttle back and forth to town. Arrive by 10 A.M. and there should be no problem.

the May and December Open Studios event offered by **Laguna Canyon Artists,** 949/494-8672, www.lagunacanyonartists.com, and **Laguna Plein-Air Painters Association,** exhibits and sales; call 949/376-3635 for details.

There is more to Laguna Beach art than what you find in galleries, too, including the award-winning **Laguna Playhouse** repertory company, 606 Laguna Canyon Rd., 949/497-2787, www.lagunaplayhouse.com, which often presents original work by local playwrights. The playhouse was founded by actors including Bette Davis and Gregory Peck; more recently Harrison Ford got his professional start here. **Ballet Pacifica** occasionally performs at the Festival Forum Theater, 650 Laguna Canyon Rd.; for details, call 949/851-9930 or see www.balletpacifica.org.

Laguna Art Museum

These days Laguna Beach is hardly recognizable as "SoHo by the Sea." But at the turn of the century—the last century—scores of American artists arrived here determined to paint in the open air *(en plein air)* like the French impressionists and Hudson River School. The legacy of artists of the Plein-air School, including Joseph Kleitsch, William Griffith, and Frank Cuprien, has been lasting. Which explains the fact that, while other high school football teams have long identified themselves as "cougars" or "chargers," until 2002 the big bruisers here were known as the Laguna Beach Artists. Presumably the name is not quite enough to strike fear into the heart of opponents, so the Artists are now the Laguna Beach Breakers, a name that at least honors the subject matter of much local art.

The Laguna Art Museum, 307 Cliff Dr. (at Coast Hwy.), 949/494-6531, www.lagunaartmuseum.org, has earned renown as the only Southern California art museum to focus exclusively on American art—contemporary California art in particular, along with avant-garde special shows. After a short-lived merger with the Orange County Museum of Art, the Laguna Art Museum is once again a local institution. Recent exhibits have included Greetings from Laguna Beach: Our Town in the Early 1900s, a selection of plein-air classics, and In and Out of California: Travels of American Impressionists. The museum is open daily 11 A.M.–5 P.M., and until 9 P.M. the first Thursday of the month (free evening admission). Free docent-guided tours are offered at 2 P.M. Regular admission is $7 adults, $5 seniors and students, free for children age 12 and under.

RECREATION

Despite the human onslaught, the natural beauty and community charm that inspired early plein-

GREETERS CORNER

While wandering toward Main Beach, take note of Greeters Corner in **Main Beach Park** at the end of Forest Avenue. The statue in front of the **Greeters Corner Restaurant**, 329 S. Coast Hwy., 949/494-0361, commemorates the town's long tradition of greeters—and, in particular, Eiler Larsen. A Danish immigrant and World War I veteran, Larsen arrived in Laguna Beach in the 1930s to serve as "the Laguna greeter," a title (and unpaid job) he held for 30 years. An organized attempt to silence Larsen failed in 1959, once a local survey established that almost 90 percent of the citizenry wanted him to stay—and to continue waving and bellowing at passing cars.

Someone has served in the role of local greeter since the late 19th century, when Laguna Beach was known as Lagona—a variation of "Lagonas," a coastal territory named in the 1500s by local native peoples. In the 1880s, for example, Portuguese fisherman Joe Lucas would holler at passing stagecoaches. At last report, the town's greeting duties fall to a fellow by the name of Number One Archer.

air painters still abide. Folks here can help you find it. The self-guided **Heritage Walk** and bus tour (pick up the brochure at the visitor bureau) showcases area historic homes and other attractions. Among the few historic homes remaining downtown is the **Murphy-Smith Bungalow** at 278 Ocean Ave., 949/497-6834, open Fri.–Sun. 1–4 P.M. for free tours. **Laguna Outdoors,** 949/874-6620, offers guided tidepool tours. **La Vida Laguna,** 949/275-7544, www.lavida laguna.com, offers guided area hikes as well as kayak, mountain bike, and catamaran tours. For information on the area's wilderness parks, contact the **Laguna Canyon Foundation,** 303 Broadway, 949/855-7275, www.lagunacanyon .org; brochures and maps are also available at the visitors bureau.

Main Beach

Main Beach is, well, the city's main beach, dominating the ocean side of downtown between the

Laguna Art Museum and Hotel Laguna near Park Avenue. You'll know you've arrived when you spot the imposing glassed-in lifeguard tower, something of a local landmark. Most of the year you also can't miss the pick-up basketball players, almost as competitive as the volleyballers. A wooden boardwalk snakes along the beach, with its youngsters, oldsters, and rollerbladers. At this intriguing if tamer version of Muscle Beach in Venice, everyone and everything hangs out.

South of Main Beach, overseen by high-priced real estate, are Laguna's "street beaches." Sections of this slim one-mile strand of sand are known by the names of intersecting streets, from **Sleepy Hollow Lane** and **Thalia** to **Oak** and **Brooks.** Farther south still is half-mile **Arch Cove,** popular for sunbathing, its section again named after relevant streets (Bluebird Canyon, Agate, Pearl, etc.).

Since the coast (actually, the beach) is clear between Laguna Beach and South Laguna, you might find a completely private cove if you're willing to walk, surf-dodge, and rock-hop the distance—not advisable at high tide.

Water Sports

North of Main Beach, atop the bluffs along Cliff Dr., is the **Heisler Park** promenade, a fine place for lolling on the lawn, picnicking, and people-watching (public restrooms are here, too). Down below are two rocky coves with nice tidepools, **Picnic Beach** at the end of Myrtle St. and **Rockpile Beach** at the end of Jasmine.

Nearby are three inlets that manage to combine the best of the beach scene with the best of beach scenery: **Shaw's Cove, Fisherman's Cove,** and **Diver's Cove.** Needless to say, the area is beloved by locals and often crowded. The path down to Shaw's Cove is on Cliff Dr. at the end of Fairview; entrances to Fisherman's and Diver's coves are close together on Cliff, in the 600 block.

Half-moon **Crescent Bay Beach** (entrance at Cliff and Circle Dr.) is quite enticing, and usually offers some privacy for sunning, swimming, and skindiving. To reach **Crescent Bay Point Park** (great views) from Cliff Dr., turn left onto the highway and left again onto Crescent Bay Drive.

Popular for bodysurfing yet quite private by Laguna Beach standards, **Victoria Beach** is a local

favorite. To get here, take Victoria Drive from the highway and then turn right onto Dumond. Tiny fan-shaped **Moss Beach** at the end of Moss St. is one of the best around, well-protected for swimming, also popular for scuba diving. The three rocky fingers of **Wood's Cove** have helped create the pocket beaches here, plus providing a pounding-surf sideshow, great swimming, good scuba diving. (To get here, take the steps down from the intersection of Ocean Way and Diamond Street.) None of these beaches have public restrooms—the price of privacy—but at last report lifeguards were on duty, at least in summer.

If you bring Fido or Fifi along on this trip, you'll soon discover that dogs are not welcome at the beach (not to mention most other places). Laguna Beach offers some consolation, though. The city's Dog Park out on Laguna Canyon Road (near El Toro Road), known by locals as the Bark Park, is one of very few public areas in Orange County where people can legally let their dogs run off-leash. Open dawn to dusk, closed Wednesday.

Several miles south of Laguna Beach proper is the area aptly known as South Laguna. The main attraction here is **Aliso Creek Beach Park** at the mouth of Aliso Creek. In the late 1800s Helena Modjeska—the Shakespearean actress for whom Orange County's Modjeska Canyon was named—camped out with her entourage here in the coastal wilderness to beat the summer heat. Though houses are now the dominant feature of the surrounding landscape, until recently another noted local character was the minimalist 1970s Aliso Pier, which looked like a gargantuan arrow about to be shot out to sea. Severely damaged in 1999 storms and ultimately torn down, the pier may never reappear, since people in these parts find they like the beach—and the ocean view—just fine without it. But take time to explore the small sandy coves here and the rocky tidepools beyond.

SHOPPING

Shopping is a serious local pastime, a primary draw in Laguna Beach, where you'll find the tackiest of tourist bric-a-brac as well as fine art and jewelry. Laguna Beach boasts some 90 art galleries. Unlike special exhibits and collections on display at the local art museum, however, much of the gallery fare is far from cutting edge—or local, for that matter. To be sure you're buying local art, to support the health and welfare of artists still managing to survive in high-rent Orange County, attend local arts and craft fairs, mentioned above. And when in doubt, don't hesitate to ask. Otherwise, to find out what's what and where it might be, pick up the current gallery guide, available in most shops.

Art

The **Esther Wells Collection,** 1390 S. Coast, 949/494-2497, www.estherwellscollection.com, is noted for its impressionistic watercolors (always some local art on display) as well as sculpture and jewelry. For a nice introduction to Laguna Beach's Plein-air School, stop by the highly regarded **Redfern Gallery,** across from the Surf & Sand Hotel at 1540 S. Coast Hwy., 949/497-3356, www.redferngallery.com. Work by California impressionists is the specialty here, including paintings by contemporary plein-air

artists. (There's a second Redfern gallery at the Montage Resort, 30801 S. Coast Highway.) There is also fabulous historic California impressionism on display at the **Joan Irvine Smith Fine Arts Gallery,** 1550 S. Coast Hwy., 949/494-0854 or 800/449-5401, www.jisfine arts.com. (For a better appreciation of Joan Irvine Smith's contribution to the preservation of plein-air art, don't miss the spectacular collection at the **Irvine Museum** in Irvine, www.irvinemuseum.org.) Back in Laguna Beach, another important plein-air gallery is **De Ru's Fine Arts,** 1590 S. Coast Hwy., 949/376-3785, www.derusfinearts.com, the firm that cleans and restores paintings in the Irvine Museum collection. Alas, here and elsewhere, if you have to ask how much it costs you probably can't afford it.

Many local galleries will help you appreciate just how much disposable income some people have these days, including the grand **Sherwood Gallery,** on Gallery Row at 460 S. Coast Hwy., 949/497-2668, www.sherwoodgallery.com, with its contemporary and pop art, sculpture (some kinetic), jewelry, and unusual furnishings.

MADAME MODJESKA IN AMERICA

Susan Sontag's novel *In America* was inspired by Orange County's own Helena Modjeska, the noted 19th-century actress who renounced her European stage career and emigrated from Poland to the United States to start a utopian farming venture with her husband. In its fictionalized facts, the book parallels Modjeska's story. A star of the Warsaw stage married to the aristocratic Count Bozenta—in revolt against his family and dreaming of his own agricultural Eden—in 1876 Modjeska and her husband arrived in California with an accomplished entourage that included Henryk Sienkiewicz, who later won the Nobel Prize for literature.

In the book, as in real life, they all settled down in what was then the Wild West of Orange County—European overlords determined to wring both civilization and crops out of the wily Mexican-American wilderness.

And in the book, as in the course of actual events, none of the privileged Poles knew beans about farming. As Modjeska would later recall in her autobiography: "The most alarming feature of this bucolic fancy was the rapid disappearance of cash and the absence of even a shadow of income."

So Helena Modjeska resumed her career—and soon became one of the most accomplished actresses on the American stage during the golden age of theater.

"It felt like, an escapade; like leaving home; like telling lies—and she would tell many lies," reflects Sontag's protagonist as she arrives in San Francisco. "She was beginning again; she was rejoining her destiny, which conferred on her the rich sensation that she had never gone astray."

As Modjeska's star ascended in America, she crisscrossed the country in her own private rail-

The first Southern California gallery to offer Australian aboriginal art is **Kakadu Dream Time,** 1100 S. Coast Hwy., 949/464-9646. **Kyber Pass,** 1970 S. Coast Hwy., 949/494-5021, specializes in jewelry, clothing, and art from Afghanistan. **The Vintage Poster,** 1476 S. Coast Hwy., 949/376-7422, www.thevintageposter .com, is fabulous for antique posters, everything from surfing, circus, and *Saturday Evening Post* posters to war propaganda.

Clothing and Jewelry

Thee Foxes' Trot, 264 Forest Ave., 949/494-4997, is a good stop for bath and homewares and a limited selection of unusual women's clothing. Also good for gifts and homewares is **Areo,** 207 Ocean Ave., 949/376-0535, www.areohome.com, where some of the vases, candles, candlesticks, and jewelry are locally made (ask). For pre-1940s Northern American Indian art and artifacts, the place is **Indian Territory, Inc.,** 305 N. Coast Hwy., 949/497-5747, www.indianterritory.com, offering everything from Indian basketry and blankets to Navajo, Hopi, and Zuni jewelry. Need a toe ring or other foot jewelry? Try **Shelby's,**

577 S. Coast Hwy. (at Legion), 949/494-7992, www.shelbysfootjewels.com. (The **Laguna Village Café** here in the Laguna Village, 949/494-6344, is a good bet for a beer-and-breakers break, out on the patio overlooking the ocean.) Try **Tippecanoes,** 648 S. Coast Hwy., 949/494-1200, for antique oddities and vintage clothing.

ACCOMMODATIONS

"Inexpensive" and "expensive" are relative terms, but it's safe to say that nothing in Laguna Beach is truly inexpensive. Here, and down the coast at the Ritz-Carlton, expensive really is expensive. If a low-rent stay is a must, see if the rustic visitor cabins at Crystal Cove State Park (see above) are finally available for rent ($100 and less). If you're heading south, try camping in Dana Point or a lower-rent motel farther south.

Most Laguna Beach lodging rates go up for "the season" either in mid-June or on July 1—just in time for the local arts festivals—and then dive again in mid-September. If you're willing to miss the summer arts pageantry and attendant crowds, come in early June (it can be foggy) or just about

---

road car and eventually played opposite Edwin Booth and Maurice Barrymore, the greatest actors of the day. She became Camille, and Ophelia. She was Nora in the premiere of Ibsen's *A Doll's House.* Yet her most famous role was Rosalind in Shakespeare's *As You Like It.*

Equally adept at besting the twists and turns of fate, in the 1880s the now wealthy Madame Modjeska and Count Bozenta returned to Orange County to build a more theatrical version of their earlier dream. The grand rambling home they built here, complete with a small stage extending out into the garden, was called Arden, as Modjeska later wrote, "because, like the Forest of Arden in *As You Like It,* everything that Shakespeare speaks of was on the spot—oak trees, running brooks, palms, snakes, even lions." She and the count lived here for 18 happy years, from 1888 to 1906.

Mountain lions still roam the Santa Ana Mountains, though they are not so common these days. And Modjeska's home still stands in a live oak grove on the banks of Santiago Creek, its original Forest of Arden—English yews, palms, white lilac, and crown of thorns—still thriving. Now a National Historic Landmark known as **Modjeska House Historical Park,** 29042 Modjeska Canyon Rd., about 10 miles east of Lake Forest via Santiago Canyon Road, the estate is owned by the county of Orange. The home and gardens are open to the public only for docent-guided tours, which at last report were offered by advance reservation only at 10 A.M. on Saturday, at last report. (The canyon road is narrow, the area residential, and gawkers are discouraged.) Tour fee is $5. For more information and reservations, call 949/923-2230 or 949/855-2028 and see www.ocparks.com.

Orange County Coast

any other time. For better value, look for establishments "close to" (not on) the beach and "near" (not in) town. Contact the visitors bureau for a fairly complete accommodations listing.

Cottages and B&Bs

There's something quite comforting about the predictability of motels, but other styles of accommodation offer more *romance*. Or something.

Cottages are *so* Laguna Beach. The beautifully restored 1920s  **Manzanita Cottages,** 732 Manzanita Dr., 949/661-2533 or 877/661-2533, are tucked into a garden complete with wishing well. How romantic is that? Exquisite attention to detail, full kitchens, charming bathrooms, and all for $195 per night (apartment $135). In summer, though, the cottages are available only by the week ($1,550 plus $75 cleaning fee), and an apartment stay requires a two-night minimum and a higher rate. Also inviting are the bungalow-style **Arabella Laguna Vintage Garden Guest**

bathing at the Casa Laguna

Cottages, 506 N. Coast Hwy., 949/376-5744 or 866/376-5744, www.arabellalaguna.com, a small selection of cozy suites and cottages with private baths and kitchens, garden setting. Rates are $175–400, though most sleep four or five. Weekly rates available.

The classic local charmer and a long-running favorite is the Mediterranean-style **M Casa Laguna Inn** bed-and-breakfast at 2510 S. Coast Hwy., 949/494-2996 or 800/233-0449, www .casalaguna.com, an updated ode to 1930s' California. Paths wander past the bell tower and courtyard and throughout the terraced gardens, connecting the 20 rooms and suites. Also here is a one-bedroom cottage with private ocean view, fireplace, and full kitchen. Rooms are small, suites are spacious; some have views; and all are tastefully furnished with antiques and overhead fans. Even the pool has a view. Head to the library in the morning for continental breakfast; tea is served in the afternoon, wine and hors d'oeuvres in the evening. In July and August there's a two-night minimum on weekends. Rooms are $125 and up, suites $175 and up, the rates much higher during summer and at other peak times. The rest of the year, though, modest rooms here are a best bet for budget romance.

Among Laguna Beach hotels the grande dame—and the only place around with a private beach—is the landmark **M Hotel Laguna,** practically on Main Beach at 425 S. Coast Hwy., 949/494-1151 or 800/524-2927 (reservations, calls from California only), www.hotellaguna.com. Most rooms are modern, with ceiling fans and the basics, and some afford ocean views. Since the Hotel Laguna was Humphrey Bogart's favorite Laguna Beach hideaway, two suites—the **Bogart Suite** and **Bacall Suite**—get special treatment, complete with canopy beds. Room rates run $110–250 in summer (mini-suites $275), free valet parking. Onsite you'll find a good seafood restaurant, **Claes Seafood, Etc.,** and **Le Bar,** complete with ocean view. Or take your cocktail out on the beachside terrace and just drink in the view.

The stylishly redone 1927 **Hotel La Casa del Camino,** 1289 S. Coast Hwy., 949/497-2446 or 888/367-5232, www.casacamino.com, offers 41 rooms just a stroll from Cress Beach. Four

Orange County Coast

room styles, from standard (queen beds) to "Euro studio suites," feature antiques, unique details, luxurious linens, down comforters and pillows, and Pro-Terra bath products. Continental breakfast. Pets allowed in some rooms. Rooftop deck, private beach access. Great onsite bistro, **Savoury's,** 949/376-9718. High-season rates start at $150.

Bed-and-breakfast fans, otherwise consider the nearby **Carriage House Inn,** 1322 Catalina St., 949/494-8945, www.carriagehouse.com, the historic 1920s French-Mediterranean colonial home once owned by film czar Cecil B. DeMille. In a residential neighborhood just two blocks from the beach, the two-story Carriage House features a lushly landscaped brick courtyard and six one- and two-bedroom guest suites. All include a living room and private bathroom; all but one feature kitchens and refrigerators; some have in-room coffeemakers. Most suites (year-round) are $150 or $175 ($20 per additional person for the two-bedroom suites), though the Lilac Time Suite is $140. Weekly rates available. To get here: About one mile south of Laguna Beach turn east onto Cress Street, go two blocks to Catalina, then turn left.

High-End Hotels

The Surfriders and other environmental organizations tend to fight hard against golf courses, luxury subdivisions, and ritzy hotels proposed for sensitive coastal "view" areas. Here as elsewhere in California, they often lose. So if money is absolutely no object, just south is Dana Point and the luxurious **Ritz-Carlton Laguna Niguel** and **St. Regis Monarch Bay Resort.** (For information on both, see below.) You can spend plenty even here in Laguna Beach, though, especially at the new **M Montage Resort & Spa,** 30801 S. Coast Hwy., 949/715-6000 or 888/715-6700, www.montagelagunabeach.com, an Arts and Crafts-inspired luxury development on a bluff overlooking the ocean. Rooms, suites, and bungalows feature every imaginable amenity, from the latest technological necessities, feathertop beds, and 400-thread count cotton sheets to marble bathrooms with oversized soak tubs. Business center, showplace 20,000-square-foot spa and

fitness facilities, three swimming pools, and on-site restaurants including the exceptional **Studio,** more casual **The Loft,** and the **Mosaic Bar & Grille.** Rates $250 and up—way up.

To park yourself quite comfortably *on* the beach, the place is light and airy **M Surf & Sand Hotel,** 1555 S. Coast Hwy. (at Bluebird Canyon Dr.), 949/497-4477 or 800/524-8621 for reservations, www.jcresorts.com. Rooms in the nine-story tower have the most breathtaking views, of course, but you won't go wrong elsewhere here, since most rooms are within 30 feet of the beach and include a private balcony looking out over the surf, surfers, and heated pool. Decor is understated in a day-at-the-beach palette, with sand-colored walls and raw-silk upholstery, shuttered windows and naked wood. The fun indoor-outdoor **Splashes** restaurant sits right on the beach. The art deco lounge is a choice spot for cocktails at sunset. Rates are $250 and up, but ask about specials and packages.

FOOD
Breakfast

Locals' choice for artsy minimalist breakfast is the very cool **M Cafe Zinc,** 350 Ocean Ave. (at Forest), 949/494-6302, though on weekends be prepared to wait at the counter and to fight for a table. The morning repast here is as simple as a huge hot cappuccino with a muffin. The frittatas are also good, not to mention the huevos rancheros with papaya salsa. If you come late, order a salad and some homemade soup—very good here—and do lunch. No credit cards. Next door is the equally cool **Cafe Zinc Market,** where you can load up on bread and baked goods, salads, cookbooks, even sundry kitchen items.

The **Beach House Inn,** centrally situated between Main Beach and PCH behind Vacation Village at 619 Sleepy Hollow Ln., 949/494-9707, is a Laguna Beach institution. This is the onetime home of Slim Summerstone, one of the original Keystone Cops. The ambience here is quite casual, and every table offers an ocean view—definitely a fine start for any day. The Beach House is best known for its lobster, steamed clams, and fresh fish specials, yet the all-American breakfast is also a best-bet. Beloved locally for breakfast, especially al fresco, is **The Cottage**, 308 N. Coast Hwy., 949/494-3023. Yes, the wait is worth it. For see-and-be-seen Sunday brunch right on the beach, head to **Splashes** outside at the Surf & Sand Hotel, 1555 S. Coast Hwy. (at Bluebird Canyon Dr.), 949/497-4477. If it's foggy or cool, the food's just as good when served indoors.

Lunch

Many of the more upscale eateries around town also serve lunch, often a variation of the dinner menu but with smaller servings at lower prices. See the listings below for possibilities. If you'll be near the Sawdust Festival grounds, stop by the **Laguna Culinary Arts Gourmet Cheese and Wine Shop & Café**, 845 Laguna Canyon Rd., 949/494-4006, for great house-made soups, salads, and sandwiches, plus an enticing selection of cheeses, olives, oils, and other uptown goodies. Open Mon.–Sat. 10:30 A.M.–5:30 P.M.

Beloved here and elsewhere in Orange County is **Wahoo's Fish Taco**, 1133 S. Coast Hwy. (PCH about a mile south of Main Beach, between Oak and Brook Streets), 949/497-0033. Also tops in the *very casual* cheap-eats fast-food category is **Taco Loco**, 640 S. Coast Hwy. (PCH between Cleo and Legion), 949/497-1635, where the ambience is asphalt-meets-the-sea-breeze and surfers scarf down fish tacos—such things as fresh lobster or mahi-mahi on blue corn tortillas—as quickly as possible. Vegetarians, don't despair. Taco Loco also serves a killer tofu burger.

For imaginative Napoli-style pizza, *the* place is **Z Pizza**, with the "best crust on the planet" according to *Los Angeles Times* readers. The original location is here, well south near Aliso Creek, 30902 S. Coast Hwy., 949/499-4949. Of course there's a **Ruby's** here too, on South Coast Highway at Nyes, 949/497-7829, the nostalgic diner-style choice for burgers, shakes, fries, and all those other things we all know we shouldn't eat.

Late in the afternoon or before dinner, stop for a drink at **Las Brisas**, 361 Cliff Dr. (N. Coast Hwy.), 949/497-5434, a place still known among old-timers as the Victor Hugo Inn. The main reason to dawdle here is to drink in the views—while considering the possibility that Orange County hasn't overhyped the "Riviera" angle after all.

Dinner

For romantic noshing, the Northern Italian **Ti Amo**, 31727 S. Coast Hwy. (near Third Street), 949/499-5350, is the perfect spot, perched as it is on a bluff overlooking the sea. The place has been lavishly decorated with sponge-painted walls and rich drapes. Entrées include paella, homemade pasta, and wonderful seafood. Or, create an appetizing light meal from several selections on the appetizer menu. Reservations wise at dinner. Another possibility if you're craving pasta at dinner is the stylish two-story **Sorrento Grille**, 370 Glenneyre St. (near Mermaid), 949/494-8686, a see-and-be-seen Italian bistro with American attitude and "martini bar."

For great food sans pretense, the place is tiny, fun, and funky **Café Zoolu**, 860 Glenneyre St., 949/494-6825, serving New American—a mighty fine cowboy steak, a swordfish sampler, and other surprises—in hugely generous portions. Do try the Zoolu chocolate cake.

Fine Dining

Stylish **Hush**, located upstairs at 858 S. Coast Hwy. where Mark's used to be, 949/497-3616, is elegant yet understated, the culinary creation of Jonathan Pflueger, former executive chef at Montage. Along with an exceptional wine cellar, expect such things as veggie-wrapped sea bass with ginger-jasmine rice and jumbo diver sea scallops with whipped potatoes. Open daily for dinner and late-night dining.

Five Feet refers to Laguna Beach's elevation. But this local hotspot at 328 Glenneyre, on the corner of Forest and Glenneyre, 949/497-4955, is actually more famous for fine nouvelle Chinese served up with pop art and pink neon. A must for first-timers: the catfish. It's open for dinner nightly, for lunch on Fridays only. David Wilhelm's fun, fairly pricey 1940s-style **French 75** bistro and champagne bar, 1464 S. Coast Hwy., 949/494-8444, is immensely popular at dinner and Sunday brunch. Starters might include wild mushroom fricassée and shrimp en cassoulet, entrées grilled rack of lamb and slow-roasted salmon with roasted tomato risotto.

Look into high-end hotels for other high-end dining options.

Dana Point and Vicinity

Given the modern-day dominance of subdivisions, shopping malls, and rush-hour traffic, one might forget that before the United States claimed the territory, pioneers from Spain and the new nation of Mexico made their homes in a much quieter California. For a glimpse into that brave old world, pick up a copy of *Two Years Before the Mast,* published in 1840 by Richard Henry Dana Jr. On leave from his studies at Harvard University to recover from measles-related afflictions, Dana put to sea onboard the *Pilgrim,* a small square-rigged Boston brig that delivered East Coast fineries to California in exchange for tanned cowhides carted over from the mission at San Juan Capistrano and other ports. San Juan Cove—now Dana Cove, which includes Dana Point Harbor, all within Capistrano Bay—was the only safe anchorage between San Diego and Santa Barbara. When Dana returned to Boston and an eventual career as a noted maritime attorney, he recalled the cove, with its rocky harbor and striking 200-foot cliffs, as "the only romantic spot in California."

And perhaps it was. "There was grandeur in everything around," Dana said. In those days the ocean surf swept all the way in to dramatic, sculptured cliffs. Huge prehistoric vultures—California condors, carrion eaters now all but extinct—launched themselves from these cliffs; birds of prey, ravens and herons, perched here as well. And long before swallows discovered the Capistrano mission, they nested in cliff crevices here.

More recently Dana Point has celebrated the grandeur of local surf, surfing, and surf-related innovations. Several times each year, when storms drove classic long-angled 30-foot waves around Dana Point from the west, hard-core surfers from far and wide assembled here to brave the "Killer Dana." Just like the local cattle hide trade, Killer Danas are history; harbor construction altered the offshore terrain. But to pay homage to those days of yore, stop by **Hobie Sports** in Lantern Bay Village, 24825 Del Prado, 949/496-2366, where rare and historic surfboards from the collection of Hobie Alter—local inventor of the foam-core surfboard and the Hobie Cat catamaran—are on display.

South from Dana Point and Laguna Niguel along the coast, just before you reach San Diego County, are San Juan Capistrano and San Clemente

DANA POINT

A city only since 1989, Dana Point today combines boat harbor, beaches, and Boston saltbox condominium developments. This stylistic twist testifies to popular identification with Richard Henry Dana's East Coast origins yet is odd, given the area's more enduring Spanish and Mexican roots. To sample original local architectural styles, explore older streets, including Chula Vista, Ruby Lantern, Blue Lantern, El Camino Capistrano, and Santa Clara. Come in March for the **Festival of Whales and Street Faire,** September for the **Tallships Festival** (including Pirate Camp) and the **Doheny Day Music Festival,** and November for the state's largest Thanksgiving race, the **Dana Point Turkey Trot.** Santa even shows up in December for the harbor **Parade of Lights.**

The cultural focal point for Dana Point is **Dana Point Harbor,** 949/496-1094, where breakwater construction began in 1966. Here, about 2,500 yachts bob and sway with the tides. The harbor also features a man-made island park—reached via Island Way—an inner breakwater created during the harbor's unusual cofferdam construction. Of particular interest is the

DANA POINT'S "LANTERN" STREETS

This peculiar local street-name phenomenon is not a recent affectation. In the 1920s Dana Point's "downtown" was defined by the Spanish-style plaza, and by streets intersecting Pacific Coast Highway—then known as the Roosevelt Coast Highway—which were named for the rainbow collection of ship's lanterns that marked them, the latter inspiration attributed to Anna Walters Walker, Dana Point's first developer. Most of the original copper street lanterns are long gone, but about 15 of the originals light the newly spiffed-up plaza park.

Ocean Institute, 24200 Dana Point Harbor Dr., 949/496-2274, www.ocean-institute.org, noted for its educational programs onboard the *Sea Explorer* research vessel and the *Spirit of Dana Point* tallship. Most Sundays, tour the brig *Pilgrim,* 10 A.M.–2:30 P.M. Public programs include marine mammal cruises and nighttime "bioluminescence cruises."

Other harbor diversions include kayaking, canoeing, parasailing, fishing, sportfishing, whale-watching (in winter), and tidepooling. **Dana Wharf Sportfishing** on the harbor's eastern edge, 949/496-5794, www.danawharfsportfishing.com, handles sportfishing trips, whale-watching (whales guaranteed), and other scenic excursions. Or try **Captain Dave's Dolphin & Whale Safari,** 949/488-2828, www.dolphinsafari.com.

For more complete information about the area, contact: **Dana Point Chamber of Commerce,** 24681 La Plaza, Ste. 15, 949/496-1555, www.danapoint-chamber.com.

Doheny State Beach

Just east of the harbor is Doheny State Beach, donated to the state in the 1930s by L.A. oil man Edward Lawrence Doheny in honor of his son, Ned. The local surf made a bigger cultural splash, though, especially when Doheny made it into the lyrics of the Beach Boys' classic *Surfin' USA.*

Head to the broad white-sand beach for the usual fun. The rocky area at the harbor end draws divers and anglers. At night beach bonfires are quite popular, if not nearly as wild as they once were (alcohol consumption has been banned). With the exception of surfing, nothing is as popular here as the grunion run, typically good. Doheny also features acres of lawn, a cool change when the sand really cooks. Worth a special stop is the **marine life museum** inside the visitor center, with its 3,000-gallon native fish aquarium and tidepool "touch tank."

Bike riding is actually quite feasible in and beyond Dana Point. The **San Juan Creek Bike Trail** starts just north of the beach; dart under PCH and take the trail all the way into San Juan Capistrano. Alternatively, take the Doheny bike path south along the sand to Capistrano Beach Park and, at Beach Road, merge into the PCH bike lanes. You can ride south into San Clemente, or north as far as Laguna Beach.

Developed campsites (hot showers, picnic tables, fire rings,) are tucked into the landscape; some are more sheltered than others. Day-use facilities lie to the west of San Juan Creek. The entrance to Doheny State Beach is just off PCH at 25300 Dana Point Harbor Dr.; follow the signs. Day use is $10. Full-facility camping (no hookups) is available—beachfront sites $26–31, inland sites $16–21—as are group camps. For more information, call 949/496-6171 (recorded information) or 949/496-6172, or see www.dohenystatebeach.org. To reserve campsites through ReserveAmerica, call 800/444-7275 or see www.reserveamerica.com.

Salt Creek Beach and Park

Almost an adjunct to the Ritz-Carlton Laguna Niguel resort, Salt Creek Beach north of Dana Point proper has long been noted for its good surfing. Two of the best "breaks" around, not often personally appreciated by Ritz-Carlton guests, include "The Point" just below the hotel and "The Beach" to the north. On windy days hang gliders surf the thermals. And on a clear day you'll see Catalina Island.

The 18-acre Salt Creek Park, above the beach at 33333 S. Coast Hwy., 949/923-2280, www.ocparks.com, is just off the highway, with access at both Selva Road and Ritz-Carlton Drive.

Technically the beach stretches both north and south of the Ritz-Carlton, yet the southern strand is also referred to as **Laguna Niguel Beach.** (Most everyone thought this stretch of coastline would be incorporated into the new city of Laguna Niguel, thus the name. Instead, the area was included in the new city of Dana Point.) Above the beach is a blufftop park, with vast ocean views. Here you'll find picnic tables and barbecue pits, showers, even a basketball court. A natural amphitheater created by the dramatic slope of the lawn provides a popular venue for summer performances.

Accommodations

To mind the budget, camp at Doheny—but only if you remembered to reserve well in advance. For bed-and-breakfast charm and comfort try 29-room **Ⓝ Blue Lantern Inn,** 34343 Blue Lantern, 949/661-1304 or 800/950-1236, www.foursisters.com, perched on a bluff overlooking the harbor. Built in the fashion of a traditional Cape Cod inn, the Blue Lantern serves up salt air and some spectacular views (Tower and some Pacific Edge rooms). Yet each room has its merits, featuring a fireplace, sitting area, small refrigerator stocked with soft drinks, and in-room whirlpool tub. Full breakfast and afternoon hors d' oeuvres are served in the library. Rates are $175–500.

The area boasts some spectacular full-service resorts. Newest is 172-acre **St. Regis Monarch Bay Resort,** 949/234-3200 or 800/722-1543, www.stregismonarchbeach.com, located just 10 mile south of Laguna Beach and boasting grand columns, royal airs, and hundreds of large guest rooms and suites. According to Zagat, this is one of the nation's top 50 resorts. Rooms feature dramatic décor, down comforters, and all the electronic amenities, from high-speed Internet and three phones to huge flat-screen TVs with in-room movies and Web-TV. Butler service is available on the Astor Floor. The resort also offers tennis courts, full fitness and spa facilities, and the onsite 18-hole Monarch Beach Golf Links designed by Robert Trent Jones, Jr. Room rates are $475 and up. Onsite restaurants include the French-Asian **Aqua,** the international **Motif** for

"small plates" and Sunday brunch, the **Lobby Lounge & Terrace** for drinking in the views, and the **Crust** bakery and sandwich/coffee shop.

In the same neighborhood but right on the beach is the **Ritz-Carlton Laguna Niguel,** 949/240-2000 or 800/241-3333, www.ritzcarlton.com, a gem for those who can afford it; room rates start at $395, suites go as high as $3,200. The Ritz here is a long, low Mediterranean villa enthroned on cliffs overlooking the beach and ocean. The northern wing faces Salt Creek Beach; the Dana Point wing overlooks ocean, palm trees, and sunset scenery. Resort amenities include four outdoor tennis courts, two heated pools with whirlpool tub, and a complete fitness center with exercise and steam room, sauna, and massage. Golf at various area courses is available. The grounds are gorgeous, too; sign on for a garden tour. All rooms have small private terraces, and are attractive and comfortable in the somewhat staid Ritz-Carlton style. Amenities include Frette linens, color TV with on-demand video, in-room honor bars and safes plus, in the bathrooms, European toiletries, lighted makeup mirrors, scales, hair dryers, an extra telephone, and thick terry bathrobes. As is typical at Ritz-Carlton hotels, services are top drawer. In the afternoon, take tea in the mahogany-paneled library. Casual meals, breakfast, lunch, and dinner, are served at the Ritz's seasonal **Ocean Terrace** café (outside on the terrace, overlooking the ocean). Grand but pricey Sunday brunch, too. Another possibility is the romantic, supper club-style **Club Grill and Bar,** which also serves live jazz and blues in the evening. When cost is no object, **The Dining Room** is truly exceptional, one of the best restaurants in Orange County. And though a dressed-down dress code is otherwise strictly enforced in Dana Point and Laguna Beach, the Ritz-Carlton insists on some semblance of formality. Jackets and ties are required even in the bar, semi-formal attire in The Dining Room.

Food

At **Jon's Fish Market,** 34665 Golden Lantern (Harbor Drive), 949/496-2807, sit outside on the red picnic tables and enjoy a casual seafood feast. For something considerably fancier and a tad more expensive in the same harbor neighborhood, try **Gemmell's,** serving fine French at 34471 Golden Lantern 949/234-0064. Warm up with the French onion or soup du jour, dive into the blackened salmon or crab meat salad, and dig into specialties including New York steak with mushrooms and creamy Bordelaise sauce and Gemelli pasta, served with gulf shrimp in Dijon mustard cream sauce. Elegant Italian **Luciana's,** south of Blue Lantern in a 1930s European-style building at 24312 Del Prado (PCH south bound) 949/661-6500, is most famous for its pastas—rigatoni al pesto, spinach lasagna with eggplant and cheeses, penne pasta with capers and Kalamata olives, even house-made gnocci. Open nightly for dinner.

Though the Ritz-Carlton and the St. Regis offer classier bar scenes, more fun is the **Mugs Away Saloon,** 27324 Camino Capistrano in Laguna Niguel, 949/582-9716, the local answer to attitude bars everywhere. In this one, you drink, dance, and admire the bare-behinds photo collection. These Mugs Away "mugs" commemorate the bar's annual day-and-night "Moon Amtrak" event—the second Saturday in July—at which patrons drop their drawers to titillate and/or terrorize train travelers. At last report commemorative T-shirts were available at www.moonamtrak.org.

SAN JUAN CAPISTRANO

A schmaltzy song started it all. The 1939 Leon Rene tune *When the Swallows Come Back to Capistrano* is responsible for the excited flutter here every year on March 19, St. Joseph's Day, when tourists flock to town to welcome the return of the cliff swallows from their annual Argentina migration.

Identifiable by their squared-off cleft tails and propensity for nesting under overhangs and in other protected high-altitude spots, the swallows' first official return was in 1776—the year the United States became a nation and the year Father Junípero Serra established the mission. Serra recorded the event in his diary.

Nowadays, though, on March 19 tourists typically far outnumber the swallows, which never

did respect that particular day much anyway. (According to ornithologists, the swallows return in the spring, March 19 being close enough to the spring equinox, though "scouts" can be spotted quite early in March.) Modern life has created confusion for the mission's mythic swallows. Too many people and too much hubbub scare them off, for one thing. Earthquakes, and earthquake repairs, have knocked down hundreds of old swallow nests, for another, and subsequent scaffolding put up to protect the mission has discouraged still more birds. As a result visitors are as likely to see cliff swallows nesting in the high nooks and crannies of taller buildings as at the mission.

All that aside, San Juan Capistrano does what it can to help the swallows do their historical duty—by setting out a buffet of ladybugs and green lacewing larvae in the rose garden in March. It also plans most of its **Fiesta de las Golondrinas,** with parade, fun runs, and people dressed up in swallow costumes, for the week framing March

the Mission in San Juan Capistrano

19. Putting local politicians and other volunteers to good use, the festivities culminate later in the month with a "mud-slinging" contest—with the mud and straw slapped onto old adobes to help preserve them.

Though there isn't yet a song to serve as a swallow send-off, Capistrano's birds are supposed to depart on St. John's Day, October 23.

For more information on the area, contact: **San Juan Capistrano Chamber of Commerce,** 31781 Camino Capistrano, Ste. 306, 949/493-4700, www.sanjuanchamber.com.

Mission San Juan Capistrano

Its crumbling church walls steadied by scaffolding and surrounded by very contemporary California, Mission San Juan Capistrano is not the most vigorous survivor of the state's 21-mission chain. Yet it's impressive nonetheless. The **quadrangle,** with its storerooms and workshops for making clothing, candles, soap, and pottery, was the center of mission life. Today, exhibits, a 12-minute film, and museum displays (including the piano on which the famous swallow song was composed) tell the basic story. Most evocative, though—if you can imagine the scaffolding

desaparecido—are the ruins of the **Great Stone Church,** built in 1797 and destroyed by an earthquake in 1812. (The nonprofit Mission Preservation Foundation is now raising funds—an estimated $7.5 million is needed—to restore the original stone church.) To get an exact idea of what the old church looked like, visit the Spanish Renaissance **New Church of Mission San Juan Capistrano** on Camino Capistrano, with its stunning interior murals and artwork. Next door—draped in spectacular color when the bougainvillea is in bloom, and still in use after all these years—is the mission's original **Serra Chapel,** the only one remaining in California in which Father Serra said mass. Capistrano's chapel, constructed in 1777, is also the oldest building standing in the Golden State. Quite striking inside is the ornate "golden altar," made of cherry wood more than 300 years ago and brought here from Barcelona, Spain, in 1922. Wander the grounds, with its ancient gardens, ponds, and Native American cemetery, to complete a thoughtful tour of San Juan Capistrano, once considered "the jewel of the missions."

Mission San Juan Capistrano is on Camino Capistrano at Ortega Hwy. (Hwy. 74) and

ORANGE COUNTY'S MISSION DAYS

Few reminders remain of the area's first known people, named by conquistadores the "Juañeno" after the mission at San Juan Capistrano. The Juañenos' 10-month combined solar and lunar calendar—unique in California but common among the Pueblo people in the American Southwest—was one remnant of native culture that survived mission influences long enough to be noted.

Today's Orange County travelers navigate by freeway the desert landscape of cactus, sagebrush, and native grass trod by Captain Gaspar de Portolá and the first inland incursion of Spanish in 1769. Padre Fermí Francisco de Lasuén, one of the far-ranging Franciscan fathers, came in 1775 to select a mission site, San Juan Capistrano. Father Junípero Serra showed up to dedicate the mission in 1776, the same year Juan Bautista de Anza ar-

rived with the region's first livestock. As was their custom elsewhere, missionaries soon planted gardens, orchards, and vineyards, establishing a foundation for the region's very rich agriculture.

Then began the much-romanticized era of the Californios, the California-born descendants of early Spanish and Mexican settlers. Though only one of the 20 original Spanish land grants was located here—the Yorba family's 30,000-acre Santiago de Santa Ana, which included part of the land now incorporated into the cities of Orange, Santa Ana, and Newport Beach—under Mexican rule the region was divided into six major ranchos. The holdings of the Peralta, Sepulveda, and Yorba families would later form the 93,000-acre Irvine Ranch, from which sprouted the cities of Santa Ana and Tustin and, later, the meticulously planned city of Irvine.

accessible either from PCH or I-5. Advance reservations are required. Docent-guided tours are $7 per person. Self-guided tours are $6 adults, $5 seniors, and $4 children 3–11 (under 3 free). It's open daily 8:30 A.M.–5 P.M. Call 949/234-1300 or see www.missionsjc.com for current information. Special events are scheduled year-round. **Living History Day** is held at the mission on the first Saturday of the month. **The Capistrano Pageant,** www.thecapistranopageant.com, is scheduled from late July into early August and features reenactors, encampments, demonstrations, the costumed California Heritage Ball, and performances of *Capistrano,* an outdoor musical celebrating early area history and culture.

Other Sights

Across from the mission's new church is another local newcomer—the postmodern mission-style **San Juan Capistrano Regional Library,** 31495 El Camino Real (at Acjachema), 949/493-1752, designed by Princeton University architect Michael Graves. The courtyard and gardens offer peaceful and private retreats for reading. Call for current hours.

Nearby is the **O'Neill Museum,** 31831 Los Rios St., 949/493-8444, a petite 19th-century Victorian with local memorabilia on display. Pick up the local **historic walking tour** map here (or at the chamber office) to discover San Juan Capistrano's **Los Rios Historic District,** the oldest residential neighborhood in California, with its surviving adobes and other venerable ancients. Marvelous, modest **Ramos House Café,** across from the railroad platform at 31752 Los Rios St., 949/443-1342, is a snazzy yet still reasonably priced New American (Spanish, Creole, Southern influences) tucked into a historic neighborhood home. Eat outside on the shaded patio. Breakfast—all the best in season, such as wild mushroom omelettes—is well worth the search to find the place, and people swoon for the smoked chile and crab Bloody Marys. For lunch, there might be basil-cured salmon or fried chicken and crawfish etouffee. For dessert, try some raspberry-buttermilk pie or delectable house-made ice cream. Open for breakfast and

lunch only, closed Monday. The 1894 Spanish revival **Capistrano Depot,** 26701 Verdugo, is a stunning stop for Amtrak.

Not everything in the area is ancient, though even some youngsters are getting a bit gray. One of Orange County's coolest;ong-running clubs is here—**The Coach House,** tucked into a warehouse at 33157 Camino Capistrano, 949/496-8930, www.thecoachhouse.com, known for good—sometimes great—live music acts. For the best seats, make dinner reservations. And if you find yourself near Santa Ana, also well worth tracking down is the Coach House's sister club, **The Galaxy Concert Theater,** 714/957-0600, www.galaxytheatre.com.

SAN CLEMENTE

This isn't much of a tourist town. The people of San Clemente prefer it that way—and you'll be glad, too, if peace and quiet have eluded you elsewhere. The well-guarded solitude of this red-tile-roofed Republican town was its primary appeal for ex-President Richard M. Nixon and his wife, Pat, who retreated here to La Casa Pacifica, the **Western White House,** overlooking the beach. The best view of Nixon's former estate, a palm-shrouded 25-acre compound, is from San Clemente State Beach. Otherwise, the most exciting scene around is at the San Clemente Pier adjoining the city beach, reached via Avenida Del Mar, where crewcut Marines from nearby Camp Pendleton cavort alongside civilians.

For more information about the area, contact: **San Clemente Chamber of Commerce,** 1100 N. El Camino Real, 949/492-1131, www.scchamber.com.

San Clemente State Beach

Backed by craggy white sandstone bluffs and wind-warped coastal chaparral, mile-long San Clemente State Beach, with its fine white sand, is still one of the best things in town—comparatively uncrowded when every other beach in the county is overrun. Reached via various trails, the beach is popular for skin diving, surfing, and just plain sunning and swimming. Up on the landscaped bluffs are picnic areas and a devel-

THE SURFRIDERS: SURFING GOES GREEN

You'd never guess it, to watch competitive young surfers duke it out for ocean elbow room, but surfing has *traditions,* concerns much more lasting than who gets there first, fastest, or with the most finesse.

One surfing tradition is caring about coastal waters and fighting environmental decline, whether from oil and sewage spills or impending development. Surfing is increasingly endangered, a development directly related to human activity as well as human efforts to correct the problem. Flood-control dams upriver, for example, prevent sand from flowing to sea to replenish beaches. The coastal breakwaters and jetties built to trap existing sand have the unfortunate side effect of aggravating sand erosion—the ocean continues to suck it out to sea—while destroying waves.

But even surfers were shocked in February of 1990 when the British Petroleum-chartered oil tanker *American Trader* impaled itself on its own anchor about a mile offshore. About 400,000 gallons of oil spilled, much of it scooped up or dispersed at sea but a substantial amount washing ashore to foul 15 miles of beaches and wetlands and kill seabirds from Anaheim Bay in L.A. County

to the Newport Beach peninsula. In one of those ironies of fate—since Huntington Beach is still Orange County's main oil producer—most of the oil came ashore near Bolsa Chica and Huntington Beach. Along with the professional crews, hundreds of Orange County volunteers turned out to stop the oil and then to clean things up.

Since 1984 the Surfrider Foundation, which began in surf-happy Huntington Beach, has been on the front lines of the battle to protect the oceans and the coastline. Originally a handful of long-haired locals—the group began educating the public by spray painting storm drains with the message "Drains to Ocean," and it is still famous for its guerrilla theater—the Surfrider Foundation is now a national organization. In addition to some notable local victories, national wins include restoring natural dune habitat on the Outer Banks in North Carolina and, in Hawaii, successfully suing Honolulu for dumping raw sewage into Kailua Bay.

For more information about the organization, or to join, contact the **Surfrider Foundation** headquarters in San Clemente, 949/492-8170, www.surfrider.org.

---

oped campground with 157 sites (72 with hookups). Day use (parking) is $12; camping, $16–21 and $25–30 (hookups), the higher rates in peak season. For camping reservations, call ReserveAmerica at 800/444-7275 or see www.re serveamerica.com. To get here, from I-5 exit at Avenida Calafia near the south side of town and follow the signs. For more information, call 949/492-3156.

Accommodations

San Clemente has a surprising number of decent motels with what are, by Orange County standards, quite reasonable rates. One best bet—right on the beach, with a peerless pier view—is the **Beachcomber Motel,** 533 Avenida Victoria, 949/492-5457 or 888/492-5457, www.beach combermotel.com, where you can park that lawn chair right out on the lawn and watch the sun set. Nothing fancy but clean and functional, kitch-

enettes too. All rooms and suites feature a sofa bed in addition to the bed, and sleep at least four. Rates vary according to day of the week and season but range $100–300 per night, weekly rates also available.

Practically on the beach is the tiny, hill-hugging **Casa Tropicana,** right across from the pier at 610 Avenida Victoria, 949/492-1234 or 800/492-1245, www.casatropicana.com. This beachfront bed-and-breakfast hotel has a festive "tropical paradise" ambience, an attitude also animating the Tropicana Bar & Grill downstairs. Rooms are themed—Coral Reef, Key Largo, Out of Africa—and most feature in-room whirlpool tubs. Full breakfast is included, either in your room or downstairs in the restaurant. Also enjoy the loaner beach chairs and umbrellas. Rates $120–280 (weekday and off-season rates much lower), two-night minimum on summer weekends.

Food

You won't starve in San Clemente, but in general the eating-out options are less abundant than elsewhere along the coast. The **Beach Garden Cafe** across from the pier at 618 ^{1}/2 Avenida Victoria, 949/498-8145, is a best bet for breakfast. Next door, at Casa Tropicana, is Rick's **Tropicana Bar & Grill,** 610 Avenida Victoria, 949/498-8767, serving burgers, pasta, and salads along with live music on weekend nights. Hottest California grill around, though, is **BeachFire,** 204 Avenida Del Mar, 949/366-3232, a Spanish California-style venue with funky tropical attitude, serving such things as coconut shrimp tempura, Bali rolls, fish and chips in Sierra Nevada Pale Ale batter, and rum butter jerk chicken. **Iva Lee's,** 555 N. El Camino Real, 949/361-2855, serves upscale Cajun, from Sweet Georgia Peach tomato soup and shrimp hush puppies to New Orleans-style barbecued shrimp and pan-fried pork chops with collard greens and black-eyed peas. For dessert, consider bourbon pecan pie topped with vanilla bean ice cream. The three-course dinner is a pretty good deal. Open for dinner every night—come on Thursday nights for live blues—and for brunch Sunday 9 A.M.–2 P.M.

To the South

Before freeway traffic slithers south into San Diego County, it all becomes one with I-5. The area near the new city of Lake Forest, once known as El Toro, is where I-5 and the 405 suddenly join, condensing into the I-5 leg of the San Diego Freeway. This traffic nightmare is known as the "El Toro Y." (Heads up.) Just north of San Clemente, Pacific Coast Highway (Hwy. 1) also becomes one with I-5.

Driving south from San Clemente, note the daunting seven-mile freeway barrier marking the center divide—intended to deter illegal aliens heading north on foot from San Diego, as they're all too frequently killed while dashing across the freeway.

Just across the county border lies **San Onofre State Beach,** part of a larger state park complete with campground. The most imposing coastal neighbor is the **San Onofre Nuclear Power Plant,** looming at the end of the beach. Next is the massive acreage of **Camp Pendleton,** the largest open-space coastal acreage remaining in San Diego County and a symbolic introduction to regional military culture.

San Diego Coast

To discover San Diego, discover its coast. To discover San Diego County's northern coastline, exit the freeway and amble along the ocean. You can exit anywhere, of course, but for the longest coastal cruise start just south of the Orange County border and head south to La Jolla. The street name changes in each community—becoming Carlsbad Boulevard in Carlsbad, for example, and Camino del Mar in Del Mar—so old Hwy. 101 is also known, prosaically, as County Road S21.

First stop for most people, just after the old highway separates from I-5, is Oceanside, with a nice pier and beach, urban adjunct to the sprawling Camp Pendleton U.S. Marine base. Just inland is Mission San Luis Rey, "King of the Missions." Farther north along the coast, just south of the county line, is San Onofre State Beach (san on-OH-free), technically in San Diego County but geopolitically more connected to San Clemente and other Orange County locales. An unavoidable feature of remote San Onofre is its

Must-Sees

Look for **M** to find the sights and activities you can't miss and **N** for the best dining and lodging.

M Legoland: With more than 40 rides, shows, and attractions on 128 acres of rolling parkland, Legoland offers a full and exciting day out for children and their families (page 598).

M San Diego Wild Animal Park: Affiliated with the San Diego Zoo, 2,200-acre San Diego Wild Animal Park exhibits endangered species in their own wide open spaces (page 603).

M San Diego Natural History Museum: Along Balboa Park's central El Prado promenade, this natural history museum is a standout (page 620).

M San Diego Aerospace Museum: This is another excellent museum, beyond Balboa Park's El Prado, appealing to flight and space buffs (page 622).

M San Diego Zoo: This world-class zoo sprang from animals left behind by the Panama-California International Exposition. Part of the zoo's appeal is the near absence of prison-bar-style cages and pens, allowing the animals to be "captivating instead of captive." (page 624).

M Old Town: The old adobe survivors of Old Town San Diego, the state's most popular historic park, are intertwined with—and clearly outnumbered by—commercial enterprises that now surround Old Town Plaza. Still, these streets of early California settlement include some great buildings—especially the 1827 La Casa de Estudillo (page 629).

M Gaslamp Quarter: San Diego's downtown has managed to preserve and polish what remained of the area's historic character. Lively Gaslamp Quarter is aglitter with striking buildings, stylish shops, great restaurants and clubs (page 632).

M Coronado: Across from San Diego's Embarcadero is Coronado, an "island" connected to the mainland only by a sandy isthmus and a sky-skimming arched bridge. Coronado is famous for its grand 1888 **Hotel del Coronado**, a national historic landmark (page 634).

M San Diego Maritime Museum: You can climb aboard the historic ships collected here, including the three-masted *Star of India* (page 638).

M Torrey Pines State Reserve: Not to be missed is the Torrey Pines State Reserve, a refuge for the rarest pine trees in the United States. Close by is the village of La Jolla, a seven-mile stretch of sublime coastline (page 647).

SAN DIEGO COAST

0   5 mi

0   5 km

Oceanside
Carlsbad
Escondido
San Diego Wild Animal Park
M Legoland
Del Mar
Torry Pines State Reserve **M**
La Jolla
Old Town **M**   San Diego
Coronado **M**   San Diego Zoo **M**
Coronado **M**   San Diego Natural History Museum
San Diego Maritime Museum   San Diego Aerospace Museum/International Hall of Fame
The Gaslamp Quarter
PACIFIC OCEAN   Imperial Beach
Tijuana

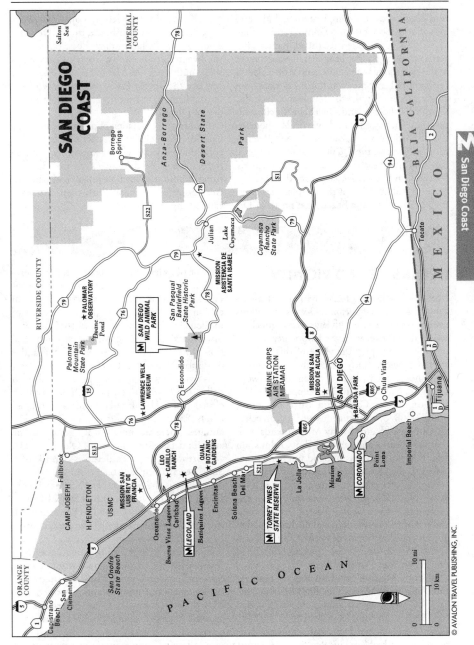

San Diego Coast

© AVALON TRAVEL PUBLISHING, INC.

mid-beach nuclear power plant, though the area also offers good spots for swimming and surfing.

South of Oceanside is Carlsbad, named after Karlsbad, Bohemia, for the similar mineral content in the local spring water, most famous these days as the home of Legoland. Next stop is Encinitas—including, technically, the communities of Leucadia, Cardiff-by-the-Sea, and Olivehain. Encinitas is historically famous for its flower fields—poinsettias in particular—the downtown Self-Realization Fellowship, the Quail Botanical Gardens, San Elijo State Beach (and the area's various locals' beaches), and Leucadia's galleries and shops.

For a full measure of the simpler pleasures, stop in sunny Solana Beach, just north of Del Mar. Known for its celebrities and chic shopping, Del Mar is also home to the Del Mar Thoroughbred Club summer horse races—and the beach here is dandy. Torrey Pines Road leads south from Del Mar to La Jolla. Along the way are the Torrey Pines reserve, beach, and coastal lagoon, technically still part of the city of San Diego.

A thorough exploration of northern San Diego County also includes excursions inland to Escondido and vicinity, best known as home to the San Diego Wild Animal Park; the apple-pie American frontier town of Julian; and fabulous Anza-Borrego Desert State Park, most inviting in early spring.

South Along the Coast

OCEANSIDE AND VICINITY

Immediately north of Carlsbad and almost a suburb of Camp Pendleton is Oceanside, with its own pier, a nice beach with largely crew-cut clientele, and an active, attractive harbor area. It's impossible to overplay the value of this 17-mile stretch of wide, sandy beach, the only significant undeveloped stretch of oceanfront between Orange County and San Diego proper. A local attraction is the **California Surf Museum,** 760/721-6876, www.surfmuseum.org, an eclectic, almost offhand display of surfboards with themed exhibits and zany gift shop. Admission free. Considerably less offhand but sometimes offbeat is the **Oceanside Museum of Art,** in an Irving Gill-designed building at 704 Pier View Way, 760/721-2787, www.oma-online.org. Exhibits range from *Snowy Day & Smoky Night* children's book illustrations and the hand-painted guitars and skateboards of *Rock & Roll*, to *Ethel Greene: Surrealistic Painter*, paying homage to one of San Diego's own.

Historic **Mission San Luis Rey de Francia,** the "King of the Missions" at 4050 Mission Ave., 760/757-3651, www.sanluisrey.org, was founded in 1798 but not completed until 1815. In 1893 the mission became a Franciscan seminary. Wander the grounds of San Luis Rey, the state's largest but one of its less visited missions, for an appreciation of early California culture—and the enduring wonder of adobe construction. Museum exhibits and displays reveal the rough reality of mission life. The mission's original 1815 *reredos* or ornamental altar screen was recently returned from the Oakland Museum of California and is on display. Mission San Luis Rey is four miles east of I-5 via Hwy. 76 (Mission Ave.) and is open daily 10 A.M.–4:30 P.M. for self-guided tours, closed major U.S. holidays. Admission is $5 adults, $3 students (children under 7 free), $18 families. There are other historic adobes in the area; for details, see Whispers of Old California.

North of Camp Pendleton is **San Onofre State Beach,** open daily 6 A.M.–sunset. The odd detail here is the **San Onofre Nuclear Power Plant,** about five miles south of San Clemente, serving as the Mason-Dixon line between north and south beaches though the two are connected by a public walkway along the seawall. The north is known for excellent surfing—San Onofre Surf Beach—and the south for good swimming and bodysurfing. **San Onofre Bluffs Campground** (no hookups but dump station) is open only May through September. **San Mateo Campground,** open year-round with hookups and hot showers, is 1.5 miles inland from the beach. very nice "primitive" campground (for both tents and

RVs, no hook-ups). It's open daily 6 A.M.–sunset. Beach day use is $10 per vehicle. Camping is $16–30. For more information about the beaches here, call 949/492-4872. For camping reservations, call ReserveAmerica at 800/444-7275 or see www.reserveamerica.com.

Another area attraction is the **Buena Vista Lagoon** and associated **Audubon Society Nature Center** south of town at 2202 S. Coast Hwy., 760/439-2473, www.bvaudubon.org, straddling the border with Carlsbad, a great spot for birders to augment their life lists. Guided nature walks are offered; call for current details.

For more information about the area, contact the **Oceanside Visitors Center,** also a California Welcome Center, at 928 N. Coast Hwy., 760/722-1534, www.oceansidechamber.com. If you're heading south, the center also distributes publications of the **Highway 101 Association,** www.drivethe101.com.

CARLSBAD

According to local lore, Carlsbad was named after Karlsbad, Bohemia (Karlovy Vary in today's Czech Republic), since its "waters" had a composition identical to the mineral waters of the Ninth Spa. Little wonder, then, that the spa trade was also hot here, beginning in the 1880s. You can see remnants and mementos of that era at the picturesque stone **Alt Karlsbad** day spa at 2802 Carlsbad Blvd., 760/434-1887, www.carls badmineralspa.com. In addition to excellent massage and fascinating ambience, the onsite spa offers Roman mud facials, "total body facials," salt exfoliation, herbal wraps and carbonated mineral water baths (all by appointment only). Adjacent are the original wells, capped after World War II.

Present-day Carlsbad is best known as an affluent, family-friendly beach town cum San Diego bedroom community, populated by surfers, eccentrics, entrepreneurs, and high-technology firms. This genuinely laid-back coastal escape exploded with hustle, bustle, and new business when the 128-acre **Legoland** children's theme park and affiliated resort opened here in 1999. Carlsbad wows the crowds every spring at California's largest street fair, the **Carlsbad Village Faire.**

PANCHO RIDES AGAIN

The historic 27-acre **Leo Carrillo Ranch** in southeast Carlsbad, also known as Rancho de Los Kiotes, was once a 2,538-acre working ranch and onetime home of noted California actor and civic leader Leo Carrillo, better known as sidekick Pancho to Duncan Renaldo's Cisco in the popular *Cisco Kid* 1950s TV series.

Leo Carrillo was also a conservationist and preservationist, a descendant of a noted Californio family rooted in Old Town San Diego. As a wedding present to his grandparents Josefa (Bandini) and Boston-educated Pedro Carrillo, Governor Pio Pico awarded them title to Coronado Island. (They sold it 23 years later for the total sum of $1,000. "I think the family let it go too soon," Carrillo often joked.) An 18-year member of the California Beaches and Parks Commission, Carrillo was pivotal in creating L.A.'s Olvera Street complex, the Los Angeles Arboretum, Anza-Borrego Desert State Park, and Hearst Castle at San Simeon. Leo Carrillo State Park in Malibu is named for him, and, while serving as the state's official Ambassador of Good Will, Governor Edmund G. Brown called him "Mr. California."

Thanks to the city of Carlsbad and Friends of Carrillo Ranch, you can visit Leo Carrillo's Old Califoria–style world. Stop by the **Caretaker's Cottage,** now park visitor center at 6200 Flying LC Ln., to pick up a free park guide before setting out to explore the grounds, complete with **Hacienda,** pool and cabana, **Dede's House,** cantina, tack room, bunkhouse, and more. The park is open in winter (Standard Time) Tues.–Sat. 9 A.M.–5 P.M. and Sun. 11 A.M.–5 P.M., in summer (daylight savings time) until 6 P.M. "Tour hours," when most buildings are open, are Sat. at 11 A.M. and 1 P.M., and Sun. at noon and 2 P.M. Closed Mondays. Park entrance and self-guided tours—which can take up to two hours—are free. For more information, call 760/476-1042 or see www.carrillo-ranch.org.

Visitors attracted to homegrown pleasures can sunbathe and swim at the beach, stroll along the seawall (Carlsbad's beach promenade), explore local lagoons, and loll around in coffeehouses and the casual, sometimes eclectic restaurants and shops collected along Carlsbad Boulevard.

Lined with antique shops selling heavy silver jewelry, country quilts, and estate furniture, the three blocks of **State Street** between Oak and Beech is an oasis of retro charm. Stroll over to **Aanteek Aavenue Mall,** 2832 State St., 760/434-8742, for an excellent variety of wares under one roof, including vintage china, glass, and jewelry. Find more vintage wares at **Black Roads Antiques,** 2988 State St., 760/729-3032.

Wind-driven winter waves tend to batter Carlsbad-area beaches, so Carlsbad State Beach and others are typically closed in winter and spring. They're also typically rockier than the southstate stereotype. Of the two local state beaches, small **Carlsbad State Beach** (County Road S21 at Tamarack) is usually the best bet for sandy sunbathing. Farther south on Carlsbad Boulevard (at but not accessible from Poinsettia Lane) is **South Carlsbad State Beach,** popular for ocean swimming as well as its large blufftop campground ($16–31, reservations mandatory). For more area beach information, call 760/438-3143.

Then there are Carlsbad's lagoons. South of Poinsettia along the shore is the quarter-mile interpretive walkway for the 610-acre **Batiquitos Lagoon,** now being revivified and reconnected with the ocean as a Port of Los Angeles wetlands mitigation project. For more information, stop by the nature center at 7380 Gabbiano Ln., call the Batiquitos Foundation at 760/931-0800, or see www.batiquitosfoundation.org. North of downtown is the **Buena Vista Lagoon,** with an Audubon Society nature center. Call the Audubon Society at 760/439-2473 or look up the Buena Vista chapter's website, www.bvaudubon.org, for information about scheduled birding and other events. Carlsbad nature has a tamer face, too, one that shines forth from its flower fields. Visit the 50-acre **Carlsbad Ranch** fields, 760/431-0352, www.theflowerfields.com, best for the ranunculus bloom from early March through May.

For more information about the community, contact the **Carlsbad Convention and Visitors Bureau** housed in the old Santa Fe Depot, 400 Carlsbad Village Dr., 760/434-6093 or 800/227-5722, www.visitcarlsbad.com. It's open Mon.–Fri. 9 A.M.–5 P.M., Saturday 10 A.M.–4 P.M., and Sunday 10 A.M.–3 P.M.

Legoland

With more than 40 rides, shows, and attractions on 128 acres of rolling parkland, **Legoland Carlsbad,** just 30 miles north of San Diego, offers a full and exciting day out for children and their families.

Opened in 1999, Legoland Carlsbad is one of four Lego-themed parks in the world inspired by the original in Denmark (other parks are in England and Germany). Like the first Legoland, this one is as expansive in scope as it is small in scale. There are fantastically detailed Lego models to admire, including 1:20 scale Lego brick reproductions of famous cities like San Francisco, Paris, and New York, each complete with moving vehicles and small-scale people scurrying about the streets. Also quite striking, and fun as

MUSING ON MUSIC

Carlsbad's **Museum of Making Music** celebrates the innovations that shaped popular music, from the player piano to digital grooves—because popular music has progressed in synch with instrument design and development. Located on the ground floor of the International Music Products Association at 5790 Armada Dr., 760/438-5996 or 877/551-9976, www.museumofmakingmusic.org, the museum features intriguing exhibits. Among past special shows: Handcrafted Artistry, historic archtop guitars; Wood Vibrations, chronicling the impact of acoustic guitars; and Hands on the Future, a hands-on encounter with futuristic music. Come on Saturday for guided **Tours @ Two,** a good introduction to the history of American popular music offered at 2 P.M. Admission is $5 adults, $3 seniors (60 and older), and $3 students and active military.

educational tools, are replicas of favorite national landmarks; New Orleans, San Francisco's Alamo Square, New York's Empire State Building, and Mount Rushmore were built using more than 30 million Lego bricks. Five new attractions debuted in 2004 to commemorate the park's fifth birthday, including the Block of Fame, the Fun Town Fire Academy, Miniland Florida, Dino Island, and the dino-inspired Coastersaurus.

What sets Legoland apart from other California theme parks is its absence of white-knuckle rides. Rides and attractions here—including a boat ride, a gravity coaster, a mini excursion tour, and a DUPLO building area—appeal instead to the two-to-eight-year-old crowd. Older kids will enjoy the Volvo driving school and the Bionicle Blaster, an intense Tilt-a-Whirl type ride. Even the food differs from regular theme park fare, with a European twist. Expect fresh fruit, applesauce, salads, and breadsticks along with homemade pizzas, popcorn, and chicken sticks.

Legoland, 1 Lego Dr. (at Cannon Rd.), 760/918-5346, www.lego.com, is open daily 10 A.M. to dusk, which translates into 10 A.M.–5 P.M. in winter, 9 A.M.–9 P.M. in summer. At last report admission was $43.95 adults, $34.95 children (ages 3–12) and seniors. Parking, available in the adjacent lot, is $7. To get here from I-5, take the Cannon exit east. To beat the traffic, take Amtrak to Oceanside then hop the Pal Shuttle to Legoland; for current details, call 760/720-9400 or see www.palomarlimo.com/palshuttle.

ENCINITAS

Known as "Flower Capital of the World," Encinitas is losing some floral ground to encroaching suburbia. **Quail Botanical Gardens,** a local horticultural star, is still going strong, however. Here you can wander 30 acres of canyon appreciating thousands of species: tropical and subtropical immigrants from Central and South America, Australia, Africa, and the Himalayas, also drought-resistant native plants. The **Seeds of Wonder Children's Garden,** new in 2003, is a total sensory experience, where kids can dig, plant, water, and even explore the baby dinosaur forest.

Quail Botanical Gardens is closed the first Monday of every month, otherwise open daily 9 A.M.–5 P.M. (closed Thanksgiving, Christmas, and New Year's Day). It offers general tours (free/every Saturday at 10 A.M. and free children's tours on the first Tuesday of every month. (Group tours are offered only by appointment.) Admission is free on the first Tuesday of every month, otherwise it's $8 adults, $5 seniors, $3 children ages 3–12 (under 3 free). For plant and gift shop purchases, come between 10 A.M. and 4 P.M. daily. Quail Botanical Gardens, 230 Quail Gardens Dr., 760/436-3036, www.qbgardens.com, is approximately 20 miles north of San Diego between Leucadia and Encinitas Boulevards. To get here from I-5, exit at Encinitas Boulevard and head east. Turn left (north) onto Quail Gardens Drive. The gardens are on the left.

Everybody's favorite surfers' park is **Swami's Beach** in Encinitas, immortalized by the Beach Boys in their 1963 *Surfin' U.S.A.* Swami's is so named because the entrance is just south of the golden-lotus towers of Paramhansa Yogananda's 1937 Self-Realization Fellowship Temple on First Street (Hwy. 101). Take the steep flight of stairs down to the beach, or watch the sunset from the blufftop park.

CARDIFF-BY-THE-SEA AND SOLANA BEACH

Head south for local beaches. The main attraction in Cardiff-by-the-Sea is **San Elijo State Beach,** Hwy. 101 at Chesterfield Drive, 760/753-5091, with lots of sand, surf, and great beachfront camping. Reservations are site-specific—beachfront sites are "premium"—so have a campground map at hand when you call, or reserve online. Campsites are $26–39, and day use is $10 (for day use, park at the north end of the campground). For reservation details, see Accommodations.

Solana means "sunny spot" in Español, and Solana Beach is still fun and funky in laid-back beach town style yet starting to try on civic phrases such as "chic" and "stylish." To sample the eclectic commercial side of this confusion, stroll the business district, more or less concentrated between Lomas Santa Fe Drive to the north and Via de la Valle to the south, Old Hwy. 101 to the west, and Cedros Avenue to the east. The **Cedros Design District,** or Cedros south of Lomas Santa Fe Drive, has become a destination in its own right, an intriguing collection of galleries, shops, and restaurants. If you'll be staying awhile, see what's shakin' at the **Belly Up Tavern,** 143 S. Cedros Ave., 858/481-9022, the local jazz and blues venue. Or take in a play at the very good **North Coast Repertory Theatre,** 987-D Lomas Santa Fe, 858/481-1055 or 888/776-6278, www.northcoastrep.org. Still, the beach in Solana Beach is the big thing, though finding a way down to it is something of a challenge. (Hint: Look for the "pillbox.") For more information about the area, contact the **Solana Beach Visitor Center,** 103 N. Cedros Ave., 858/350-6006, www.solanabeachchamber.com. For more coastal funk consider Leucadia north along the coast, once rudely nicknamed "Quaaludia" for its seriously laid-back surf-hippie society; shops such as **Ducky Waddle's Emporium** celebrate the good ol' countercultural days.

ACCOMMODATIONS

Camping is the best bet for true budget travelers, but plan ahead and make reservations. State beach parks offering camping include the two campgrounds at **San Onofre State Beach** in Oceanside and both oceanfront and inland campgrounds at **San Elijo State Beach** in Cardiff-by-the-Sea. Advance reservations are essential; call ReserveAmerica at 800/444-7275 or see www.reserveamerica.com. In addition to beach camping, Rancho Guajome Adobe County Park is a good choice (see Whispers of Old California for details). Contact local visitors bureaus for more camping options.

Well-located across the street from the beach is the attractive, Tudor-style **Carlsbad Inn Beach Resort,** 3075 Carlsbad Blvd., 760/434-7020 or 800/235-3939, www.carlsbadinn.com, once a 1920s mansion and now a 62-room hotel tucked in amid the timeshare townhouses. All rooms have TV and VCR (rental movies available), refrigerator, and coffeemaker; many have kitchenettes, and some feature fireplaces and whirlpool

tubs. Resort amenities include a large swimming pool, outdoor hot tub, steam sauna, fully-equipped exercise room, and children's play area. High-season room rates start at $200. For the ultimate Carlsbad luxury stay, head for **La Costa Resort and Spa** or the new **Four Seasons Resort–Aviara,** which overlooks Batiquitos Lagoon; see below for details on both.

Like Oceanside, Carlsbad has inexpensive motels too, including a Motel 6. A good mid-range choice for value-conscious families is the recently restyled **Ocean Palms Beach Resort,** 2950 Ocean St., 760/729-2493 or 888/802-3224, www.ocean-palms.net, where rates start at $100–150. Most rooms and suites include fully-equipped kitchens, color TV with cable (VCRs and movies available), and phones with voice mail and modem. Children's playground, heated outdoor pool, sauna, whirlpool tub, and picnic areas with barbecues.

The **Ocean Inn** in Encinitas at 1444 N. Hwy. 101 (between La Costa Avenue and Leucadia Boulevard), 760/436-1988 or 800/546-1598, www.oceaninnhotel.com, is a best bet for a base camp, just a five-minute walk to the beach. Rooms come with all the motel basics plus kitchenette—in-room refrigerator and microwave, but bring your own cookware and utensils—and color TV, cable, and video players. Some feature in-room whirlpool tubs. Midweek and off-season rates are $50–150, high-season/weekend rates $150–250.

Resorts

Got the urge to splurge? Carlsbad offers two accommodating possibilities. Noteworthy newcomer, perched on the north bank of the Batiquitos Lagoon, is the world-class Spanish colonial-style **Ⅶ Four Seasons Resort–Aviara,** 7100 Four Seasons Point, 760/603-6800, www.fourseasons.com. Sip a tall one from the shade of your poolside cabana, head for the tennis courts (open for night play), or sign up for a round of golf at the signature Arnold Palmer course. Full fitness facilities, spa services, huge family pool, and quiet pool, not to mention great restaurants. And on the off chance you're here with the kids to do Legoland, rooms at Aviara come furnished with Playstations. But don't get too comfortable: Midweek rack rates start at $315.

Otherwise, for tennis, golf, and letting go of worldly cares, the place in Carlsbad is **La Costa Resort and Spa,** luxurious yet relaxed and low-key. Almost a self-contained city, this 400-acre spread comes complete with its own movie theater. Carlsbad's La Costa features elegant rooms, wonderful restaurants, world-class spa and fitness facilities, swimming pools, tennis courts, racquetball courts, and two PGA championship 18-hole golf courses. (Inquire about special golf and tennis packages.) La Costa is also now home to the **Chopra Center,** www.chopra.com, Dr. Deepak Chopra's renowned wellness center. To keep it simple, rent bikes here and cruise on down to the beach. Room rates are $300 and up—way, way up. For more information call 760/438-9111 or 800/854-5000, or see www.la costa.com. To get here, drive two miles east of I-5 via La Costa Avenue then continue north for a quarter-mile on El Camino Real.

FOOD

Surf's up in Oceanside, and so is retro sentiment. A genuine old timey roadhouse is the 1928 **101 Café,** 631 S. Coast Hwy., 760/722-5220, and there's a **Ruby's Diner** at the pier, 1 Pier View Way, 760/433-7829. **Johnny Mañana's,** just up Mission Avenue, 760/721-9999, is a surfers' favorite, famous for its breakfast burrito special. Good for omelettes is the **Beachbreak Café,** 1902 S. Coast Hwy, 760/439-6355. For healthy staples and deli fare, head for **Cream of the Crop,** 2009 S. Coast Hwy, 760/433-2757. Inexpensive yet grand for Baja-style seafood is **Mariscos Ensenada,** 1405 El Camino Real, 760/967-6024, from fish tacos and burritos to seafood salads and soups.

As might be expected, Carlsbad is rich with restaurants. Grand for sandwiches is **Tip Top Meats** German-style deli, 6118 Paseo Del Norte, 760/438-2620. For stew, shepherd's pie, and Guinness, head for **Tom Giblin's Irish Pub,** 640 Grand Ave., 760/729-7234. Some okay choices in the Village Faire Shopping Center, 300 Carlsbad Village Dr., include: for southwestern, the

Coyote Bar & Grill, 760/729-4695; for Mexican, **Fidel's Norte,** 760/729-0903; and for burgers and brew, **Mr. Peabody's Burgers & Ale,** 760/434-4412. People come from miles around just for the unbelievable Sunday champagne brunch at **Neimans,** along the waterfront at 300 Carlsbad Village Dr., 760/729-4131, inside the grand Queen Anne mansion once owned by local "waters" promoter Gerhard Schutte.

Noteworthy for its Tuscan flair and Californian fare—from potato ale chowder and barbecue chicken pizza to honey-cured pork chops—consider **Bellefleur Winery & Restaurant** at the Carlsbad Company Stores outlet mall, 5610 Paseo Del Norte, 760/603-1919. The Four Seasons Resort–Aviara also has a nice California-style bistro, though for a superb dress-up dinner head for the Four Seasons' **Vivace** contemporary Northern Italian restaurant, 7100 Four Seasons Point, 760/603-6800.

Or head south to Encinitas, where you'll be lucky to get a reservation at super-star neighborhood-style **N Savory,** 267 N. El Camino Real (at Mountain Vista), 760/634-5556, where Chef Pascal Vignau serves up roasted garlic chicken, peppered ribeye steak, and superbly prepared fish and seafood. Open Tues.–Fri. for lunch, Tues.–Sun. for dinner. Reservations advised. Encinitas boasts a number of good restaurants. For French-Caribbean, try **Café Calypso,** 576 N. Hwy. 101, 760/632-8252, where seafood and spicy seafood pastas are specialties. For Manhattan-style clam chowder, cioppino, shrimp Louie, and an endless selection of broiled fresh seafood served up in a kid-friendly setting, the place is casual **Chesapeake,** 1060 El Camino Real, 760/943-0177, open daily for lunch and dinner.For genuine Oaxaca-style Mexican, everything very reasonably priced, the place is **El Oaxaqueño,** 1464 Encinitas Blvd., 760/632-1512. Wander the **First Street** area in downtown Encinitas to see what's new and appetizing.

Just south in Cardiff-by-the-Sea, **Ki's Juice Bar and Restaurant,** 2591 S. Hwy. 101 (near Chesterfield), 760/436-5236, is not strictly vegetarian—but if that's what you're looking for, this is where you'll find it. Everything here is fresh and healthy, including organic seven grain cereal and tofu scramble at breakfast and veggie stir fry, egg salad sandwiches, and Ki's salmon salad at lunch. Expect more of the same at dinner, plus pasta. Juice bar choices include fruit and ice cream smoothies—a chance to try a decent date shake—and fresh juices and blends, including orange and grapefruit, carrot and watermelon. Ki's serves food for the soul, too—live jazz on Friday and Saturday nights (no cover with dinner).

For California-style eclectica in Solana Beach's Cedros Design District, settle in at the **Ⓜ Wild Note Café** next to the Belly Up Tavern at 143 S. Cedros Ave., 858/259-7310. Another possibility is the **Zinc Café**, 132 S. Cedros Ave., 858/793-5436. The fare at **Solana Beach Brewery and Pizza Port**, 135 N. Hwy. 101 (at Loma Santa Fe), 858/481-7332, includes good pizza and salads—simple, straightforward flavors intended to complement the local brew. Offerings here include Ale Nino, 101 Nut Brown, Swamis India Pale Ale, Sharkbite Red Ale, as well as a selection of Belgian-style beers and Porters. If you can't decide, ask for the "taster"—four four-ounce glasses, a sample of each. While you're sampling, the kids can visit the arcade area.

Two-story **Fidel's**, 607 Valley Ave. (near Stevens) in Solana Beach, 858/755-5292, is the place for Mexican food—and lots of it. A com-bination plate, with rice, beans, and entrées of your choice, should satisfy even the most boisterous beach appetite (children's plates available). If at all possible, grab a table out on the patio. There's another Fidel's on Carlsbad Boulevard in Carlsbad, 760/729-0903. Fidel's is open daily 11 A.M.–9:30 P.M., sometimes later on weekends, and closed Christmas. Reservations taken only for groups of 10 or more.

Fun for families, a steak and prime rib kind of place, is the **Roadhouse Grill**, 937 Lomas Santa Fe, 858/794-0142, where prime rib chili is the house specialty. The Roadhouse also serves live music—and peanuts, big bowls full of unshelled peanuts. The practice here is to just toss the shells on the floor, definitely something most kids don't get to do at home.

EXCURSIONS INLAND: ESCONDIDO AND VICINITY

An intriguing drive inland from Del Mar is via County Road S6, which begins as Via de la Valle, or "By Way of the Valley," a reference to the route through the San Dieguito River Valley. This route passes the polo fields, equestrian centers, and golf resort before wending its way through the eucalyptus groves and horse corrals of 1920s-vintage **Rancho Sante Fe**, which got its start as the Santa Fe Railroad's

LAWRENCE WELK MUSEUM

The Lawrence Welk Resort north of Escondido, just off I-15 at 8860 Lawrence Welk Dr., 760/749-3000, www.welkresort.com, is quite contemporary and well-appointed, though in a sense it seems like something straight out of the 1950s. Most of Lawrence Welk's elderly fans come to his namesake resort to golf, swim, play tennis, just loaf, and take in a Broadway-style musical. Featuring stars from the long-running *Lawrence Welk Show*, the **Lawrence Welk Theater's** performance schedules include shows such as *I Love You, You're Perfect, Now Change, Bye Bye Birdie* and the annual *Welk Musical Christmas*. For a free look at memorabilia and a short lesson in television history, stop by the free **Lawrence Welk Museum** here. It's open daily 9:30 A.M.–5 P.M. Increasingly, though, this is a popular destination for family reunions, especially now that the **Boulder Springs Club House and Waterslide** have opened.

To get here: from I-15 northbound, exit at Deer Springs/Mountain Meadow Rd., turn right on Mountain Meadow, then left onto Champagne Boulevard. From I-15 southbound, exit at Gopher Canyon Road, turn left (it becomes Old Castle Road), then right onto Champagne Boulevard.

failed attempt at eucalyptus forestry—eucalyptus being a poor choice for railroad ties, as it turned out. According to the 2000 census, Rancho Santa Fe is now the wealthiest community in the U.S., with an average per capita income of $113,132. Before reaching "the ranch," though, there's a more significant stop—the **Chino Ranch Vegetable Shop,** just off Via de la Valle at 6123 Calzada del Bosque, 858/756-3184, a family-run roadside fruit and vegetable stand that's been attracting fresh food fans for more than 50 years (closed Monday). Beyond Rancho Santa Fe is **Lake Hodges,** a mountain-biking mecca, and the town of **Del Dios,** where **Hernandez' Hide-away,** 19320 Lake Dr., 858/756-8000, everyone's favorite Mexican food fueling stop.

Escondido

Escondido, which means "hidden" in Spanish, is far from invisible these days. Center of the vast inland territory north of San Diego and its suburbs, Escondido is home to the remarkable San Diego Wild Animal Park—where visitors "visit" Africa and Asia, and exotic animal and plantlife in open-air "natural" habitats, via monorail. Adjacent to this world tour of natural history is a monument to the hurried march of local history—the San Pasqual Battlefield State Historic Park. Here in 1846 a small band of "Californios," or California-born Mexican citizens, vanquished legendary scout Kit Carson and U.S. Army troops in one of the more infamous battles of the Mexican-American War. In more recent history Escondido has added high culture to its list of assets, with the $74 million California Center for the Arts, Escondido.

Radiating from Escondido like the spokes of a roughed-up wagon wheel are roads leading to other attractions—including the Lawrence Welk Resort, with its own theater for Broadway-style musical productions. Local vineyards and wineries are also a major draw.

From Escondido, intrepid travelers can set out on multiple "loop" daytrips—to Palomar Mountain State Park and the Palomar Observatory and then on to Julian, for example, or to Julian via Hwy. 78, and then on into Anza-Borrego or Rancho Cuyamaca State Parks before looping back. For more information on Palomar Mountain State Park and the observatory, see immediately below. Julian and the surrounding area are equally accessible from San Diego, and for that reason are listed under San Diego below.

For more information on the region, contact the **San Diego North County Convention and Visitors Bureau,** 720 N. Broadway in Escondido, 760/745-4741 or 800/848-3336, www.sandiegonorth.com.

San Diego Wild Animal Park

The main modern-day attraction in San Pasqual Valley is the 2,200-acre San Diego Wild Animal Park, affiliated with the San Diego Zoo. Here, the collected endangered species are exhibited in their own wide open spaces, the separate habitats representing Asian plains, Asian marshlands and swamps, North Africa, South Africa, and East Africa. Hikers can hoof it into East Africa on the hilly 1.75-mile **Kilimanjaro Safari Walk,** with observation platforms that allow spying on

the tram at San Diego's Wild Animal Park

San Diego Coast

the lions and elephants below. Cages are still cages, of course, no matter how aesthetic, so what you see here is far from "natural," in any meaningful sense. But here people are penned up, too—onboard the **Wgasa Bush Line** monorail, the park's main event. The five-mile monorail ride—sit on the right side if at all possible—traverses the prairies and canyonlands. Especially during summer heat, the best time to hop aboard is early evening, when the park's creatures are up and about and eating. Even better, in summer, are the after-dark treks, when all the park's a stage—lit by sodium-vapor lamps.

The kids will probably insist on extra time at **Nairobi Village,** the center of everything, complete with "petting kraal" (remarkably toddler-tolerant sheep and goats here); the interactive **Mombasa Lagoon** exhibit; the indoor **Hidden Jungle,** with tropical creatures not typically seen; the interactive **Lorikeet Landing,** an Australian rainforest where people can feed the nectar-loving birds all day long; and the long-running **Bird Show Amphitheater,** starring birds of prey and other performers. Exotic gardens here showcase more than 3,000 botanical specimens.

The park's most exotic activity—a must for photographers—is the **photo caravan tour,** which allows shutterbugs to get up close and personal from *inside* the animal compounds, snapping shots from an open-air truck. The tours run daily, and cost between $85–145, depending on the tour. For information and reservations, call 619/718-3030 or 800/934-2267. Family-friendly **Roar and Snore** and **Beastly Bedtime overnight campouts** are also offered, seasonally.

The San Diego Wild Animal Park is open daily from 9 A.M., with gates closing at 4 P.M. in winter and 8 P.M. in summer (grounds close two hours later). At last report admission was $29.50 adults, and $22 children ages 3–11 (parking extra). A "combination pass," $55.65 adults, $37.85 children, also covers one day's admission to the San Diego Zoo (to use within five days of purchase). Wheelchairs and strollers are available for rent. Parking is $6 ($8 for RVs). To get here: exit I-15 in Escondido at Via Rancho Parkway and follow the signs east; it's about six miles to the park. From I-5, exit at Hwy. 78 and head east to I-15; continue south on I-15, then exit east at Via Rancho Parkway. For current information (pre-recorded), call the San Diego Wild Animal Park at 760/747-8702, TTY/TDD 760/738-5067, or see www.sandiegozoo.org.

San Pasqual Battlefield State Historic Park

Near the San Diego Wild Animal Park is the historic **San Pasqual Battlefield,** 15808 San Pasqual Valley Rd., 760/737-2201, with multiple historic sights and monuments. Even with the nice visitor center here, the social and territorial skirmishes leading to California statehood don't titillate visitors as much as the animal park. Open Fri.–Mon. only, but come for living history events and the annual December reenactment of the Battle on San Pasqual.

The area's roadside produce stands do excite visitors. Keeping in mind that more than half of the U.S. avocado crop comes from San Diego County, take in more of the area's agricultural riches by meandering north toward Pauma Valley, Pala, or Fallbrook via back roads. **Fallbrook** is considered the avocado capital of the U.S. To wear the avocado green, show up in late April for the annual **Avocado Festival,** where festivities include the Avo Olympics and the Little Miss and Mr. Avocado Pageant.

Wineries

The **Ferrara Winery,** 1120 W. 15th Ave. in Escondido, 760/745-7632, is a favorite wine stop. In honor of San Diego County's oldest winemaking and grape-growing family, the Ferrara enterprise has been designated a state historical point of interest. Of particular interest to travelers: the wonderful red wines, white wines, dry wines, and dessert wines. The tasting room also features fresh grape juice, wine marinades, and wine vinegars. All Ferrara grape products are crushed, aged and/or brewed, bottled, and sold only on the premises. Self-guided tours (15–20 minutes/and wine-tasting are free.) The tasting room is open daily 10 A.M.–5 P.M., closed Christmas Day. To get here: From I-15 exit east at Ninth Ave., turn south onto Upas, then west onto 15th.

© ROBERT HOLMES/CALTOUR

the Mount Palomar Observatory

Orfila Vineyards and Winery, 13455 San Pasqual Rd., 760/738-6500 or 800/868-9463, www.orfila.com, formerly Thomas Jaeger Vineyards, is a popular stop on Gray Line and other organized tours. Orfila's wine specialties include cabernet, merlot, chardonnay, and tawny port. The very pleasant picnic area here, overlooking vineyards and valley, is the site of many weddings and other celebrations. Custom gift baskets are available at the gift shop. Tours and tastings are free for individuals; for groups (fee) reservations are required. Orfila is open daily 10 A.M.–6 P.M. One guided tour is offered daily, at 2 P.M., but visitors can take the self-guided tour any time. The winery is closed Thanksgiving, Christmas, and New Year's Day. To get here: exit I-15 at Via Rancho Parkway. Follow the signs toward the San Diego Wild Animal Park, but turn right onto Pasqual Valley Rd. and continue one mile.

The **Bernardo Winery,** 13330 Paseo del Verano Norte, south of Escondido in the Rancho San Bernardo area, 858/487-1866, www.bernardowinery.com, is one of the oldest continuously operating wineries in Southern California. The wine-tasting room, something of a general store, also features gourmet foods, olive oil, and private-label wines.

Self-guided winery tours take about 10 minutes. Lunch is served in the patio dining room daily (except Monday) 11 A.M.–3 P.M. The wine-tasting room is open daily 9 A.M.–5 P.M., gift shops 10 A.M.–5 P.M. (shops closed Monday and major holidays). To get here from I-15: exit at Rancho Bernardo Road, turn north onto Pomerado Road, then east onto Paseo del Verano Norte (just past the Oaks North Golf Club). Continue for 1.5 miles.

PALOMAR MOUNTAIN STATE PARK

This mile-high park at the edge of the Cleveland National Forest offers a refreshing pine-scented change from the scrubbier foothills below. Aside from the fine conifers and oaks, the park's easy hikes, meadows, fishing pond, great campground, and just general remoteness are its main attractions. Visitors ascend from Hwy. 76 east of Pauma Valley via the "Highway to the Stars" (County Rd. S6), built for access to the famous Mount Palomar Observatory, which is just east of the park. The park is open for day use, 8 A.M. to sunset, for camping year-round. Day use is $6 per car. Campsites at Doane Valley Family Camp are

CALIFORNIA CONDORS: BORN TO BE WILD

The world can be a dangerous place. And no one, certainly no non-human species, can keep all attendant hazards of the civilized world out of their neighborhood. The latest local symbol of this struggle is the California condor *(Gymnogyps californianus)*, the powerful and primal vulture known to Native Americans as the thunderbird. The largest land bird in North America, until 10,000 to 12,000 years ago the California condor flew and foraged across the southern reaches of what is now the United States, from the Pacific to the Atlantic Oceans. Pre-Columbian hunters soon dispatched most of the mammoths and other large animals on whose carcasses the condor fed. By the time of early European exploration the species had retrenched along the North American coastline from British Columbia to Baja California; condors were sometimes observed feeding on beached whales.

In more recent California history the California condor soared inland from the San Rafael Mountains to Sequoia National Park, protected from harm by the land's inaccessibility. Now most of the species' survivors live in protective custody—in "condorminium" cages at California zoos—because the condor's natural environment can no longer assure the bird's survival. Research suggests the precipitous recent decline of the condor was caused by lead shot and bullets, inadvertently consumed by feeding condors, in addition to the increasing incursions of civilization, in the form of power lines, antifreeze, and other hazards.

In 1987 the last wild California condors were captured and packed off as breeders for the captive breeding program, a last, fairly desperate attempt to save the species from extinction; at the time the total world Condor population was 27. For the

$14–19. Call for current reservation information. For more information, call the park directly at 760/742-3462 (sometimes a recorded information message), see www.palomar.statepark.org, or contact regional park headquarters at Cuyamaca Rancho State Park in Descanso, 760/765-0755, www.cuyamaca.statepark.org. For camping reservations, call ReserveAmerica at 800/444-7275 or see www.reserveamerica.com.

Mount Palomar Observatory

Something of a reluctant tourist attraction, the world-famous Mount Palomar Observatory was built in 1928 to take astronomical advantage of its elevation (6,100 feet), distance from coastal fog, and absence of urban light pollution. No longer boasting the world's largest reflecting telescope, this is still a serious research facility of the California Institute of Technology (Cal Tech) in Pasadena. Visitors can view the 200-inch Hale Telescope and study deep-space photos and other memorabilia at the small museum. The observatory, 760/742-2119, www.astro.caltech.edu/palomar, and museum are open daily 9 A.M.–4 P.M.; no admission fee. The small gift shop is open daily in summer, otherwise only on weekends.

Consider staying for lunch at *the* place to eat on the mountain, the vegetarian **Mother's Kitchen,** 760/742-4233. If you're not camping, the place to stay in these parts is the **Lazy H Ranch,** down the mountain in Pauma Valley, 760/742-3669; singles and doubles are $50–100.

Accommodations and Food

The comfortable **Best Western Escondido,** 1700 Seven Oakes Rd. east of I-15 (exit at El Norte Parkway), 760/740-1700 or 800/528-1234, www.bestwestern.com, is a very good value, with rooms $100–150. An appealing option for families is the **Circle of Quiet Bed and Breakfast,** just a stroll from downtown at 115 E. Seventh Ave., 760/432-8781 or 866/432-8781, www.cir cleofquietbedandbreakfast.com. And who wouldn't love a place named after one of Madeleine L'Engle's books? Rates are quite reasonable—$50–100, for rooms with shared and private baths—but the family-friendly feature here is the special kids' guest room, adjacent to the parents' room and stuffed with kid-sized beds, teddy bears, dolls, and toys that glow in the dark. The undisputed upscale star of local lodgings is south of town in the Rancho Bernardo

coastal Chumash people—haunted by what they were witnessing—the condor round-up suggested the end of the condor, and the end of the condor signaled the end of the world, the "time of purification" when the earth would shake and all life would end then begin again.

But the California condor hasn't yet disappeared. Though the species is still teetering on the edge of extinction, captive breeding and some success in releasing the birds into remote areas of their original range offer hope that the end of the world has been postponed. Today there are 220 condors and counting.

To get up-close and personal with the California condor—not something likely to happen in nature—stroll through the San Diego Wild Animal Park's **Condor Ridge** habitat.

A dozen species of rare and endangered North American animals are exhibited here, beginning with the endangered thick-billed parrots once thriving in the pines of Arizona, New Mexico, and northern Mexico. At the base of the pines here, darting among the shrubs, are western greater roadrunners. Next come the grasslands, where northern porcupines accompany the rare, steel-gray aplomado falcons. The prairies habitat is home to endangered black-footed ferrets, desert tortoises, black-tailed prairie dogs, western burrowing owls, American magpies, and western Harris hawks.

At the end of the trail is an observation deck and interpretive center concerning recovery efforts on behalf of the California condor and desert big horn sheep, the latter observed here scrambling around on steep hillsides. Several California condors can also be seen, in their six-story cage.

area—the **Rancho Bernardo Inn,** 17550 Bernardo Oaks Dr., 858/675-8500 or 877/517-9342, www.jcresorts.com, 265 acres of exquisite tile-roofed rooms, two restaurants, and exceptional resort facilities including a total of 108 holes of golf (45 on site), tennis, health spa, two swimming pools, rental bikes, the works. Rates are $250 and up. If that's too rich for you, Rancho Bernardo boasts many other nice motels and hotels, most quite reasonably priced.

If you're freeway flyin',' some good choices concentrate along Centre City Parkway, the I-15 business loop, including the **Fireside Restaurant,** 439 W. Washington St., 760/745-1931, for steaks and such, and **The Brigantine,** 421 W. Felicita Ave., 760/743-4718, for seafood.

For finer fare, romantic **Vincent's Sirino's,** 113 W. Grand Ave. (at Broadway), 760/745-3835, is locally famous for its bistro specialties, including pepper steak, rack of lamb, and poached salmon. Wonderful desserts. Open for dinner Tues.–Sat., closed major holidays. Also great, just across the street, is adventurous **150 Grand,** fortunately located at 150 W. Grand, 760/738-6868, open for lunch weekdays, for dinner nightly.

The regional dress-up dining destination s the elegant French **El Bizcocho** at the Rancho Bernardo Inn (see above), 858/675-8500.

EXCURSIONS INLAND: JULIAN AND VICINITY

This slice of apple-pie Americana, easily reached from either San Diego or Escondido, really does know its apples; small orchards climb the area's hillsides. Julian sprang to life as a hill-country mining town during Southern California's gold rush in the 1890s, and then declined into near ghost-town status until the area's affinity for apple growing was actively cultivated. Since then the town's Wild West character has been spruced up and tamed, as apples (also peaches and pears), fresh-squeezed apple cider, homemade apple pie, and the wistful American desire for simpler times have transformed tiny Julian into a major tourist draw. Bushels of visitors tumble into town during the desert's spring wildflower show, in summer, and for its **Apple Days** and **Fall Harvest Festival** celebrations—also peak seasons for local parking problems. Other main events in the fall include the **Julian Weed and Craft**

Show and the ever-popular annual **Bluegrass Festival.** Otherwise, poking into the town's museums and peering into lace-curtained curio and gift shops are Julian's primary attractions, along with some prime area hiking. Or plan a visit—advance reservations required—to the **California Wolf Center,** 619/234-9653, www.californiawolfcenter.org.

Another reason to tarry here—especially for intrepid desert and high-country explorers who prefer a bed to starry nights in a sleeping bag—is the town's proximity to spectacular Anza-Borrego Desert State Park.

For current information about the community, contact the **Julian Chamber of Commerce,** 2129 Main St., 760/765-1857 or visit the chamber's website at www.julianca.com.

Julian Pioneer Museum

Just over a block south of Main at 2811 Washington St., 760/765-0227, the Julian Pioneer Museum memorializes the hardrock mining and hardscrabble living—as well as the lace curtains and high-button shoes—so prominent in this tiny town's past. This onetime brewery showcases Julian's homage to its pioneering past, with clothing, familiar household items, photographs, and stuffed samples of area wildlife. Native American artifacts are also on display. It's open from Tues.–Sun. 10 A.M.–4 P.M. from April through November, otherwise open only on weekends and national holidays (same hours) except New Year's Day, Thanksgiving, and Christmas. Admission is $2 adults, $1 children 7–18, free for children 6 and under.

A listing of local historic buildings and sites ("Historic Sites") is available on the chamber's website.

Eagle Mining Company

Notable at the north end of C St., 760/765-0036, is a rare opportunity to tour the inner workings of a gold mine. Dug into a mountainside, the old Eagle Mine and High Peaks Mine ceased commercial operation in 1942, but the mine tunnels and plenty of mining paraphernalia are still in place. The tour explains local gold mining history and demonstrates various mining techniques; during the school year, school tours tend to overrun the place, so come late in the day. The kids even get the chance to pan for gold—but if they find some, they have to leave it at the mine. Hourly tours are offered daily 10 A.M.–3 P.M., weather permitting, not counting time spent in "rock shop." Admission is $8 adults, $4 children ages 6–15, $1 age 5 and under.

Recreation

Particularly good for guided weekend wildflower hikes in spring is 2,800-acre **Volcan Mountain Wilderness Preserve,** which may one day grow into 80,000-acre San Dieguito River Park, www.sdrp.org, a 55-mile-long parkway meandering all the way to the ocean. Guided walks to Volcan Mountain are offered on weekends. To get to the preserve: From Hwy. 78 north of Julian (past the town cemetery) take Farmer Road for 2.2 miles to Wynola Road; turn right and continue 100 yards, then turn left onto a continuation of Farmer Road. The stone gates mark the trailhead. For current hiking details, call 760/765-2300 or see www.volcanmt.org. A Julian gem—complete with a great campground, even wilderness cabins—is 900-acre **William Heise County Park,** 4945 Heise Park Rd., 858/565-3600, where the **Kelly Ditch Trail** connects with both Lake Cuyamaca and Cuyamaca state park trails. (Contact the park for current trail information.) Campsites are $12–16, cabins $35. Camping and hiking options are limited due to devastating 2003 wildfires but the welcome mat is also out at **Cuyamaca Rancho State Park,** 760/765-0755, www.cuyamaca.statepark.org. See below for more information

Anza-Borrego Desert State Park

The largest state park in the contiguous United States, reaching south from the Santa Rosa Mountains almost to the Mexican border, Anza-Borrego Desert State Park consists of 600,000 acres of Colorado Desert. "Anza" refers to Juan Bautista de Anza, the Spanish captain who explored the area in 1774, establishing a viable land route from Mexico to California coastal settlements; "borrego" is Spanish for bighorn sheep. Some sights in this spectacular vastness can be ap-

from beach to desert: Anza-Borrego Desert State Park

COURTESY OF JOANNE DIBONA/SAN DIEGO CVB

San Diego Coast

preciated from the road—the **Borrego Badlands,** the **Carrizo Badlands,** and the **Salton Sea** off in the distance—but other wonders, including **Borrego Palm Canyon, Hellhole Canyon,** and other palm oases, require the effort of a hike. In a good rain year, the park's spring wildflower bloom—usually starting in January, peaking in March or April—can be spectacular. Since remote here is *remote,* most visitors are advised to stay close to paved roads. Fortunately, a variety of half- and full-day park-approved **backroads ecotours** are offered—by the park's former naturalist, in conjunction with La Casa del Zorro Resort in Borrego Springs, 760/767-5323 or 800/824-1844, www.lacasadelzorro.com.

An excellent **visitor center** near park headquarters (it's *under* the desert garden, not visible from the road), 760/767-4205, is the best place to start an Anza-Borrego exploration. Call the park's wildflower hot line, 760/767-4684, for peak spring wildflower bloom predictions. The park is open 24 hours and admission is free (except for the Palm Canyon Trail, where hikers are charged $4 at the gate). The visitor center is open daily 9 A.M.–5 P.M. from October through May; only on weekends 9 A.M.–5 P.M. in the blistering hot months of June through September. For additional information, contact park headquarters at 200 Palm Canyon Dr., 760/767-5311, www.anzaborrego.statepark.org.

There are two developed campgrounds in Anza-Borrego, at **Borrego Palm Canyon** ($12–26) and **Tamarisk Grove** ($12–17). Reserve sites at these campgrounds through ReserveAmerica, 800/444-7275, www.reserve america.com. Also at Anza-Borrego: a group camp at Borrego Palm Canyon; a small (seven sites) primitive campground at Bow Willow; and an equestrian camp at the mouth of Coyote Canyon. Free backcountry camping is also an option; ask park staff for the rules.

Cuyamaca Rancho State Park

A high-country surprise on the edge of the desert east of San Diego, 25,000-acre Cuyamaca Rancho State Park (KWEE-uh-MACK-uh) is known for both lowland chaparral and fairly lush conifer and oak woodlands—or at least it was, until the devastating Cedar Fire of late 2003. Like the nearby town, the state park has been devastated, the shocking loss including forests and the historic 1920s visitor center and

1930s buildings built by the Civilian Conservation Corps. Most of the area is still designated as wilderness, however; camping, nature study, and serious hiking will again be the park's major attractions as the slow, painful process of rebuilding and restoration continues. As Cuyamaca is one of the few areas in Southern California with marked seasonal change, come for spring wildflowers, summer thunderstorms, fall colors, and, in winter, snow-dusted mountain peaks. But do call first, for updated information; many areas of the park—including some of its 110 miles of hiking and horseback riding trails—are not yet open to the public. The park is open for day use—still on a limited basis, at last report—from sunrise to sunset ($6 per vehicle). A temporary visitor center has opened near Paso Picacho Campground, but its relocation was a possibility, at last report. At least one family camping area, Green Valley Campground ($14–19), is open year-round. For current park information contact Cuyamaca Rancho State Park, 760/765-0755, www.cuyamaca.statepark.org.

Much of the rest of San Diego County's mountain wilderness is just to the east—the **Mount Laguna Recreation Area** in **Cleveland National Forest,** also home of the **Mount Laguna Observatory,** with still more hiking, camping, and picnicking potential. Though urbanites come east via I-8 and then amble north from Pine Valley via Laguna Mountain Road, the area is also accessible from Julian. Instead of following Hwy. 79 to Cuyamaca, turn onto the **Sunrise Highway** (County Road S1) just before Lake Cuyamaca, and keep climbing for some of the county's most spectacular desert views.

Accommodations

Bed and breakfasts are the thing in these parts. *The* place since forever is the fine and funky old-time **Julian Gold Rush Hotel** right in the middle of everything at 2023 Main St., 760/765-0201 or 800/734-5854, www.julianhotel.com, built during Julian's heyday by Albert and Margaret Robinson, freed slaves. Historical authenticity is the keynote here, since the hotel is listed on the National Register of Historic Places. Most rooms are quite nice if small, with shared baths, though a one-room cottage, the honeymoon suite, and several rooms do feature private baths. Most rooms are $100–150, cottages $150–250 (two-night minimum stay on weekends).

Not part of the town's Wild West heritage but looking the part is the **Julian Lodge,** 2720 C St. (at Fourth and C, just south of Main), 760/765-1420 or 800/542-1420. This two-story wood frame hotel boasts modern amenities beneath its 19th-century charm, expressed in attractive period-style rooms (fairly small, as in the good ol' days). All rooms have cable TV but no phone; some have refrigerators and radios. A friendly fireplace beckons from downstairs in the breakfast parlor. Most rooms are $100–150.

In need of pampering? Quite elegant yet welcoming is the **Orchard Hill Country Inn,** 2502 Washington St., 760/765-1700 or 800/716-7242, www.orchardhill.com, with a grand stone veranda overlooking the town. The lodge, with its great room and fireplace, also includes a game room (impressive video library) and "sky's the limit" dining room. Lodge rooms are $150–250, with occasional mid-week specials; cottage rooms are $250 and up. Rates include full breakfast plus afternoon hors d'oeuvres and beverages. By separate reservation, wonderful four-course dinner is served Saturday, Sunday, Tuesday, and Thursday nights.

La Casa del Zorro Desert Resort

One of those classic California desert resorts, La Casa del Zorro started out as an adobe ranch house, built in 1937. Since then, whitewashed adobe-style "casitas" have spread out over 32 tree-shaded acres. Rooms here are beautifully decorated and comfortable. Resort amenities include putting green, tennis courts, three swimming pools, rental bikes, and volleyball. (Child care can be arranged.) Two good restaurants are also part of the complex. Rates start at $250 for patio rooms and poolside deluxe rooms (all recently renovated); the separate two- to four-bedroom "casitas" are $540 and up in season, somewhat lower in summer, with a two-night minimum stay on weekends. For more information: La Casa del Zorro, 3845 Yaqui Pass Rd. in Borrego Springs, 760/767-5323 or 800/824-1844, www.lacasadelzorro.com.

Food

Julian isn't known for its great restaurants, though you'll find plenty of places for pie, coffee, even tea. **Julian Tea & Cottage Arts,** 2124 Third St., 760/765-0832, is open every day for lunch and afternoon tea—finger sandwiches, scones, and all. A good choice for candlelit dinner is **Romano's Dodge House,** 2718 B St., 760/765-1003, famous for its pork Juliana, loin chops in a whiskey, apple cider, and cream sauce. Also consider the **Orchard Hill Country Inn** (see above). Otherwise, if a genuinely good meal is mandatory, get ready to drive—all the way to Borrego Springs, in the middle of Anza-Borrego Desert State Park. **La Casa del Zorro Restaurant** at the resort, 3845 Yaqui Pass Rd., 760/767-5323, is the place for dress-up dinners out in the desert, as well as a more casual breakfast and lunch.

Dinner entrées include chicken *cordon bleu,* prime rib, scampi, Alaskan salmon, and vegetable curry. Lighter a la carte specials and the changing early bird specials are the real deals. La Casa del Zorro also offers a feast for the spirit—Old California ambience with candlelit whitewashed walls reminiscent of 1930s Palm Springs. The restaurant is open daily 7 A.M.–3 P.M., Friday and Saturday 5–10 P.M., and on Sunday 4:30–10 P.M.

But don't miss **Dudley's Bakery,** 30218 Hwy. 78, an area institution near the junction with Hwy. 79 in Santa Ysabel, 760/765-0488 or (800/225-3348, open daily 8 A.M.–5 P.M. California history aficionados may stop in Santa Ysabel to peek into **Mission Asistencia de Santa Isabel,** a small 18th-century mission outpost reconstructed in more recent times. But everyone stops at Dudley's across the street before heading into the wilderness or back into the city. This is the place to load up on specialty breads—how about jalapeño loaf?—breakfast pastries, and other goodies. Dudley's offers deli fare, too.

San Diego

In 1542 Captain Juan Rodríguez Cabrillo stepped out onto Point Loma, the tip of what is now San Diego Bay, and claimed the territory for Spain. His footfall has echoed through contemporary time as California's first and original point of discovery.

The U.S. military discovered San Diego earlier this century and settled in for a long stay, drawn by the area's sublime weather, its fine natural port, and its high-flying wide open spaces.

Despite its straitlaced military tradition, San Diego is no longer a simple social montage of battleship gray and camouflage green, no longer a predictable bastion of conservatism. New people, new high-tech industries, and new ideas have moved in.

Visitors to San Diego discover, and rediscover, a salubrious endless summer of beaches and balmy breezes along with world-class enclaves of culture and equally surprising moderate prices. They discover San Diego's relaxed, casual approach to day-to-day life and find that, here, just about

anyone can feel comfortable. The oldest city in California and the state's second largest, San Diego somehow still retains a simpler, small-town sensibility—beyond the freeway traffic, that is.

THE LAND

Though first-time visitors may see little beyond the harbor and the white-sand beaches of San Diego the city, San Diego the county offers much, much more in terms of diverse land forms. Almost one-third of San Diego County is publicly owned and accessible to the public, including 802-square-mile Anza-Borrego Desert State Park, an additional 700-plus square miles of federal land within Cleveland National Forest and federal Bureau of Land Management (BLM) preserves, and numerous county and city parks. Not open to the public but invaluable for creating de facto wildlife sanctuaries and "corridors" on the fringes of urban Southern California is the vast acreage included within U.S. military bases,

San Diego Coast

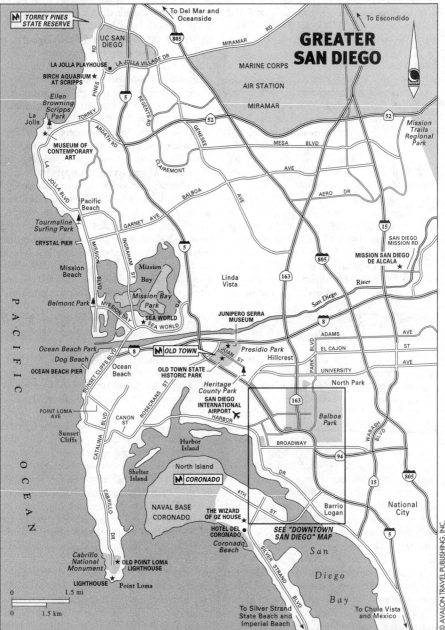

TORREY PINES STATE RESERVE

GREATER SAN DIEGO

To Del Mar and Oceanside

To Escondido

UC SAN DIEGO

MIRAMAR RD

805

LA JOLLA VILLAGE DR

LA JOLLA PLAYHOUSE
BIRCH AQUARIUM AT SCRIPPS

MARINE CORPS

AIR STATION

MIRAMAR

Ellen Browning Scripps Park

La Jolla

5

REGENTS RD

TORREY

52

Mission Trails Regional Park

52

MUSEUM OF CONTEMPORARY ART

ARDATH RD

GENESEE

MESA BLVD

LA JOLLA

CLAIREMONT

AVE

Pacific Beach

BALBOA AVE

AVE

AERO DR

15

Tourmaline Surfing Park

GARNET AVE

SAN DIEGO MISSION RD

CRYSTAL PIER

INGRAHAM ST

5

MISSION BLVD

Mission Beach

Mission Bay

Linda Vista

163

River

MISSION SAN DIEGO DE ALCALA

San Diego

Belmont Park

Mission Bay Park

MISSION BAY DR

805

SEA WORLD
SEA WORLD

JUNIPERO SERRA MUSEUM

8

Ocean Beach Park
Dog Beach

8

M OLD TOWN

JUAN ST

Presidio Park
Hillcrest

ADAMS AVE

EL CAJON ST

PACIFIC

OCEAN BEACH PIER

SUNSET CLIFFS BLVD

Ocean Beach

OLD TOWN STATE HISTORIC PARK

UNIVERSITY AVE

POINT LOMA AVE

ROSECRANS ST

CANON ST

Heritage County Park

163

North Park

SAN DIEGO INTERNATIONAL AIRPORT

Balboa Park

Sunset Cliffs

CATALINA BLVD

HARBOR

BROADWAY

W. ASH BLVD

Harbor Island

94

OCEAN

CABRILLO DR

Shelter Island

North Island

M CORONADO

15

DR

805

NAVAL BASE CORONADO

4TH

ST

Barrio Logan

National City

THE WIZARD OF OZ HOUSE

HOTEL DEL CORONADO

SEE "DOWNTOWN SAN DIEGO" MAP

5

Coronado Beach

San

Cabrillo National Monument

OLD POINT LOMA LIGHTHOUSE

Diego

LIGHTHOUSE

Point Loma

SILVER STRAND BLVD

Bay

0   1.5 mi

0   1.5 km

To Silver Strand State Beach and Imperial Beach

To Chula Vista and Mexico

© AVALON TRAVEL PUBLISHING, INC.

most notably Camp Pendleton in northern San Diego County.

Inland, or eastward, from the ocean and the beaches, the San Diego landscape becomes one of lowlands and valleys—with the area's only truly "Mediterranean" climate—flanked by the western foothills of the north-south-trending Peninsular Ranges. Most of the county is included, geographically speaking, within the hilly and mountainous Peninsular Range, which reaches to just above 6,000 feet in elevation. The range's eastern slope is high desert, rapidly descending toward the low desert of the Salton Sea and surrounding sink.

Just about everyone in San Diego will tell you the climate here is perfect. And so it usually is, if perfection is measured in the 60–70° F range in summer, in the mid-40s to mid-60s in winter. In late summer and fall, however, "Santa Anas" sometimes blow in—several-day events created by inland high pressure. In a reversal of the usual weather pattern—winds blow east, or inland, from the cool, moist coastal plain—desiccated desert winds blow west to the ocean. During strong Santa Ana conditions heat-wave mirages shimmer up and down the coastline, with temperatures reaching 100° F or higher; inland, grassland and wilderness wildfire danger becomes extreme. Milder Santa Anas, however, chase away the coastal fog and create wonderful dry weather and temperatures in the mid-80s, often sublime in October and November. What little rainfall there is along the coast and in the foothills—an average of 10–15 inches in a typical year—falls primarily from December into March.

Farther inland, the climate becomes somewhat less predictable. Mild temperatures and low rainfall predominate throughout the foothills in most years, but atop higher Peninsular Range peaks—including Cuyamaca, Laguna, and Palomar—expect cool summer temperatures and substantially more rain, even some snow, in winter. The high-desert climate just beyond the mountains is hot in summer yet cool, sometimes quite cold, in winter. Farther east the low desert begins—an environment isolated from the moderating effects of the ocean, with 100-plus summertime temperatures and mild winters. Though desert rainfall is typi-cally negligible, in some years an astonishingly intense *chabusco* or tropical storm will dump as much as 10–16 inches of rain in a single day.

HISTORY

The first known San Diego residents, called the Diegueños by the Spanish, populated the area for thousands of years before European settlement. The Ipai people living north of the San Diego River and the Tapai people to the south shared a linguistic heritage with the Yuma. Foragers who relied on the abundance of the land—particularly the acorn harvest from oak groves and other plantlife—the Ipai and Tapai also ate fish, shellfish, and small mammals. They made pottery, unusual in California, for storing both water and food. Well-developed arts included abstract rock art painting, sand painting, and ceramic etching.

Yet the characteristic most noted by the Spanish, in the words of California's first Spanish governor, Pedro Fages, was a "natural and crusty pride," an attitude "absolutely opposed to all rational subjection and full of the spirit of independence." Some historians suggest that if the Ipai and Tapai had possessed any semblance of organized social structure, their resistance to the Spanish *conquistadores* might have succeeded—and might have sent the first explorers packing. Settlement deterred might have meant settlement denied, or at least delayed long enough for England or France to claim California and otherwise radically alter the march of modern history across the New World's western landscape.

Though they repeatedly attacked the local mission and other Spanish outposts, the Diegueños did not succeed in their insurrections. So, officially, California was discovered by Spain. Hernán Cortés spotted the land he called California in 1535, but it was a man history has dubbed Captain Juan Rodríguez Cabrillo—actually a Portuguese named João Rodrigues Cabrilho—who first sailed the California coast, in search of the mythic Straits of Anian, or the Northwest Passage, to the Spice Islands. On September 28, 1542, Cabrillo stepped out onto "The Point of California," present-day Point

Loma, and named the harbor it protected San Miguel, after Saint Michael. Then, on November 10, 1602, the more adequately equipped Sebastián Vizcaíno arrived. He declared Cabrillo's records too sketchy to positively identify the area (and other areas), and two days later, on the feast day of Franciscan San Diego de Acalá, he renamed the bay after the saint and, perhaps incidentally, after his own flagship, the *San Diego*.

It would be 167 years before the Spanish returned to San Diego, spurred by the territorial threat of Russians moving south from Alaska. Fearing that the Russian fur traders and settlers might soon control California's harbors, endangering Spain's hold on Mexico, King Charles insisted that royal forces move north from their Mexican bases to formally take possession of—to colonize—California, an enterprise called "The Sacred Expedition of 1769."

Five expedition parties set out, two by land and three by sea. The seafarers fared the worst. One ship never arrived, and the crews of those that did were decimated by scurvy and other diseases. The first overland party set up its bivouac—and de facto hospital for the sickened sailors they

found by the bay—in what is now Old Town, thereby locating the city. The second overland party, led by Gaspár de Portolá, commander of the colonization forces and California's first governor, arrived in late June.

California's First Mission

The ceremonial establishment of San Diego as Spanish colony came on July 16, 1769, when the assembled multitudes ascended the hill above their encampment. The first official European foothold in California, this "Plymouth Rock of the West Coast" was chosen as the site for both California's first mission and its associated military presidio for its commanding views of the valley and the bay. After a solemn mass Father Junípero Serra, the "father president" of California's not-yet-founded mission chain, dedicated the site to the glory of God.

But because of the poor quality of surrounding soils, the mission failed to thrive. The Diegueño people were considered so dangerous that no one was allowed to leave the walled presidio compound surrounding the mission for any purpose without an armed military es-

Mission San Diego de Alcala

cort. Native peoples distrusted the military in equal measure, making it difficult for missionaries to attract neophytes—the workforce necessary for both the agricultural success and cultural transformation (some would say genocide/central to California mission society). So in 1774 the mission relocated about five miles up the valley—disastrously, at first, since the unprotected, unfinished mission was soon attacked and burned by 400 or so Diegueño. Things had settled down considerably by 1777, when the new mission complex was consecrated. It soon flourished, with olive, date, and pear orchards, lush gardens, vineyards, and vast herds of sheep, cattle, and horses. Mission life was good, and fairly uneventful—at least until 1812, when a powerful earthquake shattered the mission church. The modern Mission San Diego owes much of its present appearance to the reconstruction work of 1813.

Though San Diego was the first Spanish settlement in California, it wasn't the most influential. Monterey to the north soon became California's capital city and cultural center. But after the Mexican revolution, San Diego gained new prestige as de facto capital of both Alta and Baja California because of the personal preference of the governor.

Under Mexican rule, mission days ended and the oft-romanticized era of the ranchos began, supported by brisk Yankee trade for cattle hides, known as "California bank notes." When California was finally included within United States territory after 1848, San Diego barely noticed. With the world's attention focused on booming San Francisco and the Northern California gold rush, San Diego remained a solidly Mexican town, with fiestas and bullfights and other cultural traditions in full flower. U.S. sensibilities established themselves here quite slowly, aided by stagecoach and steamer and the eventual arrival of the railroad. Otherwise business boomed and busted, along with the rest of Southern California, into the 20th century. In 1900, the population of the entire county was 15,000.

The American Military Moves In

San Diego's presence as a major American city coincided with the arrival of the U.S. military, the Navy in particular. The Navy's Pacific Fleet, based in National City, has long been at home on San Diego Bay. The modern military presence began almost unnoticeably, however, with the humble U.S. Naval Coaling Station built in 1907 on the bay side of Point Loma. San Diego's now-famous aircraft and aerospace industries, largely related to defense, started in 1917, with the World War I-era establishment of the North Island U.S. Naval Air Station on Coronado Island—the air base that served as the actual starting point of Charles Lindbergh's famous transatlantic solo flight in 1927. More famous in modern times, the Miramar Naval Air Station just north of San Diego inspired the macho-guy-in-the-sky movie *Top Gun.* Though there have been other cutbacks and changes, San Diego's most dramatic post-Cold War downsizing denouement came in 1996, when the Navy's Top Gun school moved to Fallon, Nevada, and Miramar became a Marine base. Camp Pendleton, once a Mexican rancho, more recently a U.S. Marine base, still dominates northern San Diego County, while Naval Base Coronado, comprised of the Naval Air Station North Island and Naval Amphibious Base Coronado is the Navy's largest aerospace-industrial complex, occupying 57,000 acres on the peninsula.

Everyone Else Arrives

Throughout World War II the local tuna industry was an economic mainstay. In 1950 San Diego was the top fishing port in the U.S., producing about $30 million in fish. By 1960, because of stiff competition from Japanese and South American fishing fleets, that chapter in San Diego history was all but over. Maritime markets soon sailed in new directions, however, with increases in port exporting and shipbuilding.

After World War II the aircraft and defense industries also took off, the latter fueled by generous federal government funding. Until economic diversification began, fairly recently, almost 80 percent of local income was derived from defense, both directly and indirectly.

Scientific and technological research facilities also benefited, at least by regional association, along with high-tech industry and

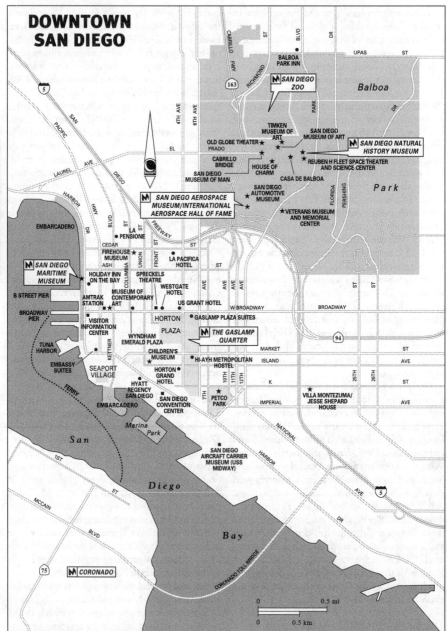

DOWNTOWN SAN DIEGO

UPAS ST

BALBOA PARK INN

Balboa

San Diego Zoo

TIMKEN MUSEUM OF ART

OLD GLOBE THEATER

SAN DIEGO MUSEUM OF ART

SAN DIEGO NATURAL HISTORY MUSEUM

PRADO

CABRILLO BRIDGE

HOUSE OF CHARM

SAN DIEGO MUSEUM OF MAN

REUBEN H FLEET SPACE THEATER AND SCIENCE CENTER

CASA DE BALBOA

SAN DIEGO AUTOMOTIVE MUSEUM

Park

SAN DIEGO AEROSPACE MUSEUM/INTERNATIONAL AEROSPACE HALL OF FAME

VETERANS MUSEUM AND MEMORIAL CENTER

EMBARCADERO

LA PENSIONE

CEDAR ST

FIREHOUSE MUSEUM

ASH

LA PACIFICA HOTEL

ST

SAN DIEGO MARITIME MUSEUM

HOLIDAY INN ON THE BAY

SPRECKELS THEATRE

WESTGATE HOTEL

B STREET PIER

AMTRAK STATION

MUSEUM OF CONTEMPORARY ART

US GRANT HOTEL

W BROADWAY

BROADWAY

BROADWAY PIER

VISITOR INFORMATION CENTER

HORTON PLAZA

GASLAMP PLAZA SUITES

THE GASLAMP QUARTER

TUNA HARBOR

WYNDHAM EMERALD PLAZA

CHILDREN'S MUSEUM

MARKET

EMBASSY SUITES

SEAPORT VILLAGE

HI-AYH METROPOLITAN HOSTEL

ISLAND

HORTON GRAND HOTEL

HYATT REGENCY SAN DIEGO

EMBARCADERO

SAN DIEGO CONVENTION CENTER

PETCO PARK

IMPERIAL

VILLA MONTEZUMA/ JESSE SHEPARD HOUSE

Marina Park

San

SAN DIEGO AIRCRAFT CARRIER MUSEUM (USS MIDWAY)

1ST ST

Diego

MCCAIN

BLVD

Bay

75

CORONADO

CORONADO TOLL BRIDGE

0   0.5 mi

0   0.5 km

© AVALON TRAVEL PUBLISHING, INC.

academic institutions. But the intelligentsia here is not entirely dedicated to military and industrial pursuits. La Jolla, for example, hosts the internationally renowned Salk Institute and the University of California at San Diego, with its famed Scripps Institution of Oceanography.

Retirees and tourists—both drawn by the sun, the sand, the sea, and the sublime weather—also have a notable presence in and around San Diego.

Not everything is copacetic in San Diego these days, however, and not everyone is welcome. California's current war against illegal immigrants who cross the border from Mexico is fought quite fiercely here—a fact that at first seems ironic, considering San Diego's Spanish and Mexican roots, and odd, considering the community's long-cherished "sister city" relationship with Tijuana, Mexico. Illegal immigration has always occurred here to some degree, yet in recent years San Diego has been literally and figuratively overrun—though that trend has slowed some as the immigrant war has been pushed inland by more successful deterrence on the San Diego County/Tijuana border.

The City Today

San Diego has always had great weather, sand and palm trees, but now it has a lot more to offer than leaping whales and sunny beaches. After almost two decades of urban redevelopment, the 2.2 square mile heart of San Diego has shown a remarkable rebirth, embracing everything from the core business district and the new Ballpark District—site of the new Padres baseball stadium, PetCo Park—to Little Italy, first settled over 100 years ago by Italian fishing families. Here new mixes with old in a fairly compact area, and you can rediscover the joy of exploring on foot or by trolley car.

ORIENTATION

As predictable as the ocean tides, tourists tend to flow toward San Diego's major attractions: Sea World, the San Diego Zoo, and, in the north county, the San Diego Wild Animal Park. But San Diego—the sunny city, the county, and the endless sky and seashore—reveals its deeper na-

ture only to those who take time to explore its neighborhoods and less advertised attractions.

Downtown's brightest light is Balboa Park, home of the San Diego Zoo and the most impressive concentration of world-class museums in any California city. Though new freeway interchanges make it more difficult to connect with the rest of downtown, the effort is worth it. The modern downtown mainstay is Horton Plaza, a stunning and stylish shopping mall disguised as a virtual city. Adjacent is San Diego's Gaslamp District, its Victorian buildings newly gussied-up and glittering with shops, restaurants, and nightlife.

Along the bay is the Embarcadero, offering a quick visual cruise of the city's maritime heart and military soul. Near here is the San Diego Convention Center and, just a stroll inland, the San Diego Padres' new Petco Park baseball stadium. Across the bay, reached by ferry or bridge, is Coronado, home of the historic Hotel Del Coronado, the North Island Naval Station, and neighborhoods of military retirees (Coronado is said to be home to the highest number of retired Admirals in the nation). Look for some astounding public art and the largely Latino Barrio Logan on the way to Coronado and in the shadow of the soaring San Diego–Coronado Bay Bridge.

Head uptown to Old Town San Diego, a state historic park where shopping and fairly commercial diversions attract most visitor interest. Technically, though, "uptown" is centered along Washington Street in artsy Hillcrest (from First to Fifth Streets), a San Diego version of San Francisco's Castro Street; eventually Washington becomes Adams Avenue, "Antiques Row." Also worth exploring: the India Street Art Colony near Washington Street and "Little Italy," along India just north of Date Street. The Linda Vista and North Park neighborhoods, not far away, are home to San Diego's large Asian communities and to many of the city's most authentic (and least expensive)Asian restaurants.

Along the coast are San Diego's beach communities, from Ocean Beach, Mission Beach, and Pacific Beach to the distinct, and distinctly affluent, La Jolla and nearby Del Mar—all included within San Diego city limits.

Balboa Park

San Diego's cultural heart and soul, home to its renowned zoo, magnificent museums, and much of the city's thriving theater program, Balboa Park is also an architectural and horticultural masterpiece, one of the largest urban parks in the country. Unimaginatively known as City Park when its original 1,400 acres of chaparral and scrub brush were set aside by the city in 1868, Balboa Park began to develop its Spanish colonial revival character in preparation for the 1915-1917 Panama-California International Exposition, a massive cultural coming-out party sponsored by the city to celebrate the completion of the Panama Canal.

The elaborate exuberance of the original buildings, intended to be temporary, can be credited to New York architect Bertram G. Goodhue, who personally designed the Fine Arts Building, the California State Building (now the Museum of Man), and the Cabrillo Bridge along El Prado—the formal entrance into the park's beaux arts center. Goodhue also set the stage for other architects.

With the arrival of World War I and San Diego's sudden centrality to the war effort, the exhibition buildings were conscripted for service. In the 1920s, as the military settled into permanent San Diego quarters, the city wisely established the precedent that makes present-day Balboa Park possible—donating the exposition buildings to various nonprofit cultural institutions.

The development of Balboa Park's cultural center continued with construction of the 1935 California-Pacific International Exposition, which added still more buildings, these by architect Richard Requa, with Aztec, Mayan, and Southwestern motifs.

Balboa Park

© ROBERT HOLMES/CALTOUR

ORIENTATION

San Diego's huge central park is lush and inviting, perfect for picnics and aimless ambling. Yet it's almost impossible to *be* aimless, given Balboa Park's astonishing array of attractions. Most visitors start at the San Diego Zoo, at the north end of the park just off Park Boulevard; the zoo can eas-

ily become a daylong adventure. Between the zoo and El Prado is the Spanish Village Art Center, studio space for artists and artisans who also sell their wares (open daily 11 A.M.–4 P.M., free). At the eastern end of El Prado begins Balboa Park's endless parade of museums. Fairly new ones, such as the Reuben H. Fleet Space Theater and Science Center and the Museum of Photographic Arts, stand beside longtime favorites, including the San Diego Natural History Museum, the San Diego Museum of Art, and the Museum of Man. Adjacent and just north, along Old Globe Way, is the rebuilt Old Globe Theatre—the original Shakespearean venue was torched in a 1978 arson fire—and the other two theaters of the Simon Edison Centre for the Performing Arts. Another don't-miss destination: the 1915 Botanical Building, with its lotus pond and impressive collection of tropical and subtropical plants.

Attractions south of El Prado include the Japanese Friendship Garden and the Spreckels Organ Pavilion, with its 1914 Spreckels Organ, featuring 4,445 pipes or 72 ranks. (Free concerts are offered year-round on Sunday afternoons at 2 P.M. and, in July and August, on Monday evenings at 7:30 P.M.) Still more museums farther south include the San Diego Automotive Museum and the excellent San Diego Aerospace Museum, as well as the Centro Cultural de la Raza, "the people's cultural center." The World Beat Center on Park Boulevard, www.worldbeatcenter.org, offers an impressive array of events and activities in support of African and indigenous cultures.

ALONG EL PRADO

Reuben H. Fleet Space Theater and Science Center

Two blocks south of the zoo at 1875 El Prado, just off Park Boulevard near the fountain in Plaza de Balboa, the Reuben H. Fleet Space Theater and Science Center is ever-popular—especially with more precocious kids. The main attraction here is the Omnimax theater, the world's first, which projects movies through a fish-eye lens onto the 76-foot Imax tilted dome. The space theater premieres you-could-be-there space, science, art, nature, and exploration films such as *Bugs!* and *Forces of Nature.* (Save time waiting in line by purchasing tickets in advance.) Fun even for adults is the 9,500-square-foot science center, with dozens of well-done interactive and hands-on exhibits including Deep Sea, a simulator ride that voyages to the bottom of the ocean and the worlds of science and biology. Other popular exhibits include Chinese resonant bowls and the Bernoulli Effect beachball. Don't miss the gift shop, with an unusually good selection of books, games, and toys.

Theater admission varies, depending on the movie/s, but is typically $11.50–15 for adults,

San Diego Coast

PRACTICAL BALBOA PARK

If at all possible, spend at least two full days in Balboa Park. Entering the park is free, but the majority of its attractions—the zoo, most museums, the theater program—charge admission. The most economical option for touring the museums is the multiple-museum Balboa Park passport—good for an entire week and including admission to 13 attractions—$30 at last report, usually a bargain even if you won't be seeing them all. The Best of Balboa Park passport includes admission to 13 attractions plus "best value" admission to the San Diego Zoo for $55. Most museums also offer a "free Tuesday" once each month, with some free on the first Tuesday of the month, others free on the second Tuesday, and so forth. Most museums are open daily from 10 A.M. to at least 4 P.M., but schedules can vary throughout the year; if your time in town is tight, call ahead to verify hours.

For more detailed information on the zoo, museums, and major attractions, see the Balboa Park listings. For additional information on the park and its current programs and events and to buy park passports, contact the very helpful **Balboa Park Information Center** in Balboa Park, inside the House of Hospitality at 1549 El Prado, 619/239-0512, www.balboapark.org, open daily 9 A.M.–4 P.M. Also quite hospitable here is impressive **The Prado** restaurant, 619/557-9441, serving Mediterranean-Latin fare, the likes of crab quesadillas and skirt-steak tacos—just the thing before an evening at the Old Globe. Great garden patio. For sushi lunch and an international selection of teas, try the **Tea Pavilion** at the Japanese Friendship Garden, 2215 Pan American Way, 619/232-2721.

If you're coming by car, the traditional entrance to Balboa Park is from downtown, heading east via Laurel Street and over the Laurel Street Bridge (the Cabrillo Bridge) spanning Hwy. 163. Once over the bridge, the street becomes El Prado, which soon becomes the park's primary pedestrian mall. Parking is a particular challenge on summer weekends, so come early in the day; you'll discover that the first lot, at Plaza de Panama, is almost always full. Continue south to find others. The other main route into the park, much more convenient if the zoo is your first or primary destination, is via Park Blvd. From Hwy. 163, exit at Park Boulevard; from I-5, exit at Pershing Drive and follow the signs.

$9.50–13 for seniors, and $8.50–12 for children ages 3–12. Center admission is free on the first Tuesday of every month, otherwise it's $6.75 adults, $6 seniors, $5.50 kids. The center is open Monday, Tuesday, and Thursday 9:30 A.M.–5 P.M., Wednesday until 8 P.M., Friday until 9:30 P.M., Saturday until 8 P.M., and Sunday until 6 P.M. For current movie and other information, call 619/233-1233 or see www.rhfleet.org.

San Diego Natural History Museum

This imposing museum at 1788 El Prado, newly reconstructed and expanded, chronicles the earth's wonders, among them shore ecology, seismography, and local gemstones. Of the "all natural ingredients" on exhibit, kids most savor the live insect displays along with the dinosaur skeletons and other fossils. And just inside the main entrance, swinging from a 43-foot cable, the museum's Foucault Pendulum verifies that the planet is, in fact, rotating on its axis. New attractions include the museum's "giant screen" natural history films. Coming permanent exhibits, all focused on peninsular California, will include Journey Through the Past (fossil mysteries), Journey Through the Present (area habitats), and a hands-on Discovery Room. Special traveling exhibits, films, lectures, and nature outings—including winter whale-watching tours—are always big draws.

Museum admission is $8 adults, $6 seniors and active military, $5 children ages 3–17, free on the first Tuesday of every month. Hours sometimes vary, but the museum is typically open daily 10 A.M.–5 P.M., closed on Thanksgiving, Christmas, and New Year's Day. The San Diego Natural History Museum is located near the fountain in Plaza de Balboa, just south of the San Diego Zoo and Village Place off Park Boulevard. For more information call 619/232-3821 or visit www.sdnhm.org.

Museum of Photographic Arts

The recently expanded Museum of Photographic Arts inside the Casa de Balboa, 1649 El Prado, focuses on both photography as art and the history of photographic arts. The permanent collection showcases the works of well-known photographers such as Ansel Adams, Edward Weston, and Henri Cartier-Bresson along with those of newer artists. The museum sponsors six to eight special gallery exhibits each year, such as Another America: Robert Weingarten's Testimonial to the Amish and Frida Kahlo: Portraits of an Icon. The museum's affiliated **Joan & Irwin Jacobs Theatre** (dig that ceiling) showcases classic, experimental, and art films, and even sponsors an annual cult film festival. Don't miss the museum store, with fine prints, posters, calendars, cards, and the largest selection of photography books in the western U.S. Gallery admission is $6 adults; $4 students, seniors, and active military; free for museum members, children under age 12, and for all visitors on the second Thursday of the month. Theatre admission is $7 adults, $6 students, seniors and children. It's typically open daily 10 A.M.–5 P.M., Thursdays until 9 P.M., closed on major holidays. For current and upcoming shows and other information, call 619/238-7559 or see www.mopa.org.

Museum of San Diego History

Another prominent resident of Casa de Balboa at 1649 El Prado, the history museum features rotating thematic exhibits from the San Diego Historical Society's permanent collection plus national traveling exhibits—almost always something of interest, even for the kids. Also take time to take in at least one of the historical society's other local outposts—the Arts & Crafts **Marston House** in Balboa Park, for example, or **Junípero Serra Museum** in Old Town, or the marvelous **Villa Montezuma/Jesse Shepard House** near the Gaslamp Quarter. The Museum of San Diego History is open daily 10 A.M.–5 P.M., Thursday until 8 P.M., closed Thanksgiving, Christmas, and New Year's Day. Admission is free on the second Tuesday of every month, otherwise $6 for adults; $5 for seniors, students, and active military; and $2 for children ages 6–17. For more information, call 619/232-6203 or visit www.sandiegohistory.org.

San Diego Model Railroad Museum

Down in the Casa de Balboa basement at 1649 El

OLD GLOBE THEATRE AND FRIENDS

First there was San Diego's Old Globe Theatre; dramatic outdoor Shakespeare productions were its original claim to fame. Now joining the 581-seat Old Globe are two more theaters in Balboa Park's performing arts center—the 225-seat **Cassius Carter Centre Stage** and the 612-seat **Lowell Davies Festival Theatre.** The performance calendar for this major-league regional repertory is full almost year-round.

The Old Globe and fellow theaters are in Balboa Park, near the Museum of Man, and reached via Park Blvd. and Old Globe Way. The regular theater season runs from January into June. The **Old Globe Festival,** showcasing Shakespeare, other classics, and modern works, both indoors and out, officially runs from July into September but summer shows can—and usually do—extend through November. No performances are scheduled on major U.S. holidays.

Advance ticket purchases are recommended. Admission varies, in the $25–55 range. For pre-recorded ticket information, call 619/239-2255. For bargain same-day tickets to these and other area theaters, as well as to music and dance events, contact the **Times Arts Tix** ticket center at Horton Plaza, 619/497-5000, or check the San Diego Performing Arts League website at www.sandiegoperforms.com.

Backstage tours of the theatre are offered year-round by appointment. For more information, contact the Old Globe Theatre, 619/231-1941 (administration), www.theoldglobe.org. Call for current performance schedule and box office hours.

Prado is the San Diego Model Railroad Museum, boasting the world's largest collection of mini-gauge trains—paradise for toy train lovers. Six separate, and intricate, scale-model exhibits, including the bustling Southern Pacific/Santa Fe route over Tehachapi Pass, come complete with sound effects: bells, whistles, and screeching brakes. With any luck, maybe one of the museum's train buffs will hand over the controls. The museum is open Tues.–Fri. 11 A.M.–4 P.M., and on Saturday and Sunday until 5 P.M. Admission is free for children under age 15—and for everyone the first Tuesday of every month—otherwise $5 adults and $4 for seniors, $3 students, and $2.50 active military. For more information, call 619/696-0199 or see www.sdmodel railroadm.com.

San Diego Museum of Art

On the park's Plaza de Panama at 1450 El Prado, the San Diego Museum of Art is best known for its European Renaissance and Dutch and Spanish Baroque paintings, including works by Goya, El Greco, Rubens, and Van Ruisdale. The collection also includes impressive collections of Dali, Matisse, O'Keeffe, and Toulouse-Lautrec. The cutting-edge contemporary California art in the Frederick R. Weisman Gallery alone is well worth the trip. Blockbuster traveling exhibits are often shown here, and the museum's interactive computer-image system allows visitors to locate works from the permanent collection and even design their own personal "tour." Great new museum store, with an impressive selection of art-related jewelry, books, and gifts. Another draw here is the sculpture garden and, for lunch, **Waters Cafe.**

Though some special exhibits are priced higher, regular admission is $8 adults; $6 seniors, active military, and students (with ID); and $3 children ages 6–17. Free admission on the third Tuesday of every month. It's open Tues.–Sun. 10 A.M.–6 P.M., open Thursday until 9 P.M. For current exhibits and other information, call 619/232-7931 or check www.sdmart.com.

Timken Museum of Art

Just east of the San Diego Museum of Art at 1500 El Prado, near the Lotus Pond, is the Timken Museum of Art, at home in an attractive building that is Balboa Park's most noticeable architectural anomaly. The collection here is intriguing, dominated by lesser-known works of significant 18th- and 19th-century artists from both Europe and America. It's open Tues.–Sat. 10 A.M.–4:30 P.M., Sunday 1:30–4:30 P.M., closed

Monday and the month of September. Admission is free, with free guided tours offered Tuesday 10 A.M.–noon and 1–3 P.M., Weds.–Thurs. 10 A.M.–noon. For more information call 619/239-5548 during regular museum hours or visit www.timkenmuseum.org.

Mingei International Museum of World Folk Art

The marvelous Mingei Museum—which means the "art of the people" in Japanese—is at home in Balboa Park's remodeled House of Charm at 1439 El Prado, devoted to pottery, toys, jewelry, textiles, paintings and sculpture—all crafted from natural materials. Over the years the changing exhibits here have included Origami Masterworks, Wearable Folk Art, and Heirlooms of the Future: Art of Contemporary American Designer Craftsmen. Call for current exhibit information.

The House of Charm sits on the southwestern corner of the Plaza de Panama. At last report the Mingei was open Tues.–Sun. 10 A.M.–4 P.M., closed on all national holidays. Admission is $6 adults, $3 children. For more information, call 619/239-0003 or check www.mingei.org.

San Diego Museum of Man

The grand Museum of Man, west of the Plaza de Panama at 1350 El Prado, under the California Tower, is striking enough from the outside. The anthropological collection here, one of the finest in the country, made its debut during the 1915 Balboa Park exposition. Expanded and updated over the years, exhibits chronicle human development but emphasize Mexican, Native American (particularly Southwestern), and South American societies. Egyptian artifacts are among recent acquisitions. Equally intriguing, though, is the museum's **Native Californians** exhibit, reflecting the dazzling diversity of San Diego's own society.

The San Diego Museum of Man is open daily 10 A.M.–4:30 P.M., closed Thanksgiving, Christmas, and New Year's Day. Admission is $6 adults, $5 military and seniors, $3 children ages 6–17, free for children under age 6. It's free for everyone on the third Tuesday of every month. For current program and other information, call 619/239-2001 or check www.museumofman.org.

BEYOND EL PRADO

San Diego Aerospace Museum and International Aerospace Hall of Fame

These days Balboa Park's exquisite art deco Ford Building—one of the finest remaining examples of its species in the United States, trimmed at night in blue neon—houses an equally impressive and artistic display of aeronautical history makers. Local history is represented by a replica of Charles Lindbergh's *Spirit of St. Louis,* and by a glider on loan from the National Air and Space Museum, first flown in 1883 near San Diego. Especially compelling: the ersatz aircraft carrier flight deck with its World War II–vintage planes. There's much more—about 70 aircraft, with displays arranged artfully and chronologically, accompanied by helpful historical and technical facts. The gift shop here is particularly worthwhile, since proceeds support the museum and its ongoing aircraft assembly and restoration projects.

The San Diego Aerospace Museum is in the southern section of Balboa Park at 2001 Pan American Plaza, most easily reached via Park Blvd. and then President's Way. Admission is free on the fourth Tuesday of the month, otherwise $9 adults, $7 seniors and students, $4 "juniors" ages 6–17, and free for children under 6 and active-duty military; behind-the-scenes Restoration Tours are an additional $3 per person. It's open daily 10 A.M.–4:30 P.M., until 5:30 P.M. in summer (last admission a half-hour before closing). Closed Thanksgiving, Christmas, and New Year's Day. For current exhibits and other information, call 619/234-8291 or check www.aerospacemuseum.org.

San Diego Automotive Museum

Nearby, at 2080 Pan American Plaza, this was the Palace of Transportation during Balboa Park's 1935-36 exposition. Car-loving kids of all ages will enjoy this particular garage. About 80 classics and exotics—Hollywood's cars, roadsters, and an exceptional motorcycle collection—make up the permanent collection. On a visit you might see a 1966 Bizzarini—one of only three ever built with the "spider" body

HIGH-FLYING SAN DIEGO

The development of San Diego has been shaped more by its aerial history—commingled with U.S. military history—than by any other factor.

In the early days of aviation, the industry's pioneers took flight in San Diego to take full advantage of the superb flying weather. Charles Lindbergh, the first man to cross the Atlantic Ocean in an airplane, is perhaps the most famous of these fanatical fly boys. In 1927 Lindbergh commissioned San Diegan T. Claude Ryan to build a plane based on Ryan's M-1 design (with wings above the fuselage). Within months, after very few test flights, "Lucky Lindy" left San Diego in his *Spirit of St. Louis*—touching down only briefly on the East Coast before flying off into the history books.

The U.S. military has had a distinguished aerial history in San Diego as well, beginning with test flights made by Glen Curtiss from Coronado's North Island Naval Station in 1911. Special air shows and other public events are scheduled at North Island and at Marine Corps Air Station Miramar, which hosts the annual Miramar Air Show in October.

To get up to speed on San Diego's high-flying history, visit the San Diego Aerospace Museum in Balboa Park.

Hall of Champions Sports Museum

Worth a stop for sports fans particularly interested in local heroes, the new San Diego Hall of Champions is located at the restored and renovated 1935 Federal Building at 2131 Pan American Plaza. In 1999 the Hall of Champs traded 17,000 square feet in its old home at Casa de Balboa for this new 71,000 square-foot facility. Over 40 sports are represented through displays and memorabilia, and there's a hands-on interactive area where visitors can test their own agility and endurance. Other benefits of the new facility include expanded exhibit space and a gift shop, a café and terrace, and a theatre.

The San Diego Hall of Champions Sports Museum is open daily 10 A.M.–4:30 P.M. It's closed Thanksgiving, Christmas, and New Year's Day. Admission is free on the fourth Tuesday of every month, otherwise $6 adults, $4 seniors and active military, $3 children ages 7–15, free for children 6 and under. For current exhibits and other information, call 619/234-2544 or see www.sdhoc.com.

Veterans Museum and Memorial Center

Housed in the World War II-vintage former San Diego Naval Hospital Chapel at Balboa Park's Inspiration Point, the Veteran's Museum honors veterans of all U.S. wars and includes unique artifacts, memorabilia, a library of 1,000-plus volumes, and veterans' collected papers. Exhibits include Civil War memorabilia, the first American flag to fall in the Philippines, the history of women in the military, and artifacts—representing all branches of military service—from World War I, World War II, Pearl Harbor, the Korean and Vietnam conflicts, and Desert Storm. Notable are military-themed murals and paintings by local artists, including striking works by Donald Schloat, a survivor of the Bataan Death March, and Richard de Rosset's D-Day mural of Omaha Beach, illuminated by one of the building's stained-glass windows. Living history tours are offered by "docents who have been there." For more information, contact the Veterans Museum and Memorial Center, 2115 Park Blvd., 619/239-2300, www.veteranmuseum.org, open Tues.–Sat. 9:30 A.M.–3 P.M.

style, or the ill-fated 1948 Tucker Torpedo, and the 1981 DeLorean. Special shows and events—such as the muscle car exhibit featuring a 1968 Chevrolet Camaro and 1964 Pontiac Tempest—are often quite fun. The gift shop, with unusual and one-of-a-kind items, is a cornucopia for car fanatics.

The San Diego Automotive Museum is open daily 10 A.M.–5 P.M., last admission one-half hour before closing. It's closed Thanksgiving, Christmas, and New Year's Day. Admission is free on the fourth Tuesday of every month, otherwise $7 adults, $6 seniors and active military, $3 children ages 6–15, free for children 5 and under. For current exhibits and other information—like details on the annual June **Auto Show on the Lawn**—call 619/231-2886 or check www.sdautomuseum.org.

ⓜ SAN DIEGO ZOO

The world-class San Diego Zoo sprang from very humble beginnings. Its original animals were chosen from those left behind by the Panama-California International Exposition. Now famous for its large exotic and endangered animal population and its lush, complex tropical landscape, the 100-acre San Diego Zoo is immensely popular—the city's top visitor draw, attracting more than three million people each year.

Part of the zoo's appeal is the near absence of prison-bar-style cages and pens. Most animals here—the zoo refers to them as "captivating instead of captive"—are kept in naturally landscaped, moated enclosures, very large walk-through aviaries, and other fairly innovative environments. Rarities among the zoo's 4,000 animals (800 species) include Australian koalas—the first exhibited outside Australia—New Zealand long-billed kiwis, Sichuan takins from China, wild Mongolian or Przewalski's horses—forerunners of all domesticated horses—and Komodo dragons from Indonesia. The San Diego Zoo also boasts the world's largest collection of parrots and parrot-like birds.

The zoo's big stars are two **giant pandas** on loan from the People's Republic of China, which arrived in 1996 to begin a 12-year conservation study. The pandas were an instant hit with the public, and on August 21, 1999, the "large bear-cats" as they're called in China, Shi Shi and Bai Yun, gave birth to a perfect cub, Hua Mei, the first giant panda born in the Western Hemisphere since 1990. In 2003, Shi Shi traveled back to China, and Gao Gao (whose name means "big big") arrived. Zoo officials hope he'll hit it off with Bai Yun, and help produce some more baby pandas. For the latest news on the zoo's panda family, call the giant panda hotline at 888/697-2632.

The natural habitats—the Polar Bear Plunge, Ituri Forest (hippopotamus habitat), Gorilla Tropics, Tiger River, Sun Bear Forest, Absolutely Apes, and the Reptile Mesa—are most impressive, designed as distinct "bioclimatic zones" with characteristic combinations of plant and animal species. Still underway at last report was the zoo's The New Heart of the Zoo project which, start-

ing with Absolutely Apes, will entirely transform the zoo's heart, from the flamingo lagoon to new "habitat" enclosures for clouded leopards, bearded pigs, pygmy hippos, mandrills, guenons, and other exotic creatures.

The San Diego Zoo is also noteworthy for its ongoing research, starting in 1916 with the Zoological Hospital and Biological Research Institute, now known as the Center for Reproduction of Endangered Species (CRES). Almost 30 years old, CRES is dedicated to managing species survival—helping endangered and threatened species to mate and produce young successfully, in captivity and in their natural habitats. The California condor captive-breeding program, artificial insemination and other reproductive research, including the "Frozen Zoo" sperm, egg, and embryo bank, behavioral studies at the Giant Panda Research Station, and ongoing disease prevention work, are among notable CRES accomplishments.

Since we're all on this big round spaceship together, research done at the San Diego Zoo to save individual animal species, no matter how obscure, may one day save us all.

Polar Bear Plunge

The Polar Bear Plunge is one of the largest polar bear exhibits in the world and a fairly complex arctic kingdom. Chillin' here with the bears are Siberian reindeer, arctic foxes, snowy owls, and a dozen other bird species. The polar bear pond here, near the Skyfari tram station at the zoo's western end, is actually an Olympic-sized pool. The two-level underwater viewing area, with a huge five-inch-thick acrylic window, and other viewing windows allow visitors to watch the bears play all day. In a necessary concession to climatic reality, the 50-plus species of plants integrated into the environment here are not tundra natives, though these immigrants from around the world look like summertime tundra plantlife.

Ituri Forest

A Central African rain forest simulation, this lush, four-acre area is home to okapis, forest buffaloes, spotted-necked otters, and a variety of colorful birds and acrobatic monkeys. The big stars are the hippopotamuses—the thrill here is

San Diego Coast

an inhabitant of the San Diego Zoo

being able to go nose-to-nose with the two-ton herbivores and get a fish-eye view of their astonishing underwater "ballets"—thanks to the 105-foot long underwater viewing window that flanks the 150,000 gallon pool. The landscape, built to recreate daily life in the rain forest, includes many authentic African plants, including papyrus, four species of bamboo, two types of banana tree, taro, African lilies and giant birds of paradise. There's even a recreation of a Mbuti village with leaf-covered houses (built for temporary shelter during hunting and gathering expeditions), visitors can tour the village to learn more about the Mbuti people native to the Republic of Congo.

Tiger River

A complex Asian rainforest with computer-controlled misting and irrigation systems to simulate 100 inches of annual rainfall, Tiger River was the zoo's first bioclimatic undertaking. Starting near the zoo's Flamingo Lagoon, wander down the ersatz dry riverbed and into the canyon below under a canopy of fig, coral, and orchid trees, flowering ginger, palms, along with 400 other exotic species of

bamboo, shrubs, and ferns. First you'll encounter a false gavial, a large crocodile relation, then the slithering ropes of pythons, then the web-footed fishing cats. The reeds and cattails in the marsh are home to pygmy geese, white-breasted kingfishers, and other rainforest birds. Next are the Malayan tapirs, piglike creatures related to both the horse and rhinoceros. Then comes the rainforest royalty, the kings and queens of cats, the tigers— allowed here to play in the ponds or just lounge around in the grass. Rare white tigers and Indochinese tigers alternate in this exhibit. What you won't see is the sophisticated behind-the-scenes scene developed for this aspect of the zoo's ongoing captive-breeding efforts.

Gorilla Tropics

The rainforest extends to Gorilla Tropics, a remarkable simulation of a lush African habitat. Guests encounter the gorillas—four adults and three youngsters, at last count—happily settled onto a hillside planted with figs, bananas, and bamboo. (Here as elsewhere in the San Diego Zoo, the animals eat and otherwise fully enjoy their environment; forests of replacement plants are always on hand.) The jungle sounds, most notable here and throughout nearby aviaries, are provided by a compact disc system with speakers cleverly camouflaged throughout the landscape.

Not smaller than common chimpanzees yet equally entertaining, the **pygmy chimps**—also known as "bonobos" in their native Zaire—are located within Gorilla Tropics. They may be the zoo's most clownish characters, whether playing in the oddly twisted palm forest here or making funny faces at humans on the other side of the glass. These chimps, yet another seriously threatened species, are the first ever exhibited in a U.S. zoo. Also hereabouts are Angolan colobus monkeys and Garnett's galagos, or "bush babies," both arboreal or "treetop" species; rare African crowned eagles, current captive-breeding candidates; and a baboon spider, Africa's largest tarantula.

Absolutely Apes

This lush Asian rainforest habitat, complete with dozens of live and fallen trees, termite mounds, and caves, allows tree-loving orangutans and siamangs plenty of room to climb, swing, and explore their landscape—as these endangered apes would in their native environments. More than twice the size of the previous orangutan enclosure, Absolutely Apes adds siamangs to the social mix for the first time in the zoo's history. The towering glass observation window offers surprising up-close experiences. Since January 2004, you can watch these amazing animals even from home, thanks to the live Ape Cam, accessible from the website.

Scripps Aviary

Just as grand as the gorilla show is a slow stroll through this huge multilevel free-flight aviary, home to hundreds of exotic African birds, including jicanas and the rare Waldrapp ibis. The sound of thunder signals imminent "rain"—in this rainforest it's provided by misting pipes. To avoid other surprises from the sky, heads up. Smaller aviaries nearby shelter carmine bee-eaters, hornbills, and softbill species.

Sun Bear Forest

In the zoo's central canyon, this ersatz corner of Malaysia is home to playful Malayan sun bears—long-clawed, pigeon-toed tree dwellers that could instead be "moon bears," since the striking gold on their chests is crescent-shaped. The smallest bears in the world, sun bears are hardly cuddly teddy-bear types. Zoologists consider them pound for pound the world's meanest, most aggressive bears. But they're also clownish and quite agile, and willing, like Winnie the Pooh, to do almost anything for honey. Also at home in this particular rainforest are dozens of lion-tailed macaques, a critically endangered species native to India. These arboreal acrobats take advantage of special rubberized monkey-proof "vines" for their impromptu performances. Note the impressive and irreplaceable 40-foot-tall ficus, the only one of its kind at the zoo. Nearby, in a small aviary, are still more exotic birds.

Children's Zoo

Though even the restrooms here are designed for four-year-olds, the Children's Zoo is immensely appealing to "kids" of all ages. Most popular are the two baby animal nurseries, where human babies peer through the glass at animal babies—these rejected by their mothers, injured, or otherwise sickly—as they are bottle-fed and reared by their human caretakers.

At the petting zoo, sheep, goats, and pot-bellied pigs are on parade. Other animals exhibited at the Children's Zoo include exotic birds, spider monkeys, tree kangaroos, small-clawed otters from Asia, lesser pandas, and the always popular—"Ooooh, mom, what's *that?*"—naked mole-rats. Zookeepers also personally present other animals, from lesser anteaters to meerkats, throughout the day.

Practicalities

The zoo is vast and spread out—a moderately challenging four- to five-mile hike if you're in a big hurry and determined to see it all. With some forethought, occasional backtracking, and strategic use of the zoo's two central moving staircases, it's possible to do most of your walking on flat ground or heading downhill (a free shuttle bus operates inside the zoo for guests with limited mobility). The upper mesa levels are less shaded, so see these areas first, particularly during hotter autumn weather.

If all-out zoo trekking is not feasible, take the guided **double-decker bus tour** for a general introduction—not a bad idea anyway, considering the valuable overview, informationally, and the great view from the open-air upper deck— then walk only to the must-see attractions on your list. (Spanish-language bus tours are offered daily at noon.) Alternatively, take the **Express Bus**, and hop on and off all day for short-distance explorations. Get the big picture on the **Skyfari aerial tram,** which crosses the zoo just above the treetops, from near the Reptile House to the Horn and Hoof Mesa.

Most zoo animals are most active, and entertaining, in the mornings and late afternoon, so plan to lunch and take in various animal shows— The Wild Ones, for example, and the Wegeforth National Park Sea Lion Show—during mid-day siesta time.

The zoo is open daily from 9 A.M. to dusk, which means entrance gates close at 4 P.M. from fall through spring and at 9 P.M. in summer (visitors can stay an hour longer). At last report— prices increase regularly—general admission, which includes admission to the Children's Zoo and all shows, was $21 adults, $14 for children ages 3–11, free for age 2 and under. Deluxe admission, which includes the guided bus tour plus the two-way fare for the Skyfari aerial tram: $32 for adults and $19.75 for children 3–11. A two-park ticket (deluxe zoo admission and Wild Animal Park general admission): $55.65 for adults and $37.85 for children 3–11. And a Balboa Park Passport with admission to 13 museums/attractions plus deluxe zoo admission, was $55.

Strollers, wheelchairs, and motorized scooters are available for rent on the front plaza next to the clock tower. Film is available at the nearby information booth (as are video camera rentals), but bring your own—more than you think you'll need—since it's expensive here. If you run short of cash, a real possibility if you venture into the zoo's great gift shops, you'll find an ATM in front of the Reptile House. For parking excess baggage, coin-operated lockers are behind the Reptile House. To save money on meals, pack your own picnic, though snack stands and eateries abound (vegetarian fare available). Best bet for a

simple sit-down meal is the **Sydney's Grill** between the koala and elephant exhibits.

For more information, contact the San Diego Zoo, 619/234-3153 (recorded) or 619/231-1515. To study up on the web, the address is www.sandiegozoo.org. For information on specialty walking and bus tours, call 619/685-3264. For information on the zoo's various education programs, including lectures, workshops, and the popular parent-participation pre-schooler program, call 619/557-3969. For information about the many benefits of membership in the Zoological Society of San Diego, which operates both the zoo and the San Diego Wild Animal Park near Escondido, call 619/231-0251.

HILLCREST AND VICINITY

Just north of Balboa Park and its fairly traditional ambience is Hillcrest, the one San Diego neighborhood noted for its eccentricities. This conservative city's gay district, centered along Washington and University Avenues between First and Fifth, Hillcrest plays host to coast-to-coast visitors during the annual summer Lesbian, Gay, Bisexual, and Transgender Pride Parade, which brings as many as 250,000 visitors to the area. This is also the place to sample the artsy bohemian life, San Diego-style—the small record and bookshops, stylish thrift stores, eclectic art films, small theaters, and good casual restaurants. Redevelopment is the watchword here, though, as elsewhere in San Diego—so hurry, before it all gets too upscale and safely cool.

For music classics and what's new internationally, spin into **Off The Record,** 3849 Fifth Ave. (at University), 619/298-4755, or **Music Trader,** 630 University Ave. (at Sixth Ave.), 619/543-0007. For retro kitsch duds, head to **Wear It Again Sam** at 3823 Fifth Ave. (between Robinson and University), 619/299-0185, which is packed to the rafters with vintage clothing dating from the '20s to the '60s. And some of San Diego's best independent bookstores are located in Hillcrest, including **Bountiful Books,** 3834 Fifth Ave. between University and Robinson, 619/491-0664, which boasts more than 20,000 new, used and rare titles, and **Fifth Avenue Books,** 3838 Fifth

SWINGIN' ON SPRUCE STREET

A well-known neighborhood secret in Hillcrest is the 1912 **Spruce Street Bridge,** a steel-cable suspension footbridge through the treetops of steep Kate Sessions Canyon. To get here from University Avenue in the Hillcrest neighborhood—it's an easy stroll—head south on First Avenuethen turn west onto Spruce Street, which deadends at the footbridge. On the other side of the bridge is the historic Bankers' Hill neighborhood: in the early 20th century, the area's mansions were connected via the footbridge to San Diego's new streetcar system.

Ave., 619/291-4660, which offers collectible first editions. One of the best bookstores in town, though, is a storefront that has housed used bookshops for over 30 years, now incarnated as **Bluestocking Books** across the street at 3817 Fifth, 619/296-1424, specializing in rare and out-of-print books and locally appreciated for its poetry readings and literary events.

The local Landmark Theatres flagship is the five-screen **Hillcrest Theater,** 3965 Fifth Ave., 619/819-0236, showing artsy independent and foreign films, a prominent feature at colorful **Village Hillcrest,** a neo-retro-looking contemporary complex at Fifth and Washington. Underground public parking is available here, if you're having little luck elsewhere. For original plays, head over to tiny **6th @ Penn Theatre,** 3704 Sixth Ave. (at Pennsylvania), 619/688-9210, www.sixthatpenn.com, which stages controversial and quirky plays like *Denial of the Fittest,* a one woman show written and performed by Judith

Sloan and Tim Miller's controversial, NEA-funded play *My Queer Body.* Just FYI, the theater was originally named 6th @ Penn, then renamed for the late Quentin Crisp, who performed here several times before his death in 1999, and is now once again known as 6th @ Penn.

For coffee and philosophical conversation, *the* place is **The Coffee Bean & Tea Leaf** at 3865 Fifth Ave. (at University), 619/298-5908, and, for drinks, **Nunu's Cocktail Lounge** at 3537 Fifth Ave. (near Walnut), 619/295-2878, the ultimate in neo-hip dive bars, with a red and brown interior seemingly unchanged since it opened in 1961. Standing across the street from the Hillcrest Cinema, **The Wine Lover** at 3968 Fifth Ave. (between University and Washington), 619/294-9200, offers over 70 wines by the taste, glass, or bottle, along with a selection of hors d'oeuvres and light meals. Good neighborhood eateries include, for breakfast, **Hash House A Go Go** at 3628 Fifth Ave. (between Brookes and Pennsylvania), 619/298-4646, serving heavenly flapjacks and scrambles at breakfast. Kids will enjoy the faux-'50s **Corvette Diner** at 3946 Fifth Ave. between University and Washington, 619/542-1001, and, more for grown-ups, fun **Kemo Sabe,** 3958 Fifth between University and Washington, 619/220-6802, with its contemporary twists on ethnic favorites. You'll also find Thai food and taco shops on and around University near Fifth.

Farther east along University, at Eighth, is the **Uptown District** complex, another emblem of neighborhood redevelopment. For an eclectic collection of antiqueries, continue east on Washington, north on Park and Mission until it becomes **Adams Avenue.**

Old Town and Downtown

⚂ OLD TOWN

The old adobe survivors of Old Town San Diego, the state's most popular historic park, are intertwined with—and clearly outnumbered by—a wide variety of minimalls, gift shops, restaurants, and other commercial enterprises that now surround Old Town Plaza. Even if you want to check out other neighborhoods, Old Town is a good place to start because of its central location and access to public transportation. The **San Diego Trolley,** 619/595-4949, stops at the Old Town Transit Center, 4005 Taylor St. (near Old Town State Park) every 15 minutes, with service to downtown, the harbor, and the International border.

Modern consumerism didn't doom Old Town's old-timers. It was fate, in the form of a devastating fire in 1872. Most of Old Town's surviving historic buildings, among the earliest outposts of early California settlement history, are clustered in the six-block area bounded by Juan Street on the north, Congress Street on the south, Wallace Street on the west, and Twiggs Street on the east.

Walking Tour

Highlights of an Old Town history walk include the **Seeley Stables** at Calhoun and Twiggs Streets, 619/220-5427, Old Town San Diego's transportation center until the 20th century, now a museum of horse-and-buggy rolling stock and western memorabilia. (Small admission.) On Mason at Calhoun is the 1829 **La Casa de Bandini,** center of the young city's social life during Mexican rule, and then after the Yankees arrived, the **Cosmopolitan Hotel.** The ground-floor rooms and walled gardens are now inhabited by a popular Mexican restaurant, **Casa de Bandini,** 619/297-8211, where strolling mariachi bands serenade diners on the patio.

A visit to adobe **La Casa de Estudillo,** 619/220-5426, on Mason Street between Calhoun and San Diego Avenue, is a must. (Small admission.) Built in 1827 by Captain José M. Estudillo, commander of the presidio, this was one of the finest homes in Mexican California. Note the leather-tied beams, and the exquisite furnishings, from the Steinway spinet pianos to the blue Duncan Phyfe sofa and elegant oriental rugs. Yet it was the courtyard, with its gardens, well, and outdoor *horno* (bake oven), that served as the center of family life—still serene and meditative, at least on slower days. Family members continued to live here until 1887, after which the home gradually declined. Bought in 1905 by local mover and shaker John D. Spreckels, who restored its grandeur, the house was opened to the public in 1910—promoted as "Ramona's Marriage Place," since the small chapel here reportedly inspired the wedding scene in Helen Hunt Jackson's wildly popular 19th-century novel *Ramona.* The house was eventually deeded to the state; its current restoration began in 1969.

Also worth exploring: the 1847 **San Diego Courthouse,** the **Wells Fargo Museum,** the 1865 **Mason Street School,** and the local **Dental Museum.** Inside the tiny **San Diego Union Newspaper Building** is a once-modern marvel of the journalism trade—an ancient Blickensderfer typewriter, complete with wood carrying case.

Just outside Old Town proper is the **Mormon Battalion Visitors Center** at 2510 Juan St., 619/298-3317, free admission, which tells the story of the longest infantry march in history. Also worth a stop for history aficionados is the two-story brick 1857 **Whaley House Museum,** 2482 San Diego Avenue, 619/297-7511, one of the few homes in the country ever declared by the U.S. government to be haunted. It served as county courthouse and government center in the 1870s. Artifacts and period memorabilia collected here include one of six "life masks" made of Abraham Lincoln. Admission $5 adults, $4 seniors, $3 children 3–12 (closed Tuesday).

Practicalities

The park itself is free, as is admission to most of its historic buildings, though a few other Old

San Diego Coast

Town-area attractions charge admission. Most of the park's historic buildings are open daily from 10 A.M. to at least 4 P.M., closed Thanksgiving, Christmas, and New Year's Day. Restaurants and some shops have extended hours.

Free Old Town walking tours depart daily at 11 A.M. and 2 P.M. from the state park visitor center, the Robinson-Rose House at 4002 Wallace St. (between Calhoun and Juan Streets), 619/220-5423, also the source for self-guided tour brochures, if you're lucky, as well as special event schedules and other current info. On the first Saturday of each month and every Wednesday, from 10 A.M.S2 P.M. in the Machado y Stewart Adobe and other historic buildings, park staff and other local history buffs don period costumes to demonstrate various domestic arts and, next to La Casa de Bandini, the village smithy plies his trade. For more information contact: **Old Town San Diego State Historic Park** headquartered at the Robinson-Ross House, 4002 Wallace St., 619/220-5422; the **Boosters of Old Town** (BOOT) group, also located here, www.ot -boot.com, offers a variety of guided Boot Tours, some including lunch in Old Town. See the website for a current events schedule.

Old Town San Diego is wedged into the shadows of two major freeways, just east of I-5 and just south of I-8. From I-5, exit at Old Town Avenue. From I-8, exit at Taylor Street, head south, then turn left onto San Diego Avenue. If coming from Point Loma and vicinity, take Rosecrans Avenue east all the way to Old Town.

Parking can be a nightmare near Old Town, so if you're driving come as early as possible. Taking the **San Diego Trolley** is definitely a safe and sane alternative. For a guided get-around—a good general introduction to San Diego, with the option of hopping off at various points and catching a later trolley to continue the tour— try **Old Town Trolley Tours,** 619/298-8687, which stops at the tiny Old Town theater on Twiggs Street (at San Diego) every 30 minutes between 9 A.M. and 5 P.M. daily. Stops include Balboa Park, Downtown, and Coronado.

Up the Hill from Old Town

Most notable in **Presidio Park,** just up the hill

from Old Town via Taylor Street and Presidio Drive, is the imposing 1929 mission revival-style **Junípero Serra Museum,** 2727 Presidio Dr., 619/297-3258, which many visitors mistake for San Diego's mission. Run by the local historical society on behalf of the city, the Serra museum does mark the hill climbed by Father Serra and his party to lay claim to the territory, and almost marks the site of the Royal Presidio of San Diego and the original mission. Museum exhibits emphasize San Diego's Spanish period, including a fascinating furniture collection and artifacts from presidio excavations. Climb the museum tower for breathtaking panoramic views. The Junípero Serra Museum is open Fri.–Sun. 10 A.M.–4:30 P.M., with extended hours during summer, Tues.–Sun. 10 A.M.–4:30 P.M. Admission is $5 adults, $4 seniors, students, and military, $2 children 6–17, free for kids age 5 and under.

The entire park, actually, serves as a museum, with various statues, memorials, and the Serra Cross—built in 1913 from presidio floor tiles— telling various parts of the story. The presidio site, directly below the Serra museum, is a National Historic Landmark, where excavations have been ongoing since 1965. The presidio's chapel, sundry walls, tile floors, and thresholds, even cannonballs, have been discovered.

Presidio Park is perfect for picnics, by the way, but parking is fairly limited, so consider walking up—or come anytime but on a summer weekend.

If you've got the time, worth exploring beyond Old Town proper is **Heritage Park,** 619/291-9784, up Juan Street near Harney. Here you'll find a collection of seven brazenly bright Victorians moved here from their original locations and given new uses. One mansion houses a B&B, another an antique store, and yet another a gift shop, and San Diego's first synagogue, which hosts bar mitzvahs, weddings, and receptions.

To the San Diego Mission

This isn't the most exciting or evocative of California's 21 missions, but it is the first. First founded by Father Junípero Serra in 1769, atop what is now Presidio Hill, the mission was moved to this location in 1774. The new site promised more water and improved agricultural prospects, but it didn't provide peace. Threatened by the mission's territorial incursions, in 1775 native peoples declared war—burning the mission, destroying religious paraphernalia, and killing one priest (Luis Jayme, California's first Catholic martyr, who is honored here). Wander the garden, stop by the museum, and visit the original chapel—California's first church—for a peek into the mission's past and present lives.

To get to Mission San Diego, located at 10818 San Diego Mission Rd., from Presidio Park, follow Presidio Drive down the hill and bear right onto Taylor; at the first light, turn left and merge onto I-8 (heading east). Exit at Mission Gorge Road and turn left; turn left again onto San Diego Mission Road. The museum and gardens are open daily 9 A.M.–5 P.M. Admission is $3 adults, $2 seniors (over age 55), and $1 for children (under age 12). "Tote-a-tape" tours are available for an additional $2. For more information, call 619/281-8449 or see www.missionsandiego.com.

DOWNTOWN

Until fairly recently San Diego was known as the city with no downtown, since even residents preferred to be anywhere but. All that has changed after more than two decades of serious redevelopment work that managed to preserve and polish, rather than destroy, what remained of the area's historic character. San Diego now has a lively, people-friendly downtown that segues quite neatly into the Embarcadero and the bay, not to mention the newly cool neighborhood surrounding the San Diego Padres new stadium, Petco Park.

Downtown San Diego got its start in 1867, the day Alonzo Erastus Horton strolled off a sidewheel steamer onto the "New Town" wharf, at the foot of what is now Fifth Street. Horton saw immediately that San Diego the city should be here, along the bay, not near the Old Town site chosen for security reasons by the Spanish. So Horton soon bought from the city 960 acres of "downtown" land for 27.5 cents an acre-a foolish outlay of $260 for jackrabbits, dust, and fleas, in the minds of lesser civic visionaries.

Nicknamed "Short Block Horton" for the short city blocks he laid out south of Broadway—shorter blocks made for more corner lots, which went for premium prices—Alonzo E. Horton sold so much land so fast he claimed to grow weary from handling all that money, day after day. Yet in the midst of San Diego's first real estate boom, Horton's fatigue failed to stop him. His developments in what was then known as Horton's Addition continued, with a pier, a de facto town hall, and facilities for the railroad, though his grandest accomplishment was the two-story brick Horton House hotel, built for the extravagant sum of $150,000, near the present-day U.S. Grant Hotel. There seemed to be no end to Horton's success.

Yet it did end, thanks to John D. Spreckels, the sugar magnate associated in local lore with Coronado Island. Building on Horton's original vision, Spreckels built a better pier and started developing downtown land north of Broadway—soon the most stylish business districts and neighborhoods in town.

Horton's development empire, known today as the Gaslamp Quarter, deteriorated into shabby "Stingaree," named after offshore stingrays and noted for its flophouse hotels, brothels, "prostitution cribs," and just general vice (with a capital V). Despite the San Diego Ladies Purity League's determination to clean things up in 1914, in preparation for the Pan-American International Exposition, the neighborhood continued its decline—a trend finally reversed in the 1970s, as San Diego got serious about redevelopment, renovation, and historic preservation.

Horton Plaza

Horton Plaza rises out of old-fashioned downtown San Diego like a Mediterranean or Middle Eastern version of the Emerald City—a jumble of odd open-air plazas, tiled courtyards and fountains, sculptures, stairways, cupolas, and towers all splashed with bold colors and draped in fluttering banners. This architectural marvel, designed by Jon Jerde and presented to the world in 1985, is clearly not your run-of-the-mill shopping mall. Yet as a mall, anchored by Nordstrom and Macy's and stuffed to its ramparts with

San Diego Coast

COURTESY OF JOANNE DIBONA/SAN DIEGO CVB

the walking tour in the Gaslamp Quarter

shops, restaurants, and movie theaters, it's a wild success. Particularly good reasons to start your downtown exploration here range from Bebe and Baby Gap to Victoria's Secret but also include the **Arts Tix Ticket Center** as well as the **Travelex** outlet (formerly Thomas Cook Foreign Exchange); the **Horton Plaza Farmers' Market** at Horton Plaza Square, 225 Broadway, held Thursday 11 A.M.–3 P.M. from March to mid-October, just the place for uptown picnic fixings, good wines, and wonderful bakery goods; and the impressive **San Diego Repertory Theater Company,** 619/544-1000, www.sandiegorep.com, with two stages here.

Horton Plaza inhabits the entire downtown "block" between Broadway and G Street and First and Fourth Avenues. The mall is regularly open Mon.–Fri. 10 A.M.–9 P.M., Saturday 10 A.M.–7 P.M., and Sunday 11 A.M.–6 P.M. (with later Saturday hours in summer and before Christmas). Restaurants, theaters, and some shops have extended hours. Walk here or take the trolley or bus, if at all possible, since parking in the

underground lot is often nonexistent. For information on what's up, contact: Horton Plaza, 324 Horton Plaza, 619/239-8180, www.westfield.com.

The Gaslamp Quarter

Most of San Diego's venerable Victorian business buildings, constructed between the Civil War and World War I, are in the city's Gaslamp Quarter, the downtown area just east of Horton Plaza, between Fourth and Sixth Streets and Broadway and L Street. Notorious for "nefarious activity" during decades of decline, the quarter has been undergoing a Renaissance of sorts—with historic hotels, new shops, art galleries, trendy restaurants, and nightclubs at the forefront of this particular downtown revival.

Gaslamp District highlights include the **Horton Grand Hotel,** at Island and Third, a Victorian-style creation dating from the 1980s—or the 1880s, if you count original construction dates. The Horton Grand is a re-creation done in the spirit, if not the architectural truth, of two old downtown hotels otherwise doomed by redevelopment—the old Horton Grand Hotel on E Street and the Saddlery Hotel, also known as the Kahle Saddlery and even earlier, when Wyatt Earp stayed there, as the Brooklyn Hotel. (The bricks and balustrades on Fourth are from the Horton Grand, those on the other side from the Saddlery.) If you don't stay at the Horton Grand, at least wander the lobby areas and visit the small Chinese museum commemorating San Diego's vanished Chinatown.

Other neighborhood landmarks include the baroque revival-style **Louis Bank of Commerce**—known as the Golden Poppy when it served as a whorehouse—on Fifth between E and F Sts., the **Backesto Building** on Fifth at Market, and the Romanesque revival **George J. Keating Building** on F Street at Fifth.

One of Southern California's most popular hip urban events, the annual three-day food and music festival **San Diego Street Scene** takes over the Gaslamp Quarter on three consecutive days in September. Come in February for **Mardi Gras,** May for the Memorial Day weekend **Jazz Festival,** and October for both the **City Arts** wine and art festival and the Halloween **Monster Bash.** To find out about other happenings in the neighborhood, call the **Gaslamp Quarter Association,** 619/233-5227 or see www.gaslamp.org.

For guided and self-guided historic tours, contact the **Gaslamp Quarter Historical Foundation** headquarters, inside the 1850 saltbox William Heath Davis House at 410 Island (at Fourth), 619/233-4692, www.gaslampquarter .org—the office is open weekdays 9 A.M.–3 P.M.—or pick up a tour brochure/map at area visitor information centers. There's also a printable map online, with almost 100 entries. The foundation's guided Heath Davis House museum tours ($3) are offered Tues.–Sun. 11 A.M.–3 P.M. The foundation's fun self-guided audio tours can be arranged for almost any time, and guided Gaslamp District tours leave from the Davis house every Saturday at 11 A.M. An $8 donation is requested for each guided tour, $6 for seniors, active-duty military, and students.

Villa Montezuma

After Balboa Park it might be tough convincing the kids they want to do another museum, and, after Horton Plaza, that this old house has entertainment value. But it does. Gaudy and splendid, Villa Montezuma is one of the strangest, most opulent "High Victorians" remaining in California. Built for internationally renowned musician, writer, and spiritualist Jesse Shepard, it's something of a monument to the 1880s' theosophy movement. Shepard and his followers held musical seances and otherwise communed with the spirits here, providing an early—and elegant—example of California's historic fascination with unorthodox spiritual orthodoxy. Villa Montezuma, 1925 K St. (at 20th), is open Friday, Saturday and Sunday only (closed major holidays) 10 A.M.noon–4:30 P.M. Admission is $5 adults, $4 seniors, active military, and students, $2 children 6–17, free for children under age 6. For more information, call 619/239-2211.

Other Sights

Across from Horton Plaza's south side at 777 Front Street and adjacent to the haute shopping heaven is the **Paladion** shopping center, 619/232-1685. North of Horton's Plaza, along Broadway at Kettner Drive, is the 1915 **Santa Fe Train Depot,** the city's Amtrak station these days, notably overshadowed by the 34-story **1 American Plaza** office tower. A notable part of the plaza is the **Museum of Contemporary Art San Diego Downtown,** 1001 Kettner Blvd. (at Broadway), 619/234-1001, www.mcasd.org, housing part of the museum's 3,000 works. For more information on both museums, see La Jolla and Vicinity, below.

Farther east on Broadway, between First and Second Avenues, is the grand old **Spreckels Theatre,** 121 Broadway, 619/235-9500, a popular local concert and theatrical venue. Across the street and one block farther is the 1910 **U.S. Grant Hotel,** 326 Broadway, 619/232-3121, San Diego's most classically elegant hostelry, commissioned by Grant's widow. The U.S. Grant was restored to its original grandeur—do stop to see the lobby—in the 1980s after a painstaking $80 million renovation.

Another time-honored presence a bit farther afield is Little Italy's **Firehouse Museum,** 1572

San Diego Coast

Columbia St. (near Cedar), 619/232-3473, with fire-fighting technology representing handcart and horse-drawn engine eras as well as the earlier ages of internal combustion engines. The museum is open Wed.–Fri. 10 A.M.–2 P.M., on weekends until 4 P.M. Admission is $2 adult, free for children under 12.

Children's Museum/ Museo de los Niños of San Diego

Since moving downtown from La Jolla in 1994, San Diego's children's museum went interactive in a big way—and that's no technological toss-off. The idea was that children need to "plug in" to the real world, not just virtual ones. The museum's lessons in real life have included Identity/Identidad and other bilingual exhibits, along with hand puppet shows and other performances held in conjunction with hands-on workshops. **The Box Show,** a series of boxlike exhibits dedicated to both artistic and educational ends, included Cora's Rain House, a giant tin building nestled into a recycled-water rainforest.

Museum changes keep coming. A new, three-story building and whimsical neighboring park at the existing Island Avenue site will include 50,000 square feet of museum space—plenty of room for new versions of museum favorites plus art studio, music room, a play theater, computer lab, indoor and outdoor interactive galleries, two magical birthday party rooms, a garden, even an interior atrium and café.

The new, improved children's museum will be located on W. Island Ave. between Front and Union Streets. For current information call 619/233-879 or see www.sdchildrensmuseum.org.

Petco Park and East Village

Just a few blocks from the Gaslamp Quarter, with its impressive roster of hotels, bars, and restaurants, is the warehouse district rapidly being refashioned as a stylish setting for the San Diego Padres' new Petco Park stadium. Modeled after Camden Yards, Coors Field, and other "retro" ballparks, Petco Park features a natural stone and stucco exterior, seats 46,000 fans, and is configured asymmetrically. The Padres have been playing ball here since spring 2004. The historic Western Metal Supply building is incorporated into the park's left field seats, and also houses bleacher seats on the roof, suites, and restaurants. The opening behind center field peers deep into downtown San Diego; fans can also feast on views of Balboa Park, the mountains, and the bay. Parking is available in city lots near the stadium, though mass transit options abound. The new, 512-room Omni Hotel connects to the ballpark's main concourse via pedestrian sky bridge; among baseball memorabilia on display at the Omni are Willie Mays' autographed broken bat and Babe Ruth's 1932 New York Yankees contract. For more information about the stadium, contact the downtown visitor center—or walk on over during business hours on weekdays and on Saturday 10 A.M.–4 P.M. To purchase Padres' tickets for upcoming home games, call 877/374-2784 or see www.padres.com.

Head for the Gaslamp Quarter for some of San Diego's best restaurants, bars, and clubs. The 26-block East Village redevelopment area surrounding the stadium is still a work in progress but there are some finds closer to the stadium, including **Bread on Market,** 730 Market St., 619/795-2730, which serves up some spectacular sandwiches on fresh-baked artisan breads.

CORONADO: CROWN OF THE BAY

Across from San Diego's Embarcadero is Coronado, an "island" connected to the mainland only by a sandy isthmus and by a sky-skimming arched bridge. A separate city reached from downtown San Diego either by ferry or via the San Diego-Coronado Bay Bridge, Coronado boasts the North Island U.S. Naval Air Station—Charles Lindbergh's departure point for his famous round-the-world flight—and, on the east, the U.S. Naval Amphibious Base, home for the elite Navy SEALS.

Not too surprisingly, the military has, in a sense, created the community here, a culture that revolves around the sound and fury of naval air technology and the needs and interests of retired naval officers and their families. Well-heeled tourists and celebrities are also well attended on

Coronado, however, and have been for over a century. The local roll-call of fame includes Charles Lindbergh, the Duke and Duchess of Windsor, 14 U.S. presidents, and a dizzying number of stars from both the stage and the silver screen. The list also includes Frank Baum, who wrote *The Wizard of Oz* while living here. **The Wizard of Oz House** still stands, at 1101 Star Park Circle.

Hotel del Coronado

The island's historic centerpiece is the astonishing Hotel del Coronado—known affectionately as the "Hotel Del" or, simply, "the Del"—one of California's grand old hotels, built in 1888, a national historic landmark. When it opened, this sprawling barn-red-and-white Victorian, with its wood shingles, turrets, and cupolas, was the largest structure outside New York City to be lighted with electricity. (Thomas Edison himself officiated at the switch-on ceremony for the hotel's first Christmas tree.) Among other movies, the 1959 comedy *Some Like It Hot*, starring Tony Curtis, Jack Lemmon, and Marilyn Monroe, was filmed at the Hotel Del.

Meander through the lobby and along darkwood downstairs corridors, where photographs and other mementos tell the hotel's story, and stroll the gorgeous grounds. Fairly recent additions include the craftsman-style **Duchess of Windsor Cottage.** Now a meeting hall, the cottage was onetime Coronado home of Wallis Warfield Spencer—the Duchess of Windsor after King Edward abdicated the English throne to marry her.

John D. Spreckels, the sugar-refining millionaire, bought the Coronado Beach Company and its in-progress Hotel del Coronado in 1887—just as San Diego's first boom days were busting. But Spreckels, whose San Diego–area development projects included water engineering, railroads, and Coronado's unique "tent city" resort, survived even the dark days in style. The entire Spreckels family relocated here from San Francisco after the 1906 earthquake and fire; their former home is now the center of Coronado's **Glorietta Bay Inn.**

Guided tours inside the Hotel del Coronado are offered to hotel guests only. Call the hotel at 619/435-6611, or try www.hoteldel.com, for details and reservations.

For the entire Coronado story, stop by the free **Coronado Historical Museum** on Loma Avenue, 619/435-7242, open Mon.–Fri. 9 A.M.–5 P.M., Sat. 10 A.M.–5 P.M., and Sun. 11 A.M.–4 P.M. The historical society sponsors tours of area landmarks ($8); tours meet at the Glorietta Bay Inn Tues., Thurs., and Sat. at 11 A.M. for

San Diego Coast

the world-famous Hotel del Coronado

COURTESY OF JOANNE DIBONA/SAN DIEGO CVB

a tour of the historic house, then go across to the Hotel Del Coronado grounds, and conclude at the Wizard of Oz house.

Beaches

Coronado's spectacular white-sand beaches are almost equally revered. Just oceanward from the Hotel Del is unbelievably broad **Coronado Beach,** typically uncrowded even in summer, since locals prefer beaches just north and south. On the island's bay side are several smaller, more protected beaches.

Silver Strand State Beach, 619/435-5184, extends the entire length of Coronado's sandy isthmus, with beaches on both sides of Silver Strand Boulevard (Hwy. 75), from near Hotel del Coronado to Imperial Beach. This popular family beach, great for swimming, was named for the small silver sea shells washed up along the shoreline. Beyond lifeguards, restrooms, and other basic services, facilities here include first-come RV campsites (self-contained only; no hook-ups), $13 per night in the summer. Silver Strand is open daily, 8 A.M.–9 P.M. in summer, until 8 P.M. during the spring, until 7 P.M. during winter. Beach use is free, though there is a parking fee (free from Labor Day through March). For more information about Silver Strand and other area state parks and beaches, contact **California State Parks, San Diego Coast District Headquarters,** 7575 Metropolitan Dr., Ste. 103, in San Diego, 619/767-2370.

Sights, Shopping, and Recreation

Coronado's other present-day pleasures include sun, sand, sailing, windsurfing, 15 miles of shoreline bikepaths—you can ride all the way to Imperial Beach—and specialty shopping along downtown Coronado's revitalized **Orange Avenue** and at the Seaport-Village like **Ferry Landing Marketplace.** In addition to its city pool, its 130-acre municipal golf course, its 18 parks, and its 18 public tennis courts, Coronado offers other diversions. **Gondola Cruises,** 619/429-6317, shoves off from the Loews resort on Venetian-style tours of the Coronado Cays canals. Or take a **Coronado Walking Tour,** 619/435-5993. And you can always see what's playing at the

Coronado Playhouse on Strand Way, 619/435-4856, or the **Lamb's Players Theatre** on Orange Ave., 619/437-0600.

Coronado also sponsors an almost endless series of special events—from the downhome **Coronado Flower Show** in Spreckels Park every spring and **Art in the Park** on the first and third Sunday of each month to a dazzling **Fourth of July** parade and fireworks. A **Coronado Christmas** is quite eventful, from the treelighting ceremonies at the Hotel Del and Santa Claus (sometimes in sunglasses) to caroling, choirs, and—reminiscent of a tradition started locally by Frank Baum—children's story hours. Or pay a visit to the lobby of the Loews Coronado Bay Resort, where readings of Dr. Seuss' *The Grinch Who Stole Christmas* has become a tradition starting the week before Christmas, and they even serve complimentary juice and cookies. Coronado's Christmas **Parade of Lights,** with every boat in sight decked out in Christmas finery, is usually scheduled for one week in mid-December.

Information and Transportation

For more information about Coronado, contact the very helpful **Coronado Visitor Information** office, 1100 Orange Ave., 619/437-8788, www.coronadovisitors.com.

Getting around Coronado is fun—except on particularly hectic weekends—thanks to its walkable streets lined with trees and bungalows, its paved bikepaths, and the **Coronado 904 Shuttle,** 619/233-3004, www.sdcommute.com, $1 fare.

Getting to Coronado is even more fun, especially if you take the **Bay Ferry,** 619/234-4111, from the Broadway Pier in San Diego to Coronado's Ferry Landing at First and B Streets. Ferries leave San Diego every hour on the hour 9 A.M.–9 P.M. Sun.–Thurs. (until 10 on weekend nights), and return from Coronado every hour on the half-hour, from 9:30 A.M.–9:30 P.M. Sun.–Thurs. (until 10:30 P.M. on weekend nights). Ferry fare is $2 (pedestrians and bicyclists only), 50 cents extra if you BYOB (bring your own bike). **San Diego Harbor Excursion water taxi,** 619/235-8294, travels to Ferry Landing Marketplace, the Hotel Del, and Le Meridien from Seaport Village on the mainland.

It's also fairly exciting to drive over. It's like riding a rainbow, gliding up and then over the soaring arch of the **San Diego-Coronado Bay Bridge** (Hwy. 75). The toll is $1 heading into Coronado—free with two or more people in the car—and free returning to the mainland.

AROUND SAN DIEGO BAY

A superlative harbor, San Diego Bay begins at Point Loma, where Cabrillo stepped ashore. Its fairly narrow mouth is created by the "island" city of Coronado, which is connected to San Diego's South Bay area by a narrow isthmus of sand. This seemingly tenuous connection actually forms the long, protected bay.

Starting at Point Loma, major features along the bay's long inland curve include the Cabrillo National Monument, an impressive land's end complete with venerable lighthouse, whale-watching platform, excellent visitor center, bayside trails, even tidepools.

Next come Shelter Island and Harbor Island, not natural islands but onetime shoals built into bayside real estate with the help of harbor dredging.

Fronting San Diego Bay and increasingly integrated with most everyone's idea of "downtown" is the Embarcadero, a bayside walkway along Harbor Drive that winds its way past an armada of vessels—some of them tour boats and cruise ships, others converted into gift shops and restaurants—and other harbor attractions. While exploring the port area, keep an eye out for evidence of the **Port of San Diego Public Art Program,** an impressive tour. Download details and a walking tour from the website, www.portof sandiego.org.

Particularly noteworthy in the bayside attractions category is the San Diego Maritime Museum, floating at 1492 N. Harbor Dr. (at the foot of Ash Street), 619/234-9153. About a half-mile south is the art deco B Street Pier, also known as the Cruise Ship Pier, local port for major cruise ship lines. Next south is the Broadway Pier, also known as the Excursion Pier, largely dedicated to sportfishing, whale-watching, and harbor tour companies. This is also the place to catch the San Diego-Coronado Ferry to Coronado Island.

Though San Diego's tuna fishing heyday is long gone, the next stop south is Tuna Harbor, headquarters for the American Tunaboat Association and also home to the very popular Fish Market restaurant and fresh-fish market. Navy ships may be tied up nearby; if so, on weekends they're usually open for tours.

Usually getting most of the neighborhood attention, though, is Seaport Village, a seafaring-themed shopping and restaurant development with turn-of-the-century style. For shoppers, a memorable stop might be the **San Diego City Store** here, 803 W. Harbor Dr., 619/234-2489, www.sandiegocitystore.com, where you might find civic artifacts including street signs—perhaps a genuine Swimsuits Optional sign from Black's Beach—plus parking meters, seats from Jack Murphy Stadium, fire hydrants, traffic lights—your name it, you just might find it here. For children and nonshoppers, the best thing here goes 'round and 'round—the 1890 Looff Broadway Flying Horses Carousel, originally stabled at Coney Island. Worth a stroll nearby is the Embarcadero Marine Park North, a grassy public park angling out into the bay.

Seaport Village ends at the San Diego Marriott Hotel and Marina, though the walkway wanders on. The striking San Diego Convention Center at the foot of Fifth, designed by Arthur Erickson and built by the Port of San Diego, is just beyond the hotel. With its fiberglass "sails" and wavelike walls, the convention center could only be confused with a choppy day at the America's Cup. A quick stroll inland leads to the San Diego Padres' new Petco Park; see Other Downtown Draws above for details. South of the convention center is the Embarcadero Marina Park South and the stunning Coronado Bay Bridge. South of the bridge and east of I-5 begins the region's South Bay.

Cabrillo National Monument

Here's a bit of history with open-air flair. This breathtaking 144-acre vantage point on the ocean edge of San Diego Bay commemorates Cabrillo's exploration of the California coastline in 1542. What actually marks the spot is the Point Loma Lighthouse (no longer in operation but open to

© ROBERT HOLMES/CALTOUR

San Diego Coast

Cabrillo National Monument

the public), a newer lighthouse, various viewpoints, plus a winter whale-watching station, tidepools (explorable at low tide), trails, and a good visitor center. There are no food concessions, however, so bring a picnic or snacks if you'll be staying awhile.

Fully appreciate the breathtaking bay views by hiking the **Bayside Trail,** an asphalt road threading through old World War II military installations, meandering east along the bay. Watch sailboats and ships, not to mention the soaring sea birds—and, on aerially active days, U.S. Navy aircraft taking off from the North Island Naval Air Station across from the trail on Coronado Island. This two-mile roundtrip (easy) begins near the lighthouse and typically takes just over one hour.

One of San Diego's best bets for **tidepooling** lies within a stone's throw of San Diego Bay, on the rocky western edge of the Point Loma Peninsula. At low tide, the tidepools near the Coast Guard station teem with ocean creatures tossed ashore at high tide—crabs, sometimes an octopus

or jellyfish—and also reveal more stationary residents of the rocks, including anemones and starfish. It's okay to look, but not touch, since the tidepools are protected reserves. Ask park rangers about expected low tides. To reach the tidepools, go north from the visitor center. The first road to the left leads to the Coast Guard station and the peninsula's western shore.

Cabrillo National Monument, 1800 Cabrillo Memorial Dr. (the southern end of Cabrillo Memorial Drive, Hwy. 209), is open in winter daily 9 A.M.–5:15 P.M., though the Bayside Trail is open only 9 A.M.–4 P.M. In summer the park is open until sunset, with extended trail hours. Admission is $5 per vehicle, $3 per person entering by bicycle or on foot, and free for seniors with Golden Age Passports, the disabled, and children age 16 and under. For more information, contact: Cabrillo National Monument, 619/557-5450, www.nps.gov/cabr.

Shelter and Harbor Islands

Shelter Island's main claim to fame is as the yacht-harbor home of the America's Cup international sailing competitions, www.americascup.com, sponsored by the San Diego Yacht Club. But Shelter Island, centered at Rosecrans Street and Shelter Island Drive, has its charms even without the America's Cup hubbub, most notably a family-friendly fishing pier, yachters' hangouts such as the Fiddler's Green and the Brigantine, and "tiki" resort hotels and restaurants noted for their Polynesian and faux-Polynesian style. At the island's "end" is **Pearl of the Pacific** sculpture park, perfect (on a still day) for picnics. **Seabreeze Nautical Books & Charts,** 1254 Scott St., 619/223-8989, is great for new and used books and seafaring gifts. And if you can't find it there, try **Downwind Marine,** 2804 Canon St., 619/224-2733, the "the cruiser's chandlery."

Harbor Island is another yachter's haven, this one close to the San Diego Airport and not coincidentally filled to the gills with waterfront hotels and restaurants.

San Diego Maritime Museum

Star of the show here is the three-masted *Star of India*—the oldest iron-hulled merchant ship

USS MIDWAY MUSEUM

The **San Diego Aircraft Carrier Museum** on San Diego Bay, the city's first major new attraction in more than 25 years, open since June 2004, is a floating "city at sea" now doing duty as the nation's fifth and largest naval aviation museum. Debut exhibits onboard the decommissioned 1945-vintage USS *Midway,* which last served as an aircraft carrier during Desert Storm, encompass the hangar, mess, and flight decks, also "island" flight control. The audio-guide recording leads visitors through more than 30 onboard stations—including the waterworks, radio and TV stations, daily newspaper office, post office, hospital, bomb assembly area, and jail—to explain the sailors' onboard life and work. Peer into the captain's spartan cabin, sample a galley and crew mess, and imagine 40 winks in those cramped enlisted berths. Explore the bridge—sit in the captain's chair—and wander the four-acre flight deck and the mission-preparation "bird farm." *Midway* veterans are on hand to answer questions, tell tales, and otherwise interpret what you'll see. Restored aircraft on display include an A-6 Intruder, an A-7 Corsair, an E-2C Hawkeye, a McDonnell Douglas F-4 Phantom II, and a Grumman F-14 Tomcat. Climb into flight simulators to fully comprehend the *Midway* experience.

The aircraft carrier museum is located at Navy Pier 11A, just three blocks from the Santa Fe Depot transit center at 910 N. Harbor Dr. Wear sensible shoes and sunscreen but bring a light jacket for the flight deck; no large parcels allowed. Docent-guided tours are offered. The *Midway* is open daily, except major holidays, 10 A.M.–5 P.M. Admission is $13 adults, $10 seniors (62 and older), military ID, and college ID); and $7 youth (6–17); and free for children 5 and younger as well as for active duty military in uniform. There's a gift shop on board, also the Fantail Café. The *Midway* is available for private parties and special events; a children's sleepaboard program and other educational activities are offered. For current information, see www.midway.org.

still afloat, first launched from the Isle of Man in 1863 as the *Euterpe.* The 1904 *Medea,* a relative youngster hailing from Scotland, was quite a beauty in her day—with imported teak decks and housing, finished inside with quarter-sawn English oak. The museum's gift shop is holed up next door inside the *Berkeley,* an 1898 ferry most famous for serving as rescue ship during the 1906 San Francisco earthquake and fire. Also part of the permanent collection here is the 1914 *Pilot* and the schooner *Californian,* a replica of a mid-19th-century revenue cutter and the state's official Tall Ship. The *Californian* is available to take passengers on day sails, weekend trips to Catalina, and an extended summer journey along the California coast. Visiting exhibits might include superstars such as **HMS *Surprise,*** from the Academy Award-winning film *Master and Commander: The Far Side of the World,* and the historic **SS *Lane Victory.***

The San Diego Maritime Museum, 1492 N. Harbor Dr. at the foot of Ash Street (find the *Star of India* at the foot of Grape) is open daily 9 A.M.–8 P.M. (until 9 P.M. in summer). Admission is $8 adults, $6 seniors and "juniors" (ages 13–17), $5 children ages 5–12. The museum is supported entirely by private contributions, making this a particularly good place for seafaring history buffs to make an extra donation. For more information, call 619/234-9153 or visit www.sdmaritime.com.

South Bay

National City is known for its **Naval Station San Diego,** a.k.a. the 32nd Street Naval Base, home port of the U.S. Pacific Fleet, not to mention the area's shipbuilding yards and the **National City Marine Terminal.**

The South Bay's **Chula Vista** is famous for its **ARCO Training Center** for Olympic athletes, the country's first year-round, warm-weather, multisport Olympic training complex. It's one of only three United States Olympic Committee training centers in the U.S.—the other two (in Lake Placid, New York and Colorado Springs, Colorado) are dedicated to winter sports. Visitors can see athletes training, take a narrated tour (1.5 mile walk) of the campus, and shop at the Olympic Spirit Store. Call 619/656-1500 or visit www.usolympicteam.com for more information. Chula Vista is also known for **Sweetwater Marsh National Wildlife Refuge,** one of San Diego's endangered species refuges, home to populations of light-footed clapper rail, Belding's savannah sparrows, and California least terns. The **Chula Vista Nature Center** within the refuge, 1000 Gunpowder Point Dr. at the foot of E Street, 619/409-5900, www.chulavistanature center.org, features aviaries, aquaria (including the David A. Wergeland Shark & Ray Experience), native plant gardens, and guided walking tours. Open Tues.–Sat. 10 A.M.–5 P.M. Admission is $5 adults; $3 seniors, juniors, and students; and $2 children 6–11.

Imperial Beach, in the same-named community, stars the **Imperial Beach Pier** and plenty of warm, white sand—the most essential ingredient for its fabulous **U.S. Open Sandcastle Competition** held here each year. For more information contact the **Imperial Beach Chamber of Commerce,** 877/640-3020, www.ib-chamber.biz. Following the sand from Imperial Beach northwest onto the strand leads to **Silver Strand State Beach,** a superb swimming beach on the way to Coronado, justifiably popular with fam-

ilies. For more information on Coronado-area beaches, see Coronado: Crown of the Bay.

Southernmost, adjacent to the U.S.-Mexican border, is **Border Field State Park and Beach.** People avoid the beach here like the plague, since chronic sewage contamination from Tijuana has made swimming unsafe. And beyond the beach this otherwise serene wetlands preserve along the U.S.-Mexican border seems like a war zone, with Border Patrol helicopters slicing the air overhead in search of, and to deter, illegal immigrants. It's difficult to ignore the intensity of this daily San Diego-area drama. The state park is adjacent to the **Tijuana River National Estuarine Sanctuary National Wildlife Refuge,** with visitor center, guided walks and trails, and ongoing research facilities in Imperial Beach.

BEACH TOWNS AND BEACHES

Beyond downtown, starting north of Point Loma, are the oceanside communities of Ocean Beach, Mission Beach, and Pacific Beach. Still farther north are the fairly exclusive and expensive communities of La Jolla and Del Mar, also included within San Diego's city limits.

Ocean Beach

Strung out along Sunset Cliffs Boulevard just north of Point Loma is Ocean Beach, "O.B." in locals' lingo. Sitting just beyond the western end of the I-8 Freeway, Ocean Beach is San Diego's "farthest out" community—an unusual and unusually settled beach neighborhood with a hip (and hippie) history, an unusual collection of old-timers, surfers, young families, hipsters of all ages, and a smattering of ne'er-do-wells. To get a feel for the place, head for the **Ocean Beach Pier** (though beaches nearest the pier are sometimes unsavory) and stroll the **Newport Avenue** commercial district., which has become quite the antique-lovers destination. Dog lovers, note that Ocean Beach's **Dog Beach** is one of only three in the county (along with Coronado and Del Mar) where canines can cavort sans leash. (Watch your step.) For more seclusion, head south to the cove beach at **Sunset Cliffs,** on the Point Loma Peninsula—popular with locals and

---

CALIFORNIAN ON THE WATERFRONT

The newest addition to the San Diego Maritime Museum's fleet is the tall ship *Californian,* built in 1984 as a replica of the *C. W. Lawrence,* an 1847 revenue cutter used by the Coast Guard's precursor, the Revenue Service. The 145-foot-long double-masted wooden schooner, recently renovated, has been honored as the "official tall ship of the state of California." In 1997, it was used by Stephen Spielberg as the centerpiece of his movie *Amistad,* the story of 53 African slaves who revolted off the coast of Cuba in 1839. These days the *Californian* is used for educational and public programs, including onboard tours and coastal sailing adventures. For more information, call 619/234-9153 or visit www.sdmaritime.com.

MISSION TRAILS PARK

Take a hike in San Diego's "secret" gem, 5,800-acre Mission Trails Regional Park, made up of both natural and developed areas and bisected by the San Diego River. Located just eight miles northeast of downtown San Diego, these rugged oak-dotted hills and valleys suggest San Diego prior to Cabrillo's arrival in San Diego Bay. Indeed, here you'll find remnants of the Old Mission Dam and flume completed in 1816 by Spanish missionaries and Kumeyaay Indians—engineering that was essential for the survival of Mission San Diego. You can also hike some 40 miles of trails—most inviting in early spring—boat on **Lake Murray,** climb Bongo Fury, or camp at primitive **Kumeyaay Lake**

Campground ($13) just two miles east of the visitor center. Though some 2,800 acres of parklands in the East and West Fortuna areas were burned in fall 2003 wildfires, most of the park has been reopened for public use.

For more information, contact the **Mission Trails Regional Park Visitor Center,** One Fr. Junipero Serra Trail (off Mission Gorge Rd.), 619/668-3275, www.mtrp.org, open daily 9 A.M.–5 P.M. (closed major holidays). For campground reservations, see the website or call 619/668-274 for information. Also see the website for guided hike and events information, and for specific instructions on how to get to various areas of the park.

surfers, accessible at low tide and only via slippery sandstone pathways or from the stairways at the feet of Bermuda and Santa Cruz Avenues. For more information about the area contact the **Ocean Beach Main Street Association,** www.oceanbeachsandiego.com.

Mission Beach and Mission Bay

Next stop north, beyond the San Diego River, is Mission Beach—about 17 miles of ocean beach and boardwalk plus Mission Bay, onetime wetlands refashioned, in the 1960s, into a faux bay resort area with man-made beaches, hotels, motels, marinas, and condominiums. When passing through in 1542, Cabrillo himself called it a "false bay," since the outlet led straight into the swamp.

Inland, Mission Bay Park is largely "natural"—meaning, in this case, undeveloped—and a de facto park popular with San Diegans looking for bracing saltwater breezes and open space for jogging, walking, biking, kite-flying, and watersports. If you're interested in the view from the water but are without your own boat, get around via the **Harbor Excursion** water taxi, 619/234-4111 or 800/442-7847, www.sdhe.com, $6 one-way. Or take a tour—the full bay tour is $20 adult—or a brunch or dinner cruise. Popular for its sunset cruise is the *Bahia Belle,* 858/539-7779, docked at the Bahia Hotel on West Mission Bay Drive (no cruises in December and January).

Attractions along the ocean include both **South Mission** and **North Mission Beaches,** waterfront walkways, and grassy parks. The **Belmont Park** area is home to the landmark 1925 **Giant Dipper** roller coaster and equally venerable **The Plunge** swimming pool. After being abandoned for a number of years, the historic roller coaster, with 13 hills and over 2,600 feet of track, was renovated and reopened to the public in 1990. The boardwalk now includes shops in addition to the rides, open March through September Sun.–Thurs. 11 A.M.–10 P.M., Fri.–Sat. 11 A.M.–11 P.M. The Giant Dipper is $4 per ride, $13.95 for unlimited ride wristband (riders must be at least 50 inches tall). For more information call the park at 858/488-1549 or see www.gi antdipper.com.

Sea World

People either love or hate Mission Bay's Sea World, an Anheuser-Busch amusement park with an ocean animal theme. Those who love Sea World say it offers families the chance to see unusual or endangered sealife up close and personal, a positive experience that increases environmental awareness. Those who hate it point out that with friends such as these—and with an excellent aquarium just north, in La Jolla, not to mention San Diego County's exceptional zoos—the beleaguered and endangered creatures of the sea hardly need enemies.

San Diego Coast

A recent controversy here, for example, involved the Behind-the-Scenes killer whale exhibit, interactive in the sense that park guests feed, pet, and participate in training Sea World's killer whales. All in all, this is the water-park equivalent of a petting zoo, animal rights activists say. They believe that rather than capturing, breeding, and training whales to perform tricks, Sea World should dedicate its considerable resources to making the real world safe for whales—these captive whales, for starters—and other wild things. Sea World officials respond that whale participation is "voluntary," that whales can swim away—albeit only so far as the next pool—if they wish to avoid their fans.

Of course the traditional star performers of the Sea World show, here and elsewhere, are **Shamu** the killer whale and **Baby Shamu,** actually stage names for a half-dozen or more individual whales. The **Shamu Adventure** encounter is adjacent to Shamu Stadium; visitors view the whales through a 70-foot window in the 1.7 million gallon pool while waiting in line to touch them. And if that's not enough Shamu to-do, the kids can pose for pictures with an ersatz Shamu and Baby Shamu in two-acre **Shamu's Happy Harbor,** an active—and interactive—playground. You can even **Breakfast with Shamu** or **Dine With Shamu,** poolside.

Increasingly, "encounter" and "interactive" are the watchwords at Sea World, because more than anything else, people want to touch—or almost touch—animals they would never see, even at a distance, in real life.

So there's **Shark Encounter,** a three-part exhibit that permits visitors to commune with captive sharks from above, below, and "within" their habitat. A transparent acrylic tunnel allows you to "walk through" the shark tank. At **Penguin Encounter,** a moving sidewalk takes you through a glassed-in Arctic and the hundreds of emperor penguins gliding over glacier-like ice and into the water. At **Rocky Point Preserve,** visitors interact with—feed, pet, and talk to—bottlenose dolphins. Sea World also includes a **California Tide Pool** touch pool and a **Forbidden Reef**—kids love anything that's forbidden—with bat rays and moray eels.

OUT OF YOUR GOURD

Every June squash fans head for **Fallbrook and the Welburn Gourd Farm,** 40787 De Luz Murietta Rd., 760/728-4271, www.welburngourdfarm.com, the world's largest supplier of organic hard-shell gourds in the United States—some 375,000 gourds each year, especially canteen and bottle types. Late June is when the wonderful **Welburn Gourd Art Festival** is held, a two-day celebration of gourd greatness, complete with classes, demonstrations, and competitive judging. Admission is $7 adults (children under 12 free), and parking is free.

But for those who can afford it, none of the "encounter" exhibits come close to the popularity of Sea World's **Dolphin Interaction Program,** where an extra $140 buys you the chance to don a wetsuit, do a little dolphin training, and then take a dip in the dolphin pool. Space is limited, so reservations are required; call 877/436-5746 (619/225-3291 for international calls). Children must be 6 or older to participate. Sea World's **Day Camps,** special **Sleepovers,** and accredited week-long **Resident Camps** offer still more up-close marine animal encounters.

There's more to see and do at Sea World, too—including rides, from **Journey to Atlantis** and **Shipwreck Rapids** to Southwest Airlines' **Skytower.** Sea World is open daily from at least 10 A.M. to dusk, from 9 A.M. in summer (call for current summer schedule). As you might expect, the experience is expensive, with admission $49.75 adults, $39.75 children ages 3–11, plus food, high-priced mementos, and parking ($4 motorcycles, $7 cars, and $9 RVs). Behind-the-scenes tours, in addition to other educational activities and the dolphin interaction program, are available by arrangement.

Sea World is in Mission Bay; to get here from I-5, exit at Sea World Drive and follow the signs. For more information, call Sea World at 800/380-3203 or see www.seaworld.com. **Security Note:** Please leave unneeded belongings in your hotel room or vehicle; all backpacks, bags, and packages are subject to inspection. The following items in particular are not permitted: weapons, knives, other sharp objects, straws, coolers, and any hazardous items or materials.

Pacific Beach

Hippest of all local beach towns these days is Pacific Beach or "P.B." in the local vernacular, where surf, surfers, skates, skaters, hip shops and just hangin' out define local culture. Most of the action is at the beach—and at the **Lahaina Beach House** at 710 Oliver (at Ocean), 858/270-3888, where almost everything is less than $5 (now also open for break-

fast); at **Garnet Street** shops; and, after dark, at the **Society Billiard Café,** 1051 Garnet Ave. (near Cass St.), 858/272-7665. Unique in P.B. is the **Crystal Pier,** the only pier in California to include a hotel. Social historians and surf scene voyeurs can visit **Tourmaline Surfing Park** (Tourmaline Street at La Jolla Boulevard), the only stretch of local coastline dedicated exclusively to worshippers of the next wave, however grizzled some may be. For more information see **Discover Pacific Beach,** www.pacificbeach.org, a website that also features some great local history.

La Jolla and Vicinity

Along the coast just north of Pacific Beach is the village of La Jolla, a seven-mile stretch of sublime coastline that serves as San Diego's answer to the Riviera. Local commerce cultivates, quite profitably, a sophisticated, red-tile-roofed Mediterranean image, one that attracts old-money minions as well as movie stars.

La Jolla (La HOY-yah, though people here say, simply, "the Village") means "jewel" in Spanish, or, according to local Native American tradition, "hole" or "cave." Both meanings are fitting. Hammered for eons by the relentless surf, the coastal bluffs beneath La Jolla's dazzling real estate are laced with caves, large and small, some explorable by land, some by sea. Other natural attractions are local beaches—including the infamous Windansea Beach, the top-notch but highly territorial surf scene described by Tom Wolfe in *The Pump House Gang*—and area parks, including Torrey Pines State Reserve, sanctuary for about 6,000 very rare pine trees.

Not rare, however, is the human imperative to see, be seen, and make the scene. These, as well as shopping, are major pastimes in and around La Jolla's upmarket downtown. Any and all downtown adventures are best undertaken on foot, since finding a place to park can be all but impossible.

For more information about La Jolla, and for friendly practical assistance from the volunteer staff, contact the San Diego Convention and

Visitor Bureau's **La Jolla Visitor Center,** 7966 Herschel Ave., 619/236-1212, www.sandiego.org. Hours vary by season, but the center is open at least 11 A.M.–4 P.M. on weekdays and Sunday, 10 A.M.–6 P.M. on Saturday (closed Thanksgiving, Christmas, and New Year's Day). Or drop by the office of the **La Jolla Town Council,** 7734 Herschell, Ste. F, 858/454-1444, www.lajolla tc.org, for a map and other local direction.

SIGHTS

Ellen Browning Scripps Park

La Jolla's aqua-blue ocean and adjacent beaches are beautiful but unbelievably popular. If personal space and peace are on your agenda, you won't find either here. Instead, head north along the coast.

Nonetheless, one of La Jolla's jewels is **Ellen Browning Scripps Park** overlooking La Jolla Cove, a palm-lined promenade where everyone goes to see the sea scene (and be seen). Even children regularly dip into the Scripps legacy; a wonderful local diversion is the **Children's Pool** at the park's south end, with shallow waters and a curved beach protected by a seawall. In recent years, sea lions basking on **Shell Beach** just to the north have provided free entertainment; in summer spotted leopard sharks enjoy La Jolla's balmy waters. South toward Pacific Beach is San Diego's surfing paradise, an area including mythic **Windansea**

COURTESY OF JOANNE DIBONA/SAN DIEGO CVB

La Jolla Cove

Beach and **Tourmaline Surfing Park,** neither particularly fun for "outsiders."

North from Children's Pool, starting offshore just south of Point La Jolla, is the **San Diego-La Jolla Underwater Park.** Most popular for skindiving and snorkeling is northern **La Jolla Cove.** Lining La Jolla Bay north of the cove are the town's famed **La Jolla Caves.** Sonny Jim Cave (small fee) is accessible via a stairway starting at the La Jolla Cave and Shell Shop on Coast Boulevard. The best **tidepools** around are along the coast north of the Scripps Pier at the Scripps Institution of Oceanography on La Jolla Shores Drive, the former site of the Scripps aquarium. **La Jolla Shores beaches,** including those below residential areas, are among the best for swimming and sunbathing, along with Torrey Pines State Beach and Del Mar Beach farther north. Between La Jolla Shores and Torrey Pines is an almost inaccessible, unauthorized nude beach known as **Black's Beach,** best reached from Torrey Pines at low tide. For more on that area, see Torrey Pines State Reserve and Beach, below.

And girls, if you're interested in surfing lessons, La Jolla's **Surf Diva Surf School** is the first to emphasize instruction for women and girls—including Girl Scout troops—offered by the twin Tihanyi sisters (lessons also available for "guys on the side"). For more information, contact Surf Diva at 2160 Avenida de la Playa, 858/454-8273, www.surfdiva.com.

Museum of Contemporary Art

This restyled 1915 Irving Gill original, once home to Ellen Browning Scripps, is the primary location of San Diego's Museum of Contemporary Art, 700 Prospect St., 858/454-3541, www.mcasd.org. The museum's permanent collection intentionally blends U.S. and Latin American culture and includes galleries exhibiting works by Frida Kahlo and Diego Rivera, Latin American art, works from every major art movement since 1950, including minimalism and pop art, installation art, and conceptual art from the 1960s to the present. Traveling exhibits tend toward the provocative and cutting edge—or, simply, "edge," as they say in L.A. (Call for current program information.) Don't miss the outdoor sculpture garden. A smaller museum branch in downtown San Diego, on Kettner Boulevard at Broadway, 619/234-1001, is also well worth a stop (free).

Both museums are open daily except Wednesday 11 A.M.–5 P.M., closed Thanksgiving, Christmas, and New Year's Day. The La Jolla museum is also open Thursday night until 7 P.M. Admission is $6 for adults, $2 for seniors (ages 65 and older), military, and students (ages 12–18), and free for children under age 12. Both museums are free on the third Tuesday and first Sunday of every month.

While you're in the neighborhood, a little-known arts attraction in La Jolla is the **Athenaeum Music & Arts Library** in central La Jolla at 1008 Wall St., 858/454-5872, founded in 1899. There's a small gallery, and thick stacks of music and art reference books. To look at the rare, artist-made books, you'll have to slip on those little white gloves. The library is open

COURTESY OF JOANNE DIBONA/SAN DIEGO CVB

Museum of Contemporary Art

Tues.–Sat., but check the schedule here for upcoming classical music and jazz performances.

Birch Aquarium at Scripps

The Birch Aquarium at Scripps is the public information center for the University of California's renowned **Scripps Institution of Oceanography.** Aquarium exhibits include a replica of Scripps Canyon, the underwater valley just off the La Jolla coast, and an abundance of re-created marine habitats—a kelp forest, for example, and aquatic homes for creatures such as the bioluminescent "flashlight fish." Exhibits in the adjacent building, collected under the banner **Exploring the Blue Planet,** delve into oceanography as science. The simulated submarine dive has major kid appeal, as does the fairly new, 13,000-gallon shark tank, now available for public diving, Another fascination: the "ocean supermarket" display of everyday items derived from the ocean. The **Morphis Movieride** (extra fee) in the Smargon Courtyard offers 20-minute virtual adventures. Every bit as fun are the aquarium's many organized real-life natural history activities, from seahorse rodeos and "guided" summer grunion runs to kayak tours and winter whale-watching trips.

The Birch Aquarium at Scripps, 2300 Expedition Way, 858/534-3474, is on the edge of the University of California, San Diego campus. The museum is open daily 9 A.M.–5 P.M. (last admission at 4:30 P.M.), closed on Thanksgiving, Christmas, and New Year's Day. This is a popular place, so to avoid the crush on weekends come early in the morning; to avoid school groups on weekdays, come in the afternoon. Admission is $10 adults, $8.50 for seniors (age 60 and older), $6.50-7 students and children (ages 3–17). Three hours of validated parking. Visit the aquarium website at www.aquarium.ucsd.edu.

La Jolla Playhouse and Vicinity

The Tony Award-winning La Jolla Playhouse was founded in 1947 by Gregory Peck and like-minded theater buffs. By producing original musicals and plays that subsequently made a name for themselves, such as *Big River, A Walk in the*

THE SCRIPPS LEGACY

San Diego Coast

Ellen Browning Scripps was half-sister of newspaper publisher Edward Wyllis Scripps, founder of the United Press (UP) newspaper syndicate. A respected journalist too, Ellen Browning Scripps also made millions in real estate—good fortune she shared with Southern California by founding Scripps College in Claremont and by endowing, with her brother, the Scripps Institution of Oceanography in La Jolla. Part of the genteel community of artists, writers, scientists, and just plain wealthy people that settled La Jolla at the turn of the century, she was also a patron of architecture—in particular local architect Irving J. Gill, who designed her 1915 home, now San Diego's Museum of Contemporary Art, and various public buildings here.

In a sense the Scripps family's philanthropic contributions to the community set the stage for present-day La Jolla's cultural influence, with its renowned Salk Institute and the sprawling University of California at San Diego, which now includes the Scripps Institution of Oceanography, the Scripps-affiliated Stephen Birch Aquarium-Museum, and the nationally recognized La Jolla Playhouse theater program.

Woods, The Who's *Tommy,* and various Neil Simon works, the La Jolla Playhouse has established itself in the past decades as one of the most innovative regional theaters in the country. Thanks to a capital campaign launched in 1999 by the late Gregory Peck, since fall 2004 the Playhouse has had a new permanent home—the $42 million **Joan and Irwin Jacobs Center for La Jolla Playhouse.** The theater's performance season runs from May through October. Admission varies, but tickets are typically in the $35–50 range. Call for box office hours, which change throughout the year. For current program information and directions to the new "theatre village," call 858/550-1010 or see www.lajollaplayhouse.com.

Also worth a stop on campus, even if you're just passing through, is the **Stuart Collection** of outdoor art. Many of the outdoor pieces stand within an easy walk of the whimsical Theodore Geisel Library, named after the late La Jolla resident better known as Dr. Seuss. Enter the campus at Gilman Drive (from La Jolla Village Drive) and request a sculpture guide at the information kiosk.

Other Sights

Girard Avenue downtown is prime-time for La Jolla shopping. Among the multitude of cool shops here—not all of them expensive, by the way—is **Gallery Alexander,** 7925 Girard (between Prospect and Wall), 858/459-9433, with whimsical and unusual items in home furnishings, ceramics, glassware, and jewelry. Also try **Gallery Eight,** 7464 Girard (near Pearl), 858/454-9781. Poke around too in search of unbeatable places such as **John Cole's Book Shop,** in a historic house overlooking the ocean at 780 Prospect (at Eads), 858/454-4766, and **Artful Soul,** 1237-C Prospect St. (between Ivanhoe and Cave), 858/459-2009, locally owned and operated and quite casual, showcasing good work by about 20 local artists and artisans. Jewelry is the mainstay, each piece identified by artist, along with small gift items.

If you're out and about after dark, a "new" local jazz venue in La Jolla is romantic **Elario's Bistro & Sky Lounge,** in the 11th-floor penthouse at Hotel La Jolla, 7955 La Jolla Shores Dr., 858/551-3620, www.elarios.com—reinventing one of San Diego's most famous cultural destinations. The original Elario's hosted the PBS *Club Date* jazz series, which showcased live acts on more than 120 affiliates. The new Elario's, however, is a modern lounge scene, and books local acts and up-and-coming talent in addition to classic jazz acts.

To get the big picture of La Jolla and vicinity, head to **Mount Soledad,** reached by following Nautilus Street east. From the summit of this tinder-dry hill, the area's traditional site for outdoor Easter Sunday services, at night the headlights and taillights of the traffic flow below on I-5 seem like endless dazzling strands of diamonds and rubies.

TORREY PINES STATE RESERVE AND BEACH

Here's a story of endangered species that doesn't star human beings as the culprits, for a change. Protected in this small preserve are about 10,000 Torrey pines *(Pinus torreyana)*. The rarest pine trees in the United States, these beautifully primeval, strange, and scraggly five-needle pines represent an Ice Age species endangered by too-specific climatic and soil needs. Get oriented at the attractive 1923 adobe-style **Torrey Pines Lodge** museum and visitor center, once a private restaurant, located near the trailhead for the precipitous Beach Trail. On cool, foggy days, there might even be a fire blazing in the fireplace. Short and easy hiking trails wind through the semi-desert forests. Guided walks are offered on weekends and some holidays. Bring your own water; drinking fountains are available in the parking lot. Food and drink are otherwise not allowed in the preserve.

Below the heavily eroded bluffs is **Torrey Pines State Beach,** one of the most beautiful in San Diego County. Adjacent, technically in Del Mar, and forming the reserve's northern reach is **Los Penasquitos Lagoon,** wetlands that serve as wildlife refuge and bird sanctuary, an area first damaged by Santa Fe Railroad construction then almost destroyed in the 1960s by the construction of the Pacific Coast Highway.

Torrey Pines is north of La Jolla Village, just off N. Torrey Pines Road. To reach the preserve from I-5, exit at Genesee Avenue and head west. Turn north (right) onto N. Torrey Pines Road. To reach the beach from I-5, exit at Carmel Valley Road and head west. One parking lot is near the beach, another near the preserve's visitor center. Admission is free, but parking is $6. The beach is open daily, 8 A.M. to sunset; the visitor center is open 9 A.M. to sunset. For more information, contact Torrey Pines State Reserve and Beach, 858/755-2063, www.torreypine.org.

A natural high at Torrey Pines, not an official reserve activity, is offered by the **Torrey Pines International Gliderport,** 2800 Torrey Pines Scenic Dr. (behind the Salk Institute), 858/45-9858, www.flytorrey.com, which launches hang

WHISPERS OF OLD CALIFORNIA

The story of early California settlement is whispered by area missions. Also worth a peek are three 19th-century homes.

Most evocative of mission-era California is the 28-room adobe at **Rancho Guajome Adobe County Park,** 3000 Guajome Lake Rd. in Oceanside, 760/724-4082, open only for docent-led tours (small fee) on Sat. and Sun. at 11 A.M., 12:30 P.M., and 2 P.M., at last report. Both a state and national historic landmark, the Guajome Adobe features period furniture and appliances. Come in July for the annual Civil War reenactment. Near the adobe is the **Antique Gas and Steam Engine** museum, open daily, a surprising array of working antique farm equipment. The 557-acre Rancho Guajome is also a local hiking, equestrian, and bird-watching hotspot. Camping ($16) is popular too; all sites have electrical and water hookups, and amenities include hot showers, toilets, fire rings, and a dump station. For camping reservations call 858/565-3600 or 877/565-3600.

In nearby Vista is the Monterey-style **Rancho Buena Vista Adobe** compound, 651 East Vista Dr., 760/639-6164 or 760/639-6139 (recorded, for upcoming events), featuring regularly changing furnishings, art gallery, and gift shop. Tours (small fee) are offered only Wed.–Fri. 10 A.M.–2:15 P.M., and Sat. 10 A.M.

The city of San Diego's **Los Peñasquitos Canyon Preserve,** stretching between the I-5 and I-15 freeways near Del Mar, includes two large coastal canyons—the preserve will one day include 4,000 protected acres—and San Diego's oldest surviving residence. **Rancho Santa Maria de los Peñasquitos,** built in 1823, is part architectural monument, part museum, and part events venue. Tours are offered on Saturday at 11 A.M. and Sunday at 1 P.M. The preserve is headquartered at 12020 Black Mountain Rd.; just north of the stables, turn onto Canyonside Park Driveway. For more information, including guided hike information—there's a lovely waterfall here—call Friends of Los Peñasquitos Canyon Preserve at 858/484-3219.

gliders and paragliders who blithely cruise the updrafts above the beach. Ask about kite surfing.

DEL MAR

For Del Mar's surf, head for **Del Mar Beach.** To watch the sunset, locals and visitors alike gather up top, on the bluffs at the end of 15th Street. For Del Mar's turf, head to the fairgrounds. Del Mar is most famous for its elegant art deco Spanish colonial **Del Mar Race Track** at the Del Mar Fairgrounds, "Where the Turf Meets the Surf." Recently reconstructed, the track is the place for some serious thoroughbred racing from late July into mid-September. The show here has always been something of a star-studded affair. The Del Mar Thoroughbred Club was organized in the 1930s by entertainer Bing Crosby and some of his cronies, because Crosby wanted some of the glitz and glitter of glamour racing close to his home in Rancho Santa Fe. Mostly serious gamblers and more sedate business types make up the crowd these days. But you can pony up on the ponies even in the off-season, thanks to the new age of satellite betting. Who can resist a place where you buy mementos at **The Gift Horse?** Admission to the Del Mar Race Track, 2260 Jimmy Durante Blvd. (Via de la Valle Road at Coast Boulevard), is $5 ($10 for grandstand seats). Parking is $5. For more information, call 858/755-1141 (recorded information 858/793-5533) or visit www.dmtc.com.

Upscale accommodations and restaurants aren't hard to find in and around Del Mar; there are also some great deals. (For local suggestions, see Accommodations in San Diego.) Shopping opportunities also aren't hard to find, either, especially in upscale malls such as the **Del Mar Plaza.** Good deals can be found here, too. For example: relatively inexpensive for all-occasion natural-fiber women's wear is **Chico's,** 858/792-7080. Contact the **Del Mar Chamber of Commerce,** 1104 Camino del Mar, 858/755-4844, www.delmarchamber.org, for more area information.

Recreation

The sun always shines in San Diego County, powerfully enough, most of the time, to dry up even the chance of rain. Since even San Diego's major tourist attractions are out in the open air, it's little wonder then that, here, life is lived outdoors. Recreation and sports are central to local life, which explains the area's endless variety of outdoor activities. Begin with aerial sports—skydiving, sky sailing, aerial barnstorming. Then beach combing, bicycling, birdwatching, boating—every imaginable type of boat and water sport—and even bocce ball. There's golfing—lots of it, with lush green courses spread out everywhere—and Frisbee golf in Balboa Park. And hiking. Horseback riding. Kayaking. Kite-flying. Racquetball. Recreational working-out, at the legion of local health and fitness clubs. Rock climbing. Inline skating. Sportfishing, swimming, surfing, snorkeling, shark diving, scuba diving, sailing, and sailboarding. Tennis. Volleyball at the beaches. Waterskiing. Whale-watching. You name it, chances are San Diego does it—and has at least one outfitter offering the necessary equipment and/or service.

A great place to start is **Hike Bike Kayak San Diego** in La Jolla, 858/551-9510, www.hikebikekayak.com, which offers all kinds of tours—family bike rides as well as challenging mountain bike trips; hikes in Torrey Pines or in Mission Hills Park; kayak tours of La Jolla's Sea Caves, even surfing lessons. The specialty, though, is the full-day Hike Bike Kayak Tour outing.

CRUISES

Inexplicably, nonathletic types sometimes find themselves in San Diego. For them, the local love affair with aerobic exercise, buff bodies, and too-dark tans can be a bit intimidating. For the record, however, you *can* come to San Diego, have a good time, and leave the exercise to someone else. At last report there was no law—no official law, anyway—stating otherwise.

COASTING ON THE COASTER

If you'd rather leave the driving to everyone else in San Diego, you can get to San Diego—and get all around San Diego—by train. From north county you can take Amtrak into downtown, then get around on the San Diego Trolley light-rail system. But you can also climb aboard the North San Diego County Transit District's **Coaster commuter trains** in either Oceanside (195 S. Tremont St.) or Carlsbad (2775 State St.) or destinations farther south for the quick trip into downtown San Diego. Coming soon: the 22-mile **Sprinter** high-speed transit link connecting Oceanside with Vista, San Marcos, and Escondido along the Hwy. 78 corridor.

For more information about the Coaster, call 800/262-7837; for Sprinter details, 760/599-8332; for transit schedules, maps, fares, and other current information, see www.gonctd.com.

Sign on for a San Diego Bay tour, for example. **Hornblower Cruises** at the Cruise Ship Pier, 1066 N. Harbor, 619/234-8687 or 888/467-6256, www.hornblower.com, offers mainstream one- and two-hour harbor tours, brunch and dinner cruises, even whale-watching trips, with rates $15 and up. The cheapest water trip around, something of a self-designed tour, is the **Coronado Ferry**, which departs from the nearby Broadway Pier, $2 each way (plus 50 cents if you bring a bike), 619/234-4111 for information and schedules.

TRAIN TOURS

Design your own train trip—or a self-designed train-oriented nostalgia trip—with help from San Diego's **San Diego Trolley** light rail system. Take the trolley to Tijuana, for example, or east to old-hometown-style La Mesa, for example, for a visit to the **Pacific Southwest Railway Museum** (open weekends only), 619/465-7776. (For current trolley information, see www.sdcommute.com.) A more ambitious weekend possibility: the 16-mile roundtrip

backcountry boogie aboard a vintage steam- or diesel-powered train on the **San Diego & Arizona Railway,** starting at **Campo Depot,** 619/478-9937 (weekends), www.sdrm.org, well east of San Diego in Campo, near the Mexican border. In winter and early spring, you can also take a trip from Campo to Tecate, Mexico.

HOT-AIR BALLOON

Or, how 'bout an aerial excursion? For hot-air ballooning, **Skysurfer Balloon Company** in Del Mar, 858/481-6800 or 800/660-6809, www.skysurferballoon.com, is one good possibility. To fly higher and faster, climb into a beautifully restored open-cockpit biplane and go for an easy 20-minute spin or a high-flying "Sunset Snuggler" tour with **Barnstorming Adventures.** If you're feeling dangerous, stay out for an hour long aerial roller-coaster ride with dogfight maneuvers. Vintage plane rides start at $60 per person for 20 minutes, when two people fly together. Flights usually depart from either Palomar Airport near Carlsbad or Gillespie Field, only as scheduled (reservations required). For more information and to make reservations, call 760/438-7680 or 800/759-5667 or see www.barnstorming.com, sometimes featuring notable Internet specials.

SPECTATOR SPORTS

Non-participatory sports are ever-popular with San Diego's armchair athletes. For pro baseball, the National League **San Diego Padres** fill the bill at new Petco Park near the Gaslamp Quarter downtown. For current info, see www.padres.com; for schedule information call 619/283-4494; for tickets, 619/29-PADRES. The new stadium is within walking distance of major downtown hotels and is also well-served by public transit. The city's Qualcomm Stadium ("the Q") at 9449 Friars Rd. in Mission Valley (intersection of I-8 and I-805) is now strictly for football, home to the **San Diego Chargers,** 619/280-2111 or 877-CHARGERS, www.chargers.com. For Chargers' home games, consider taking the **Express** bus, 619/233-3004, which picks up fans at several locations throughout the city beginning two hours before the game.

In addition to major entertainment performances, the **San Diego Sports Arena,** 619/224-4171, www.sandiegoarena.com, hosts the U.S. International Hockey League **San Diego Gulls,** 619/224-4625 or www.sandiegogulls.com, from October through April, and the rock 'em-sock 'em **San Diego Sockers** professional indoor soccer team, 619/224-GOAL, www.sockers.com, October–May.

To watch Sunday polo matches from June through October, head to Rancho Santa Fe and the **San Diego Polo Club,** 858/481-9217. In late July through mid-September, you'll find horse-racing action at the **Del Mar Race Track** in Del Mar, 858/755-1141.

Entertainment and Events

San Diego is renowned for the art museums and other cultural riches collected in **Balboa Park,** and for both the **Old Globe Shakespeare Festival** and **La Jolla Playhouse** theater programs. The **California Ballet Company, San Diego Opera, San Diego Symphony,** and **San Diego Civic Light Opera** are also center stage on the local arts scene. And the **La Jolla Symphony & Chorus,** the **La Jolla Chamber Music Society,** and other music groups are still going strong. Touring concerts and other national troupes perform both at downtown venues and at area college and university campuses—the University of California at San Diego, San Diego State University, local community colleges, and private colleges and universities, which are also good bets for guest speakers and eclectic special events. Pick up local newspapers to find out what's going on where. Local papers also publish listings of local art galleries; many are concentrated in the Gaslamp Quarter, in La Jolla, and elsewhere along the coast.

Though Balboa Park's three stages and the La Jolla Playhouse are local theatrical stars, smaller repertory groups and venues abound—including the contemporary **San Diego Repertory Theater,** 79 Horton Plaza, 619/235-8025, and the cabaret-style **Coronado Playhouse,** 1775 Strand Way, 619/435-4856.

Mainstream movie theaters are everywhere; multiple multiplexes cluster at area malls and elsewhere. Often the most challenging cinema is served forth from smaller, sometimes historic theaters. Happening in Hillcrest, for example, is the **Hillcrest Cinemas** multiplex, 3965 Fifth Ave., 619/819-0236, showing foreign and art films. The art-revival house **Ken Cinema** on Adams Avenue, 619/819-0236, and the **La Jolla Village Cinemas,** are brought to you by the same folks. The 500-seat **Sherwood Auditorium** at the Museum of Contemporary Art in La Jolla, 700 Prospect, 858/454-0267 (box office), 858/454-3541 (administration), also screens classic and foreign films.

MUSIC, CLUBS, AND BARS

San Diego is entertaining, from its distinctive neighborhood bar scenes and dance clubs to respectable jazz and rock venues. Again, local newspapers are the best source for what's going on while you're in town. **Dizzy's,** 344 Seventh Ave. (between J and K), "where the music matters most," is in the up-and-coming East Village, an easy throw from the San Diego Padres' new Petco Park. Dizzy's is a jazz club sans alcohol, TV, restaurant, and every other modern distraction, so patrons focus on the music. All ages are welcome. For more information, call 858/270-7467 or see www.dizzyssandiego.com.

The Gaslamp Quarter has become the scene for the younger set, at places including the sleek **Gaslamp Billiard Palace** and pub, 379 Fourth Ave., 619/230-1968; the **Blue Tattoo** dance club, downstairs at 835 Fifth Ave., 619/238-7191; and the **Dublin Square Irish Pub & Grill** at 554 Fourth Ave., 619/239-5818, a quick trip all the way to Grafton Street. In order to stand a chance of getting into the painfully hip **Zen Café** sushi bar and night club in the On Broadway

Event Center, 615 Broadway, 619/231-0011, open only on Friday and Saturday nights, reservations are required. For bourgeois vodka specialties and other expensive mockery of the U.S.S.R., head for black and red **Red Circle Café**, 420 E St., 619/234-9211.

An eclectic around-town club-scene cruise for older hipsters might include, for acoustic jazz and R&B, **Croce's** in the Gaslamp Quarter, 802 Fifth Ave., 619/233-4355; the top-flight jazz venue **Elario's** on the top floor of the Hotel La Jolla in La Jolla, 7955 La Jolla Shores Dr., 858/459-0541; and, for live rock, R&B, reggae, and whatever, the Quonset-hut-chic **Belly Up Tavern** in Solana Beach, 143 S. Cedros Ave., 858/481-9022. And there's always the loud **Hard Rock Cafe** in La Jolla, 858/454-5101. If the arthritis and bursitis aren't giving you too much grief, consider headin' out for a country-western stomp at **In Cahoots** in Mission Valley, 5373 Mission Center Rd., 619/291-8635. Otherwise, it's safe to settle in at the bar at the **U.S. Grant Hotel** downtown, 619/232-3121, for great local blues and jazz, or soak up some classy piano-bar comfort at the **Westgate Hotel** downtown, 619/238-1818, and at **Hotel del Coronado** across the water, 619/522-8496.

EVENTS

With the sublime weather here, it's little wonder that so many San Diego events, among them open-air theater and street festivals, are staged outdoors. Unique or oddball local events can be the most fun, so while you're here ask around and study local newspapers. Museums, colleges, and universities also sponsor a variety of unusual activities.

Mid-December through mid- March is **whale-watching** season, when California gray whales make their northern migration. And in January, catch the **San Diego Marathon** as it winds 26.2 miles down the coast from Carlsbad. The ever-popular **Festival of Animation** collection of shorts is a long-running favorite staged in La Jolla at the Museum of Contemporary Art's Sherwood Auditorium from mid-January through March; the *Sick and Twisted*

series arrives later in the summer. Major San Diego spring events include the **Ocean Beach Kite Festival** in March; the **San Diego Crew Classic**, the **Downtown ArtWalk**, and the **Coronado Flower Show** in April; and the **Pacific Beach Block Party**, the Olympic-caliber **Del Mar National Horseshow**, and Old Town's **Cinco de Mayo** festivities in May.

In June, come for the **San Diego County Fair** at the fairgrounds in Del Mar, the **Mostly Mozart Festival** downtown in the Spreckels Theater, the annual **Ocean Beach Street Fair and Chili Cook-Off**, the **San Diego International Triathlon**, and the **Rock n' Roll Marathon.** Also in June, the **Twilight in the Park** summer concert series at Spreckels Organ Pavilion in Balboa Park begins, continuing through August. In July, the annual **San Diego Lesbian and Gay Pride Parade** is a huge draw, with a rally and festival well into the night. Also in July, **Sand Castle Days** at the Imperial Beach Pier is a big hit, fun in the sun along with serious competitive sand castle construction, along with the **Sizzling Summer Jazz Festival** on Coronado and the immensely popular **San Diego Comic Convention** at the convention center in downtown San Diego. The convention pays homage to comic books, cartoon and comic art, and comic artists. The **Hillcrest Cityfest Street Fair** comes in August, part of America's finest city week festivities.

The biggest big deal in September is the Gaslamp Quarter's **Street Scene** fall food and music festival (sometimes scheduled in late August), while the **Adams Avenue Street Fair,** a right neighborly neighborhood block party, is much more laid-back. In October, when admission is free for children all month, **Zoo Founder's Day** makes a human zoo out of the San Diego Zoo, with the typical zoo crowd of 20,000 easily zooming past 50,000. All kinds of Halloween fun—including the **Haunted Museum of Man** in Balboa Park, and an **Underwater Pumpkin Carving Contest** in La Jolla—round out the year's foremost month of fright. For animals on the march, head to El Cajon with kids in tow in November for the annual **Mother Goose Parade** or to the **Carlsbad Village Faire** in Carlsbad. Magical among

San Diego Coast

the multitude of holiday events in December is **Christmas on El Prado** in Balboa Park and, along the bay downtown, the **San Diego Harbor Parade of Lights.**

SHOPPING

You're not looking very hard if you can't find something to buy in San Diego. Major malls are the obvious places to start parting with your hard-earned cash—places such as **Horton Plaza** and the nearby **Paladion** downtown, **Fashion Valley** and the **Mission Valley Center** near Hotel Circle, the huge **University Town Center** in La Jolla's Golden Triangle, and Del Mar's cunningly camouflaged **Del Mar Plaza.** The **San Diego Factory Outlet Center,** 619/690-2999, in San Ysidro, near the Mexican border, is also immensely popular. Savvy shoppers can pick up bargains at **Carls-**bad **Company Stores,** 760/804-9000, with bargains from Barney's New York, Kenneth Cole and The Gap, among others. The traditional bargain-hunter's bonanza, however, is **Kobey's Swap Meet** at the Sports Arena parking lot, 3500 Sports Arena Blvd., 619/226-0650. Fun and funky, it's open Thurs.–Sun. 7 A.M.–3 P.M. (admission $1).

For specialty items, migrate to the most likely neighborhoods. **Hillcrest,** for example, is a good bet for trendy clothes, gifts, and good bookstores and music shops, as is **La Jolla,** also known for homewares, home fashions, and art galleries. For tourist-grade international arts and crafts and Mexican memorabilia, head for Old Town and **Bazaar del Mundo, La Esplanade,** and **Old Town Mercado.** (Do comparison shop here; some places are substantially less expensive than others.) To hunt down seafaring wares, look around on and near both **Harbor Island** and **Shelter Island.**

Accommodations

A pleasant surprise in San Diego is the range of surprisingly decent accommodation options, from dirt cheap to definitely expensive. You'd expect to find upscale hotels, inns, and resorts along the coast, downtown, and elsewhere, but the surprise is that prime visitor areas also feature hostels, very inexpensive hotels, and reasonably priced, pleasant motels. The following suggestions are arranged by general locale. For more choices, see also Coronado: Crown of the Bay and contact the local visitors bureau (see Practical San Diego). For bed-and-breakfast listings, contact the **San Diego Bed & Breakfast Guild,** 619/523-1300 or 888/863-4325, www.bandbguildsandiego.org, or the county-wide **Bed & Breakfast Directory for San Diego,** 619/297-3130 or 800/619-7666, www.sandiegobandb.com.

The area's "off season" is September through mid-June. Why summer is still prime time for vacationers to San Diego, considering the marvelous year-round climate, remains something of a mystery—but don't complain, since everyone else's shortsightedness can save you from the crowds *and* save you money. For summertime bargains, head inland; away from the moderate coastal climate, temperatures soar and prices drop. Larger hotels, resorts, and motel chains almost always offer discounts, with special deals and packages during slow periods. As elsewhere in California and the U.S., members of the American Automobile Association (AAA) and the American Association of Retired Persons (AARP) qualify for sometimes substantial discounts, as do corporate customers. For major deals—savings as much as 50 percent, in some cases—consider booking even resort accommodations through **San Diego Hotel Reservations,** 619/627-9300 or 800/SAVE-CASH, or www.sandiegohotel res.com. While making travel plans, be aware of the city's all-out conventioneering—and be flexible about trip timing, if at all possible. San Diego's success at attracting major conventions and staging major events is great for the hotel business but bad news for savvy travelers suddenly unable to get a bargain rate.

DOWNTOWN

Hostels

Affiliated with Hostelling International, the **HI-USA San Diego Downtown Hostel** is in the heart of the Gaslamp Quarter, on the corner of Fifth Avenue and Market. Fully renovated, the Downtown Hostel features private and dorm rooms, laundry facilities, lockers, a common kitchen, pool table, and rental bikes. A bed in a dorm room is under $25 per person, a private room in the $50 range. For more information, contact the hostel at 521 Market St., 619/525-1531, www.sandiegohostels.org. Groups welcome. Children (under age 18) are welcome if accompanied by an adult. Reservations are essential in summer (through September). The office is open daily 7 A.M.–midnight.

Also in the midst of the downtown action, "run by backpackers for backpackers," is **USA Hostels San Diego,** nearby at 726 Fifth Ave., 619/232-3100 or 800/438 8622 (in the U.S. and Canada), www.usahostels.com. A dorm bed (four to six per room) is $16–19, a private room (with a double bed or two bunkbeds) is $40–44. All-you-can-eat pancake breakfast and all-day tea and coffee are included. Reception is open 24 hours, too, a real plus for hardcore sightseers.

Motels

A comfortable downtown area budget hotel, on India Street at Date, residential-style **La Pensione** is contemporary and clean. Especially appealing if you'll be staying awhile—the general ambience here, plus onsite laundry, make that an attractive idea—each cozy room (two people maximum) features a private bath, a kitchenette with microwave and refrigerator, and adequate space for spreading out work projects or tourist brochures. Daily rates are $50–100, single or double. Ask about weekly and monthly rates. For more information, contact: La Pensione, 1700 India St., 619/236-8000, www.lapensionehotel.com. For reservations, call 800/232-4683.

Downtown San Diego's **Motel 6** is another San Diego bargain—a well-located property with great rates. Amenities include private baths, telephone,

color TV with cable and some rooms even have a harbor view. Other pluses: daily maid service, onsite laundry, and nearby public parking. In summer rates are $50–100. Motel 6 is downtown at 1546 Second Ave. (between Beech and Cedar), 619/236-9292 or 800/466-8356, www.motel6.com.

Definitely a find—one of those places where you'll find a bed even when conventioneers have taken every other place in town—is the landmark **Embassy Hotel** just north of Balboa Park at 3645 Park Blvd., 619/296-3141, these days primarily a residential home for the elderly. Rooms, $50–100 per night, are fairly basic but quiet and roomy, with private bathrooms and in-room phones. Free laundry facilities. You can even eat with the residents, in the decent cafeteria-style dining room.

U.S. Grant Hotel

Downtown's most dignified and time-honored presence, the landmark U.S. Grant Hotel was built in 1910 by Ulysses S. Grant, Jr., son of the former Civil War general and U.S. president. After decades of decline mid-century, the 11-story U.S. Grant reopened in 1985 after an impressive $80 million renovation, and is now on the National Register of Historic Places. The classy classic lobby, with its Palladian columns, marble floors, crystal chandeliers, Old World art, and Chinese porcelain, sets the tone for the guest rooms, decorated in a style more often found on the East Coast. Regular rooms are somewhat small but tastefully done in Queen Anne-style mahogany, even the armoire hiding the TV (cable provided; movies available). Marble and tile bathrooms offer other modern comforts, such as terrycloth robes and handmilled soaps. High-speed Internet access and ergonomic chairs connect visitors to contemporary times. Official room rates are in the $150–250 range and up but look for specials, packages, and discounts. One of downtown's best restaurants is the **Grant Grill** here, 619/232-3121, surprisingly reasonable, serving breakfast, lunch, and dinner. Other facilities include exercise room (massage extra), business center, and conference rooms.

The U.S. Grant, downtown at 326 Broadway,

inhabits an entire city block. Its formal entrance is directly across from Horton Plaza but, unless on foot, most guests enter the lobby from the parking lot (valet parking). For more information, call 619/232-3121 or check www.wyndham.com. For reservations, call 800/237-5029.

Horton Grand Hotel

Another notable downtown presence is the genteel Horton Grand Hotel in the Gaslamp Quarter, on Island Street between Third and Fourth. The ambience here is historic yet new, a neat trick achieved by building what amounts to a new hotel from the old-brick bones of two time-honored neighborhood hotels otherwise doomed by redevelopment—including the original Horton Grand, which stood in the way of Horton Plaza. Rooms here are cozy, in the Victorian style, with neat touches such as gas fireplaces and TV sets cleverly tucked into the wall (behind a mirror). Rates run $150–250, with various discounts and special packages often available. For more information, contact: Horton Grand Hotel, 311 Island Avenue (at Fourth Avenue), 619/544-1886 or 800/542-1886 for reservations, www.hortongrand.com.

Other Hotels

There are more upscale hotels downtown than ever—the likes of the **W Hotel San Diego** at 421 W. B St., 619/231-8220, www.starwood.com, and the 21-story **Omni Hotel San Diego**, connected to the ball park via skybridge at 675 L St., 619/231-6664, www.omnihotels.com—with more on the way, especially now that Petco Park stadium has joined the convention center as an area draw. Coming soon: the seriously cool boutique **Hotel Solamar,** with onsite restaurants and all the comforts, www.kimptongroup.com, a Kimpton Hotels property.

Colorful and fresh, the jazzy boutique **M Bristol Hotel San Diego** 1055 First Ave., 619/232-6141 or 800/662-4477, www.thebristolsandiego.com, offers an impressive pop-art collection—Andy Warhol, Peter Max, Roy Lichtenstein, Keith Haring, and Guy Buffet—along with Daisies Bistro and an inviting bar. Bright, spacious guest rooms include abundant conve-

niences, from plush robes and plenty of work space to high-speed Internet access, dataports, voice mail, web TV, in-room coffee, hair dryers, irons and ironing boards. And meeting planners, when was the last time you enjoyed a ballroom with a retractable roof? Room rates are $200–250 but can drop to $99 for special promotions.

The 19-story **Westgate Hotel** is a classic modern American study in contrast—in this case, the contrast between somewhat formal Old World luxury and the ubiquitous, thoroughly modern downtown high-rise in which it hides. The lobby sparkles with Baccarat crystal chandeliers; high tea is served every afternoon. The theme of classical opulence continues through on-site restaurants and into the antique-furnished guest rooms, where bathrooms come with Italian marble and gold-plated fixtures. From the ninth floor up, rooms come with a view, too. Rack rates run $250 and up, with considerable price flexibility depending on what's going on. Weekends are usually the best deal, with $149 the typical rate. The Westgate is at 1055 Second Ave. (at C Street), 619/238-1818 or www.westgatehotel.com. For reservations, call 800/221-3802.

The **Wyndham Emerald Plaza,** formerly the Pan Pacific Hotel, caters to the business trade, but with swimming pool, full fitness facilities, and abundant other extras, it's quite comfortable for tourists who prefer a downtown base. Rates are $150–250, generally lowest on the weekend, sometimes starting at $159; ask about other discounts and specials. And if you're meeting someone, rendezvous under the "emerald" in the lobby. The Wyndham Emerald Plaza is at the Emerald-Shapery Center (between Columbia and State), 400 W. Broadway, 619/239-4500, www.wyndham.com. For reservations, call 800/996-3426.

Bed-and-Breakfasts

The friendly **Balboa Park Inn,** right across the street from Balboa Park, is a stylistic complement to the park's 1915 exposition architecture. All rooms at the inn—actually, four Spanish colonial homes interconnected by courtyards—are tasteful yet simple suites with either one or two bedrooms; fun "specialty" suites include the Paris in the 30s, Orient Express, and Nouveau Ritz suites. Amenities vary (as does room décor) but include kitchens, fireplaces, patios, in-room whirlpools, and wetbars. Continental breakfast and the morning newspaper are delivered to your door. The inn is on the north end of Balboa Park, and you can walk to park attractions. Rates are $100–150. For more information, contact Balboa Park Inn, 3402 Park Blvd., 619/298-0823 or 800/938-8181, www.balboaparkinn.com.

Though a summertime stay often requires considerable advance booking, another great deal is the impeccably restored 1913 **Gaslamp Plaza Suites** just a block from Horton Plaza at 520 E St. (corner of Fifth Avenue), 619/232-9500 or 800/874-8770, www.gaslampplaza.com, a timeshare complex that also rents out rooms as available. The building itself, with a lovely lobby chiseled from marble and mosaic tiles, is San Diego's first high-rise, circa 1913, and listed on the National Register of Historic Places. The suites—larger ones feature a separate bedroom— are attractive and named famous writers including Shelley, Fitzgerald, and Emerson, with various amenities, some including microwaves, refrigerators, coffeemakers, color TV, the works. Standard rooms are $100–150, deluxe rooms $150–250, depending on room size and amenities, and include continental breakfast—served on the roof, weather permitting. The view is free.

CORONADO

If planning to splurge, stay at least one night at the historic **Hotel del Coronado,** the city's crowning glory. The legendary and eclectic Queen Anne "Hotel Del" features a classic dark-wood lobby, with a still-functioning birdcage elevator and a spectacular support-free formal dining room, the latter used only on special occasions. Guest rooms in the original wooden section of the hotel, with its marvelous quirky corridors, boast all modern amenities yet a Victorian sensibility—all the more dazzling following the Hotel Del's $50 million renovation, completed in 2000. Newer hotel units near the beach include the Ocean Towers, the California Cabanas, and the Beach House. And if you aren't

sufficiently entertained by the hotel's grandeur, its Olympic-size swimming pool, tennis courts, and pristine white-sand Coronado Beach—beach chairs, umbrellas, towels, even boogie boards provided—then watch the hotel's closed-circuit TV, showing movie after movie filmed at the Hotel Del. Other amenities include wonderful on-site restaurants, from the stunningly Victorian Crown-Coronet dining room, complete with chandeliers designed by *Wizard of Oz* author Frank Baum, to the romantic Prince of Wales Grill and the new Sheerwater (formerly the Ocean Terrace), serving California coastal cuisine. (For very Victorian High Tea, head for the Palm Court on Sunday afternoon.) Not to mention various business services, shopping, complete spa services (extra), and rental bikes, sailboards, and sailboats. Summer room rates are $250 and up, with a two-night minimum on weekends, though ask about packages and off-season deals. For more information, contact: Hotel del Coronado, 1500 Orange Ave., 619/435-6611, www.hoteldel.com. For reservations, call 800/468-3533 or reserve online.

Another top choice is the 15-acre **Loews Coronado Bay Resort,** 4000 Coronado Bay Rd., 800/235-6397 or 619/424-4000, www.loewshotels.com, a lovely contemporary hotel with light and airy view rooms—every room has a view, be it of the ocean, the bay, or the marina (moor your own). All the usual luxuries, on-site restaurants, fitness and business facilities, even a kid's program are provided. Room rates are $150–250, suites $250 and up, but ask about specials.

Also appealing in the pricier category is the **Coronado Island Marriott Resort,** formerly Le Meridien San Diego, 16 acres fronting the bay directly across from downtown, with lush landscaping, lagoons full of fish and flamingos, tennis courts, pools, health and fitness facilities, business services, and great restaurants. Rooms, suites, and villas, all with a balcony or patio, open onto either a bay or lagoon view. Room rates are $150–250, suites $250 and up, but look for off-season specials and packages. The Coronado Island Marriott is at 2000 Second St. (at Glorietta), 619/435-3000, www.marriott.com.

Thankfully for just plain folks and most families, Coronado also offers budget-friendly choices, including the **Crown City Inn,** 520 Orange Ave. (between Fifth and Sixth), 800/422-1173 or 619/435-3116, www.crowncityinn.com. Every room at this attractive Mediterranean-style motel has a refrigerator, microwave, and coffeemaker, in-room modem hookup, ironing board and iron, plus color TV and cable with free movies. Heated pool, complimentary bikes, on-site laundry facilities. Even better, from here it's just a 10-minute walk to the beach. The **Crown City Bistro** here is open for breakfast, lunch, and dinner and provides impressive room service. Summer rates are $100–150 for standard rooms (discounts in the off-season).

If there's no room at that inn, **La Avenida Inn,** 1315 Orange, 619/435-3191, www .laavenidainn.com, and the **Best Western Suites Coronado Island,** 235 Orange, 800/528-1234 or 619/437-1666, www.bestwestern.com, are good alternatives; summer rates are $150–250 at both properties. Contact the local visitor center (see below) for more suggestions.

MISSION BAY AND VICINITY
Hostels
Most surprisingly, San Diego boasts three hostels at, or very near, the beach. Thoroughly renovated, affiliated with the American Association of International Hostels, bustling **Banana Bungalow San Diego** is right on the beach—on Reed Avenue at Mission Boulevard—and right in the middle of the way-cool, way-young Pacific Beach scene. Most accommodations are dormitory style, with four to eight beds per room. Rates are under $25 for dormitory rooms; semi-private rooms start at $49. Jungle-themed décor; generous common areas; breakfast, sand volleyball, and beach bonfires are included. Laundry facilities, storage lockers, Internet access, and pay phones are available. For more information, contact: Beach Banana Bungalow San Diego, 707 Reed Ave., 858/273-3060 or 800/546-7835, www.bananabungalow.com.

The newest place around, though, is also the oldest—the **Ocean Beach International**

Backpacker Hostel, at home in the historic Hotel Newport in Ocean Beach, on Newport Ave. between Cable and Bacon. This 80-bed hostel is just one block from the beach in San Diego's most laid-back and "local" beach community, and there are no curfews, no chores and no lockouts. Accommodations include a few small but private "couples rooms," with two beds and a bathroom. Most rooms are semi-private with four or six beds per room; most of these also have private bathrooms. (More bathrooms are in the hallways) Rates under $25—including pastries for breakfast. For more information, contact: Ocean Beach International Backpacker Hostel, 4961 Newport Ave., 619/223-7873 or 800/339-7263, www.californiahostel.com.

The **HI-USA San Diego Point Loma Hostel,** affiliated with Hostelling International, is in a pleasant Point Loma residential neighborhood—close to the ocean but not particularly close to San Diego's other attractions. Yet this 60-bed hostel, on Udall Street, off Voltaire between Warden and Poinsettia, is a reasonably good base for wanderings farther afield. Draws include full kitchen (just a stroll to the People's Market), laundry facilities, bike rentals, a travel library, and baggage storage. The basic dormitory rate is under $25 for members and non-members. Private rooms (one or two people) are $38; family rooms (three adults or a family with one or two adults and children) are $45. Children under age 18 are welcome if accompanied by an adult. Check-in is 8 A.M.–10 P.M., with 24-hour access. For more information, contact: HI-USA San Diego Point Loma Hostel, 3790 Udall St., 619/223-4778, www.sandiegohostels.com. Reservations are advisable from April through September.

Resorts
If you prefer contemporary big-hotel ambience with the usual amenities plus an indoor pool and gym, consider the contemporary **Embassy Suites,** 601 Pacific Hwy. (at N. Harbor Drive), 619/239-2400 or 800/EMBASSY, www.em bassysuites.com. This is a better setup for families, too, since all suites feature a separate bedroom plus conveniences like refrigerators, hairdryers,

coffeemakers, and microwaves. All rooms have city or bay views. Full breakfast, as you like it (served in the restaurant), is included, along with free cocktails. Rates run $150–250, with various discounts and specials often available.

Shelter Island naturally attracts the sailing set but also draws wannabe yachters, what with all those pretty, high-priced boats bobbing around everywhere. The spectacular bay views attract everyone else. Still, attractive Hawaii-like tropical landscape and the endless "tiki" on parade is the real appeal of **Humphrey's Half Moon Inn** on Shelter Island, making for comfortable California coastal kitsch complete with in-room refrigerators and coffeemakers. In the midst of San Diego's bustling boat harbor, Humphrey's provides a private boat dock, huge heated pool, and whirlpool spa; for tooling around, rental bikes are available; special events, such as the great **outdoor jazz, folk, and easy-rock concerts** in summer, keep everyone coming back. (For cool jazz—indoors—during the rest of the year, show up on Sunday and Monday nights.) High-season rates are $150–250, depending on the view, with a two-night minimum on weekends from Memorial Day through Labor Day. For more information, contact Humphrey's Half Moon Inn & Suites, 2303 Shelter Island Dr., 619/224-3411 or 800/542-7400, www.halfmooninn.com.

Hotels

Mission Beach, Mission Bay, and Pacific Beach are filled to the gills with resorts and large hotels, many quite pricey and, in summer, overrun by fellow travelers. But the coastal areas also offer some nice midrange motel-style stays; a motel sitting literally above the surf, on a pier; and several hostels. For more on inexpensive hostel stays, see below.

Mission Bay's classic family getaway is the lush and lovely ꡒ **San Diego Paradise Point Resort,** a 44-acre island originally opened in the 1960s as Vacation Village South Seas Paradise. Recently updated to modern standards, the hotel still retains its '60s bungalow charm. The 462 tropical-style rooms and suites are housed in single-story buildings located across the island (complete with private patios, refrigerators, and coffeemakers). Its perfect for those who prefer a self-contained resort, as the endless recreation here is the real draw—including paddleboats, water sports, croquet, and volleyball. Rent bikes and cruise over to the beach, an easy few miles away, with or without the kids; in summer, the organized kids' program gives grown-ups a break, too. Guests have access to five heated swimming pools, a new exercise room, and a luxurious Indonesian-themed spa which opened in 2001. Restaurants include the family-friendly Barefoot Bar on the beach, and the upscale Baleen restaurant fronting Mission Bay. Rates run $250 and up in summer, but inquire about off-season rates and other specials. For more information, contact: San Diego Paradise Point Resort, 1404 W. Vacation Rd., 858/274-4630 or 800/344-2626, www.paradisepoint.com.

One of the best values around is the **Bahia Resort Hotel,** 998 W. Mission Bay Dr., 858/488-0551 or 800/576-4229, www.bahia hotel.com, semi-tropical and attractive, right across the street from a grassy park area and just a stroll from the beach. A bay beach and marina, where the paddlewheeler *Bahia Belle* is berthed (bay cruises, even dinner-theatre cruises, available), augment the backyard view from some rooms. Standard rooms are $100–150, deluxe rooms and suites $150–250, often discounted on a space-available basis.

The *classic* Pacific Beach stay, though, is right in the middle of the local action—out on the Crystal Pier, at the landmark 1930s ꡒ **Crystal Pier Hotel,** 4500 Ocean Blvd., 858/483-6983 or 800/748-5894, www.crystalpier.com, actually a pier-long collection of motel-style cottages. Guests can drive right out on the pier and park next to their cottages, a big plus on crowded weekends. The Crystal Pier Hotel features 26 white-and-blue cottages with Cape Cod–style décor, kitchenettes, and surf-view patios—nothing fancy but unique and immensely popular. Rates are $150–250 mid-June to mid-Sept., $100–150 mid-Sept. to mid-June. Make reservations well in advance for summer (three-day minimum stay in summer, two-night otherwise). Weekly and monthly rates are available in the off-season.

OLD TOWN

Old Town San Diego offers some of the best lodging bargains around, including the all-suites **Ⓜ Best Western Hacienda Hotel Old Town.** Once a mission-style minimall, it's now a multilevel hillside motel—a quite clever renovation albeit a bit baffling at first, with multiple patios, passageways, stairways, terraces, and elevators to navigate. Wheelchair-accessible rooms are reached via elevators. Once you do find your way around—and find the on-site restaurants and pleasant pool area—you're set for an enjoyable stay. The mood here is San Diego-style Southwestern, with lovely landscaping outside; some rooms open onto terraces, with partially private patios. Inside, most rooms are smallish but quite adequate, with all the usual amenities plus ceiling fans, in-room coffeemakers, microwaves, and refrigerators. Great harbor views at night, especially from upper levels. Rates are $150–250 in summer, somewhat lower at other times, but weekdays rates can go as low as $135. Ask about packages and seasonal specials. The Hacienda Hotel Old Town is at 4041 Harney St. (just off Juan), 619/298-4707 or 800/888-1991, www.ha ciendahotel-oldtown.com.

"Hotel Circle" refers to the low-priced and midrange motels that flank I-8 between Old Town and Mission Valley—not a bad location given the instant freeway access, assuming you have a car and don't mind doing the freeways to get around. Among the cheaper choices in the neighborhood is good old **Motel 6 Hotel Circle,** 2424 Hotel Circle N., San Diego, 619/296-1612, or, for reservations at any Motel 6 nationwide, 800/466-8356, www.motel6.com. This one features a swimming pool and the usual basics for $50–100. A remarkable value for sporting types is the 20-acre **Mission Valley Resort,** 875 Hotel Circle S., 619/298-8281 or 800/362-7871, www.missionvalleyresort.com. Try to land a room away from the freeway noise, and then plunge into any of the three swimming pools (one's heated) or head to the adjacent tennis, racquetball, and health club facilities. Rooms here are in the $100–150 range in summer.

If you can't yet swing that trip to Hawaii, consider a stay at the very pleasant **Red Lion Hanalei Hotel,** 2270 Hotel Circle N., 619/297-1101 or 800/882-0858, www.hanaleihotel.com, yet another of San Diego's Polynesian-themed sleep palaces. Since Hanalei is Hawaiian for "valley of the flowers," the lush tropical foliage fits—as do the extravagant summertime luaus staged in the courtyard and the pool area, watched over by a huge Easter Island Tiki. Everything here has a fantastically '60s tropical theme-the Islands Restaurant has Disneyland-like Polynesian decor with an array of floats, outriggers, and lamps-but the rooms feature refreshingly contemporary decor and conveniences, and each have a private patio or balcony. Room rates start at $150–250 in summer, and $100–150 in the off season.

LA JOLLA

Motels

As you'd guess in such exclusive neighborhoods, life can get quite pricey in La Jolla and adjacent Del Mar. Because parking space is also a local luxury, many establishments charge extra for parking; be sure to inquire. **La Jolla Town Council** volunteers, 858/454-1444, can be very helpful if you'd like some personal assistance in making local lodging arrangements.

Low-rent accommodations don't exist in and around upscale, conservative La Jolla. Quite decent midrange motels are available, however, and to find them look inland, away from the ocean-front views.

Nothing fancy, **La Jolla Cove Suites** is stylin' it circa the 1950s but still a sweet deal. Quite well-situated—right across the street from Scripps Park and La Jolla Cove, as advertised—here you'll get views at a fairly reasonable price. In most units you'll also get a full kitchen, so you can eat in anytime you want. Rates run $150–250 depending on view and amenities, one and two bedroom suites $250 and up. Find La Jolla Cove Suites at 1150 Coast Blvd., 858/459-2621 or 888/525-6552, www.lajollacove.com. And if there's no room here, there may be space at the **Shell Beach Apartment Motel,** 981 Coast Blvd., run by the same folks.

Hotels and Resorts

La Jolla's oldest hotel is the still-dignified, wonderfully luxurious four-story **The Grande Colonial La Jolla,** a 1913-vintage belle overlooking the cove and close to everything downtown at 910 Prospect (between Fay and Girard), 858/454-2181 or 888/530-5766, www.thegrande colonial.com, Pool, restaurant, and full bar. High-season rates are $250 and up. Downtown's traditional darling, though, is the historic **La Valencia Hotel and Ocean Villas,** 1132 Prospect (at Herschel), 858/454-0771 or 800/451-0772, www.lavalenciahotel.com. Art deco La Valencia, still pretty in pink, was one of those legendary Hollywood celebrity destinations in the 1930s and '40s—*the* place to be, in the classic style of European luxury, as La Jolla began making a name for itself. And it still is, for those who can afford it. Rates start at $275, with some of the cheaper rooms not all that stellar. The layout of this Mediterranean-style pleasure palace *is* stellar, however. "Street level" happens to be the fourth floor, with the floors below on the way down to the ocean, and the others above. Even the elevator—with a human being at the controls!—is straight out of an old classic movie. Three restaurants—one with a 10th-floor view—a swimming pool and gardens terraced into the hillside, and a small spa are also modern classics.

One of *Condé Nast Traveler's* Top 20 Small Hotels in America in 2002, the stylish **Hotel Parisi** in the heart of the village at 1111 Prospect, 858/454-1511, www.hotelparisi.com, has it all, from feng shui design and intimacy—just 20 suites here—to custom-designed furnishings, original art, and excellent service. Rates start at $300, but look for off-season specials and packages.

Just north of the village, adjacent to the 18th green of the Torrey Pines Golf Course and the state's stunning botanical reserve, **N The Lodge at Torrey Pines,** 11480 N. Torrey Pines Rd., 858/453-4420 or 888/826-0224, www.lodge torreypines.com, boasts one of the best "view" locations around. The spectacular lodge is a modern-day example of Craftsman design, inspired by the architects Greene and Green. The 175

rooms and suites at this decidedly swank resort provide either an ocean or golf course view, and some have fireplaces. Restaurants include everpopular The Grill for casual dining, and the upscale A.R. Valentien restaurant, named for the early 20th-century artist whose works adorn the room. Rooms epitomize understated luxury, and start at $500. Except for the price tag, what's not to love?

The neighborhood's newest enclave of luxurious accommodation and upmarket dining is 210-room **Estancia La Jolla Hotel & Spa,** once the Black Family Horse Farm, located at 9700 N. Torrey Pines Rd., 858/550-1000 or 877/378-2624, www.estancialajolla.com, and scheduled to open in the summer of 2004.

DEL MAR

Motels

A genuine gem in Del Mar, literally *on* the beach, is the minimalist **N Del Mar Motel,** close to the racetrack and just a stroll into downtown at 1702 Coast Blvd., 858/755-1534 or 800/223-8449, www.delmarmotelonthebeach.com. Rooms come with refrigerators, color TV, and courtesy coffee; outdoor showers (essential for sandy feet) and barbecue grills available. Rates from $150–250 in the high season, $100–150 otherwise. **N Les Artistes,** 944 Camino Del Mar in Del Mar (between Ninth and 10th Streets), 858/755-4646, www.lesartistesinn.com, offers unique bed-and-breakfast rooms decorated in styles evoking particular artists, from the western-themed Remnington and Santa Fe-style O'-Keefe to the Mexican-style Diego Rivera and striking art-deco Erte rooms. Rates are $100–200 in summer, and start at $85 in winter.

L'Auberge Del Mar Resort and Spa

Right in the middle of everything in Del Mar, this luxury resort with a hillside ocean view graces the site of the famed Hotel Del Mar, a playground for the Hollywood celebrity set from the 1920s through the 1940s. The architecture of this Victorian-style beachhouse mimics the original, and the lobby still serves as the resort's social center. Guest rooms are country French, with marble bathrooms and the usual luxury amenities. Also here: full European-style spa and fitness facilities—affordable, by separate fee, for just about anyone, if lodging at the hotel is a bit too rich—plus tennis courts, two pools, great restaurants. Best of all, it's only one block to the beach. July, August, and September—race season at the Del Mar Race Track—is the high season, with rates $405 and up. Much lower rates are available at other times, standard doubles in the $150–250 range. L'Auberge Del Mar Resort and Spa is at 1540 Camino del Mar, 858/259-1515 or 800/245-9757, www.laubergedelmar.com. To get here from I-5, head west on Del Mar Heights Road for one mile, then turn north onto Camino del Mar. The resort is one mile farther.

Rancho Santa Fe

Often a real deal for a special-occasion escape is the **M Inn at Rancho Santa Fe,** a San Diego classic with 20 acres of terraced gardens, vine-draped cottages, croquet courses, tennis courts, pool, exercise facilities, and on-site restaurant, with golf and horseback riding available nearby. Another perk here: daytime access to an inn-owned beach cottage in Del Mar with patio tables for dining as well as showers and changing rooms inside. The inn's main building dates from 1923, and was originally built as a guesthouse for

prospective real estate buyers after the Santa Fe Railroad's local experiment with eucalyptus trees failed. (Santa Fe had hoped eucalyptus would produce quality wood for railroad ties; instead, the trees grew up to produce shade for the very exclusive residential neighborhoods here.) Quiet and relaxed, it's not particularly oriented toward families though kids are welcome. A good deal, with rates $150–250 (discounts and other specials often available). To get here, exit I-5 at Loma Santa Fe Dr. (Hwy. 58) and continue east four miles. For more information Inn at Rancho Santa Fe, 5951 Linea del Cielo (at Paseo), 858/756-1131 or 800/843-4661, www.theinnatrsf.com.

Privileged sibling to La Jolla's lovely La Valencia Hotel, the contemporary Old California–style **Rancho Valencia Resort,** near Del Mar in Rancho Santa Fe, has it all—40 acres of serenity, celebs, red-tiled roofs, bougainvillea-draped walkways, fountains, romantic and luxurious suites tucked into the lush landscape—not to mention the 18 tennis courts, exercise facilities, championship croquet lawn, pool, whirlpool tubs, sauna, and adjacent 18-hole golf course. Official rates are $500 and up, but ask about midweek and off-season specials. For more information: Rancho Valencia Resort, 5921 Valencia Circle, 858/756-1123 or 800/548-3664, www.ranchovalencia.com.

Food

DOWNTOWN

Even for those who avoid shopping malls as a matter of principle, the **Panda Inn** at Horton Plaza, 619/233-7800, merits an exception. Open daily for lunch and dinner, this good Chinese restaurant offers an impressive list of Mandarin and Szechuan selections. From noodle dishes and twice-cooked pork to fresh seafood, nothing here disappoints. There are other choices at Horton Plaza; study the directory to appreciate your choices.

Good and quite reasonable west of Horton Plaza is **Athens Market** in the Senator building, 109 W. F St., 619/234-1955, beloved for its

Greek classics, from roast lamb and chicken to moussaka. Also just across the street from hustle-bustle Horton Plaza, the **Grant Grill** at the venerable U.S. Grant Hotel, on Broadway between Third and Fourth, 619/232-3121, is a sure bet for escaping the tourist hordes. The hotel's elegant, dignified, and historically correct decor lends a men's club sensibility to the surprisingly good food—from American standards at breakfast and good salads, sandwiches, and specials at lunch to French specialties and steak and lobster dinners. Full bar. The Grant Grill is open daily for breakfast, lunch, and dinner.

Affordable and unpretentious yet sophisticated **Café Cerise** bistro, 1125 Sixth Ave. (between B and C Streets), 619/595-0153, serves meatloaf, warm brie sandwiches, a good Caesar salad, wonderful buckwheat crêpes, and entrées from mushroom and fennel soup to smoked trout. Grand desserts. The romantic **Candelas,** 416 Third Ave., 619/702-4455, serves stylish Mexican cuisine, from spectacular grilled red snapper and halibut in corn sauce to savory cactus salad. For uptown Italian at dinner, the place is stylish **Salvatore's,** 750 Front St., 619/544-1865, where the specialties include homemade ravioli filled with goat cheese, mascarpone, and walnuts, and marinated grilled lamb chops.

Rainwater's, 1202 Kettner (next door to the Santa Fe Depot), on the second floor, 619/233-5757, is a very uptown downtown establishment and one of the best steakhouses around. Steaks here are huge, side dishes simple but artfully selected. Grilled seafood is also prominent on the menu. If you can manage dessert—and here, that's typically a challenge—locals swear by the hot-fudge sundaes. Rainwater's is also a popular lunchtime rendezvous for the suit and tie set, during the week. Open nightly for dinner, weekdays for lunch. Call for holiday schedules (they vary from year to year).

GASLAMP QUARTER

In San Diego's Gaslamp Quarter you could easily eat your way around the globe, several times over, but would you be alive to tell about it? This is seriously hip and trendy territory, especially along foodie-friendly Fifth Avenue. Not everything is très expensive, though. The genuine article amid all the clone, faux, and retro on display throughout the Quarter is the **Cheese Shop** deli at 627 Fourth Ave. (between G Street and Market), 619/232-2303, where you can get a good all-American breakfast, grand sandwiches, and all the essentials for a picnic. Open daily for breakfast and lunch. The more stylish yet unstuffy **M Café 222,** 222 Island Ave. (at Second), 619/236-9902, stars spoon chandeliers—just part of the fun and funky post-industrial vibe. Breakfast is the big deal. People practically swoon over the famous pumpkin waffles, once featured in *Gourmet* magazine, and the banana-stuffed French toast, eggs Benedict Arnold, and pork tamales and eggs. Kids and pooches are welcome, too, so long as parents and pet owners remain well behaved.

Also affordable, open daily for lunch and dinner, is **Alambres** at 756 Fifth Ave., 619/698-2267, the place for Mexican-style grilled skewers. The place for hearty Irish fare, from potato-leek soup to shepherd's pie, is **The Field,** 544 Fifth Ave., 619/232-9840. A favorite for sushi is **Kiyo's,** just off overwhelming Fifth Avenue at 531 F St., 619/238-1726, which also serves a traditional Japanese menu. Also good and a notable bargain is Persian **Bandar,** 825 Fourth Ave., 619/238-0101. Brazilian barbecue, anyone? **Rei do Gado,** 939 Fourth Ave. (near Broadway), 619/702-8464, does meat—lamb, beef, pork, chicken, and beef—prepared in multiple ways; servers circulate with sizzling skewers to offer patrons sizzling slices of this and that. If there's any room, balance all that protein with salads, side dishes, and desserts.

And there are outposts of downhome Western exotica, such as the gussied-up **Dakota Grill and Spirits,** 901 Fifth (at E St.), 619/234-5554, specializing in "cowboy steak" and other surprises, and **5ifth Qtr,** (at Fifth and F Streets), 619/236-1616, where the 'cue is as good as the country-western, and dancing begins around 9 P.M. to a mix of live bands plays everything from reggae and rock to '60s soul. Just west of the Gaslamp Quarter and north of the convention center is **Kansas City Barbecue,** 610 W. Market St. (near W. Harbor), 858/231-9680, whose Hollywood claim to fame is as film location for the "sleazy bar scene" in the movie *Top Gun.* But the 'cue is the real reason to stop by.

Even the good ol' U.S. of A. can seem exotic. At the **Bayou Bar and Grill,** 329 Market St. (between Third and Fourth), 619/696-8747, if you didn't know it was San Diego you'd swear you'd somehow stumbled into Louisiana, what with the ceiling fans and color scheme. Once inside, keep it simple. Whether you choose seafood gumbo, another fresh fish dish, or rice and beans accompanied by homemade sausage, do leave room for dessert. Suitably decadent selections include Cajun velvet pie (chocolate and peanut butter) and Creole pecan pie. It's open for lunch and dinner daily, closed major holidays.

If it has to be Italian, **Fio's,** 801 Fifth Ave. (at F Street), 619/234-3467, is tried and true among the Gaslamp Quarter's trendy Fifth Avenue restaurants—a cheery contemporary Italian place looking down on the fray from its seasoned-brick setting. Those with smaller appetites and/or the budget-minded should stick to pastas and salads—or split one of those great pizzas fresh from the wood-fired oven. This a very popular place, so reservations are advisable at dinner. It's open weekdays for lunch, nightly for dinner, closed major holidays. **Ristorante Acqua Al 2,** 322 Fifth Ave., 619/230 0382, is a Tuscan-style bistro serving pizza Margherita, panini, baked eggplant with mozzarella, and both pasta and meat entrées.

Other excellent choices in the neighborhood: **Bella Luna,** with all those pretty moons, at 748 Fifth Ave. (between F and G), 619/239-3222, open daily for both lunch and dinner, and the stylish Tuscan **Trattoria La Strada,** 702 Fifth Ave. (at G), 619/239-3400, open daily for lunch and dinner. More casual than its Italian neighbors, bistro-style **Osteria Panevino,** 722 Fifth Ave. (at G), 619/595-7959, open daily for lunch and dinner, serves wonderful vegetable focaccia, spinach ravioli, and pizzas. Great for Italian san pretension at lunch and dinner daily is Sicilian **Trattoria Mamma Anna,** 644 Fifth Ave., 619/235-8144, serving such things as grilled Portobello mushrooms, pastas to those unbelievable proscuitto pizzas.

Another shining light in downtown's Gaslamp Quarter is **Croce's,** 802 Fifth Ave. (at F Street), 619/233-4355, a noted jazz club named in honor of the late singer Jim Croce and operated by his family. The music continues, these days with a pretty jazzy dinner menu, too, on which imaginative international riffs include pastas, salads, and seafood entrées. Best of all, Croce's is open late every night—for dinner, 5:30 P.M.–midnight (closed Thanksgiving and Christmas).

Fine Dining

Ⓜ Lou & Mickey's, 224 Fifth Ave., 619/237-4900, is the Quarter's hot new all-American steak and seafood destination, a kissing cousin to L.A.'s downtown Water Grill. Seafood is succulent, steaks are a specialty, and side dishes are the ultimate in comfort food, like the house-made desserts, ice creams, and sorbet. For something light, consider the garlic meatloaf po' boy sandwich. Impressive wine list, martinis, and exotic drinks—the likes of Horny Monkey, Taboo for Two, and Witch Doctor.

Excellent for contemporary seafood dinner served up in white-tablecloth, supper-club style is **Ⓜ Blue Point Coastal Cuisine,** 565 Fifth Ave., 619/233-6623, complete with traditional oyster bar and old-fashioned full bar. It's all good, from starters including crab with white corn chowder and "tart of the day" to entrées such as lobster pot pie, pan-seared dayboat scallops, and horseradish-crusted salmon.

Chichi **Chive,** 558 Fourth Ave. (near K Street), 619/232-4483, is minimalist stainless-steel style with welcoming orange neon, adventurous cocktails, and a globetrotting wine list. The fare is pretty hip too, which means organic and regional, as much as possible. (That doesn't have to mean expensive too, but it often does.) Stylish east here include mac and cheese with merguez sausage, bell pepper, and tomato in a cumin crust, Niman Ranch pork porterhouse with white-cheddar grits and marinated cabbage, and Atlantic skate with fingerling potatoes, braised bacon, English peas, and pearl onions.

For that massive martini, 48-ounce porterhouse steak, and eclectic Italian dishes like buffalo ravioli and crab linguine, the place is stylish and expensive **Greystone the Steakhouse,** 658 Fifth Ave. (near G), 619/232-0225, where your host may be restaurant partner and former San Diego Padre Kevin Wade.

NEAR HILLCREST

Beyond the usual tourist definition of downtown, look for **Little Italy** along India Street, just north of Date. The 1700 block of India (between Cedar and Grape Streets) is still the center of San Diego's historic Italian district, first settled more than 100 years ago by fishing families. Savory stops here include **Mimmo's Italian Village Deli & Bakery,** 1743 India St., 619/239-3710, great for pizza; **Caffe Italia,** 1704 India St., 619/234-6767, for sandwiches, coffee, and such; and **Filippi's Pizza Grotto** 1747 India St., 619/232-5094, where you walk through the Italian deli—complete with hanging salamis, mascarpone, and orechetti—to get to the dining room, adorned with red-checked-tablecloths and dozens of Chianti bottles. The menu is straightforward Italian with no pretense—huge portions of lasagne, pasta with marinara sauce, and some of the best pizza in town.

The dramatic **Indigo Grill,** a relative of Hillcrest's Kemo Sabe at 1536 India St. (at W. Cedar), 619/234-6802, serves high-style New Western, from ceviche bar to entrées such as glazed hickory- and apple-smoked pork ribs with Indian cord pudding and pecan-crusted rainbow trout with roasted corn salsa and oven-roasted fennel potatoes. The full bar here includes an impressive selection of mescals, tequilas, and rums. Open weekdays for lunch, nightly for dinner.

Hob Nob Hill, just blocks from Balboa Park at 2271 First Ave. (at Juniper), 619/239-8176, is a long-running neighborhood favorite—serving heaping helpings of all-American favorites, such as pot roast and fried chicken, at very reasonable prices. Breakfast here is one of the best deals in town, and on Sunday everyone shows up (reservations wise).

One of San Diego's legendary fine dining destinations is **N Laurel,** just west of Balboa Park at 505 Laurel St. (at Fifth), 619/239-2222, sibling of the famous WineSellar and beloved for its Mediterranean and Southern French specialties, such things as provençal chicken roasted in a clay pot and grilled pork from Pipestone Family Farms. Laurel offers complimentary shuttle service to the Old Glove theatres, too.

Farther north, in an area overrun with freeway on- and off-ramps, another section of downtown's India Street marks the turn-off to Hillcrest, with additional worthy (and inexpensive) eateries. An institution in San Diego, the original "uptown" **N El Indio,** 3695 India St. (at Washington), 619/299-0333, is where locals go for Mexican. El Indio claims to have invented the term "taquito," so be sure to try a few. But save space for the killer fish tacos and cheese enchiladas, the burritos, the tostadas. Abundant vegetarian choices, everything inexpensive. And if you're in a hurry, call ahead for takeout. The casual **Saffron,** 3731 India St. (at Washington), 619/574-0177, specializing in imaginative Thai fare at both lunch and dinner, is another good neighborhood choice, also popular for takeout.

HILLCREST

The **Corvette Diner Bar and Grill** in Hillcrest at 3946 Fifth Ave. (near Washington), 619/542-1001 or 619/542-1476, is one of San Diego's best bets for kids, a raucous rock-out joint complete with DJs and singing wait staff. They'll also like the burgers, shakes, and fries. A rollicking imitation of a 1950s-style diner, the Corvette is known, too, for its meatloaf and other baby-boomer-era comfort foods. Very popular, so expect to wait (no reservations taken). It's open daily Sun.–Thurs. 11 A.M.–10 P.M., until midnight on weekend nights, closed Thanksgiving (and on Christmas if it falls on a weekday). Another hot spot for burgers is **Hamburger Mary's,** 308 University (at Third Ave.), 619/491-0400.

This is it, pizza fans—San Diego's best. **Pizzeria Arrivederci,** 3739 Fourth Ave. (at Robinson), 619/542-0293. Since you're in the neighborhood, try the University Avenue, with mascarpone, mozzarella, arugula and toasted walnuts, though the Prosciutto Funghi—yes, ham and mushrooms—is mighty tasty too. Otherwise best bet for pizza is **Pizza Nova** in the Village Hillcrest, 3955 Fifth Ave. (between Washington and University), 619/296-6682. Always cheap and also good is the down-to-earth Japanese **Ichiban** in Hillcrest at 1449 University, 619/299-7203. A great Italian, popular for patio dining, is **Busalacchi's,** 3683 Fifth Ave. (at Pennsylvania), 619/298-0119.

Refreshingly, San Diego still doesn't entirely cotton to the faddish and overly fancy in food, which explains the popularity of casual yet cutting

San Diego Coast

edge M **Kemo Sabe,** 3958 Fifth Ave. (between Washington and University), 619/220-6802, with its imaginative and witty Mexican and multiethnic cuisine—"Skirts on Fire," for example, starring charbroiled skirt steak with rice sticks. Then there's **Seven,** "an American grill" at 1421 University (between Richmond and Normal), 619/297-0722, fueled by grilled everything and some incredible desserts.

For tapas and other Spanish selections, head to very friendly **Tapas Picasso,** 3923 Fourth Ave. (between Washington and University), 619/294-3061, open nightly for dinner, Tues.–Fri. for lunch. Garlic lovers will do well here, whether they choose the garlic lamb, garlic shrimp, or garlic mushrooms. The affordable French **Café Eleven,** 1440 University Ave., 619/260-8023, is famous for its $10 dinner specials. Casual and open daily for lunch and dinner, **Aladdin Mediterranean Café** at 1220 Cleveland Ave., 619/573-0406, offers vegetarian falafel, chicken, and lamb dishes along with wood-fired pizzas.

Farmhouse-style **Region,** at the onetime site of Mixx, 3671 Fifth Ave. (at Anderson Place), 619/299-6499, serves the San Diego region's best and freshest. The menu changes nightly, but it might include fresh ricotta cheese and smoked prosciutto salad or goat cheese, beet, and apple salad (simple and delicious), puréed squash soup, roast chicken, or duck confit.

The **Gulf Coast Grill** in University Heights, 4130 Park Blvd. (near Washington), 619/295-2244, serves up genuine Southern-style fried chicken on its tasty Baja-Creole fusion menu, with veggie quesadillas, seafood chiles rellenos, Creole shrimp etouffée, jambalaya, Baja clam chowder, and crab cakes withcorn and black bean and corn salsa. Very stylish **Parallel 33,** 741 W. Washington St, 619/260-003, features a circumnavigating menu, touching down in Baghdad, India, Shanghai. Have some savory Moroccan *bisteeya,* or curried lamb, or duck in five-spice sauce.

And no matter where you have your meal, at some point try **Karen Krasne's Extraordinary Desserts,** 2929 Fifth Ave. (at Palm), 619/294-7001, a truly inviting, somewhat expensive sweet feast, from the cookies, gateaux, and tarts to the grand cakes.

CORONADO

For fresh produce and flowers, show up on Tuesday for the **Coronado Certified Farmers' Market,** 760/741-3763, held at the Ferry Market Landing, First Street and B Avenue. Microbrewery fans, you'll find Coronado's own at the **Coronado Brewing Company,** 170 Orange, 619/437-4452. For Pacific Rim-style Asian cuisine, the place is the **Bistro d' Asia,** 1301 Orange Ave., 619/437-6677. Delightful for French bistro fare is **Chez Loma,** near the history museum at 1132 Loma Ave. (at Orange), 619/435-0661.

Generally speaking, though, seafood is the thing in Coronado. For good seafood at lunch and dinner and a chance to appreciate America's Cup memorabilia, head for the **Bay Beach Cafe** at Ferry Market Landing, 619/435-4900. Another best bet for seafood—not to mention the macadamia nut pie—is **Pehoe's,** nearby at 1201 First St., 619/437-4474, with bay views, patio tables, and a good Sunday brunch. For a bit of remodeled history with your seafood and steaks, **The Boat House** is at home in the Hotel del Coronado's onetime boathouse at 1701 Strand Way, 619/435-0155 (casual, children's menu, dinner only, reservations required).

If you're prepared to spend some real money, stars of the local fine dining scene tend to cluster at Coronado's luxury hotels. The elegant **Crown-Coronet Room** at the Hotel del Coronado is being remodeled, though it still serves an excellent brunch banquet on Sunday—probably enough calories to fuel the entire naval air base for a week. The hotel offers astounding contemporary style at the **Prince of Wales,** 619/522-8490, fresh from its multi-million-dollar renovation, and the more casual **Sheerwater,** with spacious outside terraces and gigantic fireplaces. Other hotel hot spots include **Azzura Point** at Loews Coronado Bay Resort, 619/424-4000, and the charming **L'Escale** brasserie and jazzy **La Provence** at the Coronado Island Marriott, 619/435-3000.

MISSION BAY AND VICINITY

Buster's Beach House Grill & Longboard Bar at Seaport Village, 807 W. Harbor Dr.,

619/233-4300, is the place to eat, where patrons can delight themselves with Bloody Mary shrimp cocktails, lobster quesadillas, fried coconut shrimp, and Jamaican jerk chicken. A dining room with a view, too. Happy hour is longboard-sized, too, 2–6 P.M.

A local favorite is the **Fish Market,** 750 N. Harbor Dr. (near Broadway), 619/232-3474. Here, parents can enjoy good seafood—even with young children in tow—along with one of the best waterfront views in town. Most grownups go for the mesquite-grilled fish and seafood selections. Most kids are happy with fish and chips, though the children's menu also includes burgers and other American standards. There's a fish market downstairs, plus sushi and shellfish bars and a cocktail lounge. Upstairs is the dressier, more expensive **Top of the Market** dinner restaurant, 619/234-4867, also popular for self-indulgent Sunday brunch. The Fish Market is open daily for lunch and dinner, closed Thanksgiving and Christmas.

Another seafood hot spot is **Anthony's Fish Grotto** downstairs at 1360 N. Harbor (at Ash), 619/232-5105, part of a popular regional chain. The dress-up destination is upstairs at the **Star of the Sea,** 619/232-7408, which holds its own bayside with beautiful views and an even grander international seafood selection.

Wildly popular near Shelter Island is **Point Loma Seafoods,** 2805 Emerson, 619/223-1109, seafood market also great for takeout. Nearby is casual **Hudson Bay Seafood,** 1403 Scott, 619/222-8787, famous for its seafood sandwiches.

Of course, Coronado Island has its share of bayside bounty—including the elegant French **Chez Loma** 1132 Loma (off Orange Ave.), 619/435-0661, set in an 1889 Victorian cottage and one of San Diego's most romantic restaurants in any category. For other suggestions, see *Coronado: Crown of the Bay.*

OCEAN BEACH, MISSION BEACH, PACIFIC BEACH

San Diego's classic beach towns have their share of classic burger and taco joints—and a few outstanding options, such as **Caffe Bella Italia** in Ocean Beach, 1525 Garnet Ave. (between Ingraham and Haines), 858/273-1224, where the authentic Italian food is consistently excellent (try not to fill up on the homemade bread). It's not only the food that brings people here; inside the bland strip-mall exterior the decor is soothing, with sheer curtains and warm earth tones, and the mostly Italian-accented staff is always welcoming and friendly. Each and every item on the menu is draws on the freshest local ingredients—the pastas, risottos, and pizzas are all made from scratch. Top dessert picks are any of the Italian sorbets, tartufo, and tiramisu. Kids menu available, and there's a terrific wine list featuring selections from California and Italy. It's open Tues–Fri. 11 A.M.–2:30 P.M., Tues.–Sun. 5:30–10:30 P.M., closed major holidays.

For a romantic night out, try **3rd Corner,** at 2265 Bacon St. (near Lotus), 619/223-2700, formerly the legendary Belgian Lion, and just as well-regarded locally. The Corner specializes in colorful Mediterranean fare and lighter seafood and fresh fish. It's open daily for dinner; reservations recommended. For German at either lunch or dinner, head for **Kaiserhof,** 2253 Sunset Cliffs Blvd. (at W. Point Loma), 619/224-0606, closed Monday. For something more exotic, try the buffet lunch at the very good **Star of India,** 1820 Garnet (near Jewel), 858/459-3355, a popular place. If you come for dinner, make reservations.

OLD TOWN

The colorful **Old Town Mexican Cafe,** 2489 San Diego Ave. (at Congress), 619/297-4330, is famous for its humongous portions of just about every Mexican standard and a popular place for locals and tourists alike. And if the kids don't know how tortillas are made, here they can watch. It's open daily for both lunch and dinner.

But **Berta's Latin American Restaurant,** 3928 Twiggs St. (at Congress), 619/295-2343, ranges far beyond predictable Old Town south-of-the-border fare. High points of this Latin American tour include pastas, stews, Peruvian chicken with chiles and feta cheese, and seafood *vatapa* from Brazil—all good opportunities for the kids to move beyond tacos and burritos. The wine list is also

© ROBERT HOLMES/CALTOUR

making tortillas in Old Town

international. You'll be pleasantly surprised by this friendly respite from the tourist hordes. In balmy weather, the patio is perfect. Berta's is open for lunch and dinner daily, closed major holidays.

California-style **Cafe Pacifica,** 2414 San Diego Ave. (between Arista and Linwood), 619/291-6666, a longstanding local choice for uptown dining in Old Town, specializes in seafood. Entrée choices change daily, but count on mesquite-grilled fresh fish selections served with house-made salsa, fruit chutney, or herbed sauces. For smaller appetites: fish tacos, crab cakes, and surprising salads and pastas. It's open for dinner nightly 5:30–10 P.M.

LA JOLLA
Inexpensive

If you're looking to pack a food-lover's picnic— a basket brimming with garden-fresh produce and fresh fruit—look no farther than **Chino**

Farms, 6123 Calzada del Bosque in Rancho Santa Fe, 858/756-3184. This vegetable stand supplies some of the best restaurants in California, including Berkeley's Chez Panisse. It's open Mon.–Sat. 10 A.M.–4 P.M., on Sunday 10 A.M.–1 P.M., closed Christmas Day. Or come to the **La Jolla Certified Farmers' Market,** held on Sunday 9 A.M.–1 P.M. at Girard and Genter, La Jolla Elementary School.

Who could resist a place called **Porkyland?** This porcine food palace, at 1030 Torrey Pines Rd., 858/459-1708, specializes in carnitas, or Mexican-style lard-tenderized pork, in its various final incarnations. For good coffee and a simple breakfast the place—packed on weekends—is the coffeehouse-style **Brockton Villa,** 1235 Coast Blvd. (near Prospect), 858/454-7393. For lunch, consider a grilled salmon BLT on sourdough. Open daily for breakfast and lunch, **Harry's** at 7545 Girard St., 858/454-7381, is La Jolla's down-home coffeeshop, the place for eggs and omelettes at breakfast, all-American sandwiches at lunch. Excellent across the street—and an excellent value at lunch and dinner—is the **India Palace** at La Jolla Market Place, 7514 Girard, 858/551-5133, emphasizing Northern Indian dishes—lamb vindaloo, chicken pasanda—as well as seafood. Unbelievable all-you-can-eat lunch buffet.

Affordable yet featuring good food and a priceless view at breakfast and lunch, all-American **Cody's** at 8030 Girard Ave., 858/459-0040, serves everything from applewood-smoked bacon and mozzarella omelettes, blue crabs eggs Benedict, and blueberry pancakes to grilled Portobello sandwiches, fish and chips, and grilled burgers with white Canadian cheddar.

Also quite reasonable, serving cool food in a quaint setting, is **The Cottage** at 7702 Fay Ave., 858/454-8409, open for breakfast, lunch,, and dinner. French toast stuffed with mascarpone cheese and strawberry compote, anyone? Or a breakfast burrito, or fresh veggie fritatta? Try the fish tacos or the tuna melt at lunch, Laura's meatloaf, chicken pot pie, or "rasta pasta" at dinner. Sit inside or people-watch streetside. Wine and beer. Just down the street is **Bali,** 7660 Fay Ave., 858/454-4540, the area's only Indonesian restaurant, quite good.

Wonderful for homey Italian—and just about everything here is house-made—is **La Taverna,** 927 Silverado St., 858/454-0100, open for dinner Mon.–Sat. and for lunch on weekdays only. Quite reasonable and good is family-owned **Spice & Rice Thai Kitchen,** 7734 Girard Ave. (at Klein), 858/456-0466.

Fine Dining

Relaxed **Trattoria Acqua,** downstairs in the Coast Walk Center, 1298 Prospect, 858/454-0709, serves up cove views and good Cal-Italian. Great place for Sunday brunch. Open daily for lunch and dinner, bustling **M Barbarella** in La Jolla Shores at 2171 Avenida de la Playa, 858/454-7373, has become quite the relaxed yet stylish La Jolla hangout, a place well on its way to becoming a beloved neighborhood fixture. Whether you choose the steak-frites, daily-changing mixed seafood-veggie fry, or fresh fish special, you won't go wrong here. For sophisticated Mexican, **La Fonda** at 5752 La Jolla Blvd., 619/456-7171, serves the real deal—wonderful regional dishes, from spiced lamb to *chalupitas poblanas.*

Then there are the pricier places. One of San Diego's hottest dining destinations these days is **A.R. Valentien** at The Lodge at Torrey Pines, 11480 N. Torrey Pines Rd., 858/777-6635, open for breakfast, lunch, and dinner and named after the artist whose nature studies and other original art works are exhibited here. The exquisite Craftsman-style dining room is a fitting setting for such culinary artistry, which at dinner might include entrées such as roasted halibut in herbed tomato sauce with chanterelles, leeks, and basil; roasted chicken on leeks in butter sauce; and king salmon with green garlic and morels. Daily changing menu, reservations essential at dinner. Tucked inside The Grande Colonial at 910 Prospect St., **M Nine-Ten,** 858/964-5400, sets the local standard for fine dining without fussy attitude. The experience is rooted in reliance on the freshest local produce—gorgeous greens from Chino Farms, Good Faith Organic, and other local farms, regional meats and poultry, and the day's catch flown in fresh

daily—to create "evolving contemporary American cuisine." Menu specialties include the house-smoked salmon, Maine scallops, and Niman Ranch New York strip steak. Don't hesitate to try the tasting menu at either lunch or dinner. Nine-Ten is open for breakfast, lunch, and dinner. Sunday brunch is also memorable.

George's at the Cove, 1250 Prospect St. (near Ivanhoe), 858/454-4244, is also at the top of La Jolla's seafood food chain, and is beloved for its contemporary American cuisine as for its spectacular local views. You'll have to dress up some for the dining room (reservations), but not for the **Ocean Terrace Cafe** upstairs, which is more relaxed (no reservations taken, so be prepared for a wait). Simpler fare includes soups, salads, shellfish pastas, fish tacos, even seafood sausages. George's is open daily for lunch and dinner.

The excellent, very expensive **Top o' the Cove,** 1216 Prospect St. (near Ivanhoe), 858/454-7779, a long-running local institution, serves classic French fare and romantic ambience with a grand view. **The Sky Room,** nearby at La Valencia Hotel, 1132 Prospect (at Herschel), 858/454-0771, is tiny (12 tables) and specializes in contemporary French and spectacular views of both sea and sky. La Valencia's continental **The Whaling Bar,** open for both lunch and dinner, is another option. For classical, fairly formal French in the heart of La Jolla, **Tapenade,** 7612 Fay Ave., 858/551-7500, is superb.

Another La Jolla classic is **The Marine Room** at La Jolla Beach & Tennis Club, 2000 Spindrift Dr., 858/459-7222, famous for its truly exceptional seafood and the thrill of watching those big waves coming straight at you, from the other side of those thick glass windows.

Another dine-around destination is La Jolla's "Golden Triangle," rich real estate reared on biotechnology and other high-tech enterprise wedged into the triangle created by I-5, I-805, and Hwy. 52. The **On Tap!** microbrewery at La Jolla's University Town Center (between Broadway and Robinson's May), 4353 La Jolla Village Dr., 858/587-6677, enlivens its shopping mall setting with high-test homemade beers—Brewer's Blonde, Red Moon Raspberry, Alt-er-Ego Amber, and Grateful Red ales plus Hop Manic India Pale Ale and Steamroller Stout. The Brewmaster's Special changes. The food's also quite good, imaginative but not too eclectic California-style bistro fare, wood-fired pizza and such, everything under $14. Patio dining available. It's open daily for lunch and dinner, closed major holidays. Other culinary attractions at and near University Town Center include the Italian **Tutto Mare,** 4365 Executive Dr. (reached via Town Center Drive, north from Jolla Village Drive), 858/597-1188, where roasted seafood and seafood pastas star.

Center stage at the theatrical **Aventine Center** nearby, on University Center Lane, are a number of great restaurants, including the very stylish and expensive **Cafe Japengo,** 858/450-3355, offering trendy Pacific Rim cuisine and sushi, and an extensive list of creative desserts. Other dining hotspots include **808 La Jolla** at Aventine Plaza, 858/552-1048, serving French-Hawaiian, and Bradley Ogden's **Arterra** at Marriott Del Mar, east of I-5 at 11966 El Camino Real (at Carmel Valley Road), 858/369-6032, which makes exceptional use of local produce and the freshest regional ingredients, to the delight of San Diego foodies.

The ultimate destination for foodies in San Diego County however, is the **WineSellar & Brasserie** in an industrial park at 9550 Waples St., 858/450-9557, whose wine list has been declared one of the top 100 in the world by *Wine Spectator.* And that's just the beginning of the superlatives. The seasonally changing contemporary French menu might include pan-roasted pheasant, black pepper-roasted rack of venison, Szechuan pepper and coriander-cured pork loin, and Pacific scallops. For dessert, try the Valrhona bittersweet chocolate terrine with hazelnut praline sauce and caramel. Open Tues.–Sat. for dinner nightly, for lunch Thurs.–Sat. only.

DEL MAR

Nugent's Seafood Grille on the southside at 2282 Carmel Valley Rd., 858/792-6100, serves fresh grilled fish, cioppino, and fish and chips. **Sbicca's** in Del Mar, 215 15th St. (at Camino del Mar), 858/481-1001, is an inventive California bistro serving brunch—crepes, omelets, *huevos rancheros,* and eggs benedict—on weekends until 3 P.M. Count on healthy items like the free-range turkey burger, vegetable lasagna, or grilled ahi at lunch. For dinner, consider the salmon au poivre or the asian-jalapeno flat iron steak. Hours vary, so call ahead.

Other best bets in Del Mar hold forth from the Del Mar Plaza mall at 1555 Camino del Mar (at 15th Street), including the **Harvest Ranch Market** gourmet grocery store on the second floor, 858/847-0555, with a sandwiches, prepared foods, and deli items. More trendy in the neighborhood, all on the third floor and all serving spectacular ocean views from their outdoor patios: **Epazote,** 858/259-9966, serving California-style Mexican and southwestern cuisine; ever-popular northern Italian **Il Fornaio,** 858/755-8876; and **Pacifica Del Mar,** 858/792-0476, serving exotic California-style Cajun, Italian, southwestern, and Pacific Rim fare. All are open daily for lunch and dinner, with dinner reservations advisable. Downstairs from Pacifica Del Mar, the **Pacifica Breeze Café,** 858/509-9147, serves breakfast, sandwiches, and dinners in the $7–10 range. And the bar draws a fun, trendy crowd on the weekends.

For dress-up dining in nearby Rancho Santa Fe, serving somewhat pricey but casual California-style American fare is **Delicias,** 6106 Paseo Delicias, 858/756-8000, open for dinner daily except major holidays. At the top of the local food chain, though, is the fancy French **Mille Fleurs** just a stroll away at 6009 Paseo Delicias, 858/756-3085, open Mon.–Fri. for lunch and dinner and dinner only on weekends.

Information and Services

For current visitor information, including major attraction and tour tickets, contact the San Diego Convention and Visitor Bureau's multilingual **San Diego International Visitor Information Center** at its new downtown location, 1040 1/3 W. Broadway (at Harbor Drive), 619/236-1212, www.sandiego.org, open Mon.–Sat. 9 A.M.–5 P.M. and on Sunday, at least in summer, 10 A.M.–5 P.M., or its **La Jolla Visitor Center,** 7966 Herschel Ave. (at Prospect) in La Jolla, also 619/236-1212. Hours vary by season, but the La Jolla center is open every day of the week. Both are closed Thanksgiving, Christmas, and New Year's Day. To request information via email, the address is sdinfo@sandiego.org.

If you're rolling into town on the spur of the moment, stop off at the **Mission Bay Visitor Information Center** on E. Mission Bay Drive (exit I-5 at Clairemont), 619/276-8200, open daily, where you can get enough info to get you around.

The San Diego Union-Tribune is the local newspaper of record but not all that impressive a rag, though even a cursory read will give you some sense of just how conservative this city is. The Thursday "Night and Day" section is useful for figuring out what's going on, but all in all the weekly *San Diego Reader* is a better information source, particularly for entertainment and restaurant listings. Entertaining alternative publications pop up, too; look for them in hip bookstores, music shops, and coffeehouses.

TRANSPORTATION

Airport

Everybody calls it Lindbergh Field, but the official name is the **San Diego International Airport,** and it lies just three miles northwest of downtown San Diego (closer to Harbor Island) near the bay, just off Harbor Drive. Expanded in 1997 and served by all major U.S. carriers—including **America West, American,** **Continental, Delta, Frontier, Northwest, United,** and the ever-popular **Southwest Airlines.**—the airport is also served by **Aeromexico,** and smaller commuter lines. You can't store anything at the airport (no lockers), but it is open 24 hours, with restaurants, snack stops, and ATMs. Free terminal-to-terminal transportation is provided via Red Bus. The airport is well-served by public transportation, and private van and bus shuttle service picks up and drops off at Terminals 1 and 2. For general airport information, call 619/400-2400 or see the website, www.san.org.

Shuttles

By Bus: San Diego's Metropolitan Transit System (MTS) Route 992 provides service from the airport and downtown San Diego with stops outside each terminal. Buses run every 10 minutes during the week and every 15 minutes on weekends, though if you're traveling on a holiday be sure to check the holiday schedule. Fare is $2.25; for more information call 619/233-3004 or visit www.sdcommute.com. **By Shuttle:** One of the easiest ways to get where you're going is via shuttle. The 24-hour **Cloud 9 Shuttle,** 800/9-SHUTTLE, is the most popular shuttle service, and charges $6–10 to major points in the city. **By Taxi:** Taxis line up outside the terminal and charge $8–10 for the trip downtown, usually a 5–10 minute ride.

Train

In many ways, the most civilized way to get here is by train. San Diego is easily reached by **Amtrak,** 619/239-9021 or 800/872-7245 for recorded information, www.amtrak.com, with daily trains coming and going from Los Angeles, Santa Barbara, and San Luis Obispo; you can also get to Solana Beach and other coastal San Diego County stops on one train or another.

Amtrak trains pull in to the attractive, mission-style **Santa Fe Depot** downtown, 1050 Kettner Blvd. (at Broadway), which is open all

San Diego Coast

night; the ticket office is open daily 5 A.M.–9 P.M. The **San Diego Trolley** light-rail lines start here, too, making it quite easy to get around, at least between 5 A.M. and midnight. For public transit details, see www.sdcommute.com and also see Getting Around.

Popular with north county commuters and, increasingly, visitors is the San Diego **Coaster,** darling of the North San Diego County Transit District, www.gonctd.com, which connects coastal communities (Oceanside to Sorrento Valley) with Old Town and the Santa Fe Depot in downtown San Diego—even Petco Park. Regular fares start at $3.50, though 10-trip and monthly fares are also available. The Coaster does not operate on Sundays or on major holidays. Validated Coaster tickets are good for a free transfer to the "Airport Flyer," the San Diego MTS Bus Route 992 to San Diego International Airport; Route 992 buses leave the Santa Fe Depot (at the corner of Kettner and Broadway).

Bus

The **Greyhound** bus station, open 24 hours, is downtown, just a few blocks east of the train station at 120 W. Broadway, 619/239-3266 or 800/231-2222, www.greyhound.com. From here, L.A. is the major destination, though you can also trek east. Since the bus station is in an unsavory neighborhood, by San Diego standards, don't plan to walk the streets late at night—and keep an eye on your luggage. Lockers are available.

Getting Around

San Diego's public **Metropolitan Transit System (MTS),** 619/685-4900 (recorded), www.sdcommute.com, also provides around-town bus service. Pick up a transit map at the visitor information center at Horton Plaza or call the MTS **Information Line,** 619/233-3004 or TTY/TDD 619/234-5005 (5:30 A.M.–8:30 P.M.), to figure out which bus will get you where. Another resource is the **Transit Store,** downtown at 449 Broadway (at Fifth), 619/234-1060, where you can pick up free brochures, route maps, and schedules. This is

also the place to buy a variety of passes: the **Day Tripper** pass, for example, buys all-day access to local buses, the trolley system, and the ferry to Coronado—such a deal, making mass transit a viable way for visitors to get around. A one-day Day Tripper pass is $5; two-day, $9; three-day, $12; and four-day, $15.

More fun by far is the **San Diego Trolley** light-rail transit system, 619/231-8549 for current route and fare information (recorded) or see www.sdcommute.com. For assistance call 619/233-3004 or 619/234-5005 TTY/TDD. Several lines are now up and running—the **Blue Line** connects the Old Town transit center to Qualcomm Stadium and Mission San Diego but also heads south from the transit center to the Santa Fe Depot, other downtown stops, then south through National City and Chula Vista to the U.S./Mexico border. The **Orange Line** stops in the Gaslamp Quarter, at the convention center, at Seaport Village, the civic center, San Diego City College, and also heads east and northeast to Lemon Grove, La Mesa, El Cajon, and Santee. Call or see the website for current schedule information, or pick up a schedule at the Transit Store on Broadway. At last report one-way trolley fare downtown was $1.25 for up to two hours, otherwise $1.50–3, depending on the distance traveled, for a maximum of two hours. Buy your ticket at the relevant transit center vending machines—some require exact change, others accept $1 and $5 bills and Susan B. Anthony dollars—or buy a Day Tripper pass at the Transit Store.

If they didn't drive into town, to get farther faster most people "go local" and rent a car. San Diego is served by the usual car rental agencies—the visitor center can provide you with a current listing—and some allow their cars to be driven into Mexico. If you don't particularly care about appearances, save some money with **Rent-a-Wreck,** 800/535-1391. Rent-a-Wreck even rents motor homes, along with new and used cars, trucks, and vans. Other options include **Avis,** 800/331-1212 and TDD 800/331-2323, and **Payless Car Rental,** 800/PAYLESS.

Driving

Most people drive here—a fact quite obvious once you're on the local freeways, where traffic is typically nightmarish. The straight shot into downtown is provided by I-5, which dead-ends at the Mexican border; I-5 is also the main thoroughfare for reaching San Diego beach towns, Old Town, and Coronado Island. Inland, I-15 creates the city's de facto eastern edge; if you follow it north it'll eventually deliver you to Las Vegas. The area's major east-west freeway is I-8, which slithers in out of the desert and slides to a stop at Mission Bay (after crossing paths with both I-15 and I-5). Heads up. And good luck, especially when merging—or trying to merge.

Know Coastal California

The Land

California's isolated, sometimes isolationist human history has been shaped more by the land itself than by any other fact. That even early European explorers conceived of the territory as an island is a fitting irony, since in many ways—particularly geographically, but also in the evolutionary development of plant and animal life—California was, and still is, an island in both space and time.

The third-largest state in the nation, California spans 10 degrees of latitude. With a meandering 1,264-mile-long coastline, the state's western boundary is formed by the Pacific Ocean. Along most of California's great length, just landward from the sea, are the rumpled and eroded mountains known collectively as the Coast Ranges.

But even more impressive in California's 158,693-square-mile territory is the Sierra Nevada range, which curves like a 500-mile-long spine along the state's central-eastern edge. Inland from the Coast Ranges and to the north of California's great central valley are the state's northernmost mountains, including the many distinct, wayward ranges of the Klamaths—mountains many geologists believe were originally a northwesterly extension of the Sierra Nevada. Just east of the Klamath Mountains is the southern extension of the volcanic Cascade Range, which includes Mt. Shasta and Lassen Peak.

This great partial ring of mountains around California's heartland (with ragged eastern peaks reaching elevations of 14,000 feet and higher) as well as the vast primeval forests that once almost suffocated lower slopes, have always influenced the state's major weather patterns—and have also created a nearly impenetrable natural barrier for otherwise freely migrating plant and animal species, including human beings.

But if sky-high rugged rocks, thickets of forest, and rain-swollen rivers blocked migration to the north and east, physical barriers of a more barren nature have also slowed movement into California. To the south, the dry chaparral of the east-west Transverse Ranges and the northwest/

southeast-trending Peninsular Ranges impeded northern and inland movement for most life forms. The most enduring impediment, however, is California's great southeastern expanse of desert—including both the Mojave and Colorado Deserts—and the associated desert mountains and high-desert plateaus. Here, only the strong and well-adapted survive.

GEOLOGY

Perched along the Pacific Ring of Fire, California is known for its violent volcanic nature and for its earthquakes. Native peoples have always explained the fiery, earth-shaking temperament of the land quite clearly, in a variety of myths and legends, but the theory of plate tectonics is now the most widely accepted scientific creation story. According to this theory, the earth's crust is divided into 20 or so major solid rock (or lithospheric) "plates" upon which both land and sea ride. The interactions of these plates are ultimately responsible for all earth movement, from continental drift and landform creation to volcanic explosions and earthquakes.

Most of California teeters on the western edge of the vast North American Plate. The adjacent Pacific Plate, which first collided with what is now California about 250 million years ago, grinds slowly but steadily northward along a line more or less defined by the famous San Andreas Fault (responsible for the massive 1906 San Francisco earthquake and fire as well as the more recent shake-up in 1989). Plate movement itself is usually imperceptible: at the rate things are going, within 10 million years Los Angeles will slide north to become San Francisco's next-door neighbor. But the steady friction and tension generated between the two plates sometimes creates special events. Every so often sudden, jolting slippage occurs between the North American and Pacific Plates in California—either along the San Andreas or some other fault line near the plate border—and one of the state's famous earthquakes occurs. Though most don't amount to much, an average of 15,000 earthquakes occur in California every year.

A still newer theory augments the plate tectonics creation story, suggesting a much more fluid local landscape—that California and the rest of the West literally "go with the flow," in particular the movement of hot, molten rock beneath the earth's crust. "Flow" theory explains the appearance of earthquake faults where they shouldn't be, scientists say, and also explains certain deformations in the continental crust. According to calculations published in the May 1996 edition of the journal *Nature,* the Sierra Nevada currently flows at the rate of one inch every three years.

In ancient times, some geologists say, the American Southwest was connected to Antarctica. This theory, presented in 1991 by researchers at the University of California at Davis and the University of Texas, suggests that 500–700 million years ago a "seam" connected the two continents; Antarctica's Transatlantic Mountains were contiguous with the western edge of the Sierra Nevada, parts of Idaho, and the Canadian Rockies. The geological similarities between the now far-flung rock formations are unmistakable. Yet at that time the North American continent was missing California. Some geologists theorize that California came along later; certain rock formations now found south of the equator match those of California's Coast Range.

Wherever its raw materials originally came from, California as land was created by the direct collision, starting about 250 million years ago, of the eastward-moving Pacific Plate and the underwater western edge of the North American Plate—like all continents, something like a floating raft of lighter rocks (primarily granite) attached to the heavier, black basalt of the earth's mantle. At first impact, pressure between the two plates scraped up and then buckled offshore oceanic sediments into undulating ridges of rock, and an eventual California shoreline began to build.

But the Pacific Plate, unable to follow its previous forward path against such North American resistance, continued on its way by first plunging downward, creating a trough that soon began filling with oceanic basalts, mud, and eroded sediments from what is now Nevada. Sinking (or subducting) still farther beneath the North American Plate, some of these trench sediments slipped into the hot core (or athenosphere) beneath the earth's lithosphere and melted—transformed by heat into the embryonic granitic backbone of the Sierra Nevada and other metamorphic mountains that slowly intruded upward from the inner earth.

Approximately 140 million years ago, the northern section of what would later be the Sierra Nevada started to shift westward along the east-west tectonic fault line known as the Mendocino Fracture, the genesis of the Klamath Mountains. The Pacific Ocean, sloshing into the area just north of the infantile Sierra Nevada, brought with it the sediments that would create California's northeastern Modoc Plateau—a high-plains landscape later transformed by volcanic basalt flows and "floods."

About 60 million years ago, California's modern-day Sierra Nevada was a misshapen series of eroded ridges and troughs sitting on the newly risen edge of the continent. The violent forces generated by continuing plate confrontation, including sporadic volcanism and large-scale faulting, pushed the state's mountains slowly higher. Remaining ocean sediments later rose to create first the Coast Ranges, as offshore islands about 25 to 30 million years ago, and eventually an impressive, 450-mile-long inland sea, which, once filled with sediment, gradually evolved into the marshy tule wetlands recognizable today as California's fertile central valley.

Though California's creation has never ceased—with the land transformed even today by volcanic activity, earthquake shifts, and erosion—the landscape as we know it came fairly recently. According to the widely accepted view, about 10–16 million years ago the Sierra Nevada stood tall enough (approximately 2,000 feet above sea level) to start changing the continent's weather patterns: blocking the moisture-laden winds that had previously swept inland and desiccating the once-lush Great

Basin. Then, one million years ago, the Sierra Nevada and other fault-block ranges "suddenly" rose to near their current height. By 800,000 years ago, the mountains had taken on their general modern shape—but fire was giving way to ice. During the million-year glaciation period, particularly the last stage from 100,000 to 30,000 years ago, these and other California landforms were subsequently carved and polished smooth by slow-moving sheets of ice. Vestigial glaciers remain in some areas of the Sierra Nevada and elsewhere.

A "countercultural" view of Sierra Nevada creation is emerging, however. According to this theory, based on research done in the southern Sierra Nevada, the range reached its zenith about 70 million years ago—massive mountains, as tall as the Andes, looming large during the last days of the dinosaurs. The height of the Sierra Nevada, once reaching 13,000 feet, has been declining ever since—a loss of about a quarter-inch in the course of a single person's lifetime—because erosion has proceeded faster than the forces of ongoing creation.

Though vegetation typical of the late ice age has largely vanished and mastodons, saber-toothed cats, and other exotic animals no longer stalk the land, the face of the California landscape since those bygone days has been transformed most radically by the impact of humanity—primarily in the past century and a half. Building dams and "channeling" wild rivers to exploit water, the state's most essential natural resource; harvesting state-sized forests of old-growth trees; hunting animals, to the edge of extinction and beyond, for fur and pelts; digging for, and stripping the land of, gold and other mineral wealth; clearing the land for crops and houses and industrial parks: all this has changed California forever.

CLIMATE

California's much-ballyhooed "Mediterranean" climate is at least partially a myth. Because of extremes in landforms, in addition to various microclimatic effects, there are radical climatic

differences within the state—sometimes even within a limited geographic area. But California as a whole does share most of the classic characteristics of Mediterranean climates: abundant sunny days year-round, a cool-weather coast, dry summers, and rainy winters. California, in fact, is the only region in North America where summer drought and rainy winters are typical.

Between the coast and the mountains immediately inland, where most of the state's people live, temperatures—though cooler in the north and warmer to the south—are fairly mild and uniform year-round. Because of the state's latitudinal gradation, rain also falls in accordance with this north-south shift: an average of 74 inches falls annually in Crescent City, 19–22 inches in San Francisco, and less than 10 inches in San Diego. When warm, moist ocean air blows inland over the cool California Current circulating clockwise above the equator, seasonal fog is typical along the California coast. Summer, in

A day for swimming in San Diego . . .

other words, is often cooler along the coast than autumn. (Just ask those shivering tourists who arrive in San Francisco every June wearing Bermuda shorts and sandals.)

Inland, where the marine air influence often literally evaporates, temperature extremes are typical. The clear, dry days of summer are often hot, particularly in the central valley and the deserts. (With occasional freak temperatures above 130° Fahrenheit, Death Valley is aptly named.) In winter, substantial precipitation arrives in Northern California—especially in the northwest "rain belt" and in the northern Sierra Nevada—with major storms expected from October to May. California's northern mountains "collect" most Pacific Ocean moisture as rain; in the High Sierra, the average winter snowpack is between 300 and 400 inches. Wrung out like sponges by the time they pass over the Sierra Nevada and other inland mountains, clouds have little rain or snow for the eastern-slope rainshadow.

Since the 1970s, California's climate patterns have been increasingly atypical—which may be normal, or may be early local indications of global warming. The reason no one knows for sure is because the state's "average" weather patterns were largely defined between the 1930s and the 1970s, a period of unusually stable weather conditions, it now appears. Complicating the question further is new scientific research suggesting that California climate has been characterized, since ancient times, by alternating cycles of very wet and very dry weather—200- to 500-year cycles. Epic droughts have been traced to the Middle Ages, and just 300 years ago California experienced a drought lasting 80–100 years. California's last century and a half, it turns out, represents one of the wettest periods in the past 2,500 years.

The increasing scientific consensus is that global warming is indeed having a major impact on California weather. Researchers at the University of California at Santa Cruz conclude that

. . . could be drastically chilly in San Francisco.

the state most likely will see warmer temperatures and a smaller snowpack during the next 50 years. Temperature increases could range as high as 15 degrees for the Sierra Nevada and five to six degrees for coastal Los Angeles. In addition, rising sea levels may erode the state's coastline and increase salinity in the critical Sacramento–San Joaquin Delta, degrading much of the state's drinking water. Since the late 1970s, El Niño "events" have increased noticeably, bringing warmer offshore waters and heavy storms in California and the Southwest. But in other years—drought times for California—"La Niña" occurs, with colder offshore waters and storms tracking into the Pacific Northwest. Being whipsawed between periods of torrential rains and flooding (yet subnormal snowpack) and devastating drought seems to be California's future—a future almost certain to feature disrupted water supplies, even without a 100-year drought.

FLORA

"In California," observed writer Joaquin Miller, "things name themselves, or rather Nature names them, and that name is visibly written on the face of things and every man may understand who can read." When explorers and settlers first stumbled upon California's living natural wonders, they didn't "read" landforms or indigenous plants and animals in the same way native peoples did, but they were quite busy nonetheless attaching new names (and eventually Latin terminology) to everything in sight. From the most delicate ephemeral wildflowers to California's two types of towering redwoods, from butterflies and birds to pronghorns, bighorn sheep, and the various subspecies of grizzly bear, the unusual and unique nature of most of the territory's life forms was astonishing. California's geographical isolation—as well as its dramatic extremes in landforms and localized climates—was (and still is) largely responsible for the phenomenal natural divergence and diversity found here.

Former President Ronald Reagan, while still governor of California and embroiled in a battle over expanding redwood parks, unwittingly ex-

© ROBERT HOLMES/CALTOUR

California poppy

pressed the old-and-in-the-way attitude about the state's resources with his now-famous gaffe, widely quoted as: "If you've seen one redwood, you've seen 'em all." (What Reagan actually said was: "A tree is a tree—how many more do you need to look at?") But his philosophy, however expressed, is the key to understanding what has happened to California's trees, other native flora, and animal species.

Even today, the variation in California's native plantlife is amazing. Nearly 5,200 species of plants are at home in the Golden State—symbolized by the orange glow of the California poppy—and more than 30 percent of these trees, shrubs, wildflowers, and grasses are endemic. (By comparison, only 13 percent of plantlife in the northeastern U.S., and one percent of flora in the British Isles, are endemic species.) In fact, California has greater species diversity than the combined totals of the central and northeastern

U.S. and adjacent Canada—an area almost 10 times greater in size.

But to state that so many plant species survive in California is not to say that they thrive. The economic and physical impacts of settlement have greatly stressed the state's vegetative wealth since the days of the gold rush, when the first full-scale assaults on California forests, wetlands, grasslands, and riparian and oak woodlands were launched. The rate of exploitation of the state's 380 distinct natural communities has been relentless ever since. Half of the state's natural terrestrial environments and 40 percent of its aquatic communities are endangered, rare, or threatened. Human settlement has eliminated 85 percent of old-growth redwoods, 91 percent of the state's wetlands, and 99 percent of its grasslands.

Some of the state's most notable natural attractions are its unique trees—entire forests nearly toppled at the edge of extinction. California's *Sequoiadendron giganteum,* or giant sequoia, grows only in limited surviving stands in the Sierra Nevada—saved as much by the brittleness of its wood as by the public outcry of John Muir and other enlightened 19th-century voices. But the state's remaining virgin forests of *Sequoia sempervirens,* the "ever-living" coast redwoods, are still threatened by clearcutting, a practice that also eliminates the habitat of other species. The same conservation-versus-economic expediency argument also rages over the fate of the few remaining old-growth outposts of other popular timber trees. And decades of fire suppression, logging, grazing, and recreational development in California's vast forests of ponderosa pines, combined with increasing air pollution and the state's recent drought, have led to insect infestations, tree disease, and death—and a tinder-dry, fuel-rich landscape more vulnerable than ever to uncontrollable fires. Even trees without notable economic value are threatened by compromises imposed by civilization. Among these are the ancient bristlecone pines near the California-Nevada border—the oldest living things on earth, some individuals more than 4,000 years old—now threatened by Los Angeles smog, and the gnarled yet graceful valley oak. An "indicator

plant" for the state's most fertile loamy soils, even the grizzled veteran oaks not plowed under by agriculture or subdivision development are now failing to reproduce successfully. The Bush administration's 2002 decision to allow U.S. Forest Service managers to revise long-term, ecosystem-based plans for individual forests means that California's remaining forests are even more vulnerable to the ax.

And while the disappearance of trees is easily observed even by human eyes, other rare and unusual plants found only in California disappear, or bloom at the brink of extinction, with little apparent public concern. A subtle but perfectly adapted native perennial grass, for example, or an ephemeral herb with a spring blossom so tiny most people don't even notice it, are equally endangered by humankind's long-standing laissez-faire attitude toward the world we share with all life.

COURTESY OF THE NATIONAL PARK SERVICE

a misty morning in Redwoods National Park

Only fairly recently, with so much of natural California already gone for good, have public attitudes begun to change. No matter what Ronald Reagan says, and despite the very real economic tradeoffs sometimes involved, most Californians—and usually the state's voters—strongly support conservation, preservation, and park expansion proposals whenever these issues arise. Yet urban and suburban sprawl and commercial development continue unabated throughout California, with little evidence that the general public connects its personal and political choices with a sense of shared responsibility for the state's continued environmental decline.

FAUNA

The Golden State's native wildlife is also quite diverse and unique. Of the 748 known species of vertebrate animals in California, 38 percent of freshwater fish, 29 percent of amphibians, and nine percent of mammals are endemic species; in-vertebrate variation is equally impressive. But with the disappearance of quite specific natural habitats, many of these animals are also endangered or threatened. Nearly six out of 10 fish species native to California are now extinct, and one in five of the state's land bird species is endangered.

One notable exception is the intelligent and endlessly adaptable coyote, which—rather than be shoved out of its traditional territory even by suburban housing subdivisions—seems quite willing to put up with human incursions, so long as there are garbage cans to forage in, swimming pools to drink from, and adequate alleys of escape. Yet even the coyote's lonely late-night howl is like a cry for help in an unfriendly wilderness.

The rapid slide toward extinction among California's wild things is perhaps best symbolized by the grizzly bear, which once roamed from the mountains to the sea, though the wolf, too, has long since vanished from the landscape.

WATCHING THE CALIFORNIA GRAYS

A close-up view of the California gray whale, the state's official (and largest) mammal, is a life-changing experience. As those dark, massive, white-barnacled heads shoot up out of the ocean to suck air, spray with the force of a firehose blasts skyward from blowholes. Watch the annual migration of the gray whale all along the California coast—from "whale vistas" on land or by boat.

Despite the fascination they hold for Californians, little is yet known about the gray whale. Once endangered by whaling—as so many whale species still are—the grays are now swimming steadily along the comeback trail. Categorized as baleen whales—which dine on plankton and other small aquatic animals sifted through hundreds of fringed, hornlike baleen plates—gray whales were once land mammals that went back to sea. In the process of evolution, they traded their fore and hind legs for fins and tail flukes. Despite their fish-like appearance, these are true mammals: warm-blooded, air-breathing creatures who nourish their young with milk.

Adult gray whales weigh 20–40 tons, not counting a few hundred pounds of parasitic barnacles. Calves weigh in at a hefty 1,500 pounds at birth and can expect to live for 30–60 years. They feed almost endlessly from April to October in the arctic seas between Alaska and Siberia, sucking up sediment and edible creatures on the bottom of shallow seas, then squeezing the excess water and silt out their baleen filters. Fat and sassy with an extra 6–12 inches of blubber on board, early in October they head south on their 6,000-mile journey to the warmer waters of Baja in Mexico.

Pregnant females leave first, traveling alone or in small groups. Larger groups make up the rear guard, with the older males and nonpregnant females engaging in highly competitive courtship and mating rituals along the way—quite a show for human voyeurs. The rear guard becomes the frontline on the way home: males, newly pregnant females, and young gray whales head north from February to June. Cows and calves migrate later, between March and July.

The last wild wolf in California was killed in Lassen County in 1924. The Sierra Nevada bighorn sheep, the San Joaquin kit fox, the desert tortoise, and the California condor—most surviving birds maintained now as part of a zoo-based captive breeding program—are among many species now endangered. Upward of 550 bird species have been recorded in California, and more than half of these breed here. But the vast flocks of migratory birds (so abundant they once darkened the midday sky) have been thinned out considerably, here and elsewhere, by the demise of native wetlands and by toxins. The 12 million ducks that traditionally migrated along the California flyway recently are now estimated to number two million (and shrinking).

The fate of the state's once-fabled fisheries is equally instructive. With 90 percent of salmon spawning grounds now gone because of the damming of rivers and streams, California's commitment to compensatory measures—fish hatcheries and ladders, for example—somehow misses the point. Now that humans are in charge of natural selection, the fish themselves are no longer wild, no longer stream-smart; many can't even find their way back to the fisheries where they hatched out (in sterile stainless steel trays). California's once-fabled marine fisheries are also in dire straits because of the combined effects of overfishing, pollution, and habitat degradation, a subject of only very recent political concern. Rockfish species in particular have been so heavily harvested by both commerical and sporting interests that a fishing moratorium has been imposed along the entire state's coast.

However, some California animals almost wiped out by hunters, habitat elimination, and contamination are starting out on the comeback trail. Included among these are native elk and the antelope-like pronghorn populations, each numbering near 500,000 before European and American settlement. Also recovering in California is the native population of desert bighorn sheep. Among marine mammals almost hunted into oblivion but now thriving in California's offshore ocean environments are the northern elephant seal and the sea otter. And in 1994 the California gray whale was removed from the federal endangered species list—the first marine creature ever "delisted"—because its current population of 21,000 or so is as high, historically speaking, as it ever was.

Until recently, California's predators—always relatively fewer in number, pouncing from the top of the food chain—fared almost as poorly as their prey, preyed upon themselves by farmers, ranchers, loggers, and hunters. Though the grand grizzly hasn't been seen in California for more than a century, California's black bear is still around—though increasingly tracked and hunted by timber interests (for the damage the bears inflict on seedling trees) and poachers out to make a fast buck on gall bladders popular in Asian pharmacology. Of California's native wildcats, only the mountain lion and the spotted, smaller bobcat survive. The last of the state's jaguars was hunted down near Palm Springs in 1860.

Know Coastal California

History

Europeans generally get credit for having "discovered" America, including the mythic land of California. But a dusty travel log tucked away in Chinese archives in Shenshi Province, discovered in the 19th century by an American missionary, suggests that the Chinese discovered California—in about 217 B.C. According to this saga, a storm-tossed Chinese ship—misdirected by its own compass, apparently rendered nonfunctional after a cockroach got wedged under the needle—sailed stubbornly for 100 days in the direction of what was supposed to be mainland China. (The navigator, Hee-li, reportedly ignored the protests of his crew, who pointed out that the sun was setting on the wrong horizon.) Stepping out into towering forests surrounding an almost endless inlet at the edge of the endless ocean, these unwitting adventurers reported meetings with red-skinned peoples—and giant red-barked trees.

Conventional continental settlement theory holds that the first true immigrants to the North American continent also came from Asia—crossing a broad plain across the Bering Strait, a "bridge" that existed until the end of the ice age. Archaeologists agree that the earliest Americans arrived more than 11,500 years ago, more or less in synch with geologists' belief that the Bering bridge disappeared about 14,000 years ago. Circumstantial support for this conclusion has also come from striking similarities—in blood type, teeth, and language—existing between early Americans and Asians, particularly the northern Chinese. But recent discoveries have thrown all previous American migration theories into doubt.

In 1986, French scientists working in Brazil discovered an ancient rock shelter containing stone tools, other artifacts, and charcoal that was at first carbon-dated at approximately 32,000 years old. (A subsequent announcement, that the discovery was actually more than 45,000 years old, shocked archaeologists and was widely discredited.) Then in 1989 University of California at Berkeley linguist Johanne Nichols took a systematic look at Native American languages. She found 150 languages families in North and South America and, knowing that languages take a long time to develop, suggested that humans had lived on the two continents for the last 30,000 or 40,000 years. Wall paintings suggest that cave art developed in the Americas at about the same time it did in Europe, Asia, and Africa. Preliminary evidence of very early human habitation (possibly as long ago as 33,000 years) has also been found in Chile. Subsequent Chilean finds at Monte Verde, dated authoritatively to 10,900 to 11,200 years ago, were announced in 1997—setting off a flurry of searches for still earlier sites of human habitation.

So the question is: if migration to the Americas was via the Bering Strait, and so long ago, why hasn't any similar evidence been discovered in North America? The mummified, mat-wrapped body of an elderly man discovered in 1940 in Spirit Cave near Fallon, Nevada, has subsequently been dated as 9,415 years old—making this the only Paleonoid (more than 8,500 years old) ever found in North America; the body was particularly well preserved by the desert climate. And a human skull dated as 9,800 years old has been discovered on Canada's Prince of Wales Island. But both of these finds are thought to bolster the Bering Straits land bridge theory—as does the Monte Verde discovery in Chile, if the first American arrivals were fishing people who worked their way down the continental coastline to settle, first, in South America. Some suggest that signs of earlier human habitation in North America have been erased by climatic factors, or by glaciation. But no one really knows. One thing is certain: most archaeologists would rather be buried alive in a dig than be forced to dust off and reexamine the previously discredited "Thor Heyerdahl theory" of American settlement: that the first immigrants sailed across the Pacific, landed in South America, and then migrated northward.

FIRST PEOPLE

However and whenever they first arrived in California, the territory's first immigrants gradually created civilizations quite appropriate to the land they had landed in. "Tribes" like those typical elsewhere in North America did not exist in California, primarily because the political unity necessary for survival elsewhere was largely irrelevant here. Populations of California native peoples are better understood as ethnic or kinship or community groups united by common experience and shared territory.

Though no census takers were abroad in the land at the time, the presettlement population (about 500 groups speaking 130 dialects) of what is now California is estimated at about 250,000—a density four to eight times greater than early people living anywhere else in the United States. Before their almost overnight decimation—from settlement, and attendant disease, cultural disintegration, and violence—California's native peoples found the living fairly easy. The cornucopia of fish, birds, and game, in addition to almost endlessly edible plantlife, meant that hunting and gathering was not the strict struggle for survival it was elsewhere on the continent. Since abundance in all things was the rule, at least in nondesert areas, trade between tribal groups (for nonlocal favorite foods such as acorns, pine nuts, or seafood and for nonlocal woods or other prized items) was not uncommon. Plants and animals of the natural world were respected by native peoples as kindred spirits, and a deep nature mysticism was the underlying philosophy of most religious traditions and associated myths and legends.

Most California peoples were essentially nonviolent, engaging in war or armed conflict only for revenge; bows and arrows, spears, and harpoons were used in hunting. The development of basketry, in general the highest art of native populations, was also quite pragmatic; baskets of specific shapes and sizes were used to gather and to store foods and for cooking in. Homes, boats, and clothing were made of the most appropriate local materials, from slabs of redwood bark and animal hides to tule reeds.

Time was not particularly important to California's first immigrants. No one kept track of passing years, and most groups didn't even have a word for "year." They paid attention, however, to the passage of the moons and seasons—the natural rhythm of life. Many native peoples were seminomadic, moving in summer into cooler mountain regions where game, roots, and berries were most abundant, and then meandering down into the foothills and valleys in autumn to collect acorns, the staff of life for most tribes, and to take shelter from winter storms.

But there was nowhere to hide from the whirling clouds of change that started sweeping into California with the arrival of early explorers and missionaries, or from the foreign flood that came when the myth of California gold became a reality. Some native peoples went out fighting: the 19th-century Modoc War was one of the last major Indian wars in the United States. And others just waited until the end of their world arrived. Most famous in this category was Ishi, the "last wild man in America" and believed to be the last of his people, captured in an Oroville slaughterhouse corral in 1911. Working as a janitor as a ward of the University of California until his death five years later from tuberculosis, Ishi walked from the Stone Age into the industrial age with dignity and without fear.

FOREIGNERS PLANT THEIR FLAGS

The first of California's official explorers were the Spanish. Though Hernán Cortés discovered a land he called California in 1535, Juan Rodríguez Cabrillo—actually a Portuguese, João Rodrigues Cabrilho—first sailed the coast of Alta California ("upper," as opposed to "lower" or Baja California, which then included all of Mexico) and rode at anchor off its shores.

But the first European to actually set foot on California soil was the English pirate Sir Francis Drake, who in 1579 came ashore somewhere along the coast (exactly where is still disputed, though popular opinion suggests Point Reyes) and whose maps—like others of the day—reflected his belief

RESCUE MISSIONS

California's 21 adobe missions, the legacy of Spanish territorial settlement dating to 1769, are the state's most recognizable cultural and historic symbols. That history is not universally celebrated, particularly among native California peoples, yet mission architectural features, from whitewashed walls to red tile roofs, still influence California style. But the original California icons, attracting 5.5 million visitors each year, are fading fast. Cracking and crumbling adobe, earthquake and termite damage, water leaks, structural failures, art and ar- tifacts in need of restoration—the list of needed re- pairs is so long and so significant that the U.S. Congress has finally taken action, allocating $10 million in federal funds to match state funds and private contributions.

For current information about the current rescue of California's missions—and to contribute much- needed cash—contact the **California Missions Foundation,** 4129 Main Street, Suite 207, River- side, 909/369-0440 or 877/632-3623, www.mis- sionsofcalifornia.org.

that the territory was indeed an island. Upon his return to England, Drake's story of discovery served primarily to stimulate Spain's territorial appetites. Though Sebastián Vizcaíno entered Monterey Bay in 1602 (18 years before the Pil- grims arrived at Plymouth), it wasn't until 1746 that even the Spanish realized California wasn't an island. It wasn't until 1769 and 1770 that San Francisco Bay was discovered by Gaspar de Portolá and the settlements of San Diego and Monterey were founded.

Though the Spanish failed to find Califor- nia's mythical gold, between 1769 and 1823 they did manage to establish 21 missions (some- times with associated presidios) along El Camino Real or "The Royal Road" from San Diego to Sonoma. And from these busy mission ranch outposts, maintained by the free labor of "hea- then" natives, Spain grew and manufactured great wealth.

But even at its zenith, Spain's supremacy in California was tenuous. The territory was vast and relatively unpopulated. Even massive land grants—a practice continued under later Mexican rule—did little to allay colonial fears of success- ful outside incursions. Russian imperialism, spreading east into Siberia and Central Asia, and then to Alaska and an 1812 outpost at Fort Ross on the north coast, seemed a clear and present danger—and perhaps actually would have been, if the Russians' agricultural and other enterprises hadn't ultimately failed. And enterprising Amer- icans, at first just a few fur trappers and traders, were soon in the neighborhood.

As things happened, the challenge to Spain's authority came from its own transplanted population. Inspired by the news in 1822 that an independent government had been formed in Baja California's Mexico City, young Cali- fornia-born Spanish ("Californios") and in- dependence-seeking resident Spaniards declared Alta California part of the new Mex- ican empire. By March 1825, when California proper officially became a territory of the Re- public of Mexico, the new leadership had al- ready achieved several goals, including secularizing the missions and "freeing" the as- sociated native neophytes (not officially achieved until 1833), which in practice meant that most became servants elsewhere. The Cal- ifornios also established an independent mil- itary and judiciary, opened the territory's ports to trade, and levied taxes.

During the short period of Mexican rule, the American presence was already prominent. Since even Spain regularly failed to send supply ships, Yankee traders were always welcome in Califor- nia. In no time at all, Americans had organized and dominated the territory's business sector, es- tablished successful ranches and farms, married into local families, and become prominent citi- zens. California, as a possible political conquest, was becoming increasingly attractive to the United States.

Gen. John C. Frémont, officially on a scientific expedition but perhaps acting under secret orders from Washington (Frémont would never say), had been stirring things up in California since 1844—engaging in a few skirmishes with the locals or provoking conflicts between Californios and American citizens in California. Though the U.S. declared war on Mexico on May 13, 1846, Frémont and his men apparently were unaware of that turn of events and took over the town of Sonoma for a short time in mid-June, raising the secessionist flag of the independent—but very short-lived—Bear Flag Republic.

With Californios never mustering much resistance to the American warriors, Commodore John C. Sloat sailed unchallenged into Monterey Bay on July 7, 1848, raised the Stars and Stripes above the Custom House in town, and claimed California for the United States. Within two days, the flag flew in both San Francisco and Sonoma, but it took some time to end the statewide skirmishes. It took even longer for official Americanization—and statehood—to proceed. The state constitution established, among other things, California as a "free" state (but only to prevent the unfair use of slave labor in the mines). This upset the balance of congressional power in the nation's anti-slavery conflict and indirectly precipitated the Civil War. Written in Monterey, the new state's constitution was adopted in October 1849 and ratified by voters in November.

GOLD RUSH

California's legendary gold was real, as it turned out. And the Americans found it—but quite by accident. The day James Marshall, who was building a lumber mill on the American River for John Sutter, discovered flecks of shiny yellow metal in the mill's tailrace seemed otherwise quite ordinary. But that day, January 24, 1848, changed everything—in California and in the world.

As fortune seekers worldwide succumbed to gold fever and swarmed into the Sierra Nevada foothills in 1849, modern-day California began creating itself. In the no-holds-barred search for

personal freedom and material satisfaction (better yet, unlimited wealth), something even then recognizable as California's human character was also taking shape: the belief that anything is possible, for anyone, no matter what one's previous circumstances would suggest. Almost everyone wanted to entertain that belief. (Karl Marx was of the opinion that the California gold rush was directly responsible for delaying the Russian revolution.) New gold dreamers—all colors and creeds—came to California, by land and by sea, to take a chance on themselves and their luck. The luckiest ones, though, were the merchants and businesspeople who cashed in on California's dream by mining the miners.

Because of the discovery of gold, California skipped the economically exploitive U.S. territorial phase typical of other western states. With almost endless, indisputable capital at hand, Californians thumbed their noses at the Eastern financial establishment almost from the start: they could exploit the wealth of the far West themselves. And exploit it they did—mining not only the earth, but also the state's forests, fields, and water wealth. Wild California would never again be the same.

Almost overnight, "civilized" California became an economic sensation. The state was essentially admitted to the union on its own terms—because California was quite willing to go its own way and remain an independent entity otherwise. The city of San Francisco grew from a sleepy enclave of 500 souls to a hectic, hell-bent business and financial center of more than 25,000 within two years. Other cities built on a foundation of prosperous trade included the inland supply port of Sacramento. Agriculture, at first important for feeding the state's mushrooming population of fortune hunters, soon became a de facto gold mine in its own right. Commerce expanded even more rapidly with the completion of the California-initiated transcontinental railroad and with the advent of other early communications breakthroughs such as the telegraph. California's dreams of prosperity became self-fulfilling prophecies. And as California went, so went the nation.

SOUTHERN CALIFORNIA'S GOLDEN AGE

There was gold in Southern California, too—and it was actually discovered first, at Placerita Canyon not far north of Mission San Fernando. But the subsequent discovery at Sutter's Mill soon dwarfed Southern California's gold rush-era mining finds. The bonanza here came from inflated beef prices and otherwise supplying the booming northstate gold fields. The boom went bust in the mid-1850s, and depression came to California. Only the arrival of the railroads awakened Southern California from its social and economic slumber. Lured by well-promoted tales and photographs of the salubrious sunny climate—a place where oranges grew in people's backyards, where even roses bloomed in winter—migrants arrived by the trainloads, particularly from the Midwest, throughout the 1880s. Soon agriculture, with orchards and fields of crops stretching to every horizon, became Southern California's economic strength. Real estate developments and grand hotels, often built on land owned by the railroad barons, soon boomed as well. In the late 1800s oil was discovered throughout the greater Los Angeles basin, creating still more regional wealth.

As a land with little annual rainfall, its vast underground aquifers already well on the way to depletion because of agricultural irrigation and urban use, by the early 1900s Los Angeles was quickly running out of water. Yet the inventiveness of self-taught water engineer William Mulholland, soon an international celebrity, eliminated any prospect of enforced limits on growth. When the floodgates of the famed Los Angeles Aqueduct first opened, to great public acclaim, in 1913, Southern California had made its first monumental step toward eliminating the very idea of limits. Mulholland's engineering miracle, which successfully tapped into Owens Valley water supplies that originated 250 miles to the north, also tapped into the southstate's social imagination. In no time at all the "desert" was in full bloom, landscaped with lush lawns, ferns, roses, and palm trees and populated by happy, healthy families frolicking in the sunshine.

That image, translated to the world's imagination via Hollywood's movie industry in the 1920s and subsequent years, essentially created the Southern California of today. Massive growth followed World War II, when Los Angeles began to create itself as an industrial and technological superpower—one soon beset by traffic, pollution, and social problems befitting its size.

Yet for all its current challenges Southern California is still a surprisingly optimistic place. For every problem there is a solution, according to traditional southstate thinking.

DREAMING THE NEW GOLD DREAM

California as the land of opportunity—always a magnet for innovation, never particularly respectful of stifling and stodgy tradition—has dictated terms to the rest of the country throughout its modern history. Even with the gradual arrival of what the rest of the world could finally recognize as civilization, which included the predictable phenomenon of personal wealth translated into political power, California's commitment to prosperity and change—sometimes for its own sake—has never waned.

From the founding of the Automobile Club of Southern California in 1900 to the construction of Yosemite's Hetch Hetchy Dam (to slake San Francisco thirst) in 1923; from the establishment of the first Hollywood movie studio in 1911 to the 1927 transmission, from San Francisco, of the first television picture; from the completion in 1940 of the world's first freeway to the opening of Disneyland in 1955; from the 1960s' Free Speech Movement, the rise of Black Power in the wake of the Watts riots in 1965, and the successes of César E. Chávez's United Farm Workers Union to the Beat poets, San Francisco's Summer of Love, and the oozing up of New Age consciousness; from California's rise as leader in the development of nuclear weapons and defense technology to the creation of the microchip and personal computer: California history is a chronicle of incredible change, a relentless double-time march into the new.

"All that is constant about the California of my childhood," writes Sacramento native Joan Didion in an essay from *Slouching Towards Bethlehem,* "is the rate at which it disappears."

Politics and Economy

California's political structure is quite confusing, with thousands of tax-levying governmental units—including special districts, 58 county governments, and hundreds of cities both large and small—and a variety of overlapping jurisdictions. Based on the federal principle of one person, one vote and designed with separate executive, judicial, and legislative (Assembly and Senate) branches, the game of state-level California government is often quite lively, almost a high form of entertainment for those who understand the rules. The use and abuse of public resources is the ultimate goal of power-brokering in the Golden State, affecting statewide and local economies as well as the private sector and creating (or abandoning) commitments to social justice and various human rights issues many Californians still hold dear.

The popularity of unusually affable, charismatic, and highly visible California politicians,

from Ronald Reagan to Jerry Brown, would suggest that Golden State politics generally takes place in the entertainment arena. Nothing could be further from the truth. Though Californians are committed to the concept of public initiatives and referenda on major issues—politicians be damned, basically—most decisions affecting life in California are still made in the time-honored behind-the-scenes tradition of U.S. politics, with backroom deal-making conducted something like a poker game. In order to know the score, you must know the players and what cards they hold.

Those in the know contend that the California Legislature, considered the best state-level legislative body in the nation as recently as 1971, has steadily been careening downhill, in terms of effectiveness and ethics, ever since—largely because of "juice," or the influence of lobbyists and special interest money. According to veteran *Sacramento Bee* political reporter and columnist Dan Walters: "Votes are bought, sold, and rented by the hour with an arrogant casualness. There are one-man, one-vote retail sales as well as wholesale transactions that party leaders negotiate for blocs of votes."

Though from some perspectives California voters—and nonvoters—are largely responsible for the seemingly insoluble problems the state now faces, polls indicate that Californians increasingly distrust their politicians. From his years observing the species from the 19th-century Washington, D.C., press gallery, Mark Twain offered this fitting summary, a quote from a fictitious newspaper account in his novel, *The Gilded Age:* "We are now reminded of a note we received from the notorious burglar Murphy, in which he finds fault with a statement of ours

DUCK THE BUDGET BLUES

Heads up, California travelers. Present and future circumstances have become decidedly uncertain as a direct result of California's ongoing budget crisis. When will state parks be open, and how much is admission? Public libraries? Will there be lifeguards at public pools and beaches? Will mass transit trains and buses run on time—or run at all? Will there be adequate police and fire protection? Every effort was made to corral current details, but it's likely that circumstances will keep changing, as California's budget crisis continues. For the sake of a pleasant and fruitful visit *please* call ahead to verify essential details.

that he had served one term in the penitentiary and one in the U.S. Senate. He says, 'The latter statement is untrue and does me great injustice.'"

Given California voters' current penchant for taking matters into their own hands, no matter how disastrously, it came as no surprise in 1992 when California became one of the first states in the nation to pass a "term limitations" law, restricting its Assembly members to maximum six-year terms in office and limiting the terms of governor, state senators, and other constitutional officers to eight years. Another initiative, put before the voters in 1990 as Proposition 140, cut the Legislature's operating budget by $70 million, about 38 percent. It has been upheld as constitutional by the state supreme court.

ECONOMY

If the lure of gold brought pioneers to California, the rich land, its seemingly endless resources, and the state's almost anarchistic "anything goes" philosophy kept them here. The Golden State has essentially become a nation-state—an economic superpower, the the fifth-largest (or sixth or seventh, depending on the comparison data) economy in the world. A major international player in the game of Pacific Rim commerce, California's cry is usually "free trade," in contrast to the philosophy of high-tariff trade protectionism typically so strong elsewhere in the United States. With so much financial clout, until George W. Bush ascended to the U.S. presidency California was often the tail that wagged the dog of U.S. domestic and foreign economic and political policy. Even in the Bush-Cheney-Rove years, with California all but tossed aside due to its Democratic political leanings, the state could easily have seceded from the union, able to compete as an independent entity in the world market.

Though industry of every sort thrives in California, agriculture has long been the state's economic mainstay. ("The whole place stank of orange blossoms," observed H.L. Mencken on a Golden State visit.) Though most Southern California citrus groves have long since been paved

over for parking lots and shopping malls—those disturbed by California's proclivity for bulldozing the past in the name of progress have coined a verb for it: "to californicate"—agriculture in pockets of Southern California and in Northern California is still going strong. Because of the large size and concentrated ownership of farm and ranch lands, helped along by public subsidies of irrigation engineering projects, agriculture in California has always been agribusiness. In its role as agricultural nation-state, California produces more food than 90 percent of the world's nations, a $25 billion annual business. But with farmers caught between rising production costs and declining crop prices due to global competition, some state economists say that food production can no longer be regarded as the profitable business it once was. And population increases continue to put pressure on limited water resources as well as productive farmland.

The economic spirit of the northstate, suggested philosopher George Santayana in a 1910 Berkeley speech, is best summed up by the immense presence of nature in Northern California—nature in tandem with engineering and technology. Now that the roughshod, rough-and-tumble days of man against nature are no longer widely condoned, Californians increasingly expect technology to respect nature's standards. In Northern California particularly, but increasingly in Southern California, information is the cleanest industry of all. It seems no coincidence that both the microchip and the personal computer were born here.

Yet California, northern and southern, is industrious in all ways. Travel and tourism is a major industry—now promoted, in good budget years, at least, since California has started to lose ground in the tourist sweeps to other Western states—with annual revenues in the $52 billion range. Growth itself is a growth industry in California, with all aspects of the construction trade generating an average $30 billion in business annually. Revenues generated by California's top 100 privately held companies—including Bechtel Group, Hughes Aircraft, USA Petroleum (and other oil companies), Twentieth-Century Fox

Films (and other media giants), Purex Industries, Denny's Inc., Raley's, both the AAA-affiliated Automobile Club of Southern California and the California State Automobile Association, and a long string of agricultural cooperatives as well as health- and life-insurance companies—approach $100 billion annually.

A U.S. capital of finance and commerce, the state is also the world's high-technology headquarters. Helped along by state-supported University of California labs and research facilities, California has long been a leader in the aerospace and weapons development industries. Including military bases and research, testing, and surveillance sites, about 80 outposts of nuclear weaponry are—or were—based in California; recent federal cuts in defense spending have slowed business considerably.

California is number one in construction-related business contracts and leads the nation in number of millionaires, though it no longer tops the nation's lists for livable cities or average personal incomes-and in fact falls behind the rest of the nation in the latter category. Despite the crush of its urban population, California usually makes more money in agriculture than any other state, and produces—and consumes—most of the country's wine.

The People

Native peoples had many explanations for how the land and life in California came to be, almost as many stories as there were villages. But it's a stranger-than-fiction fact that California as a concept was concocted in Europe, by a Spanish soldier turned romance writer.

The rocky-shored island paradise of California, according to the 1510 fictional *Las Sergas de Esplandían* by Garcí Ordóñez de Montalvo, overflowed with gold, gems, and pearls, was inhabited by griffins and other wild beasts, and "peopled by black women, with no men among them, for they lived in the fashion of Amazons" under the great Queen Calafia's rule. With such fantastic images seared into the European imagination, it's no wonder that Cortés and his crew attached the name California to their later territorial claims from Baja California north to Alaska.

THE MYTHS OF NORTHERN AND SOUTHERN CALIFORNIANS

While California is still a destination of the imagination and a rich land indeed, its true wealth is (and always was) its breathtaking beauty, its cultural creativity, and its democratic dreams.

The primary political fact of life here is that California is one state. Technically indisputable, this fact is nonetheless widely disputed. Californians themselves generally view the state as two distinct entities: Northern California, centered in sophisticated San Francisco, and the continuous sprawl of Southern California south of the Tehachapi Mountains, its freeways spreading out from its Los Angeles heart like the spokes of a bent and broken wheel.

According to the myth that successfully populated Southern California, simple, neighborly, nature-oriented living amid sunny gardens and citrus groves would save civilization from the mass-production mind-set of industrialism—almost shocking to contemplate now, when one sees what's become of that idea. Yet this is also the land of the American dream made manifest, where the sun always shines—on the deserving and deserving alike, the ultimate in California-style social democracy—and where even the desert itself is no limitation since, thanks to the wonders of modern engineering, water can be imported from elsewhere. In the newer Southern California myth, style is more important than substance and image is everything, cultural truths shaped in large part by Hollywood and the movies. Life itself is defined by humanity—by an artificial environment of pavement and plastic technologies manufactured by human need and vanity, by the worship of physical beauty in human form, and by the relentless search for the ultimate in hedonistic diversion and novelty. An engineered Eden ruled by Midwestern social and political mores, Southern California worships everything new—from new beliefs and ideas and commercially viable images transmitted via its own film and media industries to art and innovation for their own sakes—and rarely questions the intrinsic value of cosmetic change. The main moral question in the southstate is not "Is it important?" or "Is it right?" but: "Is it new?"

Northern California's mythic soul is represented by nature in all its contradictions—the rugged outdoors in tandem with the rugged individualist struggling for survival, the simple beauty of humanity in nature as well as more complicated relationships that result from humanity's attempts to change and control nature's inherent wildness. The collective and personal histories of Northern California suggest secessionism, rebellion, and the high-technology innovations largely responsible for today's global culture. Northern California is also about human awareness in nature, and a modern consciousness seemingly sprung fully formed from nature worship: holistic health and get-in-touch-with-yourself psychological trends; mandatory physical fitness, as if to be ready at a moment's notice to embark upon ever more challenging outdoor adventures; natural foods and a regionally focused appreciation for fresh produce and fine wines. Life in Northern California is defined by outdoor-oriented, socially responsible narcissism—and symbolized by an upwardly mobile young professional couple nudging their new, gas-guzzling four-wheel drive onto well-engineered highways leading out of the city and into the wilderness.

Yet in many ways the two ends of the state are becoming one. Despite regional chauvinism, southstate-style growth, with all its attendant problems, is fast becoming a fact of life in the north; within several decades, almost as many people will live in Northern California as in Southern. In all parts of the state, growth is moving away from major cities and into the suburbs—a fact that is influencing political trends as well. Northern California, traditionally more

liberal than Southern California, is becoming more Republican, while the southstate's increasing concerns over health and environmental issues are liberalizing urban political trends. And though Northern California politicians tend to openly oppose any increased water shipments to Southern California (unless their districts are paid well for private water sales), most are much quieter about supporting water engineering feats designed to meet the needs of the northstate's own suburban growth.

Californians themselves still see most statewide social, political, and "style" differences in terms of north versus south regionalism. The time-honored historical issue of politically splitting California into two separate states—an idea now at least rhetorically quite popular in the rural north, though the state's first secessionism arose in the south—still comes up regularly. But the actual facts about modern-day California suggest a different reality. Life here is, and will be continue to be, defined by the conflicting cultures of minority-dominated urban areas, more conservative Sun Belt suburbs created by "white flight," and declining, truly rural resource-based communities.

"FIRST IN THE NATION"

California's most obvious "first" is its population. Half of the people living in the West, the fastest-growing region of the nation, live in California. Number one in the nation now—with almost 36 million people—California's population at current growth rates will be nearly 40 million by the year 2005, nearly 50 million by 2030 (some say 2020 or 2025), and 60 million by 2040. Or more. The state has been growing so rapidly during the past decade, largely because of legal and illegal immigration, that demographers can't keep up (After the 2000 census, for instance, state head-counters added another million to the feds' estimate). Keeping tabs on Californians has been complicated further by their increasing migration, in recent years, to other states; more than 1.1 million left in the early 1990s, though that trend has slowed.

The sheer heft of California humanity makes it first in the nation in immigration (both legal and illegal), first in bomb threats and investigations, first in firearm-related violent crime, and first in prison budgets. Largely because of Southern California population pressures, California also ranks shockingly high for endangered and threatened species. Yet California boasts more Nobel Prize laureates than any other state, more engineers and scientists, and more research labs, colleges, and universities.

Common wisdom in the U.S. holds that "as California goes, so goes the nation." As with most California legends, there is at least some truth to this. California is quite often the national trendsetter, from fads and fashions in political or social beliefs to styles in cars and clothes. In its endless pursuit of style, California searches for its identity, for some explanation of itself. California is constantly inventing and reinventing its own mythology. Yet California was among the last states in the U.S. to emerge from the latest recession, and few states so far are following California's lead in eliminating affirmative action programs and attempting to withhold public services from immigrants.

The Free Speech Movement, the philosophical foundation supporting both civil rights and anti–Vietnam War activism, took root in California. But so did the New Republicanism (best represented by Richard Nixon and Ronald Reagan), a reactionary trend toward social control that arose at least as an indirect result. California is usually first in the nation for new religious and spiritual trends, too, from New Age consciousness to televangelism.

California is the birthplace of the motel, the climate-controlled shopping mall, suburban sprawl, and a lifestyle almost entirely dependent upon cars and elaborately engineered highway and freeway systems. But California is also first in the nation in car thefts and in marijuana cultivation. It's home to the back-to-the-land culture and spawning ground for the philosophy of bioregionalism, too, decrying all things homogenized, unnatural, unnecessarily imported, and plastic. For every action in California, there is also a reaction.

CONTEMPORARY FACTS AND FANCY

Among common misconceptions about the state is the one the rest of the world tenaciously clings to—that everyone in California is laid-back, liberal, blond, rich, and well educated.

Californians as Laid-Back

California may be casual, but it's not exactly relaxed. Despite the precedents set by native peoples and early Californios (those of Spanish descent born in the pre-U.S. period), most of the state's modern residents are hardly content to live in leisure. In their frantic rush to accumulate, to stay in style, to just keep up with the state's sophisticated survival code and incredible rate of change, Californians tend to be tense and harried. And now that Californians have remembered—and reminded the rest of the world—that rest and relaxation are necessary for a well-rounded life, people here pursue recreation with as much determination as any other goal. Just sitting around doing nothing isn't against the law in California, but it's definitely déclassé.

Californians as Liberal

If people in California aren't particularly laid-back, they aren't particularly liberal either. After all, California created both Richard Nixon and Ronald Reagan. The truth is, California has never committed itself to any particular political party. Democratic legislators still predominate in California's Senate and Assembly—a surprise in 1996, considering the general Republican drift elsewhere—and Democrats, after losing ground in 1994, regained strength in the U.S. House of Representatives in 1996. Some blame former Republican governor Pete Wilson, described by national columnist Anthony Lewis as "the premier gutter politician of our day," since Wilson's reactionary anti-immigrant reelection campaign of 1994 and his activist anti-affirmative action stance in 1996 made Latino citizens—and other voters—angry enough to vote Democratic in a big way. Perhaps it was only fitting that Fresno's Cruz Bustamante, the first Latino speaker of the state Assembly, took

Know Coastal California

office in 1996. Subsequently, there was a rapid decline in the Republicans' recent race-baiting politicking—but not enough to slow the statewide decline in Republican influence.

Republican influence in California continued its steady decline until Arnold Schwarzenegger became governor in October 2003, following the successful, rather shocking recall of Democratic governor Gray Davis.

In November 1998, California elected a Democratic governor, Gray Davis, by a whopping 20-point margin, though the state had supported only Republicans in that office since the departure of "Governor Moonbeam," Jerry Brown, in the late 1970s. And Cruz Bustamante was elected lieutenant governor, the first Latino in the 20th century elected to statewide office. In the same election, the previously ascendant Christian conservatives in the Republican Party lost big—and the state also elected its first Green Party candidate, Audie Bock, to the state Assembly.

Yet even in 1992, when Republicans otherwise dominated state politics, California was first in the nation to elect women—both Democrats, Barbara Boxer and Dianne Feinstein—to fill its two U.S. Senate seats, outdoing all other states, cities, and municipalities in paying homage to "the year of the woman." (Ten years later, in a trickle-up effect, U.S. House Democrats enthusiastically elected veteran San Franciscan politician Nancy Pelosi to lead their party.) And California overwhelmingly supported Gov. Bill Clinton, a Democrat, in the 1992 presidential election. President Clinton's support, though still a majority, was substantially less in the 1996 election. Yet the Democrats' previous declines and Republican dominance on the national level have diminished the state's traditional political clout in the U.S., at least in the short term, because of the loss of key committee chairs and committee rankings once held by California Democrats.

The tattered terms of Governor Gray Davis, beset by a manufactured energy crisis and fiscal fallout from the dotcom bomb, and the election of Schwarzenegger don't bode well for the Democrats. Republicans are equally ill-prepared to manage the massive scale of problems now facing

California, though in 2002 they had gained back a handful of seats at the capitol and sought to further strengthen their position by skirmishing over California's perennially pressing issues: education, energy, and the economy.

Occasional flamboyant public figures and long-standing double-edged jokes about the land of "fruits and nuts" aside, predicting the direction in which political winds will blow here is difficult. Until recently, pollsters detected a steady trend toward increasing identification with the Republican party among the state's voting-age population. Generally speaking, the political labels of Democrat and Republican mean little in California. People here tend to vote on the basis of enlightened economic interest, personal values, and "political personality."

But if the New Republicanism is quite comfortable in California, so is the orthodoxy of no orthodoxy. Values, political and social, are discarded as easily as last year's fashions. (Californians don't oppose tradition so much as they can't find the time for it.) The state's legendary liberalness is based on the fact that, like social voyeurs, Californians tolerate—some would say encourage—strangeness in others. Rooted in the state's rough-and-tumble gold rush history, this attitude is almost mandatory today, considering California's phenomenal cultural and ethnic diversity.

Californians as Blond

Despite the barrage of media and movie images suggesting that all Californians are blond and tan and live at the beach, not much could be further from the truth. Though Caucasians or "Anglos" predominate ethnically, California's population has represented almost every spot on the globe since the days of the gold rush. More than 240 identified cultures or ethnicities have been identified in California. Blacks, Asians, and those of Hispanic descent have the highest numbers among the state's diverse minority populations. Already, California's collective "minority" populations have become the majority. This has long been true in major cities, including Los Angeles, East Los Angeles, Fresno, Oakland, and San Francisco, and in many public school classrooms.

California's Asian population, now representing almost 10 percent of the total, will grow slightly. Its Latino population, now approximately 28 percent, will increase to 50 percent by the year 2040 (some say this demographic event will occur much sooner). Blacks in California will remain at a fairly stable population level, demographers project, about 7 percent of the population, as will Native Americans at around 1 percent.

No matter what color they started out, people in paradise have been getting a bit gray; throughout the 1980s, retirees were California's fastest-growing age group. But just as it seemed the Golden State's stereotypical golden glow of youth was on the wane came the news that the population is actually getting younger, helped along by the arrival of five million preschoolers since 1990. And that trend underscores the others. According to the most recent U.S. census—already inadequate for keeping pace with the state's fast-changing face—in 1990, 70 percent of the state's 60 year olds were white and 55 percent of the 10 year olds were ethnic minorities.

Californians as Rich

Though California is the richest state in the union, with a bustling economy of nation-state status and an average per-capita personal income of $22,000, the gap between the very rich and the very poor is staggering—and shocking to first-time visitors in major urban areas, since the despair of homelessness and poverty is very visible on city streets.

The news in 1995 that the U.S. is now the most economically stratified of all industrialized nations—with the top 20 percent of the population controlling 80 percent of the nation's wealth—barely raised an eyebrow in California. Neither did the word in 1996 from the Public Policy Institute of California that, with the state's economy once again booming, California has the largest gap between rich and poor in the world because of precipitous declines in wages and income among the working poor. That income gap was still growing in 2000, with the widest income disparities in Los Angeles.

Interpretations of U.S. census data suggest that California is becoming two states—or at least two states of mind. One California is educated, satisfied, and safe. The other is young, uneducated, immigrant (many do not speak English), restless, and impoverished. The ranks of the upper-income professional class (household income $50,000 or above) increased almost 10 percent between 1980 and 1990, to 33 percent—a phenomenon partly attributed to greater numbers of working women. (It's also striking to note that 18 percent of all U.S. households with an annual income of $150,000 or more are in California.) During that same decade, the state's middle-income households shrank from 35 percent to 33 percent, and the number of low-income households also declined, from 41 percent to 34 percent. But the numbers of the actual poor increased, from 11.4 percent to 12.5 percent.

Contradicting the skid row-alcoholic image of street life, nearly one-third of the homeless in California are under age 18. But almost more disturbing is California's unseen poverty. Not counting those who are turned away because there isn't enough to go around, more than two million people—almost one in every ten Californians—regularly require food from public and private charitable organizations just to survive; on any given day in the Golden State, half a million people stand in line to get a free meal at a soup kitchen or commodity pantry. Minors, again, are California's largest class of hungry people. More than one in every four children in the Golden State live in poverty.

Californians as Well Educated

California has long been committed to providing educational opportunity to all citizens—a commitment expressed in once-generous public school funding as well as public financing for the nine (soon 10) campuses of the prestigious University of California, 23 California State University (CSU) campuses (CSU recently acquired the Maritime Academy), and the 106 independent California Community College (CCC) campuses. But because of the obvious educational impacts of increased immigration—80 separate languages are

Know Coastal California

spoken at Los Angeles schools, at least 40 at Hollywood High alone—and the unofficial reality of socially segregated schools, uneven early educational opportunities are a fact of life even in well-intentioned California. Until recently the situation has been steadily worsening, with California spending $900 less per public school student than the national average; ranked 40th in per-pupil spending; and burdened with the nation's highest student-teacher ratios. Faced with a projected 18 percent enrollment increase in elementary and high schools by 2006, California has lately turned its attention to improving public schools—both with increased levels of funding and increased performance testing. The state's entrenched economic crisis, however, threatens that recent progress.

Previous declines in public school performance, coupled with increasingly stringent entrance requirements at both University of California and California State University campuses, have led critics such as former state Senator Tom Hayden of Santa Monica to suggest that California's current public education policies are creating a "de facto educational apartheid." Though California's two-year community colleges are providing more four-year college preparation courses and are increasingly encouraging students to transfer to state universities, most minority groups in California are vastly underrepresented even in public universities.

The state's ongoing budget crisis has meant significant cuts in public financial support for education, and fees at public universities (California educators and legislators never say "tuition") have increased rapidly. The state's enduring budget crisis suggests far worse news still to come. Yet even with the general public financing a diminishing share of the cost of each student's college education, there still isn't enough opportunity to go around. Just to keep pace with current and anticipated demand early in the coming century, the University of California needs three new campuses, the California State University system needs five, and the California Community Colleges need 28. According to a gloomy 1996 report by the nonprofit RAND think tank in Santa Monica, all three levels of California public higher education will be in deep financial crisis yet challenged to absorb a record 2.3 million potential students by 2010.

Overall trends in education, economics, and employment patterns suggest that California is evolving into a two-tiered society dominated by an affluent and well-educated Anglo-Asian "overclass." Those who make up the underclass and who compete for relatively low-paying service jobs will increasingly be immigrants or the functionally illiterate. According to Bill Honig, former state superintendent of public instruction, about 60 percent of California's public school students leave school without being able to read well enough to compete in California's increasingly complex, technology-oriented job market.

PEOPLE ON THE MOVE

Everyone is moving to California and vicinity, it seems. According to *American Demographics,* the geographic center of the U.S. population moves 58 feet farther west and 29 feet to the south every year. (Recent bad times in California slowed that trend temporarily, as nearly one million Californians left to find jobs elsewhere, but that loss has been overshadowed by increased immigration.) Be that as it may, some people consider Californians among the most obnoxious people on earth, and this is not necessarily a new phenomenon.

To some, the state is a kind of cultural purgatory, settled (in the words of Willard Huntington Wright) by "yokels from the Middle West who were nourished by rural pieties and superstitions." Others consider, and have always considered, Californians as somehow inherently unstable. "Insanity, as might be expected, is fearfully prevalent in California," Dr. Henry Gibbons stated before San Francisco's local medical society in 1857. "It grows directly out of the excited mental condition of our population, to which the common use of alcoholic drink is a powerful adjunct." The general outside observation today is that if Californians aren't talking about themselves—and about accomplishing their latest career, financial, fitness, or psychospiritual goals—they talk about California. New Englander Inez

Hayes Irwin defined those afflicted with Californoia in her 1921 book *Californiacs:*

> *The Californiac is unable to talk about anything but California, except when he interrupts himself to knock every other place on the face of the earth. He looks with pity on anybody born outside of California, and he believes that no one who has ever seen California willingly lives elsewhere. He himself often lives elsewhere, but he never admits that it is from choice.*

There may be more than a shred of truth in this, even today; pollsters say one out of every four Californians would rather live elsewhere—for the most part, either in Hawaii or Oregon. But many who live and work in California are not native Californians. This is almost as true today as it ever was; at least one-third of contemporary Californians were born somewhere else. Somehow, California's amazing cultural and ethnic diversity is the source of both its social stability and its self-renewal.

Perhaps because of misleading portrayals of California's past, in the media and the movies as well as the history books, a common misconception is that the impact and importance of California's ethnic populations is relatively recent, a post–World War II phenomenon. But many peoples and many races have made significant contributions to California culture and economic development since the days of the gold rush—and since the decimation of native populations.

Blacks and Latinos, despite attempts (official and otherwise) to prevent them from dreaming the California dream, were among the first to arrive in the gold fields. The Chinese, who also arrived early to join the ranks of the state's most industrious citizens, were relentlessly persecuted despite their willingness to do work others considered impossible—including the unimaginable engineering feat of chiseling a route over the forbidding Sierra Nevada for the nation's first transcontinental railroad. And when the state's boom-bust beginnings gave way to other possibilities, including farming, ranching, and small business enterprises, California's minorities stayed—helping, despite the realities of subtle discrimination and sometimes overt racism, to create the psychological pluralism characteristic of California society today.

CALIFORNIA FROM THE AIR

Anyone can visit the California coastline—even strand of sand, every craggy cove or promontory, every seastack—even without leaving home, thanks to Ken and Gabrielle Adelman's photographic hobby. Their **California Coastal Records Project,** some 13,000 digital photographs of the California coastline available free for viewing, is not universally popular, however. The folks at Vandenberg Air Force Base near Lompoc successfully prevented aerial images of their stretch of coastline. Actress Barbra Streisand sued to bar photographs of her coastal Malibu estate, a lawsuit she lost in 2004. Not only did Streisand have to pay the Adelmans' legal fees; adding insult to alleged injury, her lawsuit provided almost endless international publicity for the website.

There is so much more to see than Barbara Streisand's backyard—and from offshore perspectives most landlubbers would never see. The intrepid Point Reyes Lighthouse. The serene University of California campus in Santa Barbara. The haunting beauty of Point Lobos, the equally craggy Mendocino coast. Cher's ostentatious Malibu estate, miscellaneous millionaire and billionaire homes, the "XOX House" next to Frank O. Gehry's place. The website allows visitors to search by caption, by general area, by latitude and longitude, or frame by frame, for an almost endless visual tour of the California coast.

More than just a sightseeing tool, however, the coastal photography documents every inch of coastal land and landscape—an invaluable tool for land use planners, scientists, environmentalists, and community activists.

To sample the California coastline online, see www.californiacoastline.org.

Entertainment and Shopping

Not even the sky's the limit on entertainment in California. From air shows to harvest fairs and rodeos, from symphony to opera, from rock 'n' roll to avant-garde clubs and theater, from strip shows (male and female) to ringside seats at ladies' mud-wrestling contests, from high-stakes bingo games to horse racing—anything goes in the Golden State. Most communities offer a wide variety of special, often quite unusual, annual events; many of these are listed by region or city elsewhere in this guide.

Most stores are open during standard business hours (weekdays 8 A.M.–5 P.M. or 9 A.M.–5 P.M.) and often longer, sometimes seven days a week, because of the trend toward two-income families and ever-reduced leisure time. This trend is particularly noticeable in cities, where shops and department stores are often open until 9 P.M. or later, and where many grocery stores are open 24 hours.

Shopping malls—almost self-sustaining cities in California, with everything from clothing and major appliances to restaurants and entertainment—are the standard California trend, but cities large and small with viable downtown shopping districts often offer greater variety and uniqueness in goods and services. Also particularly popular in California are flea markets and arts-and-crafts fairs, the former usually held on weekends, the latter best for handcrafted items and often associated with the Thanksgiving-through-Christmas shopping season and/or festivals and special events. California assesses a 7.25 percent state sales tax on all nonfood items sold in the state, and many municipalities levy additional sales tax.

Recreation

With its tremendous natural diversity, recreationally California offers something for just about everyone. Popular spring-summer-fall activities include hiking and backpacking; all water sports, from pleasure boating and water-skiing to sailing, windsurfing, kayaking, and swimming; whitewater rafting, canoeing, and kayaking; mountain and rock-climbing; even hang gliding and hunting. In most years, winter activities popular in Northern California can also be enjoyed in Southern California, at least to a certain extent. These include both Alpine and Nordic skiing, snowshoe hiking, sledding and tobogganing, and just plain snow play. Also high on the "most popular" list of outdoor California sports: bicycling, walking and running; coastal diversions from beachcombing to surfing; and the increasingly popular statewide diversion, bird-watching. The most likely places to enjoy these and other outdoor activities are mentioned throughout this book.

And where do people go to re-create themselves in the great outdoors? To Northern California's vast public playgrounds—to the rugged coast and almost endless local, regional, and state parks as well as national parks and forest lands. In Southern California, where wide-open spaces are all but gone, outdoor recreation still centers on local beaches, some nice local and regional parks as well as state parks and beaches, national forests—and the vast expanse of the state's deserts. For more information on the national parks, national forests, and other state- and federally owned lands (including Bureau of Land Management wilderness areas) mentioned in this book, contact each directly.

NATIONAL PARKS INFORMATION AND FEES

For those planning to travel extensively in national parks in California and elsewhere in the U.S., a one-year Golden Eagle Passport provides unlimited park access (not counting camping fees) for the holder and family, for the new price of $50. Though the Golden Eagle pass has recently doubled in price, it can still be worth it in California, where fees at certain national parks have recently increased; admission to Death Valley is now $10 (for up to a one-week stay) and Yosemite is $20. Those age 62 or older qualify for the $10 Golden Age Passport, which provides free lifetime access to national parks, monuments, and recreation areas, and a 50 percent discount on RV fees. Disabled travelers are eligible for the $10 Golden Access Passport, with the same privileges. You can buy all three special passes at individual national parks or obtain them in advance, along with visitor information, from: **U.S. National Park Service,** National Public Inquiries Office, U.S. Department of the Interior, 1849 C St., P.O. Box 37127, Washington, DC 20013, www.nps.gov. For regional national parks information covering California, Nevada, and Arizona, contact: **Pacific West Region U.S. National Park Service,** One Jackson Center, 1111 Jackson St., Ste. 700, Oakland, CA 94607, 510/817-1300, or see the website: www.nps.gov/pwro.

Campgrounds in some national parks in California—including Sequoia–Kings Canyon and Whiskeytown National Recreation Area, along with Southern California parks including Channel Islands, Death Valley, and Joshua Tree—can be reserved (with MasterCard or Visa) through the **National Park Reservation Service,** website: reservations.nps.gov, or by calling 800/365-2267 (365-CAMP) at least eight weeks in advance. The total cost includes both the actual camping fee plus a $8–9 reservations fee. From California, call 7 A.M.–7 P.M. (10 A.M.–10 P.M. Eastern time). If you're heading to **Yosemite,** make campground reservations via the Internet (see address above) or by calling 800/436-7275 (436-PARK). And to cancel your reservations, call 800/388-2733. To make national park camping reservations from outside the U.S., call 619/452-8787.

To support the protection of U.S. national parks and their natural heritage, contact the nonprofit **National Parks and Conservation Association** (NPCA), 1300 19th St. N.W., Ste. 300, Washington, DC 20036, 800/628-7275, ext. 213, or 202/223-6722, www.npca.org. Both as a public service and fundraiser, the NPCA sells sweatshirts, T-shirts, and books about national

Know Coastal California

COURTESY OF THE NATIONAL PARK SERVICE

there is no lack of National Parks in California

park history. You can also sign up for tours and keep abreast of regional conservation events.

NATIONAL FORESTS AND OTHER FEDERAL LANDS

For general information about U.S. national forests, including wilderness areas and campgrounds, contact: **U.S. Forest Service,** U.S. Department of Agriculture, Publications, P.O. Box 96090, Washington, DC 20090, 202/205-8333. For a wealth of information via the Internet, try www.fs.fed.us. For information specifically concerning national forests and wilderness areas in California, and for maps, contact: **U.S. Forest Service, Pacific Southwest Region,** 1323 Club Drive, Vallejo, CA 94592, 707/562-8737, www.fs.fed.us/r5. Additional California regional offices are mentioned elsewhere in this guide.

Some U.S. Forest Service and Army Corps of Engineers campgrounds in California can be reserved through ReserveAmerica's **National Recreation Reservation Service** (with MasterCard or Visa) at the website: www.reserveusa.com, or call 877/444-6777 (TDD: 877/833-6777), a service available 5 A.M.–9 P.M. (8 A.M.–midnight Eastern time) from April 1 through Labor Day and otherwise 7 A.M.–4 P.M. (10 A.M.–7 P.M. Eastern time). From outside the U.S., call 518/885-3639. Reservations for individual campsites can be made up to eight months in advance, and for group camps up to 360 days in advance. Along with the actual costs of camping, expect to pay a per-reservation service fee of $8–9 for individual campsites (more for group sites). In addition to its first-come, first-camped campgrounds, in some areas the U.S. Forest Service offers the opportunity for "dispersed camping," meaning that you can set up minimal-impact campsites in various undeveloped areas. For detailed current recreation, camping, and other information, contact specific national forests mentioned elsewhere in this book.

Anyone planning to camp extensively in national forest campgrounds should consider buying U.S. Forest Service "camp stamps" (at national forest headquarters or at ranger district stations) in denominations of 50 cents, $1, $2,

$3, $5, and $10. These prepaid camping coupons amount to a 15 percent discount on the going rate. (Many national forest campgrounds are first-come, first-camped; without a reserved campsite, even camp stamps won't guarantee one.) Senior adults, disabled people, and those with national Golden Age and Golden Access recreation passports pay only half the standard fee at any campground and can buy camp stamps at half the regular rate as well.

For wannabe archaeologists, the U.S. Forest Service offers the opportunity to volunteer on archaeological digs through its **Passport in Time** program—certainly one way to make up for stingy federal budgets. To receive the project's newsletter, which announces upcoming projects in various national forests, contact: Passport in Time Clearinghouse, P.O. Box 31315, Tucson, AZ 85751, 800/281-9176 or 520/722-2716, www.passportintime.com.

Some Northern California public lands and vast expanses of Southern California are managed by the **U.S. Bureau of Land Management** (BLM). For general information, contact: U.S. Bureau of Land Management, Office of Public Affairs, 1849 C St. NW, LS 406, Washington, DC 20240, 202/452-5125, fax 202/452-5124, www.blm.gov. For information specifically related to California, contact: **California BLM,** 2800 Cottage Way, Ste. W1824, Sacramento, CA 95825, 916/978-4400, www.ca.blm.gov. If you plan to camp on BLM lands, be sure to request a current *California Visitor Map,* which includes campgrounds and other features; the BLM also allows "dispersed camping" in some areas (ask for details). For detailed information on all 69 of the BLM's new desert wildernesses in California, contact the BLM's **California Desert District Office,** 22835 Calle San Juan de Los Lagos, Moreno Valley, CA 92553, 909/697-5200, www.ca.blm.gov/cdd.

For information on national wildlife reserves and other protected federal lands, contact: **U.S. Fish and Wildlife Service,** Division of Refuges, Arlington Square, 4401 N. Fairfax Dr., Room 670, Arlington, VA 22203, 800/344-9453 or 703/358-1744, www.fws.gov.

STATE PARKS

California's 275 beloved state parks, which include beaches, wilderness areas, and historic homes, have recently been going through bad times—the unfortunate result of increasing public use combined with budget cuts. State beach and park fees, cut in half when California coffers overflowed, were increased substantially in 2004.

Day-use (parking) fees for admission to California state parks now range from $2 to $14 per vehicle, with extra fees charged for extra vehicles and other circumstances. In highly congested areas, it may be more attractive to park elsewhere and walk or take a bus. Admission fees for museums, historic sites and most tours are $2–8. Tours of Heasrt Castle (San Simeon State Historic Park) are $20–30 adults, $10–15 children. For information on special assistance available for individuals with disabilities or other special needs, contact individual parks—which make every effort to be accommodating, in most cases.

Annual passes (nontransferable), which you can buy at most state parks and at the State Parks Store in Sacramento (see below), are $125 for day use. Golden Bear passes, for seniors age

THE CALIFORNIA COASTAL TRAIL

Californians love their Pacific Ocean coastline. Love of the coast has inspired fierce battles over the years concerning just what does, and what does not, belong there. Among the things most Californians would agree belong along the coast are hiking trails—the reason for the existence of the nonprofit educational group **Coastwalk,** which sponsors group walks along the **California Coastal Trail** to introduce people to the wonders of the coast.

The California Coastal Trail seems to be an idea whose time has come. Now a Millennium Legacy Trail, honored at special White House ceremony in October 1999 that recognized 50 unique trails in the U.S., Washington, D.C., Puerto Rico, and the Virgin Islands, in March 2000 the California Coastal Trail also received a special $10,000 Millennium Trails Grant from American Express.

Yet in some places, the trail is still just an idea. It doesn't yet exist everywhere along the California coastline—and changing that fact is the other primary purpose of this unique organization. That's why members of Coastwalk set out in June of 2003 to walk the entire length of California's coastline—and its coastal trail-to-be—pointing out various "missing links" along the way, from Sea Ranch in Sonoma County to David Geffen's beachfront Malibu estate. Since 1983, Coastwalk's mission has been to establish a border-to-border California Coastal Trail as well as preserve the coastal environment.

You can join the coastwalking club. Guided four- to six-day Coastwalk trips, typically covering 5–10 miles each day, include in the far north the Del Norte coastline, Redwood National Park in Humboldt County, the rugged Medocino shoreline, and Sonoma and Marin Counties. Always popular, too, is the eight-day Lost Coast Backpack in Humboldt and Mendocino Counties. In central California, coastwalks are offered near San Francisco Bay, along the San Mateo and Santa Cruz coasts, in Monterey and San Luis Obispo Counties, and along the Ventura coast. Southern California coastwalks cover Los Angeles (the Santa Monica Mountains) and Catalina Island, Orange County, and San Diego County.

Accommodations, arranged by Coastwalk as part of the trip, include state park campgrounds and hostels with hot showers. "Chuckwagon" dinners, prepared by volunteers, are also provided; bring your own supplies for breakfast and lunch. All gear—you'll be encouraged to travel light—is shuttled from site to site each night, so you need carry only the essentials as you walk: water bottle, lunch, camera, and jacket. Daily coastwalk fees, actually assessed on a per-walk basis, work out to about $50 adults and $25 full-time students—all in all a very reasonable price for a unique vacation.

For more information and to join up—volunteers are always needed—contact Coastwalk, 7207 Bodega Ave. (across from the Sebastopol Library at Bodega Ave. and High St.), Sebastopol, 707/829-6689, www.coastwalk.org. The California coastal trail's website is www.californiacoastaltrail.org.

62 and older with limited incomes and for certain others who receive public assistance, are $5 per year and allow day-use access to all state parks and off-road vehicle areas except Hearst/San Simeon, Sutter's Fort, and the California State Railroad Museum. For details on income eligibility and other requirements, call 916/653-4000. "Limited use" Golden Bear passes, for seniors age 62 and older, allow free parking at state parks during the nonpeak park season (usually Labor Day through Memorial Day) and are $10 per year; they can be purchased in person at most state parks. Senior discounts for state park day use and camping (but only if the discount is requested while making reservations) are also offered. Special state park discounts and passes are also offered for the disabled and disabled veterans/POWs (prisoners of war). For more information, contact state park headquarters (see below).

Detailed information about California's state parks, beaches, and recreation areas is scattered throughout this guide. To obtain a complete parks listing, including available facilities, campground reservation forms, and other information, contact: **California State Parks,** Public Information, P.O. Box 942896, Sacramento, CA 94296, 800/777-0369 or 916/653-6995 (recorded, with an endless multiple-choice menu), www.parks.ca.gov.

Also available through the state parks department is an annually updated "Sno-Park" guide to parking without penalty while cross-country skiing or otherwise playing in the snow; for a current Sno-Park listing, write in care of the program at the state parks' address listed above or call 916/324-1222 (automated hotline). Sno-Park permits (required) cost $5 per day or $25 for the entire season, Nov. 1–May 30; you can also buy them at REI and other sporting goods stores and at any AAA office in California. Another winter-season resource, free to AAA members, is the annual *Winter Sports Guide* for California, which lists prices and other current information for all downhill and cross-country ski areas.

California state parks offer excellent campgrounds. In addition to developed "family"

campsites, which usually include a table, fire ring or outdoor stove, plus running water, flush toilets, and hot showers (RV hookups, if available, are extra), some state campgrounds also offer more primitive "walk-in" or environmental campgrounds and very simple hiker-biker campsites. Group campgrounds are also available (and reservable) at many state parks. If you plan to camp over the Memorial or Labor Day weekends, or the July 4th holiday, be sure to make reservations as early as possible.

Make campground reservations at California state parks (with MasterCard or Visa) through **ReserveAmerica,** website: www.reserveamerica.com, or call 800/444-7275 (444-PARK) weekdays 8 A.M.–5 P.M. For TDD reservations, call 800/274-7275 (274-PARK). And to cancel state park campground reservations, from the U.S. call 800/695-2269 (TDD 800/274-7275) or see www.reserveamerica.com. To make reservations by telephone from Canada or elsewhere outside the U.S., call 916/638-5883. As in other camping situations, before calling to make reservations, know the park and campground name, how you'll be camping (tent or RV), how many nights, and how many people and vehicles. In addition to the actual camping fee, which can vary from $9–15 for undeveloped campsites (without showers and/or flush toilets) to $11–25 for developed campsites, there is a $3–6 peak-season surcharge, a $10 "premium site" fee, and an additional reservations fee. State-owned cabins are $35–60. You can make camping and cabin reservations up to seven months in advance. (Be advised: popular coastal and other prime destinations often sell out for summer on "opening day"— seven months in advance—for reservations.) Certain campsites, including some primitive environmental and hiker/biker sites (now just $3) can be reserved only through the relevant state park.

To support the state's park system, contact the nonprofit **California State Parks Foundation,** 800 College Ave., P.O. Box 548, Kentfield, CA 94914, 800/963-7275 or 415/258-9975, fax

415/258-9930, www.calparks.org. Through memberships and contributions, the foundation has financed about $100 million in park preservation and improvement projects in the past several decades. Volunteers are welcome to contribute sweat equity, too.

OTHER RECREATION RESOURCES

For general information and fishing and hunting regulations, usually also available at sporting goods stores and bait shops where licenses and permits are sold, call the **California Department of Fish and Game** in Sacramento at 916/653-7664 or 916/445-0411; for license information or to purchase licenses online, call 916/227-2244, www.dfg.ca.gov. For additional sportfishing information, call 800/275-3474 (800/ASK-FISH).

For environmental and recreational netheads, the California Resources Agency's CERES website: ceres.ca.gov (aka the California Environmental Resources Evaluation System) offers an immense amount of additional information, from reports and updates on rare and endangered species to current boating regulations. The database is composed of federal, state, regional, and local agency information as well as a multitude of data and details from state and national environmental organizations—from REINAS, or the Real-time Environmental Information Network and Analysis System at the University of California at Santa Cruz, The Nature Conservancy, and NASA's Imaging Radar Home Page. Check it out.

Worth it for inveterate wildlife voyeurs is the *California Wildlife Viewing Guide* (Falcon Press), produced in conjunction with 15 state, federal, and local agencies in addition to Ducks Unlimited and the Wetlands Action Alliance. About 200 wildlife viewing sites are listed—most of these in Northern California. Look for the *California Wildlife Viewing Guide* at local bookstores, or order a copy by calling 800/582-2665. With the sale of each book, $1 is contributed to California Watchable Wildlife Project nature tourism programs.

To support California's beleaguered native plantlife, join, volunteer with, and otherwise contribute to the **California Native Plant Society** (CNPS), 1722 J St., Ste. 17, Sacramento, CA 95814, 916/447-2677, www.cnps.org. In various areas of the state, local CNPS chapters sponsor plant and habitat restoration projects. The organization also publishes some excellent books. Groups including the **Sierra Club, Audubon Society,** and **The Nature Conservancy** also sponsor hikes, backpack trips, birdwatching treks, backcountry excursions, and volunteer "working weekends" in all areas of California; call local or regional contact numbers (in the telephone book) or watch local newspapers for activity announcements.

Know Coastal California

Accommodations and Food

CAMPING

Because of many recent years of drought, and painful lessons learned about extreme fire danger near suburban and urban areas, all California national forests, most national parks, and many state parks now ban all backcountry fires—with the exception of controlled burns (under park supervision), increasingly used to thin understory vegetation to prevent uncontrollable wildfires. Some areas even prohibit portable campstoves, so be sure to check current conditions and all camping and hiking or backpacking regulations before setting out.

To increase your odds of landing a campsite where and when you want one, make reservations (if reservations are accepted). For details on reserving campsites at both national and state parks in California, see relevant listings under Recreation, immediately above, and listings for specific parks elsewhere in this book. Without reservations, seek out "low-profile" campgrounds during the peak camping season—summer as well as spring and fall weekends in most parts of California, late fall through early spring in Southern California desert areas—or plan for off-season camping. Some areas also offer undeveloped, environmental, or dispersed "open camping" not requiring reservations; contact relevant jurisdictions above for information and regulations.

Private campgrounds are also available throughout California, some of these included in the current *Campbook for California and Nevada*, available at no charge to members of the American Automobile Association (AAA), which lists (by city or locale) a wide variety of private, state, and federal campgrounds. Far more comprehensive is Tom Stienstra's *California Camping: The Complete Guide* (Foghorn Outdoors), available in most California bookstores. Or contact **California Travel Parks Association,** 530/823-1076, fax 530/823-5883, www.campgrounds.com/ctpa, which features a great online campground directory. Request a complimentary copy of the association's annual *California RV and Campground Guide* from any member campground, or order one by mail—send $4 if you live in the U.S., $7 if outside the U.S.—by writing to: ESG Mail Service, P.O. Box 5578, Auburn, CA 95604.

Two Internet sites worth visiting for campground information are FreeCampgrounds.com, to track down free sites, and Campsites411.com, which lists campgrounds throughout the United States, including California.

HOSTELS, YMCAS, AND YWCAS

Among the best bargains around, for travelers of all ages, are the **Hostelling International-USA** (HI-USA) scattered throughout California—in major urban areas, at various scenic spots along the coast, and in other appealing locations. Most are listed separately throughout this guide, but the list continually expands (and contracts); the annual Hostelling International *Hostelling North America* guide, available free with membership (or for $6.95 plus tax at most hostels), includes updated listings. Most affiliated hostels offer separate dormitory-style accommodations for men and women (and private couple or family rooms, if available), communal kitchens or low-cost food service, and/or other common facilities. Some provide storage lockers, loaner bikes, even hot tubs. At most hostels, the maximum stay is three nights; most are also closed during the day, which forces hostelers to get out and about and see the sights. Fees are typically $10–16 ($25–30 in big cities) for HI members, usually several dollars more for nonmembers. Since most hostels are quite popular, especially during summer, reservations—usually secured with one night's advance payment—are essential. Contact individual hostels for details (or see listings elsewhere in this book), since reservation requirements vary. Guests are expected to bring sleeping bags, sleepsacks, or sheets, though sheets or sleepsacks are sometimes available; mattresses, pillows, and blankets are provided.

For membership details and more information about hostelling in the U.S. and abroad, contact: **Hostelling International USA,** 8401 Colesville Rd., Ste. 600, Silver Springs, MD 20910, 301/495-1240, fax 301/495-6697, www.hiayh.org. For more information on Northern California hostels, contact the **HI Golden Gate Council,** 425 Divisadero St., Ste. 307, San Francisco, CA 94117, 415/863-1444 or 415/701-1320, fax 415/863-3865, www.norcalhostels.org, and the **HI Central California Council,** P.O. Box 2538, Monterey, CA 93942, 831/899-1252, fax 831/465-1553, http://westernhostels.org/centralcalifornia.

You'll find other reputable hostels in California, some independent and some affiliated with other hostel "chains" or umbrella organizations (such as the Banana Bungalow group, now well represented in Southern California). For current comprehensive U.S. listings of these private hostels, contact: **BakPak Travelers Guide,** 670 West End Ave., Ste. 1B, New York, NY 10025,/fax 718/504-5099, http://bakpakguide.com, and **Hostel Handbook of the U.S. and Canada,** c/o Jim Williams, 722 St. Nicholas Ave., New York, NY 10031. Copies of both these guides are also usually available at affiliated hostels.

Particularly in urban areas, the **Young Men's Christian Association** (YMCA) often offers housing, showers, and other facilities for young men (over age 18 only in some areas, if unaccompanied by parent or guardian), sometimes also for women and families. **Young Women's Christian Association** (YWCA) institutions offer housing for women only. Life being what it is these days, though, many of these institutions are primarily shelters for the destitute and homeless; don't steal their beds unless absolutely necessary. For more information, contact: **YMCA Guest Room Reservations,** 224 E. 47th St., New York, NY 10017, 212/308-2899 (Mon.–Fri. 9 A.M.–5 P.M. Eastern time), or contact local YMCA outposts. Another low-cost alternative in summer is on-campus housing at state colleges and universities; for current information, contact individual campuses (the student housing office) in areas you'll be visiting. For seniors, the **Elderhostel** program, www.elderhostel.org, links up the perennially curious with bargain study programs and accommodations not only in California but worldwide.

MOTELS AND HOTELS

California, the spiritual home of highway and freeway living, is also the birthplace of the motel, the word a contraction for "motor hotels." Motels have been here longer than anywhere else, so they've had plenty of time to clone themselves. As a general precaution, when checking into a truly cheap motel, ask to see the room before signing in (and paying); some places look much more appealing from the outside than from the inside. Midrange and high-priced motels and hotels are generally okay, however. In addition to the standard California sales tax, many cities and counties—particularly near major tourism destinations—add a "bed tax" of 5–18 percent (or higher). To find out the actual price you'll be paying, ask before making reservations or signing in. Unless otherwise stated, rates listed in this guide do not include state sales tax or local bed taxes.

Predictably reliable on the cheaper end of the accommodations scale, though there can be considerable variation in quality and service from place to place, are a variety of budget chains fairly common throughout California. Particularly popular is pet-friendly **Motel 6,** a perennial budget favorite. To receive a copy of the current motel directory, from the U.S. and Canada call 800/466-8356, which is also Motel 6's central reservations service, or try the website at www.motel6.com. (To make central reservations from outside the U.S., call 817/355-5502; reserve by fax from Europe and the United Kingdom at 32-2-753-5858.) You can also make reservations, by phone or fax, at individual motels, some listed elsewhere in this book. Other inexpensive to moderately priced motels are often found clustered in the general vicinity of Motel 6, these including **Comfort Inn,** 800/228-5150, www.comfortinn.com; **Days Inn,** 800/329-7466, www.daysinn.com; **Econo Lodge,** 800/553-2666, www.econolodge.com;

Rodeway Inn, 800/228-2000, www.rode-wayinn.com; and **Super 8 Motels,** 800/800-8000, www.super8.com. You can also pick up a current accommodations directory at any affiliated motel.

You'll find endless other motel and hotel chains in California, most of these more expensive—but not always, given seasonal bargain rates and special discounts offered to seniors, AAA members, and other groups. "Kids stay free," free breakfast for families, and other special promotions can also make more expensive accommodations competitive. Always reliable for quality, but with considerable variation in price and level of luxury, are **Best Western** motel and hotel affiliates, 877/237-8802 in the U.S., www.best-westerncalifornia.com. Each is independently owned and managed, and some are listed in this guide. Though the gold rush is over, the West's amenities rush is in full swing. There are many upmarket hotels and chains in California, with the **Four Seasons,** www.fshr.com, and **Ritz-Carlton,** www.ritzcarlton.com, hotel and resort chains at the top of most people's "all-time favorite" lists of places to stay if money is no object.

For members of the **American Automobile Association** (AAA), the current *Tourbook for California and Nevada* (free) includes an impressive number of rated motels, hotels, and resorts, from inexpensive to top of the line, sometimes also recommended restaurants, for nearly every community and city in both Southern and Northern California. Nationwide, AAA members can also benefit from the association's reservations service, 800/272-2155; with one call, you can also request tour books and attractions information for any destination. Other travel groups or associations offer good deals and useful services, too.

Even if you don't belong to a special group or association, you can still benefit from "bulk-buying" power, particularly in large cities—which is a special boon if you're making last-minute plans or are otherwise having little luck on your own. Various room brokers or "consolidators" buy up blocks of rooms from hoteliers at greatly discounted rates and then broker them through their own reservations services. Sometimes, brokers still have bargain-priced rooms available—at rates 40–65 percent below standard rack rates—when popular hotels are otherwise sold out. Lately, though, in an attempt to outbid brokers, hotel chains are touting prices equal to or lower than those offered by brokers. Consequently, prices shift rapidly and no one source has the corner on cheap rates. You'll have the best luck by checking all relevant sources-brokers as well as hotels' websites and reception desks.

That said, for hotel deals try **Hotel Discounts,** 800/715-7666, www.hoteldiscount.com. Particularly helpful for online reservations is the discounted **USA Hotel Guide,** 888/729-7705, www.usahotelguide.com. For other bargain hotel prices in San Francisco, Los Angeles, San Diego, and sometimes also Santa Barbara and Palm Springs, contact **Hotel Reservations Network,** 800/364-0801, www.180096hotel.com, and **Room Exchange,** 800/846-7000, www.hotel-rooms.com. If you're willing to bid for a hotel bargain, try **Revelex,** www.revelex.com. Other popular websites for hotel booking include **hotels.com, quikbook.com,** and **1800USAHotels.com.** Two general-purpose broker sites, which handle accommodations as well as transportation and other travel-related bookings, are **expedia.com** and **travelocity.com.** You can download hotel coupons at **www.roomsaver.com.**

BED-AND-BREAKFASTS

Another hot trend, particularly in Northern California, is the bed-and-breakfast phenomenon. Many bed-and-breakfast guides and listings are available in bookstores, and some recommended B&Bs are listed in this book. Unlike the European tradition, with bed-and-breakfasts a low-cost yet comfortable lodging alternative, in California these inns are actually a burgeoning small-business phenomenon—usually quite pricey, in the $100–150-plus range (occasionally less expensive), often more of a "special weekend getaway" for exhausted city people than a mainstream accommodations option. In some areas, though, where motel and hotel rooms are on the high end, bed-and-breakfasts can be quite competitive.

For more information on what's available in all parts of California, including private home stays, contact **California Association of Bed and Breakfast Inns,** 2715 Porter St., Soquel, CA 95073, 831/462-9191, fax 831/462-0402, www.cabbi.com. This group also maintains a search engine at www.innaccess.com that lists all bed-and-breakfasts in the state. **International Bed and Breakfast Pages,** P.O. Box 50594, Denton, TX 76206, www.ibbp.com, claims to include every bed-and-breakfast in the world. It can help with information gathering but doesn't make reservations.

FOOD

One of the best things about traveling in California is the food: They don't call the Golden State the land of fruits and nuts for nothing. In agricultural and rural areas, local "farm trails" or winery guides are often available—ask at local chambers of commerce and visitor centers—and following the seasonal produce trails offers visitors the unique pleasure of gathering (sometimes picking their own) fresh fruits, nuts, and vegetables direct from the growers.

This fresher, direct-to-you produce phenomenon is also quite common in most urban areas, where regular farmers markets are *the* place to go for fresh, organic, often exotic local produce and farm products. Many of the most popular California farmers markets are listed elsewhere in this book—but ask around wherever you are, since new ones pop up constantly. For a reasonably comprehensive current listing of California Certified Farmers Markets (meaning certified as locally grown), contact: **California Federation of Certified Farmers Markets,** P.O. Box 1813, Davis, CA 95617, 707/756-1695, www.cafarmersmarkets.com.

Threaded with freeways and accessible on-ramp, off-ramp commercial strips, particularly in urban areas, California has more than its fair share of fast-food eateries and all-night quik-stop outlets. (Since they're so easy to find, few are listed in this guide.) Most cities and communities also have locally popular cafés and fairly inexpensive restaurants worth seeking out; many are listed here, but also ask around. Genuinely inexpensive eateries often refuse to take credit cards, so always bring some cash along just in case.

The northstate is also famous for its "California cuisine," which once typically meant consuming tastebud-tantalizing, very expensive food in very small portions—almost a cliché—while oohing and aahing over the presentation throughout the meal. But the fiscally frugal early 1990s restrained most of California's excesses, and even the best restaurants offer less-pretentious menus and slimmed-down prices. The region's culinary creativity is quite real, and worth pursuing (sans pretense) in many areas. Talented chefs, who have migrated throughout the region from Los Angeles and San Francisco as well as from France and Italy, usually prefer locally grown produce, dairy products, meats, and herbs and spices as basic ingredients. To really "do" the cuisine scene, wash it all down with some fine California wine.

Know Coastal California

Information and Services

Visitors can receive free California travel-planning information from the **California Travel & Tourism Commission** website, www.visitcalifornia.com, and by calling 800/462-2543 (800/GO-CALIF). Most California tourism publications, in addition to regional and local publications, are also available at the various roadside volunteer-staffed **California Welcome Centers,** a burgeoning trend. The first official welcome center was unveiled in 1995 in Kingsburg, in the San Joaquin Valley, and the next four—in Rohnert Park, just south of Santa Rosa; in Anderson, just south of Redding; in Oakhurst in the gold country, on the way to Yosemite National Park; and at Pier 39 on San Francisco's Fisherman's Wharf—were also in Northern California. There are others in Northern California, too, including the fairly new one in Arcata, and several in Southern California. Eventually the network will include virtually all areas of California; watch for signs announcing new welcome centers along major highways and freeways.

Most major cities and visitor destinations in California also have very good visitor information bureaus and visitor centers, listed elsewhere in this book. Many offer accommodations reservations and other services; some offer information and maps in foreign languages. Chambers of commerce can be useful, too. In less populated areas, chambers of commerce are something of a hit-or-miss proposition, since office hours may be minimal; the best bet is calling ahead for information. Asking locals—people at gas stations, cafés, grocery stores, and official government outposts—is often the best way to get information about where to go, why, when, and how. Slick city magazines, good daily newspapers, and California-style weekly news and entertainment tabloids are other good sources of information.

ACCESS FOR THE DISABLED

Well worth checking out is **Access Northern California,** 1427 Grant St., Berkeley, CA 94703, 510/524-2026, which publishes its own guide-book, **Access San Francisco,** and also offers a very useful website: www.accessnca.com. Similarly helpful in the southstate is **Accessible San Diego,** P.O. Box 124526, San Diego, CA 92112-4526, 858/279 0704, www.accessandiego.org, which publishes a helpful San Diego area guide-book. Useful in a more general sense is **Access-Able Travel Source,** P.O. Box 1796, Wheat Ridge, CO 80034, 303/232-2979, fax 303/239-8486, www.access-able.com, which also manages the Travelin' Talk Network at www.travelintalk.net, an international network of disabled people available "to help travelers in any way they can." Membership is only $19.95, a bargain by any standard, since by joining up you suddenly have a vast network of allies in otherwise strange places who are all too happy to tell you what's what. Also particularly useful is the **Society for Accessible Travel & Hospitality** (SATH), P.O. Box 382, Owatonna, MN 55060, 507/451-5005, www.sath.org, dedicated to making barrier-free travel a reality. Primarily an educational group, SATH provides useful travel tips and consumer travel information on its website and in *Open World* magazine.

For current information about the **Americans with Disabilities Act,** which spells out U.S. laws regarding accessibility at public and other buildings, see www.usdoj.gov/crt/ada. Information specific to accommodations and transportation for the disabled is also available. Before plotting transportation logistics, get a free copy of *Access Amtrak,* a booklet published by Amtrak that lists its accessible services; call 800/872-7245 for details. Also helpful is *The Disabled Driver's Mobility Guide* put out by the American Automobile Association (AAA) and available by calling 800/637-2122.

Flying Wheels Travel, 800/535-6790, www.flyingwheelstravel.com, is a travel agency that specializes in independent vacations for the disabled. **1-888-Inn-Seek,** an online search engine, lists wheelchair-accessible bed-and-breakfasts. Access it either via phone, 888/466-7355, or online at www.1-888-Inn-Seek.com.

Mobility International USA, P.O. Box 10767, Eugene, OR 97440, and TDD 541/343-1284, fax 541/343-6812, www.miusa.org, provides two-way international leadership exchanges. Disabled people who want to go to Europe to study theater, for example, or British citizens who want to come to California for Elderhostel programs—anything beyond traditional leisure travel—should call here first. The individual annual membership fee is $25 for individuals, $35 for organizations.

SENIOR CITIZENS

Senior adults can benefit from a great many bargains and discounts. A good source of information is the *Travel Tips for Older Americans* pamphlet published by the U.S. Government Printing Office, 202/275-3648, www.gpo.gov, available for $1.25. (Order it online at the website: www.pueblo.gsa.gov/travel.) The federal government's Golden Age Passport offers free admission to national parks and monuments and half-price discounts for federal campsites and other recreational services; state parks also offer senior discounts. Discounts are also frequently offered to seniors at major tourist attractions and sights as well as for many arts, cultural, and entertainment destinations and events in Southern California. Another benefit of experience is eligibility for the international **Elderhostel** program, 11 Avenue de Lafayette, Boston, MA 02111, 877/426-8056 or 617/426-7788, www.elderhostel.org, which offers a variety of fairly reasonable one-week residential programs in California.

For information on travel discounts, trip planning, tours, and other membership benefits of the U.S.'s largest senior citizen organization, contact the **American Association of Retired Persons** (AARP), 601 E St. NW, Washington, DC 20049, 800/424-3410, fax 501/451-1685, www.aarp.org. Despite the name, anyone age 50 and older—retired or not—is eligible for membership. Other membership-benefit programs for seniors include **Senior Citizens America,** 8403 Colesville Rd., Ste. 1200, Silver Springs, MD 20910, 301/578-8800, fax 301/578-8999.

MAPS

The best all-around maps for general California travel, either in the city or out in the countryside, are those produced by the **American Automobile Association,** which is regionally organized as the California State Automobile Association (CSAA) in Northern and Central California, and as the Automobile Club of Southern California in the southstate. The AAA maps are available at any local AAA office, and the price is right (free, but for members only). In addition to its California state map and Southern California map, AAA provides urban maps for most major cities, plus regional maps with at least some backcountry routes marked (these latter maps don't necessarily show the entire picture, however; when in doubt about unusual routes, ask locally before setting out). For more information about AAA membership and services in Northern California, contact the **California State Automobile Association;** the main office address is 150 Van Ness Ave., P.O. Box 429186, San Francisco, CA 94102, 415/565-2012 or 415/565-2468, www.csaa.org, but there are also regional offices throughout the northstate. Members can also order maps, tour books, and other services online. If you'll also be visiting Southern California, the AAA affiliate there is the **Automobile Club of Southern California,** 2601 S. Figueroa St., Los Angeles, CA 90007, 213/741-3686, www.aaa-calif.com. For AAA membership information, from anywhere in the U.S. call 800/222-4357, or try www.aaa.com.

The best maps money can buy, excellent for general and very detailed travel in California, are the **Thomas Bros. Maps,** typically referred to as "Thomas guides." For the big picture, particularly useful is the *California Road Atlas & Driver's Guide,* but various other, very detailed spiral-bound book-style maps in the Thomas guide street atlas series—San Francisco, Monterey County, Los Angeles, Orange County, San Diego—are the standard block-by-block references, continually updated since 1915. Thomas guides are available at any decent travel-oriented bookstore, or contact the company directly. In

Know Coastal California

Southern California, you'll find a major Thomas Bros. Maps store at 521 W. Sixth St., Los Angeles, CA 90017, 888/277-6277 or 213/627-4018; the map factory and other store is in Orange County, at 17731 Cowan in Irvine, 800/899-6277 or 949/863-1984, fax 949/852-9189. In Northern California, stop by Thomas Bros. Maps, 595 Market St., San Francisco, CA 94105, 800/969-3072 or 415/543-8020. Or order any map by calling, from anywhere in California, 800/899-6277—or by trying, from anywhere in the world, www.thomas.com.

When it comes to backcountry travel—where maps quickly become either your best friend or archenemy—the going isn't nearly as easy. U.S. Geological Survey quadrangle maps in most cases are reliable for showing the contours of the terrain, but U.S. Forest Service and wilderness maps—supposedly the maps of record for finding one's way through the woods and the wilds— are often woefully out of date, with new and old logging roads (as well as disappearing or changed trail routes) confusing the situation considerably. In California, losing oneself in the wilderness is a very real, literal possibility. In addition to topo maps (carry a compass to orient yourself by landforms if all else fails) and official U.S. maps, backcountry travelers would be wise to invest in privately published guidebooks and current route or trail guides for wilderness areas; the Sierra Club and Wilderness Press publish both. Before setting out, compare all available maps and other information to spot any possible route discrepancies, then ask national forest or parks personnel for clarification. If you're lucky, you'll find someone who knows what's going on where you want to go.

Aside from well-stocked outdoor stores, the primary California source for quad maps is: **U.S. Geological Survey,** 345 Middlefield Rd., Menlo Park, CA 94025, 650/853-8300 (ask for the mapping division); an index and catalog of published California maps is available upon request. Or try the USGS website: info.er.usgs .gov, or call 888/275-8747. Also contact the U.S. Forest Service and U.S. National Park Service. The best bet for wilderness maps and guides is **Wilderness Press,** 1200 Fifth St., Berkeley, CA 94710, 510/558-1666 or 800/443-7227 (for orders), www.wildernesspress .com. Most Wilderness Press titles are available in California bookstores.

Not necessarily practical for travelers are the beautiful yet utilitarian maps produced by **Raven Maps & Images,** 34 N. Central, P.O. Box 850, Medford, OR 97501, 541/773-1436, or (for credit-card orders) 800/237-0798, www.raven-maps.com. These beauties are big, and—unless you buy one for the wall and one for the road— you'll never want to fold them. Based on U.S. Geological Survey maps, these shaded relief maps are "computer-enhanced" for a three-dimensional topographical feel and incredible clarity— perfect for planning outdoor adventures. Raven's *California* map measures 42 by 64 inches, and *Yosemite and the Central Sierra* is 34 by 37 inches. Wonderful for any California-lover's wall is the three-dimensional, five-color *California, Nevada, and the Pacific Ocean Floor* digital landform map, which offers three aerial oblique views: now, five million years ago, and five million years in the future. Fabulous. All Raven maps are printed in fade-resistant inks on fine quality 70-pound paper and are also available in vinyl laminated versions suitable for framing.

CONDUCT AND CUSTOMS

Smoking is a major social sin in California, against the law in public buildings and on public transport, with regulations particularly stringent in urban areas. Even smoking outdoors can be problematic. Smoking has been banned outright in California restaurants and bars; smoking is not allowed on public airplane flights, though nervous fliers can usually smoke somewhere outside airline terminals. Many bed-and-breakfasts in California are either entirely nonsmoking or restrict smoking to decks, porches, or dens; if this is a concern, inquire by calling ahead. Hotels and motels, most commonly in major urban areas or popular tourist destinations, increasingly offer nonsmoking rooms (or entire floors). Ask in advance.

DIGITAL CONSERVATION

Map fans will be over the moon once they tap into the online **California Digital Conservation Atlas,** early fruit of the California Resources Agency and the interagency California Legacy Project. This comprehensive atlas maps California's natural resources data—everything from land trusts and toxic sites to rare species, roads and highways, rivers and lakes, floodplains, and urban growth projections—and is available free to anyone with Internet Explorer and a reasonably powerful computer.

Most significantly, website visitors can even overlay various aspects of land use and resource data—to see where urban growth may affect productive farmland or rare species, say. To check it out, see http://legacy.ca.gov.

The legal age for buying and drinking alcohol in California is 21. Though Californians tend to (as they say) "party hearty," public drunkenness is not well tolerated. Drunken driving—which means operating an automobile (even a bicycle, technically) while under the influence—is definitely against the law. California is increasingly no-nonsense about the use of illegal drugs, too, from marijuana to cocaine, crack, and heroin. Doing time in local jails or state prisons is not the best way to do California.

English is the official language in California, and even English-speaking visitors from other countries have little trouble understanding California's "dialect" once they acclimate to the accents and slang expressions. (Californians tend to be very creative in their language.) When unsure what someone means by some peculiar phrase, ask for a translation into standard English. Particularly in urban areas, many languages are commonly spoken, and—even in English—the accents are many. You can usually obtain at least some foreign-language brochures, maps, and other information from city visitor centers and popular tourist destinations. (If this is a major concern, inquire in advance.)

Californians are generally casual, in dress as well as etiquette. If any standard applies in most situations, it's common courtesy—still in style, generally speaking, even in California. Though "anything goes" just about anywhere, elegant restaurants usually require appropriately dressy attire for women, jacket and tie for men. (Shirts and shoes—pants or skirt too, usually—are required in any California restaurant.)

By law, public buildings in California are wheelchair-accessible, or at least partially so. The same is true of most major hotels and tourist attractions, which may offer both rooms and restrooms with complete wheelchair accessibility; some also have wheelchairs, walkers, and other mobility aids available for temporary use. Even national and state parks, increasingly, are attempting to make some sights and campgrounds more accessible for those with physical disabilities; to make special arrangements, inquire in advance. But private buildings, from restaurants to bed-and-breakfasts, may not be so accommodating. Those with special needs should definitely ask specific questions in advance.

TIPPING

For services rendered in the service trade, a tip is usually expected. Some say the word is derived from the Latin *stips,* for stipend or gift. Some say it's an 18th-century English acronym for "to ensure promptness," though "to ensure personal service" seems more to the point in these times. In expensive restaurants or for large groups, an automatic tip or gratuity may be included in the bill—an accepted practice in many countries but a source of irritation for many U.S. diners, who would prefer to personally evaluate the quality of service received. Otherwise, 15–20 percent of the before-tax total tab is the standard gratuity, and 10 percent the minimal acknowledgment, for those in the service trade—waitresses and waiters, barbers, hairdressers, and taxi drivers. In fine-dining circumstances, wine stewards should be acknowledged personally, at the rate of $2–5 per bottle, and the maitre d' as well, with $5 or $10. In very casual buffet-style joints, leave $1 each for the people who clear the dishes and pour your coffee after the meal. In bars, leave $1 per drink, or 15 percent of the bill if you run a tab. At airports, tip skycaps $1 per bag (more if they transport your baggage any distance); tip more generously for extra assistance, such as helping wheelchair passengers or mothers with infants and small children to their gates.

At hotels, a desk clerk or concierge does not require a tip unless that person fulfills a specific request, such as snagging tickets for a sold-out concert or theater performance, in which case generosity is certainly appropriate. For baggage handlers curbside, $1 tip is adequate; a tip of at least $1 per bag is appropriate for bell staff transporting luggage from the lobby to your room or from your room to the lobby. For valet parking, tip the attendant $2–3. Tip the hotel doorman if he helps with baggage or hails a cab for you. And tip swimming pool or health club personnel as appropriate for extra personal service. Unless one stays in a hotel or motel for several days, the standard practice is not to tip the housekeeper, though you can if you wish; some guests leave $1–2 each morning for the housekeeper and $1 each evening for turn-down service.

BASIC SERVICES

Except for some very lonely areas, even backwater areas of California aren't particularly primitive. Gasoline, at least basic groceries, laundries of some sort, even video and DVD rentals are available just about anywhere. Outback areas are not likely to have parts for exotic sports cars, however, or 24-hour pharmacies, hospitals, and garages, or natural foods stores or full-service supermarkets, so you should take care of any special needs or problems before leaving the cities. It's often (though not always) cheaper to stock up on most supplies, including outdoor equipment and groceries, in urban areas.

MEDICAL CARE AND GENERAL HEALTH

In most places in California, call 911 in any emergency; in medical emergencies, life support personnel and ambulances will be dispatched. To make sure health care services will be readily provided,

health insurance coverage is almost mandatory; carry proof of coverage while traveling in California. In urban areas and in many rural areas, 24-hour walk-in health care services are readily available, though hospital emergency rooms are the place to go in case of life-threatening circumstances.

To avoid most health and medical problems, use common sense. Eat sensibly, avoid unsafe drinking water, bring along any necessary prescription pills—and pack an extra pair of glasses or contacts, just in case. Sunglasses, especially for those unaccustomed to sunshine, as well as sunscreen and a broad-brimmed hat can help prevent sunburn, sunstroke, and heat prostration. Drink plenty of liquids, too, especially when exercising and/or in hot weather.

No vaccinations are usually necessary for traveling in California, though here as elsewhere very young children and seniors should obtain vaccinations against annually variable forms of the flu virus; exposure, especially in crowded urban areas and during the winter disease season, is a likelihood.

As in other areas of the United States and the world, the AIDS (Acquired Immune Deficiency Syndrome) virus and other sexually transmitted diseases are a concern. In mythic "anything goes" California, avoiding promiscuous or unprotected sex is the best way to avoid the danger of contracting the AIDS virus and venereal disease—though AIDS is also transmitted via shared drug needles and contaminated blood transfusions. (All medical blood supplies in California are screened for evidence of the virus.) Sexually speaking, "safe sex" is the preventive key phrase, under any circumstances beyond the strictly monogamous. This means always using condoms in sexual intercourse; oral sex only with some sort of barrier precaution; and no sharing sex toys.

CITY SAFETY

Though California's wilderness once posed a major threat to human survival, in most respects the backcountry is safer than the urban jungle of modern cities. Tourism officials don't talk about it much, but crimes against persons and property are a reality in California (though the state's overall crime rate has dropped sharply in recent years). To avoid harm, bring along your street-smarts. The best overall personal crime prevention includes carrying only small amounts of cash (inconspicuously, in a money belt or against-the-body money pouch); labeling (and locking) all luggage; keeping valuables under lock and key (and, in automobiles, out of sight); being aware of people and events, and knowing where you are, at all times; and avoiding dangerous, lonely, and unlighted areas after daylight, particularly late at night and when traveling alone. If you're not sure what neighborhoods are considered dangerous or unsafe, ask locals or hotel or motel personnel—or at the police station, if necessary.

Women traveling alone—not generally advisable, because of the unfortunate fact of misogyny in the modern world—need to take special care to avoid harm. For any independent traveler, self-defense classes (and/or a training course for carrying and using Mace) might be a worthwhile investment, if only to increase one's sense of personal power in case of a confrontation with criminals. Being assertive and confident, and acting as if you know where you are going (even when you don't), are also among the best deterrents to predators. Carry enough money for a phone call—or bus or taxi ride—and a whistle. When in doubt, don't hesitate to use it, and to yell and scream for help.

OUTDOOR SAFETY

The most basic rule is, know what you're doing and where you're going. Next most basic: whatever you do—from swimming or surfing to hiking and backpacking—don't do it alone. For any outdoor activity, be prepared. Check with local park or national forest service officials on weather, trail, and general conditions before setting out. Correct, properly functioning equipment is as important in backpacking as it is in hang gliding, mountain climbing, mountain biking, and sailing. (When in doubt, check it out.)

Among the basics to bring along for almost any outdoor activity: a hat, sunscreen, and lip balm (to protect against the sun in summer, against heat loss, reflective sun, and the elements in winter); a whistle, compass, and mylar "space blanket" in case you become lost or stranded; insect repellent; a butane lighter or waterproof matches; a multipurpose Swiss Army-type knife; nylon rope; a flashlight; and a basic first-aid kit (including bandages, ointments and salves, antiseptics, pain relievers such as aspirin, and any necessary prescription medicines). Hikers, backpackers, and other outdoor adventurers should bring plenty of water—or water purification tablets or pump-style water purifiers for long trips—at least minimal fishing gear, good hiking shoes or boots, extra socks and shoelaces, "layerable" clothing adequate for all temperatures, and a waterproof poncho or large plastic garbage bag. (Even if thunderstorms are unlikely, any sort of packable and wearable plastic bag can keep you dry until you reach shelter.) The necessity for other outdoor equipment, from campstoves to sleeping bags and tents, depends on where you'll be going and what you'll be doing.

Poison Oak

Poison oak (actually a shrublike sumac) is a perennial trailside hazard, especially in lowland foothill areas and mixed forests; it exudes oily chemicals that cause a strong allergic reaction in many people, even with only brief contact. (Always be careful what you're burning around the campfire, too; smoke from poison oak, when inhaled, can inflame the lungs and create a life-threatening situation in no time flat.) The best way to avoid the painful, itchy, often long-lasting rashes associated with poison oak is to avoid contact with the plant—in all seasons—and to immediately wash one's skin or clothes if you even suspect a brush with it. (Its leaves a bright, glossy green in spring and summer, red or yellow in fall, poison oak can be a problem even in winter—when this mean-spirited deciduous shrub loses its leaves.) Learn to identify it during any time of year.

Once afflicted with poison oak, never scratch, because the oozing sores just spread the rash.

Know Coastal California

Very good new products on the market include Tecnu's **Poison Oak-n-Ivy Armor** "pre-exposure lotion," produced by Tec Laboratories, Inc., of Albany, Oregon, 800/482-4464 (800/ITCHING). Apply it before potential exposure to protect yourself. Another excellent product, quite helpful if you do tangle with poison oak, is Tecnu's **Poison Oak-n-Ivy Cleanser,** the idea being to get the toxic oils off your skin as soon as possible, within hours of initial exposure or just after the rash appears. The cleanser—which smells suspiciously like kerosene—also helps eliminate the itching, remarkably well. (But do *not* apply after oozing begins.) Various drying, cortisone-based lotions, oatmeal baths, and other treatments can help control discomfort if the rash progresses to the oozing stage, but the rash itself goes away only in its own good time.

Lyme Disease and Ticks

Even if you favor shorts for summer hiking, you had better plan on long pants, long-sleeved shirts, even insect repellent. The weather may be mild, but there's an increasing risk—particularly in California coastal and foothill areas, as in other states—that you'll contract Lyme disease, transmitted by ticks that thrive in moist lowland climates.

A new ailment on the West Coast, Lyme disease is named after the place of its 1975 discovery in Old Lyme, Connecticut. Already the most common vector-transmitted disease in the nation, Lyme is caused by spirochetes transmitted through blood, urine, and other body fluids. Research indicates it has often been wrongly diagnosed; sufferers were thought to have afflictions such as rheumatoid arthritis. Temporary paralysis, arthritic

pains in the hands or arm and leg joints, swollen hands, fever, fatigue, nausea, headaches, swollen glands, and heart palpitations are among the typical symptoms. Sometimes an unusually circular red rash appears first, between three and 30 days after the tick bite. Untreated, Lyme disease can mean a lifetime of suffering, even danger to unborn children. Treatment, once Lyme disease is discovered through blood tests, is simple and 100 percent effective if recognized early: tetracycline and other drugs halt the arthritic degeneration and most symptoms. Long-delayed treatment, even with extremely high doses of antibiotics, is only about 50 percent effective.

Outdoor prudence, coupled with an awareness of possible Lyme symptoms even months later, are the watchwords when it comes to Lyme disease. Take precautions against tick bite: the sooner ticks are found and removed, the better your chances of avoiding the disease. Tuck your pants into your boots, wear long-sleeved shirts, and use insect repellent around all clothing openings as well as on your neck and all exposed skin. Run a full-body "tick check" daily, especially checking hidden areas such as the hair and scalp. Consider leaving dogs at home if heading for Lyme country; ticks they pick up can spread the disease through your human family.

Use gloves and tweezers to remove ticks from yourself or your animals—never crush the critters with your fingers!—and wash your hands and the bitten area afterward. Better yet, smother imbedded ticks with petroleum jelly first; deprived of oxygen, they start to pull out of the skin in about a half hour, making it easy to pluck them off without tearing them in two and leaving the head imbedded.

Transportation

DRIVING

This being California, almost everyone gets around by car. Urban freeway driving in California, because of congestion and Californians' no-nonsense get-on-with-it driving styles, can inspire panic even in nonlocal native drivers. It doesn't help that California's aging highways are ranked worst in the nation in terms of condition and upkeep. If this is a problem, plan your trip to skirt the worst congestion—by taking back roads and older highways, if possible, or by trying neighborhood routes—but only if you know something about the neighborhoods. Alternatively, plan to arrive in San Francisco, other Bay Area destinations, Sacramento, and anywhere in Southern California well after the day's peak freeway commute traffic, usually any time after 7 or 8 P.M.

A good investment for anyone traveling for any length of time in California is a membership in the American Automobile Association (see above) since—among many other benefits, including excellent maps and trip-planning assistance—a AAA card entitles the bearer to no-cost emergency roadside service, including five gallons of free gas and at least limited towing, if necessary.

Gasoline in California is typically more expensive than elsewhere in the U.S., up to 40 cents per gallon more, only in part because of California's new cleaner-burning "reformulated" fuels, the world's cleanest gasoline. The effect of using the new gasoline is roughly equivalent to the effect of taking 3.5 million cars off the road on any given day—or sucking about three million pounds of toxins and particulate matter out of the air. The clean fuels are designed to reduce vehicle emissions and improve air quality, which seems to be working, but a new concern is that clean fuel residues (particularly from the additive MTBE) are polluting California's water. Though MTBE will soon be banned, the Golden State's pollution solutions are, clearly, ideas that still need work.

To check on current **California road conditions** before setting out—always a good idea in a state with so much ongoing road construction and such variable regional weather—call **Caltrans** (California Department of Transportation) from anywhere in California at 800/427-7623, and from outside California at 916/445-7623. The road-condition phone numbers are accessible from touch-tone and pay phones as well as cellular phones. Or check road conditions for your entire trip via real-time travel maps available on the Caltrans website: www.dot.ca.gov/traffic.

Though every municipality has its own peculiar laws about everything from parking to skateboarding or roller skating on sidewalks, there are basic rules everyone is expected to know and follow—especially drivers. Get a complete set of regulations from the state motor vehicles department, which has an office in all major cities and many medium-sized ones. Or contact **California Department of Motor Vehicles**, 2415 First Ave., P.O. Box 942869, Sacramento, CA 94269, www.dmv.ca.gov. Foreign visitors planning to drive should obtain an **International Driver's License** before leaving home (they're not available here); licensed U.S. drivers from other states can legally drive in California for 30 consecutive days without having to obtain a California driver's license. Disabled travelers heading for California can get special handicapped-space parking permits, good for 90 days, by requesting applications in advance from the DMV and having them signed by their doctors (there is an application fee). If you'll be renting a car, ask the rental car agency to forward a form to you when you make reservations.

Among driving rules, the most basic is observing the posted speed limit. Though many California drivers ignore any and all speed limits, it's at their own peril should the California Highway Patrol be anywhere in the vicinity. The statewide speed limit for open highway driving varies, typically posted as somewhere between 55 and 70 miles per hour; freeway speeds can vary at different points along the same route. Speed limits for cities and residential neighborhoods are substantially slower. Another avoidable traffic ticket is *not* indulging in what is colloquially known as the "California stop," slowing down and then rolling right through intersections without first making a complete stop.

Once arrived at your destination, pay attention to parking notices, tow-away warnings, and curb color: red means no parking under any circumstances; yellow means limited stops only (usually for freight delivery); green means very limited parking; and blue means parking for the disabled only. In hilly areas of California—and most necessarily in San Francisco—always turn your front wheels into the curb (to keep your car from becoming a rollaway runaway) and set the emergency brake.

Driving while under the influence of alcohol or drugs is a very serious offense in California—aside from being a danger to one's own health and safety, not to mention those of innocent fellow drivers and pedestrians. Don't drink (or do drugs) and drive.

Rental Cars

Renting a car—or a recreational vehicle—in California usually won't come cheap. Rates have been accelerating, so to speak, in recent years, especially when consumers put the kibosh on mileage caps. Turns out people really liked the idea of unlimited "free" mileage. So now the average car rental price is just above $60 a day (lower for subcompacts, higher for roadhogs). Still, bargains are sometimes available through small local agencies, though rates can vary, from city to city and company to company, by as much as 80 percent. It definitely pays to comparison shop for car rentals. Among national agencies, National and Alamo often offer the lowest prices. But in many cases, with weekly rentals and various group-association (AAA, AARP, etc.) and credit-card discounts ranging from 10–40 percent, you'll usually do just as well with other major rental car agencies. According to the *Consumer Reports* June 1996 national reader quality survey, **Hertz, Avis,** and **National** were rated

highest by customers for clean cars, quick and courteous service, and speedy checkout.

Beware the increasingly intense pressure, once you arrive to pick up your rental car, to persuade you to buy additional insurance coverage. In some companies, rental car agents receive a commission for every insurance policy they sell, needed or not, which is why the person on the other side of the counter is so motivated (sometimes pushy and downright intimidating). Feel free to complain to management if you dislike such treatment—and to take your business elsewhere. This highly touted insurance coverage is coverage you probably don't need, from collision damage waivers—now outlawed in some states, but not in California—to liability insurance, which you probably don't need unless you have no car insurance at all (in which case it's illegal to drive in California). Some people do carry additional rental-car collision or liability insurance on their personal insurance policies—talk to your agent about this—but even that is already covered, at least domestically, if you pay for your rental car with a gold or platinum MasterCard or Visa. The same is true for American Express for domestic travelers, though American Express recently rescinded such coverage on overseas car rentals; it's possible that Visa and MasterCard will soon follow suit. (Check your personal insurance and credit-card coverage before dealing with the rental car agencies.) And bring personal proof of car insurance, though you'll rarely be asked for it. In short—buyer beware.

For current information on options and prices for rental cars in Northern California, Southern California, and elsewhere in the U.S., contact **Alamo,** 800/462-5266, www.alamo.com.; **Avis,** 800/831-2847, www.avis.com; **Budget,** worldwide 800/527-0700, www.budget.com; **Dollar,** 800/800-3665, www.dollar.com; **Enterprise,** 800/736-8222, www.enterprise.com; **Hertz,** worldwide 800/654-3131, www.hertz.com; **National,** 800/227-7368, www.nationalcar.com; and **Thrifty,** 800/847-4389, www.thrifty.com. You can also make rental car arrangements online otherwise, through virtual travel agencies and reservations systems such as **Travelocity,** www.travelocity.com, and **The Trip,** www.thetrip.com.

Though some rental agencies also handle recreational vehicle (RV) rentals, travelers may be able to get better deals by renting directly from local RV dealers. For suggestions, contact area visitor bureaus—and consult the local telephone book.

AIR TRAVEL

Following the September 11, 2001, terrorist attacks, airport security measures are now strictly enforced. For travelers, this means extra time for air travel. To reduce the chances of delays or problems, keep in mind the following. A couple of days before your flight, contact your travel agent or the airline for an update on departure time, ID requirements, and luggage rules. Don't bring wrapped gifts. Pack any instruments capable of puncturing or cutting (such as nail files, knives, scissors, box cutters, etc.) in your checked luggage. Arrive two hours early to ensure you'll have time to check your luggage and get through security inspections before your flight.

Airfares change and bargains come and go so quickly in competitive California that the best way to keep abreast of the situation is through a travel agent. Or via the Internet, where major U.S. airlines regularly offer great deals—discounts of up to 90 percent (typically not *quite* that good). Popular home pages include **American Airlines,** www.aa.com; **Continental,** www.flycontinental.com; **Delta,** www.delta-air.com; **Northwest,** www.nwa.com; **TWA,** www.twa.com; **United,** www.ual.com; and **US Airways,** www.usairways.com. Also look up the people's favorite, **Southwest,** at www.iflyswa.com. Have your credit card handy. To find additional websites, know your computer—or call any airline's "800" number and ask.

Online travel brokers offer cheap fares as well. A recent Consumer Reports study concluded that **Expedia,** www.expedia.com, **Travelocity,** www.travelocity.com, and airlines-owned **Orbitz,** www.orbitz.com, offer the best ratio of low fares to viable itineraries (such as single-carrier flights and fewer connecting flights and lengthy lay-

overs). However, the smaller online brokers often advertise the lowest-though generally nonrefundable-fares. Among these, **Cheap Tickets,** www.cheaptickets.com, **One Travel,** www.onetravel.com, and **TravelNow,** www.travelnow.com are reputable. **Travelzoo,** www.travelzoo.com, searches the 20 major airline websites for the deep-discounted fares and posts them, so you don't have to spend hours looking for the best deals. **Hotwire,** www.hotwire.com, offers airline tickets at a 40 percent discount (though with limited consumer routing control), with hotel rooms and rental car discounts added to the mix in late 2000. For possibly great deals on last-minute departures, try **Savvio,** www.savvio.com.

Another good information source for domestic and international flight fares: the travel advertisements in the weekend travel sections of major urban newspapers. Super Saver fares (booked well in advance) can save fliers up to 30–70 percent and more. Peak travel times in and out of California being the summer and the midwinter holiday season, book flights well in advance for June–August and December travel. The best bargains in airfares are usually available from January to early May.

Bargain airfares are often available for international travelers, especially in spring and autumn. Charter flights are also good bargains, the only disadvantage usually being inflexible departure and return-flight dates. Most flights from Europe to the U.S. arrive in New York; from there, other transcontinental travel options are available. Reduced-fare flights on major airlines from Europe abound.

Keep in mind, too, if you're flying, that airlines are getting increasingly strict about how much baggage you're allowed to bring with you. They mean business with those prominent "sizer boxes" now on display in every airport. Only two pieces of carry-on luggage are allowed on most carriers—some now allow only one—and each must fit in the box. Most airlines allow three pieces of luggage total per passenger. (Fortunately for parents, diaper bags, fold-up strollers, and—at least sometimes—infant carrier seats don't count.) So if you are philosophically opposed to the concept of traveling light, bring two massive suitcases—and check them through—in addition to your carry-on. Some airlines, including American, charge extra for more than two checked bags per person. Contact each airline directly for current baggage guidelines.

TRAINS

An unusually enjoyable way to travel the length of the West Coast to California, or to arrive here after a trip west over the Sierra Nevada or across the great desert, is by train. Within Northern California, travel along the coast on Amtrak's immensely popular and recently spiffed up **Coast Starlight,** which now features more comfortable tilt-back seats, a parlor car with library and games, and California-style fare in its dining cars. (From the south, the two-way route continues north to Oakland, across the bay from San Francisco, and eventually continues all the way to Seattle.) If you'll eventually arrive in Southern California, from grand Union Station near downtown L.A. you can head east to New Orleans on the **Sunset Limited,** to San Antonio on the **Texas Eagle,** and to Chicago on the **Desert Wind** and the **Southwest Chief.** Regional trains operated by Amtrak within California include the **Pacific Surfliner** (formerly the San Diegans) along the state's central and south coasts, and the **San Joaquins** connecting Sacramento with the greater San Francisco Bay Area.

For **Amtrak** train travel routes (including some jogs between cities in California by Amtrak bus), current price information, and reservations, contact a travel agent or call Amtrak at 800/872-7245 (USA RAIL), www.amtrak.com or amtrakwest.com. For the hearing impaired, Amtrak's TTY number is 800/523-6590 or 91.

BUSES

Most destinations in California are reachable by bus, either by major carrier, by "alternative" carrier, or in various combinations of long-distance and local bus lines. And if you can't get *exactly* where you want to go by bus, you can usually get close.

EURAIL-STYLE TRAIN PASSES

Much of the California coastline is easily accessible by train. Amtrak now sells passes for unlimited train travel in the Golden State. For $159 ($80 for children 2–15), the **California Rail Pass** allows holders to board, on any seven days during a 21-day period, *Capitol* trains between Sacramento and the Bay Area; other local trains such as the *Pacific Surfliner* between San Diego and San Luis Obispo; and the California portions of the *Coast Starlight* route that runs between Los Angeles and Seattle. The price includes any available Thruway bus routes to connecting trains.

Similar five-in-seven-days passes are available for Southern California as far north as San Luis Obispo, and for Northern California as far south as Santa Barbara. These cost $99 for adults, $50 for children. All three passes are available from travel agents or Amtrak, 800/872-7245. For more information, visit either of the company's two websites: www.amtrak.com or www.amtrakwest.com.

Greyhound is the universal bus service. Obtain a current U.S. route map by mail (see below), but check with local Greyhound offices for more detailed local route information and for information about "casino service" to Reno and other local specials. Greyhound offers discounts for senior adults and disabled travelers, and children under age 12 ride free when accompanied by a fare-paying adult (one child per adult, half fare for additional children). The **Ameripass** offers unlimited travel with on-off stops for various periods of time, but it is usually more economical for long-distance trips with few stopovers. International travelers should inquire about the **International Ameripass.** For more information, in the U.S. contact Greyhound Bus Lines, Inc., at 800/232-9424, or www.greyhound.com.

Then there are alternative bus options, most notably **Green Tortoise,** the hippest trip on wheels for budget travelers, combining long-distance travel with communal sightseeing. Sign on for a westbound cross-country tour to get to California, an eastbound trip to get away—seeing some of the most spectacular sights in the U.S. along the languid, looping way. As the motto emblazoned on the back of the bus says: "Arrive inspired, not dog tired." Unlike your typical bus ride, on Green Tortoise trips you bring your sleeping bag—the buses are converted sleeping coaches, and the booths and couches convert into beds come nightfall. And you won't need to stop for meals, since healthy gourmet fare (at a cost of about $10 a day) is usually included in the freight; sometimes the food charge is optional, meaning you can bring your own. But Green Tortoise also offers a weekly three-day **California Coast Tour,** with departures from both Los Angeles and San Francisco, making it easy—and fairly entertaining—to get from one end of the state to the other. From San Francisco, you can also get to Southern California on the Green Tortoise **Death Valley National Park** tour; dropoffs can be arranged in either Bakersfield or Mojave, and Greyhound can get you to Los Angeles. For more information, contact: Green Tortoise Adventure Travel, 494 Broadway, San Francisco, CA 94133, 415/956-7500 or, from anywhere in the U.S. and Canada, 800/867-8647, www.greentortoise.com.

BICYCLING

Many parts of California are not much fun for cyclists. Let's face it: cities are car (and bus and Mack truck) country. Cycling on public roadways here usually means frightening traffic; brightly colored bicycle clothing and accessories, reflective tape, good lights, and other safety precautions are mandatory. And always wear a helmet. Only the brave would pick this part of the world—or at least the urban part of this world—for bicycle touring, though some do, most wisely with help from books such as *Bicycling the Pacific Coast* (The Mountaineers) by Tom Kirkendall and Vicky Spring. Yet there are less congested areas, and good local bike paths here and there, for more timid recreational bikers; rental bike shops abound, particularly in beach areas. For those who hanker after a little two-wheel backroads sightseeing, many areas aong the central and north coasts, throughout the Sonoma and Napa County "wine countries," and in the Sierra Nevada foothills, are still sublime. Southern California has bicycling possibilities, too, including paved beachfront bike paths and reasonably untraveled backcountry routes.

Various good regional cycling guides are available, though serious local bike shops—those frequented by cycling enthusiasts, not just sales outlets—and bike clubs are probably the best local information sources for local and regional rides as well as special cycling events. For upcoming events, other germane information, and referrals on good publications, contact: **California Association of Bicycling Organizations** (CABO), P.O. Box 26864, Dublin, CA 94568, www.cabobike.com. The **Adventure Cycling Association,** P.O. Box 8308, Missoula, MT 59807, 406/721-1776 or 800/755-2453, www.adv cycling.org, is a nonprofit national organization that researches long-distance bike routes and organizes tours for members. Its maps, guidebooks, route suggestions, and *Cyclist's Yellow Pages* can be helpful. For mountain biking information via the Internet, also try the **International Mountain Bicycling Association** at www.imba.com.

Suggested Reading

The virtual "publisher of record" for all things Californian is the **University of California Press,** 510/642-4247 or 800/777-4726, www.ucpress.edu, which publishes hundreds of titles on the subject—all excellent. The UC Press California and the West series and its Food and Wine titles are quite useful. Exiting news came in 2003: UC Press is undertaking the immense (and expensive) task of re-releasing the 60-some titles in its venerable California Natural History series. Other publishers offering California titles include **Chronicle Books,** 415/537-3730 or 800/722-6657, www.chronbooks.com, and **Heyday Books,**510/549-3564, www.heydaybooks.com. California's own **Avalon Travel Publishing,** 510/595-3664, www.travelmatters.com, offers **Moon Handbooks** to California (including this one), **The Dog Lover's Companion** titles, and numerous **Foghorn Outdoors** California recreation guides, including camping, fishing, hiking, biking, and "getaways" guides. Contact these and other publishers, mentioned below, for a complete list of current titles relating to California.

COMPANION READING

Baldy, Marian. *The University Wine Course.* San Francisco: The Wine Appreciation Guild, 1992. Destined to be a classic and designed for both instructional and personal use, this friendly book offers a comprehensive education about wine. *The University Wine Course* explains it all, from viticulture to varietals. And the lips-on lab exercises and chapter-by-chapter examinations help even the hopelessly déclassé develop the subtle sensory awareness necessary for any deeper appreciation of the winemaker's art. Special sections and appendixes on reading (and understanding) wine labels, combining wine and food, and understanding wine terminology make it a lifelong personal library reference. Definitely "do" this book before doing the California wine country.

For college wine appreciation instructors and winery personnel, the companion *Teacher's Manual for The University Wine Course* (1993) may also come in handy.

Bierce, Ambrose Gwinnet, wickedly illustrated by Gahan Wilson. *The Devil's Dictionary.* New York: Oxford University Press, 1998. According to *The Devil's Dictionary,* a saint is a "dead sinner revised and edited," and a bore is a "person who talks when you wish him to listen." The satiric aphorisms included herein earned Ambrose Bierce the nicknames Bitter Bierce and the Wickedest Man in San Francisco, though—considering his talent for heaving his witty pitchfork at any and all he happened to encounter in life—it's clear that Bierce was born way too soon. He would have a field day in contemporary California.

Brautigan, Richard. *A Confederate General from Big Sur, Dreaming of Babylon, and the Hawk-line Monster.* New York: Mariner Books, reissue edition, 1991. Did you miss the sixties? If so, you probably also missed Richard Brautigan, whose literary star ascended then flamed out too quickly.

Bright, William O. *1,500 California Place Names: Their Origin and Meaning.* A revised version of the classic *1,000 California Place Names* by Erwin G. Gudde, first published in 1949. Berkeley: University of California Press, 1998. Though you can also get the revised edition of Gudde's original masterpiece (see below), this convenient, alphabetically arranged pocketbook—now in an expanded and updated edition—is perfect for travelers, explaining the names of mountains, rivers, and towns throughout California.

Buckley, Christopher, and Gary Young, eds. *The Geography of Home: California's Poetry of Place.* Berkeley: Heyday Books, 1999. This contemporary anthology showcases the work of 76 California poets. In addition to multiple selections of each poet's work, the poets also talk about their history in California, and the state's influence on their poetry.

Chandler, Raymond. *The Big Sleep.* New York: Vintage Books, 1992. The first mystery writer to be initiated into the Library of America—the U.S.A.'s literary hall of fame—Raymond Chandler and his legacy have been all but put to sleep by successors in the genre, including parodies such as the film *Dead Men Don't Wear Plaid.* But if one hasn't succumbed to today's trendy nihilism—if one understands that pain hurts and life matters—then *The Big Sleep,* first published in 1939, is still a spellbinding and fresh introduction to L.A.'s underlying ideas about itself. And Philip Marlowe, Chandler's alter ego and private-eye protagonist, is still the L.A. insider's outsider. (As James Wolcott puts it, to Marlowe the rich are risen scum.) Lesser works by Chandler include *Farewell, My Lovely, The Long Goodbye,* and *The Little Sister.*

Clark, Donald Thomas. *Monterey County Place Names: A Geographical Dictionary.* Carmel Valley, CA: Kestrel Press, 1991. This marvelous resource, meticulously researched and guaranteed to enlighten all who dip into it, is a gift from the UC Santa Cruz University Librarian, Emeritus. Also well worth searching for, though out of print at last report, is the author's *Santa Cruz County Place Names* (1986).

Dana, Richard Henry, Jr. *Two Years Before the Mast.* New York: New American Library, 1990. A classic of early California literature. After recovering from a bout with the measles, young Harvard man Richard Henry Dana sailed off to complete his convalescence—not as a privileged ship passenger but as a sailor. On August 14, 1834, he boarded the *Pilgrim* in Boston Harbor and was underway on what was to be the greatest adventure of his life. This realistic depiction of life on the high seas

offers an accurate firsthand account of what it was like to see the California coastline for the first time—and to tie up in San Francisco *before* the gold rush. Some of the earliest written descriptions of California—and still an exceptional read.

De La Pérouse, Jean François, with commentary by Malcolm Margolin. *Monterey in 1786: The Journals of Jean François de La Pérouse.* Berkeley: Heyday Books, 1989. On September 14, 1786, two ships sailed out of the fog and into Monterey Bay. The ships were French, *L'Astrolabe* and *La Boussole,* the first foreign vessels to visit the Spanish colonies in California. Onboard, as Malcolm Margolin tells us in his introduction, "was a party of eminent scientists, navigators, cartographers, illustrators, and physicians" sent by King Louis XVI to explore the western coast of North America, look for sea otters (for the fur trade), and report on Spain's colonies. Leader of the expedition was Jean François de La Pérouse, whose journal describes the presidio at Monterey, the mission at Carmel, Indian customs, and the land and its abundant plant and animal life. Reading his journals, as Margolin points out, allows to unfold before us "not a tale of a distant fantasy land, but the far more gripping story of our place, of our times, the story of 'us.'" The journals are greatly enhanced by Margolin's historical introduction and his careful annotations.

Fisher, M.F.K. *The Art of Eating.* Foster City, CA: IDG Books Worldwide, 1990. Reprint ed. John Updike has called her "the poet of the appetites." According to the *Chicago Sun-Times,* "M.F.K. Fisher is to literary prose what Laurence Olivier is to acting." And that point is hard to argue. Often characterized as California's premier food writer, particularly after she settled into the Sonoma County wine country, Mary Frances Kennedy Fisher was actually a *writer*—one who understood that the fundamental human needs are food, love, and security. She wrote about them all, in more than 20 books and countless other essays, letters, and stories. Five of her most beloved book-length essays—*An Alphabet of Gourmets, Consider the Oyster, The Gastronomical Me, How to Cook a Wolf,* and *Serve It Forth*—are all included in this collection.

Gilbar, Steven. *Natural State: A Literary Anthology of California Nature Writing.* Berkeley: University of California Press, 1998. This hefty and dazzling collection includes many of the writers you'd expect—Gretel Ehrlich, M.F.K. Fisher, John McPhee, John Muir, Gary Snyder, and Robert Louis Stevenson—but also a few surprises, including Joan Didion, Jack Kerouac, and Henry Miller.

Gudde, Erwin G. Edited by William O. Bright. *California Place Names: The Origin and Etymology of Current Geographical Names.* Berkeley: University of California Press, 1998. Did you know that *Siskiyou* was the Chinook word for "bobtailed horse," as borrowed from the Cree language? More such complex truths await every time you dip into this fascinating volume—the ultimate guide to California place names (and how to pronounce them). A revised and expanded fourth edition, building upon the masterwork of Gudde, who died in 1969.

Hammett, Dashiell. *The Maltese Falcon.* New York: Vintage Books, 1992. Reissue ed. More *noir* than even Humphrey Bogart, who starred in the Hollywood version of this classic mystery, Sam Spade is Dashiell Hammett's tough-as-nails San Francisco private dick. Also central to Hammett's *The Dain Curse* and *The Glass Key,* in this story Spade attempts to unravel the enigma of the Maltese Falcon, a solid-gold statuette originally crafted as a tribute to the Holy Roman Emperor Charles IV. While trying to find the falcon, Spade's partner is murdered, the coppers blame him for it, and the bad guys are determined to get him, too. Then, of course, there's also the beautiful redhead, who appears and just as mysteriously disap-

pears. Whodunnit? And why? Other classic Hammett reads include *The Continental Op* and *The Thin Man.*

Hansen, Gladys. *San Francisco Almanac.* Second revised ed. San Francisco: Chronicle Books, 1995. Finally back in print after a too-long hiatus, this easy-to-use source for San Francisco facts was written by the city archivist. Contains a detailed chronology, maps, and bibliography. Also fun: what some famous people have said about San Francisco.

Hart, James D. *A Companion to California.* Berkeley: University of California Press. Revised and expanded, 1987 (OP). Another very worthy book for Californiacs to collect, if you can find it, with thousands of brief entries on all aspects of California as well as more in-depth pieces on subjects such as literature.

Herron, Don. *The Literary World of San Francisco and its Environs.* San Francisco: City Lights Books, 1985 (OP). A well-mapped "pocket guide" for do-it-yourself walking and driving tours to sites where literary lights shine in and around San Francisco, their homes and haunts. This is the companion guide to the excellent *Literary San Francisco* by Lawrence Ferlinghetti and Nancy J. Peters. Also by Herron: *The Dashiell Hammet Tour: A Guidebook.*

Hong Kingston, Maxine. *The Woman Warrior: Memoirs of a Girlhood Among Ghosts.* New York: Vintage Books, 1989. Reissue ed. Fictionalized memoir about growing up Chinese-American in Stockton, California. In China, ghosts are supernatural beings, but in California they become everyone who is not from China. This is an elliptical and powerful story about finding a place in American society, though still raising ire in some quarters for its representations of Chinese culture.

Houston, James D. *Californians: Searching for the Golden State.* Santa Cruz, CA: Otter B Books, 1992. 10th reprint ed. Good prose, good points in this collection of personal essays about Californians in their endless search for the meaning of their own dream.

Huxley, Aldous. *After Many a Summer Dies the Swan.* London: Chatto and Windus, 1939. As an expatriate in Southern California, Huxley never did entirely warm up to the place. But he understood it, as he so deftly demonstrated in this literary masterpiece, inspired by the larger-than-life life of William Randolph Hearst.

Jackson, Helen Hunt. *Ramona.* New York: New American Library, 1988. The author was an early activist on behalf of California's native peoples. Despairing that so few cared about the Indians' plight, Jackson decided to tell the story as a romance—an interracial romance. As she herself put it: "I am going to try to write a novel, in which will be set forth some Indian experiences in a way to move people's hearts. People will read a novel when they will not read serious books." The resulting *Ramona* was a national sensation when it was first published in 1884. It is the now the official California State Play, staged since 1923 at the annual outdoor Ramona Pageant near Hemet.

Jeffers, Robinson. *Selected Poems.* New York: Random House, 1965. The poet Robinson Jeffers died in 1961 at the age of 75, on a rare day when it actually snowed in Carmel. One of California's finest poets, sophisticated yet accessible, many of his poems pay homage to the beauty of his beloved Big Sur coast. Poems collected here are selections from some of his major works, including *Be Angry at the Sun, The Beginning and the End, Hungerfield,* and *Tamar and Other Poems.*

Jeffers, Robinson, with an introduction by James Karman, photography by Morley Baer. *Stones of the Sur.* Stanford, CA: Stanford University, 2001. A coffeetable book for people who don't even have coffee tables, this stunning work is crafted from the words of the Carmel poet Robinson Jeffers and the brilliant black-and-

white photos of Morley Baer. As a general introduction to the significance of Jeffers's work and his connection to Carmel, scholar James Karman's contribution is invaluable.

Kahrl, William. *Water and Power: The Conflict over Los Angeles' Water Supply in the Owens Valley.* Berkeley: University of California Press, 1982. Perhaps the best book available for anyone who wants to understand the politics of water and power in California, and how water and political power have transformed the state's economy and land. To keep up with new twists and turns in this meandering tale, read the *Sacramento Bee* (where Kahrl is now an editor).

Karman, James. *Robinson Jeffers: Poet of California.* Brownsville, OR: Story Line Press, Inc., revised second ed., 1995. This marvelous critical biography details the life and times of the reticent poet Robinson Jeffers, for whom the Big Sur coast was once named. "It is not possible to be quite sane here," Jeffers wisely observed. Though here Karman also sympathetically introduces us to Jeffers's wife Una, also of interest to Jeffers fans is Story Line's *Of Una Jeffers* by Edith Greenan.

Kerouac, Jack. *Subterraneans.* New York: Grove Press, 1989. Considered by some to be Kerouac's masterpiece and first published in 1958, this is a Beat exploration of life on the fringes, a novel largely set in the San Francisco Bay Area. Others, however, prefer *The Dharma Bums* (1958) and *Big Sur* (1962).

Le Guin, Ursula K. *Always Coming Home.* Berkeley: University of California Press, 2001. Unbelievably, this book was out of print for a time. Thanks to UC Press, it's back. Ms. Le Guin gained fame as a science fiction writer, for novels including *The Left Hand of Darkness* and *The Dispossessed.* Her formal literary recognition includes the Hugo, Gandalf, Kafka, Nebula, and National Book awards. *Always Coming Home* is perhaps Le Guin's masterwork, and a special treat for those who love California—particularly Northern California, and even more particularly the Napa Valley, where the landscape happens to coincide with the geographical borders of the land she describes (and maps) in this imaginative exploration of "futuristic anthropology."

London, Jack, ed. by Gerald Haslam. *Jack London's Golden State: Selected California Writings.* Berkeley: Heyday Books, 1999. The first major U.S. writer to use California as his base, Jack London has finally come home—so California can reclaim him. Included here are some of London's finest works, from *John Barleycorn: or Alcoholic Memoirs* and *Star Rover* to *Valley of the Moon,* along with journalism, short stories, and letters.

MacDonald, Ross. *The Moving Target.* New York: Alfred A. Knopf, 1967. In this, one of MacDonald's many Southern California intrigues, private dick Lew Archer encounters Los Angeles criminals at their most entertaining.

Michaels, Leonard, David Reid, and Raquel Scherr, eds. *West of the West: Imagining California.* New York: HarperCollins Publishers, 1991. Though any anthology about California is destined to be incomplete, this one is exceptional—offering selections by Maya Angelou, Simone de Beauvoir, Joan Didion, Umberto Eco, Gretel Ehrlich, M.F.K. Fisher, Aldous Huxley, Jack Kerouac, Maxine Hong Kingston, Rudyard Kipling, Henry Miller, Ishmael Reed, Kenneth Rexroth, Richard Rodriguez, Randy Shilts, Gertrude Stein, John Steinbeck, Octavio Paz, Amy Tan, Gore Vidal, Walt Whitman, and Tom Wolfe.

Miller, Henry. *Big Sur and the Oranges of Hieronymus Bosch.* New York: W.W. Norton & Co., 1978. First published in 1958, the famed writer shares his impressions of art and writing along with his view of life as seen from the Big Sur coastline—the center of his personal universe in his later years, and the first real home he had ever found.

Norris, Frank. *McTeague: A Story of San Francisco.* New York: New American Library, 1997. Reissue ed. The basis for the classic silent film *Greed,* Norris's novel is, in a way, the ultimate Western. First published in 1899, a retelling of an actual crime, *McTeague* tells the story of a dimwitted dentist and his greedy wife—all in all a bleak, low-brow tour of life in San Francisco at the turn of the 20th century, ending with McTeague stumbling off into the desert.

Paddison, Joshua, ed. *A World Transformed: Firsthand Accounts of California Before the Gold Rush.* Berkeley: Heyday Books, 1999. According to popular California mythology, the Golden State was "born" with the onrushing change that came with the gold rush of 1848. But this collection of earlier California writings gathers together some intriguing earlier observations—from European explorers and visitors, missionaries, and sea captains—that reveal pre-gold rush California.

Parker, T. Jefferson. *Laguna Heat.* New York: St. Martin's Press, 1985. So, who says only L.A. does down and dirty whodunits? Orange County's own T. Jefferson Parker, in his bestselling national debut, certainly did Laguna Beach proud. And when you're done untangling this tale, there's always *Little Saigon, Pacific Beat,* and *Summer of Fear,* not to mention more recent works.

Sinclair, Upton. *Oil!* Berkeley: University of California Press, 1997. Reprise of the original 1927 edition, in which journalist and socialist gadfly Sinclair fictionally recreates the Signal Hill oil fields of Long Beach and the Teapot Dome oil reserve scandals.

Stegner, Wallace Earle. Edited and with a preface from the author's son, Page Stegner. *Marking the Sparrow's Fall: Wallace Stegner's American West.* New York: H. Holt, 1998. This brilliant collection of Stegner's conservation writings traces his development as a Westerner—and as a Western writer—starting with his seemingly inauspicious beginnings as an avid reader, hunkered down in small-town libraries in places almost no one's ever heard of. The first collection of Stegner's work since the author's death in 1993, *Marking the Sparrow's Fall* includes 15 essays never before published, his best-known essays on the American West—including *Wilderness Letter*—and a little-known novella.

Stegner, Wallace Earle. *Where the Bluebird Sings to the Lemonade Springs: Living and Writing in the West.* New York: Penguin USA, 1993. Reprint ed. It's certainly understandable that, at the end of his days, Wallace Stegner wasn't entirely optimistic about the future of the West, bedeviled as it is, still, by development pressures and insane political decisions. In these 16 thoughtful essays, he spells out his concerns—and again pays poetic homage to the West's big sky and bigger landscapes. In the end, he remains hopeful that a new spirit of place is emerging in the West—and that within a generation or two we will "work out some sort of compromise between what must be done to earn a living and what must be done to restore health to the earth, air, and water."

Steinbeck, John. *Cannery Row.* New York: Penguin USA, 1993. Reprint ed. Here it is, a poem, a stink, a grating noise, told in the days when sardines still ruled the boardwalk on Monterey's Cannery Row. Also worth an imaginative sidetrip on a tour of the California coast is Steinbeck's *East of Eden,* first published in 1952, the Salinas Valley version of the Cain and Abel story. Steinbeck's classic California work, though, is still *The Grapes of Wrath.*

Stevenson, Robert Louis. *The Complete Short Stories of Robert Louis Stevenson: With a Selection of the Best Short Novels.* New York: Da Capo Press, 1998. It's hard to know where to start with Stevenson, whose California journeys served to launch his literary career. Da Capo's collection is as good a place as any.

West, Nathanael. *The Day of the Locust.* New York: New Directions, 1962. Before West and his wife were killed in a car accident, he published this surreal novel of L.A. apocalypse. This 1939 tale of terror premieres in Hollywood, naturally, but the story is about the troublesome troupes no longer needed by the silver screen.

WPA Guide to California: The Federal Writers Project Guide to 1930s California. New York: Pantheon Press (an imprint of Random House), 1984. The classic travel guide to California, first published during the Depression, is somewhat dated as far as contemporary sights but excellent as a companion volume and background information source.

HISTORY AND PEOPLE

Atherton, Gertrude. *My San Francisco, A Wayward Biography.* Indianapolis and New York: The Bobbs-Merrill Company, 1946. The 56th book—written at the age of 90—by the woman Kevin Starr has called "the daughter of the elite" whose career of historical fiction "document[ed] . . . itself . . . in a careless but vivid output. . . ." A delightfully chatty browse through the past, filled with dropped names and accounts of Atherton's own meetings with historic figures.

Brands, H.W. *The Age of Gold: The California Gold Rush and the New American Dream.* New York: Doubleday, 2002. Turns out the California gold rush was a turning point in American and world history, and this brilliant new history explains why.

Cleland, Robert Glass. *A History of California: The American Period.* Westport, CT: Greenwood Press, 1975. Originally published in 1922. Also try to find Cleland's *From Wilderness to Empire: A History of California.*

Dreyer, Peter. *A Gardener Touched with Genius: The Life of Luther Burbank.* Berkeley: University of California Press, 1985.

Farquhar, Francis P., ed. *Up and Down California in 1860-1864: The Journal of William H. Brewer.* Berkeley: University of California Press, 1974. Reprint of 1966 edition.

Frémont, John Charles. *Memoirs of My Life.* New York: Penguin, 1984. Originally published in Chicago, 1887. The old Bearflagger himself tells the story of early California—at least some of it.

Gutiérrez, Ramon A., and Richard J. Orsi, eds. *Contested Eden: California Before the Gold Rush.* Berkeley: University of California Press, 1998. In this first volume of a projected four-part series, essays explore California before the gold rush.

Harlow, Neal. *California Conquered: The Annexation of a Mexican Province, 1846-1850.* Berkeley: University of California Press, 1982.

Heizer, Robert F. *The Destruction of the California Indians.* Utah: Gibbs Smith Publishing, 1974.

Heizer, Robert F., and Albert B. Elsasser. *The Natural World of the California Indians.* Berkeley: University of California Press, 1980. As an adjunct to the rest of Heizer's work, this fact-packed volume provides the setting—the natural environment, the village environment—for California's native peoples.

Heizer, Robert F., and M.A. Whipple. *The California Indians.* Berkeley: University of California Press, 1971. A worthwhile collection of essays about California's native peoples, covering general, regional, and specific topics—a good supplement to the work of A.L. Kroeber (who also contributed to this volume).

Holliday, J.S. (James). *The World Rushed In: The California Gold Rush Experience: An Eyewitness Account of a Nation Heading West.* Norman, OK: University of Oklahoma Press, 2002. Holliday labored for decades to compile and recast as narrative history diary entries

and letters of William Swain, a young man from near Niagara Falls who came to California to pan for gold at Bidwell's Bar.

Hutchinson, W.H. *California: The Golden Shore by the Sundown Sea.* Belmont, CA: Star Publishing Company, 1988. The late author, a professor emeritus of history at CSU Chico known as Old Hutch to former students, presents a dizzying amount of historical, economic, and political detail from his own unique perspective in this analysis of California's past and present. Hutchinson saw the state from many sides during a lifetime spent as "a horse wrangler, cowboy, miner, boiler fireman, merchant seaman, corporate bureaucrat, rodeo and horse show announcer, and freelance writer."

Jackson, Mrs. Helen Hunt. *Century of Dishonor: A Sketch of the US Government's Dealings (with some of the Indian tribes).* Temecula, CA: Reprint Services, 1988. Originally published in Boston, 1881.

Kroeber, Alfred L. *Handbook of the Indians of California.* New York: Dover Publications, 1976 (unabridged facsimile version of the original work, *Bulletin 78* of the Bureau of American Ethnology of the Smithsonian Institution, published by the U.S. Government Printing Office). The classic compendium of observed facts about California's native peoples by the noted UC Berkeley anthropologist who befriended Ishi—but also betrayed him, posthumously, by allowing his body to be autopsied (in violation of Ishi's beliefs) then shipping his brain to the Smithsonian Institution.

Lewis, Oscar. *The Big Four.* Sausalito, CA: Comstock Editions, 1982. Originally published in New York, 1938.

Margolin, Malcolm. *The Way We Lived.* Berkeley: Heyday Books, 1981. A wonderful collection of California native peoples' reminiscences, stories, and songs. Also by

Margolin: *The Ohlone Way,* about the life of California's first residents of the San Francisco-Monterey. Bay Area.

McDonald, Linda, and Carol Cullen. *California Historical Landmarks.* Sacramento, CA: California Department of Parks and Recreation, 1997. Revised ed. Originally compiled in response to the National Historic Preservation Act of 1966, directing all states to identify all properties "possessing historical, architectural, archaeological, and cultural value," this updated edition covers more than 1,000 California Registered Historical Landmarks, organized by category—sites of aboriginal, economic, or government interest, for example—and indexed by county. A wide variety of other publications is available from the Department of Parks and Recreation. To order, call toll-free (800) 777-0369.

McWilliams, Carey, with a foreword by Lewis H. Lapham. *California, the Great Exception.* Berkeley: University of California Press, 1999. Historian, journalist, and lawyer Carey McWilliams, editor of *The Nation* from 1955 to 1975, stepped back from his other tasks in 1949 to assess the state of the Golden State at the end of its first 100 years. And while he acknowledged the state's prodigious productivity even then, he also noted the brutality with which the great nation-state of California dealt with "the Indian problem," the water problem, and the agricultural labor problem— all issues of continuing relevance to California today. McWilliams' classic work on the essence of California, reprinted with a new foreword by the editor of *Harper's* magazine, is a must-read for all Californians.

Monroy, Douglas. *Thrown Among Strangers: The Making of Mexican Culture in Frontier California.* Berkeley: University of California Press, 1990.

Nasaw, David. *The Chief: The Life of William Randolph Hearst.* New York: Mariner Books, 2001. *The Chief* draws on papers and interviews that were previously unavailable, as well as on newly released documentation of interactions with such figures as Hitler, Mussolini, Churchill, every president from Grover Cleveland to Franklin Roosevelt, and movie giants Louis B. Mayer, Jack Warner, and Irving Thalberg. David Nasaw completes the picture of this colossal American "engagingly, lucidly and fair-mindedly," according to Arthur Schlesinger, Jr.

Perry, Charles. *The Haight-Ashbury: A History.* New York: Rolling Stone Press (an imprint of Random House), 1984. A detailed chronicle of events that began in 1965 and led up to the Summer of Love, with research, writing, and some pointed observations by the author, a *Rolling Stone* editor.

Pitt, Leonard. *Decline of the Californios: A Social History of the Spanish-Speaking Californians, 1846-1890.* Berkeley: University of California Press, 1966.

Reisner, Marc. *Cadillac Desert: The American West and Its Disappearing Water.* New York: Penguin Books, 1993. Revised ed. Inspiration for the four-part 1997 PBS documentary, this is the contemporary yet classic tale of water and the unromantic West—a drama of unquenchable thirst and reluctant conservation, political intrigue and corruption, and economic and ecological disasters. How Los Angeles got its water figures prominently—the histories of William Mulholland and the Owens Valley as well as the Colorado River. A must-read book. Reisner's apocalyptic *A Dangerous Place: California's Unsettling Fate,* which he hurried to finish before he died, explores the omnipresent danger of earthquakes and California's heedlessness.

Robinson, W.W. *Land in California: The Story of Mission Lands, Ranchos, Squatters, Mining Claims, Railroad Grants, Land Scrip, Homesteads.* Berkeley: University of California Press, 1979.

Know Coastal California

Rowland, Leon. *Santa Cruz the Early Years.* Santa Cruz, CA: Otter B Books, OP. A great little history if you can find it, originally privately published as four separate tracts in the 1940s by Santa Cruz newspaper reporter Leon Rowland.

Royce, Josiah. *California from the Conquest in 1846 to the Second Vigilance Committee in San Francisco 1856.* New York: AMS Press. Originally published in Boston, 1886.

Sinclair, Upton. *I, Candidate for Governor: And How I Got Licked.* Berkeley: University of California Press, 1994. Reprint of the original edition. This is a genuine treasure of California history—a first-person account of California's liveliest and most notorious gubernatorial race, in which California business employed Hollywood's tools to defeat muckraking journalist and socialist Democratic candidate Sinclair in the too-close-to-call 1934 campaign. Sinclair's platform was EPIC—End Poverty in California—and he almost got the chance to try.

Starr, Kevin. *Americans and the California Dream: 1850-1915.* New York: Oxford University Press, 1973. A cultural history, written by a native San Franciscan, former newspaper columnist, onetime head of the city's library system, professor and historian, and current California State Librarian. The focus on Northern California taps an impressively varied body of sources as it seeks to "suggest the poetry and the moral drama of social experience" from California's first days of statehood through the Panama-Pacific Exposition of 1915 when, in the author's opinion, "California came of age." Starr's 1985 *Inventing the Dream: California Through the Progressive Era,* second in his Americans and the California Dream series, and *Material Dreams: Southern California Through the 1920s,* his third, primarily tell the southstate story. Annotations in all three suggest rich possibilities for further reading.

Starr, Kevin. *Endangered Dreams: The Great Depression in California.* New York: Oxford University Press, 1996. "California," Wallace Stegner has noted, "is like the rest of the United States, only more so." And so begins the fourth volume of Starr's imaginative and immense California history, in which the author delves into the Golden State's dark past—a period in which strikes and unions were forcibly suppressed, soup kitchens became social institutions, and both socialism and fascism had their day. Also worthwhile: *The Dream Endures: California Enters the 1940s,* fifth title in Starr's California history series, aand *Embattled Dreams: California in War and Peace, 1940-1950,* sixth.

Stevenson, Robert Louis. *From Scotland to Silverado.* Cambridge, MA: The Belknap Press of Harvard University Press, 1966. An annotated collection of the sickly and lovelorn young Stevenson's travel essays, including his first impressions of Monterey and San Francisco, and the works that have come to be known as *The Silverado Squatters.* Contains considerable text—marked therein—that the author's family and friends had removed from previous editions. A useful introduction by James D. Hart details the journeys and relationships behind the essays.

Stone, Irving. *Jack London: Sailor on Horseback.* New York: Doubleday, 1986. Originally published in Boston, 1938.

Stone, Irving. *Men to Match My Mountains.* New York: Berkeley Publishers, 1987. A classic California history, originally published in 1956.

Walton, John. *Western Times and Water Wars: State, Culture, and Rebellion in California.* Berkeley: University of California Press, 1992. Winner of both the Robert Park and J.S. Holliday Awards, Walton's compelling chronicle of the water wars between Los Angeles and the farmers and ranchers of the Owens Valley is a masterpiece of California history.

NATURE AND NATURAL HISTORY

Bakker, Elna. *An Island Called California: An Ecological Introduction to Its Natural Communities.* Berkeley: University of California Press, 1985. Expanded revised ed. An excellent, time-honored introduction to the characteristics of, and relationships between, California's natural communities. New chapters on Southern California, added in this edition, make *An Island* more helpful statewide.

Barbour, Michael, Bruce Pavlik, Susan Lindstrom, and Frank Drysdale, with a foreword by Pulitzer Prize-winning California poet Gary Snyder. *California's Changing Landscapes: Diversity and Conservation of California Vegetation.* Sacramento: California Native Plant Society Press, 1993. Well-indexed lay guide to California's astonishing botanical variety. The society also publishes some excellent regional floras and plant keys.

California Coastal Commission, State of California. *California Coastal Resource Guide.* Berkeley: University of California Press, 1997. This is the revised and expanded fifth edition of the California coast lover's bible, the indispensable guide to the Pacific coast and its wonders—the land, marine geology, biology—as well as parks, landmarks, and amusements. But for practical travel purposes, get the commission's *The California Coastal Access Guide,* listed under Enjoying the Outdoors below.

Collier, Michael. *A Land in Motion: California's San Andreas Fault.* Berkeley: University of California Press, 1999. An intriguing geologic tour of the world's most famous fault, which runs the entire length of western California—and right through the San Francisco Bay Area. Wonderful photographs.

Duremberger, Robert. *Elements of California Geography.* Out of print but worth searching for. This is the classic work on California geography.

Fix, David, and Andy Bezener. *Birds of Northern California.* Auburn, WA: Lone Pine Publishing, 2000. Already the bible of beginning birders.

Grinnell, Joseph, and Alden Miller. *The Distribution of the Birds of California.* Out of print but worth looking for, this is the definitive California birder's guide—for those interested in serious study.

Hickman, Jim, ed. *The Jepson Manual: Higher Plants of California.* Berkeley: University of California Press (with cooperation and support from the California Native Plant Society and the Jepson Herbarium), 1993. Hot off the presses but at least 10 years in the making, *The Jepson Manual* is already considered the bible of California botany. The brainchild of both Jim Hickman and Larry Heckard, curator of the Jepson Herbarium, this book is a cumulative picture of the extraordinary flora of California, and the first comprehensive attempt to fit it all into one volume since the Munz *A California Flora* was published in 1959. The best work of almost 200 botanist-authors has been collected here, along with exceptional line drawings and illustrations (absent from the Munz flora) that make it easier to identify and compare plant species. This book is the botanical reference book for a California lifetime—a hefty investment for a hefty tome, especially essential for serious ecologists and botanists, amateur and otherwise.

Hill, Mary. *California Landscape: Origin and Evolution.* Berkeley: University of California Press, 1984. An emphasis on the most recent history of California landforms. Also by Hill: *Geology of the Sierra Nevada.*

Jaeger, Edmund C., and Arthur C. Smith. *Introduction to the Natural History of Southern California.* Berkeley: University of California Press, 1966. A must-have for the southstate naturalist's bookshelf.

Know Coastal California

Kaufman, Kenn. *Lives of North American Birds.* New York: Houghton Mifflin Co., 1997. Sponsored by the Roger Tory Peterson Institute. A bit bulky for a field guide but already considered a classic, this 674-page hardbound tome focuses less on identifying features and names and more on observing and understanding birds within the contexts of their own lives. Now, there's a concept.

Le Boeuf, Burney J., and Stephanie Kaza. *The Natural History of Año Nuevo.* Santa Cruz, CA: Otter B Books, 1985. Reprint ed. An excellent, very comprehensive guide to the natural features of the Año Nuevo area just north of Santa Cruz.

McCauley, Jane, and the National Geographic Society staff. *National Geographic Society Field Guide to the Birds of North America.* Washington, D.C.: National Geographic Society, 1993. One of the best guides to bird identification available.

Munz, Phillip A., and David D. Keck. *A California Flora and Supplement.* Berkeley: University of California Press, 1968. Until quite recently this was it, the California botanist's bible—a complete descriptive "key" to every plant known to grow in California—but quite hefty to tote around on pleasure trips. More useful for amateur botanists are Munz's *California Mountain Wildflowers, Shore Wildflowers,* and *California Desert Wildflowers,* as well as other illustrated plant guides published by UC Press. Serious amateur and professional botanists and ecologists are more than ecstatic these days about the recent publication of the *new* California plant bible: *The Jepson Manual,* edited by Jim Hickman. (For more information, see above.)

Pavlik, Bruce, Pamela Muick, Sharon Johnson, and Marjorie Popper. *Oaks of California.* Santa Barbara: Cachuma Press, 1991. In ancient European times, oaks were considered spiritual beings, the sacred inspiration of artists, healers,

and writers since these particular trees were thought to court the lightning flash. Time spent with this stunning book will soon convince anyone that this truth lives on. Packed with photos and lovely watercolor illustrations, maps, even an oak lover's travel guide, this book celebrates the many species of California oaks.

Peterson, Roger Tory. *A Field Guide to Western Birds.* Boston: Houghton Mifflin Co., 1990. The third edition of this birding classic has striking new features, including full-color illustrations (including juveniles, females, and in-flight birds) facing the written descriptions. The only thing you'll have to flip around for are the range maps, tucked away in the back. Among other intriguing titles in the Peterson Field Guide series: *A Field Guide to Western Birds' Nests* by Hal Harrison.

Schmitz, Marjorie. *Growing California Native Plants.* Berkeley: University of California Press, 1980. A handy guide for those interested in planting, growing, and otherwise supporting the success of California's beleaguered native plants.

Schoenherr, Allan A. *A Natural History of California.* Berkeley: University of California Press, 1992. With introductory chapters on ecology and geology, *A Natural History* covers California's climate, geology, soil, plant life, and animals based on distinct bioregions, with almost 300 photographs and numerous illustrations and tables. An exceptionally readable and well-illustrated introduction to California's astounding natural diversity and drama written by an ecology professor from CSU Fullerton, this 700-some page reference belongs on any Californiac's library shelf.

Sibley, David Allen. *The Sibley Guide to Birds.* New York: Knopf, 2000. Already a birding bestseller, Sibley's guide is a tad unwieldy for some. But it is durable, detailed, profusely illustrated with watercolors, and accurate. More portable and to the point: *The Sibley Field Guide to Birds of Western North America.* A companion: *The Sibley Guide to Bird Life and Behavior.*

Starker, Leopold A. *The California Quail.* Berkeley: University of California Press, 1985. This is the definitive book on the California quail, its history and biology.

RECREATION AND TRAVEL

Bakalinsky, Adah. *Stairway Walks in San Francisco.* Berkeley: Wilderness Press, 1998. Third revised ed. This updated San Francisco classic offers 27 neighborhood walks connecting San Francisco's 200-plus stairways, choreographed by a veteran city walker and walking tour guide.

California Coastal Commission, State of California. *The California Coastal Access Guide.* Berkeley: University of California Press, 2003. Sixth revised ed. According to the *Oakland Tribune,* this is "no doubt the most comprehensive look at California's coastline published to date." A must-have for serious Californiacs.

California Coastal Conservancy, State of California. *San Francisco Bay Shoreline Guide.* Berkeley: University of California Press, 1995. This is it, the definitive guide to the entire 400-mile Bay Trail shoreline route, from its piers to its paths and parks. Comprehensive and user-friendly, with full-color maps and illustrations.

Clark, Jeanne L. *California Wildlife Viewing Guide.* Helena, MT: Falcon Press, 1996. Second ed. This revised and expanded guide tells you where to go for a good look at native wildlife, and what to do once you're there. Color photos, overview maps.

Jeneid, Michael. *Adventure Kayaking: Trips from the Russian River to Monterey.* Berkeley: Wilderness Press, 1998. Tired of fighting that freeway traffic around the Bay Area? Try a kayak.

Under decent weather conditions—and with an experienced kayaker to clue you in—you can get just about everywhere. If you'll be shoving off a bit farther south, try *Adventure Kayaking: Trips from Big Sur to San Diego,* by Robert Mohle (1998).

Kirkendall, Tom, and Vicky Springs. *Bicycling the Pacific Coast.* Seattle: The Mountaineers, 1998. Third ed. A very good, very practical mile-by-mile guide to the tricky business of cycling along the California coast (and north).

Lorentzen, Bob. *The Hiker's Hip Pocket Guide to the Mendocino Coast.* Mendocino, CA: Bored Feet Publications, 1998. Third ed. One of the stars in Lorentzen's excellent hiking series, this best-selling, easy-to-follow hiking guide now includes 100 more miles of trails. Coverage includes all Mendocino area state parks, Jackson State Forest, Sinkyone Wilderness State Park, and little-known coastal access points. Also by Lorentzen: *The Hiker's Hip Pocket Guide to the Humboldt Coast* and *The Hiker's Hip Pocket Guide to Sonoma County.*

Lorentzen, Bob, and Richard Nichols. *Hiking the California Coastal Trail, Volume One: Oregon to Monterey.* Mendocino, CA: Bored Feet Publications, 1998. The first comprehensive guide to the work-in-progress California Coastal Trail, America's newest and most diverse long-distance trail. Published in conjunction with Coastwalk—which receives a hefty percentage of the proceeds, to support its efforts to complete the trail—this accessible guide describes 85 sections of the California Coastal Trail's northern reach. Keep an eye out, too, for *Hiking the California Coastal Trail, Volume Two: Monterey to Mexico,* published in 2000.

McKinney, John. *Coast Walks: 150 Adventures Along the California Coast.* Santa Barbara: Olympus Press, 1999. The new edition of McKinney's coast hiking classic contains plenty of new adventures, from Border Field State

Park at the Mexican Border north to Damnation Creek and Pelican Bay. Along the way, you'll also learn about local lore, history, and natural history—a bargain no matter how you hike it. Maps and illustrations.

McMillon, Bill, and Kevin McMillon. *Best Hikes With Children: San Francisco's North Bay.* Seattle: The Mountaineers, 1992. Also consider the McMillons' hiking guides to the South Bay and Sacramento.

National Register of Historic Places, *Early History of the California Coast.* Washington, D.C.: National Conference of State Historic Preservation Officers, 1997. Map. This fold-out introduction to the California coast serves as a travel itinerary with 45 stops illustrating the coast's earliest settlement and culture.

Pomada, Elizabeth. *Fun Places to Go with Children in Northern California.* San Francisco: Chronicle Books, 2003. Ninth ed. This long-running guide is based on the premise that, as important as it is to find a comfortable place to eat with kids, equally important is finding appropriate places to take them before and after meals. For aficionados of California's Victorian homes and buildings, the author's *Painted Ladies* series, co-authored with Michael Larsen, is also quite charming.

Rusmore, Jean. *The Bay Area Ridge Trail: Ridgetop Adventures Above San Francisco Bay.* San Francisco: Wilderness Press, 2002. Second ed. Abundant adventures for hikers, bikers, and horseback riders, along completed segments of this in-progress trail. Includes area maps, trailhead directions, and complete trail descriptions.

Rusmore, Jean, et al. *Peninsula Trails: Outdoor Adventures on the San Francisco Peninsula.* Berkeley: Wilderness Press, 1999. This updated third edition covers all parks and open-space preserves from Fort Funston south to

Saratoga Gap. Also by Rusmore, and Frances Spangle: *South Bay Trails: Outdoor Adventures Around the Santa Clara Valley.*

Schad, Jerry. *Afoot and Afield in San Diego.* Berkeley: Wilderness Press, 1998. Third ed. Well-written, informative hiking guide offering a wide variety of hikes (rated for difficulty) along the coast and inland both in mountainous areas and desert. Also by Jerry Schad: *Afoot and Afield in Los Angeles* and *Afoot and Afield in Orange County.* (1988).

Schaffer, Jeffrey. *Hiking the Big Sur Country: The Ventana Wilderness.* Berkeley: Wilderness Press, 1988.Soares, Marc J. *Best Coast Hikes of Northern California: A Guide to the Top Trails from Bug Sur to the Oregon Border.* San Francisco: Sierra Club Books, 1998. There's something for everyone here—75 scenic trails, organized north to south, suited for all skill levels (including mention of those that allow dogs).

Socolich, Sally. *Bargain Hunting in the Bay Area.* San Francisco: Chronicle Books, 2000. The ultimate shop-til-you-drop guide, now in its 13th edition, including discount stores, outlets, flea markets, and the year's best sales.

Stevens, Barbara, and Nancy Conner. *Where on Earth: A Guide to Specialty Nurseries and Other Resources for California Gardeners.* Berkeley: Heyday Books, 1997, but OP at last report. Ever wondered where to get that unusual color of iris or that exotic azalea, or where to find the state's best native plant nurseries? Wonder no more. California gardeners won't be able to live for long without *this* essential resource.

Stienstra, Tom. *Foghorn Outdoors California Camping.* Emeryville, CA: Avalon Travel Publishing, 14th ed., 2005. This is undoubtedly the ultimate reference to California camping and campgrounds, public and private. Every single one is in here. Also included here are Stienstra's "Secret Campgrounds," an invaluable list when the aim is to truly get away from it all. In addition to a thorough practical introduction to the basics of California camping—and reviews of the latest high-tech gear, for hiking and camping comfort and safety—this guidebook is meticulously organized by area, starting with the general subdivisions of Northern, Central, and Southern California. Even accidental outdoorspeople should carry this one along at all times.

Stienstra, Tom. *Foghorn Outdoors California Fishing.* Emeryville, CA: Avalon Travel Publishing, 2004. Seventh ed. This is it, *the* guide for people who think finding God has something to do with strapping on rubber waders or climbing into a tiny boat; making educated fish-eyed guesses about lures, ripples, or lake depths; and generally observing a strict code of silence in the outdoors. As besieged as California's fisheries have been by the state's 30 million-plus population and the attendant devastations and distractions of modern times, fisherfolk can still enjoy some world-class sport in California. This tome contains just about everything novices and masters need to know to figure out what to do as well as where and when to do it.

Stienstra, Tom. *Foghorn Outdoors Easy Camping in Northern California.* Emeryville: Avalon Travel Publishing, 1999. Second ed. A great guide for beginning campers, detailing 100 easily accessible campgrounds and cabin getaways.

Wach, Bonnie. *San Francisco as You Like It: 20 Tailor-Made Tours for Culture Vultures, Shopaholics, Neo-Bohemians, Fitness Freaks, Savvy Natives, and Everyone Else.* Berkeley: Ulysses Press, 2004. A hefty helping of more than the usual tourist fare, from The Politically Correct and Avant-Garde Aunts tours to Current and Former Hippies, and Queer and Curious. And a good time will be had by all.

Weintraub, David. *North Bay Trails: Outdoor Adventures in Marin, Napa, and Sonoma Counties.* Berkeley: Wilderness Press, 1999. Once you get there, this substantial guide to North Bay trails will help you get around.

Whitnah, Dorothy L. *Point Reyes.* Berkeley: Wilderness Press, 1997. Third revised ed.. but OP at last report. A very good and comprehensive guide (with an introduction by John Carroll) including trails, campgrounds, and picnic areas.

Winnett, Thomas, and Melanie Findling. *Backpacking Basics.* Berkeley: Wilderness Press, 1994. Fourth ed. Everything you need to know about going the distance on foot—with an emphasis on getting (and staying) in shape, the principles of low-impact camping, and how to save money on just about everything you'll need.

Zagat Survey. *Zagat San Francisco Bay Area Restaurant Survey.* New York: Zagat Survey. This annually updated collection, a compilation of "people's reviews" of regional restaurants, is a fairly reliable guide to what's hot and what's not in San Francisco and surrounding Bay Area destinations. If you'll be in Southern California, you'll want to get the *Los Angeles/Southern California* and/or *Orange County* guides.

Know Coastal California

Index

Children's Activities

Redwoods

Surfing

Whale-Watching

U.S.~Metric Conversion

1 inch	=	2.54 centimeters (cm)
1 foot	=	.304 meters (m)
1 yard	=	0.914 meters
1 mile	=	1.6093 kilometers (km)
1 km	=	.6214 miles
1 fathom	=	1.8288 m
1 chain	=	20.1168 m
1 furlong	=	201.168 m
1 acre	=	.4047 hectares
1 sq km	=	100 hectares
1 sq mile	=	2.59 square km
1 ounce	=	28.35 grams
1 pound	=	.4536 kilograms
1 short ton	=	.90718 metric ton
1 short ton	=	2000 pounds
1 long ton	=	1.016 metric tons
1 long ton	=	2240 pounds
1 metric ton	=	1000 kilograms
1 quart	=	.94635 liters
1 US gallon	=	3.7854 liters
1 Imperial gallon	=	4.5459 liters
1 nautical mile	=	1.852 km

To compute Celsius temperatures, subtract 32 from Fahrenheit and divide by 1.8. To go the other way, multiply Celsius by 1.8 and add 32.

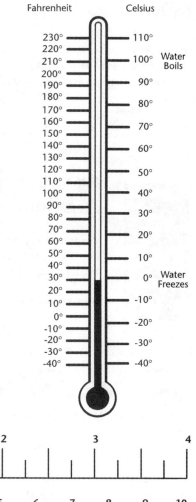

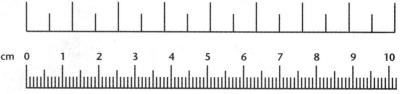

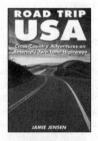

Keeping Current

Although we strive to produce the most up-to-date guidebook humanly possible, change is unavoidable. Between the time this book goes to print and the moment you read it, a handful of the businesses noted in these pages will undoubtedly change prices, move, or even close their doors forever. Other worthy attractions will open for the first time. If you have a favorite gem you'd like to see included in the next edition, or see anything that needs updating, clarification, or correction, please drop us a line. Send your comments via email to atpfeedback@avalonpub.com, or use the address below.

Moon Handbooks Coastal California
Avalon Travel Publishing
1400 65th Street, Suite 250
Emeryville, CA 94608, USA
www.moon.com

Editor: Ellen Cavalli
Series Manager: Kevin McLain
Acquisitions Manager: Rebecca K. Browning
Graphics Coordinator: Deb Dutcher
Production Coordinator: Justin Marler
Cover Designer: Kari Gim
Interior Designer: Amber Pirker
Freelance Designer: Karen Heithecker
Map Editor: Kevin Anglin
Cartographers: Mike Morgenfeld, Kat Smith, Kat Kalamaras
Proofreader: Elizabeth McCue
Indexer: Rachel Kuhn

ISBN: 1-56691-651-8
ISSN: 1531-1325

Printing History
1st Edition—2000
2nd Edition—March 2005
5 4 3 2 1

Text © 2005 by Kim Weir
Maps © 2005 by Avalon Travel Publishing, Inc.
All rights reserved.

Avalon Travel Publishing is an imprint of Avalon Publishing Group, Inc.

AVALON
publishing group incorporated

Poems by Gary Thompson are © 1999 by Gary Thompson. All rights reserved. All of these poems are included in the collection *On John Muir's Trail* (1999), which is available from Bear Star Press, 185 Hollow Oak Dr., Cohasset, CA 95973, www.bearstarpress.com.

Some photos and illustrations are used by permission and are the property of the original copyright owners.

Front cover photo: © Terry Donnelly

Printed in U.S.A at Malloy